Tolley's Corporate Insolvency

by

Shashi Rajani MSPI

partner,
Nicholson Graham & Jones, solicitors

Tolley Publishing Company Limited
A UNITED NEWSPAPERS PUBLICATION

Whilst every care has been taken to ensure the accuracy of the contents of this work, no responsibility for loss occasioned to any person acting or refraining from action as a result of any statement in it can be accepted by any of the authors or the publishers.

Coventry University

PO 3914

Published by
Tolley Publishing Company Ltd
Tolley House
2 Addiscombe Road
Croydon CR9 5AF England
081-686 9141

Typeset in Great Britain
by Phoenix Photosetting, Chatham, Kent

Printed in Great Britain
by The Bath Press, Avon

ISBN 0 85459 748–4

Foreword by the Honourable Mrs Justice Arden DBE

The Insolvency Act 1986 will shortly reach its tenth anniversary, and this comprehensive guide to it demonstrates well the volume of case law that it has generated since it came into force. The recession which gave rise to much of this case law may now be waning and so the pace of change can be expected to slacken. But there will still be significant changes—see for example the changes to the corporate voluntary provisions announced in the Budget this Autumn and the progress made this year on the EEC Bankruptcy Convention. Hopefully some of the lessons of the recession will be learnt.

In a field of law where there has been so much case law and where the law continues to change, another textbook of this quality is very welcome. I have known the author for many years. His work is in the very engine room of insolvency law. Anyone who has to venture into this subject in depth (whether as a newcomer or not) will benefit from this comprehensive work and from the skill, experience and industry of its author.

Mary Arden
5 December 1994

Preface

The first edition of this work, which was published in 1990 and ran to 500 pages, was called *Tolley's Corporate Insolvency Handbook*. Even at that time a number of readers remarked that the substantial size of the book made the description *Handbook* inappropriate.

There has since been a record number of insolvencies in the wake of the economic recession, in addition to some mega insolvencies, such as BCCI and Maxwell, which had very little, if anything, to do with the economy.

A substantial body of case law has developed. This includes some landmark decisions, such as *Paramount Airways* (currently subject to appeal to the House of Lords) on the meaning of 'adopted' in relation to preexisting contracts of employment, *British and Commonwealth Holdings* as to the efficacy of pre-liquidation subordination of debt and *BCCI* as to the availability of a set-off in respect of a debt due to a guarantor against his guarantee liability so as to reduce the debt due by the principal debtor. A number of further cases on section 236 (which has come to be known as the 'Star Chamber clause') have been decided; and some further interesting developments on the subject may be in store following the recent judgment of the European Commission on Human Rights in Strasbourg in the case of *Ernest Saunders* to the effect that he had been deprived of a right to fair trial by having been compelled to make incriminating statements. Directors' disqualification has been another active area; and, following the very helpful advice of a reviewer of the first edition, I have included in this new edition a new Part I containing detailed chapters on the subject.

The year 1994 also saw the passing of two Insolvency Acts, one of them aimed at partially mitigating the effect of the *Paramount* decision and, the other, clarifying the position of a third party in a transaction challengeable as a preference or as a transaction at an undervalue. Schedule 5 to the Deregulation and Contracting Out Act 1994 has introduced a new regime for the striking off of companies by the Registrar at the instance of directors, perhaps ironically giving rise to overregulation rather than deregulation. Further, the new Insolvent Partnerships Order, running to over 120 pages, came into force on 1 December 1994. It is only marginally less obscure than its predecessor.

All this has meant that the second edition has substantially grown in size and changed in complexion; and the publishers and I have finally been forced to shed our veil of modesty and drop the word 'Handbook' from its title.

In the preface to the first edition, I alluded to certain imperfections of the current insolvency law. One of my complaints was that the administration and company voluntary arrangement procedures were being under-utilised as instruments of corporate rescue due to, firstly, the overriding position of banks as holders of all-embracing fixed and floating charges and, secondly, the unavailability of a statutory interim moratorium. I also questioned the necessity for a corporate voluntary arrangement scheme to be approved by a meeting of shareholders. These concerns were shared widely, and I am gratified that early this year the Department of Trade and Industry issued a Consultative Document addressing these and other concerns. I had the privilege of being on the committees of some of the organisations which made representations on the Consultative Document.

In his budget speech on 29 November 1994, the Chancellor of the Exchequer Mr Kenneth Clarke claimed to herald a new 'rescue culture' when he announced the Government's intention to introduce a 28-day moratorium procedure 'binding on all parties'. This, he said, would enable rescue prospects to be evaluated and, if possible, creditors to be persuaded to agree to a scheme. He also revealed that further consultations were being held on a possible mechanism for converting debts due by an insolvent company into equity.

The first proposal has had a mixed reception. The British Bankers Association is concerned at the wider implication of the resulting curb on the powers of floating charge holders. There is also uncertainty as to how a business would be funded during the moratorium period. On the other hand, groups representing ordinary creditors and some insolvency practitioners have welcomed the proposal. The second proposal, based on a paper published by some leading academics, is more idealistic than practical and would require an extremely complex set of rules and a considerable change in attitudes.

On 1 December 1994, a committee of JUSTICE under the chairmanship of David Graham QC published a report entitled 'Insolvency Law—an Agenda for Reform'. The report makes some far-reaching proposals aimed at achieving a fairer system of insolvency administration. The proposals include an Insolvency Ombudsman, more advice for small debtors including advice on a pro bono basis, a two-tier bankruptcy system to separate serious and fraudulent cases from ordinary small cases, a permanent specialised committee to formulate and review national insolvency strategy and a Creditors' Charter.

At the end of the day, for a true rescue culture to develop there needs to be a change of attitudes, which can mainly be brought about by leadership and education rather than by legislation.

In the last preface, I also mentioned the uncertainty of the effect of Rule 4.90 regarding set-off in an insolvent liquidation, and the Government's ambivalent attitude towards it. Recently, while the Government's reluctance to clarify the position by legislation continued, the Financial Law Review Panel, backed by some of the leading lawyers in the City, boldly came out with a statement of law placing a robust interpretation on the

Rule, at least as far as it applies to certain types of sophisticated financial transaction. This has come as a breath of fresh air to those who were feeling exasperated by the Government's inaction.

I further expressed regret at the absence of express statutory recognition of the efficacy of pre-liquidation debt subordination or anti-set-off agreements. Fortunately, the *British and Commonwealth Holdings* case has now resolved the uncertainty in favour of subordination, and it is hoped that future court decisions will recognise anti-set-off agreements as well.

I also referred to the special regime for insolvencies in the financial markets set up by Part VII of the Companies Act 1989 and the possible conflicts which it might give rise to between the interests of market creditors and non-market creditors. So far, that regime has been little used and we await, with interest, development of case law and practice in that area.

International insolvency was another area that I mentioned. Progress towards achieving better co-ordination between different jurisdictions has been painfully slow. This is quite understandable in view of the inherent conflict of interests between local creditors and overseas creditors and, generally, historic and cultural differences. Those involved in the efforts have, quite rightly, recognised the harsh reality that the best the international commercial community can realistically aspire to, at least for the foreseeable future, is an administrative regime which avoids a multiplicity of procedures in different jurisdictions in relation to the same debtor. This can be achieved by giving exclusive control of the administration of the insolvency to that jurisdiction with which the matter has the closest connection, but so that the continued diversity of substantive laws of all the jurisdictions involved is respected and accommodated.

At the European Community level, the Council of Europe Convention (or the Istanbul Convention) is currently lying in a dormant state. It represents a set of principles assumed to have widespread acceptability, but with a complex set of reservations, so as to enable signatory states to adopt the Convention in varying degrees. The Convention was opened for signing in Istanbul on 5 June 1990. It has so far been signed by Belgium, France, Germany, Greece, Italy, Luxembourg, Cyprus and Turkey but ratified by only Cyprus. At least two more signatory states must ratify it before it can come into force. Meanwhile, substantial progress appears to have been made in respect of the draft EEC Convention which is regarded as an improvement on, and intended to supersede, the Council of Europe Convention.

On a wider international front, a new taskforce formed by Committee J of the International Bar Association is endeavouring to develop a set of general guidelines, in the form of a draft 'Concordat', for use by lawyers and courts in different jurisdictions on a case-by-case basis. The Concordat is no more than an initial effort to provide a framework for discussion of principles and is not intended to be used as, or as a substitute for, an international treaty. In each individual case, there would need to be court orders or formal agreements or informal understanding with a view to achieving a just and practical solution to the problems involved. This approach, which has the merit of being pragmatic, informal and flexible, is to be highly commended. It may well encourage development, in the course of time, of more judicial 'comity' between different jurisdictions.

If at all this book is worthy of being dedicated, I would like to dedicate it to all those legislators, judges, practitioners, commentators and academics, past and present, and the reviewers and readers of the first edition, the cream of whose collective wisdom this book, in its humble way, attempts to encompass.

More specifically, I am deeply grateful that the Hon Mrs Justice Arden DBE has done me the honour of writing the Foreword to this edition.

I am also indebted to my partners John Garbutt and Jenny Cottrell for their expert advice and assistance in relation to the chapters dealing with environmental issues and taxation respectively.

Once again, it has been a pleasure for me to work with the editor, Stephen Barc of Tolley Publishing Co Ltd, for whose patience, skill and efficiency I have nothing but praise and gratitude.

On a more personal note, I am yet again grateful to my wife Chandrika and my daughters Rita, Priya and Nina for their continued support, indulgence and sacrifice.

Shashi Rajani
Nicholson Graham & Jones

25–31 Moorgate
London
EC2R 6AR

December 1994

Contents

Table of Statutes	*xi*
Table of EC Legislative Material	*xxii*
Table of US Legislation	*xxii*
Table of Statutory Instruments	*xxiii*
Table of Cases	*xxxv*

Part A: General — **1**
Preliminary — 3
The new insolvency legislation — 7
Options available to a financially distressed company — 11
Insolvency practitioners and office-holders — 14
Jurisdiction and court procedure in insolvency matters — 35
Meetings in insolvency matters — 42
Table — 44

Part B: Administration Orders — **47**
Preliminary — 49
Conditions which must be satisfied — 53
Application and order — 59
Effects of application and order — 67
Manner of administration — 79
Adminstrator's powers affecting the rights of secured
    creditors and owners of assets — 90
Position and general powers and duties of the administrator — 96
Protection of creditors' and members' interests — 110
Adjustment of antecedent transactions — 113
International elements — 118

Part C: Liquidations — **121**
Introduction — 125
Pre-liquidation considerations — 129
Initiation of members' voluntary winding up — 132
Initiation of creditors' voluntary winding up — 138
Initiation of winding up by the court — 144
Effect of winding up: general — 219
Effect of voluntary winding up — 220
Effect of compulsory winding up — 222
Effect of all forms of winding up — 233
Adjustment of prior transactions — 243
Conduct of winding up: general administrative aspects — 261
Conduct of winding up: realisation of assets — 290
Malpractice — 317
Conduct of winding up: establishment of liabilities — 340
Marshalling and distribution of assets — 370
Conclusion of the winding up — 379

Contents

Part D: Receivers **385**
Preliminary 387
Pre-appointment considerations 396
Appointment of receiver 411
Procedural matters following appointment 414
General effects of receivership 421
Fixed charges and floating charges 430
Matters affecting assets available in receivership 441
Post-appointment liabilities 493
Realisation of assets 526
Conclusion of receivership 559
Receivership in Scotland 566
International aspects of receivership 572

Part E: Voluntary Arrangements **575**
Preliminary 577
Creditors' and members' meetings for approval 581
Procedure after and effect of approval 587
Taxation aspects 592

Part F: Special Provisions for Financial Markets **593**
Introduction 595
Insolvency-related problems before CA 1989, Part VII 598
Use of special contracts to minimise problems 604
Use of market default rules to minimise problems 607
Residual problems before CA 1989, Part VII 608
CA 1989 Part VII—effect on general law of insolvency 610
Overall effect of Part VII 628

Part G: Dissolution and Revival **631**
Dissolution 633
Effect of dissolution 638
Revival of a dissolved company 641

Part H: Taxation **649**
Introduction 651
Tax planning 652
Tax liabilities in insolvency 657

Part I: Disqualification of Directors **665**
Preliminary 667
Circumstances triggering the disqualification process (section 1) 670
Scope of the court's discretion 676
Test of unfitness (section 9) 677
Principles for determining unfitness and length of disqualification 679
Some cases on unfitness and periods of disqualification 685
Consequences of disqualification order 695
Procedural aspects 699

Index 711

Table of Statutes

1677	**Statute of Frauds**	
	s 4	D2.8
1838	**Judgments Act**	
	s 17	C3.2, C14.19, C15.2, C15.5
1844	**Joint Stock Companies Act**	C5.7
1852	**Common Law Procedure Act**	
	s 210	D7.14
1856	**Joint Stock Companies Act**	C5.7
1856	**Mercantile Law Amendment Act**	C14.24
	s 5	D7.4, D10.4
1857	**Joint Stock Banking Companies Act**	C5.7
1857	**Joint Stock Companies Act**	C5.7
1862	**Companies Act**	C5.7
1875	**Explosives Act**	D8.26
1878	**Bills of Sale Act**	D7.23
1879	**Companies Act**	C5.7
1890	**Partnership Act**	
	s 3	C14.35
1893	**Industrial and Provident Societies Act**	D1.4
1893	**Sale of Goods Act**	
	s 26	C9.3
1894	**Merchant Shipping Act**	D7.23
1908	**Companies (Consolidation) Act**	C5.7
	s 57	C5.7
1908	**Law of Distress Amendment Act**	D7.13
	s 6	D2.6, D7.13
1914	**Bankruptcy Act**	
	s 25(6)	A4.19
	s 31	C14.26
	s 44	C10.4
	s 122	C5.6
1925	**Land Registration Act**	D9.17
	s 24(1)(b)	C14.19
	s 30	D9.3
	s 49	D2.5
1925	**Law of Property Act**	A4.1, D1.3, D5.3
	s 40	D9.7
	ss 52, 53	D2.4, D9.7
	s 54	D9.7
	s 74	D2.4
	ss 76, 78	D9.8
	s 86(1)	C12.6
	s 87	C12.6
	s 91(2)	D7.31, D9.17
	s 94	D9.3
	s 99	D2.13
	s 101(1)(iii)	D3.1, D3.2
	s 104	D5.3, D9.17
	s 105	D10.1
	s 109(2)	D5.2
	(3)	D10.1
	(6)	D4.9
	(8)	D8.1, D8.5, D8.11, D10.1
	(8)(v)	C14.33
	s 110(1)	C14.32
	s 136	G2.1
	s 146	C8.3, C12.18, D7.14
	(2)	C12.18
	(9)	B1.1, D7.14
	(10)	C12.18
	s 172	C5.8, C10.10
	s 181	G2.1
	s 205(1)	C12.18
	(i)	C8.3, C14.32
	(xxi)	D2.4
	(9)	C8.3
1925	**Trustee Act**	
	s 40	D8.17
	s 44(2)(c)	G2.1
	s 51(2)(c)	G2.1
1927	**Landlord and Tenant Act**	
	s 1	D7.14
1927	**Moneylenders Act**	C10.7
1929	**Companies Act**	C5.7
	s 16	C5.7
1930	**Finance Act**	
	s 42	D9.12, H2.7
1930	**London Building Act**	
	s 5	D8.10
1930	**Third Party (Rights Against Insurers) Act**	C12.22, C14.24, C14.26, G2.1
1934	**Law Reform (Miscellaneous Provisions) Act**	
	s 1(2)(c)	G3.2
1936	**Public Health Act**	D8.9
	s 294	D8.8
	s 343	D8.8, D8.10
1937	**Factories Act**	D8.26
1939	**London Building Acts (Amendment) Act**	
	Pt V	D8.10
	Pt XII	D8.10
	s 33	D8.10
1947	**Crown Proceedings Act**	
	s 35(2)(g)	D7.6
1948	**Companies Act**	
	s 16	C5.7
	s 94(1)	D1.4
	s 223	C14.26
	(d)	C5.22
	s 270	C11.22
	s 325(1)	C9.3
	s 353	G1.5
1958	**Agricultural Marketing Act**	
	Sch 2	C5.4, C5.8, C5.12, C5.27, C12.20
	para 4	C5.24
1961	**Companies (Floating Charges) (Scotland) Act**	D11.1

1961	**Factories Act**	D9.16
	s 29(1) D8.8	s 101(2) D7.1
1965	**Industrial and Provident Societies**	**1975 Policyholders Protection Act** C9.12,
	Act C16.5, D1.4, D7.3	C14.23
	s 55 C5.3, C5.8, C5.13	**1975 Social Security Pensions Act** D9.16
1967	**Companies Act**	s 57C D8.17
	s 44 C5.7	s 57D(5) D8.17
1967	**Criminal Justice Act**	Sch 3 C14.34, D7.4
	s 8(1) C13.1	**1976 Civil Liability (Contributions)**
1967	**Finance Act**	Act C13.2
	s 27(2) D9.12	**1976 Damages (Scotland) Act** G3.2
	(3) D9.12, H2.7	**1976 Fatal Accidents Act** G3.2
1967	**General Rates Act**	**1976 Insolvency Act** A2.1
	Sch 1 D8.11	**1976 Restrictive Trade Practices**
1967	**Leasehold Reform Act**	Act A4.23
	s 23(3) D7.15	**1977 Torts (Interference with**
1967	**Misrepresentation Act**	Goods) Act D8.15
	s 3 D9.14	**1977 Unfair Contract Terms Act** D8.4
1968	**Civil Evidence Act** I8.5	s 8 D9.14
1970	**Administration of Justice Act**	s 10 D7.26
	s 36 D2.8	s 13 D7.5
	s 44 C3.2, C14.19	(1)(b),(c) D7.5
1970	**Income and Corporation Taxes Act**	**1978 Employment Protection**
	s 267 C2.4	(Consolidation) Act C14.24
	(3A) C2.4	ss 12–17 D7.2
	s 272(4) C2.4	s 19 D7.2
1970	**Taxes Management Act** A4.19	s 31(3) D7.2
	ss 61, 62 D7.13	s 31A(4) D7.2
	s 108 H3.4, H3.5, H3.7, H3.8, H3.12	s 49 D7.2
1971	**Power of Attorney Act**	s 57(3) D9.16
	s 4 C9.8	s 72 D7.2
	(1) D5.2	s 106(1A),(1B) D7.2
1971	**Town and Country Planning Act**	s 107 D7.2
	ss 87–91 D8.9	ss 122–127 D7.2
	ss 96–99 D8.9	s 125(2) D7.2
	s 290 D8.9	s 153 D7.4
1972	**Companies (Floating Charges**	Sch 13 para 17(2) D9.16
	and Receivers) (Scotland) Act A2.1,	**1978 Interpretation Act**
	D11.1	Sch 1 I2.1
1972	**Defective Premises Act** D7.28	**1978 State Immunity Act**
1972	**European Communities Act**	s 1 C15.4
	s 9 C12.18	s 3(1)(a) C15.4
	(4) C12.18	s 6(3) C15.4
1972	**Land Charges Act** D7.21	**1979 Charging Orders Act**
1972	**Road Traffic Act**	s 1 C9.3
	s 60 D9.8	s 2(2) D7.11
1973	**Fair Trading Act** C5.31	s 3(5) D7.11
1974	**Consumer Credit Act**	(7) D7.11
	s 138 C10.7	**1979 Credit Unions Act**
1974	**Control of Pollution Act** D8.26	s 20(2) C5.8, C5.15, C5.27
1974	**Health and Safety at Work etc Act**	**1979 Sale of Goods Act** D7.25
	s 2(1) D8.8	ss 17, 18 D7.18
	s 3(1) D8.8	s 19(1) D7.18
	s 4(2) D8.8	s 21(2)(b) C9.3
	s 21 D8.23	s 25 D7.18
	s 22 D8.23	**1980 Limitation Act**
1974	**Insurance Companies Act** C5.17	s 9(1) C5.29
1974	**Solicitors Act**	s 11 G3.2
	s 69 C5.29	s 29(7) C9.5
	s 73 D7.7	s 33 G3.2, G3.3
1975	**Employment Protection Act** D7.1,	s 39(1) C5.29

1980	**Local Government Planning and Land Act**		
	s 42	D8.11	
1981	**Betting and Gaming Duties Act**		
	s 12(1)	D7.4	
	s 14	D7.4	
	Sch 2	D7.4	
1981	**Supreme Court Act**	A4.19	
	s 16	A5.1	
	s 51	E3.1	
	s 51(1)	D8.16	
1982	**Civil Aviation Act**	B4.1	
1982	**Civil Jurisdiction and Judgments Act**	C5.2, F6.27	
1982	**Companies Act**		
	s 56	C12.13	
1982	**Insurance Companies Act**	B2.1, C14.23	
	Pt II	C1.5, C5.17, C15.4	
	s 15	C1.5	
	s 53	C5.27	
	s 54	C5.17	
	(1)	C5.27	
	(4)	C5.27	
	s 55	C15.4	
	(2)	C1.5	
	s 56	C11.29	
1982	**Iron and Steel Act**		
	Sch 4 para 9	C5.14	
1982	**Stock Transfer Act**		
	Sch 1	F6.18	
1984	**County Courts Act**	D7.13	
	Pt VI	I2.9	
	s 99	C9.3	
	s 138(7)	D7.14	
	(9A)	D7.14	
	(9C)	D7.14	
	s 429	I2.9	
1984	**Data Protection Act**	A4.8	
	s 20	D8.15	
1984	**General Rates Act**		
	Sch 1	D8.11	
1984	**Police and Criminal Evidence Act**		
	s 78	A4.19	
1985	**Administration of Justice Act**		
	s 55	D7.14	
1985	**Bankruptcy (Scotland) Act**	A2.1, C1.3, C10.3, F6.6, F6.27	
	s 42	F6.14	
	s 75	B9.3	
1985	**Companies Act**	B7.4, C1.1, D9.9	
	Pt II	C5.7	
	Pt XII	D2.5	
	Pt XIII	E1.2	
	s 3A	D2.2	
	s 4	D5.3	
	s 22(2)	C5.30	
	s 35	D2.2, D2.3	
	s 35A	D2.3	
	s 35B	D2.2, D2.3	
	s 36A	D2.4, D9.17	

s 36B	D2.4, D9.17	
(2)	D11.2	
s 42	C6.1, C12.18	
s 83	I2.6	
s 107	C11.25	
s 111A	C12.20	
s 117	C5.10	
s 143(1)	C11.25	
ss 151–157	D4.8, D9.15	
s 155	A1.2, C11.23	
s 156	A1.2	
s 168(2),(3)	C11.24	
(5)	C11.24	
s 196	A2.1, C14.34, D7.2, D7.3	
(1)	D1.4	
s 221	A4.12, I4.1	
s 222	I4.1	
ss 226, 227	A4.12, D5.5, D8.18, I4.1	
s 233	A4.12, D5.5, D8.18, E1.2, I4.1	
ss 234–238	D5.5, D8.18	
s 234	A4.12	
s 234A	A4.12	
s 235(2)	A4.12	
ss 237, 238	A4.12	
s 241	A4.12, D5.5, D8.18	
s 242	A4.12, D5.5, D8.18	
(5)	I2.2	
s 242A	A4.12, D5.5, D8.18	
s 245B	I2.2	
ss 247–249	E1.2	
s 250(3)	C9.1	
s 251	E1.2	
s 263	C12.9	
s 288	I4.1	
s 303(1)	C3.1	
s 310	C13.5	
s 311	C12.9	
s 317	D2.7	
ss 320–322	D2.7	
s 330	C12.9, D2.7, I6.1	
s 349(4)	C13.3	
s 352	I4.1	
s 353	I4.1	
s 363	A4.12, D5.5, D8.18, I4.1	
s 366	A4.12, D5.5, D8.18	
s 369(1)(b)(i),(ii)	C4.5	
(3),(4)	C4.5	
s 370	C3.7	
s 371	C3.7	
s 375	A6.1, C3.7, C11.12	
s 378	C3.7	
(2)	C3.1	
(3)	C3.1, C3.7	
s 380	C3.8	
s 381A–C	C3.7, C4.5	
s 382A	C3.7, C4.5	
s 386	E1.2	
s 387	E1.2	
ss 388–398	E1.2	
s 390	C3.7	
s 395	B9.12, C12.10, C14.25,	

1985	Companies Act	
		C14.31, D7.23, F4.3
	s 396	C12.10, D7.23
	(1)(c)	D7.18
	(2)(g)	D7.23
	s 397(5)	D2.5
	s 399	D2.5, I4.1
	s 400	D2.5
	s 401(2)(b)	D2.5
	s 404	B4.1
	s 405	A2.1, D4.1
	(2)	D10.6
	s 406	D2.5
	ss 408–500	A2.1
	s 409	C12.10, D4.1
	s 410	B6.4, C12.10, D6.3
	(4)	D7.18
	ss 411–414	E1.2
	s 415	I4.1
	s 416	B6.4
	s 419	E1.2
	ss 423–425	E1.2
	s 425	B2.1, B8.3, C11.26, E2.5
	ss 426–444	E1.2
	s 427	G1.1, G3.1
	s 435	C11.24, E1.2
	s 436	E1.2
	s 437	I2.6
	s 440	C5.27
	s 447	C5.29, C5.31, G3.2, I2.6, I8.5
	s 448	I2.6
	s 458	A1.2, C13.1, I2.3
	s 459	C3.1, C5.2, C5.30, C5.33
	s 460	C5.33
	s 461	C5.30, C5.33
	s 462	A2.1, B6.1, D1.4, D11.1
	ss 463–466	A2.1, D11.1
	ss 467–487	A2.1, D11.1
	s 497	D5.5
	s 518(1)(e)	C5.22
	s 519(7)	C5.32
	ss 563, 564	C11.22
	s 580(1)	C11.27
	s 612(1)	C14.26
	s 615	C10.4, D2.6
	s 616(3)	C10.4
	s 617	C10.4, C10.9, D2.6
	s 619(3)	C12.6
	s 630	C13.1
	s 641	C11.25
	s 651	G2.1, G3.1, G3.2, G3.3
	(3)	G3.2
	(4)–(7)	G3.2
	s 652	G1.1, G1.5, G3.1, G3.2, G3.3
	(1), (3)	G1.2
	(4), (5)	G1.2, G1.3, G1.4
	(6)(b)	G2.1
	s 652A–C	G3.3
	s 652A–F	G1.1, G1.7
	s 652A	G1.7
	(1)	G3.3
	s 652B(1)–(6)	G1.7
	(3)	G3.3
	s 652C	G1.7
	s 653	G2.1, G3.1, G3.3
	(2A)–(2D)	G3.3
	(3)	G3.3
	s 654	G2.1
	s 655	G2.1, G3.3
	s 656	G2.1
	(5)	G2.1
	s 657(2)	G2.1
	(3)–(7)	G2.1
	s 658	C16.5, G2.1
	s 671(2)	C5.8
	ss 675–677	C5.7
	s 680	C8.2
	s 689	C5.7
	s 691	C5.24
	s 695	C5.35
	s 711	C12.18
	(1)(p)	C6.1
	(q)	C16.9
	(r)	C16.9
	(2)	C6.1
	s 712	G2.1
	s 713	I2.2
	s 719	C15.9
	s 726	C5.30, D8.16
	s 727	B7.5, C13.3–C13.5, D5.3, I5.6
	(2)	D5.3
	s 735	5.2, B1.1, C3.1, C5.7, D1.4, E1.3
	s 735A	C5.7
	s 740	I1.1, I7.4
	s 741	C13.2
	s 744	A5.1, C1.6, G1.2, I7.4
	Sch 4 Pt III para 10	A1.3
	para 12	A1.3, C11.24
	Sch 7 Pt I para 1(2)	C5.30
	Sch 15A	C3.7
	Sch 21 para 6	C5.7
1985	Companies Consolidation (Consequential Provisions) Act	C5.10
	s 17	C7.4
1985	Housing Act	
	Pt IV	D9.7
1985	Insolvency Act	A2.1, A2.2, A2.4, B1.1, C13.2
1985	Reserve Forces (Safeguard of Employment) Act	D7.4
1986	Agricultural Holdings Act	C10.10
1986	Company Directors Disqualification Act	A3.1, A4.2, C2.7, C5.50, C8.5, D9.6, I1.1
	s 1	D3.3
	(1)	I7.1
	s 2	I2.1
	s 3	A4.7, I2.2
	s 4	C11.25, I2.3

1986 Company Directors Disqualification Act	
s 5	I2.4
ss 6–10	I1.1, I8.10
s 6	A1.2, I2.5, I5.7, I8.2
(1)	A4.9, I1.1
(b)	I5.5
(2)	I4.1
s 7	I1.1, I2.5, I8.8, I8.10
(1)	I8.3
(2)	I8.2
(3),(4)	A4.9
(8)	I8.3
s 8	I1.1, I2.6, I8.8, I8.10
(6)	I8.5
s 10	I2.7
s 11	I1.1, I2.8, I7.1, I7.4
s 12	I2.9, I3.1, I7.1
(2)	I7.4
ss 13–15	I7.4
s 14	I1.1
s 15	I1.1, I8.10
s 16	I8.3, I8.6
s 17	I7.2
s 19	I1.1
(c)	I1.1, I8.10
s 20	I1.1, I8.10
s 21(2)	I8.10
s 22(2)	I1.1
(4),(5)	I1.1
(6)	I1.1, I7.4
(7)	A4.7, C11.25
s 22A	I1.1
s 23(1)	I1.1
Sch 1	I1.1, I8.10
Pts I, II	I4.1
Schs 2, 3	I1.1
1986 Drug Trafficking Offences Act	D7.5
s 1	C14.13
1986 Financial Services Act	A4.6, C12.13, F1.3, F6.1, F6.22
s 6(3)(a),(b)	C14.13
s 39(4)	F6.3
s 40(2)	F6.3
s 45	A4.6
(2)	C12.14
s 54	F6.30
s 55	F6.4
s 61(3)(a),(b)	C14.13
s 67	C12.21, F6.29
s 72	C5.8, C5.18, C5.27, F6.29
s 74	B3.1, F6.29
s 94	I2.6
s 105	I2.6
s 114	C5.27
s 177	I2.6
Sch 1 paras 7–9, 11	F6.2
Sch 4	F6.3
1986 Insolvency Act	A1.1, A2.1, A2.4
Pts I–VII	I8.10
Pt II	B3.1, D1.4
Pt III	D1.4
Pts IV–VII	C1.2
Pt IV	D1.4
Pt V	A4.1, C5.8, I1.1
Pts XII–XVII	C1.2
Pts XVI	I4.1
ss 1–7	E1.2
s 1(1)	E3.3
(3)	E1.2
s 2	E1.4
(4)	E3.2
s 3	E2.1
s 4(1)	E2.1
(2)	E2.1, E3.2
(3),(4)	E2.7
(6)	E3.1
s 5(2)	E3.1
(3),(4)	E3.4
s 6	E3.3
s 7	E3.3
(2),(3)	E3.2
(4)	E3.3
(b)	C5.27
s 8	A5.2, B1.1, B5.4
(1)	B3.2
(a)	A1.2, B2.1
(b)	B2.1
(2)	B3.2
(3)	B2.1, B3.1
(4)	B2.1
s 9	D2.9
(1)	B3.1
(2)(a)	B3.1, D2.10
(b)	B3.1
(3)	B1.1, B2.1, B3.2, D2.9
(4)	B1.1, B3.2
(5)	B3.2
s 10(1)	B4.2
(a)	B4.1
(b)	B4.1, D2.9, F6.20
(c)	B4.1, F6.11
(2)(b),(c)	D2.9
s 11	B4.2, B7.7, H3.12
(1)(b)	D2.10
(2)	D2.10, F6.20
(3)	B4.2, B7.2, C8.2, F6.11
(b)	D2.10
(c)	B4.1, B4.2, D2.10, F6.20
(d)	B4.1, B4.2
s 12	B5.1
s 13	B7.1
s 14	C5.27, D5.3
(1),(2)	B7.2
(3)	B4.2, B5.4, B5.15, B7.3, B7.5
(4)	B7.4
(5)	B7.5
(6)	B7.8
s 15	B4.1, B7.2
(1)	B6.1, F6.20
(2)	B6.1, F6.20
(3)–(7)	B6.1

1986 *Insolvency Act*	
(9)	B6.1
s 16	B6.1
s 17	B4.2
(2)(a)	B5.2
(b)	B5.15
(3)	B8.2
s 18	B7.2, B8.3
s 19	D8.3
(1),(2)	B7.1
(4)	B5.4, B7.1, B7.2, B7.7
(5)	B5.4, B7.1, B7.2, B7.7, D8.3
s 20(1)–(3)	B7.1
s 21(1)(a),(b)	B3.3
s 22	I4.1
(1)–(4)	B5.3
s 23	B5.2, B5.3–B5.7, B5.11, B7.2, B7.6
(1)	B5.4, B5.7, B5.9
(b)	B5.7
(2)(b)	B5.4
s 24	B8.3, H2.2
(1),(2)	B5.5
(4)	B5.11, B5.13
(5),(6)	B5.14
s 25	B5.15, B6.1, B8.3
(2)	B5.7
(b)	B5.7
s 26	B8.1
s 27	B7.6, B7.7, H3.12
(1)–(4)	B8.3
(6)	B5.16, B8.3
s 29	D1.4, D3.1
(2)	D12.1
(a)	D1.4
s 31	D3.3, I7.1
s 32	D1.4, D3.1
s 33	D3.2
s 34	D2.14
s 35	D4.8
s 36	D4.9
s 37	B7.7, D8.2, D8.3
(1)(b)	D8.1
s 38	D4.10, D5.5
(3)(b)	D10.6
s 39	D4.12
s 40	C14.34, D1.4, D7.2, D7.3, D10.2, D10.3
(3)	D7.3, D10.2
s 41	D4.11, I2.2
s 42	C5.27, C9.8, D5.3
(3)	D5.2, D8.4
s 43	D5.3, F6.20
s 44	B7.7, C9.8, D5.2, D8.2, D8.3
(1)(a)	C9.8
(c)	D8.1
s 45	D5.2, D8.2
(4)	D10.6
s 46(1)	D4.1
(2)	D4.1, D4.4, D4.5
s 47	I4.1
(1)–(5)	D4.2
s 48(1)	D4.3, D4.4
(2)	D4.3, D4.5
(3)	D4.5
(4)	D4.3
(5)–(7)	D4.4
s 49(1),(2)	D4.6
ss 50–71	D11.1
s 51	D1.4, D11.1
(3)	D11.2
s 52(1)–(6)	D11.2
s 53(7)	D11.3
s 54	D11.2
(6)	D11.3
s 55	D11.4
s 56	D11.5
s 57	C9.8, D11.6
s 58	D11.7
s 59	D11.8
ss 60(1)–(3)	D11.9
s 61	D11.10, F6.20
ss 62–65	D11.11
s 66	D11.11, I4.1
ss 67–69	D11.11
s 72	D11.1
s 73	C1.5, C5.7
ss 74–83	C5.8, C5.30
s 74(2)(a)–(d)	C12.20
(2)(f)	C14.13, C14.35
s 75(2)(b)	C12.20
s 79	C5.30
s 84	C1.5
(1)	G1.7
(b)	C3.1, C4.1
(c)	C4.1
(3)	C3.8
s 85	C3.8
s 86	B7.2, C3.1, C6.1
s 87	C7.1
s 88	C7.3
(2)	C12.6
s 89	A1.2, C1.5, C3.1, C3.2
(1), (4), (5)	C3.2
s 90	C1.5, C3.2
s 91	C12.1
(1)	C3.3
(2)	C7.2
s 92	C11.28
s 93	A4.25, C11.18
s 94	C11.28, C16.1, C16.2, G1.1
s 95	A1.2, C4.12, C11.19
s 96	C4.12, C11.18, C16.1, C16.2
s 98	C4.6, C4.9, C4.12, C7.2, C11.11, C11.15, C11.19, C14.26, C15.2, F6.13, I4.1
(1)(a)	C4.6
s 99	C4.6, C4.7, C4.9, C7.2, C15.2, I4.1
(1)(c)	C4.1, C11.5
s 100	C4.8, C11.11
(1)	C4.3, C12.1

1986 Insolvency Act

s 101	C4.4, C4.11
s 102	C4.12
s 103	C7.2
s 104	C11.28
s 105	C11.18
s 106	C11.28, C16.1, C16.2, G1.1
s 107	C12.1, C15.9
s 108	C11.28
s 109	C3.8, C6.1
s 110	C3.5, C12.3, H2.5
(3)(a)	C3.5
s 111	C3.5, C12.3
s 112	C1.2, C5.46, C7.4, C7.6, C11.19, C11.26, C11.27, C12.1, C12.4, C14.1, C15.2, C15.8
s 113	C7.4
s 114	C7.2
s 115	C11.27, C15.2, D10.3
s 116	C5.30
ss 117–119	C5.2
s 117	C5.8
s 120	C5.3
(1)	D11.1
(3)	C5.3
s 121	C5.3
s 122	C5.1, C5.9, C5.10, C5.14, C5.16, C5.17, C5.23
(1)	C5.14
(a)	C5.28
(b)	C5.27
(f)	A1.2, C5.22
s 123	B2.1, B9.2, C5.9, C5.14, C5.16, C5.17, C5.18, C5.20, C5.22, C5.23, C10.2, C10.8, F2.2, F3.3, F6.29
(1)(a)	C5.27, C5.29
(e)	A1.2, C5.22
(2)	A1.2, C5.22, C5.23
s 124	B3.1, C5.1, C5.32
(1)	C5.27–C5.29
(2)	C5.30
(4)	C5.31
(5)	C5.27, C5.29, C5.32
s 124A	C5.10, C5.25, C5.27
s 125	C5.19
(1)	C5.42
(2)	C5.26, C5.30
s 126	C7.4, C8.2, C11.19, F6.11
s 127	C5.30, C5.36, C5.38, C8.3, C8.4, C9.8, C14.25, D2.6, D2.8, D5.2, D7.7, F2.7, F3.7, F6.15, F6.21, I4.1
s 128	C8.3, F6.11
s 129	C5.1, C6.1
s 130	C5.43, F6.11
(2)	B7.5, C8.2, C8.3
(3)	C8.2
(4)	C15.9
s 131	C5.48, I4.1

s 132	B7.1, C5.47, C5.50, C8.5
s 133	A4.19, C11.22
(3)	C11.22
s 134	C11.22
s 135	C5.41
s 136	C5.49, C11.4
(2)	C5.47
(3)	C5.47, C11.28
(5)	C5.50, C11.3
(6)	C11.28
s 137	C5.50
(4),(5)	C5.51
s 138	C5.50, C16.8
(1),(2)	C5.47
(3),(4)	C5.49
s 139	C5.50
(3)	C11.16
(4)	C5.50, C11.16
(a)	C11.28
s 140	B7.2, C5.27, C5.50
(1)	C11.28
s 141	C5.51
(3)	C5.51
s 144(1),(2)	C12.1
s 145	C9.9, C12.4
s 146	C11.18, C11.28, C16.3
s 147	C5.46, C11.19
s 148	C12.1, C12.20, C15.9
s 149(2),(3)	C12.1
s 151	C12.1
s 152(1),(2)	C12.1
s 153	C14.1
s 154	C12.20, C15.9
s 156	C11.27, C15.2
s 157	C11.8
s 158	C12.20
s 160	C12.20
(2)	C12.20
ss 161, 162	C12.20
s 165	C4.9, C11.26, C12.1, C12.2, C12.20
(4)	C11.26, C12.1
(a),(b)	C12.20
(c)	C12.14
(6)	C11.26, C12.2
s 166	C4.9, C11.26, C12.1, C12.2
(5)	C4.6
ss 167–169	C12.3
s 167	C11.26, C12.2, C12.20
(3)	B7.1, C11.26
s 168	C11.19
(3)	C14.1, C14.14
(4)	C11.26
(5)	C12.6, C14.14
s 169(1),(2)	C11.26
s 170	I2.2
s 171	C11.28
(2)–(3)	C11.28
(6)	C11.28, C16.2
s 172(2), (4), (7)	C11.28
(8)	C11.28, C16.3, C16.4, C16.6

1986 Insolvency Act

s 173(2)	C16.2
s 174	C16.4
(3)	C16.4
s 175	C14.34, D7.2, D7.3, D10.2, D10.3
(2)(a)	C15.2
(b)	D10.2
s 176	C14.34, D7.2
s 177	C11.29
ss 178–182	C12.6
s 178	C12.6, F2.3, F6.14
(4)	C12.6, G2.1
(b)	C12.6
(5)	C12.6, F2.3
(6)	C12.6
ss 179–182	G2.1
s 180	C12.6, G2.1
s 181	C12.6
(3)	C12.6
s 182	C12.6
s 183	C9.3, C9.4, D7.9
(2)(b)	C9.3
(c)	C9.4
(3)	C9.3
s 184	C9.4
(1)–(4)	C9.2
(5)	C9.4
s 185	C9.2, C9.3, F6.11
s 186	C12.7, F2.3, F6.14
s 187	C15.9
s 188	C11.1
s 189	C14.19
(2)	C14.13
(4)	C3.2
s 190	C12.5, H3.13
s 191	C12.20
s 192	C11.18, C11.25
s 193	C16.11
s 194	C11.15
s 195	C11.19, C11.26
ss 197, 198	C5.6
s 199	C8.2
s 201	C16.2, G1.1, G1.5
ss 202–205	G1.1, G1.5
s 202	C16.7
(5)	C16.7
s 203	C16.7
s 204	C11.28, C16.8
s 205	C16.6
(3)	C16.7
ss 206–211	C9.13
s 212	A5.2, B7.1, B7.6, C13.2, C13.4, C16.2, C16.4, D5.3, G2.1, I5.4
(1)(b)	D5.2, D8.14
(c)	A4.8
(3)	C13.4
s 213	A1.2, A5.2, C5.8, C13.1, I2.7, I5.4
s 214	A1.2, A5.2, B3.1, C5.8,

	C13.2, D9.1, I2.7, I5.4
(4)	C13.2, C13.4
(6)	A1.2, C13.2
(7)	C13.2
s 215	C13.1, C13.2
s 216	C9.1, C12.14
(4)	C9.1
(6)	C9.1
s 217	C9.1
s 218	C8.5, C9.13
(4)–(6)	C7.2
s 219	C9.13
ss 220–222	C5.27
ss 220–229	A2.4, C5.12
s 220	C5.4, C5.8
s 221	C5.4, C5.11, C5.13, C5.15, C5.16, C5.18, C5.30, F6.29
(4)	C5.8
(5)	C5.9
(7)	C5.9, C5.27
ss 222–224	C5.9, C5.11, C5.15, C5.16, C5.17, C5.24
s 222	C5.13
(2)	C5.25
s 223	C5.12
(2)	C5.25
s 224	C5.13
s 225	C5.8, C5.9
s 226	C5.30
(2)	C5.8
s 230	A4.5
(2)	D1.4
(3)	C4.8
s 231	A4.5, C3.3, D3.1, D5.3
s 232	A4.5, D1.4, D5.2, D8.4
s 233	A4.15, D7.30
ss 234–236	D1.4
s 234	C12.1, I4.1
(2)	A4.16
(3)	A4.8, A4.17, B7.6, D8.15
(4)	A4.8, A4.17, B7.6
(a),(b)	D8.15
s 235	A4.18, A4.19, I4.1, I8.5
s 236	A4.19, A4.20, A4.21, C5.6, D7.7, I8.5
(2)–(6)	A4.19
s 237	A4.19
(1),(2)	A4.21
(3)	A4.19
s 238	A1.2, A3.1, A5.2, B9.2, B10.1, C10.10, C14.25, D2.6, D9.1, F2.2, I4.1
(4)(a),(b) (5)	C10.2
s 239	A1.2, A5.3, B9.4, B10.1, C10.4, C10.9, C13.2
s 240	B9.2, B9.4, C10.2, C10.4
(2),(3)	A1.2
s 241	B9.6, C10.6
(1)	C10.6
(2)	B9.6, C10.2, C10.6, C10.10
(2A)–(3A)	B9.6

1986	*Insolvency Act*	
	s 242	A3.1, B9.3, C10.3, I4.1
	s 243	B9.5, C10.5, C10.9, I4.1
	s 244	B9.7, C10.7, D2.6
	(4)	B9.7, C10.7
	(5)	C10.7
	s 245	A1.2, C10.8, C10.9, C14.25,
		D2.6
	(2)	B9.8
	(a),(b)	C10.9
	(3)	B9.9
	(4), (5)	A1.2
	(a)	B9.9
	(6)	B9.10
	s 246	A4.19, A4.20, B9.11, C10.11
	(3)	D7.7
	s 247	A1.2, C13.2, C14.19
	(2)	B2.1, C10.7
	s 248	B4.1, C14.29
	s 249	B5.13, B9.2, C10.2, D8.17,
		E2.5
	s 251	A1.2, A5.1, A5.2, B1.1, B6.4,
		C1.6, C3.1, C3.2, C5.7, C10.9,
		C13.2, D1.4
	ss 252–262	E1.2
	s 262(1)(a)	E3.3
	s 271	C5.19
	(1)	C5.19
	(2A)	C5.19
	s 323	C14.26
	s 328(6)	C14.35
	s 329	D7.2
	s 342	C10.6
	s 348	D7.2
	ss 366, 367	A4.19
	s 375(2)	A5.1
	ss 383, 385(1)	C14.29
	s 386	C14.34, D7.2, D7.4, D11.8
	s 387	C14.34, D7.4
	(2)(a)	B7.2
	(3)(a)	B7.2
	(c)	B7.2
	s 388	A4.1, A4.5
	(1)	D1.4
	(a)	D3.3
	(4)	A4.1
	s 389	A4.1, A4.5, D3.3
	s 390(1),(2)	A4.2
	(3)	A4.3
	(4)	A4.2
	s 391	A4.2, A4.10
	s 392	A4.2
	s 393	A4.2
	(3)	A4.2
	(4)	A4.2, A4.10
	ss 394, 395	A4.2
	ss 396–398	A4.2
	ss 399–401	C5.47
	s 400	I2.5
	s 411	I8.10
	s 416	C5.2, C5.22

	s 417	C5.24
	s 419(2)(b)	A4.10
	s 420	C5.19
	s 422	B2.1, C5.6
	s 423	C10.2, C10.10
	(2)	C10.10
	s 424	C10.10
	s 425	C10.10
	(2)	C10.10
	s 426	A4.19, A5.3, B1.1, B10.1,
		C13.6, D12.1, F6.27
	(1), (2)	C5.6
	(4)	A5.2, C5.6
	(5)	A5.2, A5.3
	(10)	A5.2
	(11)	A5.2, C5.6
	s 428	A4.23
	s 433	A4.19, C5.48, I8.5
	s 434	A2.4
	s 435	A6.1, B5.13, B9.2, C10.2,
		D8.17, E2.5
	s 436	B4.1
	s 440	A2.4, C10.7
	s 441	C5.6
	(2)	C5.4
	s 442	A2.4
	Sch 1	B5.2, B7.2, D5.3, D5.4
	para 2	B5.4, C9.8, D5.3
	para 3	B7.2, D5.3, D9.3
	para 8	C9.8, D5.3
	para 9	C9.8
	para 11	D5.3
	para 12	D5.3, D9.3
	para 13	B7.2, B7.7, D8.1
	paras 14, 15	D5.3
	para 16	D5.3, H2.2
	para 19	D9.1
	para 21	B7.2, C5.27, D5.3
	para 23	B7.2
	Sch 2	D11.4
	Sch 4	C1.2, C12.3
	Pts I–III	C11.26
	Pt I paras 2, 3	C11.26
	para 3(a)	C12.20
	Pts II, III	C12.1
	para 6	C12.2, C12.4,
		C12.13, C12.14
	para 7	C12.4
	Sch 6	C14.34, D7.2, D7.4, D11.8
	Sch 7	A4.2
	Sch 10	D3.1
	Sch 11 para 1(1)	B6.3, D2.8
	para 4(1)	C5.32
	Sch 13	D7.3
	Sch 14	C5.24, D7.2
1986	**Policyholders Protection**	
	Act	A3.1
1986	**Wages Act**	D8.3
	s 1(1)	D8.3
	(5)	D8.3
	(e)	D8.3

1987	**Banking Act**	B2.1, B3.1, C5.34,
		C11.3
	Pt II	A3.1
	s 49	C14.13
	ss 50–66	C14.24
	s 58	C4.11, C5.51, C9.12, C11.5
	s 92	C5.8, C5.16, C5.27, C5.42
1987	**Criminal Justice (Scotland) Act**	
	s 1	C14.13
	s 52	I2.6
1987	**Criminal Justice Act**	
	s 2	I2.6
	(2)	A4.19
	(8)–(10)	A4.19
	s 3(3)	A4.19
1987	**Landlord and Tenant Act**	
	Pt I	D7.15
1988	**Court of Session Act**	
	s 45	F6.17
1988	**Income and Corporation Taxes**	
	Act	H1.1
	s 12(7)	C2.4, H2.4
	s 23(7)	D8.12
	s 74	E4.1
	s 94	E4.1
	s 203	D7.4
	s 209(1)	C15.9
	s 343	D9.5, D9.7
	ss 349, 350	H3.12
	s 394	C2.4
	s 410	H2.2
	s 559	D7.4, H3.12
	s 768	D9.5, D9.7
1988	**Landlord and Tenant Act**	
	s 1(5), (6)	D9.7
1988	**Local Government Finance**	
	Act	D8.11
	Pt III	D8.11
	s 17	D8.11
	s 43	D8.11
	s 65	D8.11
	Sch 4 para 7	D7.13
	Sch 9 para 3	D7.13
1988	**Road Traffic Act**	D9.8
1989	**Companies Act**	C3.7, C4.5, C12.20,
		C14.25, D4.1, D7.2, D7.18,
		D8.18, D9.9, D11.1
	Pt IV	D2.5, F4.3
	Pt VII (ss 158–165)	C1.2, F1.1, F2.2,
		F5.1, F6.1, F6.2, F6.5, F6.27–
		F6.30, F7.1, F6.17
	s 27(1)	C13.4
	s 60	C5.10, C5.27, C5.31
	s 78	C8.5
	ss 92–104	C12.10
	s 93	D7.23
	ss 94, 95	D2.5
	s 100	B6.4, D6.3
	s 103	B6.4
	s 108	D2.2, D2.3
	s 110	D2.2

	(2)	D5.3
	ss 113, 114	C3.7
	s 120	C3.7
	s 130	D2.4, D9.17
	s 137	C13.5
	s 141	G3.2
	(4),(5)	G3.2
	s 154	F6.1
	s 155(1)	F 6.1, F6.2
	(2),(2A)	F6.2
	(3)	F6.2
	s 156	F6.3, F6.4
	s 157	F6.4
	s 158	F6.5
	(2)	F6.5
	ss 159–165	F6.5
	s 159	F6.6
	(4),(4A)	F6.6
	(5)	F6.6
	s 160	F6.7
	(4)	F6.7
	s 161	F6.27
	(1)	F6.8
	(2)	F6.9
	(3)	F6.10
	(4)	F6.11
	s 162	F6.12
	(1)	F6.6
	(1A)	F6.12
	s 163(2),(3)	F6.13
	(4)	F6.6, F6.13
	(5),(6)	F6.13
	s 164	F6.27
	(1),(2)	F6.14
	(3)	F6.14, F6.21
	(4)	F6.6, F6.15, F6.21
	(5),(6)	F6.15
	s 165	F6.16
	(1),(2)	F6.6, F6.16
	(3),(4)	F6.6
	(4)	F6.16
	s 166	F6.17
	(2)(a)	F6.17
	s 167(3)	F6.17, F6.20
	(4),(5)	F6.17
	s 168	F6.5
	s 169	F6.3
	ss 170–172	F6.2, F6.22
	ss 173–176	F6.1, F6.18
	s 173	F6.18
	(2)	F6.19
	s 174	F6.18, F6.19
	(1)	F6.19
	s 175	F6.20, F6.27
	(2)	F6.20, F6.27
	(4)–(6)	F6.21
	s 176	F6.22
	s 177	F6.1, F6.22, F6.23
	ss 178, 179	F6.24
	s 180	F6.25
	s 181	F6.22

1989	*Companies Act*	
	s 182	F6.26, F6.27
	s 183	F6.27
	s 184	F6.28
	s 188	F6.4, F6.5–F6.7
	s 189	F6.6
	s 193	C12.10
	ss 238, 239	F6.16
	ss 242, 243	F6.16
	ss 395, 396	C12.10
	s 401(2)(b)	C12.10
	s 409	D10.6
	s 423	F6.16
	Sch 21 Pts I–III	F6.3
	para 1(4)	F6.19
	para 2(1)	F6.4
	para 5	F6.28
	para 9(2)(a)	F6.19
	para 12	F6.28
	Sch 22	F6.26
1989	**Employment Act**	D7.2
1989	**Finance Act**	D7.13
1989	**Law of Property (Miscellaneous Provisions) Act**	
	s 1	D2.4, D9.17
	(2)	D9.17
	(5)	D9.17
	s 2	D9.7, D9.17
1989	**Water Act**	
	s 115	D8.24
1990	**Courts and Legal Services Act**	D7.13
	s 4	C5.29
1990	**Environmental Protection Act**	
	Pt I	D8.23
	Pt II	D8.23
	Pt III	D8.22, D8.23
	s 6	D8.20
	ss 13, 14	D8.20
	s 23	D8.20
	ss 26, 27	D8.20
	ss 33, 34	D8.21
	s 36	D8.21
	s 59	D8.21, D8.26
	s 61	D8.21
	s 79	D8.22
	s 80	D8.8, D8.22
	s 81	D8.22
	s 143	D8.23
	s 157(1)	D8.26
	s 158	D8.26
	Sch 1	D8.20
1990	**Law Reform (Miscellaneous Provisions) (Scotland) Act**	
	s 72	D2.4, D11.2
	(1)	D9.17
	s 74	D11.2
1990	**Social Security Act**	
	s 11(3)	D9.1
	Sch 4	D8.17
1990	**Town and Country Planning Act**	
	s 215	D8.23
1991	**Water Resources Act**	D8.23
	s 85	D8.24
	s 161	D8.24
	s 217	D8.26
1992	**Local Government Finance Act**	D8.11
1992	**Social Security Contributions Act**	D7.4
1992	**Social Security Contributions and Benefits (Northern Ireland) Act**	D7.4
1992	**Taxation of Chargeable Gains Act**	
	s 26(2)	H3.10
	s 139	H2.5
	(5)	H2.5
	s 170(11)	H2.3
	s 171	H2.3
	s 178	D9.7
1992	**Trade Union and Labour Relations (Consolidation) Act**	
	s 169	D7.2
	s 188	B7.5
	ss 188–192	D7.1
	s 189	D7.1, D7.2, D9.16
	s 194	D7.1
1993	**Bankruptcy (Scotland) Act**	A2.1
1993	**Charities Act**	
	s 63(1)	C5.27
1993	**Railways Act**	A2.1
1993	**Trade Union Reform and Employment Act**	D7.1, D9.10
	s 33	D9.16
1994	**Deregulation and Contracting Out Act**	G3.3
	Sch 5	G1.1
1994	**Finance Act**	
	s 144	E4.1
1994	**Insolvency Act**	D7.1, D11.6
	s 1	B7.7
	s 2	D8.3
1994	**Insolvency (No 2) Act**	C10.6, F2.2
	s 1(2)	B9.6
1994	**Law of Property (Miscellaneous Provisions) Act**	D9.8
1994	**Value Added Tax Act**	
	s 36	B5.18, H3.15
	s 46(4)	H3.15
	s 49(1)(b)	D9.17
	s 76	D7.4
	s 81	D7.6, H3.15
	Sch 4 para 7	D8.5
	Sch 9	D8.5
	Sch 9 Group 1	D9.13
	Sch 10	D8.5
	Sch 11 para 5	D9.13
	(4)	D7.13

Table of European Community Material

Decision 3/52/ECSC

Art 6   D7.4

Dir Proposal for a Directive on civil liability for damage

caused by waste (COM (91) 219)   D8.25

Dir 68/151/EEC First Company Law Directive

Art 12(3)   G1.6

Dir 75/129/EEC Collective Redundancies Directive   D7.1

Dir 77/187/EEC Acquired Rights Directive   D9.10, D9.16

Art 1   D9.16

Dir 89/654/EEC Safety and Health in Workplace   D8.8

EC Treaty of Rome 1957

Art 86   D7.30

ECSC Treaty of Paris 1952

Art 49   D7.4

Art 50   D7.4

(3)   D7.4

Table of United States Legislation

Bankruptcy Code 1984   D12.1

Ch 11   C5.6

s 304   A5.3

s 362   A5.3

s 547   A5.3, B10.1

Bankruptcy Reform Act 1978

s 101   D12.1

s 303(b)(4)   D12.1

s 304(a)   D12.1

Comprehensive Environmental Response Compensation and Liability Act   D8.26

Table of Statutory Instruments

1949	**Companies (Winding–up) Rules**	
	SI 1949, No 330	
	r 106	C14.2, G2.1
	r 172(3)	C11.19
	r 195	C15.2, D10.3
1952	**Bankruptcy Rules**	
	SI 1952, No 2113	
	r 86	A4.19
1965	**Rules of the Supreme Court**	
	SI 1965, No 1776	
	Appendix A, Form 10	I8.3
	Appendix A, Form 15	I8.4
	Ord 11	C5.35
	r 1(b)	C5.30
	(d)(i)	C5.30
	(iii)	C5.30
	Ord 14	C5.29
	Ord 15 r 6(2)(b)(i)	G3.2, G3.3
	Ord 18 r 19	I8.7
	Ord 24	I8.5
	Ord 28 r 10	C13.4
	Ord 38 r 2A	C13.5
	Ord 39 r 1	C5.6
	r 2	C5.6
	Ord 45 r 3	C8.2
	Ord 59	I8.10
	r 13(1)	I8.8
	r 19(5)	I8.8
	Ord 62	C5.44
	r 2(4)	D8.16
	r 11	C5.44
	Ord 65 r 5(1)	D2.8
	Ord 77	D7.6
	Ord 102 r 2	G3.4
1967	**Rating (Exemption of Unoccupied Property) Regulations**	
	SI 1967, No 954	D8.11
1972	**Solicitors Remuneration Order**	
	SI 1972, No 1139	
	art 3(2)	C5.29
1975	**Bankruptcy (Fees) Order**	
	SI 1975, No 1350	A6.2
1977	**Companies (Register of Disqualification Orders) (Fee) Regulations**	
	SI 1977, No 776	I1.1
1980	**Unoccupied Property Rate (Variation of Current Ceiling) Order**	
	SI 1980, No 2012	D8.11
1981	**County Court Rules**	
	SI 1981, No 1687	I8.3
	Ord 42	D7.6
1981	**Transfer of Undertakings (Protection of Employment) Regulations**	
	SI 1981, No 1794	C2.6, D7.1, D7.4
	reg 5	D9.10, D9.16
	(2),(3)	D9.16
	reg 8(1)	D9.16

1983 Protection of Training Interests (US Antitrust Measures) Order
SI 1983, No 900   A5.3

1985 Companies (Department of Trade and Industry) (Fees) Order
SI 1985, No 1784   A6.2

1985 Companies (Disqualification Orders) Regulations
SI 1985, No 829   I1.1

1985 Companies (Forms) Regulations
SI 1985, No 854   A6.2, C1.3
Sch 3 Form 405(1)   D4.1
      (2)   D10.6

1985 Companies (Tables A–F) Regulations
SI 1985, No 805
Table A art 12   D9.1
    art 40   C3.7
    art 53   C3.7
    art 117   C3.4

1985 Insurance Companies (Winding Up) Rules
SI 1985, No 95   A6.2, C1.3, C5.27, C11.19, C11.27,
            C12.13, C14.1, C14.23, C15.2
r 5   C15.4
r 6   C14.23
r 24   C15.4
Sch 1 para 1   C14.23
    para 2   C14.23

1985 Rating (Exemption of Unoccupied Industrial and Storage Hereditaments) Regulations
SI 1985, No 258   D8.11

1985 Value Added Tax (General) Regulations (Amendment) Regulations
SI 1985, No 1650   D7.13
reg 11   D8.5, H3.15
    (2)   A4.11
reg 59   D8.5
reg 63   H3.15
reg 65   D7.13

1986 Act of Sederunt (Rules of Court Amendment No 11) (Companies)
SI 1986, No 2298   A5.1, A6.2

1986 Act of Sederunt (Sheriff Court Company Insolvency Rules)
SI 1986, No 2297   A5.1, A6.2

1986 Administration of Insolvent Estates of Deceased Persons Order
SI 1986, No 1999   A6.2

1986 Administrative Receivers (Value Added Tax Certificates) (Scotland) Rules
SI 1986, No 304   A6.2

1986 Administrative Receivers (Value Added Tax Certificates) Rules
SI 1986, No 385   A6.2

1986 Co–operation of Insolvency Courts (Designation of Relevant Countries and Territories) Order
SI 1986, No 2123   A5.2, A6.2, C5.6

1986 Companies (Disqualification Orders) Regulations
SI 1986, No 2067   A6.2, I1.1

1986 Companies (Unfair Prejudice Applications) Proceedings
SI 1986, No 2000   A6.2, C5.26, C5.35
Sch   C5.33

1986 County Court Fees (Amendment) (No 2) Order 1986
SI 1986, No 2143   A6.2

1986 Insolvency (Amendment of Subordinate Legislation) Order
SI 1986, No 2001 — A6.2

1986 Insolvency (Land Registration Rules) Order
SI 1986, No 2245 — A6.2

1986 Insolvency (Scotland) Rules
SI 1986, No 1915 — A2.1, A6.2, B1.1, E1.2
Pt III — D11.1
Pts IV–VII — C1.3
r 3.1 — D11.2
rr 3.1–3.14 — D11.11
rr 4.1–4.6 — C5.41
rr 4.7–4.9 — C5.48
r 4.12 — C11.4
r 4.13(1) — C11.18
    (2) — C11.24
r 4.14 — C11.8
r 4.15 — C11.13–C11.15, C14.1, C14.12
r 4.16 — C11.13–C11.15, C14.1, C14.12, C14.13
r 4.17 — C14.13, C14.17
r 4.18–4.21 — C5.50
r 4.22 — C12.1
rr 4.23–4.30 — C11.28
rr 4.32–4.35 — C11.27
rr 4.36, 4.37 — C11.28
rr 4.38, 4.39 — C11.24
rr 4.40–4.65 — C4.11, C5.51
rr 4.66–4.68 — C15.1
rr 4.69–4.73 — C11.29
rr 4.74, 4.75 — C11.22
r 4.76 — C5.33
r 4.79 — C9.1
rr 4.80–4.82 — C9.1
rr 7.1–7.13 — C11.2
r 7.7 — C11.12
rr 7.14–7.20 — A6.1, C11.2
r 7.27 — A4.22
r 7.28 — A4.3
r 12.19 — C9.2
Sch 5 — C1.3

1986 Insolvency Act 1985 (Commencement No 1) Order
SI 1986, No 6 — A6.2

1986 Insolvency Act 1985 (Commencement No 2) Order
SI 1986, No 185 — A6.2

1986 Insolvency Act 1985 (Commencement No 3) Order
SI 1986, No 463 — A6.2

1986 Insolvency Act 1985 (Commencement No 4) Order
SI 1986, No 840 — A6.2

1986 Insolvency Act 1985 (Commencement No 5) Order
SI 1986, No 1924 — A6.2

1986 Insolvency Fees Order
SI 1986, No 2030 — A6.2, B7.2, C5.34, C11.27, C12.15
art 11 — C5.34

1986 Insolvency Practitioners (Recognised Professional Bodies) Order
SI 1986, No 1674 — A4.2, A6.2

1986 Insolvency Practitioners Tribunal (Conduct of Investigations) Rules
SI 1986, No 952 — A4.2, A6.2
r 4 — C5.50

1986 Insolvency Proceedings (Monetary Limits) Order
SI 1986, No 1996 — A6.2, C9.2, D7.4

1986 Insolvency Regulations
SI 1986, No 1994   A6.2, C11.18, C11.27, C12.15
1986 Insolvency Rules
SI 1986, No 1923   A2.1, A6.2, D1.3, E1.2
Pt II   B1.1
Pt IV   C1.3
Pt VII–XIII   C1.3
r 1.1(3)   E1.3
r 1.2   E1.3
r 1.3   E1.3
r 1.4   E1.3
r 1.7   E1.4
r 1.9   E2.2
r 1.10   E1.3
       (2)   E1.3
r 1.11   E2.2
r 1.12   E1.3, E2.2
r 1.13   E2.2
rr 1.14, 1.15   E2.3
r 1.16   E2.4
r 1.17(1)(2)   E2.5
r 1.18(1)–(3)   E2.5
r 1.19   E2.5
       (1)   E2.2, E2.5
       (3)   E2.2
       (4)   E2.2, E2.5
       (7)   E2.5
r 1.20(1), (2)   E2.5
r 1.21(1), (2)–(5), (6)   E2.6
r 1.22   A4.5, E2.5
r 1.23(1),(2)   E3.5
r 1.24   E3.1
r 1.25   E3.3
rr 1.26–1.29   E3.7
r 2.1   B3.1
r 2.2   B2.1, B3.1, I8.5
r 2.3   B3.1
r 2.4(3), (6)   B3.1
r 2.5   B3.1
r 2.6A   B3.1
r 2.7(1),(2), (4A)   B3.1
r 2.8   B3.1
r 2.9(1),(2)   B3.2
r 2.10   B3.3
       (5)   B3.2
r 2.11   B5.3
r 2.12(6)   B5.3
r 2.13–2.15   B5.3
r 2.16(1),(2)   B5.4
r 2.17   B5.4
r 2.18   B5.7
       (4)   B5.9
r 2.19   B5.15
       (2)–(5)   B5.7
       (6),(7)   B5.9
r 2.20   B5.8
r 2.21   B5.7, B8.2
r 2.22   B5.11
       (1)–(5)   B5.10
r 2.23   B5.11
rr 2.24–2.27   B5.10, B5.12

1986 *Insolvency Rules*

r 2.28	B5.9
(1A)	B5.13
r 2.30(1),(2)	B5.14
rr 2.32–2.46	B8.1
r 2.33(2)	B8.1
rr 2.47–2.50	B7.1, B7.9
r 2.47(7)	B7.9
r 2.51	B6.1
r 2.52	B7.10
r 2.53(1)–(3)	B7.1
r 2.54	B7.1
r 2.55	B7.1
r 3.1	D3.2
r 3.2(2)	D4.1
r 3.3	D4.2
r 3.4(1)–(3)	D4.2
r 3.5	D4.3
r 3.6	D4.2
r 3.7	D4.2
r 3.8(1)–(4)	D4.3
rr 3.9–3.15	D4.5
rr 3.16–3.30	D4.6
r 3.18(1)	D4.6
r 3.28	D4.6
r 3.32	D4.10, D5.5, D10.6
rr 3.33–3.34	D4.1, D5.2
r 3.35(2)	D10.6
r 3.36	D4.7
r 3.37	D4.7
r 4.1	C11.27
(1)(g)	C11.18
r 4.3	C5.45
rr 4.4–4.6	C5.22
r 4.7	C5.2, C5.33, C5.34
(2)	B7.2
(7)–(10)	C5.33
(7)	B7.2, C5.50
r 4.8	C5.35
(4)	C5.35
r 4.9	C5.35
r 4.10	C5.34
r 4.11(4), (5)	C5.36
r 4.12	C5.34
r 4.14	C5.36
r 4.15	C5.37
rr 4.16, 4.17	C5.39, C5.40
r 4.18	C5.39
r 4.19	C5.38
r 4.20	C5.43
r 4.21	C5.33, C5.40, C5.43
r 4.21A	C5.40
rr 4.22–4.24	C5.33
r 4.22	C5.40
(1A)	C5.40
r 4.23	C5.40
(1)(c)	C5.36
r 4.24	C5.40
rr 4.25–4.31	C5.41
r 4.30	C5.31
rr 4.32, 4.33	C5.48

1986 Insolvency Rules
    r 4.34   C4.7, C4.12

r 4.34	C4.7, C4.12
rr 4.35–4.37	C5.48
r 4.38	C15.2
r 4.42	C5.48
r 4.43	C4.10, C11.19
r 4.43A	C4.10
rr 4.44–4.47	C11.19
r 4.48	C5.46
r 4.49	C11.19
r 4.50	C11.3
(6)	C5.49, C5.50
(7)	C5.49
(8)	C11.3
r 4.51	C11.3
(3)	C11.3
r 4.52	C11.4
r 4.53	C11.4
r 4.53A	C11.15
r 4.53B	C4.7
r 4.54	C11.5, C11.7, C11.19, C11.24
rr 4.55, 4.56	C11.7
r 4.57	C5.49, C5.50
r 4.58	C11.8
r 4.59	C11.6
r 4.60(1),(2)	C11.9
(3)	C11.10
r 4.61	C11.11
r 4.62	C4.6, C11.11, C15.2
r 4.63	C11.15
(2A)	C11.15
r 4.65	C11.16
r 4.66	C11.12
r 4.67–4.69	C11.13
r 4.70	C11.13, C11.14
r 4.71	C11.17
r 4.72	C11.3
r 4.73	C14.12
r 4.74	C14.11
rr 4.82, 4.83	C14.5
r 4.84	C14.7
r 4.85	C4.12, C14.6
r 4.86	C14.14
r 4.87	C14.15
r 4.88	C14.32
r 4.89	C14.16
r 4.90	C9.10, C12.6, C14.26, D6.2, D7.6, F2.4, F3.5, F3.6, F6.13
(3)	C14.3, C14.26
r 4.91	C14.17
r 4.92	C14.18
r 4.93	C14.19
r 4.94	C14.20
r 4.95(1),(2)	C14.32
r 4.96–4.99	C14.32
r 4.100	C5.50
r 4.101	C4.8
r 4.102	C5.50
r 4.103	C4.8, C11.28
r 4.104–4.106	C5.50
r 4.107	C5.50, C12.1

1986 Insolvency Rules

r 4.108	C11.28
r 4.113(3)	C11.16
r 4.114(3)	C11.16
r 4.123	C11.28
r 4.124	C16.4
r 4.125	C16.3, C16.4
(5)	C11.18
r 4.126	C16.1, C16.2
rr 4.127–4.131	C11.27
r 4.127	C15.2
(4)	C11.27
rr 4.132–4.138	C11.28
r 4.138(2)	C16.10
r 4.139	C11.27
r 4.140	C11.28
rr 4.148, 4.148A	C11.27
r 4.149	C11.19, C11.24
r 4.150	C11.24
rr 4.151, 4.152	C4.11, C5.51
r 4.152	C5.51
(2)–(7)	C4.11
(7)	C4.11, C5.51
r 4.154	C5.51
r 4.155	C11.20
r 4.159	C5.51
rr 4.161–4.164	C11.19
r 4.172	C15.8
rr 4.173–4.175	C5.51
r 4.178	C4.11, C5.51
r 4.179	C11.25
(1),(2)	C12.1
r 4.180	C15.5, C15.7
(2)	C14.2
(3)	C15.7
r 4.181	C15.4
r 4.182	C14.3
(1)	C15.5
(3)	C15.5
r 4.182A	C14.2, C14.3
r 4.183	C15.8
r 4.184(1),(2)	C11.26
r 4.185	C12.1
r 4.186	C15.6
rr 4.187–4.190	C12.6
r 4.191–4.194	C12.6
rr 4.195–4.201	C12.20
rr 4.202–4.205	C12.20
r 4.205(2)	C12.20
r 4.206(5)	C11.29
rr 4.206–4.210	C11.29
rr 4.211–4.216	C11.22
r 4.217	C11.22, C15.2
rr 4.218–4.220	C11.27
r 4.218	C11.27, C15.2, D10.3
(1)	H3.8, H3.10
(l),(m)	C12.18
(o)–(q)	C15.2, H2.3
r 4.219	C15.2
r 4.220	C15.2
r 4.221	C15.9

1986 *Insolvency Rules*

r 4.222	C15.9
r 4.223	C11.18, C16.1
rr 4.224, 4.225	C16.6, C16.7
r 4.227	C9.1
r 4.228(2)	C9.1
r 4.228–4.230	C9.1
r 4.229	C9.1
r 5.18(3)(b)	E2.5
r 6.1(5)	C14.29
r 7.1	A5.1, C5.2, C11.23, C11.24
rr 7.3, 7.4	C5.41
r 7.4(6)	C5.41
r 7.7(1)	C5.36
r 7.10	C11.24
rr 7.14–7.19	B5.10
r 7.20	A4.18, B5.10
r 7.31	A5.1
r 7.33	C5.44
rr 7.33–7.42	C15.2
r 7.47	A5.1, B5.16, C 5.2, I8.10
(1)	C5.45, I8.10
(2)	A5.1, I8.10
(4)	C5.45
r 7.49	I8.10
r 7.49(1)	A5.1
r 7.51	I8.8
r 7.55	C5.22
r 7.61	A5.1, C5.2, C11.23, C11.24
rr 8.1–8.7	A6.1, C11.2, E2.5
rr 9.1–9.6	A4.19
rr 10.1–10.4	C5.47
r 11.1(2)(b)	C14.2
r 11.2	C14.2, C15.6, C15.7
(1A)	C14.2
r 11.3	C14.4
(2)	C14.3, G2.1
rr11.4	C15.7
r 11.5(2)	C15.7
r 11.6	C15.7
r 11.7	C15.6, C15.7
r 11.8(1)–(3)	C14.7
r 11.9	C14.32
rr 11.10, 11.11	C15.4
r 11.12	C14.2
r 11.13	C14.20
r 12.2	A5.1, C15.2
r 12.3	C14.13, F2.4
(2A)	C14.13, C14.35
r 12.4A	A6.2, C11.12, D4.5
r 12.7	C1.3, C5.33
r 12.8(1)–(3)	A4.3
r 12.9	B3.1, C5.45
r 12.12	A4.19
r 12.13	C11.19, C14.21
(4)	A4.22
r 12.15	C11.19
r 12.16	C11.16, C11.19, E3.1
r 12.18	C11.19
r 13.2	C11.23
rr 13.3–13.5	A5.1

r 13.12	C14.13, C14.21, C14.26, F2.4
Sch 4	A1.1
1986 Insolvent Companies (Disqualification of Unfit Directors)	
Proceedings Rules	
SI 1986, No 612	I1.1
1986 Insolvent Companies (Report on Conduct of Directors) Rules	
SI 1986, No 611	I1.1
1986 Insolvent Companies (Report on Conduct of Directors)	
(No 2) Rules	
SI 1986, No 2134	A6.2, I1.1
r 3	A4.9
1986 Insolvent Companies (Report on Conduct of Directors)	
(No 2) (Scotland) Rules	
SI 1986, No 1916	A6.2
1986 Insolvent Partnerships Order	
SI 1986, No 2142	A6.2, C1.3, C5.8, C5.19, C11.22, E1.2
art 2	C5.19
1986 Insurance Companies (Winding Up) (Amendment) Rules	
SI 1986, No 2002	A6.2, C1.3, C5.27, C5.50, C14.23
1986 Insurance Companies (Winding Up) (Scotland) Rules	
SI 1986, No 1918	A6.2, C1.3, C5.27, C11.19, C12.13,
	C14.1, C14.23, C15.2
r 5	C15.4
r 23	C15.4
1986 Land Registration (Companies and Insolvency) Regulations	
SI 1986, No 2116	A6.2
1986 Receivers (Scotland) Regulations	
SI 1986, No 1917	A6.2, D11.1
reg 4	D11.2
reg 6	D11.11
reg 7	D11.11
1986 Supreme Court (Fees) (Amendment) (No 2) Order	
SI 1986, No 2144	A6.2
1986 Value Added Tax (Bad Debt Relief) Regulations	
SI 1986, No 335	B5.18, C14.8, D4.7
1986 Value Added Tax (General) (Amendment) (No 2) Regulations	
SI 1986, No 305	D7.13
1987 Companies (Forms) (Amendment) Regulations	
SI 1987, No 752	A6.2
Sch 2	C1.3, C3.8
1987 Counterfeit Goods (Customs) Regulations	
SI 1987, No 2097	A6.2
1987 Financial Services (Clients' Money) Regulations	F6.2
1987 Financial Services Act 1986 (Delegation) Order	
SI 1987, No 942	C5.27
1987 Insolvency (Amendment of Subordinate Legislation) Order	
SI 1987, No 1398	A6.2
1987 Insolvency (Amendment) Regulations	
SI 1987, No 1959	A6.2
1987 Insolvency (Amendment) Rules	
SI 1987, No 1919	A1.1, A2.1, A6.2, B1.1, B3.1, B5.4,
	C1.3, D1.3, E1.2, E2.5
1987 Insolvency (ECSC Levy Debts) Regulations	
SI 1987, No 2093	A6.2, D7.4
1987 Insolvency (Scotland) (Amendment) Rules	
SI 1987, No 1921	A2.1, A6.2, B1.1, D11.1, E1.2
r 3	C1.3
Schs 1, 2	C1.3
1987 Insolvent Companies (Disqualification of Unfit Directors)	
Proceedings Rules	
SI 1987, No 2023	A6.2, I1.1

r 1(3) — I8.8, I1.10
r 2 — I8.3, I8.8
r 3 — I8.3, I8.4, I8.6, I8.7
r 4 — I2.5, I8.3
r 5 — I1.1, I8.4
r 6 — I8.4, I8.6
r 7 — I8.6, I8.10
r 8(2) — I6.1
r 9 — I8.8

1987 Stamp Duty (Exempt Instruments) Regulations
SI 1987, No 516 — C15.9

1988 Companies (Forms) (Amendment) Regulations
SI 1988, No 1359 — C1.3

1988 Department of Trade and Industry (Fees) Order
SI 1988, No 93 — A6.2

1988 Distress for Rent Rules
SI 1988, No 2050 — D7.13

1988 Insolvency (Amendment) Regulations
SI 1988, No 1739 — A6.2

1988 Insolvency Fees (Amendment) Order
SI 1988, No 95 — A6.2, B7.2, C11.27

1989 Banks (Administration Proceedings) Order
SI 1989, No 1276 — A6.2, B3.1
Sch — B2.1

1989 Community Charges (Administration and Enforcement)
Regulations
SI 1989, No 438 — D7.13

1989 Companies (Northern Ireland) Order
SI 1989, No 2404 — I1.1

1989 Insolvency (Amendment) Rules
SI 1989, No 397 — A1.1, A2.1, A6.2, B1.1, C1.3, D1.3, E1.2

1989 Insolvency (Northern Ireland) Order
SI 1989, No 2405 — A2.4, A6.2, C5.6

1989 Insolvency Act (Guernsey) Order
SI 1989, No 2409 — A2.4, A5.2, A6.2, C5.6

1989 Non–Domestic Rating (Collection and Enforcement) Regulations
SI 1989, No 1058
reg 4 — D7.13
reg 14 — D7.13
Sch 13 — D7.13

1989 Non–Domestic Rating (Unoccupied Property) Regulations
SI 1989, No 2261 — D8.11

1990 Bankruptcy and Companies (Department of Trade and Industry)
(Fees) (Amendment) Order
SI 1990, No 559 — A6.2

1990 Companies Act 1989 (Commencement No 8 and Transitional and
Saving Provisions) Order
SI 1990, No 2569
art 7 — D2.2, D2.3

1990 Companies (Forms) Amendment Regulations
SI 1990, No 572 — A6.2, C1.3

1990 Companies (Unregistered Companies) (Amendment No 3)
Regulations
SI 1990, No 2571 — D2.2, D2.3

1990 Insolvency Fees (Amendment) Order
SI 1990, No 560 — A6.2, C5.34, C11.27

1990 Insolvency Practitioners Regulations
SI 1990, No 439 — A6.2
Pt III — A4.3
Pt IV — A4.4
regs 4, 5–8, 10 — A4.2

	reg 12	A4.3
	(1)(c)	A4.3
	regs 13–15	A4.3
	reg 15A	A4.3
	reg 20	A4.4
	Sch 2 Pt I	A4.2, A4.3
	Pt II	A4.3
	Sch 3	A4.4
1990	**Land Registration (Execution of Deeds) Order**	
	SI 1990, No 1010	D9.17
1991	**Bankruptcy and Companies (Department of Trade and Industry) Fees (Amendment) Order**	
	SI 1991, No 494	A6.2
1991	**Companies Act 1989 (Commencement No 9 and Saving and Transitional Provisions) Order**	
	SI 1991, No 488	F1.1
1991	**Companies Act 1989 (Commencement No 10 and Saving Provisions) Order**	
	SI 1991, No 878	F1.1, F6.4, F6.19, F6.20, F6.23–F6.25
1991	**Environmental Protection (Prescribed Processes and Substances) Regulations**	
	SI 1991, No 472	
	Sch 1	D8.20
1991	**Financial Markets and Insolvency Regulations**	
	SI 1991, No 880	F1.1
	reg 3	F6.2
	reg 5	F6.7
	reg 6	F6.12
	reg 7	F6.18
	reg 8	F6.19
	reg 9	F6.18
	reg 10(1)	F6.19
	(2)–(4)	F6.19
	regs 11–13	F6.19
	regs 14, 15	F6.18, F6.20
	reg 17	F6.3, F6.4
	reg 18	F6.20
	reg 19	F6.27
1991	**Insolvency (Amendment) Regulations**	
	SI 1991, No 380	A6.2
1991	**Insolvency (Amendment) Rules**	
	SI 1991, No 495	A1.1, A2.1, A6.2, B1.1, C1.3, D1.3, E1.2
1991	**Insolvency Fees (Amendment) Order**	
	SI 1991, No 496	A6.2, C5.34, C11.27
1991	**Value Added Tax (Refunds for Bad Debts) Regulations**	
	SI 1991, No 371	B5.18, C14.8, D4.7
1992	**Companies Single Member Private Limited Companies Regulations**	
	SI 1992, No 1699	C5.10
1992	**Council Tax (Administration and Enforcement) Regulations**	
	SI 1992, No 613	D7.13
1992	**Employment Protection (Variation of Limits) Order**	
	SI 1992, No 312	D7.2
1992	**Financial Markets and Insolvency (Amendment) Regulations**	
	SI 1992, No 716	F1.1
1992	**Insolvency Fees (Amendment) Order**	
	SI 1991, No 34	A6.2, C11.27, C12.15
1992	**Insurance Companies (Amendment) Regulations**	
	SI 1992, No 445	C14.23
1992	**Transfer of Functions (Financial Services) Order**	
	SI 1992, No 1315	F6.1

1992 Value Added Tax (Accounting and Records) Order
SI 1992, No 2248 — D9.17

1992 Value Added Tax (Special Provisions) Order
SI 1992, No 3129 — D8.5
art 5 — D9.13, H2.8

1992 Workplace (Health, Safety and Welfare) Regulations
SI 1992, No 3004 — D8.8

1993 County Court Fees (Amendment) Order
SI 1993, No 2762 — A6.2

1993 Income Tax (Employments) Regulations
SI 1993, No 744
reg 4(1) — H3.12
reg 54 — D7.13

1993 Income Tax (Sub–contractors in the Construction Industry) Regulations
SI 1993, No 743
reg 19 — D7.13

1993 Insolvency (Amendment) Rules
SI 1993, No 602 — A1.1, A2.1, A6.2, B1.1, C1.3

1993 Insolvency Practitioners (Amendment) Regulations
SI 1993, No 221 — A4.2, A4.3

1993 Judgment Debts (Rate of Interest) Order
SI 1993, No 564 — C3.2, C14.19

1993 Unfair Dismissal (Increase of Compensation Limit) Order
SI 1993, No 1348 — D7.2

1994 Insolvency Fees (Amendment) Order
SI 1994, No 2541 — C11.27

1994 Insolvency Regulations
SI 1994, No 2507 — C11.27, C12.15
reg 11 — C11.18
reg 13 — C16.10
reg 14 — C11.18
reg 16(1),(2) — C16.10
reg 18 — C16.11

1994 Insolvent Partnerships Order
SI 1994, No 2421 — C5.2, C5.4, C5.8, C5.19, C5.20, C5.27, C5.35, C5.41, C5.42, C5.47–C5.51, C9.10, C11.1, C11.22, C11.25, C11.26, C13.5, C14.34, C14.37, C15.2, E1.2
arts 2, 3 — C9.13
art 4 — E1.2
art 5(1),(2) — E1.2
art 7 — C5.19, C5.27
art 8 — C5.19, C5.27, C5.30. C15.4
art 9 — C5.19, C5.27
art 10 — C5.19, C5.27, C5.30, C15.4
(2),(3) — C5.23
art 12 — C5.19
art 16 — I1.1
Sch 1 — E1.2
Sch 3 — C5.19, C5.25, C5.27, C5.30, C5.33, C15.4
Pt I — C5.23
Sch 5 — C5.25
Sch 6 — C5.19, C5.25, C5.27, C5.30, C5.33, C15.4
Sch 8 — I1.1
Sch 9 — C5.33, C5.34

Table of Cases

A & B C Chewing Gum Ltd, Re [1975] 1 WLR 579 — C5.26
ABC Coupler and Engineering Co Ltd, Re [1961] 1 WLR 243 — C5.26
ABC Coupler and Engineering Co Ltd, Re (No 2) [1962] 1 WLR 1236 — C5.34
ABC Coupler and Engineering Co Ltd, Re (No 3) [1970] 1 All ER 650 — C12.18
AE Realisations Ltd, Re [1987] BCLC 486 — C12.6
AEG (UK) Ltd, Re [1994] STI 135 — E4.1
AEVO Ltd v D & A MacLeod Co (Canada) (1991) 7 CBR (3d) 33 — C14.35
AGB Research plc, Re [1994] EGCS 73 — B4.1, D7.14
AIB Finance Ltd v Bank of Scotland [1994] BCC 184 — D6.2, D11.1
ARV Aviation Ltd, Re (1988) 4 BCC 708 — B6.1
AT & T Istel Ltd, Re [1992] 3 WLR 344, HL — A4.19
Abbey Leisure Ltd, Re [1990] BCC 60 — C5.30
Abrahams & Others v Nelson Hurst and Marsh Ltd The Times,
  9 June 1989 — C14.24
Accurist Watches v King [1992] FSR 80 — D7.18
Acli Metals (London) Ltd, Re [1989] BCLC 749 — A4.19, A4.21
Adam Eyton Ltd, Re (1887) 36 Ch D 299 — C11.28
Adams (A J) (Builders) Ltd, Re [1991] BCC 62 — C11.27
Adelaide Truss & Frame Ltd v Bianco Hiring Services Ltd (Australia)
  (1993) 1 ACLC 192 — C8.4
Advance Insulation Ltd, Re (1989) 5 BCC 55 — G3.3
Adviser (188) Ltd, Re; Trachtenburg, ex parte [1993] BCC 492, CA — A4.19
African Farms Ltd [1906] TS 373 — A5.3
Aga Estate Agencies Ltd, Re [1986] BCLC 346 — G3.2, G3.3
Agip (Africa) Ltd v Jackson [1989] 3 WLR 1367 — D7.22
Agricultural Mortgage Corporation plc v Woodward and Another
  [1994] BCC 688 — C10.2, C10.10
Aiden Shipping Co Ltd v Interbulk Ltd [1986] AC 965, HL — C5.44
Air Ecosse Ltd v Civil Aviation Authority (1987) 3 BCC 492 — B4.1
Air India v Balabel (1990) 30 EG 90 — D9.7
Airline Airspares Ltd v Handley Page Ltd [1970] Ch 193 — D7.24, D8.15, F2.3
Aldermanbury Trust plc, Re [1993] BCC 598 — I8.6
Allan v Stirling District Council [1994] IRLR 208 — D9.16
Allobrogia Steamship Corporation, Re [1978] 3 All ER 423 — C5.8
Alsop v Star Vehicle Contracts Ltd [1990] IRLR 83 — D8.3
Aluminium Industrie Vaasen BV v Romalpa Aluminium Ltd [1976]
  2 All ER 552 — D7.18
Amalgamated Investment & Property Co Ltd v Texas Commerce
  International Bank Ltd [1982] QB 84 — D2.12
Amalgamated Investment and Property Co Ltd, Re [1984]
  3 All ER 272 — C14.19, C14.33
Amalgamated Properties of Rhodesia Ltd, Re (1914) 30 TLR 405 — C11.28
American Cyanamid Co v Ethicon Ltd [1975] 1 All ER 504 — A5.3, C5.30
American Express International Banking Corporation v Hurley
  [1985] 3 All ER 564 — D8.14
Anderson v Dalkeith Engineering Ltd [1984] IRLR 429 — D9.16
Andrabell Ltd (in liquidation), Re [1984] 3 All ER 407 — D7.18
Anglo-Austrian Printing and Publishing Union [1895] 2 Ch 891 — C13.4
Anglo-Baltic Bank v Barber & Co [1924] 2 KB 410 — C7.4
Anglo-Italian Bank v Davies (1878) 9 Ch D 275 — C14.30
Angus Jowett & Co Ltd v NUTGW [1985] IRLR 326, EAT — D7.1, D9.16
Anvil Estates Ltd, Re (1994) Unreported — C5.29
Apex Leisure Hire v Barratt [1984] IRLR 224 — D9.16

Aquila Design (GRB) Products Ltd v Cornhill Insurance plc [1988]
BCLC 134   A4.24, D8.16
Arab Bank plc v Mercantile Holdings Ltd [1994] 2 WLR 307   D9.17
Arbuthnot Leasing International Ltd v Havelet Leasing Ltd [1990]
BCLC 802   C5.34
Arbuthnot Leasing International Ltd v Havelet Leasing Ltd (No 2) [1990]
BCC 636   C10.10
Arch Joinery Contracts Ltd v Arcade Building Services Ltd 1992
SLT 755   A4.24
Arctic Engineering Ltd and Others, Re (1985) 1 BCC 99, 563, [1986]
BCLC 253, [1986] 1 WLR 686   A4.7, C11.25, I2.2
Argentum Reductions (UK) Ltd, Re [1975] 1 WLR 186   C5.30, C8.4
Armagh Shoes Ltd, Re [1984] BCLC 409   D6.2
Armorduct Manufacturing Co v General Incandescent Co [1911]
2 KB 143   C8.3, C9.4
Armour v Thyssen [1990] 3 All ER 481   D7.18
Armstrong v Coopers & Lybrand Ltd (Canada) (1987) 65 CBR (NS)
258, Ont CA   D6.2
Armstrong Whitworth Securities Co, Re [1947] Ch 673   G2.1, C14.1
Armvent Ltd, Re [1975] 1 WLR 1679   C5.31, C5.34
Arnold (R M) & Co Ltd, Re [1984] BCLC 535   C12.10
Aro Co Ltd, Re [1980] Ch 196, [1980] 2 WLR 453   C14.30, D7.12
Arrow Leeds Ltd, Re [1986] BCLC 538   C5.44
Arrows Ltd, Re [1992] BCC 446   A4.19
Arrows Ltd, Re (No 1) [1992] BCC 121   C11.28
Arrows Ltd, Re (No 2) [1992] BCC 125   A4.19
Arrows Ltd, Re (No 3) [1992] BCC 131   B2.1
Arrows Ltd, Re (No 4) [1994] BCC 641, aff'g [1993] BCC 473, rev'g
[1992] BCC 987   A4.19
Art Reproduction Co Ltd, Re [1952] Ch 89   C14.13
Artistic Colour Printing Co, Re (1880) 14 Ch D 502   C8.2
Ashberg (C & M), Re The Times, 17 July 1990   C5.19
Ashley & Smith Ltd, Re [1918] 2 Ch 378   D7.4
Ashley Guarantee plc v Zacaria [1993] 1 All ER 254   D1.5, D2.8, D7.5
Asiatic Electric Co Pty Ltd, Re (Australia) (1970) 92 WN (NSW) 361   C13.4
Aspen Property v Ratcliffe (1993) Unreported, 24 July, CA   D8.15
Asphaltic Limestone Concrete Co v Glasgow Corporation 1907 SC 463   C9.6
Associated British Ports Ltd v C H Bailey plc [1990] 1 All ER 929,
Financial Times, 27 March 1990, HL   B4.1, D7.14
Association of Patternmakers & Allied Craftsmen v Kirvin Ltd
[1978] IRLR 318   D7.1
Astor Chemicals Ltd v Synthetic Technology Ltd [1990]
BCC 97   A5.1, B3.1, B7.5
Atlantic Computer Systems plc, Re [1992] 2 WLR 367,
[1992] 1 All ER 476, CA   B4.1, B4.2, B7.7, D6.2
Atlantic Medical Ltd, Re [1992] BCLC 653   D6.2
Attorney-General for Hong Kong v Reid [1994] 1 AC 324   D7.22
Auchtertyre Farmers EDN/87/109 No 2822   D9.13
Augustus Barnett & Son Ltd, Re [1986] BCLC 170   C13.1
Ault v Gregory (1967) 2 ITR 301   D9.16
Auriferous Properties Ltd, Re (No 1) [1898] 1 Ch 691   C12.1
Auriferous Properties Ltd, Re (No 2) [1898] 2 Ch 428   C12.1
Austinsuite Furniture Ltd, Re [1992] BCLC 1047   C13.2, I5.4, I6.1
Australian Home Finance Pty Ltd, Re (Australia) [1956] VLR 1   C15.4
Aveling Barford Ltd v Perion Ltd (1989) 5 BCC 677   C12.9, C13.4, D9.1

Aveling Barford Ltd, Re [1989] 1 WLR 360, (1988) 4
   BCC 448   A4.19, A4.20, D7.7
Ayala Holdings Ltd, Re [1993] BCLC 256   C10.10, C13.4
Ayerst v C & K Construction Ltd [1976] AC 167, [1975]
   3 WLR 16   C2.4, C9.9, C9.10, D9.5, H2.2
Ayres and Moore, Re [1989] LMCLQ 281   C13.2
Ayres v Evans (Australia) (1981) 39 ALR 129, aff'g (1981) 34 ALR 582   C14.13
Azoff-Don Commercial Bank, Re [1954] Ch 315   C5.6, C5.8

BSB Holdings Ltd, Re [1993] BCLC 246   C5.30
Baby Moon (UK) Ltd, Re [1985] PCC 103   C5.2
Bacal Contracting Ltd v Modern Engineering (Bristol) Ltd [1980]
   2 All ER 655   C9.8, D8.16
Baku Consolidated Oilfields Ltd, Re [1993] BCC 653   C15.9
Baltic Real Estate Ltd, Re (No 1) [1993] BCLC 498   C5.30
Baltic Real Estate Ltd, Re (No 2) [1993] BCLC 503   C5.30
Bamford Publishers Ltd, Re The Times, 4 June 1977   C5.31
Banco de Portugal v Waddell (1880) 5 App Cas 161   C5.6, C14.27
Banister v London Borough of Islington (1972) 71 LGR 239   D8.11
Bank of Baroda v Panessar and Others [1986] BCLC 497   D2.8
Bank of Boston Connecticut v European Grain Shipping Ltd;
   (The Dominique) [1989] 1 All ER 545   D7.5
Bank of Credit and Commerce International SA, Re [1992]
   BCC 83   C5.42, C9.10
Bank of Credit and Commerce International SA, Re [1994]
   IRLR 282   C14.22
Bank of Credit and Commerce International SA, Re (No 2)
   [1992] BCC 715   C11.26, C15.4
Bank of Credit and Commerce International SA, Re (No 3)
   [1994] BCC 462 (also reported as No 8 [1994] 1 BCLC 758)   C14.26, F2.8
Bank of Credit and Commerce International SA; Bank of Credit
   and Commerce (Overseas) Ltd, Re [1993] BCC 787   A5.2, C10.1, C13.6
Bank of England v Riley [1992] 1 All ER 769   A4.19
Bank of Montreal v Titan Landco Inc (Canada) (1989) 72 CBR (NS)
   262, BCSC   D6.2
Bank of Scotland v Pacific Shelf (Sixty Two) Ltd (1988) 4
   BCC 457   C10.3, C10.5
Bank of Scotland v Wright [1991] BCLC 244   D2.8, D2.12
Bank of South Australia, Re [1895] 1 Ch 578   C5.8
Banking, Insurance and Finance Union v Barclays Bank plc
   [1987] ICR 495   D9.16
Banner, ex parte (1881) 17 Ch D 480   C14.10
Banque Brussels Lambert SA v Australian National Industries Ltd
   (Australia) (1990) International Business Lawyer, Jul/Aug, p.289   C13.2
Banque des Marchands de Moscou v Kindersley [1951] Ch 112   C5.8
Banque Indoseuz SA v Ferromet Resources Inc [1993] BCLC 112   A5.3
Barbor v Middleton (1988) 4 BCC 681   C5.30
Barclays Bank Ltd v Quistclose Investments Ltd [1970] AC 567   D7.22
Barclays Bank plc v Homan [1992] BCC 757   A5.3, B10.1
Barclays Bank plc v Waterson [1989] CLY 2505   D1.5
Barclays Bank plc v Willowbrook Ltd [1987] BCLC 717   D6.2
Barclays Bank v TOSG Trust Fund [1984] 2 WLR 650, HL, aff'g (1983)
   127 SJ 130, CA   C14.9
Barclays Mercantile Business Finance Ltd v Sibec Developments Ltd
   [1992] 1 WLR 1253   B4.1, B7.1

Barleycorn Enterprises Ltd, Re [1970] 2 All ER 155 — D10.3
Barlow Clowes (Gilt Managers) Ltd, Re [1991] 4 All ER 385 — A4.19, C11.24
Barlow v Whittle [1990] IRLR 79 — D8.3
Barn Crown Ltd, Re [1994] BCC 381 — C8.4
Barnett, ex parte; Deveze, Re (1874) 9 Ch App 293 — C14.26
Barratt Apartments Ltd, Re (Ireland) [1985] IR 350 — C14.31, D7.22
Barrow Borough Transport Ltd, Re (1989) 5 BCC 646 — B4.1, C12.10
Barrows v Chief Land Registrar The Times, 20 October
1977 — C8.4, C9.8, D5.2, D8.11
Barton Thompson & Co Ltd v Stapling Machines Co [1966] 1 Ch 499 — D7.14
Barton-on-Humber Water Co, Re (1889) 42 Ch D 585 — C5.8
Bascal Contracting Ltd v Modern Engineering (Bristol) Ltd [1980]
2 All ER 655 — C5.44
Bateson (John) & Co Ltd, Re [1985] BCLC 259 — C11.24, C12.10
Bath Glass Ltd, Re (1988) 4 BCC 130 — I2.5, I5.2, I6.1
Bathampton Properties Ltd, Re [1976] 1 WLR 1685 — C5.44
Beacon Leisure Ltd, Re [1991] BCC 213 — C10.4
Beale v Worth [1993] EGCS 135 — D9.7
Beeton & Co Ltd, Re [1913] 2 Ch 279 — D7.4
Belfast Tailors Company Partnership, Re [1909] 1 IR 49 — C5.8
Belhaven Brewery Co Ltd v Berekis and Others (1993) Industrial
Relations Law Bulletin 484, 9 — D9.16
Bell v Lothinsure (in liquidation) The Times, 2 February 1990 — C14.24
Belmont & Co Ltd, Re [1952] Ch 10 — G3.1, G3.2, G3,4
Berg and Busschers v Besselen [1989] IRLR 447 — D9.16
Bergsoe Metal Corp, Re (USA) 910 F 2d 668 (9th Cir 1990) — D8.25
Berkeley Applegate (Investment Consultants) Ltd (1988) 4 BCC 274 — D7.22
Berkeley Applegate (Investment Consultants) Ltd, Re (No 2) (1988)
4 BCC 279 — C11.25
Berkeley Applegate (Investment Consultants) Ltd, Re (No 3) (1989)
5 BCC 803 — C11.25
Berry (Herbert) Associates Ltd, Re [1976] 1 WLR 783 — C9.4
Bethell v Trench Tubeless Tyre Co [1900] 1 Ch 408 — C3.3
Bhogal v Punjab National Bank [1988] 2 All ER 296 — D7.5
Bi-Print Ltd, Re (1989) 22 June; (1989) 2 Insolvency Intelligence 76 — C5.29
Biddencare Ltd, Re [1993] BCC 757 — D7.22
Biggerstaff v Rowatt's Wharf Ltd [1896] 2 Ch 93 — D7.13
Bill Hennessey Associates Ltd, Re [1992] BCC 386 — C5.36
Billson v Residential Apartments Ltd [1992] 1 AC 494, [1992]
1 WLR 15, HL rev'g [1991] 3 All ER 265, CA — B1.1, D7.14
Billson v Residential Apartments Ltd [1993] EGCS 150, re-Trial — D7.14
Bishop v Bonham (1988) 4 BCC 347, CA — D8.14
Bishopsgate Investment Management Ltd (in liquidation) v Maxwell
[1993] BCC 120 — C13.4
Bishopsgate Investment Managent Ltd, Re: M G N v Maxwell [1992]
BCC 222, aff'g [1992] BCC 214 — A4.19
Blackburn (W) and Co, Re [1899] 2 Ch 725 — C10.4
Blackpool and Fylde Aero Club Ltd v Blackpool Borough Council
[1990] 1 WLR 1195 — D9.15
Blakeley, Re (1892) 9 Mor 173 — C14.33
Blakely Ordnance Co, Re; Brett's Case (1873) 8 Ch App 800 — C12.20
Bletchley Boat Co Ltd, Re [1974] 1 WLR 630 — A4.19
Blue Jeans Ltd, Re [1979] 1 All ER 641 — C8.2
Blum v OCP Repartition SA [1988] BCLC 170 — C13.3
Bold v Brough, Nicholson & Hall Ltd [1963] 3 All ER 849 — C14.22

Bolland, ex parte (1834) 1 M CA 570 — C14.13

Bolton (H L) Engineering Co Ltd, Re [1956] Ch 577 — C5.30

Bolton Metropolitan District Council v Malrod Insulations Ltd [1993] ICR 658 — D8.6

Bond Worth Ltd, Re [1979] 3 All ER 919 — D7.18

Bonsor v Patara (1967) 2 KIR 23 — D9.16

Bonus Breaks Ltd, Re [1991] BCC 546 — C9.1

Borax Co Ltd, Re [1901] 1 Ch 326 — D6.2

Borden (UK) Ltd v Scottish Timber Products Ltd [1979] 3 All ER 961 — D7.18

Bork (P) International A/E (in liquidation) v Foreningen Arbejtsledere I Danmark (ECJ) [1989] IRLR 41 — D9.16

Borough of Portsmouth Tramways Co, Re [1892] 2 Ch 362 — C5.29

Boston Timber Fabrications Ltd, Re [1984] BCLC 328 — C5.42

Botibol, Re; Botibol v Botibol [1947] 1 All ER 26 — B7.7, D5.2, D8.3, D8.15

Bovey Hotel Ventures Ltd, Re (1981) Unreported, 31 July — C5.30

Bradley v Eagle Star Insurance Co Ltd [1989] 2 WLR 568 — G2.1, G3.2

Bradman v Trinity Estates plc (1989) 5 BCC 33 — C3.7

Braemar Investments Ltd, Re (1988) 4 BCC 366 — C12.10

Bratton Seymour Service Co v Oxborough [1992] BCC 471 — D2.3

Briant Colour Printing Co Ltd, Re [1977] 1 WLR 942 — D8.11

Bridge v Campbell Discount Co Ltd [1962] 1 All ER 385 — C8.3

Brightlife Ltd, Re [1986] BCLC 418 — B6.4, D6.2, D6.3

Brinsmead (T E) & Sons, Re [1897] 1 Ch 406 — C5.26

Bristol Airport plc v Powdrill [1990] 2 WLR 1362, [1990] BCLC 585, sub nom Paramount Airways Ltd, Re [1990] BCC 130 — B4.1, B4.2, C8.2, D7.7

British Airways Board v Laker Airways Ltd [1985] 1 AC 58, HL — A5.3, B10.1

British and Commonwealth Holdings plc, Re (No 2) [1992] BCC 977, HL, aff'g [1992] BCC 165 & 172, CA — A4.19

British & Commonwealth Holdings plc, Re (No 3) [1992] BCC 58, [1992] BCLC 322, [1992] 11 JIBL 471 — B2.1, E2.5

British Columbia v Gilbertson (Canada) 597 F 2d 1161 (1979) — C14.13

British Eagle International Airlines Ltd v Compagnie Nationale Air France [1975] 1 WLR 758, [1975] 2 All ER 390 — C8.3, C12.10, C12.19, C15.4, D6.2, F2.9, F3.3, F3.5, F3.6, F5.3, F6.6

British Steel plc v Elliott (1991) Industrial Relations Legal Information Bulletin 425, 24 May — D8.3

British Transport Commission v Gourley [1956] AC 185 — C14.22, D7.2

Britton & Millard, Re (1957) 107 LJ 602 — C5.29

Bromley Park Garden Estates Ltd v Moss [1982] 2 All ER 890 — D9.7

Brompton Securities Ltd, Re (1988) 4 BCC 189 — C8.2

Brompton Securities Ltd, Re (No 2) (1988) 4 BCC 436 — C12.17

Brook Lane Finance Co Ltd v Bradley [1988] IRLR 283, EAT — D9.16

Brook Martin and Co (Nominees) Ltd, Re [1992] EGCS 138 — A4.19

Brooke Marine Ltd, Re [1988] BCLC 546 — B2.1

Brooks Transport (Purfleet) Ltd, Re [1993] BCC 766 — I8.9

Brown v Cork [1985] BCLC 363, CA — C12.17, D10.4

Brown v Gregory [1904] 1 Ch 627, 2 Ch 448 — C14.26

Brown v Gregory [1904] 1 Ch 410 — D7.5

Brown v Southall & Knight [1980] IRLR 130 — D9.16

Brown's Estate, Re [1893] 2 Ch 300 — C14.26

Brown, Bayley & Dixon, Re (1881) 17 Ch D 649 — C12.18

Buchanan (Peter) Ltd v McVey (Ireland) [1955] AC 520 — C14.13

Bulawayo Market and Offices Co Ltd, Re [1907] 2 Ch 458 — C13.2, I1.1

Bulteel and Colmore v Parker and Bulteel's Trustee (1916) 32
 TLR 661   C10.4
Bunbury Foods v National Bank of Australia (Australia) [1954]
 ALJ 199   D2.8
Burford Midland Properties Ltd v Marley Extrusions Ltd
 [1994] BCC 604   E3.1
Burnham Marketing Services Ltd, Re [1993] BCC 518   I5.4, I6.1
Burston Finance Ltd v Speirway Ltd [1974] 3 All ER 735   D7.23
Burton & Deakin Ltd, Re [1977] 1 WLR 390   C8.4
Business Computers International Ltd v Registrar of Companies
 and Others [1987] BCLC 621   C5.36
Business Computers Ltd v Anglo-African Leasing Ltd [1977]
 2 All ER 741   D7.5, F2.4
Business Properties Ltd, Re (1988) 4 BCC 684   B2.1, B3.1, B3.2, C13.2
Busytoday Ltd, Re [1992] 4 All ER 61   A5.1
Butler and Another v Broadhead and Others [1974] 3 WLR 27   G2.1
Butterfield, ex parte (1811) 1 Rose 192   C14.10
Byblos Bank SAL v Al Khudhairy [1987] BCLC 232   C5.22, D2.4
Byng v London Life Association Ltd [1989] 2 WLR 737   C11.16

CCA v Brecht (Australia) (1989) 7 ACLC 40   I7.1
CCG International Enterprises Ltd, Re [1993] BCC 580   D6.2
CIBL v Coopers & Lybrand Ltd (Canada) [1989] 3 JIBL N-98,
 Alberta CA   D6.2
CIN Properties Ltd v Gill (1993) EG, 27 September   D9.7
CU Fittings Ltd, Re (1989) 5 BCC 210   I6.1
Cairney v Back [1906] 2 KB 746   D7.4, D7.10, D8.6
Calgary & Edmonton Land Co, Re [1975] 1 WLR 355   C5.46
Callaghan (Myles J) Ltd v City of Glasgow District Council (1987)
 3 BCC 337   D11.3
Callendar Sykes & Co v Lagos Colonial Secretary [1891] AC 460   C5.6
Calmex Ltd, Re (1988) 4 BCC 761   C5.45
Calor Gas Ltd v Piercy and Others [1994] BCC 69   E2.5
Cambridge Coffee Room Association Ltd, Re [1952] 1 All ER 112   G2.1
Cambridge Water Company v Eastern Counties Leather plc [1994]
 1 All ER 53, HL   D8.26
Camburn Petroleum Products Ltd, Re [1979] Ch 297   C5.29
Camden Breweries Ltd, Re (1912) 106 LT 598, CA   D6.2
Campbell Coverings Ltd, Re (No 1) [1953] Ch 488   C11.22
Campbell Coverings Ltd, Re (No 2) [1954] Ch 225   C11.22
Campbell Meads plc (in administration), Re (1991) Unreported,
 24 September   B1.1
Canada Deposit Insurance Corporation v Canadian Commercial Bank
 (Canada) [1993] 1 JIBL N-7   C14.35
Canadian Land Reclaiming and Colonising Co (1880) 17 Ch D 660   C13.4
Canniford v Smith and Others, Financial Times, 21 December 1990   C5.30
Cannon Screen Entertainment Ltd, Re [1989] BCLC 660   C5.44
Canon (Scotland) Business Machines Ltd, Noter [1992] BCC 620   C8.2
Capital Cameras Ltd v Harold Lines Ltd [1991] 1 WLR 54   D8.16
Capital Finance Co Ltd v Stokes [1969] 1 Ch 261   D7.23
Carecraft Construction Co Ltd, Re [1993] BCC 336   I8.6
Cargo Agency Ltd, Re [1992] BCC 388   I6.1, I7.3
Caribbean Products (Yam Importers) Ltd, Re [1966] Ch 331   C9.3, C9.4
Carlos Federspeil & Co SA v Charles Twigg & Co Ltd [1957] 1
 Lloyd's Rep 240   D7.25

Carr v British International Helicopters Ltd [1993] BCC 855 — B4.1
Carreras Rothmans Ltd v Freeman Mathews Treasure Ltd [1985]
    Ch 207, [1984] BCLC 420 — C15.4, D7.22
Carrington Viyella plc, Re (1983) 1 BCC 98,951 — C5.30
Carroll Group Distributors Ltd v G & JF Bourke Ltd (Ireland)
    [1990] ILRM 285 — D7.18
Cases of Taff Wells, Re [1992] BCLC 11 — C9.5
Casson Beckman & Partners v Papi [1991] BCLC 299 — C11.27
Castle New Homes Ltd, Re [1979] 1 WLR 1975 — A4.19
Castle Phillips Finance Company v Williams Unreported, Current
    Law 12/86 — C10.7
Caterleisure Ltd v Scottish Citybank Coaches Ltd EAT 182/91 — D9.16
Cavco Floors Ltd, Re [1990] BCC 589 — B3.1
Cedac, Re. See Secretary of State for Trade and Industry v Langridge;
    Cedac, Re
Centrebind Ltd, Re [1966] 3 All ER 889 — C4.9
Cerro Colorado, The [1993] 1 Lloyd's Rep 58 — D7.23
Chadwick v Chadwick (1852) 22 LJ Ch 329 — A4.19
Chancery plc, Re [1991] BCLC 712 — B3.1, B3.2
Chandles-Chandles v Nicholson [1942] 2 KB 321 — D7.14
Charge Card Services Ltd, Re [1986] 3 WLR 697, [1986]
    3 All ER 289 — C14.26, D6.2, D7.5,
    D9.1, F2.4, F2.8, F3.5-F3.7, F4.3, F6.4, F7.1
Charles Forte (Investments) Ltd v Amanda [1964] Ch 240 — C5.26
Charnley Davies Business Services Ltd and Others, Re (1987)
    3 BCC 408 — B5.2, B5.4, B5.16, B7.2, B7.9
Charnley Davies Business Services Ltd and Others, Re (No 2)
    [1990] BCC 605 — B7.6
Charterfield Goldfields Ltd, Re (1909) 26 TLR 132 — C11.24, C11.28
Chartmore Ltd, Re [1990] BCLC 673 — I7.3
Chase Manhattan (Asia) Ltd v First Bangkok City Finance Ltd
    (Hong Kong) (1988) FTLR, 15 July — C12.10, D7.23
Chase Manhattan (Asia) Ltd v Official Receiver and Liquidator of
    First Bangkok City Finance Ltd (Hong Kong) [1990] 1 WLR 1181 — D7.23
Chase Manhattan Bank NA v Israel-British Bank (London) Ltd [1979]
    3 All ER 1025 — D7.22
Chavasse, ex parte (1865) 34 LJ Bcy 17 — C14.13
Cheah Theam Swee v Equiticorp Finance Group Ltd (New Zealand)
    [1992] 1 AC 472, [1992] 2 WLR 108, PC — D10.4
Chelmsford City Football Club (1980) Ltd, Re [1991] BCC 133 — B3.2
Chelsea Cloisters Ltd, Re 41 P & CR 98 — D7.22
China and South Sea Bank Ltd v Tan Soon Gin [1990] 1 AC 536 — D8.14
Chohan v Saggar [1994] BCC 134, CA aff'g [1992] BCC 750 — C10.10
Choudri v Palta [1992] BCC 787, CA — D4.9, D7.23
Christonette International Ltd, Re [1982] 3 All ER 225 — D5.2, D7.3, D10.3
Churchill Hotel (Plymouth) Ltd, Re (1988) 4 BCC 112 — I6.1
Circle Freight International Ltd v Medeast [1989] 2 Lloyd's
    Rep 427, CA — D7.18
Circle Holidays International plc, Re [1994] BCC 226 — I8.5
City Equitable Fire Insurance Co Ltd, Re [1925] 1 Ch 407 — C13.2, C13.4, I5.4
City Equitable Fire Insurance Co Ltd, Re (No 2) [1930] 2 Ch 293 — C14.26
City Investment Centres Ltd, Re [1992] BCLC 956 — I6.1, I8.5
City of London Corporation v Bourn [1989] EGCS 136 — D9.7
City of London Insurance Co Ltd, Re [1932] 1 Ch 226 — C12.20
Cladrose Ltd, Re [1990] BCC 11 — I6.1

Clandown Colliery Co, Re [1915] 1 Ch 369 — C5.29
Clark v May (1852) 16 Beav 273 — C12.6
Clark, Re [1975] 1 WLR 599 — C11.24
Clarke Pipe & Supply Co Inc, Re (USA) 893 F 2d (5th Cir 1990);
  [1990] 7 JIBL N-175 — C14.35
Clarkes of Hove Ltd v Bakers Union [1978] IRLR 366 — D7.1
Clarkson (H) (Overseas) Ltd, Re (1987) 3 BCC 606 — G3.3
Clasper Group Services Ltd, Re (1988) 4 BCC 673 — C10.4, I7.1
Clay & Sons, Re (1896) 3 Mans 31 — C10.4
Claybridge Shipping Co SA, Re [1981] Com LR 107 — C5.29
Clayton's Case (1816) 1 Mer 572 — C10.9, D7.22
Clifton Place Garage Ltd, Re [1970] Ch 477 — C8.4
Clough Mill Ltd v Martin [1984] 3 All ER 982 — D7.18
Cloverbay Ltd v Bank of Credit and Commerce International
  [1990] 3 WLR 574, [1991] 1 All ER 894, CA — A4.19, C11.24
Cloverbay Ltd, Re (1988) Unreported and Undecided — D2.8
Cloverbay Ltd, Re (1989) 5 BCC 732 — A4.19, B3.2
Cloverbay Ltd, Re (No 3) [1990] BCLC 471 — A4.19
Clyde Football Co Ltd, Re (1901) 8 SLT 328 — D7.4
Coastplace Ltd v Hartley and Another [1987] 2 WLR 1289 — C12.6
Cock, Re; Shilson, ex parte (1887) 30 QBD 343 — C12.6
Coghlan v SH Lock (Australia) (1987) 3 BCC 183, PC — D2.12
Columbian Fireproofing Co, Re [1910] 2 Ch 120 — C10.9
Combined Weighing and Advertising Machine Co, Re (1889) 43 Ch D 99 — D8.6
Commercial and Industrial Insulations Ltd, Re [1986] BCLC 191 — C5.30
Commercial Bank of Australia v Official Assignee [1893] AC 181 — C14.33
Commercial Bank of South Australia, Re (1886) 33 Ch D 174 — C5.6
Commission v United Kingdom (ECJ) [1994] IRLR 392 — D7.1, D9.16
Commonwealth of Australia v Verwayen (Australia) (1990)
  95 ALR 321 — D7.25
Commonwealth v Amann Aviation Pty Ltd (Australia)
  (1991) 66 ALJR 12 — D9.15
Compania de Electricidad, Re [1980] 1 Ch 146 — C14.13
Compania Merabello San Nicholas SA, Re [1973] Ch 75 — C5.8
Companie de Electricidad de la Provincia de Buenos Aires, Re
  [1980] 1 Ch 146 — C9.5
Company, A, Re [1894] 2 Ch 349 — C5.36
Company, A, Re [1980] 1 All ER 284 — C13.4
Company, A, Re (No 002567 of 1982) [1983] 2 All ER 854 — C5.30
Company, A, Re (No 003729 of 1982) [1984] 1 WLR 1090 — C5.29
Company, A, Re (No 1573 of 1983) [1983] BCLC 492 — C5.36
Company, A, Re (No 006794 of 1983) [1986] BCLC 261 — C5.22
Company, A, Re [1984] BCLC 307 — C5.33
Company, A, Re (No 002612 of 1984) [1985] BCLC 430 — C5.30
Company, A, Re [1985] BCLC 37 — C5.22, C5.29
Company, A, Re (No 007339 of 1985) [1986] BCLC 127 — C5.36
Company, A, Re (No 008699 of 1985) (1986) 2 BCC 99,024 — B7.6, C5.30
Company, A, Re (No 007523 of 1986) [1987] BCLC 200 — C8.4
Company, A, Re (No 007623 of 1986) [1986] BCLC 362 — C5.30
Company, A, Re (No 00175 of 1987) [1987] BCLC 467 — B1.1, B2.1, B3.1, B3.2
Company, A, Re (No 00359 of 1987) [1987] 3 WLR 339 also reported
  as International Westminster Bank plc v Okeanos Maritime Corp
  [1987] BCLC 450 — C5.8
Company, A, Re (No 00370 of 1987), ex parte Glossop [1988] BCLC 570 — C5.30
Company, A, Re (No 00789 of 1987), ex parte Nuneaton Borough AFC

Ltd (1989) 5 BCC 92 — C5.30
Company, A, Re (No 003028 of 1987) [1988] BCLC 282 — C5.29
Company, A, Re (No 003318 of 1987) (1987) 3 BCC 564 — A4.19
Company, A, Re (No 005009 of 1987), ex parte Copp [1989] BCLC 13,
 (1988) 4 BCC 424 — C10.4, C13.2
Company, A, Re (No 001363 of 1988) (1989) 5 BCC 18 — C5.30
Company, A, Re (No 001418 of 1988) [1991] BCLC 197 — C13.1
Company, A, Re (No 001992 of 1988) (1988) 4 BCC 451 — B2.1, B4.1, C5.36
Company, A, Re (No 005685 of 1988), ex parte Schwartz [1989]
 BCLC 424 — C5.30, C8.4
Company, A, Re (No 001448 of 1989) [1989] BCLC 715, (1989) 5
 BCC 706 — B4.1, C5.36
Company, A, Re (No 001029 of 1990), ex parte F Ltd [1991]
 BCLC 567 — C5.34
Company, A, Re (No 003079 of 1990) [1991] BCLC 235 — C5.29
Company, A, Re (No 008790 of 1990) [1991] BCLC 561 — C5.22
Company, A, Re (No 009681 of 1990) (1990) Unreported, 23 November — C5.29
Company, A, Re (No 0010656 of 1990) [1991] BCLC 464 — C5.29
Company, A, Re, ex parte N D Pritchard Financial Times,
 22 November 1991 — C5.29
Company, A, Re (No 00687 of 1991) [1992] BCLC 133 — C5.30, C5.36, C8.4
Company, A, Re (No 00928 of 1991), ex parte City Electrical
 Factors Ltd [1991] BCLC 514 — C5.33
Company, A, Re (No 00962 of 1991), ex parte Electrical Engineering
 Contracts (London) Ltd [1992] BCLC 248 — C5.36
Company, A, Re (No 001259 of 1991), ex parte Medialite Ltd [1991]
 BCLC 594 — C5.29
Company, A, Re (No 001946 of 1991), ex parte Fin Soft Holding SA
 [1991] BCLC 737 — C5.29
Company, A, Re (No 003102 of 1991), ex parte Nyckeln Finance Co
 Ltd [1991] BCLC 539 — C5.8, C5.41
Company, A, Re (No 004055 of 1991) (See also Record Tennis Centres
 Ltd, Re) [1991] 1 WLR 1003 — C5.44
Company, A, Re (No 11102 of 1991) [1992] EGCS 79, [1992] 1 Re
 LR 288 — C5.29
Company, A, Re (No 0012209 of 1991) [1992] 1 WLR 351 — C5.29
Company, A, Re (No 0013734 of 1991) [1993] BCLC 59, [1992]
 2 Lloyd's Rep 415 — C5.29, C12.22
Company, A, Re (No 0013925 of 1991), ex parte Rousell [1992]
 BCLC 562 — C5.36
Company, A, Re, ex parte Burr [1992] BCLC 724 — C5.30
Company, A, Re (No 00751 of 1992), ex parte Avocet Aviation Ltd
 [1992] BCLC 869 — C5.29
Company, A, Re (No 00792 of 1992) [1992] EGCS 32 — C12.6
Company, A, Re (No 009080 of 1992) [1993] BCLC 269 — C5.29, C5.36
Company, A, Re (No 006273 of 1992) [1992] BCC 794 — C5.22, C5.29
Company, A, Re (No 0022 of 1993) (See also Philex plc v Golban)
 [1994] BCC 390, rev'ing [1993] BCC 726 — C5.29
Company, A, Re (No 007946 of 1993) The Times, 18 November 1993 — C5.4
Compaq Computer Ltd v Abercorn Group Ltd [1991] BCC 484 — D7.18
Compass Airlines Pty Ltd, Re (Australia) (1992) 10 ACLC 1380 — A4.19
Competitive Insurance Co Ltd v Davies Investments Ltd [1975] 1
 WLR 1240 — C11.24
Connaught Restaurants Ltd v Indoor Leisure Ltd [1994] 1 WLR 501 — D7.5
Connolly Brothers Ltd [1912] 2 Ch 25 — D7.23

Constellation, The [1966] 1 WLR 272 — C8.2, C14.31

Consumer and Industrial Press Ltd, Re [1988] BCLC 177 — B2.1

Consumer and Industrial Press Ltd, Re (No 2) (1988) 4 BCC 72 — B5.2, B5.15

Contract Corp, Re; Gooch's Case (1872) LR 7 Ch App 207 — C11.19, C11.24

Contract Corporation, Re (1866) 2 Ch App 95 — C12.20

Cook v 'X' Chain Patents Co Ltd [1960] 1 WLR 60 — C8.2

Cooke v Thomas (1876) 24 WR 427 — D1.5

Cooper v Cartwright (1860) John 679 — C12.6

Coopers & Lybrand Ltd v National Carters Ltd (Canada) 47 CBR
(NS) 57, BC SC — D7.10

Copecrest Ltd, Re [1993] BCLC 1118 — I8.2

Coptic Ltd v Bailey [1972] 1 All ER 1242 — D7.23

Corbenstoke Ltd, Re [1989] BCLC 496 — C5.35, C5.36

Corbenstoke Ltd, Re (No 2) (1989) 5 BCC 767 — C11.28

Coregrange Ltd, Re [1984] BCLC 453 — C8.2

Cornhill Insurance plc v Cornhill Financial Services Ltd [1992]
BCC 818, CA — B3.1, B5.16

Cornhill Insurance plc v Improvement Services Ltd [1986]
1 WLR 114 — C5.22, C5.36

Coulson Sanderson & Ward v Ward (1986) 2 BCC 99, CA — C5.36

Court Lodge Development Co Ltd, Re [1973] 1 WLR 1097 — G3.3

Courtney and Fairbairn Ltd v Tolani Bros (Hotels) Ltd [1975]
1 WLR 297 — D9.15

Cox Moore v Peruvian Corporation Ltd [1908] 1 Ch 604 — D6.2

Coxon v Gorst [1891] 2 Ch 73 — G2.1

Crago v Julian [1992] 1 All ER 744 — D9.7, D9.17

Craig v Iona Hotels Ltd 1988 SCLR 131 — C5.22

Cranley Mansions Ltd, Re; Saigol v Goldstein [1994]
BCC 576 — A6.1, C11.13, E2.5

Crawford v Swinton Insurance Brokers Ltd [1990] IRLR 42 — D9.16

Creasey v Breachwood Motors Ltd [1992] BCC 638 — C10.10

Creative Handbook Ltd, Re [1985] BCLC 1 — C5.38

Crestjoy Products Ltd, Re [1990] BCC 23 — I8.2

Crigglestone Coal Co, Re [1906] 2 Ch 327 — C5.26

Cripps (Pharmaceuticals) Ltd v Wickenden [1973]
1 WLR 944 — D2.8, D3.2, D5.2

Croftbell Ltd, Re [1990] BCLC 844 — B3.2, D1.4

Crossmore Electrical and Civil Engineering Ltd, Re [1989]
BCLC 137, (1989) 5 BCC 37 — C5.30, C8.4

Crowther & Nicholson Ltd, Re (1981) L S Gaz, 22 July — C14.22

Cryne v Barclays Bank plc [1987] BCLC 548 — D2.8

Crystal Reef Gold Mining Co, Re [1892] 1 Ch 408 — C5.30

Cuckmere Brick Co Ltd v Mutual Finance Ltd [1971] 2 All ER 633 — D8.14

Cullen (R A) Ltd v Nottingham Health Authority The Times,
1 August 1986 — D7.6

Cummings Trustee v Glenrinnes Farms Ltd 1993 SLT 904 — C5.30

Currie v Consolidated Kent Collieries Corporation Ltd [1906] 1 KB 134 — C8.2

Currie v Cowdenbeath Football Club Ltd [1992] BCLC 1029 — C3.1

Curtain Dream plc v Churchill Merchanting Ltd [1990]
BCC 341 — C12.10, D7.23

Curtis (D H) (Builders) Ltd, Re [1978] Ch 162 — C14.26, D7.6

Cushla Ltd, Re [1979] 3 All ER 415 — C11.24, C14.26, D7.6

Customs & Excise Commissioners v Derawood Ltd [1986] STC 327 — D9.13

Cutts, Re [1956] 1 WLR 728 — C10.4

Cyona Distributors Ltd, Re [1967] Ch 889 — C13.1

D (In liquidation), Re [1985] PCC 279 — C5.6
DFC Financial Services Ltd v Coffey [1991] BCC 218 — D2.8
DKG Contractors Ltd, Re [1990] BCC 903 — C10.4, C13.2, C13.4
DMG Realisations Ltd, Re (1990) Unreported, August — D9.16
DPR Futures Ltd, Re [1989] 1 WLR 778 — C11.23, C11.26
D'Jan of London Ltd, Re [1993] BCC 691 — C13.4, C13.5
D'Urso v Ercole Marelli Elettromeccanica Generale SpA [1992]
    IRLR 136 — D9.16
Daintrey, Re [1900] 1 QB 546, CA — C14.26
Dallhold Estates (UK) Ltd, Re [1992] BCC 394 — A5.2, B1.1, B10.1, E1.3
Dansk Metalarbejderforbund v H Neilson and Son (in liquidation)
    (ECJ) [1985] 1 CMLR 91 — D7.1
Darlington Borough Council v Denmark Chemists Ltd The Times,
    12 May 1992 — D7.14
Darlington Borough Council v Wiltshier Northern Ltd The Times,
    4 July 1994 — D9.11
David Lloyd & Co, Re (1877) 6 Ch D 339 — C8.2, C9.4
David Meek Access Ltd, Re [1993] BCC 175 — B4.1, B4.2
Davies Chemists Ltd, Re [1992] BCC 697 — C14.14
Davies v Directloans Ltd [1986] 1 WLR 823 — C10.7
Davis Investments (East Ham) Ltd, Re [1961] 1 WLR 1396, CA — C5.34
Davis v Richards & Wallington Industries Ltd [1990] 1 WLR
    1511 — C12.17, C15.9, D9.1
Dawson Print Group Ltd, Re [1987] BCLC 601 — I6.1
De Beers Consolidated Mines Ltd v British South Africa Co
    [1912] AC 52 — D12.1
De Courcey v Clement [1971] Ch 693 — C3.2
De Mattos v Gibson (1858) 4 De G & J 276 — D7.22, D8.15
Deanplan Ltd v Mahmoud [1992] 3 All ER 945 — D9.7
Debtor, A, Re [1927] 2 Ch 367 — C14.10
Debtor, A, Re; Debtor v Trustee of Property of Waite [1956]
    1 WLR 1226 — C14.26
Debtor, A, Re; Viscount of the Royal Courts of Justice, ex parte [1980]
    3 All ER 665 — C5.6
Debtor, A, Re (No 59 of 1987) The Independent,
    1 February 1988 — A5.1
Debtor, A, Re (No 310 of 1988) [1989] 1 WLR 453 — C14.29, C14.31
Debtor, A, Re (No 222 of 1990), ex parte The Bank of Ireland and
    Others [1992] BCLC 137 — E2.5, E3.3
Debtor, A, Re (No 222 of 1990), ex parte The Bank of Ireland and Others
    (No 2) [1993] BCLC 233 — E2.5
Debtor, A, Re (No 259 of 1990) [1992] 1 WLR 226 — E3.3
Debtor, A, Re (No 51-SD-1991) [1992] 1 WLR 1294 — C5.22
Debtor, A, Re (No 88 of 1991) [1992] 4 All ER 301 — C5.26
Debtor, A, Re (No 490-SD-1991), ex parte Debtor v Printline (Offset) Ltd
    [1992] 2 All ER 664 — C5.22
Debtor, A, Re (No 517 of 1991) The Times, 25 November 1991 — D2.8
Debtor, A, Re (No 64 of 1992) [1994] 1 WLR 264 — E3.1
Debtor, A, Re (No 340 of 1992) The Independent, 13 September 1993,
    The Times, 19 July 1992 — C5.22, D7.9
Debtor, A, Re (No 90 of 1992) The Times, 12 July 1993 — C5.29
Deering v Lord Winchelsea (1787) 29 ER 1184 — D10.4
Delabole Slate Ltd v Berriman [1985] IRLR 305, CA — D9.16
Delaney v R J Staples [1992] 1 All ER 944, HL — D8.3

Dempsey & National Bank of New Zealand v Traders' Finance
    Corp Ltd (New Zealand) [1933] NZLR 1258   D6.2
Denby (William) & Sons Ltd Sick and Benevolent Fund, Re [1971]
    1 WLR 973   C5.5
Denetower Ltd v Toop [1991] 3 All ER 661   D7.15
Denney v John Hudson & Co Ltd [1992] BCLC 901   C8.4
Derek Randall Enterprises Ltd, Re [1990] BCC 749, CA   C13.4
Destone Fabrics Ltd, Re [1941] Ch 319   C10.9
Devon and Somerset Farmers Ltd, Re [1993]
    BCC 410   C13.5, D1.4, D12.1, E1.3
Devon General Ltd v Seeney (1994) Industrial Relations Law
    Bulletin 499, 9   D8.3
Diamond Fuel Co, Re (No 2) (1879) 13 Ch D 400   C5.30
Dicetrade Ltd, Re [1994] BCC 371   I7.2
Dines Construction Ltd v Perry Dines Corporation Ltd (New Zealand)
    (1989) 4 NZ CLC 65, 298   D7.22
Dines v Initial Health Care Services Ltd [1994] IRLR 336   D9.16
Diplock, Re [1951] AC 251, HL aff'g [1948] 1 Ch 465, CA   D7.18, D7.22
Dirassar v Kelly Douglas & Co Ltd (Canada) (1966) 59 DLR (2d) 452   D8.15
Discount Tobacco and Confectionery Ltd v Williamson [1993] ICR 371   D8.3
Distributors and Warehousing Ltd, Re [1986] BCLC 129   C12.6
Dixon (C W) Ltd, Re [1947] Ch 251   G3.2
Dole Dried Fruit and Nut Co v Trustin Kerwood Ltd [1990] 2 Lloyd's
    Rep 309, CA   D7.5
Dombrowski, Re (1923) 92 LJ Ch 415   D8.15
Donald Kenyon Ltd, Re [1956] 1 WLR 1397   G3.3
Dorchester Finance Company Ltd v Stebbing and Another [1989]
    BCLC 498   C13.2, C13.3, I5.4
Douglas Construction Services Ltd, Re [1988] BCLC 397,
    (1988) 4 BCC 553   C13.2, I5.1
Downer Enterprises, Re [1974] 1 WLR 1460   C12.18
Downs Wine Bar Ltd, Re [1990] BCLC 839   C3.7
Downsview Nominees Ltd v First City Corporation Ltd (New Zealand)
    [1993] BCC 46, PC   D8.14
Dramstar, Re The Times, 30 October 1980   C5.44, C6.1
Driffield Gas Light Co, Re [1898] 1 Ch 451   C12.20
Dubai Bank Ltd v Galadari (1989) 5 BCC 722   A4.19
Dublin City Distillery Ltd v Doherty [1914] AC 823   C12.10, D7.25
Duffy v Yeomans and Partners (1994) Unreported, 12 July, CA   D7.1
Duke Group Ltd v Arthur Young (Reg) (Australia) (1991) 9 ACLC 380   C14.4
Duncan (W W) & Co, Re [1905] 1 Ch 307   C14.13
Duncan, Fox & Co v North and South Wales Bank (1880) 6 App Cas 1   D10.4
Dynamics Corporation of America, Re [1973] 1 WLR 63   C8.2
Dynamics Corporation of America, Re (No 2) [1976] 1 WLR 762   C14.13

ECM (Europe) Electronics Ltd, Re [1991] BCC 268   I6.1
ECSG Ltd LON/88/580 No 5204   D9.13
ELS Ltd, Re, sub nom Ramsbottom and Another v Luton Borough
    Council and Another [1994] BCC 449   D7.13
EVTR Ltd, Re (1987) 3 BCC 389   D7.22
Easiwork Homes Ltd v Redbridge London Borough Council
    [1970] 2 QB 406   D8.11
Eastern Capital Futures Ltd, Re (1989) 5 BCC 223   C11.25, D7.22
Eastern Holdings Establishment of Vaduz v Singer & Friedlander
    Ltd [1967] 1 WLR 1017   C8.2

Eastern Telegraph Co, Re [1947] 2 All ER 104   C5.26
Eaton v Robert Eaton and Secretary of State for Employment [1988]
   IRLR 83   D7.4
Ebrahimi v Westbourne Galleries Ltd [1973] AC 360   C5.26, C5.30
Eddystone & Marine Insurance Co, Re; Western Insurance Co,
   ex parte [1892] 2 Ch 43   C12.22
Edwards, Re; Chalmers, ex parte (1873) 8 Ch App 289   D7.30
Edwin Hill and Partners v First National Finance Corporation
   The Times, 3 August 1988, CA   D8.15
El Ajou v Dollar Land Holdings plc [1994] BCC 143, CA   D7.22
El Jawhary v Bank of Credit and Commerce International SA
   [1993] BCLC 396   A4.8
Electro-Optieck and Communicatie BV, Re [1981] 2 All ER 1111   C5.8
Eller v Grovecrest Investments Ltd [1994] EGCS 28   D7.13
Ellesmere Brewery Co, Re [1896] 1 QB 75   D10.4
Ellis (Alan) (Transport & Packing) Services Ltd, Re (1989)
   5 BCC 835   C11.25
Ellis (W A) Services Ltd v Stuart Wood (1993) 31 EG 78   D8.15
Elphinstone (Lord) v Monkland Co (1886) 11 App Cas 332   C12.17
Emerald Stainless Steels Ltd v South Side Distribution Ltd
   1983 SLT 162   D7.18
Emmandart Ltd, Re [1979] 1 All ER 599   B3.1, C5.28, D5.3
Emmerson's Case (1866) 1 Ch App 433   C6.1
Engineering Industry Training Board v Samuel Talbot (Engineers) Ltd
   [1969] 2 QB 270   C9.2
English, Scottish and Australian Chartered Bank, Re [1893]
   3 Ch 385   A6.1, C5.6
Equiticorp International plc, Re (1989) 5 BCC 599   B3.1, C5.26, C13.2
Equus Financial Services Ltd v Boambee Bay resort Property
   Ltd (in liquidation) (Australia) (1991) 9 ACLC 779   D6.2
Eren v Tarmac Ltd (1993) Unreported, 25 November   D7.13
Eric Audio Visual Ltd, Re, The Times, 13 May 1981   C5.44
Eric Ltd, Re [1928] Ch 861   C13.4
Eros Films Ltd, Re [1963] Ch 565   C14.26
Esal Commodities Ltd, Re (1988) 4 BCC 475, CA   A4.10, A4.19
Esal Commodities Ltd, Re (No 2) [1990] BCC 708   C11.22
Esal Commodities Ltd, Re; London and Overseas (Sugar) Co v
   Punjab National Bank [1993] BCLC 872   C13.1
Esanda Finance Corporation Ltd v Jackson (Australia) (1993)
   11 ACLC 138   F2.8
Euro RSCG SA v Conran The Times, 2 November 1992   C13.2, I5.4
Euro-Diam v Bathurst [1987] 2 WLR 1368   C14.13
Europa Holdings Ltd v Circle Industries (UK) Plc [1992] CILL 781 D8.16
European Life Assurance Society, Re (1869) LR 9 Eq 122   C5.22, C14.26
Evans (C) & Sons Ltd v Spritebrand Ltd [1985] BCLC 105, CA   C11.24
Evans v Clayhope Properties Ltd [1988] BCLC 238   D4.9
Evans v Rival Granite Quarries Ltd [1910] 2 KB 979   D6.2
Evans v South Ribble Borough Council [1992] 2 WLR 429   D7.13
Exchange Securities & Commodities Ltd and Others, Re
   [1983] BCLC 186   C8.2
Exchange Securities & Commodities Ltd, Re [1987] 2 WLR 893   C14.10
Exchange Travel (Holdings) Ltd, Re [1992] BCC 954   B7.1, C5.50
Exchange Travel Agency Ltd v Triton Property Trust plc
   [1991] BCC 341   B4.1
Exeter Trust Ltd v Screenways Ltd [1991] BCLC 888,

[1991] BCC 477, CA — C12.10, D2.5

Exmouth Docks, Re (1873) Comm 181 — C5.29

Expro Services Ltd v Smith [1991] IRLR 156 — D9.16

FLE Holdings Ltd, Re [1967] 1 WLR 1409 — C10.4

FMS Financial Management Services Ltd, Re (1989) 5 BCC 191 — C14.13, E3.3

FSA Business Software Ltd, Re [1990] BCC 465 — C5.29

Fairclough Building Ltd v Borough Council of Port Talbot
(1992) Unreported, 16 July, CA — D9.15

Fairfield (Allen) & Sons Ltd, Re (1971) 115 SJ 244 — C10.4

Fairfield v Skinner [1992] ICR 837 — D8.3

Fairmont Tours (Yorkshire) Ltd, Re (1989) Insolvency Law and
Practice, p 184 — C13.2

Fairway Magazines Ltd, Re [1992] BCC 924 — C10.4, C10.9

Falcon (R J) Developments Ltd, Re [1987] BCLC 437 — C5.29

Fanti, The [1987] 2 Lloyd's Rep 299 — C12.22

Fargo Ltd v Godfroy and Others [1986] 1 WLR 1134 — C12.11

Farley v Housing and Commercial Developments Ltd [1984]
BCLC 442 — C14.26

Farr (AE) Ltd, Re [1992] BCC 150 — A4.19

Farrar v Farrars Ltd (1888) 40 Ch D 395 — D9.17

Farrell v Federated Employers Insurance Association Ltd [1970]
1 WLR 1400 — C14.24

Fastframe Franchises Ltd v Lohinski (1993) Unreported, 3 March — D7.5

Fearman (WF) Ltd, Re (1988) 4 BCC 139 — B2.1, B3.1, C5.41

Fearman (WF) Ltd, Re (No 2) (1988) 4 BCC 141 — C5.41

Federal Bank of Australia Ltd, Re (1893) 68 LT 728 — C5.6

Felixstowe Dock & Railway Co v United States Lines Inc Financial
Times, 7 April 1987 — C5.6

Felt and Textiles of New Zealand v R Hubrick Ltd (New Zealand)
[1968] NZLR 716 — D7.5

Fenton, Re [1931] 1 Ch 85 — C14.26

Ferguson and Skilling v Prestwick Circuits Ltd [1992] IRLR 266 — D7.1

Finley Ltd, Re; Clothworkers' Co, ex parte (1888) 21 QBD 475 — C12.6

Finnegan (J F) Ltd v Ford Seller Morris Developments Ltd (No 1)
[1991] CILL 672 — D7.22

Finnegan (J F) Ltd v Ford Seller Morris Developments Ltd (No 2)
[1991] CILL 679 — D7.22

Firedart Ltd, Re (1994) 138 SJ 16 — I6.1

Firma-C-Trade v Newcastle Protection and Indemnity Association
[1990] 2 All ER 705 — C14.24

First National Securities Ltd v Jones [1978] 2 All ER 221 — D2.4

Fitness Centre (South East), Re [1986] BCLC 518 — C5.29

Fleetwood & District Electric Light & Power Syndicate, Re
[1915] 1 Ch 486 — C14.13

Fletcher, Re (1891) 9 Mor 8 — C10.4

Fletcher Hunt (Bristol) Ltd, Re [1988] BCLC 703 — C5.44

Flint (A Bankrupt), Re [1992] 2 WLR 537 — C8.4

Forte's (Manufacturing) Ltd, Re [1994] BCC 84 — G3.2

Foster Wheeler (London) Ltd v Jackson [1990] ICR 757 — D8.3

Foster Yates & Thom Ltd v H W Edghill Equipment Ltd
(1978) 122 SJ 860 — G2.1

Fosters and Rudd Ltd, Re (1986) 2 BCC 98 — D2.12

Four Point Garage Ltd v Carter [1985] 3 All ER 12 — D7.18

Fowler v Broad's Patent Night Light Co [1893] 1 Ch 724 — C8.1

Fowler v Fowler [1963] P 311 — A4.19

Francovich (Andrea) and Bonifaci (Danila) v Italy (ECJ Cases C-6 & 9/90) [1992] IRLR 84 — D9.16

Freevale Ltd v Metrostore (Holdings) Ltd [1984] 1 All ER 495 — D7.26, F2.3

French's (Wine Bar) Ltd, Re [1987] BCLC 499 — C8.4

Fulham Football Club Ltd v Cabra Estates plc [1992] BCC 863, CA — C13.4

GMB v Rankin and Harrison [1992] IRLR 514 — D7.1

Galahurst Ltd, Re [1989] BCLC 140 — C5.2

Galbraith v Grimshaw [1910] AC 508 — D7.10

Galden Properties Ltd (in liquidation), Re (Ireland) (1988) ILRM 599 — D7.7

Gallidoro Trawlers Ltd, Re [1991] BCLC 411 — B1.1

Gamelstaden plc v Brackland Magazines Ltd [1993] BCC 194 — C5.44

Garage Door Associates Ltd, Re [1984] 1 WLR 35 — C5.30

Garden Cottage Foods Ltd v Milk Marketing Board [1984] 1 AC 130 — D7.30

Garton (Western) Ltd, Re [1989] PCC 428 — C5.35

Gattopardo Ltd, Re [1969] 1 WLR 619 — C5.30

Gee & Co (Woolwich) Ltd, Re [1974] 2 WLR 515 — C9.5

Geisse v Taylor [1905] 2 KB 658 — D7.10

General Communications Ltd v DFC (New Zealand) (1987) Unreported, CP 634/86, NZ High Ct — D7.22

General Radio Co Ltd, Re [1929] WN 172 — D7.4

General Rolling Stock Co, Re; Joint Stock Discount Co's Claim (1872) 7 Ch App 646 — C9.5, C14.3, G3.2

General Store and Trust Co v Wetley Brick and Pottery Co (1882) 20 Ch D 260, CA — C8.2, C11.24

George Barker (Transport) Ltd v Eynon [1974] 1 WLR 462 — D7.7, D7.13

Gerald Cooper Chemicals Ltd, Re [1978] 2 WLR 866 — C13.1

Gersten v Municipality of Toronto (Canada) (1973) 41 DLR (3d) 464 — D8.26

Gertzenstein Ltd [1937] Ch 115 — C11.24

Ghyll Beck Driving Range Ltd, Re [1993] BCLC 1126 — C5.30

Gibbons, Re [1960] Ir Jur Rep 60 (Ireland) — C14.13

Gibson v Motortune Ltd [1990] ICR 740 — D9.16

Gibson's Executor v Gibson 1980 SLT 2 — C12.9, C15.9

Gilbert-Ash (Northern) Ltd v Modern Engineering (Bristol) Ltd [1974] AC 689 — D7.5

Gilham v Kent County Council (No 2) [1985] ICR 233 — D9.16

Gill's Case (1879) 12 Ch D 755 — C12.1

Gillett Pressings (Cardiff) Ltd [1994] STI 113 — D9.13

Glamorgan Coal Co Ltd v South Wales Miners' Federation [1903] 2 KB 545 — D8.15

Glaser (W & A) Ltd, Re [1994] BCC 199 — C5.51

Godwin Warren Control Systems plc, Re [1993] BCLC 80, [1992] BCC 557 — I2.5, I6.1, I7.3, I8.9

Goff v Gauthier (1991) 62 P & CR 388 — D9.14

Goker v NWS Bank plc The Times, 23 May 1990 — B4.1, D7.14

Gold Co, Re (1879) 12 Ch D at 85 — A4.19

Goldburg, Re (No 2) [1912] 1 KB 606 — D8.15

Goldcorp Exchange Ltd, Re (New Zealand) [1994] 2 All ER 806, PC — D7.22, D7.25

Golden Chemical Products, Re [1976] Ch 300 — C5.31

Gomba Holdings (UK) Ltd v Homan [1986] 1 WLR 1301 — D1.5, D5.3, D5.5

Gomba Holdings (UK) Ltd v Minories Finance Ltd [1992] BCC 877 — D4.9, D5.5

Gorringe v Irwell India Rubber Works (1886) 34 Ch D 128 — C8.4

Gosling v Gaskell [1897] AC 575, HL   D7.3
Gosscott (Groundworks) Ltd, Re [1988] BCLC 363   B3.1, C11.25
Gothard v Mirror Group Newspapers Ltd [1988] ICR 729   D8.3
Gough's Garage v Pugsley [1930] 1 KB 615   D5.2
Government of India v Taylor [1955] AC 491   C5.6, C14.13
Grassby & Sons Ltd [1994] STI 133   D9.13
Gray's Inn Construction Ltd, Re [1980] 1 WLR 711, CA   C8.4
Green v Wavertree Heating and Plumbing Co Ltd [1978] ICR 928   D9.16
Green v Weaver (1827) 1 Sim 404   A4.19
Green-Wheeler v Onyx (UK) Ltd (1993) Industrial Relations Law
    Bulletin 484, 8   D9.16
Greening & Co, Re; Marsh's Case (1871) LR 13 Eq 388, 41 LJ Ch 111   C12.20
Greg May (CF & C) Ltd v Dring [1990] IRLR 19, EAT   D8.3
Griffiths v Secretary of State for Social Services [1974] QB 468   D7.1
Grissell's Case (1866) 1 Ch App 528   C12.1
Grosvenor Metal Co, Re [1950] Ch 63   C9.4
Grovewood Holdings plc v James Capel & Co Ltd The Independent,
    20 September 1994   C12.1
Guinness plc v Saunders [1990] BCC 205, HL   C12.9
Gunsberg, Re [1920] 2 KB 426   D8.15

HBM Abels v Administrative Board (Netherlands) (ECJ) [1987]
    2 CMLR 406   D9.16
Hailey Group Ltd, Re [1993] BCLC 459   C5.30
Halesowen Presswork Assemblies Ltd v Westminster Bank Ltd [1970]
    1 All ER 33   D6.2, D7.4
Hall (William) (Contractors) Ltd, Re [1967] 2 All ER 1150   C10.4, C14.26
Hall v Second Nature Ltd (1988) IDS Brief 380, September   D8.3
Hallett's Estate, Re (1880) 13 Ch D 696, CA   D7.18
Halls v O'Dell [1992] 2 WLR 308, CA   C13.4
Hamer v London, City & Midland Bank Ltd (1918) 87 LJKB 973   D6.2
Hamilton's Windsor Ironworks, Re (1879) 12 Ch D 707   D6.2
Hans Place Ltd, Re [1992] BCC 737   C12.6
Hargreaves (B) Ltd v Action 2000 Ltd [1993] BCLC 1111, CA,
    (1993) 6 Insolvency Intelligence 34   C14.26, D1.5, D6.3, D7.5
Harold Meggitt Ltd v Discount and Finance Ltd (Australia)
    (1938) 56 WN (NSW) 23   D2.1
Harris Simons Construction Ltd, Re [1989] 1 WLR 368   B2.1
Harrods (Buenos Aires) Ltd, Re [1991] BCC 249, CA, rev'g
    [1990] BCC 481   C5.2, C5.35
Hartlebury Printers Ltd, Re [1993] BCLC 902, [1992] BCC 428   B7.5, D7.1
Hartshorn v Slodden (1801) 2 B & P 582   C10.4
Harvela Investments Ltd v Royal Trust Company of Canada (CI) Ltd
    [1986] AC 207   D9.17
Harvey v Ventilatoren Fabrik Oelde GmbH Financial Times,
    11 November 1988, CA   D7.18
Hastie and Jenkerson v McMahon [1990] 1 WLR 1575, [1991]
    1 All ER 255, CA   C5.22, D2.8
Hawtin v Pugh (1975) Unreported   D2.8
Haycraft Gold Reduction and Mining Co, Re [1900] 2 Ch 230   C5.30
Hayter (A E) & Sons (Porchester) Ltd, Re [1961] 1 WLR 1008   C5.44
Headington Investments Ltd, Re [1993] BCC 500   A4.19
Hedley Byrne and Co Ltd v Heller and Partners [1964] AC 465   C13.3
Helbert v Banner; Barned's Bank, Re (1871) LR 5 HL 28, 40
    LJ Ch 410   C12.20

Henderson v Atwood [1894] AC 150 — D9.3

Hendy Lennox (Industrial Engines) Ltd v Grahame Puttick Ltd [1984]
2 All ER 152 — D7.18

Henry Pound, Son & Hutchins, Re (1889) 42 Ch D 402 — D2.10, D2.11, D5.2

Hercules Security Fabrications Ltd, Re (1987) Unreported — B7.2

Herman, Re [1915] HBR 41 — D8.15

Heron International Ltd v Lord Grade [1983] BCLC 244 — C13.2

Hewitt Brannan (Tools) Co Ltd, Re [1990] BCC 354 — C5.29, C5.32

Hi-Fi Equipment (Cabinets) Ltd, Re (1987) 3 BCC 478 — D6.2

Higginshaw Mills & Spinning Co, Re [1896] 2 Ch 544 — C12.18

High Street Services Ltd and Others v Bank of Credit and Commerce
International SA. See MS Fashions v Bank of Credit and Commerce
International SA

Highfield Commodities Ltd, Re [1984] 3 All ER 884 — C5.31, C5.41

Highgrade Traders Ltd, Re [1984] BCLC 151, CA — A4.19

Hilger Analytical Ltd v Rank Precision Industries Ltd [1984]
BCLC 301 — D2.12

Hill Samuel & Co Ltd v Laing (1988) 4 BCC 9 — D8.2

Hill, Re; ex parte Bird (1883) 23 Ch D 695 — C10.4

Hindcastle Ltd v Barbara Attenborough Associates Ltd [1994]
BCC 705 — C12.6

Hockerill Athletic Club Ltd, Re [1990] BCLC 921 — C5.46

Hodson v Dears [1903] 2 Ch 647 — D9.17

Hoey, Re (1919) 88 LJKB 273 — C14.9

Hoffman-La Roche (F) & Co AG v Secretary of State for Trade and
Industry [1975] AC 295 — C5.31

Hoffman-La-Roche v Commission (ECJ Case 85/76) [1979] ECR 461 — D7.30

Holiday Stamps Ltd, Re The Times, 11 July 1985, CA — C5.29

Holliday (L B) & Co Ltd, Re [1986] 2 All ER 367 — C14.35

Holmes (Eric) (Property) Ltd, Re [1965] Ch 1052 — C10.4

Holt Southey Ltd v Catnic Components Ltd [1978] 1 WLR 630 — C5.36

Home and Overseas Insurance Co Ltd v Mentor Insurance Co (UK) Ltd
[1989] 1 Lloyd's Rep 473 — C12.22

Home Assured Corporation plc, Re [1993] BCC 573 — I8.5

Home Office v Ayres [1992] IRLR 59 — D8.3

Home Remedies Ltd, Re [1943] Ch 1; [1942] 2 All ER 552 — C5.29

Home Treat Ltd, Re [1991] BCLC 705 — B7.5, D5.3

Hong Kong and Shanghai Banking Corporation v Kloeckner & Co AG
[1989] 3 All ER 513 — D7.5

Hood's Trustees v Southern Union General Insurance Co of Australasia
[1928] Ch 793 — C14.24

Hopkins v Norcros plc [1994] IRLR 18, CA — C14.22

Hornal v Neuberger Products Ltd [1956] 3 All ER 970 — C13.1

Hough (A Bankrupt), Re (1990) Unreported, 10 April — C5.19

Hough v Leyland DAF Ltd [1991] IRLR 194 — D7.1

Houldsworth v City of Glasgow Bank (1880) 5 App Cas 317 — C12.20

House Property and Investment Co, Re [1954] Ch 576 — C12.17, C14.21

Howard v Boddington (1877) 2 PD 203 — I8.1

Howell v Montrey The Times, 17 March 1990 — D7.11

Hughes (CW & AL) Ltd, Re [1966] 1 WLR 1369 — D7.4

Hull & County Bank, Re; Burgess's Case (1880) 15 Ch D 507 — C12.20

Humber Ironworks and Shipbuilding Company (1869) LR Ch App 643 — C14.13

Humberstone (Jersey) Ltd, Re (1977) 74 LSG 711 — C5.26

Huntingdon Poultry Ltd, Re [1969] 1 WLR 204 — G3.3

Hydrodan (Corby) Ltd, Re [1994] BCC 161 — C13.2

IBL v Coussens [1991] 2 All ER 133   D8.15
ISS Mediclean v Searle and Wilson EAT 711/91   D9.16
Ian Chisholm Textiles Ltd v Griffiths [1994] BCC 96   D6.2, D7.18, D7.19
Ibex Trading Co Ltd v Walton [1994] IRLR 564   D9.16
Icarus (Hertford) Ltd v Driscoll [1990] PLR 1   D9.1
Illingworth v Houldsworth [1904] AC 355   D6.3
Imperial Group Pension Trust Ltd v Imperial Tobacco Ltd [1991]
    1 WLR 589   D9.1
Imperial Motors (UK) Ltd, Re (1989) 5 BCC 214   B2.1, B3.2
Ince Hall Rolling Mills Co v Douglas Forge Co (1882) 8 QBD 179   C9.6, F2.3
Indian Oil Corporation Ltd v Greenstone Shipping Co SA [1987]
    3 All ER 893   D7.18
Industrial and Commercial Securities Ltd, Re (1989) 5 BCC 320   A5.1
Industrial Design & Manufacture Ltd (1984) Unreported 25 June,
    NI Ch D   C10.4
Industrial Development Authority Ltd v William T Moran (Ireland)
    (1978) IR 159   D9.1
Inglis v Robertson & Baxter [1898] AC 616   D11.1
Initial Supplies Ltd v McCall 1991 SLT 67   D9.16
IRC v Goldblatt [1972] Ch 498   D7.3
IRC v Olive Mills Ltd [1963] 1 WLR 712   D9.5, H2.2
IRC v Pollock & Peel [1957] 1 WLR 822   C15.9
Insituform (Ireland) Ltd v Insituform Group Ltd The Times,
    27 January 1992   D7.5
Instrumentation Electrical Services, Re (1988) 4 BCC 301   B3.1, C5.26, C13.2
Intermain Properties Ltd, Re [1986] BCLC 265   C5.45
International Bulk Commodities Ltd, Re [1993] Ch 77, [1992]
    3 WLR 238   C13.5, D1.4, D12.1, E1.3
International Drilling Fluids Ltd v Louisville Investments
    (Uxbridge) Ltd [1986] 1 All ER 332, CA   D9.7
International Sales & Agencies Ltd v Marcus [1982] 3 All ER 551   C12.9
International Tin Council, Re [1989] Ch 309, CA; aff'g [1987] Ch 419,
    [1987] BCLC 272   C5.5, C5.6, C5.8
International Westminster Bank plc v Okeanos Maritime Corp. See
    Company, A, Re (No 00359 of 1987)
Ipcon Fashions Ltd, Re (1989) 5 BCC 773   I6.1
Iperion Investments Corporation v Broadwalk House Residents Ltd
    (1992) Estates Gazette, 12 & 19 September   D7.14
Irish Aerospace (Belgium) NV v European Organisation for the Safety of Air
    Navigation The Times, 23 July 1991   D7.7
Irish Oil and Cake Mills Ltd v John Donnelly (Ireland) (1984) Unreported, 27
    March   D5.5

JN2 Ltd, Re [1977] 3 All ER 1104   C5.30
Jaffre Ltd (in liquidation), Re; Jaffre v Jaffre (No 2) (New Zealand)
    [1932] NZLR 195   D2.1
James Roscoe (Bolton) Ltd v Winder [1915] 1 Ch 62   D7.22
James, ex parte (1874) 9 Ch App Cas 609   C11.24
Janeash Ltd, Re [1990] BCC 250   C5.22
Jarvis Conklin Mortgage Co Ltd, Re (1895) 11 TLR 373   C5.6
Jaymar Management Ltd, Re [1990] BCC 203   I8.1
Jazzgold Ltd, Re [1992] BCC 587   I8.7
Jeffrey S Levitt Ltd, Re [1992] BCLC 250   A4.19
Jesner v Jarrad Properties Ltd [1993] BCLC 1032   C5.30

John Crowther Group plc v Carpets International plc [1990]
  BCLC 460 — C13.4
John Snow & Co Ltd v DBG Woodcroft & Co Ltd [1985] BCLC 54 — D7.18
John Willment (Ashford) Ltd, Re [1979] 2 All ER 615, [1979]
  STC 288 — D8.5, D8.6, H3.7
Johnson (B) & Co (Builders) Ltd, Re [1955] Ch 634 — C13.4, D1.5, D8.14
Jones v Bernstein [1900] 1 QB 100, CA — D7.13
Jones v Williams; Dan Jones (Porth) Ltd Employees Pension Fund
  [1989] PLR 21 — D9.1
Joshua Shaw and Sons Ltd, Re (1989) 5 BCC 188 — C5.29
Justfern Ltd v D'Ingerthorpe [1994] IRLR 164 — D9.16

K, Re [1990] 2 All ER 562 — D7.5
K/9 Meat Supplies (Guildford) Ltd, Re [1966] 1 WLR 1112 — C5.30
Karamelli and Bennett Ltd, Re [1917] 1 Ch 203 — C11.28
Karnos Property Co Ltd, Re (1989) 5 BCC 14 — C5.29
Karsberg (B) Ltd, Re [1955] 3 All ER 854 — C5.29, C11.22
Katherine et Cie, Re [1932] 1 Ch 70 — C12.6
Katsikas v Konstantinidas (ECJ) [1993] IRLR 179 — D9.16
Kayford Ltd, Re [1975] 1 WLR 279 — D7.22
Keenan Bros Ltd, Re (Ireland) [1986] BCLC 242 — D6.2
Kenmir Ltd v Frizzell [1968] 1 WLR 329 — D9.13, D9.16
Kenny v South Manchester College [1994] IRLR 265 — D9.16
Kent Management Services Ltd v Butterfield [1992] IRLR 394 — D8.3
Kentish Homes Ltd and Others (1989) Unreported, 31 July — B2.1, B3.1, B3.2
Kentish Homes Ltd, Re [1993] BCC 212 — C12.18, C14.13, D8.11
Kentwood Constructions Ltd, Re [1960] 2 All ER 655 — C14.5
Kenyon Swansea Ltd, Re [1987] BCLC 514 — C5.26, C5.30
Kestongate Ltd v Miller The Times, 28 May 1986 — D9.16
Keypak Homecare Ltd, Re [1987] BCLC 409 — C11.28
Keypak Homecare Ltd, Re (No 2) [1990] BCLC 440 — I6.1, I8.5
Kidd, Re (1861) 4 LT 344 — C5.6
Killick v Second Covent Garden Property Co Ltd [1973] 1 WLR 658 — D9.7
King Township v Rolex Equipment Co Ltd (1992) 90 DLR (4th)
  442, 8 OR (3d) 457 — D8.26
Kinsela v Russell Kinsela Pty Ltd (Australia) (1986) 4 NSWLR 722,
  CA — C13.4
Kirby's Coaches Ltd, Re [1991] BCLC 414 — C13.5
Kitson & Co Ltd, Re [1946] 1 All ER 435 — C5.26
Kleinwort Benson Ltd v Malaysia Mining Corporation BhD [1989]
  1 WLR 379, CA — C13.2
Knight v Lawrence [1991] BCC 411 — D8.14
Knights v Wiffen (1870) LR 5 QB 660 — D7.25
Knightsbridge Estates Trust plc v Byrne [1940] 2 All ER 401 — C12.10, D1.4
Knitwear (T H) (Wholesale) Ltd, Re [1987] BCLC 86 — C11.24
Knowles v Scott [1891] 1 Ch 717 — C11.24
Koscot Interplanetary (UK) Ltd, Re; Koscot AG, Re [1972] 3 All
  ER 829 — C5.34
Kournavous v JR Masterton & Sons (Demolition) Ltd [1990]
  IRLR 119 — D8.3
Kumar (A Bankrupt), Re; Lewis v Kumar [1993] 1 WLR 224 — C10.2
Kushler Ltd, Re [1943] Ch 248 — C10.4
Kuwait Asia Bank EC v National Muntual Life Nominees Pty Ltd
  (New Zealand) [1990] BCC 567, PC — C13.2

Laceward Ltd, Re [1981] 1 All ER 254 — C5.26, C5.36
Ladd v Marshall [1954] 1 WLR 1489 — I8.2
Lamplugh Iron Ore Co Ltd, Re [1927] 1 Ch 308 — D7.4
Lanaghan Bros Ltd, Re [1977] 1 All ER 265 — C5.44
Lancashire Cotton Spinning Co, Re (1887) 35 Ch D 656 — C12.18
Land and Property Trust Co plc, Re [1991] BCC 446, [1991] BCC 459, CA — B2.1, B3.1, C5.44
Land and Property Trust Co plc, Re (No 2) [1993] BCC 462, CA — B3.1, B3.2, C5.44
Landbase Nominee Co Ltd, Re (New Zealand) (1989) 4 NZCLC 65, 093 — C15.4
Langley Constructions (Brixham) v Wells [1969] 2 All ER 46 — C14.26
Langley Marketing Services Ltd, Re [1991] BCLC 584 — I8.10
Larner v British Steel plc [1993] 4 All ER 102 — D8.6
Larsen v Henderson [1990] IRLR 512 — D8.3
Laser Control Ltd, Re (1987) Unreported — B7.2, B7.3
Lathia v Dronsfield Bros Ltd [1987] BCLC 321 — D5.2, D7.24, D8.15, F2.3
Lathom v Greenwich Ferry (1895) 72 LT 790 — D8.15
Laurie v Dudin & Sons [1926] 1 KB 223 — D7.25
Law Guarantee Trust and Accident Society Ltd, Re [1914] 2 Ch 677 — C12.22
Law v James (Australia) [1972] 2 NSWLR 573 — C14.26
Lawrence v European Credit Co Ltd [1992] BCC 792 — A5.1
Ledingham-Smith, Re [1992] 5 Insolvency Intelligence 65 — C10.4
Lee-Parker v Izzet [1971] 1 WLR 1688 — D7.5
Leeds Permanent Building Society v Kassai (1992) Current Law Digest, September — D1.5
Leeds Twentieth Century Decorators, Re (1962) CLY 365 — D7.4
Leigh Estates (UK) Ltd, Re [1994] BCC 292 — C5.29, D8.11
Leisure Study Group Ltd, Re (1993) Unreported, 26 January, Ch D — D7.22, E2.7, E3.3
Leitch (William C) Bros, Re [1932] 2 Ch 71 — C13.1
Leon v York-O-Matic Ltd [1966] 1 WLR 1450 — C11.24, C11.25
Leslie (J) Engineers Co Ltd, Re [1976] 1 WLR 292 — C8.4
Levasseur v Mason & Barry Ltd (1891) 63 LT 700 — A5.3
Lever Finance Ltd v Trustee of the Property of LN and HM Needleman [1956] Ch 375 — D2.5
Levy (A I) (Holdings) Ltd, Re [1964] Ch 19 — C8.4
Lewis Merthyr Consolidated Collieries Ltd, Re [1929] 1 Ch 498, CA — D7.3
Leyland DAF Ltd v Automotive Products plc [1993] BCC 389 — D7.30
Leyland DAF Ltd, Re; Ferranti International plc, Re [1994] BCC 658 — B7.7, D8.3
Linda Marie Ltd, Re (1988) 4 BCC 463 — C12.18
Linden Gardens Trust Ltd v Lenesta Sludge Disposals Ltd; St Martins Property Corporation Ltd v Sir Robert McAlpine & Sons Ltd [1993] 3 WLR 408 — D9.11
Lindsay Bowman Ltd, Re [1969] 1 WLR 1443 — G3.3
Lines Bros Ltd, Re [1982] 2 WLR 1010, [1982] 2 All ER 183, aff'g [1981] Com LR 214 — C9.10, C14.13, C14.17
Lines Bros Ltd, Re (No 2) [1984] 2 WLR 905 — C14.17
Linvale Ltd, Re [1993] BCLC 654 — I6.1
Lipe Ltd v Leyland DAF Ltd [1993] BCC 385 — D7.19
Lipkin Gorman v Karpnale Ltd [1991] 2 AC 548, HL — D7.22, D8.3
Litster v Forth Dry Dock & Engineering Co Ltd [1989] IRLR 161 — D9.16
Liverpool and District Hospital for Diseases of the Heart v Attorney-General [1981] 1 All ER 994 — C15.9

Liverpool Commercial Vehicles Ltd, Re [1984] BCLC 587 — D8.5
Liverpool Corporation v Hope [1938] 1 KB 751 — D8.5, D8.11, D10.1
Lloyds & Scottish Finance Ltd v Cyril Lord Carpet Sales Ltd
   [1992] BCLC 609, HL — C12.10, D7.22
Lloyds & Scottish Finance Ltd v Prentice (1977) 121 SJ 847, CA — C12.10
Llynvi & Tondu Co, Re (1889) 6 TLR 11 — C11.24
Lo-Line Electric Motors Ltd, Re [1988] BCLC 698 — I5.1, I7.3
Loch v John Blackwood Ltd [1924] AC 783 — C5.26
Lockley v National Blood Transfusion Service [1992] 1 WLR 492 — C14.14
Lombard Finance Ltd v Brookplain Trading Ltd and Others
   [1991] 1 WLR 271 — D2.4
Lombard Shipping and Forwarding Ltd, Re [1992] BCC 700 — I8.5
London and Norwich Investments Ltd, Re [1988] BCLC 226 — C5.41
London Casino Ltd, Re [1942] WN 138 — D7.4
London Iron and Steel Co Ltd, Re [1990] BCLC 372 — A4.16
London Pressed Hinge Co Ltd, Re [1905] 1 Ch 576 — D2.8, D7.9
London United Investments plc, Re [1992] BCC 202 — A4.19
London Wine Company (Shippers) Ltd, Re [1986] PCC 121 — D7.25
Longden v Ferrari Ltd and Kennedy International Ltd [1994]
   IRLR 157 — D7.1, D9.16
Looe Fish Ltd, Re [1993] BCC 348 — I6.1
Lord Advocate v Aero Technologies Ltd (in receivership) 1991
   SLT 134 — D8.26
Lovell Construction Ltd v Independent Estates plc (in liquidation)
   (1992) Unreported, 25 June, QBD — C12.10
Lowerstoft Traffic Services Ltd, Re [1986] BCLC 81 — C5.29
Lowston Ltd, Re [1991] BCLC 570 — C5.46
Lubin, Rosen and Associates Ltd, Re [1975] 1 WLR 122 — C5.29, C5.31
Lundy Granite Co, Re (1871) LR 6 Ch App 462 — C12.18

MC Bacon Ltd, Re [1990] BCC 78 — C10.2, C10.4
MC Bacon Ltd, Re (No 2) [1990] BCC 430 — C10.2, C10.4, C15.2
MCH Services Ltd, Re [1987] BCLC 535 — C5.29
MEPC plc v Scottish Amicable Life Assurance Society
   [1993] 36 EG 133 — C12.6
MS Fashions Ltd and Others v Bank of Credit and Commerce
   International SA [1992] BCC 571, CA — C14.26, D2.8
MS Fashions Ltd and Others v Bank of Credit and Commerce
   International SA (No 2) [1993] BCC 360, CA aff'g [1993] BCC 70 — C14.26
McCarthy (M) & Co (Builders) Ltd, Re (No 2) [1976] 2 All ER 339 — C5.44
McCree v London Borough of Tower Hamlets [1992] IRLR 56 — D8.3
McGuiness Bros (UK) Ltd, Re (1987) 3 BCC 571 — C8.4
McIsaac and Another, Petitioners, joint liquidators of First Tokyo
   Index Trust Ltd [1994] BCC 410 — A4.19
MacJordan Construction Ltd v Brookmount Erostin Ltd [1992]
   BCLC 350 — C12.19, D7.22, D7.25, D8.15
McKillop and Walters The Times, 14 April 1994 — D8.11
McKinnon v Armstrong (1877) 2 App Cas 531 — C14.26
McLean v Secretary of State for Employment (1992) 455 IRLIB 14 — D7.4
McMullen & Sons Ltd v Cerrone [1994] BCC 25 — B4.1
McNulty's Interchange Ltd, Re (1988) 4 BCC 533, [1989]
   BCLC 709 — C13.2, I6.1
McQuillan, Re (1989) 5 BCC 137 — I7.3
McRuary v Washington Irvine Ltd (1994) Industrial Relations
   Law Bulletin 499, 9 — D8.3

Mace Builders (Glasgow) Ltd v Lunn [1986] 3 WLR 921, CA aff'g
    [1985] 3 WLR 465   C10.9, D2.5
Macer v Abafast Ltd [1990] IRLR 137   D9.16
Mack Trucks (Britain) Ltd, Re [1967] 1 WLR 780   D7.1
Macrae (P & J) Ltd, Re [1961] 1 WLR 229   C5.29
Magna Alloys & Research Pty Ltd, Re (Australia) (1975) CLC 40-227   I7.1
Maidstone Building Provisions Ltd, Re [1971] 3 All ER 363   C13.1
Majestic Recording Studios Ltd, Re (1988) 4 BCC 519   I6.1, I7.2, I7.3
Mancetter Developments Ltd v Garmanson Ltd [1986] BCLC 196   D7.14
Manlon Trading Ltd, Re (1988) 4 BCC 455   B2.1, C5.36
Manlon Trading Ltd, Re The Times, 15 August 1994   I8.7
Mann v Abruzzi Sports Club Ltd (Australia) (1994) 12 ACLC 137   B5.4
Mannin Management Services Ltd v Ward The Times, 9 February, CA   D9.16
Manurewa Transport Co Ltd, Re (New Zealand) [1971] NZLR 909   D6.3
Marcel v Commissioner of Police of the Metropolis [1991] 1 All ER 845   C11.24
Mardas v Official Receiver and Halls (1989) Insolvency Law and
    Practice Vol 5, Vol 6, 187   C11.16
Mareva Compania Naviera SA of Panama v International Bulk Carriers
    SA [1975] 2 Lloyd's Rep 509   D7.12
Margart Property Ltd, Re; Hamilton v Westpac Banking Corporation
    (Australia) [1985] BCLC 314   C8.4
Marleasing v La Commercial Internacional de Alimentacion (ECJ
    Case C-106/89) [1993] BCC 421   D9.16
Marley Tile Co v Burrows [1978] QB 241   C9.2
Marr, Re [1990] 2 All ER 880, CA   C5.19
Marriage, Neave & Co, Re [1896] 2 Ch 663   D7.13
Martin Coulter Enterprises Ltd, Re [1988] BCLC 12   C5.29
Marwalt Ltd, Re [1992] BCC 32   D7.5, D7.22
Matheson Brothers Ltd, Re (1884) 27 Ch D 225   C5.6
Matthews (D J) (Joinery Design) Ltd, Re (1988) 4 BCC 513   I7.3
Matthews (FP & CH) Ltd, Re [1982] 1 All ER 338   C10.4
Maude, ex parte (1870 LR 6 Ch App 51   C12.20
Maudsley Sons and Field, Re [1900] 1 Ch 602   D11.1, D12.1
Maurice v Tempany v Royal Liver Trustees Ltd and Others
    (Ireland) [1984] BCLC 568   C12.6
Mawcon Ltd, Re [1969] 1 WLR 78   C8.1
Maxwell Communications Corporation, Re (No 2); Barclays Bank
    plc v Homan and Others [1992] BCC 757   A5.3, B10.1
Maxwell Communications Corporation plc, Re (No 3) [1993]
    BCC 369   C14.36, C15.4
Meadrealm Ltd and Another v Transcontinental Golf Construction
    Ltd and Others (1991) Unreported, 29 November   D1.4
Measures Bros Ltd v Measures [1910] 2 Ch 248   C9.7
Medical Battery Co, Re [1894] 1 Ch 444   C5.29
Medisco Equipment Ltd, Re [1983] BCLC 305   C5.29
Meesan Investments Ltd (1988) 4 BCC 790   B4.1
Meigh v Wickenden [1942] 2 KB 160   D8.26
Melcann Ltd v Marmion Holdings Pty Ltd (Australia) (1991)
    9 ACLC 678   C5.36
Melcast (Wolverhampton) Ltd, Re [1991] BCLC 288   I6.1
Mellor v Mellor [1992] BCC 513   D4.9, D5.2
Melon v Hector Powe Ltd [1981] 1 All ER 313   D9.16
Memco Engineering Ltd, Re [1985] 3 All ER 267   C8.2, C9.4, C14.33, D7.13
Mercantile Bank of Australia, Re [1892] 2 Ch 204   C5.8
Merchant Navy Supply Association Ltd, Re [1947] 1 All ER 894   C15.9

Merrett v Capital Indemnity Corporation [1991] 1 Lloyd's Rep 169   C14.24

Mersey Steel & Iron Co v Naylor Benzon & Co (1882) 9 QBD
648, CA   C9.6, C14.26, F2.3

Mesco Properties Ltd, Re [1980] 1 All ER 117, [1979]
STC 788   C15.2, H2.3, H3.5, H3.8, H3.10

Metcalfe, Re; Hicks v May (1879) 13 Ch D 236   C14.3

Metropolitan Life Assurance Company of New Zealand Ltd v Essere
Print Ltd (in receivership) (New Zealand) (1990) 66 NZCL 775, CA   D7.13

Mettoy Pension Trustees Ltd v Evans and Others [1990]
1 WLR 1587   C12.17, C15.9, D8.17, D9.1

Mid-Kent Fruit Factory, Re [1896] 1 Ch 567   C14.26

Midland Bank plc v Chart Enterprises Inc [1990] 2 EGLR 59   D9.7

Midland Bank plc v Laker Airways Ltd [1986] QB 689   A5.3, B10.1

Mikkelsen v Danmols Inventar A/S (ECJ) [1986] 1 CMLR 316   D9.16

Milgate Developments Ltd, Re [1993] BCLC 291   C5.30

Millward (James), Re [1940] Ch 333   C5.29

Minna Craig Steamship Co v Chartered Mercantile Bank of India
London and China [1897] 1 QB 460   C5.6

Mirror Group (Holdings) Ltd, Re [1992] BCC 972   C14.21, D8.13

Mixhurst Ltd, Re [1993] BCC 748   G3.2

Mobil Oil Co Ltd v Rawlinson (1981) 43 P & CR 221   D1.5, D2.8, D7.5

Modiwear Ltd v Wallis Fashion Group EAT 535/80   D9.16

Mohammed Naeem, Re [1989] LS Gaz, 20 December, 37   E3.3

Moon v Franklin FTLR, June 1990   C10.10

Moonbeam Cards Ltd, Re [1993] BCLC 1099   I8.5

Moor v Anglo-Italian Bank (1879) 10 Ch D 681   C5.6

Moore (Sir John) Gold Mining Co, Re (1879) 12 Ch D 325   C11.24, C11.28

Morel (E J) (1934) Ltd, Re [1962] Ch 21   C14.26, D7.4

Morison (G H) & Co Ltd, Re (1912) 106 LT 731   D7.4

Morris Angel & Son Ltd v Hollande [1993] IRLR 169   D9.16

Morris v Director of Serious Fraud Office [1992] BCC 934   A4.19

Morris v Harris [1927] AC 252   G3.2, G3.3

Morris' Case (1871) LR 7 Ch App 200   C12.20

Mortgage Corporation Ltd v Nationwide Credit Corporation Ltd
[1993] 3 WLR 769   D2.5

Moss, Re [1905] 2 KB 307   C14.9

Mountforest Ltd, Re [1993] BCC 565   C3.1

Movitex Ltd, Re [1992] 1 WLR 303, [1992] BCC 101, CA rev'g
[1990] BCLC 785   A4.8, C11.19, C15.2

Multi Guarantee Co Ltd, Re [1987] BCLC 257, CA   D7.22

Multinational Gas and Petrochemical Co v Multinational Gas
and Petrochemical Services Ltd [1983] BCLC 461   C13.3

Munday v Secretary of State for Employment EAT 618/88   D7.2

Murray v Legal & General Assurance Society Ltd [1970]
2 QB 495   C14.24, C14.26

Murray v Strathclyde Regional Council [1992] IRLR 396   D8.3

NL Electrical Ltd, Re [1994] 1 BCLC 22   D4.8

NRG Vision Ltd v Churchfield Leasing Ltd (1988) 4 BCC 56   D2.8

NS Distribution Ltd, Re [1990] BCLC 169   B5.2, B5.4

NV Slavenburgs Bank v International Natural Resources Ltd
[1980] 1 All ER 955   D2.5

Nadler Enterprises Ltd, Re [1980] STC 457   D7.4

Napier (Lord) v Ettrick and Hunter [1993] AC 713, [1993] 1
All ER 385, HL   C14.24, D7.22

National Arms and Ammunition Co, Re (1885) 28 Ch D 474   C9.4, C12.18

National Bank of Australasia v United Hand in Hand and Band
  of Hope Co (1879) 4 App Cas 391   D9.17
National Bank of Canada and McArthur, Re (Canada) (1986) 53 OR
  (2d) 385   D6.2
National Bank of Greece SA v Pinios Shipping Co (No 1) [1989]
  3 WLR 1330   D2.12
National Benefit Assurance Co, Re (Canada) (1927) 3 DLR 289   C5.6
National Jazz Centre Ltd, Re (1988) 38 EG 142   C12.17
National Livestock Insurance Co, Re [1917] 1 Ch 628   C12.1
National Provincial Bank Ltd v Ainsworth [1965] AC 1175   B2.1
National Provincial Bank of England v United Electric Theatres Ltd
  [1916] 1 Ch 132   D6.2
National Union of Pulic Employees (1993) Unreported, 5 May
  (Scots Law report)   D9.16
National Westminster Bank Ltd v Halesowen Presswork and
  Assemblies Ltd [1972] AC 785   C14.26, C15.4
National Westminster Bank plc v Hornsea Pottery Company Ltd
  and Others (1984) Unreported, 11 May, CA   D7.26
National Westminster Bank plc v Skelton [1993] 1 All ER 242   D1.5, D7.5
Neale v Hereford & Worcester County Council [1986] ICR 471   D9.16
New Bullas Trading Ltd, Re [1994] BCC 36, CA   D4.8, D6.2
New Centurion Trust Ltd v Welsh [1990] IRLR 123, EAT   D8.3
New Gas Co, Re (1877) 5 Ch 703   C6.1
New Generation Engineers Ltd, Re [1993] BCLC 435   I5.7
New Oriental Bank Corporation, Re (No 2) [1895] 1 Ch 753   C14.21
Newfoundland Government v Newfoundland Railway Co (1887)
  13 App Cas 199   D7.5
Newhart Developments Ltd v Co-operative Commercial Bank Ltd
  [1978] 2 All ER 896, CA   D5.5
Newman and Howard Ltd, Re [1962] Ch 257   C5.26, C5.30
Newman Shopfitters (Cleveland) Ltd, Re [1991] BCLC 407   B6.1
Newport County Association Football Club Ltd, Re [1987] BCLC 582   B5.4
Newspaper Proprietary Syndicate Ltd, Re [1900] 2 Ch 349   D7.4
Nicholas v Soundcraft Electronics Ltd and Another [1993] BCLC 360   C5.30
Nicholson v Permkraft (NZ) Ltd (New Zealand) [1985] 1 NZLR 242, CA   C13.4
Noble (R A) (Clothing) Ltd, Re [1983] BCLC 273   C5.30
Noble Trees Ltd, Re [1993] BCC 318   I8.7
Nocoll v Cutts [1985] BCLC 322, CA   D8.2
Nokes v Doncaster Amalgamated Collieries Ltd [1940] AC 1014   D9.16
Norfolk House plc v Respol Ltd 1992 SLT 235   D11.1
Norman and Another v Theodore Goddard and Others [1991]
  BCLC 1028   I5.4
Norman Hartnell Ltd, Re (1987) Unreported   B4.1
Norman Holding Co Ltd, Re [1990] 3 All ER 757   C14.26
Norman v Theodore Goddard [1991] BCLC 1028   C13.2, C13.4
Normid Housing Association Ltd v Ralph [1989]
  1 Lloyd's Rep 265   C14.24
Norris v Checksfield [1991] 4 All ER 327, CA   D7.15
Norse Self Build Association Ltd, Re [1985[] BCLC 219   C5.8
North Australian Territory Co v Goldsborough Co (1889) 61 LT 716   C5.8
North Brazilian Sugar Factories, Re (1887) 37 Ch D 83   C11.19
North Bucks Furniture Depositories, Re [1939] Ch 690   C5.29
North Carolina Estate Co, Re (1889) 5 TLR 328   C5.6
Northern Bank Ltd v Ross [1990] BCC 883, NI CA   D6.2
Northern Counties of England Fire Insurance Co Ltd, Re;

MacFarlane's Claim (1880) 17 Ch D 337   C14.13
Northern General Hospital National Health Service Trust v Gale
  [1994] ICR 426   D9.16
Norton v Yates [1906] 1 KB 112   D7.9, D8.6
Norton Warburg Holdings and Another, Re [1983] BCLC 235   A4.19
Norwich Union Fire Insurance Society Ltd v William H Price Ltd
  [1934] AC 455   C11.24
Noyes v Pollock (1888) 32 Ch D 53   D1.5
Nugent v Nugent [1908] 1 Ch 546   D9.17
Number 1 London Ltd, Re [1991] BCLC 501   C12.6, G2.1
Nuneaton Borough Association Football Club Ltd, Re (1989)
  5 BCC 377   C5.30

O (Restraint Order: Disclosure of Assets), Re [1991] 2 QB 520   A4.19
O'Connor v Brian Smith Catering Services Ltd (1992) Unreported,
  18 March, EAT   D9.16
O'Loaire v Jackel International Ltd [1991] IRLR 170   C14.22
Oak Pits Colliery Co, Re (1882) 21 Ch D 322   C12.18
Oakwood Group plc v Renton and Others (1990) Unreported,
  22 February   D2.12
Official Custodian for Charities v Parway Estates Developments
  [1985] 1 Ch 151, [1984] 3 WLR 525, [1984] 3 All
  ER 679, CA   B1.1, C6.1, C8.4, C12.17, D7.14
Offshore Ventilation Ltd, Re (1989) 5 BCC 160, CA   D7.13
Ogdens v Nelson [1905] AC 109, HL   C9.6
Olympia & York Canary Wharf Ltd, Re [1993] BCC 154   B4.1
Ontario v Tyre King Recycling Ltd (Canada) (1992) 9 OR (3d) 318   D8.26
Opera Ltd, Re [1891] 3 Ch 260, CA   D7.9
Opera Photographic Ltd, Re [1989] BCLC 763   C3.7
Orakpo v Manson Investments Ltd [1977] 3 All ER 1   D7.23
Oriental Bank Corporation, Re (1884) 28 Ch D 634   C5.8, C6.1, C8.4
Oriental Credit Ltd, Re [1988] 2 WLR 172   A4.19
Oriental Inland Steam Co, Re (1874) 9 Ch App 557   C5.6
Orion Finance Ltd v Crown Financial Management Ltd (1994)
  Unreported, 30 March   B9.12, C12.10
Orlanda Investments Ltd v Grosvenor Estate Belgravia (1989)
  Unreported   D9.7
Osmondthorpe Hall Society, Re [1913] WN 243   C5.8
Ottotcha v Voest Alpine Intertrading GmbH The Times,
  21 September 1992   D8.16
Overmark Smith Warden Ltd, Re [1982] 3 All ER 513   C9.5
Oxted Motor Co Ltd [1921] 3 KB 32   C3.7

P & C and R & T (Stockport) Ltd, Re [1991] BCC 98   B7.2, B7.5
Packaging Direct Ltd, Re [1994] BCC 213   I8.2
Padre Island, The [1987] 2 Lloyd's Rep 529   C12.22
Palk v Mortgage Services Funding plc [1993] Ch 330, CA   D7.31
Palmer Marine Surveys Ltd, Re [1986] 1 WLR 573   C5.29
Pamstock Ltd, Re [1994] BCC 264   I6.1, I8.5
Panamericana de Bienes y Servicios SA v Northern Badger
  Oil & Gas Ltd (Canada) (1991) 81 DLR (4th) 280, (1991) 5
  WWR 577, 1 Alta LR (2d) 49, 2 OR (3d) 31, CA   D8.26
Parameters Ltd, Re (1988) Unreported, 9 May   B7.2
Paramount Airways Ltd, Re [1990] BCC 130   D7.7
Paramount Airways, Re (No 1). See Bristol Airport v Powdrill

Paramount Airways, Re (No 2) [1992] 3 WLR 690, [1992] 3 All ER 1,
   [1992] BCC 416 CA   A4.19, B9.4, B10.1, C10.1, C10.2, C10.4, I1.1
Paramount Airways, Re (No 3) [1994] BCC 172, CA, aff'g [1993]
   BCC 662   B7.7, D8.2, D8.3, D11.6
Park, Ward and Co, Re [1926] Ch 828   C8.4
Parker and Cooper Ltd v Reading [1926] Ch 975   C3.7
Parker, Re; Morgan v Hill [1894] 2 Ch 400   D10.4
Parker-Tweedale v Dunbar Bank plc (No 1) [1990] 2 All ER 577   D8.14
Parker-Tweedale v Dunbar Bank plc (No 2) [1990] 2 All ER 588   D2.12, D10.4
Parkes Garage (Swadlincote) Ltd, Re [1929] 1 Ch 139   C10.9, D2.5
Patrick & Lyon Ltd, Re [1933] Ch 786   C13.1
Paul v Speirway Ltd [1976] 2 All ER 587   D7.23
Peachdart Ltd, Re [1984] 1 Ch 131   D7.18
Peake and Hall, Re [1985] PCC 87   C13.1
Pearce Duff and Co Ltd, Re [1960] 3 All ER 222   C3.7
Peat v Gresham Trust [1934] AC 252   C10.4
Peat v Jones (1881) 8 QBD 147   C14.26
Pellicano v MEPC plc (1994) 19 EG 138   C12.6
Pename Ltd v Patterson [1989] IRLR 195   D8.3
Pennington & Owen Ltd, Re [1925] 1 Ch 825   C12.1, C14.26
Perak Pioneer Ltd v Petroliam Nasional BhD [1986] 3 WLR
   105, PC   C5.38
Perfectaire Holdings Ltd, Re [1990] BCLC 423   C5.30
Perkins, Re [1898] 2 Ch 105   C14.21
Permanent House Holdings Ltd, Re (1989) 5 BCC 151   D6.2
Perry v Intec Colleges Ltd [1993] IRLR 56   D9.16
Perry v Walker (1855) 3 Eq Rep 721   D1.5
Peruvian Amazon Co, Re (1913) 29 TLR 384   C5.26
Peruvian Railway Construction Co, Re [1915] 2 Ch 144   C12.1
Pfeiffer (E) Weinkellerei-Weineinkauf GmbH & Co v Arbuthnot Factors
   [1988] 1 WLR 150   D7.18
Philex plc v Golban. See also Company, A, Re (No 0022 of 1993)
   [1994] BCC 390, rev'g [1993] BCC 726   C5.29
Philipson, Re (1993) Unreported, 10 & 13 September   A6.1
Phillip and Lion Ltd, Re [1994] BCC 261   I8.2
Phoenix Oil and Transport Co Ltd, Re (No 2) [1958] Ch 565   C1.6
Phoenix Properties Ltd v Wimpole Street Nominees Ltd [1992]
   BCLC 73   D3.1
Phonographic Equipment (1958) Ltd v Muslu [1961] 3 All ER 626   C8.3
Piggin, Re; Dicker v Lombank Ltd The Law Journal, Vol CXII
   (29 June 1962)   C8.3
Pitman (Harold M) & Co v Toip Business Systems (Nottingham) Ltd
   [1984] BCLC 593   C11.25
Pitt v PHH Asset Management Ltd [1993] 4 All ER 961, CA   D9.15
Pittman v Davis Build plc (in liquidation) EAT 122/90   D9.16
Pleatfine Ltd, Re [1983] BCLC 102   C5.2
Pollitt, Re [1893] 1 QB 455   C14.26
Polly Peck International plc (in administration), Re (1991) Unreported,
   27 June   B7.7
Polly Peck International plc, Re [1991] BCC 503   B5.10, B8.1
Polly Peck International plc, Re (No 2) [1993] BCC 890   I2.5, I5.5, I8.2
Polly Peck International plc v Nadir (No 3) The Times, 22
   March 1993   B10.1
Port Talbot Engineering Co Ltd v Passmore [1975] IRLR 156   D9.16
Portafram Ltd, Re [1986] BCLC 533   G3.3

Portbase (Clothing) Ltd, Re [1993] BCC 96   D10.3, D10.4
Porter v Queens Medical Centre [1993] IRLR 486   D9.16
Post Office v Norwich Union Fire Insurance Society Ltd [1977]
   1 All ER 577   C14.24
Potel v IRC [1971] 2 All ER 504   C14.26
Potter v Hunt Contracts Ltd [1992] IRLR 108   D8.3
Potters Oils Ltd, Re [1985] PCC 148   C12.6
Potters Oils Ltd, Re (No 2) [1986] 1 WLR 201   D4.9
Pound (Henry) Son and Hutchings, Re (1889) 42 Ch D 402   B4.1
Practice Direction [1986] 1 WLR 1428   C5.42
Practice Direction [1986] 1 WLR 545   C5.42
Practice Direction [1988] 1 WLR 998   C5.36
Practice Direction (Companies Court) [1987] 1 All ER 107, [1987]
   1 WLR 53   A5.1, C5.36, C5.42, C11.23
Practice Direction (Insolvency Appeals: Hearings outside London)
   [1992] 3 All ER 921, [1992] 1 WLR 791   A5.1
Practice Direction No 1 of 1990 (Companies Court:
   Contributory's Petitions) [1990] BCC 292   C5.26, C5.30, C5.34, C8.4
Practice Note (1976) 120 SJ 317   C5.44
Practice Note [1928] WN 218   G3.4
Practice Note [1931] WN 199   G3.4
Practice Note [1971] 1 WLR 4   C5.45
Practice Note [1971] 1 WLR 757   C5.45
Practice Note [1974] 1 WLR 1459   C5.42
Practice Note [1980] 1 WLR 657   C5.36
Practice Note [1994] 1 All ER 324   B3.1
Pratt, Re [1951] Ch 225   D7.4
Precision Dippings Ltd v Precision Dippings Marketing Ltd [1985]
   3 WLR 812, CA   C12.9
Premier Motors (Medway) Ltd v Total Oil Great Britain Ltd [1983]
   IRLR 471   D9.16
Prescott, ex parte (1840) 1 MD BD 199   C14.10
Price Waterhouse v BCCI Holdings (Luxembourg) SA [1992]
   BCLC 583   A4.19
Priestly v Clegg (South Africa) 1985 (3) SA 955   C14.13
Prime Metal Trading Ltd, Re [1984] BCLC 543   C11.14
Primlaks (UK) Ltd, Re (1989) 5 BCC 710   B2.1
Primlaks (UK) Ltd, Re (1989) Unreported, December   E3.3
Primrose (Builders) Ltd, Re [1950] 1 Ch 561   D7.4
Printing and Numerical Registering Co, Re (1878) 8 Ch D 535   C14.30
Pritchard v National Westminster Bank Ltd [1969] 1 WLR 547, CA   D7.11
Probe Data Systems Ltd, Re (1989) 5 BCC 384   I2.5, I8.2
Probe Data Systems Ltd, Re (No 2) [1990] BCC 21   I8.2
Probe Data Systems Ltd, Re (No 3) [1992] BCC 110, aff'g [1991]
   BCC 428, [1991] BCLC 586   A5.1, I8.2, I8.10
Produce Marketing Consortium Ltd, Re (1989) 5 BCC 569   D9.1
Produce Marketing Consortium Ltd, Re (No 2) [1989] BCLC 520   C13.2, C13.5
Pulsford v Devenish [1903] 2 Ch 625   C14.1, G2.1
Purcell v Queensland Public Curator (Australia) (1922) 31
   CLR 220   D7.13
Purpoint Ltd, Re [1991] BCLC 491; (1990) Unreported,
   18 July 1990   C13.2, C13.4

Queen v Customs and Excise (1988) Digest of Cases, Issue 49, p 839   D7.6
Quest Cae Ltd, Re [1985] BCLC 266   D2.12

Quintex Australia Finals Ltd v Schroeders Australia Ltd (Australia)
(1991) 9 ACLC 109, 111   C15.4

R v Appleyard (1985) 81 Cr App R 319   I2.1
R v Associated Octel Co Ltd [1994] IRLR 540, CA   D8.6
R v Austen (1985) 1 BCC 99, 528   I7.1
R v Brockley [1994] BCC 131   I2.8
R v Campbell [1984] BCLC 83   I7.1
R v Clowes and Others (1991) Unreported, 21 June   C11.24
R v Corbin (1984) 6 Cr App R (S) 17   I2.1
R v Esal Commodities Ltd, ex parte Central Bank of India [1986]
1 All ER 105, CA   D2.5
R v Georgiou (1988) 4 BCC 322   I2.1
R v Goodman [1992] BCC 625   I2.1
R v Grantham [1984] BCLC 270, CA   C13.1
R v Kansal [1992] BCC 615   A4.19
R v Kemp [1988] BCLC 217   C13.1
R v Philippou (1989) 5 BCC 665   C13.1
R v Registrar of Companies, ex parte Attorney-General [1991]
BCLC 476   G1.6
R v Registrar of Companies, ex parte Central Bank of India [1986] 1 All
ER 105   G1.6
R v Registrar of Companies, ex parte Esal (Commodities) Ltd [1986]
2 WLR 177   C9.10
R v Robinson [1990] BCC 656, CA   C6.1
R v Secretary of State for Trade and Industry, ex parte Lonrho plc [1992]
BCC 325   I3.1
R v Seillon [1982] Crim LR 676   C13.1
R v Sinclair [1958] 1 WLR 1246   C13.2
R v Young [1990] BCC 549   I2.1
RMC Roadstone Products Ltd v Jester [1994] IRLR 330, DC   D8.6
RR Realisations Ltd, Re [1980] 1 All ER 1019   C14.1
Rackham v Peek Foods Ltd [1990] BCLC 895   C13.4
Rae, Re (1994) Unreported, 15 July   B4.1
Rafidain Bank, Re [1992] BCC 376   C5.6, C8.4, C15.4
Rafsanjan Pistachio Producers Co-operative v Reiss [1990]
BCC 730   C13.3
Railways and Canal Commission, Re The Times, 1 June 1892   D7.7
Rainbow v Moorgate Properties Ltd [1975] 1 WLR 788, [1975]
2 All ER 821, CA   C9.3, D7.11
Rampgill Mill Ltd, Re [1967] 1 Ch 1138   D7.4
Rank Film Distributors Ltd v Video Information Centre [1982]
AC 380   A4.19
Rask and Christensen v ISS Kantinservice A/S [1993] IRLR 133   D9.16
Rastill v Automatic Refreshment Services Ltd [1978] ICR 289   D9.16
Ratford v Northavon District Council [1986] BCLC 397, CA   D8.11, D8.26
Rawlings v Barclays Bank plc [1900] EGCS 50, CA   D8.14
Real Estate Development Co, Re [1991] BCLC 210   C5.8
Record Tennis Centres Ltd, Re (See also Company, A, Re
(No 004055 of 1991)) [1991] BCC 509   C5.29, C5.44
Record v Bell [1991] 1 WLR 853, [1991] 4 All ER 471   D9.7, D9.17
Redmond (Dr. Sophie) Stichting v Bartol (ECJ Case C29/91)
[1992] IRLR 366   D9.16
Reeves v Pope [1914] 2 KB 284   B2.1
Regent Insulation Co Ltd, Re The Times, 5 November 1981   G3.3

Registered Securities Ltd, Re (New Zealand) [1991] 1 NZLR 545   C15.4
Reliance Wholesale (Toys) Ltd, Re; Patterson v Mills (1979) LS Gaz
   18 July   C13.4
Rencoule Joiners and Shopfitters Ltd v Hunt (1967) 2 ITR 475   D9.16
Rendell v Doors and Doors Ltd (in liquidation) (New Zealand)
   [1975] 2 NZLR 191   D7.5
Reprographics Exports (Euromat) Ltd, Re (1978) 122 SJ 400   C5.44
Rex Williams Leisure Ltd, Re [1994] BCC 551, CA, [1993] BCC 79   I8.5, I8.6
Reynolds Bros (Motor) Pty Ltd v Escanda (Australia) (1983)
   8 ACLR 422   D6.2
Rhodes (JT) Ltd, Re [1987] BCLC 77   A4.19
Rhodes v Allied Dunbar Pension Services Ltd; Offshore Ventilation Ltd,
   Re (1989) 5 BCC 160   D6.2
Rhodesia Goldfields Ltd, Re [1910] 1 Ch 239   C14.14
Rica Gold Washing Co, Re (1879) 11 Ch D 36   B3.2
Richards v Kidderminster Overseers [1896] 2 Ch 212   D8.11
Rickard v B B Glass Supplies Ltd [1990] ICR 150   D8.3
Riddeough, Re; Vaughan, ex parte (1884) 14 QBD 25   D8.15
Ringtower Holdings Ltd, Re (1989) 5 BCC 82   C5.30
Riviera Pearls, Re [1962] 1 WLR 722   C5.26
Robbie (N W) & Co Ltd v Witney Warehouse Co Ltd [1963] 1
   WLR 1324, [1963] 3 All ER 614, CA   C10.2, C10.4, D7.5, D7.13, F2.5, F2.7
Robert Stephenson & Co Ltd, Re [1913] 2 Ch 201, CA   D6.2
Roberts Petroleum Ltd v Bernard Kenny Ltd [1983]
   1 All ER 564, [1983] BCLC 28, HL   C4.9, C8.2, C9.3, C9.10, D7.11
Robertson (A Bankrupt), Re [1989] 1 WLR 1139   C5.46
Robinson v Kitchin (1856) 8 De GM & G 88   A4.19
Robson v Smith [1895] 2 Ch 188   D7.9
Roburn Construction Ltd v William Irwin (South) and Co Ltd
   [1991] BCC 726   D8.16
Roehampton Swimming Pool Ltd, Re [1968] 1 WLR 1693   G3.2
Rolled Steel Products (Holdings) Ltd v British Steel Corporation
   [1985] 2 WLR 908, [1985] 3 All ER 52, CA   C10.2, C12.9, D2.3
Rolls Razor Ltd v Cox [1967] 1 QB 552, [1967] 2 WLR 241   C12.17, C14.26
Rolls Razor Ltd, Re (No 2) [1970] Ch 576   A4.19, I8.10
Rolus Properties Ltd, Re [1988] BCC 446   I5.1, I6.1
Rome v Punjab National Bank (1989) 5 BCC 785   C5.24, C5.35
Roselmar Properties Ltd (No 2), Re (1986) 2 BCC 99   C5.29
Rosemary Simmons Memorial Housing Association v United
   Dominions Trust Ltd [1986] 1 WLR 1440   C12.9
Ross v Taylor 1985 SLT 387   C10.4, C13.1, D6.2
Rosseel NV v Oriental Commercial and Shipping (UK) Ltd
   [1991] 2 Lloyd's Rep 625   D7.11
Rother Iron Works Ltd v Canterbury Precision Engineers Ltd [1974]
   QB 1, CA   D7.5, D7.30
Rottenberg v Monjack [1992] BCC 688   D5.3, D8.14
Roundwood Colliery Co, Re [1897] 1 Ch 373   D7.13
Rowbotham Baxter Ltd, Re [1990] BCC 113   B2.1, B3.1, B3.2, B5.16
Rowlands (Mark) v Berni Inns Ltd [1985] 3 All ER 473   C14.24
Royal Bank Trust v Buchler [1989] BCLC 130   B4.1, B4.2
Rubber Improvements Ltd, Re The Times, 5 June 1962   C5.29
Rubber Investment Co, Re [1915] 1 Ch 382   C11.24
Rubber Produce Investment Trust, Re [1915] 1 Ch 382   C11.28
Rudd & Sons Ltd, Re [1984] Ch 237   C14.33
Runciman v Walter Runciman plc [1992] BCLC 1084   D2.7

Rushingdale Ltd SA v Byblos Bank SAL [1985] PCC 342   B7.2
Russell (J) Electronics Ltd, Re [1968] 1 WLR 1252   C5.32
Ryder Installations, Re [1966] 1 WLR 524   C5.29
Rylands v Fletcher (1868) LR 3 HL 330   D8.26

SCL Building Services Ltd, Re (1989) 5 BCC 746   B2.1
SEIL Trade Finance Ltd, Re [1992] BCC 538   A4.20
SIP Industrial Products Ltd v Swinn [1994] IRLR 323   D8.3
SN Group plc v Barclays Bank plc [1993] BCC 506   C5.36
Sabre International Products Ltd, Re [1991] BCLC 470   B4.1
Safety Explosives Ltd, Re [1904] 1 Ch 226   C14.30
Said v Butt [1920] 3 KB 497   D8.15
Saint Clair Sampson Ltd, Re (1984) Unreported, 20 July   D10.4
Saint Ives Windings Ltd, Re (1987) 3 BCC 634   B5.17
Saint James' Club, Re (1852) 2 De GM & G 383   C5.8
Saint Piran Ltd, Re [1981] 3 All ER 270   C5.34
Salcombe Hotel Developments Co Ltd, Re (1989) 5 BCC 807   C4.6
Sam Weller Ltd, Re [1989] 3 WLR 923   C5.30
Samuel Keller (Holdings) Ltd v Martins Bank Ltd [1971]
    1 WLR 43   D1.15, D2.8, D7.5
Samuel Sherman plc, Re [1991] 1 WLR 1070   I6.1
Sandwell Copiers Ltd, Re [1989] PCC 413   C15.2
Sarflex Ltd, Re [1979] 1 All ER 529   C13.1
Sargent v Customs & Excise Commissioners [1994] 1 WLR 235,
    [1994] STC 11   D8.5, H3.15
Saul D Harrison & Sons plc, Re [1994] BCC 475   C5.30
Saunders (G L) Ltd, Re [1986] 1 WLR 215   C12.1, D7.3
Sauter Automation Ltd v H C Goodman (Mechanical Services) Ltd
    FTLR, 14 May 1986   D7.18
Saxton v Miles [1983] BCLC 70   C4.9
Scher and Ackman v Policyholders Protection Board [1993]
    3 All ER 384   C14.23
Scher and Ackman v Policyholders Protection Board (No 2) [1993]
    4 All ER 840   C14.23
Schmidt v Spar und Leihkasse der früheren Amter Bordesholm,
    Kiel und Cronshagen (ECJ) [1994] IRLR 302   D9.16
Scholey v Peck (1893) 1 Ch 709   D7.7
Scientific Research Council v Nasse [1980] AC 1028   B4.2
Scotlane Ltd, Re (1987) Unreported, 31 July   B7.2
Scottish Co-operative Wholesale Society Ltd v Meyer [1959]
    AC 324   C5.30, C13.2
Scottish Exhibition Centre Ltd, Noters [1993] BCC 529   B4.1
Scottish Granite Co, Re (1868) 17 LT 533   C11.24, C11.28
Scottish Poultry Journal Co, Re (1896) 4 SLT 167   D7.4
Seagull Manufacturing Co Ltd, Re [1993] BCC 241   A4.19, C11.22, I1.1
Seagull Manufacturing Co Ltd, Re (No 2) [1993] BCC 833   I1.1
Secretary of State for Employment v Anchor Hotel (Kippford) Ltd
    [1985] IRLR 452   D9.16
Secretary of State for Employment v Cooper [1987] ICR 766   D7.2
Secretary of State for Employment v Spence and Others [1986]
    IRLR 248, CA   D9.16
Secretary of State for India, Re (1859) 13 Moo PC 22   C5.8
Secretary of State for Trade and Industry v Checketts and Another;
    Southbourne Sheet Metal Co Ltd, Re [1992] BCC 797, CA, rev'g
    [1991] BCC 732   I8.9

Secretary of State for Trade and Industry v Langridge; Cedac, Re [1991]
BCC 148, CA, rev'g [1990] BCC 555   I8.1
Secretary of State for Trade and Industry v Palmer The Times, 4
November 1994, aff'g [1993] BCC 650   I8.2
Secretary of State for Trade and Industry v Sananes [1994] BCC 375   I2.5
Secure & Provide plc, Re [1992] BCC 405   C5.31
Securities and Investments Board v Lancashire and Yorkshire
Portfolio Management Ltd [1992] BCC 381   C5.26, C5.29
Security Trust Co v Royal Bank of Canada [1976] 1 All ER 381   D7.23
Sedgwick Collins and Co Ltd v Russia Insurance Co of Petrograd
[1926] 1 KB 1   C5.6
Selangor United Rubber Estates Ltd v Cradock [1967] 1 WLR 1168   C13.4
Selangor United Rubber Estates Ltd v Cradock (No 4) [1969]
1 WLR 1773   C14.14
Serene Shoes Ltd, Re [1958] 1 WLR 1087   C11.22
Servers of the Blind League, Re [1960] 1 WLR 564   G3.2
Sevenoaks Stationers (Retail) Ltd, Re [1991] Ch 164, [1990] 3 WLR
1165, CA   I5.3, I5.7, I6.1, I8.5
Shamji and Others v Johnson Matthey Bankers Ltd and Others
[1986] BCLC 278, [1991] BCLC 36, CA   D2.8
Shanley (MJ) Contracting Ltd, Re (1979) 124 SJ 239   C3.7
Sharp v Jackson [1899] AC 419   C10.4
Sharpe, Re [1980] 1 WLR 219   D7.25
Sharps of Truro Ltd, Re [1990] BCC 94   B3.1
Shepherd v Spanheath Ltd [1988] EGCS 35   D1.5
Sheridan Securities Ltd, Re (1988) 4 BCC 200   B7.1
Sherratt (W A) Ltd v John Bromley (Church Streeton) Ltd [1985]
QB 1038, [1985] BCLC 170, CA   C14.30, D7.23
Sherry, Re; London and County Banking Company v Terry (1884)
25 Ch D 692   C14.33
Shilena Hosiery Co Ltd, Re [1979] 2 All ER 6   C10.10
Shizelle, The [1992] 2 Lloyd's Rep 444   D7.23
Shoe Lace Ltd, Re [1993] BCC 609, CA aff'g [1992] BCC 367   C10.9
Shorrock Ltd v Meggitt plc [1991] BCC 471   D9.3
Shusella Ltd, Re [1983] BCLC 505   C5.44
Siebe Gorman & Co Ltd v Barclays Bank Ltd [1979] 2 Lloyd's
Rep 142   D6.2
Signland Ltd, Re [1982] 2 All ER 609   C5.36
Silkstone Coal Co v Edey [1900] 1 Ch 167   C11.24
Silver Valley Mines Ltd, Re (1882) 21 Ch D 381, CA   C11.24
Simm v Anglo-American Telegraph Co (1879) 5 QBD 188   D7.25
Simmonds v Heffer and Others [1983] BCLC 298   C12.9
Simms, Re [1934] Ch 1   D8.15
Sinclair v Brougham [1914] AC 398, HL   D7.22
Singlehurst v Tapscott Steamship Co Ltd (1899) 107 LT Jo 347   C13.5
Skeats' Settlement, Re (1889) 42 Ch D 522   D8.17
Sklan Ltd, Re [1961] 1 WLR 1013   C5.29
Smalley v Hardinge (1881) 7 QBD 524   C12.6
Smallman Construction Ltd, Re (1988) 4 BCC 784   B5.15
Smith (M H) (Plant Hire) Ltd v D L Mainwaring [1986] BCLC 342   G2.1
Smith (W H) Ltd v Wyndham Investments Ltd [1994] BCC 699   C12.6
Smith v Lord Advocate (No 2) 1981 SLT 19   D7.6
Smith v Phillips (1837) 1 Keen 694   C12.6
Smith v Wood [1929] 1 Ch 14   D10.4
Smiths Ltd v Middleton [1979] 3 All ER 842   D5.5

Smoker v London Fire and Civil Defence Authority; Wood v British
   Coal Corporation [1991] 2 All ER 449, HL   C14.22
Snowden, ex parte (1881) 17 Ch D 44   D10.4
Société Nationale Industrielle Aerospatiale v Lee Kui Jak [1987]
   AC 871   A5.3, B10.1
Solar (Sales) Ltd MAN/87/428 No 2988   D9.13
Solomons v Gertzenstein [1954] 2 QB 243   D8.6
Somes, Re (1896) 3 Mans 131   C5.6
Sonido International Ltd v Peters 1991 SCLR 874   B3.2
Sonnethal v Newton (1965) 109 SJ 333   D9.7
Sorge (A V) & Co Ltd, Re [1986] BCLC 490   C11.27
South Australian Baryates Ltd v Wood (Australia) (1978) SASR 527   D9.1
South London Fish Market, Re (1888) 39 Ch D 324   C5.8
Southard & Co Ltd, Re [1979] 1 WLR 546   C5.29
Southern Cross Commodities Pty Ltd v Marlin 1991 SLT 85   D7.22
Sovereign Distribution Services v TGWU [1989] IRLR 334   D7.1
Sowman v David Samuel Trust Ltd [1978] 1 WLR 22, [1978]
   BCLC 1   C8.4, C9.8, D5.2, D8.11
Space Investments Ltd v Canadian Imperial Bank of Commerce
   Trust Company (Bahamas) Ltd [1986] 1 WLR 1072, PC   D7.22
Specialised Mouldings Ltd (1987) Unreported, 13 February   B7.7, D8.3
Specialist Plant Services Ltd v Braithwaite [1987] BCLC 1, CA   D7.18
Spedley Securities Ltd v Bond Growing Investments Pty Ltd
   (Australia) (1991) 9 ACLC 522   A4.19
Spijkers v Gebroeders Benedik Abbatoir CV (ECJ Case 24/85)
   [1986] 2 CMLR 296   D9.13, D9.16
Spiraflite Ltd, Re [1979] 1 WLR 1096   A4.19
Spiro v Glencrown Properties Ltd [1991] 2 WLR 931   D9.7
Stacey v Hill [1901] 1 KB 660, CA   C12.6
Standard Chartered Bank v Walker [1982] 1 WLR 1410, [1982]
   3 All ER 938   B7.6, D8.14
Standard Chartered Bank v Walker and Another [1992]
   BCLC 603   A3.1
Standard Insurance Co, Re (Australia) [1968] Qd St R 118   C5.6, C14.27
Standard Manufacturing Co, Re [1891] 1 Ch 627, CA   D7.9
Stanford Services Ltd, Re (1987) 3 BCC 326   I6.1
Stanlake Holding Ltd v Capital Investment Ltd FTLR, 25 June
   1991, CA   D7.22
Stanton (F & E) Ltd, Re [1929] 1 Ch 180   C10.9
Starside Properties Ltd v Mustapha [1974] 1 WLR 816   D7.14
Steel Linings Ltd v Bibby & Co The Times, 30 March 1993   D7.13
Steel Wing Co, Re [1921] 1 Ch 349   C5.29
Stein v Blake [1993] BCC 587   C14.26
Stetzel Thomson & Co Ltd, Re (1988) 4 BCC 74   C11.25
Stewart Gill Ltd v Horation Meyer & Co Ltd [1992] QB 600,
   [1992] 2 All ER 257   D7.5
Stirling v Dietsmann Management Systems Ltd [1991] IRLR 368   D9.16
Stockloser v Johnson [1954] 1 All ER 630   C8.3
Stockton Iron Company, Re (1875) 2 Ch D 101   C14.26
Stonegate Securities Ltd v Gregory [1980] 1 All ER 241, CA   C5.29, C5.36
Stoneleigh Finance Ltd v Phillips [1965] 2 QB 537   C12.10
Strathblaine Estates, Re [1948] Ch 228   G2.1
Stroud Architectural Systems Ltd v John Laing Construction Ltd
   (1993) Building LM 4.93, 3   D7.18
Stuart, Re [1897] 2 Ch 583   C13.5

Sugar Properties (Drisley Wood) Ltd, Re [1988] BCLC 146 — C8.4
Suidair International Airways Ltd, Re [1951] Ch 165 — C5.6
Sunderland Polytechnic v Evans [1993] ICR 392 — D8.3
Surplus Properties (Huddersfield) Ltd, Re [1984] BCLC 89 — C5.29
Swain (J D) Ltd, Re [1965] 1 WLR 909 — C5.29
Swift 736 Ltd, Re; Secretary of State for Trade & Industry v
    Ettinger [1993] BCC 312 — I6.1
Swiss Bank Corporation v Lloyds Bank Ltd [1981] 2 All ER 449,
    HL aff'g [1980] 2 All ER 19, CA rev'g [1979] Ch 548, [1979]
    2 All ER 853 — D7.22, D8.15
Synthetic Technology Ltd, Re [1990] BCLC 378 — B5.4, B7.3
Synthetic Technology Ltd, Re [1993] BCC 549 — I6.1, I8.9

T & D Services (Timber Preservation & Damp Proofing Contractors)
    Ltd, Re [1990] BCC 592 — I6.1, I8.8
TCB Ltd v Gray [1986] 1 All ER 587 — D2.3, D2.4
TH Knitwear (Wholesale) Ltd, Re [1987] BCLC 86 — C14.8
Taggs Island Casino Hotel Ltd v London Borough of
    Richmond-upon-Thames (1968) 14 RRC 119 — D8.11
Tailby v Official Receiver (1888) 13 App Cas 523 — D6.2
Tansag Haulage Ltd v Leyland DAF Finance plc [1994] BCC 350 — D7.14
Tansoft Ltd, Re [1991] BCLC 339 — I5.1, I5.7, I6.1
Tasbian Ltd, Re [1990] BCC 318, CA, aff'g (1989) 5 BCC 729 — I2.5, I8.2
Tasbian Ltd, Re (No 2) [1990] BCC 322 — I8.10
Tasbian Ltd, Re (No 3) [1992] BCC 358, CA, aff'g [1991]
    BCC 435 — C13.2, I1.1, I8.2, I8.10
Tatung (UK) Ltd v Galex Telesure Ltd (1989) 5 BCC 25 — D7.18
Taunton v Sheriff of Warwickshire [1895] 2 Ch 319 — D7.9
Tay Bok Choon v Tahanson Sdn Bhd [1987] BCLC 472 — C5.26
Tay Valley Joinery Ltd v CF Financial Services Ltd (1987) 3 BCC 71 — D11.1
Taylor v Pace Developments Ltd [1991] BCC 406, CA — C5.44
Taylor, Note r [1992] BCC 440 — C11.26
Taylors Industrial Flooring Ltd v M & H Plant Hire (Manchester)
    Ltd [1990] BCC 44 — C5.22, C5.29
Tejani v Official Receiver [1963] 1 WLR 59 — C11.22
Telecom Australia v Russel Kumar & Sons (1993) 10 ACSR 24 — D5.1
Telematrix plc v Modern Engineers of Bristol (Holdings) plc and
    Others [1985] BCLC 213 — D8.15, D8.16
Telescriptor Syndicate Ltd, Re [1903] 2 Ch 174 — C5.46
Tellfa Furniture Pty Ltd v Glendave Nominees Pty Ltd (Australia)
    (1987) 13 ACLR 64 — C8.4
Telsen Electric Co Ltd v J J Eastick & Sons [1936] 3 All ER 266 — C9.6
Test Holdings (Clifton) Ltd, Re — G3.3
Thomas Saunders Partnership v M A Harvey The Times, 10 May 1989 — C13.3
Thomas v Patent Lionite Co, Re (1881) 17 Ch D 250 — C14.31
Thomas v Todd [1926] 2 KB 511 — D5.2
Thompson and Cottrell's Contract, Re [1943] 1 All ER 169 — C12.6
Thompson and Riches Ltd, Re [1981] 2 All ER 477 — G3.3
Thompsons Soft Drinks Ltd v Quayle EAT 12/81 — D9.16
Thorne (H E) & Sons Ltd, Re [1914] 2 Ch 438 — C12.1
Thorpe (William) & Son Ltd, Re (1989) 5 BCC 156 — C5.29
Thrells v Lomas [1993] 2 All ER 546 — D9.1
Thundercrest Ltd, Re [1994] BCC 857 — D2.8, E3.1
Time Utilising Business Systems Ltd, Re (1989) 5 BCC 851 — I8.10
Todd (L) (Swanscombe) Ltd, Re [1990] BCC 125 — C13.1

Tong Aik (Far East) Ltd v Esatern Minerals & Trading (1959) Ltd
    (Malaya) [1965] 2 MLJ 149   C5.6
Tootal Clothing Ltd v Guinea Properties Management Ltd [1992]
    41 EG 117   D9.17
Tout & Finch, Re [1954] 1 WLR 178   C12.19
Townreach Ltd, Re [1994] 3 WLR 983   G3.2
Traders' North Staffordshire Carrying Co, Re (1874) LR 19 Eq 60   C9.4
Tramway Building & Construction Co Ltd, Re (1987) 3 BCC 443   C8.4
Transit Casualty Co v Policyholders Protection Board [1991]
    1 Re LR 49   C14.23
Travel Mondial (UK) Ltd, Re [1991] BCLC 120, [1991] BCC 224   I6.1, I8.8
Trepca Mines Ltd, Re [1960] 3 All ER 304   C14.5
Trident International Freight Services Ltd v Manchester Ship Canal
    Co [1990] BCLC 263, CA   A4.24
Trinity Insurance Co Ltd, Re [1990] BCC 235   C5.29
Trix Ltd, Re [1970] 1 WLR 1421   C11.26
Trustee Savings Bank plc v Kantz The Times, 2 May 1994   C10.10
Tse Kwong Lam v Wong Chit Sen (Hong Kong) [1983] BCLC 88   D9.17
Tuck (A & G) Ltd v Bartlett [1994] IRLR 162, EAT   D9.16
Tucker, Re [1988] 1 All ER 603   A4.19
Tudor Grange Holdings Ltd v Citibank [1991] 4 All ER 1   D5.5, D7.26
Tunbridge (G E) Ltd, Re [1994] BCC 563   D6.2
Turner (P) (Willesden) Ltd, Re [1987] BCLC 149, CA   C5.41
Turner, Petitioner [1993] BCC 299   D7.6
Tweeds Garage Ltd, Re [1962] Ch 406   C5.29
Tymans Ltd v Craven [1952] 2 QB 100, CA   G3.3

UCKATT v Brain [1981] ICR 452   D9.16
UK Security Services (Midland) Ltd v Gibbons EAT 104/90   D9.16
US Ltd, Re (1983) L S Gaz, 9 November   C11.29
Union Accident Insurance Co Ltd, Re [1972] 1 WLR 640   C8.1
Union Bank of Calcutta, Re (1850) 3 De G & SSM 253   C5.6
Unisoft Group Ltd, Re [1994] BCC 11   C5.30
Unit 2 Windows Ltd, Re [1985] 1 WLR 1383   C14.26, D7.4, D7.6
United Dominions Trust Ltd v Shellpoint Trustees Ltd [1993]
    4 All ER 310, CA   D7.14
United States v Fleet Factors Corporation (USA) 901 F 2d 1550
    11th Cir 1990, (1991) 111 S Ct 752   D8.25, D8.26
Universal Thermosensors Ltd v Hibben [1992] 3 All ER 257   D9.15
Urethane Engineering Products Ltd, Re (1989) 5 BCC 614, CA   D7.2
Urman, Re (Canada) (1983) 48 CBS (NS) 129, Ont CA   D6.2
Urmston Grange Steamship Co, Re (1901) 17 TLR 553   C11.28
Usdaw v Leancut Bacon Ltd [1981] IRLR 295   D7.1
Utlamchandami v Central Bank of India The Independent,
    31 January 1989   D7.5

VIP Insurance Ltd, Re (Australia) (1978) 3 ACLR 751   D7.4
Van Haarlam v Kasner Charitable Trust [1992] NPC 11   D7.14
Vartex Petroleum Industries Pty Ltd, Re (Australia) [1990]
    5 JIBL N-1133   D9.17
Vautin, Re [1900] 2 QB 325   C10.4
Vedmay Ltd, Re The Independent, 4 October 1993   C12.6
Vehicle & General Insurance Co Ltd v Elmbridge Insurances [1973]
    1 Lloyd's Rep 325   C12.17
Victoria Society, Knottinglery, Re [1913] 1 Ch 167   C5.8

Virgo Systems Ltd, Re (1989) 5 BCC 833 — C5.45
Vivian (H H) & Co Ltd, Re [1900] 2 CH 654 — D6.2
Vocalion (Foreign) Ltd, Re [1932] 2 Ch 196 — C5.6
Vujnovich v Vujnovich [1990] BCLC 227, PC — C5.30
Vuma Ltd, Re [1960] 1 WLR 1283 — C5.29

Wait, Re [1927] 1 Ch 606 — D7.25
Wala Wynaad Indian Gold Mining Co, Re (1882) 21 Ch D 849 — C5.30
Walden Engineering Co Ltd v Warrener [1993] IRLR 420, EAT — D9.16
Walford v Miles [1992] 1 All ER 453, HL — D9.15
Walkden Sheet Metal Co Ltd, Re [1960] Ch 170 — C9.2, C9.3
Walker v Wimbourne (Australia) (1976) 137 CLR 1 — C13.4
Wallace Smith Trust Co Ltd, Re [1992] BCC 707 — A4.18
Walsh v Lonsdale (1882) 21 Ch 9 — C12.6
Walter L Jacob & Co Ltd, Re [1993] BCC 512 — I8.2
Walter L Jacob & Co Ltd, Re (1989) 5 BCC 244 — C5.31
Walter Wright, Re [1923] WN 128 — G3.4
Waltons Stores (Interstate) Ltd v Maher (Australia) (1988)
   164 CLR 387 — D7.25
Ward v Haines Watts [1983] ICR 231 — D9.16
Warnford Investments Ltd v Duckworth [1978] 2 All ER 517 — C12.6
Washington Diamond Mining Co [1893] 3 Ch 95 — C13.4
Waters v Widdows (Australia) [1984] VR 503 — D10.4
Wates Construction (London) Ltd [1991] 3 Constr LJ, CA — D7.22
Watts v Midland Bank plc [1986] BCLC 15 — D5.5
Wayfarer Leisure Ltd v Commissioner of Customs and Excise
   [1985] VATTR 174 — D4.7
Wear Engine Works Co, Re (1875) 10 Ch App 188 — C5.33
Webb Electrical Ltd, Re (1988) 4 BCC 230 — C8.4
Webb v EMO Air Cargo (UK) Ltd [1993] IRLR 27, HL — D9.16
Webb v Whiffin (1872) LR 5 HL 711 — C12.20
Welch v Birrane (1974) 29 P & CR 102 — D9.7
Weldtech Equipment Ltd, Re [1991] BCLC 393 — D7.18
Welfab Engineers Ltd, Re [1990] BCC 600 — C13.2, C13.4, C13.5
Welsh Development Agency v Export Finance Co Ltd
   [1992] BCC 270, CA — A4.17, C12.10, D6.2, D7.24, D8.15, D9.1, F2.8
Welsh Highland Light Railway Co, Re [1993] BCLC 338 — C5.30
Welsh Irish Ferries Ltd, Re [1986] Ch 471 — D7.23
Wendleboe v LJ Music ApS (ECJ) [1986] 1 CMLR 476 — D9.16
West Mercia Safetywear Ltd v Dodd (1988) 4 BCC 30 — C10.4, C13.4
West-Tech International Lrd, Re [1989] BCLC 600 — B2.1
Westdock Realisations Ltd, Re (1988) 4 BCC 192 — C11.25, D7.22
Western Welsh International System Buildings Ltd, Re (1988)
   4 BCC 449 — I6.1
Westminster City Council v Hastie [1950] Ch 442 — D7.3
Westwood v Secretary of State for Employment [1984] IRLR 209 — D7.2
Wheeler & Partners Ltd (1990) Unreported, February — B7.2
Wheeler v Patel [1987] IRLR 211, EAT — D9.16
White & Osmond (Parkstone) Ltd, Re (1960) Unreported, 30 June — C13.1
White v Metcalfe [1903] 2 Ch 567 — C14.33
Whitehouse v Frost (1810) 12 East 614 — D7.25
Whyte (G T) & Co Ltd, Re [1983] BCLC 311 — C10.9
Willcocks (W R) & Co Ltd, Re [1973] 3 WLR 669 — C5.30, C5.34
William Gaskell Group Ltd v Highley [1993] BCC 200 — D6.2
William Hall (Contractors) Ltd, Re [1967] 2 All ER 1150 — D7.4

Williams & Glyn's Bank v Barnes (1980) Unreported, 26 March   D2.8
Wilson (D) (Birmingham) Ltd v Metropolitan Property Developments Ltd
  [1975] 2 All ER 814, CA   C9.3, D7.10
Wilson (E K) & Sons Ltd, ReBostels Ltd, Re [1972] 1 WLR 791   C5.44
Wilson v Banner Scaffolding Ltd The Times, 22 June 1982   C8.2
Wimbledon Village Restaurant Ltd, Re [1994] BCC 753   I6.1
Windsor Mortgage Nominees Pty Ltd v Cardwell (Australia) (1979)
  CLC 32   C15.4
Windsor Refrigerator Co Ltd v Branch Nominees Ltd [1961]
  Ch 375, CA   D3.1
Winkworth v Edward Baron Development Co Ltd [1987] BCLC 193   C13.4
Winter Garden German Opera Ltd, Re (1907) 23 TLR 662   D7.4
Wisepark Ltd, Re [1994] BCC 221   E3.1
Witney Town Football and Social Club, Re [1993] BCC 874   C5.5, C5.8
Wolverhampton Steel & Iron Co Ltd, Re [1977] 1 WLR 860   C5.30
Wood and Martin (Bricklaying Contractors) Ltd, Re [1971]
  1 WLR 293   G3.2
Wood Preservation Ltd v Prior (1968) 45 TC 112, CA   D9.5
Woodhouse Applebee v Joseph Allnatt Centre EAT 292/80   D9.16
Woodhouse v Peter Brotherhood Ltd [1972] 2 QB 520   D9.16
Woodroffes (Musical Instruments) Ltd, Re [1985] 2 All ER 908,
  [1985] BCLC 227   B6.4, D4.8, D6.3, D10.4
Woodruff v Hambro (1991) Estates Gazette, 30 March   D7.15
Woodstead Finance Ltd v Petrou and Another The Times,
  23 January 1986   C10.7
Workvale Ltd, Re [1992] 1 WLR 416   G3.2
Wren v Eatsbourne Borough Council and UK Waste Control Ltd
  [1993] IRLR 425   D9.16
Wrightson v McArthur and Hutchisons [1921] 2 KB 807   C12.10
Wyvern Developments Ltd, Re [1974] 1 WLR 1097   C11.24, C11.25

Xyllyx plc, Re (No 2) [1992] BCLC 378   C5.31

Yagerphone Co Ltd, Re [1935] Ch 392   C10.2, C10.4, C13.1, C13.4, D6.2, D9.1
Yarmarine (I W) Ltd, Re [1992] BCC 28   C12.6
Yenidje Tobacco Co, Re [1916] 2 Ch 426   C5.26
Yeovil Glove Co Ltd, Re [1965] Ch 148   C10.9
Yorkshire Joinery Co Ltd, Re (1967) 111 SJ 701   C14.31
Yorkshire Woolcombers Association Ltd, Re [1903] 2 Ch 284   D6.2
Your Size Fashions Ltd, Re (New Zealand) [1990] 3 NZLR 727   C11.24
Yourell v Hibernian Bank [1918] AC 372   D2.12, D9.17

Zafiro, The [1959] 3 WLR 123   C14.31
Zinotty Properties Ltd, Re [1984] 1 WLR 1249   C5.30
Zurich Insurance Company and Troy Woodworking Ltd, Re (Canada)
  (1984) 50 CBR (NS) 1, 61 OR (2d) 129, CA   D6.2

Part A: General

1. Preliminary   **3**

Scope   3
Meaning of insolvency   3
Commercial and accountancy test   5
Insolvency as a general term   5

2. The new insolvency legislation   **7**

Introduction   7
Background to the new legislation   8
Aims of the new legislation   8
Scope of the new legislation   10

3. Options available to a financially distressed company   **11**

Administrative receivership   11
Administration procedure   11
Voluntary arrangement   12
Scheme of arrangement or composition   12
Disposal of going concern outside formal procedures   12
'Hive-down' within or outside formal procedures   12
Informal rescue   12

4. Insolvency practitioners and office-holders   **14**

Qualification and conduct of insolvency practitioners   14
Office-holders—position and liabilities   18
Office-holders—statutory aids available   24
Office-holders—guidance notes   34

5. Jurisdiction and court procedure in insolvency matters   **35**

Proceedings   35
Co-operation between courts   36

6. Meetings in insolvency matters   **42**

Proxies and corporate representation   42
Quorum at meeting of creditors or contributories   44

Table   **44**

Part A: General

Chapter 1: Preliminary

Scope

A1.1   This Part is intended to serve as a general introduction to the following separate Parts on specific areas of corporate insolvency, namely PART B: ADMINISTRATION ORDERS, PART C: LIQUIDATIONS, PART D: RECEIVERS and PART E: VOLUNTARY ARRANGEMENTS. It also deals with particular aspects which are common to all or most of those specific areas, such as insolvency practitioners, jurisdiction and court procedure, cross-frontier insolvencies and representation at insolvency meetings. By contrast, PART F: SPECIAL PROVISIONS FOR FINANCIAL MARKETS deals with situations where the effect of the general insolvency provisions is substantially modified in the case of insolvencies in the financial markets. PART H: TAXATION addresses taxation aspects relevant to insolvency.

Unless otherwise stated, the provisions referred to are those of the Insolvency Act 1986 ('the Act') and, in the case of 'Rules', to those of the Insolvency Rules 1986 (SI 1986 No 1925), as amended by the Insolvency (Amendment) Rules 1987 (SI 1987 No 1919), 1989 (SI 1989 No 397), 1991 (SI 1991 No 495) and 1993 (SI 1993 No 602). The forms referred to are those contained in Schedule 4 to the Rules (as amended). (It should be noted that the Insolvency Rules 1986 apply only to England and Wales. For a detailed explanation of the new insolvency legislation, as it affects England and Wales and Scotland, see A2.1 *et seq.* below.)

Meaning of insolvency

Specific statutory tests

A1.2   The expressions 'insolvency' and 'insolvent' have no uniform or comprehensive legal meaning. Case law and legislation have dealt with the concept of insolvency only in the context of various specific statutory provisions. The following examples will illustrate this point.

(*a*)   For the purposes of a declaration of solvency (a pre-requisite to the initiation of a winding-up as a members' voluntary winding-up), the test of a company's solvency is whether, in the opinion of its directors, the company will be able to pay its debts in full, together with interest at the official rate (as defined in section 251), within such period, not exceeding twelve months from the commencement of the winding-up, as may be specified in the declaration (section 89;

see also section 95 and C4.12 PART C: LIQUIDATIONS). The form of declaration (Form 4.70) requires, *inter alia*, the amount at which any contingent liabilities are estimated to rank to be taken into account.

(*b*) For the purposes of section 122(1)(f) (inability to pay debts as one of the grounds on which a company may be wound up by the court), a company is unable to pay its debts if, *inter alia*, it is proved to the satisfaction of the court that—

   (i)   it is unable to pay them *as they fall due* (section 123(1)(e)); or

   (ii)   the value of its assets is less than the amount of its liabilities, taking into account its contingent and prospective liabilities (section 123(2)).

(See C5.22 PART C: LIQUIDATIONS.)

This test is akin to the commercial and accountancy test mentioned in A1.3 below.

(*c*) One of the conditions which must be satisfied before the court makes an administration order (see PART B: ADMINISTRATION ORDERS) in relation to a company is that the company is *or is likely to become* unable to pay its debts within the meaning of section 123 (see (*b*) above) (section 8(1)(a)).

(*d*) As the cases referred to in C13.1 PART C: LIQUIDATIONS indicate, a person is liable under what is now section 213 (fraudulent trading antecedent to liquidation) (see also section 458 of the Companies Act 1985) if he was knowingly party to the company incurring liabilities at a time when he knew that there was no (or, arguably, was recklessly indifferent as to whether there was any) reasonable prospect that those liabilities would be discharged as they fell due *or shortly afterwards*.

(*e*) For the purposes of section 214 (which makes a director or shadow director of a company which goes into insolvent liquidation personally liable for its debts in certain circumstances—see C13.2 PART C: LIQUIDATIONS), a company goes into insolvent liquidation if it goes into liquidation at a time when its assets are insufficient for the payment of its debts and other liabilities *and the expenses of the winding-up* (section 214(6)).

(*f*) For the purposes of sections 238, 239 and 245 (transactions at undervalue in England and Wales, preferences in England and Wales, and avoidance of certain floating charges—see C10.2, C10.4 and C10.8 PART C: LIQUIDATIONS), 'the relevant time' is defined by reference to various periods between the time a company was (or, in consequence of the act complained of, became) unable to pay its debts and the onset of insolvency. Inability to pay debts has the same meaning as in (*b*) above (sections 240(2) and 245(4)). 'Onset of insolvency' is defined as the date of the presentation of the petition on which an administration order was made or the commencement of a winding-up (sections 240(3) and 245(5)).

(*g*) By section 247 (general interpretation), 'insolvency' has been defined, except insofar as the context otherwise requires, to *include* the approval of a voluntary arrangement (see PART E: VOLUNTARY ARRANGEMENTS), the making of an administration order (see PART B: ADMINISTRATION ORDERS) or the appointment of an administrative receiver.

(*h*) Under section 6 of the Company Directors Disqualification Act 1986 (disqualification of directors of insolvent companies) a company is treated as becoming insolvent if (i) it goes into liquidation at a time when its assets are insufficient for the payment of its debts and other liabilities and the expenses of the winding-up or (ii) an administration order is made in relation to it or (iii) an administrative receiver of it is appointed.

(*j*) The statutory declaration referred to in sections 155 and 156 of the Companies Act 1985 (as a condition precedent to a private company giving financial assistance for the purposes of the acquisition of its own shares) requires the inclusion of statements (1) that in the directors' opinion there will be no ground on which the company could be found to be unable to pay its debts (taking into account the liabilities as in (*b*)(ii) above) and (2) that it will be able to pay its debts as they fall due during the year immediately following the date on which the assistance is proposed to be given or (if it is intended to commence a winding-up within twelve months from that date) that it will be able to pay its debts in full within twelve months of the commencement of the winding-up. The declaration is required to be supported by the auditors' report stating that they have enquired into the state of affairs of the company and they are not aware of anything to indicate that the opinion expressed by the directors is unreasonable in all the circumstances. In its effect this test is closest to the commercial and accountancy test (see A1.3 below).

Commercial and accountancy test

A1.3   In a commercial and accountancy sense, the expression 'insolvency' connotes actual or anticipated deficiency of assets ('the balance sheet test') and/or inability to pay debts as they fall due ('the cash flow test'). (See also A1.2 (*b*) and (*j*) above.) The two tests may impact on each other: for example, a deficiency of assets may eventually result in an adverse cash flow and, conversely, an adverse cash flow may eventually reduce the going-concern value of the assets (see paragraphs 10 and 12 of Schedule 4 to the Companies Act 1985, as amended by the Companies Act 1989) to a break-up value.

Insolvency as a general term

A1.4   Lastly, the expression is also used as a convenient general label for various formal procedures applicable in the case of a company in financial difficulties (and even for solvent liquidations) which an insolvency practitioner would normally handle as part of his practice. It is in this sense that the Insolvency Act 1986 and this book cover the following subjects:

(*a*)   members' voluntary winding-up, creditors' voluntary winding-up and winding-up by the court (see PART C: LIQUIDATIONS);

(*b*)   administration orders (see PART B: ADMINISTRATION ORDERS);

(*c*)   receivership, including administrative receivership (see PART D: RECEIVERS);

(*d*)   voluntary arrangements (see PART E: VOLUNTARY ARRANGEMENTS);

(*e*)   insolvency practitioners (see A4.1 *et seq.* below);

(*f*)   special provisions for insolvencies in financial markets (see PART F: SPECIAL PROVISIONS FOR FINANCIAL MARKETS); and

(*g*)   taxation in insolvencies (see PART H: TAXATION).

Chapter 2: The new insolvency legislation

Introduction

A2.1   The Companies Act 1985 (the bulk of which came into force on 1 July 1985) consolidated the 1948 to 1981 Companies Acts, the Insolvency Act 1976, the Companies (Floating Charges and Receivers) (Scotland) Act 1972 and certain other enactments. Sections 501 to 674 of the 1985 Act dealt with liquidation, sections 462 to 466 with floating charges in Scotland, sections 467 to 487 with receivership in Scotland, and sections 196, 405 and 488 to 500 with receivership in England and Wales.

The Insolvency Act 1985 made substantial amendments to the provisions of the Companies Act 1985 relating to liquidation and receivership and introduced new insolvency procedures (such as administration orders and voluntary arrangements). It strengthened and enlarged the provisions of the Companies Act 1985 relating to disqualification of directors and transactions antecedent to insolvency. The provisions of the Insolvency Act 1985 relating to disqualification of directors and wrongful trading came into force on 28 April 1986.

Before the Insolvency Act 1985 became fully effective, two consolidating Acts were enacted: the Insolvency Act 1986, and the Company Directors Disqualification Act 1986.

The Insolvency Act 1986 incorporated the whole of the Insolvency Act 1985 (except the provisions relating to disqualification of directors) and all the provisions of the Companies Act 1985 (as amended) relating to liquidation and receivership, except sections 405 (notices to Registrar of receiver's appointment and its cesser—England and Wales) and 462 to 466 (floating charges in Scotland). The Company Directors Disqualification Act 1986 incorporated all the provisions of the Insolvency Act 1985 and the Companies Act 1985 relating to disqualification of directors. Tables of derivations are contained within the two consolidation Acts and tables of destinations have been separately published. Both the consolidation Acts came into force on 29 December 1986 and thereby repealed the Insolvency Act 1985 which, insofar as it was not already in force, had theoretically come into force on the same day. Subsequently, the Companies Act 1989, which *inter alia* amends and modifies the insolvency legislation particularly as regards insolvencies in financial markets and registration of charges, received Royal Assent on 16 November 1989.

The present principal legislation relating to company insolvency is therefore contained in the Insolvency Act 1986 (as read with the Company Directors Disqualification Act 1986) and sections 405 and 462 to 466 of the Companies Act 1985 (as amended by the Companies Act 1989; some of the amendments are not yet in force). The Act is supplemented or modified by other enactments in relation to special types of companies and bodies such as insurance companies, banks, investment businesses and industrial and provident societies or in relation to special categories of claimants such as employees—see PART B: ADMINISTRATION ORDERS to PART E: VOLUNTARY ARRANGEMENTS. The Railways Act 1993, for example, contains special provisions, including those relating to railway administrators, in respect of the insolvency of a railway undertaking. In relation to companies registered in Scotland, some of the provisions of the Bankruptcy (Scotland) Act 1985 (as amended by the Bankruptcy (Scotland) Act 1993 with effect from 1 April 1993) also apply, as provided by the principal legislation and by the delegated legislation referred to below.

The principal legislation referred to above is supplemented by delegated legislation which comprises numerous sets of orders, regulations and rules made by statutory instruments, mostly pursuant to powers conferred by the Insolvency Act 1986. The most important are the Insolvency Rules 1986 (SI 1986 No 1925), as amended by the Insolvency (Amendment) Rules 1987 (SI 1987 No 1919), 1989 (SI 1989 No 397), 1991 (SI 1991 No 495) and 1993 (SI 1993 No 602), which *inter alia* set out the detailed procedure for the conduct of insolvency proceedings in relation to companies registered in England and Wales; and the Insolvency (Scotland) Rules 1986 (SI 1986 No 1915), as amended by the Insolvency (Scotland) Amendment Rules 1987 (SI 1987 No 1921), which make similar provision in relation to companies registered in Scotland. A table setting out the statutory instruments in force relating to insolvency, as at 1 November 1994, can be found at the end of this Part.

Background to the new legislation

A2.2   The new legislation resulted in part from the report of the Review Committee chaired by Sir Kenneth Cork entitled 'Insolvency Law and Practice' (Cmnd 8558), which was presented to Parliament in June 1982. The Government published a White Paper entitled 'A Revised Framework for Insolvency Law' (Cmnd 9175) in February 1984, based on the Cork Committee Report. The White Paper was preceded and followed by extensive consultations with interested bodies, and a number of significant amendments were made to the Insolvency Bill (which later became the Insolvency Act 1985) during its passage through Parliament.

Aims of the new legislation

A2.3   The aims of the new legislation were stated by the Government to be to:

(*a*)   ensure that those who act as insolvency practitioners are fit to do so;

(*b*)   combat the abuse of limited liability by those whose actions undermine the legitimate purpose for which it was established;

(c) encourage directors to take a closer interest in the affairs of their companies and to take early action when financial difficulties loom;

(d) clarify the law on receivership;

(e) create a new insolvency mechanism, known as company administration, specifically designed to facilitate company rescue and reorganisation; and

(f) simplify and reform corporate and personal insolvency law and procedures and reduce unnecessary involvement of the courts and the Government insolvency service.

As regards (a), a system of licensing and control of insolvency practitioners has been introduced (see A4.1 *et seq.* below).

As to (b) and (c), the provisions regarding the disqualification of unfit directors have been tightened; restrictions have been imposed against directors and shadow directors of a company which has gone into insolvent liquidation starting a new company with the same or similar name (the 'Phoenix syndrome') without the leave of the court (see C9.1 PART C: LIQUIDATIONS); a new form of civil liability on the part of directors and shadow directors called 'wrongful trading' (see C13.2 PART C: LIQUIDATIONS) has been introduced; and the provisions relating to misfeasance have been modified.

With reference to (d), the contractual agency and powers of a receiver usually contained in a general charge have now received statutory recognition; certain further powers have been conferred on a receiver appointed under such a charge; and unsecured creditors have been given additional rights to information in such a receivership (see D4.1 *et seq.* and D5.2 *et seq.* PART D: RECEIVERS).

The new administration procedure (see PART B: ADMINISTRATION ORDERS) referred to in (e) is akin to a receivership on behalf of unsecured creditors, and has some similarity to the Chapter 11 procedure in the USA. Receivers under a general charge have, in the past, been able to turn some insolvent companies round to viability whilst a *de facto* 'freeze' on the rights of unsecured creditors operated. The administration procedure is designed to impose a wider statutory 'freeze' or moratorium on enforcement remedies of creditors and others and provide a formal framework within which, even in the absence of a receiver, a rescue of the company, or at least an unhurried, orderly and more beneficial realisation of its assets, can be facilitated, particularly when the procedure is used in conjunction with another new procedure called 'voluntary arrangement' (see PART E: VOLUNTARY ARRANGEMENTS).

Finally, with regard to (f), the new legislation introduces new types of voidable transactions, such as transactions at an undervalue, fraudulent dispositions and extortionate credit transactions, and modifies the old provisions relating to fraudulent preference and invalid floating charges (see B9.1 *et seq.* PART B: ADMINISTRATION ORDERS and C10.1 *et seq.* PART C: LIQUIDATIONS). In addition, it modifies procedural aspects of winding-up, particularly a winding-up by the court (see generally PART C: LIQUIDA-TIONS).

Scope of the new legislation

A2.4 In broad terms, the Insolvency Act 1986 applies to insolvencies or antecedent events occurring after the relevant provisions of the Act (or the corresponding provisions of the Insolvency Act 1985) came into force (Schedule 11). The Act applies to companies incorporated under the Companies Act 1985 (or its predecessor Acts) whether they have been incorporated before or after the coming into force of its provisions. Some or all of its provisions can be made applicable (with or without modification) to any of the Channel Islands or any colony by means of an Order in Council (section 442; see now, as to Guernsey, the Insolvency Act (Guernsey) Order 1989 (SI 1989 No 2409)). With certain exceptions, the provisions of the Act relating to company insolvency apply to Scotland (section 440) but the Act does not, except for a few specified sections, apply to Northern Ireland (section 441; see now the Insolvency (Northern Ireland) Order 1989 (SI 1989 No 2405)). The provisions of the Companies Act 1985 relating to the winding-up of unregistered and oversea companies are now embodied in sections 220 to 229 of the Insolvency Act 1986. Whether the provisions of the Act relating to administration, receivership and corporate voluntary arrangements apply to oversea companies (except where section 442 applies) is currently the subject of judicial controversy. The provisions of the Act which derive from the Insolvency Act 1985 bind the Crown so far as affecting or relating to remedies against, or against the property of, companies or individuals, priority of debts, transactions at an undervalue, preferences and voluntary arrangements (section 434).

Chapter 3: Options available to a financially distressed company

A3.1 As will be seen in C13.2 PART C: LIQUIDATIONS (Wrongful trading), a positive duty is imposed on directors to take every step which, applying the 'dual test' of a 'reasonably diligent person', they ought to take to minimise the potential loss to the company's creditors, after they become or (applying the same test) ought to have become aware of the inevitability of the company's insolvent liquidation. Their conduct in relation to the company's affairs may also come under scrutiny by virtue of the provisions of the Company Directors Disqualification Act 1986 (see PART I: DISQUALIFICATION OF DIRECTORS).

Even apart from the statutory requirements, directors owe a duty of care to the company under the general law, although such duty is perhaps not as high as that under the Act. Therefore, when financial difficulties loom, they must explore and implement the best means of dealing with them, so far as practicable.

What course is most appropriate will depend on the nature and extent of the problems. Outright liquidation may not necessarily be the best course, because it normally leads to the disintegration of the business as a going concern and, eventually, to the dissolution of the company; but the problems may be of such a magnitude that liquidation may be the only feasible course. Subject to this, among other courses, in various combinations, which may be considered, are the following.

(1) *Administrative receivership*

This is only possible if the company has created a general charge and the holder has become entitled, or the company requests him, to appoint, and he decides to appoint, an administrative receiver. As stated in A2.3 above, receivership brings about a *de facto* general freeze on the rights of unsecured creditors and thus allows a breathing space for an unhurried, orderly and most beneficial realisation of the assets or, perhaps, for a formal or informal rescue to be launched. (See PART D: RECEIVERS.)

(2) *Administration procedure*

Subject to certain exceptions, this new procedure can only be used where the company has not created a general charge under which an administrative receiver can be appointed. It would not be appropriate unless the result is likely to be better than in a liquidation. Once the procedure is invoked, there is a *de jure* freeze (which is wider than the *de facto* freeze which operates in an administrative receivership) on the rights of secured and unsecured creditors, thus again affording a breathing space. (See PART B: ADMINISTRATION ORDERS.)

(3) *Voluntary arrangement*

This is another new form of formal rescue. It stands a better chance of success if it is promulgated during a receivership or administration procedure whilst there is a *de facto* or a *de jure* freeze. (See PART E: VOLUNTARY ARRANGEMENTS.)

(4) *Scheme of arrangement or composition*

This is another form of formal rescue but is likely to fall into disuse and be replaced in practice by (3) above. (See PART E: VOLUNTARY ARRANGEMENTS.)

(5) *Disposal of going concern outside formal procedures*

Subject to the provisions of the company's memorandum and articles of association and the provisions of sections 238 (transactions at an undervalue) and 242 (gratuitous alienations—Scotland), the company may dispose of its assets as a going concern or on a break-up basis without first invoking any of the formal procedures, if such disposal is likely to achieve a better result than that which would be achieved under the formal procedures. The directors must, however, carefully weigh the relative advantages and disadvantages, having regard to the interests of the company and any other courses available. Where the assets have been charged, the disposal can only be effected by appropriate arrangements with the holder of the charge. Unless the net proceeds of the disposal are sufficient to discharge all the liabilities in full, the disposal would have to be followed by a liquidation and/or a voluntary arrangement so as to ensure a fair distribution of the proceeds.

(6) *'Hive-down' within or outside formal procedures*

A business may be preserved as a going concern from the ravages of execution creditors by hiving it down to a 'clean' subsidiary. This can be done independently or as part of, or in anticipation of, a receivership, administration or liquidation with a view to presenting an attractive corporate package, perhaps (except where the hive-down is effected in a liquidation) with the benefit of potential tax advantages, to a prospective purchaser. For details, see D9.4 *et seq.* PART D: RECEIVERS; and see also PART H: TAXATION. A hive-down outside these formal procedures may require prior arrangements with any holder of a charge over the assets. A hive-down within these procedures can only be carried out by the responsible insolvency practitioner.

(7) *Informal rescue*

This, in a suitable case, may prove to be by far the least traumatic and disruptive, and the most beneficial, course. On the other hand, it carries substantially greater risks. If it is ill-conceived or is not successful, the company may end up being in a worse position than it would have been in a formal procedure. The rescue is contractual in form and is by way of an informal moratorium (perhaps under the supervision of an informal committee of creditors) or an arrangement with only the loan creditors. In the latter case, the lenders may not only defer their rights to recover the existing loans but also continue to provide financial facilities (perhaps in return for a security) to enable trading to be continued. Because of the need to achieve unanimity among the creditors or the lenders, this form of rescue may be difficult to achieve. The company would almost certainly be expected to accept a stringent financial discipline, reporting obligations and events of default. Where any security given covers existing loans as well, the provisions as to preferences (see C10.4 PART C: LIQUIDATIONS) must be borne in mind. The lenders must carefully avoid unwittingly becoming 'shadow directors' (see, for example, C13.2 PART C: LIQUIDATIONS (Wrongful trading)). In suitable cases of sufficient importance, the Bank of England may be prepared to assist informally in maintaining co-ordination between the lenders or creditors involved.

In choosing any particular course of action, the interaction between the provisions relating to wrongful trading and those relating to fraudulent trading (see C13.1 *et seq.* PART C: LIQUIDATIONS) must be borne in mind. On the one hand, the directors have a duty to minimise a potential loss to the creditors. On the other hand, they should so conduct the affairs of the company that its position does not deteriorate and that it does not incur new liabilities which cannot be discharged as they fall due or shortly afterwards. In summary, in reaching a decision the directors must not be unduly cowardly nor unduly rash, but must be prudently realistic in commercial terms. In *Standard Chartered Bank v Walker and another* *[1992] BCLC 603*, certain restructuring proposals in respect of a company in grave financial difficulties were to be put to a general meeting of the shareholders. Vinelott J granted an application of a lending bank for an injunction restraining a shareholder and his associates, who together held between five and ten per cent of the voting rights, from voting against the proposals. Although as a general rule, a shareholder is free to exercise his voting rights in any way he chooses and owes no duty to the company in doing so, Vinelott J said that there would be a point beyond which the conduct of a debtor in relation to his property would be so plainly injurious to a creditor that the court would have a power to intervene.

Finally, it should be noted that in the case of the insolvency of an authorised insurance company, or an authorised institution or former authorised institution (as defined in the Banking Act 1987), financial assistance or other relief under statute may be available to it or to certain classes of its creditors in certain circumstances. See the Policyholders Protection Act 1985 and Part II of the Banking Act 1987.

Chapter 4: Insolvency practitioners and office-holders

Qualification and conduct of insolvency practitioners

A4.1 Under the previous legislation, a person did not need any professional qualification to act as a receiver or liquidator or to act in other similar capacity. One exception was that in a winding-up by the court it was the practice of the court to appoint as liquidator (other than the Official Receiver) only a practising accountant of at least five years' standing (unless his practical experience in the administration of insolvency matters made up for his shorter standing). There was no statutory provision against a person acting in a matter in which he might have a conflict of interest, although the codes of ethics of certain professional bodies, such as the Institute of Chartered Accountants in England and Wales and the Insolvency Practitioners Association, prohibited their members from acting in such matters. The only statutory sanction against an unfit person acting as a liquidator in a compulsory or voluntary winding-up was that the court could remove a liquidator for good cause.

Under the Act, a person first of all requires a basic authorisation to act as an insolvency practitioner (see A4.2 below), that is (in relation to a company, including a company which may be wound up under Part V (unregistered companies)—see section 388(4)), as liquidator, provisional liquidator, administrator or administrative receiver, supervisor of a voluntary arrangement or (in relation to an individual) as trustee in bankruptcy, or as a holder of certain other offices (section 388). In addition, before acting he must not be under any disability mentioned at the end of A4.2 below; and he must also satisfy the requirements as to security or caution mentioned in A4.3 below. A person (other than the Official Receiver) who acts as an insolvency practitioner when he is not qualified to do so is liable to imprisonment or to a fine, or to both (section 389).

It should be noted that:

(*a*) 'in-house' members' voluntary liquidations, for example the winding-up of a solvent dormant subsidiary, by way of group tidying up, under the liquidatorship of a group company secretary, are no longer possible; and

(*b*) an ordinary receiver, as distinct from an administrative receiver (see D1.4 PART D: RECEIVERS), is not subject to any prescribed qualification requirement. In the depressed property market during the current recession, there has been a number of appointments of surveyors, who are not qualified insolvency practitioners, as 'LPA receiver' (i.e. Law of Property Act receiver) under fixed charges over commercial property. Such appointments have been regarded by the chargeholders as more cost-effective and satisfactory in view of the surveyors' expertise in managing and marketing property.

Basic authorisation to act as insolvency practitioner

A4.2   Only an individual can be qualified to act as an insolvency practitioner (section 390(1)). He may acquire his basic authorisation as an insolvency practitioner in two ways:

(*a*)   by being authorised so to act by virtue of his membership of a recognised professional body (under and subject to the rules of that body); or

(*b*)   by a direct authorisation from a competent authority (as defined by section 392) (section 390(2)).

Before according recognition to a professional body, the Secretary of State must be satisfied that it:

(i)   regulates the practice of a profession; and

(ii)   maintains and enforces rules for securing that such of its members as are permitted by or under its rules to act as insolvency practitioners are fit and proper persons so to act, and meet *acceptable* requirements with respect to education and practical training and experience (section 391).

The professional bodies so far recognised by the Secretary of State under section 391 are: The Chartered Association of Certified Accountants, The Insolvency Practitioners Association, The Institute of Chartered Accountants in England and Wales, The Institute of Chartered Accountants in Ireland, The Institute of Chartered Accountants of Scotland, The Law Society and The Law Society of Scotland (see the Insolvency Practitioners (Recognised Professional Bodies) Order 1986 (SI 1986 No 1764)).

In the case of a direct authorisation by a competent authority, it must be satisfied that the applicant is similarly a fit and proper person and meets the *prescribed* requirements with respect to education and training and experience (section 393). These requirements which came into force on 1 April 1990 (replacing the previous statutory instruments) are set out in Regulations 5 to 8 of the Insolvency Practitioners Regulations 1990 (SI 1990 No 439). Regulation 4 includes matters which in particular are to be taken into account in determining whether an applicant is a fit and proper person to act as an insolvency practitioner.

With effect from 1 April 1990, a new applicant, unless exempted under Regulation 5, must, in addition to having an academic qualification set out in Part I of Schedule 1 to the Regulations (as amended by the Insolvency Practitioners (Amendment) Regulations 1993 (SI 1993 No 221)) have passed the Joint Insolvency Examination set by the Joint Insolvency Examination Board or must have a corresponding overseas professional or vocational qualification.

The function of monitoring professional standards of authorised insolvency practitioners is primarily the responsibility of, in the case of a practitioner authorised by the Secretary of State, the Insolvency Service (an executive agency within the Department of Trade and Industry) and, in the case of a practitioner authorised by a recognised professional body (see above), that body. A joint insolvency monitoring unit (JIMU) has been set up by arrangements between the Insolvency Service and the recognised professional bodies to carry out monitoring visits to insolvency practitioners and to report back to the Secretary of State or the relevant recognised body, as the case may be, on any lapse in standards discovered during such a visit. Issue number 28 (December 1993) of 'Dear IP' (a bulletin from time to time issued by the Insolvency Service—see A4.25 below) sets out the minimum standards applicable to all insolvency practitioners, whether authorised by the Secretary of State or a recognised professional body, which have been agreed in this regard.

The competent authority must give written notice to the applicant of the grant of authorisation or, as the case may be, that it proposes to refuse an application for authorisation or to withdraw an authorisation previously granted. In the case of a proposed refusal or withdrawal, the written notice must set out particulars of the grounds on which the competent authority proposes to act (section 394). An applicant on whom such a notice is served has a right to make written representations to the competent authority (section 395), and a right of reference to the Insolvency Practitioners Tribunal, against a refusal or withdrawal of authorisation by the authority (sections 396–398; see also Schedule 7 and the Insolvency Practitioners Tribunal (Conduct of Investigations) Rules 1986 (SI 1986 No 952)). The maximum period for which a direct authorisation may be granted by a competent authority is three years (section 393(3) and Regulation 10 of the Insolvency Practitioners Regulations 1990). An authorisation previously granted may be withdrawn in certain circumstances (specified in section 393(4)).

Even where he has obtained the basic authorisation, a person is not qualified to act as an insolvency practitioner if at the time he acts:

(A) he has been adjudged bankrupt or sequestration of his estate has been awarded and (in either case) he has not been discharged;

(B) he is subject to a disqualification order made under the Company Directors Disqualification Act 1986; or

(C) he is a mental health patient (section 390(4)).

Requirement to provide security or caution

A4.3 A person is also not qualified to act as an insolvency practitioner at any time unless there is at that time security or (in Scotland) caution for the proper performance of his functions in accordance with the prescribed requirements (section 390(3)). The requirements are prescribed by Part III of the Insolvency Practitioners Regulations 1990 (SI 1990 No 439), as amended by SI 1993 No 221. Regulation 12 requires a two-fold bond in a form approved by the Secretary of State:

(*a*) there must be in force, at the time when the insolvency practitioner is appointed to any relevant office in any particular case, a general bond (which complies with the requirements set out in Part I of Schedule 2 to the Regulations) in the sum of £250,000; and

(*b*) subject to the exceptions set out in Regulation 13 (as amended), there must be in force, in relation to that bond with effect from the time when he is so appointed, a specific penalty in respect of his so acting in that particular case of an amount equal to the value of the assets involved in that case (estimated in accordance with Part II of Schedule 2, subject to a minimum of £5,000) or £5,000,000 (whichever is the less).

With effect from 1 April 1993, the liability under the bond in relation to the general penalty and specific penalty sums is limited to a sum equivalent to the losses caused by the fraud *or* dishonesty of the practitioner 'whether acting alone or in collusion with one or more persons, or the fraud or dishonesty of any persons committed with the connivance of the practitioner'.

Regulation 12(1)(c) contains 'topping-up' provisions whereby the practitioner is required, where he forms the view that the estimated value of the assets is higher than the penalty sum under the current specific penalty (being a penalty sum of less than £5,000,000), to obtain a further specific penalty so that the penalty sum is equal to the higher value or £5,000,000, whichever is the less.

In England and Wales before 1 April 1993, a copy of every certificate of specific bond was required to be filed with (in the case of a liquidator in a voluntary winding-up or an administrative receiver) the Registrar of Companies or (in any other case) the court having jurisdiction over that case (Reg 14). With effect from 1 April 1993, this requirement has been replaced by new provisions which require every practitioner to maintain a 'bordereau', i.e. a form containing certain details in relation to his every appointment including the name of the case, the estimated value of the assets comprised in that case, any increase in his estimation of the value of those assets, particulars of the specific penalty obtained (and any further specific penalty) and the date of his release or discharge from the appointment. The practitioner must submit a copy of the bordereau in respect of each calendar month (even if it contains no particulars in respect of that month) to his authorising body (Reg 15A, inserted by SI 1993 No 221). A copy of the bordereau must also be produced for inspection on demand to any person reasonably appearing to him to be a creditor or contributory of the debtor concerned, to the debtor himself or, where the debtor is a partnership or a company, to any partner or director of the debtor. The practitioner must retain the copy of the bordereau for two years after his release or discharge from the appointment (Reg 14, substituted by SI 1993 No 221).

There are different inspection and retention requirements in Scotland (Reg 15), but the requirement to maintain a bordereau and to submit a copy of it to the practitioner's authorising body under the new Regulation 15A, referred to above, also applies in Scotland.

In England and Wales, there are further provisions relating to the insolvency practitioner's security in the Insolvency Rules 1986 (SI 1986 No 1925, as amended). The costs of obtaining the specific bond may be paid out of the assets of the company (Rule 12.8(3)). Any person appointing, or certifying the appointment of, an insolvency practitioner must satisfy himself that the appointee has the necessary security (Rule 12.8(1)). The creditors' committee or the liquidation committee in any insolvency must from time to time review the adequacy of the security (Rule 12.8(2)). (In Scotland, there are similar provisions relating to the insolvency practitioner's caution in Rule 7.28 of the Insolvency (Scotland) Rules 1986 (SI 1986 No 1915).)

Records to be kept by insolvency practitioners

A4.4 Part IV of the Insolvency Practitioners Regulations 1990 (SI 1990 No 439) requires a record to be kept by an insolvency practitioner in respect of each case in which he acts, in the form set out in Schedule 3 to those Regulations. Every record must be preserved for ten years from the date on which he is granted his release or the date on which the bond in respect of that case ceases to have effect, whichever is the later (Regulation 20). All such records must be available for inspection, on reasonable notice, by the professional body by virtue of membership of which the insolvency practitioner is authorised to act, or the competent authority which granted his authorisation, as the case may be.

Office-holders—position and liabilities

Qualification

A4.5 A person appointed as an administrator, administrative receiver, liquidator or provisional liquidator of a company must be a person who is qualified to act as an insolvency practitioner (see A4.1 to A4.4 above) *in relation to that company* (section 230—see, however, sections 388 and 389, the effect of which is to treat even a supervisor of a voluntary arrangement as an insolvency practitioner and to require him to be so qualified). Where more than one person is appointed or nominated to any of those offices, the appointment or nomination must declare whether any act required or authorised under any enactment to be done by the administrator, administrative receiver, liquidator or provisional liquidator is to be done by all or any one or more of the persons for the time being holding the office in question (section 231). (As to supervisors of a voluntary arrangement, see Rule 1.22 and E2.5 PART E: VOLUNTARY ARRANGEMENTS.) Section 232 makes it clear that the acts of an individual as such office-holder are valid notwithstanding any defect in his appointment, nomination or qualifications. The section does not, however, apply to a supervisor.

Position under financial services legislation

A4.6 An office-holder must consider his position under the Financial Services Act 1986 (the 'FSA') where he is appointed in relation to a company which has been carrying on investment business or has among its assets 'investments' as defined in the FSA.

An insolvency practitioner, such as a receiver, administrator or liquidator will usually be a chartered accountant or a solicitor. Provided he or his firm has obtained authorisation under the FSA by holding a certificate from the appropriate self-regulating organisation ('SRO') such as FIM-BRA, or recognised professional body such as one of the Institutes of Chartered Accountants or one of the Law Societies, then he may carry on investment business which arises from his acting as an insolvency practitioner in accordance with the SRO's or RPB's conduct of business rules.

In certain circumstances, however, an insolvency practitioner will be an exempted person under the FSA.

Section 45 of the FSA exempts the Official Receiver and is also relevant in relation to partnerships. It provides that if a winding-up order is made in respect of a partnership which is authorised under the FSA, then the liquidator is an exempted person. He will therefore not require to be authorised when he carries on investment business when acting as liquidator. However, because as an exempt person he would, in principle, not be obliged to observe any of the FSA's conduct of business rules, he will be bound by the SIB conduct of business rules and financial resource rules to the extent that they bound the partnership. He will, in addition, be subject to the rules of any SRO or RPB which authorised the insolvent person or partnership.

So far as the position generally is concerned, the Department of Trade and Industry has made a number of statements with regard to the position of insolvency practitioners in relation to companies which are authorised under the FSA. While these statements are not legally authoritative it is understood that they do represent the views of a number of insolvency practitioners. It is considered that an administrator, administrative receiver, liquidator or supervisor of a voluntary arrangement of a company authorised under the FSA will not require to be authorised under the FSA or, if so authorised, will not be governed by the rules of his SRO or RPB when acting as such, because he will not thereby be carrying on investment business. He will, instead, be acting as the agent of the company and may rely on, and will be bound by, that company's authorisation.

(1) Where an authorised investment business is being wound up, the authorisation does not lapse automatically on its going into liquidation. It continues unless it is specifically withdrawn.

(2) Where the company is not concerned with investment business, the mere fact that the office-holder sells off shares or carries out some other transaction with investments would not constitute the carrying on of investment business. He is in those circumstances engaging in the activity of being an insolvency practitioner and not an activity constituting investment business.

Liability to be disqualified

A4.7 An office-holder may be subject to a disqualification order under, *inter alia*, section 3 of the Company Directors Disqualification Act 1986 (see PART I: DISQUALIFICATION OF DIRECTORS) if he is persistently in default under the companies legislation (defined by section 22(7) of that Act to include the Insolvency Act 1986) of his duty to file with, or deliver, send or give notice of any matter to, the Registrar of Companies. In *Re Arctic Engineering Ltd and others [1986] 1 WLR 686*, decided under the old legislation, the court refused to make a disqualification order against a liquidator because of the special circumstances of the case and because although his serious defaults could not be considered other than culpable, he was neither dishonest nor incompetent.

Personal liability generally

A4.8 Under section 212, a liquidator, administrator or administrative receiver or (if he falls within section 212(1)(c)) supervisor of a voluntary arrangement can become personally liable to pay money or damages in the liquidation of the company (see C13.4 PART C: LIQUIDATIONS), subject to the relieving provisions referred to in C13.5 PART C: LIQUIDATIONS. In *Re Movitex Ltd [1992] BCC 101*, a former director of the company, who had successfully defended an action brought against him by the liquidators of the company, was held entitled to inspect and copy books, records and documents in the liquidators' possession relating to the action (including counsel's opinion), with a view to the company instituting misfeasance proceedings against them. (In that case, the liquidators did not have sufficient funds of the company to meet the order for costs which was made in the director's favour.) Under the general law, an office-holder can also be personally liable for any tortious acts or omissions or any breach of statutory or fiduciary duties (for some examples, see D8.2 to D8.26 PART D: RECEIVERS), subject to the limited immunity and indemnity he has under section 234(3) and (4) (see A4.17 below). Personal liability may further arise in respect of contracts entered into or adopted by him, subject to any right of recourse he may have against the assets of the company, as will appear from the chapters which follow. (See also A4.10 below.)

Where the insolvency office he holds relates to a bank, the office-holder needs to consider the law relating to a banker's duty of confidentiality to its customers. However, in *El Jawhary v Bank of Credit and Commerce International SA [1993] BCLC 396*, the court varied an injunction against the liquidators so as to permit disclosure when in the interests of the bank, but warned the liquidators to err on the side of caution and, if in doubt, to seek the consent of the customers or the leave of the court.

The office-holder must also consider the provisions of the Data Protection Act 1984, which impose a number of compliance requirements. These include notifying the Data Protection Registrar of any change of address of a registered data user (for example, where the address of the company's registered office changes). It should also be noted that the renewal of registration is required at the end of every three years.

Duty to report on directors' conduct

A4.9   Section 7(3) of the Company Directors Disqualification Act 1986, as read with Rule 3 of the Insolvent Companies (Report on Conduct of Directors) No 2 Rules 1986 (SI 1986 No 2134), requires the official receiver in a compulsory winding-up, a voluntary liquidator, an administrative receiver or an administrator to report to the Secretary of State (in the case of an office-holder other than the official receiver, on an appropriate prescribed form) if it appears to him that the conditions mentioned in section 6(1) of that Act are satisfied in relation to any person. Those conditions are that the person is or has been a director of the company which has at any time become insolvent (whether while he was a director or subsequently) and that his conduct as a director of that company (either taken alone or taken together with his conduct as a director of any other company or companies) makes him unfit to be concerned in the management of a company. Rule 4 provides for reporting on an appropriate form during the period of six months from the relevant date in respect of every person who was, on the relevant date, a director or shadow director of the company or had been a director or shadow director of the company at any time in the three years immediately preceding that date. Such a report must in any case be furnished not later than the expiry of the period of six months from the relevant date, where no return has been so furnished by a date one week before the expiry of that period.

For these purposes a company becomes insolvent if it goes into liquidation at a time when its assets are insufficient for the payment of its debts and other liabilities and the expenses of the winding-up or if an administration order is made in relation to it or if an administrative receiver of it is appointed. 'Relevant date' means the date of the passing of the resolution for a creditors' voluntary winding-up or, in the case of a members' voluntary winding-up, the date on which the liquidator forms the opinion that at the time of the liquidation the company was insolvent, or the date of the appointment of the administrative receiver or the date of the administration order, as the case may be.

When the reporting procedure was introduced, it was agreed between the Department of Trade and Industry and representatives of insolvency practitioners that payment would not be made for reports submitted under section 7(3) or in straightforward cases for basic information provided in response to the statutory duty under section 7(4). The cost of this work was regarded as an overhead on the practice to be recovered generally from all work and not chargeable to the particular estate unless exceptionally agreed with the creditors concerned. However, when, following the submission of a defence where proceedings are taken, an insolvency practitioner is called upon to undertake investigations, provide further evidence or attend a court hearing for possible cross-examination, reimbursement at reasonable rates would be made by the Department of Trade and Industry.

Professional conflict of interest

A4.10   It should also be noted that the rules of the professional body by which an insolvency practitioner is authorised, or of which he is a member, may contain restrictions preventing him from acting in particular categories of cases, e.g. where a conflict of interest may arise, notwithstanding that the requirements set out at A4.2 to A4.4 above are satisfied. The Secretary of State is also empowered to make regulations *inter alia* providing for a similar prohibition (section 419(2)(b)). In *Re Esal Commodities Ltd (1988) 4 BCC 475* (see A4.19 below), Dillon LJ referred, in passing, to potential conflicts of interest which can exist when the same persons act as liquidators of a parent company and its subsidiaries but went on to say '. . . these sort of potential conflicts do not in practice give rise to any serious difficulty because they are well known to the experienced insolvency practitioners . . .'. The repercussions for an insolvency practitioner who accepts an appointment as an office-holder in a matter in which he has a conflict of interest by reason of his past or continuing involvement can be serious.

Firstly, his authorisation as an insolvency practitioner is liable to be withdrawn by the competent authority which had granted him the authorisation (see section 393(4)) or by the professional body by virtue of the membership of which he has been authorised as an insolvency practitioner, if the conflict is such as is prohibited by the disciplinary rules of that body. As to the latter, the rules as to conflict contained in the 'Guide to Professional Conduct and Ethics' issued on 25 April 1990 by the Society of Practitioners of Insolvency (itself not a recognised professional body for the purposes of section 391 but an 'umbrella' organisation of various recognised professional bodies) and adopted by the English, Irish and Scottish Institutes of Chartered Accountants and the Chartered Association of Certified Accountants, are relevant.

Secondly, he may incur civil financial liability in tort or otherwise to anyone suffering loss or damages as a result of the insolvency practitioner having acted in such a situation.

The provisions of section 230A of the Act, as set out in its modified form in Part II of Schedule 4 to the Insolvent Partnerships Order 1994 (SI 1994 No 2421) may also be noted here. The section, in its application to cases where there are winding-up/bankruptcy orders against a partnership and one or more of its members on the current petitions of a creditor, enables the insolvency practitioner appointed in respect of the partnership and member/s, to apply to the court for, and the court to make, appropriate orders where the insolvency practitioner is in a conflict of interests situation.

VAT

A4.11   It should be noted that under Regulation 11(2) of the VAT (General) Regulations 1985 (VAT Guide, paragraph 84), office-holders are normally required to advise HM Customs and Excise of their appointment within 21 days. The notification should be given by completing form VAT 769 and sending it to the local VAT office responsible for the VAT registration of the company with a copy of the statement of affairs (if available). VAT Leaflet 700/49/93, Notifying Customs and Excise of

Insolvency, provides detailed guidance. As to claims for input tax, a form VAT 426, specifically designed for use by insolvency practitioners, has been introduced for completion and submission without invoices. (See VAT Leaflet 700/48/93, Insolvent VAT Traders: Claims for Input Tax after De-registration.) Any enquiries are to be addressed, as regards any policy or general issues, to VAT Registration and Collection Policy Branch 7 (VRCP 7) and, as regards casework, to VAT Operations (VOPS), both at Queens Dock, Liverpool L74 4AA. Telephone enquiries from insolvency practitioners may be made on 051 703 8711 or 051 703 8743 from Monday to Friday between 10 a.m. and 4 p.m.

Duties of office-holders and directors as to filing of accounts and returns

A4.12   The question of whether upon a formal insolvency of a company the obligations of the directors under the Companies Act 1985 as regards the production and filing of annual accounts and returns and other similar obligations continue, and whether the office-holder, on his appointment, becomes liable to comply with those obligations, has been the subject of some debate. From the directors' point of view, the question assumes importance in administrative receiverships and administrations, inasmuch as they continue to have residual functions. It is arguable that their obligations go into abeyance during the continuance of the receivership or administration, as it could not have been intended by the legislature that the Companies Act requirements and the requirements of the Insolvency Act 1986, as regards the filing of various types of accounts and returns by the office-holder, should be co-extensive. In any case, it would appear that the directors would have a valid defence if the reason for their non-compliance is that they had no full access to the books and records of the company in the possession of the office-holder nor to the funds of the company to defray the expenses involved in complying with the requirements. Among the relevant provisions of the Companies Act 1985 are sections 221, 226, 227, 233, 234, 234A, 235(2), 237, 238, 241, 242 and 242A, 363 and 366.

It is submitted that the obligations do not pass to the office-holder for two reasons. First, because the requirements are imposed primarily on the directors and the objects of those requirements are superseded by the objects of the insolvency procedures and the peculiar requirements of the Insolvency Act 1986 as to the provision of information. Secondly, in any case, the office-holder would not be justified in diminishing the funds in his hands by either himself complying with the requirements or providing funds to the directors to enable them to do so, inasmuch as there is no benefit to the parties for whose benefit the formal insolvency is being administered.

It is understood that the Registrar of Companies has indicated that he will not pursue company officers in respect of their obligations to file accounts, so long as the company is in administrative receivership or administration, as regards subsidiaries of the company which are not subject to any insolvency procedure. The Registrar's view appears to be that the obligation to comply with the requirements lies on the officers of those subsidiaries and not upon the parent company or its officers. In the Autumn

1990 issue of 'Insolvency Practitioner' (at page 8) it was reported that the Registrar was setting up a procedure to prevent companies and their directors getting into difficulties because of non-compliance with the requirements as to the filing of annual returns and accounts and that administrators were not required to file them; on receipt of the required notification of an administration order, the Registrar would put a computer 'stop' on default pursuits. The Registrar would then write to the administrator and ask for comments as to whether the directors are able to comply with the requirements and, depending on the response, the 'stop' would either be lifted or maintained. It would be open to administrators to indicate the position when they filed the administration documents, thus making it unnecessary for the Registrar to make the enquiry.

Pension scheme

A4.13   As to the duty of an office-holder to ensure that there is at least one independent trustee of any pension scheme of the company, see D8.17 PART D: RECEIVERS.

Office-holders—statutory aids available

A4.14   The Act contains provisions designed to facilitate the functions of and give a measure of protection to the various office-holders in an insolvency. The following are the main examples.

(a) Utility supplies

A4.15   Section 233 applies where a request is made by or with the concurrence of an administrator, administrative receiver, supervisor of a voluntary arrangement, liquidator or provisional liquidator for the supply of gas, electricity, water or telecommunication services (excluding cable programme services) by the relevant public undertakings specified in that section. The supplier may make it a condition of the giving of the supply that the office-holder personally guarantees the payment of any charges in respect of the supply; but it must not make it (or do anything which has the effect of making it) a condition of the giving of the supply that any outstanding charges are paid in respect of the supply given to the company before the effective date (broadly, the date of the relevant insolvency or the date when the voluntary arrangement was approved). As will be seen, this provision is intended to stop the practice of the public undertakings using their monopoly position to obtain priority over other creditors in respect of past supplies.

(b) Recovery of property and records

A4.16   Section 234(2) enables an administrator, administrative receiver, liquidator or provisional liquidator (as to whom, see also Rule 4.185) to apply to the court for an appropriate order against any person who has in his possession or control any property, books, papers or records to which the company *appears to be entitled*. Such an order may require that person to pay, deliver, convey, surrender or transfer the property, books, papers or records to the office-holder. The court has jurisdiction under the section to order property to be handed over to the office-holder, instead of leaving the matter to be determined by way of an ordinary action, even though there is a dispute as to its ownership (*Re London Iron & Steel Co Ltd [1990] BCLC 372*). As to the position of any person claiming lien, see A4.19 below.

(c) *Immunity and indemnity re third party property*

A4.17 Where the office-holder (excluding a supervisor) seizes or disposes of any property which is not property of the company, and at the time of seizure or disposal believes, and has reasonable grounds for believing, that he is entitled (whether in pursuance of an order of the court or otherwise) to seize or dispose of that property, the office-holder is not liable to any person in respect of any loss or damage resulting from the seizure or disposal except insofar as that loss or damage is caused by the office-holder's own negligence. The office-holder has a lien on the property, or the proceeds of the sale, for such expenses as were incurred in connection with the seizure or disposal (section 234(3) and (4)). The section does not apply to any third party *intangible* property (*Welsh Development Agency v Export Finance Co Ltd [1992] BCC 270 (CA)*).

(d) *Right to information*

A4.18 Section 235 imposes a duty on certain classes of persons connected with the affairs of the company to give to an office-holder (including, in the case of a winding-up by the court in England and Wales, the Official Receiver, whether or not he is the liquidator) such information concerning the company and its promotion, formation, business, dealings, affairs or property as the office-holder may after the effective date of the relevant insolvency reasonably require; and to attend on the office-holder at such times as he may reasonably require. This duty may be enforced through the court under Rule 7.20 (see *Re Wallace Smith Trust Co Ltd [1992] BCC 707*).

(e) *Private examination*

A4.19 On the application of an office-holder (defined as in (*b*) and (*d*) above) the court may summon to appear before it any officer of the company, any person known or suspected to have in his possession any property of the company or supposed to be indebted to the company, or any person whom the court thinks capable of giving information concerning the promotion, formation, business, dealings, affairs or property of the company. The court may require any such person to submit an affidavit to the court containing an account of his dealings with the company or to produce any books, papers or other records in his possession or under his control relating to the company or any such matters (section 236(2) and (3)). A solicitor against whom an order for production of documents under section 236 has been obtained is not entitled to refuse their production on the ground that he has a lien over them for his costs owing and remaining unpaid by the company. This applies even where the application is made by an administrative receiver and regardless of section 246 (unenforceability of liens on books etc.) (see A4.20 below), which does not apply to a receivership (*Re Aveling Barford Ltd [1989] 1 WLR 360*).

The documents disclosed to the office-holder can be used by him for the purposes of carrying out his duties (see *Re Esal Commodities Ltd [1988] PCC 443* at *450*; see also *Re Acli Metals (London) Ltd [1989] BCLC 749*). The transcript of the examination of a director is *prima facie* privileged at the suit of the office-holder and cannot be disclosed to a person who proposes to sue the director for fraud perpetrated in the name of the company (*Dubai Bank Ltd v Galadari (1989) 5 BCC 722*).

There are powers of personal arrest and seizure of property available to the court (set out in section 236(4) to (6)) where a person without reasonable excuse fails to appear before the court when he is summoned, or there are reasonable grounds for believing that he has absconded, or is about to abscond, with a view to avoiding such an appearance. In extreme cases the court may restrain a person ordered to be examined from leaving the jurisdiction in exercise of its powers under the Supreme Court Act 1981 (*Re Oriental Credit Ltd [1988] 2 WLR 172*). The injunction may be granted even if there is no cause of action vested in the liquidator, the injunction being anticipatory of the power of arrest for failure to attend under that section (*Re a Company (No 003318 of 1987) (1987) 3 BCC 564*).

Rules 9.1 to 9.6 contain detailed procedure for applications in England and Wales; see also *Re Norton Warburg Holdings and another [1983] BCLC 235* where the court required the liquidators and receivers to submit detailed written questions to and invite comments from the persons to be examined with a view to narrowing the field of oral examination.

Section 237(3) provides that the court may order the examination of any person in any part of the United Kingdom where he may for the time being be, *or in any place outside the United Kingdom*. Rule 12.12 empowers the court to direct the mode of service of any process or order or document required to be served on a person who is not in England and Wales. However, in *Re Tucker [1988] 1 All ER 603* in the context of section 25(6) of the Bankruptcy Act 1914 and Rule 86 of the Bankruptcy Rules 1952, containing similar provisions in relation to the bankruptcy of an individual, the Court of Appeal held, *inter alia*, that the court would not make an order under section 25(6) for the examination in Belgium of a person if it could not compel him to attend and could not punish him if he refused to attend. Rule 86 merely provided the machinery for service to implement the jurisdiction conferred by section 25 and did not purport to extend the jurisdiction.

Re Tucker was distinguished in *Re Seagull Manufacturing Co Ltd [1993] BCC 241 (CA)*, a case relating to *public* examination under section 133 (see C11.22 PART C: LIQUIDATIONS). It was held that section 133 empowered the court to order that a director of an English company which was being wound up by the court in England be publically examined, notwithstanding that the director was resident and domiciled abroad. Although, as a general rule of interpretation, statutes were not considered to take effect abroad unless they contained specific words to that effect, powers to examine directors from abroad must be implied because of the legislative policy of giving the courts effective power for investigation of company failures.

When the case came before the High Court (*[1991] BCC 550*), Mummery J (with whom the Court of Appeal agreed) stated that the public examination provisions of section 133 were not territorially limited in the same way as were the private examination provisions of sections 236, 237, 366 and 367 (the latter two sections relating to individual bankrupts). The two sets of provisions were different from each other in two important respects. First, private examination extended to a much wider class of persons than public examination. The latter was restricted to bankrupts and those who had participated in a specific capacity in the affairs of the company. The former extended to third parties who were capable of giving relevant information. Secondly, the private examination provisions contained express provisions which conclusively and inevitably connoted that if the person was not in England, he was not liable to be brought before the English court (though the taking of evidence abroad could be ordered if practicable). Any such provision was conspicuously absent from section 133.

It would seem that the distinction between the two sets of provisions based on the differences in their language is not wholly convincing in view of the common general objective of both types of examination. (See also *Re Paramount Airways Ltd (No 2) [1992] 3 All ER 1 (CA)*; *McIsaac and another, Petitioners, joint liquidators of First Tokyo Index Trust Ltd [1994] BCC 410*, a Scottish case, where it was held that it was competent for the court, having regard to the intention of section 426, to make an order under section 236 for production and examination against persons out of the jurisdiction.)

The decided cases, including those in connection with a similar provision in relation to liquidations under the old legislation, have established the following.

(i) 'Person' includes a company and it can be summoned to produce documents through its appropriate officer (*Re Highgrade Traders Ltd [1984] BCLC 151 (CA)*).

(ii) Documents (such as experts' reports) brought into existence with the dominant purpose of obtaining legal advice with respect to possible litigation with the company are protected by legal professional privilege and cannot be required to be produced (*Re Highgrade Traders Ltd*).

(iii) An examination of a person can be ordered even though he is a complete outsider and wholly unconnected with the company and the information sought relates to matters arising after the company had ceased active trading and with respect to transactions of which he has no direct knowledge, provided that he is likely to have some information which would assist the liquidator in carrying out his functions (*Re Highgrade Traders Ltd*).

(iv) Although the court must attach great weight to the views of the liquidator, it should ensure that the provision is not used in an oppressive, vexatious or unfair manner. Whether the examination is sought after the office-holder has made up his mind to sue the person to be examined, and will therefore subject that person's evidence to premature scrutiny, is a factor, but not necessarily an overriding factor, to be taken into account. Examination may be allowed where its purpose is to discover whether the proposed action should be commenced and whether there were any other transactions which may lead to claims. An order for examination on condition that the office-holder pays the costs of compliance may hamper the discharge of the office-holder's duties to investigate thoroughly the affairs of the company and would only be made in exceptional circumstances. (For cases on the points made in this paragraph, see *Re Cloverbay Ltd (1989) 5 BCC 732*; see also *Re Bletchley Boat Co Ltd [1974] 1 WLR 630*; *Re Castle New Homes Ltd [1979] 1 WLR 1975*; *Re Spiraflite Ltd [1979] 1 WLR 1096*; *Re JT Rhodes Ltd [1987] BCLC 77*; *Re Aveling Barford Ltd [1989] 1 WLR 360* (where it was doubted whether an examinee was entitled to be paid the costs of compliance); *Re British and Commonwealth Holdings plc (No 2) [1992] BCC 172 (CA)* where it was not disputed that the court had power to make an order for costs and Woolf LJ took into account that an order for costs would be made by the examining court); *Re Brook Martin and Co (Nominees) Ltd [1992] EGCS 138*). However, see also (v) to (viii) below.

(v) The nineteenth century cases (see, for example, *Re Gold Co (1879) 12 Ch D at 85*; *Green v Weaver (1827) 1 Sim 404*; *Chadwick v Chadwick (1852) 22 LJ Ch 329*; *Robinson v Kitchin (1856) 8 De GM & G 88 (CA)*) which construed the meaning of the word 'oppressive' in the context of a similar section may now be obsolete. Today it is recognised that persons involved in the affairs of an insolvent company have a public duty to assist the office-holder in investigating the company's affairs in the interests of the creditors, and due weight must be given to that point (*Re J T Rhodes Ltd (above)*). In exercising the powers under the section, the court must conduct a balancing exercise between helping the office-holder on the one hand and any potential prejudice to the person ordered to be examined or to produce documents on the other hand, the balance being 'loaded' somewhat in favour of the office-holder (see *Re Esal Commodities Ltd [1988] PCC 443 at 457* and *458*).

(vi) An office-holder, who issued a protective writ pending a decision by him whether to proceed with litigation on behalf of the company, was not permitted by the court to examine the defendant, because the office-holder had had the benefit of extensive disclosure of documents and no further information was needed to enable him to reach a decision; the production of any new information would merely improve his position as a litigant (*Re Cloverbay Ltd (No 3)* [*1990*] *BCLC 471*). On appeal in *Cloverbay Ltd v Bank of Credit and Commerce International SA* [*1990*] *3 WLR 575* the Court of Appeal, whilst dismissing the office-holder's appeal, rejected the test in *Re Castle New Homes Ltd* (above) and held that the test propounded in that case, of whether the office-holder had reached a firm decision to bring an action against the party to be examined, was not the appropriate test. The court had to balance the requirements of the office-holder against possible oppression of the party to be examined, bearing in mind that the purpose of the section was to enable the office-holder to reconstitute the knowledge the company should possess in order to discharge his duties to the creditors and contributories. The case for making an order against an officer or former officer of the company would be stronger than that against a third party; and an oral examination was likely to be more oppressive than an order for production of documents. In that case the balance was clearly against making the order sought.

The point as to the nature of the information which can be required from a particular examinee was finally settled by the House of Lords in *Re British and Commonwealth Holdings Plc (No 2)* [*1992*] *BCC 977*. It was held that the use of the powers under section 236, particularly in relation to the production of documents, was not restricted to reconstituting the previous state of the company's knowledge, but could go beyond that in order to discover the true state of affairs. However, as the power under section 236 was an extraordinary power, the court's discretion had to be exercised after carefully balancing the factors involved: on the one hand, the reasonable requirement of the office-holder to carry out his task and, on the other hand, the need to avoid making an order which was wholly unreasonable, unnecessary or oppressive to the proposed examinee. An application under the section was not necessarily unreasonable because it was inconvenient or caused him a lot of work, or might make him vulnerable to future claims, or he was not an officer or employee or a contractor with the company; but all those would be relevant factors. The court's discretion was not subject to any absolute limitations.

(vii) It would appear that section 236 does not take away legal professional privilege so that information or any document which is protected by such privilege under the general principles cannot be the subject of an order under the section. A decision to this effect was made in *Re Compass Airlines Pty Ltd* by the Federal Court of Australia on 21 August 1992 ((*1992*) *10 ACLC 1380*). This point may be of particular relevance where the office-holder wishes to discover details of any legal advice that was previously given to the company and/or its directors. It is submitted that there can be no objection to the disclosure of the advice given by the legal adviser to the company itself, because the office-holder is in effect the *alter ego* of the company as the former client of the adviser. There may, however, be a borderline case where the advice was primarily sought for the benefit and at the expense of the company, but, in the process, the legal adviser was drawn into giving advice to the directors personally on their position, on the basis of information given by the directors in confidence, before the legal adviser was able to form the view that the directors needed separate legal advice. The position in such cases has not been clearly determined. In *Price Waterhouse v BCCI Holdings (Luxembourg) SA [1992] BCLC 583*, Millett J held that reports produced by a firm of accountants for the purposes of an internal investigation into their clients' problem loans, sent by them directly to the clients' solicitors, were not protected by legal professional privilege. This was because they were not part of any client/solicitor communication and were not made for the dominant purpose of litigation. Millett J also held that on the facts, confidential banking information could be produced to a non-statutory inquiry into the supervision of a bank; in this case, the public interest in confidentiality was outweighed by the public interest in disclosure which was necessary for the purposes of an inquiry into the allegedly poor performance of the Bank of England's statutory functions.

(viii) Further court decisions on ancillary aspects of section 236 may be noted here. In *Re British and Commonwealth Holdings Plc [1992] BCC 165* the Court of Appeal, reversing the decision of the High Court, granted a firm of accountants leave to inspect the confidential statements which had been filed by the administrators in obtaining an *ex parte* order against the accountants under section 236. It stated that inspection of such confidential documents should *prima facie* be allowed where the court was of the opinion that it would or might be unable fairly or properly to dispose of the application to set aside the *ex parte* order if part of the evidence was withheld from the proposed examinee. It would then be for the office-holder to satisfy the court that confidentiality in whole or in part was nevertheless appropriate (*Re Gold Co (1879) 12 ChD 77* was distinguished; see also *Re Aveling Barford Ltd [1989] 1 WLR 360*; *Re Bletchley Boat Co Ltd [1974] 1 WLR 630*; *Fowler v Fowler [1963] P 311*; *Re K [1963] Ch 381*; *Re Rolls Razor Ltd (No 2) [1970] Ch 576*).

In *Re Arrows Ltd (No 4) [1993] BCC 473*, the Court of Appeal allowed an appeal from Vinelott J's order (*[1992] BCC 987*) that the transcript of the private examination of a person be disclosed to the Serious Fraud Office only on an undertaking by that Office not to use the transcripts save in circumstances specified in section 2(8) of the Criminal Justice Act 1987. It was held that a civil court had no power to restrict the use in criminal proceedings of transcripts of interviews carried out under section 236 and disclosed to that Office (see also section 433). The Court of Appeal's decision was affirmed by the House of Lords in *Re Arrows Ltd (No 4) [1994] BCC 641*. It held that although a judge had a discretion under Rule 9.5 whether to authorise the unconditional disclosure of transcripts of an examination under section 236, he had no power to seek to prevent the use by the Serious Fraud Office of those transcripts in criminal proceedings. This was so notwithstanding that if the SFO had itself directly asked the same incriminating questions to the examinee under section 2(2) of the Criminal Justice Act 1987, the examinee's answers would not have been admissible against him in criminal proceedings. Further, an examiner obtaining information from the examinee under statutory powers owed no duty of confidentiality. Subject to limited exceptions, section 3(3) of the 1987 Act expressly overrode any duty of confidence 'imposed by or under' any statute other than the Taxes Management Act 1970. Similarly, the fact that section 2(9) and (10) of the 1987 Act expressly preserved two specific duties of confidence showed that all other common law duties of confidence were overridden. Nor did public interest immunity attach to the transcripts of the examination under section 236 (having regard to its scope, purpose and policy), although section 3(3) in itself overrode only the statutory obligation of secrecy, not obligations arising under the general law on the ground of policy. (See also *Rank Film Distributors Ltd v Video Information Centre [1982] AC 380*, where Lord Wilberforce stated: 'I cannot accept that a civil court has any power to decide in a manner which would bind a criminal court that evidence of any kind is admissible or inadmissible in that court.' See further, however, section 78 of the Police and Criminal Evidence Act 1984 which gives the criminal court a discretion to exclude such transcripts in the light of all the circumstances, including those under which they were obtained.)

In the leading judgment in *Re Arrows Ltd (No 4)*, Lord Browne-Wilkinson expressed no view as to whether the position was similar with regard to the record of information obtained pursuant to section 235 (see A4.18 above) but refused to equate the rights of the SFO to obtain that record with its right to obtain records of the examination under section 236, stating that all the leading insolvency practitioners attached much greater importance to the confidentiality of information under section 235 than to the information obtained under section 236. See also *Re Adviser (188) Ltd, ex parte Trachtenberg [1993] BCC 492 (CA)*.

Following the decisions of the Court of Appeal in *Re London United Investments plc [1992] BCC 202* and *Re Bishopsgate Investment Management Ltd [1992] BCC 222*, an appeal to the Court of Appeal by that Office against the decision of Hoffmann J in *Re Arrows Ltd (No 2) [1992] BCC 125*, that the transcript of the examination should not be disclosed by the liquidators to that Office, was allowed by consent.

In *Re Jeffrey S Levitt Ltd [1992] BCLC 250* Vinelott J held that an examinee was not entitled to refuse to answer questions on the ground that to do so would tend to incriminate him. In *Re Arrows Ltd (No 2) [1992] BCC 446*, Vinelott J went further and stated that although the courts felt the greatest anxiety at the prospect that a person who had already been charged with a criminal offence should be subjected to an examination in the course of which he might be compelled to answer self-incriminating questions, it was clear that there was no absolute bar against preventing such an examination. The court had a discretion, to be exercised in the light of the practical considerations, the proximity of the trial and the public interest in ensuring that large insolvencies were properly and fully investigated. On the facts of the case the importance of allowing the liquidators to complete their enquiries outweighed any element of unfairness or oppression. See also *Re A E Farr Ltd* *[1992] BCC 150*; *Bank of England v Riley [1992] 1 All ER 769*; *Re London United Investments Plc [1992] BCLC 91*; *MGN v Maxwell [1992] BCC 218*, *Re Arrows Ltd (No 2) [1992] BCC 125*; *Re Headington Investments Ltd (CA) [1993] BCC 500*; *Re Barlow Clowes (Gilt Managers) Ltd [1991] 4 All ER 385* (information confidentially obtained by office-holder not to be voluntarily disclosed to the defendants in collateral criminal proceedings without compelling reasons, such as an order of the Crown Court); *Re Norton Warburg Holdings Ltd [1983] BCLC 235*; *R v Kansal [1992] BCC 615*; *Morris v Director of Serious Fraud Office [1992] BCC 934*; *Re AT and T Istel Ltd [1992] 3 WLR 344 (HL)* (approving *Re O (Restraint Order: Disclosure of Assets) [1991] 2 QB 520*).

In *Re Bishopsgate Investment Management Ltd; MGN v Maxwell [1992] BCC 222*, the Court of Appeal considered there to be some similarity between the position of a company director and a bankrupt who could be compelled to give incriminating answers. Whilst the interpretation of the Act was not governed by the old statutes, the 1986 legislation was not designed to weaken the examination process. Prior to section 235 (see A4.18 above) appearing for the first time in the Act, there was no equivalent in company law to the general duty to co-operate which had long been imposed on bankrupts. In an Australian case, *Spedley Securities Ltd v Bond Growing Investments Pty Ltd (1991) 9 ACLC 522*, Cole J in the Supreme Court of New South Wales expressed the opinion that privilege from answering incriminating questions (under a provision similar to section 236) should not be permitted to be claimed by directors or senior officers of public companies or companies which received money from the public.

(f) Unenforceability of liens on books, etc.

A4.20   Section 246 provides that a lien or other right to retain possession of any books, papers or other records of the company is unenforceable to the extent that its enforcement would deny *possession* of any such records to an administrator or a liquidator or provisional liquidator of the company. The section does not apply to a lien on documents which give a title to property and are held *as such* (for example, a bill of exchange). The words 'as such' refer to the circumstances, manner or capacity in which the documents are held which give rise to the lien so as to differentiate that case from those where the documents are held by one who would sometimes be entitled to assert a lien but in circumstances, manner or capacity which do not give rise to a lien (*Re SEIL Trade Finance Ltd [1992] BCC 538*). There are two main differences between sections 246 and 236 (see A4.19 above); firstly, section 246 deals with possession whereas section 236 deals with production and disclosure and, secondly, unlike section 236, section 246 does not apply to an administrative receiver (but see the *Aveling Barford* case mentioned in A4.19).

(g) Court orders re property and debts

A4.21   If it appears to the court, on consideration of any evidence obtained under section 236 or 237, that any person has in his possession any property of the company, the court may, on the application of the office-holder, order that person to deliver the whole or any part of the property to the office-holder. If it appears to the court, on consideration of such evidence, that any person is indebted to the company, the court may, on the application of the office-holder, order that person to pay to the office-holder the whole or any part of the amount due whether in full discharge of the debt or otherwise, as the court thinks fit (section 237(1) and (2)).

It has been held that the lawful acts of a liquidator are not confined to the exercise of his statutory powers to deal with the company's assets and liabilities for the purpose of the winding-up, but include acts incidental to his custody of company documents and other assets, provided their performance costs the company nothing. Accordingly, a liquidator (L) is not precluded from disclosing non-privileged and non-confidential documents to a creditor (C) to assist C in litigation with defendants against whom L also has a claim, if it reimburses any expense, or if disclosure could benefit the winding-up in that C may reciprocate. L may disclose information in his hands to a third party for the purpose of an action without obtaining an undertaking that the information will be used only for the purposes of that action (*Re Acli Metals (London) Ltd [1989] BCLC 749*).

(h) Confidentiality of documents

A4.22   An office-holder may decline to allow any person (including a member of a liquidation committee or a creditors' committee) who is otherwise entitled, to inspect any document forming part of the records of the insolvency if he considers that it should be treated as confidential or that its disclosure would be calculated to be injurious to the interests of the creditors or contributories. The person who is refused inspection has a right of recourse to the court (Rule 12.13; as to Scotland, see Rule 7.27 of the Insolvency (Scotland) Rules 1986 which makes similar provision). The Rule does not entitle the office-holder to decline to allow the inspection of any proof or proxy (Rule 12.13(4)).

(j) Exemption from the Restrictive Trade Practices Act 1976

A4.23 In relation to insolvency services supplied, offered or obtained, the restrictions contained in the above-mentioned Act do not apply to certain matters specified in section 428. 'Insolvency services' means the services of persons acting as insolvency practitioners (see A4.1 above) or carrying out corresponding functions under the law of Northern Ireland (section 428).

(k) Relief against security for costs in recovery proceedings

A4.24 An office-holder may be able to rely on *Aquila Design (GRB Products) Ltd v Cornhill Insurance plc [1988] BCLC 134* and be allowed to bring proceedings without having to furnish security for costs (see D8.16 PART D: RECEIVERS). In *Arch Joinery Contracts Ltd v Arcade Building Services Ltd 1992 SLT 755* (a decision of the Outer House of the Court of Session in Scotland), in an action by a company in liquidation and the liquidator, an order for security for costs against them was refused. Lord Osborne stated that where a liquidator was also a pursuer (i.e. plaintiff), a Scottish court would not make such an order since he would be personally liable for any costs awarded against the pursuer. Although in that case the liquidator had since retired as a partner in his firm, there was no allegation that the liquidator, who was a reputable chartered accountant of good standing, was insolvent in any legal or practical sense. (See also *Trident International Freight Services Ltd v Manchester Ship Canal Co [1990] BCLC 263 (CA)* and 'Legal Professional Privilege' by David Hunt QC, *Solicitors' Journal,* 6 May 1992).

Office-holders—guidance notes

A4.25 An active insolvency practitioner may from time to time encounter difficulties or a dilemma as to the correct interpretation or application, in a given situation, of the provisions of the Act or the delegated legislation made under it with regard to his administrative duties. In this connection, general guidance notes issued by insolvency professional bodies and others may be of considerable practical use. Particularly noteworthy are the Statements of Insolvency Practice issued by the Society of Practitioners of Insolvency (see A4.10 above) on 18 May 1992 on such subjects as an administrative receiver's responsibility for the company's records, a liquidator's investigation into the affairs of an insolvent company, disqualification of directors, statutory reports, non-preferential claims by employees dismissed without proper notice by insolvent employers, treatment of directors' claims as 'employees' in insolvency administration, preparation of insolvency office-holders' receipts and payments accounts, and conduct of meetings of creditors held pursuant to section 93 of the Insolvency Act 1986. Further guidance notes will no doubt be issued from time to time. Equally, if not more, useful are the information notes which the Insolvency Service (an executive agency within the Department of Trade and Industry) from time to time issues to insolvency practitioners under the banner of 'Dear IP'.

Chapter 5: Jurisdiction and court procedure in insolvency matters

Proceedings

A5.1 In all proceedings under the Act, whether in relation to voluntary arrangements, administration procedure, receivership or liquidation, jurisdiction rests with the court which has jurisdiction to wind up the company (section 251 (last part), as read with section 744 of the Companies Act 1985). As to which courts have jurisdiction to wind up a company in England and Wales and in Scotland, see C5.2 *et seq.* PART C: LIQUIDATIONS.

For England and Wales, Rules 7.1 to 7.61 of the Insolvency Rules contain detailed court procedure in relation to insolvency proceedings, other than a petition for an administration order or for a winding-up order (as to which see PART B: ADMINISTRATION ORDERS and PART C: LIQUIDATIONS (Chapter 3 *et seq.*)).

Rule 7.47 provides that every court having jurisdiction under the Act to wind up companies may review, rescind or vary any order made by it in the exercise of that jurisdiction, and an appeal from a decision made in the exercise of that jurisdiction by a county court or a registrar of a High Court lies to a single judge of the High Court. An appeal from a decision of the judge on such an appeal lies, with the leave of the judge or of the Court of Appeal, to the Court of Appeal (Rule 7.47(2)). Rule 7.49(1) provides that the procedure and practice of the Supreme Court relating to appeals to the Court of Appeal apply to appeals in insolvency proceedings. By Rule 7.49(2) it is provided that in relation to any appeal to a single judge of the High Court, any reference in the Rules of the Supreme Court to the Court of Appeal is replaced by a reference to that judge.

It will be noted that under the procedure and practice of the Supreme Court, an appeal to the Court of Appeal is by way of rehearing and not a hearing *de novo*. In *Re Probe Data Systems Ltd (No 3)* [*1991*] *BCLC 586*, Harman J, on an appeal to him from a decision of the registrar, held that the appeal to him was to be by way of a rehearing and not a hearing *de novo* so that he could only interfere with the registrar's decision if the registrar had exercised his discretion on wrong principles or on some whole misapprehension of the matter. It will be noted that if the appeal was by way of hearing *de novo*, then it would have been open to Harman J to exercise his discretion independently without going into the question of whether or not the registrar had erred in law or principle or was under some whole misapprehension of the matter. See also *Re A Debtor (No 59 of 1987), The Independent, 1 February 1988; Re Industrial and Commercial Securities Ltd (1989) 5 BCC 320.*

In *Lawrence v European Credit Co Ltd* [*1992*] *BCC 792* it was held that section 375(2) (relating to bankruptcy appeals which is similar to Rule 7.47(2)) did not impliedly exclude the appellate jurisdiction conferred on the Court of Appeal by section 16 of the Supreme Court Act 1981.

Rule 7.31 regulates inspection of the court file by various interested persons. The court may impose a prohibition against inspection of any particular documents without its leave which may be sought by *inter alia* 'any party having an interest'. The expression 'party' is not confined to a party to the proceedings (*Astor Chemicals Ltd v Synthetic Technology Ltd* [*1990*] *BCC 97*). Rules 12.10 to 12.12 and 13.3 to 13.5 deal with the service of documents in such proceedings. For Scotland, the Act of Sederunt (Rules of Court Amendment No 11) (Companies) 1986 (SI 1986 No 2298) deals with the procedure for insolvency proceedings in the Court of Session, and the Act of Sederunt (Sheriff Court Company Insolvency Rules) 1986 (SI 1986 No 2297) with the procedure for such proceedings in the sheriff court. In addition, the Insolvency Court Users' Committee has issued guidelines to registrars and district registrars in the provinces to be followed in deciding whether to assign a hearing to a judge or a registrar (see the *New Law Journal*, 11 November 1988, page 320). These guidelines are not given the force of formal practice directions.

Practice Direction [*1987*] *1 All ER 107*; [*1987*] *1 WLR 53* sets out lists of applications under the Act which (unless otherwise ordered) must be heard in open court, those which in the first instance should be made to the registrar of the court and those which are authorised to be heard by the chief clerk of the Companies Court.

Practice Direction (Insolvency Appeals; Hearings Outside London) [*1992*] *3 All ER 921;* [*1992*] *1 WLR 791* lists six additional centres in which appeals from the decisions of district judges exercising insolvency jurisdiction can be heard. The additional centres are: Birmingham, Bristol, Cardiff, Liverpool, Newcastle upon Tyne and Preston.

Unlike under Rule 7.47(2) (see above), whereby leave is required in the case of an appeal from the decision of a single judge to the Court of Appeal, no leave is required to appeal from an interlocutory order of a registrar to a single judge (*Re Busytoday Ltd* [*1992*] *4 All ER 61*).

Co-operation between courts

Statutory provisions

A5.2 An order made by a court in one part of the United Kingdom in the exercise of jurisdiction in relation to insolvency law (as defined by section 426(10)) is enforceable in any other part of the United Kingdom as if it were made by a court exercising the corresponding jurisdiction in that other part; but this does not require a court in any part to enforce such an order made in relation to property situated in that part by a court in any other part. The courts having jurisdiction in relation to insolvency law in one part of the United Kingdom must assist the courts having the corresponding jurisdiction in any other part of the United Kingdom or in any of the Channel Islands or the Isle of Man or in any country or territory designated for the purpose by the Secretary of State. The countries currently so designated are: Anguilla, Australia, The Bahamas, Bermuda, Botswana, Canada, Cayman Islands, Falkland Islands, Gibraltar, Hong Kong, Republic of Ireland, Montserrat, New Zealand, St Helena, Turks and Caicos Islands, Tuvalu and Virgin Islands. (See the Co-operation of Insolvency Courts (Designation of Relevant Countries and Territories) Order 1986—SI 1986 No 2123.) (Further, subsections (4), (5), (10) and (11) of section 426 have been extended to, and thus made part of the law of, the Bailiwick of Guernsey, with modifications—see the Insolvency Act 1986 (Guernsey) Order 1989 (SI 1989 No 2409).) A request for such co-operation made to a court in any part of the United Kingdom is authority for that court to apply, in relation to any matters specified in the request, the insolvency law which is applicable by either court in relation to comparable matters falling within its jurisdiction (section 426).

In *Re Dallhold Estates (UK) Pty Ltd [1992] BCC 394*, winding-up petitions had been presented, and provisional liquidators appointed, both in Australia and England in respect of the company which was incorporated in Australia. No winding-up orders had been made in either jurisdiction. At the request of the Federal Court in Australia addressed to the High Court of Justice, Chancery Division, in England, Chadwick J held that the court in England had jurisdiction under section 426 to make an administration order in respect of the company notwithstanding that the company had not been incorporated or registered in the United Kingdom and, therefore was not a 'company' for the purposes of sections 8 to 20 of the Insolvency Act 1986 relating to administration (see the last part of section 251, as read with section 735 of the Companies Act 1985).

Section 426 has also been successfully used to apply to a company, which is being wound up in a scheduled territory, the English provisions of the Insolvency Act 1986 relating to misfeasance/breach of statutory duty (section 212), fraudulent/wrongful trading (sections 213 and 214) and transactions at an undervalue (section 238): see *Re Bank of Credit and Commerce International SA and another [1993] BCC 787*, where Rattee J acceded to the request of the Grand Court of the Cayman Islands under section 426 to apply the provisions referred to above to a company which was being wound up in the Cayman Islands and had no branch in the United Kingdom. In doing so he made the following points.

(1)   The expression 'company' used in sections 212, 213, 214 and 238 was confined to a company formed and registered in Great Britain and did not include a foreign company. However, section 426, when invoked by a court of a scheduled territory in respect of a foreign company, gave the English court a discretion to apply those sections as if the company was being wound up in England. (Note that those sections would automatically apply to an overseas company which is being wound up in England as an unregistered company (see C5.4 PART C: LIQUIDATIONS); but that was not the position in the above case.)

37

(2) The court's discretion to apply those provisions did not depend on the existence of equivalent provisions of the law of the scheduled territory concerned since, if the requesting court had the necessary powers under its local law, there would be no need for a request for assistance under section 426.

(3) It was not correct, as suggested by Chadwick J in *Re Dallhold Estates* (above), that the English court had no discretion as to which law to apply or that the discretion lay solely in the requesting court. The English court had a general discretion as to how the assistance requested should be rendered.

(4) The English court should exercise its discretion in favour of giving assistance unless there was some good reason for not doing so. Such reasons might include rules of private international law, such as the general rule against enforcing the revenue laws of another state. (Note: section 426(5) expressly provides for regard to be had to the rules of private international law.)

(5) The fact that the application of the English provisions could cause a person not liable under the local laws of the foreign country concerned to become liable under English law did not detract from the clear words of section 426 conferring a discretion on the English court as to which law to apply.

International comity

A5.3 Even where section 426 does not apply, an English court will try to do its utmost (within the ambit of the principles of private international law) to accord recognition to foreign insolvency proceedings and to co-operate with a foreign bankruptcy court so as to avoid any action which might disturb the orderly administration by the foreign court of the insolvency of a corporation which is being conducted under the foreign court's jurisdiction. In principle, such recognition 'carries with it the active assistance of the court' (*Re African Farms Ltd* [1906] *TS 373* at *377*), but it is submitted that (except where section 426 applies) the English court will stop short of giving effect to any provisions of the foreign law or any order of the foreign court relating to avoidance of pre-insolvency or post-insolvency transactions affecting English assets; but see *Levasseur v Mason & Barry Ltd* (*1891*) *63 LT 700* at *702* (on appeal, [*1891*] *2 QB 73*) which is relied upon by some commentators for suggesting to the contrary as far as English moveable assets are concerned.

A typical example is where a foreign company is being wound up both in the country of its incorporation and in England. In such a case the English court treats the English winding up as ancillary to the foreign winding up (see C5.6 PART C: LIQUIDATIONS). Even where a company is not subject to English winding-up proceedings, the English courts' position appears to have become more co-operative than was typified in the *Felixstowe Dock* case referred to at C5.6 (which has been criticised by some judges out of court).

In *Banque Indosuez SA v Ferromet Resources Inc [1993] BCLC 112*, two of the issues were

(i)   whether certain choses in action, allegedly charged to a bank by an English subsidiary (which was not subject to any insolvency process in England) of a Texan parent (in respect of which a bankruptcy petition under the US Chapter 11 procedure had been filed in Texas), beneficially belonged to the subsidiary or the parent, and

(ii)   whether the bank should be granted an injunction preventing the subsidiary from disposing of them.

Hoffmann J held on the facts that the bank had no proprietary claim as the alleged charge-holder against the subsidiary and therefore had no right to an injunction against the subsidiary as alleged owner of the assets in question. He further held that insofar as those assets beneficially belonged to the parent, the bank's claims were subject to the stay under Section 362 of the US Bankruptcy Code. The English court would do its utmost to co-operate with the US Bankruptcy Court and avoid any action which might disturb the orderly administration of the insolvency of the parent in Texas. In exercising the discretion to grant or refuse injunctive relief, the court would take into account that the proceedings in England by the bank had not been authorised by the US Bankruptcy Court. In those circumstances, the injunctions would only be maintained if the court were satisfied that any assets recovered in the proceedings would be made subject to the Chapter 11 administration and the injunctions were necessary to prevent some dissipation which would be to the prejudice of the bank's rights under the US bankruptcy law. Only if those conditions were satisfied would the court examine the balance of convenience test in *American Cyanamid Co v Ethicon Ltd [1975] 1 All ER 504*. On the facts, the banks could be adequately protected by applications in the Chapter 11 proceedings and therefore the injunctions should be discharged.

In *Barclays Bank plc v Homan [1992] BCC 757*, an administration order had been made in England in respect of Maxwell Communications Corporation plc ('MCC'). MCC was also subject to Chapter 11 bankruptcy proceedings in the USA. The English administrators and the US examiner, subject to the respective jurisdictions of their courts, had carried on the management of the insolvency of MCC in co-operation. With the consent of the courts in the two jurisdictions, they had entered into an agreement aimed at harmonisation of their work. The agreement was expressed not to affect the jurisdiction of the two courts under their respective laws. The administrators proposed to pursue proceedings in the US bankruptcy under Section 547 of the US Bankruptcy Code to set aside a payment, which MCC had made to a bank, as a preference. The reason was that it was easier to establish a voidable preference under the US Bankruptcy Code than under the English section 239, it being unnecessary in the US, unlike in England, to show any intention or motive leading up to the payment. The bank sought an order of the English court restraining the administrators from pursuing the US proceedings on the ground that such proceedings were vexatious and oppressive. The bank argued that because it was or might be at a disadvantage under Section 547 as compared with section 239, that of itself made the US proceedings oppressive or vexatious. The Court of Appeal upheld the decision of Hoffmann J to refuse such an order. Hoffmann J had said

'It seems to me that an injunction. . . could serve no purpose except to antagonise the United States court and prejudice the co-operation which has thus far prevailed between the Chapter 11 and the English administration. . . If the United States judge does not think that there is a sufficient connection with America to justify a preference action against [the bank], she will dismiss the company's suit. . . If she does think so, she will not be deflected from securing the prosecution of that claim by any injunction I may make'.

Glidewell LJ in the Court of Appeal approved the following principles laid down by the Privy Council in *Societe Nationale Industrielle Aerospatiale v Lee Kui Jak [1987] AC 871*:

'(1) If the only issue is whether an English or a foreign court is the more appropriate forum for the trial of an action, that question should normally be decided by the foreign court on the principles of *forum non conveniens* and the English court should not seek to interfere with that decision.

(2) However, if, exceptionally, the English court concluded that the pursuit of the action in the foreign court would be vexatious and oppressive and that the English court is the natural forum, i.e. the more appropriate forum for the trial of the action, it could properly grant an injunction preventing the plaintiff from pursuing his action in the foreign court.

(3) In deciding whether the action in the foreign court is vexatious and oppressive, account must be taken of the possible injustice to the defendant if the injunction be not granted and the possible injustice to the plaintiff if it is. In other words, the English court must seek to strike a balance.'

Glidewell LJ went on to state that it was true that American law was different from English law in relation to voidable preferences, but there was nothing inherently oppressive about the difference. He also agreed with Hoffmann J that the facts of the present case were distinguishable from those of *Midland Bank plc v Laker Airways Ltd [1986] QB 689*. (Compare *British Airways Board v Laker Airways Ltd [1985] 1 AC 58 (HL)* which involved interaction with the Protection of Trading Interests Act 1980 and the Protection of Training Interests (US Antitrust Measures) Order 1983 (SI 1983 No 900)).

On the subject of the position of an English office-holder in relation to the company's affairs in the USA, Section 304 of the US Bankruptcy Code (of which there is no equivalent in England) can be of considerable assistance to the office-holder. That section permits a 'foreign representative' (defined as a 'duly selected trustee, administrator, or other representative of an estate in a foreign proceeding') appointed in a 'foreign insolvency proceeding', i.e.

'any proceeding in a foreign country in which the debtor's domicile, residence, principal place of business, or principal assets were located at the commencement of such proceeding, for the purpose of liquidating an estate, adjusting debts by composition, extension or discharge, or effecting reorganisation',

to file ancillary proceedings in the USA, that is, a petition to enjoin any action against the debtor with respect to property involved in such ancillary foreign proceeding, to seek turnover of assets located in the US, or for other appropriate relief. A US court considering a request for such relief applies the standard of 'what will best assure an economical and expeditious administration of [the] estate' and takes into account six factors:

(*a*) just treatment of all claimants;

(*b*) protection of domestic US claimants against prejudice and inconvenience in processing claims in the foreign proceedings;

(*c*) prevention of preferential or fraudulent transfers of assets;

(*d*) distribution of proceeds substantially in accordance with the US scheme;

(*e*) comity; and

(*f*) if possible, a fresh start for the foreign debtor.

An English liquidator or administrator clearly falls within the definition of a 'foreign representative' but an administrative receiver does not appear to do so as his appointment is not derived from a 'foreign proceeding' of the type mentioned above.

(See also B10.1 PART B: ADMINISTRATION ORDERS, C5.6 PART C: LIQUIDATIONS, and D12.1 PART D: RECEIVERS.)

Chapter 6: Meetings in insolvency matters

Proxies and corporate representation

A6.1   In England and Wales, Rules 8.1 to 8.7 deal with representation of a creditor (individual or corporate) by proxy or (where the creditor is a corporation) by a representative at meetings of creditors of the company, or of contributories summoned or held under the Act or the Rules. These provisions are described below. (There are similar, but not identical, provisions applicable to Scotland in Rules 7.14 to 7.20 of the Insolvency (Scotland) Rules 1986.)

A proxy is an authority, given by the principal to the proxy-holder, to attend and speak and vote as his representative at such a meeting. Only one proxy may be given for any one meeting. It may only be given to one person, being an individual aged at least 18, but the principal may specify one or more other such individuals in the alternative, in the order in which they are named in the proxy. A proxy may be given to the chairman of the meeting or (in a compulsory winding-up) to the Official Receiver; and neither of them can decline to act as proxy-holder. In the case of the latter, his deputy or any other official of the Department of Trade and Industry who is authorised in writing, may use the proxy. A proxy given to the responsible insolvency practitioner to be used by him as chairman may be used by any other person who acts as chairman.

A proxy requires the holder to give the principal's vote on matters arising for determination at the meeting, or to abstain, or to propose, in the principal's name, a resolution to be voted on at the meeting, either as directed or in accordance with the holder's own discretion. A direction in the proxy to vote for the appointment or nomination of a particular person as responsible insolvency practitioner is, unless the proxy states otherwise, deemed to include authority to the proxy-holder to vote for or against (as he thinks fit) that person's appointment or nomination jointly with another or others. Further, unless the proxy states otherwise, the proxy-holder may vote for or against any resolution, not dealt with in the proxy, which may be put to the meeting.

When forms of proxy are sent with the notice of meeting, no such form must have inserted in it the name or description of any person. Only the form sent out with the notice, or a substantially similar form, must be used at the meeting (see Forms 8.1 to 8.5).

The form must be signed by the principal, or by some other person authorised by him (either generally or with reference to a particular meeting). In the latter case, the nature of the person's authority must be stated.

It is not clear whether a proxy (or proof of debt) sent by facsimile transmission is valid for this purpose. The Department of Industry has, by its letter of 3 August 1989, informed insolvency practitioners that it has instructed the Official Receiver not to accept such a proxy (or proof). One reason it gave was that facsimile documents tend to fade with time. Many practitioners believe that it cannot be valid, since the faxed copy cannot be said to bear the original signature. However, in *Re Philipson, 10 and 13 September 1993 (unreported)*, Judge Hunt in the Harrogate County Court had no doubt that it could be. In *Re Cranley Mansions Ltd [1994] BCC 576*, Ferris J declined to express a view on a submission in favour of its validity (based partly on *Re English, Scottish and Australian Chartered Bank [1893] 3 Ch 385*), since the issue was not crucial to that case.

A proxy given for a particular meeting may be used at any adjournment thereof.

All proxies used must be retained by the chairman and delivered to the responsible insolvency practitioner forthwith after the meeting.

The responsible insolvency practitioner must, so long as the proxies are in his hands, allow them to be inspected at all reasonable times, on any business day, by the creditors (that is, those who, in a compulsory winding-up, have proved their debts or, in any other case, submitted a written claim, and whose proofs or claims have not been wholly rejected for the purposes of voting or dividend), members or contributories, as the case may be. The right of inspection is also exercisable by the directors of the company, if it is insolvent. Any person attending the meeting is entitled, immediately before or in the course of the meeting, to inspect proxies and associated documents (including proofs) sent or given, in accordance with the directions contained in any notice convening the meeting, to the chairman or any other person by a creditor, member or contributory for the purposes of that meeting.

A proxy-holder must not vote in favour of any resolution which would directly or indirectly place him, or any associate (as defined by section 435) of his, in a position to receive any remuneration out of the company's assets, unless the proxy specifically directs him to vote in that way. This prohibition applies to any person acting as chairman of the meeting and using proxies in that capacity; and in its application to him the proxy-holder is deemed to be the chairman's associate. Where the proxy has been signed by the proxy-holder himself as being authorised to do so by his principal and the proxy specifically directs him to vote in the way mentioned above, the restriction nevertheless applies to him unless he produces to the chairman a written authorisation from his principal sufficient to show that the proxy-holder was authorised to sign the proxy.

Where a person is authorised under section 375 of the Companies Act 1985 to represent a corporation, he must produce to the chairman a copy of the relevant resolution, which must be under the corporation's seal or certified by its secretary or director to be a true copy. This does not mean that the authority of a person who has signed a proxy on behalf of a corporate principal must be in the form of a resolution of that principal.

Quorum at meeting of creditors or contributories

A6.2 Any meeting of creditors or contributories in insolvency proceedings is competent to act if a quorum is present. In the case of a creditors' meeting, the quorum is at least one creditor entitled to vote present or represented by proxy by any person (including the chairman) or by corporate representative (see A6.1 above). In the case of a contributories' meeting the quorum is at least two contributories present or so represented. However, where (in either case) the quorum is constituted by the chairman alone or one other person in addition to the chairman, and the chairman is aware, by virtue of proofs and proxies received or otherwise, that one or more additional persons would, if attending, be entitled to vote, the meeting must not commence until at least the expiry of 15 minutes after the time appointed for its commencement. (Rule 12.4A as inserted by SI 1987 No 1919).

Table

Statutory instruments relating to corporate insolvency in force as at 1 November 1994

(In force from 29 December 1986 unless otherwise stated.)

SI 1985 No

95	Insurance Companies (Winding Up) Rules 1985 (1 March 1985) (as amended by SI 1986 No 2002 with effect from 29 December 1986)

SI 1986 No

6	Insolvency Act 1985 (Commencement No 1) Order 1986 (1 February and 1 March 1986)
185	Insolvency Act 1985 (Commencement No 2) Order 1986 (1 March and 1 April 1986)
304	Administrative Receivers (Value Added Tax Certificates) (Scotland) Rules 1986 (1 April 1986)
385	Administrative Receivers (Value Added Tax Certificates) Rules 1986 (1 April 1986)
463	Insolvency Act 1985 (Commencement No 3) Order 1986 (1 and 28 April 1986)
840	Insolvency Act 1985 (Commencement No 4) Order 1986 (1 June and 1 July 1986)
952	Insolvency Practitioners Tribunal (Conduct of Investigations) Rules 1986 (1 July 1986)

1764	Insolvency Practitioners (Recognised Professional Bodies) Order 1986 (10 November 1986)
1915	Insolvency (Scotland) Rules 1986 (as amended by the Insolvency (Scotland) Amendment Rules 1987 (SI 1987 No 1921) with effect from 11 January 1988)
1916	Insolvent Companies (Reports on Conduct of Directors) (No 2) (Scotland) Rules 1986
1917	Receivers (Scotland) Regulations 1986
1918	Insurance Companies (Winding-Up) (Scotland) Rules 1986
1924	Insolvency Act 1985 (Commencement No 5) Order 1986
1925	Insolvency Rules 1986 (as amended by the Insolvency (Amendment) Rules 1987 (SI 1987 No 1919) with effect from 11 January 1988, 1989 (SI 1989 No 397) with effect from 3 April 1989, 1991 (SI 1991 No 495) with effect from 2 April 1991, and 1993 (SI 1993 No 602) with effect from 5 April 1993)
1996	Insolvency Proceedings (Monetary Limits) Order 1986
1999	Administration of Insolvent Estates of Deceased Persons Order 1986
2000	Companies (Unfair Prejudice Applications) Proceedings Rules 1986
2001	Insolvency (Amendment of Subordinate Legislation) Order 1986 (as amended by SI 1987 No 1398 with effect from 1 September 1987)
2002	Insurance Companies (Winding-up) (Amendment) Rules 1986 (to be read with SI 1985 No 95)
2030	Insolvency Fees Order 1986 (as amended by SI 1988 No 95 with effect from 16 February 1988, SI 1990 No 560 with effect from 2 April 1990, SI 1991 No 496 with effect from 2 April 1991, SI 1992 No 34 with effect from 14 January 1992, and SI 1994 No 2541 with effect from 24 October 1994)
2067	Companies (Disqualification Orders) Regulations 1986
2116	Land Registration (Companies and Insolvency) Rules 1986
2123	Co-operation of Insolvency Courts (Designation of Relevant Countries and Territories) Order 1986
2134	Insolvent Companies (Reports on Conduct of Directors) No 2 Rules 1986
2142	Insolvent Partnerships Order 1986 (replaced by the 1994 Order with effect from 1 December 1994—see below)
2143	County Court Fees (Amendment No 2) Order 1986, as further amended by SI 1993 No 2762
2144	Supreme Court Fees (Amendment No 2) Order 1986

2245   Insolvency (Land Registration Rules) Order 1986

2297   Act of Sederunt (Sheriff Court Company Insolvency Rules) 1986

2298   Act of Sederunt (Rules of Court Amendment No 11) (Companies) 1986

SI 1987 No

2023   Insolvent Companies (Disqualification of Unfit Directors) Proceedings Rules 1987 (11 January 1988)

2093   Insolvency (ECSC Levy Debts) Regulations 1987 (1 January 1988)

SI 1988 No

93   Department of Trade and Industry (Fees) Order 1988 (22 January 1988) (as read with SI 1975 No 1350, SI 1985 No 1784 and as amended by SI 1990 No 559 with effect from 2 April 1990 and SI 1991 No 494 with effect from 2 April 1991)

SI 1989 No

1276   Banks (Administration Proceedings) Order 1989 (23 August 1989)

2405   Insolvency (Northern Ireland) Order 1989 (in part 16 May 1990)

2409   Insolvency Act (Guernsey) Order 1989 (1 February 1990)

SI 1990 No

439   Insolvency Practitioners Regulations 1990 (1 April 1990), as amended by SI 1993 No 221 with effect from 1 April 1993

SI 1994 No

2421   Insolvent Partnerships Order 1994 (1 December 1994)

2507   Insolvency Regulations 1994 (24 October 1994)

N.B. See also the Companies (Forms) ((Amendment) Regulations 1987 (SI 1987 No 752, as read with SIs 1985 No 854 and 1986 No 2097 as amended by SI 1990 No 572) particularly Forms 600 and 600a in Schedule 2).

Part B: Administration Orders

1. **Preliminary**   **49**

2. **Conditions which must be satisfied**   **53**

3. **Application and order**   **59**

   Making and serving the application   59
   The hearing of the application   64
   Notice and advertisement of administration order   66

4. **Effects of application and order**   **67**

   Leave applications   75

5. **Manner of administration**   **79**

   Notice on stationery   79
   Initial control and management   79
   Statement of affairs   80
   Administrator's proposals   80
   Creditors' meetings under section 23   83
   Procedure for creditors' meetings generally   83
   Administrator's reports   86
   Implementation and revision of proposals   87
   Discharge or variation of order   88
   No preferential creditors or distribution to any creditors   89
   VAT bad debt relief   89
   Taxation in the administration   89

6. **Administrator's powers affecting the rights of secured creditors and owners of assets**   **90**

   Power of disposal   90
   Implications of power of disposal   92
   Transitional provisions regarding floating charges   92
   Some practical points for holders of general charges   93

7. **Position and general powers and duties of the administrator**   **96**

   Vacancy in office of administrator, and his release   96
   General powers   97
   Right to apply to court for directions   102
   Conflict with powers of company and its officers   102
   Administrator's agency   102
   Administrator's liability   103
   Post-administration expenses and liabilities   105
   Parties dealing with administrator   108
   Administrator's remuneration   109
   Abstracts of receipts and payments   109

8. Protection of creditors' and members' interests   **110**

Creditors' committee   110
Right of creditors to requisition meeting   111
Right of a creditor or member to apply to court   111

9. Adjustment of antecedent transactions   **113**

Transactions at an undervalue (England and Wales)   113
Gratuitous alienations (Scotland)   113
Voidable preferences (England and Wales)   114
Unfair preferences (Scotland)   114
Court's powers   115
Extortionate credit transactions (Great Britain)   115
Avoidance of certain floating charges (Great Britain)   116
Unenforceability of lien on books, etc. (England and Wales)   116
Void unregistered charges   117

10. International elements   **118**

Part B: Administration Orders

(This chapter should be read in conjunction with PART A: GENERAL and PART F: SPECIAL PROVISIONS FOR FINANCIAL MARKETS.)

Chapter 1: Preliminary

B1.1   The concept of the administration order for companies was introduced for the first time by the Insolvency Act 1985 and is now embodied in the Insolvency Act 1986. Sections 8 to 27 of the Insolvency Act 1986 (as amended by the Insolvency Act 1994) apply to England and Wales and to Scotland. More detailed aspects of the procedure are mainly dealt with, in relation to companies registered in England and Wales, in Part 2 of the Insolvency Rules 1986 (SI 1986 No 1925), as amended by the Insolvency (Amendment) Rules 1987 (SI 1987 No 1919), 1989 (SI 1989 No 397), 1991 (SI 1991 No 495) and 1993 (SI 1993 No 602), and, in relation to companies registered in Scotland, in Part 2 of the Insolvency (Scotland) Rules 1986 (SI 1986 No 1915), as amended by the Insolvency (Scotland) (Amendment) Rules 1987 (SI 1987 No 1921). Unless otherwise stated, the sections referred to in this chapter are those of the Insolvency Act 1986, the Rules referred to are the Insolvency Rules 1986, as amended (applicable to England and Wales) and the Forms are those contained in Schedule 4 to the Rules. The Insolvency (Scotland) Rules 1986, as amended, contain equivalent, but not identical, provisions.

The procedure came into effect on 29 December 1986 but is available only in respect of companies (other than insurance companies) registered under the present and the previous companies legislation. The procedure is not available in the case of oversea companies or other bodies not registered under that legislation (see section 735 of the Companies Act 1985 and the concluding part of section 251 of the Insolvency Act 1986); except in cases where section 426 (co-operation between courts) applies (see *Re Dallhold Estates (UK) Pty Ltd [1992] BCC 394*, discussed at A5.2 PART A: GENERAL). (See also B10.1 below.) The provisions of the Insolvency Act 1986 relating to this procedure interact with certain other provisions of that Act relating to other types of insolvency.

With effect from 1 December 1994, the administration procedure, as it applies to companies, has also been made applicable, with modifications, to insolvent partnerships. The Insolvent Partnerships Order 1994 (SI 1994 No 2421), replacing the Insolvent Partnerships Order 1986 (SI 1986 No 2142), provides that sections 8 to 27 of the 1986 Act, in their modified form as set out in Schedule 2 to the 1994 Order, apply to an insolvent partnership (Article 6). The following sections, in so far as they relate to administration orders, also apply: 212 (misfeasance etc.), 230 to 232 (insolvency office-holders), 233 to 237 (statutory aids for insolvency office-holders), 238 to 246 (adjustment of prior transactions), 247, 248, 249 and 251 (interpretation), 388 to 398 (insolvency practitioners), 411, 413, 414 and 419 (subordinate legislation), 423 to 425 (debt avoidance), 426 to 434 (miscellaneous and general), 435 and 436 (interpretation) and 437 to 444 (final provisions) (Article 6).

One noteworthy feature of the modified provisions is that which deals with an agricultural charge within the meaning of the Agricultural Credits Act 1928, that is, a floating charge over agricultural assets created by an individual or a partnership (etc.), as permitted by that Act. The effect which the administration procedure has on an agricultural charge, on its holder and on a receiver (agricultural receiver) appointed under it, is similar to that which that procedure has on a charge created by a company which carries an entitlement to appoint an administrative receiver, on its holder and on an administrative receiver appointed under it.

The remainder of this part of the book deals with administration orders in relation to registered companies only. For detailed provisions on partnership administration orders, the reader should refer to the 1994 Order in full.

Under the previous legislation, there was no statutory mechanism which summarily imposed a general moratorium on the rights of secured and unsecured creditors whilst a scheme of arrangement or composition or other rescue package was being worked out as an alternative to immediate liquidation, which usually reduces the realisable value of assets and proliferates liabilities. A rescue attempt could be undermined by a creditor taking precipitate action resulting in the break-up of the company, unless the company had created a general charge and a receiver appointed thereunder was able to preserve the viable parts of the business by a hive-down or otherwise.

Under this new procedure, which enables the court, in certain circumstances, to make an administration order and thereby put the affairs of the company into the hands of a qualified insolvency practitioner, a creditor will be subject to severe restrictions against 'stealing a march' over the other creditors once an administration order has been applied for.

The insolvency practitioner appointed under such an order is called the 'administrator', which title must be distinguished from that of the 'administrative receiver' (see D1.4 PART D: RECEIVERS). The difference between the two is that whereas an administrative receiver is appointed (usually out of court) by the holder of a general charge, such as a debenture, for the holder's own benefit, an administrator is appointed by the court for the benefit of the creditors generally.

There may be cases where even from the standpoint of the holder of a general charge, the administration procedure is more beneficial than the administrative receivership. This is because administration provides a more extensive moratorium than the limited *de facto* 'freeze' available in the administrative receivership. More particularly, under the administration procedure, third party owners of assets in the company's possession are under a restriction against repossessing those assets, and landlords of leasehold premises of the company are under a restriction against forfeiting the leases, without the leave of the court. Thus, where such assets or leases comprised in a general charge are vital to the continuation of the company's business with a view to a better realisation, the restriction can help to prevent a rapid deterioration of the value of the general charge.

In *Campbell Meads plc (in administration) Chancery Division (Companies Court), 24 September 1991 (unreported)*, the bulk of the company's assets consisted of wine bars operated on leasehold premises. A bank had a fixed and floating charge over all the assets of the company, including the leasehold premises. There was no real likelihood of any surplus remaining for unsecured creditors. An administration order for the purpose of a better realisation of the company's assets had been made but the administrators' proposals for achieving that purpose had been rejected by the meeting of creditors. There was also pending against the company a petition for its compulsory winding up. If the court were to discharge the administration order and thereby allow a winding-up order to be made, the forfeiture clauses contained in the leases would be triggered. Unlike in an administration, a landlord is not under any restriction in a liquidation or an administrative receivership against forfeiting a lease although, in certain situations, the court has power to grant relief against forfeiture. Unfortunately, in the instant case such relief would not have been available in view of section 146(9) of the Law of Property Act 1925 which expressly excludes relief against forfeiture in respect of public houses (including wine bars) (see *Official Custodian for Charities v Parway Estates Developments [1984] 3 WLR 525* and *Billson v Residential Apartments Ltd [1992] 1 AC 494 (CA)* (reversed on appeal by the House of Lords ([1992] 1 AC 494) on different grounds) which make it clear that the section is exhaustive and excludes any inherent jurisdiction of the court to grant relief in such cases). This is an instance where an administration order was successfully applied for, in effect, for the sole benefit of a secure creditor.

In *Re Gallidoro Trawlers Ltd [1991] BCLC 411*, the company had mortgaged some of its ships to a bank. The company was in financial difficulties and the bank was concerned that valuable fishing licences attached to the ships, granted by the Ministry of Agriculture, Fisheries and Food, might be transferred by the company to another party or might be otherwise jeopardised, thus reducing the realisable value of the ships. The bank intended to present a petition for the making of an administration order in respect of the company on the ground of a more advantageous realisation. The bank applied for the appointment of a manager to manage the affairs of the company pending the presentation, service and hearing of the petition, and also for an abridgement of the time for the hearing of the petition. In addition, the bank sought an order restraining the company and its directors from disposing of the licences without the consent of the proposed interim manager. Harman J, approving the observations of Vinelott J in *Re a Company (No 00175 of 1987)* [*1987*] *BCLC 467*, held that the court was entitled to abridge time for service but that there was no power to appoint an interim administrator. The only power was to appoint an administrator or refuse to do so. Further, although under section 9(4) the court had a specific power to make an interim order or other order as it thought fit (including the appointment of an interim manager), and under section 9(3) to make orders restricting the exercise of powers, in the instant case there was no need to make such an appointment, however, there was a need to impose a restriction on any attempt to dispose of the assets of the company, such as those licences. On the bank giving an appropriate cross-undertaking in damages in favour of the company, Harman J made the restraining order and also abridged the time for service.

Chapter 2: Conditions which must be satisfied

B2.1   Before the court makes an administration order, it must be satisfied that the company is, or is likely to become, unable to pay its debts as
they fall due or that the value of its assets is, or is likely to become, less
than the amount of its liabilities, taking into account its contingent and
prospective liabilities (sections 8(1)(a) and 123). Thus, the court has
jurisdiction to make an administration order where a company is 'asset
solvent' but 'cash insolvent' (see *Re Business Properties Ltd (1988) 4 BCC
684*); see also *Re Imperial Motors (UK) Ltd (1989) 5 BCC 214*). The court
must also consider (section 8(1)(b)) that the making of the order would be
likely to achieve one or more of the following purposes:

(*a*)   the survival of the company, and the whole or any part of its undertaking, as a going concern;

(*b*)   the approval of a voluntary arrangement (see PART E: VOLUNTARY
ARRANGEMENTS) or the sanctioning of a scheme of arrangement or
compromise under section 425 of the Companies Act 1985; and

(*c*)   a more advantageous realisation of its assets than would be effected
on a winding up (section 8(3)).

A proposal for a 'hive-down' of the business and assets of a company,
aimed at ensuring that the hived-down company survives as a going concern, does not fall within (*a*) above, because this does not ensure the
survival of the company itself (*Re Rowbotham Baxter Ltd [1990] BCC
113*). Such a proposal may, however, fall within (*c*) above.

In *Re Consumer and Industrial Press Ltd [1988] BCLC 177*, Peter Gibson
J held that the words 'would be likely to achieve' mean that the achievement of the purpose or purposes concerned is probable, rather than possible. (See also *Re Manlon Trading Ltd (1988) 4 BCC 455*). However, in
Re Harris Simons Construction Ltd [1989] 1 WLR 368, Hoffmann J
expressed the view that Peter Gibson J had set the standard of probability
too high in the context of the language used in section 8(1). Hoffmann J
made an administration order on being satisfied that there was a real prospect (which means no more than 'a modest threshold of probability') that
one or more of the stated purposes may be achieved. The purposes could
be mutually exclusive and they did not all have to be capable of the same
degree of probability (see also *Re Primlaks (UK) Ltd (1989) 5 BCC 710*).
In a later case, *Re SCL Building Services Ltd (1989) 5 BCC 746*, Peter
Gibson J followed the 'real prospect' test. Where the purpose concerned
is a more advantageous realisation of the assets than would be effected on
a winding up, and the court is satisfied that that purpose is likely to be
achieved, it may make an administration order notwithstanding that allegations of fraudulent or wrongful trading require to be investigated by a
liquidator. The allegations are a matter to be taken into account in deciding whether to grant the administration order but the court would also

have regard to the possibility that following the disposal of the assets by the administrator, the company would be put into liquidation whereupon the allegations would be investigated (see *Re Consumer Industrial Press Ltd* (above)).

As to purpose (*b*) above, it was originally believed that the voluntary arrangement procedure, as introduced for the first time by the 1986 Act, would, because of its simplicity and cost-effectiveness, largely supersede the old scheme of arrangement or compromise procedure as a means of effecting a formal corporate rescue. However, experience has shown certain limitations and technical problems in the voluntary arrangement procedure, largely created by unsatisfactory legislative drafting, particularly where large companies with complex affairs, including contingent, future and unknown claims and a proposal for the restructure of the share capital, are involved. Notwithstanding these problems, the successful reconstruction of Chancery PLC by means of a voluntary arrangement during the operation of the administration procedure demonstrates that most of these problems are capable of being resolved in practice. (See 'Reconstruction of Chancery PLC: Part 2' by Colin Bird and Alan Perry in (*1992*) *5 Insolvency Intelligence* at page 83 where some of these problems are summarised.) The scheme of arrangement continues to be a viable formal rescue option in an administration as is demonstrated by the case of *Re British & Commonwealth Holdings plc*. In particular, the cause of such formal rescues was substantially advanced by the decision in *Re British & Commonwealth Holdings plc (No 3)* [*1992*] *BCLC 322* in which the court upheld the validity of contractual subordination of debts (thus settling a long-existing controversy among lawyers) and dispensed with the need for a meeting of subordinated creditors in a proposed scheme of arrangement on the ground that they had no tangible interest in the outcome of the scheme. (See also the very helpful article of Scott Slorach of Nottingham Law School, the Nottingham Trent University, entitled 'Proposed Scheme of Arrangement within an Administration: The Decision in *Re British & Commonwealth Holdings plc (No 3)*' in [*1992*] *11 JIBL 471*.)

In considering whether to grant an administration order the court has taken various factors into account, particularly

  (i) the degree of support which the petition has from the creditors, directors and shareholders (*Re Imperial Motors Ltd, Re Harris Simons Ltd* and *Re Consumer and Industrial Press Ltd* (above), although it is not helpful for the court to indulge in head-counting (*Re Rowbotham Baxter Ltd* (above));

 (ii) whether the sale of the assets as a going concern is likely to realise a better price than the sale on a break-up basis in a liquidation (*Re Consumer and Industrial Press Ltd* (above));

(iii) whether requisite funds would be available for the purposes of the administration (*Re Consumer and Industrial Press Ltd* and *Re Harris Simons Ltd* (above));

(iv) the likelihood of redundancies and costs connected with them in a liquidation as opposed to in an administration (*Re Harris Simons Ltd* (above) and *Re Brooke Marine Ltd [1988] BCLC 546)*;

(v) the speed with which the sale of the assets could be achieved in an administration as opposed to in a liquidation (*Re Imperial Motors (UK) Ltd* (above));

(vi) the likelihood of additional losses arising from continuation of the business during the administration (*Re Consumer and Industrial Press Ltd* (above)); and

(vii) the existence of profitable on-going contracts which could be saved in an administration, as opposed to in a liquidation (*Re Harris Simons Ltd* and *Re Brooke Marine Ltd* (above)).

Among other matters, the court necessarily places considerable reliance on the views of the reporting insolvency practitioner (*Re Primlaks*, above). Where administration petitions are presented in relation to a number of companies in the same group, the question of whether any of the purposes of the administration is likely to be achieved must be looked at in relation to each company independently. In *Kentish Homes Ltd and Others (31 July 1989, unreported)*, petitions in relation to a number of companies in a group were opposed by holders of fixed charges (who, unlike holders of floating charges, were not entitled to frustrate an administration application by appointing receivers). Harman J dismissed the petitions on the ground that there was no real prospect that any of the purposes was likely to be achieved, looking at each company independently, as there was too much uncertainty and there had been too much change since the applications were first contemplated.

In *Re Manlon Trading Ltd (1988) 4 BCC 455*, the company was subject to both a winding-up petition and an administration petition. The judge in the Vacation Court had made an order restraining advertisement of the winding-up petition on the basis that a report under Rule 2.2 of the Insolvency Rules 1986 would be prepared by an insolvency practitioner with a view to presentation of a petition for an administration order. The restraining order was continued by Harman J (see *Re a Company (No 001992 of 1988) (1988) 4 BCC 451*) at a time when a Rule 2.2 report had been prepared and an administration petition presented. The report, based on statements made by the company's 'general manager', stated that a better realisation of assets would be achieved in an administration than in a winding up. The court refused the petition for an administration order, stating that:

(A) the judge in the Vacation Court should not have restrained advertisement of the winding-up petition—that petition was properly presented, was not challenged and there was no countervailing administration order petition pending at that time nor any undertaking that one would be presented but merely a contemplation that one might be; and

(B) nothing in the report or the evidence showed that there was a probability (which was the test the court had to apply) that the only object of an administration order put forward would be achieved if the order was made.

Re West-Tech International Ltd [1989] BCLC 600 was an example where a petition for an administration order was presented by the directors following the presentation of a petition for a winding-up order and the appointment of provisional liquidators before the winding-up order. The evidence of the liquidators indicated a state of affairs that was at best chaotic and at worst thoroughly dishonest. On an application by one of the directors to stand over both the petitions to enable sufficient material to be put before the court, the court, refusing the application, held that there had been ample time and opportunity for the directors to adduce sufficient evidence in support of the administration petition. It could not be said that an administrator would be in a better position to recover assets in the form of foreign debts than a liquidator.

Re Arrows Ltd (No 3) [1992] BCC 131 involved both a creditor's winding-up petition supported by other creditors and a petition for an administration order presented by the sole director and shareholder of the company and opposed by creditors. Pending the hearing of the winding-up petition, a provisional liquidator had been appointed. The court dismissed the administration petition and granted the winding-up petition on two grounds. First, there was no evidence before the court justifying a conclusion that there was a real prospect of a more advantageous realisation of assets. The Rule 2.2 report submitted in support of the administration petition was based on the misapprehension that the company had a right of set-off against the mortgagees of the property of certain associated companies in respect of head lease rentals due by the company to those associated companies (see *National Provincial Bank Ltd v Ainsworth [1965] AC 1175*; *Reeves v Pope [1914] 2 KB 284*). Secondly, since a majority of creditors in value opposed administration, it seemed unlikely that the proposals which the administrators might put forward on the lines of the report would be approved by the creditors' meeting. Although the court had a discretion to appoint administrators despite opposition by a majority of the creditors, in the circumstances of the case the interests of the creditors would be better served by an investigation into the company's affairs in the course of a compulsory winding up.

Re Land and Property Trust Company plc [1991] BCC 446 was another case where the court had before it both a creditor's winding-up petition supported by other creditors and the company's petition for an administration order opposed by creditors. The purposes for which the administration order was sought were first, a voluntary arrangement and, secondly, more advantageous realisation of assets which depended on a voluntary arrangement being approved and a disputed amount of tax losses being achieved. The court dismissed the administration petition on the ground that there was no evidence that the voluntary arrangement envisaged would be acceptable to creditors—such evidence as there was suggested the opposite. The view of Peter Gibson J in *Re SCL Building Services Ltd (1989) 5 BCC 746* that there must be some evidence which gives reality to the prospect of a voluntary arrangement being acceptable to creditors was cited with approval.

In *Re Imperial Motors (UK) Ltd* (above), the petition for an administration order was presented by a secured creditor. The sole purpose for which the order was sought was a more advantageous realisation (see (*c*) above). The petition was opposed by the company, but was supported by an unsecured creditor. Both the petitioning and supporting creditors had made demands on the company for repayment which had not been complied with, but there was an undertaking that the supporting creditor's debt would be paid by a director. A debt owed to the director himself had been subordinated. If the subordinated debt and the debt due to the supporting creditor to be discharged by the director were excluded, the company was solvent on the balance-sheet test. It was held that:

(1)   as the company was insolvent on the cash-flow test, the court had power to make an administration order;

(2)   there could be a more advantageous realisation of the assets in an administration than in a winding up, notwithstanding that the company appeared to be solvent on a balance-sheet test;

(3)   in considering whether to make an administration order, as a matter of discretion, the interests of secured creditors weighed lighter in the scales than the interests of other creditors, because the secured creditors did not stand to lose so much; and

(4)   balancing the interests of the petitioner in achieving a more advantageous realisation against the interest of the company, its shareholders and management in not having the business taken out of their hands and sold to a third party, it was right to refuse to make an administration order.

Where it is clear that the purpose of the administration order will fail and there is a winding-up petition pending, the court may, instead of making an administration order, exercise its discretion to appoint a provisional liquidator in the winding up without notice to other parties (*Re W F Fearman Ltd (1988) 4 BCC 139*).

The court will normally be reluctant to make an administration order where there has been a breakdown of trust and there is a deadlock among the shareholders as a winding up would be more appropriate (*Re Business Properties Ltd (1988) 4 BCC 684*). (As to winding up on this ground see C5.26 PART C: LIQUIDATIONS.)

The court may not make an administration order if the company has gone into liquidation (i.e. if a voluntary winding-up resolution has been passed or a winding-up order has been made by the court in respect of the company—section 247(2)) (section 8(4)), or if there is an administrative receiver (see D2.9 PART D: RECEIVERS) in respect of the company (section 9(3); and see *Re a Company (No 00175 of 1987) [1987] BCLC 467*) (unless his appointor consents to the making of the administration order or unless the security under which the appointment has been made is vulnerable under the provisions relating to transactions at an undervalue, voidable preferences, gratuitous alienations (Scotland), or invalid floating charges or under any rule of law in Scotland (see B9.1 *et seq.* below)) (section 9(3)). The court may also not make an administration order in respect of an insurance company within the meaning of the Insurance Companies Act 1982. By the Banks (Administration Proceedings) Order 1989 (SI 1989 No 1276), made pursuant to section 422, the administration procedure has been made applicable to authorised and former authorised institutions within the meaning of the Banking Act 1987 with effect from 23 August 1989, subject to the modifications specified in the Schedule to that Order.

Chapter 3: Application and order

Making and serving the application

B3.1   An application for an administration order must be by petition (see Rule 2.4 and Form 2.1) presented to the court either by the company itself or its directors or any one or more of its creditors (including contingent or prospective creditors), or by all or any of these parties, together or separately (section 9(1)). (Under section 74 of the Financial Services Act 1986, it is possible for a recognised self-regulating organisation or a recognised professional body or the Secretary of State to make such an application in relation to a company which is an authorised person or whose authorisation has been suspended or which is an appointed representative under that Act.) The petition may not be withdrawn except with the leave of the court (section 9(2)(b)).

'Directors' in the preceding paragraph means all the directors—see *Re Instrumentation Electrical Services Ltd (1988) 4 BCC 301*, decided under section 124 which relates to a petition by the directors for a winding up; and see *Re Business Properties Ltd (1988) 4 BCC 684*. See also *Re Equiticorp International Ltd (1989) 5 BCC 599*, where it was held that although 'the directors' in section 9(1) meant all the directors, once a proper board resolution had been passed it became the duty of all the directors to implement it and the petition by five of the seven directors had been properly presented.

In the matter of the *Kentish Homes* group (*31 July 1989, unreported*) the administration petitions had been presented in the names of the companies themselves pursuant to their board resolutions. Following *Re Emmadart Ltd [1979] 1 All ER 599*, Harman J expressed the view that the companies were not entitled to present the petitions without authorising resolutions of the shareholders of those companies. However, since the directors of each company had passed the necessary resolution and had power to present the petition in their own names, and since by Rule 2.4(3), once the directors' petitions were presented they became the petitions by the company, Harman J granted leave to amend the petitions to the effect that they were the petitions of the directors.

In *Re W Fearman Ltd (No 2) (1988) 4 BCC 141*, Harman J ordered the costs of an unsuccessful, but *bona fide*, administration petition of the directors to be borne by them instead of being paid as an expense of the winding up out of the company's assets. However, in *Re Gosscott (Groundworks) Ltd [1988] BCLC 363*, the court held that it would be unfair to order the directors or their professional advisers to meet the costs of an unsuccessful petition for an administration order, where it had been presented in good faith on the advice of an insolvency practitioner.

The right of a company to present an administration petition in respect of itself was challenged, and the *locus standi* of directors to present such a petition was discussed, in *Re Land and Property Trust Company plc [1991] BCC 446*. The company's petition was opposed by a creditor on the ground that it had no *locus standi* in the absence of 'sufficient interest' in the outcome (in the sense of a prospect of advantage or avoiding some disadvantage) and that a hopelessly insolvent company could have no such interest. In rejecting the objection, Harman J stated that the analogy of winding-up petitions by contributories (see B3.2 below) was not appropriate. Winding-up petitions by insolvent companies (as distinct from by their contributories) had never been refused on such a ground. An insolvent company did have an interest in 'having its affairs properly conducted and adequately wound up and in satisfying its duty to pay its debts, or at least to have them met *pari passu* out of its assets. . .'. An insolvent company's directors would also have *locus standi* to present a winding-up petition provided that in their capacity as directors they showed sufficient interest. It is submitted that in view of their positive duty to explore all reasonable options to minimise the potential loss to the company's creditors which is implicit in the provisions of section 214 (wrongful trading—see C13.2 PART C: LIQUIDATIONS below), the directors would normally have sufficient *locus standi*.

At a subsequent hearing of the administration petition in the *Land and Property Trust* case referred to above (see *[1991] BCC 449 et seq.*), Harman J refused to grant a further adjournment to enable the directors to prepare evidence, dismissed that petition and made a winding-up order on a creditor's petition, and ordered the directors to pay the costs personally. He said 'to present an administration petition seems to me to have had no independent support at all and not to have been the act of persons making desperate efforts in all good faith to save the company. . . this is a wholly exceptional case where the petition was resolved upon without proper consideration of its purposes and was persisted in in the face of overwhelming opposition and without reason'. However, on appeal (*Re Land and Property Trust Co plc (No 2) [1993] BCC 462*), the Court of Appeal set aside the order for costs. It held that his refusal to grant an adjournment was wrongful and that his failure to ensure that he had adequate evidence before him, on which he could reach a decision, caused him to err in principle in holding the directors personally liable for the costs.

The petition must be supported by an affidavit (Rule 2.1) complying, as to contents and exhibits, with Rules 2.3 and 2.4(6) (see Forms 2.1 and 2.3). The prescribed contents include a statement of the company's financial position. The prescribed exhibits include a written consent (Form 2.2) by the proposed administrator to accept the appointment if an administration order is made. An optional exhibit is a report by an independent person (which includes the proposed administrator but excludes any director or other officer or employee of the company) having adequate knowledge of the company's affairs to the effect that the appointment of an administrator is expedient. The court now regards it as good practice for such a report to be included (but see the *Practice Note* referred to in the next paragraph). Any such report must specify one or more of the purposes referred to in section 8(3) (see B2.1 above) which, in the opinion of its author, may be achieved by the making of the administration order (Rule 2.2). In any event, the affidavit itself must do so (Rule 2.3).

In connection with the optional report under Rule 2.2 referred to in the preceding paragraph, Sir Donald Nicholls V-C has issued the following *Practice Note* (*[1994] 1 All ER 324*) on behalf of the Chancery Division:

'Administration orders under Part II of the Insolvency Act 1986 are intended primarily to facilitate the rescue and rehabilitation of insolvent but potentially viable businesses. It is of the greatest importance that this aim should not be frustrated by expense, and that the costs of obtaining an administration order should not operate as a disincentive or put the process out of the reach of smaller companies.

Rule 2.2 of the Insolvency Rules 1986, SI 1986/1925, provides that an application for an administration order may be supported by a report by an independent person to the effect that the appointment of an administrator for the company is expedient. It is the experience of the court that the contents of the rule 2.2 report are sometimes unnecessarily elaborate and detailed. Because a report of this character is thought to be necessary, the preliminary investigation will often have been unduly protracted and extensive and, hence, expensive.

The extent of the necessary investigation and the amount of material to be provided to the court must be a matter for the judgment of the person who prepares the report and will vary from case to case. However, in the normal case, what the court needs is a concise assessment of the company's situation and of the prospects of an administration order achieving one or more of the statutory purposes. The latter will normally include an explanation of the availability of any finance required during the administration.

Every endeavour should be made to avoid disproportionate investigation and expense. In some cases a brief investigation and report will be all that is required. Where the court has insufficient material on which to base its decision, but the proposed administrator is in court, he may offer to supplement the material by giving oral evidence. In such a case he should subsequently provide a supplemental report covering the matters on which oral evidence was given so that this can be placed on the court file.

In suitable cases the court may appoint an administrator but require him to report back to the court within a short period so that the court can consider whether to allow the administration to continue or to discharge the order. In some cases the court may require the administrator to hold a meeting of creditors before reporting back to the court, both within a relatively short period.

It is the experience of the judges who sit in the Companies Court that, in general, a rule 2.2 report is valuable as a safeguard in assisting the court to see whether the application has a sound basis. However, there may be straightforward cases in which such a report is not necessary because it would provide little assistance. Practitioners are reminded that the 1986 Rules do not require that a rule 2.2 report must be provided in every case.'

An application for an administration order is made *ex parte*, although at the hearing the parties mentioned in B3.2 below may appear. The general rule in all *ex parte* applications, that material non-disclosure may result in the court setting aside any order, applies with even more force to administration applications, the administrator being the only person who can apply for the discharge of the administration order. Where material facts are not brought before the court, the court may direct the administrator to apply for his discharge (see *Re Sharps of Truro Ltd* [1990] *BCC 94*).

The evidence in support of the application must disclose, fully and frankly, all facts relevant to the exercise by the court of its discretion, even though to do so may be embarrassing to the applicant. In *Astor Chemicals Ltd v Synthetic Technology Ltd* [1990] *BCC 97*, after Peter Gibson J had made an administration order, proceedings were brought before Vinelott J to prevent the administrator from terminating a sole distributorship agreement which the company had entered into prior to the administration order. A number of matters that were not before Peter Gibson J came to light, which Vinelott J considered to be sufficiently serious to require the administration proceedings to be restored to the Companies Court. He said that if the information that the future of the company depended on its being able to terminate the distribution agreement and the availability of fresh finance, and the history of the company (which was the 'Phoenix' company of a previous company with a similar name, and under the control of the same person, which had gone into compulsory liquidation) had been brought to the notice of Peter Gibson J, 'there must at the lowest be very serious doubt whether he would have made the administration order'. (See also the Court of Appeal guidelines in *Cornhill Insurance plc v Cornhill Financial Services Ltd* [1992] *BCC 818*, discussed at B5.16 below.)

Section 9(2)(a), Rules 2.5 to 2.8 and Form 2.3 deal with the procedure for the filing and service of the petition or copies of the petition and the affidavit and exhibited documents in support. They are required to be served on (i) any person who has appointed, or is or may be entitled to appoint, an administrative receiver, (ii) any administrative receiver already in office, (iii) any person who has presented a pending winding-up petition, (iv) any provisional liquidator in office under a pending winding-up petition, (v) the proposed administrator and (vi) where the petition is presented by creditors, the company. In addition, where the company is an authorised institution under the Banking Act 1987, service must also be effected on the Bank of England (Banks (Administration Proceedings) Order 1989 (SI 1989 No 1276)).

The manner of effecting service is laid down in Rule 2.7(1) and (2). The service must be effected not less than five days before the date fixed for the hearing (Rule 2.7(1)). However, by virtue of Rule 12.9 the court has power to abridge that period provided that the circumstances of the case so require (for example, where the assets are in jeopardy) and, in the case of a service on the person mentioned in (i) above, that he has adequate opportunity to consider the position before the hearing (*Re a Company (No 00175 of 1987)* [*1987*] *BCLC 467*) (which, as a matter of practice, can be ensured by liaising with him and obtaining his agreement in advance).

In *Re Chancery plc* [*1991*] *BCLC 712*, Harman J held that the circumstances of the case were so exceptional as to justify dispensing with the normal requirements of notice to all the parties concerned. The exceptional circumstances concerned the fact that the company was a bank recognised as an authorised institution under the Banking Act 1987 and that confidence, which was essential to a banking venture, could quickly be lost, with disastrous consequences, during a period of uncertainty when it was known that an administration petition was pending. Moreover, he was satisfied that the other requirements relating to the presentation of a petition had been satisfied; in particular, that the Bank of England (on which service was required—see above) had been notified and had agreed to short notice, that the proposed administrators had signified their consent to act as such, that there was no person entitled to appoint an administrative receiver and that it had been demonstrated to the court that the company was likely to be unable to pay its debts. In that case, the petition had been presented at about 2.50 p.m. following a board resolution passed at 12.10 p.m. on the same day and the petition was dealt with and an order made the same afternoon. Harman J referred to his observations in *Re Rowbotham Baxter Ltd* [*1990*] *BCLC 397* (see B3.2 below) that it was in general undesirable for administration petitions to be brought or to be proceeded with without the participation of all persons interested in their outcome. However, in the instant case, he stated, the circumstances were exceptional.

Harman J also found the circumstances in *Re Cavco Floors Limited* [*1990*] *BCC 589* exceptional and abridged the usual timetable. Those circumstances were that the company had a number of profitable building sub-contracts. In practice, in the building trade sub-contracts are swiftly terminated by prime contractors if the sub-contractor fails to perform. He was of the view that no injustice would be done to anyone, including the creditor who had issued a statutory demand. Counsel had placed before the court an accountants' report under Rule 2.2, a comprehensive affidavit from a director and a letter from the company's bank, which held a general charge, waiving its right to the usual five days' notice of the hearing. Counsel also undertook to present the petition forthwith after the hearing.

Rule 2.6A (as inserted by SI 1987 No 1919) requires the petitioner to give notice of the filing of the petition forthwith to (*a*) any sheriff or other officer who is to his knowledge charged with an execution or other legal process against the company or its property and (*b*) any person who to his knowledge has distrained against the company or its property. For the significance of this, see B4.1(*c*) below. Another new Rule, 2.7(4A), is aimed at ensuring that where the person who has appointed or is, or may be, entitled to appoint an administrative receiver is a bank, the service is effected at its appropriate branch (wherever applicable).

The hearing of the application

B3.2 There may appear or be represented at the hearing (i) the petitioner, (ii) any of the parties required to be served with the petition as stated in B3.1 above (and the company, whether or not so required), and (iii) with the leave of the court, any other person who appears to have an interest justifying his appearance (Rule 2.9(1)), for example, the holder of a fixed charge (as in *Re Imperial Motors* and *Kentish Homes* referred to in B2.1 above). This means that if counsel for the petitioner and the parties required to be served (as in (ii) above) appear before the court forthwith upon the administration petition being presented or an undertaking being given to present it, and before the petition is advertised, this would deprive other parties having an interest in the application of an opportunity of applying to the court for leave to appear. The court would hear only one side of the argument and this might lead to a serious risk of injustice. In *Re Rowbotham Baxter Ltd [1990] BCLC 397*, Harman J stated that such a practice, which had been developing, was undesirable and should not continue. (See, however, his decision in *Re Chancery plc* referred to in B3.1 above.)

A shareholder who does not have sufficient interest in the petition will not be granted leave to appear. In *Re Chelmsford City Football Club (1980) Ltd [1991] BCC 133*, a petition for an administration order presented by the directors for the purpose of securing the survival of the company was supported by the administrator designate's report which contained a proposal to redevelop the football ground. The petition was opposed by certain unsecured creditors who claimed to be majority shareholders and offered to refinance the company. Harman J, in making an administration order, held that since the company was plainly insolvent, the shareholders had no interest sufficient to justify being heard on the petition even if they had some interest in what happened in the future. Although, as creditors, they could be heard, there was still a strong case for the making of an administration order—an administrator, once appointed, would be bound to consider the refinancing proposal in any event (see *Re Rica Gold Washing Co (1879) 11 ChD 36*). This decision to exclude shareholders follows the analogy of the liquidation cases which, for over a century, have rejected winding-up petitions by contributories holding fully paid shares in an insolvent company on the ground that because they have neither the prospect of any return on capital nor any liability to contribute, they have no tangible interest in winding-up petitions. (See C5.30 PART C: LIQUIDATIONS below.)

The court must dismiss the petition if it is satisfied that there is an administrative receiver of the company unless it is also satisfied as to the existence of the consent of the appointor or as to the vulnerability of the appointor's security under section 9(3) (see B2.1 above). As to the meaning of 'administrative receiver', see D1.4 PART D: RECEIVERS. In *Re*

Croftbell Ltd [1990] BCLC 844, referred to there, the court dismissed the administration petition on the ground that the receiver who had been appointed under a charge expressed to be a fixed and floating charge was an administrative receiver, notwithstanding that at the time of the appointment the company had no floating charge assets. It is debatable whether for this purpose the expression is confined to an administrative receiver whose appointment is valid in every respect. It is not clear whether the court has jurisdiction to make an administration order where the validity of the security or the administrative receiver's appointment thereunder is challenged on grounds other than those mentioned in section 9(3). Would the court be willing to hold a 'trial within a trial' to determine the question of validity? Would it make an order until the question is determined in a separate action? Or would it simply dismiss the application? These questions arose in an application before Millett J in 1989 for an administration order in respect of the *Cloverbay Ltd* case but eventually the matter was otherwise resolved. Subject thereto, the court may dismiss the petition, adjourn the hearing conditionally or unconditionally or make an interim or any other order as it thinks fit, including an interim order restricting the exercise of any powers of the directors or of the company, whether by reference to the need for the consent of the court or of a qualified insolvency practitioner or otherwise (section 9(4) and (5)). Where the court makes any such other order, it must give directions as to the persons to whom and how notice of it is to be given (Rule 2.10(5)).

The court will not normally wish to make an administration order where there has been a breakdown of confidence among the shareholders or directors of a *quasi partnership* company, as a winding up may be more appropriate (see, for example, *Re Business Properties Ltd (1988) 4 BCC 684*).

Whether the hearing should be adjourned so as to give the person who is entitled to appoint an administrative receiver more than five days within which to consider his position (see B3.1 above) will depend on the circumstances of the case (*Re a Company (No 00175 of 1987)*, cited in B2.1 above).

The power of the court to make 'an interim order' does not include a power to appoint an 'interim administrator' pending the hearing, as no administrator can be appointed before an administration order has been made. However, it does include a power to appoint the proposed administrator or other suitable person to take control of the property of the company and manage its affairs pending the hearing, if the court is satisfied that the assets or business are in jeopardy, and there exists a *prima facie* case for the making of an administration order. Such an appointment would be analogous to the appointment of a receiver of a disputed property which is in jeopardy. In Scotland, there have been cases where interim appointments have been made, apparently for such limited purposes, although the persons have been described as interim administrators (see, for example, *Sonido International Ltd v Peters 1991 SCLR 874 (Sh Ct)*). Where there is a person who is entitled to appoint an administrative receiver, the interim order will be limited to a period to enable him to decide whether to appoint an administrative receiver and with a view to the person appointed under the interim order either being superseded by an administrative receiver or continuing as or being supplanted by an administrator. The remuneration of the person appointed under the interim order can be paid out of the assets, as it would relate to the period prior to the appointment of the administrative receiver (*Re a Company*, above).

If the court is satisfied as to the existence of the circumstances mentioned in B2.1 above, it may (which in practice presumably means 'must') make an administration order in relation to the company (section 8(1)). An administration order is an order directing that for its duration the affairs, business and property of the company are to be managed by an administrator appointed for the purpose by the court (section 8(2)).

If the court makes an administration order (Form 2.4), the costs of the petitioner, and of any person appearing whose costs are allowed by the court, are payable as an expense of the administration (Rule 2.9(2)).

As mentioned in B3.1 above, in *Re Land and Property Trust Co plc (No 2)* [1993] BCC 462, where the directors' petition for an administration order had been successfully opposed by creditors, the Court of Appeal refused to award the creditors' costs against the directors personally. They had acted throughout in good faith and in the interests of the company. They had observed all the requirements of the Rules and had been supported by experienced insolvency practitioners.

Notice and advertisement of administration order

B3.3   Forthwith upon the making of the order, the court must give notice thereof to the administrator. Upon notice being received, the administrator must forthwith advertise the making of the order once in the *London* (or in Scotland, *Edinburgh*) *Gazette*, and once in such newspaper as he thinks most appropriate for ensuring that the order comes to the notice of the company's creditors (Form 2.5) and give notice of its making to (*a*) each of the other parties who were required to be served with notice of the petition (see B3.1 above), (*b*) the company, whether or not so required, and (*c*) the Registrar of Companies (on Form 2.6). Two sealed copies of the order must be sent by the court to the administrator, one of which must be sent by him to the Registrar of Companies (together with Form 2.7) within 14 days after the making of the order (section 21(I)(a) and (2), Rule 2.10). Within 28 days after the making of the order, the administrator must, unless the court otherwise directs, send such a notice to all the creditors of the company, so far as he is aware of their addresses (section 21(1)(b)).

Chapter 4: Effects of application and order

B4.1 From the presentation of the petition for an administration order (or, where there is already an administrative receiver and his appointor has not consented to the making of the order, from the time the appointor so consents) until the making of the order or the dismissal of the petition:

(*a*)   no resolution may be passed or order made for the winding up of the company (section 10(1)(a));

(*b*)   no steps may be taken to enforce any security over the company's property, or to repossess goods in the company's possession under any hire purchase agreement (including a conditional sale, chattel leasing or retention of title agreement), except with the leave of the court and subject to such terms as the court may impose (section 10(1)(b)); and

(*c*)   no other proceedings and no execution or other legal process may be commenced or continued, and no distress may be levied (or, in Scotland, diligence carried out or continued) against the company or its property, except with the leave of the court and subject to such terms as aforesaid (section 10(1)(c)).

(*a*) above does not, however, prevent (and no leave is necessary for) the *presentation* of a winding-up petition or the appointment of an administrative receiver or the carrying out by such a receiver (whenever appointed) of his functions (section 10). Nevertheless, a winding-up petition must not be advertised without leave, as the advertisement may damage the company and would be contrary to section 10 (see *Re a Company (No 001992 of 1988) (1988) 4 BCC 451*). Even an undertaking by the intending petitioner to present an administration petition may suffice to make an order restraining advertisement of the winding-up petition (*Re a Company (No 001448 of 1989) (1989) 5 BCC 706*).

With regard to (*b*) and (*c*) above, it would appear that save in very exceptional circumstances, the court would not be willing to grant leave, *a fortiori* an unconditional leave, pending the making of an administration order (see B4.2 below), because to grant the leave might be to pre-empt any proposals or representations which the administrator might have wished to make.

As to the meaning of 'property' in (*b*) and (*c*) above, see section 436; see also *Re Rae* (*15 July 1994*, Warner J, referred to in the *Technical Bulletin of the Society of Practitioners of Insolvency*, Issue No 18, August 1994 at 18.7), where the entitlement of a bankrupt to fishing licences attached to his vessels was held to be property. This was because although the interest in the licences was not enforceable in a court of law (because of its discretionary nature), it was nevertheless marketable and capable of being turned into money.

The restrictions referred to under (*a*), (*b*) and (*c*) above continue after an administration order has been made and whilst it remains in force, with the following modifications (section 11):

(i)   no administrative receiver may be appointed;

(ii) any administrative receiver already appointed must vacate office, and any receiver of part of the property of the company must vacate office on being required to do so by the administrator; but the remuneration of such administrative or other receiver and any indemnity to which he is entitled out of the company's assets will be a first charge on the assets, and he ceases to be under a duty to pay preferential debts (see D7.3 PART D: RECEIVERS) (normally, no administration order may be made where there is already an administrative receiver but there are exceptions—see B2.1 and B3.2 above);

(iii) as regards the restrictions referred to under (*b*) and (*c*) above, the court's leave is not required if the administrator has consented to the taking of the steps referred to there; and

(iv) any pending winding-up petition will be dismissed.

For general observations on applications to the court for leave under (iii) above, see B4.2 below.

After an administration order has been made, although it is not essential to show some criticism of the administrator's conduct, the court would only grant leave under (*b*) above where the creditor has shown that in all the circumstances it is appropriate to do so. In *Royal Trust Bank v Buchler [1989] BCLC 130* (also cited as *Re Meesan Investments Ltd (1988) 4 BCC 790*) the company had borrowed £560,000 from a bank to purchase and refurbish property with a view to letting it. The loan was secured by a charge over the property entitling the bank to appoint a receiver. The administrator took the view that it would be best to let the premises and then sell them. The letting programme failed and the administrator decided to sell the premises as they stood. A bid was made for the property for £850,000. The court refused the bank's application for leave to enforce its security and held that the bank had failed to discharge the onus of showing that it was a proper case to give leave. There were no grounds for criticising the administrator's decision to delay the sale of the property in an attempt to sell it fully let and that there was every likelihood that it would now be sold, realising sufficient amount to pay the bank in full. If the leave were granted, the bank would have to appoint a receiver, increasing costs and reducing the proceeds of the sale. (See B6.1 below as to the circumstances in which an administrator may be allowed to dispose of secured property.)

The restrictions in (*b*) above apply to an airport authority's statutory power to detain aircraft, including leased aircraft, pending payment of charges due, so that the power is not exercisable without the leave of the court. In *Bristol Airport plc v Powdrill [1990] 2 WLR 1362* (also reported as *Re Paramount Airways Ltd [1990] BCC 130*), where the aircraft detained by the airport's authority were held by the company under chattel leases, the Court of Appeal held that (1) the aircraft were 'property' as defined by section 436, and not merely contractual rights, (2) the right of detention was 'other security', if not 'lien' within the definition of 'security' in section 248, and (3) the exercise of the statutory right of detention was a 'step taken to enforce' a security under (*b*) above, notwithstanding that the overt act of perfecting the security and the act of enforcing it by detention constituted the same single act. However, contrary to what the judge in the court of first instance had held, the detention did not constitute the levying of a distress under (*c*) above.

It was further held that the judge had rightly exercised his discretion not to grant leave to enforce the security. Sir Nicolas Browne-Wilkinson V-C said that if at the outset of an administration, a secured creditor wished to enforce a security in a way inconsistent with the achievement of the statutory purpose of the administration, he should have made his position clear at the outset. To stand by and accept all the benefits of an administration and then at the eleventh hour seek to enforce a right which was inconsistent with the achievement of the statutory purpose was unacceptable. The position in the instant case was worse in that it was only as a result of the operations of the administrators that the aircraft came to be at the airports in question. The airport authorities were seeking to achieve an outcome where, as a result of the administration, they achieved greater rights than they would have done had the company gone into liquidation. While the administration procedures should not be used so far as possible to prejudice those who were secured creditors at the time when the administration order was made in lieu of a winding-up order, neither should they be used so as to give the unsecured creditors at that time security which they would not have enjoyed had it not been for the administration.

It appears from the above decision that where no leave to detain is granted, the airport authority can be in a worse position than the holder of an ordinary form of security to whom no leave to enforce it is granted. Unlike such holder, the authority may not have its security when the administration order is discharged as the administrator may have disposed of the aircraft in the meantime or it may never land again at that airport and the authority will not be entitled to any payment in respect of its disposal by the administrator pursuant to section 15 (see B6.1 below). This is because, until the aircraft is physically detained, the airport authority has no lien and, hence, no security.

Where the company's goods are held by another party who claims a lien over those goods, a continued detention of those goods by that party amounts to enforcement of security within the meaning of (*b*) above (i.e. within section 11(3)(*c*)). Therefore, unless that other party obtains the consent of the administrator or the leave of the court he must deliver up the goods to the administrator (*Re Sabre International Products Ltd [1991] BCLC 470*). Any failure to effect delivery, even in the absence of any special order of the court to do so, may constitute a contempt of the court on the ground of interference with the possession or right to possession of the administrator as an officer of the court (*Re Sabre International* (above); *Re Henry Pound Son & Hutchings* (*1889*) *42 ChD 402*). However, sections 10 and 11 are not intended to deprive a creditor of his security. As Sir Nicolas Browne-Wilkinson V-C observed in *Bristol Airport plc v Powdrill* [*1990*] *2 WLR 1362* (referred to above), it cannot be right that the appointment of an administrator has the effect of turning a secured creditor into an unsecured creditor. The onus is, however, on that creditor to take appropriate steps at the earliest possible stage to preserve his security by applying for the consent of the administrator or the leave of the court to continue to hold the goods (since the loss of possession would result in the loss of a lien) or to seek alternative security. (*Re Sabre International* (above)). That administrator must act reasonably and fairly on any application to him. Woolf LJ in *Bristol Airport plc v Powdrill* (above) stated:

'The administrator can give his consent . . . and I would expect the administrator to consent to that detainor exercising his rights until an application could be made to the court [where an application was necessary].'

In *Re Sabre International* (above) Harman J stated:

'Administrators are officers of the court. There are rights clearly given by the statute to security holders to apply for leave. Many such applications are made. Plainly I entirely agree with, and in any event must follow and accept, the Court of Appeal's observations in *Bristol Airport v Powdrill* [above] that if reasonable proposals are put to administrators they ought to agree to them . . . .'.

In relation to hire-purchase agreements, it will be noted that section 10 refers to goods 'in the company's possession' (see (*b*) above). In *Re Atlantic Computer Systems plc* [*1992*] *2 WLR 367 (CA)*, it was held that for the purposes of section 10, goods which were in the possession of a third party under a sub-lease granted by the company were nevertheless deemed to be in the company's possession and that, therefore, the owner of the goods needed the leave of the court (the administrator not having given his consent—see B4.2 below) before he could repossess the goods in exercise of his rights under the hire-purchase agreement. Delivering the judgment of the court, Nicholls LJ said, 'In our judgment the answer emerges once one considers the purpose of section 11(3)(c) . . .' (which corresponds to section 10(1)(b) (see (*b*) above) '. . . The paragraph is dealing with goods which, as between the company and its supplier, are in the possession of the company under a hire-purchase agreement. Those goods are to be protected from repossession unless there is either consent . . .' (see (iii) above) '. . . or leave. It is immaterial whether they remain on the company's premises, or are entrusted by the company to others for repair, or are sub-let by the company as part of its trade to others. We do not see that such a construction does any violence to the language of the paragraph, or is more purposive than is warranted by the current approach of the English courts to statutes which are neither fiscal nor penal, even though it is said that a breach of the paragraph is a contempt of court . . . In the present case, the computer equipment, as between the funders and the company, remains in the possession of the company . . . It cannot be repossessed save with consent or leave'.

As noted above, sections 10(1)(b) and (c) and 11(3)(c) and (d) merely impose a moratorium on the enforcement of the creditor's legal right and does not alter or destroy those rights. The third party owner's right to possession of his goods is not removed by the section. In *Barclays Mercantile Business Finance Ltd v Sibec Developments Ltd [1992] 1 WLR 1253*, rental payments in respect of goods taken by the company on hire purchase were in arrears, and the hire purchase agreements were terminated, either automatically on the making of the administration order or shortly afterwards by letter. The hire-purchase company requested the administrators to consent to it repossessing the goods forthwith, but the administrators refused. The hire-purchase company applied to the court pursuant to section 11(3)(c) and (d) for leave to repossess the goods, or alternatively for leave to commence proceedings against the company or the administrators for delivery up of the goods and/or damages for wrongful interference with them, or for payment of the hire charges in respect of the goods as an expense of the administration. The administrators subsequently allowed the hire-purchase company to repossess the goods, and the alternative claims were adjourned generally, with liberty to restore. The administration order was subsequently discharged and a compulsory winding-up order was made under which the administrators were appointed as liquidators. The order provided for the release of the administrators on the expiration of a specified period after they had filed their receipts and payments account. On the application for the administrators' release to be postponed until after the adjourned alternative claims had been dealt with, Millett J, in ordering postponement of their release stated:

'In my judgment, the administrators remain exposed to a claim so long as they have not been released, whether they committed the tort of conversion or not. That is because the administrators are officers of the court and at all times subject to the court's direction. If they wish to make use of another party's property for the purpose of the administration and cannot agree terms, they can seek the directions of the court. If administrators wrongly retain goods otherwise than for the proper purposes of the administration, for example, to use them as a bargaining counter, the owner can apply to the court to direct the administrators to hand over the goods without the need for action, and to pay compensation for having retained them in the meantime. Only in a case where there was a triable issue as to the ownership of the goods would the question of giving leave to take proceedings for possession arise. I can see no difference between the amount of compensation that the administrators should be directed to pay for having wrongfully retained goods properly demanded and for having wrongfully refused leave to repossess them. Accordingly, in my judgment, whether or not the company, and possibly the administrators, may be liable to a claim for damages for conversion, the administrators, until their release, remain liable at the direction of the court to pay not only for the use of the goods of another, but also for compensation for having wrongfully refused leave to the owner to retake the goods.'

In the *Barclays Mercantile* case (above), the claim against the administrators personally was based on the principle that an administrator acts as agent of the company and if he procures his company to commit a tort he may be made personally liable for it. Millett J extended the scope of the personal liability by virtue of their being officers of the court. It is important, therefore, that administrators should carefully apply the *Atlantic Computer* principles (see B4.2 below) in considering any request from third party owners of assets for the return of their goods.

The restriction in (*b*) above against repossession of any goods held under a hire-purchase agreement applies notwithstanding that the relevant hire-purchase agreement had been terminated prior to the presentation of the administration petition (*Re David Meek Access Ltd* [*1993*] *BCC 175*, where the hire-purchase agreements were expressed to terminate upon the presentation or the drafting of an administration petition).

The exercise, even out of court, by a landlord of the right to re-entry (even by peaceful means) to forfeit the lease granted by the company is caught by the restrictions in (*b*) above because such exercise is a 'step taken to enforce . . . security': *Exchange Travel Agency Ltd v Triton Property Trust plc* [*1991*] *BCC 341*. Harman J, in that case, went on to hold that such exercise also amounted to 'other legal process' and was, therefore, caught by the restrictions in (*c*) above. However, in *Re Olympia & York Canary Wharf Ltd* [*1993*] *BCC 154*, Millett J declined to follow that decision because in his view the expression was confined to a process requiring the assistance of the court. Of course, if the landlord wishes to commence or continue any proceedings in court to complete the forfeiture and obtain possession, he would need the leave of the court under (*c*) above or the consent of the administrator (see B4.2 below); and the administrator would have a right to apply for relief against forfeiture. The court would normally grant such leave and refuse such relief, unless the administrator is prepared to pay the rent and observe the other terms and conditions of the lease whilst he continues to retain the premises (see, for example, *Re Norman Hartnell Ltd, 1987, unreported*) and there is unlikely to be any significant diminution in the value of the landlord's interest (see, for example, *Associated British Ports v C H Bailey plc, FT Law Reports, 27 March 1990*).

In *Scottish Exhibition Centre Ltd, Noters* [*1993*] *BCC 529*, a landlord was successful in obtaining leave of the court to bring proceedings to terminate a lease held by a company in administration, the administrators having unsuccessfully endeavoured for over 18 months to sell the business, including the lease which was the principal asset, as a going concern. The lease had been charged by the company to a third party who was owed by the company more than what the lease was worth and who had indicated that he would contest the landlord's attempt to terminate the lease. The court upheld the landlord's argument that since the chargee was the only party with a degree of interest in the administration, a refusal of the leave to proceed would deny to the landlord its proprietary right and cause it to suffer significant loss by being unable to regain its property; that it would remain burdened with an unsatisfactory tenant whose liability for rent was based on a turnover which had been diminishing; and that the administrator had had sufficient time to try and sell the business. The court was of the view that the landlord had a 'seriously arguable case' and that administration was supposed to be only an interim and temporary regime. The grant of further time to the administrator was unlikely to achieve anything.

Thus, it will be seen that the making of an application for an administration order has the effect of imposing a wide-ranging moratorium on the rights of creditors, security holders and third party owners of assets. One notable limitation of the moratorium is that the right of a party to a contract with the company to terminate the contract pursuant to the terms thereof is not affected. If he were to exercise such a right in relation to a contract which is vital to the success of the administration, for example a building contract or a hire-purchase agreement, then the purpose of the administration order could be undermined. However, again, in certain circumstances relief against such termination may be available to the administrator on the analogy of the principles applicable to forfeiture of leases (see, for example, *Goker v NWS Bank plc, The Times, 23 May 1990*), provided that the administrator is prepared to observe the terms thereof and there is unlikely to be a significant prejudice to the other party. *Re Olympia & York* (above) involved an intended service, by a party to a contract with the company, of a notice electing to treat the contract as terminated by reason of the company's repudiatory breach. Millett J held that such notice was not 'legal process' and did not fall within restriction (*c*) above. The expression did not extend to the service of a contractual notice, whether or not the service was a pre-condition to the bringing of legal proceedings.

It is not clear whether the restrictions in (*b*) above will apply to any security created *by the administrator* on behalf of the company to secure any borrowing made by him for the purpose of discharging his functions. It is submitted that the better view must be that the words 'security over the company's property' means security which had been created over the company's property before the administration order. However, the possibility that the court may adopt a more literal construction and hold that the leave of the court or the consent of the administrator (see (iii) above) is necessary cannot be ruled out. If the leave of the court is required, it would almost certainly be granted, because otherwise in future cases administrators might find it impossible to obtain financing. The secured lender may also be assisted in this regard if the charging document expressly provides that the lender's rights and remedies as mortgagee will arise and become exercisable immediately upon the execution of the charge. It is difficult to envisage circumstances in which the court would refuse such leave if by its terms the charge has become enforceable. However, a further provision containing the administrator's prospective consent to the enforcement of the charge under section 11(3)(c) is unlikely to be held to be effective, as the administrator must exercise his discretion at the time of enforcement in the light of the circumstances then obtaining and must not commit himself in advance to exercising his discretion in a certain way.

An application under section 404 of the Companies Act 1985 for leave to register a charge outside the normal period of 21 days is not 'proceedings against a company or its property' under (*c*) above and is not subject to the restriction. However, on such an application, the court should not exercise its discretion under section 404 to grant the leave after an administration order has been made even if failure to register the charge was due to inadvertence (*Re Barrow Borough Transport Ltd (1989) 5 BCC 646*).

'Proceedings' in restriction (*c*) above includes a complaint by an employee of the company to an industrial tribunal for unfair dismissal (*Carr v British International Helicopters Ltd [1993] BCC 855*; see also the *Hartlebury* case referred to in B7.5 below). This expression does not include an application under the Civil Aviation Act 1982 by an airline (not being a creditor of the company) to the Civil Aviation Authority for an order revoking the company's licence to operate a particular route, and granting a licence to that airline to operate it itself: *Air Ecosse Ltd v Civil Aviation Authority (1987) 3 BCC 492*. 'Legal process' in that restriction does not include a landlord's distress, as it does not involve the intervention of the court (see *McMullen & Sons Ltd v Cerrone [1994] BCC 25*, decided under section 252(2) relating to the effect of an interim order under the voluntary arrangement procedure for individuals; see also the *Olympia & York* case above). However, such a distress is expressly caught by the language of restriction (*c*) above (not included in section 252(2)).

A party cannot rely on his own breach of the above restrictions to assert any rights which he would otherwise have had against the company in administration. In *Re AGB Research Ltd (22 April 1994, unreported*, Vinelott J), a landlord, having unilaterally purported to forfeit a lease held by a company in administration, re-entered the premises and granted a new lease to another tenant company which went into liquidation owing certain sums under the new lease. The landlord's claim under the original lease against the company in administration, on the ground that the forfeiture was ineffective because of the breach of the restrictions, failed. The judge held that while an administrator could argue that actions in breach of the restrictions were ineffective, it was not open to the person committing the breach to use such an argument. (The administrators also sought to avoid liability on the ground that the forfeiture was effective as they had given their consent retrospectively.)

For general observations on applications for leave under (*b*) above, see B4.2 below.

Leave applications

B4.2 In *Re Atlantic Computer Systems plc*, referred to in B4.1 above, Nicholls LJ, delivering the judgment of the Court of Appeal, made the following observations (*[1992] 2 WLR 367* at *394*) on the subject of applications for leave under section 11(3), which are also relevant to applications for leave under section 10(1).

'In the course of argument we were invited to give guidance on the principles to be applied on applications for the grant of leave under section 11. It is an invitation to which we are reluctant to accede, for several reasons: first, Parliament has left at large the discretion given to the court, and it is not for us to cut down that discretion or, as it was put in argument, to confine it within a straitjacket. However much we emphasise that any observations are only guidelines, there is a danger that they may be treated as something more. Secondly, section 11(3)(c) and (d) applies to a very wide range of steps and proceedings, and the circumstances in which leave is sought will vary almost infinitely. Thirdly, it is the judges who sit in the Companies Court who have practical experience of the difficulties arising in the working out of this new jurisdiction, not the members of this court.

However, we have already drawn attention to the important role of the administrator in this field. He should respond speedily and responsibly to applications for consent under section 11. Parliament envisaged that in the first place section 11 matters should be dealt with by him. It is to be hoped, in the interests of all concerned, that applications to the court will become the exception rather than the rule. But we recognise that for this to be so, authorised insolvency practitioners and their legal advisers need more guidance than is available at present on what, in general, is the approach of the court on leave applications. We feel bound therefore to make some general observations regarding cases where leave is sought to exercise existing proprietary rights, including security rights, against a company in administration.

(1) It is in every case for the person who seeks leave to make out a case for him to be given leave.

(2) The prohibition in section 11(3)(c) and (d) is intended to assist the company, under the management of the administrator, to achieve the purpose for which the administration order was made. If granting leave to a lessor of land or the hirer of goods (a "lessor") to exercise his proprietary rights and repossess his land or goods is unlikely to impede the achievement of that purpose, leave should normally be given.

(3) In other cases when a lessor seeks possession the court has to carry out a balancing exercise, balancing the legitimate interests of the lessor and the legitimate interests of the other creditors of the company (see Peter Gibson J in *Royal Trust Bank v Buchler [1989] BCLC 130, 135*).

The metaphor employed here, for want of a better, is that of scales and weights. Lord Wilberforce adverted to the limitations of this

metaphor, in *Scientific Research Council v Nasse [1980] AC 1028, 1067*.
It must be kept in mind that the exercise under section 11 is not a mechanical one; each case calls for an exercise in judicial judgment, in which
the court seeks to give effect to the purpose of the statutory provisions,
having regard to the parties' interests and all the circumstances of the
case. As already noted, the purpose of the prohibition is to enable or
assist the company to achieve the object for which the administration
order was made. The purpose of the power to give leave is to enable
the court to relax the prohibition where it would be inequitable for the
prohibition to apply.

(4) In carrying out the balancing exercise great importance, or weight,
is normally to be given to the proprietary interests of the lessor. Sir
Nicolas Browne-Wilkinson V-C observed in *Bristol Airport plc v Powdrill [1990] 2 WLR 1362, 1379* that, so far as possible, the administration procedure should not be used to prejudice those who were secured
creditors when the administration order was made in lieu of a winding-
up order. The same is true regarding the proprietary interests of a
lessor. The underlying principle here is that an administration for the
benefit of unsecured creditors should not be conducted at the expense
of those who have proprietary rights which they are seeking to exercise, save to the extent that this may be unavoidable and even then this
will usually be acceptable only to a strictly limited extent.

(5) Thus it will normally be a sufficient ground for the grant of leave if
significant loss would be caused to the lessor by a refusal. For this purpose loss comprises any kind of financial loss, direct or indirect, including loss by reason of delay, and may extend to loss which is not
financial. But if substantially greater loss would be caused to others by
the grant of leave, or loss which is out of all proportion to the benefit
which leave would confer on the lessor, that may outweigh the loss to
the lessor caused by a refusal.

Our formulation was criticised in the course of the argument, and we
certainly do not claim for it the status of a rule in those terms. At
present we say only that it appears to us the nearest we can get to a
formulation of what Parliament had in mind.

(6) In assessing these respective losses the court will have regard to
matters such as: the financial position of the company, its ability to pay
the rental arrears and the continuing rentals, the administrator's proposals, the period for which the administration order has already been
in force and is expected to remain in force, the effect on the administration if leave were given, the effect on the applicant if leave were
refused, the end result sought to be achieved by the administration, the
prospects of that result being achieved, and the history of the administration so far.

(7) In considering these matters it will often be necessary to assess
how probable the suggested consequences are. Thus if loss to the
applicant is virtually certain if leave is refused, and loss to others a

76

remote possibility if leave is granted, that will be a powerful factor in favour of granting leave.

(8) This is not an exhaustive list. For example, the conduct of the parties may also be a material consideration in a particular case, as it was in the *Bristol Airport* case. There leave was refused on the ground that the applicants had accepted benefits under the administration, and had only sought to enforce their security at a later stage: indeed, they had only acquired their security as a result of the operations of the administrators. It behoves a lessor to make his position clear to the administrator at the outset of the administration and, if it should become necessary, to apply to the court promptly.

(9) The above considerations may be relevant not only to the decision whether leave should be granted or refused, but also to a decision to impose terms if leave is granted.

(10) The above considerations will also apply to a decision on whether to impose terms as a condition for refusing leave. Section 11(3)(c) and (d) makes no provision for terms being imposed if leave is refused, but the court has power to achieve that result. It may do so directly, by giving directions to the administrator: for instance, under section 17, or in response to an application by the administrator under section 14(3), or in exercise of its control over an administrator as an officer of the court. Or it may do so indirectly, by ordering that the applicant shall have leave unless the administrator is prepared to take this or that step in the conduct of the administration.

Cases where leave is refused but terms are imposed can be expected to arise frequently. For example, the permanent loss to a lessor flowing from his inability to recover his property will normally be small if the administrator is required to pay the current rent. In most cases this should be possible, since if the administration order has been rightly made the business should generally be sufficiently viable to hold down current outgoings. Such a term may therefore be a normal term to impose.

(11) The above observations are directed at a case such as the present where a lessor of land or the owner of goods is seeking to repossess his land or goods because of non-payment of rentals. A broadly similar approach will be applicable on many applications to enforce a security: for instance, an application by a mortgagee for possession of land. On such applications an important consideration will often be whether the applicant is fully secured. If he is, delay in enforcement is likely to be less prejudicial than in cases where his security is insufficient.

(12) In some cases there will be a dispute over the existence, validity or nature of the security which the applicant is seeking leave to enforce. It is not for the court on the leave application to seek to adjudicate upon that issue, unless (as in the present case, on the fixed

or floating charge point) the issue raises a short point of law which it is convenient to determine without further ado. Otherwise the court needs to be satisfied only that the applicant has a seriously arguable case.'

In the *Atlantic Computers* case itself, the Court of Appeal granted finance companies leave to terminate the leases of computers to the company (which had, in turn, sub-leased them to end-users) and to re-possess them. The discretion conferred on the court by section 11(3) was unfettered and, in reaching its decision, the Court of Appeal took into account various factors, including the nature of the leases and sub-leases, the company's insolvency, the fact that it did not have proper records and did not produce a statement of affairs; the administrators' proposals, which mainly involved a formidable task of re-negotiating the leases; the effect of granting the leave to re-possess, involving probably a 'wholesale collapse' of the administrators' proposals if all the finance companies terminated the leases; the effect on the finance companies of refusal to grant leave, including significant loss to them and the weakening of their position in re-negotiations; the prospects of a successful outcome if leave was refused; the likelihood or otherwise of the finance companies consenting to any new terms; and the conduct of the parties, the finance companies having applied early for leave to terminate and the administrators not having been dilatory. The Court of Appeal went on to observe that the administration was a prelude to winding up and that the administrators were primarily seeking by their proposals to negotiate a reduction in the claims of the unsecured creditors, who were largely the end-users and the finance companies themselves. Any re-negotiations would take place at the expense of the finance companies because they would, if leave to re-possess was refused, have to modify their existing proprietary rights without being able to rely on their original rights. In the court's view, this was not a case where leave should be refused on terms that the sub-rentals be paid over to the finance companies. Even if the flow of money could be re-started, the sub-rentals were lower than the contractual head rents.

In *Re David Meek Access Ltd [1993] BCC 175*, the administrators had resisted the application of several finance houses for leave to repossess goods which were subject to hire-purchase agreements on the ground that the company's entire business was that of hiring goods out, that they were proposing to hive-down the business into a new company with a view to preserving it as a going concern and that if the goods were repossessed the whole purpose of the administration would be defeated and the creditors would suffer. Applying the principles of *Re Atlantic Computer Systems plc*, the court held that it must balance any loss suffered or to be suffered by the finance houses against the benefit to the creditors and to the company as a whole. The administrators' fears as to the consequences of repossession were well founded; and they had already proposed an orderly return of goods to those finance houses not wishing to participate in the hive-down. Accordingly, leave to repossess was refused except to those two finance houses which had unsuccessfully sought to repossess the relevant goods on the day before the presentation of the administration petition.

Chapter 5: Manner of administration

Notice on stationery

B5.1   Section 12 requires that every invoice, order for goods or business letter issued during the time an administration order is in force by or on behalf of the company or the administrator, on which the company's name appears, must also contain the administrator's name and a statement that the affairs, business and property of the company are being managed by the administrator.

Initial control and management

B5.2   The administrator must, on his appointment, take into his custody or under his control all the property to which the company is or appears to be entitled. Until the proposals referred to in B5.4 below have been approved at a section 23 meeting, he must manage the affairs, business and property of the company in accordance with any directions given by the court (section 17(2)(a)). Where before such approval, he needs to sell any asset of the company (for example, because he has received an offer not to be missed), he must, notwithstanding his power of disposal contained in Schedule 1 (see B7.2 below), seek the directions of the court authorising such disposal. (See the *Charnley Davies* case referred to in B5.4 below.) The leave of the court would be more readily available in the case of a single asset than in the case of the whole or substantially the whole undertaking.

In *Re Consumer and Industrial Press Ltd (No 2) (1988) 4 BCC 72*, Peter Gibson J stated that where the goodwill and business of the company was being sold prior to the meeting, quite exceptional circumstances would be required before the court would approve such sale; otherwise the function of the meeting could be undermined. In *Re NS Distribution Ltd [1990] BCLC 169*, Harman J granted leave to sell a single asset among a number of other assets, stating, 'It is plain that administrators can, and indeed should, sell individual assets of the company . . . and (still) be in a position to make sensible proposals to the creditors' meeting. The mere disposal of one asset in no way prevents there being a need for a sensible creditors' meeting in the usual case'. He went on to suggest that where one asset was being sold at a good price under great pressure of time, and to do so would not frustrate the purposes of the Act or a creditors' meeting, the administrator should decide for himself without the direction of the court. He was not saying that the administrator would be beyond criticism if he proceeded to enter into the contract, but there was a strong *prima facie* case that what he was doing was an ordinary and sensible step in the administration. It was not right for the court to be asked to bless such steps, because, if it were, the court would be inundated with such applications.

As to the position after any such proposals have been approved, see B5.15 below. As to the administrator's powers, see B6.1 and B7.2 below.

Statement of affairs

B5.3   Forthwith on his appointment, the administrator must require some or all of the persons in the categories specified in section 22(3) (in broad terms, the company's past and present officers, employees (including persons under a contract for *services*), and promoters) to make out and submit to him a statement in prescribed form as to the affairs of the company. The statement of affairs must be verified by affidavit by the deponents and, if so required by the administrator, supported by an affidavit of concurrence (which may be appropriately qualified) by any of the others (section 22(1) and (2), Rules 2.11, 2.12, and Forms 2.8, 2.9). The persons so required must submit the statement to the administrator within 21 days from the day after that on which the notice of the requirement is given to them; but the administrator or, should he refuse, the court may release a person from his obligation or extend the period (section 22(4) and (5), Rule 2.14).

A verified copy of the statement of affairs and the related affidavit must be filed by the administrator in court (Rule 2.12(6)); but the court may on his application make appropriate orders to prevent or restrict disclosure of it or any part of it to other persons (Rule 2.13).

A person making the statement of affairs and affidavit must be allowed, and paid by the administrator out of his receipts, any expenses incurred by him in doing so which the administrator considers reasonable; but this does not relieve that person of his obligation to submit the statement and provide information (see A4.18 PART A: GENERAL) to the administrator. The administrator's decision regarding expenses is subject to appeal to the court (Rule 2.15).

Administrator's proposals

B5.4   Within three months (or such longer period as the court may allow) after the making of the administration order, the administrator must send to the Registrar of Companies and all the creditors and members (so far as he is aware of their addresses), and must lay before a meeting of creditors summoned for the purpose, a statement of his proposals for achieving the purpose or purposes for which he was appointed (section 23). Annexed to the proposals must be a statement by him containing information specified in Rule 2.16(1), including:

(*a*)   the purposes for which the administration order was applied for and made and any subsequent variation of those purposes;

(*b*)   a copy of the statement of affairs or, if none has been submitted, details of the company's financial position at the latest practicable date (being not earlier than the date of the administration order unless the court otherwise orders);

(*c*)   an account of the circumstances giving rise to the application for the order;

(*d*)   the manner in which the affairs of the company (i) have since the date of the administrator's appointment been managed and financed and (ii) will, if the administrator's proposals are approved, be managed and financed (*Note*: (i) above was inserted by SI 1987 No 1919 with effect from 11 January 1988); and

(*e*) any other information necessary to enable creditors to reach a decision.

It is advisable to include in the proposals express provisions as to payment of all costs, expenses and liabilities incurred in the implementation of the proposals and in the discharge by the administrator of his other functions out of the administration funds (subject to the provisions discussed in B6.1 below) and as to how the implementation is to be financed. This is because section 19(4) and (5) applies only when he vacates his office (see B7.1 below).

The administrator must, within the period of three months mentioned above, also publish a notice, in the *London* (or in Scotland, *Edinburgh*) *Gazette* and the newspaper in which the administration order was advertised, stating an address to which the members should apply for copies of the statements (section 23(2)(b), Rule 2.17).

For instances where the period of three months mentioned above was extended, see *Re Newport County Association Football Club Ltd* [*1987*] *BCLC 582* (legitimate hopes, though not expectations, of salvage; further five weeks allowed for exploration); *Re Charnley Davies Business Services Ltd and others* (*1987*) *3 BCC 408* (time extended to the date of the hearing, followed immediately by discharge of the administration order, so as to relieve him of any criminal liability for failure to lay a report within the three-month period—see also below), and *Re N S Distribution Ltd* [*1990*] *BCLC 169* (time taken up in important negotiations with the parent company).

Where no proposals can be formulated within the time allowed, the court may direct that a report to that effect be sent to the creditors: see, for example, *Re Synthetic Technology Ltd* [*1990*] *BCLC 378*.

Although the company, acting through its directors, has *locus standi* to make the application for an extension of the period, it is not the most suitable applicant. It should normally be made by the administrator himself. It is he on whom the statutory duty to report is imposed and who is exposed to criminal penalties if he fails to discharge that duty. He is the most vitally interested person and also the only person who can offer an up-to-date and detached view: see the *Newport* case above. In that case the company's application was supported by an affidavit of one of its directors who, Harman J said, was inevitably *parti pris* and could not be expected to be dispassionate about the chances of salvage. Very large additional expenses out of the assets would be incurred during the further three-month period for which the extension was desired. Accordingly, Harman J restricted the extension to a further period of five weeks.

Section 23 requires the proposals to be made *within* three months and not *at the expiry* of three months. Where the purposes of the administration order are (i) the survival of the company and (ii) more advantageous realisation of the assets (see B2.1 above) and the administrator forms the view that purpose (i) cannot be achieved but purpose (ii) can be, it is desirable for him to send at once to the Registrar of Companies and the creditors a statement as to his conclusions and as to the realisation proposals: see the *Charnley Davies* case cited above. In that case the administrator had failed to send such a statement or lay it before a meeting of the creditors and proceeded to sell the assets. He then applied to the court for the discharge of the administration order (see B5.16 below) but not for his release (see B7.1 below) and for an extension of time for the performance of his mandatory duty under section 23, and also caused the company to petition the court for its own winding up and for the appointment of himself as liquidator (see B7.2 below).

Without going into the propriety of such a sale, Harman J held that the purposes for which the administration order was made having apparently been achieved, it was pointless to have any meeting of creditors under section 23 when there were no proposals which could conceivably be sensibly considered. There could not be a meeting simply to consider a report of what had happened or the administrator's proposals about winding up. No meeting under section 23 could be held for any purposes other than to consider section 8 purposes (see B2.1 above). Accordingly, exercising its discretion, the court discharged the administration order notwithstanding that there had been a failure to comply with section 23. The court also, in the circumstances of the case, extended the time as applied for. (As regards the winding-up petition in that case, see B7.2 below.) A decision under the Australian legislation relating to extension of time (of 21 days) for holding a creditors' meeting, under the administration procedure of that country, may be noted here. In *Mann v Abruzzi Sports Club Ltd* (*1994*) *12 ACLC 137*, it was held that it would be contrary to the whole spirit of that procedure to allow the time limit to be over-extended or to over-encourage administrators to apply to the court for an extension. However the courts' power should be exercised with the aims of the procedure in mind, that is maximisation of the chances of the company's continued existence or a better return to the creditors. On the facts, the administrator was doing his best to deal speedily with the process and there would be no prejudice to the creditors or members. An extension was granted.

It is suggested that in *Re Charnley Davies* it would have been preferable for the administrator to seek the directions of the court under section 14(3) (see B7.3 below) when faced with the opportunity to sell the assets on the one hand and the risk of losing the opportunity, if he waited for his proposal for such sale to be approved by the creditors' meeting, on the other hand. He could have sought directions to the effect that the time for presenting his proposals be appropriately extended, that in the meantime he should sell the assets pursuant to his powers contained in paragraph 2 of Schedule 1 and that thereafter, but before the expiration of the extended time, he should apply to the court to discharge the administration order.

Rule 2.16(2), inserted by SI 1987 No 1919 with effect from 11 January 1988, now attempts to deal with the sort of situation which arose in the *Charnley Davies* case. It provides that where the administrator intends to apply to the court under section 18 for the administration order to be discharged before he has sent a statement of his proposals to creditors in accordance with section 23(1), he must, at least 10 days before he makes such an application, send to all the creditors (so far as he is aware of their addresses) a report containing the information specified in Rule 2.16(1) except that mentioned in (*d*)(ii) and (*e*) above.

Creditors' meetings under section 23

B5.5 The meeting of creditors summoned under section 23 (see B5.4 above) may approve the administrator's proposals without modification or with such modifications as the administrator approves or may reject the proposals (section 24(1) and (2)). As to the procedure for the meeting, see B5.6 to B5.13, and for that following the meeting, see B5.14 *et seq.* below.

Procedure for creditors' meetings generally

B5.6 The procedure for the section 23 meeting referred to in B5.4 and B5.5 above and the other meetings of creditors referred to in B5.15, B7.2, and B8.2 below is laid down in Chapter 3 of Part 2 of the Rules. This procedure is summarised below. As to the appointment of a creditors' committee by a meeting of creditors, see B8.1 below.

Notice of meeting

B5.7

(1) Notice of the section 23 meeting (Form 2.11) must be given to all creditors who are identified in the statement of affairs, or are known to the administrator and had claims at the date of the administration order. It must also (unless the court otherwise directs) be given by advertisement in the newspaper in which the administration order was advertised. Notice to attend (Form 2.10) must be sent out at the same time to any present or past directors or officers whose presence is, in the administrator's opinion, required (Rule 2.18). As regards any other meeting of creditors, notice of the meeting (Form 2.11) must be given to all creditors who are known to the administrator and had claims at the date of the administration order (Rule 2.19(4)).

(2) The notice must be accompanied by forms of proxy (Rule 2.19(5), Form 8.2; see also A6.1 PART A: GENERAL).

(3) In fixing the venue, the administrator must have regard to the convenience of the creditors (Rule 2.19(2)). The time of the meeting must commence between 10.00 and 16.00 hours on a business day, unless the court otherwise directs (Rule 2.19(3)).

(4) In the case of a meeting summoned under section 23(1) or 25(2) to consider the administrator's proposals or proposed revisions thereto (see B5.15 below), at least 14 days' notice must be given (sections 23(1)(b) and 25(2)(b)). In the case of any other meeting, at least 21 days' notice of the meeting must be given (Rule 2.19(4A)).

(5) As to a meeting requisitioned by creditors, see Rule 2.21.

Chairman

B5.8 The chairman of the meeting is the administrator or a person nominated by him who must be a qualified insolvency practitioner in relation to the company or an employee of the administrator or his firm who is experienced in insolvency matters (Rule 2.20).

Adjournment and quorum

B5.9 A meeting may from time to time be adjourned, if the chairman thinks fit, but not for more than 14 days from the date on which it was fixed to commence (Rule 2.19(7)). As regards a section 23(1) meeting, if there is no requisite majority for the approval of the administrator's proposals (with modifications, if any) the chairman may, and shall if a resolution is passed to that effect, adjourn the meeting for not more than 14 days (Rule 2.18(4)). It is not clear what 'requisite majority' means in this context. Rule 2.28 requires a majority in value of those *present and voting* (in person or by proxy) for the passing of a resolution. Presumably, the quoted expression is confined to a situation where votes are evenly divided (see B5.10(4) below). If within 30 minutes no person is present to act as chairman, the meeting stands adjourned to the same time and place in the following week or, if that is not a business day, on the following business day (Rule 2.19(6)). The quorum for any meeting of creditors is at least one creditor entitled to vote, present or represented by a proxy or corporate representative subject as stated in A6.1 and A6.2 PART A: GENERAL.

Entitlement to vote—general

B5.10

(1) A person is only entitled to vote if he has given written details of his claim to the administrator no later than noon on the business day before the day of the meeting, the claim has been admitted for the purposes of voting, and any proxy has been lodged with the administrator. (For detailed provisions relating to proxies and corporate representation at meetings see A6.1 PART A: GENERAL above and Rules 7.14 to 7.20.) Details of the claim must include any calculation for the purposes of Rules 2.24 to 2.27 (see B5.12 below) (Rule 2.22(1)). Normally, a creditor would wish to vote in the same way in respect of the entire amount of the debt due to him; and it would appear that he is not entitled to split his vote in more than one way by reference to different parts of the debt. However, where the

amount of the debt due to him represents sums due to him for the benefit of different parties (for example, where he is a trustee for a number of beneficiaries, or otherwise owes fiduciary or contractual obligations to them, and different beneficiaries want him to vote in different ways in relation to their beneficial interests in the debt), it would be unjust if in that situation he was not allowed to split his votes. In *Re Polly Peck International plc [1991] BCC 503*, the administrators successfully applied to the court for directions allowing a trustee for bondholders to split its vote in respect of the debt due to it in accordance with the wishes of the bondholders to the extent of their respective beneficial interests in the debt.

(2)   The chairman may allow a creditor to vote even if he has failed to comply with the above requirements, if satisfied that the failure was due to circumstances beyond the creditor's control (Rule 2.22(2)).

(3)   The administrator or chairman may call for further evidence for the purpose of substantiating the whole or any part of the claim (Rule 2.22(3)).

(4)   Votes are calculated according to the amount of a creditor's debt at the date of the administration order, deducting any amounts paid in respect of the debt after that date (Rule 2.22(4)).

(5)   A creditor is not entitled to vote in respect of a debt for an unliquidated amount, or any debt whose value is not ascertained, except where the chairman agrees to put upon it an estimated minimum value for the purposes of voting and admits the claim for that purpose (Rule 2.22(5)).

Admission and rejection of claims for voting

B5.11   The general position (set out in Rule 2.23) is outlined below.

(1)   The chairman may admit or reject the whole or part of a claim for the purposes of voting.

(2)   If he is in doubt whether a claim should be admitted or rejected, he must mark it as objected to and allow the creditor to vote, subject to the vote being subsequently declared invalid if the objection is sustained.

(3)   The chairman's decision in respect of the matters arising under Rule 2.23 or Rule 2.22 (see B5.10 above) is subject to appeal to the court by any creditor. If, on appeal, the decision is reversed or varied, or a creditor's vote is declared invalid, the court may order that another meeting be summoned or make such other order as it thinks just. In the case of a section 23 meeting, the appeal must be lodged not later than 28 days after the delivery of the administrator's report under section 24(4) (see B5.14 below). Neither the administrator nor the chairman is personally liable for costs incurred by any person in respect of any such appeal, unless the court makes an order to that effect.

Entitlement to vote—specified categories of creditor

B5.12   Rules 2.24 to 2.27 set out special provisions in relation to the following specified categories of creditor.

Secured creditors. A secured creditor may vote only in respect of the balance (if any) of his debt after deducting the value of his security estimated by him (Rule 2.24).

Holders of negotiable instruments. A creditor in respect of a debt on, or secured by, a current bill of exchange or promissory note must treat the liability to him of every party who is liable on it antecedently to the company (and against whom a bankruptcy order has not been made or, being a company, which has not gone into liquidation) as a security in his hands, must deduct the value of such security from his claim and may vote only in respect of the balance (Rule 2.25).

Retention of title creditors. A seller of goods to the company under a retention of title agreement must deduct from his claim the value, as estimated by him, of any rights arising under that agreement in respect of goods in possession of the company (Rule 2.26).

Hire-purchase (etc.) agreements. An owner of goods under a hire-purchase or chattel leasing agreement, or a seller of goods under a conditional sale agreement, is entitled to vote in respect of the amount of debt due and payable to him as at the date of the administration order. In calculating the debt, no account is to be taken of any amount attributable to the exercise of any right under the agreement, so far as the right has become exercisable solely by virtue of the presentation of the petition for an administration order or any matter arising in consequence of that, or of the making of the order (Rule 2.27).

Resolutions and minutes of creditors' meeting

B5.13   A resolution is passed when a majority (in value) of those present and voting, in person or by proxy, have voted in favour of it. However, a resolution is invalid if those voting against it include more than half in value of the creditors to whom notice of the meeting was sent and who are not, to the best of the chairman's belief, persons connected with the company (as defined by section 249, read with section 435)—see Rule 2.28(1A). The chairman must cause to be entered in the company's minute book minutes of the proceedings, which must include a list of the creditors who attended personally or by proxy and, if applicable, the names and addresses of those elected to be members of the creditors' committee (as to which, see B8.1 below) (Rule 2.28).

Administrator's reports

B5.14   After the conclusion of the creditors' meeting held to consider the proposals referred to above, or any substantial revisions thereof (see B5.15 below), the administrator must give notice of the result to the

Registrar of Companies and to every creditor who received notice of the meeting, and any other creditor of whom he has since become aware (section 24(4), Rule 2.30(1), Form 2.12). The administrator must also report the result to the court. Any such report or notice must have annexed to it details of the proposals, and of any revisions and modifications, which were considered by the meeting (section 24(4), Rule 2.29). If the meeting has declined to approve the proposals (with or without modifications), the court may by order discharge the administration order and make any other consequential provision, or may adjourn the hearing, or may make an interim order or any other order that it thinks fit (section 24(5)). An office copy of any such discharge order must be sent by the administrator to the Registrar of Companies within 14 days of the making of that order (section 24(6)).

Rule 2.30(2) contains requirements regarding six-monthly progress reports and a final report by the administrator on vacating office.

Implementation and revision of proposals

B5.15 After the proposals are approved, it is the duty of the administrator to manage the affairs, business and property of the company in accordance with the proposals as from time to time revised, whether by him or his predecessor (section 17(2)(b)). In discharging this duty, he is assisted by wide powers conferred upon him—see, for example, B6.1 and B7.2 to B7.5 below. Any substantial revisions of the approved proposals which the administrator proposes to make are required to be approved by a creditors' meeting (section 25, Rule 2.19, Forms 2.11 (as amended) and 2.22). The procedure to be followed after such a meeting is similar to that to be followed in respect of the meeting held to consider the original proposals.

The court has a residual discretion to direct the conduct of administrators where a course of action approved by the creditors has proved impracticable and there is no time to put revised proposals to a creditors' meeting. In *Re Smallman Construction Ltd (1988) 4 BCC 784*, when the proposals approved by a meeting of creditors proved impractical, a substitute scheme, beneficial to the company and approved by the creditors' committee, was put forward by the administrators but, as a matter of commercial reality, it was not possible to wait until the revised proposal was approved by a meeting of creditors for which at least 14 days' notice was necessary. In making an order authorising the scheme, the court said that in the very exceptional circumstances such as those in this case, there was a residual jurisdiction in the court to authorise the administrators to implement the scheme under section 14(3) (power of the court to give directions to an administrator in relation to any particular matter arising in connection with the carrying out of its functions—see B7.3 below), since that involved only filling in a lacuna in the scheme and not overriding the proposals originally approved by the creditors.

In *Re Consumer and Industrial Press Ltd (No 2) (1988) 4 BCC 72*, before the meeting of the creditors had been held to consider the administrators' proposals (see B5.4 above), the administrators applied to the court for leave to sell certain assets on the ground that a creditors' meeting would be pointless because even the best offer received for the assets would not realise sufficient money to discharge the sums due to the secured creditors and there would be no money left for the unsecured creditors. The court refused to grant the order, stating that its jurisdiction under section 15(2) should only be exercised in circumstances in which it could readily be seen that the sale was really the only sensible course to be adopted and when the unsecured creditors had had a chance to consider the proposals. It would require exceptional circumstances for the court to override the requirement of a creditors' meeting. There did not appear to be a real need for the sale to be concluded immediately and the administrators could have called the meeting earlier, on or shortly after the deadline for receipt of offers had expired.

Discharge or variation of order

B5.16   The administrator may at any time apply to the court to discharge or vary the administration order and must do so if the purpose or each of the purposes of the order either has been achieved or is incapable of achievement (as to which see, for example, the *Charnley Davies* case referred to in B5.4 above), or if a creditors' meeting requires him to make the application. The court may make various orders on such an application. The court may also discharge an administration order if the creditors' meeting has declined to approve the administrator's proposals with or without modifications (see B5.14 above). An office copy of any discharge or variation order must be sent to the Registrar of Companies within 14 days after its making (section 18; see also section 27(6) and B8.3 below).

Further, the court also has general jurisdiction under Rule 7.47 (power of court having winding-up jurisdiction to review, rescind or vary its order and to hear appeals from a county court or a registrar) to set aside an administration order on an application by a creditor. In making an administration order the court is exercising its jurisdiction to wind up companies and Rule 7.47 is available to the creditor as the party aggrieved by an oppressive order made *ex parte*: see *Cornhill Insurance plc v Cornhill Financial Services Ltd [1992] BCC 818 (CA)*. In that case, assurances had been given to the judge at the time of the *ex parte* application that certain assets would be transferred back to the company and that certain claims against it would be released. Those assurances were not in a binding form and could only be fulfilled with the co-operation of other parties. The court was of the view that those assets were necessary to achieve the purpose of the administration and were incapable of being secured to the administrators. The creditor's application to set aside the administration order was granted by the judge on the ground of material non-disclosure and prejudice to the creditor concerned. The Court of Appeal dismissed an appeal against the judge's decision, and went on to provide the following general guidelines in relation to *ex parte* applications:

(1)   the applicant must provide full information including matters which might be embarrassing to the applicant himself;

(2)   the court must look critically at all material put before it and, if necessary, should take time for further consideration;

(3)   it was not a good practice for the court to grant administration orders on undertakings by applicant to file petitions forthwith after the hearing (per Dillon LJ, approving Harman J in *Re Rowbotham Baxter Ltd [1990] BCLC 397* (see B3.2 above)).

As to the power of the court to make a winding-up order upon the discharge of the administration order and to appoint the administrator as liquidator, see B7.2 below.

No preferential creditors or distribution to any creditors

B5.17   It is not the purpose of the administration procedure to enable a distribution of funds to be made among the creditors. This can only be done in a liquidation or a voluntary arrangement (see *Re St. Ives Windings Ltd (1987) 3 BCC 634, per* Harman J). Unlike in the case of the appointment of a receiver under a floating charge or of a liquidation, there are no provisions in the case of an administration order for the payment of preferential debts. The object of an administration order is either to achieve a better realisation of assets or to effect a voluntary arrangement (see PART E: VOLUNTARY ARRANGEMENTS) or a compromise or arrangement and then to terminate the administration. Unless the company is then solvent, or a voluntary arrangement or a compromise or arrangement is in place, such termination will normally be followed by a liquidation which will trigger the rights of preferential creditors. Where a voluntary arrangement is to be effected its terms would have to provide for the discharge of preferential debts in priority to other debts (see PART E: VOLUNTARY ARRANGEMENTS). In the case of a compromise or arrangement, the requirement to secure the approval of each class of creditors separately and the sanction of the court will in practice ensure that provision is made for such a priority.

VAT bad debt relief

B5.18   Rule 2.56 deals with the requirement of the issue by the administrator of a certificate enabling creditors to obtain relief of VAT on bad debts. However, this provision has become largely redundant in view of the provisions of section 36 of the Value Added Tax Act 1994, supplemented by the Value Added Tax (Bad Debt Relief) Regulations 1986 (SI 1986 No 335) and the Value Added Tax (Refunds for Bad Debts) Regulations 1991 (SI 1991 No 371)).

Taxation in the administration

See PART H: TAXATION.

Chapter 6: Administrator's powers affecting the rights of secured creditors and owners of assets

Power of disposal

B6.1   The administrator has power to dispose of (*a*) without the leave of the court, assets which are subject to a charge which *as created* (as to the meaning of which, see D6.1 *et seq*. PART D: RECEIVERS) was a floating charge (including a floating charge within section 462 of the Companies Act 1985 (Scottish floating charges)) (section 15(1)) and (*b*) with the leave of the court, assets subject to any other form of charge or to any hire-purchase, conditional sale, chattel leasing or retention of title agreement (section 15(2)). (Of course, this power becomes irrelevant where the holder of the charge or owner of the assets has already been granted leave or consent under section 11 to enforce the charge or repossess the assets, as the case may be (see B4.1 and B4.2 above).) The court may grant the leave referred to in (*b*) if it is satisfied that such disposal (with or without other assets) would be likely to promote the purpose or one or more of the purposes specified in the administration order. An office copy of such an order must be sent by the administrator to the Registrar of Companies within 14 days after the making of the order (section 15(1), (2), (3), (7) and (9)). The additional procedure, including notice of application to the holder or owner, is dealt with in Rule 2.51.

The disposal takes place as if the assets were not subject to any such charge or as if all the rights of the owner of the assets comprised in any such agreement were vested in the company (section 15(1) and (2)). In Scotland, the administrator must grant an appropriate conveyance or transfer to the disponee and that document or, where applicable, any recording, intimation or registration thereof, has the effect of disencumbering the property or freeing it from the security; and any disposal of goods subject to any agreement mentioned above has the effect of extinguishing, as against the disponee, all rights of the owner of the goods under that agreement (section 16).

In the event of a disposal of assets which were subject to a floating charge, the holder of that charge has the same priority to any property of the company which directly or indirectly represents the assets disposed of as he would have had to such assets (section 15(4)). With regard to the disposal of assets subject to any other form of charge or to any agreement of the types mentioned above, it will be a condition of a court order granting the leave that the net proceeds of disposal or, where the net proceeds are less than the net amount (as determined by the court) which would have been realised on a sale in the open market by a willing vendor, the amount realisable on such notional sale, must be applied towards discharging the sums secured by the security or payable under such an agreement (section 15(5)). Where there are successive securities, the amount must be applied in order of their priorities (section 15(6)). The court will not dispense with this condition and instead order the net proceeds to be held in suspense merely because the administrators are contemplating the possibility of challenging the validity of the charge (*per* Judge O'Donoghue in *Re Newman Shopfitters (Cleveland) Ltd [1991] BCLC 407*).

In *Re ARV Aviation Ltd (1988) 4 BCC 708*, where the administrator applied for leave under section 15(2) to dispose of part of the land which was subject to a fixed charge, together with the remaining assets and the undertaking of the company, Knox J held as follows.

(1) Assuming the intention of section 15(5) to be the protection to the maximum practical extent of the rights of a secured creditor, the court had to balance the prejudice that would be felt by the secured creditor if the order was made, against the prejudice that would otherwise be felt by those interested in the promotion of the purposes specified in the administration order.

(2) The existence of a *bona fide* dispute between the administrator's and the security holder's valuers would clearly call into operation the discretion of the court under section 15(2), but was not necessarily the only circumstance in which that discretion could be exercised and was not a prerequisite of the existence of the jurisdiction.

(3) The expression 'the sums secured by the security' in section 15(5) covered not only the capital sum secured but all interest properly payable and any costs which the security holder was entitled to add to his security in accordance with the general law and the terms of the instrument in question (subject to the overriding discretion of the court in relation to the costs of any particular application).

(4) In principle, it was desirable for proper valuation evidence to be put in by the administrators before the court exercised its discretion under section 15(2). In the present case the court exercised its discretion in making the order in spite of, rather than because of, the administrators' evidence. Although the valuation evidence put in by the holder of the charge would not necessarily remain unchallenged as the evidence upon which any deficiency under section 15(5)(b) was ascertained, it did enable the court to see that the amount available in respect of the sale of the remainder of the assets of the company was adequate security to prevent prejudice to the holder of the charge.

(5) The court had no power to make an interim order under section 15(2), but there was clearly power for there to be a final order involving a two-stage process, namely, the disposal of the property and directing an enquiry to be made for evaluating precisely what sum the holder of the charge was entitled to, bearing in mind that subsection (5) provided for the security holder to receive not only the net proceeds of the disposal of the property charged, but also any excess of the market value over the value realised, towards the discharge of the sum due under the security.

(6)   It was not the intention of section 15(5)(b) to introduce as the figure
      for the amount which would be realised on the sale of the property
      in the open market by a willing vendor, anything which was signifi-
      cantly less than what one would anticipate a secured creditor could
      himself realise (*obiter*).

(See also B4.1 above as to the circumstances in which a secured creditor
may be allowed to enforce his security after the administration order.)

Implications of power of disposal

B6.2   The provisions referred to in B6.1 above, though they could, in
certain circumstances, adversely affect the rights of the holder of the
security or owner of the goods to a material extent, appear to go a considerable way towards protecting the holder or owner. The main disadvantage for him is that the disposal may be effected at a time which in
his view is not the most propitious. If he had control over the assets concerned, he might have preferred to receive income from the assets before
they are disposed of, or to take a view as to the best time for disposing of
it. There is no express provision to the effect that if the administrator
makes any income from the assets, he should account for it to the holder.
Where the assets disposed of have been subject to a floating charge, difficult questions might arise as to what property 'indirectly' represents the
assets disposed of, but it seems that the administrator will be accountable
to the holder in the same way as he would have been if he were a receiver
under that charge including, presumably, for any sum which the administrator may have, through his negligence, failed to realise. It should also
be noted that unless the floating charge has crystallised before or by
reason of the administration order, or the application therefor, or, in any
case, before the disposal, the holder's priority may be adversely affected
(see D5.1 *et seq*. PART D: RECEIVERS).

Because of possible adverse effects of the new administration procedure
on his rights, a creditor holding a general charge may decide to take pre-
emptive action to forestall an administration order by appointing an
administrative receiver before the hearing of the adminstration application (see B2.1 above). Such an appointment, hastened by the fear of an
administration order, might itself destroy any chances of normal recovery
or an informal rescue that may have existed for the company.

Transitional provisions regarding floating charges

B6.3   Paragraph 1(1) of Schedule 11 to the 1986 Act provides that
where, in a debenture or floating charge created *before* the provisions
relating to the administration procedure came into force (29 December
1986), a right to appoint an administrative receiver is conferred, the conditions precedent to the exercise of that right are to be deemed to include
the presentation of a petition for an administration order in respect of the
company. The effect is to imply, in such a debenture or floating charge,
the filing of a petition for an administration order as an event which automatically entitles the holder to appoint a receiver under the debenture or

floating charge and thereby to frustrate an administration order. The following limitations of this provision must be noted.

(*a*)   No such entitlement is implied in debentures or floating charges which are created *on or after* 29 December 1986; it will be necessary to include expressly such an entitlement in such documents.

(*b*)   No such entitlement is implied in a charge which is wholly a fixed charge *ab initio* or which does not extend to the whole or substantially the whole of the company's property (see the meaning of 'administrative receiver' in D1.4 PART D: RECEIVERS). Where it is partly a fixed charge and partly a floating charge, and contains common receivership provisions, the entitlement will, it seems, apply to the whole charge.

(*c*)   Only the right to appoint a receiver is implied. No right to enforce the security by any other means, for example, by the holder himself selling or entering into possession of the charged assets or deriving income therefrom, is implied, nor is the repayment of the money secured necessarily triggered—this would depend on the contractual terms of payment.

(*d*)   The mere fact that the right to appoint a receiver arises may not necessarily mean that without the actual appointment of a receiver the floating charge automatically crystallises. This would depend on the express terms of the charge and on whether the concept of automatic crystallisation is recognised by the courts (see D5.1 *et seq.* PART D: RECEIVERS).

Some practical points for holders of general charges

B6.4   To derive the maximum protection that may be available, a creditor obtaining a general charge from a debtor company would be well advised to consider the following suggestions (as appropriate or practicable, and subject to any considerations of commercial fairness).

(*a*)   To continue the current practice of providing in the charging document that all assets of the debtor company, present and future, with the exception of stock-in-trade and work-in-progress (which, of necessity, can only be subject to a floating charge as otherwise the company cannot carry on its business) are, from the inception of the charge, subject to a fixed, rather than a floating, charge. (It will be useful to include in the fixed charge all present and future contractual and other rights and choses-in-action under all present and future retention of title, leasing, hire-purchase, conditional sale, intellectual property licensing, franchise, distributorship and other similar agreements.) Assets which are subject to a fixed charge from the beginning will not only have priority over preferential debts (see C14.34 PART C: LIQUIDATIONS and D7.4 PART D: RECEIVERS) but also ensure for the holder the right to receive not less than a net market value from any administrator who disposes of those assets and, possibly, a better priority over subsequent chargees or purchasers of assets.

(*b*) To provide, as most well-drafted charging documents securing moneys payable on demand currently do, that at any time the holder may at his discretion by notice to the company convert any floating charge comprised in his security into a fixed charge. If such conversion notice is actually given at the first signs of trouble, for example, before (or even after) a petition for an administration order or a winding up is filed, this could again give the holder a better priority against subsequent chargees or purchasers of the assets with actual or constructive notice of the conversion and may also disentitle the company from making any disposals. In this connection it will be noted that section 410 of the Companies Act 1985, as inserted by section 100 of the Companies Act 1989 (not yet in force), enables regulations to be made providing for the registration of the crystallisation of a floating charge. Section 416 of the Companies Act 1985, as inserted by section 103 of the Companies Act 1989 (also not yet in force), deals with what matters on the register of charges constitute notice. It would seem that notwithstanding such conversion, even if it extends to all the assets, the holder will still be able to frustrate an administration by appointing an administrative receiver before an administration order is made, because the charge, *as created*, was still a floating charge (see D1.4 PART D: RECEIVERS). However, such conversion will not give him priority over preferential debts (as was available under the previous legislation—see *Re Woodroffes (Musical Instruments) Ltd* [*1985*] *BCLC 227*; *Re Brightlife Ltd* [*1986*] *BCLC 418*) in the event of receivership or liquidation or the right to receive *market value* (see B6.1 above) from an administrator who disposes of the assets. This is because under the definition of 'floating charge' in section 251 (see D1.4 PART D: RECEIVERS) a subsequent crystallisation of a floating charge does not alter its character as a floating charge for the purposes of the Act.

(*c*) To provide in all charges, fixed and floating, and in all loan documents, a further event of default. This would be to the effect that upon an application for an administration order being filed, or steps being taken towards such filing, all the moneys due by the debtor company to the holder under the hoan document or charged under the charging document shall forthwith (or upon the holder or lender making a demand) become due and payable and the security enforceable, whether by appointment of a receiver or otherwise.

(*d*) To insert in such documents stronger pre-insolvency events of default, particularly those relating to financial discipline.

(*e*) To enforce any general charge held, by appointing an administrative receiver, not later than the making of an administration order. As regards any other type of charge, if its enforcement is well advanced before an administration order is applied for, the court may be more likely to grant leave to continue and complete its enforcement despite the order or application for the order (although the court may be less willing to grant the leave pending the appointment of an administrator, as it may not wish to pre-empt his position). It will carefully strive to strike a balance between the interests of the holder and those of the unsecured creditors (see B4.1 and B6.1 above).

(*f*) If step (*e*) has not been taken or if fixed charge assets are involved, to obtain an independent valuation of the assets charged as soon as there are indications that the administrator is taking steps to sell the assets. This may assist the holder in any subsequent dispute with the administrator as to what was the proper value of the assets for which the administrator is accountable or how the proceeds actually realised, and any accretion thereto, should be apportioned between various types of assets sold.

Chapter 7: Position and general powers and duties of the administrator

Vacancy in office of administrator, and his release

B7.1   If a vacancy occurs by death (as to which see also Rule 2.54), resignation or otherwise, the court may by order fill the vacancy (see also Rule 2.55) on the application of any continuing administrator or (if there is no administrator) of the creditors' committee (see B8.1 below) or (if there is no continuing administrator and no creditors' committee) of the company or of the directors or of any creditor or creditors (section 13).

The administrator may at any time be removed from office by order of the court and may, in the prescribed circumstances (ill health, intention to cease practising as an insolvency practitioner, conflict of interest, or change of personal circumstances—Rule 2.53(1)), resign his office by giving notice of his resignation to the court (section 19(1)). He may also resign on any other ground with the leave of the court. Seven days' prior notice of his intention to resign, or to apply to the court for leave to do so, must also be given to any continuing co-administrator, or the creditors' committee, or the company and its creditors (as the case may be) (Rule 2.53(2) and (3)). He must vacate office if he ceases to be qualified to act as an insolvency practitioner (see PART A: GENERAL) in relation to the company or if the administration order is discharged (section 19(2)).

Where he ceases to hold office, his remuneration (as to which see B7.9 below, and Rules 2.47 to 2.50) and any expenses properly incurred by him are to be charged on and paid out of any property of the company which is in his custody or under his control at that time, in priority to any security which as created was a floating charge (section 19(4)), as also are any sums payable in respect of debts or liabilities incurred, while he was administrator, under contracts entered into or contracts of employment adopted by him or a predecessor of his in the carrying out of his or his predecessor's functions (section 19(5)). However, he is not to be taken to have adopted any contract of employment by reason of anything done or omitted to be done within 14 days after his appointment (as to which see B7.7 and D7.1 *et seq.* PART D: RECEIVERS).

A person who has ceased to be the administrator has his release, where he has died, from the time at which notice of his death is given under Rule 2.54 or, in any other case, from such time as the court may determine (section 20(1)). With effect from the time of such release, he is discharged from all liability both in respect of his acts or omissions in the administration and otherwise in relation to his conduct as administrator, but not from any liability which may attach to him under section 212 (summary remedy against delinquent directors, liquidators, administrators, administrative receivers, etc. for misfeasance, etc.) (section 20(2) and

(3)). In *Re Sheridan Securities Ltd* (*1988*) *4 BCC 200*, where the administrator had unsuccessfully pursued the purpose of achieving a voluntary arrangement not authorised by the administration order, the court postponed the administrator's release for two months to allow the creditor who objected to the release time to consider his position with the Official Receiver and the other creditors following a winding-up order (which was about to be made). For another instance of postponement of the administrator's release, see *Barclays Mercantile Business Finance Ltd v Sibec Developments Ltd*, discussed in B4.1 above.

In *Re Exchange Travel (Holdings) Ltd [1992] BCC 954*, the release of the administrators following the discharge of the administration order, the making of a winding-up order and their appointment as liquidators was opposed by some of the former directors and beneficiaries of the pension fund of the company on the ground of several instances of failure on the part of the administrators. The applicants also applied for the appointment of an additional liquidator to investigate the complaints. The deputy High Court judge held that he could not appoint an additional liquidator solely for the purpose of investigation. The court should be guided by the wishes of the majority of the creditors and the views of the creditors' committee unless there was some reason that indicated that their wishes should be overruled. The creditors and the committee opposed investigation. On the evidence, the judge could not feel justified in ordering the former administrators (now liquidators) to co-operate in an investigation under section 167(3) (control of the court over liquidators' powers). However, the court granted the release of the administrators only so as to take effect three months from the date of the order, so that the former directors could take steps to put evidence before the Official Receiver to enable him to decide whether to commence an investigation under his powers contained in section 132.

General powers

B7.2   The administrator may do all such things as may be necessary for the management of the affairs, business and property of the company and has also all the powers specified in Schedule 1 to the Act (section 14(1)). The Schedule 1 powers include most of the powers usually conferred on a receiver and manager by a general charge, and it is submitted that, as in the case of a receiver and manager, these powers will be construed broadly (see *Rushingdale Ltd SA v Byblos Bank SAL [1985] PCC 342*). The administrator also has power to use the company seal, to remove any director and to appoint any person as a director, whether to fill a vacancy or otherwise, and to call any meeting of the members (as to which see Rule 2.31) or creditors of the company (section 14(2)). Although these powers, which are quite wide-ranging, are exercisable from the time of his appointment, even before the section 23 meeting referred to at B5.4, subject to any restrictions imposed by the court under section 17 (see B5.2) (*Re Charnley Davies Ltd*, referred to at B5.4; *Re Hercules Security Fabrications Ltd* (*1987, unreported*); *Re Laser Control Ltd* (*1987, unreported*)), it is submitted that they must be exercised only in the context of the specified purposes for which the administration order has been made and, when approved, of the administrator's proposals (see B5.4).

One notable limitation of the administrator's powers is that, unlike a liquidator (see C12.6 PART C: LIQUIDATIONS), he has no statutory power to disclaim an onerous property or an unprofitable contract. Indeed, in certain situations he can be restrained from causing the company to breach a pre-administration contract (see, for example, B7.5 below). On the other hand, in some special situations he may be able to achieve a result which is similar to or even better than that resulting from a statutory disclaimer by the liquidator.

In *Re P & C and R & T (Stockport) Ltd [1991] BCC 98*, the company was a joint venture company formed to develop a business park. Two of the parties to the joint venture agreement entered into an agreement with the local council for the grant of a lease to one of those parties and for the lease obligations to be guaranteed by the other party. The agreement for the lease, and the lease itself, contained the development obligations of the joint venturers to the council. The rights and obligations of the joint venturers *inter se* were governed by a separate joint venture agreement. That agreement provided, *inter alia*, that the lease granted to one of the parties was to be novated to the company and that pending such novation those two parties were to hold the lease on trust for the benefit of the company. The company was to make certain payments to the party in whom the lease was vested and for that party to act as the project co-ordinator, receiving fees for its services. Before the novation of the lease, the development was unsuccessful and administrators were appointed to the company. The administrators wished to raise finance to complete at least the first phase of the development, without which the company would have no realisable assets. A bank was willing to provide such finance on the security of a legal charge over the lease that was still vested in one of those parties. The administrators contended that the company was entitled to require the party holding the lease to transfer it to the company. That party argued, however, that since the company did not propose, and was not in a position, to perform its contractual obligations to that party under the joint venture agreement, the company was not entitled to call for performance by that party of its obligations, or to ignore that party's contractual rights, including the right to provide services as project co-ordinator in return for the agreed fees. Finding in favour of the administrators, Scott J held that in the circumstances of the case the administrators had a power similar to that of disclaimer because

(*a*)   the joint venture agreement was, in effect, one of quasi-partnership (notwithstanding that the joint venture agreement expressly excluded partnership),

(*b*)   the insolvency of the joint venture project had frustrated the purpose of the joint venture company,

(*c*)   accordingly, the party in whom the lease was vested had no equity to enforce the contract, and (*d*) to allow enforcement of the contract would be inconsistent with the spirit and purpose of the administration order (namely survival as a going concern or a more advantageous realisation) and section 14.

The effect of enforcement would be to place that party in the position of a secured creditor to the detriment of the company's other creditors. The administrators were held to be entitled to have the lease vested in the company provided that a release from all obligations of the joint venture company, under the agreement for the lease or under the lease itself, was obtained from the owner of the reversion.

In the performance of his functions, the administrator may need to borrow money, whether on an unsecured basis or on the security of any property of the company. This power is given to him by paragraph 3 of Schedule 1. Where the property is already subject to a legal or other fixed charge created by the company, it would appear that the security to be created by the administrator will, in the absence of an agreement to the contrary with the holder of the existing charge, rank after that charge. The same may apply where the property is subject to an existing *floating* charge, particularly if by its terms (or, where applicable, by virtue of the transitional provisions referred to in B6.3 above) the floating charge has crystallised or (arguably) the floating charge contains a prohibition against the creation of any prior or *pari passu* charges and the prohibition is expressly noted in the particulars filed with the Registrar of Companies. However, any liability in respect of such borrowing would fall under section 19(5), as to which see B7.7 below.

It is submitted that section 15, which gives an administrator power to dispose of or otherwise exercise his powers in relation to the property, as if it were not subject to the existing charge (subject to the court granting him leave where the existing charge is a fixed charge), does not apply to the *creation* by the administrator of *a security*. The reference to a disposal in that section, when construed with the section as a whole, appears to be a reference to an outright disposal rather than by way of the creation of a security and the words 'or otherwise exercise his powers in relation to any property' must also be construed in that context. (See B6.1 and B6.2 above.) However, regardless of the question of priorities between the existing *floating charge* and the charge created by the administrator, or of whether a charge is created by him, the amount of his borrowing would, by virtue of section 19(5), as read with section 19(4), be payable as an expense of the administration in priority to the floating charge (see B7.7 below).

The administrator, as agent of the company, may find it necessary, in the performance of his functions, to give a guarantee for the borrowing or other fresh obligations of a subsidiary of the company.

Schedule 1 does not contain an express power to give a guarantee but it is submitted that by the combined effect of paragraph 3 (borrowing and grant of security) and paragraph 23 (power to do all other things incidental to the exercise of the other powers in the Schedule) he does have such a power.

In common with office-holders in certain other types of corporate insolvency, the administrator can enforce the provision of information and assistance by others (see PART A: GENERAL).

The administrator has a power to present a petition for the winding up of the company (Schedule 1, paragraph 21), although no winding-up order can be made during the administration period (see B4.1(*a*) and B4.2 above). Where a winding-up order is made immediately upon the discharge of an administration order, the court may appoint the administrator as liquidator (section 140—see also C5.50 PART C: LIQUIDATIONS). In the *Charnley Davies* case referred to at B5.4 above, the court made a winding-up order immediately upon the discharge of the administration order but reached its decision to appoint the administrator as liquidator reluctantly, since the liquidator would be reviewing his own acts as administrator. The factors which influenced its decision were *inter alia*:

(i) the time lapse involved if the Official Receiver were appointed,

(ii) the fact that there was no other nominee before the court,

(iii) the right of the creditors in any case to appoint at a later date another liquidator in his place and a liquidation committee to supervise his acts, and

(iv) the need in the interim to manage moneys and pursue claims.

It should be noted that before the court can make a winding-up order upon the discharge of the administration order, there should be before the court a winding-up petition which complies with the Rules. In the case of a winding-up petition by the administrator, the petition must comply with Rule 4.7(7) and, in particular, contain an application under section 18 for the discharge of the administration order. Section 140 does not envisage that the court can make a winding-up order upon the discharge of the administration order without the need for a winding-up petition or without an appropriate deposit being paid to the court as required by Rule 4.7(2). (See 'Dear IP', No 20, January 1992, issued by the Insolvency Service, as to which see A4.25 PART A: GENERAL.)

Sometimes it may be more advantageous to have a creditors' voluntary winding up than a winding up by the court, when the administration order is discharged. Among the advantages are that lower fees are payable in a voluntary winding up than in a compulsory winding up in respect of the funds deposited into the Insolvency Services Account at the Bank of England, and the period of six months allowed before they are so deposited (see the Insolvency Fees Order 1986 (SI 1986 No 2030), as amended by the Insolvency Fees (Amendment) Order 1988 (SI 1988 No 95)) and that a voluntary winding up is much less cumbersome than a compulsory winding up. However, as stated in B4.1 and B4.2 above, no winding-up resolution can be passed whilst an administration application or order is in force. Therefore, any resolution by the members for a voluntary winding up would have to await the discharge of that administration order.

There are two possible disadvantages of the hiatus (though it may be of a short duration) between the discharge of the administration order and the passing of the voluntary winding-up resolution. Firstly, during the hiatus the control of the company is, at least technically, in the hands of the directors and, secondly, for the purposes of the determination of preferential claims, the 'relevant date' under section 387 would be the time of the passing of the resolution, unlike in the case of a compulsory winding-up order made immediately upon the discharge of the administration order, where the 'relevant date' is the date of the making of the administration order (see section 387(3)(a) and contrast this with section 387(3)(c)). If it were possible to pass a voluntary winding-up resolution before the discharge of the administration order, then, as provided by section 387(2)(a), the relevant date would, again, be the date of the administration order and may therefore produce more equitable results for the preferential creditors.

In an attempt to get round this problem, Harman J made an order in *Re Scotlane Limited (31 July 1987, unreported)* to the effect that the discharge of the administration order be conditional upon the passing of a winding-up resolution. In the subsequent case of *Re Parameters Limited (9 May 1988)*, he did not follow his decision in *Re Scotlane* and instead discharged the administration order but directed that the order be not drawn up until a copy of the resolution had been lodged at the Court Office with a letter from the administrators' solicitors certifying that the resolution was duly passed and that those documents be lodged either on the same day or the following day.

Another possible solution is to pass, before the discharge of the administration order, a voluntary winding-up resolution conditional upon the discharge of the administration order, on the basis of the argument that 'resolution' referred to in section 11(3) must mean 'effective resolution'. It is submitted, however, that this is not a sound solution as, equally for the purposes of section 86 (which provides that a voluntary winding up is deemed to commence at the time of the passing of the resolution), 'resolution' must mean 'effective resolution'. Further, it is debatable whether a conditional voluntary winding-up resolution is valid at all, unless the condition is fulfilled on the same day as the day on which the resolution is passed (see C3.1 and C4.1 PART C: LIQUIDATIONS). In *Wheeler and Partners Ltd, February 1990 (unreported)*, Warner J appears to have approved the conditional resolution route.

It is debatable whether the problem could be got round by the creditors passing a resolution directing the liquidator in the creditors' voluntary liquidation or the administrator in the administration to pay preferential creditors on the basis that the date of the administration order be treated as the relevant date. The argument against such a course is that since the court itself does not appear to have jurisdiction to alter the relevant date, the creditors cannot have better powers unless, of course, the resolution of the creditors has been assented to by all the creditors. However, in suitable cases it may be possible to persuade the court that payment of preferential claims on that basis is in the larger interests of a 'better realisation' or is a 'necessary or incidental' payment in the terms of paragraph 13 of Schedule 1.

Right to apply to court for directions

B7.3   The administrator may apply to the court for directions in relation to any particular matter arising in connection with the carrying out of
his functions (section 14(3)). This is a wide and useful provision and has
been used, for example, to apply for the leave of the court to sell assets
before the approval of the administrator's proposals or revised proposals
if the circumstances are exceptional (see B5.15 above). However, the
provision must not be lightly used as in an *inter partes* hearing the costs
can be a considerable drain on the administration funds. Further, the
court is unlikely to make a commercial decision for him on a matter which
the creditors have not considered (see *Re Control Laser Ltd (1987, unreported)*) or to act as legal adviser to the administrator on a matter which
has not been considered by counsel. The issues on which directions are
sought must clearly be set out. In *Re Synthetic Technology Ltd [1990]
BCLC 378*, on an application by the administrators for directions as to the
future conduct of the administration, Harman J stated that applications
for directions should set out the type of directions sought and, if appropriate, the options available.

Conflict with powers of company and its officers

B7.4   Any power conferred on the company or its officers whether by
the Insolvency Act 1986 or the Companies Act 1985 or by the memorandum and articles of association, which could be exercised in such a way as
to interfere with the exercise by the administrator of his powers, is not
exercisable except with the consent of the administrator. The consent
may be given either generally or in relation to particular cases (section
14(4)).

Administrator's agency

B7.5   In exercising his powers, the administrator is deemed to be the
company's agent (section 14(5)). It would seem that an administrator is in
no better position than is the company itself as regards repudiation of outstanding contracts entered into by the company before his appointment.
In *Astor Chemicals Ltd v Synthetic Technology Ltd [1990] BCC 97*, an
injunction granted before the administration order, against the company
breaching a distribution agreement, was continued after the administration order. In this respect an administrative receiver is in a better position
(see D7.24 *et seq.* PART D: RECEIVERS). However, in certain circumstances,
the administrator may be able to obtain the direction of the court to
ignore a pre-administration contract affecting its assets. See, for
example, *Re P & C and R & T (Stockport) Ltd*, discussed at B7.2 above.

In relation to employees of the company, an administrator is in no
different position than any other employer in respect of the duty under
what is now section 188 of the Trade Union and Labour Relations (Consolidation) Act 1992 to consult with a recognised trade union (*see Re Hartlebury Printers Ltd [1993] BCLC 902* where, however, the court refused
leave under section 130(2) for the trade union involved to proceed before

an industrial tribunal because the redundancies had not been proposed by the administrators but resulted from the court's decision to put the company into compulsory liquidation).

An administrator is an officer of the company. He cannot cause the company to carry on a business which the company is not authorised to carry on under the objects clause of its memorandum of association; but, like any other officer of the company, he is entitled to apply for relief under section 727 of the Companies Act 1985 (see C13.5 PART C: LIQUIDATIONS). In *Re Home Treat Ltd [1991] BCLC 705*, the company had a nursing home business which had been running at a substantial loss. Although, after their appointment, the administrators had the assent of the shareholders and the creditors' approval for keeping the company trading with a view to its sale as a going concern, the company was probably not empowered by its objects clause to carry on such a business. The administrators applied for direction of the court under section 14(3) to enable them to carry on the business and for relief under section 727 in respect of any potential allegation of negligence, fault or breach of duty. It was held that as an administrator appointed by the court to conduct the business of the company with a view to better realisation of its assets or, indeed, with a view to the survival of the undertaking as a going concern, he must, even more than a liquidator, be a person properly within the context an officer of the company. This was so although he was also an officer of the court, there being in that context no conflict of duties. In both capacities his duties were to manage the business and property of the company in the interests of the creditors and, in the instant case, possibly eventually also of the shareholders of the company. There had been an informal alteration of the relevant objects clause to which all the members of the company had consented before the business had begun to be carried on. Accordingly, directions should be given to the administrators validating their conduct in relation to the affairs of the company. Further, the administrators were entitled to relief from any future claim against them since they plainly were acting honestly, reasonably and in pursuance of the order of the court, and ought fairly to be excused.

Administrator's liability

B7.6   Like anyone with a power, contractual or statutory, to sell property which does not belong to him, an administrator owes a duty to the company to take reasonable steps to obtain a proper price for its assets. His duty is 'to take reasonable care to obtain the best price that the circumstances permit' (*Standard Chartered Bank v Walker [1982] 1 WLR 1411*, a receivership case). That means the best price that circumstances, *as the administrator reasonably perceives them*, permit. He is not liable because his perception was wrong, unless it was unreasonable. It must be established that he had made an error which a reasonable, skilled and careful insolvency practitioner would not have made. (Re *Charnley Davies Ltd (No 2) [1990] BCC 605*).

In *Re Charnley Davies Ltd (No 2)* above, the company in respect of which an administration order was made, had carried on an insurance broking business. In a previous application to the court for directions, the court had confirmed the advice which the administrator had received from counsel that he could sell the entire undertaking of the company in advance of the section 23 creditors' meeting (see B5.4 and B5.5 above). He told those who had expressed an interest in buying the business that its value was at risk and was diminishing, and that offers must be submitted by a certain date. When the deadline expired, no offers had been received, except one, and he decided to accept it. Subsequently, other parties expressed an interest and another offer was received which he decided not to pursue, because it contemplated a deferred purchase, was not sufficiently attractive and would delay negotiations on and jeopardise the offer which he had accepted. The accepted offer, on which he proceeded to exchange contracts, was far below what the major insurance company creditors had been expecting. Some of those creditors petitioned the court under section 27 (see B8.3 below) for appropriate relief, claiming that the company's affairs had been managed by the administrator in a manner unfairly prejudicial to them. In substance, the petition was an action for professional negligence.

Millett J held that the administrator had not acted negligently or with undue haste in selling the business when he did, nor in the manner in which he conducted the sale, neither had he realised less than fair value. He had treated each post-deadline enquiry on its merits and could not fairly be criticised for following the old adage about a bird in the hand. He had a judgment to make. In any case, the proper course for the creditors was to have the administration order discharged and to have the company put into compulsory liquidation, so that the liquidator could, if he so decided, bring a claim under section 212 (misfeasance etc.—see C13.4 PART C: LIQUIDATIONS). A sale of assets by administrators at negligent undervalue was not sufficient, without more, to establish a claim to relief under section 27 on the ground of unfair prejudice to the 'interests' of creditors. 'Interests' was wider than 'rights' (see *Re a Company (No 008699 of 1985) (1986) 2 BCC 99,024*). An allegation that acts complained of were unlawful or infringed the petitioners' legal rights was not a necessary or sufficient averment in a section 27 petition. Millett J went on to state

> '. . . it would be misuse of language to describe an administrator who has managed the company's affairs fairly and impartially and with a proper regard for the interests of all . . . , conscientiously endeavouring to do his best for them, but who has, through oversight or inadvertence, fallen below the standards of a reasonably competent insolvency petitioner in the carrying out of some particular transaction, as having managed the affairs of the company in a manner which is unfairly prejudicial to the creditors'.

On a successful claim against an administrator for misfeasance etc. under section 212, his liability to pay money or damages is personal, subject to the relieving provision referred to in C13.5 PART C: LIQUIDATIONS.

Like other office-holders under the Act, he can also incur personal liability in respect of any tortious act or omission or for breach of fiduciary or statutory duty, subject to the limited protection he has under section 234(3) and (4). He may also be personally liable on any contracts entered into or contracts of employment adopted by him, subject to his right of recourse to the assets of the company (see B7.1 above; and see B7.7 below).

Post-administration expenses and liabilities

B7.7   All debts and liabilities incurred by the administrator (whether as agent of the company or as principal, as it seems) under contracts entered into or contracts of employment adopted by him or his predecessor in carrying out the administrator's functions are, like his remuneration and any expenses properly incurred by him, charged on and to be paid out of any property of the company which is in his custody or under his control at the time (section 19(5)). This includes any such property which is subject to any charge which, as created, was a floating charge. Such debts and liabilities rank before his remuneration and expenses—see section 19(4) and (5). Although section 19 deals with the position when a person ceases to be administrator, it appears to have more general application and operates not only for the benefit of that person but also for the benefit of the parties to whom the debts or liabilities are incurred. (See *Re Atlantic Computer Systems plc [1992] 2 WLR 367 (CA)*).

In the matter of *Polly Peck International plc (in administration)* (*27 June 1991, unreported*), on an application for directions made by the administrators, Mervyn Davies J granted the administrators liberty to cause the company to enter into a revolving credit facility agreement with certain lenders for the borrowing by the company of substantial sums and to treat the company's liability thereunder as an administration expense and ordered that such liability be charged on the property of the company as provided by section 19.

It will be noted that section 19(5) is confined to contracts (including contracts of employment) entered into by the administrator and contracts of employment adopted by him. It does not apply to outstanding pre-administration order contracts (other than contracts of employment) 'adopted' by the administrator.

The meaning of the word 'adopted' in section 19(5), in relation to contracts of employment, was considered in *Re Paramount Airways (No 3) [1993] BCC 662*. On their appointment, the administrators wrote a circular letter to those of the existing employees of the company whose services they wished to continue. The circular letter was in the form of a 'Specialised Mouldings' type letter (see D8.3 PART D: RECEIVERS), stating that by continuing with their services they were not adopting their contracts and were not accepting any personal liability in respect of them. The administrators applied to the court for directions as to whether the amounts payable to the employees in respect of the services provided by them after the date of the administration order were to be treated as priority payments in the terms of section 19(5). Evans-Lombe J held that the circular letter did not have the effect of taking those payments out of the scope of that section. To 'adopt' simply meant to 'procure the company to carry out', even if the administrators were not going to accept personal liability or the contracts were not to be novated to them. The court did, however, go on to express the view that the section did not prevent the administrators from contracting out of the effect of the adoption of the contracts and thus preventing the liabilities incurred under those contracts from ranking in priority to the remuneration and expenses of the administrators; but it was necessary for such contracting out to be clear and unequivocal. The letter to the employees must be drafted with section 19(5) specifically in mind. (The Court of Appeal (see below) disagreed with Evans-Lombe J on this point.) The court also directed that the debts covered by the section should, like any other expenses of the administrators, be paid as they fall due, that is forthwith.

In the *Paramount Airways* case Evans-Lombe J held that holiday pay, pay in lieu of notice and pension contributions for the notice period relating to the employees whose services had been continued fell under section 19(5), as they were part of the adopted employment contracts. However, a loyalty bonus which had been offered by the administrators for the notice period was not part of the adopted contract and was therefore outside the section. Further, a claim for unfair dismissal was not 'under' the employment contract; rather it was a statutory claim and, therefore, outside the section.

On appeal (*Re Paramount Airways Limited (No 3)* [*1994*] *BCC 172*), the Court of Appeal, in upholding the decision of Evans-Lombe J in the Chancery Division ([*1993*] *BCC 662*) held, in effect, that if any administrator continues, after the 14-day period of grace mentioned in section 19(5) (in common with sections 37 and 44 relating to ordinary and administrative receivers respectively—see D8.3 PART D: RECEIVERS), to employ staff, and pays them in accordance with their previous contracts, he (like receivers by virtue of similar language in sections 37 and 44) will be held *impliedly* (emphasis supplied) to have adopted their contracts of employment (*per* Dillon LJ). The Court of Appeal's decision, in effect, gives the expression 'adopted' a meaning different from that previously understood. For example, in *Botibol v Botibol* [*1947*] *1 All ER 26*, Evershed J dealing with the position of a court-appointed receiver, remarked '. . . it may be difficult to say that a receiver, acting strictly as such, can ever be sued in contract. On the other hand, a receiver may . . . adopt as his own a contract and render himself liable as on a novation of it'.

The expression 'impliedly', emphasised above, might suggest that an administrator (or a receiver) can negative an implied adoption by express words to the contrary. However, Dillon LJ, in a later part of his judgment, referred to the practice of receivers and administrators of using such express 'non-adoption' language, following the *Specialised Mouldings* case (above) (which he did not find a helpful authority because of the absence of any report, transcript or note of reasons by which Harman J reached his conclusion). Dillon LJ said that the mere assertion (or 'ritual incantation') by an administrator *or* receiver that he is not adopting the contract was 'mere wind with no legal effect', because adoption was a matter not merely of words but of fact. (It is relevant to note here that in the *Leyland Daf* case (below), Lightman J expressed the view that in order validly to avoid personal liability from the effect of adoption, an administrative receiver would need to achieve a variation of the existing contract excluding his personal liability through the 'offer and acceptance' route.)

At the time of the revision of this chapter, an appeal to the House of Lords by the administrators in the *Paramount Airways* case (which was subsequently followed by Lightman J in *Re Leyland Daf Ltd; Re Ferranti International plc [1994] BCC 658*, an administrative receivership case, also subject to an appeal) was pending. Meanwhile, in view of the far-reaching implications of that decision for administrators (and receivers), who might be left with no choice but to close the business and dismiss the employees before the expiry of the 14-day grace period, emergency legislation was rushed through Parliament to counteract partially the harsher effects of that decision on administrators and administrative receivers. The result was the Insolvency Act 1994, which came into force on 24 March 1994 but is retrospective to contracts of employment adopted on or after 15 March 1994. Insofar as it applies to administrators, it amends section 19(5) of the 1986 Act by restricting the priority treatment of liabilities incurred in respect of contracts of employment adopted by them to 'qualifying liabilities'. A liability is a qualifying liability if:

(*a*)   it is a liability to pay a sum by way of wages or salary or contribution to an occupational pension; and

(*b*)   it is in respect of services rendered wholly or partly after the adoption of the contract.

Where a qualifying liability relates to services rendered partly before and partly after the adoption of the contract, it only extends to so much of the sum as is payable in respect of services rendered after the adoption. Wages or salary payable in respect of a period of holiday or absence from work through sickness or other good cause are deemed wages or salary in respect of services rendered in that period. A sum payable in lieu of holiday is deemed to be wages or salary in respect of services rendered in the period by reference to which the holiday entitlement arose. Here, the reference to wages or salary payable in respect of a period of holiday includes any sums which, if they had been paid, would have been treated for the purposes of the enactments relating to social security as earnings in respect of that period (section 1 of the 1994 Act).

It will be noted that the 1994 Act does not protect administrators (or administrative receivers) in respect of potential liability under contracts of employment adopted by them before 15 March 1994. Their only hope is that the House of Lords overrules the Court of Appeal in *Paramount Airways* on the meaning of 'adopted'.

Creditors have no automatic preference or priority in respect of the contracts to which section 19(5) applies. Nor is there room in administrations for the application of a rigid principle (which applies in liquidations) that 'if land or goods in the company's possession under an existing lease or hire purchase agreement are used for the purposes of an administration, the continuing rent or hire charges will rank automatically as expenses of the administration and as such are payable by the administrators ahead of the pre-administration creditors'. (See *Re Atlantic Computer Systems plc*, above).

'Section 19(5) does not impose personal liability on the administrator. In that respect, he is in a better position than an administrative receiver, even though his status resembles that of an administrative receiver in that in exercising his powers he is deemed to act as the company's agent . . . One of the primary functions of an administrator is that frequently, if not normally, he will continue to carry on the company's business and, hence will continue to use the land and goods currently being used by the company for the purposes of its business. Indeed, it is of the essence of his appointment that an administrator should do these very things in cases where the purpose sought to be achieved by the administration order is purpose (a) in section 8(3), namely, the survival of the company, and the whole or any part of its undertaking as a going concern' (*Re Atlantic Computer Systems plc* [1992] 2 WLR 367 at 380).

An administrator undoubtedly has power (as distinct from obligation), in an appropriate case, to pay rent and hire charges in respect of land and goods used by him for the purposes of the administration. This is so both as to arrears and as to amounts continuing to fall due. Under the Act he has power to make any payment which is necessary or incidental to the performance of his functions (paragraph 13 of Schedule 1). (*Re Atlantic Computer Systems plc*, above).

An administrator has neither an automatic personal liability to pay, nor an automatic obligation to discharge as an expense of the administration, post-administration outgoings in respect of third party property which he continues to use pursuant to a pre-administration contract. However, the court may, on an application by the owner of the property for leave to repossess the property under section 11 (see B4.2 above) or under section 27 for relief against unfair prejudice (see B8.3 below), order the administrator to pay such outgoings as an expense of the administration to compensate the owner for his inability to exercise his rights in relation to the property.

Parties dealing with administrator

B7.8   A person dealing with the administrator in good faith and for value is not concerned to enquire whether the administrator is acting within his powers (section 14(6)).

Administrator's remuneration

B7.9   The administrator is entitled to receive remuneration for his services. The remuneration is to be fixed by reference either to a percentage of the value of the property with which he has to deal or to time properly spent by him and his staff in attending to the matters arising in the administration. It is fixed by the creditors' committee (see B8.1 below) (subject to a right of recourse to a meeting of creditors or the court) or, if a committee has not been appointed or fails to fix it, by a meeting of creditors (subject to a right of recourse to the court) or, failing that, by the court on the administrator's application. (In the *Charnley Davies* case referred to at B5.4 above, on discharging the administration order, the court ordered that the administrator's remuneration be determined in Chambers in the way in which receivers and other officers of the court appointed for such purposes have always had their remuneration fixed.) Any creditor, with the concurrence of at least 25 per cent in value of creditors (including himself), may apply to the court for the reduction of the remuneration (Rules 2.47 to 2.50). Where there are joint administrators, it is for them to agree between them as to how the remuneration should be apportioned, but any dispute may be referred to the committee, a creditors' meeting or the court. Where the administrator is a solicitor and employs his own firm, or any partner in it, profit costs cannot be paid unless this is authorised by the committee, the creditors or the court (Rule 2.47(7)).

Abstracts of receipts and payments

B7.10   The administrator is required to send to the court, the Registrar of Companies and each member of the creditors' committee six-monthly and final accounts of receipts and payments of the company. (See Rule 2.52 and Form 2.15.)

Chapter 8: Protection of creditors' and members' interests

Creditors' committee

B8.1   Where the meeting of creditors referred to in B5.5 above has approved the administrator's proposals (with or without modifications), it may establish a creditors' committee, consisting of not less than three and not more than five creditors elected at that meeting, to exercise the functions conferred upon it by the Act and the Rules. No person may act as a member of it unless and until he has agreed to do so. The proxy or corporate representative present may consent to the agreement on behalf of the creditor whom he represents, unless the instrument of proxy or authorisation contains a statement to the contrary (Rule 2.33(2), as amended). The committee does not come into being and cannot act until the administrator has issued a certificate of its due constitution.

The committee is to assist the administrator in discharging his functions, and act in relation to him in such manner as may be agreed from time to time. The committee may, on giving not less than seven days' notice, require the administrator to attend before it at any reasonable time and furnish it with such information relating to the carrying out of his functions as it may reasonably require.

The establishment of the committee is a two-stage process. First, the meeting determines by a majority in value whether there is to be a committee and, if so, whether it is to consist of three or five creditors. Secondly, nominations are invited for membership of the committee consisting of the number determined by the first resolution. If there are more candidates than that number (say three), then those three obtaining the most support in value are elected. It is not necessary that each candidate alone has to obtain a majority of votes in value; otherwise it would require a succession of ballots, at the end of each of which the candidate obtaining the least support would be eliminated (see *Re Polly Peck International plc* [*1991*] *BCC 503*).

Membership of the committee does not prevent a person from dealing with the company provided that the transaction concerned is in good faith and for value. However, the court may, on the application of any person interested, set aside any transaction which appears to it to be contrary to the above proviso, and may give appropriate directions for compensating the company for any loss which it may have incurred in consequence of the transaction.

(See section 26, Rules 2.32 to 2.46, as amended (which also contain the detailed procedure for proceedings of the committee, including representation of a committee member by an authorised person), and Forms 2.13 and 2.14.)

Right of creditors to requisition meeting

B8.2   The administrator must summon a meeting of creditors if so requested in accordance with the Rules (see Rule 2.21) by one-tenth in value of the creditors, or if directed to do so by the court (section 17(3)).

Right of a creditor or member to apply to court

B8.3   A creditor or shareholder may apply by petition to the court for an order on the ground that:

(*a*)   the company's affairs, business or property are being, or have been, managed by the administrator in a manner unfairly prejudicial to the interests of its creditors or members generally, or some part of its creditors or members (including at least the applicant); or

(*b*)   any actual or proposed act or omission of the administrator would be so prejudicial (section 27(1)).

In the *Charnley Davies (No 2)* case referred to in B7.6 above, Millett J commented that to say that an administrator's conduct had to be 'inequitable' or 'partial' for relief under section 27 to be available would be to distort the meaning of 'unfairly prejudicial'. However, he said that while it was difficult to envisage a situation where negligent or inadvertent conduct could fall within the section, it would be unwise to dismiss the possibility altogether. He would also not wish to rule outside the section a case where the company's affairs were managed by the administrator in a manner which unfairly subordinated the interests of its creditors to those of another company in the same group of which he was also administrator.

On such an application the court may make such order as it thinks fit for giving relief, or adjourn the hearing conditionally or unconditionally, or make an interim order or any other order that it thinks fit (section 27(2)). However, any order so made must not prejudice or prevent (*a*) the implementation of a voluntary arrangement (see PART E: VOLUNTARY ARRANGEMENTS) or any compromise or arrangement sanctioned under section 425 of the Companies Act 1985 or (*b*) where the application for the order was made more than 28 days after the approval of any proposals or revised proposals under section 24 or 25 (see B5.5 and B5.15 above, respectively), the implementation of those proposals or revised proposals (section 27(3)).

Subject as stated above, an order under section 27 may in particular:

(*a*)   regulate the future management by the administrator of the company's affairs, business, and property;

(*b*)   require the administrator to refrain from doing an act complained of, or to do an act which the petitioner complained he omitted to do;

(*c*)   require the summoning of a creditors' or members' meeting to consider such matters as the court directs; and

(*d*)   discharge the administration order and make such consequential provision as the court thinks fit (section 27(4)). (See also B5.16

above as to the general right of a creditor to apply to the court to set aside the administration order.)

Where the administration order is discharged, the administrator must send an office copy of the discharge order to the Registrar of Companies within 14 days after its making (section 27(6); see also section 18 and B5.16 above).

Chapter 9: Adjustment of antecedent transactions

B9.1   The 1986 Act enables the effect of certain types of transaction entered into by the company which may be detrimental to the company's creditors generally to be set aside or adjusted if subsequently the company goes into liquidation or becomes subject to an administration order. In relation to liquidation, the provisions replace the previous provisions relating to fraudulent preference and invalid floating charges. In this chapter the provisions are dealt with briefly only in the context of an administration order. For a more detailed treatment of this subject generally, see C10.1 *et seq.* PART C: LIQUIDATIONS.

Transactions at an undervalue (England and Wales)

B9.2   On the application of the administrator, the court must, subject to what is stated in this section and B9.6 below, set aside any gift made by the company or any other transaction entered into by it that provides for the company to receive no consideration if (i) a petition for an administration order is presented within two years following the transaction and (ii) at the time of or in consequence of the transaction the company was unable to pay its debts within the meaning of section 123 (see C5.22 PART C: LIQUIDATIONS) (which in the case of a transaction with a 'connected person' (as widely defined by section 249, read with section 435) is, unless the contrary is shown, presumed to have been the case). The same applies to a transaction entered into by a company for a consideration the value of which is significantly less than the value provided by the company. The court will not set aside any such gift or transaction if it was entered into by the company in good faith *and* for the purposes of carrying on its business and in the reasonable belief that the transaction would benefit the company (sections 238 and 240).

Gratuitous alienations (Scotland)

B9.3   The administrator may challenge any alienation by which any part of the company's property is transferred or any claim or right of the company is discharged or renounced, provided that the alienation has become effectual on one of the following days (whether occurring before or after 1 April 1986, when section 75 of the Bankruptcy (Scotland) Act 1985 came into force):

(*a*)   where the alienation has the effect of favouring a person who is an associate (within the meaning of that Act) of the company, on a day not earlier than five years before the date of the administration order; or

(*b*)   where the alienation has the effect of favouring any other person, on a day not earlier than two years before that date.

Where such a challenge is made, the court must grant decree of reduction or for such restoration of property to the company's assets or other redress as may be appropriate, unless it is shown—

(i) that immediately, or at any other time, after the alienation the company's assets were greater than its liabilities, or

(ii) that the alienation was made for adequate consideration (which does not include an alienation in implementation of a prior obligation to the extent that the prior obligation was undertaken for no or no adequate consideration), or

(iii) that the alienation was a birthday, Christmas, or other conventional gift or was a gift made for a charitable purpose to a person who is not an associate of the company which, having regard to all the circumstances, it was reasonable for the company to make (section 242).

Voidable preferences (England and Wales)

B9.4 The court must also, subject to what is stated in this section and B9.6 below, set aside a preference, i.e. anything done or suffered to be done by the company which has the effect of putting one of its creditors, or any surety or guarantor for the company's debts, into a position which, in the event of the company going into insolvent liquidation, would be better than the position in which such person would have been if that thing had not been done. However, (i) it must be shown to the court that the company was influenced in deciding to give the preference by a desire to produce the above effect (which in the case of a 'connected person' (see B9.2 above) is, unless the contrary is shown, presumed to have been the case) and (ii) the provisions will not apply unless (*a*) at the time or in consequence of that act the company was unable to pay its debts (see B9.2 above) (which, again in the case of a 'connected person' is, unless the contrary is shown, presumed to have been the case), and (*b*) a petition for an administration order is filed within six months (or, in the case of a 'connected person', within two years) following that act (sections 239 and 240).

(See also *Re Paramount Airways Ltd (No 2)* discussed at B10.1 below.)

Unfair preferences (Scotland)

B9.5 Under section 243, the administrator may challenge a transaction entered into by the company (whether before or after 1 April 1986) which has the effect of creating a preference, in favour of a creditor to the prejudice of the general body of creditors, being a preference created not earlier than six months before the making of the administration order. Certain transactions are excluded (for example, a transaction in the ordinary course of trade or business, or payment in cash for a debt which had become due unless the transaction was collusive with the purpose of prejudicing the general body of creditors). Where the court is satisfied that the transaction is one to which section 243 applies, it must grant decree of reduction or for such restoration of property to the company's assets or other redress as may be appropriate.

Court's powers

B9.6   The court in England and Wales has very wide powers (set out in section 241, as amended by section 1 of the Insolvency (No 2) Act 1994 with effect from 26 July 1994) to make appropriate orders to counteract the effect of the transactions and acts described in B9.2 and B9.4 above. It is provided that an order of the court may not affect a third party in relation to any interest in property acquired or any benefit from a transaction or preference received in good faith and for value (section 241(2), as amended).

Where at the time of any such acquisition or receipt, a third party—

(a)   had notice of the relevant surrounding circumstances and of the relevant proceedings, or

(b)   he was connected with, or was an associate of, either the company in question or the person with whom that company entered into the transaction or to whom that company gave the preference,

then, unless the contrary is shown, it will be assumed for the purposes of section 241(2) that the interest was acquired or the benefit was received otherwise than in good faith (section 241(2A), inserted by section 1(2) of the 1994 Act).

For the purposes of (a) above, the *relevant surrounding circumstances* are (as the case may require) the fact that the company entered into the transaction at an undervalue, or the circumstances which amounted to a giving of the preference by the company (section 241(3), substituted by section 1(2) of the 1994 Act). Where an administration order has been made, a person has notice of the *relevant proceedings* if he has notice of the fact that a petition on which the administration order is made has been presented, or that the administration order has been made (section 241(3A), inserted by section 1(2) of the 1994 Act).

(The powers of the court in Scotland are not set out in detail in the Act, but see B9.3 and B9.5 above.)

Extortionate credit transactions (Great Britain)

B9.7   Provision has also been made (in section 244) for relief to be granted to the company at the instance of the administrator in respect of any transaction for the provision of credit to the company entered into within three years preceding the administration order which the court regards as extortionate, i.e. if, having regard to the risk accepted by the provider of the credit, the terms require grossly exorbitant payments or otherwise grossly contravene ordinary principles of fair trading. A transaction with respect to which relief is sought will be presumed to be extortionate unless the contrary is proved. Section 244(4) specifies the terms which may be included in an order under that section.

Avoidance of certain floating charges (Great Britain)

B9.8   A floating charge created on the company's undertaking or property is invalid in the circumstances set out in B9.9 below except to the extent of the aggregate of:

(*a*)   the value of so much of the consideration for the creation of the charge as consists of money paid or goods or services supplied (see B9.10 below) to the company at the same time as, or after, the creation of the charge;

(*b*)   the value of so much of that consideration as consists of the discharge or reduction, at the same time as, or after, the creation of the charge, of any debt of the company; and

(*c*)   the amount of such interest, if any, as is payable on the amount falling within (*a*) or (*b*) above, in pursuance of any agreement under which the money was so paid, the goods or services were so supplied or the debt was so discharged or reduced (section 245(2)).

Circumstances in which floating charge is invalid

B9.9   The circumstances referred to in B9.8 above are the following:

(*a*)   in the case of a charge created in favour of a connected person (see B9.2 above), if it was created within the period of two years ending with the date on which a petition for an administration order is filed; or

(*b*)   in the case of a charge created in favour of any other person, if it was created—

　　(i)   at a time the company was unable to pay its debts (see B9.2 above) or became unable to pay its debts in consequence of the transaction under which the charge was created, and

　　(ii)   within the period of twelve months ending with the date on which the petition is filed; or

(*c*)   in either of the cases (*a*) and (*b*) above, if it was created at a time between the presentation of a petition and making of such an order on that petition (section 245(3) and (5)(a)).

Value of goods or services

B9.10   The value of goods and services referred to in B9.8 above is the amount in money which at the time of the supply could reasonably have been expected to be obtained for the supply in the ordinary course of business and on the same terms (apart from the consideration) as those on which they were supplied to the company (section 245(6)).

Unenforceability of lien on books, etc. (England and Wales)

B9.11   A lien or other right to retain possession of any books, papers or other records of the company is unenforceable to the extent that its enforcement would deny possession thereof to the administrator. This does not apply to a lien on documents which give a title to property and are held as such (section 246).

Void unregistered charges

B9.12   It should be noted that section 395 of the Companies Act 1985 (as amended), which requires the registration of certain categories of charges created by a company, makes an unregistered charge void not only as against a liquidator and creditors of the company, but also against its administrator. For an example of where a transaction was held to be a registered charge which was void against an administrator for non-registration, see *Orion Finance Ltd v Crown Financial Management Ltd, 30 March 1994 (unreported)*. In that case, the transaction in question was an assignment by the company to a finance company, which had funded the acquisition by the company of computer equipment, of sub-lease rentals of the equipment receivable by the company from end-users. (See further C12.10 PART C: LIQUIDATIONS.)

Chapter 10: International elements

B10.1 It will be useful to mention here some points relating to international aspects of the administration procedure.

Although generally the administration procedure is available only to companies formed and registered under the companies legislation of the United Kingdom, it was held in *Re Dallhold Estates (UK) Pty Ltd [1992] BCC 394* that the English court had jurisdiction under section 426 to make, at the request of the relevant foreign court, an administration order in respect of a company incorporated in a scheduled territory (in this instance, Australia) and in respect of which winding-up petitions were pending in both jurisdictions. (See further A5.2 PART A: GENERAL.) Presumably, the English court will not exercise the jurisdiction under section 426 unless the court first has winding-up jurisdiction over the company as an unregistered company (see C5.4 PART C: LIQUIDATIONS).

In *Re Paramount Airways Ltd (No 2) [1992] 3 All ER 1*, the administrators sought to recover certain sums which the company (incorporated in Great Britain) had transferred from England to an account held by a Jersey company in Jersey with the bank incorporated in Jersey. The basis of the claim was that the transfers constituted transactions at an undervalue under section 238. The Court of Appeal, in granting the administrators leave to serve the proceedings out of the jurisdiction, stated that where a foreign element was involved, the court would need to be satisfied that the defendant was sufficiently connected with England for it to be just and proper to make the order against him. In considering whether there was sufficient connection, the court had to look at all the circumstances of the case. If the proceedings were to go ahead in England, the bank would not be precluded from raising the issue of whether there was sufficient connection with England as a defence. Thus, the Court of Appeal appears to have recognised the principle that the provisions of the Act relating to the 'claw-back' of antecedent transactions (see B9.1 *et seq.* above) could affect foreign assets and foreign parties subject to there being sufficient connection between the two jurisdictions.

Re Maxwell Communications Corporation (No 2), Barclays Bank plc v Homan and others [1992] BCC 757, involved a past payment in the USA by an English company in the Maxwell group to an English bank. The company was in administration in the United Kingdom and under Chapter 11 proceedings in New York. The basis for the claim was a preference. The validity of a preference claim under section 239 depended on the subjective intention of the company making the payment; and the bank contended that it had a valid defence under that section as the payment was not made in order to improve its position in the event of the company's insolvency. By contrast, a preference claim could succeed under paragraph 547 of the US Bankruptcy Code regardless of the desire or motive on the part of either party, provided that the payment had been made within 90 days before the filing of the Chapter 11 petition. The bank applied to the English court for an injunction restraining the administrators from pursuing the preference claim in the USA. It argued that this would be unjust because the transaction had no sufficient connection with the US and the natural forum for deciding whether the transaction was a preference was England. Until its collapse, the company had been managed in London and the main basis for the US Bankruptcy Court's Chapter 11 jurisdiction was that the company's principal assets were shares in American companies. The injunction also sought to restrain the administrators from instructing, encouraging or permitting the US examiner under Chapter 11 to pursue the claim in the USA. The court held that English courts, like those of the US, had jurisdiction in appropriate circumstances to grant an 'anti-suit injunction' to restrain persons subject to their jurisdiction from prosecuting proceedings before a foreign court. But this was a jurisdiction to be exercised with great circumspection. An anti-suit injunction should be granted only where the foreign proceedings were 'unconscionable' or 'vexatious or oppressive' (see *British Airways Board v Laker Airways Ltd [1985] 1 AC 58* at *81, 95* and *Societe Nationale Industrielle Aerospatiale v Lee Kui Jak [1987] 1 AC 871* at *896*).

The normal assumption was that an English court had no superiority over a foreign court in deciding what justice between the parties required and, in particular, that both comity and common sense suggested that the foreign court was usually the best forum to decide whether in its own court it should accept or decline jurisdiction, stay proceedings or allow them to continue. The bank had relied on *Midland Bank plc v Laker Airways Ltd [1986] 1 QB 689*, where the Court of Appeal granted an injunction to stop Laker joining Midland Bank as a defendant to an anti-trust suit in Washington DC. In support of the application the bank argued that although it had a presence in the USA and was subject to the personal jurisdiction of the US Bankruptcy Court, the circumstances of the payments had so little contact with the USA that, according to English notions of international law, the US court lacked subject-matter jurisdiction. The fact that the payment was in respect of an overdraft facility drawn in US dollars, and that it was routed through the bank's New York branch was, it argued, irrelevant. However, in the view of Hoffmann J at first instance (with whom the Court of Appeal agreed), the instant case was quite different from *Midland Bank v Laker*. The *situs* of the assets from which the payment was derived was a connecting factor, which could legitimately be taken into account, particularly in view of the fact that the whole of the sum paid was derived from the proceeds of sale of an American asset. Arguably, it was appropriate that paragraph 547 should be invoked to recover it. Moreover, for the US court to assert jurisdiction would not involve, according to English notions, so egregious a claim of extra-territoriality that justice required that it should be prevented by injunctions.

In *Polly Peck International plc v Nadir (No 3), The Times, 22 March 1993*, the administrators were refused leave by the Court of Appeal to serve proceedings out of the jurisdiction on the Central Bank of the Turkish Republic of Northern Cyprus in which the administrators sought to recover from the bank as constructive trustees the sum of £371 million. The administrators claimed that Mr Nadir, who controlled the company, had fraudulently misappropriated sums totalling that amount, that he had owed a fiduciary duty to the company, that payments to the bank were in breach of that duty and that the bank knew, or ought to have known, about the alleged fraud. The Court of Appeal stated that to justify the invocation of extra-territorial jurisdiction against a foreign bank, a sufficiently strong case had to be shown. In the light of the evidence, the mere fact that payments had been transferred on a large scale ought not necessarily have put the bank on enquiry. The bank might have wondered what kind of business the company or Mr Nadir was pursuing but there were no grounds for saying that it should have suspected dishonesty.

Part C: Liquidations

1. Introduction   **125**

Preliminary   125
Principal legislation   125
Delegated legislation   126
Solvent and insolvent companies   127
Modes of winding up   127
The 'court' and cross-frontier recognition   128

2. Pre-liquidation considerations   **129**

Just distribution   129
Termination of company's existence   129
Taxation   130
Alternatives to liquidation   130
Pre-liquidation 'hive-down'   130
Timing of liquidation   131

3. Initiation of members' voluntary winding up   **132**

Members' meeting and resolutions   132
Declaration of solvency   134
Appointment of a liquidator   134
Authority to make distribution in specie   135
Authority to transfer assets for consideration in specie   135
Liquidator's indemnity   135
Procedure of members' winding up meeting   135
Filing and notification requirements   137

4. Initiation of creditors' voluntary winding up   **138**

Members' meeting and resolutions   138
Creditors' meeting   139
Position of 'caretaker liquidator'   141
Filing and notification requirements   141
Appointment of liquidation committee   142
Conversion of members' to creditors' voluntary winding up   142

5. Initiation of winding up by the court   **144**

Introduction   144
Jurisdiction in a winding up   145
Bodies which may be wound up by the court   150
Grounds for the petition   155
Grounds most frequently relied on   161
Who may petition   170
Presentation of the petition and ensuing proceedings
    up to winding-up order   195

6. Effect of winding up: general   **219**

7. Effect of voluntary winding up   **220**

Cessation of business   220
Cesser of directors' powers and investigation   220
Transfer of shares, etc.   220
Stay of actions and proceedings   220
Execution, distress, etc.   221

8. Effect of compulsory winding up   **222**

Cesser of directors' powers   222
Stay of actions and proceedings   222
Execution, distress, forfeiture, defeasance etc.   224
Disposition of property, etc.   225
Investigation by Official Receiver and Secretary of State   232

9. Effect of all forms of winding up   **233**

Restriction on re-use of company name   233
Goods and chattels taken in execution   234
Execution over goods, land or debt   235
Power of court to grant relief to execution or
    distraining creditors   236
Period of limitation   237
Contracts generally   238
Employees   239
Agents   239
Ownership of property   240
Assets and liabilities   240
Ultimate dissolution   241
Banks, deposit takers and insurance companies   241
Investigation of prior transactions and malpractice   242

10. Adjustment of prior transactions   **243**

Introduction   243
Transactions at an undervalue (England and Wales)   244
Gratuitous alienations (Scotland)   246
Preferences (England and Wales)   247
Preferences (Scotland)   251
Court's powers in respect of transactions at an
    undervalue and preferences, and position of third parties   252
Extortionate credit transactions (Great Britain)   253
Avoidance of certain floating charges (Great Britain)   253
Practical application of section 245 (floating charges)   254
Debt avoidance (England and Wales)   256
Unenforceability of lien on books, etc. (England and Wales)   260
Disposition of property after commencement of
    compulsory winding up   260

11. Conduct of winding up: general administrative aspects   **261**

Notification on stationery   261
Meetings and accounts   261
Involvement of creditors and contributories   271
Involvement of liquidation committee   274
Involvement of company's officers and others   275
Involvement of the court   276
The liquidator   277
Special manager   289

12. Conduct of winding up: realisation of assets   **290**

General aspects   290
Recission of contracts by the court   301
Recovery of assets in respect of antecedent transactions
     or matters   301
Recovery in respect of malpractice   305
Derivative action   305
Dealing with specific types of assets   306

13. Malpractice   **317**

Fraudulent trading   317
Wrongful trading   321
Negligence or breach of statutory duty   330
Misfeasance   331
Relieving provision   337
Extra-territorial application   339
Liability for contravening 'anti-Phoenix' restrictions   339
Liability to be disqualified   339

14. Conduct of winding up: establishment of liabilities   **340**

General aspects as to proofs of debt   340
Creditors' claims generally   347
Ordinary creditors   362
Secured creditors   362
Concurrent claims in two or more liquidations   365
Preferential creditors   366
Deferred creditors   368
Creditors of a partnership   369

15. Marshalling and distribution of assets   **370**

Payment of costs and expenses of the winding up   370
Payment to preferred creditors   372
Dividends to ordinary creditors   373
Dividend on post-liquidation interest   377
Dividend to deferred creditors   377
Distribution of surplus to members   377

16. Conclusion of the winding up   **379**

Members' and creditors' voluntary winding up   379
Compulsory winding up   380
Dissolution in a compulsory winding up   381

Part C: Liquidations

(This part is to be read in conjunction with PART A: GENERAL and PART F: SPECIAL PROVISIONS FOR FINANCIAL MARKETS.)

Chapter 1: Introduction

Preliminary

C1.1   In this part, the expressions 'winding up' and 'liquidation' are used interchangeably, and 'company' is mainly used in the context of the winding up in England and Wales of a company formed and registered in England and Wales under the Companies Act 1985 or the previous companies legislation. Wherever appropriate, mention has been made of provisions affecting companies incorporated in Scotland, companies or bodies formed outside but having a relevant connection with Great Britain, and special enactments applicable to the winding up of companies or bodies carrying on particular types of business or activities. However, the treatment of these is not comprehensive. This part does not deal with the law relating to the winding up of companies in Northern Ireland.

Principal legislation

C1.2   The principal legislation is mainly contained in Parts IV to VII and XII to XVIII (sections 73 to 251 and 386 to 436) of the Insolvency Act 1986. The scheme of those parts is as follows:

Sections	Subject
73– 83	Preliminary
84– 90	Voluntary winding up (Introductory)
91– 96	Members' voluntary winding up
97–106	Creditors' voluntary winding up
107–116	Provisions applicable to both types of voluntary winding up
117–162	Winding up by the court
163–251	Provisions applicable to every mode of winding up (and other company insolvency procedures)
386–436	Provisions applicable to every mode of winding up (and other company and personal insolvency procedures)

Some provisions applicable to a winding up by the court may be invoked in a voluntary winding up (of either type) by virtue of section 112, which empowers the court, on an application by the liquidator or any contributory or creditor, to determine any question arising in the voluntary winding up or to exercise, as respects the enforcing of calls or any other matter, all or any of the powers exercisable if the company were being wound up by the court.

Schedule 4 to the Act sets out the powers of a liquidator in every mode of winding up.

The Act applies to winding up in Scotland, subject to the variations or special provisions contained therein.

The provisions mentioned above are subject to provisions of certain enactments which regulate the winding up of various special types of companies and bodies (see C5.11 *et seq.* below).

Part VII of the Companies Act 1989 modifies the law of insolvency (including winding up) as it applies to a corporate member or designated non-member of certain financial markets (see PART F: SPECIAL PROVISIONS FOR FINANCIAL MARKETS).

Delegated legislation

C1.3   The main delegated legislation relating to winding up in England and Wales is contained in Parts 4 and 7 to 13 of the Insolvency Rules 1986 (SI 1986 No 1925), as amended by the Insolvency (Amendment) Rules 1987 (SI 1987 No 1919), the Insolvency (Amendment) Rules 1989 (SI 1989 No 397), the Insolvency (Amendment) Rules 1991 (SI 1991 No 495) and the Insolvency (Amendment) Rules 1993 (SI 1993 No 602) ('the Rules'); the prescribed forms ('the Forms') are contained in Schedule 4 to those Rules, as supplemented by Forms 600 and 600a in Schedule 2 to the Companies (Forms) (Amendment) Regulations 1987 (SI 1987 No 752), which Regulations, together with the Companies (Forms) (Amendment) Regulations 1988 (SI 1988 No 1359) and 1990 (SI 1990 No 572), amend the Companies (Forms) Regulations 1985 (SI 1985 No 854); see also Rule 12.7 as amended for transitional provisions. Special provisions relating to the winding up of insolvent partnerships as unregistered companies are contained in the Insolvent Partnerships Order 1994 (SI 1994 No 2421), replacing with effect from 1 December 1994, the Insolvent Partnerships Order 1986 (SI 1986 No 2142). The other statutory instruments mentioned in the Table at the end of PART A: GENERAL are also relevant in varying degrees. The special provisions relating to the winding up of insurance companies in England and Wales, contained in the Insurance Companies (Winding up) Rules 1985 (SI 1985 No 95) and made before the Insolvency Act 1986 came into force, continue to apply subject to the amendments made by the Insurance Companies (Winding up) (Amendment) Rules 1986 (SI 1986 No 2002).

Delegated legislation in respect of winding up in Scotland is contained in Parts 4 to 7 of the Insolvency (Scotland) Rules 1986 (SI 1986 No 1915). Those rules, as modified by Schedules 1 and 2 thereto in the case of creditors' voluntary winding up and members' voluntary winding up, and as amended by the Insolvency (Scotland) (Amendment) Rules 1987 (SI 1987 No 1921), are referred to below as 'the Scottish Rules'. In certain respects these rules apply, with modifications, to the Bankruptcy (Scotland) Act 1985. For insurance companies there are special provisions in the Insurance Companies (Winding up) (Scotland) Rules 1986 (SI 1986 No 1918). The prescribed forms for Scotland ('the Scottish Forms') are contained in Schedule 5 to the Scottish Rules. Forms 600 and 600a referred to above also apply to Scotland (see also Rule 3 in SI 1987 No 1921). The other statutory instruments mentioned in PART A: GENERAL as relating to Scotland are also relevant.

Solvent and insolvent companies

C1.4   The company to be wound up may be solvent or insolvent. The relevance of this distinction is two-fold: first, the reasons for winding up a solvent company and those for winding up an insolvent company may be different; secondly, the mode of winding up may depend on whether the company is solvent or insolvent.

Modes of winding up

C1.5   A company may be wound up voluntarily or by the court (section 73). A voluntary winding up may be a members' voluntary winding up or a creditors' voluntary winding up (section 90). In either type of voluntary winding up, the decision to initiate it is taken solely by the company (see section 84). A creditors' voluntary winding up is so called not because the creditors have a say in the initiation, but because they have a say in the choice of the liquidator and the conduct of the winding up. A members' voluntary winding up is, however, available only if the directors of the company are able to make and file with the Registrar of Companies a statutory declaration of solvency within the prescribed time limits (sections 89 and 90). Voluntary winding up (of either type) is not available for certain types of companies, e.g. insurance companies to which Part II of the Insurance Companies Act 1982 applies and which carry on long-term business (as defined) within the United Kingdom (sections 15 and 55(2) of the Insurance Companies Act 1982); companies and bodies incorporated outside Great Britain; and bodies (including partnerships) formed in Great Britain otherwise than under the existing or previous companies legislation. These can only be wound up by the court (section 221; and the Insolvent Partnerships Order 1994 (SI 1994 No 2421), containing a modified version of section 221). A winding up by the court is often referred to as a compulsory winding up.

The applicable practice and procedure and, to a lesser extent, the substantive provisions, may differ depending on the mode of winding up. Under the previous legislation, the procedure in a compulsory winding up was more cumbersome than in a voluntary winding up because of the detailed involvement of the court and the government insolvency service. The Insolvency Act 1986 and the secondary legislation made thereunder has considerably rationalised the procedures. Nevertheless, where a choice is available, voluntary winding up is likely to continue to be preferable because it continues to be more convenient and simpler.

The 'court' and cross-frontier recognition

C1.6   In relation to *any* mode of winding up (voluntary or compulsory), the 'court' means the court having jurisdiction to wind up a company compulsorily (section 744 of the Companies Act 1985, as read with section 251 of the Insolvency Act 1986). The subject of jurisdiction, including the position regarding cross-frontier recognition, is dealt with in C5.2 *et seq.* below. The court has jurisdiction in all forms of winding up; but the degree of its involvement varies between voluntary winding up (of either type) and compulsory winding up. This was explained by Wynn-Parry J in *Re Phoenix Oil and Transport Co Ltd (No 2) [1958] Ch 565* at *570* as follows:

> 'In the case of a voluntary winding up, the jurisdiction of the court is not invoked in order to place a company in liquidation. In the case of a creditors' liquidation, the creditors, through the committee of inspection. . .' [now called the liquidation committee] '. . . are in control as against the contributories. . .' [that is, members] '. . . while in the case of a members' voluntary winding up, it is the members who are in control. In both cases the court is given a certain degree of jurisdiction, but I think that it can be accurately, though shortly, be said that in both forms of voluntary winding up, the court is in the background to be referred to if the necessity should arise. In the case of winding up by the court, however, different considerations arise.'

Chapter 2: Pre-liquidation considerations

C2.1   The winding up of a company is generally initiated for either or both of the following reasons:

(*a*)   to ensure a just distribution of its assets; and

(*b*)   to terminate its existence by its eventual dissolution.

In the case of an insolvent company a just distribution is the primary objective, the termination of existence being merely a by-product. Where the company is solvent, the reverse may be the case.

Just distribution

C2.2   A winding up may bring about a just distribution in the following ways.

(1)   The company's assets and affairs pass into the hands of an independent and experienced liquidator whose powers, duties and functions are regulated by statute, and his conduct is also subject to the disciplinary rules applicable to his authorisation as insolvency practitioner, including those of the professional body which has granted the authorisation. He is in a fiduciary position *vis-à-vis* the company's creditors and members generally, and certain statutory aids facilitate his task.

(2)   The rights of unsecured creditors against the company's assets are virtually 'frozen' upon the commencement of the winding up. Further deterioration of its financial position and proliferation of its liabilities may thus be averted. Ordinary liabilities are discharged on a *pari passu* basis.

(3)   It may be possible for the liquidator to 'claw back' some of the advantages received from the company by a creditor or another party at the expense of the other creditors.

(4)   The liquidator may be able to call into question the past conduct of the company's officers and others in relation to the company's affairs and make appropriate recovery from them.

Termination of company's existence

C2.3   The winding up of a solvent company, with the primary object of terminating its existence, may be desired, for example, as part of a corporate or financial restructuring of the group to which the company belongs, or (subject to anti-avoidance provisions) as a subsidiary device to minimise tax liabilities or maximise tax advantages for the group, or may be a natural sequel to the winding down or disposal of its business or cessation of its activities.

Some other considerations which could affect the decision as to whether or when to commence a winding up are summarised below.

Taxation

C2.4   In the case of a solvent company, particularly as part of a scheme of reconstruction, tax questions may be important. The following tax points (which are by no means exhaustive) might affect the decision on whether or when to liquidate a solvent company.

(1)   On commencement of liquidation a new accounting period starts (Taxes Act 1988, s 12(7)).This may affect the company's ability to make use of group relief and capital allowances, and the calculation of losses available for set-off against profits and gains, etc.

(2)   Liquidation may entail cessation of trading, if not immediately then by the end of the winding up. Terminal loss relief under section 394 of the Taxes Act 1988 may not be as attractive as the relief which might have been available on the basis of continued trading.

(3)   Liquidation severs a group relationship with subsidiaries and that traced through the company (*IRC v Olive Mills Ltd [1963] 1 WLR 712; Ayerst v C & K (Construction) Ltd [1976] AC 167*). This could affect group relief and the ability to transfer losses within the group and, possibly, the non-close company status of a subsidiary. (However, the severing of the group relationship does not trigger a deemed disposal for the purposes of corporation tax on capital gains —see section 272(4) of the Taxes Act 1970.) Payment of dividends within the group without ACT may no longer be possible.

(4)   Where the liquidation is to be part of a reconstruction under section 267 of the Taxes Act 1970 (that is where assets are transferred on a 'no gain, no loss' basis) it may be advisable to obtain from the Inland Revenue a clearance under section 267(3A) of that Act.

(5)   The anti-avoidance provisions of that Act may need to be watched carefully.

For detailed treatment of this subject, see PART H: TAXATION.

Alternatives to liquidation

C2.5   In the case of an insolvent or potentially insolvent company, a liquidation may not necessarily be the best solution for the company's creditors and shareholders, and alternative courses may have to be explored by the directors (as to which see A3.1 PART A: GENERAL above). In the case of a defunct company without any assets, the cheapest and speediest course may be to have it struck off the register by the Registrar of Companies (see PART G: DISSOLUTION AND REVIVAL).

Pre-liquidation 'hive-down'

C2.6   It may be possible to improve the prospects of selling the profitable parts of the company's business as a going concern if they are 'hived down' into a clean subsidiary before the commencement of winding up. This, to some extent and in some circumstances, may also enable the tax benefit of any accumulated trading losses to be preserved for the benefit of the subsidiary and, hence, the purchaser thereof. Assets on the disposal of which a chargeable gain would arise may be left in the parent to enable the gain to be set off against any available losses. This subject is discussed in more detail in D9.4 *et seq*. PART D: RECEIVERS below. The effect of the Transfer of Undertakings (Protection of Employment) Regulations 1981 (referred to in D9.10 and D9.16 PART D: RECEIVERS below) would be that the transferee company would succeed to the transferor company's liabilities and obligations to its employees (except in respect of an occupational pension scheme). This would happen either immediately upon the hive-down or, if the hive-down is effected by a receiver of the transferor company (or its liquidator in a creditors' voluntary winding up), when the transferee company ceases to be the subsidiary of the transferor company.

Timing of liquidation

C2.7   As explained, tax considerations may have an important bearing on the timing of liquidation. But, in the case of an insolvent company, it may not be possible to delay commencement of liquidation without the risk of falling foul of the provisions relating to fraudulent trading, wrongful trading and misfeasance (see C13.1 to C13.4 below) or the provisions of the Company Directors Disqualification Act 1986. In fact, the urgency of the situation might make it necessary to put an insolvent company into a creditors' voluntary winding up immediately. This may in some cases be achieved by the use of the short notice procedure (as to which, see C4.5 and C4.9 below).

Chapter 3: Initiation of members' voluntary winding up

Members' meeting and resolutions

C3.1   This form of winding up is only available to a 'company', that is, a company formed and registered under the Companies Act 1985 or under the previous companies legislation (see section 735 of that Act, as read with the last part of section 251 of the Insolvency Act 1986).

Winding up commences upon the members at their general meeting passing a special resolution under section 84(1)(b) (see section 86) that the company be wound up voluntarily. (Paragraph (a) of section 84(1) is rarely applicable in practice; and paragraph (c), by its very nature, is only appropriate to a creditors' voluntary winding up (see C4.1 below)). The first step would be for the company's board of directors to meet to direct the convening of the requisite extraordinary general meeting of the company. In certain circumstances, the court may, on application by a shareholder under section 459 of the Companies Act 1985 (relief against unfair prejudice—see C5.30 below) restrain the passing of a voluntary winding-up resolution; for example, where the company is a 'quasi partnership' and the winding up is proposed in the context of a proposal by the other shareholders to make a transfer, by means of a self-dealing transaction, of the company's undertaking to another company, which transaction the court considers should be restrained: *Re Mountforest Ltd* [*1993*] *BCC 565*.

The directors may specify in their direction two dates in the alternative; an early date if the requisite consent to short notice under section 378(3) of the Companies Act 1985 is received by that date or, otherwise, a later date which allows time to give the usual 21 days' notice under section 378(2) of that Act. They may make the necessary declaration of solvency (see C3.2 below) at that board meeting or may postpone that step until a later board meeting held before the general meeting.

(As to the procedure for a members' meeting, see C3.7 below.)

In certain cases it may be thought necessary to pass a voluntary winding-up resolution conditional upon the happening of certain events, for example, in cases involving corporate restructuring conditionally upon the receipt of a tax clearance. However, the validity of a conditional winding-up resolution is not beyond doubt. There are no clear judicial authorities on the point, but the following may be the arguments against such validity.

(1)   A voluntary winding up can only be effective as and to the extent expressly provided by statute. Section 84 exhaustively lays down the circumstances in which a company may be wound up voluntarily. Among them are: if the company resolves by special resolution that

it be wound up voluntarily; or if the company resolves by extra-ordinary resolution to the effect that it cannot by reason of its liabilities continue its business, and that it is advisable to wind up. The section appears to require an absolute unconditional resolution.

In this connection, the case of *Currie v Cowdenbeath Football Club Ltd [1992] BCLC 1029* may be relevant. It concerned section 303(1) of the Companies Act 1985 which provides: 'A company may by ordinary resolution remove a director . . .'. The respondents had already brought a petition in which they claimed that certain persons had resigned as directors. The respondents had been granted an interdict against those persons holding themselves out as directors. The respondents had now called an extraordinary general meeting to consider a proposed resolution which stated: 'That if, as a matter of fact, [the persons concerned are] presently [directors] of the company (which contention is subject to dispute involving action within the Court of Session) [they] be removed as [directors]'. Lord Penrose, sitting in the Outer House of the Court of Session, held the resolution to be incompetent. In his opinion the section did not contemplate action depending upon a contingency of that kind. The procedure under that section was designed exclusively for the removal of persons who were at the material time directors.

(2) Section 86 provides that a voluntary winding up is deemed to commence at the time of the passing of the resolution for voluntary winding up. Arguably, a resolution (conditional or unconditional) is 'passed' when it is actually passed and not (if conditional) when the condition is satisfied (that is, the resolution becomes effective).

(3) Upon the passing of a winding-up resolution, certain statutory provisions as to notification, rights of creditors and dealing with assets are irrevocably triggered. In this connection, it is also relevant to note that section 89 lays down a maximum period of twelve months from the commencement of the winding up for payment of debts for the purposes of a declaration of solvency. The declaration must be made within five weeks immediately preceding the date of the passing of the resolution or on that date but before the passing of the resolution. If the fulfilment of the condition is delayed beyond twelve months, or if the resolution is deemed to be passed when the condition is fulfilled and the fulfilment is delayed beyond five weeks, the declaration would become invalid.

(4) A condition may, in extreme cases, take years to be satisfied. In the meantime, there would be uncertainty. Passing a winding-up resolution requires a degree of judgment to be made in the light of the circumstances prevailing at the time the winding up becomes effective. A deferred resolution deprives the members of the opportunity to look at the situation prevailing at the time of the expiration of the period of deferment.

(5) The statutory provisions do not enable a winding-up resolution deferred for a long time to be distinguished from a resolution deferred for a short time.

However, if a conditional resolution becomes unconditional on the same day as it is passed, it may be possible to rely on the principle that courts do not take account of fractions of the same day. Further, most of the objections referred to above would lose their significance.

As to problems involved in effecting a voluntary winding up immediately following the discharge of an administration order, see B7.2 PART B: ADMINISTRATION ORDERS.

Declaration of solvency

C3.2   The process does not qualify as a members' voluntary winding up (and will be treated as only a creditors' voluntary winding up—section 90) unless, within the period of five weeks immediately preceding the date of the passing of the resolution for winding up, or on that date but before the passing of that resolution, the majority of the directors (or all of the directors where there are no more than two) at their meeting have made a statutory declaration as to the company's solvency in the pre-scribed form (Form 4.70; see section 89). 'Solvency' in this context means that in the directors' opinion, formed after having made a full enquiry into the company's affairs, the company would be able to pay its debts in full, together with interest at the 'official rate', within a period specified in the declaration not exceeding twelve months from the commencement of the winding up (section 89(1)). (The 'official rate' means the contractual rate, if any, or the rate specified for the purposes of section 17 of the Judgments Act 1838 (currently eight per cent per annum—see the Judgment Debts (Rate of Interest) Order 1993 (SI 1993 No 564) and see also section 44 of the Administration of Justice Act 1970) on the day of commencement of the winding up, whichever is the greater—sections 189(4) and 251.) A director making the declaration as to solvency without reasonable grounds for his opinion renders himself liable to imprisonment or a fine or both (section 89(4)). If the company is wound up pursuant to a resolution passed within five weeks after the making of the declaration, and the debts and interest are not paid or provided for in full within the period specified in the declaration, it will be presumed (unless the contrary is shown) that the director had no reasonable grounds for his opinion (section 89(5)). It is advisable for the directors to consult the company's auditors and to obtain a 'comfort letter' from them before making the declaration. An error in the statement of assets and liabilities embodied in the declaration does not render the declaration void provided that the statement can reasonably and fairly be described as such a statement (*De Courcy v Clement [1971] Ch 693*).

Appointment of a liquidator

C3.3   Section 91(1) *requires* the company in general meeting to appoint one or more liquidators. This can be done at the same meeting, even without notice, as soon as the resolution to wind up has been passed (*Bethell v Trench Tubeless Tyre Co [1900] 1 Ch 408*). The appointment can be made by an ordinary resolution but is usually made as part of the special resolution for winding up. A separate ordinary resolution may be considered preferable where, for example, votes as to the choice of liquidator (but not as to the decision to wind up) are likely to be divided. Where two or more persons are appointed as liquidators, the resolution must state whether they are to exercise their functions jointly or separately or otherwise (section 231); but it would appear that the only consequence of a failure to comply with this requirement is that their functions can only be exercised jointly. The person(s) appointed must be qualified insolvency practitioner(s) in relation to the company (see PART A: GENERAL).

Authority to make distribution in specie

C3.4   The articles of association of a company usually provide that the liquidator may, with the sanction of an extraordinary resolution of the company (and any other sanction required by the Companies Act 1985), divide among the members *in specie* or kind the whole or any part of the assets of the company and for such purposes set a fair value on the property (see, for example, article 117 of Table A). It is usual to pass such an authorising resolution contemporaneously with, or as part of, the special resolution to wind up, although it can also be passed at a later date.

Authority to transfer assets for consideration in specie

C3.5   Where appropriate, a special resolution may also be similarly passed under section 110(3)(a) authorising the liquidator to transfer the business or assets for consideration *in specie* receivable by the members in accordance with sections 110 and 111. See also C12.3 below.

Liquidator's indemnity

C3.6   A liquidator so authorised may wish to obtain appropriate indemnities from the shareholders in respect of (i) any distribution *in specie*, or any transfer for consideration *in specie*, which he may make, (ii) in respect of his remuneration, costs and expenses, and (iii) any liability which he may incur by reason of any act which he does or omits to do at the shareholders' request or otherwise, which is not attributable to fraud or negligence on his part.

Procedure of members' winding up meeting

C3.7   For a meeting of the members referred to in C3.1 above, the company's articles apply, subject to sections 369 to 375 and 378 of the Companies Act 1985 (as amended, with effect from 1 April 1990, by the Companies Act 1989) as regards (i) notice of the extraordinary general meeting, (ii) the procedure thereat, and (iii) the requisite majority for the special resolution. (The Insolvency Rules do not apply here.) The meeting can be validly held at short notice as permitted by section 378(3) of that Act. A special resolution approved by all the members (or, where the company has an article similar to article 53 of Table A, a special resolution in writing signed by all the members having a right to vote) would have the same effect as if it was duly passed at a meeting (*Re M J Shanley*

Contracting Ltd (1979) 124 SJ 239). There are now statutory provisions regarding written resolutions (see sections 381A to 381C and 382A of, and Schedule 15A to, the Companies Act 1985, as inserted by sections 113 and 114 of the Companies Act 1989 with effect from 1 April 1990).

It should be noted that

(*a*)   notice of the meeting (whether convened at short notice or otherwise) must be given to the company's auditors as required by section 390 of the 1985 Act (as inserted by section 120 of the 1989 Act with effect from 1 April 1990), and

(*b*)   a written resolution has no effect unless a notification of the resolution is given to the auditors, and either seven days have passed since the notification, or in the meantime the auditors have notified the company that in their opinion the resolution does not concern them (or does concern them but need not be considered by a general meeting or class meeting of the company).

(*Quaere* whether the requirement in (*b*) above can be circumvented if the written resolution is passed pursuant to express provisions in that regard contained in the company's memorandum of association instead of pursuant to the statutory provisions referred to above—see, for example, *Re Oxted Motor Co Ltd [1921] 3 KB 32; Parker and Cooper Ltd v Reading [1926] Ch 975; Re Pearce Duff and Co Ltd [1960] 3 All ER 222*.)

Where the company's articles provide that delivery of a notice sent by post is deemed to be effected 24 hours after it is posted, but give the company an option to use an alternative method of service if, by reason of the total suspension or curtailment of postal services within the UK, the company is unable effectively to convene the meeting by notices sent through the post, the posting of notice during a strike action will not necessarily enable it to rely on the '24 hours deemed service' provision (*Bradman v Trinity Estates plc (1989) 5 BCC 33*).

If for any reason it is impracticable to call a meeting of the members, for example due to a dispute between the directors or the members, or because of any difficulty in securing a quorum for that meeting or for a meeting of the board of directors to authorise the convening of that meeting (see C3.1 above), the court may, of its own motion or on the application of any director or any member entitled to vote, order a meeting to be called, held and conducted in any manner the court thinks fit (CA 1985, s 371; for examples, see *Re Opera Photographic Ltd [1989] BCLC 763; Re Downs Wine Bar Ltd [1990] BCLC 839*). Further, section 370 of the Companies Act 1985 provides that, insofar as the articles do not make other provision in that behalf, two or more members holding not less than one-tenth of the issued share capital (or, if the company does not have a share capital, not less than five per cent in number of the members) may call a meeting of the company; and the members present at the meeting may elect a chairman of the meeting.

The quorum requirements for such a meeting of members are governed by the articles. Article 40 of the 1985 Table A lays down a quorum of two persons entitled to vote, each being a member or a proxy for a member or a duly authorised representative of a corporate member. If the articles are silent then section 370 applies which provides for a quorum of 'two members personally present'.

Filing and notification requirements

C3.8   The declaration of solvency and the winding-up resolution must be filed by the company with the Registrar of Companies within 15 days after the passing of that resolution (section 84(3) of the Insolvency Act 1986 and section 380 of the Companies Act 1985). The company must also advertise the resolution in the *Gazette* within 14 days after it is passed (section 85). Further, the liquidator must, within 14 days after his appointment, publish in the *Gazette* and file with the Registrar of Companies a notice of his appointment (section 109; Forms 600 and 600a in Schedule 2 to the Companies (Forms) (Amendment) Regulations 1987, SI 1987 No 752).

Chapter 4: Initiation of creditors' voluntary winding up

Members' meeting and resolutions

C4.1   This form of winding up is, again, only available to a 'company' formed and registered under the Companies Act 1985 or under the previous companies legislation (see C3.1 above).

Winding up commences when the members, at a meeting convened as authorised by the board of directors, pass an extraordinary resolution under section 84(1)(c), 'that the company cannot by reason of its liabilities continue its business, and that it is advisable to wind up' and that, accordingly, the company be wound up voluntarily. This form of winding up is appropriate where the company is insolvent. It is possible to commence a creditors' voluntary winding up by a special resolution in the same form as for a members' voluntary winding up under section 84(1)(b), that is, 'that the company be wound up voluntarily'. However, the text of that resolution could create a misleading impression that the winding up is either a solvent or a members' voluntary winding up. Consequently, this course is rarely followed.

Unlike in the case of a members' voluntary winding up, no declaration of solvency is made, and the creditors *do* have a say in the choice of liquidator and the conduct of the winding up and a right to appoint a liquidation committee to oversee the liquidator's activities. The creditors' wishes generally override the members' wishes.

The members' meeting will be preceded by the board of directors' meeting to authorise and direct the convening of the members' and creditors' meetings. That board meeting or a subsequent board meeting, to be held before the meeting of the creditors, must appoint one of the directors to preside at the creditors' meeting (section 99(1)(c)) and will approve the statement of affairs and list of creditors to be laid before the creditors' meeting (see C4.7 below).

As to the validity or otherwise of a conditional winding-up resolution, see C3.1 above.

Authority to make distribution in specie

C4.2   Such an authority to the liquidator will not generally be appropriate where the company is clearly insolvent; but if it is deemed desirable to give such an authority in case the company eventually turns out to be solvent, the procedure as in C3.4 above may be followed.

Nomination of liquidator by members

C4.3   The members at their meeting at which the winding-up resolution is passed may also nominate a person to be liquidator (section 100(1);

see also C4.8 below). This may be done by an ordinary resolution but is usually done as part of the extraordinary resolution referred to in C4.1 above.

Nomination for liquidation committee by members

C4.4　The winding up meeting of members or any subsequent meeting of the members may also appoint, by ordinary resolution or as part of the extraordinary resolution to wind up, up to five persons to act as members of any liquidation committee that may be appointed by the creditors. This is subject to the right of a creditors' meeting to resolve that the persons appointed by the members should not be members of the committee (section 101; see also C4.11 below).

Procedure for members' meeting

C4.5　Unless the short notice or written resolution procedure referred to in sections 369(3) and (4), 381A to 381C and 382A of the Companies Act 1985 (as amended by the Companies Act 1989) (see also C3.7 above) is used, at least 14 days' prior notice of the members' meeting specifying the intention to propose the winding-up resolution as an extraordinary resolution must be given (section 369(1)(b)(i) and (ii) of that Act). The rest of the requirements and procedure are as in the case of a special resolution for a members' voluntary winding up (see C3.7 above).

Creditors' meeting

C4.6　A creditors' meeting is required to be convened by the company for a day not later than the 14th day after the day on which the winding up meeting of the members is to be held (section 98(1)(a)). However, the failure to comply with this requirement, though it may entail criminal penalties, does not invalidate the winding up commenced by the members' resolution mentioned in C4.1 (see C4.9 below and the cases mentioned there). The director appointed by the board of directors for the purpose under section 99 (see C4.1 above) must act as chairman. However, if he is not present and one of the creditors present or his solicitor accompanying him takes the chair, the proceedings of the meeting are not invalidated. (See also section 166(5) which provides that the liquidator 'shall' apply to the court for directions as to the manner in which a default by the directors under section 99 is to be remedied; but the word 'shall' is permissive rather than mandatory.) Under the general law relating to meetings, if the person nominated to preside is absent, it is open to those who are entitled to attend and are present to appoint their own nominee to preside (*Re Salcombe Hotel Developments Co Ltd* (*1989*) *5 BCC 807*).

The requirements of section 98 as to notice of the meeting must be complied with. The notice must contain certain particulars such as the name and address of an insolvency practitioner from whom creditors may obtain further information concerning the company's affairs and the address where they can inspect a list of creditors. The notice must be sent by post to the creditors not less than seven days before the date of the meeting. Notice of the meeting must also be advertised once in the *London Gazette* (or, in Scotland, the *Edinburgh Gazette*) and at least once in two newspapers circulating in the locality in which the company's principal place of business in Great Britain was situated during the preceding six months. If the principal place was situated in different localities at different times during that period, the notice must be so advertised in relation to each of those localities or, if there was no such place within that period, in relation to the locality of the company's registered office (section 98). For details of the procedure at the meeting, see C11.2 *et seq.* below. As to the expenses of convening, advertisement and holding of the meeting, see Rule 4.62. See also C15.2 below and note in particular the duty of the chairman of the meeting to give details of any such expenses paid before the commencement of the winding up.

Statement of affairs and list of creditors

C4.7 The directors must lay before the creditors' meeting a full statement of the company's affairs and a list of creditors as required by section 99. (See also Rule 4.34, as amended, and Forms 4.19 and 4.20 which contain detailed procedure, including provisions as to expenses of preparing the statement. See also C15.2 below and note in particular the duty of the chairman of the meeting to give details of such expenses paid before the commencement of the winding up. Note also that Rule 4.53B requires the presiding director to report to the meeting on any material transaction occurring between the date of the statement and the date of the meeting.)

Appointment of liquidator

C4.8 The creditors' meeting may nominate a person to be the liquidator (who must be an authorised insolvency practitioner in relation to the company—section 230(3)). Subject to any application to the court, as below, the person so nominated will be the liquidator notwithstanding the nomination of any other person by the members' meeting. Where no person is nominated by the creditors' meeting, the person (if any) nominated by the members' meeting (see C4.3 above) will be the liquidator. Where different persons are nominated by the two meetings, any director, member or creditor may within seven days after the date of the nomination by the creditors, apply to the court for an order that the person nominated by the members should be the liquidator instead of or jointly with the creditors' nominee, or that some other person should be the liquidator (section 100).

The chairman of the members' (or, as the case may be, creditors') meeting by which the liquidator is appointed must certify the appointment after the appointee has confirmed in writing that he is an insolvency practitioner duly qualified to be the liquidator and that he consents so to act. The appointment is nevertheless effective from the date of the passing of the resolution for that appointment (Rule 4.101, as amended). A certificate from the chairman of the members' meeting is not necessary where the liquidator appointed by that meeting is replaced by another liquidator appointed on the same day by a creditors' meeting. The certificate must be delivered by the chairman to the liquidator and will form part of the records of the liquidation (Rule 4.101, Forms 4.27 to 4.30). In the case of a court appointment under section 100 (see above), it takes effect from the date of the order, but the order will not be issued unless and until he has given a similar confirmation (Rule 4.103).

As to (i) the authority of the liquidator to transfer assets for consideration *in specie*, see C12.3 below, and (ii) the appointment of a liquidation committee, see C4.11 below.

Position of 'caretaker liquidator'

C4.9   Where the members' meeting is held at short notice (see C3.7 and C4.5 above), there can be a gap of several days between that meeting and the creditors' meeting. Under the previous legislation it was held in *Re Centrebind Ltd [1966] 3 All ER 889* (see also *Roberts Petroleum v Kenny [1983] BCLC 28 (HL)* and *Saxton v Miles [1983] BCLC 70*) that pending the creditors' meeting, the person appointed as liquidator by the members had all the powers of a liquidator. Now there is a provision to prevent the liquidator appointed by the members from pre-empting the position of any other person whom the creditors might appoint as substantive liquidator and of the liquidation committee which may subsequently be appointed. Section 166 provides that the liquidator nominated by the members must not, except with the sanction of the court, during the period before the holding of the creditors' meeting exercise any of the powers conferred on a liquidator by section 165 (see C11.26 below) except the power to (*a*) take into his custody or under his control all the property to which the company is or appears to be entitled, (*b*) dispose of perishable goods or other goods, the value of which is likely to diminish if they are not immediately disposed of, and (*c*) do such other things as may be necessary for the protection of the company's assets. He must attend the creditors' meeting and report to it on *any* exercise by him of his powers. If the company fails to comply with its obligations as regards the convening of a creditors' meeting or the laying of a statement of affairs in accordance with sections 98 and 99 (see C4.6 and C4.7 above) the liquidator must, within seven days from the day of his nomination by the members or from the day on which he becomes aware of the default, whichever is the later, apply to the court for directions as to the manner in which the default is to be remedied (section 166).

Filing and notification requirements

C4.10   The requirements for the filing and advertisement of the winding-up resolution and the appointment of the liquidator are similar to those for a members' voluntary winding up as outlined in C3.8 above. Further, when a liquidator is appointed, the statement of affairs referred to in C4.7 above must be delivered by the directors to him; and he must file it with the Registrar of Companies within seven days (Rules 4.34 and 4.34A, and Form 4.20).

Appointment of liquidation committee

C4.11   The creditors at their meeting referred to above, or at any subsequent meeting, may appoint a liquidation committee of not more than five persons ('creditor members') in addition to any persons ('contributory members') appointed by the members' meeting; but the creditors may by resolution exclude from the committee all or any of the contributory members (in which case, those persons so excluded are disqualified from membership of the committee, unless the court otherwise directs). The court may on application appoint other persons to act as members of the committee in the place of the persons so excluded (section 101). As to the role of the committee, see C11.20 below. The committee must have at least three members before it can be established. Any creditor (other than one who is fully secured) is eligible for its membership so long as he has lodged a proof of his debt and the proof has not been wholly disallowed or rejected for the purposes of voting or dividend. No person can be a member both as a creditor and a contributory (as to the meaning of which see C5.30 below). A body corporate can only act by a person who has been duly authorised as its representative. Any other member of the committee may act by such a representative. Where a representative of the Deposit Protection Board exercises the right under section 58 of the Banking Act 1987 to be a member, he is regarded as an additional creditor member (Rule 4.152(2) to (7)). For further provisions see Rules 4.151 to 4.178 (including the new Rule 4.172A) and Forms 4.47 to 4.52 generally, and, for Scotland, Scottish Rules 4.40 to 4.65 and Forms 4.20 (Scot) to 4.24 (Scot). As to the right of the Deposit Protection Board to be represented on the committee in the winding up of a recognised bank or licensed deposit taker (now known as an 'authorised institution' under the Banking Act 1987), see section 58 of that Act and also Rule 4.152(7).

Conversion of members' to creditors' voluntary winding up

C4.12   Where, during the course of a winding up which has been initiated as a members' voluntary winding up (see C3.1 *et seq.* above), the liquidator forms the opinion that the company will be unable to pay its debts in full (together with interest at the official rate) within the period stated in the directors' declaration of solvency, he must summon a creditors' meeting for a day not later than the 28th day after the day on which he has formed that opinion. The requirements as to notices of the meeting are similar to those in the case of a creditors' voluntary winding up *ab initio* (see C.4.6 above). During the period before the day of the creditors' meeting, the liquidator must furnish creditors free of charge with such information concerning the company's affairs as they may reasonably require, which duty must be referred to in the notice of the meeting. He must also lay a statement of affairs (see Rule 4.34, and Forms 4.18 and 4.20) before the creditors' meeting and preside thereat (section 95). As from the day on which that meeting is held, the winding up becomes a creditors' voluntary winding up and the meeting is treated as if it was held under section 98 (see C4.6 above) (section 96) and as if any resolutions passed thereat for any appointment of a liquidator or establishment of a committee were resolutions of a section 98 creditors' meeting (section 102). Any appointment of a liquidator at that meeting is likewise required to be certified, filed and advertised. For detailed procedure as to the creditors' meeting, see C11.2 *et seq.* below.

Chapter 5: Initiation of winding up by the court

Introduction

C5.1   The initiation of a winding up by the court involves the presentation of a winding-up petition to the court under section 124 by the company itself (including any administrative receiver, administrator, or supervisor of a voluntary arrangement), the directors, a creditor, a contributory or, in certain cases, a Government department or independent authority on one or more of the grounds specified in section 122. A petition founded upon the company's inability to pay its debts may have been preceded by the service upon the company by a creditor, to whom a sum exceeding the prescribed amount (which at present is £750 but may be altered by statutory instrument) is due, of three weeks' notice of demand in the prescribed form under section 123 and the failure by the company to comply therewith. Inability to pay can, however, be proved by other means as well (see C5.22). The petition is followed by the court at its discretion making a winding-up order some weeks after the presentation. If the petition is dismissed or (subject to what is stated in C5.38) withdrawn, the proceedings lapse. Between presentation and the making of the winding-up order the court may appoint a provisional liquidator.

Upon the making of a winding-up order the Official Receiver becomes liquidator (as he also does during any vacancy in the office of liquidator), and he continues in office until another person becomes liquidator as stated in C5.47 below. However, in certain cases, the court may directly appoint as liquidator any person who is the administrator, or supervisor of a voluntary arrangement, in relation to the company (see C5.50 below). The winding-up order is followed by separate meetings of the creditors and contributories for the appointment of a substantive liquidator and, perhaps, a liquidation committee (see C5.49 and C5.50 below). Alternatively, the meetings can in certain circumstances be dispensed with and a liquidator may be appointed by the Secretary of State. The date of the presentation, the date of the appointment of a provisional liquidator and the date of the winding-up order are each relevant for different purposes of the winding up. As will be seen later, the procedure in Scotland is somewhat different.

The winding up is deemed to have commenced upon the presentation of the petition or, if the company was already in voluntary liquidation at that date, upon the passing of the voluntary winding-up resolution (section 129). (As to the significance of this relation back as regards the commencement of the winding up, see, for example, C5.38 below.)

Jurisdiction in a winding up

Companies registered in England and Wales

C5.2   The High Court has jurisdiction in all cases to wind up a company registered (as to the meaning of which see C5.7 below) in England and Wales. But, where the amount of its paid-up share capital does not exceed £120,000 (which limit may be varied by order under section 416) the county court of the district in which the company's registered office has been situated for the longest period during the preceding six months has concurrent jurisdiction, unless winding-up jurisdiction has been taken away from that county court and conferred on another by statutory instrument. A provincial district registry of the High Court has no jurisdiction to hear ordinary winding-up petitions unless it has been given specific power to do so (*Re Pleatfine [1983] BCLC 102*). Any appeal from the decision of the county court or a Registrar of the High Court lies to a single judge of the High Court and, thence, with the leave of the Court of Appeal, to the Court of Appeal (sections 117 to 119; Rules 7.1 to 7.42, 7.47 to 7.61; Forms 7.1 to 7.13). (See also *Re Galahurst Ltd [1989] BCLC 140.*)

In *Re Harrods (Buenos Aires) Ltd [1990] BCC 481*, which concerned an English company that traded exclusively in Argentina and whose only shareholders were two Swiss companies, one of the Swiss companies petitioned the High Court for relief under section 459 of the Companies Act 1985 (unfair prejudice) or alternatively, for a winding-up order, and the other Swiss company applied for the proceedings to be stayed on the ground that Argentina was the more appropriate forum for the proceedings. The High Court refused a stay and held that the jurisdiction of English courts with respect to a company registered in England is not affected by the fact that the acts giving rise to the grounds for the petition occurred in a foreign domicile. However, the Court of Appeal (*[1991] BCC 249*), in granting a stay, held that

(*a*)   the Civil Jurisdiction and Judgments Act 1982 (enacting the 1968 Brussels Convention), which obliges an English court to accept jurisdiction where the company concerned is 'domiciled' in England, did not apply as Argentina was not a party to the Brussels Convention,

(*b*)   the forum with which the proceedings had the most connection was Argentina, where the management of the company was conducted and the witnesses were based, and

(*c*)   justice did not require that a stay should not be granted even though there was no equivalent procedure to section 459 in Argentinian law.

A company registered in Scotland cannot be wound up in England and Wales. However, where the Registrar of Companies has issued a certificate of registration to the effect that the company is registered in England, the certificate is conclusive and the company can be wound up in England, notwithstanding that the certificate should not have been issued because the company had a registered office in Scotland instead of England (*Re Baby Moon (UK) Ltd [1985] PCC 103*).

In the case of a petition for the winding up of a company which is already under an administration order or a voluntary arrangement, the court in which it should be filed is that which made the order or to which the report of the nominee under the voluntary arrangement was filed (Rule 4.7 as amended; see also C5.33 below). As to the jurisdiction of the court in respect of a corporate member (being a registered company) of an insolvent partnership, see the Insolvent Partnerships Order 1994 (SI 1994 No 2421); see also C5.4 below.

Companies registered in Scotland

C5.3   The Court of Session has jurisdiction in all cases to wind up a company registered (as to the meaning of which see C5.7 below) in Scotland. When it is in vacation, its jurisdiction may be exercised by the vacation judge. Sheriff courts have concurrent jurisdiction corresponding to the jurisdiction of county courts in England and Wales (section 120), subject as stated in paragraphs (*a*), (*b*) and (*c*) of section 120(3) and in section 121. In the winding up of a society registered under the Industrial and Provident Societies Act 1965, the court having jurisdiction is the sheriff court within whose jurisdiction the society's registered office is situated (section 55 of that Act). A company registered in England and Wales cannot be wound up in Scotland.

Unregistered companies

C5.4   Partnerships and certain types of bodies, and oversea companies, not registered under the Companies Act 1985 or the previous companies legislation, may be wound up compulsorily as unregistered companies (as to the meaning of which see C5.8 below) in England and Wales or Scotland under the Insolvency Act 1986. For the purposes of determining jurisdiction as between England and Wales and Scotland, the body concerned (other than a partnership, as to which see the Insolvent Partnerships Order 1994 (SI 1994 No 2421)) is deemed to be registered in that part of Great Britain where its principal place of business is situated. (The principal place of business of an agricultural marketing board (see C5.8 below) is the address of its office as registered by the Minister—Agricultural Marketing Act 1958, Schedule 2.) If it is situated in both parts of Great Britain, the body is deemed to be registered in both parts. If, however, the body has a principal place of business in Northern Ireland it cannot be wound up under the Insolvency Act 1986 *unless* it also has a principal place of business in England and Wales and/or Scotland (sections 220 and 221, notwithstanding section 441(2) which provides 'subject . . . to any provision *expressly* relating to companies incorporated elsewhere than in Great Britain, nothing in this Act extends to Northern Ireland or applies to or in relation to companies registered or incorporated in Northern Ireland': *Re a Company (No 007946 of 1993), The Times, 18 November 1993*). This subject is dealt with further in C5.11 *et seq*. and C5.24 *et seq*. below.

Bodies other than registered companies

C5.5   Bodies other than registered companies (see C5.2 and C5.3 above) and those which may be wound up as unregistered companies (see C5.4 above) may, in appropriate circumstances, be wound up by the High Court under its inherent jurisdiction without bringing in all the detailed provisions of the 1986 Act or the Rules (*per* Morritt J in *Re Witney Town Football and Social Club* [*1993*] *BCC 874*; compare *In re William Denby & Sons Ltd Sick and Benevolent Fund* [*1971*] *1 WLR 973*; see also the discussion in *Re International Tin Council* [*1989*] *Ch 309*).

Cross-frontier recognition

C5.6   An order made by a court in any one part of the United Kingdom can be enforced in any other part as if it were made by a court exercising a corresponding jurisdiction in that other part; but this does not require the court in that other part to enforce any such order in relation to property situated in that other part (section 426(1) and (2); see also sections 197 (commission for receiving evidence in England and Wales, Scotland or Northern Ireland) and 198 (examination of persons in Scotland)).

The courts having jurisdiction in relation to insolvency law in any one part of the United Kingdom are required to assist courts having the corresponding jurisdiction in any other part of the United Kingdom or 'any relevant country or territory'. The quoted expression means any of the Channel Islands or the Isle of Man or any country or territory designated for the purpose by delegated legislation (section 426(4) and (11)). So far, the following have been so designated (SI 1986 No 2123): Anguilla, Australia, The Bahamas, Bermuda, Botswana, Canada, Cayman Islands, Falkland Islands, Gibraltar, Hong Kong, Republic of Ireland, Montserrat, New Zealand, St Helena, Turks and Caicos Islands, Tuvalu and Virgin Islands. As to the Channel Islands, it was held, in the context of the Bankruptcy Act 1914 (now repealed), that *désastre* proceedings in Jersey (which also apply to companies incorporated there and to assets outside Jersey) were 'matters of bankruptcy' for the purposes of section 122 of that Act (orders in aid): *Re a debtor, ex parte Viscount of the Royal Courts of Justice* [*1980*] *3 All ER 665*. (For an excellent summary of the present insolvency law of Jersey, including cross-border aspects, see 'Jersey insolvency law and practice' by Michael Wilkins, Viscount of the Royal Courts of Justice, in *Insolvency Law and Practice 1989*, page 98.)

Upon receipt of a request for assistance from any such foreign court, the court in the relevant part of the United Kingdom may apply, in relation to any matters specified in the request, the insolvency law which is applicable by either court in relation to comparable matters falling within its jurisdiction. Further, pursuant to section 442, certain provisions of the Act have been extended to Guernsey by SI 1989 No 2409; and by section 441, as supplemented by SI 1989 No 2405, a limited number of provisions of the Act have been extended to Northern Ireland.

Subject as above, the general attitude of courts in England to foreign insolvency proceedings appears to be as follows.

(1) Where such proceedings are pending in a court of the country in which the company is incorporated, that court is regarded as the principal forum for controlling winding up. The English court carries out any winding up commenced in England as an ancillary winding up in accordance with English law, while working in harmony with the foreign court.

(2) Until there is a winding up in England, the English court will probably recognise the status of the foreign liquidator or trustee as having the same authority to represent the company in England as he has in the foreign country.

(3) No other effect of the foreign winding up affecting assets in England is likely to be recognised. For example, the effect of the foreign insolvency law on antecedent or subsequent transactions or a stay under that law on creditors' rights is unlikely to be recognised in relation to English assets.

In *Felixstowe Dock & Railway Co v United States Lines Inc* (*FT Com Law Reports, 7 April 1987, QBD Commercial Court*), a plaintiff had obtained a *Mareva* injunction against the defendant, a USA corporation, restraining it from removing its assets out of the jurisdiction. The court was requested to set aside the injunction on the ground that reorganisation proceedings in bankruptcy under Chapter 11 of the USA Federal Bankruptcy Code had been commenced in the USA in respect of the defendant and this had the effect of restraining all creditors from enforcing their claims by judicial action. It was submitted that without the English assets the administration of the Chapter 11 scheme would be prevented and that the English court should accede to the request on the ground of international comity. The court declined to do so stating that irreparable harm would be done to the English creditors if the assets were removed from the country and that it appeared unlikely that in a reverse situation the US court would vacate local claims in favour of the English court.

In *Re D (In Liquidation)* [1985] *PCC 279*, a company was being wound up under the laws of the Cayman Islands. The liquidators applied, pursuant to the provisions of the companies legislation of the Islands corresponding to section 236 (private examination—see A4.19 PART A: GENERAL above) and RSC Ord 39, rr 1 and 2, for an order issuing letters to judicial authorities in Switzerland requesting assistance for the examination of the company's auditors in Switzerland. The application was refused on the ground that the court had no power to make the request. The powers under those provisions were of a purely fact-finding nature and were not susceptible to such a request. In any event, if a similar request was received from the Swiss court, the Cayman Islands court would have refused it.

Where a foreign corporation is in liquidation under the law of the place of incorporation, the English court may, under the principles of private international law, either (i) order a winding up in England but direct that the English winding up be ancillary to the main winding up in the place of incorporation, or (ii) refrain from making an English winding-up order but recognise the authority of the liquidator appointed by the foreign court to deal with assets and claims in England. The latter course may be appropriate only in relatively straightforward cases.

Where the winding up is ancillary, the court may restrict the powers of the English liquidator to collecting the English assets, settling a list of creditors and paying preferential creditors and making other approved payments, with a direction that the balance of the funds realised in England be remitted to the foreign liquidator with the intent that the claims of the other creditors, including English creditors, be dealt with on an equal footing in one single liquidation.

In suitable cases, the English court may refuse to make a winding-up order and instead allow the foreign liquidator to recover the assets in England (*Re Jarvis Conklin Mortgage Co* (*1895*) *11 TLR 373*).

However, before ordering an ancillary winding up or recognising the authority of the foreign liquidator (instead of making a full winding-up order in England), the English court must be satisfied that the foreign court is, in the interests of justice, the appropriate forum for the liquidation and that the English creditors will be able to rank *pari passu* with the other creditors of the same class in the foreign liquidation.

(See *Dicey and Morris, The Conflict of Laws* (twelfth edition, 1993) particularly Rule 160 in that book; *Re English, Scottish and Australian Chartered Bank* [*1893*] *3 Ch 385*; the *Felixstowe* case (above); *Re Matheson Brothers Ltd* (*1884*) *27 Ch D 225*; *Re National Benefit Assurance Co* [*1927*] *3 DLR 289*; *Tong Aik* (*Far East*) *Ltd v Eastern Minerals & Trading* (*1959*) *Ltd* [*1965*] *2 MLJ 149*; *Re Union Bank of Calcutta* (*1850*) *3 De G & SSM 253*; *Re Federal Bank of Australia Ltd* (*1893*) *68 LT 728*; *Re Commercial Bank of South Australia* (*1886*) *33 Ch D 174*; *Sedgwick Collins and Co Ltd v Russia Insurance Co of Petrograd* [*1926*] *1 KB 1*. Cf. *Re Suidair International Airways Ltd* [*1951*] *Ch 165*, where the English winding up was ancillary to the South African liquidation, and it was held that the court should administer the assets of the South African company within the jurisdiction in accordance with the relevant English law. This case appears to be inconsistent with *Re Commercial Bank of South Australia*, *Re Federal Bank of Australia Ltd* and *Sedgwick Collins and Co Ltd* (above) which were not referred to in that case and which reveal a more restrictive scope of ancillary winding up. For an excellent analysis of this subject, see 'International Insolvency: Ancillary Winding-up and the Foreign Corporation' by P St.J Smart in *International and Comparative Law Quarterly*, volume 39, page 827, October 1990.)

An English court will not seek to enforce extra-territorially the effect of an English winding up on foreign assets or proceedings, but may restrain any person within its jurisdiction, irrespective of whether he has lodged his claim in the English winding up, from ignoring the effect by continuing foreign proceedings (except insolvency proceedings) or seeking to recover foreign funds or assets. See, for example, *Re Vocalion (Foreign)*

Ltd [1932] 2 Ch 196; *Re North Carolina Estate Co (1889) 5 TLR 328*; see also the *Paramount* case referred to at C10.2 below and the comments thereon. Such a person may, in certain circumstances, also be required to surrender to the English liquidator any funds or assets of the company recovered by means of foreign legal proceedings, particularly where he has lodged his claim in the English winding up (*Re Oriental Inland Steam Co (1874) 9 Ch App 557*; cf. *Re Kidd (1861) 4 LT 344*; see also *Banco de Portugal v Waddell (1880) 5 App Cas 161*; *Re Standard Insurance Co [1968] Qd St R 118 (Australia)*. This does not, however, apply to any recovery made abroad under a mortgage, charge, lien or other security (*Moor v Anglo-Italian Bank (1879) 10 Ch D 681*; *Minna Craig Steamship Co v Chartered Mercantile Bank of India, London and China [1897] 1 QB 460*), or under any attachment or execution proceedings completed before the commencement of the English winding up (*Re Somes (1896) 3 Mans 131*; *Callender Sykes & Co v Lagos Colonial Secretary [1891] AC 460*). See also A5.3 PART A: GENERAL and C14.27 below.

Subject to the preceding paragraph, English winding-up law follows the approach of universality of assets (wherever situated) (*Re International Tin Council [1987] Ch 419 at 447*)—although the extent to which a foreign court will recognise this in relation to assets within its jurisdiction may be limited—and universality of assets (wherever arising) (*Re Azoff-Don Commercial Bank [1954] Ch 315*) on a *pari passu* basis (*Re Rafidain Bank [1992] BCC 376*) except that claims of foreign states of a fiscal or penal nature are not enforced (*Government of India v Taylor [1955] AC 491*).

Bodies which may be wound up by the court

Registered companies

C5.7   The following may be wound up under the Insolvency Act 1986 as 'companies' (as distinct from unregistered companies).

(*a*)   A company (whether limited by shares or by guarantee, or unlimited) formed and registered under the Companies Act 1985, the Companies Act 1929 or the Companies Acts 1948 to 1983 (sections 675, 735 and 735A of the 1985 Act and sections 73 and 251 (last part) of the Insolvency Act 1986).

(*b*)   A company (whether limited by shares or by guarantee or unlimited) formed and registered under the Joint Stock Companies Act 1856; the Joint Stock Companies Acts 1856, 1857; the Joint Stock Banking Companies Act 1857, the Act to enable Joint Stock Banking Companies to be formed on the principle of limited liability (but not the Joint Stock Companies Act 1844); the Companies Act 1862; or the Companies (Consolidation) Act 1908—not being a company registered thereunder in what was then Ireland (sections 675, 735 and 735A of the Companies Act 1985 and section 251 (last part) of the Insolvency Act 1986).

(*c*)   A company (whether limited by shares or by guarantee, or unlimited) registered but not formed under either of the 1929 and

1948 Acts mentioned in (*a*) above or any of the Acts up to and including the 1908 Act mentioned in (*b*) above (other than the 1985 Act), not being a company registered in what was then Ireland (sections 676 and 735A of the 1985 Act).

(*d*) An unlimited company registered or reregistered as limited in pursuance of the Companies Act 1879, section 57 of the 1908 Act, section 16 of the 1929 Act, section 16 of the 1948 Act or section 44 of the Companies Act 1967 or Part II of the 1985 Act (sections 677 and 735A of the 1985 Act).

(*e*) A company in existence on 2 November 1862, including any company registered under any of the Joint Stock Companies Acts referred to in (*b*) above or formed after that date in pursuance of any Act (other than the 1985 Act) or of letters patent or being otherwise duly constituted according to law, which has been reregistered under the 1985 Act (sections 680 *et seq.*, including 689, and section 735A, of the 1985 Act and paragraph 6 of Schedule 21 thereto).

Unregistered companies

C5.8   An unregistered company may be wound up by the court under Part V (sections 220 to 229) but cannot be wound up voluntarily (section 221(4)). Subject to certain variations (and further variations in the case of partnerships and oversea companies and certain special types of bodies), all the provisions of the Insolvency Act 1986 and the Companies Act 1985 regarding winding up apply to the winding up of unregistered companies.

'Unregistered company' includes any insolvent partnership if the Insolvent Partnerships Order 1994 (SI 1994 No 2421), replacing, with effect from 1 December 1994, the Insolvent Partnerships Order 1986 (SI 1986 No 2142), applies, any association and any company except (i) a railway company incorporated by Act of Parliament and (ii) a company registered in any part of the United Kingdom under any of the enactments referred to in (*a*) to (*e*) under C5.7 (*Registered companies*) above or any other past or present legislation relating to companies in Great Britain (section 220 as modified by the 1994 Order and, previously, the 1986 Order).

The definition of 'unregistered companies' mentioned above is not exhaustive. Among the bodies which have been ordered to be wound up as unregistered companies are the following.

(*a*) Companies incorporated by special Acts of Parliament (*Re South London Fish Market (1888) 39 Ch D 324*; *Re Barton-upon-Humber Water Co (1889) 42 Ch D 585*), except railway companies (see above).

(*b*) Companies incorporated by Royal Charter (*Re Oriental Bank Corporation (1884) 28 Ch D 634*; *Re Bank of South Australia [1895] 1 Ch 578*).

(*c*) Foreign and colonial companies with assets and liabilities in England (*Re Mercantile Bank of Australia [1892] 2 Ch 204*; *North Australian Territory Co v Goldsborough Co (1889) 61 LT 716*).

(*d*) Friendly Societies (*Re Victoria Society, Knottingley* [*1913*] *1 Ch 167*).

(*e*) An association for purchase and division of an estate (*Re Osmondthorpe Hall Society* [*1913*] *WN 243*).

By contrast, in *Re International Tin Council* [*1987*] *BCLC 272*, Millett J held that the International Tin Council, a body comprising sovereign states and constituted under the International Tin Agreement, which provided that the Council should have a legal personality, could not be wound up as an unregistered company. His reasons were as follows.

(1) Parliament could not have intended an English court to enforce con-tributions from member states under section 671(2) of the Com-panies Act 1985 (now section 226(2) of the Insolvency Act 1986) since that would require the court to interpret and enforce a treaty between sovereign states. This was outside the court's jurisdiction (*Re Secretary of State for India (1859) 13 Moo PCC 22* at 75).

(2) To make a winding-up order would mean one member state assum-ing the management of the enterprise subject to its domestic law.

(3) The treaty did not have the force of law in the United Kingdom as it had not been enacted as part of domestic law by Parliament. The Council's status was derived from English domestic law and was governed only by a statutory instrument made in 1972 which granted the Council immunity from legal proceedings except where an arbi-tration award was being enforced. The winding-up petition was not an enforcement of the award since the petition precluded creditors from enforcing awards and substituted instead the right to partici-pate in the distribution of assets on insolvency.

Millett J's decision was upheld by the Court of Appeal (see [*1989*] *Ch 309*).

A football and social club is not, depending on its constitution, rules and activities, 'any association' and cannot be wound up under the 1986 Act (*In Re St James' Club (1852) 2 De GM & G 383*) even if it is not simply a social club but a body set up for the purpose of professional association football (*Re Witney Town Football and Social Club* [*1993*] *BCC 874*); but see C5.5 above.

The Insolvency Act 1986 also enables the following to be wound up by the court as unregistered companies.

(A) *A partnership*, whatever the number of its partners, provided that it has, or at any time had, in England and Wales either a principal place of business or (in the case of a creditors' petition) a place of business at which business is or has been carried on in the course of which the petition debt (or part thereof) arose; but so that if it has not carried on business in England and Wales at any time in the period of three years ending with the date of the presentation of the petition it cannot be wound up there, unless it has a place of busi-ness in Scotland or Northern Ireland and it had a place of business in England and Wales or any time in the period of one year or three years respectively ending with the date of the presentation of the petition (sections 117 and 220, as modified by the Insolvent Partnerships Order 1994 (SI 1994 No 2421), replacing, with effect from 1 December 1994, the Insolvent Partnerships Order 1986 (SI 1986 No 2142)). Where a partnership is wound up, its partners would become contributories (see sections 74 to 83 and also C5.30, C12.1 and C12.20 below) but their liability to contribute might be unlimited. (*Note:* in addition, or alternatively, its individual members may be made bankrupt and its corporate members can be wound up; but see the *Marr* case referred to in C5.19 below.)

(B)   *An oversea company*, being a company incorporated outside Great Britain which has been carrying on but ceases to carry on business in Great Britain. Such a company may be wound up notwithstanding that it has been dissolved or has otherwise ceased to exist under or by virtue of the laws of the country of its incorporation (section 225). It would appear that section 225 is not exhaustive, and an oversea company may also be wound up by virtue of what is stated in(*c*) above notwithstanding that it has not been carrying on or has not ceased to carry on business in Great Britain, provided that it has not been dissolved (see also C5.11 below). It is not necessary to show that the oversea company has a principal place of business within Great Britain (although the location of a place of business may help to determine the part of Great Britain whose court has jurisdiction—see C5.2 *et seq.* (*Jurisdiction in a winding up*) above). A petitioner must show that the company has some assets within the jurisdiction and that there are claimants for those assets over whom the court has jurisdiction. He need not show that the assets will be distributable by a liquidator among creditors generally; it is sufficient that the relevant assets will be available to the petitioning creditor (*Re Compania Merabello San Nicholas S A [1973] Ch 75*).

Where the only alleged asset is a cause of action, that is sufficient to give the court jurisdiction without proof that the action is certain to succeed (*Re Allobrogia Steamship Corporation [1978] 3 All ER 423*). The asset does not have to be in the company's ownership. It is sufficient if there is a reasonable possibility of the petitioner obtaining payments from a source of assets directly related to his employment by the company, such as the Redundancy Fund (now part of the National Insurance Fund) (*Re Eloc Electro-Optieck and Communicatie B V [1981] 2 All ER 1111*). These points have been summed up in *Re a Company (No 00359 of 1987) [1987] 3 WLR 339* (also reported as *International Westminster Bank Plc v Okeanos Maritime Corp [1987] BCLC 450*): there should be a proper connection with the jurisdiction, for example, a reasonable possibility of benefit to some or all of the creditors (see also *Re Azoff-Don Commercial Bank [1954] Ch 315*; cf. *Banque des Marchands de Moscou v Kindersley [1951] Ch 112*).

In the *Okeanos* case referred to above, the court held that the presence of assets in England was not essential to confer jurisdiction on the court to wind up a foreign company. The court could wind up a foreign company if there was sufficient connection with England and a reasonable possibility that benefit would accrue to the company's creditors from the winding up. On the facts, there was evidence indicating that the company had sufficient connection with England to confer jurisdiction, since, in particular, the loan agreement with the bank was negotiated and executed in England and required performance in England, and there was evidence to suggest that the company was effectively managed in England either directly or through another company and that it carried on business in England. Moreover, no other jurisdiction was more appropriate for the winding up of that company, since the connection with England was closer than with the country of incorporation (Liberia), or with the country where the vessel was registered (Greece). Furthermore, there was a reasonable possibility that the liquidator might be successful in bringing an action under sections 213 (fraudulent trading) and 214 (wrongful trading) against some members of the family who controlled the company resident in England which would benefit the creditors.

In *Re a Company (No 003102 of 1991), ex parte Nyckeln Finance Co Ltd* [1991] *BCLC 539*, a winding-up petition founded on a large debt was presented against a company incorporated in Guernsey. The petition alleged that a large part of its business was carried on in England through a representative resident in England, although it had not delivered particulars of its place of business in England to the Registrar of Companies. It had substantial assets, largely in Portugal. The petition debt represented loans made by the petitioner to the company which had been negotiated and drawn down in London. The company's business was conducted from premises in England. It was held that the court had jurisdiction to wind up the company. The fact that the business was carried on in England was a sufficiently close connection between the company and England. It was not necessary to show that the company had assets within the jurisdiction. No other jurisdiction would be appropriate for the winding up of the company. The winding-up process in Guernsey was outmoded and there was no connection with Portugal apart from the presence of assets there. The English jurisdiction was more appropriate since not only the representative of the company was present and resident in England but also the petitioner was present in England. There was a reasonable possibility of benefit accruing to the creditors since the petitioner would be unlikely to recover anything if a winding-up order were not made, whereas if it were made there was a reasonable chance that the petitioner would recover something.

The core requirements for the court's jurisdiction to wind up an overseas company were summarised in *Re Real Estate Development Co* [1991] *BCLC 210* as follows:

(1)   there must be sufficient connection with England and Wales but this does not necessarily have to consist in the presence of assets within the jurisdiction;

(2)   there must be a reasonable possibility that a winding-up order would benefit those applying for it;

(3)   the court must be able to exercise jurisdiction over one or more persons interested in the distribution of the company's assets.

In that case, on the facts the only connection with England and Wales was the foreign judgment which had been registered with the High Court, shares held by the overseas company in an English company which had non-UK assets and directors, and which carried on a non-UK business, and the possibility of an action under section 172 of the Law of Property Act 1925 (transfer of property with intent to defraud creditors). It was held that those facts were not sufficient to confer jurisdiction on the court to wind up the overseas company.

Certain United Kingdom and overseas bodies may be wound up by virtue of special enactments notwithstanding that they are not 'companies'. The following are some examples.

(i)   *Agricultural Marketing Boards* established as bodies corporate under the Agricultural Marketing Act 1958 (see Schedule 2 thereto). These can be wound up as unregistered companies.

(ii)   *Co-operative societies* registered under the Industrial and Provident Societies Act 1965. These may be wound up as if they are 'companies' (see section 55 of that Act; and see, as to the position under the previous insolvency provisions, *Re Norse Self Build Association Ltd* [1985] *BCLC 219*; *Re Belfast Tailors Company Partnership* [1909] *1 IR 49*).

(iii)   *Credit unions*, i.e. saving and mutual benefit societies registrable under the Industrial and Provident Societies Act 1965 (section 20(2) of the Credit Unions Act 1979) (see also (ii) above).

(iv)   *Authorised institutions or former authorised institutions* under the Banking Act 1987. Section 92 empowers the Bank of England to present a winding-up petition in certain circumstances (see C5.16 below).

(v)   *Investment businesses.* Under section 72 of the Financial Services Act 1986 a petition for winding up may in certain circumstances be presented by the Secretary of State in respect of, *inter alia*, an 'authorised person' or 'appointed representative' which is a registered company, an unregistered company (including a partnership) or an oversea company.

Grounds for the petition

C5.9   Subject to the enactments applicable to special types of companies or bodies (see C5.12 *et seq*. below), the petition must be founded on one or more of the grounds specified in section 122 (as read with section 123) or, in relation to an unregistered or oversea company, in section 221(5) and (7) (as read with sections 222 to 224—see also section 225).

Registered companies—grounds in ordinary cases

C5.10   The grounds specified in section 122, as read with section 124A, inserted by section 60 of the Companies Act 1989 (which came into force on 21 February 1990, and extends to Scotland) are as follows.

(1)   (*a*)   that the company has by special resolution resolved that the company be wound up by the court;

    (*b*)   that, being a public company which was registered as such on its original incorporation, the company has not been issued with a certificate under section 117 of the Companies Act 1985 (public company share capital requirements) and more than a year has expired since it was so registered;

    (*c*)   that it is an old public company, within the meaning of the Companies Consolidation (Consequential Provisions) Act 1985;

    (*d*)   that the company does not commence its business within a year from its incorporation or suspends its business for a whole year;

    (*e*)   that (except in the case of a private company limited by shares or by guarantee, by virtue of SI 1992 No 1699) the number of members is reduced below two;

    (*f*)   that the company is unable to pay its debts (see C5.22 *et seq.* below); or

    (*g*)   that the court is of the opinion that it is just and equitable that the company should be wound up (see C5.26 below).

(2)   Where the petition is presented by the Secretary of State under section 124A referred to above, that it is expedient in the public interest that the company should be wound up, his view to be based on the reports and information referred to in that section.

(3)   In Scotland, that the company is one which the Court of Session has jurisdiction to wind up, and there is subsisting a floating charge over property comprised in the company's property and undertaking, and the court is satisfied that the security of the creditor entitled to the benefit of the floating charge is in jeopardy (which is deemed to be the case if the court is satisfied that events have occurred or are about to occur which render it unreasonable in the creditor's interests that the company should retain power to dispose of the property concerned).

Unregistered companies and oversea companies—grounds in ordinary cases (excluding partnerships)

C5.11   The grounds mentioned in section 221 (which extends to Scotland) are as follows.

(1) (*a*)   That the company is dissolved, or has ceased to carry on business, or is carrying on business only for the purposes of winding up its affairs;

  (*b*)   that the company is unable to pay its debts within the meaning of section 222, 223 or 224 (see C5.22 *et seq.* below); or

  (*c*)   that the court is of the opinion that it is just and equitable that the company should be wound up (see C5.26 below).

(2) In Scotland, in the case of an unregistered (including an oversea) company which the Court of Session has jurisdiction to wind up, that there is a subsisting floating charge over property comprised in the company's property and undertaking, and the court is satisfied that the security of the creditor entitled to the benefit of the floating charge is in jeopardy (which is deemed to be the case if the court is satisfied that events have occurred or are about to occur which render it unreasonable in the creditor's interests that the company should retain power to dispose of the property concerned).

Registered, unregistered and oversea companies—grounds in special cases

(1) *Agricultural Marketing Boards*

C5.12   The boards are corporate bodies set up under regulatory 'schemes' established by the Agricultural Marketing Act 1958. The 'schemes' must provide for the winding up of the boards and, for that purpose, may apply sections 220 to 229, except section 223. Thus, if those sections are applied, a board may be wound up as an unregistered company on any of the grounds mentioned in C5.11 above except that the reference to section 223 should be ignored (see also C5.24 below). A board is not automatically deemed dissolved merely by virtue of revocation of the appropriate 'scheme' (Schedule 2 to the 1958 Act).

(2) *Registered co-operative societies*

C5.13   These can be wound up as unregistered companies on any of the grounds mentioned in section 221 (see C5.11 above) (as read with sections 222 and 224). A society may also be wound up by an instrument of dissolution signed by at least three-quarters in number of the members (section 55 of the Industrial and Provident Societies Act 1965) (see also C5.24 below).

(3) *Subsidiaries of the British Steel Corporation*

C5.14   These are registered companies and can be wound up as such on any of the grounds mentioned in section 122 (see C5.10 above) (as read with section 123) save that ground (*e*) (number of members reduced below two) in section 122(1) does not apply (Schedule 4, paragraph 9 of the Iron and Steel Act 1982) (see also C5.22 below).

(4) *Credit unions*

C5.15 These can be wound up as unregistered companies on any of the grounds mentioned in section 221 (see C5.10 above) (as read with sections 222 to 224). Further, they can also be wound up on a petition by the Registrar of Friendly Societies based on any of the following grounds:

(*a*) that the union cannot pay sums due to its members other than by obtaining further subscriptions or defaulting on its obligations to other creditors;

(*b*) that it does not comply with the provisions of the Industrial and Provident Societies Acts 1965 to 1978 (see C5.8 above) or the Credit Unions Act 1979;

(*c*) that there is no longer a common bond between its members; or

(*d*) that it appears to the Registrar that a winding up would be in the public interest or be just and equitable having regard to the interests of the union.

(Section 20(2) of the Credit Unions Act 1979). (See also C5.24 below.)

(5) *Authorised or former authorised institutions*

C5.16 These (which before the coming into force of the Banking Act 1987 on 1 October 1987 were known as 'recognised banks and licensed deposit takers') can be wound up as registered companies or unregistered or oversea companies, including partnerships and limited partnerships (as the case may be) on any of the grounds applicable (that is, those mentioned in section 122 (see C5.10 above) as read with section 123, or those mentioned in section 221 (see C5.11 above) as read with sections 222, 223 and 224, as the case may be). (See also C5.22 *et seq*. below). In addition, they can (notwithstanding that they have ceased to be authorised) be wound up on the petition of the Bank of England if—

(*a*) the institution is unable to pay its debts within the meaning of section 123 or, as the case may be, section 221; or

(*b*) the court is of the opinion that it is just and equitable that the institution should be wound up.

For the purposes of (*a*) above, the institution is deemed to be unable to pay its debts if it defaults in an obligation to pay a sum due and payable to a depositor (section 92 of the Banking Act 1987 (as amended)).

(6) *Insurance companies*

C5.17 These can be wound up as registered companies or unregistered companies (including partnerships—see C5.19 below) or oversea companies (as the case may be) on any of the grounds applicable (that is, those mentioned in section 122 (see C5.10 above) as read with section 123, or those mentioned in section 221 (see C5.11 above) as read with sections 222, 223 and 224, as the case may be). (See also C5.22 *et seq.* below.) Further, an insurance company to which Part II of the Insurance Companies Act 1982 (as amended) applies (i.e. one which is not a member of Lloyds, or a friendly society or the insurance business of a trade union or employers' association, and which does not pay any benefits in kind) may be wound up on the petition of the Secretary of State based on any of the following grounds:

(*a*)   that the company is unable to pay its debts within the meaning of section 123 or sections 222 to 224 (as the case may be) of the Insolvency Act 1986 (see C5.22 *et seq.* below);

(*b*)   that it has failed to comply with its obligations under the Insurance Companies Act 1974 or 1982 or the Insurance Companies Acts repealed by the 1982 Act (including, for example, requirements as to maintenance of assets and as to other financial discipline);

(*c*)   that it has failed to keep or produce accounts under the companies legislation and the Secretary of State cannot ascertain its financial position; or

(*d*)   that the Secretary of State thinks it expedient, and the court thinks it just and equitable, that it be wound up.

(Section 54 of the Insurance Companies Act 1982 (as amended)).

(7)   *Investment businesses*

C5.18   These can be wound up as registered companies or unregistered companies (including partnerships—see C5.19 below) or oversea companies on any of the grounds applicable (see C5.10 and C5.11 above). Under section 72 of the Financial Services Act 1986, the Secretary of State has power (in the case of a member of a recognised self-regulating organisation or a recognised professional body, only with its consent) to present a winding-up petition in respect of an 'authorised person' or an 'appointed representative' (being a registered company, unregistered company (including oversea company) or a partnership—see C5.19 below) on any of the following grounds:

 (i)   that it is unable to pay its debts (within the meaning of section 123 or 221 (as the case may be) of the Insolvency Act 1986—see C5.22 *et seq.* below);

 (ii)   that it has defaulted in an obligation to pay a sum due and payable under an investment agreement—this is deemed to be inability to pay debts; or

(iii)   that the court considers that winding up would be just and equitable (see C5.26 below).

(8)   *Partnerships*

C5.19   A partnership (provided that it validly exists, as distinct from one presumed to exist by estoppel—see *Re C & M Ashberg (CA), The Times,*

17 July 1990) may be wound up in England and Wales as an unregistered company, regardless of the number of partners (section 420, and section 220, as modified by the Insolvent Partnerships Order 1994 (SI 1994 No 2421) ('the Order'), replacing, with effect from 1 December 1994, the Insolvent Partnerships Order 1986 (SI 1986 No 2142)). In addition, or in the alternative, there may be presented against the partners separately an 'insolvency petition' (i.e. a winding-up petition in the case of a corporate partner, being a registered company, or a bankruptcy petition in the case of an individual partner—article 2 of the Order).

Some of the provisions of the Act relating to the winding up of an unregistered company have, in their application to a partnership, been modified by the 1994 Order. They have been differently modified to deal with the following different situations:

(*a*)   a winding-up petition by a creditor, a responsible insolvency practitioner or the Secretary of State, where no 'insolvency petition' (that is, a winding-up petition or a bankruptcy petition, as the case may be) is presented by the petitioner against a member or former member of the partnership in his capacity as such (Article 7 of the 1994 Order);

(*b*)   a winding-up petition by a creditor where insolvency petitions are also presented by him against one or more members or former members of the partnership in their capacity as such (Article 8 of the 1994 Order);

(*c*)   a winding-up petition by a member where no insolvency petition is presented by him against a member of the partnership in his capacity as such (Article 9 of the 1994 Order);

(*d*)   a winding-up petition by a member where insolvency petitions are presented by him against the partnership and against all its members in their capacity as such (Article 10 of the 1994 Order).

The provisions as modified by Articles 8 and 10 (see (*b*) and (*d*) above) also apply to an insolvent partnership being wound up as an unregistered company where another partnership or other body which may be wound up as an unregistered company is a member of the first mentioned partnership. In that case, the other partnership or body is treated as a corporate member of the first mentioned partnership (Article 12 of the 1994 Order).

The grounds on which a partnership may be wound up are as follows.

In situations (a) and (c) above. If

(i)   it is dissolved, or has ceased to carry on business, or is carrying on business only for the purposes of winding up its affairs;

(ii)   it (i.e. as an entity, as distinct from any individual member of it—*Re Hough (a bankrupt) (Ch D), 10 April 1990*) is unable to pay its debts; or

(iii)   the court is of the opinion that it is just and equitable that the partnership should be wound up.

In situations (*b*) *and* (*d*) *above.* If it is unable to pay its debts.

Under the now superseded Insolvent Partnerships Order 1986, it was
held in *Re Marr [1990] 2 All ER 880 (CA)* that a creditor whose debt and
costs had been paid in full by the partnership since the winding-up order
against the partnership was not entitled to a bankruptcy order against the
individual partners. Giving judgment in that case, Nicholls LJ said that on
the facts, subsections (1) and (2A) of section 271 of the Insolvency Act
1986, as amended by the Insolvent Partnerships Order 1986, led to opposite results. Under subsection (1), the court was precluded from making a
bankruptcy order where the debt had been paid off, whereas subsection
(2A) provided that once a winding-up order was made, a court had no
discretion but to make bankruptcy orders against the partners. The
proper inference was that subsection (1) was intended to apply to
bankruptcy petitions brought for the concurrent winding up of an insolvent partnership and the making of insolvency orders against its
members, in the same way as it normally applied to bankruptcy petitions.
To read subsection (2A) as qualifying subsection (1), so that a bankruptcy
order had to be made even when the partnership debt on which the
bankruptcy petition was founded had been paid, would be to render the
scope of subsection (1) negligible. In his Lordship's view section 271, as
modified, was to be construed and applied as follows. When the court was
hearing a bankruptcy petition it had to consider first whether it was satisfied in the terms set out in subsection (1) (i.e. that a debt has been neither
paid nor secured or compounded for). If it was not so satisfied, then the
petition failed at the first hurdle.

The new Insolvent Partnerships Order 1994 (SI 1994 No 2421) has
modified section 125 (power of court on hearing winding-up petition—
see C5.42 below) and section 271 (see the previous paragraph) so as to
give the court considerable flexibility in rationalising a multiplicity of
insolvency proceedings against an insolvent partnership and against its
members (see Schedules 4 and 6 to that Order).

(9)   *Corporate members of an insolvent partnership*

C5.20   A registered company which is a member of an insolvent partnership ('corporate member') (or an insolvent partnership or other body
which the court has jurisdiction to wind up as an unregistered company
and which is itself a member of an insolvent partnership being so wound
up) may be wound up if the corporate member (or the member) is unable
to pay its debts within the meaning of section 123 (see C5.22 and C5.23
below), as specially modified in this context by the 1994 Order referred to
in C5.19 above.

Grounds most frequently relied on

C5.21   The grounds most frequently relied on are inability to pay debts
and the 'just and equitable' ground. These grounds (with modifications in

some of the special cases) are examined below in greater detail by reference to the various types of companies and bodies mentioned above.

Inability to pay debts

(1) *Registered companies—all cases*

C5.22 Section 123, as read with section 122(1)(f), applies (subject to the modifications of insolvency-related grounds in special cases of registered companies dealt with in C5.12 to C5.20 above). Section 123 defines inability to pay debts as follows:

'(1) A company is deemed unable to pay its debts—

(*a*) if a creditor (by assignment or otherwise) to whom the company is indebted in a sum exceeding £750 then due has served on the company, by leaving it at the company's registered office, a written demand (in the prescribed form) requiring the company to pay the sum due and the company has for three weeks thereafter neglected to pay the sum or to secure or compound for it to the reasonable satisfaction of the creditor, or

(*b*) if, in England and Wales, execution or other process issued on a judgment, decree or order of any court in favour of a creditor of the company is returned unsatisfied in whole or in part, or

(*c*) if, in Scotland, the *induciae* of a charge for payment on an extract decree, or an extract registered bond, or an extract registered protest, have expired without payment being made, or

(*d*) if, in Northern Ireland, a certificate of unenforceability has been granted in respect of a judgment against the company, or

(*e*) if it is proved to the satisfaction of the court that the company is unable to pay its debts as they fall due.

(2) A company is also deemed unable to pay its debts if it is proved to the satisfaction of the court that the value of the company's assets is less than the amount of its liabilities, taking into account its contingent and prospective liabilities.

(3) The money sum for the time being specified in subsection (1)(*a*) is subject to increase or reduction by order under section 416 in Part XV.'

With regard to subsection (1)(*a*) above, the form of statutory demand prescribed is Form 4.1 and must comply with Rules 4.4, 4.5 and 4.6 as to content. Where the debt is in a foreign currency, the demand is valid notwithstanding that it is not made in sterling or the rate of exchange or the date of conversion into sterling is not specified (see *In re a Debtor (No 51-SD-1991) [1992] 1 WLR 1294*, a bankruptcy case where Morritt J was considering corresponding provisions). The debt must be undisputed (see

C5.29 below). It will be noted that the statutory demand is required to be served 'by leaving it at the company's registered office'. This raises the question as to whether sending it by post is sufficient. In *Craig v Iona Hotels Ltd 1988 SCLR 131 (Scotland),* a statutory demand sent to the company's registered office by recorded delivery was held to be ineffective. However, in *Re a Company (No 008790 of 1990)* [1991] *BCLC 561*, where a statutory demand, sent by post to the company's registered office, was proved to have been received by the company, Morritt J held the service to have been effective. He did not follow the decision to the contrary by Nourse J in *Re a Company* [1985] *BCLC 37* (where Nourse J had not regarded the service of a statutory demand by telex as effective) and stated that it made no difference whether the act of leaving the demand at the registered office was carried out by the creditor personally or by his employee, or by a security firm engaged for the purpose, or by the postman. All that was required to be proved was that the demand was left at the registered office. See also *Hastie & Jenkerson v McMahon* [1991] *1 All ER 255* where the Court of Appeal held service by fax, of a list of documents ordered to be delivered in an action, to be valid. Woolf LJ said that apart from exceptional instances, such as documents initiating legal proceedings, there seemed to be no need for ceremony. In ordinary cases the purpose of serving a document was to ensure that its contents were available in a legible form to the recipient. There was however a risk in using a fax, without the recipient's consent, in case a legible copy was not printed on his fax machine.

The expression 'neglected' in subsection (1)(a) does not mean 'failed' or 'omitted' to pay. It means 'failed or omitted to pay *without reason*'. The mere existence of a cross-claim by the company which has not been or is not being established by litigation is not a good reason for refusing to pay an undisputed quantified claim (*Re a Company (No 006273 of 1992)* [1992] *BCC 794*).

A demand which does not constitute an effective statutory demand can, if not met, still be relied upon as evidence of the company's inability to pay under subsection (1)(e) above (see the last paragraph under this heading, below). However, the mere fact that a statutory demand overstated the amount of the debt does not invalidate the demand. In *Re a Debtor (No 490-SD-1991), ex parte the Debtor v Printline (Offset) Ltd* [1992] *2 All ER 664*, Hoffmann J refused to set aside a demand (made under the provisions of the 1986 Act relating to individual bankruptcies) on that ground. He stated that the purpose of a statutory demand was to activate the presumption of inability to pay debts on which to found a creditor's petition.

Although, unlike the provisions relating to the bankruptcy of an individual, the provisions relating to the winding up of a company do not expressly contain machinery for setting aside a statutory demand, the court does have jurisdiction to set it aside. The jurisdiction will only be exercised, however, if there is a genuine dispute as to the existence of the debt (see *Re Janeash Ltd* [1990] *BCC 250*, where Browne-Wilkinson V-C refused to set aside a statutory demand because he felt that the attempt to have it set aside was really no more than a device to keep creditors at bay).

As to subsection (1)(b), a writ of *fieri facias* is not deemed to have been returned unsatisfied if all that the sheriff has done is to call at the debtor's premises and reported his inability to gain access to the premises. A writ which is returned unsatisfied should have been properly executed. Such a failure to execute cannot be treated as 'a formal defect or irregularity insolvency proceedings', so as to be capable of remedy under Rule 7.55. The Act allows a petition to be presented only if its requirements are complied with. An irregularity must be some error leading to a failure by the creditors to satisfy some condition or other in the insolvency proceedings. A failure by a sheriff to comply with what the writ commands him to do is a failure not in the insolvency proceedings but in the process of execution: see *Re a Debtor (No 340 of 1992), The Times, 19 July 1992*.

Subsections (1)(*e*) and (2) of section 123 enable a petitioner to adduce wider evidence, based on the company's financial position generally, which tends to show *as a fact* that the company is unable to pay its debts. These provisions represent a noteworthy change from the corresponding provisions contained in the previous legislation, section 223(d) of the Companies Act 1948 and, subsequently, section 518(1)(e) of the Companies Act 1985, which read as follows:

'if it is proved to the satisfaction of the court that the company is unable to pay its debts (and, in determining that question, the court shall take into account the company's contingent and prospective liabilities)'.

The new provisions have thus split the previous test more distinctly into two separate tests, namely, the 'cash flow test' and the 'assets/liabilities test'. Failure by the company to meet either is sufficient. It is debatable, however, whether this represents a substantive change in practice.

In *Byblos Bank SAL v Al Khudhairy [1987] BCLC 232*, decided under the old legislation, it was held that a company's inability to pay its debts (for the purposes of section 223 of the Companies Act 1948) was to be assessed by having regard to its position at the time and that the prospect of future assets (e.g. an injection of loaned cash funds) unaccompanied by a right to such assets must be disregarded (see also *Re European Life Assurance Society (1869) LR 9 Eq 122*). In another case (*Cornhill Insurance PLC v Improvement Services Ltd [1986] 1 WLR 114*) it was held that the failure by an apparently solvent company to pay an undisputed debt within the statutory period of three weeks gives rise to a proper inference that the company is unable to pay its debts notwithstanding that the petitioner is aware of the high financial standing of the company; and the court will not restrain such a petition as an abuse of process of the court. Where immediate payment of a debt which has become due is demanded, but payment remains outstanding, though the demand does not constitute a statutory demand under subsection 1(a), and the statutory period of three weeks has not expired, that may be sufficient evidence of inability to pay (see *Taylors Industrial Flooring Ltd v M & H Plant Hire (Manchester) Ltd [1990] BCC 44*, where the Court of Appeal stated that from a creditor's point of view, the extra three weeks required under a statutory demand gives the company time to dissipate the assets in trying to keep the company going). However, the fact that the company can only pay its debts with borrowed money does not necessarily show that it is unable to pay its debts, although if it has persistently failed or neglected to pay them until forced to do so then in an appropriate case the court can find that it is unable to pay its debts (*Re a Company (No 006794 of 1983)* [*1986*] *BCLC 261*).

(See further C5.29 below.)

(2)   *Corporate member of an insolvent partnership*

C5.23   Apart from its liability to be wound up on the ground of its inability to pay its debts (or any of the other grounds mentioned in section 122 or any special enactment applicable to it) in relation to its own affairs, a corporate member or former corporate member (being a registered company) of an insolvent partnership may, by virtue of the Insolvent Partnerships Order 1994 (SI 1994 No 2421) ('the 1994 Order'), replacing SI 1986 No 2142 with effect from 1 December 1994):

(1)   where situation (*b*) referred to in C5.19 above exists, be wound up on the ground that 'it is unable to pay its debts', in a special sense of that expression, that is, if there is a creditor, by assignment or otherwise, to whom the partnership is indebted in the sum exceeding £750 (the limit may be varied by statutory instrument) then due for which that corporate member or former corporate member is liable and:

  (*a*)   the creditor has served on that member and the partnership a written demand in Form 4 in Schedule 9 to the 1994 Order, in the manner set out in section 123(2) as modified by Schedule 4 to that Order, requiring that member and the partnership to pay that sum, and

  (*b*)   that member and the partnership have for three weeks after the service of the demands (or of the last one) neglected to pay that sum or to secure or compound for it to the creditor's satisfaction (Part I of Schedule 4 to the Order); or

(2)   where situation (*d*) referred to in C5.19 above exists, be wound up on any of the grounds stated in section 123 of the Act (in its unmodified form—see C5.22 above) (Article 10(2) and (3) of the 1994 Order).

(3)   *Unregistered* (*including oversea*) *companies—all cases* (*excluding partnerships*)

C5.24   Section 222, 223 or 224 applies (except that section 223 does not apply to Agricultural Marketing Boards), subject to the modifications of insolvency-related grounds in special cases of unregistered companies dealt with in C5.12 to C5.20 above. These sections define inability to pay debts as follows.

Section 222

'(1)   An unregistered company is deemed (for the purposes of section 221) unable to pay its debts if there is a creditor, by assignment or otherwise, to whom the company is indebted in a sum exceeding £750 then due and

(*a*)   the creditor has served on the company, by leaving at its principal place of business, or by delivering to the secretary or some director, manager or principal officer of the company, or by otherwise serving in such manner as the court may approve or direct, a written demand in the prescribed form [Form 4.1] requiring the company to pay the sum due, and

(*b*)   the company has for three weeks after the service of the demand neglected to pay the sum or to secure or compound for it to the creditor's satisfaction.

(2)   The money sum for the time being specified in subsection (1) is subject to increase or reduction by regulations under section 417 in Part XV; but no increase in the sum so specified affects any case in which the winding-up petition was presented before the coming into force of the increase.'

(As to (1)(*a*), note that in the case of an oversea company, service of the notice on the persons stated in the documents delivered to the Registrar of Companies, pursuant to section 691 of the Companies Act 1985, to be authorised to accept service of process or notice is not expressly prescribed for the purposes of section 222—thus the decision in *Rome v Punjab National Bank (1989) 5 BCC 785* (valid service of writ on such persons even after the company has ceased to have a place of business in Great Britain and has notified the Registrar accordingly) may not automatically apply here.)

Section 223

'An unregistered company is deemed (for the purposes of section 221) unable to pay its debts if an action or other proceeding has been instituted against any member for any debt or demand due, or claimed to be due, from the company, or from him in his character of member, and—

(*a*)   notice in writing of the institution of the action or proceeding has been served on the company by leaving it at the company's principal place of business (or by delivering it to the secretary, or some director, manager or principal officer of the company, or by otherwise serving it in such manner as the court may approve or direct), and

(*b*)   the company has not within three weeks after service of the notice paid, secured or compounded for the debt or demand, or procured the action or proceeding to be stayed or sisted, or indemnified the defendant or defender to his reasonable satisfaction against the action or proceeding, and against all costs, damages and expenses to be incurred by him because of it.'

Section 224

'(1)   An unregistered company is deemed (for the purposes of section 221) unable to pay its debts—

(*a*)   if in England and Wales execution or other process issued on a judgment, decree or order obtained in any court in favour of a creditor against the company, or [except in the case of an Agricultural Marketing Board—see paragraph 4 of Schedule 2 to the Agricultural Marketing Act 1958 as amended by Schedule 14 to the Insolvency Act 1986] any member of it as such, or any person authorised to be sued as nominal defendant on behalf of the company, is returned unsatisfied;

(*b*)   if in Scotland the *induciae* of a charge for payment on an extract decree, or an extract registered bond, or an extract registered protest, have expired without payment being made;

(*c*)   if in Northern Ireland a certificate of unenforceability has been granted in respect of any judgment, decree or order obtained as mentioned in paragraph (*a*);

(*d*)   if it is otherwise proved to the satisfaction of the court that the company is unable to pay its debts as they fall due.

(2)   An unregistered company is also deemed unable to pay its debts if it is proved to the satisfaction of the court that the value of the company's assets is less than the amount of its liabilities, taking into account its contingent and prospective liabilities.'

(4)   *Partnerships*

C5.25   The provisions whereby an insolvent partnership is deemed unable to pay its debts vary depending upon which of situations (*a*) to (*d*) in C5.19 above is applicable. Each of these situations is dealt with in turn.

(A) Where situation (a) in C5.19 above applies. The partnership is deemed to be unable to pay its debts if there is a creditor, by assignment or otherwise, to whom the partnership is indebted in a sum exceeding £750 (the limit may be varied by statutory instrument) and:

(*a*)   the creditor has served on the partnership, in the manner specified in section 222(2) as modified by Schedule 3 to the 1994 Order, a written demand in the prescribed form requiring it to pay that sum; and

(*b*)   the partnership has for three weeks after such service neglected to pay that sum or to secure or compound it to the creditor's satisfaction.

The partnership is also deemed to be unable to pay its debts if an action or other proceeding has been instituted against any member for any debt or demand due, or claimed to be due, from the partnership, or from him in his character of member, and:

(*a*)   notice in writing of the institution of the action or proceeding has been served in the manner specified in section 223(2) (as modified by Schedule 3 to the 1994 Order); and (*b*)   the partnership has not within three weeks after service of the notice paid, secured or compounded for the debt or demand, or procured the action or proceeding to be stayed or sisted, or indemnified the defendant or defender to his reasonable satisfaction against the action or proceeding, and against all costs, damages and expenses to be incurred by him because of it.

(Sections 222, 223 as modified by the 1994 Order, Sch 3).

A partnership is also deemed to be unable to pay its debts if the conditions in section 224 (unmodified) are satisfied (as to which, see C5.24 above). It can also be wound up on a petition of the Secretary of State under section 124A of the Act (unmodified).

(B)   Where situation (b) in C5.19 above applies. The partnership is deemed to be unable to pay its debts if there is a creditor, by assignment or otherwise, to whom it is indebted in a sum exceeding £750 then due and:

(*a*)   the creditor has served on the partnership, in the manner specified in section 222(2) (as modified by Schedule 4 to that Order), a written demand in Form 4 in Schedule 9 to the 1994 Order requiring the partnership to pay that sum;

(*b*)   the creditor has also served on any one or more members or former members of the partnership liable to pay the sum due (in the case of a corporate member, by leaving it at its registered office, and in the case of an individual member, by serving it in accordance with the rules) a demand in Form 4 in Schedule 9 to that Order, requiring that member or those members to pay the sum so due, and

(*c*)   the partnership and its members have for three weeks after the service of the demands, or the service of the last of them if served at different times, neglected to pay the sum or to secure or compound for it to the creditor's satisfaction.

(Section 222, as modified by the 1994 Order, Sch 4).

(C) Where situation (c) in C5.19 above applies. The partnership is deemed unable to pay its debts in the same circumstances as those set out under situation *(A)* above. In this situation, the partnership can be wound up on a member's petition only if the partnership consists of not less than eight members, with one exception. The exception is that irrespective of the number of members, a member's winding-up petition may be presented (with the leave of the court), if the court is satisfied that:

(*a*)   the member has served on the partnership, by leaving at a principal place of business of the partnership in England and Wales, or by delivering to an officer of the partnership, or by otherwise serving in such manner as the court may approve or direct, a written demand in Form 10 in Schedule 9 to the 1994 Order in respect of a joint debt or debts exceeding £750 then due from the partnership but paid by the member, other than out of partnership property;

(*b*)   the partnership has for three weeks after the service of the demand neglected to pay the sum or to secure or compound for it to the member's satisfaction; and (*c*) the member has obtained a judgment, decree or order of any court against the partnership for reimbursement to him of the amount of the joint debt or debts so paid and all reasonable steps (other than insolvency proceedings) have been taken by the member to enforce that judgment, decree or order.

(1994 Order, Sch 5).

(D) Where situation (d) in C5.19 above applies. The position is as in (*B*) above.

(1994 Order, Sch 6).

'*Just and equitable*' ground

C5.26 This ground is interpreted flexibly and is not confined to particular instances nor construed *ejusdem generis* with the other grounds (*Ebrahimi v Westbourne Galleries Ltd [1973] AC 360*). Some examples are given below.

(1) Fraudulent, *mala fide* or other improper element in the formation or running of the company or the need for full investigation (*Re T E Brinsmead & Sons [1897] 1 Ch 406; Re Peruvian Amazon Co (1913) 29 TLR 384*).

(2) Disappearance of the justification for the company's continued existence (see e.g. *Re Eastern Telegraph Co [1947] 2 All ER 104; Re Kitson & Co Ltd [1946] 1 All ER 435*).

(3) Refusal by majority shareholder to produce accounts or pay dividends (*Loch v John Blackwood Ltd [1924] AC 783*; see also *Re Newman and Howard Ltd [1962] Ch 257*).

(4) Complete deadlock in the management of the company (*Re Yenidje Tobacco Co [1916] 2 Ch 426*).

(5) In the case of a small company which is formed or continued on the basis of personal relationship involving mutual confidence and is in substance a partnership (a 'quasi-partnership' case), if the petitioning contributory is excluded from all participation in the business or if such relationship or confidence is broken and the facts are such as would have justified the dissolution of a partnership (*Ebrahimi v Westbourne Galleries* above; *Re A & B C Chewing Gum Ltd [1975] 1 WLR 579; Re Yenidje Tobacco Co* above; see also *Tay Bok Choon v Tahanson Sdn Bhd [1987] BCLC 472*).

A petitioner on this ground must come with clean hands; for example, the breakdown in confidence must not be due to his own misconduct (*Ebrahimi v Westbourne Galleries*, above). Refusal by directors holding half the shares to register as members the executors of a deceased shareholder holding the other half, in exercise of their discretion under the articles, does not necessarily constitute a 'just and equitable' ground (*Charles Forte Investments Ltd v Amanda [1964] Ch 240*).

It is sufficient to show that an act has been proposed which, if carried out or completed, would be prejudicial to the petitioner (*Re Kenyon Swansea Ltd [1987] BCLC 514*).

The winding up of a profitable company may not be in the best interests of an aggrieved shareholder. In the case of a registered company, he may wish to consider the alternative of invoking sections 459 to 461 of the Companies Act 1985 (power of court to grant relief where any shareholder is unfairly prejudiced). (For procedure, see the Companies (Unfair Prejudice Applications) Proceedings Rules 1986 (SI 1986 No 2000)). In any case where the petition is presented by members on the 'just and equitable' ground, the court may, in exercise of its power under section 125(2), refuse to make a winding-up order if it is of the opinion both that some other remedy is available to the petitioner (e.g. under sections 459 to 461 above referred to) and that the petitioner is acting unreasonably in seeking the winding-up order instead of pursuing that other remedy. In *Practice Direction No 1 of 1990 [1990] BCC 292* (reproduced in C5.30 below), Browne-Wilkinson V-C drew the attention of practitioners 'to the undesirability of including as a matter of course a prayer for winding-up as an alternative to a section 459 order. It should be included only if that is the relief which the petitioner prefers or if it is considered that it is the only relief to which he is entitled'.

(See also C5.30 below.)

Who may petition

C5.27   Subject as stated below, the petition may in all cases (in addition to the right of any particular person(s) to present it in specified circumstances), be presented by any one or more of the following (in the case of (1) to (4) below, together or separately).

(1)   The company (section 124(1)).

(2)   The directors (section 124(1)). 'Directors' means all the directors and not one or a majority of them (*Re Instrumentation Electrical Services Ltd (1988) 4 BCC 301*). However, once a proper resolution of the board has been passed for the presentation of a winding-up petition, a petition presented pursuant to that resolution is properly presented, since once it is passed, it becomes the duty of all the directors, including those who took no part in the deliberations of the board and those who voted against the resolution, to implement it (*Re Equiticorp International Plc (1989) 5 BCC 599*, a case relating to an administration petition under section 9(1) the language of which is similar).

(3)   Any creditor or creditors, including any contingent or prospective creditor or creditors (section 124(1)) and a creditor by assignment (section 123(1)(a)).

(4)   Any contributory or contributories (section 124(1)); but see (13) below in the case of a petition by a partner against the partnership.

(5)   The Secretary of State, if the ground of the petition is that laid down in section 122(1)(b) (public company share capital requirements) or (c) (old public company) (see C5.10 above), or in a case falling within the former section 440 of the Companies Act 1985 (replaced by section 124A of the Insolvency Act 1986, as inserted by section 60 of the Companies Act 1989, which came into force on 21 February 1990) (expedient in the public interest, following report of inspectors, etc.).

(6)   Where the company is being wound up voluntarily in England and Wales, the Official Receiver as well as any of the parties mentioned in (1) to (5) above (section 124(5)).

(7)   Any administrator or administrative receiver (as to which, see generally the cases referred to at C5.29 below) of the company and any supervisor of a voluntary arrangement in relation to the company (sections 14 and 42 and Schedule 1, paragraph 21, and section 7(4)(b); see also section 140, empowering the court to appoint as liquidator a person who has been an administrator or a supervisor of the company).

(8)   In the case of a charity, the Attorney-General (section 63(1) of the Charities Act 1993).

(9)   In the case of a credit union, the Registrar of Friendly Societies (see C5.15 above) (section 20(2) of the Credit Unions Act 1979) and, in the case of an Agricultural Marketing Board, the Minister (Schedule 2 to the Agricultural Marketing Act 1958, as amended).

(10) In the case of an authorised or former authorised institution, the Bank of England, where the ground of the petition is one of those mentioned in C5.16 above (section 92 of the Banking Act 1987).

(11) In the case of an insurance company which is not a member of Lloyds, or a friendly society, or the insurance business of a trade union or of an employers' association:

(a)   (with the leave of the court and subject to a *prima facie* case being established to its satisfaction and security for costs being furnished as required by it) any ten or more policyholders owning policies with an aggregate value of at least £10,000 (section 53 of the Insurance Companies Act 1982); or

(b)   the Secretary of State, where the petition is based on any one or more of the grounds mentioned in C5.17 above (section 54(1) and (4) of the Insurance Companies Act 1982; see also the Insurance Companies (Winding up) Rules 1985 (SI 1985 No 95), as amended by SI 1986 No 2002, and the Insurance Companies (Winding up) (Scotland) Rules 1986 (SI 1986 No 1918)).

(12) In the case of an 'authorised person' or 'appointed representative' (as defined by the Financial Services Act 1986), the Secretary of State (whose functions in this regard are exercisable concurrently with the Securities and Investments Board Limited ('SIB') by virtue

of section 114 of that Act and the Financial Services Act 1986 (Delegation) Order 1987 (SI 1987 No 942)), where the petition is based on any one or more of the grounds mentioned in C5.18 above (section 72 of that Act). (For an example where the power was successfully invoked, see *Securities and Investments Board v Lancashire and Yorkshire Portfolio Management Ltd [1992] BCC 381.*)

(13) In addition to a creditor and others who may be entitled to present one under the Act, as modified by the Insolvent Partnerships Order 1994 (SI 1994 No 2421), in the case of a winding-up petition against a partnership—

(*a*)   where no 'insolvency petition' (as to the meaning of which see C5.19 above) is also presented by the petitioner against any of the partners:

(i)   if the ground for the petition is one of the circumstances set out in section 221(7), as modified by Schedule 3 to the Insolvent Partnerships Order 1994 (SI 1994 No 2421):

(*aa*)   the liquidator or administrator (if any) of a corporate partner or former corporate partner;

(*bb*)   the administrator of the partnership;

(*cc*)   the trustee in bankruptcy (if any) of an individual partner or of a former individual partner;

(*dd*)   the supervisor of a voluntary arrangement of a corporate member, or of the partnership, or of an individual member;

(ii)   if the partnership consists of at least eight partners, any member of the partnership; or

(iii)   whether or not the partnership consists of less than eight partners, any partner who:

(*aa*)   has paid a joint debt or debts exceeding £750 (which limit may be varied by statutory instrument) due by the partnership, other than out of partnership property;

(*bb*)   has obtained a court order or judgment against the partnership for reimbursement in respect of such payment;

(*cc*)   has taken reasonable steps to enforce the order or judgment;

(*dd*)   has in the prescribed manner served a written demand on the partnership in the prescribed form (Form 10 in Schedule 9 to the Insolvent Partnerships Order 1994 (SI 1994 No 2421));

(*ee*)   for three weeks after such service has not received payment of such debt, or security or composition to his satisfaction; *and* (*ff*) (where there are less than eight partners) has obtained the leave of the court to present the petition

(the Insolvent Partnerships Order 1994, articles 7 and 9 and Schedules 3 and 5, modifying sections 220, 221 and 222);

(*b*) where an insolvency petition is also presented by the petitioner against all the members of the partnership, any member of the partnership, provided that petitions against every member are presented on the same day and to the same court as the winding-up petition against the partnership (except where, in the case of petitions against the members, the court directs that they are presented only against those members as are specified by the court) (the Insolvent Partnerships Order 1994, article 10 and Schedule 6).

(14) In the case of a corporate member or former corporate member of an insolvent partnership, any creditor or creditors to whom the partnership is indebted in a sum exceeding £750 (the limit may be varied by statutory instrument) then due for which that corporate member is liable, provided that:

(i) a written demand in Form 4 in Schedule 9 to the 1994 Order has been served on that corporate member and the partnership, and both have for three weeks failed or neglected to pay the sum due or to secure or compound for it to the creditor's satisfaction, and

(ii) the petition is presented in the same court and on the same day (unless the court otherwise directs) as the winding-up petition against the partnership.

(the 1994 Order, Article 8 and Sch 4).

Company's own petition

C5.28 Under the previous legislation directors could not, as a general rule, exercise the right of the company to present a winding-up petition without the authority of a special resolution contemplated in what is now section 122(1)(a) (or, if the articles of association allowed, an ordinary resolution of the company in general meeting). This rule was recognised in, *inter alia, Re Emmandart Ltd [1979] 1 All ER 599* where, however, a receiver was held to be entitled to cause the company to present a petition without such authority. Directors are now expressly authorised by section 124(1) to present a petition (see C5.27 above). Thus, the options are: a petition in the company's name following the special resolution of its members; a petition by all the directors; or a petition by one or more of the directors following their board resolution.

Creditor's petition

C5.29 Here 'creditor' includes—

(i) the assignee of the whole or part of a debt, whether at law or in equity (section 123(1)(a); *Re Steel Wing Co [1921] 1 Ch 349*);

(ii) a secured creditor even if he has obtained the appointment of a receiver in an action (*Re Borough of Portsmouth Tramways Co [1892] 2 Ch 362*, although the weight to be attached to his voice, as against the voices of other interested parties, may depend on the circumstances—see *Re Leigh Estates Ltd [1994] BCC 292* and *Re Anvil Estates Ltd (unreported)*, both referred to in *Insolvency Law and Practice*, Vol 10 (1994) at page 47, and compare and contrast with *Re Exmouth Docks (1873) Comm 181* and *Re Borough of Portsmouth* (above));

(iii) a local authority in respect of rates remaining unpaid after an unsuccessful distress (*Re North Bucks Furniture Depositories [1939] Ch 690*), but not if the rates have become time-barred under what is now the Limitation Act 1980, sections 9(1) and 39(1), by reason of six years having expired since they became due, notwithstanding that the local authority may be entitled to execute a distress warrant previously obtained but not executed (*Re Karnos Property Co Ltd (1989) 5 BCC 14*); and

(iv) a contingent or prospective creditor (section 124(1)).

However, the expression 'creditor' does not include a creditor whose claim has become time-barred. For the purposes of the Limitation Acts, a winding-up petition is an 'action', because, if successful, it would result in the creditors receiving a dividend (see *Re Karnos Property Co Ltd* above; and *Re Joshua Shaw and Sons Ltd (1989) 5 BCC 188*, where the period of limitation expired during the receivership of the company, which continued for a long period).

The general rule is that an unpaid creditor is entitled *ex debito justitiae* (i.e. as of right) to a winding-up order (*Re Sklan Ltd [1961] 1 WLR 1013; Re James Millward [1940] Ch 333*). This rule is, however, subject to the overriding principle that the power of the court to make the order is discretionary (*Re P & J Macrae Ltd [1961] 1 WLR 229*), the exercise of the discretion depending on the circumstances of the case with decided cases being only a guide rather than laying down strict principles. Among the relevant considerations are the following.

(1) *Disputed or unmatured debt*

    (*a*) It is a general rule of practice that a person whose claim is disputed by the company in good faith and on substantial grounds (as distinct from 'a thoroughly bad reason . . . put forward honestly' (*Taylor's Industrial Flooring Ltd v M & H Plant Hire (Manchester) Ltd [1990] BCC 44*)) may be refused an order (and may even be restrained from presenting or advertising a petition—see C5.36 below). A winding-up petition is not a legitimate means of enforcing payment of such a claim as the company cannot be said to have 'neglected' to pay (*Re a Company (No 003729 of 1982) [1984] 1 WLR 1090*, see also *Stonegate Securities Ltd v Gregory [1980] 1 All ER 241 (CA)*). It is an abuse of the process of the court to present a winding-up petition against a company based on the non-payment of a debt where there is a *bona fide* dispute as to whether the debt is payable. In such a case the court would grant an injunction to restrain its advertisement and could order the petitioner to pay costs to be taxed on an indemnity basis, even though it had not been necessary to investigate the question of the company's insolvency, because the petition was doomed to failure on the ground of the dispute (*Re a Company (No 00751 of 1992), ex parte Avocet Aviation Ltd [1992] BCLC 869*, where the company had previously disputed the claim in writing giving reasons, and the petition had been presented without any statutory demand or formal or informal warning; Mummery J held that there had been a serious abuse of the process of the court). However, in the absence of substantial grounds on which liability is disputed, the failure by a company to pay a debt is sufficient evidence of its inability to pay the debt (*Taylor's Industrial Flooring Ltd v M & H Plant Hire (Manchester) Ltd [1990] BCC 44*). Where part of a debt is disputed and no agreement has been reached on the amount of the undisputed part at the date of the statutory notice, the petitioner cannot rely on the fact that the undisputed part was not paid until after the expiration of the period of notice (*Re a Company (No 003729 of 1982)* (above); and *Re a Company (No 11102 of 1991) [1992] EGCS 79, [1992] 1 Re LR 288*) (see also below).

In *Re Record Tennis Centres Ltd [1991] BCC 509*, Hoffmann J found, on the facts, that the debt was not disputed on *bona fide* grounds and that the dispute was being used by the company in an attempt to stave off liquidation. The company's claim to set off part of the debt was very small in comparison with the total debt due by it. The set-off issue had not been raised by the company until several months after the debt had become due, and had not been substantiated by the company in the correspondence with the creditor. Further, the only source from which the company could pay the petition debt was financial assistance from another company which was in administrative receivership; and the first company itself was, by its own admission, insolvent. The application to strike out was dismissed. *Re a Company (No 001946 of 1991), ex parte Fin Soft Holding SA [1991] BCLC 737* was another case where a similar result ensued. Harman J found, on the facts, that there was no substantial dispute, and the lateness of the allegation that the promissory note (on the dishonour of which the petition was based) had been obtained by fraudulent misrepresentation, and the evidence of the company's insolvency, indicated that the company was looking for any defence to avoid payment of the promissory note.

(b) In *Re a Company, ex parte N D Pritchard, FT Law Reports, 22 November 1991,* the company concerned was a re-insurer and the petitioners were members of three Lloyds' syndicates who claimed that the company owed them £59,911 under a re-insurance contract. The contract allowed for inspection by the company of the syndicates' books and papers. The syndicate managers refused to allow inspection until payment had been received whereas the company was not willing to make payment until it had the opportunity to inspect. Granting an *ex parte* injunction to restrain the petitioners from pursuing the petition, Hoffmann J held that the debts were disputed in good faith on substantial grounds. It would be unfair to allow the syndicates to enforce their claim by winding-up petition when they had flatly refused to allow any inspection at all.

In exceptional circumstances, the court may refuse to entertain a winding-up petition based on a dishonoured cheque. In *Re a Company (No 0010656 of 1990) [1991] BCLC 464,* a creditor's petition was based on non-payment of a debt incurred in connection with the publication of certain brochures and the dishonour by the bank of a cheque issued by the company in payment of that debt. The cheque had been dishonoured on the instructions of the company. The company alleged that the brochures were defective and were wholly unfit for the purpose for which they were designed. Harman J struck out the petition. This was because the debt, and the company's liability on the cheque, were disputed on substantial grounds and there was no evidence of the company's financial position which would indicate that it was insolvent. It was more appropriate for the matter to proceed by ordinary action.

In *Re a Company (No 001259 of 1991) ex parte Medialite Ltd [1991] BCLC 594,* a cheque for £3,231 issued by a company in payment of a debt was returned to the payee by the bank with the remarks 'refer to drawer please re-present'. The creditor re-presented the cheque but petitioned for a winding up the following day. The cheque was cleared the day after. Harman J held that it was an abuse of the process of the court to present a petition whilst the cheque was going through the clearing system which the petitioner hoped would result in payment of the cheque. He therefore ordered that the petition be removed from the file.

In the case of a disputed debt, not only is the petition liable to be dismissed at the hearing but also the court may exercise its inherent jurisdiction before then to strike out the petition on the ground that, when the matter comes to a substantive hearing, it is bound to be dismissed because the *locus standi* of the petitioner is disputed. The test for determining whether the petition should be struck out is the same as that where there is an application to restrain the presentation or advertisement of a petition on the ground that there is a *bona fide* dispute on substantial grounds as to the company's liability to pay the debt on which the winding-up petition is based. In particular, a petition can be struck out if it is without hope of success and therefore represents an abuse of the process of the court (*Re a Company (No 003079 of 1990)* [*1991*] *BCLC 235*; see also *Re Martin Coulter Enterprises Ltd* [*1988*] *BCLC 12*; *Re a Company (No 003028 of 1987)* [*1988*] *BCLC 282*; *Stonegate Securities Ltd v Gregory* [*1980*] *1 All ER 241 at 243*).

In *Re a Company (No 0012209 of 1991)* [*1992*] *1 WLR 351* Hoffmann J dismissed a winding-up petition which was based on a statutory demand for a clearly disputed debt. He held that the petition was an abuse of the process of the court and awarded indemnity costs against the petitioning creditor. He said '. . . if, as in this case, it appears that the defence has a prospect of success and the company is solvent then I think that the court should give the company the benefit of the doubt and not do anything which would encourage the use of the Companies Court as an alternative to the RSC Order 14 procedure . . . I think that it should be made clear that abuse of the petition procedure in these circumstances is a high risk strategy . . .'. A similar result followed in *Philex Plc v Golban, The Times, 9 July 1993* (reported as *Re a Company (No 0022 of 1993)* [*1993*] *BCC 726*) where, in addition, a 'wasted costs' order was also made against the petitioning creditor's solicitors pursuant to section 4 of the Courts and Legal Services Act 1990 (although this was set aside, on the facts, by the Court of Appeal: [*1994*] *BCC 390*). Although, in essence the court applies the 'triable issue' test of the Order 14 proceedings, the court has no jurisdiction, unlike in the Order 14 proceedings, to order the company to pay the disputed sum into court (see, for example, *Re a Debtor (No 90 of 1992), The Times, 12 July 1993*).

By contrast, where a company refuses to pay an undisputed debt, or fails to put forward any defence to a claim for a debt even though it is solvent, the court can properly infer that the company is unable to pay its debts and refuse to interfere with the right of the unpaid creditor to a winding-up order. It should be noted, however, that where a creditor has issued a winding-up petition in abuse of the process of the court, the company may well have a claim for damages against the petitioner for malicious institution of the proceedings, provided that the petition is eventually dismissed, or was presented without reasonable cause, or its presentation was actuated by malice.

In *Re Trinity Insurance Co Ltd [1990] BCC 235*, it was held that a petitioner was entitled to present a winding-up petition in respect of the amount which the insurance company knew it owed the petitioner, notwithstanding that there was a *bona fide* dispute in respect of other debts allegedly due from the company to the petitioner. However, in *Re a Company (No 0013734 of 1991) [1993] BCLC 59*, a winding-up petition against a reinsurance company, presented by a reinsured (which itself was being wound up in Bermuda) in respect of the non-payment of settled or actuarily valued, but as yet unpaid, insurance claims, was struck out. This was because although, in a simple case, the contractual wording imposed an obligation on the reinsurer to indemnify the reinsured for unpaid claims, the liability in the instant case was disputed in good faith and on substantial grounds, raising issues inappropriate for resolution on the petition.

The mere fact that the company has made a cross-claim against the creditor in a separate action does not necessarily *prevent* that creditor from presenting a winding-up petition against the company based on a debt in respect of which he brought an action against the company and applied for a summary judgment under Order 14. Such a petition is not an abuse of the process of the court meriting an injunction (*Re a Company (No 009681 of 1990), 23 November 1990 (unreported)*); when such a petition comes up for hearing (and it had not been reasonably possible to litigate a genuine cross-claim which, if established, exceeded the petition debt) the court has a discretion whether to dismiss or stay the petition, or to make a winding-up order if inability to pay debts is established (see *Re FSA Business Software Ltd [1990] BCC 465*).

The court may also refuse to grant a stay of advertisement for a winding-up petition on the ground of a cross-claim, even if it might exceed the amount of the petition debt, if the company is, in any case, insolvent. In *Re a Company (No 009080 of 1992) [1993] BCLC 269*, during a protracted litigation costs were awarded against and in favour of the company at different hearings. Shortly afterwards, administrative receivers were appointed to the company, and the other party to the litigation presented a winding-up petition against the company on the ground of a dishonoured statutory demand in respect of the costs awarded in favour of that party. The court refused to stay the advertisement of the petition, despite the company's contention that it had a larger claim for costs against the other party. The court held that as, on the facts, the company was not engaged in active trading, it would not be unduly harmed by the advertisement and, as it was insolvent, there would be further losses incurred if the stay was granted. *Re a Company (No 006273 of 1992) [1992] BCC 794* is another example where the existence of an alleged counterclaim by a solvent company, which was not the subject of any impending litigation, was held not to be a bar to a winding-up petition being presented against the company which was based on an otherwise undisputed claim.

(*c*)   The petitioner may also fail where the court is unable to say that there is no *bona fide* dispute on substantial grounds *(Re Fitness Centre (South East)* [*1986*] *BCLC 518*) or where, on the facts, it is impossible to conclude that there is debt the existence or quantum of which cannot be *bona fide* disputed on substantial grounds *(Re a Company* [*1985*] *BCLC 37*).

(*d*)   On the other hand, the court does have a discretion in appropriate cases to determine the dispute so as to preserve the petitioning creditor's remedy where, for example, there is a danger of the company's assets being put out of reach of its creditors. In such a case it is sufficient if the creditor has a 'good arguable case' or there is doubt whether there is a substantial dispute. The rule of practice referred to in (*a*) above is only a rule of practice and should be overridden when its application might result in injustice (see *Claybridge Shipping Co SA* [*1981*] *Com LR 107*). Where only the amount of the debt is disputed, the court may make a winding-up order without requiring the petitioner to quantify his debt precisely (*Re Tweeds Garage Ltd* [*1962*] *Ch 406*). Whether the court should exercise a discretion to dismiss or stay (see C5.42 below) when there is a genuine cross-claim which it has not been reasonably possible to litigate and, which, if established, would exceed the debt due to the petitioner, is governed by the facts and circumstances of each case (*Re FSA Business Software Ltd* [*1990*] *BCC 465*).

(*e*)   If the debt is not immediately due, or there is dispute as to whether it is so due, the petitioner will not be allowed to proceed except as a contingent creditor (see *Stonegate Securities Ltd v Gregory* (above) and C5.29 (iv) above). A creditor is not entitled to base his petition solely on a claim for damages or for an unquantified sum (*Re Humberstone (Jersey) Ltd* (*1977*) *74 LSG 711*); he may, however, proceed as a contingent or prospective creditor. Such a creditor has a heavier onus to discharge. This is because (1) in the absence of the statutory notice (which can only be given in respect of a debt exceeding the specified amount, at present £750, 'then due'), he would need to establish the company's inability to pay its debt by other evidence and (2) he cannot rely on the *ex debito justitiae* rule—he may have to invoke the *Claybridge* principles (see (*d*) above).

(*f*)   A petition based on a solicitor's bill of costs before it is taxed may be disallowed (*Re Laceward Ltd* [*1981*] *1 All ER 254*). A statutory demand for payment of a solicitors' bill of costs is not an 'action' within the meaning of section 69 of the Solicitors Act 1974. Accordingly, such a demand can validly be made before the expiration of one month after delivery of the bill, the minimum period which must elapse before an 'action' is brought (*Re a Debtor (No 88 of 1991) [1992] 4 All ER 301*). However, a winding-up petition cannot be presented before the expiration of that period, as the petition amounts to 'proceedings' (where the bill relates to non-contentious business) within the meaning of article 3(2) of the Solicitors' Remuneration Order 1972 (*Re Lacewood Ltd [1981] 1 All ER 254*) and (in other cases) section 69 (*Re a Debtor* (above)).

(g) A secured creditor may petition without deducting the value of his security, although subsequently in his proof of debt he would have to make full deduction (see C14.32 below).

(2) *Class rights of the majority of creditors*

(a) The petitioning creditor is regarded as exercising a class right belonging to all creditors of the class of which he is a member (Buckley J in *Re Crigglestone Coal Co [1906] 2 Ch 327*). Accordingly, the wishes of the majority of the creditors of that class is an important, though not necessarily a decisive, factor. Section 195 enables the court to have regard to their wishes and provides that in ascertaining their wishes regard must be had to the value of their debts. (See also *Re Riviera Pearls [1962] 1 WLR 722* where it was suggested that, *prima facie*, greater value carries more weight than numerical majority.)

(b) Where a majority both in number and in value of the creditors oppose the petition, ordinarily their wishes will prevail (*Re Crigglestone Coal Co* (above)). The court may refuse a winding-up order if a majority in value of the creditors oppose the petition for some good reason (*Re A B C Coupler and Engineering Co Ltd [1961] 1 WLR 243*). However, the nature and quality of their debts is also a material consideration (*Re P & J Macrae Ltd* (above); see also *Re Southard & Co Ltd [1979] 1 WLR 546* at *550* and *Re Vuma Ltd [1960] 1 WLR 1283*). Where the opposition comes from secured creditors, the court may favour the unsecured creditors who support the petition even if they are in the minority, since to refuse the order may rob them of their only remedy (*Re Rubber Improvements Ltd, The Times, 5 June 1962*). Further, the wishes of the majority of creditors may not prevail where they are 'domestic' or 'associated' creditors, such as the parent company or companies in the same group (*Re Southard & Co Ltd* (above)). The views of 'domestic' creditors are not, however, to be completely discounted, though they carry less weight than ordinary outside trade creditors (*Re Medisco Equipment Ltd [1983] BCLC 305*).

(c) The court's decision does not depend solely on the wishes of the creditors. If the facts disclose a strong *prima facie* case for an investigation into the company's affairs, a winding-up order may be made in the interests of commercial morality irrespective of the creditors' opposition (*Re Clandown Colliery Co [1915] 1 Ch 369*). The discretion must be exercised judicially on sufficient evidence. Where, for example, evidence suggests that assets have been transferred for inadequate value, a liquidator, who is manifestly independent, should be appointed to investigate (*Re Palmer Marine Surveys Ltd [1986] 1 WLR 573*).

(3)   *Voluntary winding up in progress*

(*a*)   A winding-up order will not necessarily be refused merely because the company is already in voluntary liquidation, but the court will not make the order unless satisfied that the voluntary winding up cannot be continued with due regard to the interests of the creditors or contributories (section 124(5)). The 'class rights' considerations (see (2) above) apply with greater force here (if a majority of the creditors oppose the petition) as the petitioning creditor will not *prima facie* be robbed of his remedy. Greater weight is attached to the creditors' wish to have a voluntary liquidation instead of a compulsory liquidation than to their wish to have no liquidation at all (*Re Southard & Co Ltd* (above); see also *Re J D Swain Ltd [1965] 1 WLR 909* and *Re Bi-Print Ltd, 22 June 1982 (1989) 2 Insolvency Intelligence 76* (Nourse J)). Again, however, the objections or wishes of independent outside creditors will have greater weight than those of interested parties such as directors or contributories (*Re Holiday Stamps Ltd, The Times, 11 July 1985 (CA)*).

(*b*)   Thus the burden of establishing a case for a compulsory winding up to replace the voluntary winding up is on the petitioner and is particularly heavy where a majority in value of independent creditors favour continuation of the voluntary winding up. In *Re Home Remedies Ltd [1943] Ch 1, [1942] 2 All ER 552*, a judgment creditors' petition for a compulsory winding up against a company which was already in a voluntary liquidation was opposed by all except three creditors. In dismissing the petition, Simmonds J said, 'If the creditors wish to continue the voluntary liquidation and no valid reason is shown why effect should not be given to their wishes the court will not make a winding-up order'. In *Re B Karsberg Ltd [1955] 3 All ER 854*, the Court of Appeal upheld the wishes of the majority of the creditors who opposed a compulsory winding up, whilst a voluntary liquidation was in progress. The petitioners' argument was that only in a compulsory winding up could a proper investigation of the circumstances leading to the company's insolvency, particularly by way of a public examination (see C11.22 below) take place. The court stated that even in a voluntary liquidation, a public examination could be ordered. However, in *Re Lubin, Rosen and Associates Ltd [1975] 1 WLR 122*, where an overwhelming majority of the creditors opposed a winding-up petition by the Secretary of State in respect of a company which was in voluntary liquidation, but were ignorant of the discoveries which had been made by the

Department of Trade and Industry inspector from documents obtained by him pursuant to what is now section 447 of the Companies Act 1985, Megarry J granted the petition, stating that a petition by the Secretary of State, acting in the public interest, was different from one presented by a creditor, although that was not the main reason why he was granting the petition.

Notwithstanding an existing voluntary liquidation, a winding-up order was also granted on the ground of a public interest element in investigating the company's affairs in *Securities and Investments Board v Lancashire & Yorkshire Portfolio Management Ltd [1992] BCC 381*. It was submitted by the SIB that the extra powers to investigate in a compulsory winding up, and the automatic involvement of the Official Receiver, would ensure a more thorough enquiry into the activities of the company. The voluntary liquidator had put information before the court showing that the costs of a compulsory winding up would be very much greater than the costs that would be incurred in a voluntary winding up, and that the unsecured creditors would recover correspondingly less. Hoffmann J held that if, on reasonable material being presented, it was the view of the SIB that a compulsory liquidation was preferable, then the winding-up order ought to be made. The balance of convenience and expense in favour of a voluntary winding up might be appropriate for an ordinary trading company where nothing really required investigation, but was not necessarily so in the case of an investment company where there was a public interest element in investigating the company's affairs. It is submitted that it was unfair that the unsecured creditors in that case should bear the expenses of the investigation in the public interest, as distinct from an investigation aimed solely at realising more funds for the unsecured creditors.

(*c*)   Where a majority in number and value of the creditors favour the voluntary winding up, the court may dismiss the petition and permit the company to proceed to validate any irregularities associated with the voluntary winding-up resolution (*Re Fitness Centre (South East) Ltd [1986] BCLC 518*). The petition may also be dismissed if evidence shows that the remedy under the voluntary winding up will be better for all creditors than it would be under the petition (*Re Medisco Equipment Ltd [1983] BCLC 305*, where the petitioner had a majority in value but the opposing creditors a majority in number and the only complaint was that the voluntary liquidator had not declared a dividend quickly enough); see also *Re J D Swain Ltd* (above) and *Re Lubin, Rosen and Associates Ltd [1975] 1 WLR 122*.

(*d*)   On the other hand, the court may look beyond the mere wishes of the majority of creditors and make a winding-up order despite their opposition if there is any suggestion of bias and/or incompetence on the part of the voluntary liquidator. The voluntary liquidator is entitled to appear at the hearing by counsel and can, and perhaps should, to assist the court, appear to give evidence of what he has found and of what the position is, but he can have no actual say in advocating one conclusion or the other. Partisan management by a voluntary liquidator, for example, by facilitating creditor opposition, is frowned upon by the courts (see *Re Medisco Equipment Ltd* (above); *Re Roselmar Properties Ltd (No 2) (1986) 2 BCC 99, 157)*. It is regarded as undesirable for a voluntary liquidator to take steps which appear to be designed to secure support for himself or to discourage creditors who take a different view. Where he attempts only to whip up opposition this would make any judge extremely doubtful as to the liquidator's good sense (*Re Lubin, Rosen and Associates Ltd*; and *Re Medisco Equipment Ltd* (above)). Whose appointee the voluntary liquidator is, is a factor to be taken into account in determining his fitness (*Re Medical Battery Co [1894] 1 Ch 444*; *Re Britton & Millard (1957) 107 LJ 602*; *Re Ryder Installations [1966] 1 WLR 524*).

(*e*)   There is no general rule that a winding-up order would only be made where there is doubt as to the voluntary liquidator's competence or probity. The court should take into account the number, value and quality of the creditors who favour a winding- up order. An appropriate discount can properly be made in weighing the views of the opposing creditors who are closely associated with the management of the company. It is in the public interest that creditors should have confidence in the liquidator's independence, and where there is suspicion of wrong doing, he should not only be independent but be seen to be independent (*Re Lowerstoft Traffic Services Ltd [1986] BCLC 81*; see also *Re Falcon RJ Developments Ltd [1987] BCLC 437*). A winding-up order may also be granted where the creditors would be left with a justifiable sense of grievance that they have been deprived of an opportunity to have the company's affairs investigated by a more independent liquidator (*Re MCH Services Ltd [1987] BCLC 535*). In *Re William Thorpe & Son Ltd (1989) 5 BCC 156*, a company in members' voluntary liquidation incurred substantial post-liquidation losses in the course of completing outstanding contracts. A creditor presented a petition for compulsory winding up which was supported by certain other creditors, as they desired an independent investigation into how the directors had come to swear a declaration of solvency and into the conduct of the liquidator. The court made a compulsory winding-up order, stating that it would be for the meeting of creditors, which would be held following the order, to decide whether it wanted another liquidator. The wishes of a majority of the creditors would usually be followed unless they were being 'perverse or masochistic'. (See also *Re Falcon R J Developments [1987]*

BCLC 437; and *Re Medisco Equipment Ltd [1983] BCLC 305*). In *Re Hewitt Brannan (Tools) Co Ltd [1990] BCC 354*, Harman J refused to follow the unanimous wishes of the creditors who opposed the Official Receiver's compulsory winding up in favour of a voluntary winding up and who argued that there would be a higher dividend in the latter than in the former. He stated that having regard to the 'really disgracefully unsatisfactory conduct of the voluntary liquidator', the interests of creditors and the public cried out for investigation by the Official Receiver.

(f)   A situation may arise where a winding-up petition is presented against a company which is in voluntary liquidation and, before the hearing of the petition, an application is made by the petitioner for the appointment of a provisional liquidator. In considering whether or not to make the appointment, the court would need to take a view, without the benefit of knowing the views of the other creditors, as to whether or not the winding-up petition is likely to be successful.

In *Securities and Investments Board v Lancashire and Yorkshire Portfolio Management Ltd [1992] BCC 381*, the company carried on investment business and was a member of FIMBRA. In October 1991, FIMBRA, in accordance with its rules, made directions restricting the company's activities and requiring that all the assets of the company and of investors be transferred to a trustee to be appointed by FIMBRA. The company then resolved to go into members' voluntary liquidation. The SIB, under its statutory powers, appointed accountants to investigate the company. The accountants concluded that the company was insolvent (particularly as a result of the value of certain investments having dropped since the declaration of solvency). The SIB presented a winding-up petition and applied for the appointment of a provisional liquidator. The voluntary liquidator submitted that there should not be a compulsory winding-up because continuing the voluntary winding-up would be a great deal cheaper and, therefore, in the interests of unsecured creditors. Hoffmann J, ordering the appointment of a provisional liquidator, stated that the kind of balance of convenience and expense, which would be appropriate in the case of an ordinary trading company where there was no suggestion of matters which particularly required it to be investigated, was not necessarily appropriate in the case of a company carrying on investment business, where there was a public interest in a parallel investigation of the affairs of any such company which became insolvent. Without any personal reflection on the voluntary liquidator, if the regulatory authorities wished to have the sort of investigation which would follow upon a compulsory winding-up, and if that view appeared to be based upon reasonable material, then such an order should be made.

(g) The fact that a voluntary winding-up resolution followed the presentation of the petition may strengthen the case for a compulsory winding up (*Re Lubin Rosen Associates Ltd*; and *Re D J Swain Ltd* (above)), particularly where it is a members' voluntary winding up with the company's director as liquidator with no special expertise and the contributories fail to show that they will be prejudiced by the making of a compulsory winding-up order (*Re Surplus Properties (Huddersfield) Ltd* [*1984*] *BCLC 89*).

(4) *Contributories' wishes*

The views of contributories are also to be taken into account particularly where they have a tangible interest in the result or where there is evidence of wrong doing (see C5.30 below). As to the court's attitude where a creditor's petition is opposed by contributories, see *Re Camburn Petroleum Products Ltd* [*1979*] *Ch 297*.

Contributory's petition

C5.30 The term 'contributory' (which also occurs in the provisions relating to voluntary winding up) is not necessarily synonymous with 'member' or 'shareholder'. It has a wider meaning. A 'contributory' is a person liable to contribute to the assets of the company in the event of its being wound up, and the expression includes a person alleged to be a contributory before the names of contributories are determined (section 79). Sections 74 to 83 set out the extent and the circumstances in which various categories of persons are liable to contribute as contributories.

Where a winding-up order has been made against a partnership, and insolvency orders have been made against its members, by virtue of Article 8 or 10 of the Insolvent Partnerships Order 1994 (SI 1994 No 2421) and the provisions contained in Schedule 4 or 6 to that Order, those members are not, unless the contrary intention appears, to be treated as contributories (see the modified section 221 contained in each of those Schedules).

The categories include present and past members. Section 22(2) of the Companies Act 1985 defines a member as including 'every other person who agrees to become a member of a company, and whose name is entered in its register of members'. The expression 'agrees' does not mean that a bilateral contract is necessary. The requirement is satisfied if the person concerned assents to become a member and the company sees fit to register him as a member (*Re Nuneaton Borough Association Football Club Ltd* (*1989*) *5 BCC 377*). In *Barbor v Middleton* (*1988*) *4 BCC 681* (*Court of Session, Outer House*), the petitioner discovered that she was included in the register of members of an unlimited company as the owner of shares. The company was in financial difficulties and the petitioner sought rectification of the register to the effect of having her name removed. The court pronounced an interlocutor directing the register to be so rectified. Subsequently, the company went into creditors' voluntary liquidation and the respondent was appointed liquidator. He included the petitioner in the list of contributories on the basis that the order for rectification was not retrospective and that therefore the petitioner was liable to contribute as a past member. The petitioner maintained that she had never been a member of the company. The court determined the question in favour of the petitioner. Although the order for rectification made no reference to any particular date, there was no reason why it should do so; it was in the usual form and was pronounced upon a petition which proceeded upon a narrative that the petitioner had never been a member of the company. It would make little sense and could lead to manifest injustice in such a situation for an order directing rectification to be effective only from the date of the order. The order was to be interpreted by reference to the state of facts disclosed in the petition and the order directing rectification in effect recognised that the petitioner had never been a member of the company.

In the case of an unregistered company, apart from their potential liability to contribute and potential rights of adjustment as against other contributories, the involvement of the contributories (as to the meaning of which, see section 226) who are not existing members is tenuous. For an example of where a party not on the register was held not to be the contributory of an unregistered company, see *Re Welsh Highland Railway Light Railway Co [1993] BCLC 338*).

A contributory cannot present a petition unless the number of members is reduced below two or the shares in respect of which he is a contributory (or some of them) either were originally allotted to him or have been held by him and registered in his name for at least six months during the eighteen months before the commencement of the winding up, or have devolved on him through the death of a former holder (section 124(2)). Where the shares held by a contributory satisfy the requirement of registration for six months, a trustee in his bankruptcy in whom the shares vest is competent to present the petition without the shares being registered in his name (*Cumming's Trustee v Glenrinnes Farms Ltd 1993 SLT 904 (Court of Session, Outer House)*).

The shares must be standing in the name of the petitioner (*Re Wala Wynaad Indian Gold Mining Co (1882) 21 ChD 849*), but if the company itself is in default in allotting shares or registering a transfer it is arguable that the allottee or transferee is entitled to bring the petition (see *Re Gattopardo Ltd [1969] 1 WLR 619*). If the allotment or the allottee's entry on the register is disputed he would not be allowed to petition (*Re JN2 Ltd [1977] 3 All ER 1104*). As to a bankrupt shareholder, see *Re Wolverhampton Steel & Iron Co Ltd [1977] 1 WLR 860*; *Re K/9 Meat Supplies (Guildford) Ltd [1966] 1 WLR 1112*; and *Re H L Bolton Engineering Co Ltd [1956] Ch 577*.

The principles governing the right of a contributory to obtain a winding-up order are as follows—

(1) If his shares are fully paid, he must show some tangible interest in the winding up, such as the probability that there will be a substantial surplus for distribution among the shareholders (*Re W R Willcocks & Co Ltd [1973] 3 WLR 669*; *Re Commercial and Industrial Insulations Ltd [1986] BCLC 191*), or that because of the failure by the company to supply accounts and information he is unable to say whether there will be such surplus, or that the company's affairs require an investigation that is likely to produce such surplus (see *Re Newman and Howard Ltd [1962] Ch 257; Re Argentum Reductions (UK) Ltd [1975] 1 WLR 186*). This means that ordinarily, the petition must be founded on the 'just and equitable ground' rather than on the company's inability to pay its debts. If his shares are partly paid, he may not have to show the possibility of a surplus, but only that his interest would be prejudiced if the company continued to trade.

(2) Mismanagement by directors is not necessarily a good ground, particularly if the petitioner has not exhausted his other remedies (see sections 459 to 461 of the Companies Act 1985).

(3) A petitioning contributory who is in arrears of calls may be required to pay the calls into court or give appropriate undertakings in respect thereof (*Re Diamond Fuel Co (No 2) (1879) 13 Ch D 400*; *Re Crystal Reef Gold Mining Co [1892] 1 Ch 408*).

(4) Where a voluntary winding up is already in progress, the court may refuse to grant the contributory's petition if the voluntary winding up represents an honest exercise of the shareholders' wishes (*Re Haycraft Gold Reduction and Mining Co [1900] 2 Ch 230*). However, this does not apply where the court is satisfied that the rights of the contributories will be prejudiced by the voluntary winding up (section 116; see also *Re Zinotty Properties Ltd [1984] 1 WLR 1249*).

(5) In the case of a contributories' petition on the 'just and equitable' grounds (see C5.26 above) the court must make a winding-up order if it is of the opinion that the petitioners are entitled to relief either by winding up or by other means and that in the absence of any other remedy it would be just and equitable to wind up the company; but it will not make a winding-up order if in its opinion some other remedy is available to them (for example under sections 459 to 461 of the Companies Act 1985) *and* they are acting unreasonably in seeking the winding up instead of the other remedy (section 125 (2); see also *Re a Company (No 002567 of 1982) [1983] 2 All ER 854* and *Ebrahimi v Westbourne Galleries Ltd [1973] AC 360*). Where a contributory seeks both to wind up a company and relief under sections 459 to 461 of the Companies Act 1985, the petition is not an abuse of the process of the court (*Re Garage Door Associates Ltd [1984] 1 WLR 35*).

In a 'quasi-partnership' case (see C5.26(5) above), the court will not generally strike out a contributory's petition before its substantive hearing if it is not plain and obvious whether, at such a hearing, he would be more likely to get section 459 relief than a winding up. The availability (or probable availability) of a remedy under section 459 does not negate the right established by the House of Lords in *Ebrahimi v Westbourne Galleries Ltd* (above) for shareholders to petition for a winding up when they are genuinely aggrieved. Petitioning for winding up might be damaging to the company, but it does not necessarily follow that the petitioner who claims that his position as a 'quasi-partner' has been infringed and seeks a winding-up order instead of exercising his right to have his shares purchased by the other members is behaving unreasonably, even where he himself is partly responsible for the circumstances giving rise to his petition: *Re a Company (No 001363 of 1988) (1989) 5 BCC 18*; see also *Re Abbey Leisure Ltd [1990] BCC 60; Vujnovich v Vujnovich [1990] BCLC 227 (PC)*, a New Zealand case. It has been held that for the purposes of section 459 referred to above, the fact that the conduct complained of prejudices the interests of those responsible for it and affects all members' rights equally does not prevent relief being granted under that section. The expression 'interests' in this section is wider than 'rights', and members of a company might have different interests even though their rights are identical (*Re Sam Weller Ltd [1989] 3 WLR 923*; see also *Scottish Co-operative Wholesale Society v Meyer [1959] AC 324; Re a Company (No 007623 of 1986) [1986] BCLC 362*; cf. *Re a Company (No 00370 of 1987), ex parte Glossop [1988] BCLC 570*). Where it was known to the proposers of a rights issue that some members would be unable to afford to purchase their entitlement of the issue, so that their relative positions would be weakened, this could amount to unfairly prejudicial conduct (*Re a Company (No 002612 of 1984) [1985] BCLC 430*). Further, where there was a risk that the valuation of the petitioner's 40% shareholding under the pre-emption provisions to be carried out by an accountant might be carried out at a discount because he was a minority shareholder, the court made a winding-up order instead of holding that the petitioner was acting unreasonably in preferring a winding-up order to relief under section 461 of the Companies Act 1985 (*Re Abbey Leisure Ltd [1990] BCC 60 (CA)*).

In *Nicholas v Soundcraft Electronics Ltd and another [1993] BCLC 360*, the company's parent company, which held 75 per cent of its share capital and exercised strong control over its finances, withheld payment of a debt due to the company because of its own (the parent's) financial difficulties. It was held that such withholding constituted acts in the conduct of the company's affairs for the purposes of section 459 but that, in the circumstances, such acts were not unfairly prejudicial to the other shareholders.

A minority shareholder in a 'quasi-partnership' may be entitled to a winding-up order on the 'just and equitable' ground where a share purchase order under section 459 is not appropriate (*Jesner v Jarrad Properties Ltd [1993] BCLC 1032*).

The test of unfairness is objective, so that intentions are irrelevant (*Re RA Noble (Clothing) Ltd [1983] BCLC 273 at 290*, citing *Re*

Bovey Hotel Ventures Ltd (31 July 1981, unreported); Re Sam Weller Ltd (above); *Re a Company (No 007623 of 1986) [1986] BCLC 362* at *367*).

(6)   Where, in a quasi-partnership case, a contributory seeks relief under section 459 of the Companies Act 1985 on the ground of unfair prejudice and, in the alternative, seeks a winding-up order, the company's involvement in the petition can be restrained by the court, except in respect of any application under section 127 of the Insolvency Act 1986 to validate any disposition of the company's property (see C8.4 below) if there is no justification for the company's incurring the expense of what is, in essence, a dispute between the shareholders (*Canniford v Smith & others, Financial Times, 21 December 1990*; see also *Re Kenyon Swansea Ltd [1987] BCLC 514*; *Re Crossmore Electrical and Civil Engineering Ltd [1989] BCLC 137*; *Re a Company (No 005685 of 1988), ex parte Schwarcz [1989] BCLC 424*; *Re Milgate Developments Ltd [1993] BCLC 291*). In considering whether to grant a restraining order, the court must consider the balance of convenience and other matters referred to in *American Cyanamid Co v Ethicon Ltd [1975] AC 396*.

(7)   The court in its discretion may allow a dispute about the ownership of the contributory's shares to be resolved at the substantive hearing as a matter of procedural convenience instead of depriving the contributory of his standing to petition.

(8)   It is a valid ground for the obtaining of a winding-up order by a contributory that the principal objects of the company as set out in its memorandum can no longer be achieved. In *Re Perfectair Holdings Ltd [1990] BCLC 423*, although the company had the necessary cash to continue in business, the majority of the shareholders, by their agreement, had been content to get in the assets of the company and wind it up. Although there was a pending action against the subsidiary which was to be sold to one of the shareholders, it was not being prosecuted for the purpose of trading but for the purpose of liquidation. Scott J, in granting the winding-up order, said that the directors could not claim to be kept in office for the purpose of liquidating the company and, in all the circumstances of the case, it was appropriate that the liquidation should be carried out by a liquidator.

(9)   Where there is a dispute between shareholders in a 'quasi partnership' company, it is becoming increasingly common for the aggrieved shareholder to apply to the court under section 459 of the Companies Act 1985 (as amended by the Companies Act 1989) for appropriate relief, such as an order requiring the other shareholders to purchase his shares, and, alternatively, for a winding-up order. An application under that section can be made by a member on the ground that the company's affairs are being or have been conducted in a manner which is unfairly prejudicial to the interests of its members generally or some part of its members (including at least himself) or that any actual or proposed act or omission of the company, including an act or omission on its behalf, is or would be so prejudicial.

The test for determining what amounts to unfairly prejudicial conduct is an objective one. The test is 'whether a reasonable bystander observing the consequences of the conduct would regard it as having unfairly prejudiced the petitioner's interests' (*Re RA Noble & Son (Clothing) Ltd [1983] BCLC 273*, citing Slade J in *Re Bovey Hotel Ventures Ltd (31 July 1981, unreported)*). The reference to the interest of a member is not confined to his interest in the shares held by him (*Re a Company (No 008699 of 1985) (1986) 2 BCC 99, 024*). Bad faith or intent to cause harm on the part of the respondent is not an essential requirement (*Re RA Noble & Son (Clothing) Ltd* (above)). A mere infringement of the petitioner's rights under the company's articles is not sufficient; rather it must be shown that the infringement itself constitutes conduct which is unfairly prejudicial (*Re Carrington Viyella plc (1983) 1 BCC 98, 951*). A persistent failure to hold general meetings, lay accounts and file statutory returns, and the failure to give notices of extraordinary general meetings at which further shares are invalidly issued to members, including the petitioner, may be sufficient to amount to unfairly prejudicial conduct (see, for example, *Re a Company (00789 of 1987) (Nuneaton Borough AFC Ltd) (1989) 5 BCC 92*).

For further examples of proposed prejudicial acts and past acts which, though remedied, continue to be prejudicial, see *Re Kenyon Swansea Ltd [1987] BCLC 514*. However, conduct which is prejudicial may not necessarily constitute *unfairly* prejudicial conduct (see, for example, *Re Ringtower Holdings Ltd (1989) 5 BCC 82*, where there was a single example of laying the company's accounts before the general meeting out of time).

In *Re a Company, ex parte Burr [1992] BCLC 724*, a petition under section 459 was based on an allegation that the directors had failed to keep adequate accounting records and that the company's property had been carried into the balance sheet at the historic cost instead of being revalued and shown at a new valuation. The petition also alleged that excessive remuneration was being paid to the directors (including payments made to their wives) and that the directors were continuing the business of the company when it was not making a profit. Vinelott J held that there was no evidence that the directors had failed to keep adequate accounting records. Paragraph 1(2) of Part I of Schedule 7 to the 1985 Act did not impose an unqualified duty to revalue the property and, therefore, the directors were not in breach of their statutory obligations. Further, there was no evidence that the remuneration paid to the directors (including payments made to their wives) was out of line with what would have been paid to replacements or what was paid to executive directors of other comparable companies. As to the continuation of the business, in certain circumstances the court might draw the inference that a decision by directors to continue to trade when a company was failing to make a profit was influenced by a desire to remain in office; but there had to be some evidence which, if substantiated at trial, could justify that inference. In the instant case, there was evidence that although the company had made a trading loss on its core business, the company was diversifying into more profitable areas and also that it would benefit from the acquisition of new custom-built premises. The petition for relief was dismissed.

The expression 'unfairly prejudicial' is deliberately imprecise, to replace an earlier attempt to provide a similar remedy using the word 'oppressive', which had been too restrictively construed. The starting point is to ask whether the conduct complained of is in accordance with the company's articles. A finding that the conduct was not in accordance with the articles does not necessarily mean that it was unfair, still less that the court will exercise its discretion to grant relief. The articles might not fully reflect the understandings upon which the shareholders were associated: *Re Saul D Harrison & Sons plc [1994] BCC 475*, where the court found, on the facts, no equitable considerations to be superimposed on the articles in the absence of bad faith.

Once an administrative receiver of a company is appointed, that may make it impossible for its affairs to be conducted in a manner unfairly prejudicial to a minority shareholder. However, an order for relief would be appropriate in such a case if the unfairly prejudicial conduct had prevented a sale of the minority shareholder's shares, or if the minority shareholder had sought an order for the purchase of his shares at a time when the company was solvent (*Re Hailey Group Ltd [1993] BCLC 459*).

Where a corporate shareholder brings an unfair prejudice petition, the court has power to order that shareholder to provide security for costs under section 726 of the Companies Act 1985 (*Re Unisoft Group Ltd [1994] BCC 11*).

For further cases on section 459, see *Re Ghyll Beck Driving Range Ltd [1993] BCLC 1126* (petitioner unjustifiably excluded from management and justifiably not trusting respondents); *Re Baltic Real Estate Ltd (No 1) [1993] BCLC 498* (majority shareholder with voting control not necessarily barred from seeking relief; ex-members cannot be proper respondents); *Re Baltic Real Estate Ltd (No 2) [1993] BCLC 503* (court had power under RSC Ord 11 rule 1(b), but not under RSC Ord 11 rule 1(d)(i) and (iii), to grant leave to serve a section 459 petition on respondents out of the jurisdiction where the order sought was for the transfer of shares within the jurisdiction; but since the petitioner as a controlling shareholder could remove the respondents as directors for their allegedly unfair prejudicial conduct and thus put an end to that conduct, he had not made out a case for relief); *Re BSB Holdings Ltd [1993] BCLC 246* (not only persons responsible for the alleged unfair prejudicial conduct but also those likely to be affected by relief rectifying that conduct may be respondents); *Re Welsh Highland Railway Light Railway Co [1993] BCLC 338* (definition of contributory in relation to unregistered company; a person not within the definition (in section 226 of the Insolvency Act 1986) cannot petition).

In connection with a contributory's petition, *Practice Direction No 1 of 1990* [*1990*] *BCC 292* issued by the Chancery Division (Companies Court) should be noted. It reads as follows:

'(1) Practitioners' attention is drawn to the undesirability of including as a matter of course a prayer for winding up as an alternative to a s 459 order. It should be included only if that is the relief which the petitioner prefers or if it is considered that it may be the only relief to which he is entitled.

(2) Whenever a prayer for winding up is included in a contributory's petition, the petition shall include a statement whether the petitioner consents or objects to a s 127 order in the standard form, and if he objects the affidavit in support shall contain a short statement of his reasons.

(3) If the petitioner objects to a s 127 order in the standard form but consents to such an order in a modified form, the petition shall set out the form of order to which he consents, and the affidavit in support shall contain a short statement of his reasons for seeking the modification.

(4) If the petition contains a statement that the petitioner consents to a s 127 order, whether in the standard or a modified form, but the petitioner changes his mind before the first hearing of the petition, he shall notify the respondents and may apply on notice to a judge for an order directing that no s 127 order or a modified order only (as the case may be) shall be made by the registrar, but validating dispositions made without notice of the order made by the judge.

(5) If the petition contains a statement that the petitioner consents to a s 127 order, whether in the standard or a modified form, the registrar shall without further inquiry make an order in such form at the first hearing unless an order to the contrary has been made by the judge in the meantime.

(6) If the petition contains a statement that the petitioner objects to a s 127 order in the standard form, the company may apply (in cases of urgency ex parte) to the judge for an order.

Section 127 order

Standard form

ORDER that notwithstanding the presentation of the said petition,

(1) payments made into or out of the bank accounts of the company in the ordinary course of the business of the company, and

(2) dispositions of the property of the company made in the ordinary course of its business for proper value,

between the date of presentation of the petition and the date of judgment on the petition or further order in the meantime shall not be void by virtue of the provisions of s 127 of the *Insolvency Act 1986* in the event of an order for the winding up of the company being made on the said petition.'

In view of the concern the bank holding the account may feel as to the extent of its obligation to be satisfied as to whether any such payment is in the ordinary course of business, Harman J in *Re a Company (No 00687 of 1991)* [1992] *BCLC 133* suggested the addition of the following proviso:

'Provided that [the relevant bank] should be under no obligation to verify for itself whether any transaction through the company's bank accounts is in the ordinary course of business, or that it represents full market value for the relevant transaction.'

Petition by Secretary of State

C5.31   The Secretary of State may present a petition on any of the grounds referred to in C5.10(1)(*b*)(*c*) and (2) above (section 124(4), as amended by section 60 of the Companies Act 1989). As to the court's attitude to a petition by the Secretary of State, see *inter alia, Re Lubin, Rosen and Associates Ltd [1975] 1 WLR 122* (referred to in C5.29(3)(*b*) above); *Re Armvent Ltd [1975] 1 WLR 1679*; *Re Bamford Publishers Ltd, The Times, 4 June 1977*; and *Re Golden Chemical Products [1976] Ch 300*. In *Re Walter L Jacob Ltd (1989) 5 BCC 244*, the court made an order for a winding up on the petition of the Secretary of State on the ground of public interest in respect of a financial services company which had publicised its services in a misleading way, whose records had been badly kept and whose further trading had been prohibited by FIMBRA. The fact that the company had ceased to trade before presentation of the petition was no reason to preclude a winding-up order.

Where the petition has been presented on the 'public interest' ground, it is not appropriate, in the absence of special circumstances, to require the Secretary of State to give an undertaking in damages which may result from the appointment of a provisional liquidator or special manager in the event of the petition being dismissed, if the appointment has been properly made on the facts (*Re Highfield Commodities Ltd [1984] 3 All ER 884*; see also *Hoffman-La Roche (F) AG v Secretary of State [1975] AC 295*).

In *Re Xyllyx plc (No 2) [1992] BCLC 378*, on 8 February 1990 the Secretary of State for Trade and Industry presented a winding-up petition against the company on the 'just and equitable' ground, because he had formed the opinion that it would be in the public interest that the company should be wound up. On 15 July 1991, he informed the court that he did not intend to pursue the petition which, accordingly, was dismissed. On the question of costs, Harman J stated that if a petition by the Secretary of State on public interest grounds failed, he should not automatically be ordered to pay the company's costs. Since the petition was presented at the public expense and in the public interest, the proper approach was to ask whether the petition was properly presented on the basis of information available to him. On the facts, there was sufficient material to justify the Secretary of State's opinion that it was in the public interest to present and pursue the petition until May 1990. However, he had failed to assess objectively events since May 1990, in particular the removal of the sole director of the company, who appeared to have conducted its affairs with disregard for the interests of the company, and his replacement by two independent directors who were making strenuous efforts to promote the company's interests. Accordingly, Harman J ordered that the company pay the Secretary of State's costs down to and including May 1990 and the Secretary of State should pay the company's costs from the end of May 1990 onwards, the costs to be set off one against the other.

Re Secure & Provide plc [*1992*] *BCC 405* was another instance of a petition presented by the Secretary of State on public interest grounds. The company had been specifically incorporated by an individual for the purpose of promoting a scheme for selling insurance. The method of marketing the insurance was described in the evidence as 'pyramid selling'. The Secretary of State did not allege that any aspects of the company's marketing scheme or its literature contravened the provisions of the Fair Trading Act 1973 or the regulations covering pyramid selling; but the petition was based on a number of allegedly fraudulent representations. Inspectors had been appointed to conduct enquiries into the company's affairs under section 447 of the Companies Act 1985, and the Official Receiver had been appointed provisional liquidator on the Department of Trade and Industry's *ex parte* application. Hoffmann J dismissed the petition with a direction, under Rule 4.30, that the provisional liquidator should not retain the company's property to meet his remuneration and expenses; those costs were to be borne by the petitioner. Certain statements were exaggerated or wrong, but they were made in good faith. The public interest did not require the winding up of the company. The evidence was not sufficient to justify the appointment of the provisional liquidator without giving the individual any opportunity to put his case or offer undertakings. This case demonstrates that the court is becoming increasingly prepared to subject the evidence on which the Secretary of State's petition is based, and his assumptions and opinions, to a close scrutiny, and less averse to making an order for costs against the Secretary of State in appropriate cases where the petition is dismissed.

Petition by Official Receiver

C5.32   Where a company is being wound up voluntarily, the court will make an order for a compulsory winding up on a petition by the Official Receiver (or any other party entitled) only if it is satisfied that the voluntary winding up cannot be continued with due regard to the interests of the creditors or contributories (section 124; and see *Re J Russell Electronics Ltd* [*1968*] *1 WLR 1252*). Where a petition was brought by the Official Receiver after 29 December 1986 (the date on which the

Insolvency Act 1986 relating to winding up of companies came into force) to wind up a company in respect of which a voluntary winding up had already commenced before that date, it was held that the position was governed by section 124(5) of the 1986 Act and not by the Companies Act 1985, section 519(7) (both of which sections are identical apart from the deletion of the reference to a winding up subject to the supervision of the court). (*Re Hewitt Brannan (Tools) Co Ltd [1990] BCC 354*; see also the 1986 Act, Schedule 11, paragraph 4(1)).

Presentation of the petition and ensuing proceedings up to winding-up order

Introduction

C5.33 A winding-up petition must be made on the relevant prescribed form with such variations as circumstances may require (Rule 12.7), and must comply with the relevant rules (including the requirement for the payment of a deposit on presentation of the petition—see below). For the procedure as regards the petition and ensuing proceedings, see Rules 4.7 to 4.21 and Forms 4.2 to 4.13 (creditor's petition), Rules 4.22 to 4.24 and Form 4.14 (contributory's petition), or in relation to partnerships, Schedules 3 to 6 and 9 to the Insolvent Partnerships Order 1994 (SI 1994 No 2421), and the forms contained in Schedule 9. Special procedural requirements apply where there is an administration order or a voluntary arrangement or where the administrator or the supervisor of the arrangement is the petitioner or the proposed liquidator (see Rule 4.7(7) to (10), as amended; as to partnerships, see the provisions of the 1994 Order).

Where winding up is sought by a member or the Secretary of State under sections 459 and 460 of the Companies Act 1985 as an alternative to other reliefs under section 461 of that Act, the applicable procedure is set out in the Companies (Unfair Prejudice Applications) Proceedings Rules 1986 (SI 1986 No 2000) and in the form contained in the Schedule thereto. Where reliefs are sought with respect to a number of companies in the same group and include in the alternative a winding-up order, a single petition in respect of those companies may be permissible; but otherwise there must be a separate winding-up petition in respect of each company (*Re a Company [1984] BCLC 307*).

If the petition does not allege a case for winding up within the relevant statutory provisions it is liable to be dismissed with costs unless the court allows it to be amended (*Re Wear Engine Works Co (1875) 10 Ch App 188*). For Scotland, see *inter alia*, Scottish Rule 4.76.

Where the petitioning creditor and the company agree that a petition, founded on a disputed debt, be withdrawn but the costs of the petition be costs in the cause in the Queen's Bench proceedings to be taken by the petitioning creditor to recover the debt, and the petition is dismissed at its hearing due to the petitioning creditor's absence, the court may restrain him from presenting a second petition founded on the same debt. (See *Re a Company (No 00928 of 1991), ex parte City Electrical Factors Ltd [1991]*

BCLC 514, where in such a situation Harman J stated that it was necessary to imply a term into the agreement that no further winding-up petition would be presented in respect of the same debt.)

The following paragraphs (C5.34 to C5.39 below) describe the procedure applicable to a winding-up petition, other than a petition by a contributory. However, certain aspects of this procedure do also apply to a contributory's petition—see C5.40 below.

Form and presentation of petition

C5.34   The petition, verified by affidavit, must be filed in the appropriate court (see C5.2 *et seq*. above), together with the requisite number of copies of the petition. The prescribed form of the petition is set out in Form 4.2. The forms of petition against a partnership in various situations are contained in Schedule 9 to the Insolvent Partnerships Order 1994 (SI 1994 No 2421). The affidavit (Form 4.3) must be made by the petitioner (or one of the petitioners) or a director, company secretary or similar company officer, or a solicitor who has been concerned in the matter giving rise to the presentation of the petition, or by some responsible person who is duly authorised to make the affidavit and has requisite knowledge of those matters (Rule 4.12). The requisite copies comprise one for service on the company (unless it is its own petition), one to be exhibited to the affidavit, and a sufficient number of others for service on (where applicable) any voluntary liquidator, administrator, administrative receiver, the supervisor of any voluntary arrangement in force and (in the case of an authorised institution or former authorised institution within the meaning of the Banking Act 1987) the Bank of England (unless it is the petitioner) (Rule 4.10). There must also be produced to the court the receipt for the deposit payable on presentation (currently £500—the Insolvency Fees Order 1986, SI 1986 No 2030 (as amended by SI 1990 No 560, SI 1991 No 496 and SI 1994 No 2541)) as security for the Official Receiver's administration fees (currently £640—SI 1986 No 2030, as amended by SI 1991 No 496). The deposit is refundable if the petition is dismissed or withdrawn or to the extent that assets of the company are available to pay the administration fee (SI 1986 No 2030, article 11). The prescribed form must be adhered to as far as possible. Longer or supplementary affidavits, notice of which must be given to the company, may be necessary where:

(*a*)   fraud or misconduct is alleged (*Re A B C Coupler and Engineering Co Ltd (No 2) [1962] 1 WLR 1236)*; or

(*b*)   the quasi-partnership analogy is invoked or a deadlock in the management is claimed (*Re Davis Investments (East Ham) Ltd [1961] 1 WLR 1396, CA; Re W R Willcocks & Co Ltd [1973] 3 WLR 669*) (see C5.26(5)); or

(*c*)   the Department of Trade and Industry inspector's report is relied upon (as to which see *Re Armvent Ltd [1975] 1 WLR 1679* and *Re St Piran Ltd [1981] 3 All ER 270*).

Unreasonably or unnecessarily long affidavits or hearsay statements on substantive matters are generally discouraged (see *Re Koscot Inter-planetary (UK) Ltd*; *Re Koscot AG [1972] 3 All ER 829*).

(As to the contents of a contributory's petition, see *Practice Direction No 1 of 1990 (Companies Court: Contributory's Petitions) [1990] BCC 292*, reproduced in C5.30 above.)

The court fixes a venue for the hearing of the petition, and this is endorsed by the court on the copies of the petition. The seal of the court is then applied to the copies, which are returned to the petitioner for service (Rule 4.7).

A petition must be endorsed by a solicitor. When it is issued by the company itself, it cannot be endorsed by one of its directors (see *Re a Company (No 001029 of 1990) ex parte F Ltd [1991] BCLC 567*, where a petition by a company was struck out due to non-compliance with RSC Ord 5, r 6, which requires a company to conduct proceedings through solicitors; although in a special situation, Scott J in *Arbuthnot Leasing International Ltd v Havelet Leasing Ltd [1990] BCLC 802* at *811* had allowed a director to conduct proceedings on his company's behalf).

Service of petition

C5.35   Service on the company is effected at its registered office by the petition being handed (*a*) to a person who there and then acknowledges himself to be — or to the best of the server's knowledge, information and belief is — a director or other officer or employee of the company, or (*b*) to a person who there and then acknowledges himself to be authorised to accept service. If no such person is present, it may be deposited at or about the registered office in such a way that it is likely to come to the notice of a person attending the office. If service in any of those ways is not practicable, or the company has no registered office or is an unregistered company, service may be effected (according to Rule 4.8(4), as amended) by leaving it at its last known principal place of business in such a way that it is likely to come to the attention of the person attending there, or by delivering it to the secretary or some director, manager or principal officer of the company, wherever that person may be found. In the case of an oversea company, service may be effected in any manner provided for by section 695 of the Companies Act 1985, i.e. by leaving it or sending it by post to any person mentioned in particulars delivered to the Registrar of Companies at the address so mentioned (see also *Rome v Punjab National Bank* referred to in C5.24 above which may apply here) or, failing such service, by leaving it or sending it by post to any place of business established by the company in Great Britain (Rule 4.8; as to proof of service, see Rule 4.9 and Forms 4.4 and 4.5). Neither the Insolvency Rules 1986 nor the Companies (Unfair Prejudice Applications) Proceedings Rules 1986 require that leave of the court be obtained under RSC Order 11 before service of a winding-up petition out of the jurisdiction (*Re Harrods (Buenos Aires) Ltd [1990] BCC 481*).

If for any reason it is impracticable to effect service as mentioned above, the petition may be served in such other manner as the court approves or directs. Application for this purpose may be made *ex parte* with an affidavit stating what steps have been taken to effect service and why the service is impracticable (Rule 4.8).

In *Re Corbenstoke Ltd [1989] BCLC 496*, where the petitioner served the petition at the address registered at Companies House which proved to be out of date, Hoffmann J refused to strike out the petition, stating that the petitioner had done all it could to search for the correct address; in any event, supporting creditors had appeared so that the company was not prejudiced. (See also *Re Garton (Western) Ltd [1989] PCC 428.*)

For variations of the procedure in the case of a partnership, see the Insolvent Partnerships Order 1994 (SI 1994 No 2421).

Advertisement of petition and restraining orders

C5.36   Unless the court otherwise directs, the petition must be advertised by the petitioner once in the *Gazette* so as to appear (if the company is the petitioner) not less than seven business days before the day appointed for the hearing or (where someone other than the company is the petitioner) not less than seven business days after service on the company nor less than seven business days before the appointed day. If compliance with these requirements is not reasonably practicable, the court may direct the advertisement to be placed in a specified newspaper, instead of in the *Gazette* (Rule 4.11).

The advertisement must be in Form 4.6 or (in partnership cases) Form 8 in Schedule 9 to the Insolvent Partnerships Order 1994 and must contain particulars specified in Rule 4.11(4) or (in partnership cases) Form 8 referred to above. If the petition is not duly advertised, the court may dismiss it (Rule 4.11(5)) or order the petitioner to bear part of his costs or, where the advertisement was in the wrong form and readvertisement in the correct form is dispensed with, deprive the petitioner's solicitor of his profit costs in respect of the advertisement and make him bear them personally (*Practice Note [1980] 1 WLR 657*).

The petitioner or his solicitor must, at least five days before the hearing, file in court a certificate of compliance with the rules relating to service and advertisement together with a copy of the advertisement. Failure to do so may result in dismissal of the petition (Rule 4.14, Form 4.7). The power to strike out a petition for failure to allow sufficient time between service of the petition and its advertisement is intended to be disciplinary, and would not be used where the petitioner was faultless, for example, where the petitioner served the petition at the original registered office of the company, the change of its registered office as notified to the Registrar of Companies not having been noted on the Registrar's file due to a mistake (*Re Corbenstoke Ltd [1989] BCLC 496*; see also *Re Signland Ltd [1982] 2 All ER 609*).

Delaying the advertisement of a petition (other than one by the company itself) for at least seven days after the service enables the company, if it alleges the petition to be vexatious, groundless or an abuse of the process of the court, to apply to restrain the advertisement of the petition, as the advertisement may seriously damage the company's business and financial position even if the petition is subsequently rejected (see *Stonegate Securities Ltd v Gregory [1980] 1 All ER 241*, and *Holt Southey Ltd v Catnic Components Ltd [1978] 1 WLR 630*). The fact that the debt on which the petition (or the statutory demand preceding it) is founded is disputed on *bona fide* and substantial grounds may be sufficient to justify a restraining order. In *Re a Company (No 1573 of 1983) [1983] BCLC 492*, the petitioner was an alleged prospective creditor in respect of costs of an earlier action which had not been fixed or agreed. Harman J, granting an injunction, held that (1) it was arguable that until the costs were taxed or agreed, they were in the nature of a disputed debt, (2) it was not a proper use of the Companies Court to present a petition based on an unascertained debt which had never been demanded and which the company had never had a chance to pay and (3) a petitioning creditor was invoking a class right and if the petition was brought for a purpose other than the benefit of the petitioner's class, then it was improperly brought. (See also *Re a Company [1894] 2 Ch 349*; *Re Laceward Ltd [1980] 1 WLR 133*.)

In *Re a Company (No 009080 of 1992) [1993] BCLC 269*, at different stages of litigation costs had been awarded against and in favour of the company, and those awarded in favour of the company were likely to exceed, according to the company's contention, those awarded against it. However, the court refused to restrain advertisement of a winding-up petition presented by the other party based on the costs awarded in its favour. The court was influenced by the point that as the company was already insolvent and in administrative receivership, and had ceased trading, the balance was in favour of allowing the petition to proceed. Among the relevant factors to be considered were the respective prejudice to the parties, whether the creditors would be prejudiced if the petition did not proceed, whether the petitioner would suffer some special prejudice and the effect on the company in either case.

However, a petition is not an abuse of process, whatever the motive behind its presentation, so long as there are legal grounds for its presentation. This is so even if other legal remedies exist to deal with some of the presenter's complaints (*Coulson Sanderson & Ward v Ward (1986) 2 BCC 99, 207 (CA)*; see also the *Cornhill Insurance* case referred to in C5.22 above).

The court may restrain advertisement of a winding-up petition if there is pending an administration petition, as it would be quite contrary to the whole essence of the administration procedure that anything be done, while an administration petition is pending, to continue legal proceedings or to do anything which may be seen in public to damage the company (*Re a Company (No 001992 of 1988) (1988) 4 BCC 451*). Where an administration petition is merely being *contemplated* but no petition has actually been issued, and an undertaking is given to the court to issue one immediately, the court may, as part of its *quia timet* jurisdiction, order cancellation of an advertisement, as the advertisement might damnify the company (*Re a Company (No 001448 of 1989) [1989] BCLC 715*). However, if no such undertaking is given, then, unless the petitioner for winding up is guilty of abuse of the process of the court, the advertisement of a winding-up petition will not be restrained (*Re Manlon Trading Ltd (1988) 4 BCC 455*).

Where advertisement of a contributory's petition has been expressly restrained, it is not open to the petitioner's solicitors to refer to the petition in a letter to a third party, for example, a company's bank. In the context of Rule 4.23(1)(c) relating to a contributory's petition, the meaning of the word 'advertised' includes 'notified' (*Re a Company (No 00687 of 1991) [1992] BCLC 133*, Harman J; see also the Australian case of *Melcann Ltd v Marmion Holdings Pty Ltd (1991) 9 ACLC 678*). In that case, upon receipt of such a letter the bank froze the company's account, notwithstanding that the registrar had made an order validating all future payments into and out of the account in the ordinary course of business. This necessitated an application by the company, as a result of which the order was varied to the effect that the bank would not be obliged to verify for itself whether the transactions through the account were in the ordinary course of business or at full market value; the solicitors were ordered to pay the costs of that application. (See also C5.30 (final paragraph) above and C8.4(C)(*h*) below.)

The court may not only expressly restrain advertisement but also expressly, by order, restrain the petitioner from otherwise publishing the petition (*Re a Company (No 007339 of 1985) [1986] BCLC 127*). In *Re Bill Hennessey Associates Ltd [1992] BCC 386* (also cited as *Re a Company (No 0013925 of 1991), ex parte Rousell [1992] BCLC 562*), on the day a creditor presented a winding-up petition, and the petition was served, by hand, on the company, her solicitors faxed a copy of the petition to the company's bankers with a covering letter stating 'We enclose a copy of the winding-up petition which has today been presented against the above company who we believe holds an account with you.' The bank immediately froze the company's account which happened to be in credit. The judge stated that the decision of Harman J in *Re a Company (No 00687 of 1991)* (above), where he had construed the meaning of 'advertisement' as being 'a notification to an outsider of the existence of the petition' was not applicable in the instant case, as that decision had been made in the context of an order prohibiting advertisement and not in the context of Rule 4.11 (which, as stated above, prohibits advertisement of the petition in the *Gazette* before the expiry of seven days from the date of its service on the company). The judge relied, however, on *Re Signland Ltd [1982] 2 All ER 609* where Slade J had expressed the purpose of what is now Rule 4.11 as being

'(1)   to give the company the opportunity to discharge the debt in question, if it is undisputed, before advertisement takes place, with all the necessary potentially damaging consequences to the company, and

(2) to enable the company, if it wishes to dispute the debt, to apply to the court to restrain advertisement'.

The judge said that he would go further and say that the seven days gave the company the opportunity of considering its position in general with regard to the petition, including the possibility of an application under section 127. In *Re Signland*, Slade J, who was dealing with a case where the advertisement in fact took place two days before the petition was served, had gone on to say: 'it seems to me to have been a flagrant and serious breach and one of a type which the court must take every step to discourage'. In the instant case, the judge accordingly dismissed the petition on a more general ground. He stated:

'However I have no doubt that the interference with the company's bank account . . . was a principal purpose of giving virtually simultaneous notice of the petition to the company's bank. . . . It has had a serious consequence on the conduct of the company's business. In my judgment the right inference is that the sequence of events was designed to put pressure on the company, and that appears to me to be a wrong use of the Companies Court jurisdiction and procedures. It would, I think, be deplorable if creditors could select for the purpose of maximising pressure on a company whom they would inform, and how, and how quickly. I am reinforced in my view by the approach of Slade J in the *Signland* case.'

The above cases may be contrasted with *SN Group plc v Barclays Bank plc* [1993] *BCC 506* where Jonathan Parker J held that 'advertisement' in Rule 4.11 referred to the advertisement in the Gazette. If that were not the case, it would follow that notification to the company's bank would be a breach of the rule. (It is submitted that this reasoning would defeat the very purpose of the restriction in the rule against advertisement within seven days after service. Publication of the petition in other newspapers and by other means can cause equal or even more harm to the company.) However, the judge was also influenced by the fact that the company was indisputably insolvent and a notification of the petition to the company's bank did not amount to publication for an improper purpose.

A petitioner owes no duty of care to the company in regard to service of process or any other step in the proceedings and is not liable in negligence if a winding-up order would not have been made but for a defective service or other step (*Business Computers International Ltd v Registrar of Companies and others* [1987] *BCLC 621*).

The court has power not only to restrain the advertisement of a petition but also to restrain *presentation* of a petition, as recognised by the *Practice Directions* referred to below.

On an interlocutory motion, the court should not interfere with what would otherwise appear to be a legitimate right to present a petition unless there is evidence sufficient to establish *prima facie* that the company would succeed in establishing that the presentation would constitute an abuse of the process (see e.g. the *Cornhill Insurance* case referred to in C5.22 above).

As provided by *Practice Direction [1987] 1 All ER 107*, an application to restrain the presentation or advertisement of a winding-up petition must be made direct to the judge of the Companies Court and, unless otherwise ordered, must be heard in open court. A *Practice Direction ([1988] 1 WLR 998)*, issued on 11 July 1988, by the Chief Chancery Master under the authority of the Vice-Chancellor, directs that from 3 October 1988 every application to restrain presentation of a winding-up petition should be made by originating motion in the Companies Court instead of, as under the previous practice, by motion in an action commenced by writ in the Chancery Division.

Where a restraining order is applied for on the ground that the petition debt is disputed, the court would practically never make an order pursuant to Rule 7.7(1) for cross-examination of the deponents of the affidavits tendered in support of the application. The court is only required to determine whether there is a substantial case to be argued either way and is not required to make a finding of fact: *Re a Company (No 00962 of 1991), ex parte Electrical Engineering Contracts (London) Ltd [1992] BCLC 248.*

Withdrawal

C5.37 The court may on any *ex parte* application allow the petitioner to withdraw the petition on such terms as to costs as the parties may agree, if at least five days before the hearing the petitioner satisfies the court that the petition has not been advertised, that no notice in support of or opposition to the petition has been received by him and that the company consents to the withdrawal (Rule 4.15, Form 4.8).

Substitution of petitioner

C5.38 Rule 4.19 empowers the court (on such terms as it thinks just) to substitute as petitioner any other creditor or contributory who would have a right to present a winding-up petition against the company and who is desirous of prosecuting it, if the circumstances mentioned in the Rule relating to the original petitioner's default, or unwillingness or inability to proceed, exist. Following substitution, the winding up is still deemed to have commenced from the date of presentation of the petition by the original petitioner. This provision has an important practical significance. If the original petitioner has received payment of his debt after the presentation (perhaps as an inducement not to prosecute his petition) the payment may be set aside under section 127 (see C8.4 below). It also prevents time running between the date of the presentation and substitution for the purposes of the Limitation Acts (see C9.5 below), the execution process referred to in C9.2 to C9.4 below and the antecedent transactions and events referred to in C10.1 *et seq.* below. It is the almost invariable practice of the court to ensure that the winding up of a company is subject to one petition only. Convenience and the saving of costs are also in favour of the substitution rather than a separate petition. Where the original petition has already been advertised, the court may order readvertisement, amendment and re-service: *Re Creative Handbook Ltd [1985] BCLC 1*.

The court has jurisdiction to permit an assignee of a debt, upon which the winding-up petition was based, to be substituted as a petitioner even if the assignment had taken place after the presentation of the petition (*Perak Pioneer Ltd v Petroliam Nasional BhD [1986] 3 WLR 105 PC*).

Appearances

C5.39 Every person intending to appear at the hearing to support or oppose the petition must give the petitioner or his solicitor notice of the intention on Form 4.9 to arrive not later than 4 p.m. on the business day before the day of the hearing or adjourned hearing. A person failing to observe this requirement may appear only with the leave of the court (Rule 4.16).

The petitioner must hand to the court before the hearing a list of appearances in Form 4.10. Particulars of any other party whom the court allows to appear must be added to the list (Rule 4.17, Form 4.10).

If the company intends to oppose the petition, its affidavit in opposition must be filed in court not less than seven days before the hearing date. A copy must be sent forthwith to the petitioner (Rule 4.18).

Variations in procedure in the case of a contributory's petition

C5.40 The petition must specify the grounds on which it is presented. According to Rule 4.22 (1A), the petition must be accompanied by the deposit payable on presentation (see C5.34 above). It must be filed in court with one copy for service.

The court fixes a 'return day' on which, unless it otherwise directs, the petitioner and the company must attend before the Registrar in Chambers for directions as to the procedure on the petition. The petitioner must serve a sealed copy of the petition on the company at least 14 days before the return day (Rule 4.22, Form 4.14). On the return day, the court gives directions with respect to the matters specified in Rule 4.23. Subject as above, Rules 4.16 (notice of appearance), 4.17 (list of appearances), 4.21 (transmission and advertisement of order), and 4.21A (expenses of voluntary arrangement) apply, with necessary modifications, to a contributory's petition as they apply to a creditor's petition (see Rule 4.24).

Appointment of provisional liquidator

C5.41 The court may on application appoint a provisional liquidator at any time after the presentation of the petition and before a winding-up order against a company. This also applies to a foreign company or an unregistered company (see below). The Official Receiver or any fit person may be appointed. The provisional liquidator must carry out such functions in relation to the company's affairs as the court may confer on him, and the court may limit his powers on appointment. Where the proceedings are in Scotland, the appointment of a provisional liquidator may be made at any time before the first appointment of liquidators. The applicant must furnish a deposit or security in respect of the remuneration and expenses of the Official Receiver, where the latter is appointed provisional liquidator (section 135; Rules 4.25 to 4.31; Form 4.15; and as to Scotland, see Scottish Rules 4.1 to 4.6 and Form 4.9 (Scot)).

The applicant must also comply with the provisions of Rule 7.3 and 7.4 as to the form of application and the service of notice at least 14 days before the date of the hearing. However, in an urgent case, the court may dispense with those requirements and proceed to hear the application forthwith or authorise a shorter period for service: Rule 7.4(6); and see *Re W F Fearman Ltd (1988) 4 BCC 139*. In that case, the court had before it both a creditors' petition for winding up and the directors' petition for an administration order and was minded to dismiss the latter. On the making of the winding- up order, it preferred to appoint provisional liquidators and (at the request of the Official Receiver) to appoint them special managers (see C11.29 below) rather than substantive liquidators (see C5.50 below). To appoint substantive liquidators would have been to pre-empt the right of the creditors at their meeting to choose the person or persons for that office (*Re W F Fearman Ltd (No 2) (1988) 4 BCC 141*).

An application for the appointment of a provisional liquidator may, in exceptional circumstances, be ordered to be heard *in camera* where the presentation of the winding-up petition has not been advertised and there is a risk of irreparable harm to the company's business and goodwill, it being not certain at that stage whether a winding-up order will eventually be made (*Re London and Norwich Investments Ltd [1988] BCLC 226*).

Where a winding-up petition has been presented against a company which is already in creditors' voluntary liquidation, a provisional liquidator may be appointed if the voluntary liquidator is in a position of conflict of interest, for example, if he is also a voluntary liquidator of an associated company and the affairs of the two companies are inextricably intertwined (*Re P Turner (Wilsden) Ltd [1987] BCLC 149 (CA)*). The court's power to appoint a provisional liquidator is not restricted to cases where the company consents or where the company is obviously insolvent or its assets are in jeopardy. Such a restriction would not cover the case of a well-run and prosperous company thriving on frauds (*Re Highfield Commodities Ltd [1984] 3 All ER 884*). The Secretary of State, acting on the 'public interest ground' (see above), will not in the absence of special circumstances be required, as the price of obtaining the appointment of a provisional liquidator or resisting his removal, to give an undertaking in damages in the event of his petition for winding up being dismissed (*Re Highfield Commodities Ltd (above)*).

An appointment of a provisional liquidator may be made in respect of an unregistered or a foreign company. Such an appointment was made in *Re a Company (No 003102 of 1991), ex parte Nyckeln Finance Co Ltd [1991] BCLC 539* where although a Guernsey-incorporated company's substantial assets were largely situated in Portugal, a large part of its business was carried on in England. The Official Receiver did not object to the appointment of a provisional liquidator and there was a real risk that in the absence of such an appointment, the assets would be dissipated by distribution otherwise than rateably amongst the creditors.

As to the appointment of a provisional liquidator in respect of a partnership, see the Insolvent Partnerships Order 1994 (SI 1994 No 2421).

Powers of court on hearing petition

C5.42   The court may dismiss the petition, adjourn the hearing conditionally or unconditionally or make any interim or other order that it thinks fit. A winding-up order cannot be refused merely because the company has no assets or its assets have been mortgaged to an amount equal to or in excess of those assets (section 125(1)). For variations of the court's powers in relation to a petition against a partnership, see the Insolvent Partnerships Order 1994 (above), which also contains provisions aimed at co-ordinating multiple petitions against the partnership and its members. The court is reluctant to grant adjournments of petitions for long or indefinite periods or repeatedly (*Re Boston Timber Fabrications Ltd [1984] BCLC 328*) even if they are unopposed (see statement of Brightman J [1977] 1 WLR 1066). As to adjournments to allow defaulting companies to file annual returns and the like, see *Practice Note [1974] 1 WLR 1459*. See also *Practice Directions [1986] 1 WLR 1428* (hearing of petitions by the Registrar in open court; solicitors' right of audience), *[1986] 1 WLR 545* (solicitors' right of audience in open court), and *[1987] 1 All ER 107* (applications to court). (As to some of the considerations which determine whether or not a petition should be granted, see C5.29 and C5.30 above.)

An example where, in the special circumstances of the case, the court granted a long adjournment was *Re Bank of Credit and Commerce International SA [1992] BCC 83*. The Bank of England presented a winding-up petition in respect of BCCI under section 92 of the Banking Act 1987 based on two grounds: first, that it was in the public interest to wind up BCCI and, second, that BCCI was insolvent. Previously the court had granted an adjournment for eight days so that three matters could be considered. The first was that the provisional liquidators appointed by the court and a commissaire appointed by the courts in Luxembourg were encountering difficulties in obtaining information from the majority shareholders in Abu Dhabi. The second was the position of the employees of BCCI in the United Kingdom whose situation during a prolonged adjournment could be very difficult. The third matter was the position of sterling depositors in England, who would not enjoy the benefits of the Deposit Protection Scheme established under the Banking Act 1987 until a winding-up order was made.

At the resumed hearing, the majority shareholders, supported by the provisional liquidators and the commissaire, sought a further adjournment of the hearing of the petition for a substantial period to allow for further investigation into the position of BCCI and the possibility of formulating a scheme whereby at least a partial rescue could be achieved. The Bank of England opposed the application on the grounds that BCCI was insolvent and that the interests of small depositors would be prejudiced, as payment of the compensation to them under the Deposit Protection Scheme would be delayed. The court rejected the Bank of England's opposition and granted an adjournment for six months for the following reasons:

(1)   The interim scheme for partial compensation out of a trust fund set up by the majority shareholders would alleviate immediate financial hardship to the small depositors during the adjournment period.

(2)   As the best prospect of any substantial recovery by the creditors of BCCI worldwide was the restructuring proposals which the majority shareholders might put forward, it would not be in the interests of the depositors of BCCI to stand in the way of the possibility of a rescue. The Bank of England was putting undue stress on the interests of English sterling creditors at the expense of other creditors worldwide.

(3)   BCCI might very well be insolvent but that had not been proven and a further adjournment would allow detailed investigation.

(4)   Although the allegations of fraud made by the Bank of England, if true, would certainly make a winding up of BCCI in the public interest, the appointment of provisional liquidators meant that no further fraud could take place during the adjournment period. While the Bank of England's desire to demonstrate that banks which act in a way BCCI was alleged to have acted must not survive was understandable, it was not essential to the immediate interest of the public or of the depositors that that should be demonstrated at this stage.

(5)   In view of the major task of ascertaining the extent of the problems within BCCI and formulating any rescue plan, a six-month period of adjournment was not inordinate.

In the case of a petition against a partnership, where the petitioner also presents an insolvency petition against one or more partners, the court order may contain directions as to the future conduct of any insolvency proceedings against any partner against whom an insolvency order has been made (the Insolvent Partnerships Order 1994 (SI 1994 No 2421)).

Formalities regarding winding-up order

C5.43   When a winding-up order has been made, the procedure as to completion, notification and transmission thereof, laid down in section 130, Rules 4.20 and 4.21 and Forms 4.11, 4.12 and 4.13, must be followed. In particular, the Official Receiver must file a copy with the Registrar of Companies and advertise the order in the *Gazette* and in a local newspaper.

Costs of the proceedings

C5.44 Upon disposing of a winding-up petition, the court has a wide discretion on the question of costs of the proceedings (see Rule 7.33). Usually a successful petitioner and the company would be awarded their costs payable out of the company's assets, subject to any encumbrances. For cases on the question of costs see, *inter alia, Re A E Hayter & Sons (Porchester) Ltd [1961] 1 WLR 1008; Re Bostels Ltd [1968] Ch 346; Re E K Wilson & Sons Ltd [1972] 1 WLR 791; Re M McCarthy & Co (Builders) Ltd (No 2) [1976] 2 All ER 339; Re Bathampton Properties Ltd [1976] 1 WLR 168; Re Lanaghan Bros Ltd [1977] 1 All ER 265; Re Reprographics Exports (Euromat) Ltd (1978) 122 SJ 400; Re Dramstar, The Times, 30 October 1980.* A creditor or contributory who has not given notice in proper time will only be allowed to appear on the hearing of the petition if he undertakes not to seek an order for costs (*Practice Note (1976) 120 SJ 317*). Where, after presentation of the creditors' petition, but before its advertisement, the debt on which it was founded has been paid without an offer to pay the petitioner's costs, the petitioner must elect either to have the petition struck out with no order for costs, or to seek an adjournment to allow an advertisement to take place so that he ultimately gets his costs (*Re Shusella Ltd [1983] BCLC 505*).

In *Re Bathampton Properties Ltd* (above), the company was a one-man company which opposed a creditor's petition on the ground that the debt was disputed. After several adjournments and a three-day hearing, Brightman J decided that there was no *bona fide* dispute on substantial grounds and proceeded to make a winding-up order. The person owning the company had caused the company to resist the petition because he wanted to postpone the sale of the property which the company owned until he could get a better price, so as to generate liquid assets with which to discharge the company's liabilities. The judge said that the opposition to the petition was entirely for the benefit of that person and that there would be

> 'a great injustice in permitting the beneficial owner of all the shares in a company to oppose a winding-up petition in order to seek to secure a benefit for himself as shareholder and then, having failed in his opposition, to charge the costs of such unsuccessful opposition to the creditors of the company'.

He ordered that the company's costs of opposing the petition should not be paid out of the assets of the company in priority to the payment in full of all the unsecured creditors of the company. Obviously, the intention was to indirectly penalise the beneficial owner for such costs; however, the judge took the view that he had no power to make an order for costs directly against a person who was not a party to the proceedings, or who was a party to the proceedings but had not added to the costs. Such an indirect order for costs came to be known as 'a *Bathampton* order'.

However, since that case, the House of Lords has held in *Aiden Shipping Co Ltd v Interbulk Ltd [1986] AC 965* that the court does have jurisdiction to make an order for costs against a person who is not a party to the proceedings. *Re Land & Property Trust Co plc [1991] BCC 459* shows that this jurisdiction may be exercised in the Companies Court to make an order against directors of a company which had presented what the judge considered to have been a hopeless petition for an administration order. Nicholls LJ in that case remarked that the circumstances in which it will be just to make such an order are exceptional and that in the nature of things it will very seldom be right to order a person who is not a party to the proceedings to pay the costs of the proceedings.

In *Re Record Tennis Centres Ltd [1991] BCC 509* (also cited as *Re a Company (No 004055 of 1991) [1991] 1 WLR 1003*), Hoffmann J decided that a dispute of the petition debt on the ground of alleged set-off had been 'conjured up' at a late stage to avert liquidation, and dismissed the company's motion to strike out the creditor's petition. He ordered the company to pay the petitioning creditor's costs of the motion on the standard basis in any event, with liberty to the petitioning creditor to apply on notice to the persons affected for an order that the company's costs of the motion be paid by one or more of the directors personally, or that such costs be disallowed under the Rules of the Supreme Court, Order 62, rule 11. Hoffmann J was of the view that it was unfair to make an order in the *Bathampton* form on grounds which had no necessary connection with the conduct of the solicitors themselves. He stated:

> '*Prima facie*, solicitors representing the company are retained by the company itself and must look to the company alone for their costs. If the company is insolvent, the effect of an order in the *Bathampton* form is to deprive them of their costs . . . The court has, of course, jurisdiction under RSC O 62, r 11 to disallow the costs as between the company and its solicitors if it considers that they have been unreasonably or improperly incurred. Under that rule, however, the court must give the solicitor a reasonable opportunity to appear and show cause why such an order should not be made. The inquiry is into the conduct of the solicitor and not that of the shareholders or directors of the company.'

Hoffmann J went on to state that since the court now has power to do directly what Brightman J tried to do indirectly in *Bathampton*, he found it difficult to imagine a case in which it would be proper in future to make an order in the *Bathampton* form.

In *Taylor v Pace Developments Ltd [1991] BCC 406 (CA)*, the question was whether the company's managing director and sole beneficial shareholder, who had caused the company (which was insolvent at the time) to defend unsuccessfully an action against it, should be ordered to pay personally the plaintiff's costs. The Court of Appeal, whilst recognising the principles of the *Aiden Shipping* case (above), refused on the facts to make an order to that effect. Lloyd LJ rejected the argument that the person substantially responsible for causing the costs to be incurred should necessarily be made to bear them; otherwise, for example, in the case of a one-man company, the controlling director would always be in that position. He suggested that such an order might be appropriate

'. . . if the company's defence is not *bona fide*, as, for example, where the company has been advised that there is no defence, and the proceedings are defended out of spite, or for the sole purpose of causing the company to incur irrecoverable costs. No doubt there will be other cases. But such cases must necessarily be rare'.

There is no general rule that where a petition is dismissed on a debt being paid the court should not order the company to pay the petitioning creditors' costs. Moreover, it is a wrong exercise of judicial discretion to order the petitioner to pay the company's costs merely because the petitioner acts over-hastily and presents a petition without giving the company notice of a default judgment or of intention to petition (*Re Eric Audio Visual Ltd, The Times, 13 May 1981*). The company may be ordered to pay a petitioning creditor's costs where he withdraws the petition because a majority in number and value of the creditors oppose it but such opposition only manifests itself at the hearing which had previously been adjourned on two occasions (*Re Arrow Leeds Ltd [1986] BCLC 538*).

However, in *Re Cannon Screen Entertainment Ltd [1989] BCLC 660*, Warner J refused to grant costs to a creditor who had served a statutory demand on the company but who, on an application by the company to restrain him from presenting a winding-up petition and on seeing the company's evidence, undertook not to proceed with the petition. Warner J said that a creditor who had no notice of a substantial defence to his claim, and serves a statutory demand, does so at his own risk. This is because the normal course for a creditor to adopt, if he wants to enforce a debt by proceedings, is to issue a writ and, if he is sufficiently confident that there is no defence to his claim, he is then entitled to make use of the procedure under Order 14 of the Rules of the Supreme Court. If, instead of adopting that course, the creditor takes the 'short cut' of serving a statutory demand with a view to presenting a winding-up petition without having obtained judgment, he does so at his own risk as to costs. If it should turn out that there is a defence to his claim, he must pay the costs of the company against whom he has chosen to take such proceedings.

In *Re Fletcher Hunt (Bristol) Ltd [1988] BCLC 703*, a winding-up petition was presented by a creditor who was also a director and shareholder of the company. His co-director instructed solicitors to act for the other shareholders and the company. Those solicitors contacted the petitioner's solicitors and accepted service of the petition. After unsuccessful negotiations for a compromise, a winding-up order was made without opposition. The petitioner applied for the excess of his costs, over what they would have been if the petition had been unopposed on its first hearing, to be paid by the solicitors acting for the company, on the ground that they were never properly retained by the company. The court dismissed the application on the ground that by sending the petition for service to the company's solicitors, the petitioner, as a director having the necessary authority, did something through the agency of his solicitors which confirmed the authority.

In *Gamelstaden plc v Brackland Magazines Ltd [1993] BCC 194*, during several months preceding the presentation of the latest winding-up petition against the company, several winding-up petitions had been presented against it but in each case the petitioners had been paid off. When other petitioners were substituted in their place, they, too, had been paid off. After the presentation of the latest petition, Chadwick J granted the petitioner's application for the appointment of provisional liquidators pending a winding-up order. He held that the conduct of the directors in buying off the previous petitioners had been dishonourable and a breach of fiduciary duty. The company had been minded to oppose the appointment of the provisional liquidators but had failed to appear at the hearing. In those circumstances, Chadwick J ordered that the costs of the application for the appointment of provisional liquidators should be borne by the directors because the application had been made necessary by their breach of fiduciary duty. He also ordered the directors to pay the costs of the adjournment which they had obtained with a view to opposing the application for the appointment of provisional liquidators.

However, in *Re Land and Property Trust Co plc (No 2) [1993] BCC 462*, the Court of Appeal set aside an order for costs which had been made by Harman J (*[1991] BCC 446*) against the directors personally, in refusing an adjournment of the petition (which the directors had sought so as to enable them to apply for an administration order) and making a winding-up order. The Court of Appeal was of the view that an adjournment should have been granted. (At an earlier hearing (see *[1991] BCC 459*), the Court of Appeal had held that the directors were entitled to appeal as of right, although Harman J had refused leave to appeal.)

For the circumstances in which a receiver under a debenture may be ordered to pay the costs of an action carried on by him after the winding-up order which had been incurred after such order, see *Bascal Contracting Ltd v Modern Engineering (Bristol) Ltd [1980] 2 All ER 655*.

Proceedings subsequent to a winding-up order

Rescission of winding-up order

C5.45   The court has an inherent power to rescind a winding-up order provided an application is made promptly and, in any event, before the winding up has been perfected (see *Re Intermain Properties Ltd [1986] BCLC 265*); and now has a statutory power to rescind the order provided that an application is made within seven days after the date of the order— Rule 7.47(4). However, by virtue of Rules 4.3 and 12.9, the court has power to extend the time limit in appropriate cases. In *Re Virgo Systems Ltd (1989) 5 BCC 833*, a winding-up petition and a statutory demand were correctly served at a company's premises. The company knew nothing of the petition and did not attend the hearing at which a winding-up order was made. When the liquidator contacted the company it applied out of time for the winding-up order to be rescinded, notwithstanding the fact that no complaint was made about service, or about the order itself. The company put forward a scheme for immediate payment of debts. The court extended the time for making the application and rescinded the winding-up order, stating that on all the facts this was a proper case for the court to exercise its jurisdiction under Rule 7.47(1). The power of rescission is exercised cautiously. (See *Practice Notes [1971] 1 WLR 4* and *757*.) The fact that the winding-up order was made by mistake is a valid ground for rescission: *Re Calmex Ltd (1988) 4 BCC 761*, in which the court also stated that Rule 7.47 was expressed in general terms and gave the court jurisdiction to rescind the order notwithstanding that it had already been drawn up and the seven-day time limit (which the court has power to extend under Rule 4.3) had expired. The order in that case could properly be described as a nullity; and the court had power to order the removal of the order from the records of the Registrar of Companies (see C5.43 above). An alternative course is to apply to the court for a stay of the winding up (see C5.46 below; see also *Re Intermain Properties Ltd [1986] BCLC 265*).

Stay of winding up

C5.46   The court may, at any time after the winding-up order, on the application of the liquidator or the Official Receiver or any creditor or contributory, on appropriate proof, stay or (in Scotland) sist all the proceedings *in the winding up*, either altogether or for a limited time, on such terms and conditions as the court thinks fit (section 147). This provision should be distinguished from the provisions relating to the stay of proceedings *against the company* which is being wound up (see C8.2 below).

There seems to be no reason why this power cannot be invoked in a voluntary winding up as well, by virtue of section 112.

In exercising its discretion, the court has in the past applied the analogy of rescinding a receiving order in bankruptcy (for example, where all the debts have been discharged, provided for or compounded). The exercise of the discretion has depended not only on the wishes of the creditors but also on the interests of commercial morality. The court may refuse a stay if there is evidence of misfeasance or irregularities requiring investigation (*Re Calgary & Edmonton Land Co [1975] 1 WLR 355*). The test, as laid in *Re Telescriptor Syndicate Ltd [1903] 2 Ch 174* and approved in *Re Calgary & Edmonton* (above), is that the court must be satisfied that it is right to stay the winding up, and, if there are any matters as to which the court has doubts, then it should not order a stay. In *Re Lowston Ltd [1991] BCLC 570*, a default judgment against the company for £120,000, on which the creditor's petition and the winding-up order had been based, was subsequently set aside and was subject to serious dispute in *inter partes* litigation which was not proceeding with any speed or diligence. The applicants seeking the stay gave personal undertakings to file all the necessary statutory accounts and returns within three months. One of the applicants also undertook to postpone part of his claim against the company for a period of one year, that amount being sufficient to cover the present deficiency of assets. Harman J, in granting a stay, stated that he was satisfied that these undertakings gave proper protection to any future creditors of the company.

For a recent example of an unsuccessful application for annulment of a bankruptcy order where somewhat similar considerations apply, see *Re Robertson (a Bankrupt)* [*1989*] *1 WLR 1139* (debtor desiring time to put forward a scheme of arrangement).

In *Re Hockerill Athletic Club Ltd* [*1990*] *BCLC 921*, a case of a solvent voluntary winding up, when the liquidator proposed to make a distribution to the shareholders, some of the shareholders applied to the court for a stay of the winding up on the grounds that

(1) two of the applicants, who had been present at the winding-up meeting of the company, had not been aware that they were entitled to demand a poll,

(2) one of the applicants was willing to purchase the shares of the other shareholders,

(3) if the distribution by the liquidator was delayed, one of the applicants might be able to take steps to avoid capital gains tax,

(4) the liquidator would not conduct the dispute with the Inland Revenue about the base value of the company's land with the same vigour as the directors of the company,

(5) the minutes of the meetings of the shareholders did not record the opposition by one of the applicants to the winding up, and

(6) the Inland Revenue's opinion on the base value of the company's land had not been disclosed to the members before they voted on the resolution to wind up the company.

Warner J held that

(*a*) the company's articles required the support of three members for a poll vote whereas only two of the applicants had been present at the meeting, but, in any case, they were themselves to blame for failing to take proper legal advice before the meeting,

(*b*) the offer to purchase the shares was of no relevance as the value of the shares was so uncertain that any agreement between the parties could not be effected before any distribution, even if postponed for a short period, was made by the liquidator,

(*c*) the liquidator had to consider the interests of the members as a class and accordingly he did not have to consider the liability of one of the applicants to capital gains tax, (*d*)   there was no evidence that a liquidator would not conduct any dispute with the Inland Revenue with sufficient vigour and, even if the winding up was stayed, there was no certainty that the directors would be back in control of the company since it would be for the court to decide what was to be done as regards the management of the company,

(*e*)   the failure to record the opposition to a resolution did not invalidate the minutes of the meeting,

(*f*)   there was no obligation on directors in summoning a meeting of shareholders for the purposes of a winding-up resolution to relay all the details of the company's financial position before the meeting and, while it might have been preferable for the Inland Revenue's valuation to have been communicated to the meeting, the failure to do so did not invalidate the proceedings, and

(*g*)   accordingly, on the facts, the court would not grant the application as it would constitute an unwarranted interference with the discretion of the liquidator.

As to the procedure following a stay in a compulsory winding up, see Rule 4.48.

Official Receiver or interim liquidator in compulsory winding up

C5.47   On the winding-up order being made, the Official Receiver (or, in Scotland, the 'interim liquidator' appointed by the court at the time when the order is made) becomes liquidator and continues until he or another person becomes liquidator. The Official Receiver is, by virtue of his office, the liquidator during any vacancy in the office of liquidator (sections 136(2) and (3) and 138(1) and (2)). For detailed provisions about the Official Receiver, see sections 132, 399 to 401 and Rules 10.1 to 10.4. As to section 132, see also C8.5 below. For variations in the case of a partnership, see the Insolvent Partnerships Order 1994 (SI 1994 No 2421).

Statement of affairs, accounts and other information in compulsory winding up

C5.48   Upon the appointment of the provisional liquidator, or the making of the winding-up order by a court, various provisions relating to the submission by the company's officers and others to the Official Receiver (or, in Scotland, the liquidator or provisional liquidator) of a statement of affairs of the company and its accounts and other information become applicable (see section 131 and Rules 4.32, 4.33, 4.35 to 4.37, 4.39 and 4.42, Forms 4.16 and 4.17 and Scottish Rules 4.7 to 4.9, and Forms 4.3 and 4.4 (Scot)). These include provisions as to extension of time for the submission of the statement, release of any person from the obligation to submit it and allowance for the expenses of preparing the statement and accounts. The statement may be used in evidence against its maker (section 433). For variations in the case of a partnership, see the Insolvent Partnerships Order 1994 (above).

First meetings of creditors and contributories in compulsory winding up

C5.49 In England and Wales, at any time when he is the liquidator of the company, the Official Receiver may convene separate (first) meetings of the creditors and contributories (together called 'the first meetings in the liquidation'—Rule 4.50(7)) for the purposes of choosing a person as liquidator in the place of the Official Receiver. As soon as practicable within twelve weeks beginning with the date of the winding-up order, he must decide whether to exercise this power. If he decides not to, he must notify his decision before the end of that period to the court and the creditors and contributories. He must convene such meetings if he is at any time requested to do so by one-quarter in value of the creditors in accordance with Rule 4.57 (see also Rule 4.50(6) and Form 4.21) (section 136). As to the procedure for the meetings, see C11.3 *et seq.* below.

In Scotland, the interim liquidator *must* as soon as practicable within 28 days beginning with the date of the order summon the first meetings for a similar purpose; but he may dispense with a meeting of the contributories where the winding up is on grounds including its inability to pay debts and it appears to him that it would be inappropriate to summon it (section 138(3) and (4)). (As to the procedure for the meetings, see C11.3 *et seq.* below.)

For variations in the case of a partnership, see the Insolvent Partnerships Order 1994 (SI 1994 No 2421).

Appointment of substantive liquidator in compulsory winding up

C5.50 In England and Wales, in the case of an insolvent company, the separate meetings referred to in C5.49 above may each nominate a person (who must be an authorised insolvency practitioner in relation to the company or body) as liquidator of the company or body. The person nominated by the creditors' meeting will act as liquidator, but if none is so nominated, the person nominated by the contributories' meeting (where applicable) will so act.

Where different persons are nominated by the two meetings, any creditor or contributory may, within seven days after the date of the nomination of the liquidator by the creditors, apply to the court for the appointment as liquidator of the person nominated by the contributories instead of or jointly with the person nominated by the creditors, or for the appointment of some other person instead of the person nominated by the creditors (section 139).

In Scotland, if no person is nominated by either of the meetings as liquidator in the place of the interim liquidator, the interim liquidator must make a report to the court. The court may appoint him or some other person as liquidator. The person appointed (otherwise than by the court) in place of the interim liquidator must forthwith notify the court of that fact (section 138).

Where a winding-up order is made immediately upon the discharge of an administration order (see PART B: ADMINISTRATION ORDERS), the court may appoint as liquidator the person who has been the administrator. Where a supervisor of a voluntary arrangement (see PART E: VOLUNTARY ARRANGE-MENTS) is in office at the time of the winding-up order, the court may appoint him as liquidator. In these cases, the Official Receiver does not become liquidator and need not summon the meetings above referred to (section 140). The Official Receiver is still under a duty to perform his investigatory functions under section 132 (see C5.47 above) and under the Company Directors Disqualification Act 1986 (see A4.9 PART A: GEN-ERAL above).

The court has no power under section 140 to appoint any person who has not been an administrator or supervisor as liquidator in addition to or substitution for the administrator or supervisor (*Re Exchange Travel (Holdings) Ltd [1992] BCC 954*). It should be noted, however, that an administrator or supervisor can only be appointed as liquidator if a winding-up order is made *immediately* upon the discharge of the admin-istration order or whilst the supervisor is *in office*. The court has no power to make a winding-up order upon the discharge of an administration order unless a winding-up petition is presented, for example by the administrator on behalf of the company, and the appropriate deposit is paid (Rule 4.7(7)).

In England and Wales, an alternative procedure can be invoked by the Official Receiver for the appointment of a liquidator in his place. This may be done where he does not wish to continue as liquidator and (i) he has decided under section 136(5) (see C5.49 above) not to summon meet-ings of creditors and (where applicable) contributories or (ii) any such meetings have been held but no person has been chosen to be liquidator in his place as a result thereof. Section 137 provides that, at any time when he is the liquidator, he may apply to the Secretary of State for the appoint-ment of another person as liquidator in his place and, where (ii) above applies, he must decide whether to refer the need for such an appoint-ment to the Secretary of State. (It is understood that, in practice, the Official Receiver for this purpose maintains a rota of authorised insol-vency practitioners who are willing to accept such appointments.) The Secretary of State may or may not accede to the Official Receiver's appli-cation (section 137). Where this procedure is adopted, it is still open to the creditors to requisition a meeting of the creditors to replace that liqui-dator by one appointed by the meeting (see Rules 4.50(6) and 4.57; and C5.49 above).

In the winding up of a Part II insurance company (see C5.17 above), where the court considers the appointment of a liquidator under section 139(4) (conflict between creditors' and contributories' wishes) or section

140 (appointment following administration or voluntary arrangement), the Policyholders Protection Board is entitled to appear and make representations on the choice of the liquidator (Rule 4 of the Insurance Companies (Winding up) Rules 1985 (SI 1985 No 95), as substituted by SI 1986 No 2002).

An out of court appointment of a liquidator in a compulsory liquidation must be certified by the chairman of the meeting which makes the appointment or the Secretary of State (as the case may be) and a copy of the certificate must be filed in court by the Official Receiver. Before the certificate or, in the case of a court appointment, the order is issued, the liquidator must (except where he is appointed by the Secretary of State) deliver a statement to the effect that he is a duly qualified insolvency practitioner and consents to act. An appointment by a meeting of creditors or contributories takes effect from the date of the filing of the certificate in court; an appointment by the court from the date of the order of appointment; and an appointment by the Secretary of State from the date specified in his certificate (Rules 4.100, 4.102, 4.104 and 4.105, Forms 4.27 to 4.30; as to Scotland, see Scottish Rules 4.18 and 4.20 and Forms 4.8 and 4.9 (Scot)).

The liquidator must also advertise his appointment in such newspaper as he thinks most appropriate for ensuring that it comes to the notice of the creditors and contributories, and forthwith notify the appointment to the Registrar of Companies (Rule 4.106; Form 4.31). In Scotland, notice of the appointment to the court and to the Registrar of Companies must be given within seven days of the date of the appointment and must be advertised (as stated above or in a newspaper circulating in the area where the company has its principal place of business) within 28 days of that date (Scottish Rules 4.18 and 4.19 and Form 4.9 (Scot)). Where a liquidator has been appointed in place of the Official Receiver by the Secretary of State (see above), the liquidator must give notice of his appointment to the creditors or, if the court so allows, advertise the appointment in accordance with the directions of the court. As to some of the contents of such notice, see C5.51 below. For variations in the case of a partnership, see the Insolvent Partnerships Order 1994 (SI 1994 No 2421).

As to the handover of assets to the substantive successor liquidator, see Rule 4.107 and Scottish Rule 4.21.

Liquidation committee in compulsory winding up

C5.51 Each of the separate meetings (subject, in the case of a partnership, to the Insolvent Partnerships Order 1994 referred to above), may appoint a liquidation committee. However, the committee does not carry out its functions while the Official Receiver is the liquidator; instead its functions are vested in the Secretary of State. The liquidator (other than the Official Receiver) may, at any time, and must if requested to do so by one-tenth in value of the creditors, convene separate meetings of the creditors and contributories (or a single meeting in the case of the partnership) for the purpose of appointing a committee (section 141). If the liquidator has been appointed by the Secretary of State, the notice or advertisement referred to in C5.50 above must state whether he proposes to convene meeting(s) under section 141 for the purpose of appointing a liquidation committee and, if he does not propose to do so, must also inform the creditors of their right under that section to requisition a meeting as stated above (section 137(4) and (5)).

The final composition of the committee must be not less than three and not more than five creditors elected by the creditors' meeting and, in the case of a 'solvent winding up' (that is, a winding up on grounds which do not include inability to pay debts) up to three contributories elected at their meeting (if at all) (Rules 4.151 and 4.152). However, where (even in an insolvent winding up) the creditors' meeting does not decide (or decides not) to appoint, but the contributories' meeting wishes to appoint, a committee, the latter meeting may appoint one of their number to apply to the court for another meeting of the creditors to be convened for establishing a committee. The court may grant the application if there are special circumstances justifying this course. If the creditors' meeting so convened does not establish a committee, a meeting of the contributories may do so. In that event, the committee will consist of not less than three and not more than five contributories elected at that meeting (section 141(3); Rule 4.154).

Where a winding-up order immediately follows the discharge of an administration order (see PART B: ADMINISTRATION ORDERS), the creditors' committee (if any) established for the purposes of the administration continues as the liquidation committee for the purposes of the winding up provided that the creditors' committee consists of at least three members. (A creditor member of that committee ceases to be a member on the making of a winding-up order, if his debt is fully secured.) A meeting of creditors convened by the liquidator may appoint additional members of the committee in order to make up numbers (between three and five) or fill vacancies. In the case of a solvent winding up (for meaning, see above), the liquidator must, on not less than 21 days' notice, summon a meeting of contributories, in order to elect (if the meeting so wishes) up to three contributory members of the committee (Rules 4.173 to 4.175).

Any creditor of the company (other than a fully secured creditor) is eligible to be a member of the liquidation committee provided that he has lodged his proof of debt and his proof has not been wholly disallowed for voting purposes (see C14.12 below) or wholly rejected for dividend purposes (see C14.2 *et seq.* below). In *Re W & A Glaser Ltd [1994] BCC 199*, Harman J held that the liquidation committee was not properly constituted, despite the certificate issued by the liquidator under Rule 4.153(1), because the purported creditor members of the liquidation committee were in fact not creditors and, hence, were not qualified. In an earlier decision in that case, he had also held that documents passing between the liquidator and the DTI concerning possible disqualification proceedings against the directors (see PART I: DISQUALIFICATION OF DIRECTORS) were not documents which were within any of the statutory rights of the committee to inspect, or in relation to which the committee could properly put questions to the liquidator or ask him for a report.

No person may be a member both as a creditor and a contributory. A body corporate can only be a member of the committee through a representative duly authorised for the purpose (Rules 4.152 and 4.159). As to the role of the committee, see C11.20 below.

For further provisions see Rules 4.151 to 4.178 (including the new Rule 4.172(A)) and Forms 4.47, 4.49, 4.50 and 4.52 generally; and, for Scotland, Scottish Rules 4.40 to 4.65 and Forms 4.20 to 4.24(Scot). As to the right of the Deposit Protection Board to be represented on the committee in the winding up of an authorised institution or former authorised institution under the Banking Act 1987, see section 58 of that Act. (See also Rule 4.152(7).)

For variations in the case of a partnership, see the Insolvent Partnerships Order 1994 (SI 1994 No 2421).

Chapter 6: Effect of winding up: general

C6.1   The effect of a winding up is mainly determined, in the case of a members' or creditors' voluntary winding up, by reference to the date of the winding-up resolution (the date on which the winding up is deemed to have commenced—see section 86) and, in the case of a compulsory winding up, by reference, for some purposes, to the date of the presentation of the winding-up petition or any voluntary winding-up resolution, whichever was the earlier (which is the date on which the winding up is deemed to have commenced—see section 129) and, for some other purposes, to the date of the winding-up order. A winding-up order is valid until set aside (*R v Robinson [1990] BCC 656 (CA)*).

Until a compulsory winding-up order or an appointment of a liquidator in a voluntary winding up is officially notified (that is, published in the *Gazette* (in the case of the appointment of a voluntary liquidator, as required by section 109 of the Insolvency Act 1986—see C3.8 above; and as to a compulsory winding-up order, see C5.43 above)) the company cannot rely on such an event as against any other person except where that event is shown by the company to have been known to that person at the material time, nor can it so rely on such an event where the material time fell on or before the fifteenth day after the date of the official notification and it is shown that that person was unavoidably prevented from knowing of the event at that time (sections 42 and 711(1)(p) and (2) of the Companies Act 1985). However, these provisions are negative in their impact and cannot be read in a positive way so as to impose constructive notice to the person concerned or to the public at large (*Official Custodian for Charities v Parway Estates Developments Ltd (in liquidation) [1984] 3 WLR 525*). By contrast, the advertisement of a winding-up *petition* pursuant to the Insolvency Rules (see C5.36 above) is not subject to official notification under the above-mentioned provisions but is still, for many purposes, treated by the court as notice to all the world of the petition from the time when they may reasonably be supposed to have seen it (see *Emmerson's Case (1866) 1 Ch App 433*; *Re New Gas Co (1877) 5 Ch 703*; *Re Oriental Bank Corpn (1884) 28 ChD 634*; *Re Dramstar Ltd, The Times, 30 October 1980*).

Some of the other effects of a winding up are dealt with below, by reference to first, a voluntary winding up, then, a compulsory winding up, and finally, all forms of winding up. (See also C11.27 below.)

Chapter 7: Effect of voluntary winding up

Cessation of business

C7.1   The company must, upon commencement of the winding up, cease to carry on its business except so far as may be required for the beneficial winding up thereof. Its corporate state and powers continue until its dissolution (section 87).

Cesser of directors' powers and investigation of their conduct

C7.2   On the appointment of a liquidator all powers of the directors cease, unless these are preserved, in the case of a members' voluntary winding up, by the company in general meeting or the liquidator (section 91(2)), or, in the case of a creditors' voluntary winding up, by the liquidation committee or, if there is no such committee, the creditors (section 103). Where no liquidator has been appointed or nominated by the company, the powers of the directors are not exercisable, except with the sanction of the court or (in the case of a creditors' voluntary winding up) so far as may be necessary to secure compliance with sections 98 (duty to convene creditors' meeting—see C4.6 above) and 99 (statement of affairs—see C4.7 above), during the period before the appointment or nomination of a liquidator. However, this restriction does not affect the powers of the directors to dispose of perishable goods or other goods the value of which is likely to diminish if they are not immediately disposed of or to do all such other things as may be necessary for the protection of the assets (section 114).

If it appears to the liquidator in the course of the voluntary winding up that any past or present officer of the company, or any member of it, has been guilty of an offence in relation to the company, he must report the matter to, and co-operate with, the Director of Public Prosecutions or, in Scotland, the Lord Advocate, who may in turn refer the matter to the Secretary of State for further enquiry. If the liquidator has not made the report, the court may direct him to do so (section 218(4)–(6)).

Transfer of shares, etc.

C7.3   Any transfer of shares without the liquidator's sanction, and any alteration in the status of the members of the company, made after the commencement of the winding up is void (section 88).

Stay of actions and proceedings

C7.4   The court has, by virtue of sections 112 and 126 and its inherent jurisdiction, power to stay actions and proceedings against a company in England and Wales, Scotland and Northern Ireland (see *Anglo-Baltic*

Bank v Barber & Co [1924] 2 KB 410; see also section 17 of the Companies Consolidation (Consequential Provisions) Act 1985). In the case of a company registered in Scotland, the court may on the liquidator's application direct that no action or proceeding is proceeded with or commenced against the company except by leave of the court and subject to such terms as the court may impose (section 113). The considerations which the court will apply in deciding whether a particular action should be allowed to be commenced or continued will be similar to those which the court will apply in a compulsory liquidation in deciding, before the winding-up order, whether it should be stayed or, after the order, whether the stay on it should be lifted (as to which see C8.2 below).

Execution, distress, etc.

C7.5   After a winding-up resolution is passed, the provisions applicable to compulsory liquidation referred to in C8.3 below may be invoked by virtue of section 112.

Chapter 8: Effect of compulsory winding up

Cesser of directors' powers

C8.1   A winding-up order has the effect of dismissing the directors and terminating their powers (*Fowler v Broad's Patent Night Light Co [1893] 1 Ch 724; Re Mawcon Ltd [1969] 1 WLR 78*) except certain residuary powers such as to instruct solicitors and counsel to appeal against the winding-up order and to act in interlocutory proceedings (*Re Union Accident Insurance Co Ltd [1972] 1 WLR 640*).

Stay of actions and proceedings

C8.2   At any time after the presentation of the petition and before the making of a winding-up order, the appropriate court may, upon application, stay, sist or restrain any action or proceeding pending against the company in England, Scotland or Northern Ireland (section 126; and see *Re Dynamics Corporation of America [1973] 1 WLR 63*). The application must be made to the High Court or Court of Appeal in which the action or proceeding is pending or (if pending in any other court) the court having jurisdiction in the winding up.

'Proceedings' includes executions (*Re Artistic Colour Printing Co (1880) 14 ChD 502; The Constellation [1966] 1 WLR 272*), interpleader summonses (*Eastern Holdings Establishment of Vaduz v Singer & Friedlander Ltd [1967] 1 WLR 1017*) but, *quaere*, whether it includes distress (*Re Memco Engineering Ltd [1985] 3 All ER 267*; see, however, *Bristol Airport plc v Powdrill [1990] 2 WLR 1362* (also reported as *Re Paramount Airways Ltd [1990] BCC 130*), an administration case, where the Court of Appeal held that the words 'other proceedings' in section 11(3) did not include detention of an aircraft by the airports authority under its statutory powers, adding that the natural meaning of those words was that the proceedings in question were either legal proceedings or *quasi-legal* proceedings such as arbitration).

If a provisional liquidator is appointed before the winding up, or once a winding-up order is made, the stay is automatic and no action or proceedings may be commenced or proceeded with against the company or its property unless the court otherwise orders, subject to such terms as it may impose (section 130(2)). The same applies where a winding-up order is made in respect of a company registered under section 680 of the Companies Act 1985, the stay also extending to any action or proceeding against a contributory in respect of any debt of the company (section 130(3)). (See also section 199 for Scotland.)

A writ served on a company without the leave of the court, after a winding- up order is made, is a nullity (see *Wilson v Banner Scaffolding*

Ltd, The Times, 22 June 1982 and *Roberts Petroleum Ltd v Bernard Kenny Ltd [1983] 1 All ER 564*).

On the principle that the plaintiff is entitled to choose his tribunal, the court may allow an action to continue or be commenced unless there is sufficient reason not to, for example, that expense will be saved or that the existence of the liability is substantially admitted (*Currie v Consolidated Kent Collieries Corpn Ltd [1906] 1 KB 134*; *Cook v 'X' Chain Patents Co Ltd [1960] 1 WLR 60*). The court should do what is right and fair in all the circumstances. If the proposed action raises issues which can be conveniently decided in the course of the winding up then, in the absence of special circumstances, permission to bring the action should be refused. There is a positive benefit in having the issue decided in the liquidation proceedings as this should be less expensive and quicker than an independent action. Also, as the liquidator is obliged to act evenhandedly as between each class of claimant, the settlement of claims through the winding-up proceedings will normally not cause prejudice to any particular class of claimant (*Re Exchange Securities & Commodities Ltd and others [1983] BCLC 186*).

However, in *Canon (Scotland) Business Machines Ltd, Noter [1992] BCC 620* (a decision of the Court of Session (Outer House) in Scotland), the court granted leave to a proposed pursuer (i.e. plaintiff) to raise proceedings against a company which it claimed had, through the instrumentality of its liquidator, breached an interim interdict (i.e. injunction) against disposal of equipment supplied to the company by the proposed pursuer under retention of title terms. The court held that the winding-up process was designed to provide a fair procedure for the settlement of claims of creditors and contributories, and the party applying for leave to litigate against the company had to show special cause; but the court had to do what was right and fair according to the circumstances of each case. The winding-up process was not an appropriate place to determine a breach of interdict, particularly where the liquidator was said to have been instrumental to the breach, since the court would have less pertinent powers under the winding-up process than in the interdict process.

Secured creditors are generally allowed to proceed with any action to enforce their security (*Re David Lloyd & Co (1877) 6 ChD 339*). Where a company in liquidation has no defence to a landlord's claim for possession, the court may make an order for possession even though third parties' rights are involved, as such rights are protected by RSC Ord 45, r 3 (*General Store and Trust Co v Wetley Brick and Pottery Co (1882) 20 ChD 260 (CA)*; *Re Blue Jeans Ltd [1979] 1 All ER 641*). The possession order may be made by the court in exercise of its winding-up jurisdiction without requiring the landlord to bring an action for forfeiture (and granting him leave for the purpose); and it may be made despite the fact that the premises are in the sole occupation of a third party (*Re Blue Jeans* (above)). Before enforcing the possession order against the third party, the landlord would have to give notice to it and opportunity to it of applying for relief. The *Blue Jeans* case was followed in *Re Brompton*

Securities Ltd (1988) 4 BCC 189 where the premises had been sold to, and were in the occupation of, a guarantor in respect of the lease.

Leave to commence an action against the company for specific perform-ance will normally be given to a plaintiff who has an unimpugnable claim for specific performance of an agreement for the sale by the company of its property where the plaintiff is in equity the owner thereof, notwith-standing that questions as to the adequacy of the consideration may have to be dealt with in the action (*Re Coregrange Ltd [1984] BCLC 453*).

Execution, distress, forfeiture, defeasance etc.

C8.3   Any attachment, sequestration, distress or execution put in force against the estate or effects of a company registered in England and Wales, or against any estate or effects situated in England and Wales of a company registered in Scotland, after the commencement of a compul-sory winding up, is void (section 128). Section 128 also applies to distress levied without the aid of the court. It does not *prima facie* apply to such enforcement procedures levied but not completed before the commence-ment of the winding up. It seems, however, that where a winding-up order has been made, the combined effect of sections 127, 128 and 130(2) is that even a distress levied before the commencement of winding up is automatically stayed upon the making of a winding-up order, subject to the discretion of the court to allow it to proceed (see *Armorduct Manufac-turing Co v General Incandescent Co [1911] 2 KB 143*). (See further C9.4 below.) As to distress by a landlord within three months before the making of a winding-up order, see C14.34 below.

In relation to leasehold property, relief against forfeiture may be avail-able under section 146 of the Law of Property Act 1925, but this is subject to the law relating to re-entry or forfeiture or relief in the case of non-payment of rent. Section 146 of that Act also applies where a condition of forfeiture on the bankruptcy (which expression includes the winding-up — see section 205(1)(i) of that Act) of the lessee, or on taking in execution of the lessee's interest, is contained in the lease (other than a lease of any of the classes mentioned in subsection (9) of that section) if the lessee's interest is sold within one year from the bankruptcy or taking in execution or, if the interest is not sold before the expiration of that year, only during the first year from the date of the bankruptcy or taking in execution.

Relief may also be available against the forfeiture of a hire-purchase agreement under which the company holds an asset and other agreements (see, for example, D7.14 PART D: RECEIVERS). In a liquidation, such relief may also be available under the wider, anti-defeasance principle of the *British Eagle* case (see F2.9 PART F: SPECIAL PROVISIONS FOR FINANCIAL MARKETS below). In this connection, the county court case of *Re Piggin, Dicker v Lombank Ltd, The Law Journal Vol CXII (29 June 1962)*, relat-ing to a hire-purchase agreement under which the bankrupt had been the hirer, may be noted. In that case the court granted relief against forfeiture to the trustee in bankruptcy on two grounds. Firstly, that the relevant bankruptcy-break clause in the agreement was void as against the trustee as being an attempt to deprive the creditors of an asset of the bankrupt. The respondent had contended that the agreement provided for two entirely separate and independent contracts, that is, a simple hiring for two years and an option to purchase for £1 and, accordingly, a determination of a mere hiring upon bankruptcy was unobjectionable. The court, in disagreeing, stated that one must look at the agreement as a whole— the bankrupt was not simply hiring the van, having parted with a deposit in any case and also paid fifteen instalments in return for the full rights available. In the court's judgment any provision whereby the bankrupt sought to deprive his trustee in bankruptcy of the contractual advantages he had thus acquired for valuable consideration was void against the trustee. For many years such clauses had been accepted without challenge in leases; but there might be special reasons for that, and in any case the trustee was, in general, entitled to relief from forfeiture by reason of the bankruptcy. Secondly, equity might properly be invoked to prevent the hirer, or someone claiming through him, forfeiting the benefit of the agreement and losing all he had paid and the vehicle too when the owners were offered the full balance due to them. (The trustee had undertaken within hours to pay the balance.) (See also *Stockloser v Johnson* [1954] *1 All ER 630*; *Phonographic Equipment* (1958) *Ltd v Muslu* [1961] *3 All ER 626*; *Bridge v Campbell Discount Co Ltd* [1962] *1 All ER 385*.)

Disposition of property, etc.

C8.4   Section 127 provides that any disposition of the company's property, and any transfer of shares, or alteration in the status of the members of the company, made after commencement of winding up by the court (i.e after the presentation of the petition) shall, unless the court otherwise orders, be void. This provision is examined below under three sub-headings.

(A) *Transactions covered*

(*a*)   Payments into and out of the company's bank account are covered. The bank may be ordered to restore the diminution in the amounts, which would otherwise have been available for distribution to the creditors, less any amounts recovered from any payee who has received the payment out of the bank account, as he too is liable (*Re Gray's Inn Construction Co Ltd* [1980] *1 WLR 711* (*CA*)). However, payments into the bank account of the company, which is already *in credit*, for example, by receipt by the bank of third party cheques presented through it and by a resultant further credit to the account, do not constitute a disposition: *Re Barn Crown Ltd* [1994] *BCC 381* (not following the *obiter dicta* in *Re Gray's Inn Construction Co Ltd* (above)).

This section is a source of considerable concern to banks. After a petition is advertised, and even before the fact comes to the notice of the bank, if any credits are paid into the customer's account the bank is liable to refund them to the liquidator and cannot keep them by way of set-off. If it allows any cheques payable to third parties to go through, then the position is as follows. If the account is already overdrawn, the bank cannot claim against the company the amount of the further overdraft so created but may be able to recover it from the payees. If the account is in credit before the cheques are passed, the bank will be liable to pay the gross amount of the credit without deducting the amounts of the cheques (but subject, of course, to any other valid right of set off it may have). Most banks operate a central computerised system to keep track of winding-up petitions; but there is inevitably a time lag between the advertisement of the petition and the information going into the system.

Where the court makes an order authorising transactions through the company's bank account (see (*h*) under (C) *Circumstances meriting relief from the court* below), it would be useful from the bank's standpoint for there to be a proviso in the order to the effect that the bank would not be under an obligation to verify whether any such transaction is in the ordinary course of business (see, for example, *Re a Company (No 00687 of 1991) [1991] BCC 210*).

(*b*)   Transfers of assets even at full value are covered, although the court is more likely to validate the transfer.

(*c*)   The section also applies to an indirect disposition of the company's property by a third party; but a *bona fide* purchaser for full value without notice will not be liable (*Re J Leslie Engineers Co Ltd [1976] 1 WLR 292*).

(*d*)   A payment by the company which is part of a circular transaction, whereby the amount of the payment is replaced, is also covered. The court would only validate a payment which was made with a *bona fide* view to assisting the company (*Re Webb Electrical Ltd (1988) 4 BCC 230*).

(*e*)   A transfer of property pursuant to an order of the court in any proceedings, regardless of whether the order was a consent order or made in the face of opposition by the debtor (*In re Flint (a bankrupt) [1992] 2 WLR 537*, decided under similar provisions of the 1986 Act relating to bankruptcy).

(B) *Transactions not covered*

(*a*)   A payment to the holder of a charge (even a floating charge), in reduction of the amount secured thereby, is not caught by section 127. The holder of such a charge has a sufficient beneficial interest in the property charged to him. 'Disposition' does not include the process by which a person with a beneficial interest in the property obtains that property or the proceeds of its realisation. A disposition normally requires a change of beneficial ownership (*Re Margart Property Ltd, Hamilton v Westpac Banking Corporation [1985] BCLC 314 (New South Wales)*). However, depending on the circumstances, the payment may constitute a preference to the extent that it reduces the amount available to preferential creditors who would have ranked before the floating charge.

(*b*)   The disposal of charged assets by the chargee or a receiver appointed by him is not caught by the section, because the disposition in effect dates back to the date of the creation of the charge (*Sowman v David Samuel Trust Ltd [1978] BCLC 1*; *Barrows v Chief Land Registrar, The Times, 20 October 1977*; see also *Re Margart* (above)).

(*c*)   Completion, after the commencement of the winding up, of a pre-commencement unconditional contract by the company to sell land may not constitute a void disposition (*Re French's (Wine Bar) Ltd [1987] BCLC 499*).

(C)   *Circumstances meriting relief from the court*

(*a*)   The court has power to validate any disposition otherwise caught by the section. It may validate a disposition even before a winding-up order is made (*Re A I Levy (Holdings) Ltd [1964] Ch 19*) and may authorise the making of a disposition. An example of the type of authorisation order which the court normally makes is given in *Practice Direction No 1 of 1990 [1990] BCC 292*—see C5.30 above. The court is guided by what would be just and fair in the circumstances of the case, having regard to the good faith of the person concerned (*Re Clifton Place Garage Ltd [1970] Ch 477*).

(*b*)   The court's discretion in favour of a disposition can only be exercised with a view to benefiting the creditors of the company as a whole, and not with a view to benefiting one creditor at the expense of the others (*Re Gray's Inn Construction Co Ltd [1980] 1 WLR 711 (CA)*; *Re Rafidain Bank [1992] BCC 376*).

   (i)   In *Re Gray's Inn Construction Co Ltd* (above), Buckley J explained the court's attitude on validation as follows:

   'Since a policy of the law is to procure so far as practicable rateable payment of the unsecured creditors' claims, it is, in my opinion, clear that the court should not validate any transaction or series of transactions which might result in one or more pre-liquidation creditors being paid in full at the expense of other creditors, who will only receive a dividend, in the absence of special circumstances making such a cause desirable in the interests of the unsecured creditors as a body.'

   (ii)   The principles that emerge from case law, particularly *Re Gray's Inn*, are as follows:

   (1)   Creditors have a right to a *pari passu* division of the assets at the commencement of the winding up.

   (2)   However, continuation of the company's business, and hence the position of assets and payments out in the ordinary course of business after presentation of the petition, may be beneficial to the creditors.

   (3)   On the other hand, their interests should not be prejudiced by transactions effected after the presentation of the petition. The court should carry out a balancing

exercise between the likely benefit and the likely prejudice to the creditors from post-petition transactions.

(4) Payment to one existing creditor at the expense of the
others would not normally be validated but there may be
special circumstances which may justify such payment,
for example, where without such payment continuity of
essential supplies from that particular creditor cannot be
assured.

(iii) In *Denney v John Hudson & Co Ltd [1992] BCLC 901*, the
Court of Appeal held that payments made in good faith by a
company in the ordinary course of business after commencement of its compulsory winding up in respect of supplies (of
diesel) made before presentation of the winding up petition,
could be validated by the court if there was a possibility that it
would benefit the company and its unsecured creditors in that
it would ensure that further deliveries would be made by the
supplier to enable the company to continue its business. The
policy of the courts was summarised as follows:

(1) The court's discretion was entirely at large, subject to
the general principles which applied to any kind of
discretion and also to the limitation that it be exercised
in the context of the statutory liquidation provisions.

(2) A basic principle of law governing liquidation of insolvent estate was that assets would be distributed *pari
passu* among unsecured creditors as at the date of
insolvency.

(3) There were occasions, however, when it might be beneficial, not only for the company but also for unsecured
creditors, that it should be able to dispose of some of its
property after the petition had been presented, but
before the winding-up order was made. Thus, it might
sometimes be beneficial to the company and creditors
that it should be able to continue business in its ordinary
course.

(4) In considering whether to make a validating order the
court must always do its best to ensure that the interest
of unsecured creditors would not be prejudiced.

(5) The desirability of the company being enabled to carry
on its business was often speculative. In each case, the
court must carry out a balancing exercise.

(6) The court should not validate any transaction which
might result in pre-liquidation creditors being paid in full
at the expense of other creditors, in the absence of
special circumstances. If, for example, it were in the
interests of the creditors generally that the business
should be carried on and that could only be achieved by
paying for goods supplied to the company when the

petition was presented and not yet paid for, the court might exercise its discretion to validate payment for those goods.

(7) A disposition carried out in good faith in the ordinary course of business at a time when the parties were unaware that a petition had been presented would usually be validated unless there were grounds for thinking that the transaction might involve an attempt to prefer the disponee.

(8) The general principle of securing a *pari passu* distribution had no application to post-liquidation creditors— for example, where there was a sale to the company of an asset at full market value after presentation of the petition. That was because such a transaction involved no dissipation of the company's assets for it did not reduce the value of its assets.

(iv) In *Adelaide Truss & Frame Ltd v Bianco Hiring Services Ltd (1993) 1 ACLC 192* (a decision of the full Supreme Court of Australia having only persuasive effect in England), after the presentation of a winding-up petition against it, the company had continued, in the course of trading, to buy material from a supplier and paid the supplier the sums due on normal account terms (including sums becoming due in respect of the pre-petition supplies. By a majority of two to one, the court validated the payments, notwithstanding that there was no evidence that continued supplies were essential to the company's business or that the continuance of the company benefited the company or its creditors. A majority of the court was of the view that there was no need to prove that the continued trading did in fact benefit the company's creditors; it was sufficient if there had been, at the time, perceived advantage to the creditors (for example, by keeping the business going with a view to its sale as a going concern). The supplier had received the payments honestly and in good faith and had given equally valid value for them in the form of the goods supplied after the presentation of the petition. It appears that although the payments made in respect of the pre-petition supplies were validated those payments were probably balanced by sums in respect of post-petition supplies which were still due at the date of the winding up order.

In this connection, it should also be noted that in the Australian case of *Tellfa Furniture Pty Ltd v Glendave Nominees Pty Ltd (1987) 13 ACLR 64* Mahoney J expressed the view that continuation of the business was, in effect, presumed to be for the creditors' benefit. However, in England the courts would be unlikely to accept this as a firm principle.

(c) The court's attitude varies depending on whether validation in advance of a proposed disposition is sought or whether validation is sought retrospectively after the event. Where authorisation of a *proposed* disposition is sought, the court will exercise its discretion so as to 'do equity' as between unsecured creditors and the person standing to benefit from the disposition. However, where *ex post facto* validation of a disposition already made is applied for, the court will not grant the application to the extent that the disposition can be shown to have reduced the assets in the winding up (*Re Tramway Building and Construction Co Ltd (1987) 3 BCC 443*; see also *Re Gray's Inn* ((*b*) above)).

(*d*) A disposition at a full value is caught by section 127, but where there has been no such reduction, the court will not refuse validation merely to enable unsecured creditors to earn an uncovenanted and unearned windfall (*Re Tramway Building and Construction Co Ltd (1987) 3 BCC 443*; see also *Re Gray's Inn* ((*b*) above)).

(*e*) A shareholder has sufficient *locus standi* to make an application to the court for a validation order (*Re Argentum Reductions (UK) Ltd [1975] 1 WLR 186*).

(*f*) Other things being equal, the court leans in favour of giving effect to transactions in the ordinary course of business completed after presentation of the petition but before the winding-up order (see *Re Park, Ward and Co [1926] Ch 828*, where a debenture given in return for a loan while the lender was aware of the presentation of the petition was declared valid). (See also *Re Oriental Bank Corporation (1884) 28 ChD 634*; *Gorringe v Irwell India Rubber Works (1886) 34 ChD 128*.) No claim will lie against a *bona fide* purchaser for value without notice (*Re Leslie Engineering Co Ltd*, above). However, ignorance of the petition is no justification for a validation order if it was advertised and the recipient ought to have been aware of it (contrast the *Office Custodian for Charities* case cited in C12.18 below); but a disposition in the ordinary course relating to post-petition debts may be protected (*Re McGuinness Bros (UK) Ltd (1987) 3 BCC 571*).

(*g*) In the *Tramway Building* case (above), Scott J said that the exercise of the court's discretion to validate a transaction is unfettered by any statutory criteria. Such discretion should not be used so as to allow an unauthorised disposition to reduce the assets available for unsecured creditors. It is wrong for the court to compare the position of the unsecured creditors if a validation order is made with their position if one is not. Instead, the court should have regard to the interests of the unsecured creditors on the one hand and the claimants under the unauthorised disposition on the other. As, in that case, the court would have made an order validating the transfer if an application had been made prior to the date of transfer, and since the transfer did not reduce the assets available for unsecured creditors, the court would make an order validating the transfer *ex post facto*.

(*h*) In the case of a contributory's petition, the court leans in favour of a validation order as regards future payments into and out of the company's bank account in the ordinary course of business. *Practice*

Direction No 1 of 1990 [*1990*] *BCC 292* requires the petitioner to state in his petition whether he consents to such an order being made and entitles the company to apply *ex parte* for an urgent validation order if the contributory does not consent. For further details of the Practice Direction, including the standard form of validation order, as further improved by Harman J in *Re a Company (No 00687 of 1991)* [*1992*] *BCLC 133*, see C5.30 above. In *Re a Company (No 007523 of 1986)* [*1987*] *BCLC 200*, an application by a company, against whom a contributory's petition was pending, for an order that, in the event of a winding-up order being made, no payments made from the company's bank account in the course of its business should be avoided, was opposed by the petitioner and refused by Mervyn Davies J. He accepted that great weight should given to the view of the directors, as the mere presentation of the petition should not be allowed to interfere with their management of the company's affairs and should not hamper the company from carrying out transactions which benefited those interested in the value of its assets. However, on the facts, he held that since there was a serious doubt as to the company's solvency and as continued trading would deplete the assets, the application should be rejected.

(*i*)   In *Re a Company (No 005685 of 1988)* [*1989*] *BCLC 424*, the company and its shareholders (other than the petitioners) brought a motion to strike out the petition and sought validation of payments into and out of the company's bank account pending the hearing of the motion. The petitioners argued that the validation should not extend to the costs of defending the petition or prosecuting the striking out motion, as the company's money should not be spent on litigation between shareholders. The company proposed to limit the validation so as to exclude expenditure on the costs of individuals involved in the litigation but to include the company's own costs. Hoffmann J accepted the company's proposals. In *Re Crossmore Electrical and Civil Engineering Ltd (1989) 5 BCC 37* there were two petitions before the court; one a creditor's winding-up petition and the other a petition by a shareholder for relief against unfair prejudice. The company applied for a validation order in respect of payments into and out of the company's bank account in relation to the costs of defending the petition. Hoffmann J granted a validation order in respect of the creditor's petition only, stating that the costs of defending that petition were costs incurred in the ordinary course of business but the costs of the unfair prejudice petition were not costs so incurred as that was a dispute between shareholders. It was a general principle that a company's money should not be expended on disputes between shareholders.

(*j*)   In *Re Sugar Properties (Drisley Wood) Ltd* [*1988*] *BCLC 146*, the court was asked to make a validation order for a proposed sale of shares in racehorses charged to a third party, because there was doubt about the validity of the charge in the absence of its registration. The court held that the charge was not required to be registered and was valid and granted the validation order.

231

(*k*) The court will generally approve a disposition by a solvent company where it is satisfied that the directors took the view that the disposition was in the interests of the company, provided that an intelligent and honest person could reasonably have taken that view, even if a contributory is objecting (see *Re Burton & Deakin Ltd* [*1977*] *I WLR 390*).

Investigation by Official Receiver and Secretary of State

C8.5 Following the winding-up order the Official Receiver is under a duty to investigate the causes of the company's failure (if any) and generally its promotion, formation, business, dealings and affairs and to make such report (if any) to the court as he thinks fit. Any such report is, in any proceedings, *prima facie* evidence of the facts stated in it (section 132). If it appears to the court in the course of the compulsory winding up that any past or present officer, or any member, of the company has been guilty of any offence in relation to the company, it may (on the application of a person interested in the winding up or of its own motion) direct the liquidator to refer the matter to the Director of Public Prosecutions or (in Scotland) the Lord Advocate, who may in turn refer the matter to the Secretary of State (section 218, as amended by CA 1989, s 78). The Official Receiver also has reporting functions under the Company Director Disqualification Act 1986 (see A4.9 PART A: GENERAL above).

Chapter 9: Effect of all forms of winding up

Restriction on re-use of company name

C9.1 Section 216, which is one of the provisions aimed at counteracting the 'Phoenix syndrome', becomes applicable. It imposes restrictions on certain categories of person who have been associated with a company which has gone into insolvent liquidation against being associated with another company or unincorporated business with a prohibited name. The restrictions (i) apply to all those who were directors or shadow directors of the liquidating company at any time during the twelve months preceding the liquidation and (ii) continue for five years thereafter. (For the meanings of 'shadow directors' and 'gone into insolvent liquidation' see C13.2 below).

For this purpose, a prohibited name is one by which the liquidating company was known (or any name under which the company carried on business—section 216(6)) at any time during that period of twelve months or is so similar to that name as to suggest an association with the liquidating company.

The effect of the restrictions is that no such person must, without the leave of the court or except in the prescribed circumstances (see below), be a director of, or in any way, directly or indirectly, be concerned or take part in the promotion, formation or management of, another company that is known by a prohibited name or in the carrying on of a business carried on (otherwise than by a company) under a prohibited name.

In determining an application for leave, the court may take into consideration a report from the liquidator or former liquidator of the circumstances in which the company became insolvent and the extent (if any) of the applicant's apparent responsibility for its doing so (Rule 4.227; Scottish Rule 4.79). Among the factors which the court may take into account are: whether the proposal to use a prohibited name is part of the terms under which the applicant's company is acquiring the business of the insolvent company; whether those terms are on the whole beneficial to the company; whether the acquiring company has an adequate capital base which is properly protected; whether its officers have the requisite financial management skill; whether the proposed business is viable; and the extent to which the application is supported by the creditors of the insolvent company (see, for example, *Re Bonus Breaks Ltd [1991] BCC 546*).

Rules 4.228 to 4.230 (and Scottish Rules 4.80 to 4.82) prescribe the following three cases where no such leave is necessary.

(1) Where a company ('the successor company') acquires the whole or substantially the whole of the business of the liquidating company

under arrangements made by the latter's liquidator, administrator, administrative receiver or supervisor of a voluntary arrangement *and* the successor company gives notice within 28 days from the completion of the arrangements to the liquidating company's creditors containing certain particulars as required by Rule 4.228(2) and (3) (or, as the case may be, Scottish Rule 4.80(2) and (3)), including the names of the persons who are to be the directors of or otherwise associated with the successor company and to whom the restriction would otherwise apply.

(2)   Where the person concerned applies to the court for leave not later than seven days from the date of liquidation and the matter is disposed of by the court not later than six weeks from that date. In such a case the restriction does not apply until the matter is disposed of (Rule 4.229, as amended).

(3)   Where the successor company has been known by that prohibited name for the whole of the period of twelve months preceding the liquidation of the liquidating company, and has not at any time during that period been dormant within the meaning of section 250(3) of the Companies Act 1985.

It is an offence (punishable by imprisonment or a fine or both) for anyone to contravene the restrictions (section 216(4)). Further, any person who contravenes them, or acts or is willing to act on instructions given by another whom he knows to be in contravention of the restrictions, is also personally responsible for all the relevant debts (as defined) of the other company (section 217).

Goods and chattels taken in execution

C9.2   Section 184(1) and (2) applies where *goods or chattels* of the company are taken in execution, and, before sale or completion of the execution by the receipt or recovery of the full amount of the levy, notice is served on the sheriff (or any other officer charged with the execution) that a provisional liquidator has been appointed, or that a winding-up order has been made, or that a resolution for voluntary winding up has been passed. The sheriff (or other officer) must, on being so required, deliver to the liquidator the goods and chattels, and any money seized or received in part satisfaction (see also Rule 12.19).

Section 184(3) requires the sheriff (or the other officer) who has sold a company's *goods or chattels* under an execution in respect of a judgment debt exceeding £500 (see SI 1986 No 1996: the limit may be further varied by statutory instrument), or who has received money in order to avoid the sale (as to which see *Marley Tile Co v Burrows [1978] QB 241*), to retain the proceeds of sale or such money (after deduction of the costs of execution) for 14 days. Section 184(4) provides that if within that period notice is served on him of the *presentation* of a petition for the company's winding up, or of the *convening* of a meeting of the company at which a resolution for the voluntary winding up is to be proposed, and an order is made or a resolution passed (as the case may be) he must pay it to the liquidator who is entitled to hold it as against the execution creditor.

The notice referred to in section 184(1) and (4) must be in writing and be delivered by hand at, or sent by recorded delivery to, the office of the under-sheriff or (as the case may be) the other officer charged with the execution. However, where the execution is in a county court, then the requirements as to the notice are satisfied if a winding-up petition is filed in, or a winding-up order or an order appointing a provisional liquidator is made by, that court (Rule 12.19). A notice under section 184(4) is not invalid merely because it states that a meeting of creditors has been convened 'in connection with the winding up'. The section is not to be construed literally but according to its object and intent (*per* Lord Denning MR in *Engineering Industry Training Board v Samuel Talbot (Engineers) Ltd [1969] 2 QB 270*). Where money is paid to the bailiff to avoid 'sale', the 14-day period in section 184(3) runs from the time of its receipt by the bailiff, not from the time he hands it over to the sheriff (*Re Walden Sheet Metal Co Ltd [1960] Ch 170*). Section 184 does not apply to a winding up in Scotland; instead section 185 applies.

(See also C9.4 below.)

Execution over goods, land or debt

C9.3   Section 183 prevents a creditor who has issued execution against the *goods or land* of the company or has attached any debt due to the company, from retaining the benefit of the execution or attachment unless he has completed it before the earlier of:

(*a*)   (in a voluntary winding up) the date of receipt by him of a notice of the winding up meeting of the company having been called; or

(*b*)   (in any type of winding up) the date of commencement of the winding up.

(In Scotland section 185 applies, and not section 183.)

For the purposes of the Act,

(i)   an execution against goods is completed by seizure and sale, or by the making of a charging order under section 1 of the Charging Orders Act 1979 (note: the 1979 Act does not at present apply to goods as no statutory instrument applying it has been issued),

(ii)   an attachment of a debt is completed by the receipt of the debt, and

(iii) an execution against land is completed by seizure, by the appointment of a receiver, or by the making of a charging order under section 1 of the 1979 Act (section 183(3)). The order appointing a receiver or the charging order must be final and not merely provisional or *nisi*; and the court which made the charging order *nisi* will not, in exercise of its discretion, ordinarily convert it into an absolute order if a winding up has supervened (*Roberts Petroleum Ltd v Bernard Kenny Ltd [1983] 1 All ER 564 (HL)*). In any case,

before the court to which an application is made for a charging
order on the debtor's land exercises its discretion to grant the application, it has to be satisfied that it would be proper to place the
judgment creditor at an advantage over other creditors. Where the
court is aware that the debtor is, or is likely to turn out to be, insolvent it is wrong that it should give one creditor an advantage over
other unsecured creditors by granting him a charging order which
effectively converts him into a secured creditor (*Rainbow v Moorgate Properties Ltd [1975] 2 All ER 821 (CA)*). In *D Wilson (Birmingham) Ltd v Metropolitan Property Developments Ltd [1975] 2
All ER 814 (CA)*, it was held that section 325(1) of the Companies
Act 1948 (now section 183 of the Insolvency Act 1986) did not
deprive the court of the power to make a garnishee order absolute;
what that section provided was that, if a debt were attached, the
judgment creditor would not be entitled to retain the benefit of the
attachment unless it had been completed before the commencement of the winding up, and not that the court should not make an
attachment order at all.

A *bona fide* purchaser of goods from the sheriff (or other authorised
officer) is protected by section 183(2)(b) and by the Sale of Goods Act
1979 (section 21(2)(b)), the Sale of Goods Act 1893 (section 26) and the
County Courts Act 1984 (section 99).

The 'benefit of execution' means the benefit of the charge obtained by the
issue of execution, and does not include money actually received thereunder before notice of the convening of a winding-up meeting (*Re Caribbean Products (Yam Importers) Ltd [1966] Ch 331*). Money paid to the
sheriff or his officer to avoid sale is not a 'benefit of the execution' and can
be retained by the creditor (*Re Walkden Sheet Metal Co Ltd [1960] Ch
170*), unless it falls within the provisions of section 184(3) discussed in
C9.2 above.

(See also C9.4 below.)

Power of court to grant relief to execution or distraining creditors

C9.4   The rights conferred by sections 183 and 184 on the liquidator
may be set aside by the court in favour of the creditor to such extent and
subject to such terms as the court thinks fit (sections 183(2)(*c*) and
184(5)). The court has a free hand to do what is right and fair according to
the circumstances of the case (*per* Vaisey J in *Re Grosvenor Metal Co
[1950] Ch 63 at 65*), but may insist on being satisfied that the creditor has
been unfairly treated by the company before it interferes with the ordinary rule that all unsecured creditors should rank equally (*Re Caribbean
Products (Yam Importers) Ltd [1966] Ch 331*). The sections mentioned
above do not apply to a distress but the court, in exercise of its discretion,
would not normally restrain a distress levied before the commencement
of the winding up (see *Armorduct Manufacturing Co v General Incandescent Co [1911] 2 KB 143*). The property of the company directed to be

distributed amongst its creditors (subject to preferential claims) by the winding-up provisions is subject to such rights as were exercised prior to the winding up (*Re Herbert Berry Associates Ltd [1976] 1 WLR 783*). Where distress has been levied but not completed before a winding-up order, and there has been no unconscionable conduct or delay on the part of the distraining creditor, the court may allow the distress to be completed and give its benefit to him (*Re Memco Engineering Ltd [1985] 3 All ER 267*). However, a distress may be restrained where preferential debts will exhaust the assets (*Re South Rhondda Colliery Co [1928] WN 126*). For other cases on this subject, see *Re David Lloyd & Co (1877) 6 Ch D 339, 344*; *Re Traders' North Staffordshire Carrying Co (1874) LR 19 Eq 60*; *Re National Arms and Ammunition Co (1885) 28 Ch D 474, 478*.

Period of limitation

C9.5   On the making of a winding-up order, the period of limitation ceases to run against a creditor (*Re General Rolling Stock Co, Joint Stock Discount Co's Claim (1872) 7 Ch App 646*; *Re Cases of Taff Wells Ltd [1992] BCLC 11*). In the case of the petitioning creditor, the period ceases to run against him on the presentation of the petition, as the petition constitutes an action for this purpose. However, he is acting on his own behalf and is not taken to have brought the action on behalf of all the creditors, known or unknown. The provision for other creditors to intervene and support or oppose the petition (see C5.39 above) is inconsistent with the idea of a class action. Therefore, the period does not cease to run as against the other creditors until the making of the winding-up order (*Re Cases of Taff Wells Ltd* (above)). The general reasoning in *Re General Rolling Stock Co* (above) seems to be equally applicable to a voluntary winding up.

As to the circumstances in which a company's balance sheet can be an effective acknowledgement for the purposes of the statutes of limitation see *Re Gee & Co (Woolwich) Ltd [1974] 2 WLR 515* and *Re Compania de Electricidad de la Provincia de Buenos Aires Ltd [1980] 1 Ch 146*. In *Re Overmark Smith Warden Ltd [1982] 3 All ER 513*, it was held that a liquidator's statement of affairs operated as an acknowledgment, but only as at the effective date of the statement. Where the appointment of a receiver has preceded the winding up, the inclusion in a statement of affairs prepared by him of a claim may constitute an acknowledgement of that claim; but the acknowledgement is effective only from the time the statement of affairs is made and not from any earlier date as at which it shows the position. An acknowledgement after the claim has become statute-barred is, since section 29 (7) of the Limitation Act 1980, of no avail (*Re Cases of Taff Wells Ltd* (above)). A period of limitation continues to run in favour of the company's debtor and the liquidator must take action to recover the debt before the period runs out. The period of limitation for an unclaimed dividend declared by the company before liquidation is six years, not twelve (*Re Compania de Electricidad*, above).

Contracts generally

C9.6 As a general rule, in the absence of an express term to that effect, a winding up does not of itself constitute a breach by the company of an outstanding contract or entitle the other party to refuse to perform its part; but see C12.7 below. However, the nature of the particular contract or type of contract or the special position of the parties thereto may require such a term to be implied.

If a contract continues after the winding up, the position will be as follows.

(1) The liquidator may disclaim it; this would entitle the other party to prove in the winding up for any damages suffered by him as a result (see C12.6 below).

(2) If the contract is not disclaimed, the other party may still prove as a contingent creditor (see C14.13 and C14.14 below) for estimated damages likely to be suffered by him in the event of the company not performing its part of the contract. His claim will, however, be subject to reduction or elimination if the liquidator does in fact perform the contract (see (4) below). The liquidator can be put to his election in this regard (see C12.6 (last paragraph) below).

(3) If the liquidator has declared his inability to perform the company's part, the other party may treat this as an immediate breach and prove for damages: *Ogdens v Nelson [1905] AC 109 (HL)*; see also *Telsen Electric Co Ltd v JJ Eastick & Sons [1936] 3 All ER 266.*

(4) The liquidator may choose to perform the company's part of the contract. In that event the other party will be bound to perform its part. However, the liquidator must be careful that in performing the contract he does not, in effect, give preference to the other party (in relation to any claim the other party may otherwise have under (1) or (2) above) over the other creditors, unless the preference is outweighed by an overall benefit to the other creditors. The liquidator cannot insist on the other part performing his part of the contract unless the liquidator is prepared to perform the company's part. It is submitted that by insisting on the other party performing, the liquidator would be deemed to have adopted the contract or otherwise assumed personal responsibility for its performance by the company.

(5) Any sum due by the other party in respect of post-liquidation performance by the liquidator of even a pre-liquidation contract cannot be set off by the other party against any other claim which the other party may have in the winding up (*Ince Hall Rolling Mills Co v Douglas Forge Co (1882) 8 QBD 179*; see also *Mersey Steel & Iron Co v Naylor, Benzon & Co (1882) 9 QBD 648 at 669 (CA)*).

(6) Where there are two or more contracts between the same parties, the liquidator may adopt some and enforce their performance while not performing (or disclaiming) others (*Asphaltic Limestone Concrete Co v Glasgow Corporation 1907 SC 463*). In appropriate cases,

the other party may be able to protect itself against the consequences of such 'cherry picking' by a future liquidator by stipulating in a contract with the company (i) a provision treating all contracts between them as one single contract and making mutual performance interdependent and specifying circumstances in which the contract is automatically terminated and (ii) a 'flawed asset' provision (see PART F: SPECIAL PROVISIONS FOR FINANCIAL MARKETS).

Employees

C9.7   In the case of contracts of employment, the making of a winding-up order constitutes notice of termination of employment to all employees of the company (*Measures Bros Ltd v Measures* [*1910*] *2 Ch 248*). It seems that the passing of a voluntary winding-up resolution has a similar effect since the ongoing nature of the company's business comes to an end, although the business may be temporarily continued.

Agents

C9.8   The authority of an agent will automatically determine. This also applies to a receiver's contractual agency contained in a charge and an administrative receiver's statutory agency contained in section 44, but not to the statutory agency of the receiver under a floating charge in Scotland contained in section 57.

A power of attorney under seal given to secure a proprietary interest of, or the performance of an obligation owed to, the donee or the person under whom he derives title, for example, a power contained in a mortgage or a debenture stock trust deed granted to the mortgagee or trustee, and expressed to be irrevocable, will not be revoked by the winding up (Powers of Attorney Act 1971, s 4).

A power of attorney granted to a receiver does not fall within that Act unless, perhaps, the charging instrument under seal also contains a covenant by the company, expressed to be in favour of the receiver, to do all such acts and things as either of them may require in exercise of the powers conferred on them, and the covenant is linked with the power of attorney conferred on the receiver.

However, a power (apart from a power of attorney) expressly conferred by a debenture (or other charging instrument) on a receiver to sell and convey the property charged, as agent and in the name of the company, continues to be exercisable after liquidation, independently of the Powers of Attorney Act 1971 and notwithstanding the general termination of the agency by reason of the liquidation and notwithstanding (what is now) section 127 of the Insolvency Act 1986 (avoidance of disposition of the company's property after the commencement of its compulsory winding up) (see *Sowman v David Samuel Trust Limited* [*1978*] *1 WLR 22* and *Barrows v Chief Land Registrar, The Times, 20 October 1979*, and also C8.4 above).

In the case of an administrative receiver, he now has statutory powers *inter alia* to sell, or otherwise dispose of, property of the company, to use the company's seal and to execute in the name and on behalf of the company any deed, receipt or document (see section 42 and Schedule 1, paragraphs 2, 8 and 9). It would appear, on the analogy of the *Sowman* and *Barrows* cases cited above, that those powers are not affected by liquidation and section 44(1)(a), which provides that he is deemed to be the company's agent unless and until it goes into liquidation, must be read subject to those powers. However, the receiver's agency to incur debts on behalf of the company ceases upon liquidation. He may be personally liable for costs of an action incurred after the winding up (*Bacal Contracting Ltd v Modern Engineering (Bristol) Ltd [1980] 2 All ER 655*).

Ownership of property

C9.9   A winding-up order does not divest the company of the legal ownership of its assets, unless a vesting order in favour of the liquidator is made under section 145. However, the company ceases to be the beneficial owner of its property (*IRC v Olive Mills Ltd [1963] 1 WLR 712*; *Ayerst v C & K (Construction) Ltd [1975] 3 WLR 16*). This may have important tax consequences (see C2.4 above).

Assets and liabilities

C9.10   Upon the company going into liquidation, the liquidator takes control of the affairs of the company, and the rights of its creditors are replaced by a statutory scheme for dealing with the assets and their distribution; in this sense, the winding up and the notional discharge of the liabilities are simultaneous (*Ayerst v C & K Construction Ltd* (above *per* Lord Diplock); *Roberts Petroleum Ltd v Bernard Kenny Ltd* [1983] *1 All ER 564*; *Re Lines Bros Ltd [1982] 2 WLR 1010 at 1018*). In the case of a compulsory winding up, the scheme relates back to the date of the presentation of the petition: *per* Dillon J in *R v Registrar of Companies ex p Esal (Commodities) Ltd [1986] 2 WLR 177* on Allied Arab Bank's appeal (not included in the judgment but referred to in *Insolvency Law & Practice July/August 1986* page 119). The only financial entitlement of the creditors is to a distribution of the company's assets by reference to their rights insofar as they are translated into quantified claims admitted to proof in the liquidation in accordance with statutory provisions (including the mandatory provisions of Rule 4.90 as regards set-off—see C14.26 below). The claims are generally determined as at the date of the winding-up order (see C14.13 below). Ordinary liabilities are required to be discharged *pari passu* and any pre-liquidation agreement to the contrary (excluding a debt subordination agreement) is not enforceable (see C15.4 below).

In partnership cases, a marshalling of assets and liabilities by reference to those of the partnership and those of the partners may in certain circumstances be required pursuant to the Insolvent Partnerships Order 1994 (SI 1994 No 2421).

English law follows the principle of universality of assets and liabilities in a liquidation, so that the company's assets worldwide are to be applied to payment of its creditors worldwide.It does not permit the court to erect a 'ring fence' around assets or creditors in any one jurisdiction. No class of creditors has the right to stand in the way of what is in the best interest of the creditors worldwide: *Re Bank of Credit and Commerce International SA [1992] BCC 83.*

A liquidation also triggers the provisions enabling certain antecedent transactions to be avoided or adjusted, and recoveries to be made in respect of any past malpractice on the part of those connected with the management of the company, for the benefit of the creditors (see C8.4 above and C9.13, C10.1 to C10.10 and C13.1 to C13.5 below).

Further, a winding up or its commencement gives rise to certain restrictions on the rights of execution and distraining creditors and those who have commenced or intend to commence actions or proceedings against the company (see C7.4, C7.5, C8.2, C9.2 to C9.4 above).

An unregistered charge created by the company becomes void (see C12.10 below).

Ultimate dissolution

C9.11   A winding up ultimately leads to the dissolution of the company (see C16.5 below) subject to the power of the court to stay the winding up (see C5.46 *et seq.* above) or defer the dissolution (see C16.7 to C16.8 below).

Banks, deposit takers and insurance companies

C9.12   Upon a winding-up order being made, a creditors' voluntary winding-up resolution being passed, or a members' voluntary liquidation subsequently becoming a creditors' voluntary liquidation, in respect of an authorised institution or former authorised institution, or a corresponding event occurring in the country or State of its incorporation, the Deposit Protection Board is required, subject to certain exceptions and limitations, to pay out of the Fund referred to in the Banking Act 1987 to every depositor who has a 'protected deposit' with the bank/deposit taker an amount equal to three-quarters of such deposit. To the extent of such payment the Board is subrogated to the claim of the depositor in the winding up (section 58 of that Act).

Upon a recognised insurance company going into liquidation, the Policyholders Protection Board is required, subject to certain exceptions and limitations, to provide financial assistance to policyholders and third parties having rights against the company in road traffic cases. The assistance may range from 90 per cent to 100 per cent of the benefit depending on the nature of the policy (see the Policyholders Protection Act 1975).

Investigation of prior transactions and malpractice

C9.13 Certain types of transaction previously effected by the company, and the pre-liquidation and post-liquidation conduct of the directors and others in relation to the company's creditors, come under scrutiny. This may lead to appropriate orders being made by the court to counteract the effect of such transactions or making the directors (or, in certain cases, any shadow directors) who were responsible for malpractice personally liable to contribute to the company's assets (see C13.1 *et seq.* below), or to disqualification. It may also lead to the imposition on the company's officers and others of criminal penalties (see sections 206 (fraud etc. in anticipation of winding up), 207 (transactions in fraud of creditors), 208 (misconduct in course of winding up), 209 (falsification of books), 210 (material omissions from statement of affairs) and 211 (false representations to creditors)).

These provisions apply, with modifications, to the winding up of a partnership. References in the Act to companies are to be construed as references to insolvent partnerships; those to an 'officer' are to be construed as references to a member of the partnership or a person who has the management and control of the partnership; and other expressions appropriate to companies are to be construed as references to the corresponding persons, officers, documents or organs appropriate to a partnership (Articles 2 and 3 of the Insolvent Partnerships Order 1994 (SI 1994 No 2421)).

As to investigation and prosecution of malpractice in a compulsory winding up, see sections 218 and 219.

Chapter 10: Adjustment of prior transactions

Introduction

C10.1 The new insolvency legislation has introduced significant changes to the previous provisions relating to pre-liquidation transactions entered into by a company which, on its subsequent liquidation within a specified period, could be set aside, or be made the subject of relief, for the benefit of the company's creditors generally. The changes, in broad terms, are as follows.

(1) Two new categories of vulnerable transactions are created, namely, transactions at an undervalue and extortionate credit transactions. The previous categories, namely fraudulent preference and invalid floating charge, were aimed at depriving an existing creditor of an advantage, in relation to the debt due to him, received by him to the detriment of other creditors. The new categories will catch even those parties who receive an advantage otherwise than as existing creditors.

(2) The previous category of 'fraudulent preferences' is replaced by a new category of 'preferences'. Under the former, it had to be established that the company entered into the transaction 'with a view to preferring' the creditor concerned. Under the latter it has to be established that the company was 'influenced by a desire' to produce the relevant effect. Further, the period of vulnerability has been extended in relation to transactions in favour of 'connected persons'.

(3) The previous provisions relating to invalid floating charges have been modified by removing certain anomalies and ambiguities; and, again, the period of vulnerability in relation to transactions with 'connected persons' has been extended.

(4) In terms of the burden of proof, it is now easier to establish a transaction at an undervalue, a preference or an invalid floating charge where it is in favour of a 'connected person'.

(5) All the transactions mentioned above can now be challenged not only in the event of a subsequent liquidation but also in the event of a subsequent administration order.

(6) Unlike the previous provisions relating to 'fraudulent preferences', the new provisions relating to 'preferences' and 'transactions at an undervalue' do not expressly make a transaction void as such. Instead they require the court to make appropriate orders to counteract the effect of the transaction and give the court wide powers to stipulate the terms of such orders.

Each of these new categories is considered below. (As to the application of these provisions to an overseas company where section 426 is invoked, see *Re Bank of Credit and Commerce International SA and Re Bank of Credit and Commerce (Overseas) Ltd [1993] BCC 787*; and see A5.2 PART A: GENERAL. As to the extra-territorial application of these provisions to a company which is being wound up in England, see *Re Paramount Airways Ltd (No 2)*, referred to in C10.2 below.)

Transactions at an undervalue (England and Wales)

C10.2   The court must (subject to what is stated below under this heading and in C10.6 below), on an application by the liquidator, make appropriate orders (see C10.6) to counteract the effect of any gift made by the company or any other transaction entered into by it that provides for the company to receive no consideration (section 238(4)(a)) if:

(i)   the company's winding up commences (see C6.1 above) within two years following the transaction; and

(ii)   at the time of or in consequence of the transaction the company was unable to pay its debts within the meaning of section 123 (see C5.22 above). (Where the transaction is with a connected person this is presumed to have been the case unless the contrary is shown. For this purpose, 'connected person' has the meaning ascribed to it in section 249, read with section 435, but does not include one who is such a person by reason only of being the company's employee.)

The same applies to a transaction entered into by a company for a consideration the value of which in money or money's worth is significantly less than the value in money or money's worth provided by the company (section 238(4)(b)).

The court's jurisdiction to make appropriate orders can be exercised extra-territorially in that it applies even where the transaction in question took place abroad and the recipient of the benefit of the transaction is a non-resident and is not present in England, or is a foreign company carrying on business only abroad; but there must be a sufficient connection between the transaction and England (*Re Paramount Airways Ltd (No 2) [1992] 3 All ER 1 (CA)*, reversing the decision of Mervyn Davies J). However, it is debatable whether, in the absence of mutual recognition or enforcement treaties, an order of an English court will be enforced by the foreign court against a person, company or asset within the latter's jurisdiction if its assistance is sought (see C5.6 above).

The court will not set aside any such gift or transaction referred to in section 238(4)(a) or (b) if it was entered into by the company in good faith *and* for the purposes of carrying on its business *and* in the reasonable belief that the transaction would benefit the company (section 238(5)).

(Sections 238 and 240).

The following observations arise.

(1)   Except where section 241(2) applies (see C10.6 below), a person receiving the benefit of a transaction is not protected merely because he was acting in good faith. It is hoped that in the case of a purchaser of assets, with whom the price has been freely negotiated on an arm's length basis, the court will not regard the purchase as being at an undervalue, even if it subsequently transpires that the price was in fact significantly lower than the market price.

(2)   The granting by the company of a charge to secure existing and future advances to it may not constitute a transaction at an undervalue (*Re M C Bacon Ltd [1990] BCC 78, per* Millett J).

(3)   It is debatable whether a guarantee given by a company for the indebtedness of another party is *ipso facto* a transaction at an undervalue where there is no conceivable commercial benefit to the company giving the guarantee. It is submitted that this is not the case. The operative word in section 238(4)(b) is 'consideration' and not 'benefit'. The question of benefit may be relevant for the purposes of section 238(5) mentioned above or on the question of whether the giving of the guarantee constituted malpractice (see C13.1 *et seq.* below) or an improper exercise of corporate powers (see *Rolled Steel Products (Holdings) Ltd v British Steel Corporation [1985] 2 WLR 908 (CA)* and C12.9 below); but that is a separate question. The word 'consideration' must be taken as deliberately used in the context of the law of contract so that the value of the consideration received by the guarantor is the value which the principal debtor receives. Where a fresh advance is made on the strength of the guarantee, the value of the consideration received must be the full amount of the advance. Where the guarantee secures an existing debt, the value of the forbearance shown by the creditor cannot be measured in terms of *money or money's worth*. In any case, the value of the guarantee, too, is arguably incapable of valuation in money or money's worth because from the standpoint of the guarantor, it is a contingent liability with a contingent right of recourse against the principal debtor.

In *Re M C Bacon Ltd [1990] BCC 78*, Millett J, in considering whether the giving of a debenture to a bank was a transaction at an undervalue, said that the section required comparison to be made between the two values from the company's point of view, that both values must be measurable in money or money's worth and that a transaction at an undervalue must result in the depletion of the company's assets. He stated that a company 'by charging its assets . . . appropriates them to meet the liabilities due to the secured creditor and adversely affects the rights of other creditors in the event of insolvency. But it does not deplete its assets or diminish the value . . . All it loses is the ability to apply the proceeds otherwise than in satisfaction of the secured debt. That is not something capable of valuation in monetary terms and is not customarily disposed of for value'. By analogy, this reasoning may apply to a guarantee because, in essence, it increases liabilities rather than depletes assets and the values of the guarantee and the forbearance are incapable of comparison.

(4)   In *In Re Kumar (A Bankrupt), Ex parte Lewis v Kumar [1993] 1 WLR 224*, decided under the corresponding provisions of the 1986 Act relating to bankruptcy, a transfer by a husband of his interest in the matrimonial home worth £140,000 to his wife who owned it jointly with him, in consideration of her taking over sole responsibility for the outstanding mortgage of £30,000, was held to be a transaction at an undervalue.

(5)   It would seem that on the analogy of the reasoning in the *Yagerphone, Robbie* and *M C Bacon (No 2)* cases in relation to preferences (see C10.4 below), any recovery made by the liquidator for a transaction at an undervalue will not fall within the purview of a general charge held by a third party over the company's present and future assets but will go for the benefit of the creditors generally.

Compare and contrast the above provisions with section 423 (debt avoidance), dealt with in C10.10 below. See also the case of *Agricultural Mortgage Corporation plc v Woodward*, referred to there.

Gratuitous alienations (Scotland)

C10.3   The liquidator, or any creditor, may challenge any alienation by the company provided that the alienation has taken place on one of the following days:

(*a*)   where the alienation favours a person who is an associate (within the meaning of the Bankruptcy (Scotland) Act 1985) of the company, on a day not earlier than five years before the commencement of the winding up; or

(*b*)   where the alienation favours any other person, on a day not earlier than two years before that date.

Where such a challenge is made, the court must grant a decree of reduction or for such restoration of property to the company's assets or other redress as may be appropriate, unless it is shown:

(i)   that immediately, or at any other time, after the alienation the company's assets were greater than its liabilities, or

(ii)   that the alienation was made for adequate consideration, or

(iii)   that the alienation was a birthday, Christmas or other conventional gift or was a gift made for a charitable purpose to a person who is not an associate of the company which, having regard to all the circumstances, it was reasonable for the company to make.

(Section 242).

In Scotland, the provisions of the Insolvency Act 1986 do not exclude a creditor's right to challenge a gratuitous alienation or preference outside a winding up or an administration (*Bank of Scotland v Pacific Shelf (Sixty Two) Ltd (1988) 4 BCC 457*).

Preferences (England and Wales)

C10.4   On the liquidator's application, the court must, subject to what is stated below under this heading and in C10.6 below, make appropriate orders to counteract the effect of a preference. A preference consists of anything done or suffered to be done by the company which has the effect of putting one of its creditors, or any surety or guarantor for any of its debts, into a position which, in the event of the company going into insolvent liquidation, would be better than the position which such person would have been in if that thing had not been done. However, (i) it must be shown to the court that the company, in deciding to give the preference 'was influenced by a desire' to produce the above effect (which in the case of a 'connected person' (see C10.2 above) is presumed to have been the case unless the contrary is shown) and (ii) the provisions will not apply unless:

(*a*)   at the time or in consequence of that act the company was unable to pay its debts (see C5.22 above); and

(*b*)   the winding up commences within six months (or, in the case of a 'connected person', within two years) following that act (sections 239 and 240).

It is debatable whether the words 'influenced by the desire' have the same meaning as the words 'with a view of' in the old legislation. The Cork Committee Report (Cmnd 8558) had recommended the retention of the same test (see paragraph 1256). The courts have interpreted 'view' (under the old legislation) to mean 'dominant, substantial or effectual view or intent' (as distinguished from 'motive'). There is an argument for the proposition that they should continue to hold that the influence or the desire should also be dominant, substantial or effectual and that 'desire' means 'intent' and not 'motive'.

However, in *Re M C Bacon Ltd [1990] BCC 78* it was held that, unlike under the old law, it is no longer necessary to establish a dominant intention to prefer. Millett J suggested a two-stage test. It is sufficient to prove that there was a desire to prefer and that the company's action was influenced by that desire. 'Intention' is objective, 'desire' is subjective. The requirement that desire should have influenced the decision is satisfied if it was one of the factors which operated on the minds of those who made the decision. It need not have been the only factor or even the decisive one. If there was evidence that the directors of the company perceived the consequences of the transaction as giving preference to the recipient, then it was possible to establish the requisite 'desire'. However, it could not be assumed that the directors desired the necessary consequences of their acts. Further, once 'desire' was established, it was necessary to show 'influence'. This meant showing that the perceived advantages actually operated on the directors' minds so as to be one of the factors motivating their actions. The Act did not stipulate that the desire must be dominant. It merely needed to be a desire which influenced the decision. An 'influence' was perceptible only in its effect and involved a subjective analysis of a director's state of mind. It was not necessary to prove that, if the requisite desire had not been present, the company would not have entered into the transaction. That would be too high a test. In that case, where the transaction complained of was the giving of a debenture to a bank, Millett J found on evidence that one of the directors was motivated by the desire that he should carry out his agreement to give the bank a debenture, and the other two directors by the desire to avoid the calling in of the overdraft and desire to continue to trade. The latter two were also influenced by the former. Although there might have been consequences of the decision to give the bank a debenture which were of advantage to the first director and therefore desired by him, on an analysis of his state of mind he was not influenced by such a desire in granting the debenture.

For an example of where a grantee of a debenture succeeded in disproving such influence by showing that the decision by the company to grant the debenture was solely influenced by commercial considerations, see *Re Fairway Magazines Ltd [1992] BCC 924.*

In *Re Ledingham-Smith [1992] 5 Insolvency Intelligence 65* (decided under the new legislation but under the provisions relating to preferences by individuals which are similar to those relating to preferences by companies), the debtors, who were unable to pay their debts, owed their accountants a substantial sum for work done in the past. The accountants continued to act for them in assisting them to make a beneficial disposal of their business, in consideration of the debtors' undertaking to pay the accountants £5,000 per week to cover their continuing fees and, as to any balance, towards payment of the past fees. The payments, irregularly made by the debtors, together with £1,000 per month which they continued to pay by a bankers' standing order under a previous arrangement relating to the past fees, totalled some £14,000 whereas the continuing fees totalled £11,690. Morritt J held that the surplus, which went to discharge the past fees, did not constitute a preference. The debtors were influenced by a desire to retain the accountants but not a desire to prefer them, in the absence of evidence that the payments were to benefit, as distinct from might benefit, the accountants (as regards the past fees). Whether or not the weekly £5,000 would result in any such surplus depended on the amount of new work which the accountants would do.

Subject to the above, the position under the old legislation (section 615 of the Companies Act 1985, read with section 44 of the Bankruptcy Act 1914) relating to fraudulent preference may be summarised as follows (although Millett J in the *M C Bacon* case did not think that the cases under it were of assistance in applying the new provisions).

(1)   Good faith or the state of knowledge on the part of the creditor or other party preferred was irrelevant. It was the intent on the part of the company through its directors that was material.

(2) 'View' meant intent rather than motive (*Sharp v Jackson [1899] AC 419*).

(3) Preference did not have to be the sole view but must have been the dominant, substantial or effectual view on the part of the company through its directors (*Ex p Hill; Re Bird (1883) 23 ChD 695; Sharp v Jackson* above). The fact that the company genuinely believed that it would be able to pay its debts at some future time did not in itself negative the intent to prefer (*Re FP & CH Matthews Ltd [1982] 1 All ER 338*).

(4) The act must have been voluntary on the part of the company and evidence of pressure might negative the voluntary nature of the act. The pressure must, however, have been genuine, e.g. a threat of legal proceedings. The element of 'deliberate selection' was strongly canvassed in *Re Cutts [1956] 1 WLR 728* (see also *Re Fletcher (1891) 9 Mor 8*).

(5) Where the transaction was entered into for *bona fide* overriding commercial reasons, e.g. payment to key suppliers in respect of past supplies to ensure continuity of supplies or payment to a bank so as to maintain the line of credit (see *Re F L E Holdings Ltd [1967] 1 WLR 1409*), intention to prefer might be negatived. This principle has been recognised by Millett J in the *M C Bacon* case mentioned above, decided under the new legislation.

(6) Where the company created a charge to secure new moneys advanced to it there was no preference to the extent of the new moneys, as the person preferred was not an existing creditor to the extent of the new advance.

(7) The onus of proving liability to pay and intent to prefer was on the liquidator (*Peat v Gresham Trust [1934] AC 252*). In this respect, the sections looked to the factual position at the time of the transaction in question (*Re FP and CH Matthews Ltd*, above, where intent to prefer a bank was established).

(8) On the question of intent to prefer, the following further cases gave some guidance.

Where intent established

(a) *Re W Blackburn & Co [1899] 2 Ch 725* (debtor acting from a mere moral sense of duty).

(b) *Re M Kushler Ltd [1943] Ch 248* (preference of bank for the benefit of guarantor; intent inferred from circumstances; see also section 616(3) of the Companies Act 1985, now repealed and not re-enacted).

(c) *Re Eric Holmes (Property) Ltd [1965] Ch 1052* (right to be preferred on request).

(d) *Re Allen Fairfield & Sons Ltd (1971) 115 SJ 244* (unreality of alleged pressure by directors on their own company).

(e)   *Re Industrial Design & Manufacture Ltd, Northern Ireland Chancery Division, 25 June 1984* (bank writing series of standard letters asking overdraft to be reduced; unexplained increase in level of repayments to it; managing director aware of company's inability to pay its debts but influenced by the fact that he had guaranteed the overdraft).

Where intent not established

(a)   *Sharp v Jackson [1899] AC 419* (demand by creditor; pressure; fear of legal proceedings).

(b)   *Hartshorn v Slodden (1801) 2 B & P 582* (pressure, even though debt not yet due and payable).

(c)   *Re Clay & Sons (1896) 3 Mans 31* (ordinary course of dealing and anticipation of benefit).

(d)   *Re Vautin [1900] 2 QB 325* (obligation believed to be legal).

(e)   *Bulteel and Colmore v Parker and Bulteel's Trustee (1916) 32 TLR 661* (antecedent engagement).

(f)   *Re William Hall (Contractors) Ltd [1967] 2 All ER 1150* (execution by company of legal mortgages pursuant to its obligations under memoranda of deposit of title deeds).

In *West Mercia Safetywear Ltd v Dodd (1988) 4 BCC 30*, a parent company's overdraft with a bank had been guaranteed by a director of a subsidiary and secured by a charge on the parent's book debts, including a debt owed to it by the subsidiary. The discharge by the subsidiary of the intercompany debt by payment into the overdraft account was held to be a preference by the subsidiary in favour of the parent (and, hence, misfeasance on the part of the director). See also C13.4 below (misfeasance). Likewise, where the directors caused their company to discharge its debts to them ahead of the debts due to other creditors, this was held to be a preference (*Re DKG Contractors Ltd [1990] BCC 903*). By contrast, where the company, which occupied business premises leased by one of its directors to two of its other directors, paid rent of the business premises to the landlord director about ten days before its due date, with a view to continuing its business at least temporarily to take advantage of the Christmas trade, the payment was held not to be a preference in favour of the tenant directors—in any case, it could not have been a preference in favour of the landlord director as the company had no direct or primary liability to him (*Re Beacon Leisure Ltd [1991] BCC 213*).

The whole payment made by or on behalf of the company need not refer to the preferred debt (*Re Clasper Group Services Ltd (1988) 4 BCC 673*, where a payment made to the controlling shareholder's son in respect of his employment with the company in excess of what was due to him was held to be a preference).

A debenture granted to a bank (securing past and future indebtedness) is capable of constituting a preference under the new legislation, at least in relation to the past indebtedness (section 239) (*Re a Company No 005009 of 1987, ex parte Copp* (1988) 4 BCC 424).

Money recovered by the liquidator under (what was then) section 617 of the Companies Act 1985 in respect of a preference was not covered by a floating charge, even though it had crystallised by reason of the liquidation (*Re Yagerphone Ltd* [1935] *Ch 392;* see also the *dictum* of Russell LJ in *Robbie v Watney Warehouses Ltd* [1963] *3 All ER 614* at *622;* and *N A Kratzmann Pty Ltd v Tucker (No 2)* (1988) *123 CLR 295 (High Court of Australia)*). In *Re M C Bacon Ltd (No 2)* [1990] *BCC 430,* Millett J rejected the liquidator's application for an order that the costs incurred by and awarded against him in an unsuccessful attempt to challenge the validity of a fixed and floating charge as a preference, and to recover compensation for alleged wrongful trading by the company, should be reimbursed out of the floating charge assets. The judge observed that the proceeds of any sums recovered as a preference or for wrongful trading would not have been assets of the company comprised in the charge. He stated [*1990*] *BCC* at *434:*

> 'The proceedings were not brought by or on behalf of the company nor . . . in order to recover assets belonging to the company at the date of the winding up. . . . Neither claim could have been made by the company itself.'

However, the recovery of goods by a receiver, appointed under a floating charge created by a company, from a supplier creditor to whom the company had returned the goods by way of preference in discharge of the amount due for the goods, was held in a liquidation in Scotland to be applicable for the benefit of the holder of the charge on the ground that assets coming into existence after the crystallisation of the charge (due to the receiver's appointment) were, by its terms, caught by the charge (*Ross v Taylor 1985 SLT 387 (Ct of Session)*). Interest on the money recoverable was payable from the date of commencement of the winding up (see *Re FP and CH Matthews Ltd,* above).

As to extra-territorial aspects, see the *Paramount Airways* case referred to at C10.2 above and the comments thereon.

Preferences (Scotland)

C10.5 Under section 243, the liquidator (or any creditor) may challenge a transaction, entered into not earlier than six months before the commencement of the winding up, which has the effect of creating a preference in favour of a creditor to the prejudice of the general body of creditors. Certain transactions are excluded (for example a transaction in the ordinary course of trade or business). Where the court is satisfied that the transaction is one to which section 243 applies, it must grant a decree of reduction or for such restoration of property to the company's assets or other redress as may be appropriate. (See also the *Bank of Scotland* case cited in C10.3 above).

Court's powers in respect of transactions at an undervalue and preferences, and position of third parties

C10.6 The court in England and Wales has very wide powers (set out in section 241(1)) to make appropriate orders to counteract the effect of the transactions and acts described in C10.2 and C10.4 above. Section 241(2) (as amended—see below) expressly provides that an order of the court may affect the property of, or impose any obligation on, any person (whether or not he is the person with whom the company entered into the transaction or to whom the preference was given) but that such an order must not prejudice any interest (or any interest derived from any interest) in property which was acquired, or require a payment from a person (not being a party to the transaction or a creditor receiving the preference) who received a benefit—

(*a*) in good faith, and

(*b*) for value.

The Insolvency (No 2) Act 1994, which received Royal Assent on 26 May 1994 and came into force on 26 July 1994, amends sections 241 and 342 (the latter applicable to bankruptcies) of the Insolvency Act 1986 (and related statutory instruments applying to Northern Ireland) dealing with transactions at an undervalue and preferences ('antecedent transactions'). The new Act has effect in relation to interests acquired and benefits received after the coming into force of that Act.

The main thrust of the new Act is to afford substantially greater protection to unconnected *third parties* in relation to property or assets, tainted with antecedent transactions, in which they acquire an interest in good faith and full value from a company other than the insolvent company or individual.

The concept of 'notice of the relevant circumstances' (previously defined in section 241(3) prior to its amendment by the new Act) is removed as an independent test, but is replaced by the concept of 'notice of the relevant surrounding circumstances and of the relevant proceedings' as the test for determining whether the recipient of the interest, where he is an 'unconnected person', was acting in good faith. In the case of 'connected persons' there is to be a rebuttable presumption, regardless of 'notice', that he was not acting in good faith.

It should be noted that this protection only applies to third parties (that is, parties other than those in whose favour the insolvent company or individual made the preference or entered into the undervalue transaction). A typical example is where the insolvent company makes a tainted transfer of assets to another party and that other party borrows money from a bank on the security of those assets. There, the bank would be a third party. As far as immediate counterparties are concerned, they can be liable regardless of good faith, absence of notice or the giving by them of value. In such cases, the question is whether the relevant act or omission was *in fact* an undervalue transaction or a preference, and not whether the counterparty *knew* or *ought to have known* that that was the case.

(The powers of the court in Scotland are not set out in detail in the Act, but see C10.3 and C10.5 above.)

Extortionate credit transactions (Great Britain)

C10.7 Provision has also been made (in section 244) for relief to be granted to the company at the instance of the liquidator in respect of any transaction for the provision of credit to the company entered into by the company within three years ending with the day on which the company went into liquidation (i.e. on which the winding-up resolution was passed or the winding-up order was made—section 247(2)) which the court regards as extortionate. For this purpose a transaction is extortionate if, having regard to the risk accepted by the provider of the credit, the terms require grossly exorbitant payments or otherwise grossly contravene ordinary principles of fair trading. A transaction in respect of which the relief is sought will be presumed to be extortionate unless the contrary is proved.

In *Woodstead Finance Ltd v Petrou and another, The Times, 23 January 1986* (decided in another context), the interest rate of 42.5 per cent per annum on a short term bridging loan given for the purpose of paying off the debtor's pressing business creditors on the security of his wife's property and her personal guarantee, although apparently harsh, was held on the facts to be a normal going rate for such loan, and therefore, not extortionate. In *Davies v Directloans Ltd [1986] 1 WLR 823*, decided under section 138 of the Consumer Credit Act 1974 (which defines extortionate credit bargains in similar terms), interest at the rate of 25.785 per cent per annum on the balance of the purchase price of a house, secured by a legal charge on the house which was given despite warnings by the mortgagor's solicitors and the mortgagee, was held not to be extortionate. By contrast, in *Castle Phillips Finance Company v Williams, Current Law 12/86 (unreported)* the court refused to apply to section 138 of the Consumer Credit Act 1974 the analogy of the cases interpreting the words 'harsh and unconscionable' in the Moneylenders Act 1927. It held that even a rate of interest of less than 48 per cent could be held to be extortionate under the Consumer Credit Act 1974, depending on the evidence as to interest rates prevailing at the time of the transaction and having regard to the court's own knowledge of interest rates.

Section 244(4) and (5) specifies the terms which may be included in an order under that section. Section 244 applies to Scotland (see section 440).

Avoidance of certain floating charges (Great Britain)

C10.8 Under section 245 (which applies in administrations and liquidations but is here dealt with only in the context of liquidations), a charge on the company's undertaking or property which, as created, was a floating charge, is invalid in the circumstances set out below *except* to the extent of the aggregate of:

(1) the value of so much of the consideration for the creation of the charge as consists of money paid, or goods or services supplied (see C10.9 below), to the company at the same time as or after the creation of the charge;

(2) the value of so much of that consideration as consists of the discharge or reduction, at the same time as or after the creation of the charge, of any debt of the company; and

(3) the amount of such interest (if any) as is payable on the amount falling within (1) or (2) above in pursuance of any agreement under which the money was so paid, the goods or services were so supplied or the debt was so discharged or reduced.

The circumstances referred to above are the following:

(*a*) in the case of a charge created in favour of a 'connected person' (see C10.2 above), if it was created within the period of two years ending with the commencement of winding up (see C10.9 below); or

(*b*) in the case of a charge in favour of any other person, if it was created—

(i) within the period of twelve months ending with the commencement of the winding up (or administration, if earlier), *and*

(ii) at a time when the company was unable to pay its debts within the meaning of section 123 (see C5.22 above) or the company became unable to pay its debts in consequence of the transaction under which the charge was created.

Practical application of section 245 (floating charges)

C10.9

(1) The main differences between section 245 and its predecessor (section 617 of the Companies Act 1985) are the following.

(*a*) Section 617 protected only 'cash paid to the company' at the time of or subsequent to the creation of, and in consideration for the charge, together with annual interest on that amount of five per cent. Section 245 extends the protection to certain other forms of benefit provided to the company at the same time as, or after, the creation of the charge, and created in consideration therefor. The protection is also extended to the full interest (if any) agreed between the parties in respect of the items protected.

(*b*) The vulnerable period in the case of a 'connected person' is now extended from one year to two years.

(*c*) Previously the onus of proving that at or following the creation of the charge the company was 'solvent' (which expression had not been defined) was on the holder of the charge. Now the burden appears to have shifted onto the liquidator to prove that the company was 'unable to pay debts' (as defined in section 123); but in the case of a connected person the vulnerability of the charge does not depend on whether the company was in that position.

(*d*)   Under section 245, any post-creation crystallisation of a floating charge (even if it occurs before the commencement of winding up) is irrelevant (see the definition of 'floating charge' in section 251).

(2)   Unlike section 239 (preferences), intent or desire is irrelevant.

(3)   The section applies only to a floating charge. Where the same charge contains a fixed charge over some assets and a floating charge over others it only applies to the latter. The fixed charge may, however, fall within section 239 (preferences) or 243 (unfair preferences— Scotland), depending on the circumstances.

(4)   The section invalidates only the floating charge; the debt remains, but only as an unsecured debt (*Re Parkes Garage (Swadlincote) Ltd [1929] 1 Ch 139*).

(5)   'Cash paid to the company' in the context of section 617 meant that if the charge secured moneys advanced to another party (e.g. to a parent company or a subsidiary or fellow subsidiary), it was invalid except to the extent that money was on-lent or otherwise passed to the company. The test was whether it could be said that in substance, and not merely in form, the money was paid to the company. The mere fact that it had been paid into the company's account was not conclusive; the payment must have been intended to benefit the company and not some other person (*Re Destone Fabrics Ltd [1941] Ch 319*). Cash could include cheques paid by a bank on the company's behalf out of money advanced to the company (*Re Yeovil Glove Co Ltd [1965] Ch 148*). A replacement advance by artificially moving money in a circle, even through another party, was not 'cash paid' (*Re G T Whyte & Co Ltd [1983] BCLC 311*). However, now the discharge or reduction by the chargee, at the same time as or after the creation of the charge, of the company's debt (presumably only if the debt is owed to a third party and the transaction is genuine) is expressly protected by section 245(2)(b) (see C10.8 above). However, in *Re Fairway Magazines Ltd [1992] BCC 924*, a payment made by the holder of a floating charge at the request of the company to the company's bank, in reduction of its overdraft guaranteed by the charge-holder, was held to fall foul of section 245. The reason given by the court was that it was not 'money paid . . . to the company' within section 245(2)(a). The charge-holder had not sought to rely on or argue the effect of section 245(2)(b).

(6)   The words 'at the time of or subsequently to and in consideration for the charge', in the context of section 617 of the Companies Act 1985, have been interpreted to apply to money advanced a few days before the creation of but in reliance upon a promise to create a

charge (*Re Columbian Fireproofing Co [1910] 2 Ch 120; Re F & E Stanton Ltd [1929] 1 Ch 180*). However, in *Re Shoe Lace Ltd [1992] BCC 367*, a delay of about four months between the date of passing of the directors' resolution to create the charge and the date of actual creation was held to make the charge void in relation to the moneys advanced in the interim. In affirming that decision, the Court of Appeal held (*[1993] BCC 609*) that the words 'at the same time as' were strictly a matter of contemporaneity. Delay would only be tolerated if it really was *de minimis*—such as a 'coffee break'. This decision effectively overrules the decision in *Re Fairway Magazines Ltd [1992] BCC 924* where there was a gap of at least one month between the advances and the creation of the charge and Mummery J, in upholding the validity of the charge in respect of the payments, sought to distinguish the decision of Hoffmann J at first instance in *Re Shoe Lace Ltd* (above).

(7)   Where a floating charge is given to secure an existing overdraft, and there are subsequent debits and credits therein to reflect further advances from and receipts into the account, the rule in *Clayton's case (1816) 1 Mer 572* applies and the receipts would be applied first in payment of the pre-charge indebtedness regardless of the consequence of the charge (*Re Yeovil Glove Co Ltd [1965] Ch 148*). The section would not of course apply to the post-charge advances which remain outstanding after such application but, depending on the circumstances, payments into the account could constitute a preference (see C10.4 above).

(8)   The section, when it applies, invalidates the charge only on a winding up (or an administration order—see PART B: ADMINISTRATION ORDERS) and, therefore, does not invalidate the repayment of the debt secured which has been made before the commencement of the winding up. Where a receiver appointed under the charge who is the company's agent has realised the assets and applied the proceeds towards repayment of the company's debt before the winding up, the repayment is neither invalidated nor required to be repaid (*Mace Builders (Glasgow) Ltd v Lunn [1986] 3 WLR 921*). This is, however, subject to the 'preference' point made in (7) above.

Debt avoidance (England and Wales)

C10.10   Sections 423 to 425 deal with debt avoidance and may be invoked even if there is no formal winding up or other insolvency procedure. They apply to individuals as well as bodies corporate (*Re Shilena Hosiery Co Ltd [1979] 2 All ER 6*). Here the subject is dealt with only in the context of a body corporate.

If a company has entered into a transaction at an undervalue (the basic definition of which is similar to that in C10.2 above) for the purpose of putting the assets beyond the reach of a person who is making, or may at some time make, a claim against the company or otherwise prejudicing the interests of such a person in relation to such claim or future claim, the court may, on application, make various orders under section 425 for restoring the original position and protecting the interests of the 'victim' of the transaction, that is a person who is or is capable of being prejudiced thereby.

Section 425(2) gives innocent third parties protection similar to that afforded to them under section 241(2) in respect of preferences and transactions at an undervalue (see C10.6 above). This means, for example, that section 423(2), which empowers the court to make such orders as it thinks fit for restoring the position to what it would have been and protecting the interests of the victims of the transaction, must be read as if that power were qualified by the words 'as far as possible' (*Chohan v Saggar [1992] BCC 750*, affirmed on appeal [*1994*] *BCC 134*).

For examples of such transactions, see *Moon v Franklin, FT Law Reports, June 1990* (transfer of property to wife 'as an expression of gratitude for support' at the time when the transferor was facing a criminal investigation, an action for professional negligence (with a double insurance cover) and a threat of action by creditors, including the plaintiff; the action, though brought by an individual, is a class action; a 'Mareva' order was made); and *Arbuthnot Leasing International Ltd v Havelet Ltd (No 2) [1990] BCC 636* (heavily insolvent company transferring its undertaking to another company owned by the first company's executive director).

In *Moon v Franklin* (above), the court subsequently issued an injunction against the wife restraining her from disposing of the property, having regarded the relief under section 423 as akin to *Mareva* relief. It will be noted that although the relief was applied for by one particular creditor, it was in effect a 'class relief' benefitting all victims or potential victims of the transaction, since the essence of the relief is to preserve or restore the *status quo* as far as possible.

In *Re Ayala Holdings Ltd [1993] BCLC 256*, a construction company in financial difficulties sent a letter to a bank instructing it to use certain funds, receivable by it for the company under a contract, to pay off the indebtedness to the bank of a local company whom the company had used as an agent to obtain finance for the contract in the name of the local company. Following the presentation of a winding-up petition against the company, a creditor sought by an application to the court to prevent the bank from making the payment until it was shown that the local company had become a secured creditor by virtue of that letter (which had not been registered as a charge). The creditor contended that the letter of instruction was a transaction at an undervalue for the purposes of section 423. The bank's objection that it was bound to comply with the letter of instruction was rejected on the grounds that

(i)   on a full hearing it was open to the court to reach the conclusion that there had been a transaction at an undervalue, and

(ii)   the creditor fell within the definition of 'victim' of the transaction and had *locus standi*.

On a full hearing, it was held that as a creditor he was entitled to apply for an order against the bank under section 423, subject to obtaining the court's leave, and that, since he had an arguable case, such leave should be granted.

The purpose of putting the assets beyond the reach of the creditors (etc.) must be a *dominant* purpose; but if the dominant purpose is present, the section applies whether or not any other motives exist: *Chohan v Saggar* [*1992*] *BCC 306*. See also the subsequent decision in that case, [*1992*] *BCC 750* (affirmed on appeal, [*1994*] *BCC 134*). An individual had transferred his house, worth £75,000 (or £50,000 subject to the burden of his wife's protected tenancy), to his wife upon payment to him, by his wife, of only £31,000 of which £25,000 was provided by a building society; and the wife had executed a declaration of trust in favour of a third party in return for an 'illusory' payment by the third party of £19,000 representing the balance. A creditor obtained a charging order absolute over the house which the building society sought to have set aside. He had also obtained a *Mareva* injunction over the husband's assets and a garnishee order for rent due from the wife. The court decided not to set aside the transfer but to set aside the declaration of trust, to discharge the charging and garnishee orders and declare that the wife held the equity of redemption on trust for sale, as to 19/75ths for the creditor and the balance for herself.

In *Agricultural Mortgage Corporation plc v Woodward* [*1994*] *BCC 688*, a farmer had granted a mortgage of his freehold farm to a lender. He fell into arrears with his mortgage payments and the lender granted him three months within which to regularise his position. During that period, the farmer granted an agricultural tenancy over his entire farm to his wife at the full market rent. The result, nevertheless, was that the value of the freehold to the lender was substantially reduced. The purpose of the grant was admitted to be to prevent the lender from obtaining vacant possession, and to protect the interests of the family and its farming business. The form of waiver which the wife had signed in favour of the lender related only to such rights as the wife had at the time of the loan and not to any subsequent tenancy. (No consent of the lender to the grant of the tenancy was required despite the 'negative pledge' in the mortgage, as the provisions of the Agricultural Holdings Act 1986 appear to permit the grant of an agricultural tenancy.) It was contended by the lender that this was a transaction at an undervalue because

(i) the grant of the tenancy resulted in a detriment to the value of the freehold, and/or

(ii) in spite of the rent payable by the wife being a market rent, the overall benefit she received was in excess of the value of the rent.

The Court of Appeal expressed no view on argument (i) but accepted argument (ii).

The persons who may make the application to the court are: where the company is being wound up or subject to an administration order, the liquidator or the administrator (as the case may be) or, with the leave of the court, the victim; and where there is in force a voluntary arrangement, the victim or (if the victim is bound by the arrangement) the supervisor of the arrangement (section 424(1)). An application under section 423 which is not made in the existing proceedings in the Companies Court or the Bankruptcy Court, or which is brought otherwise than by virtue of some other provision of Parts I and XI of the 1986 Act, is not confined to those particular courts and can be made in any other part of the High Court: *Trustee Savings Bank plc v Kantz, The Times, 2 May 1994*; see also section 423(4).

An application made under section 424(1) is to be treated as made on behalf of every victim of the transaction (section 424(2)). This means, in effect, that where there are several victims of the transaction, any recovery made will be shared between all those victims.

As to a claim against a stranger by way of third party proceedings under the now repealed section 172 of the Law of Property Act 1925 (fraudulent dispositions), see *Re Shilena Hosiery Co [1979] 2 All ER 6* which may have some relevance to sections 423 to 425.

It is useful here to summarise the similarities and differences between section 423 (debt avoidance) and section 238 (transactions at an undervalue—see C10.2 above).

(*a*)   Unlike section 238, section 423 applies even if at the time of, or as a result of, the transaction the company is *not* unable to pay its debts.

(*b*)   As under section 238, a transaction under section 423 must be one at an undervalue (similarly defined for the purposes of both sections).

(*c*)   Under section 238, a transaction is protected if the company entered into it in good faith *and* for the purposes of carrying on its business *and* in the reasonable belief that the transaction would benefit the company. By contrast, a transaction under section 423 would be protected *unless* the dominant purpose of the transaction, on the part of the company, was to put the assets concerned beyond the reach of a person who is making or may at some time make a claim against the company, or otherwise to prejudice the interests of such a person in relation to such claim or future claim.

(*d*)   A claim under section 238 can lie only in a liquidation or administration, but a claim under section 423 can lie regardless of any formal insolvency of the company.

(*e*)   A claim under section 238 can be made only by or at the instance of a liquidator or administrator of the company and for the benefit of the creditors generally. By contrast, a claim under section 423 can also be made (subject to the leave of the court) by or at the instance of, and (it would seem, in exceptional circumstances) for the sole benefit of, the 'victim' or all victims or potential victims of the transaction, and also by the supervisor of a voluntary arrangement in relation to the company.

(*f*)   The risk period for a transaction under section 238 is two years preceding the 'onset of insolvency', whereas there is no specific risk period under section 423 so that, as it would seem, the normal six-year period of limitation under the Limitation Acts would apply.

An example of an aggrieved creditor succeeding against a transferee of assets, even without the aid of section 423, occurred in *Creasey v Breachwood Motors Ltd [1992] BCC 638*. An insolvent company (B), against which a former employee (C) had issued a writ claiming damages for wrongful dismissal, transferred all its assets and liabilities to another company in common ownership (M). After C obtained judgment in default against B, but before damages had been assessed, B was struck off the register. The court 'short-circuited' the process of having that company restored to the register and then put into liquidation (to enable the liquidator or C to have the transfer set aside under section 423), by piercing the corporate veil and holding M in principle directly liable to C. This was done mainly on the basis of expediency and practical justice.

Unenforceability of lien on books, etc. (England and Wales)

C10.11   A lien or other right to retain possession of any books, papers or other records of the company is unenforceable to the extent that its enforcement would deny possession thereof to the liquidator. This does not apply to a lien on documents which give a title to property and are held as such (section 246).

Disposition of property after commencement of compulsory winding up (see C8.4 *et seq.* above).

Chapter 11: Conduct of winding up: general administrative aspects

(Note: some of the provisions dealt with below are, in their application to the winding up of an insolvent partnership, subject to variations contained in the Insolvent Partnerships Order 1994 (SI 1994 No 2421).)

Notification on stationery

C11.1　Every invoice, order for goods or business letter issued by or on behalf of the company or the liquidator, receiver or manager on which the company's name appears must contain a statement that the company is being wound up (section 188).

Meetings and accounts

Introduction

C11.2　In addition to the first meetings of creditors and contributories in a compulsory winding up (see C5.49 above) and the first meeting of creditors in a creditors' voluntary winding up (see C4.6 above), other types of meetings of creditors or members or contributories must or may be held for various other purposes. (For some examples see C11.8 and C11.19(6) below.) As well as the requirements stated in C4.6 and C5.49 above, and C11.18 and C11.19 below, the points made in C11.3 to C11.17 below must be noted. The Rules and Scottish Rules mentioned are supplemented by Rules 8.1 to 8.7 and Scottish Rules 7.14 to 7.20 (proxies and company representation). See also PART A: GENERAL and, as to Scotland, Scottish Rules 7.1 to 7.13 (meetings in insolvency proceedings generally).) It will also be seen in C11.18 that the liquidator has continuing obligations with regard to his accounts.

Notice of first meetings

C11.3　In a compulsory winding up where under section 136(5) the Official Receiver decides to summon meetings of the creditors and contributories (see C5.49 above), he must give notice of each meeting to the court and (in the case of the creditors' meeting) to every creditor known to the Official Receiver or identified in the statement of affairs and (in the case of the contributories' meeting) to every person appearing (by the company's books or otherwise) to be a contributory. The notice must specify the time and date (which must be not more than four days before the date of the meeting) by which the creditors or contributories (as the case may be) must lodge proofs and (if appropriate) proxies, in order to be entitled to vote. The notice is also required to be advertised (Rule 4.50, Form 4.21).

In a creditors' voluntary winding up the notice of the creditors' meeting (see C4.6 above) must specify *inter alia* the time (which must not be earlier than 12.00 hours on the business day before the day of the meeting) by which, and the place at which, the creditors must lodge proofs and (if applicable) proxies (Rule 4.51).

Where the company is an authorised institution or former authorised institution under the Banking Act 1987, notice of the first meeting of creditors and contributories in a compulsory winding up or notice of the first meeting of creditors in a voluntary winding up must also be given to the Bank of England and the Deposit Protection Board (Rules 4.50(8), 4.51(3) and 4.72).

(See also C11.5 and, as to meetings of creditors of Part II insurance companies, C11.19 below.)

Business of first meetings

C11.4   In a compulsory winding up:

(*a*)   no resolutions must be taken at the first meeting of creditors other than resolutions:

   (i)   to appoint a named insolvency practitioner to be liquidator or two or more such practitioners as joint liquidators;

   (ii)   to establish a liquidation committee;

   (iii)   (unless it has been resolved to establish a liquidation committee) specifying the terms of the liquidator's remuneration or to defer consideration of the matter;

   (iv)   (in the case of joint liquidators) specifying whether acts are to be done by both or all of them, or by only one;

   (v)   (in the case of a meeting requisitioned under section 136—see C5.49 above) authorising payment out of the assets, as an expense of the liquidation, of the costs of summoning and holding the meeting and any meeting of contributories so requisitioned;

   (vi)   to adjourn the meeting for not more than three weeks;

   (vii)   any other resolution which the chairman thinks it right to allow for special reasons:

(*b*)   the business of the first meeting of contributories is similarly restricted except that items (iii) and (v) do not apply (Rule 4.52);

(*c*)   Scottish Rule 4.12 applies as to Scotland.

In a creditors' voluntary winding up, the business of the first meeting of creditors is restricted as in (*a*) above except that item (v) does not apply (Rule 4.53).

Further requirements as to notices of meetings generally

C11.5 In the case of a meeting of creditors or contributories in a compulsory or creditors' voluntary winding up, further provisions as to notice apply, subject as stated in C4.6, C5.49, C11.3 and C11.4 above. The person summoning the meeting ('the convener') must fix a venue and then give a notice thereof, in the case of a creditors' meeting, to every creditor who is known to him or is identified in the company's statement of affairs, and in the case of a contributories' meeting to every person appearing (by the company's books or otherwise) to be a contributory.

The notice must be given at least 21 days before the date of the meeting and must specify the purpose. Additional notice may be given by public advertisement if the convener thinks fit, and must be so given if the court orders.

The notice must specify the time and date (not more than four days before the day of the meeting) by which, and the place at which, creditors must lodge proxies (where applicable) and (in a compulsory winding up) proofs in order to be entitled to vote (Rule 4.54).

As to the right of the Deposit Protection Board to attend meetings in the winding up of an authorised institution or former authorised institution, see section 58 of the Banking Act 1987.

Notice of meetings by advertisement only

C11.6 The court may order that notice of any meeting of creditors or contributories in a compulsory or creditors' voluntary winding up be given by public advertisement, and not by individual notice. In this connection, the court must have regard to the cost of public advertisement, the amount of assets available and the interests of creditors or contributories or any class of them (Rule 4.59).

Chairman

C11.7 In a compulsory winding up, the chairman of any meeting of creditors or contributories must be (where it has been convened by the Official Receiver) the Official Receiver or a person nominated by him (in writing unless such person is another Official Receiver) or (where the convener is someone else) the convener or a person nominated in writing by him. The latter must be a person qualified to act as an insolvency practitioner in relation to the company or an employee of the liquidator or his firm experienced in insolvency matters (Rule 4.55).

In a creditors' voluntary winding up, the chairman of the first meeting of creditors must be one of the directors appointed for the purpose by the company's board of directors (section 99(1)(c) and see C4.1 above). At any other meeting of creditors, the chairman must be the liquidator or a person nominated in writing by him. The latter must be a person qualified to act as an insolvency practitioner in relation to the company or an employee of the liquidator or his firm experienced in insolvency matters (Rule 4.56).

Where the chairman holds a proxy requiring him to vote for a particular resolution, and no other person proposes the resolution, he must himself propose it, unless he considers that there is a good reason for not doing so. In the latter case, he must forthwith after the meeting notify his principal of the reasons (Rule 4.64).

Attendance of company's personnel

C11.8   Rule 4.58 and Scottish Rule 4.14 contain provisions aimed at securing the attendance of certain categories of present and past officers and employees of the company at meetings of creditors and contributories in a compulsory or creditors' voluntary winding up (so that questions may be put to them, insofar as they are allowed by the chairman), or allowing them to attend voluntarily. See also section 157 (power of the court in Scotland to require attendance of company's officers at meetings of creditors, contributories or liquidation committee).

Venue

C11.9   In fixing the venue of the meeting of creditors or contributories in a compulsory or creditors' voluntary winding up, the convener must have regard to the convenience of the persons (other than the chairman) who are invited to attend. Meetings must in all cases be summoned for commencement between the hours of 10.00 and 16.00 on a business day, unless the court otherwise directs (Rule 4.60(1) and (2)).

Proxy forms

C11.10   Forms of proxy must accompany every notice of meeting of creditors or contributories in a compulsory or creditors' voluntary winding up (Rule 4.60(3); Form 8.4 or 8.5).

Expenses of summoning meetings

C11.11   In a creditors' voluntary winding up, any reasonable and necessary expenses incurred in connection with the summoning, advertisement and holding of the first meeting of creditors under section 98 (see C4.6 above) may be paid out of the company's assets, either before or after the commencement of the winding up, as part of the expense of the liquidation. Where the payment is made before the commencement of the winding up, the director presiding at the meeting must give particulars to the meeting. Where the liquidator appointed under section 100 (following the creditors' meeting) intends to make the payment, he must give at least seven days' prior notice to the liquidation committee (if any). He must not make any payment to himself or his associate without the approval of the committee, the creditors or the court (Rule 4.62).

Where in a compulsory or creditors' voluntary winding up, any meeting of creditors or contributories is summoned at the instance of any person other than the Official Receiver or liquidator, the expenses of summoning and holding it must be paid by that person, who must deposit with the liquidator security for their payment. However, any creditors' meeting so summoned may resolve that the expenses of that meeting, and of any meeting of contributories requisitioned at the same time, be paid out of the assets, as an expense of the liquidation. Where a meeting of contributories is summoned on their requisition, it may vote that the expenses of that meeting be paid out of the assets, but subject to the rights of the creditors to be paid in full, with interest (Rule 4.61).

Quorum

C11.12 In a compulsory or creditors' voluntary winding up, a meeting of creditors or contributories is competent to act if a quorum is present.

The quorum, in the case of a creditors' meeting, is at least one creditor entitled to vote, and in the case of a contributories' meeting, is at least two contributories or, if their number does not exceed two, all the contributories, entitled to vote. The creditors or contributories forming the requisite quorum must be present in person or represented by proxy by any person (including the chairman) or (in the case of corporations) their representatives under section 375 of the Companies Act 1985.

However, if the chairman alone or one other person in addition to the chairman constitutes a quorum, and the chairman is aware, by virtue of proofs and proxies received or otherwise, that one or more additional persons would, if attending, be entitled to vote, the meeting must not commence until at least fifteen minutes after the scheduled time (Rule 12.4A; see also Scottish Rule 7.7).

Entitlement to vote

C11.13 Creditors are only entitled to vote at their meeting if:

(*a*) they have lodged (in a compulsory winding up, by the time and date stated in the notice) their proofs of debt and their claims have been admitted for the purposes of entitlement to vote (see C11.14 below); and

(*b*) they have lodged by the time and date stated in the notice, any proxy requisite for that entitlement.

The court may, in exceptional circumstances, by order declare the creditors, or any class of them, entitled to vote at creditors' meetings, without being required to prove their debts. In such an event, the court may, on the application of the liquidator, make consequential orders (e.g. an order treating a creditor as having proved his debt for the purposes of a dividend).

A creditor must not vote in respect of a debt for an unliquidated amount, or any debt whose value is not ascertained, except where the chairman agrees to put thereon an estimated minimum value for the purpose of entitlement to vote and admits his proof for that purpose. The expression 'agrees' connotes mutual agreement between the creditor and chairman rather than a unilateral decision by the chairman: see *Re Cranley Mansions Ltd, Saigol v Goldstein* [*1994*] *BCC 576*, a case concerning a company voluntary arrangement where the issue was of greater importance than in a liquidation. The fact that the company might have instituted a counterclaim, or disputed or objected to the quantum of the claim, does not render the debt in question either 'for an unliquidated amount' or 'whose value is not ascertained'. The correct course for the chairman in such a case is to mark the proof as objected to and allow the creditor to vote conditionally as provided by Rule 4.70 (see C11.14 below).

A secured creditor is entitled to vote only in respect of the balance (if any) of his debt after deducting the value of his security as estimated by him. (See, further, C14.29 *et seq.* below.)

A creditor in respect of a debt on, or secured by, a bill of exchange or promissory note must treat the liability to him of every person (not being a person against whom a bankruptcy order has been made or a company which has gone into liquidation, as the case may be) on the bill or note antecedently to the company as security in his hands and deduct from his proof the value of such security as estimated by him for the purposes of his entitlement to vote (but not for dividend) (Rule 4.67).

Any decision of the chairman on any of the foregoing matters is subject to appeal to the court by a creditor or contributory (Rule 4.70). In a creditors' voluntary winding up, the chairman may allow a creditor to vote, notwithstanding that he has failed to lodge a proof in accordance with the requirements stated above, if satisfied that the failure was due to circumstances beyond the creditor's control (Rule 4.68).

As to Scotland, see Scottish Rules 4.15 and 4.16.

At a meeting of contributories, voting rights are as at a general meeting of the company, subject to any provision in the articles affecting entitlement to vote, either generally or at a time when the company is in liquidation (Rule 4.69).

Admission or rejection of proofs for voting

C11.14   At any creditors' meeting, the chairman has power to admit a creditors' proof in whole or in part for the purposes of entitlement to vote. The decision is subject to appeal to the court by a creditor or contributory. If the chairman is in doubt as to whether a proof should be admitted or rejected, he should mark it as objected to and allow the creditor to vote, subject to his vote being subsequently declared invalid if the objection to the proof is sustained. If, on an appeal, the chairman's decision is reversed or varied, or a creditor's vote is declared invalid, the court may order that another meeting be summoned, or make such other order as it thinks fit. The chairman may allow a creditor to vote on a proof for money had and received notwithstanding that it is expressed to be without prejudice to the creditor's claim to the ownership of that money as being held by the company on a constructive trust (*Re Prime Metal Trading Ltd [1984] BCLC 543*). Presumably, this is also so where the proof is without prejudice to the creditor's retention of title claim covering the amount claimed in the proof. In a compulsory winding up, the Official Receiver or the liquidator or any person nominated by him as chairman is not personally liable for costs incurred by any person in respect of the appeal; nor is any other chairman unless the court otherwise orders. In a creditors' voluntary winding up, the liquidator or his nominee is not so liable unless the court otherwise orders (Rule 4.70; as to Scotland, see Scottish Rules 4.15 and 4.16).

As to debts which are provable, the procedure for proving, quantification of claims and general principles applicable to proofs, see C14.1 *et seq.* below.

Resolutions in compulsory and creditors' voluntary winding up

C11.15 At a meeting of creditors or contributories, a resolution is passed when a majority in value of those present and voting, in person or by proxy, have voted in favour. The value of contributories is determined by reference to the number of votes conferred on each contributory by the company's articles.

In the case of a resolution for the appointment of a liquidator:

(*a*) if there are two nominees, the person who obtains the most support is appointed—the new Rule 4.63(2A) makes it clear that in a compulsory winding up this support must represent a majority in value of all those present (in person or by proxy) at the meeting and entitled to vote;

(*b*) if there are three or more nominees and one of them has a clear majority over all the others together, that one is appointed;

(*c*) in any other case, the chairman must continue to take votes (disregarding at each vote any nominee who has withdrawn and if none has withdrawn, the nominee who obtained the least support last time), until a clear majority is obtained for any one nominee;

(*d*) the chairman may at any time put to the meeting a resolution for the joint appointment of any two or more nominees.

Where a resolution proposed affects a person in respect of his remuneration or conduct as liquidator, the vote of that person, and of any partner or employee of his, must not be counted (Rule 4.63; see also Scottish Rules 4.15 and 4.16).

A resolution passed at an adjourned meeting of the creditors or contributories is treated for all purposes as having been passed at that meeting, and not earlier (section 194). The new Rule 4.53A provides that where, in a creditors' voluntary winding up, the meeting of the company at which the winding-up resolution is to be proposed is adjourned, any resolution passed at the meeting of creditors under section 98 (see C4.6 above) held before the holding of the adjourned company meeting only has effect on and from the passing by the company of the winding-up resolution.

Suspension and adjournment

C11.16 In a compulsory or creditors' voluntary winding up, once only in the course of any meeting the chairman may, in his discretion and without an adjournment, declare the meeting suspended for up to one hour. He may, in his discretion, and must, if the meeting so resolves, adjourn it to such time and place as seems to him to be appropriate in the circumstances (Rule 4.65). This does not apply to a creditors' meeting in a compulsory or a creditors' voluntary liquidation at which a resolution for the removal of the liquidator is proposed and the liquidator or his nominee is the chairman, unless at least one-half in value of the creditors present (in person or by proxy) and entitled to vote consent (Rules 4.113(3) and 4.114(3)).

If within 30 minutes from the time appointed for the commencement of the meeting a quorum is not present, the chairman may at his discretion adjourn the meeting to such time and place as may be appointed by the chairman. The chairman's discretion whether or not to adjourn the meeting must be exercised judicially. In *Mardas v Official Receiver and Halls, Insolvency Law & Practice 1989, Vol 5, No 6, 187,* the Official Receiver, in a compulsory liquidation, refused the request of a creditor to adjourn the meeting for 48 hours to enable that creditor to lodge his proof and thereby qualify to vote, he having received the notice of the meeting too late. A liquidator was appointed on the votes of the petitioning creditor and the proxies held by the Official Receiver. The aggrieved creditor applied to Millett J under section 139(4) for relief on three grounds: (i) section 139(3) provided that the creditors' nominee should prevail; (ii) the meeting was not validly convened as the creditor concerned did not receive the notice in time and his debt outweighed the aggregate of all other debts; and (iii) the refusal to adjourn was a decision no reasonable chairman could have reached. Millett J rejected the application on the ground that the court's discretion was fettered by section 139(3).

On appeal by the creditor, the Court of Appeal held that the court's discretion was unfettered. Obviously, it would only be exercised for some reason, but there was ample reason in that case. It was not through any fault of his own that the creditor did not receive the notice in time, and an adjournment to enable him to lodge the proof of debt should have been allowed. The court did not, however, accept that despite Rule 12.16 (which provided that a meeting was presumed to have been duly summoned and held, notwithstanding that not all of those to whom the notice was to be given had received it) the meeting had not been duly convened and held. The position might have been different if *no* notices were sent, and therefore no one attended. No distinction could be found in Rule 12.16 between creditors whose presence at the meeting would have been significant and those whose presence would not, in a case where neither received notice. It could not be said, in the context of the test laid down in *Byng v London Life Association Ltd [1989] 2 WLR 737*, that the refusal to adjourn was a decision no reasonable chairman could have reached (that is, that the decision was unreasonable under the '*Wednesbury*' principles). It did, however, seem to the court that the decision reached by the Official Receiver was not an intelligent exercise of the chairman's discretion in the circumstances of the case. The appeal was allowed.

If there is no person present to act as chairman, some other person present (being entitled to vote) with the agreement of others present (and so entitled) may perform this function. If there is no agreement, the adjournment will be to the same time and place in the next following week, or if that is not a business day, to the business day immediately following.

No such adjournment may be for a period of more than 21 days, and what is stated in C11.9 above applies.

At an adjourned meeting, proofs and proxies may be used if lodged at any time up to midday on the business day immediately before the adjourned meeting (Rule 4.65).

Record of proceedings

C11.17 Rule 4.71 requires minutes and other records of the meetings of creditors and contributories in a compulsory winding up to be kept. Particulars of all resolutions, certified by the chairman, are required to be filed in court not more than 21 days after the date of the meeting (Rule 4.71).

Annual meetings and accounts

C11.18 In a members' voluntary winding up which continues for one year, the liquidator must summon a general meeting of the company at the end of the first year of the commencement of the winding up and of each succeeding year, or at the first convenient date within three months of the end of the year or such longer period as the Secretary of State may allow. The liquidator must lay before the meeting an account of his acts and dealings, and of the conduct of the winding up, during the preceding year (section 93).

The same applies to a creditors' voluntary winding up, and a members' voluntary winding up which subsequently becomes a creditors' voluntary winding up, except that the accounts must be laid before both a general meeting of the company and a meeting of the creditors similarly summoned (sections 96 and 105). In Scotland, Scottish Rule 4.13(1) requires the liquidator to summon a meeting of the creditors in each year during which the liquidation (apparently including, unlike in England and Wales, a compulsory liquidation) is in force.

Where the winding up (of any type) is not concluded within one year after its commencement, the liquidator must, at prescribed intervals until the winding up is concluded, send to the Registrar of Companies a statement in the prescribed form (in duplicate) with respect to the proceedings in, and position of, the liquidation (section 192). For a creditors' and members' voluntary winding up (see Rule 4.1(1)(g)), Form 4.68 has been prescribed; and Rule 4.223 provides that the statement must be sent not more than 30 days after the expiration of the first year and thereafter not less often than six-monthly until the winding up is concluded. The final statement must be sent forthwith after the conclusion of the winding up. For these purposes, the winding up is concluded at the date of the company's dissolution, except that, if at that date any assets or funds remain unclaimed or undistributed in the hands or under the control of the liquidator, the winding up is not concluded until they are distributed or paid into the Insolvency Services Account (see C12.15 and C16.11 below).

Special provisions apply in a compulsory winding up, some of which extend to a voluntary winding up. These are set out in Regulation 14 of the Insolvency Regulations 1994 (SI 1994 No 2507, which replaced the Insolvency Regulations 1986 (SI 1986 No 1994, as amended) with effect from 24 October 1994). The 1994 Regulations have abolished the requirement under the 1986 Regulations for the liquidator in a compulsory winding up to provide annual accounts of his receipts and payments to the Secretary of State (no provision having been prescribed in the latter pursuant to section 192 for their filing with the Registrar of Companies); however, the Secretary of State has power to require such accounts to be sent to him at any time, in relation to *any type* of winding up. (Note that the requirements as regards the filing of accounts with the Registrar of Companies in a voluntary winding up under the provisions of the Act or the Rules summarised in the preceding paragraphs are not affected by the 1994 Regulations.)

In the case of a compulsory winding up, in the following circumstances the liquidator must send to the Secretary of State an account of his receipts and payments as liquidator which are not covered by any previous accounts sent by him (or if no accounts have been submitted previously, an account of such receipts and payments for the whole of his period of office):

(a) where the liquidator vacates office prior to the holding of the final general meeting of creditors under section 146, within 14 days of vacating office; or

(b) where the final general meeting referred to in (a) above has been held, within 14 days of the holding of that meeting; or

(c) where the final general meeting is deemed to have been held by virtue of Rule 4.125(5), within 14 days of his report to the court pursuant to that Rule.

In the case of a compulsory winding up, any account sent under Regulation 14 of the 1994 Regulations must be accompanied by a summary of the statement of affairs (see C5.48 above) (or, where none is available, a summary of all known assets with the value of those not realised) and showing the amounts of any assets realised and explaining the reasons for any non-realisation.

The Secretary of State may require any such account to be audited (but whether or not he does so, he may require the liquidator to send him any documents, including vouchers and bank accounts, and any information relating to the account). A statement of the liquidator's receipts and payments (or, in the case of a voluntary winding up, a copy of the statement sent to the Registrar of Companies under section 192—see also Rule 4.223 and Form 4.68) must be sent free of charge to any creditor, contributory or director who so requests, within 14 days of the receipt of the request (or, in the case of a voluntary winding up, within 14 days of the statement being sent to the Registrar, if later) (SI 1994 No 2507, Reg 11).

For Scotland, see the Scottish Rules 4.10 and 4.11 and Forms 4.5 and 4.6 (Scot).

Involvement of creditors and contributories

C11.19 Creditors and, to a lesser extent, contributories are in the position of being able to exercise some degree of influence over the proper conduct of a winding up. The provisions which particularly place them in that position are those relating to the supply to them of information on certain matters, the holding of their meetings for various purposes and their rights to apply to the court in respect of certain matters. The following are some examples.

(1) A creditor or contributory may enforce through the court the liquidator's statutory duties to file, deliver or make any return account or other document, or file, deliver, make or give any notice, if the liquidator fails to make good any default in that regard within 14 days after the service on him of a notice requiring him to do so (section 170).

(2) In a compulsory winding up, the Official Receiver is required to send to the creditors and contributories, at least once after the making of the winding-up order, a report with respect to the proceedings in the winding up and the state of the company's affairs (Rules 4.43 and 4.44). The court may relieve him of this duty or vary it after having regard to the costs involved, the assets available and the extent of the interest of creditors or contributories, or any particular class of them (Rule 4.47). Further, when a statement of affairs has been submitted and filed in court (see C5.48 above) he must send them a report containing a summary of it and his observations (if any) with respect to it or to the affairs of the company in general (Rule 4.45). Where a statement of affairs has been dispensed with by the Official Receiver or the court (see C5.48 above), he must send to the creditors a

summary of the company's affairs so far as within his knowledge, unless he has previously reported to them with respect to the affairs and nothing further is needed to be brought to their attention (Rule 4.46).

(3)   In any form of winding up, a creditor or contributory or his representative has a right to inspect proofs of debts lodged by creditors which are for the time being in the liquidator's hands (Rule 4.79).

(4)   Rules 12.15 and 12.16 give creditors and contributories a right to require copies of certain documents, including a list of creditors; but see also Rule 12.18 (offence to claim falsely status as creditor etc.). In *Re Movitex Ltd [1990] BCLC 785*, decided under the old legislation, Mervyn Davies J at first instance (overruled by the Court of Appeal—see below) refused a creditor's application for permission to inspect the books and records of the company where the inspection was desired with a view to deciding whether the creditor should pursue the liquidators personally. The judge said that this was a purpose for which the winding-up procedure could not be used. In the context of Rule 172(3) of the Companies (Winding up) Rules 1949 (which required the liquidators' books etc. to be submitted to the creditors when there was no committee of inspection), the general principle was that the liquidators were not entitled to claim as against a creditor that the liquidation was confidential. No concept of confidentiality prevented the creditors from seeing the liquidators' books. However, that did not mean that an individual creditor (as opposed to the creditors as a whole) could require the production of the books for his own personal purposes. The judge was referred to the following passage from the judgment of James LJ in *Re Contract Corp, Gooch's case (1872) LR 7 Ch App 207* at *211–212*:

'If a person interested in any such case decides to see any books or papers, it is the duty of the liquidator to give him not only access to them, but to give him every assistance and facility in finding out which are the relevant books and papers he requires; and if the liquidator has already ascertained any books or papers bearing on the subject, he should frankly place this information at the service of the party. But this is a very different thing from the liquidator being obliged, at the instance of every person interested in every question, to employ that time which, unfortunately, is so costly to the contributories, in making that fresh and careful investigation of the papers and documents in its possession which would be requisite to enable him truthfully to make the ordinary affidavit which is required from a party or *quasi* party called on to make discovery.'

Mervyn Davies J relied on *Re North Brazilian Sugar Factories (1887) 37 Ch D 83* where in the course of his judgment Cotton LJ said, 'The object of the application evidently is to obtain evidence in support of actions by individual shareholders for their own benefit against the directors, and that is not within the object of the section'. Lopes LJ said, 'Now what is the object for which inspection is sought here? Not the more beneficial winding-up of the company, but a collateral object, the obtaining of discovery to enable individual shareholders to bring actions against the directors or promoters'.

(It should be noted that under the new legislation, in common with other office-holders, a liquidator may decline to allow any person (including a member of the liquidation committee or a creditors' committee) who is otherwise entitled, to inspect any document forming part of the records of the insolvency if he considers that it should be treated as confidential or that its disclosure would be calculated to be injurious to the interests of the creditors or contributories. Any such refusal is subject to an appeal to the court (Rule 12.13; see A4.13 PART A: GENERAL).)

However, on appeal to the Court of Appeal (*[1992] 1 WLR 303*), the applicants sought to make the application to inspect on behalf of the company itself. In allowing the appeal and ordering leave to inspect the documents, including counsels' opinions and relevant reports, the Court of Appeal said it was not known whether the liquidators were at fault. If the applicants were able to inspect the documents they might be able to form a view whether a misfeasance action against the liquidators would have any prospects of success. The applicants were the only persons who could act on behalf of the company and they should be able to enquire into why a legal action continued which had resulted in the secondary insolvency.

(5) In a creditors' voluntary winding up, the liquidator must, within 28 days of the first meeting of creditors held under section 95 or 98 (see C4.6 and C4.12 above), send to the creditors and contributories a copy or summary of the statement of affairs (see C4.7 above) and a report of the proceedings of the meeting (Rule 4.49).

(6) In any type of winding up, the court may have regard to the wishes of the creditors and contributories (as proved to it by any sufficient evidence) as to all matters relating to the winding up. If it thinks fit, it can order meetings to be held for the purpose of ascertaining their wishes. In the case of creditors, regard must be had to the value of their respective debts and, in the case of contributories, to the number of votes conferred on each contributory (section 195). In a compulsory winding up, the liquidator may himself summon such meetings for this purpose; and he must do this if so directed by the previous respective meetings or requested in writing by one-tenth in value of the creditors or contributories (as the case may be) (section 168). In the case of Part II insurance companies carrying on long-term insurance business, a separate meeting of creditors in respect of the long-term business is required (see the Insurance Companies (Winding up) Rules 1985 and the Insurance Companies (Winding up) (Scotland) Rules 1986). The liquidator's decision is subject to appeal to the court by any person aggrieved thereby (section 168). Rule 4.54 empowers him to call such meetings for this purpose both in a compulsory winding up and in a creditors' voluntary winding up.

(7) Creditors and/or contributories also have a say through their respective meetings as regards:

  (i) the remuneration, removal, replacement and release of the liquidator (see C11.27 and C11.28 below);

  (ii) the removal or replacement of a creditor member or a contributory member (as the case may be) of the liquidation committee (Rules 4.161 to 4.164):

  (iii) sanctioning the continuance of directors' powers in a voluntary winding up (see C7.2 above); and

  (iv) in a voluntary winding up, authorising distribution *in specie* and transfer of assets for consideration *in specie* (see C3.4, C3.5 and C4.2 above, and C12.3 below).

(8) A creditor or contributory may make various other applications to the court; for example, applications under section 112 (determination of any question arising in the winding up, or exercise in a voluntary winding up of any powers of the court exercisable in a compulsory winding up), 126 (stay of proceedings after presentation of winding- up proceedings), 147 (stay of winding up) (see C5.46 above) and Rule 4.149 (setting aside antecedent transactions) (see C12.8 *et seq.* below). See also C11.23 below as to inspection of certain documents by creditors and contributories.

Involvement of liquidation committee

C11.20 A liquidation committee may only be appointed in a creditors' voluntary liquidation or a compulsory liquidation (see C4.11 and C5.51 above). The liquidator must report to the members of the committee all such matters as appear to him to be, or as have been indicated to him as being, of concern to them with respect to the winding up. He need not comply with any request for information where it appears to him that the request is frivolous or unreasonable or the cost of complying with it would be excessive, having regard to the relative importance of the information, or there are not sufficient assets to enable him to comply. Where the committee has come into being more than 28 days after his appointment, he must provide it with a summary of the actions taken since his appointment and answer any questions put to him regarding the conduct of the winding up. A summary of matters which previously arose must also be provided to a new member. The committee or any member of it is also entitled to have access to the liquidator's records and seek explanation of any matter within the committee's responsibility (Rule 4.155).

The committee may also be involved in sanctioning the exercise by the liquidator of certain of his powers (see C11.26 below) and the liquidator's remuneration (see C11.27 below).

A proper working relationship and communication between the liquidator and the committee is essential for the smooth conduct of the winding up. For this purpose, the liquidator generally looks upon the committee as having a *de facto* general supervisory role in relation to his main functions and consults with it before taking any major decision having a bearing on the course or result of the liquidation.

Involvement of company's officers and others

C11.21 Upon the company going into liquidation, on the one hand the powers of the company's officers cease for most practical purposes (see C7.2 and C8.1 above), except that they may be able to enforce their right to require information from the liquidator to enable them to consider taking action against him for misfeasance (see C11.19(4) above). On the other hand, they become subject to certain duties to assist in the winding up; for example, as regards submission of a statement of affairs, accounts and other information (see C11.18 above), attendance at meetings of creditors and contributories and general assistance to the liquidator (see PART A: GENERAL).

Private and public examinations

C11.22 A company's officers can also be subjected to a private or public examination in court.

As to private examination, see A4.19 PART A: GENERAL above. Public examination is governed by sections 133 and 134 as modified, in relation to partnerships, by the Insolvent Partnerships Order 1994 (SI 1994 No 2421) replacing, with effect from 1 December 1994, the Insolvent Partnerships Order 1986 (SI 1986 No 2142), where applicable. The detailed procedure is contained in Rules 4.211 to 4.217 and Forms 4.61 to 4.67 and, as to Scotland, Scottish Rules 4.74 and 4.75.

In a compulsory winding up the court may on the application of the Official Receiver or, in Scotland, of the liquidator, made at any time before the dissolution of the company, order the public examination of any person who is or has been an officer of the company, or has acted as liquidator or administrator of the company, or as receiver or manager or, in Scotland, receiver, of its property, or has been concerned with or has taken part in the promotion, formation or management of the company. Such an application may, unless the court otherwise orders, also be requisitioned by one-half, in value, of the creditors or three-quarters, in value, of the contributories. In addition to the Official Receiver, the liquidator, the special manager, any contributory, and any creditor who has tendered a proof or (in Scotland) submitted a claim, may take part in the examination.

This procedure may be invoked in a voluntary winding up by virtue of section 112 (see *Re Campbell Coverings Ltd (No 1)* [1953] *Ch 488; (No 2)* [1954] *Ch 225; Re Serene Shoes Ltd* [1958] *1 WLR 1087*, and *Re B Karsberg Ltd* referred to in C5.29 (3)(*b*) above).

The matters as to which the person concerned may be examined are those concerning the promotion, formation or management of the company or the conduct of its business and affairs, and his conduct or dealings in relation to the company (section 133(3)). Under the previous legislation (section 270 of the Companies Act 1948 and sections 563 and 564 of the Companies Act 1985) the application had to disclose at least a *prima facie* case of fraud (*Tejani v Official Receiver [1963] 1 WLR 59*). This is no longer necessary in view of the language of section 133, but it seems that a *prima facie* case for a serious need to examine the person concerned will have to be made out.

The court's power to order public examination under section 133 has no territorial limitation so long as the person to be examined falls within the criteria in that section. In *Re Seagull Manufacturing Co Ltd [1993] BCC 241 (CA)*, public examination was ordered of an officer of the company who was resident in Alderney, regardless of when the order could be enforced.

The leave of the court is required for the use in subsequent legal proceedings of material obtained in the course of a private or public examination: leave will be granted only if the proposed use will assist the beneficial winding up of the company (see *Re Esal Commodities Ltd (No 2) [1990] BCC 708, per* Millett J).

For variations in the case of the winding up of a partnership, see the Insolvent Partnerships Order 1994 (SI 1994 No 2421).

Involvement of the court

C11.23 In addition to winding-up petitions presented to it (see C5.1 above), examples of where the court may on application intervene during the conduct of both compulsory and voluntary winding up are numerous throughout this chapter.

The court procedure and practice are set out in Rules 7.1 to 7.61 and Rule 13.2 as modified, and, in the case of Scotland, by the Scottish Rules. As to the lists of applications which are to be heard in open court, those which may be made to the Registrar in the first instance and those which may be dealt with by the chief clerk of the Companies Court, see *Practice Direction, Companies Court [1987] 1 All ER 107*.

The court may make such order for inspection of the company's books and papers by creditors and contributories as the court thinks just. Without such an order the creditors or contributories have no right to inspect them, except that any statutory rights of a government department or person acting under the authority of the government department are not excluded (section 155). This power of the court is confined to books and papers of the company in the possession of the company or the liquidator and does not extend to documents held by the police. Further, a creditor or contributory can only invoke the power for the purposes connected with the winding up and not for the creditor's or contributory's defence to criminal charges (see *Re DPR Futures Ltd [1989] 1 WLR 778*).

The liquidator

Position of liquidator

C11.24 A liquidator is agent for the company and occupies a fiduciary position, but is not a trustee for each individual creditor (*Knowles v Scott [1891] 1 Ch 717, 723*). In a compulsory winding up, he is an officer, and subject to the control, of the court. A liquidator's duty is to the general body of the company's creditors and contributories; but as he is an agent employed for the purpose of winding up the company, charged with important statutory powers, duties, discretion and, to some extent, even quasi-judicial functions, he must treat each creditor and contributory fairly. He may be personally liable in damages to creditors for breach of his statutory duty if he does not use proper diligence. But a liquidator who inadvertently disposes of trust property is not liable as constructive trustee, even if he is negligent (*Competitive Insurance Co Ltd v Davies Investments Ltd [1975] 1 WLR 1240*). He must not be over-litigious and must not resist well-founded claims where there is no real defence (*Re General Store & Trust v Wetley Co (1882) 20 Ch D 260*). In a compulsory winding up, he may in exceptional circumstances be directed by the court not to enforce legal rights where it is unethical to do so (*Re Wyvern Developments Ltd [1974] 1 WLR 1097*).

As to the right of the liquidator to require and make disclosures of documents and information see A4.9, A4.10 and A4.12 PART A: GENERAL. It was held in *Re Barlow Clowes Gilt Managers Ltd [1991] 4 All ER 385* that the liquidators were under no duty to assist directors of the company in defending criminal charges brought against them by providing the directors with information given to the liquidators in confidence; to do so would be against public policy as it would jeopardise the proper and efficient functioning of the liquidation. In fact, the court, in its capacity as the Companies Court responsible for the compulsory winding up of the companies concerned in that case, directed the liquidators not to make voluntary disclosure of the transcripts of the liquidators' interviews with various witnesses which the witnesses had attended in circumstances of confidentiality on the assurance, express or implied, that any information they gave would be used solely for the purposes of the liquidation. The court also directed the liquidators to claim public interest immunity in response to any witness summons issued by the directors and not to disclose the transcripts unless ordered to do so by the Crown Court, which was the appropriate court to weigh competing interests for and against disclosure. At the criminal hearing that followed (*R v Clowes and others, 21 June 1991*), Phillips J allowed the witness summonses to stand on the ground of the gravity of the charges which, he said, tilted the balance in favour of the interests of justice rather than public interest. (See also the *dicta* of Sir Nicolas Browne-Wilkinson V-C in *Marcel v Commissioner of Police of the Metropolis [1991] 1 All ER 845* at *853* and *Cloverbay Ltd (joint administrators) v Bank of Credit and Commerce International SA [1991] 1 All ER 894* at *900*, which were applied in the *Barlow Clowes* case.)

As to his limited immunity from liability in respect of third party property, see A4.17 PART A: GENERAL. Subject to that limited immunity and, perhaps, subject to the principles of the *Competitive Insurance* case (see above), the position of a liquidator in relation to infringement of third party proprietary rights may be analogous to that of a company director. For example, a company director may be personally liable in tort if he had authorised, directed and procured the commission by the company of an infringement of copyright even if he did not know that, or was reckless as to whether, the acts were or might be tortious (*C Evans & Sons Ltd v Spritebrand Ltd [1985] BCLC 105 (CA)*.

The liquidator must act in good faith (*Re Silver Valley Mines (1882) 21 ChD 381 (CA); Knowles v Scott [1891] 1 Ch 717; Leon v York-O-Matic Ltd [1966] 1 WLR 1450*; see also *Silkstone Coal Co v Edey [1900] 1 Ch 167; Re Gertzenstein Ltd [1937] Ch 115*) and in an honourable fashion (*Ex parte James (1874) 9 Ch App Cas 609*) so as not to take advantage of a mistake of law or fact which increases the assets available for distribution (*Ex parte James* (above); *Re Cushla Ltd [1979] 3 All ER 415; Re T H Knitwear (Wholesale) Ltd [1987] BCLC 86*; cf. *Re Clark [1975] 1 WLR 599*). It appears, however, that this duty does not apply to a liquidator in a voluntary winding up who is not an officer of the court (see *Re John Bateson & Co Ltd [1985] BCLC 259*). A payment made to a liquidator under a mistake is recoverable from him where the mistake was of such a character as 'prevented there being that intention which the common law regards as essential to the making of an agreement or the transfer of money or property' (*per* Lord Wright in *Norwich Union Fire Insurance Society Ltd v William H Price Ltd [1934] AC 455 at 462*; and see *Re Cushla* (above)).

He must be impartial and not put himself in a position of conflict of interest (*Re Contract Corporation (1872) 7 Ch App 207; Re Sir John Moore Gold Mining Co (1879) 12 ChD 325; Re Rubber Investment Co [1915] 1 Ch 382; Re Llynvi & Tondu Co (1889) 6 TLR 11; Silkstone Coal Co v Edey* (above); *Re Charterland Goldfields Ltd (1909) 26 TLR 132; Re Gertzenstein Ltd* (above)). Further, he must not agree to fetter his discretion (*Re Scottish Granite Co (1868) 17 LT 533*). He cannot delegate the exercise of his discretion; and although in paragraph 12, Part III of Schedule 4, he has power to appoint an agent to do any business which he is unable to do himself, that power appears to be impliedly limited to acts and transactions of a ministerial nature not requiring the exercise of professional judgment.

It has been held in New Zealand that a [provisional] liquidator is not allowed to avoid or totally relinquish the residual duties of collecting assets and discharging the debts of a company which is subject to a winding-up order (*Re Your Size Fashions Ltd [1990] 3 NZLR 727*).

A person who has given, or agreed or offered to give, any member or creditor of the company any valuable consideration with a view to securing his own appointment or nomination as liquidator, or to securing or preventing that of another person, is liable to a fine (section 164). Where any improper solicitation has been used by or on behalf of the liquidator in obtaining proxies or procuring his appointment, the court may disallow his remuneration (Rule 4.150 and Scottish Rule 4.39). Further, a transaction entered into by him with any associate (defined by section 435) of his may be set aside and he may be ordered to compensate the company for any loss or damage suffered by it. This does not apply to a transaction entered into with the prior consent of the court or where the liquidator did not know or have any reason to suppose that the person concerned was an associate (Rule 4.149 and Scottish Rule 4.38). These provisions are without prejudice to any rule of law or (except in Scotland) equity with respect to a liquidator's or trustee's dealings with trust property or the fiduciary obligations of any person.

In a compulsory winding up, the liquidator may summon general meetings of the creditors or contributories for the purpose of ascertaining their wishes (section 168(2)). In any form of winding up, the Official Receiver or the liquidator (as the case may be) may at any time summon and conduct such meetings for the purpose of ascertaining their wishes in all matters relating to the liquidation (Rule 4.54 and Scottish Rule 4.13(2)). It is submitted that implicit in this power is an *obligation* to exercise that power where circumstances so require and to have regard to the wishes of those meetings in conducting the winding up. Any person aggrieved by the liquidator's decision under section 168 may apply to the court for a review (section 168(5)). It is also the duty of the liquidator in a compulsory winding up to convene such meetings at such times as the creditors or contributories by resolution (either at the meeting appointing the liquidator or otherwise) may direct or whenever requested in writing by one-tenth in value of the creditors or contributories (as the case may be) (section 168(2)).

The liquidator in a compulsory winding up may apply to the court for directions in relation to any particular matter arising in the winding up (section 168(3)). This provision may be invoked in a voluntary winding up by virtue of section 112 and is very useful in helping the liquidator to resolve a dilemma or difficulty faced by him where it cannot be satisfactorily resolved merely by obtaining legal or other professional advice (see Rules 7.1 to 7.10 and 7.51 to 7.61 for the procedure).

General functions of liquidator

C11.25 In a compulsory winding up, the liquidator's general functions are to secure that the company's assets are got in, realised and distributed to the company's creditors and, if there is a surplus, to the persons entitled to it (section 143(1); see the Insolvent Partnerships Order 1994 (SI 1994 No 2421) for variation). He performs these functions as an officer of the court and subject to its control. For the purposes of acquiring and retaining possession of the assets he has the same powers as a receiver appointed by the High Court (which may, on application, enforce such acquisition or retention) (Rule 4.179).

In a voluntary liquidation his general functions are similar except that he does not act as an officer and is not subject to the control of the court (although the court has power to intervene). Section 107 provides that, subject to the provisions as to preferential payments, the company's assets must be applied in satisfaction of the company's liabilities *pari passu* and then (unless the articles otherwise provide) be distributed among the members according to their rights and interests in the company.

In certain respects he exercises quasi-judicial functions, for example, in relation to dealing with proofs of debt for the purposes of voting or dividend and when acting as chairman of meetings; and his decisions are subject to review by the court. Here in particular he is expected to act impartially and fairly.

Certain administrative statutory duties of a liquidator can be enforced by a creditor or contributory through the court (see C11.24 above). The liquidator may also risk disqualification *inter alia* under section 3 (as read with section 22(7)) of the Company Directors Disqualification Act 1986) for persistent default in such duties or under section 4 thereof if he is guilty of any fraud in relation to the company or any breach of duty as liquidator of the company. As to the considerations which the court applies where persistent default is alleged, see *Re Arctic Engineering Ltd and others (No 2) [1986] BCLC 253*. A liquidator who disobeys court orders may also face committal for contempt of court. In *Re Allan Ellis (Transport & Packing) Services Ltd (1989) 5 BCC 835*, the respondent was the voluntary liquidator of three companies. He failed to deliver to the Registrar of Companies statements which (by virtue of CA 1985, s 641—now IA 1986, s 192) he was under a statutory obligation to deliver. The defaults continued, and orders made by the Registrar were disobeyed. The court sentenced him to a total of nine months' imprisonment, stating that the liquidator had persistently totally disregarded the order of the court.

An action to restrain a proposed act of the liquidator may be brought against a liquidator by a creditor or contributory. However, the court will only interfere where the liquidator is acting fraudulently, or has not exercised his discretion *bona fide*, or is proposing to do something which no reasonable man would do. It is not sufficient merely to establish negligence on his part (*Harold M Pitman & Co v Top Business Systems (Nottingham) Ltd [1984] BCLC 593*; see also *Leon v York-O-Matic Ltd [1966] 1 WLR 1450; Re Wyvern Developments Ltd [1974] 1 WLR 1097*).

A liquidator, like an administrator, administrative receiver or supervisor of a voluntary arrangement, is required to notify his appointment to HM Customs & Excise (as the authority administering value added tax); see A4.11 PART A: GENERAL.

Specific powers and duties of liquidator

C11.26 Parts I, II and III of Schedule 4 to the Act (which, in relation to the winding up of an insolvent partnership, has been modified for certain situations by the Insolvent Partnerships Order 1994 (SI 1994 No 2421)), as read with sections 165 to 167, contain the liquidator's specific powers. The Part I powers (payment in full of debts, compromise of calls and claims, etc.) are only exercisable with the sanction of (in a members' voluntary winding up) an extraordinary resolution of the company or (in a compulsory or creditors' voluntary winding up, but, in a creditors' voluntary winding up, subject to the third paragraph below) the court or the liquidation committee or (in a creditors' voluntary winding up), if there is no such committee, a meeting of the creditors. The Part II powers (institution of and defence of proceedings, carrying on of business, etc.) may, in a voluntary winding up of either type (but, in a creditors' voluntary winding up, subject to the third paragraph below), be exercised without sanction but, in a compulsory winding up, can only be exercised with the sanction of the court or the liquidation committee. The permission to exercise any of the Part I or II powers in a compulsory liquidation must be specific and not general. A person dealing with the liquidator in good faith and for value is not concerned to enquire whether any such permission has been given (Rule 4.184(1)). Where the liquidator has done anything without that permission, the court or the liquidation committee may, for the purpose of enabling him to meet his expenses out of the assets, ratify what he has done, but not unless it is satisfied that the liquidator has acted in a case of emergency and has sought ratification without undue delay (Rule 4.184(2)). The Part III powers (miscellaneous powers) may, in any form of winding up (but, in a creditors' voluntary winding up, subject to the fourth paragraph below) be exercised without sanction (sections 165 and 166).

Included in the powers mentioned above is a power to bring legal proceedings, exercisable without sanction in a voluntary winding up but with sanction in a compulsory winding up. In *Re DPR Futures Ltd [1989] 1 WLR 778*, where the liquidators sought a *Mareva* injunction against a defendant, the usual cross-undertaking as to damages which the court usually requires from a plaintiff, was in this instance restricted by the court to the assets available in the hands of the liquidators. The court stated that the liquidators were entitled not to risk their personal assets.

Further, in a voluntary liquidation (of either type), the liquidator may (i) summon a general meeting of *the company* for the purpose of obtaining its sanction by special or extraordinary resolution for any other purpose he may think fit and (ii) exercise the court's power of settling a list of contributories and making calls (section 165(4)).

However, in a creditors' voluntary winding up, the powers of a liquidator appointed by the members of the company at their meeting ('caretaker liquidator') are restricted, and their exercise is subject to reporting requirements, as stated in C4.9 above.

Further, although the liquidator has power, without any prior sanction to dispose of any property of the company and to employ solicitors, he must give notice of the exercise of any of these powers to the liquidation committee (if any) (section 165(6)).

In a compulsory winding up, the exercise by the liquidator of his specific powers above referred to is subject to the control of the court and any creditor or contributory may apply to the court with respect to any exercise or proposed exercise of any of those powers (section 167(3)). This provision may be invoked in a voluntary winding up by virtue of section 112.

As to the power of a liquidator to distribute assets *in specie* among the members and to sell or transfer assets for consideration *in specie*, see C3.4, C3.5 and C4.2 above and C12.3 below; see also C15.8 below as to distribution among creditors *in specie*.

Subject to what is stated above, and elsewhere in this chapter, the liquidator must use his own discretion in the management of the assets and their distribution among the creditors (section 168(4)).

Where the liquidator has a choice between obtaining the court's sanction and obtaining the sanction of the liquidation committee, it is submitted that he should prefer the court's sanction where the proposed exercise is likely to have a fundamental or substantial effect on the course or outcome of the winding up or where the members of the committee have some special conflict of interest in the subject matter of the exercise.

The court will generally not sanction a proposed compromise with creditors which involves the distribution of the company's assets otherwise than strictly in accordance with creditors' rights in the winding up. The proper way to do this is by a scheme of arrangement under section 425 of the Companies Act 1985 (see e.g. *Re Trix Ltd [1970] 1 WLR 1421*).

However, the court does have a residual discretion to sanction such a compromise in special circumstances, and this is so notwithstanding that the representatives of the creditors oppose it and there is no evidence as to whether it is acceptable to a majority of the creditors. In *Re Bank of Credit & Commerce International SA (No 2) [1992] BCC 715*, the liquidators applied to the court to sanction two agreements involving compromises. The contribution agreement provided for the release of cross-claims between the majority shareholders of the company and the liquidators and payment by those shareholders of a substantial sum for the benefit of the creditors. The pooling agreement provided for the pooling of the assets and liabilities of the company and another company in the same group. An informal creditors' committee (that is, appointed without a creditors' meeting—see C4.11 and C5.51 above—which it was not practicable to hold) opposed implementation of the agreements on the grounds that

(a)   the amount of contribution offered was not as large as could be recovered by further negotiations or litigation, and

(b)   further investigation was required before it could be ascertained whether the pooling agreement was in the interests of the creditors of the company.

The Court of Appeal, upholding the decision of the High Court, held that the liquidators' powers under paragraphs 2 and 3 of Schedule 4 were wide enough to permit them to enter into any compromise arrangements with creditors that might have been entered into by the company itself. That would cover a compromise by the company with the other company in the group to resolve all their mutual dealings. The affairs of the two companies were so commingled that it was not possible to say what the assets of each were. Since it was impracticable to hold creditors' meetings, it was open to the liquidators to enter into the agreements in exercise of their compromise powers rather than by way of a scheme under section 425 of the Companies Act 1985 (see *Taylor, Noter [1992] BCC 440*, referred to below). The Court of Appeal further held that, it not being practicable to convene a creditors' meeting, with any necessary class meetings, whether under section 425 of the 1985 Act or section 195 of the 1986 Act, the court was not precluded by the views of the majority of the informal creditors' committee and of the opposing creditors at the hearing from approving the agreements.

In *Taylor, Noter [1992] BCC 440* (a decision of the Court of Session (Inner House) in Scotland), where two companies were in liquidation and the person who controlled them was in bankruptcy, the court sanctioned a single scheme of ranking and division of the joint assets of the companies and the sequestrated estate on the ground that the individual had treated the companies and his own affairs as one and that, not having been able to determine which creditors had claims against the companies and which had claims against the sequestrated estate, it would not be possible to adjudicate on creditors' claims.

In Scotland, the liquidator has, subject to the Scottish Rules, the same powers as a trustee of a bankrupt estate (section 169(2)). The court may provide by order that he may, where there is no liquidation committee, bring or defend any action or other legal proceeding in the name and on behalf of the company, or carry on its business, so far as may be necessary for its beneficial winding up, without the sanction or intervention of the court (section 169(1)).

The powers and duties of a liquidator described above do not constitute an exhaustive list. As will be seen throughout this Part, he has many other powers and duties, both general and with reference to specific aspects of a winding up (see for example C12.1 *et seq.* below).

Liquidator's remuneration and costs

C11.27 In a voluntary winding up (of either type) all expenses properly incurred, including the liquidator's remuneration, are payable out of the company's assets in priority to all other claims (section 115). In a compulsory winding up, where assets are insufficient to satisfy liabilities, the court may determine the order of priority in which the expenses are to be paid out of the assets (section 156—which may also be invoked in a voluntary winding up by virtue of section 112). Subject to sections 112, 115 and 156, the costs and expenses (including remuneration) in any form of winding up are required to be discharged in the order of priority laid down in Rules 4.218 to 4.220 (see also C15.2 below).

The court may allow the liquidator to take his proper remuneration and expenses out of any trust assets in his hands in so far as such remuneration and expenses relate to dealing with those assets (*Re Berkeley Applegate (Investment Consultants) Ltd (No 2) (1988) 4 BCC 279*). In *Re Berkeley Applegate (Investment Consultants) Ltd (No 3) (1989) 5 BCC 803*, the court held that the liquidator's costs and remuneration attributable to dealing with the trust assets could not be paid out of the company's own assets, having regard to the language of section 115, and that a fair apportionment had to be made between such remuneration and costs (payable out of the trust assets) and the remuneration and costs attributable to dealing with the company's own assets.

In *Re Eastern Capital Futures Ltd (1989) 5 BCC 223*, it was held that although the liquidators were technically not entitled to remuneration for work undertaken in relation to the identification and determination of the ownership to trust assets, the court had jurisdiction to permit payment of such remuneration and costs out of the trust assets if it thought fit. The amount of remuneration which the court allowed the liquidators so to retain was that equal to the amount of remuneration and costs they would have received in relation to those assets if they had been the company's own assets.

Further, where there was a dispute between the liquidator of a company and another party as to the ownership of the surplus of funds held by a receiver of that company, and the liquidator had no funds to finance his claim to that surplus, it was held that the court had jurisdiction to order in advance of the resolution of the dispute that the costs incurred by the liquidator to pursue that claim would be met out of the surplus (*Re Westdock Realisations Ltd (1988) 4 BCC 192*). However, in *Re Stetzel Thomson & Co Ltd (1988) 4 BCC 74*, the court had refused to make an advance order for payment of the costs of the liquidators in a creditors' voluntary winding up attributable to establishing the ownership of a certain fund in his hands.

Where a company is put into liquidation following the dismissal of an administration petition, the court has jurisdiction to order that the cost of seeking the administration order should be treated as costs in the winding up (*Re Gosscott (Groundworks) Ltd [1988] BCLC 363*).

Where a compulsory winding up follows immediately on a members' or creditors' voluntary winding up, such remuneration of the voluntary liquidator and costs and expenses of the voluntary winding up as the court may allow rank in priority to all the expenses of the compulsory winding up mentioned in Rule 4.218. As to the position under the previous rules, see *Re A V Sorge & Co Ltd [1986] BCLC 490*.

In the case of a members' voluntary winding up, the Act is silent as to how and by whom the liquidator's remuneration is to be determined.

The provision under the previous legislation (part of section 580(1) of the Companies Act 1985) empowering the company in general meeting to determine remuneration has been omitted from the Insolvency Act 1986. Section D of Chapter 11 of the Rules (Rules 4.127 to 4.131—see below), regarding the liquidator's remuneration, only applies to a creditors' voluntary winding up and a compulsory winding up (Rule 4.1). Until 11 January 1988, the position was that section F of that Chapter (Rules 4.139 to 4.148) regarding liquidators which *does* apply to a members' voluntary winding up, did not deal with the liquidator's remuneration. However, since that date new Rule 4.148A makes it clear that he is entitled to receive remuneration, empowers the company in general meeting to determine it and makes provisions similar (but not identical) to those mentioned below for compulsory and creditors' voluntary winding up.

Rules 4.127 to 4.131 make the following provisions, *inter alia*, regarding the liquidator's remuneration in a creditors' voluntary and a compulsory winding up.

(1)   It may be fixed either as a percentage of the value of the assets realised or distributed (or of the one value and the other in combination) or by reference to the time properly given by him and his staff in attending to the matters.

(2)   The decision as to which way it is to be fixed rests with the liquidation committee. If there is no such committee, or if it does not so decide, or if the liquidator disagrees with its decision, a resolution of a meeting of the creditors may make the decision. If neither the committee nor a creditors' meeting makes the decision, the liquidator is remunerated in accordance with the scale laid down for the Official Receiver (see the Insolvency Regulations 1994 referred to in (4) below).

(3)   In making the decision, the committee or the creditors' meeting must have regard to the matters referred to in Rule 4.127(4).

(4)   These provisions do not apply to the Official Receiver when he is liquidator. He receives his remuneration in accordance with the statutory scale (see the Insolvency Regulations 1994 (SI 1994 No 2507), replacing the Insolvency Regulations 1986 (SI 1986 No 1994) with effect from 24 October 1994; and see also the Insolvency Fees Order 1986 (SI 1986 No 2030 as amended by SI 1988 No 95, SI 1990 No 560, SI 1991 No 496, SI 1992 No 34 and SI 1994 No 2541)).

(5)   The court has power to increase the remuneration of a liquidator (other than the Official Receiver) on his application, or to reduce it on the application of any creditor made with the concurrence of at least 25 per cent in value of the creditors (including himself).

(6)   Where the liquidator (other than the Official Receiver) sells assets on behalf of a secured creditor, he is entitled to take for himself, out of the proceeds of sale, remuneration equivalent to that which is chargeable by the Official Receiver in corresponding circumstances under the Insolvency Regulations 1994 referred to in (4) above.

(7)   In the case of joint liquidators, it is for them to agree between themselves as to how the remuneration is to be apportioned between them. Any dispute may be referred to the court or the liquidation committee or a meeting of creditors for settlement.

(8)   If the liquidator is a solicitor and employs his own firm to act on behalf of the company, profit costs may not be paid to the firm unless this is authorised by the committee, a creditors' meeting or the court.

For Scotland, see Scottish Rules 4.32 to 4.35. As to the liquidator's remuneration in the winding up of a Part II insurance company, see the Insurance Companies (Winding up) Rules 1985.

An accountant who had been appointed to the office of receiver or liquidator whilst he was an employee or partner of a firm of accountants, but who later left the firm before completion of his official duties, was under a fiduciary duty to account to the firm for any fees subsequently accruing to him from that office (*Casson Beckman & Partners v Papi [1991] BCLC 299*).

Removal and replacement of liquidator

C11.28   In a members' voluntary liquidation any vacancy occurring by death, resignation or otherwise in the office of liquidator *appointed by the company*, may be filled by the company in general meeting (subject to any arrangement with its creditors). Any such meeting may be convened by any contributory or by any continuing joint liquidator and must be held in the manner provided for by the Insolvency Act or by the articles or determined by the court on the application of any contributory or continuing joint liquidator (section 92).

In a creditors' voluntary liquidation, any such vacancy in the office of a liquidator (other than one appointed by or by the direction of the court) may be filled by a creditors' meeting (section 104).

In either type of voluntary liquidation, if for any cause there is no liquidator acting, the court may appoint a liquidator. A liquidator whose authorisation to act as an insolvency practitioner has been suspended or withdrawn automatically vacates his office as liquidator but is a proper person to apply for the appointment of another person in his place (see section 171(4) and *Re A J Adams (Builders) Ltd [1991] BCC 62*; see also A4.5 and A4.10 PART A: GENERAL). The court may also, on cause shown, remove a liquidator (section 108; see also section 171(2), Rules 4.103, 4.140, Forms 4.29 and 4.30). A liquidator may also be removed in a compulsory liquidation by the court (section 172(2)). For cases on the question of removal by the court see the following.

(1)   *Re Sir John Moore Gold Mining Co (1879) 12 Ch D 325.*

(2)   *Re Adam Eyton Ltd (1887) 36 Ch D 299.*

(3)   *Re Amalgamated Properties of Rhodesia Ltd (1914) 30 TLR 405*

(liquidator alleged to be sympathetic to the directors whose conduct was impeached but they had ceased to be directors; application was not supported by other creditors and was refused).

(4) *Re Rubber and Produce Investment Trust [1915] 1 Ch 382* (liquidator of company, which was thought to be solvent but proved to be insolvent, had disregarded wishes of creditors; application granted).

(5) *Re Charterland Goldfields (1909) 26 TLR 132* (liquidator had intimate business relations with directors; conflict of interest; application granted).

(6) *Re Karamelli and Barnett Ltd [1917] 1 Ch 203* (application granted on ground that removal would be for the benefit of the winding up).

(7) *Re Urmston Grange Steamship Co (1901) 17 TLR 553* (immoral conduct not sufficient ground).

(8) *Re Scottish Granite Co (1868) 17 LT 533* (liquidator resident abroad; could be a valid ground for removal).

(9) *Re Keypak Homecare Ltd [1987] BCLC 409* (personal misconduct or unfitness not sole ground; failure to show sufficient vigour in carrying out duties may be sufficient).

(10) *Re Corbenstoke Ltd (No 2) (1989) 5 BCC 767* (conflict of interest as between position as trustee in bankruptcy of 99 per cent shareholder (and also an alleged creditor) for the company, as director of the company and as liquidator thereof; valid ground for removal).

(11) *Re Arrows Ltd [1992] BCC 121* (funds lent to company for onward loans to traders on the security of bills of exchange actually used for property transactions with other companies controlled by the same shareholder; two partners in a firm of accountants appointed provisional liquidators of the company; one of them and another partner in the same firm appointed receivers of some of those other companies; disputes and conflict of interest between the company and the other companies in relation to right to forfeit leases and right to seek relief against forfeiture and in relation to possible proprietary claims; court refused to remove the provisional liquidators because of considerable practical disadvantages which the removal would cause and because, though the provisional liquidators and the receivers belonged to the same firm, they had separate independent legal advisers).

A liquidator may also be removed by an order of the court or:

(*a*) in a members' voluntary liquidation, by a general meeting of the company summoned specially for that purpose (section 171(2)(a));

(*b*) in a creditors' voluntary liquidation, by a general meeting of the creditors so summoned (section 171(2)(b)); and

(*c*) in a compulsory liquidation, by a general meeting of the creditors so summoned (section 172(2)).

In the case of (*a*) or (*b*) above, where the liquidator was appointed by the court, a meeting to replace him is required to be summoned only if he thinks fit or the court so directs or if a meeting is requisitioned (where (*a*) applies) by members representing at least one-half of the total voting rights or, (where (*b*) applies) by at least one-half, in value, of the creditors (section 171(3)). In the case of (*c*), where the Official Receiver is liquidator (otherwise than in succession to a substantive liquidator whose office falls vacant—see section 136(3) and C5.47 above) or where the liquidator has been appointed by the court (otherwise than under section 139(4)(a)—court intervening when different persons chosen by meetings of creditors and contributories; or section 140(1)—appointment of administrator as liquidator upon discharge of administration order—see C5.50 above) or where he has been appointed by the Secretary of State, the meeting is required to be summoned only if he thinks fit or the court so directs or if the meeting is requisitioned by at least one-quarter, in value, of the creditors (section 172(2)). A liquidator in a compulsory winding up appointed by the Secretary of State (see C5.50 above) may also be removed by the Secretary of State (section 172(4)).

A provisional liquidator in a compulsory winding up may be removed only by an order of the court. A liquidator or, in a compulsory winding up, a liquidator or provisional liquidator (not being the Official Receiver) must vacate office if he ceases to be a qualified insolvency practitioner in relation to the company.

Where in a voluntary liquidation, the creditors have sufficient grounds for seeking the liquidator's removal, they may consider the alternative course of seeking a compulsory winding up—see C5.29(3) above.

The liquidator may, in certain circumstances, resign his office by giving notice of his resignation to the Registrar of Companies (in a voluntary winding up of either type), or the court (in a compulsory winding up). The circumstances are ill-health or his intending to cease to practice as an insolvency practitioner or there being some conflict of interest or change of personal circumstances which makes impracticable the further discharge by him of his duties. A liquidator also vacates office (in a voluntary winding up) upon his filing with the Registrar of Companies a return of the final meeting(s) under section 94 or 106 or (in a compulsory liquidation) upon his filing the return of the final meeting under section 146 or, in Scotland, upon an early dissolution under section 204 (sections 171(6) and 172(7) and (8); see also C16.1 *et seq.* below).

In a compulsory winding up in England and Wales, the Official Receiver is the liquidator during any vacancy (section 136(3)).

(For detailed provisions as to removal, vacation of office and replacement of liquidator, see section 171 (voluntary winding up of either type), section 172 (compulsory winding up), Rules 4.142 to 4.148 and Forms 4.33, 4.39 to 4.41 and 4.44 to 4.46 (members' voluntary winding up) and Rules 4.108 to 4.123 and 4.132 to 4.138 and Forms 4.22, 4.32 to 4.41 and

4.44 to 4.46 (compulsory and creditors' voluntary winding up); and for Scotland, see Scottish Rules 4.23 to 4.30 and 4.36 and 4.37 and Forms 4.9 to 4.19 (Scot).)

Special manager

C11.29 A special manager may now be appointed in a voluntary as well as a compulsory liquidation. The appointment may be made by the court, on application at any time after a voluntary winding-up resolution has been passed or a compulsory winding-up order has been made or a provisional liquidator has been appointed following a winding-up petition but before a winding-up order. The application may be made by the liquidator or the provisional liquidator. The function of the special manager is to manage the company's business or property with such powers as may be entrusted to him by the court. The court may also direct that any provision of the Act which has effect in relation to a provisional liquidator or liquidator will have the like effect in relation to the special manager for the purposes of his carrying out any of the functions of the provisional liquidator or liquidator (section 177).

The special manager's remuneration is fixed from time to time by the court (Rule 4.206(5)). Where goods claimed by another party are disposed of by the special manager with the agreement of the claimant, pending the result of the claim, such remuneration as is fair may be ordered by the court to be paid out of the proceeds of the disposal notwithstanding that the goods are found to belong to the claimant. An agreement for such disposal may be implied. In any case, as an officer of the court, the special manager's responsibilities possibly extend to the disputed goods (*Re US Ltd, The Law Society's Gazette, 9 November 1983*).

The special manager must give the prescribed security and has obligations as regards the keeping and production of accounts (section 177; Rules 4.206 to 4.210; Form 4.60).

For Scotland, see Scottish Rules 4.69 to 4.73.

For special provision relating to insurance companies carrying on long-term business, see section 56 of the Insurance Companies Act 1982.

Chapter 12: Conduct of winding up: realisation of assets

General aspects

Collection

C12.1   Section 148 requires the court in a compulsory winding up to cause the assets of the company to be collected, and applied in discharge of its liabilities. (In Scotland, Scottish Rule 4.22 applies.) In a compulsory winding up the court may require any contributory for the time being on the list of contributories to pay to the company any money due from him (or from the estate of the person whom he represents), exclusive of any money payable by him or the estate by virtue of any call pursuant to the Companies Act 1985 or Insolvency Act 1986.

A contributory in a limited company cannot set off a debt due to him by the company against a call made on him by the liquidator until all the creditors have been paid in full (together with interest at the official rate—see C14.19 below) (section 149 (3); see also *Grissell's Case (1866) 1 Ch App 528; Gill's Case (1879) 12 ChD 755*). There cannot be a set-off between a debt due to the company from a *deceased* insolvent contributory and the amount due to the contributory (*Re Peruvian Railway Construction Co [1915] 2 Ch 144; Re H E Thorne & Sons Ltd [1914] 2 Ch 438*) or between a sum due from a firm in which the contributory was a member and a debt due to the contributory alone (*Re Pennington & Owen Ltd [1925] 1 Ch 825*).

Where an insolvent company is both a contributory and a creditor of another insolvent company, there is no set-off between the call and the debt (*Re Auriferous Properties Ltd (No 1) [1898] 1 Ch 691; (No 2) [1898] 2 Ch 428*) but debts are to be taken into account in arriving at the total fund for distribution.

Where two insolvent companies are indebted to each other, the court may, in certain circumstances, give the liquidators of the two companies permission to distribute their respective assets among their other respective creditors without regard to the claims of the companies against each other (see *Re National Live Stock Insurance Co [1917] 1 Ch 628*).

In the case of a contributory of an unlimited company, or a director with unlimited liability of a limited company, the court may allow him by way of set-off any money due to him or the estate on any independent dealing or contract with the company, but not any money due to him as a member of the company in respect of any dividend or profit (section 149(2)). The court may also require any contributory, purchaser or other person to pay any money due from him to a company in compulsory liquidation into the Bank of England to the account of the liquidator instead of to the liquidator (section 151). As to the making of calls and settlement of the list of contributories and adjustment of their rights, see C12.20 below.

An order on a contributory made by the court in a compulsory winding up is conclusive evidence that the money concerned is due, subject to any right of appeal (section 152(1); as to Scotland, see section 152(2)).

Where a winding-up order has been made, or a provisional liquidator has been appointed following a winding-up petition, the liquidator or the provisional liquidator must take into his custody or under his control all the property and things in action to which the company *appears* to be entitled (section 144(1)). In a compulsory winding up in Scotland, if and so long as there is no liquidator, all the property of the company is deemed to be in the custody of the court (section 144(2)).

The duties imposed on the court in a compulsory winding up with regard to the collection of the company's assets and their application are delegated to the liquidator as an officer, and subject to the control, of the court (Rule 4.179(1)). For the purposes of acquiring and retaining possession of the company's property in discharge of his duties in a compulsory winding up, the liquidator has the same powers as a receiver appointed by the High Court. The court may on his application enforce such acquisition and retention accordingly (Rule 4.179(2)).

The powers which the court has in a compulsory liquidation in relation to the matters referred to above may be invoked through the court in a voluntary winding up by virtue of section 112. The powers and duties of a liquidator in a voluntary liquidation to collect and realise the assets are also implicit in sections 91, 100(1), 107, 165 and 166. In any type of winding up, Parts II and III of Schedule 4 are also relevant in this connection. The powers of the court in a compulsory liquidation as regards settlement of the list of contributories (which is *prima facie* evidence of the liabilities of the persons named in it) and making calls are exercisable by the liquidator in a voluntary winding up (section 165(4)).

In common with the office holders in other forms of corporate insolvency, a liquidator in any type of winding up also has available to him certain statutory aids and facilities to enable him to collect and take control of assets (see A4.14 *et seq.* PART A: GENERAL above). In a compulsory liquidation the powers of the court under section 234 (enforcing delivery of company property) are exercisable by the liquidator or provisional liquidator (Rule 4.185).

Sometimes, a liquidator is inhibited from pursuing a financial claim against third parties through the courts due to the absence of adequate 'fighting funds'. There is no objection to selling and assigning the right of action to another party in return for an undertaking by the other party to pay an agreed proportion of any recovery to the liquidator. This would be regarded as the assignment of a bare cause of action. However, if the liquidator pursues the action in the name of the company under an agreement with a 'backer', whereby the latter undertakes to bear all costs in return for an undertaking by the liquidator to pay to him an agreed proportion of any sum recovered, this may be regarded as a champertous arrangement and the court may stay the action (*Grovewood Holdings plc v James Capel & Co Ltd, The Independent, 20 September 1994*).

As to the handover of assets and information from the Official Receiver to a successor liquidator in a compulsory winding up, see Rule 4.107.

The liquidator must take appropriate steps to recover any surplus of assets in the hands of any receiver of the company (see PART D: RECEIVERS). Where the surplus relates to a *fixed* charge comprised in a hybrid fixed and floating charge, the surplus does not become part of the floating charge and must be paid to the liquidator for the benefit of the creditors generally (subject to the rights of those who have preferential claims in the *liquidation*—see C14.34 below), instead of being applied to the payment of the claims of the *receivership* preferential creditors (*Re G L Saunders Ltd [1986] 1 WLR 215*).

Power of sale

C12.2   The liquidator has power to sell any of the property of the company by public auction or private contract, with power to transfer the whole of it to any person or to sell it in parcels (Schedule 4, para 6; sections 165 and 167—subject to the restrictions contained in section 166 in the case of an interim liquidator in a creditors' voluntary winding up). In a creditors' voluntary liquidation, any sale to a person who is connected with the company (within the meaning of section 249) has to be notified to the liquidation committee (if any) (section 165(6)).

Power to transfer for consideration in specie

C12.3   The liquidator may, with the sanction of (in a members' voluntary liquidation) a special resolution of the company or (in a creditors' voluntary liquidation) either the court or the liquidation committee, enter into a scheme in accordance with sections 110 and 111 under which certain types of consideration other than cash may be received for the transfer of the company's assets to another party and distributed directly to the members in proportion to their rights. These provisions are primarily suitable for company reconstructions by solvent voluntary liquidations. They do not apply to a compulsory winding up but a similar result may be achieved there by the use of sections 167 to 169 and the Schedule 4 powers.

Vesting order

C12.4   Section 145 enables the court in a compulsory winding up on the liquidator's application to vest in the liquidator in his official name any assets of the company or assets held in trust for it. It also enables the liquidator, after he has given any indemnity as directed by the court, to bring or defend in his official name any action or proceeding for the purpose of effectually winding up the company and recovering its property. (The section can also be invoked in a voluntary winding up under section 112.)

Vesting under section 145 is not normally necessary because the liquidator can deal with the assets in the name of the company and use its common seal (Schedule 4, paras 6 and 7). However, a vesting order may assist, for example, where the seal is not immediately available or an unincorporated body is being wound up as an unregistered company, or it is more convenient for the liquidator to deal with the assets in his official name, say, in relation to proceedings in a foreign country.

Exemption from stamp duty

C12.5 Certain types of documents entered into in the course of compulsory or creditors' voluntary winding up are exempt from stamp duty under section 190. The scope of the exemption is very limited.

Disclaimer

C12.6 Sections 178 to 182 deal with disclaimer but apply only to England and Wales.

They enable the liquidator to disclaim, by giving the requisite notice, an onerous property, that is, any unprofitable contract or any other property which is unsaleable or not readily saleable or is such that it may give rise to a liability to pay money or perform any other act. The general object of a disclaimer is to mitigate the claim which other parties concerned may have in the winding up in respect of the property or contract. Failure to disclaim does not necessarily make the liquidator personally liable, or require him to discharge, as an expense of the winding up in priority to other claims, any claim or obligation in respect of the subject matter. However, failure to disclaim a *contract* may expose the liquidator to the risk of being held to have adopted it if he (even unwittingly) conducts himself in such a way as can only be explained on the hypothesis that he had adopted it although (unlike under the previous legislation, section 619(3) of the Companies Act 1985), by failing to disclaim he is not, without more, necessarily deemed to have adopted it.

These new provisions also differ from the previous provisions in that (i) the liquidator does not require the court's leave to disclaim, although the court on application may set aside the disclaimer, (ii) it is sufficient if any land to be disclaimed is unsaleable or not readily saleable or is such that it may give rise to a liability to pay money or perform any other act, even if, as required by the old provisions, it is not 'land . . . burdened with onerous covenants', (iii) no general time limit is laid down for effecting a disclaimer (subject as stated below) and (iv) special provisions are made as regards the disclaimer of leasehold property.

Although the liquidator no longer needs the court's leave to disclaim, it is submitted that the disclaimer would be invalid and can be challenged in court if the contract disclaimed is manifestly not 'unprofitable' or the other property disclaimed is not 'unsaleable . . .' (etc.). In *Re Potters Oils Ltd [1985] PCC 148* (decided under the previous legislation) Harman J held that although chlorinated waste oil stored on another party's land had no commercial value, was believed to be potentially hazardous, and would have cost a substantial sum to dispose of and was 'unsaleable', it could not be disclaimed because it was not unsaleable 'by reason of its binding the possessor thereof to the performance of any onerous act'. However, the language of the new provision appears to be less restrictive. Further, in *Re Hans Place Ltd [1992] BCC 737*, Mr Edward Evans-Lombe QC, sitting as a deputy judge of the Chancery Division, in rejecting a landlord's application to set aside a disclaimer by the liquidator of a lease on the ground that the disclaimer operated to release the guarantor of the rent (see below), held that the 1986 Act required a new approach by the court in considering challenges to a liquidator's decision to disclaim onerous property. The removal of any requirement of leave of the court meant that the decision to disclaim became simply one of the many instances where a liquidator exercised powers of management and distribution of the assets of the company. If there was no challenge to the *bona fides* of the liquidator nor any suggestion that his decision could be categorised as perverse, the court could not interfere with the decision.

A disclaimer can be effected notwithstanding that the liquidator has taken possession of the property, endeavoured to sell it, or otherwise exercised rights of ownership in relation to it. To make a disclaimer, the liquidator prepares a notice on Form 4.53 and files it with a copy in court for sealing and for endorsement with the date of filing. The copy duly sealed and endorsed with the date of filing (which is the date from which the disclaimer takes effect, subject to suspension in the case of leasehold property, as stated below) is returned to the liquidator who must, within seven days thereafter, send or give copies (i) to every person who (to his knowledge) claims an interest in the disclaimed property or contract or is under any liability in respect of the property or contract (not being a liability discharged by the disclaimer) and also (ii), in the case of leasehold property, to every person who (to his knowledge) claims as underlessee or mortgagee, and (iii), in the case of a contract, to all persons who (to his knowledge) are parties thereto or have an interest under it. If the interest of any other person subsequently comes to the knowledge of the liquidator, that person too must be given a copy forthwith. Compliance with these requirements as to giving copies may, in certain circumstances, be dispensed with. The liquidator may also give notice of the disclaimer to any person who in his opinion ought, in the public interest or otherwise, to be informed of it. Further, he may require (Form 4.55) any person who claims or may claim to have an interest in the property to declare it within 14 days and may, in the absence of such declaration, assume that the person concerned has no interest which will prevent or impede the disclaimer. Particulars of all notices of disclaimer given must be notified to the court.

A disclaimer is presumed valid and effective unless a breach of duty as to giving of notices is proved.

In *MEPC Plc v Scottish Amicable Life Assurance Society [1993] 36 EG 133*, a lease was assigned by a tenant to an individual following a licence to assign. On the individual's bankruptcy, the trustee in bankruptcy, under a corresponding provision of the 1986 Act applicable to bankruptcies, purported to effect a disclaimer. However, in the notice of disclaimer he stated that he was disclaiming the bankrupt's own interest in the licence to assign. The Court of Appeal held that the notice of disclaimer was valid as a disclaimer of the lease itself. The 'onerous property' in this context was plainly the lease itself under which the rent was payable. It was quite impossible to construe the statutory provision so as to achieve the result that the trustee could disclaim the onerous liabilities in relation to the property, but retain the property itself. Where there had been an assignment, and the bankrupt was the person who became the assignee, the trustee could not disclaim the assignment without disclaiming the lease; and the link was equally close if he sought to disclaim the licence to assign without disclaiming the lease, because the covenant in the licence to assign, which was the only subsisting provision under it, related to the full term of the covenant in the lease. Accordingly, the disclaimer was to be construed as the disclaimer of all the interest of the bankrupt's estate under the lease.

(Rules 4.187 to 4.190, 4.192 and 4.193).

A disclaimer operates so as to determine, as from the date of the disclaimer, the rights, interests and liabilities of the company in, or in respect of, the property or contract disclaimed. It does not, however, 'except insofar as is necessary for the purposes of releasing the company from any liability', affect the rights or liabilities of any other person (section 178(4)). The existence in the previous legislation of an exception similar to the foregoing quoted exception led courts to refuse a leave to disclaim a lease in cases where a surety was involved on the ground that the disclaimer would release the surety (since without such release the company would remain liable by way of indemnity to the surety) and would, therefore, prejudice the landlord's interests (see *Re Katherine et Cie [1932] 1 Ch 70; Stacey v Hill [1901] 1 KB 660 CA*). However, the reasoning in those cases was not followed in *Maurice Tempany v Royal Liver Trustees Ltd and others [1984] BCLC 568 (High Court (Ireland))*. Kean J allowed a disclaimer of a lease notwithstanding that this might have the effect of releasing a surety. He held that in exercising its discretion the exclusive concern of the court was the interests of *all* persons interested in the liquidation. As far as the interests of the landlord as one such person (who stood to be adversely affected by the disclaimer) were concerned, release of the surety was not necessary 'for the purpose of releasing the company and the property of the company from liability'. As far as the others were concerned, it was obviously in their interest that the onerous lease should be disclaimed. Further, on various hypotheses one could establish situations in which continuing the surety's liability might be more or less injurious to the winding up. Whether the liability continued could determine whether both he and the landlord would have claims in the winding up and the amount of claim which the one or the other or both would have. In any case, by the terms of the guarantee in that case, the surety would be released upon the company being dissolved following the conclusion of the winding up.

This reasoning has been echoed, to some extent, in *Re Distributors and Warehousing Ltd [1986] BCLC 129*. That case demonstrates that there may be reasons why a landlord may not succeed in resisting a disclaimer on the ground of the existence of a guarantor. Firstly, where the landlord is an assignee of the reversion, as distinct from the original grantor of the lease, the benefit of the guarantee may, in the absence of express words, not have passed to him with the assignment of the reversion, although this may not apply to a carefully drafted lease and the guarantee clause therein (see, for example, *Coastplace Ltd v Hartley and another [1987] 2 WLR 1289*). Secondly, even if such benefit has passed to him, the guarantee may, by its terms, only subsist while the lease remains vested in the company as original tenant; in that case the guarantee would cease anyway upon the company's dissolution; and it can be argued that it is not the disclaimer which really prejudices his interests under the guarantee but the restrictive language of the guarantee which the parties had deliberately chosen, although *Re Katherine et Cie* and *Stacey v Hill* suggest that the right against the surety may not survive a disclaimer, since otherwise the surety would have a claim by way of indemnity against the company.

In any case, now that under the new legislation the liquidator can disclaim a lease without the leave of the court, and it has been held in *Re Hans Place Ltd* (above) that the court will not interfere with the liquidator's discretion to disclaim unless he has acted in bad faith or his decision is perverse, it has become more difficult for a landlord to argue against a disclaimer. However, in *Re Hans Place Ltd* Edward Evans-Lombe QC went on to state that for the purposes of deciding the case, it was unnecessary to depart from the decision in *Re Katherine et Cie Ltd* (above); furthermore, the wide wording of section 168(5) did not preclude the court from taking account of the interests of landlords in preserving their right to claim against guarantors, when deciding what was just. However, he held that if the court were exercising an original discretion whether or not to permit the disclaimer, it would have ruled that there were plain advantages to the general body of creditors and to the administration of the company's affairs arising from a disclaimer which the competing advantage to the landlord ought not to overrule, and the disclaimer should stand. It is not clear, however, whether he was suggesting that in appropriate cases involving guarantors, the court can disallow a disclaimer even if the liquidator's decision to disclaim was *bona fide* and not perverse. If he was instead suggesting that notwithstanding the disclaimer the court can, on an application by the landlord, make appropriate orders preserving the landlord's rights against the surety, then that would be tantamount to departing, to a large extent, from the decision in *Re Katherine et Cie Ltd*.

It is submitted that *Re Katherine et Cie Ltd* and *Stacey v Hill* should not be allowed to stand. It is true that section 178(4)(b), like its predecessor, in providing that a disclaimer ought not to affect the rights or liabilities of any other person (such as a landlord or a surety) contains the qualifying words 'except so far as is necessary for the purpose of releasing the company from any liability'. However, the argument that without the release of the surety, the company would be liable to the surety in respect of future rents cannot logically be within the purview of that qualification. Any such claim would only be an ordinary claim provable in the liquidation. After all, one of the effects of the disclaimer of a lease is to give the landlord the right to prove in the liquidation in respect of any loss or damage that he suffers (section 178(6)—see below). To the extent that he recovers payment from the surety, his claim in the liquidation would be reduced and replaced by a claim by the surety. In such a situation the surety can be said to have had at least a contingent claim as at the date of the winding up—and contingent debts are provable; see C14.13 below. It is submitted that the expression 'liabilities' in section 178(4)(b) must be interpreted as being confined to future liabilities which would be required to be paid out as an expense of the liquidation.

The risks faced by landlords under the old legislation, of losing their rights against sureties in the event of a disclaimer by a liquidator of the tenant company, led to the practice of including a special provision in the surety clause in the lease. This was to the effect that upon the liquidation of the tenant company, or a disclaimer by its liquidator, the surety could be required by the landlord to take on a lease in the surety's own name on the same terms. Such a provision would become unnecessary if, in the context of the new legislation, *Re Katherine et Cie Ltd* and *Stacey v Hill* were overruled. It should be noted in passing that in any case, such a provision contains some loopholes which need to be closed from the point of view of the landlord. For example, the provision cannot be enforced where the tenant, instead of going into liquidation, has been struck off the register with the result that the lease has vested in the Crown as *bona vacantia*, but the lease is disclaimed by the Crown. Therefore, unless the surety clause makes it clear that the obligation to take on a new lease equally applies in such a situation, the provision would not be enforceable against the surety (see *Re Yarmarine (IW) Ltd* [*1992*] *BCC 28*).

From the surety's point of view, he cannot require the landlord to grant him a new lease where there has been such a disclaimer. The clause only gives the right to the landlord to decide whether to enforce that provision, but does not give the surety the right to demand a lease in his name and thereby possibly to mitigate his liability to the landlord. Sureties would be well advised to insist that the obligation should be made mutual. However, where a surety fails to enter into a new lease where required by the landlord to do so, the landlord is entitled to claim the rent from the surety in respect of the period after the time he should have complied with the notice. A statutory demand against the surety can be founded by the landlord on a claim for such rent (*Re a company (00792 of 1992)* [*1992*] *EGCS 32*, applying *Walsh v Lonsdale (1882) 21 Ch D 9*).

A disclaimer in itself does not divest the insolvent company of the legal estate in the property disclaimed; nor does it bring to an end a charge by way of legal mortgage of the property. Section 178 does not go as far as causing such divestment. It merely terminates the company's 'rights, interests and liabilities in or in respect of the property'. The main legal estate, as distinct from any subsidiary legal estate, remains in existence 'though without an owner until a vesting order is made' (*per* Megarry V-C in *Warnford Investments Ltd v Duckworth [1978] 2 All ER 517 at 525*) or becomes a 'dormant volcano' (*per* Uthwatt J in *Re Thompson and Cottrell's Contract [1943] 1 All ER 169 at 172*).

However, if, following a disclaimer, no vesting order is made in favour of any interested party (see below), the legal estate, at least where it is a leasehold estate, is determined and, with it, any underlease or sub-lease so that the lessor takes the reversion freed from both the lease and the underlease (*per* Lindley LJ in *Re Finley, ex parte Clothworkers' Co (1888) 21 QBD 475 at 485–487*). Such a determination is necessary in order to release the company from its liabilities and obligations in relation to both.

It is arguable that in the case of a freehold, even where no vesting order is made, the freehold estate may not necessarily come to an end because the company may not have any 'liabilities . . . in or in respect of the property disclaimed' and because, unlike in the case of leasehold, there is no reversion of a freehold. In other words, whereas the disclaimer of a leasehold, in the absence of a subsequent vesting order, has been equated to a voluntary surrender of the lease (see *Smalley v Hardinge (1881) 7 QBD 524*), this analogy cannot apply to the disclaimer of a freehold. It is also arguable that where the mortgage over the freehold or leasehold is created by a charge by way of legal mortgage (see section 87 of the Law of Property Act 1925), as distinct from by way of a demise or sub-demise (see section 86(1) of that Act—a rare occurrence these days), the mortgage does not come to an end because the mortgagor company's liabilities are not liabilities 'in or in respect of the property disclaimed' but are liabilities which are capable of independent existence, and it is not necessary to destroy the charge (by way of legal mortgage) so as to release the company from those liabilities. The old cases established the principle that a sub-lessee could be required to elect whether he wanted a vesting order and that if he elected against it, his sub-lease would come to an end. This principle appears to extend to a mortgage by way of sub-demise but not to a charge by way of legal mortgage. This point appears to be implicit in Lindley LJ's remarks in *Re Finley* at *485–487*:

> 'This. . . .' [determination of a lease and sub-lease in the absence of a vesting order] 'appears to us to be the logical consequence of the [Bankruptcy] Act, and it is impossible not to see that it is a startling result. It will very seriously affect the old practice of taking securities on leasehold property by way of sub-demise, the whole object of which is to prevent the mortgagee from becoming liable to the rent and to the convenants and obligations of the original lease. If the decision of the Divisional Court in *Re Cock, ex parte Shilson (1887) 30 QBD 343* (holding that in the absence of a vesting order a mortgage by a

sub-demise came to an end upon the disclaimer of the leasehold) is right, as we think it is, this anomaly will be introduced into the practice of conveyancing in the event of the bankruptcy of a mortgagee of leasehold property by sub-demise.'

Accordingly, where the disclaimed property is subject to a charge by way of legal mortgage, all that the liquidator in effect disclaims is the company's equity of redemption, because that is the only property the company has. The chargee and any receiver appointed by it can continue to exercise their rights as if there has been no disclaimer (subject as stated above in the case of leasehold estates). However, once the company is struck off the register or dissolved, the receiver cannot dispose of the charged property, or exercise other rights, as agent or in the name of the company. Steps should be taken to have the striking off or dissolution deferred until realisation of the charged property.

The court may make a vesting order on such terms as it deems fit (section 181(3)) and will, no doubt, so tailor its order as to do justice in the spirit of section 178(4)(b) (and to avoid giving any subsequent mortgagee a windfall). Thus, the chargee's options, where the property is freehold land, are the following:

(1)   The chargee can apply to the court for a vesting order in its favour, subject to the terms that such vesting shall not have the effect of (*a*) extinguishing its mortgage by merger and the mortgage will continue to have the same priority as it had before the disclaimer, (*b*) subjecting the chargee, as the new owner of the freehold, to the covenants on the part of the mortgagor contained in any other charges over the property created by the company or (*c*) (if this is desired) extinguishing any of the existing leases. *Prima facie*, where a mortgagee acquires the equity of redemption, or where the mortgage and the equity of redemption become united by purchase in the same person, the mortgage is merged in the land (*Smith v Phillips* (*1837*) *1 Keen 694*); but that person is entitled to have both interests kept alive for his benefit (*Clark v May* (*1852*) *16 Beav 273; Cooper v Cartwright* (*1860*) *John 679*).

(2)   In addition to (1) above, and if the realisable value of the freehold is significantly less than the amount due to the chargee, and if no significant dividend is expected to be paid to the unsecured creditors in the liquidation, the chargee can apply to the court for an order of foreclosure. Such an order would extinguish any subsequent mortgages and charges (section 88(2) of the LPA 1925). It could be risky to rely solely on this remedy, as the result of this application might not be known before the time limit for seeking remedy (1) above expires. Therefore, this remedy should be sought at the same time as remedy (1) above is sought. However, this remedy would be unnecessary if there are no subsequent encumbrances. It may be that procedurally the two remedies need to be sought by separate proceedings, although at a later stage a consolidation of the two proceedings might be successfully obtained.

(3) If a subsequent mortgagee or a lessee applies for a vesting order in his favour, the chargee can make representations to the court that, as prior mortgagee, it has a better entitlement to remedy (1) above and that, in any case, any such vesting order should be subject to terms which preserve the charge and its priority and (if so desired) the existing leases.

If the chargee is to go down the 'vesting order' route (see below), it needs to consider very carefully any potential liabilities (statutory, including environmental, tortious and others) to which, as the freeholder, it might be exposed.

The court, on the application (see Rule 4.194 for procedure) of any person claiming an interest in the disclaimed property or contract (including a statutory tenant of the property: *Re Vedmay Ltd, The Independent, 4 October 1993*) or having any liability in respect thereof not discharged by the disclaimer, may vest the property or order its delivery to him or a trustee for him. This is only done, however, where it would be just to do so for the purpose of compensating the person concerned who is subject to the liability. Such vesting or delivery must be taken into account in assessing the claim in the winding up referred to above (section 181).

A surety who has guaranteed the tenant's obligations under the disclaimed lease is not entitled to have the lease vested in him since he ceases to be liable for future (though not past) breaches by the tenant and, therefore, cannot be said to have liability 'in respect of the disclaimed property', that is, the unexpired future term: *Re No 1 London Ltd [1991] BCLC 501*.

Where *leasehold property* is disclaimed, the disclaimer remains suspended for 14 days from the date of the last notice. If within that period the person interested or under the liability mentioned above does not apply for a vesting or delivery order under section 181, the disclaimer will then become effective. If he does make the application, the disclaimer will only take effect if the court so directs. Thus it seems that a landlord who wishes to resist a disclaimer because it would release a surety would initially have to apply for a vesting or delivery order and then, during the course of the hearing, submit that the disclaimer should not be allowed to proceed.

A disclaimer of a lease by the liquidator of an assignee does not absolve the assignor, or the surety for the assignor (unlike the surety for the assignee), from his liability in respect of the unexpired future term of the lease: *WH Smith Ltd v Wyndham Investments Ltd [1994] BCC 699; Hindcastle Ltd v Barbara Attenborough Associates Ltd [1994] BCC 705*.

Where the court makes a vesting order in respect of leasehold property in favour of an underlessee (as to which see, for example *Re A E Realisations (1985) Ltd [1987] BCLC 486*) or mortgagee, it must do so on terms making him subject to the same liabilities and obligations as those to which the company was subject at the commencement of the winding up or (if the court thinks fit) those to which the person would be subject if the lease had been assigned to him at the commencement of the winding up (section 182). If the underlessee or mortgagee does not accept the vesting on those terms, the court may vest the property in any person (for example, presumably, a surety except where he has undertaken with the landlord to take a direct lease from the landlord on disclaimer by the lessee—*Re A E Realisations* above) who is liable (personally or in a representative capacity, and jointly with the company or alone) to perform the lessee's covenants. Such vesting may be made freed from all estates, encumbrances and interests created by the company (including an underlessee's right of occupation). The underlessee or mortgagee who declines the vesting is excluded from all interest in the property (section 182).

A landlord's right to forfeit the disclaimed lease is not affected by the existence of an application for a vesting order, even where the landlord has indicated that he would not oppose the application. Further, a vesting order, when made, is not retrospective to the date of disclaimer: *Pellicano v MEPC plc [1994] 19 EG 138.*

Where in consequence of the disclaimer, any land subject to a rentcharge vests by operation of law in the Crown or any other person ('the proprietor'), the proprietor or its or his successors are not subject to any personal liability in respect of any sums becoming due under the rentcharges except those becoming due after the proprietor, or someone claiming under or through it or him, has taken possession or control of the land or has entered into occupation of it (section 180).

Any person sustaining loss or damage in consequence of the disclaimer may prove therefor as creditor in the winding up (section 178(6)).

A liquidator ceases to be entitled to disclaim if within 28 days (or such longer period as the court may allow) of being required in writing (Form 4.54) to make up his mind by any person interested in the property or contract, he does not give a notice of disclaimer (section 178(5); Rule 4.191).

Rescission of contracts by the court

C12.7 The court may, on the application of a person who is, as against the liquidator, entitled to the benefit of, or subject to the burden of, a contract made with the company, make an order rescinding the contract on such terms as to payment by or to either party of damages, or otherwise as the court thinks just. Any damages so payable to such person is provable by him as a debt in the winding up (section 186). (See also PART F: SPECIAL PROVISIONS FOR FINANCIAL MARKETS as to 'cherry-picking' problems.)

Recovery of assets in respect of antecedent transactions or matters

C12.8 The liquidator must consider taking appropriate action to recover any money or assets that may be claimable in respect of any antecedent transactions or events. 'Antecedent transactions and events' as used here includes the following.

(*a*)   *Execution, distress, forfeiture, defeasance, etc.* (see C8.3, C9.2 to C9.4 above, and C14.34 below)

(*b*)   *Disposition of property after commencement of compulsory winding up* (see C8.4 above)

(*c*)   *Transactions at an undervalue, gratuitous alienation, preference, extortionate credit transactions and debt avoidance transactions* (see C10.2 to C10.7, and C10.10 above)

(*d*)   *Invalid floating charge* (see C10.8 and C10.9 above)

(*e*) *Unauthorised or prohibited company transactions*

C12.9   It may be possible to obtain restitution or compensation from another party in respect of past transactions that were in breach of company law, for example, *ultra vires* transactions where third party recipients of the benefit had notice, payment of excessive dividends, or unlawful loans, quasi-loans or other payments to or transactions with directors or connected persons (sections 263 *et seq.*, 311 *et seq.* and 330 *et seq.* of the Companies Act 1985). For some cases see *International Sales & Agencies Ltd v Marcus [1982] 3 All ER 551; Simmonds v Heffer and others [1983] BCLC 298; Rosemary Simmons Memorial Housing Association v United Dominions Trust Ltd [1986] 1 WLR 1440; Rolled Steel Products (Holdings) Ltd v British Steel Corporation [1985] 2 WLR 908; Precision Dippings Ltd v Precision Dippings Marketing Ltd [1985] 3 WLR 812 (CA); Gibson's Executor v Gibson 1980 SLT 2 (Court of Session); Guinness Plc v Saunders [1990] BCC 205 (HL).* One of the latest cases in this connection is *Aveling Barford Limited v Perion (1989) 5 BCC 677* where there was a transfer of a property by a company to another company, both companies beneficially owned or controlled by the same person, at a gross undervalue at a time when the company was solvent under the 'balance sheet' test (if a debt due to an associated company was disregarded) but had no distributable reserves and had made a trading loss. The transfer was held to be in the nature of an unauthorised distribution of capital and, hence, *ultra vires* the company and not a legitimate exercise of its powers under its memorandum of association to sell property and to be incapable of subsequent ratification by the shareholders. The transferee company was held liable.

(*f*) *Unregistered charges*

C12.10   Certain charges created by a company are void as against the liquidator or a creditor of the company unless they are registered with the Registrar of Companies under sections 395, 396 and 409 and (as to Scotland) 410 *et seq.* of the Companies Act 1985. These provisions are to be amended by sections 92 to 104 of the Companies Act 1989. Examples of 'borderline' cases are—

(i) *Retention of title clauses*

A 'Romalpa' clause might constitute a registrable charge (as a limited floating charge, or a charge under the 'bill of sale' analogy or over book debts) to the extent that any proprietary interest is sought to be reserved by the vendor in assets other than the goods in their original form (and, perhaps, other than the proceeds in respect of the goods sold in their original form). See D7.17 *et seq.* PART D: RECEIVERS.

(ii) *Factored book debts*

If under a factoring agreement the assignment of book debts by the company to the factoring company is in substance a charge rather than an absolute assignment, the transaction is registrable. In *Lloyds & Scottish Finance Ltd v Cyril Lord Carpet Sales Ltd (1979) 129 NLJ 366*, assignments under a block discounting agreement were held on the facts to be absolute assignments, even though only 80 per cent of the debts were actually taken by the bank in return for the advances; see also *Lloyds & Scottish Finance Ltd v Prentice (1977) 121 SJ 847 (CA)*. In *Chase Manhattan (Asia) Ltd v First Bangkok City Finance Ltd, FT Law Reports, 15 July 1988* (a case under Hong Kong law) the sale of an interest in a loan with a provision for its repurchase at the same price was held to be an absolute sale.

(iii) *Sale and leaseback and agency agreements*

An arrangement to raise finance by selling fixed assets to a finance company for cash, and having them leased back for a periodic charge with an option to repurchase them at a price to be determined, could be held in reality to be a registrable charge (see *Stoneleigh Finance Ltd v Phillips [1965] 2 QB 537, 574, per* Russell LJ). *Curtain Dream Plc v Churchill Merchanting Ltd [1990] BCC 341* involved an application by the receivers of Curtain Dream Plc to determine whether a pre-receivership agreement for the sale of fabric by the company to a finance company, and the sale-back of the fabric by the finance company to the company subject to a reservation of title in favour of the finance company, created a registrable charge on the fabric. The court held that in determining whether the transaction was one by way of charge, with a creditor-debtor relationship between the parties, or whether there was a sale and resale with retention of title, was to be determined by ascertaining the real intention of the parties from the documents and the facts in question. In the present case, although the documents were not a sham, the transaction was intended to be a loan, and the sale and resale were mere machinery. The critical indication of a charge was the company's entitlement to redeem. (It is debatable whether, if the entitlement to redeem is postponed for such a long time as to amount to a 'clog', this would be indicative of the transaction having been intended to be other than a charge. However, it should be noted that by section

193 of the Companies Act 1985, debentures can validly be made irredeemable or their redemption date can be postponed for a long time. 'Debentures', for this purpose, includes a single mortgage (*Knightsbridge Estates Trust Ltd v Byrne [1940] 2 All ER 401*).)

However, in *Welsh Development Agency v Export Finance Co Ltd [1992] BCC 270*, the court adopted a fundamentally different approach for ascertaining the true intention of the parties. In that case, as part of an 'off balance sheet' financing arrangement in the form of a master agreement, a finance house agreed to purchase from time to time goods from the company immediately before the company, as agent of the finance house, sold the goods to overseas buyers. It was provided that the resale by the company would be on behalf of the finance house as an undisclosed principal. The Court of Appeal held that parties were entitled to structure their arrangements in a way which avoided them being construed as a secured loan transaction. Words must be given their natural and ordinary meaning, and, if they clearly established agency arrangements, other provisions inconsistent with those arrangements were immaterial unless they necessarily gave a different meaning to those words.

(iv) *'Pledge' of goods in warehouse*

A transfer by the company of its goods in a warehouse as security may, in England, constitute a registrable charge under the 'bill of sale' analogy (sections 395 and 396 of the Companies Act 1985) and be void, if not registered (and may, in Scotland, be invalid in any case if the transfer is not accompanied by actual or constructive possession of the goods (see *Dublin City Distillery v Doherty [1914] AC 823*; and *Wrightson v McArthur and Hutchisons [1921] 2KB 807*)).

(v) *Contractual set-off*

A contractual right of set-off against the company in respect of a third party's debt, (for example, a 'cross set-off' where a debt due by A to B is to be set off against a debt due by B to C) may constitute a registrable charge over book debts. Any contractual right of bilateral set-off or 'cross set-off' which is greater than that available under Rule 4.90 (see C14.26 below) may also be void as being contrary to the *pari passu* principle of the *British Eagle* case (*British Eagle International Airlines Ltd v Compagnie Nationale Air France [1975] 1 WLR 758*).

(vi) *Escrow account*

Where moneys are paid in advance by a company into an escrow account of a trustee, as the source of payments to a building contractor under the JCT form of contract against future production of interim certificates, the escrow account may not necessarily constitute a charge. This is because in essence, it may be intended to be a mere conduit for payment: *Lovell Construction Ltd v Independent Estates plc (in liquidation), QBD, 25 June 1992.*

(vii) *Assignment of equipment lease rentals*

In *Orion Finance Ltd v Crown Financial Management Ltd (1994, unreported)*, the assignment (to the funder of an equipment lease) of lease rentals receivable by the company from end-users, though expressed to be an absolute assignment, was held to be an unregistered charge.

Time for registration. The time allowed for registration of the charge is 21 days from the date of its creation but the court may on application allow registration out of time. The imminence of liquidation is a relevant factor to be taken into account. Normally, the application will not be granted after the commencement of the winding up, although even in this situation exceptional circumstances may exist justifying an extension of time (*Re R M Arnold & Co Ltd [1984] BCLC 535;* cf. *Re John Bateson & Co Ltd [1985] BCLC 259*). The court may also refuse to grant an extension where the company is in administration which is likely to result in the insolvent liquidation of the company. (*Re Barrow Borough Transport Ltd (1989) 5 BCC 646*). In *Re Braemar Investments Ltd (1988) 4 BCC 366*, the court granted an extension of time although there was a possibility of a liquidation, but granted it on the condition that in the event of liquidation commencing on or before 3 December 1986, an application could be made to it for the discharge of that order. A creditors' voluntary liquidation commenced on 2 December 1986. On an application by the liquidator, Hoffmann J refused to discharge the order.

In *Exeter Trust Ltd v Screenways Ltd [1991] BCC 477*, the county court had granted leave to register a charge out of time, on the sole condition that the registration would be without prejudice to the rights acquired by any person between the date of the creation of the charge and the date of actual registration. However, even though there was no evidence that a liquidation was not imminent, the court omitted the second standard condition ('the L H Charles order') that liberty be reserved to the company to apply to discharge the order within a specified period after a winding up, if it took place on or before a specified date. The charge was registered only a few hours before a voluntary winding-up resolution was passed in respect of the company, and the Registrar of Companies did duly issue a certificate of registration. The liquidators' application challenging the validity of the registration was dismissed by the Court of Appeal on the ground that once issued, the Registrar's certificate was conclusive by virtue of section 401(2)(b) of the Companies Act 1985. The Court of Appeal reiterated the need for courts to include, in orders granting extensions of time, the second condition as well as the first condition referred to above.

Recovery in respect of malpractice

(See C13.1 *et seq.* below.)

Derivative action

C12.11 Where a company is in liquidation, the proper plaintiff in a minority shareholders' (derivative) action against other shareholders and directors (for example alleging that they had diverted the company's assets to their own use) is the liquidator. If he is willing, he can sue in the name of the company subject to proper indemnities as to costs from the aggrieved shareholders. If he is unwilling, the aggrieved shareholders may sue in the name of the company subject to the approval of the court and a satisfactory indemnity in favour of the company (*Fargo Ltd v Godfroy and others [1986] 1 WLR 1134*).

Dealing with specific types of assets

C12.12 The following points may be of assistance in dealing with or realising specific types of assets; but it must be noted that third party property and assets held by the company in trust do not constitute the company's assets distributable among creditors (although the liquidator may be allowed to take his remuneration and expenses attributable to dealing with claims in relation to trust assets out of those assets—see C11.27 above); for some examples of such assets see D7.17–D7.22 PART D: RECEIVERS.

(a) Continuation of business

C12.13 The liquidator has power, subject to requisite sanction in a compulsory winding up (see C11.26 above), to carry on the company's business so far as may be necessary for its beneficial winding up (Sch 4, Part III, para 6). The position as to value added tax arising during trading is similar to that in a receivership—see D8.5 PART D: RECEIVERS.

In the winding up of a Part II insurance company carrying on long-term business, the liquidator is required, unless the court otherwise orders, to carry on the long-term business with a view to its being transferred as a going concern to another insurance company formed for that purpose; and, in doing so, the liquidator may agree to the variation of any contracts of insurance in existence at the time of the winding-up order but must not effect any new contracts of insurance. He must apply to the court for the appointment of a special manager (see C11.29 above) where the interests of the creditors in respect of liabilities attributable to the long-term business so require. The liquidator or the special manager may apply to the court for the appointment of an independent actuary to investigate the business and report on the desirability or otherwise of the business being continued and on any reduction of contracts that may be necessary for its successful continuation (section 56 of the Insurance Companies Act 1982) (see also C9.12 above as to the duties of the Policyholders' Protection Board). In carrying on the business the liquidator has power to do all such things as may be necessary but the Secretary of State may require him not to make investments of a specified class or description or to realise, within a specified period, investments of a specified class or description. The liquidator may accept premiums after the due date and, having regard to the general practice of insurers, compensate a policyholder under a policy which has lapsed for non-payment of premium by issuing a free paid-up policy for reduced benefits or otherwise (see the Insurance Companies

(Winding up) Rules 1985, as amended, and the Insurance Companies (Winding up) (Scotland) Rules 1986.)

(See also C12.14 below as to the relevance of the Financial Services Act 1986.)

(*b*) *Sale of business and assets*

C12.14 In dealing with or disposing of the business or assets of the company, the liquidator must (depending on the type of business or assets) bear in mind the provisions of the Financial Services Act 1986 which, subject to various exceptions and exemptions (including an exemption in favour of a trustee in bankruptcy and liquidator of a partnership referred to in section 45(2) thereof), contains restrictions against the carrying on of 'investment business' by any person who is not an 'authorised person'. Any authorisation held by the company does not automatically lapse upon its liquidation and so long as the liquidator in the name of the company does no more than what the directors could lawfully have done in its name, and observes the provisions relating to conduct of business, no difficulties may arise; but the position may not always be so simple.

In appropriate circumstances, the liquidator may find it beneficial to 'hive-down' the business and assets as a going concern so as to sell the shares in the 'hive-down' company sale (see D9.4 *et seq.* PART D: RECEIVERS). See also Schedule 4, paragraph 6. Where it is necessary for the company's name to be changed as a condition of the purchase of its business by another party, the liquidator in a voluntary winding up convenes a meeting of its members for the purpose (section 165(4)(c)). (See, however, section 216 discussed in C9.1 above.)

(*c*) *Cash*

C12.15

(1) Cash in hand or at bank may be subject to third party rights in the nature of a trust or tracing remedy. For some examples, see D7.22 PART D: RECEIVERS.

(2) In England and Wales, the liquidator must observe the provisions of the Insolvency Regulations 1994 (SI 1994 No 2507), which with effect from 24 October 1994, replaced the Insolvency Regulations 1986 (SI 1986 No 1994 as amended) with respect to the payment of moneys into and out of the Insolvency Services Account kept by the Secretary of State with the Bank of England.

In a compulsory winding up, all moneys from time to time received by the liquidator in the course of carrying out his functions must be paid without any deduction into that account. The remittance must be made once every 14 days, or forthwith if £5,000 or more has been received.

He can, on application to the Department of Trade and Industry, obtain release of money required in respect of all necessary disbursements made, and expenses properly incurred, by him in the course of the administration to the date of his vacation of office out of any money standing to the credit of the company concerned. Where the liquidator carries on the business of the company, he may obtain authorisation from the Secretary of State to open a local bank account and to make payment into and out of such account subject to a limit.

All moneys distributable among creditors by way of dividend or among contributories by way of return of capital must be paid by way of 'payment instruments' prepared by the Department.

Where the cash balance standing to the credit of the company in the account is in excess of the amount which, in the liquidator's opinion, is required for the immediate purposes of the liquidation and should be invested, the Secretary of State may, at his request, invest it in government securities. Further, under the Insolvency Regulations 1986, wherever the amount in the account exceeded £2,000 and the liquidator gave notice to the Secretary of State that the excess was not required for the immediate purposes of the winding up, the company was entitled to interest on the excess at the rate of 3 per cent per annum from the date of the notice. With effect from 24 October 1994, interest on the excess over £2,000 will be automatically allowed at the rate of 3½ per cent per annum until the liquidator advises the Secretary of State otherwise: Insolvency Regulations 1994 (SI 1994 No 2507).

It should be noted that fees at substantial percentages of the sums deposited into the account are payable to the Secretary of State in a compulsory winding up (see the Insolvency Fees Order 1986 (SI 1986 No 2030, as amended by SI 1988 No 95), the Insolvency Fees (Amendment) Order 1992 (SI 1992 No 34), the latter effective from 14 January 1992 and making certain reductions, and the Insolvency Fees (Amendment) Order 1994 (SI 1994 No 2541), effective from 24 October 1994). This levy has been the subject of severe criticisms by insolvency practitioners (see, for example, 'Insolvency Services Account' by John Willcock, *Businesses and Assets,* Issue 153, 24 November 1989).

In a voluntary winding up, the liquidator must, within 14 days of the expiration of six months from the date of his appointment and of every subsequent period of six months until he vacates office, pay into the account the balance of funds in his hands or under his control, but excluding such part as he considers necessary for the immediate purposes. Where he requires to make payments out of the money standing to the credit of the company in that account, whether by way of distribution or in respect of the expenses of the winding-up proceedings, he may obtain a release thereof on application to the Secretary of State. The provisions relating to local bank accounts, investment and allowance of interest in a compulsory winding up apply to a voluntary winding up save that (i) any money invested or deposited at interest by the liquidator is deemed to be money under his control and must, if necessary, be realised and paid into the account for the purpose of complying with the requirement as to payment into that account, but so that for this purpose he can, with the Secretary of

State's permission, have prior recourse to any funds invested by the Secretary of State in government securities on behalf of the company and (ii) where money invested in securities is required wholly or partly for the immediate purposes of the liquidation, the Secretary of State may realise the securities wholly or in part and pay the proceeds into the Insolvency Services Account to be dealt with in the normal way. (See also sections 403 to 409.)

(d) Book debts, stocks, chattels and fixtures

C12.16 Book debts and stocks may or may not be subject to valid third party rights in favour of factoring companies or 'Romalpa' suppliers (see D7.17 *et seq.* PART D: RECEIVERS). Sales of products to the public may involve defective product liability (as to which any existing insurance arrangements need to be reviewed) and plant, equipment, fixtures, motor vehicles, etc. may be subject to third party rights under hire purchase, leasing or rental agreements.

(e) Moneys and assets in the hands of agents, pension trustees and others

C12.17 See, for example:

(1)   *Vehicle & General Insurance Co Ltd v Elmbridge Insurances [1973] 1 Lloyd's Rep 325* (premiums received by insurance brokers on behalf of the company);

(2)   *Rolls Razor Ltd v Cox [1967] 2 WLR 241* (money received by and goods held by salesman—and extent of set-off claimable by him);

(3)   *Davis v Richards & Wallington Industries Ltd [1990] 1 WLR 1511; Mettoy Pension Trustees Ltd v Evans [1990] 1 WLR 1587* (surplus in the hands of the trustees of the company's contributory pension scheme, where no provision is made for the destination of the surplus or where the surplus can only be distributed at the discretion of the company, such discretion being a fiduciary discretion to be exercised in good faith so as to give effect to the intention of the scheme, and not a right to make gifts); and

(4)   *Brown v Cork [1985] BCLC 363 (CA)* (share of surplus remaining after the claim of the holder of a cross-guarantee and cross-debenture is satisfied in full—see D10.4 PART D: RECEIVERS).

(f) Freehold and leasehold property

C12.18 Where forfeiture of a lease is threatened, action should be considered to obtain relief under section 146(2) or (10) of the Law of Property Act 1925 (in which 'bankruptcy' includes liquidation—see section 205(1) of that Act).

A recent instance where relief against forfeiture was granted was where the liquidator had no funds but had contracted to assign the lease to the guarantor under the lease who had paid the premium (*Re Brompton Securities Ltd (No 2) (1988) 4 BCC 436*).

An unequivocal acceptance of rent by the landlord after, and in respect of the period after, he has notice of the ground entitling him to forfeit the lease may constitute a waiver of that entitlement. Where the ground is the liquidation of the tenant company, the fact that the winding-up petition or order is advertised in the *London Gazette* pursuant to sections 42 and 711 of the Companies Act 1985 (formerly section 9 of the European Communities Act 1972) does not constitute constructive notice to all or to the landlord: *Official Custodian for Charities v Parway Estates Developments Ltd [1985] 1 Ch 151*, in which the Court of Appeal held that on its true construction section 9 of the European Communities Act 1972 was primarily intended for the protection of persons dealing with a company rather than for the protection of the company and, accordingly, while a company could not rely on the specified events in the absence of publication, section 9(4) of that Act did not entitle a company to rely on publication of a specified event as constructive notice to all. In that case the tenant company in liquidation failed to obtain a relief against forfeiture because the landlord had commenced proceedings, in which he claimed forfeiture and the tenant company counterclaimed relief against forfeiture, more than the period of one year (mentioned in section 146 of the Law of Property Act 1925) after the tenant company had gone into liquidation and because the leasehold interest had not been sold within a year of liquidation. In those circumstances relief under section 146 of the Law of Property Act 1925 (see particularly subsections (2) and (10) thereof) could not be claimed. The Court of Appeal went on to state that where the legislature enacted particular legislation in a particular area effect had to be given to it so that any wider equitable jurisdiction was thereby ousted. Thus section 146, by subsection (10), precluded the tenant company from obtaining relief.

The mere entering into and continuation of negotiations does not, in itself, constitute a waiver if it cannot reasonably be understood to be such by any objective observer (*Re National Jazz Centre Ltd [1988] 38 EG 142*).

Where appropriate, disclaimer of the lease should be considered (see C12.6 above).

If a lease is assigned by the liquidator, the company will continue to be liable (concurrently with the assignee) to the landlord on any future breaches of covenant, unless the landlord expressly releases the company from such liability. In the absence of such release, the landlord can prove for the difference (if any) between the value of the lease with, and its value without, the benefit of the covenant by the company as original or interim lessee (*Re House Property and Investment Co [1954] Ch 576*), presumably after allowing for the value of any covenant which the landlord obtains from a new surety as a condition of his consent to the assignment. A solvent company will not be permitted to distribute its assets amongst its shareholders without regard to the landlord's right to future rent (*Lord Elphinstone v Monkland Co (1886) 11 App Cas 332*). However, such a power will be exercised sparingly. Further, if the liquidator takes or remains in possession of a leasehold property for the purposes of the better realisation of the assets, the landlord will be entitled to payment of the rent in full as part of the winding-up expenses properly incurred by the liquidator. Where the liquidator has continued to occupy or retain the company's leasehold premises, the rent payable to the landlord during the period of such occupation or retention would be a 'necessary disbursement' within the meaning of Rule 4.218(1) and (m): *Re Linda Marie Ltd (1988) 4 BCC 463*. The landlord may also distrain for rent for any period after the liquidator has made his decision to use the premises (*ABC Coupler & Engineering Co Ltd (No 3) [1970] 1 All ER 650*). Moreover, the liquidator becomes responsible for the repairs and performance of all the obligations under the lease (see *Re Downer Enterprises [1974] 1 WLR 1460*). The liquidator may also become liable in similar circumstances in respect of other outgoings on property (see, for example, *Re National Arms and Ammunition Co (1885) 28 ChD 474, 478; Re Lundy Granite Co (1871) LR 6 Ch App 462, 466; Re Oak Pits Colliery Co (1882) 21 Ch D 322, 330; Re Brown, Bayley & Dixon (1881) 17 ChD 649* (mortgage interest where mortgagee had power to distrain); *Re Lancashire Cotton Spinning Co (1887) 35 ChD 656; Re Higginshaw Mills & Spinning Co [1896] 2 Ch 544*; contrast *Re Kentish Homes Ltd [1993] BCC 212* where, a receiver appointed by a mortgagee having taken over possession of the company's property to the exclusion of the liquidator, the liquidator was held not liable to discharge community charge (now replaced by council tax) in respect of a post-liquidation period as an expense of the winding up).

(g) *Building contracts*

C12.19 Some standard forms of building contract contain provisions as to termination in the event of the liquidation of the builder and as to the valuation of works, calculation of damages, set-off and the right of the employer to use the builder's plant and machinery on the site (subject to any third party rights) following such termination. There may also be special provisions imposing a trust in favour of nominated sub-contractors in respect of any money attributable to the work done by them and included in the amount paid or payable to the builder and giving a right to the employer to pay any such money direct to the nominated sub-contractors. (See *Re Tout and Finch [1954] 1 WLR 178: quaere*, whether that case is still good in the light of the *pari passu* principle of *British Eagle* (see C12.10 (v) above and C15.4 below).) If the contract is outstanding, a disclaimer may be appropriate (see C12.6 above).

Some standard forms also require that the retention moneys, which the employer of the contract is entitled to retain from the amounts of the interim payments due to the contractor, are to be held by the employer in a fiduciary capacity as a trustee for the contractor. However, where the employer has failed to set aside such retentions and hold them *in specie*, no trust property arises and the contractor's only remedy is to rank as an unsecured non-preferential creditor in the liquidation. (See for example, *Mac-Jordan Construction Ltd v Brookmount Erostin Ltd [1992] BCLC 350*.)

(h) Unpaid share capital and contributories' liabilities

C12.20 A call made before commencement and remaining unpaid is a debt due to the company and can be recovered as such by the liquidator (see also C12.1 above). In relation to any amount remaining unpaid on issued shares which is not subject to an outstanding call, and in the case of a company limited by guarantee or an unlimited company, calls may be made in the winding up on the contributories up to the maximum amount of or (as the case may be) in accordance with their respective liabilities. This involves three stages: settlement of a list of contributories, making of calls, and (if necessary) adjusting the rights of the contributories among themselves.

(For the meaning of 'contributories' and more detailed provisions see sections 74 to 83. See also C5.30 and C12.1 above.) In the case of an Agricultural Marketing Board (see C5.8, C5.12 and C5.24 above), every person who, at any time during the relevant period, was a registered producer is liable to contribute to the payment of debts and liabilities of the Board and of the costs and expenses of the winding up as provided by the 'scheme' (Schedule 2 to the Agricultural Marketing Act 1958).

In a compulsory winding up, as soon as possible after the making of the winding-up order the court is required to settle a list of contributories (with power to rectify the register of members) unless it appears to it that it will not be necessary to make calls on, or adjust the rights of, contributories. The list must distinguish between persons who are contributories in their own right and those who are representatives of, or liable for the debts of, others (section 148). This duty is delegated to the liquidator as an officer and subject to the control of the court, but he can rectify the register only with the court's approval (see section 160). Rules 4.195 to 4.201 contain detailed procedure. The list is, in simple cases, made out in two Parts: Part A for the present members and Part B for persons who have ceased to be members during the year before the commencement of the winding up and certain other categories of past members.

Section 150 empowers the court, at any time after the making of a winding-up order, and either before or after it has ascertained the sufficiency of assets, to make calls on all or any of the contributories for the time being settled on the list of contributories, to the extent of their liability, for payment of any money which the court considers necessary to satisfy the debts and liabilities, and the expenses of the winding up, and for the adjustment of the rights of the contributories among themselves. In making a call, the court takes into consideration the possibility that some of the contributories may partly or wholly fail to pay it. The section further empowers the court to make an order for the payment of any calls made. These powers have been delegated to the liquidator in a compulsory winding up (as an officer and subject to the control of the court) pursuant to section 160 but he must not make any call without either the special leave of the court or the sanction of the liquidation committee (section 160(2)). As to procedure, see Rules 4.202 to 4.205 and Forms 4.56 to 4.59. Payment of the amount due from any contributory may be enforced by an order of the court (sections 149, 151, 152 and 158 and, as to Scotland, section 161; see also Rule 4.205(2) and Form 4.59). The court may also, at any time either before or after making a winding-up order, on proof of probable cause for believing that a contributory is about to quit the United Kingdom or otherwise to abscond or to remove or conceal any of his property for the purposes of avoiding payment of calls, cause the contributory to be arrested and his books and papers and movable personal property to be seized (section 158). As to Scotland, see sections 161 and 162. A liquidator in a compulsory or voluntary winding up may, with appropriate sanction (see C11.26 above), compromise calls and liabilities to calls (Sch 4, Part I, para 3(a); sections 165 and 167).

As stated above, 'contributory' includes certain categories of past members in relation to any amount remaining unpaid on the shares held by them at the relevant time (see *Webb v Whiffin (1872) LR 5 HL 711; Morris's case (1871) LR 7 Ch App 200; Re City of London Insurance Co Ltd [1932] 1 Ch 226*). However they will not be required to contribute:

(i) unless the existing members are unable to satisfy the contributions required (section 74(2)(c)—see also *Helbert v Banner, Re Barned's Bank (1871) LR 5 HL 28, 40 LJ Ch 410*; but a call to the past members will not be indefinitely postponed and may be made if there is an improbability of sufficient assets being obtained within a reasonable time from the existing members or other sources: *Re Contract Corpn (1866) 2 Ch App 95*); or

(ii) in respect of any debt or liability of the company contracted after they ceased to be members or, in the case of directors or managers with unlimited liability, after they ceased to hold office (sections 74(2)(b) and 75(2)(b)); or

(iii) after the approval of a scheme of arrangement providing for partial payment of creditors and releasing present members from a portion of their liability; or

(iv) if they have ceased to be members for one year or more before the commencement of the winding up (section 74(2)(a); or

(v) in the case of a company limited by shares, an amount exceeding the amount (if any) unpaid on the shares in respect of which they are liable as present or past members (section 74(2)(d).

Any excessive contribution which the contributories make will be returned to them (*Re City of London Insurance Co [1932] 1 Ch 226*). If, before the call or the distribution of the amount of the call, any of the debts or liabilities on which the call was based are released or extinguished, or satisfied or reduced by contributions recovered from present members, the liability of past members in respect of the call is *pro tanto* discharged (*Re Blakely Ordnance Co, Brett's Case (1873) 8 Ch App 800; Re Greening & Co, Marsh's Case (1871) LR 13 Eq 388; 41 LJ Ch 111; Herbert v Banner* (above)) subject to their liability for the costs of the winding up attributable to the call.

The liabilities of past members of a later date are not to be exhausted before calls are made on past members of earlier date (*Morris's case* (above)). Their liabilities under section 74(2)(a) and (b) are concurrent.

After the calls have been made, the court may have to adjust the rights of the contributories among themselves pursuant to section 154 so as to ensure that the loss of capital is borne by them in proportion to the nominal capital respectively held by them (unless the articles otherwise provide: *Ex p Maude (1870) LR 6 Ch App 51; Re Driffield Gas Light Co [1898] 1 Ch 451*). This would be necessary where shares are unequally paid up. If necessary, another call to equalise the position must, unless the articles otherwise provide, be made (*Ex p Maude*, above; see also *Re Hull & County Bank, Burgess's Case (1880) 15 Ch D 507*). This particular power does not appear to have been delegated to a liquidator in a compulsory winding up.

Formerly, a member could not bring a claim in damages against the company (e.g. for misrepresentation) in respect of his acquisition (by subscription) of shares in the company unless he also rescinded the contract. (*Houldsworth v City of Glasgow Bank (1880) 5 App Cas 317*). Possibly it was too late to rescind the contract after the winding up (*Re Hull & County Bank, Burgess's Case (1880) 15 Ch D 507*). This rule was in effect abolished by CA 1985, s 111A, inserted by CA 1989.

In a voluntary winding up the court's powers of settling a list of contributories (which list is *prima facie* evidence of the liability of the persons named in it to be contributories) and of making calls are exercisable by the liquidator. He is also required to adjust the rights of contributories among themselves (section 165(4)(a)(b), (5)).

All books and papers of the company and of the liquidator are, as between the contributories, *prima facie* evidence of all matters purporting to be recorded in them (section 191).

(i) Investment business assets

C12.21 In the case of the winding up of an investment business, the liquidator may find that its assets have been transferred to a trustee pursuant to section 67 of the Financial Services Act 1986. The liquidator may have to consider the interaction between that provision and the provisions of the Insolvency Act 1986. It is submitted that the provision is not intended to affect priorities in a winding up or other insolvency situation. See, however, PART F: SPECIAL PROVISIONS FOR FINANCIAL MARKETS.

(j) Insurance policies

C12.22 An interesting question arises where a company is insured against liability which it has incurred to a third party but has not discharged before going into insolvent liquidation. The third party will have a provable claim in the liquidation on which it may receive a small dividend. In such a situation, is the insurer liable to the company for the full gross amount of the claim or only an amount equal to the estimated amount of dividend which the third party is likely to receive? A similar question may arise in relation to any other form of indemnity against liability to a third party which the company holds from another party. In *Re a Company (No 0013734 of 1991) [1992] 2 Lloyd's Rep 415*, a clause in a reinsurance contract provided that the reinsurer should pay to the company (the reinsured) the excess of ultimate net loss 'paid' by the company to its assured. The company went into insolvent liquidation before it had made payment to the assured. It was held that the clause, properly construed in the context of the reinsurance contract as a whole, made the reinsurer liable to the company for the whole of the excess amount for which the company was liable and which the company would have been required to pay if it had not become insolvent.

In this respect, the court followed the decision of Hirst J in the Commercial Court on a preliminary issue in *Home and Overseas Insurance Co Ltd v Mentor Insurance Co (UK) Ltd [1989] 1 Lloyd's Rep 473* where he had said

'I consider it both unjust and discordant with commercial good sense that, by reason of the accident of a reinsured becoming insolvent, the reinsurer (who has accepted premiums) should go scot-free from liability under the reinsurance policy in respect of claims for which the reinsurers would unquestionably have been liable had the reinsured remained solvent. It is of no concern to the reinsurers that any claims paid will be distributed among the general body of creditors rather than paid pound for pound to the underlying assureds; and in any event those assureds, as members of the general body of creditors, will at least receive the appropriate dividend.'

Hirst J cited *Re Eddystone & Marine Insurance Co, ex parte Western Insurance Co [1892] 2 Ch 423* where, in a judgment (involving a 'pay as may be paid' clause in a reinsurance policy), subsequently approved by the Court of Appeal in *Re Law Guarantee Trust and Accident Society Ltd [1914] 2 Ch 677*, Stirling J had stated as follows:

'The words "pay as may be paid therein" do not stand in strict grammatical connection with those which immediately precede; but the effect of them is to impose an obligation as to payment on the reinsurers. The contention on behalf of the [reinsurers] comes to this— that those words make payment by the reinsured a condition precedent to payment by the reinsurer. Now, a main object of reinsurance is to relieve the reinsured from a portion of the risk previously undertaken by him; and the result of giving effect to the. . . . contention would be that, before the reinsured obtains the benefit of his reinsurance, he must have himself have paid on the original insurance, even though bankruptcy might be the result. I think that this could not be intended, and that such a construction ought not to be put on the language of the policy unless it is clearly called for. In my opinion the words do not clearly require to be so construed. They would be satisfied if they were held to amount to this—that the payment to be made on the reinsurance policy is to be regulated by that to be made on the original policy of insurance.'

(Contrast *The Fanti* [*1987*] *2 Lloyd's Rep 299* and *The Padre Island* [*1987*] *2 Lloyd's Rep 529* where there were express provisions in the contracts covering the position on liquidation.)

The following points on the general question should be noted:

(1)   The answer in any particular case turns on the interpretation of the relevant contractual document.

(2)   The interpretation may be particularly favourable to the insolvent company where it is the reinsured under a contract of reinsurance because of the presumption that, by paying the reinsurance premium, it wishes to be relieved of its liability under the original policy.

(3)   This may not necessarily apply to non-insurance contracts of indemnity where clearer language may be necessary to establish the company's entitlement to more than it may have to pay out by way of dividend.

(4)   The concept of a notional payment or discharge of a company's liability on liquidation (see C9.10 above) did not feature in the above cases; but, again, whether the obligation of the party giving the indemnity arises when the company itself becomes liable to the third party or when it makes payments to the third party, and whether the payment should be actual or can be notional (by virtue of its liquidation), are questions to be determined by reference to the language and nature of the contract.

(5)   Where the cover which the company has in respect of its liability to third parties is a policy of *insurance*, as distinct from a policy of *reinsurance*, the above questions may not arise because the third party may have a statutory right of subrogation to the rights under the policy of the company, by virtue of the Third Party (Rights against Insurers) Act 1930 (see C14.24(vi) below).

Chapter 13: Malpractice

Fraudulent trading

C13.1   Fraudulent trading is both a criminal offence (Companies Act 1985, s 458) and carries civil financial liabilities without limit (Insolvency Act 1986, s 213). Section 213 enables the court in any form of winding up to declare, on the application of the liquidator, that any persons who were knowingly party to carrying on the business of a company, with intent to defraud creditors (which expression includes potential creditors: *R v Seillon* [1982] *Crim LR 676*) of the company or creditors of any other persons or for any fraudulent purpose, are to be liable to make contributions (if any) to the company's assets as the court thinks proper.

The leading case is *Re William C Leitch Bros* [1932] *2 Ch 71*. The respondent sold his business to the company in consideration of shares and a debenture over all the assets, present and future, and had been appointed managing director. At a time when the company was making losses he continued to order goods which became subject to the charge under his debenture. He was held liable. Maugham J said 'If a company continues to carry on business and to incur debts at a time when there is to the *knowledge* of the directors no reasonable prospect of the creditor *ever* receiving payment of those debts, it is in general a proper inference that the company is carrying on business with intent to defraud'. This statement was approved and explained by Buckley J in an unreported judgment—*Re White & Osmond (Parkstone) Ltd* (*30 June 1960*)—where on the facts the directors were held not liable because they had genuinely believed that matters would improve. It is submitted that the word 'ever' may no longer reflect present judicial thinking.

In *R v Grantham* [1984] *BCLC 270 (CA)*, it was held that an intent to defraud might be inferred if the person concerned obtained credit when he knew that there was no good reason for thinking that funds would be available to pay the debt when it became due *or shortly afterwards.*

The use of the word 'knowingly' implies that if a person concerned had a reasonable expectation that things would turn out all right—for example, that financial support would be forthcoming—he would not be liable unless he continued to be concerned in carrying on the business after that expectation was disappointed. However, in an Isle of Man case (*Re Peake and Hall* [1985] *PCC 87*) it was held that a 'reckless indifference' was sufficient to make a director liable.

It must be shown that there was active or positive participation by the person concerned in the carrying on of the business. The secretary or financial adviser of a company is not so concerned merely because he fails to draw the insolvent state of the company to the attention of the directors (see *Re Maidstone Building Provisions Ltd* [1971] *3 All ER 363*).

Whether a person who merely advances money to enable a company's business to be carried on in the circumstances mentioned is a party to the 'carrying on' of the business is undecided. It is suggested that a mere provider of finance would not be caught by the section, unless he actively participated in the decision making. Where a bank has nominated directors of, and has been providing finance for, the company, it would seem that any fraudulent participation by those directors cannot be vicariously imputed to the bank, as the directors have independent functions (statutory or otherwise). Where a company has continued trading and incurred liability in reliance on its parent company's letter of financial support which the parent had no intention of honouring, the parent is not a party to fraudulent trading (even if the parent company had acted fraudulently) if the company's directors had no intent to defraud. On the other hand, a person is liable if he is knowingly party to a fraudulent act by the company though not involved in carrying on the company's business (*Re Augustus Barnett & Son Ltd* [*1986*] *BCLC 170*).

Intent to defraud creditors, or some other fraudulent purpose, must be proved and the onus is upon those seeking to prove it. The section, as read with section 458 of the Companies Act 1985 (criminal penalties for fraudulent trading), is a punitive one and 'intent to defraud' has its criminal law meaning. In this connection, section 8(1) of the Criminal Justice Act 1967 should be noted. It provides that a court or jury is not bound in law to infer that the accused intended or foresaw a result of his actions by reason only of its being a natural and probable consequence of his actions; but must decide whether he did intend or foresee that result by reference to all the evidence, drawing such inferences from that evidence as appear proper in the circumstances. However, unlike on a criminal charge of fraudulent trading, the liability of the defendant in a civil claim for fraudulent trading does not have to be established beyond reasonable doubt. In general, the standard of proof in a civil case of the commission of an offence is the civil standard, namely, on a balance of probabilities (*Hornal v Neuberger Products Ltd* [*1956*] *3 All ER 970 (CA)*). There must be evidence to justify a finding of actual dishonesty; 'chasing of the rainbow' cannot necessarily be described as an intent to defraud (*Re Patrick and Lyon Ltd* [*1933*] *Ch 786*). It was held in *Re Sarflax Ltd* [*1979*] *1 All ER 529* that a mere intent to prefer one creditor to another, where the debtor company knew or had grounds to suspect that it would have insufficient assets to pay all creditors in full, could not constitute 'fraudulent' trading.

Carrying on business with the intent of defrauding customers of the business, rather than the (existing) creditors, is sufficient to establish fraudulent trading. In *R v Kemp* [*1988*] *BCLC 217*, on a criminal charge of fraudulent trading under the predecessors of the sections mentioned above, the Court of Appeal held that if a person carried on business with the intent of defrauding customers of the business, he acted in contravention of those sections, as the mischief aimed at by those sections was fraudulent trading and not fraudulent trading *just* in so far as it affected creditors.

The section refers to carrying on 'any business', and not 'any trade', and a person was carrying on business until he had performed all the obligations imposed upon him by the fact of trade (*Re Sarflax Ltd*, above).

A single transaction may constitute fraudulent trading: see *Re Gerald Cooper Chemicals Ltd [1978] 2 WLR 866*, where it was also suggested that a creditor is a party to the carrying on of business with intent to defraud creditors if he accepts money which he knows has been procured by carrying on a business with such intent for the very purpose of making the payment. A company's obtaining, maintaining and/or renewing its Air Travel Organisation's licences from the Civil Aviation Authority constituted 'carrying on any business of the company' within the sections mentioned above (*R v Philippou* (1989) 5 BCC 665, where the accused were sole shareholders and directors of a group of three travel companies all of which went into liquidation with deficiencies, and before the liquidation they had bought a block of flats in Spain with loans from the bank account of one of the companies on 16 occasions).

Recovery under the section is not limited to debts incurred as a result of the fraud. The court may make various orders, including an order charging the person's liability against any securities held by him or on his behalf against the company (section 215).

In *Re L Todd (Swanscombe) Ltd [1990] BCC 125*, the liquidator's allegations in support of a claim for fraudulent trading included book-keeping irregularities, forgeries of cheques, a conviction for the evasion of VAT, failure to provide for PAYE and other employee deductions and misappropriation of cash. The liquidator also alleged that the company had been insolvent from 1983 until August 1985 when the company went into a creditor's voluntary liquidation. Harman J found that actual dishonesty had been proved against the director concerned and that the director had been guilty of real moral blame in having defrauded the VAT authorities and failed to account for PAYE and other employee deductions. Harman J had three choices in determining the amount which the director should be ordered to pay to the liquidator: (i) an amount equal to the amount of the debts incurred whilst the company was insolvent; (ii) the amount of the company's deficiency plus interest thereon from the date of liquidation; or (iii) the VAT liabilities which the company incurred whilst trading fraudulently plus interest thereon. Amount (i) was deemed inappropriate because it had not been proved that the director had intended to defraud all the creditors whose claims made up the amount but, more particularly, because the costs and delays of any enquiry by the registrar to ascertain the amount would be considerable. Amount (iii) was deemed inappropriate because it exceeded the amount which the liquidator was claiming. Amount (ii) was held to be the right amount in the circumstances.

In *Re a Company (No 001418 of 1988)* [1991] BCLC 197, the company went into creditors' voluntary liquidation on 6 June 1986. It had a deficiency as regards creditors of £212,681. The unsecured creditors included the Inland Revenue for PAYE and national insurance contributions and

Customs & Excise for VAT. On the liquidator's action against the chairman, managing director and majority shareholder of the company for fraudulent trading under section 630 of the Companies Act 1985 (now replaced by IA 1986, s 213), the court held on the facts that fraudulent trading had been established. A person was knowingly party to the business of the company having been carried on with intent to defraud creditors if

(*a*)   at the time when debts were incurred by the company, he had no good reason for thinking that funds would be available to pay those debts when they became due or shortly afterwards, and

(*b*)   there was dishonesty involving real moral blame according to current notions of fair trading.

A person intended to defraud a *trade* supplier if he deceived or intended to deceive the supplier that he would be paid at the time stipulated or shortly thereafter. A person intended to deceive an *involuntary creditor* (such as the revenue authorities) if he continued to incur liabilities to that creditor when he did not honestly believe that the liabilities would be discharged when they became due or shortly afterwards. As to the amount of award against him, a declaration under section 630 should specify responsibility for a definite sum and could include a *punitive* as well as a *compensatory* element, the latter being limited to the amount of the debts of the creditors proved to have been defrauded (*Re William C Leitch Bros* (above) was applied). On the facts, a punitive element of £25,000 was required in addition to compensation of £131,420. It was further held that where the application under section 630 was made by the *liquidator*, the sum for which a person was declared liable ought to be dealt with as part of the general assets in the liquidation.

It should be noted that under section 630, a creditor also had the right to apply to the court for a declaration. Under section 213 of the Insolvency Act 1986, which replaced section 630, only the liquidator can make the application. Under section 630, there were circumstances where, in the case of an application by a *creditor*, a sum recovered could be retained by the creditor for his own benefit by way of an exception to the general rule that any sum recovered usually forms part of the general assets available to the liquidator. For example, in *Re Cyona Distributors Ltd [1967] Ch 889* a creditor (the Commissioners of Customs and Excise), who had taken out a summons to make a director financially liable for fraudulent trading and had been paid by the director the amount due to the creditor before the trial, was held entitled to retain the amount of the award.

It is not clear whether any sum recovered which forms part of the general assets in the liquidation is available to the holder of a general charge over the company's present and future assets as part of his security. Where the sum recovered represents a *compensatory* award by reference to fraud committed against another creditor, it would clearly be unfair to give its benefit to the chargeholder. As to any *punitive* element of the award, the unsecured creditors generally still have a better equity than the chargeholder has, as without the fraud they would have stood to receive a better dividend in the liquidation. Of course, to the extent that the chargeholder's security is insufficient to discharge the debt due to him in full, he would rank as an unsecured creditor and thus share the benefit of the award, compensatory or punitive, *pari passu* with the other creditors. It may be that *Re Yagerphone Ltd* and *Ross v Taylor*, decided in the context of preferences and other *dicta* on the same point (see C10.4 above), will apply here by analogy.

In *Re Esal (Commodities) Ltd [1993] BCLC 872*, it was held that any recovery made under the predecessor of section 213 for fraudulent trading was for the benefit of the liquidation and not any individual creditor or shareholder. Where the liquidator's claim had received payment from the respondent in full and final settlement under a compromise, which had not been set aside or impugned, it was an abuse of the process of the court for an individual creditor, who knew of the settlement and took no proceedings to be excluded from the compromise, to proceed against the respondent for a further recovery.

Wrongful trading

C13.2   This is a new form of civil liability, introduced by the Insolvency Act 1985 and now incorporated in sections 214 and 215 of the Insolvency Act 1986. It is without prejudice to the provisions relating to fraudulent trading (see C13.1 above). Its object is to cover cases where the persons concerned have failed to exercise sufficient diligence in monitoring the company's affairs and taking corrective action when insolvency loomed, but would previously have escaped liability for fraudulent trading (because of the absence of actual knowledge or fraudulent intent or bad faith or because no new liabilities were incurred) or for negligence (because a sufficiently high standard of care was not expected of them— see C13.3 below).

Sections 214 and 215 apply to directors (and, by virtue of section 214(7), shadow directors—see (B) below) of a company which has gone into insolvent liquidation, that is, a winding-up resolution has been passed or a winding-up order has been made (section 247) at a time when its assets are insufficient for the payment of its debts and other liabilities and the expenses of the winding up (section 214(6)).

Wrongful trading is established if some time (after 28 April 1986) before the company went into insolvent liquidation, the director or shadow director at that time knew or ought to have concluded that there was no reasonable prospect that the company would avoid going into insolvent liquidation, unless the court is satisfied that thereafter he took every step with a view to minimising the potential loss to the company's creditors as (assuming that he knew that there was no such reasonable prospect) he ought to have taken.

(A)   *Standard of care required*

For the purposes of section 214, the facts which the person concerned (say A) ought to know or ascertain, the conclusions which he ought to reach, and the steps which he ought to take, are those which would be known or ascertained, or reached or taken by a reasonably diligent person (say B) having both:

(*a*) the general knowledge, skill and experience that may reasonably be expected of a person (say C) carrying out the same functions as are carried out by A in relation to the company; and

(*b*) the general knowledge, skill and experience which A has (section 214(4)).

This dual test appears to mean that A in conducting himself has to reach the standard in (*a*) or (*b*) above, *whichever is the higher*.

Thus, a higher standard of care appears to have been imposed than that expected of an ordinary person under the law of negligence. Directors and shadow directors are effectively put into a *quasi-professional* or skilled class. In the absence of any satisfactory point of reference, such as the code of conduct of a professional body or the normal working practices of a skilled vocation, uncertainties could arise until general principles are evolved by judicial decisions. It is debatable whether any 'expert evidence' would be admissible. The position could vary considerably from one case to another according to the types of functions actually performed by the person concerned and it may be difficult to treat any witness as an expert in this regard until a general standard of practice for those particular types of functions has evolved. (See also C13.3 below.)

In this connection the following statement made in Parliament on behalf of the Government during the debate on this provision may be of interest:

'The courts are accustomed to putting themselves in the shoes of decision makers at the time, faced with all the difficulties, the need for quick decisions and decisions which have to be made in the heat of the moment, whether the defendant is a company director, a surgeon or a drug company. . . . In particular all the authorities recognise that the company director has a proper role in the exercise of commercial judgment into which the court will not inquire . . . The clause as drafted should not hold any fear for the company doctors and people whose purpose in the company is quite clearly to try to assist it.' (*Hansard, 18 July 1985, Columns 568, 569*).

Hoffmann J had an opportunity to comment on section 214(4) in *Norman v Theodore Goddard [1991] BCLC 1028*. A quantity surveyor (Q) was a director of an English property company, all the issued shares in which were held by a Jersey trust administered by a lawyer (B) specialising in tax and trust work. On the advice and certain assurances of B, Q (who had no knowledge of company law or offshore financial matters) allowed the funds of the company to be invested offshore in another company without making detailed enquiries. Unknown to Q, that other company was controlled by B who subsequently stole funds from that other company. In a claim brought against Q by B's firm under the Civil Liability (Contribution) Act 1976, the question was whether Q had been in breach of his duty as director of the first company for having failed to make detailed enquiries and to take proper care. In finding him not liable, Hoffmann J held that a director was entitled to trust persons in positions of responsibility until there was reason to distrust them. He stated:

'As a director. . ., [he] owed a duty to the company to act in good faith and with reasonable care. There is no suggestion that. . . [he] acted otherwise than in good faith. The question is whether in all the circumstances he took reasonable care. The extent of the duty of care owed by a director has been discussed in a number of cases but I need mention only two principles. . . First, a director performing active duties on behalf of the company need not exhibit a greater degree of skill than may reasonably be expected from a person undertaking those duties. A director who undertakes the management of the company's properties is expected to have reasonable skill in property management, but not in offshore tax avoidance. It may be that in considering what a director ought reasonably to have known or inferred, one should also take into account the knowledge, skill and experience which he actually had in addition to that which a person carrying out his functions should be expected to have. Miss Gloster QC [appearing for B's former firm] submitted that the test was accurately stated in section 214(4) . . . I am willing to assume that the test is as [she] submits. There is, however, a second relevant principle and that is, as Romer J said in *Re City Equitable Fire Insurance Co Ltd [1925] 1 Ch 407* at *429*, "Business cannot be carried on upon principles of distrust" and men in responsible positions may be trusted until there is reason to distrust them.'

See also *Re Austinsuite Furniture Ltd [1992] BCLC 1047*, where the failure of a director, with responsibility for manufacturing and production, to press for detailed information concerning the company's financial position, though not beyond criticism, was held not sufficient to warrant his disqualification as a director.

In *Re Produce Marketing Consortium Ltd (No 2) [1989] BCLC 520*, Knox J held that the expertise expected of a director is much less extensive in a small company in a modest way of business with simple accounting procedures and equipment than in a large company with sophisticated procedures; but certain minimum obligations are assumed to be attained, for example, compliance with the requirements of the companies legislation. Knox J went on to state that the legislation required accounting records to be kept which disclosed with reasonable accuracy, at any time, the financial position of the company. It might not be enough for a director to plead ignorance of accounting facts or figures if, with reasonable diligence and an appropriate level of skill, he ought to have ascertained them. The knowledge of disastrous financial results of the company for the end of the particular year, which were in fact late and not then available, was imputed to the directors. Accordingly, he held the directors liable for depletion of the company's assets as from the time they should have known those results.

In *Euro RSCG SA v Conran, The Times, 2 November 1992*, the question was whether a consultant had breached a restrictive covenant of his engagement (to procure that no company over which he had control competed with the plaintiff) by becoming a non-executive director of a competing company. Vinelott J held that he was in breach because each director of a company, whether executive or non-executive, was responsible for the proper management of its affairs. It appears that this statement requires modification in the context of section 214 and the *Dorchester Finance* case (see C13.3 below) in that the degrees of responsibility between individual directors may vary according to their respective functions.

The *Dorchester Finance* case referred to in C13.3 below seems to indicate that even on common law negligence the courts have edged towards expecting a higher standard of duty on the part of directors. That case and the directors' disqualification cases (although the tests there are somewhat different) appear to reflect current judicial thinking on the standard of conduct for directors. *Re Douglas Construction Services Ltd [1988] BCLC 397* suggests that a director who has acted in reliance on professional advice may, in certain circumstances, escape disqualification. According to *Re McNulty's Interchange Ltd (1988) 4 BCC 533*, a director may also escape disqualification if the commercial mismanagement on his part was based on advice obtained in good faith but not if there was culpable conduct on his part.

In this connection, *Re Welfab Engineers Ltd [1990] BCC 600*, decided by Hoffmann J on a misfeasance claim against the directors, may be relevant in determining the extent of the duties of directors of an insolvent company. He suggested that in judging the propriety of the actions of the directors, they should be viewed in the context of the alternatives of receivership or liquidation. It is debatable whether the dicta would be applicable in a claim for wrongful trading, inasmuch as the standard of duty imposed on them under the provisions relating to it is higher and the provisions appear to have been framed with a view to expressly imposing a duty on them to consider the alternatives of, *inter alia*, receivership, administration or liquidation.

The dilemma which directors of a company in financial difficulties often face may be a difficult one. It seems that they are expected to be neither unduly rash nor unduly cowardly. Causing the company to cease to trade, or putting it into administration or liquidation, or calling in an administrative receiver prematurely, can be as damaging to the interests of the creditors as causing the company to carry on trading against all odds. They must act responsibly, resisting, on the one hand, their natural tendency to be over-optimistic or to refuse to accept defeat and, on the other hand, the temptation to succumb to despair without considering the options available. A careful evaluation of the situation must be carried out with the assistance of independent professional advisers. If this is done, the court would be reluctant to substitute, with the benefit of hindsight, its own commercial judgment for that of the directors, unless it considers that no reasonable director could have concluded that the action taken was in the interest of the company (see, for example, *Heron International Ltd v Lord Grade [1983] BCLC 244*; *R v Sinclair [1958] 1 WLR 1246*).

One of the questions which a director may have to consider in practice is what the realistic cash-flow and trading prospects are and whether in the light of such prospects the requisite lines of credit and/or, where applicable, the financial support of the parent company is likely to continue. It may be that the lines of credit are in the form of bank overdraft facilities terminable and repayable on demand and that the indication of support from the parent company is in the form of a comfort letter which is not legally enforceable (see, for example, in a different context, *Kleinwort Benson Ltd v Malaysia Mining Corp Bhd [1989] 1 WLR 379 (CA)*; *Ayres and Moore [1989] LMCLQ 281*; but see the Australian case of *Banque Brussels Lambert SA v Australian National Industries Ltd, International Business Lawyer, July/August 1990, page 289* where a 'comfort letter' issued during the course of business without an indication that it was intended to be otherwise than legally binding was held to be enforceable as a contract). If the directors responsibly take a view that, notwithstanding that there is no binding obligation on the part of the bank or the parent company, its support is likely to continue given the prospects as assessed by them in good faith and with due diligence, they could, conceivably, escape liability.

In *Re DKG Contractors Ltd [1990] BCC 903*, the directors of a company were held liable under section 214 for the debts which the company incurred after they ought to have known of the inevitability of the company's insolvent liquidation. That award was to be concurrent with the awards which the court made against both directors for misfeasance under section 212 (see C13.4 below), and against one of them under section 239 (preferences—see C10.4 above).

In *Re Purpoint Ltd [1991] BCLC 491 (further hearing, 18 July 1990, unreported)*, the company was a 'phoenix' company, having bought the main asset from its predecessor which later went into liquidation. The new company started trading in January 1986. The purchase of the asset was financed by a bank overdraft, guaranteed by a director, and the working capital provided by the production manager of that company from funds borrowed by him on the security of a remortgage over his house. Later in 1986, a new asset was obtained on hire purchase terms. Only one annual general meeting had been held, no accounts were ever produced, and the business records maintained were inadequate. No cash-flow forecasts and no calculation of the company's net worth were ever made. The director ought to have known that by the end of 1986 liabilities exceeded assets by a large margin, but trading continued. On 6 April 1987 the company acquired a motor vehicle on hire-purchase terms at a cost of which more than one half was paid in cash. On 28 May 1987, the company's accountants advised the director that the company was insolvent and that he might well become personally liable for the debts. The company was forced to cease trading in November 1987. The liquidator applied for orders against the director under both section 214 and section 212 (see C13.4 below).

Vinelott J held that the director should have known that liquidation was unavoidable on 28 May 1987, when he was professionally advised to that effect. All the evidence pointed to an insolvent position at a much earlier date, although this could not readily be ascertained from the previous records. His lordship said that to conclude that the company was doomed to failure from its inception, as it never had any assets other than those acquired by way of matching loans, would impose too high a test. In the absence of proper records, accounts and projections, it was impossible to ascertain the precise extent of the company's net liabilities at the end of 1986, or the extent to which the liabilities were increased by the continuance of the trading after the end of 1986. Vinelott J decided that the only solution was to quantify the award by aggregating all debts, including Crown debts, incurred after 1 January 1987. Interest at the rate of 15% per annum was ordered to be paid on the sum awarded from the date of liquidation, 25 May 1988, and at 16% from the date of the judgment. Vinelott J considered whether the misfeasance award arising out of events subsequent to 1 January 1987 might not result in an element of double-counting, but decided that as there was clear evidence that a substantial amount in respect of Crown debts was already outstanding at that date, this was not an issue, provided only that the director did not end up in a position where his total liability was more than sufficient to discharge the arm's length debts in full (that is, excluding the loan provided by the production engineer and the director's subrogated rights as guarantor of the bank account).

(See also *Re Fairmont Tours (Yorkshire) Ltd, Huddersfield County Court, 15 February 1989, Insolvency Law and Practice 1989 page 184* (accounts for two successive years showing loss; no cashflow, sales or profit forecasts; directors who continued to accept deposits for holidays ordered to pay an amount equal to deficiency as regards creditors).)

(B) *Application to 'shadow directors'*

It will be noted that the wrongful trading provisions also apply to a 'shadow director'—a shadow director is a person in accordance with whose directions or instructions the directors of the company are *accustomed to act* but not where the directors act on advice given to them by that person in a professional capacity (section 251). 'Directors' mean the board of directors *as a whole* (see, by way of analogy, *Re Instrumentation Electrical Services (1988) 4 BCC 301*; *Re Business Properties Ltd (1988) 4 BCC 684*; *Re Equiticorp International Ltd (1989) 5 BCC 599*). The expression 'director' includes a person occupying the position of a director, by whatever name called (section 741 of the Companies Act 1985). In *Re a Company (No 005009 of 1987), ex parte Copp [1989] BCLC 13*, the court on a preliminary issue refused to strike out a claim for wrongful trading against a bank as an alleged shadow director, pending full trial in subsequent proceedings. In the event the allegation was not pursued.

It therefore remains an open question as to whether there are any circumstances in which a lending bank which is not represented on the board of directors of the company, or whose representative directors exercise their functions independently, as they are required to do under the general law, may (perhaps unwittingly) render itself liable as a shadow director, for example, where either expressly or impliedly it requires, or leads the directors to believe that it requires, the directors to implement recommendations contained in an independent accountant's report commissioned by or at the behest of the bank. Perhaps the bank can derive some measure of protection if it makes it clear that it expects the directors only to implement the recommendations if, after independent legal advice, they form the view that to do so is consistent with their duties under the law. In *Kuwait Asia Bank EC v National Mutual Life Nominees Ltd [1990] BCC 567*, decided under the law of New Zealand, the Privy Council held that the bank was not a shadow director of another company on whose board the bank had nominated only two out of five directors because it could not be said that the directors were accustomed to act on the direction or instruction of the bank. It was also argued against the bank that it was vicariously liable for acts and omissions of its appointees and that, as a substantial shareholder in the holding company which controlled the company, the bank owed the plaintiff creditor and the depositors a duty of care to ensure that the company's business was not conducted negligently, recklessly or in such a manner as to materially disadvantage their interests. However, the Privy Council held that:

(*a*)   in the absence of fraud or bad faith, a shareholder or any other person who controlled the appointment of a director, owed no duty to a company's creditors to ensure that the director discharged his duties with diligence and competence;

(*b*)   the directors appointed by the bank became the agents of the company and, if they had committed any breach of the duty they owed to the plaintiff, they were acting in an individual capacity and, as directors, were bound to ignore the interests and wishes of their employer;

(*c*)   accordingly, the bank, against which no impropriety was alleged, could not be liable for the acts of those directors either as employer or as principal (see also *Scottish Co-operative Wholesale Society Ltd v Meyer [1959] AC 324*).

It was further held that, although it was in the interests of the bank as a substantial shareholder in the company's parent, to give the directors it had appointed good advice and to see that they performed their duties to the company conscientiously and competently, the bank had no duty to do so.

Where a body corporate is a *de jure, de facto* or shadow director of a company, it does not follow that that body corporate's own directors are *de facto* or shadow directors of the company. To establish that a person is a *de facto* director, it must be shown that he undertakes functions in relation to the company which can properly be discharged only by a director: *Re Hydrodan (Corby) Ltd [1994] BCC 161*. In that case, Millett J also explained the distinction between a *de facto* director and a shadow director. He said that *de facto* directorship and shadow directorship were not overlapping expressions and were perhaps always mutually exclusive. It was wrong to allege that a person was a *de facto* or shadow director without distinguishing between them. A *de facto* director claimed and purported to be a director and was held out as such by the company, although he was not validly appointed. It must be shown that such a person undertook functions in relation to the company which could properly be discharged only by a director. Merely being concerned in management or undertaking tasks which managers below board level could undertake was not enough. A shadow director, on the other hand, did not claim or purport to act as a director. He lurked in the shadows, sheltering behind others who, he claimed, were the only directors, to the exclusion of himself. He was not held out as such. Thus it was necessary to allege and prove

(1) who were the directors of the company (whether *de facto* or *de jure*);

(2) that the defendant was the person or one of the persons who directed those directors how to act in relation to the company;

(3) that those directors acted in accordance with such directions; and

(4) that they were accustomed so to act.

The expression 'accustomed to act' appears to suggest a consistent course of conduct over a significant period but, in the absence of judicial authorities, this is by no means certain.

In a talk which Mr Justice Millett gave in November 1990 at a seminar organised by Wilde Sapte, he is reported to have expressed the following views:

(1) A body corporate, such as a bank, is capable *as a matter of law* of conducting itself in a way that makes it a shadow director. In *Re Bulawayo Market and Offices Co Ltd* [*1907*] *2 Ch 458*, it was established that a body corporate could be appointed a director, and there is nothing in the statutory definition of 'shadow director' to exclude a body corporate. It was questionable whether in practice it would be the bank itself rather than the bank manager who would become the shadow director, but the point is probably academic; the bank would be vicariously liable for the acts of its agent and employees.

(2) The expression 'the directors' in the definition obviously means the board, not just one or two members of the board. The definition is not meant to cover the situation, not uncommon in family companies, where a young nephew always votes as his uncle wants him to. The situation envisaged by the provisions is one in which the board itself had abandoned its responsibility for making its own decisions and become accustomed instead to follow the directions of a third party.

(3) It is difficult to believe that it is possible for a person to be a shadow director unless he has a conscious intention to control the decisions of the board. There are two paradigm cases:

 (i) the bankrupt who installs his wife as sole director; and

(ii)   the fraudster who makes use of nominee companies as his vehicles to operate them by nominee directors (probably offshore) who simply carry out his instructions. The relationship is that of a puppet-master and his puppets.

(4)   Where a corporate customer appears to be in financial difficulty, the bank is likely to (*a*) send in an investigating team, (*b*) demand a reduction in the overdraft, (*c*) demand security or further security, (*d*) call for information, valuations of fixed assets, accounts, cashflow forecasts, etc., (*e*) request the customer's proposals for the reduction of the overdraft, including the submission of a business plan, schedule of proposed sales etc. and/or (*f*) advise on the desirability of strengthening management, seeking fresh capital, etc. (The author of this chapter would add: (*g*) impose a stricter financial discipline (including, conceivably, an arrangement for onward payments to be vetted by the bank's representative).) In doing all these things, the bank may well expect its demands to be met, first because are likely to be commercially sensible, and secondly because the customer has no option if it wants its facility continued. But that is not enough to constitute the bank a shadow director. The fact is that a bank has no business to be managing its customer's affairs, but it is entitled to attach conditions to the continuation of its support. So long as it does nothing that a bank does not normally do in telling its customers what it requires if it is to continue banking facilities, and leaves the decision to the customer whether it will comply or not, it could not be held to have become a shadow director.

(5)   In the end, the question is not asked in a vacuum. The issue is not whether the bank has become a shadow director, but whether it should be held liable because it failed to cause the company to cease trading or go into liquidation. Normally, only directors can cause the company to do either. A shadow director can also do so, because he controls the decisions of the board. Unless the relationship between the bank and its customer is such that the decision to stop trading or go into liquidation is one that the bank, and only the bank, can take, then the bank cannot be liable. And if that is the relationship, then the bank has stepped well outside the normal banker-customer relationship.

In *Re Tasbian Ltd (No 3)*, the Secretary of State issued disqualification proceedings against a 'company doctor' who had been brought in as a consultant to the company at the behest of a financier of the company's business, it being alleged that he was a *de facto* director or a shadow director. On a preliminary issue, Vinelott J, on appeal from the registrar ([*1991*] *BCC 435*), upheld the registrar's decision to allow the case to proceed to full trial. The alleged actions of the 'company doctor' included: negotiating an informal moratorium with trade creditors; monitoring the company's trading on a monthly or fortnightly basis; representing the company in its negotiations with the Department of Trade and Industry and the Inland Revenue; procuring an alteration of the company's bank mandate so as to require his counter-signature; introducing the company to a new factoring company; negotiating in connection with the possible change of the company's bankers; and proposing and implementing the adoption of group structure. The registrar had felt that the degree and nature of the consultant's alleged involvement in the affairs of the company appeared to amount to far more than a 'hopeless case'. Vinelott J held that none of the allegations taken in isolation would found the inference that the consultant was a *de facto* or shadow director but that in this type of case the factors had to be taken together. The dividing line between the position of a watchdog or adviser imposed by an outside investor and a *de facto* or shadow director was difficult to draw, and there was a serious question whether at some stage the consultant passed over it. The Court of Appeal (*[1992] BCC 358*) agreed with the registrar and Vinelott J that the evidence disclosed an arguable case that the consultant was a *de facto* or shadow director.

(C)   *Concluding points*

Section 214 relating to wrongful trading is compensatory rather than penal, and the proper measure of contribution from the directors concerned must be the amount by which the company's assets could be seen to have been depleted by the directors' conduct (*Re Produce Marketing Consortium Ltd (No 2) [1989] BCLC 520*).

The purpose of an order under section 214 is to recoup the loss to the company. The court has no jurisdiction to direct payment to a particular class of creditors (*Re Purpoint Ltd*—see (A) above).

The relieving provision referred to in C13.5 below does not apply to wrongful trading, as stated there.

Negligence or breach of statutory duty

C13.3   An action can be brought in the name of the company against its directors and other officers for any damages which the company may have suffered as a result of their past negligence in relation to the company's affairs. An example is to be found in *Dorchester Finance Company Ltd v Stebbing & another (1977) [1989] BCLC 498* (where directors who signed blank cheques were held liable in negligence and refused relief under what is now section 727—as to which, see C13.5 below) from which the following points emerge.

(1)   A director is liable in negligence if in the performance of his duties he fails to show the degree of care and skill which may reasonably be expected from a person of his knowledge and experience.

(2)   Whereas an honest error of judgment is not sufficient to make him liable, it is not necessary to establish 'gross negligence'.

(3)   Executive and non-executive directors have the same duties under the companies legislation. Even the non-executive directors must show the necessary skill and care in the performance of their duties. They may be liable, for example, if they sign blank cheques and allow the executive director to do as he pleases with them.

Section 349(4) of the Companies Act 1985 provides, in effect, that if a director signs on behalf of a company, *inter alia*, a cheque in which the company's name is not mentioned as required by that section, he is liable, in addition to a fine, to pay personally the amount of the cheque. The liability under that section arises regardless of any moral blame attaching to the director (*Rafsanjan Pistachio Producers Co-operative v Reiss [1990] BCC 730*; *Blum v OCP Repartition SA [1988] BCLC 170*). It should be noted that the liability may also arise if the company's name is not stated in full or is misspelt.

In *Thomas Saunders Partnership v M A Harvey, The Times, 10 May 1989*, a misrepresentation made by a director on the notepaper of a limited company was held to be misrepresentation of not only the company but also that of the director, such that he could be held personally liable under the principles of *Hedley Byrne and Co Ltd v Heller and Partners [1964] AC 465*.

Where the acts of directors are outside their powers, but not *ultra vires* the company, and have been validly approved or adopted by the shareholders, formally or informally, no action for negligence can lie against them even though those acts result in a loss to the company. In such a case, the company is bound by those acts and the liquidator is in no better position than the company (*per* Lawton and Dillon LJJ (May LJ dissenting) in *Multinational Gas and Petrochemical Co v Multinational Gas and Petrochemical Services Ltd [1983] BCLC 461*).

Misfeasance

C13.4 Section 212 of the Act provides a remedy against directors and others who have been delinquent. It creates no new liability, but provides a speedier procedure for enforcing certain rights which might have been enforced by an ordinary action before winding up (*Re Canadian Land Reclaiming and Colonising Co (1880) 17 Ch D 660*).

The section allows the Official Receiver, a liquidator, a creditor, or a contributory standing to benefit, to recover money or damages (or to obtain repayment or restoration of, or an account for, any money or property, with interest) for the benefit of the company in liquidation from certain classes of person who have misapplied or retained or become liable or accountable for any money or property of the company or have been guilty of misfeasance or breach of fiduciary *or other* duty in relation to the company. The classes of persons to which the section applies are those who (i) are or have been officers of the company; (ii) are or have been concerned, or have taken part, in the promotion, formation or management of the company; or (iii) have acted as liquidators, administrators or administrative receivers of the company. In the case of a person falling within (iii) above, except an administrative receiver, the section includes any misfeasance or breach of fiduciary or other duty in connection with the carrying out of his functions as liquidator or administrator; but no application may be made against him, after he has had his release, except with leave of the court. (As to (ii) above, it may be noted here that in the *Ayala Holdings* case referred to in C10.10 above, the creditor also sought to make the bank liable in misfeasance in respect of the letter of instruction. It was held that although a creditor may apply for an order under section 212, there was nothing in the creditor's points of claim to show that the bank was concerned in the management of the company. In dealing with the settlement moneys, it had acted in its own interests as a secured creditor or pursuant to the letter of instruction.)

Section 212(3) sets out the types of orders which the court may make against the person concerned. The court may examine the conduct of such persons and compel them to repay or restore the money or the property with interest, or to contribute money to the assets of the company by way of compensation.

The term 'misfeasance' does not cover every misconduct by an officer of the company for which he might be sued apart from the section. There must be a breach of duty to, and in relation to, the company the direct consequence of which is a misapplication or loss of the company's assets for which the director could have been so sued. Non-feasance is not sufficient unless it amounts to a breach of trust resulting in loss of assets. Further, it is necessary to show pecuniary loss. An ordinary claim for damages based exclusively on common law negligence has been held under the old legislation not to be within the section (*Re B Johnson & Co (Builders) Ltd [1955] Ch 634*; and see also *Re Eric Ltd [1928] Ch 861* and *Selangor United Rubber Estates Ltd v Cradock [1967] 1 WLR 1168*). *Quaere*, whether the presence in section 212 of the expression 'other duty' (see above) has now altered the position; see, for example, *Re D'Jan of London Ltd [1993] BCC 646* (below).

Subject to the above points, section 212 covers a variety of wrongs, including improper payment of dividends, application of moneys for *ultra vires* purposes, application of moneys contrary to the Companies Act, and unauthorised loans or payment of unauthorised remuneration to directors. See also the *Aveling Barford* case cited in C12.9 above. (As to unauthorised loans or remuneration to directors, see *Re Reliance Wholesale (Toys) Ltd, Patterson v Mills, LSG, 18 July 1979*.)

In the *West Mercia* case referred to in C10.4 above, the transaction which constituted a preference by the company was held also to constitute misfeasance on the part of the director, it being his duty to protect the interests of the creditors; see also *Re Washington Diamond Mining Co [1893] 3 Ch 95*, and especially the judgment of Kay LJ at *115*.

In *Walker v Wimborne (1976), 137 CLR 1 (Aus HC)*, a decision of the High Court of Australia, the directors of a company authorised payments to other companies in the same group and to a former director for past services. Shortly afterwards, the company went into liquidation, the High Court held that a number of the payments in question were made in total disregard of the company and its creditors and, therefore, the directors were liable for a breach of trust. For other Commonwealth cases see *Kinsela v Russell Kinsela Pty Ltd (1986) 4 NSWLR 722 (CA)*, and the New Zealand Court of Appeal decision in *Nicholson v Permakraft (NZ) Ltd [1985] 1 NZLR 242 (CA)*.

In *Kinsela* a family-run company, at a time when its financial position was precarious, entered into a lease with a number of the company's directors. The lease was approved by all the shareholders. A short time later, the company was wound up. The court held that the lease was not *ultra vires* but that the court was not precluded from reviewing the propriety of the transaction despite unanimous shareholder approval. Such approval could not validate a transaction to the detriment of the company's creditors. The court went on to say, 'Where a company is insolvent, the interest of the creditors intrude. They become prospectively entitled, through the mechanism of liquidation, to displace the power of the shareholders and the directors to deal with the company's assets. It is in a practical sense their assets. . .'. The court's willingness to review transactions at the behest of the creditors' representative will be in inverse proportion to the financial circumstances of the company.

In the *Nicholson* case the defendant company was restructured with the unanimous consent of the shareholders. The company at that time paid a substantial sum as a dividend. The restructuring and repayment of the dividend were done with the consent of the company's secured creditors. The company became insolvent about two years later. The court agreed that the directors owed a duty to the company's unsecured creditors. Cooke J based his decision on the ground that the concept of limited liability was a privilege and that actions prejudicing the position of creditors constituted an abuse of this privilege. Somers J stated that in the case of an insolvent company, the directors in the management of the company must have regard to the interests of creditors.

In *Re Purpoint Ltd [1991] BCLC 491 (further hearing, 18 July 1990, unreported)* (Vinelott J), (i) the purchase by a director of a car in the name of the company when it was unnecessary for the company's business (but might have been necessary for that director's relationship with another firm) and the company was insolvent, (ii) the withdrawal of cash sums by that director which he failed to account for and (iii) the loss of profits by the company on transactions entered into by him on its behalf with the other firm after his relationship with that firm had been established, were all held to be valid misfeasance claims.

In *Re Welfab Engineers Ltd [1990] BCC 600*, the liquidators' case against the directors in a misfeasance claim was that the directors had acted improperly because they had given priority to the preservation of the business and the jobs of the employees, including theirs, by accepting an offer of £110,000 for the company's business instead of accepting a higher offer of £130,000 which had been made if allowance was made for certain imponderables in the values of the assets. Hoffmann J dismissed the misfeasance summons. He stated that the evidence of the directors showed that they had never really considered the possibility of any deal other than one allowing continuation of the business or a sale as a going concern; neither had they regarded it as their function to act as informal liquidators on a winding up of the business itself. Even if they had undertaken the task of liquidating the business, there was not a great deal of difference between the two offers. There was a question of principle involved: whether the directors should be judged on the footing that it was their duty to have undertaken the task of liquidating the business in the interest of creditors. The liquidators had admitted that if the directors had decided to invite the appointment of a receiver, the chances of the creditors having done any better would have been minimal but they had said that having undertaken the task of realising the assets, they should have done so to the best advantage of creditors. That did not seem to be fair or realistic: the directors were entitled to take the view that if the business could not be saved, its liquidation was not for them. If they had decided to invite a receiver or wind up the company, with all the consequences which that would have involved, they could not possibly have been criticised. Therefore, in judging the propriety of their actions, they should be compared with the alternatives of receivership or liquidation. Hoffmann J went on to state that if he was wrong in refusing to hold the directors liable, he would consider that the directors had acted honestly and reasonably and ought fairly to be excused from liability under section 727 of the Companies Act 1985 (see C13.5 below).

In *Re Derek Randall Enterprises Ltd [1990] BCC 749(CA)*, the company, acting by its voluntary liquidator, claimed from the former managing director of the company an amount which, it claimed, had been received by the managing director as secret commission and paid into his personal account. The managing director had then paid the amount into a special guarantee account with a bank to which he had given a guarantee for the company's indebtedness to the bank. The day before the company went into liquidation, the money was paid from his special guarantee account into the account of the company in reduction of the company's indebtedness to the bank. By a majority, the Court of Appeal held that the managing director's liability to the company for misfeasance had been discharged when the money was paid to the credit of the company's account with the bank. The liquidator, therefore, could not pursue a claim for misfeasance against him.

In *Re DKG Contractors Ltd [1990] BCC 903* where an individual obtained the benefit of a groundswork sub-contract, entered into by a company of which he and his wife were the only directors and shareholders, by invoicing and obtaining payment from the company over £400,000, both of them were held liable in misfeasance in relation to the company (which subsequently went into insolvent liquidation) for that sum.

Reference was made in C13.2(A) above to *Norman v Theodore Goddard* where Hoffmann J held, following *Re City Equitable Fire*, that a director was entitled to trust persons in responsible positions until there was reason to distrust them. This does not in every situation relieve the director of his liability. There may be circumstances where he may be liable to the company in misfeasance for breach of fiduciary duty, regardless of whether he had made proper enquiries.

For example, in *Bishopsgate Investment Management Ltd (in liquidation) v Maxwell [1993] BCC 120*, a director of a company, which was trustee of the assets of pension schemes for employees of companies controlled by his late father, was held liable by the Court of Appeal for having signed

(*a*)   a transfer of publicly quoted shares, forming part of the assets of the trust, for nil consideration to a company which controlled his late father's private interests, and

(*b*)   a further blank transfer of such shares, enabling the shares to be pledged to a financial institution to secure advances for the benefit of the private interests.

Hoffmann LJ (as he had then become) said that the company had not alleged that the director had participated in or even knew of the relevant transactions. Its complaint was that he should, as a director, have taken enough interest to find out what was happening and prevent it. The transfers by the company had not been authorised by the board, and no grounds had been put forward upon which it could honestly have been thought that the transactions were for the benefit of the company as trustee of the pension funds. A company director owed a duty to act *bona fide* in the interests of the company. He had to exercise the power solely for the purpose for which it was conferred. To exercise the power for another purpose was a breach of fiduciary duty. It was for him to demonstrate the propriety of the transaction.

The directors' duty to the company extends to its creditors, particularly where the company is insolvent or potentially insolvent. The House of Lords in *Winkworth v Edward Baron Development Co Ltd [1987] BCLC 193 at 197* stated:

'. . . a company owes a duty to its creditors, present and future. The company is not bound to pay off every debt as soon as it is incurred and the company is not obliged to avoid all ventures which involve an element of risk, but the company owes a duty to its creditors to keep its property inviolate and available for the repayment of its debts. The conscience of the company, as well as its management is confided to its directors. A duty is owed by the directors to the company and to the creditors of the company to ensure that the affairs of the company are properly administered and that its property is not dissipated or exploited for the benefit of the directors themselves to the prejudice of the creditors.'

Directors must be careful not to enter into any undertaking which may place them in conflict with their fiduciary duty to the company. On the other hand, the party receiving the undertaking should bear in mind the possibility that the court might not enforce the obligation in such a situation. In *Rackham v Peek Foods Ltd (1977) [1990] BCLC 895*, as part of a conditional contract for the acquisition by a company of the business of another company, the acquiring company and its merchant banker covenanted with the other company to use their best endeavours to procure the passing of a resolution of the acquiring company's shareholders approving the acquisition. Before the shareholders' meeting, Government measures were announced adversely affecting the position of the business to be acquired. As a result, the directors of the acquiring company felt unable to recommend the resolution to the shareholders. The court held that there was no breach of the undertaking as it did not oblige the directors to give bad advice in breach of their fiduciary duty. See also *John Crowther Group plc v Carpets International plc [1990] BCLC 460* where the above case was cited and a similar qualification was read into the vendor company's undertaking to recommend its shareholders to approve the sale of a subsidiary, where subsequently the vendor company felt unable to implement the undertaking in view of the emergence of a higher bid. In *Fulham Football Club Ltd v Cabra Estates plc [1992] BCC 863*, the Court of Appeal held that it does not follow from the proposition that the directors are under a duty to act *bona fide* in the best interests of the company, that they can never contractually bind themselves to the future exercise of their powers in relation to the company in a particular manner, where the contract as a whole is substantially for the benefit of the company.

In *Re D'Jan of London Ltd [1993] BCC 646*, the liquidator issued a misfeasance summons against a former director of the company alleging that the latter had been in breach of his duty to the company in having negligently completed an insurance proposal form on behalf of the company, with the result that a claim under the insurance policy had been repudiated by the insurance company. He was held liable. Hoffmann LJ (sitting as an additional judge of the Chancery Division) stated that a director did not always have to read the whole of every document which he signed, but the proposal form was an extremely simple document asking a few questions which the director in the present case was the best person to answer. By signing the form, he accepted that he was the person who should take responsibility for its contents. The duty of care owed by a director was accurately stated in section 214(4) (see C13.2(A) above). Both on the objective test and on the subjective test, he did not show reasonable diligence when he signed the form. It was no defence to argue that he and his wife as shareholders would probably have ratified his action if they had known or thought about it before the liquidation removed their power to do so. However, this was a fit case for granting relief under section 727 of the Companies Act 1985 (see C13.5 below). Although for the purposes of the law of negligence, the company was a separate entity to which he owed a duty of care which did not vary according to the number of shares he owned, the economic reality of his 99 per cent shareholding in the company could be taken into account in exercising the court's discretionary power under section 727 to relieve the director from liability. His breach of duty in failing to read the form before he signed it was not gross. It was the kind of thing which could happen to any busy man. At that time the company was solvent, and the only persons whose interests he was foreseeably putting at risk were himself and his wife. He had certainly acted honestly. For the purposes of section 727, he had acted reasonably and ought fairly to be excused for some, though not all, of the liability.

As stated above, a *bona fide* error of judgment is not sufficient to make a person liable. The relieving provision mentioned in C13.5 below may apply.

A company secretary is an 'officer' (*per contra* in the case of fraudulent trading). Auditors may be officers where the company has articles similar to those of Table A. On the other hand, section 27(1) of the Companies Act 1989 recognises that an auditor is not necessarily an officer. An accountant may not be so where he is merely called in to audit the accounts of the company. A subordinate manager may be an 'officer', which includes anyone who exercises supervisory or management control reflecting the general policy of the company or relating to its general administration (*Re a Company [1980] 1 All ER 284*). The company's banker is not an officer; nor *prima facie*, is the company's solicitor, although he may be if he does all the work for a fixed salary.

The failure by a liquidator to pursue 'with due despatch' misfeasance proceedings begun by him is insufficient ground for dismissing the proceedings for lack of prosecution under Ord 28, r 10 of the Rules of the Supreme Court, which applies to proceedings begun by summons or originating summons as well as to an ordinary action. To warrant dismissal, the delay must be 'inordinate and inexcusable' (*Halls v O'Dell [1992] 2 WLR 308 (CA)*).

It is not clear whether any sum recovered for misfeasance forms part of the estate of the liquidation for the benefit of the unsecured creditors generally or, where a general fixed or floating charge over the company's present and future assets is subsisting, part of the security of the holder of that charge. It was held, apparently *obiter*, in *Re Anglo-Austrian Printing and Publishing Union [1895] 2 Ch 891* (see also *Re Asiatic Electric Co Pty Ltd (1970) 92 WN (NSW) 361*) that the proceeds of such recovery would fall into the floating charge, although Vaughan Williams J thought that this was 'an unwholesome state of things' and expressed the hope that the position would be changed by legislation. (Contrast *Re Yagerphone Ltd*, cited at C10.4 above, where it was held that moneys recovered in relation to a preference did not fall within a floating charge.)

No set-off is allowed to a director who is in breach of the section. For fuller discussion of the subject of misfeasance, see *Halsbury's Laws of England* (Fourth edition), Vol 7, pages 692 *et seq*. For an excellent analysis of the subject, see 'Misfeasance proceedings against company directors' by Fidelis Oditah, fellow of Merton College, Travers Smith Braithwaite Lecturer in Corporate Law, University of Oxford, in *(1992) Lloyds Maritime and Commercial Quarterly 207*.

Relieving provision

C13.5   Section 727 of the Companies Act 1985 provides that in any proceedings for 'negligence, default, breach of duty or breach of trust' against, *inter alia*, an officer of the company, the court hearing the case may wholly or partly relieve him from liability on such terms as it thinks fit if he has acted 'honestly and reasonably' and if having regard to all the circumstances of the case, including those connected with his appointment, he ought fairly to be excused. Relief from liability for misfeasance may be available under this section—see the *Welfab* case in C13.4 above.

In the second (bound) edition of Tolley's Company Law, on this subject it was stated: 'It is debatable whether this provision will apply to (2) above (wrongful trading). It probably does involve "breach of duty"; and the person concerned may have acted "honestly". However, it must also be shown that he acted "reasonably", and it would seem that the test of reasonableness will be influenced by the specific test of "reasonably diligent person" enshrined in section 214 especially in the context of wrongful trading. If the person concerned passes the latter test he will not be liable for wrongful trading and there will be no need to apply the relieving provision. If he fails that test it seems unlikely that the ordinary test of reasonableness under the relieving provision will apply to him or that the circumstances will be such that he ought fairly to be excused'. This view has been confirmed, in effect, by *Re Produce Marketing Consortium Ltd (No 2)* [*1989*] *BCLC 520*, where it was held that section 727 does not apply to wrongful trading, as section 214 exhaustively lays down its own peculiar standard of conduct.

For an example of the operation of section 727, see the *D'Jan* case referred to in C13.4 above.

A party wishing to rely on section 727 in any relevant proceedings against him is not obliged to plead the section (*Re Kirby's Coaches Ltd* [*1991*] *BCLC 414*); but he has the burden of satisfying the court that relief should be granted (*Re Stuart* [*1897*] *2 Ch 583*). By virtue of *Singlehurst v Tapscott Steamship Co Ltd* (*1899*) *107 LT Jo 347*, and subject to any order made under RSC Order 38, r 2A (exchange of witness statements), he is not liable in the normal way to give particulars.

It should also be noted that the substituted section 310 of the Companies Act 1985, as introduced by section 137 of the Companies Act 1989 which came into force on 1 April 1990, gives statutory recognition to the practice of a company insuring its directors against any liability for negligence, default, breach of duty or breach of trust. Where a company has purchased such insurance, this fact must be stated in the directors' report. The section only applies to policies effected after it came into force. Insurance policies are available for the protection of the relevant personnel of even a whole group of companies.

In relation to the winding up of an unregistered company, including a partnership, there appears to arise an anomalous situation in that the relieving provisions of the Companies Act 1985 referred to above may not apply. This is because they refer to a 'company' (meaning a registered company) and are not imported into the provisions of the Insolvency Act 1986 relating to the winding up of an unregistered company (as modified, in the case of a partnership, by the Insolvent Partnerships Order 1994 (SI 1994 No 2421)). However, the legal position is far from clear, in view of the different opinions expressed in cases such as *Re Devon and Somerset Farmers Ltd [1993] BCC 410* and *Re International Bulk Commodities Ltd [1992] 3 WLR 238* (see D1.4 PART D: RECEIVERS).

Extra-territorial application

C13.6   As to the extra-territorial application of the malpractice provisions to an overseas company in respect of which section 426 is involved, see *Re Bank of Credit and Commerce SA and another [1993] BCC 787* and see A5.2 PART A: GENERAL.

Liability for contravening 'anti-Phoenix' restrictions

C13.7   See C9.1 above.

Liability to be disqualified

C13.8   See I2.7 PART I: DISQUALIFICATION OF DIRECTORS.

Chapter 14: Conduct of winding up: establishment of liabilities

General aspects as to proofs of debt

Exclusion of late creditors

C14.1 In a compulsory liquidation, the court may on application fix a time or times within which creditors are to prove their claims or be excluded from the benefit of any distribution made before those debts are proved (section 153). It appears that, in exercise of its general powers to give directions to the liquidator in a compulsory liquidation under section 168(3), the court may also, in special circumstances, order that creditors not proving in time are excluded from all future dividends, but see *Re R R Realisations Ltd [1980] 1 All ER 1019* (where the court refused to make an order allowing the liquidators to distribute the assets without regard to late claims; the test was whether in all the circumstances of the case it was just to make the order; the presence or absence of default or delay on the part of the claimants was only a factor in determining what was fair). As to Scotland, see Scottish Rules 4.15 and 4.16. The powers under sections 153 and 168(3) may be invoked in a voluntary liquidation by virtue of section 112.

Notice to prove

C14.2 Before declaring a dividend, the liquidator must give notice of his intention to do so to all creditors whose addresses are known to him and who have not proved their claims (Rule 11.2; see also Rule 4.180(2) as applying to compulsory and creditors' voluntary winding up). The notice must specify the last date for proving (the same date must be applicable to all those creditors) which must be not less than 21 days from the date of the notice. Before declaring a first dividend he must, unless he has previously by public advertisement invited creditors to prove their debts, also give notice of intended dividend by public advertisement (Rule 11.2 (1A)). Any such notice must also state his intention to declare the dividend within four months from the last date for proving and specify whether the dividend will be final or interim (Rule 11.2). 'Creditors', in this context, means those creditors of whom the liquidator is aware or who are identified in the company's statement of affairs (Rule 11.1(2)(b)).

In a members' voluntary liquidation, the liquidator may give notice in such newspapers as he considers most appropriate for drawing the matter to the attention of the company's creditors that he intends to make a distribution. The notice must specify the last date for proving, which must be the same for all creditors and not less than 21 days from that of the notice. Where the distribution to which the notice relates is the only or the final distribution, the notice must state that the liquidator may make the distribution without regard to any debt not already so proved (new Rule 4.182A). Even though this provision is only permissive, the liquidator would be well advised to utilise it; it comes very close to the former Rule 106 of the Companies (Winding up) Rules 1949, intended to catch unknown claimants who could not be otherwise contacted.

The provisions as to notice outlined above should be contrasted with the position under the former Rule 106 mentioned above (which applied to all forms of winding up) under which, in a compulsory winding up, the requirement of notice applied only to those creditors who were mentioned in the statement of affairs but, in a voluntary winding up, it also applied to 'each person who to the knowledge of the liquidator, claims to be a creditor'; and in all cases the notice was also required to be advertised. Under the old Rule 106 'knowledge' was not necessarily confined to actual knowledge. The liquidator was expected to take such steps as were reasonably open to him to ascertain the existence and identity of creditors or possible creditors from any books, records, documents and other information in his possession or control. The documents could include, for example, those relating to (i) a lease previously assigned by the company which still left the company exposed to liability to the landlord as assignor, and (ii) former employees having a possible outstanding claim connected with their previous employment (see *Pulsford v Devenish* [*1903*] *2 Ch 625; Re Armstrong Whitworth Securities Ltd* [*1947*] *Ch 673*).

As to proofs and claims in the winding up of Part II insurance companies carrying on long-term business, see the Insurance Companies (Winding up) Rules 1985 and the Insurance Companies (Winding up) (Scotland) Rules 1986. As to notice to preferential creditors, see Rule 11.12 of the Insolvency Rules 1986 (as amended).

Position of late creditors

C14.3   The liquidator is not obliged to deal with proofs lodged after the last date for proving, but he may do so, if he thinks fit (Rule 11.3(2) and, as to members' voluntary liquidation, Rule 4.182A). A creditor who has not proved his debt before the declaration of any dividend is not entitled to disturb, by reason of the fact that he has not participated in it, the distribution of that dividend or any other dividend previously declared. However, once he proves that debt he is entitled to be paid, out of any money for the time being available for the payment of any further dividend and before such money is applied to the payment of any further dividend, the dividend or dividends which he has failed to receive (Rule 4.182; see also *Re General Rolling Stock Co* (*1872*) *7 Ch App 646; Re Metcalfe, Hicks v May* (*1879*) *13 ChD 236*). This also applies in a members' voluntary liquidation except that (i) 'before the declaration of any dividend' should read 'before the last date for proving or on or after that date increases the claim in his proof', (ii) after 'participated in it' there should be added 'either at all or (as the case may be) to the extent that his increased claim would allow' and (iii) after the words 'out of any money for the time being available for the payment of', there should be substituted 'any further distribution, any distribution or distributions which he has failed to receive' (Rule 4.182A).

See also C14.1 above, C15.4 to C15.9, and C16.1 and C16.2 below.

Final admission/rejection of proofs

C14.4   The liquidator must, within seven days from the last date for proving, deal with every proof not already dealt with by admitting or rejecting it in whole or in part or by making such provision in respect of it as he thinks fit (Rule 11.3); but, as stated above, he is not obliged to deal with proofs lodged after the last date for proving, but may do so, if he thinks fit.

In *The Duke Group Ltd v Arthur Young (Reg)* (*1991*) *9 ACLC 380* (a South Australian case), it was held that the admission by the liquidator of a proof, though conclusive as between him and the claimant (subject to a right of appeal within the time allowed) was not conclusive as against a third party, such as a firm of accountants against whom an action was brought by the company in respect of a report they had prepared prior to a takeover.

Appeal against rejection of proof

C14.5   If the liquidator rejects a proof in whole or in part, he must prepare and forthwith send to the creditor a written statement of his reasons for doing so (Rule 4.82). An appeal lies to the court against the liquidator's decision with respect to a proof (including any decision on the question of priority). An application to reverse or vary the decision must be made to the court by the dissatisfied creditor within 21 days of his receiving the statement of reasons. The appeal is by way of a rehearing *de novo*. The court's function is not confined to deciding whether the liquidator was right in reaching his decision in the light of the evidence before him. The applicant is entitled to put fuller evidence before the court and the court must decide in the light of the evidence before it to what extent (if any) the claim should be admitted (*Re Kentwood Constructions Ltd* *[1960] 2 All ER 655; Re Trepca Mines Ltd [1960] 3 All ER 304*). A contributory or another creditor may also apply for review of the liquidator's decision within 21 days of becoming aware of the decision (Rule 4.83).

Expunging of proof by the court

C14.6   The court may on the liquidator's application or, if he declines to interfere, on the application of a creditor expunge a proof or reduce the amount claimed if improperly admitted (Rule 4.85).

Withdrawal or variation of proof

C14.7   A creditor's claim may at any time, by agreement between himself and the liquidator, be withdrawn or varied as to the amount claimed (Rule 4.84).

If the amount claimed in a creditor's proof is increased after the declaration of an interim dividend, that creditor is entitled to be paid out of any money available for the payment of any further dividend (before such money is applied to payment of the further dividend), any dividend or dividends which he has failed to receive (Rule 11.8(1) and (2)). If, on the other hand, the proof admitted is reduced or expunged after he has received a dividend, he must repay the amount overpaid (Rule 11.8(3)).

VAT bad debt relief

C14.8 A creditor who has accounted to HM Customs and Excise for value added tax in respect of supplies made to the company and proves his claim in respect of such supplies is entitled to VAT bad debt relief in respect of the value added tax element in accordance with and subject to the provisions of section 36 of the Value Added Tax 1994 (as supplemented by the Value Added Tax (Bad Debt Relief) Regulations 1986 (SI 1986 No 335), and the Value Added Tax (Refunds for Bad Debts) Regulations 1991 (SI 1991 No 371)). The proof in the liquidation will be for the value of such supplies excluding the VAT element. Upon granting the relief to the creditor, HM Customs and Excise Commissioners are not subrogated to the *rights* of the creditor against the company in respect of the amount of the value added tax (*Re T H Knitwear (Wholesale) Ltd* [*1987*] *BCLC 86*). (See further PART H: TAXATION.)

Rule against double proof

C14.9 In an insolvent winding up, there cannot be more than one claim (whether from the same claimant or from different claimants) in respect of the same debt (see *Re Hoey* (*1919*) *88 LJ KB 273*). Thus, a surety cannot prove if the principal creditor has already proved (see *Re Moss* [*1905*] *2 KB 307*). A more recent example of double proof occurred in *Barclays Bank v TOSG Trust Fund* (*1983*) *127 SJ 130* (*CA*) where there was a competition between (i) a bank's claim under a counter-indemnity given to it at the outset by the company (a tour operator) in respect of money which, under a bond given by the bank, the bank was required to pay to a company (TOSG) set up to receive and dispense moneys for the benefit of a company's customers (holidaymakers) who were adversely affected by the company's collapse and (ii) an agency, established to administer a statutory fund for compensating customers of collapsed tour operators, to whom the company's customers had, as required by the scheme, assigned their rights against the company on being paid their claims. The Court of Appeal held that the bank had a prior right of proof for considerations of equity; the agency could not be in a better position than the customers. The House of Lords, on appeal ([*1984*] *2 WLR 650 HL*), went even further and held that the question of double proof did not arise where, as in that case, the claims of the competing creditors were mutually exclusive. In their lordships' view, on the true construction of the bonds, the counter-indemnity and TOSG's own memorandum of association, the effect of a payment by TOSG was to extinguish the customers' claims and to vest in the bank a claim under the counter-indemnity for the amount paid by it.

Enquiry into consideration and estoppel

C14.10 The court of insolvency, being a court of equity, is entitled to enquire into the consideration for debts and if no debt exists in equity, to reject a proof even if the debt has been reduced to a judgment debt at law. This also applies where the claim is not *bona fide*, even though it is based on a compromise (see e.g. *Ex p Butterfield (1811) 1 Rose 192; Ex p Prescott (1840) 1 MD BD 199; Re a Debtor [1927] 2 Ch 367; Ex p Banner (1881) 17 ChD 480*). Where in support of his claim the claimant relies on estoppel in respect of representations made by the company before its liquidation, the liquidator is not bound by the estoppel (*Re Exchange Securities & Commodities Ltd [1987] 2 WLR 893*).

Supply of proof forms

C14.11 In a compulsory liquidation, the liquidator or provisional liquidator must send forms of proof of debt (see Form 4.25), in accordance with Rule 4.74, to every creditor who is known to him, or is identified in the company's statement of affairs.

Meaning of 'prove' and 'proof'

C14.12 In a compulsory liquidation, to be eligible for a dividend on his claim and for voting at any meeting of creditors (subject as stated in C11.13 above) a creditor must submit his claim in writing on Form 4.25 (or a substantially similar form).

In a voluntary winding up (of either type) a creditor need not submit his claim in writing unless the liquidator requires him to do so. Where he is so required, the written claim may be in any form.

A creditor who claims (in writing or otherwise, as the case may be) is referred to as 'proving' for his debt; and the documents by which he seeks to establish his claim is his 'proof'.

In a compulsory liquidation, the proof in respect of a debt due to a Minister of the Crown or a Government Department need not be on Form 4.25, provided that there are shown all such particulars of the debt as are required in the form used by other creditors, and as are relevant in the circumstances.

In a voluntary winding up (of either type) the liquidator or the convener or chairman of a meeting of creditors may, if he thinks it necessary for the purpose of clarifying or substantiating the whole or part of the claim made in a creditor's proof, call for details of any matter which would be required to be stated on Form 4.25 in a compulsory winding up, or for the production of such documentary or other evidence as he may require.

In any type of winding up, the liquidator may, if he thinks fit, require a claim of debt to be verified by an affidavit on Form 4.26 or a substantially similar form. The affidavit may be required notwithstanding that a proof of debt has already been lodged. An affidavit would normally be required in the case of a contentious or unusual claim or if the liquidator is minded to reject it in whole or in part.

A creditor himself bears the cost of proving or providing further documents or evidence but the costs incurred by the liquidator in estimating the quantum of a debt not bearing a certain value (see C14.14 below) are payable out of the assets as an expense of the liquidation.

(Rules 4.73 to 4.85; as to Scotland, see Scottish Rules 4.15 and 4.16 and Form 4.7 (Scot).)

Debts which are and which are not provable

C14.13 In any form of winding up, all claims by creditors to debts (for the meaning of which, see below) are provable debts whether they are present or future, certain or contingent, ascertained or sounding only in damages, except the following (Rule 12.3).

(*a*) Any obligation arising under a confiscation order made under section 1 of the Drug Trafficking Offences Act 1986 or section 1 of the Criminal Justice (Scotland) Act 1987.

(*b*) Any particular kind of debt which may not be provable, whether on grounds of public policy or otherwise, for example, debts for an (arguably) illegal or immoral consideration (*Ex p Bolland (1834) 1 M CA 570; Ex p Chavasse (1865) 34 LJ Bcy 17*) or debts tainted with illegality. A claim is tainted with illegality, and unforceable, if the claimant would have needed to plead or prove illegal conduct to establish the claim brought by him, or if the claim was so closely connected with the proceeds of crime as to offend the conscience of the court. For an English claim to be unenforceable as being tainted with *foreign* illegality, the transaction from which the taint is derived has to be unenforceable in England and sufficiently connected with the claim to amount to taint (*Euro-Diam Ltd v Bathurst [1987] 2 WLR 1368*).

(*c*) Revenue claims by a foreign state; see *Government of India v Taylor [1955] AC 491; British Columbia v Gilbertson 597 F 2d 1161 (1979)* (a Canadian case)*; Peter Buchanan Ltd v McVey [1955] AC 520, note (High Court of Ireland); Re Gibbons [1960] Ir Jur Rep 60* (an Irish case)*;* cf. *Ayres v Evans (1981) 39 ALR 129 (Federal Court of Australia) affg (1981) 34 ALR 582; Priestley v Clegg 1985 (3) SA 955* (a South African case).

Further, unless and until all other debts have been paid in full with interest under section 189(2) (see C14.19 below), the following are not provable (Rule 12.3(2A)):

(i) any claim arising by virtue of section 6(3)(a) (not being one also arising by virtue of section 6(3)(b)) of the Financial Services Act 1986: or by virtue of section 61(3)(a) (not being one also arising by virtue of section 61(3)(b)) of that Act; or by virtue of section 49 of the Banking Act 1987;

(ii) any claim which by virtue of the Insolvency Act 1986 or any other enactment is a claim the payment of which in a bankruptcy or a winding up is to be postponed.

(See also C14.9 above.)

Rule 13.12 is also relevant:

(1) 'Debt' means—

    (*a*) any debt or liability to which the company is subject at the date on which it goes into liquidation (that is, passes a winding-up resolution or a winding-up order is made against it); or

    (*b*) any debt or liability to which the company may become subject after that date by reason of any obligation incurred before that date; or

    (*c*) any interest provable as stated in C14.19 below.

(2) In determining whether any liability in tort is a debt provable, the company is deemed to become subject to that liability by reason of an obligation incurred at the time when the cause of action accrued.

(3) It is immaterial whether the debt or liability is present or future, certain or contingent, or whether its amount is fixed or liquidated, or is capable of being ascertained by fixed rules or as a matter of opinion.

(4) 'Liability' means (subject to (3) above) a liability to pay money or money's worth, including any liability under an enactment, any liability for breach of trust, any liability in contract, tort or bailment, and any liability arising out of an obligation to make restitution.

Thus, provable debts are defined in the widest possible terms.

However, a debt or liability must be such as is recoverable or enforceable by action. Accordingly a statute-barred debt or liability is not provable, and the liquidator must not admit it unless, in a solvent winding up, the contributories consent to its admission (*Re Fleetwood & District Electric Light & Power Syndicate [1915] 1 Ch 486; Re Art Reproduction Co Ltd [1952] Ch 89*).

Where, following a scheme of arrangement and subsequent capital restructure of a company, existing and former shareholders are owed money by the company by way of dividends or repayment of capital, they may be treated as creditors subject to the provisions for deferment contained in section 74(2)(f) (see C14.35 below); and unidentified holders of bearer share warrants who have failed to claim their entitlement to shares may be contingent creditors rather than members of the company (even though the shares were treated as issued or, at least, allotted) if the holders have not expressly or impliedly agreed to become members (*Re Compania de Electricidad [1980] 1 Ch 146*). In *Re FMS Financial Management Services (1989) 5 BCC 191*, an administration and voluntary arrangement case, the company had been a securities dealer and had recommended certain shares to its clients. The clients received the share certificates but the shares were worthless. Other clients who did not receive share certificates or the money which they had paid to the company for their purchase were to be treated as creditors under the voluntary arrangement. On an application for directions as to whether the clients who did receive the share certificates should be treated as creditors, the court directed that they should be so treated, as they appeared to have a strong claim against the company for misrepresentation. Further, in any case, it would be unfair to treat them differently from the other clients simply because they were unfortunate enough to be identified as the clients to which particular share certificates related.

Claims are generally ascertained as at the date of the winding-up order or resolution. A notional line is drawn at that date. Liquidation and distribution (and, therefore, the discharge of liabilities) are treated as notionally simultaneous. 'The tree must lie where it falls' (*Humber Ironworks and Shipbuilding Company (1869) LR Ch App 643, 646; Re W W Duncan & Co [1905] 1 Ch 307*; see also *Re Dynamics Corporation of America (No 2) [1976] 1 WLR 762, 763; Re Lines Bros Limited [1981] Com LR 214* (affirmed on appeal [1982] 2 All ER 183); and *Re Kentish Homes Ltd [1993] BCC 212*, where community charge (now replaced by council tax) referable to a post-liquidation period on the property of the company was held to be neither a provable debt in existence at the date of the winding up nor an expense of the liquidation, the liquidator not having been in beneficial occupation of the property for the purposes of the liquidation). There are, however certain possible exceptions to those principles; for example, see C14.14, C14.19 (post-liquidation interest), C14.20 (debts due in future), and C14.26 (re Rule 4.90(3)) below and C12.6 and C12.7 above.

As to Scotland, see Scottish Rules 4.16 and 4.17.

Creditors' claims generally

(1) *Contingent and unquantified claims generally*

C14.14 The liquidator must estimate the value of any debt which, by reason of its being subject to any contingency or for any other reason, does not bear a certain value. He may revise any estimate previously made, if he thinks fit, by reference to any change of circumstances or to information becoming available to him. He must inform the creditor as to his estimate and revision of it. Where the value is estimated by him, or by the court under section 168(3) (application by liquidator for directions) or 168(5) (application by aggrieved person), the amount provable is that of the estimate for the time being (Rule 4.86). A proof based on a contingency can be increased when the contingency happens, resulting in a larger amount of claim (*Re Northern Counties of England Fire Insurance Co Ltd, McFarlane's Claim (1880) 17 Ch D 337*).

Where in any proceedings taken after liquidation, costs have been awarded against a creditor and in favour of the company or the liquidator, the creditor may be deprived by the court of the right to receive a dividend on his claim until he has paid the costs (see, for example, *Re Davies Chemists Ltd [1992] BCC 697*). The equitable principle applies that he who claims the benefit out of a fund must bear the burden of contributing to it (see *Lockley v National Blood Transfusion Service [1992] 1 WLR 492; Re Rhodesia Goldfields Ltd [1910] 1 Ch 239; Selangor United Rubber Estates v Cradock (No 4) [1969] 1 WLR 1773*).

(2) *Negotiable instruments, etc.*

C14.15   Unless the liquidator allows, a proof in respect of money owed on a bill of exchange, promissory note, cheque or other negotiable instrument or security cannot be admitted, unless there is produced the instrument or security itself or a copy of it, certified by the creditor or his authorised representative to be a true copy (Rule 4.87).

(3) *Discounts*

C14.16   There must be deducted from the claim all trade and other discounts which would have been available to the company but for its liquidation, except any discount for immediate, early or cash settlement (Rule 4.89).

(4) *Debt in foreign currency*

C14.17   For the purpose of proving a debt incurred or payable in a currency other than sterling, the amount of the debt must be converted into sterling at the official exchange rate prevailing on the date when the company went into liquidation. 'The official exchange rate' is the middle market rate at the Bank of England, as published for the date in question. In the absence of any such published rate, it is such rate as the court determines (Rule 4.91; as to Scotland, see Scottish Rule 4.17). The position was similar under the previous legislation—see *Re Lines Bros Ltd [1982] 2 All ER 183* and *Re Lines Bros Ltd (No 2) [1984] 2 WLR 905*.

(5) *Payments of a periodical nature*

C14.18   In the case of rent and other payments of a periodical nature, the creditor may prove for any amounts due and unpaid up to the date when the company went into liquidation. Where at that date any payment was accruing due, the creditor may prove for so much as would have fallen due at that date, if it was accruing from day to day (Rule 4.92).

(6) *Interest*

C14.19   Under the previous legislation a claim for unpaid contractual interest in an insolvent liquidation was restricted to five per cent per annum up to the date of the winding up and there were complicated provisions for determining the amount of the outstanding principal on which such interest was to be calculated. This is no longer the case.

Where a debt proved in the liquidation bears interest, that interest is provable as part of the debt except insofar as it is payable in respect of any period after the company went into liquidation, that is, after a winding-up resolution was passed or a winding-up order was made (as distinct from after a petition was presented as was the case under the previous legislation —see *Re Amalgamated Investment and Property Co Ltd [1984] 3 All ER 272*) (section 247). Where no interest has been previously reserved or agreed, interest may be claimed from the 'due date' to the date the company went into liquidation. 'Due date' means (*a*) if the debt is due by virtue of a written instrument, and payable at a certain date, that date, or (*b*) if the debt is due otherwise and a demand for payment of the debt was made in writing by or on behalf of the creditor stating that interest would be payable from the date of the demand to the date of payment, the date of demand.

The rate of interest for the purposes of (*a*) above is the rate specified in section 17 of the Judgments Act 1838 (see also section 44 of the Administration of Justice Act 1970) on the date when the company went into liquidation (currently 15 per cent per annum where the liquidation commenced prior to 1 April 1993 or 8 per cent per annum where it commenced after that date—see the Judgment Debts (Rate of Interest) Order 1993 (SI 1993 No 564)), and for the purposes of (*b*) is that specified in the notice, not exceeding the rate under the Judgments Act mentioned above (Rule 4.93).

Any surplus remaining after the payment of the debts proved (or, in Scotland, accepted) in a winding up must, before being applied for any other purpose, be applied in paying post-liquidation interest on those debts (including so much of each such debt as represents interest on the remainder) in respect of the periods during which they have been outstanding since the company went into liquidation. All such interest ranks equally (whether or not the underlying debts rank equally). The rate of interest is that specified in section 17 of the Judgments Act 1838 referred to above (or, in Scotland, that specified in the Scottish Rules) at the date of liquidation or the rate applicable to the debt concerned, whichever is the higher (section 189). Where the debt is expressed to be in foreign currency, interest is calculated on the amount of that debt converted into sterling at the rate prevailing at the date of liquidation (see the cases cited in C14.17 above).

(7) *Debts payable at a future time*

C14.20 If payment for a debt proved was not due on the date the company went into liquidation, the dividend payable to the creditor may be liable to be reduced to reflect a discount of five per cent per annum for any early payment (or declaration of dividend) (Rules 4.94 and 11.13).

(8) *Lessor's claims*

C14.21 Subject to what is said in C14.18 above, a lessor can only prove for rent as it accrues (*Re New Oriental Bank Corporation (No 2) [1895] 1 Ch 753*); contrast Rules 12.3 and 13.12, cited in C14.13 above. Where the lease has been assigned either before or after liquidation, the landlord can prove for the difference between the value of the lease with and without the benefit of the covenants on the part of the company (*Re House Property and Investment Co [1954] Ch 576*). The lessor is entitled to prove for damages for any breach of covenant which may have occurred. A company in liquidation, as an assignor of a lease, is entitled to recover from the assignee the full amount due to the landlord, although it would have to pay only a dividend to the landlord whose claim has triggered the recovery (*Re Perkins [1898] 2 Ch 105*).

Where L has granted a registered lease to T and there have been successive assignments of the lease, say, from T (now insolvent) to T1 (who is solvent), from T1 to T2 (the company, now insolvent), from T2 to T3 (who is solvent), and from T3 to T4 (now insolvent), L can recover any rent not paid by T4 from T1 who can in turn prove for that rent against T2 (see section 24(1)(b) of the Land Registration Act 1925); but T1 cannot compel T2 or its liquidator, receiver or administrator to assign T2's rights against T3 to T1 or to sue T3 for recovery of the rent. There is no legal nexus between T1 and T3 (*Re Mirror Group (Holdings) Ltd [1992] BCC 972*).

(9) *Damages for breach of contract*

C14.22 Damages for breach of a contract by the company before or as a result of the winding-up order or resolution are provable subject to a just estimate being made by the liquidator, and subject to the duty of the claimant to mitigate the damages. As to continuing contracts, see C9.6 above. In the case of common law damages for premature or wrongful termination of an employee's contract of employment, deduction may be made in respect of:

(*a*)   the prospects of the employee finding and retaining an alternative employment or occupation;

(*b*)   income tax saved by the employee under the 'golden handshake' statutory tax provisions (see *British Transport Commission v Gourley [1956] AC 185; Bold v Brough, Nicholson and Hall Ltd [1963] 3 All ER 849*); and

(*c*)   a discount for early notional payment of his whole claim in one lump sum;

but not in respect of money received by way of pension arising out of a termination of contract (*Hopkins v Norcros plc [1994] IRLR 18(CA)* and *Smoker v London Fire and Civil Defence Authority, Wood v British Coal Corporation [1991] 2 All ER 449 (HL)*); nor in respect of an award of an industrial tribunal for unfair dismissal where the tribunal does not allocate any part of the award to elements of the employee's total loss

(*O'Laoire v Jackel International Ltd [1991] IRLR 170*). An employee is not entitled to claim an additional head of damages on the basis that he had suffered discrimination in the employment market because of the stigma attached to his having been the employee of the company which had been wound up on the ground, *inter alia*, of fraud by its officers (*Re Bank of Credit and Commerce International SA [1994] IRLR 282*).

As to contracts of employment providing for index-linked increases in salary, see *Re Crowther & Nicholson Ltd, LSG, 22 July 1981*.

(10) *Damages for disclaimer or rescission during winding up*

See C12.6 and C12.7 above.

(11) *Policyholders' claims*

C14.23 In the case of a winding up of a Part II insurance company (see the Insurance Companies Act 1982), special detailed provisions as to the valuation of claims in respect of general business policies and long-term policies have been made in the Insurance Companies (Winding up) Rules 1985 (SI 1985 No 95 as amended by SI 1986 No 2002 and SI 1992 No 445) and the Insurance Companies (Winding up) (Scotland) Rules 1986.

In the case of a 'general business policy' (as defined) covering 'long tail' risks (that is, where the insurer's liability depends upon a specified event having taken place during the currency of the policy but the existence and extent of the liability might not be ascertained until long after the policy has expired, for example, a claim by a workman for asbestosis due to his employment during the currency of the policy), the claim in respect of the policy may fall to be dealt with as follows:

(1) In relation to the amounts which have fallen due for payment before the date of the winding-up order, his claim would be proved and admitted in the ordinary way under the Insolvency Rules 1986 (as amended).

(2) In relation to his other rights under the policy, he is to be admitted as a creditor without proof for an amount equal to the value of the policy; see Rule 6 of the Insurance Companies (Winding up) Rules 1985 (above). Schedule 1 to those Rules contains detailed provisions for determining such value. For example (see paragraphs 1 and 2 of that Schedule):

(*a*) In relation to periodic payments which fall due for payment after the date of the winding-up order, where the event giving rise to the liability in respect of them occurred before the date of the winding-up order, their value is to be determined on such actuarial principles and assumptions in regard to all relevant factors as the court directs (paragraph 1).

(*b*) In relation to liabilities which are not dealt with under (1) or (2)(*a*) above and which relate to a policy which provides for a repayment of premium upon early termination or which is expressed to run from one definite date to another or to be terminable by any of the parties from a definite date, their value is either

(i) the amount (if any) which, under the terms of the policy, would have been repayable on early termination of the policy had the policy terminated on the date of the winding-up order, or

(ii) where the policy is expressed to run from one definite date to another or is terminable by either party with effect from a definite date, such part of the last premium paid as is proportionate to the unexpired portion of the period in respect of which that premium was paid,

whichever is the higher (paragraph 2(2)(*a*)).

(*c*) In any other case not dealt with under (1), (2)(*a*) or (2)(*b*) above, the value is such as represents a just estimate of it (paragraph 2(2)(*b*)).

See *Transit Casualty Co v Policyholders Protection Board* [*1991*] *1 Re LR 49*. In that case, Hoffmann J held that Rule 6 and Schedule 1 referred to above provided a complete and exhaustive code for valuation of claims under such policies *save in relation to amounts which had fallen due for payment before the date of the winding-up order* (referred to in (1) above). This saving is important, as otherwise contingent claims already made, or in respect of events which have already taken place, before the winding-up order would be excluded and companies which have gone into insolvent liquidation could emerge substantially solvent with a healthy surplus for their shareholders, while the policyholders would be left entirely without the cover for which they had contracted. This decision was followed on appeal in *Scher and Ackman v Policyholders Protection Board* [*1993*] *3 All ER 384*. The Court of Appeal ruled that 'liability' meant actual or contingent liability consequent upon an event which occurred during the currency of the policy and before liquidation. (This issue did not form part of the appeal to the House of Lords, which is referred to below.)

The above provisions interact with the Policyholders Protection Act 1975 under which certain types of claims, determined by reference to those provisions, of every 'private policyholder' (that is, a policyholder who is either an individual or a partnership or other unincorporated body of persons all of whom are individuals) under a 'United Kingdom policy' are required to be paid by the Policyholders Protection Board on liquidation of the insurance company. In the *Scher and Ackman* case, the House of Lords held:

(*a*) that a policy was a 'United Kingdom policy', notwithstanding that the insurance arrangements had been made through agents in the USA of the insurance company operating in the United Kingdom, if, had any of its terms been performed at the relevant time, such performance would have formed part of an insurance business which the company was authorised to carry on in the United Kingdom, whether or not those obligations would have been performed here ([*1993*] *3 All ER* at *408 et seq.*); and (*b*)   that a United States professional corporation with limited liability which was trading in partnership with individuals was not a 'private policyholder' unless each individual partner was separately entitled to indemnity under the policy (*Scher and Ackman v Policyholders Protection Board (No 2) [1993] 4 All ER 840*).

(12) *Subrogated claims*

C14.24   The following are examples where a claimant may be able to prove by way of subrogation to the rights of the original creditor (subject to the rule against double proof—see C14.9 above).

 (i)   A guarantor for the company's debt (or a person who is otherwise liable for the company's debt—see Mercantile Law Amendment Act 1856) who has discharged the debt or is liable to do so.

 (ii)   The Secretary of State by virtue of the Employment Protection (Consolidation) Act 1978 (see D7.2 PART D: RECEIVERS).

(iii)   The Policyholders' Protection Board by virtue of the Policyholders' Protection Act 1975 where the company is an insurance company (see C9.12 above).

(iv)   The Deposit Protection Board by virtue of the provisions of sections 50 to 66 of the Banking Act 1987 where the company is an 'authorised institution' or 'former authorised institution' (see C9.12 above).

 (v)   A 'stop loss' insurer who has settled the insured's claim in full (except for the excess to be borne by the insured) to the extent of the amount of his maximum liability under the insurance policy, the right of subrogation against the third party extending to the whole of that amount, and the right of the insured to recover the excess from that third party being subordinated to that right of subrogation (*Lord Napier and Ettrick v Hunter [1993] 1 All ER 385 (HL)*). However, an insurance broker who 'funds' the payment of an insurance claim or premium, before the claim is paid by the insurer or the premium is paid by the insured, has no right of subrogation to the premium receivable (*Merrett v Capital Indemnity Corporation [1991] 1 Lloyd's Rep 169*).

(vi)   A third party claimant in the winding up of an insurance company pursuant to the Third Party (Rights against Insurers) Act 1930.

With regard to (vi) above it should be noted, however, that where the rules of a P&I Club contain a 'pay to be paid' clause, a third party who has a claim against a member of the Club in respect of an event which is covered by the insurance provided by the Club has no subrogated right against the Club in the event of the insolvency of the member—*Firma C-Trade SA v Newcastle Protection and Indemnity Association [1990] 2 All ER 705*. Similarly, where under an insurance policy the insured is entitled to be indemnified 'against all sums which the insured shall become legally liable to pay . . .', the third party is not subrogated to the rights of the insolvent insured unless and until he obtains a judgment against the insured; but the court will normally grant leave to the third party to bring an action against the insured which has gone into liquidation (see C8.2 above)—*Post Office v Norwich Union Fire Insurance Society Ltd [1977] 1 All ER 577*. As regards an insured company which has been dissolved, see PART G: DISSOLUTION AND REVIVAL.

As a general rule, the third party is not entitled to any better rights than the rights which the insured has against the insurance company, so that the insurer is entitled to rely on any defence arising from the terms of the policy which would be available against the insured to avoid it or mitigate responsibility to the third party (*Farrell v Federated Employers Insurance Association Ltd [1970] 1 WLR 1400*); and there is nothing to prevent the insured's liquidator or trustee in bankruptcy or (if he does not intervene, the insured itself or himself), from reaching a compromise with the insurance company to the prejudice of the third party, before the third party's subrogated right has been triggered (*Hood's Trustees v Southern Union General Insurance Co of Australasia [1928] Ch 793*); but not if the insured had taken out the insurance pursuant to a contractual obligation owed to the third party (*Mark Rowlands Ltd v Berni Inns Ltd [1985] 3 All ER 473*; see also *Normid Housing Association Ltd v Ralph [1989] 1 Lloyds Rep 265*). However, the insurer is not entitled to set off against the third party's subrogated right any premiums due but unpaid by the insured at the time the insurer's liability arose (*Murray v Legal and General Assurance Society Ltd [1970] 2 QB 495*).

In *Bell v Lothinsure Ltd (in liquidation) (Scots Law Report), The Times, 2 February 1990*, an investor suffered a loss by a combination of events, namely, a fraudulent misrepresentation by the investment company carrying on business as an insurance company, negligent recommendation by the insurance broker and the eventual insolvency of the investment company. The investor then claimed to be subrogated to the professional indemnity insurance (issued by another insurance company), which gave the broker a right to be indemnified against any liability incurred by him due to his negligence but excluded any liability arising as a result of the insolvency of any insurance company (such as the investment company). The court singled out the fraudulent misrepresentation by the investment company or the negligence of the broker as the direct or dominant cause of the loss and upheld the investor's subrogated claim if such a cause was the fraudulent misrepresentation by the investment company or the negligence of the broker.

In *Re Abrahams & Others v Nelson Hurst and Marsh Ltd, The Times, 9 June 1989*, the company in liquidation was an insurance broker and had obtained an 'Errors and Omissions' insurance through another firm of insurance brokers. The insurance cover permitted recovery if the insured was negligent in its activities or became insolvent. The court refused leave to certain creditors of the company in liquidation to bring proceedings against the other firm of insurance brokers by by-passing the liquidator. The court stated that the liquidator had the right to pursue the other insurance brokers for recovery under the policy and, accordingly, there was no compelling reason to allow the creditors to by-pass the liquidator.

(The position of HM Customs and Excise as regards subrogation in respect of VAT bad debt relief is anomalous—see C14.8 above. As to subrogation in respect of preferential claims, see C14.34 below and D7.4 PART D: RECEIVERS.)

(13) *Debt under a void charge*

C14.25 A debt secured by a charge which is void under section 395 of the Companies Act 1985 (unregistered charge), sections 238 to 243 of the Insolvency Act 1986 (transactions at an undervalue and preferences), section 245 (invalid floating charge), or section 127 (disposition of property after commencement of compulsory winding up), is provable as an unsecured debt unless the debt itself is void. Where a charge is void under section 395 of the Companies Act 1985 (to be amended by the Companies Act 1989), the money secured thereby becomes immediately payable (subsection (2)).

(14) *Mutual credit and set-off*

C14.26 Where, before the company goes into liquidation, there have been mutual credits, mutual debts or other mutual dealings between the company and any creditor proving or claiming to prove for a debt, an account must be taken of what is due from each party to the other in respect of the mutual dealings, and the sums due from one party must be set off against the sums due from the other. Only the balance (if any) is provable in the liquidation. Alternatively (as the case may be) the amount of the balance must be paid to the liquidator as part of the assets (Rule 4.90).

However, there is a significant restriction against the right of a creditor to set off a debt due by him against a debt due to him. Rule 4.90(3) provides that sums due from the company to another party must not be included in the account 'if that other party had notice at the time they became due that a meeting of creditors had been summoned under section 98 . . .' (first meeting of creditors in a creditors' voluntary winding up)' . . . or (as the case may be) a petition for the winding up of the company was pending'. This, in the case of a winding up of an insolvent company, means that if, by the time the creditor receives the notice referred to above, the debt contracted in his favour has not become due (for example, because, in the case of a loan or debt repayable on demand, he has not had a chance to make a demand or, in the case of a term loan or other debt, the due date for payment has not arrived), he would have to pay in full the debt *due by him* to the liquidator and be content with whatever dividend (if any) he may receive from the liquidator on the gross amount of the debt *due to him*.

The language of Rule 4.90(3) represents a substantial departure from that of the previous legislation. Section 31 of the Bankruptcy Act 1914, as it applied to the winding up of an insolvent company (by virtue of section 612(1) of the Companies Act 1985), only deprived a creditor of the benefit of a set-off if 'at the time of giving credit to the debtor' he had notice of an available act of bankruptcy. This *prima facie* was understandable. A creditor must blame himself if he *gave credit* at a time he was aware of the debtor's imminent formal insolvency. The logic of the new rule is difficult to understand. The creditor should not be penalised simply because by the time the debt becomes due the debtor's position, which may have been perfectly sound at the time the credit was given, has deteriorated and notice of formal insolvency steps is given.

The creditor cannot protect himself in advance against this (presumably unintended) effect by taking a charge over the debt due by him (or any money deposited with him by the debtor representing that debt) because, according to the decision of Millett J in *Re Charge Card Services Ltd* [*1986*] *3 All ER 289*, there cannot be a charge over a debt in favour of the debtor himself.

It is understood that the Department of Trade and Industry takes the view that the change in the language does not represent a change in law in this respect and that 'due' in relation to a debt means 'contracted'. It is to be hoped that this view will be shared by the courts. In the past 'due' has been construed as 'payable' or 'recoverable by action' (see *Re European Life Assurance Society (1869) LR 9 Eq 122; Re Stockton Iron Company (1875) 2 ChD 101; Potel v IRC [1971] 2 All ER 504*). On the other hand, in *Re A Debtor Ex parte the Debtor v Trustee of Property of Waite [1956] 1 WLR 1226* at *1238* the expression was more widely construed. Hodson LJ, referring to *In re Daintrey [1900] 1 QB 546 (CA)* suggested that an amount was due at the date of the receiving order although it had to be calculated at a subsequent date. In that case a business had been sold at a price to be arrived at by applying a percentage of the profits of the business during a specified future period; and yet the price was treated as 'due'. The Government did introduce an amendment to section 323 of the Insolvency Act 1986 (which relates to set off in bankruptcy and is similar to Rule 4.90 which was expected to be correspondingly amended by statutory instrument) in the Companies Bill 1989 aimed at restoring the old position; but, for reasons which are set out below, subsequently withdrew that amendment, thus continuing the uncertainty.

The explanation for the withdrawal which was given on behalf of the Government was as follows: 'Some doubt has been expressed as to whether debts that were not due and payable at the commencement of a bankruptcy could be incorporated in a set-off under section 323 of the Insolvency Act 1986 . . . The doubt particularly concerns contingent creditors such as guarantors of the bankrupts' debt since the guarantor is often called upon after the commencement of the bankruptcy. The present clause seeks to deal with that perceived doubt by omitting the word 'due'. It has also been simplified in its construction. The clause may well have clarified the position of some contingent claims, but only by potentially widening the scope of those claims capable of being included in the set-off. The extent of that widening would be considerable. It is desirable as far as possible to maintain the principle of *pari passu* or fair distribution in insolvency. To avoid creating fresh uncertainty we have decided that it would be preferable to delete the clause from the Bill. In taking that decision we have borne in mind that the current law has not been fully tested in the courts. In all the circumstances it is sensible and desirable to delete the clause and allow the existing law to develop . . .'. The explanation does not seem very convincing.

In applying section 31 of the Bankruptcy Act 1914 (now superseded by Rule 4.90) to companies, the courts have in the past held that the convening of a first meeting of creditors in a creditors' voluntary liquidation was an act analogous to 'an act of bankruptcy' (*Re Eros Films [1963] Ch 565*). However, in the Australian case of *Law v James [1972] 2 NSWLR 573*, the analogy was extended to the situation where at the relevant time the company was unable to pay its debts for the purposes of (what was then) section 223 of the Companies Act 1948, that is, taking into account its contingent and prospective liabilities. The new Rule 4.90(3) now resolves the conflict between the two cases in favour of *Re Eros*. This is to be welcomed but it has opened up the new ambiguity discussed above.

The account between mutual credits, mutual debts or other mutual dealings is to be taken as at the time of the liquidation. Any assignment (whether by the company or the creditor) of a debt to a third party after the liquidation does not operate to defeat a set-off. In *Farley v Housing and Commercial Developments Ltd [1984] BCLC 442*, Neill J held that once the liquidation takes place the only sum available for assignment is the balance (if any) due after taking such account. However, in *Stein v Blake [1993] BCC 587*, a bankruptcy case involving similar facts and statutory provisions, the Court of Appeal refused to follow the *Farley* decision and held that until an account was taken following bankruptcy, the debt due to the bankrupt was assignable; but Balcombe LJ went on to state: 'That is not to say that there may not be other grounds on which the defendant' (who had a counterclaim in separate proceedings) 'could attack the assignment which was made in this case.' It is submitted that although the assignment may be valid, the assignee, when making a claim against the debtor under the assignment, may face a defence under the counterclaim on the principle that an assignee takes subject to all equities. It should be noted that *Stein v Blake* did not involve the substantive question of whether the assigned debt was recoverable—only whether the assignment was valid and whether the bringing of the action by the assignee was an abuse of the process of the court. In *Re Charge Card Services Ltd* (see below), Millett J stated: 'Of course, a debtor to the bankrupt must not be allowed, after the date of the receiving order, to gain an advantage by buying up the bankrupt's liabilities in order to gain the benefit of a set-off.'

Where the liquidation is preceded by the appointment of an administrative receiver under a general charge, the appointment operates as a notice of the assignment of the debts due to the company in favour of the holder of the charge. Any such assigned debt, to the extent that it did not suffer a set off under the general law (as distinct from under Rule 4.90) at the time of the receiver's appointment, is not liable to be set off under Rule 4.90 against any sum due by the company to the relevant debtor at the time of liquidation (see *B Hargreaves Ltd v Action 2000 Ltd* (referred to in (*1993*)

6 Insolvency Intelligence 34; this aspect of the case was not pursued before the Court of Appeal: [*1993*] *BCLC 1111*).

Where the requisite tests are satisfied, set-off is mandatory notwithstanding any pre-liquidation agreement to the contrary (*Rolls Razor Ltd v Cox* [*1967*] *1 QB 552; National Westminster Bank Ltd v Halesowen Presswork and Assemblies Ltd* [*1972*] *AC 785*). Conversely, where the tests are not satisfied, a set-off cannot be effected pursuant to a pre-liquidation contract for a set-off. Any such contract would be ineffective as being contrary to the *pari passu* rule (see C15.4 below).

All claims provable in a winding up may be set off against similarly provable claims, provided there is mutuality, that is, the debts in the opposite directions are in the same right (see below) and each claim results in a liability to pay money (*Rolls Razor Ltd v Cox*, above; *Peat v Jones* (*1881*) *8 QBD 147*). Subject to the interpretation of the language of Rule 4.90 discussed above, it is submitted that even a contingent debt (at its fair present value) can be set off because it is provable (see Rule 13.12 summarised at C14.13 above; see also C14.14 above). In *Re Charge Card Services Ltd* [*1986*] *3 All ER 289*, Millett J stated: '. . . contingent liabilities of all kinds . . . are debts provable in the bankruptcy, and . . . in general all provable debts resulting from mutual dealings are capable of set-off'.

A secured creditor whose claim is partly preferential (see below) and partly non-preferential may appropriate the proceeds of realisation of his security (if any) to the non-preferential part first (*Re William Hall (Contractors) Ltd* [*1967*] *2 All ER 1150*).

An unsecured debt may be set off against a secured debt (*Ex parte Barnett, re Deveze* (*1874*) *9 Ch App 293* (where a creditor, on whose goods the bankrupt had a lien for the debt due to the bankrupt, was held entitled to set off that debt against the debt due to him by the bankrupt and to have the lien on the goods released); *McKinnon v Armstrong* (*1877*) *2 App Cas 531*). However, a requirement as to set-off under Rule 4.90 only arises where any creditor of the company is 'proving or claiming to prove for a debt . . .'. Where he holds security over any asset of the company and is proving for only that part of his debt which is in excess of the value of the security, the secured part of his debt is not required to be set off, in preference to the unsecured part, against any debt owing by him to the company. This is because he is not 'proving' for the secured part (*Re Norman Holding Co Ltd* [*1990*] *3 All ER 757*). A debt due to one department of the Crown has been allowed to be set off against a debt due by another (*Re Cushla* [*1979*] *3 All ER 415; Re D H Curtis (Builders) Ltd* [*1978*] *Ch 162*; see also D7.6 PART D: RECEIVERS; see also the meaning of 'debt' in C14.13 above).

Where the company, as a third party, is subrogated to the rights of another party under an insurance policy by virtue of the Third Party (Rights against Insurers) Act 1930 (see C14.24 above), the insurer cannot set off against the company's subrogated claim any arrears of premium due by the third party under the policy (see *Murray v Legal & General Assurance Society Ltd [1970] 2 QB 495*).

Where a creditor accepts post-liquidation performance by the company of a pre-liquidation (or post liquidation) contract, any sum due by the creditor as a result cannot be set off by him against the debt due to him— see C9.6 above.

It was previously thought that a party whose (unsecured) claim in the liquidation is partly preferential and partly non-preferential must first set off any debt due by him to the company against the preferential part (see *Re EJ Morel (1934) Ltd [1962] Ch 21*). But in *Re Unit 2 Windows Ltd [1985] 1 WLR 1383*, where the Crown had a claim through one of its departments which was partly preferential and partly non-preferential and owed the company a debt through another of its departments, it was held that section 31 of the Bankruptcy Act 1914 was not intended to benefit a debtor or creditor or any class of creditors at the expense of any other but to provide a means of conducting an accounting exercise. It gave no right to either the debtor or the creditor to appropriate any credit to any particular debt or part of a debt. The principle that equality is equity operated so that the credit should be set off rateably between the preferential and the non- preferential part of the debt. In certain circumstances the value of the goods of the company held by a salesman for the purposes of converting them into money may be set off against a debt owed by him to the company (*Rolls Razor Ltd v Cox*, above).

The requirement of mutuality means that a joint debt cannot be set off against a several debt (see *Re Pennington and Owen [1925] Ch 825*) and that a 'multilateral set-off' or global netting-off arrangements through a clearing house among its members will not be effective in a winding up (see the *British Eagle* case cited in C15.4 below). Money held for a specific purpose or on a trust cannot be set off against a debt (*Re City Equitable Fire Insurance Co Ltd (No 2) [1930] 2 Ch 293; National Westminster Bank Ltd v Halesowen Presswork and Assemblies Ltd*, above, *per* Lord Simon). In applying the test of mutuality, the real right to a debt will be taken into account and it is sufficient if the debts are in equity in the same right (*Brown v Gregory [1904] 1 Ch 627, 2 Ch 448*). A contingent debt may be the subject of a set-off (see *Rolls Razor Ltd v Cox*, above; *Mersey Steel and Iron Company v Naylor, Benzon & Co (1882) 9 QBD 648* and *Langley Constructions (Brixham) v Wells [1969] 2 All ER 46*); (see also meaning of 'debt' above). A contingent claim by a surety who has not paid off the principal debt cannot, however, be the subject of a set-off (*Re Fenton [1931] 1 Ch 85*). Before Rule 4.90(3) came into force, it was suggested by Millett J in *Re Charge Card Services Ltd* (above) that a debt not presently due could be the subject of a set-off; *quaere*, whether this also applied to a contingent, as distinct from a not presently payable, debt. *Quaere*, whether the Rule has now altered the position (see above).

However, where two or more parties are jointly indebted to the company as principal debtors, and one of them has a debt owed to it by the company, that debt can be set off against the debt owed to the company with the result that the liability of each of those parties to the company is reduced by the amount of the debt owed by the company. In *MS Fashions Ltd and others v Bank of Credit & Commerce International SA* [*1992*] *BCC 571* two companies had borrowed moneys from BCCI, had cross-guaranteed each other's liability to BCCI and had given an 'all-moneys' debenture to it by way of security. In addition, two individuals had each given

(*a*)   an unlimited guarantee for the liabilities of those companies to it,

(*b*)   a charge over their property in Leeds to secure the liabilities of those companies to it, and

(*c*)   a letter of charge over their deposits with it, covenanting that their liabilities would be as if they were principal debtors.

After a winding-up petition had been presented and provisional liquidators appointed in respect of BCCI, but before a winding-up order was made, the provisional liquidators served a demand on each of the two companies and each of the two individuals for payment of the sums due by the two companies to BCCI. Following the winding-up order, fresh demands were made and receivers were appointed under debentures given by the company.

Millett J refused leave to the two companies to commence proceedings against BCCI to establish that the liabilities to BCCI had been reduced by a set-off of the amounts of the deposits which BCCI had in the accounts of the two individuals. The Court of Appeal, in reversing the decision of Millett J and granting leave, expressed strong (but preliminary) views to the effect that set-off did operate in those circumstances. It observed that although release of a surety did not discharge a principal debtor, and it was open to the creditor to release the guarantee and still enforce its security against the companies, payment by the surety not only released the surety but also discharged or reduced the principal debtor's liabilities to the creditor. The set-off under Rule 4.90 operated to reduce the individuals' liability and corresponded to payment of a corresponding amount made by the individual to BCCI. Subsequently, in a substantive action before the High Court (*(No 2)* [*1993*] *BCC 70*), Hoffmann LJ (sitting as an additional Chancery judge) allowed the companies' contention that automatic set-off of the individuals' deposits operated to reduce the companies' liabilities to BCCI.

In that action there were other similar claims involved but with the variation that in those cases, demands had not been made on the individuals. Hoffmann LJ summarised the principles as to the application of Rule 4.90, as established by case law in relation to the predecessor of that Rule, as follows:

(1)   The rule was mandatory; if there had been mutual dealings before the winding-up order, which had given rise to cross-claims, only the balance could be proved or sued for ('the mandatory principle').

(2)   An account was taken as at the date of the winding-up order ('the retroactivity principle'). This was only one manifestation of the wider principle of insolvency law, that the liquidation and distribution of the assets of an insolvent company were treated as notionally taking place simultaneously on the date of the winding-up order.

(3)   In taking the account, regard had to be had to events which had occurred since the date of the winding up ('the hindsight principle').

He rejected BCCI's submission that there could be no set-off until such time as BCCI decided to sue the individuals and they pleaded a set-off by way of defence. If there were existing cross-claims arising out of mutual dealings before the winding-up order, then Rule 4.90 took effect. The question, therefore, was whether such cross-claims existed. BCCI argued that the individuals' liability was contingent upon BCCI making a demand—except in one case, no demand had been made—and contingent liability could not form the subject of a set-off. Hoffmann LJ said that if the relationship between BCCI and the individuals had been governed only by the standard form of guarantees, then liability would have remained contingent. However, the individuals were also liable to BCCI under various additional or wider instruments, which deemed them to be principal debtors. That liability was not contingent at all. It was either a joint and several liability with the companies or, at any rate, a several liability for the same debt. In two cases the letters of charge over the deposit made no mention for the need of demand. In the other cases the obligation was to pay on demand in writing. However, in the case of primary obligations, as opposed to secondary ones like guarantees, a provision for demand in writing was not regarded as creating a contingency: see *Re Brown's Estate [1893] 2 Ch 300*. The 'principal debtor' clauses had the effect of creating primary liability. For the purposes of the rule that liability was not contingent upon demand.

The decision of Hoffmann LJ was upheld on appeal by the Court of Appeal (before which the title of the case was *High Street Services Ltd and others v Bank of Credit & Commerce International SA [1993] BCC 360*). Dillon LJ observed that although the situation was tripartite rather than bipartite, all the rights were immediately enforceable so far as relevant to the question of set-off. There was set-off between the individual guarantors and BCCI, and that automatically reduced or extinguished the indebtedness to BCCI of the companies. The statutory set-off was not something which BCCI could place in a suspense account (an apparent reference to standard provisions in guarantees entitling a creditor to hold any payments received from a guarantor in a suspense account so as to enable the creditors to prove for the whole amount owed to him by the principal debtor on the latter's insolvency). It operated to reduce or extinguish the liability of the guarantor and necessarily operated as an effective payment by him to be set against the liability of the principal debtor. A creditor could not sue the principal debtor for the amount of the debt which the creditor had already received from a guarantor. Dillon LJ also rejected BCCI's argument, based on *Re City Equitable Fire Insurance Company Ltd (No 2) [1930] 2 Ch 293, Re Pollitt [1893] 1 QB 455* and

Re Mid-Kent Fruit Factory [1896] 1 Ch 567, that since the deposits had been placed with BCCI for a special purpose, namely the companies' liabilities to BCCI, they were held on a quasi trust and were outside the scope of Rule 4.90. Those cases involved surplus funds remaining after those funds had been applied towards the discharge of the liabilities as security for which the funds had been deposited. In the instant case, the question of set-off related to the liabilities which were secured by the deposits.

In *Re Bank of Credit & Commerce International SA (No 3), [1994] BCC 462*, Rattee J distinguished the *High Street Services Ltd* case referred to above, and did not allow a set-off in a somewhat similar situation, except that the depositor was *not* expressed to be a principal debtor.

As to the restrictions against a debt due by a contributory being set off and the extent to which he is allowed set-off, see C12.1 above.

(15) *Accounting for sums recovered abroad*

C14.27   A creditor is not entitled to prove in an English winding up unless he brings into the common fund any money which he may have received or recovered out of the company's assets abroad, in circumstances where he would not have been entitled to retain it if he had received or recovered it out of the company's assets in England because of the operation of the English winding-up provisions—(see for example *Banco de Portugal v Waddell (1880) 5 App Cas 161*; see also *Re Standard Insurance Co [1968] Qd St R 118 (Australia)*).

Ordinary creditors

C14.28   Creditors other than (i) secured creditors (except to the extent of their claims which cannot be discharged out of their security), (ii) preferential creditors (see C14.34 below) and (iii) deferred creditors (see C14.35 below) are referred to in this chapter as 'ordinary creditors'. The matters dealt with in C14.1 to C14.13 (general aspects as to proofs) and C14.14 to C14.27 (creditors' claims generally) particularly apply to them. Their claims rank *pari passu* (see C15.4 below).

Secured creditors

Meaning

C14.29   'Secured creditor' means a creditor of the company who holds in respect of his debt a security over property of the company; and 'security' means, in relation to England and Wales, any mortgage, charge, lien or other security and, in relation to Scotland, any security (whether heritable or moveable), any floating charge and any right of lien or preference and any right of retention (other than a right of compensation or set-off) (section 248). (See *Re a Debtor (No 310 of 1988)* [*1989*] *1 WLR 453* as to the meaning of 'security' in bankruptcy for the purposes of Rule 6.1(5) (statutory demand), as read with sections 383 and 385(1) where the language is similar.)

Creditors who are secured

C14.30 An execution creditor (including one who has obtained the appointment of a receiver of land or a charging order in respect of land by way of execution) or a creditor who has levied distress, whose claim is not defeated by any of the provisions referred to in C8.3 and C9.2 to C9.4 above, is a secured creditor (see *Re Printing and Numerical Registering Co (1878) 8 Ch D 535, 538; Anglo-Italian Bank v Davies (1878) 9 Ch D 275*); so also is a solicitor holding a lien on the company's documents (related to his claim) for his costs (*Re Safety Explosives Ltd* [*1904*] *1 Ch 226*; but see C10.10 above). A party to an action for whose benefit money has been paid into court either voluntarily or pursuant to a court order is a secured creditor (*WA Sherratt Ltd v John Bromley (Church Stretton) Ltd* [*1985*] *BCLC 170 (CA)*) as may also be a plaintiff who has issued a writ *in rem* against the company's ship (*Re Aro Co* [*1980*] *2 WLR 453*).

For further examples of secured creditors see D7.23 PART D: RECEIVERS.

Creditors who are not secured

C14.31 A landlord is not a secured creditor merely because he has a power of distress (*Thomas v Patent Lionite Co (1881) 17 Ch D 250, 257*), nor is a creditor who has arrested a ship of the company in exercise of a maritime lien (*The Zafiro* [*1959*] *3 WLR 123*; cf. *The Constellation* [*1966*] *1 WLR 272*).

A person who has paid to the company a returnable booking deposit in respect of the proposed purchase of a house is not a secured creditor where no contracts have been signed (*Re Barrett Apartments* [*1985*] *JR 350 (Ireland)*).

A creditor who has a valid reservation of title to assets (or proceeds of assets) supplied by him to the company is not a secured creditor where the effect of such reservation is that the assets continue to belong to him rather than that he has a charge over them. He cannot both prove for the amount of his debt and take the assets; the value of the assets must be set off against his debt. Where the effect of the reservation is to constitute a charge, he is a secured creditor, unless the charge is invalid for lack of registration under section 395 of the Companies Act 1985. Where building materials supplied on retention of title terms by a creditor have become annexed to the company's land and have lost their identity, the creditor ceases to have any security or other interest therein and must prove as an unsecured creditor for their value (*Re Yorkshire Joinery Co Ltd (1967) 111 SJ 701*). A creditor who holds security from a *third party* in respect of the company's debt is not a secured creditor of the company (see e.g. *Re a Debtor* referred to in C14.29 above).

Position of secured creditor

C14.32 If a secured creditor realises his security, he may prove for the balance of his debt, after deduction of the amount realised. If he voluntarily surrenders his security for the general benefit of creditors, he may prove for his whole debt as if it were unsecured (Rule 4.88).

Where he has put a value on his security in his proof of debt, he may at any time, with the agreement of the liquidator or the leave of the court, alter that value. In a compulsory liquidation, if, as a petitioner for winding up, he has put a value on the security in the petition or has voted in respect of the unsecured balance of his debt, he may revalue the security only with the leave of the court (Rule 4.95(1) and (2)).

If he omits to disclose his security in his proof of debt, he must surrender his security for the general benefit of creditors, unless the court, on application by him, relieves him from this effect on the ground that the omission was inadvertent or the result of honest mistake. If the court grants that relief, it may require or allow the creditor's proof of debt to be amended on such terms as may be just (Rule 4.96).

The liquidator may at any time give notice to a creditor whose debt is secured that he proposes, at the expiration of 28 days from the date of the notice, to redeem the security at the value put upon it in the creditor's proof. The creditor then has 21 days (or such longer period as the liquidator may allow) in which, if he so wishes, to exercise his right to revalue his security (with the leave of the court, where Rule 4.95(2) (see above) applies). If the creditor revalues his security, the liquidator may only redeem at the new value. If the liquidator redeems the security, the cost of transferring it is payable out of the assets. A secured creditor may at any time, by notice in writing, call on the liquidator to elect whether he will or will not exercise his power to redeem the security at the value then placed on it. The liquidator then has six months in which to exercise the power or determine not to exercise it (Rule 4.97). If the liquidator is dissatisfied with the value which a secured creditor puts on his security (whether in his proof or by way of revaluation) the liquidator may require any property comprised in the security to be offered for sale. The terms of sale must be such as may be agreed, or as the court may direct. If the sale is by auction, the liquidator on behalf of the company, and the secured creditor on his own behalf, may appear and bid (Rule 4.98).

Where the security is revalued at a time when a dividend has been declared, any dividend received or receivable on the revised amount of the unsecured part of the claim is adjusted; and either the creditor must repay to the liquidator any excess dividend received, or, as the case may be, the creditor is entitled to receive from the liquidator any resulting underpayment out of the funds for the time being available for payment of any further dividend; but without disturbing any dividend declared (whether or not distributed) before the date of revaluation (Rule 11.9).

If a creditor who has valued his security subsequently realises it(whether or not at the instance of the liquidator) the net amount realised must be substituted for the value previously put by the creditor on the security, and that amount is to be treated in all respects as an amended valuation made by him (Rule 4.99).

Thus, a secured creditor has several choices.

(1) He may rest on his security and not prove (at all or for the time being).

(2) He may value his security and prove as an ordinary creditor for the balance of his claim, subject to his right in certain circumstances to amend the valuation and the liquidator's right to redeem the security or require it to be realised (see above).

(3) He may realise the security and prove as an ordinary creditor for the balance of his claim after deducting the net amount realised. Where he does so after having previously valued his security and proved for the balance, the net amount realised is substituted for the assessed value and the proof is amended and any dividends paid or payable are adjusted accordingly. (Note, however, section 110(1) of the Law of Property Act 1925, as read with section 205(1)(i) thereof, which disentitles a mortgagee to sell the mortgaged property or appoint a receiver in respect thereof by reason solely of the mortgagor's liquidation, unless he has obtained the leave of the court.)

(4) He may surrender his security to the liquidator and prove as an ordinary creditor for the whole of the amount of his claim. If the secured creditor wholly relies on his security, he can appropriate the proceeds of his security to all principal and interest (including post-liquidation interest) and any other sums to which he is entitled in accordance with the terms of his security, and is only obliged to return to the liquidator the balance, if any, that remains after such appropriation. Where he proves for any deficiency on realisation, the proof cannot be admitted in respect of any post-liquidation interest which remains outstanding after such appropriation (but see C14.19 above).

Concurrent claims in two or more liquidations

C14.33 Where companies A and B, both in insolvent liquidations, are jointly and severally liable (for example, where A is the guarantor for B's debts) to C, C's position would be as follows.

(1) Subject to (2) and (3) below, C is entitled to prove for the full amount of his claim in both the liquidations and rank for dividend accordingly up to a stage when his claim is fully satisfied.

(2) In proving his claim in A's liquidation, C must (subject to (3) below) allow credit for any amount already received or recovered by him on account of the debt (see *Re Amalgamated Investment and Property Co Ltd [1984] 3 All ER 272*):

(i) from B, before B's liquidation;

(ii) from B's liquidator by way of dividend subject to C's right, in the absence of any agreement to the contrary between B and C, to appropriate that payment to any debt due by B to C on any other account (see, for example, *In re Sherry, London and County Banking Company v Terry (1884) 25 Ch D 692*);

(iii) by way of the net proceeds of any security given by B realised before or after B's liquidation;

(iv) from A, before A's liquidation;

(v) by way of the net proceeds realised from, or the estimated value of, any security given by A.

(3) C need not allow credit in A's liquidation for:

(*a*) any payment or dividends received or recovered, *after* he has proved his claim in A's liquidation, from (or from the realisation of any security given by) B (see *Re Blakeley (1892) 9 Mor 173* and *Re Amalgamated Investment* (above));

(*b*) any of the amounts referred to in (2)(i), (ii) or (iii) above if, pursuant to the terms of the relevant contract or security, C has held such amounts in a suspense account without appropriating them to the debt (see *Commercial Bank of Australia Ltd v Official Assignee [1893] AC 181*);

(*c*) any amount, realised by a receiver appointed by C under the security given by B, not yet passed by the receiver to C—realisation by a receiver is not realisation by the holder of the charge (see *White v Metcalf [1903] 2 Ch 567*). The charging document may provide that the money need only be passed when so required by the holder of the charge (see also Law of Property Act 1925, s 109(8)(v));

(*d*) the value of any security given by B to C (as distinct from any security given by A to C) not then realised and appropriated.

(4) The position in B's liquidation would be *mutatis mutandis* similar. C can thus (subject to other considerations) derive maximum advantage by proving in both liquidations as early as possible (subject to the points about valuation of securities made in C14.32 above).

Preferential creditors

C14.34 In any form of winding up, the preferential debts listed in Schedule 6 to the Act (as read with Schedule 3 to the Social Security Pensions Act 1975) are required to be paid in priority to all other debts (section 175).

PART D: RECEIVERS at D7.4 contains a detailed list of, and comments on, preferential creditors in a receivership. These equally apply to a winding up, subject to the modification that the relevant date by reference to which the rights of the preferential creditors are determined is the date of the winding-up order or of the voluntary winding-up resolution (whichever is the earlier) except that:

(*a*) where the winding-up order is made immediately after any administration order is discharged, the date is the date of the administration order;

(*b*) subject to (*a*) above, where a provisional liquidator is appointed before the winding-up order, the date is the date of such appointment (section 387).

The preferential debts rank equally among themselves after the expenses of the winding up and must be paid in full, unless the assets are insufficient to meet them in which case they abate *pro rata*. So far as the assets available for payment of general creditors are insufficient to meet the preferential debts, the preferential debts have priority over the claims of holders of debentures secured by, or holders of, any charge created by the company which, as created, was a floating charge, and must be paid accordingly out of the property comprised in or subject to that charge (sections 175 and 386). Conversely, where an administrative receiver has been appointed, or possession is taken by the holders under a floating charge, any payment made in respect of the preferential debts which *in that event* are paid out of the proceeds of that charge, as required by section 40 of the Act or section 196 of the Companies Act 1985, is required by those sections to be recouped as far as may be out of the assets available in the winding up for the payment of ordinary creditors.

Where any person (whether or not a landlord or person entitled to rent) has distrained upon the goods or effects of the company in the period of three months ending with the date of a compulsory winding-up order in respect of the company, the goods or effects, or the proceeds of their sale, are required to be applied in and charged with the payment of the preferential debts in the winding up (to the extent that the company's assets are for the time being insufficient for meeting those debts). Where the person distraining surrenders the distrained assets or proceeds to the liquidator, he effectively steps into the shoes of the preferential creditors to the extent that those creditors are discharged by reason of such surrender (section 176). 'Distraining' or 'having distrained' denotes a continuing process rather than a single act. A person is distraining who has seized goods and is holding them with a view to sale, while a person 'having distrained' has not only seized them but has also sold them (*Re Memco Engineering Ltd [1985] 3 All ER 267*). This provision is without prejudice to what is stated in C8.3 above as regards avoidance of distress in certain circumstances.

(As to set-off involving preferential debts, see C14.26 above.)

Where two companies carry on business in partnership and go into liquidation, the debts of the partnership which would have been preferential in the bankruptcy of partners if they were individuals are not preferential in the liquidation of either of the corporate partners (*Re Rudd & Sons Ltd [1984] Ch 237*). A partnership can now be wound up as an unregistered company, whatever the number of partners and whether they are individuals or bodies corporate (see C5.19 above). In such a winding up, preferential debts of the partnership would be payable out of the partnership assets. In addition, a corporate partner may in certain circumstances be wound up, *inter alia*, because of the inability of the partnership to pay its debts (see C5.23 above). Where there is concurrent winding up of the partnership and the winding up or bankruptcy of one or more of the partners, assets are marshalled and distributed in accordance with the provisions of the Insolvent Partnerships Order 1994 (SI 1994 No 2421).

Deferred creditors

Statutory deferment

C14.35 Any sum due to any member of the company, in his character of a member, by way of dividends, profits or otherwise is not deemed to be a debt payable to that member in the case of a competition between himself and any creditor not claiming his debt in his character as a member of the company; but such sum may be taken into account for the purpose of the final adjustment of the rights of the contributories among themselves (section 74(2)(f). Accumulated dividends unpaid by a subsidiary to its parent company are a deferred debt and not a loan in the absence of an express or implied agreement to convert them into a loan; the mere fact that they are shown in the accounts as a loan does not of itself give rise to such an agreement (*Re LB Holliday & Co Ltd [1986] 2 All ER 367*).

For other deferred debts (which, however, appear to rank immediately before those mentioned in the preceding paragraph), see C14.13 (i) and (ii) above. It will be noted in particular that under Rule 12.3(2A), any claim which, by virtue of the Insolvency Act 1986 or any other Act, is a claim the payment of which in a bankruptcy or a winding up is to be postponed, ranks after all other debts or interest thereon (see section 328(6)). Thus for example, section 3 of the Partnership Act 1890 (postponement of loan on which interest varies according to the profits of the borrower) may apply.

In Canada, there are certain provisions of the partnership legislation under which certain types of loan made to the company would constitute deferred loans. In *Canada Deposit Insurance Corp v Canadian Commercial Bank (C[1993] 1 JIBL N-7)*, a support group consisting of several parties entered into an arrangement with the company (a bank) to provide emergency financial assistance to the company. The group agreed to purchase from the company a portion of a portfolio of assets, on the terms that the group would receive from the company any moneys recovered on that portfolio in addition to a percentage of the company's pre-tax income plus interest until such time as the advances were repaid. It was also agreed that in the event of insolvency or the winding up of the company, any amount remaining unpaid would represent a debt from the company to the group. The group would also have an option to receive from the company warrants to purchase common shares of the company. The Supreme Court of Canada held, on the facts and on an analysis of the

Partnership Act of Ontario, that the advances represented a loan rather than capital investment and, thus, were not a subordinated debt.

Interestingly, the Supreme Court went on to consider the relevance of the US doctrine of equitable subordination (which an earlier decision of the Ontario Court of Appeal in *AEVO Co v D & A MacLeod Co (1991) 7 CBR 3d 33* had rejected). This doctrine has become an accepted principle of American bankruptcy law under which, in certain circumstances, the claim of the creditor is postponed to the claims of ordinary creditors on grounds relating to the conduct of the creditor. The test appears to be the degree of control exercised by the lender over the company (see, for example, *Re Clarke Pipe & Supply Co Inc, Court of Appeals, 893 F 2d (5th Cir 1990) [1990] 7 JIBL N-175*). In general terms, claims will be subordinated where

(*a*)   a claimant has engaged in some type of inequitable conduct,

(*b*)   the conduct has resulted in an injury to another creditor of the company or has conferred an unfair advantage on the claimant, and

(*c*)   the subordination is not inconsistent with the provisions of the Bankruptcy Code.

The mere fact that the Supreme Court of Canada went on to consider the doctrine and apply its tests, although eventually it held that the tests were not met, may be some indication that it will not be too long before the doctrine establishes itself within Canadian law. It remains to be seen whether the doctrine will ever be developed by the UK courts or whether the courts will adhere to the conventional view, which the Canadian court took in the *AEVO* case, that the position should be governed strictly by the winding-up provisions and that it is for Parliament to introduce any innovation.

Contractual deferment

C14.36 The claims of creditors which have been subordinated by contract to the claims of the ordinary creditors in the event of liquidation will normally (subject to the terms of the contract) rank after them but before the claims of the creditors whose claims are deferred by statute (see C14.35 above; see also the *Maxwell* case referred to in C15.4 below).

Creditors of a partnership

C14.37 As to the position of the creditors in the winding up of a partnership where insolvency orders have already been made against one or more of the members of the partnership, see the Insolvent Partnerships Order 1994 (SI 1994 No 2421).

Chapter 15: Marshalling and distribution of assets

C15.1 The order of priority in which the company's assets in the winding up are to be applied is as follows.

(i)   Costs and expenses of the winding up (including the liquidator's remuneration) (see C11.27 above and C15.2 below).

(ii)   Preferential creditors (see C14.34 above).

(iii)   Ordinary creditors (see C14.28 above), including secured creditors to the extent that their claims in respect of any deficiency arising on their security have been admitted to rank with the claims of the other ordinary creditors.

(iv)   Post liquidation interest on (ii) and (iii) above *pari passu* (see C14.19 above).

(v)   Deferred creditors (see C14.35 above).

(vi)   Members of the company in accordance with their rights, unless the articles otherwise provide.

For Scotland, see Scottish Rules 4.66 to 4.68.

In this connection the following points should be noted.

Payment of costs and expenses of the winding up

C15.2 These are payable in the order of priority specified in Rule 4.218, subject to the power of the court in a compulsory winding up to determine the order of priority where the assets are insufficient (section 156 (which may be invoked in a voluntary winding up by virtue of section 112); see also section 115 (voluntary winding up) and section 175(2)(a) (preferential debts 'after the expenses of the winding up') and Rules 4.217, 4.219, 4.220 and 12.2).

Also included in the expenses of liquidation are reasonable and necessary expenses of preparing the statement of affairs under section 99 (see C4.7 above and Rule 4.38) and reasonable and necessary expenses incurred in connection with the summoning, advertisement and holding of a creditors' meeting under section 98 (see C4.6 above and Rule 4.62) or section 99 (even though they may have been incurred before the commencement of the winding up). The Insolvency Service has pointed out (see 'dear IP' No 18, July 1991) that the former should represent a fee comprising the actual cost (including profit costs) involved in the preparation of the statement of affairs and should not include any element to cover other disbursements or remuneration; and that the latter should be charged on an actual basis and treated separately from the former. Under no circumstances should a fee, charged for either of these purposes, be used to augment remuneration fixed in accordance with Rule 4.127 (see C11.27 above). Both Rules 4.38 and 4.62 require that

(*a*) where such payment is made before the commencement of the winding-up, the chairman of the meeting of creditors shall inform the meeting of the amount of the payment and the identity of the person to whom it was made, and

(*b*) such payment shall not be made to the liquidator himself, or to any associate of his, other than with the approval of the liquidation committee, the creditors or the court.

It should also be noted that these expenses are not necessarily confined to those incurred by or on behalf of the liquidator, but they must have been incurred for the specific purpose of enabling the company to pass a winding-up resolution and to take other steps required by sections 98 and 99 in relation to a creditors' meeting. They do not include fees of the advising accountants for collecting debts (*Re Sandwell Copiers Ltd [1989] PCC 413*).

Also included in the expenses of liquidation is the amount of any corporation tax on chargeable gains accruing on the (post-liquidation) realisation of any asset of the company, whether the realisation is effected by the liquidator, a secured creditor or a receiver. This ranks partly immediately before and partly immediately after the substantive liquidator's remuneration (Rule 4.218(1)(o)(p) and (q), which appears to give partial statutory recognition to *Re Mesco Properties Ltd [1980] 1 All ER 117* decided in the context of the previous rules). It will be noted that the tax has no preferential status as against a secured creditor's right to the proceeds of the sale of the asset comprised in his security to which the tax relates.

Where, after going into liquidation, a company continues an action commenced before it went into liquidation, and costs are awarded against it on the action being unsuccessful, such costs take priority over the general costs of the winding up but the assets out of which they are to be paid are the company's net assets, arrived at after an allowance has been made for the costs of realising the company's assets (*Re Movitex Ltd [1990] BCLC 785*).

The expenses of the liquidation are payable out of 'the assets' (Rule 4.218). In the context of the predecessor of this Rule (Rule 195 of the Companies (Winding up) Rules 1949, which applied to a compulsory liquidation only) the expression 'assets' was construed to include assets comprised in a floating charge which had not crystallised before the winding-up order (see *Re Barleycorn Enterprises Ltd [1970] 2 All ER 155; Re Mesco Properties Ltd [1980] 1 All ER 117; Re Christonette International Ltd [1982] 3 All ER 225*). Where a liquidator's summons to set aside a floating charge held by a bank over the company's assets, and to seek an order for payment by the bank of compensation for wrongful trading, was dismissed, the court held that the liquidator was not entitled to pay the costs incurred by and awarded against him out of the floating charge assets as being 'expenses properly incurred in the winding-up' pursuant to sections 115 and 175(2)(a) or for the purposes of Rule 4.218 (*Re M C Bacon Ltd (No 2) [1990] BCC 430*). Any recovery made for preference or wrongful trading would not have formed part of the company's assets since the summons was not, and could not be, brought by or on behalf of the company or to recover assets belonging to the company at the date of the winding up.

In certain circumstances the liquidator may be able to obtain an order for the payment of part of his remuneration and costs out of trust assets held by him (see C11.27 above).

Further, where both the liquidator and a third party are claiming the surplus of funds in the hands of a receiver of the company, the court may, in certain circumstances, order in advance of the resolution of the dispute that the liquidator's remuneration and costs attributable to the prosecution of his claim be paid out of the disputed surplus (see C11.27 above).

Where the liquidator has continued to occupy or retain the company's leasehold premises, his remuneration may rank after the rent payable to the landlord for the period of the liquidator's occupation or retention (see C12.18 above).

In a compulsory winding up, any costs, charges and expenses of any person payable by the liquidator out of the company's assets may be agreed by the liquidator with that person; or the liquidator may require them to be taxed by the court to which the winding-up proceedings are allocated or, if there is no such court, by the court having jurisdiction to wind up the company. The liquidator must require such taxation if the liquidation committee so directs. The liquidator may, however, make payment on account before taxation on the basis of an undertaking by that person to repay immediately any amount which on taxation is found to have been overpaid with interest at the rate specified (as at the date of the payment on account) for the purposes of section 17 of the Judgments Act 1838 from the date of the payment on account to the date of the refund (Rules 7.33 to 7.42).

As to the apportionment of costs and expenses between the assets representing the long-term business of a Part II insurance company and its other assets, see the Insurance Companies (Winding up) Rules 1985 (as amended) and the Insurance Companies (Winding up) (Scotland) Rules 1986.

For variations in the winding up of a partnership, see the Insolvent Partnerships Order 1994 (SI 1994 No 2421).

Payment to preferential creditors

C15.3   See C14.34 above.

Dividends to ordinary creditors

(a) General

C15.4 These rank and are to be discharged *pari passu* among themselves (section 107 and Rule 4.181). The requirement is mandatory and there can be no contracting out (*British Eagle International Airlines Ltd v Compagnie National Air France [1975] 2 All ER 390*; see also *Carreras Rothmans Ltd v Freeman Matthews Treasure Ltd [1984] BCLC 420*; *National Westminster Bank Ltd v Halesowen Presswork and Assemblies Ltd [1972] AC 785*). Until the decision in *Re Maxwell Communications Corporation plc (No 3) [1993] BCC 369*, it was widely believed that this *pari passu* principle could extend to and render unenforceable an agreement whereby a creditor subordinates a debt owed by the company to him to the debts owed by the company to its other creditors in the event of the company's liquidation; and that accordingly, it could enable the subordinated creditor still to receive payment from the liquidator on a *pari passu* basis. Legal practitioners were at pains to try to achieve the desired subordination result by the creation, before the commencement of the winding up, of a carefully drafted trust. However, in the *Maxwell* case it was held that no principle of the insolvency legislation precluded the validity of a contract, freely made between the debtor and the creditor, that moneys then advanced should, in the event of the debtor's insolvency, be subordinated to the payment of the debts of other unsecured creditors.

The *pari passu* principle also applies to a creditor enjoying sovereign immunity, such as a foreign embassy. Such a creditor is not entitled to preferential treatment and is therefore not entitled to payments for state purposes at the expense of other creditors. In *Re Rafidain Bank [1992] BCC 376*, the Iraqi Embassy in London and two Iraqi state organisations had substantial credit balances with Rafidain Bank which went into insolvent liquidation. They claimed preferential payments out of those credit balances, to the extent that the payments were required for state purposes, on the ground that retention of moneys owed by the Bank to them conflicted with the rights of the state of Iraq to sovereign immunity. They relied on the general principle of public international law that UK courts would not implead [proceed against] a foreign sovereign state either directly (by permitting proceedings against such state as a defendant) or indirectly (by deciding the title to property to which the sovereign made claim). They submitted that the debts owed by the Bank on current account were choses in action and were therefore 'property' of the State of Iraq.

The claims were rejected by Sir Nicolas Browne-Wilkinson, Vice-Chancellor. In his view, section 1 of the State Immunity Act 1978 (which provides that a State is immune from the jurisdiction of UK courts except as provided by the Act) is subject to section 6(3) of that Act which provides that 'The fact that a State has or claims an interest in any property shall not preclude any court from exercising in respect of it any jurisdiction relating to . . . the winding up of companies'. Winding up did not directly implead a foreign State which was simply a creditor. The making of a winding-up order did not, by itself, call into question the title of any creditor to the debts owed to it by the company. Iraq remained fully entitled to its claim against the Bank. All that had happened was that the right immediately to enforce the payment of such debt by action had been suspended. If the winding-up order was made, the State of Iraq could remain a creditor and its chose in action (the debt) would carry the right to distribution in the winding up. The title to the debt was not affected by the administration of the property of the company in the winding up, although the value of the debt was diminished by the insolvency. Section 6(3) covered all steps to be taken by the court in the collection and division of the assets, short of initiating separate proceedings against a foreign State. On analysis, the matter was not really related to the impleading of a foreign State. It was a claim for preferential treatment in a winding up. As for the other two organisations, although they were both State-owned bodies, they were commercial enterprises and, as such, State immunity was removed by section 3(1)(a) of the 1978 Act.

In cases where the assets and/or liabilities of related companies, or separate funds, have been hopelessly intermingled, the court may authorise the liquidator to implement a pooling of assets and liabilities and the *pro rata* distribution out of the common pool (see, for example, the *Bank of Credit and Commerce International SA* case referred to at C11.26 above; see also the Australasian cases, *Windsor Mortgage Nominees Pty Ltd v Cardwell (1979) CLC 32, 197; Re Australian Home Finance Pty Ltd [1956] VLR 1; Re Landbase Nominee Co Ltd (1989) 4 NZCLC 65, 093; and Re Registered Securities Ltd [1991] 1 NZLR 545*). In *Quintex Australia Finals Ltd v Schroeders Australia Ltd (1991) 9 ACLC 109, 111*, Rogers CJ observed

> 'Liquidators of subsidiaries, or of the holding company, come to court to argue as to which of those companies bears the liability . . . Creditors of failed companies encounter difficulty when they have to select from amongst the moving targets a company with which they consider they concluded a contract. The result has been unproductive expenditure on legal costs, a reduction in the amount available to creditors, a windfall for some, and an unfair loss to others. . . It may be argued that there is justification for preserving the same attitude in relation to the demised companies as was displayed in their active commercial life.'

In certain cases different categories of assets of a company are required to be applied in the discharge of different categories of its ordinary creditors. The following are some examples.

(1) In the case of an insurance company to which Part II of the Insurance Companies Act 1982 applies, the assets representing any fund or funds maintained by the company in respect of its 'long-term business' are available first for meeting its liabilities attributable to that business. The other assets are available first for meeting its liabilities attributable to its other business (section 55 of that Act). For this purpose the two categories of liabilities are treated as though they are liabilities of separate companies (Rule 5 of the Insurance

Companies (Winding up) Rules 1985 (as amended) and the Insurance Companies (Winding up) (Scotland) Rules 1986). For special provisions as to dividends in such cases, see Rules 24 and 23 respectively of those Rules.

(2)   Where an insolvent partnership is wound up as an unregistered company and an insolvency order is also made, on the petition of the same petitioner, against two or more partners (see C5.19 above), the joint estate of the partnership must be applied in the first instance in payment of the joint debts due to the creditors of the partnership (other than those postponed under any provision of the Insolvency Act 1986 or any other Act, for example, section 3 of the Partnership Act 1890), and the separate estate of each insolvent partner must be applied in the first instance in payment of the separate debts of that member (other than those postponed as above). If any two or more members of an insolvent partnership constitute a separate partnership, the creditors of such separate partnership are treated as a separate set of creditors and subject to the same statutory provisions as the separate creditors of any member of the insolvent partnership (articles 8 and 10 of the Insolvent Partnerships Order 1994 (SI 1994 No 2421) and Schedules 4 and 6 thereto).

If any creditor has contravened any provisions relating to the valuation of securities, the court may, on the liquidator's application, by order wholly or partly disqualify the creditor from participation in any dividend (Rule 11.10).

A creditor entitled to a dividend may notify the liquidator that he wishes the dividend to be paid to another person, or that he has assigned his entitlement to another person. In that case, the liquidator must pay the dividend to that other person (Rule 11.11).

(b)   Interim dividends

C15.5   The realisation of all assets and the ascertainment of all liabilities is a lengthy process. In the meantime, the liquidator may consider paying interim dividends, but he must maintain a prudent balance between the desirability of making the maximum distribution at the earliest opportunity and the need to retain sufficient reserves for meeting (*a*) the costs of the winding up (including his remuneration and post-liquidation tax), down to the conclusion of the winding up, (*b*) all preferential claims in so far as they have not been discharged or excluded and (*c*) dividends attributable to all ordinary claims or possible claims lodged with him which have not been finally dealt with or excluded. In this connection, in a compulsory or creditors' voluntary liquidation:

(i)   Rule 4.180 provides that whenever the liquidator has sufficient funds in hand for the purpose, he must, subject to the retention of such sums as may be necessary for the expenses of the winding up, declare and distribute dividends among the creditors in respect of the debts which they have proved, having first issued a notice of his intention to declare each dividend;

(ii) Rule 4.182(1) provides that in the calculation and distribution of a dividend the liquidator must make provision for (*a*) any debts which appear to him to be due to persons who, by reason of the distance of their place of residence, may not have had sufficient time to establish their proofs, (*b*) any claims which have not been determined and (*c*) disputed proofs and claims.

As to the position of late creditors, see C14.3 above. See also C15.7 below.

No action lies against a liquidator for a dividend; but if he refuses to pay it, the court may order him to pay it and also to pay, out of his own money, interest on the dividend at the rate for the time being specified for the purposes of section 17 of the Judgments Act 1838 from the time when it was withheld and the costs of the proceedings (Rule 4.182(3)).

(*c*) Final dividend

C15.6 When the liquidator has realised all the assets or so much of them as can, in his opinion, be realised without needlessly protracting the liquidation, he must give notice under Rule 11.2 or 11.7 (as the case may be) (see C15.7 below) of his intention to declare a final dividend or that no dividend, or further dividend, will be declared. After the last date for proving claims (see C15.7 below) he must defray any outstanding expenses of the winding up out of the assets and, if a final dividend is to be declared, must declare and distribute that dividend without regard to the claims not already proved. The court may, on the application of any person, postpone the date specified in the notice (Rule 4.186).

(*d*) Formalities and restrictions re declaration of interim or final dividend

C15.7 Before he declares a dividend, the liquidator must issue a notice of his intention to do so. The notice must be given to all creditors who have not proved their debts. It must specify whether the dividend is interim or final and the last date for proving claims, which must be not less than 21 days from the date of the notice. It must also state the liquidator's intention to declare the dividend within four months from the last date for proving (Rules 4.180 and 11.2).

The liquidator may postpone or cancel a dividend if (i) in that period of four months he has rejected a proof in whole or part and an appeal against the rejection has been lodged in court or (ii) an application has been made to the court for his decision on a proof to be reversed or varied or for a proof to be expunged or its amount reduced (Rule 11.4). Further, in any case, so long as any such application is pending he must not, except with the leave of the court, declare a dividend. Where the court gives such leave, he must make such provision in respect of the proof as the court directs (Rule 11.5(2)). Unless he has not, in that four-month period, had cause to postpone or cancel the dividend, he must proceed to declare it within that period (Rule 11.5).

When a dividend is declared, he must give notice of the fact in accordance with Rule 11.6 to all creditors who have proved their debts. In a compulsory or creditors' voluntary liquidation he must also comply with Rule 4.180(3).

If he gives notice that he is unable to declare any dividend or any further dividend (see above) the notice must contain a statement as provided by Rule 11.7.

(See also C14.1 to C14.3 above.)

(e)   Division of unsold assets among creditors

C15.8   In a compulsory or creditors' voluntary winding up, the liquidator may, with the permission of the liquidation committee, divide *in specie* amongst the creditors, according to its estimated value, any property which from its peculiar nature or other special circumstances cannot be readily or advantageously sold (Rule 4.183). If there is no such committee, the permission may, in a compulsory winding up, be given by the Official Receiver on behalf of the Secretary of State (Rule 4.172); but in a creditors' voluntary winding up, it would probably have to be obtained from the court under section 112.

Dividend on post-liquidation interest (see C14.19 above)

Dividend to deferred creditors (see C14.35 above)

Distribution of surplus to members

C15.9   Any surplus remaining after payment to all the ordinary and deferred creditors must, unless the company's articles otherwise provide, be distributed among the members of the company in accordance with their rights (sections 107, 130(4), 148, 154), after the rights of the contributories among themselves are adjusted to take account of any disparity in the amounts of their contributions in respect of shares held by them (see C12.20 above). For this purpose, where foreign compensation was belatedly received for the seizure of the company's assets and resulted in a surplus for distribution among members, the members who had disposed of their share certificates to collectors were nevertheless held to be members (in preference to the collectors) as persons who were entitled to have their names placed on the register of members: *Re Baku Consolidated Oilfields Ltd [1993] BCC 653*. In a compulsory winding up, a court order is required for such a distribution because the power of the court under section 154 is not delegated to the liquidator. The procedure is set out in Rules 4.221 and 4.222. The liquidator must inform each recipient of the rate of return per share and whether any further return is expected to be made.

The words 'unless the articles otherwise provide' and 'persons entitled thereto' are subject to the general principle that the memorandum or articles cannot authorise payment of any surplus funds for purposes which cannot be said to be in furtherance of the objects of the company as a going concern. In *Parke v Daily News Ltd [1962] Ch 927* the proposal by a company after the cessation of the major part of its business and continuation of its other business, to make *ex gratia* payments to its former employees was held to be *ultra vires*. Section 719 of the Companies Act 1985 and section 187 of the Insolvency Act 1986 go a considerable way towards counteracting the effect of that case, by permitting provisions to be made for the benefit of employees or former employees in connection with the cessation of the company's undertaking out of the assets which are available to the members; but the general principle continues to apply to other cases. As to the resolution by directors on the eve of liquidation to make an *ex gratia* payment to one of their number, see *Gibson's Executor v Gibson 1980 SLT 2* (see also *Re Merchant Navy Supply Association Ltd [1947] 1 All ER 894*). In *Mettoy Pension Trustees Ltd v Evans and Others [1990] 1 WLR 1587*, it was held that an employer's absolute discretion under an occupational pension scheme to distribute surplus pension funds among beneficiaries is not a right to make gifts from the surplus as its owner but is a fiduciary and discretionary power; and when the employer's power ceases on its going into liquidation, the fiduciary power does not vest in the liquidator or receiver but will be exercised in the manner the court considers most appropriate in the circumstances to give effect to the insertion of the scheme (see also *Davis v Richards and Wallington Industries Ltd [1990] 1 WLR 1511*; and C12.17 above).

A charitable company limited by guarantee is not a trustee, in the strict sense, of its corporate assets, but is in a position analogous to that of a trustee. Where its *memorandum* provides that on a winding up the surplus should be given to another charitable institution with similar objects and not the members, the court will intervene to give effect to that provision even if the *articles* do not contain such a provision (*Liverpool and District Hospital for Diseases of the Heart v Attorney-General [1981] 1 All ER 994*).

A distribution of assets remaining after repayment of the share capital is regarded as a capital distribution irrespective of the source of the assets represented in the distribution (*I R C v Pollock & Peel [1957] 1 WLR 822*; see also section 209(1) of the Income and Corporation Taxes Act 1988). However, this may not apply to a company limited by guarantee: see the article 'Winding up—Companies limited by Guarantee' by Jonathan D Peacock, barrister, in *The Tax Journal*, 18 July 1991. Distributions in liquidations to shareholders are exempt from stamp duty subject to their being certified as provided by the Stamp Duty (Exempt Instruments) Regulations 1987 (SI 1987 No 516).

As to the distribution of assets *in specie* among the members see C3.4 and C4.2 above.

Chapter 16: Conclusion of the winding up

Members' and creditors' voluntary winding up

Calling final meetings

C16.1 As soon as the affairs of the company are fully wound up, the liquidator calls a general meeting of the members and, in the case of a creditors' voluntary winding up (including a members' voluntary winding up subsequently becoming a creditors' voluntary winding up), a meeting of creditors to lay before them his final accounts (Rule 4.223, Form 4.68) and to give an explanation of them. The meetings are called by advertisement in the *Gazette* published at least one month before the date of the meeting (sections 94, 96 and 106). In addition, at least 28 days' notice of the creditors' meeting (where applicable) must be sent to all creditors who have proved their debts (Rule 4.126, Form 4.22). In all cases, the members are presumably entitled to receive postal notice by virtue of the provisions of the articles of association.

Return of final meetings, release of liquidator and dissolution

C16.2 If there is no quorum, the meetings are not required to be adjourned to another day. Within one week after the meetings, the liquidator sends to the Registrar of Companies a copy of the account together with a return of the final meetings stating either that the account was duly presented or that no quorum was present. As soon as the returns have been filed with the Registrar of Companies, the liquidator vacates office (section 171(6)) and has his release, except that if the creditors' final meeting has resolved against his release, the Secretary of State (or, in Scotland, the Accountant of the Court) may, on an application by the liquidator, determine the time of his release. In the latter case, the release will be effective from the date of the issue of a certificate of release issued by the Secretary of State (or the Accountant) and sent by him to the Registrar of Companies (section 173(2)). With effect from the time of his release, the liquidator is discharged from all liability both in respect of acts or omissions of his in the winding up and otherwise in relation to his conduct as liquidator (without prejudice to any liability which may attach to him under section 212 (misfeasance—see C13.4 above)). On the expiration of three months from the date of registration of the documents mentioned above, the company is deemed to be dissolved; but the court may, on the application of the liquidator or any other interested person, make an order deferring the date of dissolution. Any such order is required to be filed by the applicant with the Registrar of Companies within seven days (sections 94, 96, 106 and 201; Rule 4.126; Forms 4.71 and 4.72; see also PART G: DISSOLUTION AND REVIVAL).

Compulsory winding up

Final meeting

C16.3   Where it appears to the liquidator (not being the Official Receiver) that the winding up is for practical purposes complete, he summons a meeting of the company's creditors to receive his report and determine his release. He may give notice of the meeting at the same time as giving notice of the final distribution (section 146 and Rule 4.125; Form 4.22). He must give 28 days' notice to all creditors who have proved their debts and one month's notice in the *Gazette* and must retain sufficient sums from the company's property to cover the expenses of summoning and holding the meeting.

His report must include an account of his administration of the winding up, including a summary of receipts and payments, and a statement that he has reconciled his account with that held by the Secretary of State. He must send a copy of this report to the court, together with a notice that the final meeting has been held and stating whether he has been given his release. The notice of the result of the meeting must also be sent to the Registrar of Companies (section 172(8)) and a copy to the Official Receiver. If there is no quorum, the liquidator must report this to the court; and the final meeting is deemed to have been held, and the creditors are deemed not to have resolved against his release (see C16.4 below) (Rule 4.125).

Release of liquidator

C16.4   As soon as the notice of the result of the final meeting has been given to the court and the Registrar of Companies, the liquidator vacates office (section 172(8)). He has his release from the date he vacates office except that where the final meeting has resolved against his release, the Secretary of State (in Scotland, the Accountant of the Court) may, on the application of the liquidator, determine the moment of his release. In the latter case, the Secretary of State (in Scotland, the Accountant of the Court) must certify his release which is effective from the date of the certificate. The certificate is sent to the Official Receiver to be filed in court. A copy is sent to the liquidator. The release operates to discharge the liquidator from all liability in respect of his acts or omissions in the winding up or of his conduct as a liquidator or provisional liquidator, but is subject to the court's powers under section 212 (misfeasance by liquidators and others—see C13.4 above) (section 174, Rule 4.125 and Forms 4.42 and 4.43).

Where the Official Receiver is the liquidator, he gives notice to the Secretary of State that the winding up is for all practical purposes complete. His release has effect from such time after that notice as the Secretary of State determines (section 174(3)). Before giving that notice, the liquidator must give notice of his intention to do so to all creditors who have proved their debts. The latter notice must be accompanied by a summary of the Official Receiver's receipts and payments as liquidator. When the Secretary of State has determined the date of the release, he must give notice to the court that he has done so and must send with it the summary mentioned above (Rule 4.124).

Dissolution in a compulsory winding up

Introduction

C16.5   The process of dissolution after a compulsory winding up has now been rationalised by the Insolvency Act 1986. The main change is that the liquidator need not make an application to the court for an order of dissolution. In this respect the procedure has been brought in line with that in a voluntary winding up. Subject as stated below, the dissolution is 'automatic' three months after registration by the liquidator of certain documents with the Registrar of Companies or, in the case of a society registered under the Industrial and Provident Societies Act 1965, the appropriate registrar within the meaning of that Act (section 55 thereof). Previously, to save the cost and inconvenience of applying to the court for a dissolution order, liquidators in a compulsory winding up relied on the striking-off procedure under section 658 of the Companies Act 1985 (see PART G: DISSOLUTION AND REVIVAL).

Ordinary cases of dissolution

C16.6   The company is automatically dissolved three months from registration by the Registrar of either:

(i)   a notice served on him by the liquidator for the purposes of section 172(8) (result of final meeting—see C16.3 above); or

(ii)   a notice from the Official Receiver (when he is the liquidator) that the winding up is complete (see C16.4 above).

The Secretary of State may give directions (or in Scotland, the court may make an order) deferring the dissolution on the application of the Official Receiver or an interested person. An appeal to the court lies from any decision of the Secretary of State. The applicant, or appellant, must within seven days deliver to the Registrar of Companies a copy of the direction, order or determination on appeal (as the case may be) (section 205; Rules 4.224 and 4.225; Form 4.69; and, as to Scotland, Scottish Rule 4.77).

Early dissolution (England and Wales)

C16.7   Where the Official Receiver is the liquidator and it appears to him that:

(i)   the realisable assets of the company are insufficient to cover the expenses of the winding up; and

(ii)   the affairs of the company do not require further investigation,

he may apply to the Registrar of Companies for early dissolution.

He must give 28 days' notice of the intended application to the company's creditors and contributories and to the administrative receiver (if any). On the giving of the notice he ceases to be subject to the duties imposed on him by the Act, apart from the duty to make the application. Subject as stated below, the company is automatically dissolved three months from registration of the application by the Registrar of Companies (section 202).

Before the end of the three months, the Secretary of State may, on the application of the Official Receiver or any interested person, give directions under section 203 deferring the dissolution (section 205(3)). In addition, after the 28 days' notice of the application has been given, the Official Receiver, any creditor or contributory or the administrative receiver (if any) of the company may apply to the Secretary of State for directions under section 203 on the grounds that:

(*a*)   the realisable assets of the company are sufficient to cover the expenses of the winding up; or

(*b*)   the affairs of the company do require further investigation; or

(*c*)   for any other reason the early dissolution of the company is inappropriate.

The Secretary of State may, by direction, make such provision as he thinks fit to enable the winding up of the company to proceed as if no notice of the application had been given. Where an application under section 202(5) for dissolution has already been made, the direction may include a deferral of the date of dissolution. An appeal lies to the court from any decision by the Secretary of State. The applicant or appellant must within seven days deliver a copy of the order or direction or determination on appeal (as the case may be) to the Registrar of Companies (Rules 4.224 and 4.225 apply as they do in C16.6 above).

Early dissolution (Scotland)

C16.8   Where, after a first meeting of creditors summoned under section 138 it appears to the liquidator that the realisable assets of the company are insufficient to cover the expenses of the winding up, he may apply to the court for an order that the company be dissolved. The court must make the order if satisfied that the realisable assets are indeed insufficient to cover the expenses and if it appears appropriate to do so. The liquidator forwards a copy of the order to the Registrar of Companies, who registers it. The company is automatically dissolved three months after that registration. The court may defer the dissolution on application of an interested person, and the applicant must, within seven days of the order, deliver a copy of it to the Registrar of Companies (section 204 and Scottish Rule 4.77).

Notice of dissolution and final return

C16.9   Section 711(1)(q) and (r) of the Companies Act 1985 requires the Registrar of Companies to publish in the *Gazette* any order for the dissolution of a company on a winding up and any return by a liquidator of the final meeting of a company on a winding up.

Disposal of records

C16.10 In a compulsory winding up, the liquidator, on the authorisation of the Official Receiver, and during his (the liquidator's) tenure of office or on vacating office, or the Official Receiver while acting as liquidator, may sell, destroy or otherwise dispose of the books, papers and other records of the company. In a voluntary winding up, the person who was the last liquidator of a company which has been dissolved, may do so at any time after the expiration of one year from the date of the dissolution, and does not need any authorisation. (Regulation 16(1) and (2) of the Insolvency Regulations 1994 (SI 1994 No 2507). See, however, Regulation 13 for the requirement as to the retention of certain records for six years after vacation of office.)

In a compulsory winding up the liquidator must, when the winding up is for practical purposes complete, file in court all proofs of debt remaining with him (Rule 4.138(2)).

Unclaimed funds and dividends

C16.11 A liquidator who holds, or any former liquidator who at the date of the dissolution of the company or at the date of his vacating office holds, any moneys representing unclaimed or undistributed assets of the company, or moneys held by the company in trust in respect of dividends or other sums due to any person as a member or former member of the company, must forthwith pay the moneys into the Insolvency Services Account referred to in C12.15 above (Regulation 18 of the Insolvency Regulations 1994). As to Scotland, see section 193.

Part D: Receivers

1. Preliminary   **387**

Scope/The law   387
Meanings of key expressions   388
Object of appointing a receiver   393

2. Pre-appointment considerations   **396**

Validity of proposed appointment   396
Receivers' indemnity   409
Planning   409

3. Appointment of receiver   **411**

Mode of appointment   411
Date when appointment takes effect   412
Who may not be appointed   413

4. Procedural matters following appointment   **414**

Notification of appointment, resignation, etc.   414
Statement of affairs in administrative receivership   414
Administrative receiver's report   415
Creditors' meeting in administrative receivership   416
Creditors' committee in administrative receivership   416
VAT bad debt relief in administrative receivership   417
Application to court for directions by receiver   417
Remuneration of receiver   418
Abstracts of receipts and payments in receivership   419
Enforcement of duties of receiver   419
Notification of receivership on stationery   420

5. General effects of receivership   **421**

Receiver's agency powers and position   421
Position of the company's officers in administrative receivership   427

6. Fixed charges and floating charges   **430**

Meaning of 'fixed charge' and 'floating charge'   430
What constitutes crystallisation?   438

7. Matters affecting assets available in receivership   **441**

Contracts of employment   441
Preferential debts   446
Set-off   453
Lien   457
Execution creditors   459
Distress   462

Forfeiture or termination of lease or contract 465
Retention of title claims 468
Other third party proprietary claims 477
Outstanding contracts (other than employment contracts) 484
'Duress' payments 489
Directors right to enforce early sale 491
Liquidation costs 492
Receivers' right of recourse to assets 492
Assets excluded by law from appointor's charge 492

8. Post-appointment liabilities **493**

New, novated or adopted contracts and receivership costs 493
Value added tax 500
Attachment of earnings (or deduction from earnings) orders 502
Statutory liabilities in respect of immovable property 502
Income and corporation tax 507
Rent 507
Disposal at an undervalue, negligence and misfeasance 508
Interference with third party proprietary, statutory
    or contractual rights 510
Legal proceedings 514
Duties under the companies legislation 517
Environmental law liabilities 517

9. Realisation of assets **526**

General points 526
Deriving income 530
Carrying on business or development 530
'Hive-down' 532
Sale of going concern 544

10. Conclusion of receivership **559**

Allocation, marshalling and distribution of funds 559
Procedural aspects (in either kind of receivership) 565

11. Receivership in Scotland **566**

Introduction 566
Appointment of receiver 567
Effect of appointment 569
Powers of receiver 569
Precedence among receivers 569
Receiver's agency and liability 570
Receiver's remuneration 570
Preferential debts 570
Order of distribution 570
Disposal of property 571
Miscellaneous provisions 571

12. International aspects of receivership **572**

Part D: Receivers

Chapter 1: Preliminary

D1.1   The material in this book relating to receivers should be read in conjunction with PART A: GENERAL and, where relevant, PART F: SPECIAL PROVISIONS FOR FINANCIAL MARKETS. This chapter deals with various introductory matters, including the meanings of key expressions (in particular, 'administrative receiver'), a brief explanation of the sources of law relating to receivership, and the object of appointing a receiver.

Scope

D1.2   This part is concerned with receivership under a charge created by a company over some or all of its assets. It does not deal with other forms of receivership, for example, those arising from court orders in cases where no charge has been created. More particularly, this part focuses on a receiver appointed out of court under a charge which, *as created*, is a floating charge, or a fixed and floating charge, over the whole or substantially the whole of the property, assets and undertaking, present and future, of a company ('general charge'). The subject is dealt with primarily by reference to receivership in England and Wales; but in D11.1 *et seq.* there is an attempt to highlight the main variations in Scotland.

In this part, 'receiver' is used as a generic term. It applies to both or either of a receiver (and/or manager) appointed under an *ad hoc* fixed charge over specific property and a receiver (and/or a manager) appointed under a general charge. As will be seen below, a receiver under a general charge is technically described as an 'administrative receiver' (which expression must be distinguished from 'administrator'—see PART B: ADMINISTRATION ORDERS). For convenience, a receiver who is not an administrative receiver has been described in this part as an 'ordinary receiver' and is also popularly known as a 'LPA receiver', that is, a Law of Property Act receiver. As will be seen, the régime of administrative receivership is more sophisticated than that of ordinary receivership.

The law

D1.3   Unlike the other corporate insolvency procedures dealt with in PART B: ADMINISTRATION ORDERS, PART C: LIQUIDATIONS and PART E: VOLUNTARY ARRANGEMENTS, a corporate receivership in England and Wales is not a creature of statute. The law on the subject is essentially based on contractual relationship and derives its force from the principles of common law and the rules of equity, as supplemented by the Law of Property Act 1925 and superimposed, in relation to certain administrative and substantive aspects, by the Insolvency Act 1986 ('the Act') and the Insolvency Act 1994 (effective from 24 March 1994, but retrospective, in relation to contracts of employment adopted by an administrative receiver, to 15 March 1994). Subordinate legislation is mainly contained in the Insolvency Rules 1986 (SI 1986 No 1925), as amended by the Insolvency (Amendment) Rules 1987 (SI 1987 No 1919), 1989 (SI 1989 No 397), 1991 (SI 1991 No 495) and 1993 (SI 1993 No 602) ('the Rules'). Unless otherwise stated, a section or Rule referred to is that of the Act or the Rules, as the case may be. A form referred to is one contained in Schedule 4 to the Rules.

Meanings of key expressions

D1.4   Section 29 of the Insolvency Act 1986 must be noted at the outset. It declares, *inter alia*, that:

(*a*)   any reference to a receiver (or manager) of the property of a company includes a receiver (or manager) of part only of that property and a receiver only of the income arising from the property or from part of it; and

(*b*)   'administrative receiver' means:

  (i)   a receiver or manager of the whole (or substantially the whole) of a company's property appointed by or on behalf of the holders of any debentures of the company secured by a charge which, as created, was a floating charge, or by such a charge and one or more other securities; or

  (ii)   a person who would be such a receiver or manager but for the appointment of some other person as the receiver of part of the company's property.

It is important to analyse closely this definition of 'administrative receiver'.

(1)   An administrative receiver must be a receiver (or manager) of 'the company'. The expression 'the company' is defined by section 735 of the Companies Act 1985, as applicable here by virtue of the last part of section 251 of the Insolvency Act 1986, as a company formed and registered under the Companies Act 1985 or the previous companies legislation referred to in section 735. This would *prima facie* mean, for example, that a receiver appointed under a charge (which otherwise falls within (b)(i) above) created by an *overseas* corporation or a body corporate *formed or registered under any other legislation of the United Kingdom*, such as an industrial and provident society registered under the Industrial and Provident Societies Act 1965 (as amended), is not an administrative receiver. This interpretation could have some surprising consequences. For example, the provisions applicable only to administrative receiverships (as

distinct from ordinary receiverships) as regards the payment of preferential debts (see D7.3 below), the investigative powers of receivers under sections 234 to 236 and their powers contained in Schedule 1 to the Act, the procedural matters referred to in D4.1 to D4.12 below and the transitional VAT bad debt relief provisions referred to in D4.7 below would not apply. As far as an industrial and provident society is concerned, the 1965 Act (as amended) contains separate provisions for registration of a charge created by such a society and for enforcement of such a charge. As for transitional VAT bad debt relief, special arrangements may have to be made with HM Customs and Excise in the receivership of such a society. (By contrast, such bodies may be wound up by the court as either unregistered companies or registered companies under the provisions of the Insolvency Act 1986 in substantially the same way as may ordinary companies registered under the domestic companies legislation (see C5.7 and C5.8 PART C: LIQUIDATIONS).)

However, in *Re International Bulk Commodities Ltd [1992] 3 WLR 238*, Mummery J did not consider this interpretation to be a correct one and held, in effect, that administrative receiverships were not confined to companies registered under the domestic companies legislation. He pointed out that section 735 of the Companies Act 1985 expressly stated, in subsection (4), that the definitions contained in that section applied 'unless the contrary intention appears'. In his view, a contrary intention did appear, having regard to the subject matter and manifest purpose of the relevant provisions, when construed in the context of both the immediately relevant provisions and of the Insolvency Act 1986 as a whole. Among the indications pointing to the intention that in section 29 (definition of 'administrative receiver') the word 'company' was intended to cover unregistered companies were the following:

(*a*)   The legislative concept of administrative receiver, and the statutory scheme of the provisions relating to his qualifications, functions, powers and duties, all rested on a contractual base, namely, a receiver appointed by or on behalf of debenture holders under a debenture secured by a floating charge. The underlying contractual regime was applicable both in the case of a debenture granted by a company formed and registered under the Companies Acts, and in the case of a debenture granted by an unregistered company.

(*b*)   The general purpose and scheme of the statutory superstructure was to strengthen and build on the continuing contractual foundation for the greater benefit of all affected—the company, the contributories, the creditors, both secured and unsecured, and the preferential creditors, as well as the public generally. The attainment of that general purpose and the nature of the scheme were *prima facie* as appropriate to the case of an unregistered company as they were to the case of a registered company. There was no reason why the range of companies affected by the statutory scheme of administrative receivers should not be co-extensive with the range of companies affected by the underlying contractual regime.

(c) So long as the foreign company concerned had power to and did grant the English form of debenture which, if granted by a registered company, would invoke section 29, there was no logical reason why the receiver appointed under it should not fall within the definition of an administrative receiver.

(d) The foreign element was of no particular relevance where the company in question had granted a debenture secured by a floating charge in the English form. Both registered and unregistered companies could engage in activities, conduct business and have creditors, assets and directors in England and abroad. Both were liable to be wound up by the English court.

(e) As the provisions regarding the licencing of insolvency practitioners applied to administrative receivers but not to ordinary receivers (see section 230(2) and section 388(1)), it would be illogical if a receiver appointed under an English form of debenture granted by a registered company should be an administrative receiver and be a qualified insolvency practitioner, but not a receiver appointed under the same form of debenture granted by an overseas or unregistered company, particularly when in section 388 (meaning of 'act as insolvency practitioner') the expression 'company' was expressly defined by subsection (4) to include a company which may be wound up under Part V of the Act (unregistered companies).

Mummery J's reasoning was not followed by Judge Hague QC in *Re Devon and Somerset Farmers Ltd [1993] BCC 410*. In that case, the court had to decide whether the expression 'company' in section 40, for the purposes of giving effect to the rights of preferential creditors under that section, included an industrial and provident society registered under the Industrial and Provident Societies Act 1965 (and under its predecessor Act of 1893), but not re-registered under the companies legislation. In answering the question in the negative, the judge gave the following reasons.

(a) It was doubtful whether a 'contrary intention' required by section 735 of the Companies Act 1985 (above) was evinced by the relevant provisions of the Insolvency Act 1986. If Parliament had intended that any of the sections in Part II or III of the 1986 Act should extend to unregistered companies, it was hard to understand why that was not expressly stated in the 1986 Act.

(b) Section 40 had been derived on consolidation from section 196(1) of the Companies Act 1985 (replacing section 94(1) of the Companies Act 1948) which expressly referred to 'a company registered in England & Wales'.

(c) Industrial and provident societies had their own legislation, including provisions regarding receivers. It was impossible to find that they were included within the definition of 'company' by reason of the words 'unless a contrary intention appears' in section 735.

(*d*) In *International Bulk Commodities*, Mummery J was only concerned with overseas companies and information gathering powers of administrative receivers.

(2) The administrative receiver should be receiver (or manager) of the whole or substantially the whole of a company's property. In borderline cases, a receiver appointed over only part of the company's property may be uncertain whether the part over which he is appointed is substantially the whole of the company's property and, therefore, whether he is an administrative receiver or an ordinary receiver. The Act contains no guidelines as to how the expression 'substantially the whole' is to be construed; nor is there any direct judicial authority on the point. It is submitted that the test is primarily qualitative rather than quantitative, having regard to the central legislative purpose behind the concept of administrative receivership. The central legislative aim is to introduce a special regime in cases where a receiver has control of the substratum of the company's activities or its goodwill or key assets, so that he is able, if he so wishes, to deal with the assets comprised in his appointment as a going concern. Where the company has two or more separate businesses run as separate divisions, and the receiver is appointed in respect of only one or some of those divisions, the relative estimated values of the division or divisions over which the receiver is appointed and those over which he has not been appointed could be an important factor to be considered.

(3) The charge under which the receiver is appointed must be a debenture 'secured by . . . a floating charge, or by such a charge and one or more other securities'. A situation which is increasingly encountered in practice is that a charge created by a company contains both a fixed charge over assets which, in terms of value and quantity, represent substantially the whole of its property, and a floating charge over the other assets; but the holder of the charge expressly confines the receiver's appointment to all the fixed charge assets. The question is whether, by excluding all the floating charge assets from the appointment, the holder of the charge is able to avoid making the receiver an administrative receiver.

The language of section 29(2)(a) is unhappy in this respect. It seems to suggest that so long as the assets over which the receiver is appointed represent substantially the whole of the company's property, it is immaterial whether any of those assets are subject to a floating charge so long as the charging document pursuant to which he is appointed contains a floating charge on any assets, even if they are assets over which he is not appointed. It is submitted that such an interpretation has no practical logic. The whole concept of administrative receivership essentially centres around the concept of the floating charge. It is the nature of the charge over the assets with which the receiver is dealing that is material in practice and not the nature of the charge contained in the charging document over the assets with which he is not dealing. This was one of the questions which arose in *Meadrealm Ltd & another v Transcontinental Golf Construction Ltd & others, Ch D, 29 November 1991* (Vinelott J), where the argument that a receiver appointed over fixed charged assets alone was an administrative receiver was rejected without detailed reasoning. Vinelott J said, 'I think the short answer to that is that an administrative receiver is a receiver under a charge which as created was a floating charge with or without a fixed charge and that the receiver was not appointed under the floating charge but only under the fixed charge.'

The essential feature of a floating charge is that the company is able to carry on its business before receivership or other form of insolvency intervenes, and that the receiver is able to carry on its business after his appointment. However, where, for example, in the case of a single property company, the charge is an 'anti-administration' debenture (that is, a fixed charge on the property and (merely to give the chargeholder a right to 'veto' an administration order) a floating charge over all other present and future assets), and a receiver is appointed without exclusion of any floating charge assets, the receiver is an administrative receiver even if the company does not own and has never owned any floating charge assets (*Re Croftbell Ltd [1990] BCLC 844*).

(4)   The administrative receiver should be appointed 'by or on behalf of the holders' of debentures. The expression 'on behalf of the holders' appears to include an appointment by the court on the application of the holders (see, for example, section 32). However, where a receiver is appointed by the court, even over the whole or substantially the whole of the property of the company, otherwise than by virtue of a charge over it (for example, at the instance of an unsecured creditor with a view to safeguarding the company's assets pending judgment or its execution), he is not an 'administrative receiver'. The expression 'debentures' includes a single mortgage or charge (see *Re Knightsbridge Estates Trust Ltd [1940] 2 All ER 401*).

(5)   The floating charge referred to in (3) above must be a charge which at its inception was a floating charge. Any subsequent crystallisation of that charge (as to which see D6.3 below) is immaterial for these purposes.

(6)   A situation may arise where, under the *same* charging document, one person (X) is appointed receiver over some of the assets comprised in that document and another person (Y) is appointed over the other assets comprised in it, and the two categories of assets together represent the whole or substantially the whole of the company's property. In such a case, X is (arguably) an administrative receiver if the charge contained in the document over at least some of the assets in relation to which he is appointed is a floating charge. If at least some of the assets in relation to which Y is appointed are also subject to such a floating charge, then Y, too, is (arguably) an administrative receiver. This would mean both X and

Y having to comply with the same statutory obligations, such as those relating to obtaining a statement of affairs, communicating with creditors and convening a creditors' meeting, unless the court otherwise orders.

(7) Where there are two successive floating (or fixed and floating) charges (one ranking after the other or the two ranking *pari passu* with each other) in favour of different parties over the whole or substantially the whole of the same company's property and different persons from two different professional firms are appointed receivers under the two charges, it is not clear whether both are administrative receivers. The answer seems to be in the affirmative; but this, again, would mean both having to comply with the same statutory obligations separately and incurring additional costs, unless the court otherwise orders.

For Scotland, the definition of an administrative receiver in section 29 (see above) is extended by section 251 to include a receiver appointed under section 51 where the whole (or substantially the whole) of the company's property is attached by a floating charge.

Section 251 also defines a floating charge as a charge which, as created, was a floating charge (and also includes a Scottish floating charge, i.e. a floating charge within section 462 of the Companies Act 1985).

Object of appointing a receiver

D1.5   The appointment of a receiver is one of the ways in which a secured creditor can enforce and realise his security. In the case of a general charge, it is clear that this method is the only satisfactory one. A receiver's appointment has the effect of more readily crystallising any 'floating element' of the charge (see D6.1 *et seq.* below) and thus helping to save the assets comprised therein from the ravages of execution creditors (see D7.8 *et seq.* below). Further, taking control of, running and disposing of a whole undertaking requires considerable expertise and manpower resources, and involves substantial legal responsibilities. A receiver, as a qualified insolvency practitioner, is normally better equipped to cope with all this. Even in the case of an *ad hoc* fixed charge, the mortgagee would be well advised to effect realisation through a receiver, particularly where there is no ready purchaser of the assets concerned or the assets involved are substantial.

If, instead of appointing a receiver (who is normally the agent of the mortgagor company and is therefore at less risk of liability to it), the mortgagee takes possession of the charged property, he could become liable to account to the mortgagor company not only for the rents and profits of the property which he actually receives but also for rents and profits which, but for his wilful default, he would have received. This liability to account puts him in 'a difficult and dangerous position' (*Cooke v Thomas* (*1876*) *24 WR 427*; see also *Shepherd v Spanheath Ltd* [*1988*] *EGCS 35* (best rent possible); *Perry v Walker* (*1855*) *3 Eq Rep*

721 (duty to take steps necessary to prevent forfeiture, including by complying with repairing covenants)).

'Possession' for this purpose need not be physical or actual possession. The mortgagee can be deemed to be in possession if he displaces 'for the purpose of realising the security' the mortgagor from the control and dominion of the reversion. Giving notice to tenants to pay rents to the mortgagees may suffice; but it is debatable whether the mere sale by the mortgagee of the mortgaged property, in exercise of his power as such, in itself constitutes possession if the mortgagee has not previously taken any overt steps to displace the mortgagor's control or dominion. Mere receipt of rent is not sufficient to constitute possession. A mortgagee to be in possession must take out of the mortgagor's hands the power and duty of managing the mortgaged property and dealing with the tenants (*Noyes v Pollock (1888) 32 ChD 53*).

As a general rule, a mortgagee under a legal charge has, subject to any contractual or statutory limitations, a right to seek possession at any time after the execution of the mortgage; and the existence of a cross-claim, even if it exceeds the amount of the mortgage debt, or is admitted by the landlord, does not by itself defeat that right. This applies both where the cross-claim is a mere counterclaim and where it is in the nature of unliquidated damages which, if established, would give a right by way of equitable set-off. In *Leeds Permanent Building Society v Kassai (Current Law September 1992 Digest)*, the mortgagor's cross-claim in an action by the mortgagee for possession was by way of set-off for damages for a negligent valuation report prepared by the mortgagee. The mortgagors argued that although a counterclaim did not affect a mortgagee's right to possession, a set-off impeached the mortgagee's title and that they had an arguable claim for rescission of the mortgage. It was held that (i) the existence of an arguable set-off did not affect the mortgagee's right to possession, and (ii) although an arguable counterclaim for rescission would be a ground for adjourning the possession application (see *Barclays Bank plc v Waterson [1989] CLY 2505*), there would be no arguable claim if the mortgagors (who had defaulted on payment of the mortgage instalments) were not in a position substantially to restore the mortgagee to the original position and had affirmed the mortgage. Where the mortgagor is a surety and is expressed to be a primary debtor (so that the mortgage is deemed to be primary security), any right of set-off available to the principal debtor may, in any case, be excluded (*National Westminster Bank plc v Skelton [1993] 1 All ER 242*; see also *Ashley Guarantee plc v Zacaria [1993] 1 All ER 254; Samuel Keller (Holdings) Ltd v Martins Bank Ltd [1971] 1 WLR 43; Mobil Oil Co Ltd v Rawlinson (1981) 43 P & CR 221; B Hargreaves Ltd v Action 2000 Ltd [1993] BCLC 1111*).

The main function of a receiver is to realise the assets charged in a manner which best benefits his appointor (see, for example, *Gomba Holdings Ltd v Homan [1986] 1 WLR 1301* and *In re B Johnson & Co (Builders) Ltd [1955] Ch 634* at *644*), subject, however, to his duty in the process not to sacrifice unduly the interests of the other creditors or of the company. Particularly in the case of an administrative receiver, the Act facilitates his functions in this regard by conferring on him certain powers and rights; but it also substantially increases his administrative and legal responsibilities.

Chapter 2: Pre-appointment considerations

Validity of proposed appointment

D2.1   If the charge under which a receiver is appointed, or the appointment itself, is invalid or defective, both the receiver and his appointor could, even where they have acted in good faith, incur substantial liabilities to the company (see *Re Jaffre Ltd (in liquidation), Jaffre v Jaffre (No 2) [1932] NZLR 195; Harold Meggitt Ltd v Discount and Finance Ltd (1938) 56 WN (NSW) 23*) and to others. In the case of an administrative receiver, section 232 provides that his acts are valid notwithstanding any defect in his appointment or qualification. It is doubtful, however, whether this protects him against *the company* where *the charge* under which he is appointed is invalid or where the power to make the appointment was non-existent or had not arisen. In any case, it is prudent for the receiver designate and his proposed appointor to investigate and take legal advice (preferably separately) on all matters which may impinge on the whole or any part of the charge or the appointment. A company search and a search in the Central Compulsory Winding-up Registry of the Companies Court and as to any pending administration petitions must always be carried out as a matter of course, in addition to other necessary investigations. Among the points to be considered are the following.

(a) *Company's powers*

D2.2   Was the creation of the charge within the powers of the company as contained in the objects clause of its memorandum of association in force at the time of creation? In addition to any express powers so contained, certain powers may, depending on the company's main objects and activities, be implied as being in direct furtherance of those objects and activities. Also, the absence of the requisite power is not necessarily fatal to the charge. The holder is protected by section 35 of the Companies Act 1985 if he had acted in good faith at the time (as he is presumed to have done unless proved otherwise). Section 35 was substituted by section 108 of the Companies Act 1989 which came into force on 4 February 1991 (subject to transitional and saving provisions set out in SI 1990 No 2569, article 7). As substituted, section 35 provides that the validity of an act done by a company shall not be called into question on the ground of lack of capacity by reason of 'anything in' (which expression, it is submitted, means 'anything contained in or omitted from') the company's memorandum; but the directors continue to be under a duty to observe any limitations on their powers flowing from the memorandum, and any excessive exercise of their powers can only be ratified by a special resolution of the company. Even such a ratifying resolution does not relieve the directors of their liability; any relief from such liability must be agreed to separately by special resolution. The Companies Act 1989 also inserted a new section 35B which provides that a party to a transaction with a company is not bound to enquire as to whether it is permitted by the company's memorandum or as to any limitation on the powers of the board of directors to bind the company or authorise others to do so.

The provisions of section 3A of the Companies Act 1985, as inserted by section 110 of the Companies Act 1989 (which also came into force on 4 February 1991) should also be noted. The section provides that where the company's memorandum states that the object of the company is to carry on business as a general commercial company, the object of the company is to carry on any trade or business whatsoever and the company has power to do all such things as are incidental or conducive to the carrying on of any trade or business by it.

The new provisions relating to the capacity of companies, and the absence of a duty on a third party to enquire whether a company has the requisite capacity, apply to unregistered companies by virtue of the Companies (Unregistered Companies) (Amendment No 3) Regulations 1990 (SI 1990 No 2571).

(b) Directors' powers

D2.3   Was the creation of the charge within the powers of the directors? The articles of association of some companies may contain limitations on directors' powers to borrow (or create security) without a resolution of the general meeting. There is also an implied general limitation, namely that the directors can only exercise their powers for the purposes of the company's business. If the holder was aware (or ought reasonably to have been aware) that the charge was not being created for the purposes of the company (for example, in the case of a dormant subsidiary giving a charge for the indebtedness of its parent in circumstances where there was manifestly no conceivable benefit to the subsidiary), section 35 of the Companies Act 1985 (see D2.2 above) may not assist him (see *Rolled Steel Products (Holdings) Ltd v British Steel Corporation* [*1985*] *3 All ER 52* and cf. *TCB Ltd v Gray* [*1986*] *1 All ER 587*). It should also be noted that the articles of association of a company are construed strictly, in that terms can never be implied into them on the basis of extrinsic evidence of surrounding circumstances (*Bratton Seymour Service Co Ltd v Oxborough* [*1992*] *BCC 471*).

Section 108 of the Companies Act 1989 inserts a new section 35A into the 1985 Act (which came into force on 4 February 1991, subject to transitional and saving provisions set out in SI 1990 No 2569, article 7). This new section provides that in favour of a person dealing with the company (that is, being a party to any transaction or other act to which the company is a party) in good faith, the power of the board of directors to bind the company, or authorise others to do so, shall be deemed to be free of any limitations under the company's constitution. Mere knowledge that an act is beyond the directors' power does not constitute bad faith, and a person is presumed to have acted in good faith unless the contrary is proved. However, knowledge of the circumstances indicating improper exercise by the directors of their powers in relation to the giving of the charge, or the borrowing or guaranteeing or assumption of liability on the security of the charge, may constitute bad faith. More particularly, the charge holder is still not protected against the *Rolled Steel Products* type of situation (see above). 'Limitations' include limitations deriving from a resolution of the company in general meeting or a meeting of any class of creditors or from any agreement between the members or any class of shareholders. This does not affect the liability of the directors, or any other person, by reason of the directors exceeding their powers. The new section 35B mentioned in D2.2 above is also relevant here. Thus it seems that short of actual knowledge (or shutting his eyes to the obvious) that the directors were not exercising their powers for the legitimate purposes or in the legitimate interests of the company, the holder of the charge will not be adversely affected.

The new provisions relating to the powers of directors to bind companies, and the absence of a duty on a third party to enquire whether the directors have the authority to do so, apply to unregistered companies by virtue of the Companies (Unregistered Companies) (Amendment No 3) Regulations 1990 (SI 1990 No 2571).

(c) Due execution of charge

D2.4   Was the charge validly executed? This may depend (subject to what is stated in the third paragraph below) on whether the company's seal appears to have been affixed in accordance with the formalities prescribed in the articles and whether the persons attesting to the sealing held the offices which they were described as holding. The question of whether a board resolution authorising them to attest was passed as required by the articles is a matter of internal management with which the appointor would not, in the absence of express notice, be concerned.

It may also be possible for the appointor to rely on section 74 of the Law of Property Act 1925, which provides that in favour of a purchaser (which expression includes a mortgagee—see section 205(1)(xxi) of that Act) a deed is deemed to have been duly executed by a corporation aggregate if its seal is affixed in the presence of and attested by its clerk, secretary or other permanent officer or his deputy, and a member of the board of directors, council or other governing body, and where a seal purporting to be the seal of the corporation has been affixed and attested by persons purporting to be persons holding such offices, the deed shall be deemed to have been duly executed and to have taken effect accordingly. It seems that the protection of this section is available even where the articles prescribe a different mode of execution and the holder of the charge had express or constructive notice thereof.

Here section 36A of the Companies Act 1985, inserted by section 130 of the Companies Act 1989 (which came into force on 31 July 1990, concurrently with the provisions of section 1 of the Law of Property (Miscellaneous Provisions) Act 1989 revising the formalities for execution of deeds by individuals) should be noted. The section makes provision with respect to the execution of documents by a company under the law of

England and Wales. A document is executed by a company by the affixing of its common seal. A company need not have a common seal, however. Whether it does or does not have a common seal, a document signed by a director and the secretary of a company, or by two directors of a company, and expressed (in whatever form of words) to be executed by the company has the same effect as if executed under its common seal. If the document makes it clear on its face that it is intended by the person or persons making it to be a deed, it has effect, upon delivery, as a deed; and it is presumed, unless a contrary intention is proved, to be delivered upon its being so executed. In favour of a purchaser in good faith for valuable consideration (including a lessee, mortgagee or other person who for valuable consideration acquires an interest in property), a document is deemed to have been duly executed by a company if it purports to be signed by a director and the secretary of the company, or by two directors of the company; and, where it makes it clear on its face that it is intended by the person or persons making it to be a deed, it is deemed to have been delivered upon its being executed. (For execution of documents under the law of Scotland, see section 36B of the 1985 Act, as substituted by section 72 of the Law Reform (Miscellaneous Provisions) (Scotland) Act 1990.)

Where a charge has not been validly executed as a deed, it may still operate as an agreement under hand (and, hence, an equitable charge otherwise than by way of deed) (see sections 52 and 53 of the Law of Property Act 1925). If the receiver needs to execute a deed in exercise of the power of attorney contained in the charge, the company is under an obligation to execute new documents to perfect that power (*Byblos Bank SAL v Al Khudhairy [1987] BCLC 232*). In certain circumstances, courts are willing to give effect to documents not sealed as if they are deeds, on the ground of the intention of the parties or of estoppel (see e.g. *First National Securities Ltd v Jones [1978] 2 All ER 221*; *TCB Ltd v Gray [1986] 1 All ER 587*).

Where, without the approval of all the parties, an instrument has been altered after its execution, the instrument is not rendered void thereby if the alteration is not a material one or if, although the alteration was a forgery, it did not go to the whole or to the essence of the instrument. In *Lombard Finance Ltd v Brookplain Trading Ltd and others [1991] 1 WLR 271*, in a guarantee executed personally by two directors of a company, the name of the company was later altered by someone other than the two directors, and without their authority, by the deletion of the word 'Company' in 'B Company Ltd'. The alteration was made in good faith and merely to correct the misdescription of the company. It was held that the guarantee was enforceable against the director who had challenged its enforceability.

(*d*) *Registration*

D2.5   Was the charge or any variation or crystallisation of it required to be registered under Part XII of the Companies Act 1985 (as amended by Part IV of the Companies Act 1989 with effect from a date to be fixed) and, if so, has it been duly registered? Broadly, non-registration means that the charge is void as against a liquidator, administrator or creditor who has levied execution or otherwise acquired an interest in the assets concerned. Registration means delivery of the prescribed particulars to the Registrar of Companies in accordance with the requirements of those sections and not the actual issue by the Registrar of a certificate of registration (see *N V Slavenburg's Bank v International Natural Resources Ltd [1980] 1 All ER 955*); but under section 401(2)(b) of the Companies Act 1985 (to be replaced by new provisions in the Companies Act 1989—see below) the certificate, if issued, is conclusive evidence of compliance with those requirements (*R v Esal Commodities Ltd ex parte Central Bank of India [1986] 1 All ER 105 (CA)*; and *Exeter Trust Ltd v Screenways Ltd [1991] BCLC 888 (CA)*). The effect of section 401(2)(b) will be diluted when it is replaced by the new section 397(5) of the 1985 Act, to be inserted by section 94 of the Companies Act 1989 from a date to be announced. Under the new provision, a certificate of registration will only be issued if any person requires it. The certificate will be conclusive evidence only of the fact that the specified particulars, or other information required by the new 1985 Act provisions, were delivered to the Registrar no later than the date specified in the certificate; and it will be presumed, unless the contrary is proved, that they were not delivered earlier than that date. Thus there will be no conclusiveness as to full compliance in every respect with the registration requirements. The new provisions will also expressly allow any restrictions contained in a charge against the creation of prior or *pari passu* ranking charges to be entered on the register. This may help resolve the current doubt as to whether any particulars of such a 'negative pledge', which under the current practice are included in the registered particulars of charge without any legislative requirement or authority, constitutes a constructive notice to the public or any subsequent encumbrancer (see D6.2 below, and also D11.1(3)).

If the charge is enforced and the proceeds distributed to the appointor, by the receiver as the company's agent, before the relevant events make it void, the charge (arguably) becomes a 'spent charge' and the distribution cannot be set aside by the creditors or the liquidator or administrator. This reasoning is based, by analogy, on the decision in *Mace Builders (Glasgow) Limited v Lunn [1985] 3 WLR 465* (see also *re Parkes Garage (Swadlincote) Limited [1929]1 Ch 139*). (Section 406 of the 1985 Act, as inserted by the 1989 Act, which will impose a trust on proceeds of sale of property, only applies to a charge which has 'become void'.) If the charge has not been registered, attempts may be made to register it out of time with the leave of the court. However, the court order granting leave will contain a proviso that such registration is without prejudice to the rights of any third party acquired before registration. If the company's liquidation is imminent, the order will also contain a proviso granting the company leave to apply for the discharge of registration within a specified period, so that the Registrar will delay registration until that period has expired (see *Exeter Trust* above). The new sections 399 and 400 of the Companies Act 1985, as inserted by section 95 of the Companies Act 1989 (to come into force on a date to be announced), contain new provisions as to the effects of non-registration and late registration.

In relation to registered land, a search at the Land Registry is advisable, so that if the charge is not registered there, steps may be taken by the chargeholder to lodge a notice or caution to prevent any further erosion of the priority of the charge. Ideally, a substantive registration of the charge is advisable. For an example of where an unregistered prior charge could have priority where the appointor's charge was subject to an entry only under section 49 of the Land Registration Act 1925, see *Mortgage Corporation Ltd v Nationwide Credit Corporation Ltd [1993] 3 WLR 769*. If the charge is not registered at the Land Registry, the chargeholder has no *statutory* power to appoint a receiver (*Lever Finance Ltd v Trustee of the Property of L N and H M Needleman [1956] Ch 375*), but his *express contractual* powers contained in the charging document in that regard are not affected.

(e) Vulnerability

D2.6　Is the charge vulnerable under (if created on or after 29 December 1986) sections 238 to 241 (transactions at an undervalue and preferences), 244 (extortionate credit transactions) or 245 (avoidance of certain floating charges) of the Insolvency Act 1986 (see B9.1 *et seq.* PART B: ADMINISTRATION ORDERS and C10.1 PART C: LIQUIDATIONS) or (if created before that date) sections 615 to 617 of the Companies Act 1985; or under section 127 of the Insolvency Act 1986 (disposition of property made after the commencement of compulsory winding up), for example if the charge was created after the presentation of a winding-up petition (see C8.4 PART C: LIQUIDATIONS)? The *Mace Builders* case referred to in D2.5 above may be relevant in relation to section 245 (or section 617 of the 1985 Act), as the case may be.

(f) Illegality

D2.7　Is the charge void or unenforceable for any other reason, for example, because it is tainted with illegality under the companies legislation or other law and the appointor was party to or aware of the illegality? The restrictions and prohibitions contained in sections 317 (directors to disclose interest in contracts), 320 to 322 (substantial property transactions involving directors etc), and 330 *et seq.* (loans and quasi loans to directors and connected persons) of the Companies Act 1985 should be noted in particular. To the extent that a breach of any of those provisions has the effect of rendering the transaction concerned void or voidable, the appointor's charge over the asset involved in the transaction would be protected if he was acting in good faith and without notice. It is expressly provided that, save in the circumstances set out, a breach of sections 320 to 322 and 330 *et seq.* makes the transaction voidable at the instance of the company but not where any rights acquired *bona fide* for value and without *actual* notice of the contravention would be affected by its avoidance. In relation to section 317, it was held in *Runciman v Walter Runciman plc [1992] BCLC 1084* that a purely technical breach of that section (for instance, where a director fails to disclose an interest in a proposed contract in which every director present would know he was interested in any event) will not make the contract voidable.

(g) Enforceability

D2.8   Has the holder of the charge become entitled to enforce it? This depends on whether any event giving rise to the right to appoint a receiver has occurred and (arguably) whether at least some money secured by the charge is properly due and has become payable in the terms of the charge or any other relevant document or arrangement; but in the absence of bad faith the appointor is not under a duty of care to the company or any guarantor when deciding to appoint a receiver (*Shamji and others v Johnson Matthey Bankers Ltd and others* [1986] BCLC 278; [1991] BCLC 36 (CA)). In connection with enforceability, the following should be noted.

(i) Clear-cut evidence may not be available in respect of certain types of events, such as breach of covenants relating to the maintenance of financial ratios or solvency margins or the occurrence of cross-defaults.

(ii) If there are any conditions precedent, such as the issue, by the trustee of debenture stock, of a certificate as to the jeopardy of the security or a notice declaring default, they should be complied with (see also (iii) below). For his own protection, the trustee should be satisfied that he has reasonable grounds for issuing the certificate or notice, even where it is provided that the certificate is deemed to be conclusive.

(iii) Where a demand for payment is expressed to be a prerequisite, it should be properly issued and served, any special mode of service prescribed (if mandatory or exhaustive and not merely permissive) in the charging instrument being strictly followed, and sufficient time should be allowed for its compliance. It is not clear whether, in the absence of any express provision in the charging instrument, a notice can validly be served by facsimile transmission. In *Hastie and Jenkerson v McMahon* [1990] 1 WLR 1575 (CA), it was held that for the purposes of Order 65 rule 5(1) of the Rules of the Supreme Court (which is permissive rather than exhaustive), such service constituted good service provided that it could be proved that the document, in a complete and legible state, had in fact been received by the person on whom service was to be effected. Views differ as to the minimum time that should be allowed. A charging instrument normally contains deeming provisions as regards the service of a notice of demand, for example, a provision to the effect that a notice sent by first class pre-paid post at the last known address of the company is deemed to be served at the expiration of 48 hours from the time of posting. In this connection, *Re Thundercrest Ltd* [1994] BCC 857 may be relevant, although it concerned the service of a notice of provisional allotment of shares. It was held that a provision in the company's articles that service should be deemed to have been effected at the expiration of 24 hours after due posting could not be relied upon, where a notice sent by recorded delivery had in fact been returned to the company undelivered.

(iv) *Cripps (Pharmaceuticals) Ltd v Wickenden* [1973] 1 WLR 944 (followed in the unreported case of *Hawtin v Pugh* (1975)) suggests that the time allowed need not be more than that necessary for the mechanics of payment to be completed in the ordinary course. Certain Canadian cases suggest that the time given, at least where the demand is made unexpectedly, must be reasonable having regard to the relationship between the parties, unless it is clear that the company has no resources to meet the demand. In *Bank of Baroda v Panessar and others [1986] BCLC 497*, the court followed the approach in the *Cripps* case and held that since debentures are essentially commercial matters, the debtor should be allowed a short but adequate period limited to the mechanics of payment, rather than 'wholly imprecise' reasonable time. In that case, as the companies concerned were insolvent, even if the 'reasonable time' test was applied, the end result would have been the same, but the creditor would have had to brook unnecessary delay.

(v) Another point which was decided in the *Bank of Baroda* case (following the Australian case of *Bunbury Foods v National Bank of Australia [1954] ALJ 199*) was that a demand under an 'all moneys' debenture need not specify the amount. The *Bank of Baroda* case was cited with approval in *N R G Vision Ltd v Churchfield Leasing Ltd (1988) 4 BCC 56*. In that case, the company had guaranteed 'the payment by the customer of all sums due under' an agreement for the lease by the chargeholder of equipment to the customers of the company 'and the due performance of all the customer's obligations thereunder'. Knox J held that since certain arrears of rental were indisputably due by the customer at the relevant time, a demand under the first limb of the guarantee was good at least as regards those arrears; it was not necessary to consider whether a demand for the remaining arrears could only be made once the amount of damages under the second limb of the guarantee was ascertained. It was further held by Knox J that the letter from the creditor reciting an alleged oral agreement at a recent meeting offering to accept payment by the guarantor of the specified amount of the arrears by instalments was a good demand in the absence of an acceptance of that offer.

In the majority of such cases, debtors are insolvent anyway. If in any case a debtor is not insolvent, he could always ask the creditor to specify the exact amount. Where, however, an amount is stated in the demand but there is doubt or a possible dispute as to its accuracy, for example, where the debtor may have a right of set-off, it may be advisable to err on the safe side and demand a smaller, rather than larger, amount.

Where a smaller or estimated sum is demanded, a rider may be added in the demand to the effect that the holder of the charge reserves the right to demand and/or recover out of the charged assets any further amounts which may be found to be due to him.

(vi) There may be a dispute as to whether any money at all is due on the security of the charge, for example, because the validity or effect of the underlying transactions is queried, or the sum claimed may represent debits effected by the mortgagee bank after the commencement of the mortgagor's compulsory liquidation (see section 127 and C8.4 PART C: LIQUIDATIONS), or the mortgagor, as principal or surety, may have a larger cross-claim, or a demand was a prerequisite but had not been duly served.

Two recent cases where a mortgage was sought to be enforced may be noted here. In *Ashley Guarantee Plc v Zacaria [1993] 1 All ER 254 (CA)*, a person had guaranteed the liabilities of another person and had given a mortgage to the creditor in respect of that guarantee liability, but there was no 'primary liability' clause. The principal debtor had certain claims against the creditor. The creditor successfully sought possession. Nourse LJ and Woolf LJ rejected the suggestion that the *Mobil Oil* principle (see *Mobil Oil Co Ltd v Rawlinson (1981) 43 P & CR 221*, where there was a 'primary liability' clause, and *Samuel Keller (Holdings) Ltd v Martins Bank Ltd [1971] 1 WLR 43*) would be inapplicable if the principal had an unliquidated cross-claim of which the surety could avail himself, provided that the cross-claim exceeded the amount claimed by the creditor, because then there was arguably no 'default'. (*Quaere* whether, even if a set-off is not possible, in a mortgagee's action for possession of a dwelling-house the existence of a cross-claim would be material to a judge's consideration of what order was appropriate under section 36 of the Administration of Justice Act 1970.) In *MS Fashions Ltd v Bank of Credit and Commerce International SA [1992] BCC 571 (CA)* (a liquidation case), it was suggested, on appeal on a preliminary point, that where a guarantor for the debt of another person to a bank had placed a cash deposit with the bank as security for his guarantee liability, the principal debtor could conceivably deduct the amount of that deposit from his debt to the bank where the bank sought to enforce a mortgage for that debt which had been created by the principal debtor. In connection with a guarantee, it should also be noted that although section 4 of the Statute of Frauds 1677 requires a contract of guarantee to be in writing, there can be an oral variation of an existing guarantee. In *Re A Debtor (No 517 of 1991), The Times, 25 November 1991 (Ch D)*, it was held that a subsequent oral agreement between a guarantor and the creditor that certain monies advanced by another party should go towards the reduction of the guarantee liability was binding on the creditor, and could therefore be relied upon as a defence to a statutory demand in bankruptcy. The Statute of Frauds 1677 would make the agreement unenforceable as it was made orally, but did not prevent it being used as a defence.

Where a person has guaranteed a company's debts to a bank, his guarantee liability can, depending on the language of the guarantee, include the liability of that company under a guarantee given by it in respect of the debts of a third party to that bank (*Bank of Scotland v Wright [1991] BCLC 244*).

(vii) Where the debenture is sought to be enforced in respect of an amount lent to a third party and guaranteed by the company, whether or not a demand on the company as guarantor is a pre-condition may depend on the construction of the debenture and any related documents. For an example of where such a demand was held not necessary, see the Privy Council decision on an appeal from New Zealand in *DFC Financial Services Ltd v Coffey [1991] BCC 218.*

Even where a demand is not expressed to be a prerequisite, it is advisable to make one. Where a demand is a prerequisite and an administrative receiver has been appointed pursuant to a defective demand or without a demand or before the minimum period for complying with it has expired (see (iii) above) and it is desired to rectify the position (at least for the avoidance of any doubt or dispute), a fresh demand followed by a fresh appointment would be necessary. In *Cripps (Pharmaceuticals) Ltd v Wickenden)* (cited in (iv) above) the judge suggested that in such a situation, before a fresh demand is made, the receiver must restore control of the assets and undertaking to the company to enable it to comply with the fresh demand, if it wishes or is able to. However, in practice, to make such restoration may be risky or undesirable. In the receivership of *Cloverbay Ltd (1988, unreported and undecided)* the receiver, instead of restoring control, notified the company that he was aware of the fresh demand and would not stand in the company's way if it wanted to comply with it. In subsequent litigation, the adequacy of this procedure was challenged but the matter was otherwise resolved out of court.

(viii) In the absence of a contractual right to do so, the holder of a charge (even if it is a general charge) is not entitled to appoint a receiver out of court on the ground that his security is in jeopardy (although this is a point which can be taken into account by the court where *it* is asked to appoint a receiver: *Re London Pressed Hinge Co Ltd [1905] 1 Ch 576*). Such a term can only be implied where it is necessary to give business efficacy to the contract and would not be implied where the charge contains a number of express provisions otherwise designed to protect the security (see *Cryne v Barclays Bank Plc [1987] BCLC 548*, where, on the facts, the court also refused to hold that a term loan had, by subsequent events, been varied to an on-demand loan or that the company should be estopped from denying that it had been so varied, and *Williams & Glyn's Bank v Barnes, 26 March 1980, QBD (unreported)* was distinguished on the ground that in that case the loan facility had been granted in the context of a rescue operation accompanied by a moratorium of creditors). Any provision in the charging document to the effect that the amount secured is payable on demand must be read subject to any contractual arrangements, whether written or oral and whether express or implied, subsisting between the parties providing for payment of that amount or any part of it on any specified date or upon the occurrence of any specified event (see, for example, *Cryne v Barclays Bank Plc* above). However, even where the date has passed or the event has occurred it is always advisable to make a demand as suggested in (vii) above.

(ix) In debentures or floating charges created *before* 29 December 1986, there is implied, as an event giving rise to the right to appoint an administrative receiver, the presentation of a petition for an administration order (see PART B: ADMINISTRATION ORDERS). This implied right is contained in paragraph 1(1) of Schedule 11 to the 1986 Act but has some limitations:

    (*a*)   it is not implied in debentures or floating charges created *on or after* 29 December 1986;

    (*b*)   only the right to appoint a receiver is triggered, not a right to enforce the security by any other means, nor necessarily the repayment of the money secured;

    (*c*)   the event is not implied in a charge (whether created before on or after 29 December 1986) which is wholly a fixed charge or which does not extend to the whole or substantially the whole of the company's property (see the definition of 'administrative receiver', referred to in D1.4 above);

    (*d*)   the mere fact that the right to appoint a receiver arises may not necessarily mean that without actual appointment the floating charge automatically crystallises (see D6.3 below).

(*h*) *Administration application*

D2.9   Has an application for an administration order in respect of the company been presented to the court under section 9? (See PART B: ADMINISTRATION ORDERS.) If it has been, an *ad hoc* fixed charge cannot be enforced, whether by the appointment of an ordinary receiver, by sale or otherwise, without the leave of the court (section 10(1)(b)). However, without such leave an administrative receiver under a general charge can still be appointed, and such a receiver may carry out any of his functions (section 10(2)(b) and (c)). Indeed, such an appointment, made before the order, would have the effect of frustrating the application (except where the holder of the general charge consents to the order being made, or where that charge is vulnerable as a transaction at an undervalue or as a preference or as an invalid floating charge—section 9(3)).

(*j*) *Administration order*

D2.10   Has an administration order already been made? Once such an order has been made, and whilst it is in force, no administrative receiver may be appointed. The holder of the general charge would have been served with the application for an administration order (section 9(2)(a)) and could have appointed an administrative receiver before the order was made (see D2.9 above). It would be too late to appoint one after the order is made (section 11(3)(b)). Upon the making of an administration order, any administrative receiver already in office must vacate office, and any ordinary receiver already in office may be required by the administrator to so vacate (section 11(1)(b) and (2)). After the order is made, no other steps may be taken to enforce any security (whether by the appointment of an ordinary receiver or otherwise) except with the consent of the administrator or the leave of the court (section 11(3)(c)). Taking such steps or taking possession of property comprised in the security without such consent or leave may amount to a contempt of court (see *Re Henry Pound, Son & Hutchins (1889) 42 Ch D 402 at 420, per* Cotton LJ).

(k) *Liquidation*

D2.11   Is the company in liquidation? A liquidation does not affect the holder's right to appoint a receiver or the receiver's powers; but it terminates the latter's agency in certain respects (see D5.2 *et seq.* below). The termination of agency may involve considerable risk of personal liability for the receiver where he continues the company's business. Where the company is already being wound up by the court, it appears that unless the liquidator voluntarily surrenders possession of the charged property to the receiver, the leave of the court to take possession would be necessary—the property being in possession of an officer of the court, taking possession without such leave may amount to a contempt of court (see *Re Henry Pound, Son & Hutchins* referred to in D2.10 above).

(l) *Scope of the charge*

D2.12   Does the charge contain a power to appoint a receiver, and what significant limitations (if any) are there as to the assets covered, or the amount secured thereby, or the powers of the receiver, or the nature of the charge (fixed or floating) in relation to each category of assets (see D6.1 *et seq.* below)? An 'all moneys/liabilities' charge may not necessarily extend to unsecured loan stock issued by the company to a third party and acquired by the holder of the charge (*Re Quest Cae Ltd [1985] BCLC 266*) but may, depending on its terms, include contingent liabilities of the company under a guarantee given by it to the holder of the charge (*Re Fosters and Rudd Ltd (1986) 2 BCC 98, 955*). Where the charge was acquired by the appointor from another party it may be relevant to ascertain whether the acquisition was 'free of all equities' (see e.g. *Hilger Analytical Ltd v Rank Precision Industries Ltd [1984] BCLC 301*, and the judgment of Peter Pain J in *Oakwood Group plc v Renton and others, 22 February 1990 (QBD, unreported)*) and whether the terms of the charge also secure any advances made by the appointor after the acquisition, although the validity of such security over post-acquisition advances is doubtful.

Where the charge secures advances made by a bank, the bank may be entitled to continue to charge contractual interest compounded on a quarterly basis in accordance with the usage of bankers even after the bank has demanded payment or commenced proceedings to recover it (see *Yourell v Hibernian Bank [1918] AC 372*; *National Bank of Greece SA v Pinios Shipping Co (No 1) [1989] 3 WLR 1330*). Sometimes a charge is given to secure a guarantee for the liability of a third party to a bank. A guarantee is construed strictly, but where the wording is susceptible to more than one meaning, regard may be had to the circumstances surrounding the execution of the guarantee as an aid to construction (see *Coghlan v SH Lock (Australia) (1987) 3 BCC 183 (PC); Amalgamated Investment & Property Co Ltd v Texas Commerce International Bank Ltd [1982] QB 84; Bank of Scotland v Wright [1991] BCLC 244*). In the *Bank of Scotland* case, where an individual connected with a group of companies gave a guarantee to the bank that in consideration of the bank giving inter-available facilities to the holding company, the individual would pay all sums due to the bank by the holding company 'whether solely or jointly with any other obligant or by any other firm . . . or in any other manner or way whatsoever', it was held that the guarantee, on its true construction having regard to the circumstances of its execution, was intended by the parties to secure not only the direct indebtedness of the holding company but also the indebtedness of any other company in the group which the holding company had guaranteed.

The general rule as regards a mortgagee's right to recover the costs of court proceedings out of the mortgaged property is that such a right is confined to those costs, charges and expenses which are reasonably and properly incurred in enforcing or preserving a security. A mortgagee who successfully defended an action, brought by a third party with a beneficial interest in the mortgaged property, was not entitled to add the costs of defending those proceedings to its security, although the costs were reasonably and properly incurred, even if the action impugned the title to the mortgage or the enforcement or exercise of the mortgagee's power of sale (*Parker-Tweedale v Dunbar Bank Plc (No 2) [1990] 2 All ER 588*).

(See also the last two paragraphs of D2.8(vi) above.)

(m)   Prior or subsequent charges

D2.13   Are there in existence any prior or subsequent charges in favour of other parties over the whole or part of the same assets? Although the existence of any such charges is not in itself a bar to the appointment of a receiver, their existence could affect the proposed appointor's commercial judgment as to whether to make the appointment or to adopt any other tactics. Depending on the amount due under those charges and the extent to which that amount has priority (having regard to the provisions of any deed of priority that may have been entered into between the parties, and of section 99 of the Law of Property Act 1925 (tacking of further advances)), and the amount of anticipated net realisation from the assets, it may or may not be economical to make the appointment.

Charging documents in favour of banks usually provide that upon receiving notice of any subsequent charge, the bank may open a new account in the name of the chargor through which all future debit and credit entries would be passed and that, even if the bank does not actually do so, it shall be deemed to have done so. This device is known as 'ruling off the account' and is intended to ensure that any credits received after the notice are appropriated first to post-notice debits, rather than on a first-in first-out basis in accordance with the rule in *Clayton's case*, so as to minimise the amount of debt due to the bank in respect of post-notice advances ranking after the subsequent charge by virtue of section 99 referred to in the preceding paragraph.

Among other investigations as to the existence and nature of prior and subsequent charges, searches should be made at the Companies Registry and, in relation to registered land, at the Land Registry. It is no longer necessary to obtain the registered owner's consent to the search at the Land Registry. (See also D7.23 below.)

Receiver's indemnity

D2.14 Despite all reasonable checks, it may not be possible for the receiver designate or his legal advisers to be completely satisfied on all matters referred to in D2.1 to D2.13 above. In certain respects the receiver is dependent upon information in possession of the appointor; some relevant information may have been unwittingly withheld. In other respects, detailed analyses of circumstances may be required, for which purpose sufficient time may not be available. Further, soon after his appointment, he may need to expend considerable sums and to enter into fresh commitments, without funds to cover them. He may also be exposed to personal liabilities in respect of commitments entered into after his agency has terminated—see D5.2 *et seq.* and D7.1 and D8.2 *et seq.* below. It is, therefore, normal for a receiver designate to seek from the appointor an indemnity not only against any consequences of the charge or the appointment proving to be invalid, but also against his remuneration and expenses and any liabilities which may be properly incurred in so far as they cannot be met out of the receivership funds. Normally, the indemnity excludes cases of fraud or negligence on the part of the receiver or his employees. Clearing banks, as appointors, are generally reluctant to give such indemnities, and their appointees are normally content to rely on a non-binding implicit understanding that the banks would stand by them, within reason, in case of need.

Both an administrative receiver and an ordinary receiver now have a statutory indemnity from appointors (at the discretion of the court) against any liability which arises solely by reason of the invalidity of the appointment (whether by virtue of the invalidity of the (charging) instrument or otherwise) (section 34). This indemnity obviously does not cover all the matters referred to in the preceding paragraph and will need to be augmented by express contractual indemnities. It is not clear whether any such statutory indemnity awarded against a trustee of debenture stock will be in his personal capacity or only in his representative capacity.

Planning

D2.15 Receivership under a general charge can sometimes be a saviour of a financially distressed company (see PART A: GENERAL); but it can equally prove to be very costly for the holder of the charge (see D2.14 above), if trading is continued and goes wrong or if there are substantial prior incumbrances or third party assets. Even the timing of the appointment may significantly affect, one way or the other, the amount of the preferential debts (see D7.3 *et seq*. below) and the realisable value of out-standing contracts and other assets (see D7.1 *et seq*. below generally). Usually, events leading up to the appointment occur in quick succession, leaving little time for investigation and planning; but wherever possible some thought should be given to these matters.

Chapter 3: Appointment of receiver

Mode of appointment

D3.1   The appointment out of court should be made as prescribed by the charging document. The usual mode prescribed is that it is to be made in writing, under the hand of the holder of the charge or an authorised officer of the holder. Where two or more persons are appointed as administrative receivers, the instrument of appointment must declare whether any act required or authorised under any enactment is to be done by all or by any one or by more than one of the persons for the time being holding the office in question (section 231). Although this requirement is mandatory, the consequences of failure to comply with it are not clear. No punishment is prescribed either in section 231 or Schedule 10 (punishment of offences). It is doubtful whether such failure renders the instrument of appointment invalid. Perhaps the only consequence that follows is that all acts under any enactment can only be done by both or all (as the case may be) of the administrative receivers jointly. If the document contains no express power to appoint a receiver, the appointment may only be made either (if the charge is by way of deed) pursuant to the statutory power contained in section 101(1)(iii) of the Law of Property Act 1925 (which prescribes no particular mode of appointment but, it is submitted, permits appointment in writing, even if not by way of deed) or by an order of the court. An appointment under section 101(1)(iii) or by the court has its own drawbacks. The receiver has extremely limited powers under the former; for example, he has no power of sale. In the case of a court appointment, his powers will be specified in the order and are construed strictly. Where the debenture holders' application to appoint a receiver relates to a company which is already being wound up by the court, the Official Receiver may be appointed as receiver (section 32). Where a receiver appointed by the court is an administrative receiver as defined by section 29 (see D1.4 above) he can (in addition to any express powers, but subject to any restrictions contained in the charging document) also exercise the powers contained in Schedule 1 to the 1986 Act, which are fairly extensive (see D5.2 *et seq.* below).

As stated in the preceding paragraph, the charging document usually provides that a receiver may be appointed in writing under the hand of the holder of the charge or a duly authorised officer of the holder. Sometimes it is preferred to make the appointment by way of deed on the ground that this would enable the receiver himself to execute documents by way of deed in the exercise of his functions as agent of the company or pursuant to the power of attorney in his favour contained in the charge. It is submitted that this is not necessary in cases where the charge itself is by way of deed. The receiver derives his powers from the charge rather than from the instrument of appointment, which is merely a means of triggering the powers contained in the charge. This view has now been borne out by

Phoenix Properties Ltd v Wimpole Street Nominees Ltd [1992] BCLC 737, where it was held by Mummery J that a receiver appointed by debenture holders by writing, not by deed, could convey good title to the charged property if acting in his capacity as holder of an irrevocable power of attorney granted under the debenture deed with power to sell on the company's behalf. However, it seems that an appointment made under seal would be valid, even though the charge provides for an appointment to be made under hand, on the principle that the greater includes the lesser. In *Windsor Refrigerator Co Ltd v Branch Nominees Ltd [1961] Ch 375 (CA)*, it was held that an instrument of appointment executed as a deed, but ineffective as a deed because it was not validly delivered, could nevertheless be valid as an appointment 'by writing' as required by the charging document. Furthermore, an appointment by writing could be made out (and held in escrow) before it was intended to take effect (on its delivery to the appointee) on a subsequent date.

Date when appointment takes effect

D3.2   The instrument of appointment of an ordinary receiver or an administrative receiver, duly signed or executed by the appointor (or any other person on his behalf mentioned in the charging document), must be delivered to, or to a person authorised by, the receiver. The appointment (where it is made under powers contained in the charging document) has no effect unless it is accepted by him (or, where two or more persons are appointed jointly, by each of them as if he were the sole appointee) before the end of the business day next following the day on which the instrument of appointment was received by him or on his behalf. Once it is so accepted, it dates back to the time the instrument was so received (section 33 and Rule 3.1). This gives the receiver at least 24 hours to decide whether to accept the appointment, and still enables the appointor to preserve the priority of the appointment as at the time of the delivery of the instrument. In the case of an administrative receiver appointed out of court, the acceptance made as above must (unless it was in writing) be confirmed in writing by the appointee to the appointor within seven days thereafter. Where the appointment is solely under section 101(1)(iii) of the Law of Property Act 1925 (see D3.1 above) it would seem that, following general principles (see *Cripps (Pharmaceuticals) Ltd v Wickenden [1973] 1 WLR 944*), it becomes effective from the time that the instrument of appointment is handed over to the receiver or his agent and is accepted by the receiver expressly or by conduct.

Any acceptance or confirmation under section 33 may be given on behalf of the appointee by any person duly authorised by him. The confirmation must state the date and time of receipt of the instrument of appointment and the date and time of acceptance (Rule 3.1 and Form 3.1). Where the appointment of a receiver under an *ad hoc* fixed charge or a general charge is made by the court, for example, in a pending mortgage action or a debenture holder's action, the appointment will continue to take effect from the date of the order.

Who may not be appointed

D3.3   No person who is not an authorised insolvency practitioner in relation to the company concerned may act as its administrative receiver (sections 388(1)(*a*) and 389 and see A4.1 *et seq*. PART A: GENERAL). A body corporate (section 30), or an undischarged bankrupt (except where he has been appointed by the court) (section 31), or a person against whom a disqualification order is in force pursuant to the Company Directors Disqualification Act 1986 (see section 1 thereof, discussed in PART I: DISQUALIFICATION OF DIRECTORS), may not act as an ordinary receiver or administrative receiver.

Chapter 4: Procedural matters following appointment

Notification of appointment, resignation, etc.

D4.1   When an ordinary receiver or an administrative receiver has been appointed by an order of the court or under the powers contained in the charging document, the person obtaining the order or making the appointment must, within seven days of the appointment, give notice of the fact to the Registrar of Companies who must enter the fact on the Register of Charges (section 405 of the Companies Act 1985 (to be replaced by a new section 409, to be inserted by the Companies Act 1989 with effect from a date to be fixed) and Form 405(1) in Sch 3 to the Companies (Forms) Regulations 1985 (SI 1985 No 854) (subject to any amendments pursuant to the 1989 Act)). A receiver would be well advised to notify his appointment also to all parties who had dealings with the company, including landlords, tenants and also the High Court and county courts where any execution or attachment against the company may be pending or may have been applied for (see, e.g. D5.1 *et seq*. below).

An administrative receiver must (*a*) forthwith on his appointment send to the company, and publish by advertisement once in the *Gazette* and once in such newspaper as he thinks most appropriate for ensuring that it comes to the notice of the creditors, a notice (Form 3.1A) of his appointment; and (*b*) within 28 days after his appointment, unless the court otherwise directs, send such a notice to all the creditors of the company (so far as he is aware of their addresses) (section 46(1)). These requirements do not apply to an administrative receiver appointed (presumably, only one appointed under the same charge) to act with an existing administrative receiver or in place of an administrative receiver dying or ceasing to act, except that in the latter case the requirements apply insofar as they had not been fully complied with by the predecessor (section 46(2)). The notices sent to the company and the creditors must contain all matters set out in Rule 3.2(2), and the advertisement must contain all those matters except items (*f*) and (*g*) (Rule 3.2). For the procedure concerning vacation of office by an administrative receiver, see Rules 3.33 to 3.35 and D5.2 below.

Statement of affairs in administrative receivership

D4.2   On his appointment, an administrative receiver must forthwith by notice (Rule 3.3, Form 3.1B) require some or all of certain categories of past and present officers of the company or persons under a contract of employment with the company to make out and submit to him a statement of affairs of the company in the prescribed form (section 47(1), Rule 3.4(1), Form 3.2). The statement must be verified by affidavit (section 47(2)) (and, if the administrative receiver so requires, supported by an affidavit of concurrence (Rule 3.4(2)), or qualified concurrence

(Rule 3.4(3)), from any of the other persons in those categories), and must show certain particulars mentioned in section 47(2). 'Employment' includes employment under a contract for *services* and, therefore, the requirements appear to apply also to independent contractors such as persons providing professional services (section 47(3)).

The statement must be submitted within 21 days beginning with the day after that on which the persons concerned are given notice of the requirement; but the administrative receiver (or if he refuses to exercise his power, the court) may release any persons from the obligation or extend the period when (in the case of the administrative receiver) giving the notice or (in either case) subsequently (section 47(4) and (5), Rule 3.6).

A deponent making the statement of affairs and affidavit must be allowed, and paid by the administrative receiver out of his receipts, any expenses incurred by the deponent in doing so which the receiver thinks reasonable; but this does not relieve the deponent from his obligations. The receiver's decision is subject to appeal to the court (Rule 3.7).

Administrative receiver's report

Persons to whom report must be sent

D4.3   Within three months of his appointment (or such longer period as the court may allow), the administrative receiver is required by section 48(1) to send to the Registrar of Companies, to any trustee for secured creditors and to all such creditors (so far as he is aware of their addresses) a report as to the matters set out in that subsection (see D4.4 below) and, if applicable, in Rule 3.8(2). Subject to any order of the court (see D4.4 below), the copy of the report which is to be sent to the Registrar of Companies must be accompanied (or, if then not available, followed as soon as available—Rule 3.8(4), Form 3.3) by copies of the statement of affairs and affidavits referred to in D4.2 above (Rule 3.8(3) and (4)).

Within the same period, he must either send a copy of the report to all unsecured creditors (so far as he is aware of their addresses) or publish in the newspaper in which the notice of his appointment was advertised a notice stating an address to which they should write for free copies of the report (section 48(2), Rule 3.8(1)). This requirement need not be complied with where the company has gone into liquidation and the requirement in the following paragraph is complied with within the same period.

If the company has gone into liquidation, the administrative receiver must send a copy of the report to the liquidator. This must be done within seven days after his compliance with the requirement in section 48(1) (see above) or, if later, the nomination or appointment of the liquidator (section 48(4)).

Contents of the report

D4.4   Subject to what is stated below, the report must be as to the following matters (section 48(1)).

(*a*)   Events leading up to his appointment, so far as he is aware of them.

(*b*)   The disposal or proposed disposal by him of any property and the carrying on or proposed carrying on by him of any business of the company.

(*c*)   The amounts payable to the debenture holders by whom or on whose behalf he was appointed and to preferential creditors.

(*d*)   The amount (if any) likely to be available to other creditors.

The report must also include a summary of the statement of affairs referred to in D4.2 above and the administrative receiver's comments (if any) thereon (section 48(5)).

The administrative receiver is not obliged to include in any such report any information the disclosure of which would seriously prejudice the carrying out by him of his functions (section 48(6)). He can also apply to the court for an appropriate order to limit disclosure if he thinks that the disclosure of the whole or part of the statement of affairs would prejudice the conduct of the receivership (Rule 3.5).

Section 46(2) (see D4.1 above) also applies in relation to the administrative receiver's report (section 48(7)).

Creditors' meeting in administrative receivership

D4.5   Unless the court otherwise directs (which the court may do only if the administrative receiver's report referred to above states his intention to apply for the direction and if the requirement in section 48(2) (see D4.3 above) has been complied with not less than 14 days before the hearing of the application—section 48(3)), the administrative receiver must lay a copy of the report before a meeting of the unsecured creditors summoned for the purpose. (There is, however, an exemption under section 46(2) similar to that referred to in D4.1 above.) Rules 3.9 to 3.15 deal with the procedure for the meeting, including the venue, time, period of notice, proxy (see also Form 8.3), contents of notice, chairman of the meeting, voting rights and adjournment. As to quorum, see Rule 12.4A.

Creditors' committee in administrative receivership

D4.6   Where a meeting of creditors is summoned (see D4.5 above) the meeting may establish a creditors' committee, consisting of not less than three and not more than five creditors elected at the meeting, to exercise the functions conferred on it by or under the Act (section 49(1)). The committee is required to assist the administrative receiver in discharging his functions (Rule 3.18(1)). The procedure for the committee's proceedings is contained in Rules 3.16 to 3.30 and Forms 3.4 and 3.5. The procedure includes facilities to obtain resolutions by post and for a member of the committee to appoint a representative in relation to the committee's business. Reasonable travelling expenses directly incurred by committee members or their representatives in attending committee meetings are to be allowed as an expense of the receivership. Membership of the committee does not prevent a person from dealing with the company during the receivership provided that the transaction concerned is entered into in good faith and for value. The court may, on the application of any person interested, set aside a transaction which appears to be contrary to the above proviso and may give appropriate directions for compensating the company for any loss which it may have incurred in consequence of the transaction.

The committee may, on giving not less than seven days' notice, require the administrative receiver to attend before it at any reasonable time and to furnish it with such information relating to the carrying out by him of his functions as it may reasonably require (section 49(2), Rule 3.28).

VAT bad debt relief in administrative receivership

D4.7   Rules 3.36 and 3.37 deal with the issue, by the administrative receiver, of a VAT bad debt certificate to enable creditors, who have made taxable supplies to the company, to claim from HM Customs and Excise the appropriate VAT bad debt relief. However, these rules have largely become redundant as a result of the recent legislative changes which have considerably relaxed the conditions on which relief is available. See section 36 of the Value Added Tax Act 1994, as supplemented by the Value Added Tax (Bad Debt Relief) Regulations 1986 (SI 1986 No 335) and the Value Added Tax (Refunds for Bad Debts) Regulations 1991 (SI 1991 No 371). Relief is not available in respect of a debt represented by moneys held by the company in trust for the claimant: *Wayfarer Leisure Ltd v The Commissioners of Customs & Excise [1985] VATTR 174.* As to set-off regarding value added tax, see D7.6(2) below.

Application to court for directions by receiver

D4.8   A receiver may apply to the court for directions in relation to any particular matters arising in connection with the performance of his functions. The court may give such directions, or may make such order declaring the rights of persons before the court or otherwise, as it thinks just (section 35). This is a very useful provision for a receiver, which he would be well advised to invoke in appropriate cases; but in contested matters, the costs payable out of receivership funds can be considerable.

This provision has commonly been used to obtain the court's decisions on questions relating to priorities and order of distribution (see, for example, the *New Bullas* case referred to at D6.2 and the *Woodroffes* case referred to at D10.4). In *NL Electrical Ltd [1994] 1 BCLC 22*, the receivers appointed under a debenture applied for directions concerning an apparent past breach by the company of sections 151 to 157 of the Companies Act 1985 (financial assistance for the acquisition of shares) connected with a loan secured by another debenture granted by the company. The court approved the course adopted by the receivers, stating that the receivers had not come to the court advancing a positive case but rather enquiring how they should act. They had taken the correct attitude that there were apparent irregularities which could conceivably impugn the other debenture and must take the point in the interests of the appointing debenture holder and the unsecured creditors. However, in the court's view the financial assistance had been validly given.

Remuneration of receiver

D4.9   A charging document almost invariably provides that, in addition to 'all' costs, expenses and charges incurred by the receiver, the receiver is to be entitled to be paid such remuneration out of the charged assets as may be fixed by the holder of the charge. Section 109(6) of the Law of Property Act 1925, which fixes a rate of five per cent of the gross amount of all moneys received, has very limited application and is rarely relied on. A receiver under that Act is a receiver of only the income and profits of the property charged. He has no power of sale. A professional receiver usually expects to be paid an amount arrived at by reference to the time spent by him and his staff, adjusted to take into account any other relevant factors.

Under section 36 of the Insolvency Act 1986, the court has power on the application of the liquidator (if any) to fix and review the amount of the remuneration of an ordinary receiver or an administrative receiver payable or paid to him; and may order him or his personal representatives to refund any excess remuneration received. The latter power may not be exercised as respects any period before the making of the application, unless there are special circumstances. In *Re Potters Oils Ltd (No 2)* *[1986] 1 WLR 201*, decided under the old legislation, it was held that any interference with the receiver's rights to remuneration should be confined to cases where the contractual remuneration could clearly be seen to be excessive.

In *Gomba Holdings (UK) Ltd v Minories Finance Ltd [1992] BCC 877*, the Court of Appeal allowed the mortgagor to challenge the amount of certain litigation and non-litigation costs incurred by the mortgagee bank and the receiver appointed by it. The court rejected the bank's objection that the charging document gave the bank power to recover 'all' costs 'howsoever incurred', expenses and charges (including the receiver's remuneration) and that therefore, short of fraud, the mortgagor was not entitled to challenge the amount. It was certainly the case that, while the court had the final discretion as regards litigation costs, it would normally give effect to the pre-existing agreement between the parties. However, the expression 'all costs howsoever incurred' was not to be taken literally. It meant costs on an 'indemnity basis', the scope of which was the subject of the Rules of the Supreme Court which provided, *inter alia*, that any item of costs which was unreasonably incurred, or the amount of which was unreasonable, could be challenged on taxation. As regards non-litigation costs, the position was similar.

Where a receiver is appointed by the court in litigation to protect or preserve property in dispute, and his remuneration and costs exceed the money he is appointed to receive, the court has no power to order the parties to the litigation to meet the deficit before the rights of the parties are determined (*Evans v Clayhope Properties Ltd [1988] BCLC 238*). The court will neither itself indemnify, nor order the party at whose instance such receiver is appointed to indemnify, the receiver in respect of his remuneration and costs; but it will order that he be indemnified out of the assets under the court's control or all the assets to which the appointment extends even though the receiver has not obtained actual control of them.
 This right to indemnity continues notwithstanding the discharge of the receivership or return of the assets to the defendant. The amount of the receiver's remuneration and expenses is in the discretion of the court, but the parties may challenge the remuneration and expenses where the receiver has been in breach of his duties or where the amount claimed is excessive (see *Mellor v Mellor [1992] BCC 513*). However, the court has no power to order that the receiver's remuneration or expenses be a charge on the property concerned ranking in priority to existing valid charges (*Choudhri v Palta [1992] BCC 787 (CA)*).

Abstracts of receipts and payments in receivership

D4.10   An ordinary receiver is required to deliver to the Registrar of Companies accounts of his receipts and payments within one month (or such longer period as the Registrar may allow) after the expiration of twelve months from the date of his appointment and of every subsequent period of six months (section 38). (See also D10.6 below.)

These requirements apply to an administrative receiver (Rule 3.32, Form 3.6) with the following variations—

(*a*)   'one month' should read 'two months' and 'six months' should read 'twelve months';

(*b*)   copies of the accounts should also be sent to the company, to his appointor and to each member of the creditors' committee (if any);

(*c*)   the power to extend the period (of two months) is vested in the court instead of the Registrar of Companies.

Enforcement of duties of receiver

D4.11   A receiver's duty to file, deliver or make any return, account or other document or give notice may be enforced by the court on an application by any member or creditor or the Registrar of Companies (as the case may be). Where after being so required by the liquidator, he fails to render and vouch proper accounts of receipts and payments and to pay over to the liquidator any amount properly payable to him, the court may on the liquidator's application order the receiver to make good the default (section 41).

Notification of receivership on stationery

D4.12 Every invoice, order for goods or business letter, on which the name of the company of whose property a receiver (of either type) has been appointed appears, and which is issued by or on behalf of the company, or by or on behalf of the receiver or the liquidator, must contain a statement that a receiver has been appointed (section 39).

Chapter 5: General effects of receivership

D5.1   The main general effects of the appointment of an administrative receiver or (depending on the terms of the charge) an ordinary receiver are firstly, that he is constituted the company's agent with very wide powers, and secondly, that the floating charge, if any, under which he is appointed crystallises by the operation of law, if it has not already previously crystallised. Upon crystallisation, the assets comprised in the floating charge become assigned in equity to the holder of the charge (whereas in the case of a fixed or specific charge *ab initio* the holder's legal or equitable interest arises at the time of the creation of that charge). The appointment *does not* vest the assets concerned in the receiver as he is only an agent of the company (see below; see also the Australian case of *Telecom Australia v Russell Kumar & Sons (1993) 10 ACSR 24*). These effects, and the general principle that a receiver as agent has no better rights in relation to the assets charged than the rights which the company had vis-à-vis third parties, have an important bearing on the receiver's functions in relation to the charged assets and on his dealings with third parties, as will be seen below.

Receiver's agency powers and position

Agency and position

D5.2   A charging document almost invariably provides that in the exercise of his powers and functions, the receiver shall be the agent of the company, which alone shall be responsible for his acts and defaults. This provision is usually augmented by an irrevocable power of attorney in his favour, in addition to one in favour of his appointor. In the absence of any agency provision (subject to the last sentence of this paragraph), an *ordinary* receiver will not normally be regarded as the company's agent and could be regarded as a principal or his appointor's agent. This may not only involve the receiver or his appointor in personal liability in respect of any contracts he enters into in relation to the assets charged, but also cause difficulties to the receiver in passing title to a purchaser. Under the Law of Property Act 1925, an ordinary receiver is the mortgagor's agent (see section 109(2)), but the statutory agency is of limited use, inasmuch as a receiver under that Act is essentially a receiver of only the income and profits of the property charged—he has no power to sell or convey the property.

A receiver appointed by the court, for example, by way of equitable execution, is not an agent or trustee for the party at whose instance he is appointed nor of the owner of the property concerned. He is an officer of the court (see *Mellor v Mellor [1992] BCC 513*). He may thus render himself personally liable as principal on any contracts entered into by him subject to his right of indemnity out of the property concerned (see further D4.9 (last paragraph) above). Where a person desires to bring an action against a court-appointed receiver whilst still in office in respect of anything the receiver has done as such, it is prudent for that person to apply to the court for leave to bring the action so as to avoid the possibility of being in contempt of court (*Re Botibol [1947] 1 All ER 26*).

Where the charging document confers agency on the receiver, that agency ceases upon the company going into liquidation (*Thomas v Todd [1926] 2 KB 511; Re Henry Pound, Son & Hutchins (1889) 42 ChD 402*). In a compulsory winding up, the material time (on the analogy of *Re Christonette International Ltd [1982] 3 All ER 225*) appears to be the date of the winding-up order, and not the date of the presentation of the petition. Even the power of attorney in his favour will not survive the liquidation, as it cannot be said to have been given to secure the company's obligations owed to, or any proprietary interest of, the receiver (as distinct from the holder of the charge) in the terms of section 4(1) of the Powers of Attorney Act 1971. (It is, perhaps, possible to create, by clever drafting of the charging document, an obligation in favour of the receiver, linked to an irrevocable power of attorney, and thereby enable the irrevocable power to survive liquidation.) However, notwithstanding the termination of the agency and of the power of attorney upon liquidation, and the provisions of section 127 of the Insolvency Act 1986 (avoidance of disposition of a company's property made after the commencement of a compulsory winding up), the receiver continues, after liquidation, to be entitled to dispose of and convey the charged property as agent of or in the name of the company (see *Sowman v David Samuel Trust Ltd [1978] 1 WLR 22; Barrows v Chief Land Registrar, The Times, 20 October 1977*). In practice, a purchaser may prefer to receive a conveyance from the holder of the charge rather than from the receiver (see D5.3 below; see also the second paragraph of D3.1 above), although, as far as an administrative receiver is concerned, section 42(3) provides that a person dealing with him in good faith and for value is not concerned to enquire whether he is acting within his powers, and section 232 provides that his acts are valid notwithstanding any defect in his appointment, nomination or qualifications (but see D2.1 above as to the limited effect of this provision).

The company's liquidation does not terminate the receiver's right to continue any legal proceedings as the agent and in the name of the company (*Gough's Garage v Pugsley [1930] 1 KB 615*).

The main consequence of the termination of the receiver's agency on liquidation is that he cannot contract fresh trade liabilities on behalf of the company. He may therefore become personally responsible for them, insofar as he is unable to discharge them from the receivership assets.

As far as an administrative receiver is concerned, there is no longer a real need expressly to confer agency on him. Such agency is now conferred on him by section 44 of the Insolvency Act 1986 (but, again, only unless and until the company goes into liquidation). Nevertheless, an express inclusion of the agency in the charge may have some residual advantages. In any case, there still seems to be a need to confer a power of attorney, which is not implied by the Act (but see D5.3 below).

A receiver as agent of the company does not owe a duty to the company's creditors; he owes it only to his appointor and to the company (*Lathia v Dronsfield Bros Ltd [1987] BCLC 321*—see also D7.24 below).

As to the liability of a receiver on pre-receivership and post-receivership contracts, see D7.1 and D8.2 to D8.4 below. He may also be liable for disposing of any of the assets at an undervalue (see D8.14 below) and in tort for interference with third party proprietary rights (see D8.14 and D8.15 below). An administrative receiver can also be liable for misfeasance (section 212(1)(b); see C13.4 PART C: LIQUIDATIONS).

An administrative receiver may only be removed by an order of the court (section 45). By contrast, an ordinary receiver can be, as he could be prior to the coming into force of the present legislation, removed by his appointor out of court if the charging instrument (or the instrument of appointment) so provides (or, arguably, in any case—*Cripps (Pharmaceuticals) Ltd v Wickenden [1973] 1 WLR 944*).

An administrative receiver may resign his office subject to the provisions as to prior notice of Rule 3.33. Where he dies, his appointor must comply with Rule 3.34 as to notification. On vacation of office, the administrative receiver must comply with the notification provisions of Rule 3.35 and, subject thereto, may appoint another insolvency practitioner as administrative receiver.

Neither the Act nor the Rules deal with the resignation of an ordinary receiver appointed out of court. A charging instrument usually gives the charge-holder power to remove a receiver appointed by him but is silent (as is also the instrument of appointment) as to whether the receiver can resign unilaterally (i.e. without the consent of the appointor). Some textbooks suggest that in the absence of an express provision in the charging instrument, he cannot do so. This suggestion appears to be based on the argument that there is implied, in the contractual relationship between the appointor and the receiver created by the appointment and its acceptance, a term that the receiver will continue to act until he has fully discharged his duties and functions. It is submitted that there is no warrant for such an implication unless, perhaps, there are also implied certain exceptions relating to situations where the receiver can legitimately refuse to continue to act.

Powers

D5.3   A charging document usually contains extensive powers in favour of the receiver as regards disposal of and dealing with the charged property (including, in the case of a general charge, power to carry on the company's business), in addition to the powers conferred on him by the Law of Property Act 1925 (which are extremely limited). This practice will need to be continued in the case of an *ad hoc* charge.

In the case of an administrative receiver appointed under a general charge, most of such powers, and certain additional powers, are now conferred on him by sections 42 and 43 and Schedule 1. Even in that case, there may be some residual advantages in continuing to include them expressly in the charge (see D5.4 below).

A receiver has an unrestricted right to sell the charged property at any time, and that power continues until redemption or at least until a valid tender of the redemption money. The mere claim by the mortgagor company that it is able to redeem does not restrict the receiver's powers: *Gomba Holdings UK Ltd v Homan [1986] 1 WLR 1301*. However, where the receiver has discharged his appointor's secured claim in full out of the proceeds of realisation of some of the assets, he may be temporarily restrained by the court from carrying out any further realisation, to the detriment of the charging company, merely so as to get in money sufficient to discharge that part of his remuneration which is disputed and which is not covered by the balance in his hands: *Rottenberg v Monjack [1992] BCC 688*.

Two very useful powers which an administrative receiver now has but did not, and could not, previously have are the power to use the company's seal (see paragraph 8 of Schedule 1—it seems that this power is intended to survive liquidation) and a power, with the leave of the court, to 'overreach' a prior or *pari passu* security. The latter power is contained in section 43. This provides that where, on the administrative receiver's application, the court is satisfied that the disposal (with or without other assets) of any property (i) which is (or, but for the appointment of another person as receiver of part of the company's property, would have been) comprised in his appointment and (ii) which is subject to a security (other than his appointor's security or any security over which it has priority), would be likely to promote a more advantageous realisation of the company's assets, the court may authorise the receiver to make the disposal as if the property were not subject to that security. It will be a condition of the authorisation that the net proceeds of the disposal, and, where those proceeds are less than the amount determined by the court to be the net amount which would be realised on a sale of the property in the open market by a willing vendor, such sums as may be required to make good the difference, should be applied towards discharging that security or, if there is more than one such security, towards discharging those securities in order of their respective priorities.

Before the Insolvency Act 1986 came into force, views differed as to whether a conveyance by a receiver on behalf of the company 'overreached' a *subsequent* security, as did a conveyance by a mortgagee in exercise of his power of sale by virtue of section 104 of the Law of Property Act 1925. For this reason, some purchasers preferred to take a conveyance from the holder of the charge, unless the receiver undertook to have the subsequent security discharged. This practice is likely to continue, as the new Act is silent on the point. Section 43 only applies to a prior or *pari passu* security.

By far the most important powers of the receiver are those relating to the realisation of assets (paragraphs 2, 15 and 16 of Schedule 1), carrying out of any works (paragraph 12 of Schedule 1), the carrying on of business (paragraphs 11 and 14 of Schedule 1), and the raising of money with or without security over the receivership assets (paragraph 3 of Schedule 1). These are dealt with in D9.1 *et seq.* below.

It will also be noted that an administrative receiver's power to present a winding-up petition in respect of the company, as recognised in *Re Emmadart [1979] 1 All ER 599*, is now contained in paragraph 21 of Schedule 1, which also empowers him to defend any winding-up petition against the company. (See generally the cases referred to in C5.29 PART C: LIQUIDATIONS.) He also has a power to 'hive-down' the company's undertaking (see paragraphs 15 and 16 of Schedule 1; see also D9.4 *et seq.* below). In addition, an administrative receiver has available to him certain statutory aids to facilitate his task (see A4.14 *et seq.* PART A: GENERAL).

Paragraph 11 of Schedule 1 empowers an administrative receiver to appoint any agent to do any business which he is unable to do himself, or which can more conveniently be done by an agent. It is submitted that this power is impliedly confined to delegating to an agent powers of an administrative nature and those involving activities which can be described as in the ordinary course of the company's business or the receivership, and that powers involving the exercise of discretion on important matters cannot be delegated.

It is debatable whether the receiver's powers are subject to an implied overall limitation that being an agent of the company, he cannot do anything which the company itself has no power to do under its memorandum of association. There is no judicial authority on this point in relation to receiverships, but it was dealt with in *Re Home Treat Ltd [1991] BCLC 705*, an administration case. In that case, the administrators proposed to continue to carry on a business in the name of the company which was *ultra vires* the objects of the company, and sought directions from the court. The court held that section 14 (which incorporates, in favour of administrators, the powers specified in Schedule 1) gave the administrators no powers greater than the company itself had under its memorandum of association. At common law, the consent or acquiescence of all the shareholders was as good as a special resolution altering the objects clause, but section 4 of the Companies Act 1985 (in its original wording—see below) did not permit, and would probably have rendered invalid, the adoption of a wholly new object for a wholly new business. However, in the end, the court held that it could protect the administrators as officers of the company under section 727 of the 1985 Act and would do so in that case.

(Note that on 4 February 1991—shortly after *Re Home Treat Ltd* was decided—section 110(2) of the Companies Act 1989 came into force, substituting a new section 4 of the 1985 Act. This gives a company a general power to alter the objects clause in its memorandum in place of the more limited powers which were specified in the section as previously worded.)

It will be noted that an application for relief under section 727 may be made not only in respect of an act of negligence, default, breach of duty or breach of trust already done but also an act which is proposed to be done (CA 1985, s 727(2)). Section 727 applies only to an officer or auditor of the company. It appears that for these purposes liquidators, administrators, and administrative receivers are officers of the company, as section 212 of the Insolvency Act 1986 (misfeasance, breach of fiduciary or other duty) applies to them as well as to the officers of (and other specified persons connected with) the company. It may be that the court in *Re Home Treat Ltd* had more sympathy for the administrators than it might have had for administrative receivers because, unlike administrators, administrative receivers are not officers of the court, although in its application section 727 is not confined to officers of the court. On the other hand, it is arguable that an administrative receiver is in a stronger position because he is acting pursuant to the powers contained (and/or implied by virtue of Schedule 1) in a charge created by the company as authorised by the company's memorandum of association, that one of such powers is 'to carry on the business of the company' and that the words quoted mean the business which the company actually carries on and not merely that which it has power to carry on. However, it would be safer not to rely on these arguments and to apply immediately for relief under section 727, preferably in advance of rather than after the event.

(See also section 231, and the comments thereon in D3.1 above.)

Sufficiency of Schedule 1 powers

D5.4 Depending on the type of the company's activities, the Schedule 1 powers may prove to be deficient in some respects. Careful consideration must be given, when drafting the charging document, to adding expressly such other powers as the receiver may conceivably need so as to be able to conduct the realisation of assets to the maximum advantage.

Notwithstanding that extensive powers in relation to the realisation of assets are conferred on an administrative receiver by the Act, it is advisable to confer expressly such powers on him in the charging document (either by setting them out in detail or incorporating them by reference to Schedule 1, but making it clear that they will be exercisable by him whether he is regarded as administrative receiver or ordinary receiver). This is because, although the charge may be such that if he is appointed over all the assets comprised in it, he would be an administrative receiver with all those statutory powers, there may be a possibility that, for some special reason, the appointment is (expressly or otherwise) confined only to some assets. This may happen, for example, because the charge over the other assets has previously been released or is found to be invalid, or the other assets have negative values or are problem-ridden. In such a situation, the receiver may be only an ordinary receiver without the benefit of those extensive powers, unless they have been specifically conferred by the charging document.

Position of the company's officers in administrative receivership

D5.5   Although the administrative receiver is effectively in control of the affairs and assets of the company, to the exclusion of the directors, the directors continue to have residual functions in safeguarding the interests of the company insofar as the exercise of such functions does not in any way impinge prejudicially on the position of the receiver's appointor, by threatening or imperilling the assets which are the subject of the charge: *Newhart Developments Ltd v Co-operative Commercial Bank Ltd [1978] 2 All ER 896 (CA)*. 'If in the exercise of his discretion he chooses to ignore some asset such as a right of action, or decides that it would be unprofitable from the point of view of the debenture holders to pursue it, (it is) . . . open to the directors to pursue the right of action if they think that it would be in the interests of the company . . . If there is an asset which appears to be of value, although the directors cannot deal with it in the sense of disposing of it, they are under a duty to exploit it so as to bring it to realisation which may be fruitful for all concerned' (*per* Shaw LJ in the *Newhart* case (at *900*)).

Newhart was considered in *Tudor Grange Holdings Ltd v Citibank NA [1991] 4 All ER 1*, where the directors of a group of companies in administrative receivership issued proceedings against a bank (which was not the appointor or administrative receiver) claiming misrepresentation, duress, breach of fiduciary duty and fraud in relation to a refinancing arrangement. The bank applied to have the action struck out on various grounds, including that it had not been authorised by the administrative receivers. The Vice-Chancellor distinguished the *Newhart* case (the correctness of which decision he doubted), stating that in the *Newhart* case, the action proposed (and authorised by the Court of Appeal) was against the receiver's appointor whom it would be awkward for the receiver to sue. Also, the directors in *Newhart* had promised a full indemnity for costs so that the receiver's position was not prejudiced. As there was the possibility of an indemnity being forthcoming in this case, the Vice-Chancellor would not strike out the claim on this ground alone, although the claim was in fact struck out on other grounds.

Whereas a company in receivership cannot interfere with the receiver in the proper exercise of his powers, it can maintain an action against him for the improper discharge of his duty. The proper plaintiff is the company itself. A derivative action on behalf of the shareholders cannot be maintained, particularly where due to the company's insolvency they do not stand to benefit (*Watts v Midland Bank plc [1986] BCLC 15*).

An administrative receiver, in practice, runs the company on behalf of its directors and is, therefore, answerable to the company for the conduct of its affairs. That being so, he is under a duty to keep fuller accounts than the abstracts of receipts and payments account which he is required to file (see D4.11 above), and to produce those accounts to the company when required to do so (see the headnote to *Smiths Ltd v Middleton [1979] 3 All ER 842*; see also *Gomba Holdings UK Ltd v Homan [1986] 1 WLR 1301*). In realising and managing the assets under his control in the interests of his appointor, he can refuse to disclose information contrary to the interests of the appointor; but he has also a duty to supply information to the company during his receivership in accordance with section 38 and Rule 3.32 (formerly section 497 of the Companies Act 1985) and the terms of his appointment. That duty of disclosure is not limited to those provisions; further disclosure might be required where it is demonstrated that the company has a need to know the information (*Gomba Holdings UK Ltd v Homan* (above)). In *Irish Oil and Cake Mills Ltd v John Donnelly* (a Republic of Ireland High Court judgment of 27 March 1984), it was held that the extent and nature of the receiver's equitable duty to give information was not comparable to the duty of an ordinary agent in everyday commercial transactions, and would depend on the facts of the case.

It is not entirely clear whether during the period of administrative receivership, the directors' duties under sections 226, 227, 233, 234 to 238, 241, 242, 242A, 363 and 366 of the Companies Act 1985 with regard to the preparation, filing and presentation of annual accounts, reports and returns, and the holding of annual general meetings, go into abeyance. Although there are strong arguments for the proposition that legally their duties remain in abeyance, the conventional wisdom is that technically they continue. However, as most of their powers and the control of all the funds, information and facilities would have been taken over by the administrative receiver, the directors can, to a very large extent, successfully rely on the defences available in the sections referred to above; for example, that there was no wilful default on their part, or that despite all reasonable steps taken by them, it was impossible for them to comply with the requirements. This would particularly be so if they write to the administrative receiver asking for the necessary funding, records, information and facilities to be made available to them and the administrative receiver declines, as he would be within his rights, to do so. In this connection, it is relevant to note the statement made by Companies House as reported in the Autumn 1990 issue of 'Insolvency Practitioner', in relation to administration matters, to the effect that upon receipt of notification of the appointment of administrators, Companies House would put a computer 'stop' on default pursuit in relation to the above requirements. Companies House would then write to the administrators asking for comments as to whether in their opinion the directors are able to comply with their requirements. Depending on the response received from the administrators the 'stop' would be either lifted or continued. There seems to be no reason why the same practice should not be followed in relation to administrative receiverships.

On the termination of the receivership, the company is entitled to the return of only those documents in the receiver's possession which belong to the company. Ownership depends on the capacity in which he acquired them. Documents generated or received by the receiver pursuant to a duty to manage the company's business or to dispose of the assets belong to the company. Documents containing advice and information about the receivership or about the company brought into existence to enable the receiver to advise the holder of the charge belong to the holder. Notes, calculations and memoranda prepared by the receiver, not pursuant to any duty to prepare them but to better enable him to discharge his duties, belong to the receiver. The fact that the documents were prepared at the company's expense is not decisive (see *Gomba Holdings UK Ltd v Minories Finance Ltd* [*1988*] *BCLC 60*).

Chapter 6: Fixed charges and floating charges

D6.1   As will be seen throughout these chapters, the nature of the charge at a given time, over any particular assets covered by the receiver's appointment, may affect priorities and the level of net realisation of assets by him.

At a given time, the charge

(*a*)   may be a fixed charge, having been such from its inception (although, arguably, a subsequent course of conduct between the parties may have the effect of turning it into a floating charge); or

(*b*)   may be a floating charge, having been such from its inception; or

(*c*)   having been such a floating charge, may since have crystallised.

A charge in category (*a*) is not subject to the rights of preferential creditors but that in category (*b*) or (*c*) is. The charge in (*b*) may also be adversely affected by the rights of supervening execution, distraining or secured creditors or the costs of a supervening liquidation, whereas that in (*a*) and, to a somewhat lesser degree, that in (*c*) affords a substantial measure of protection against such rights and costs.

It would help, therefore, to be clear about the meanings of 'fixed charge' and 'floating charge' and as to what constitutes crystallisation. Some of the salient points, viewed from a receiver's standpoint, may be mentioned here.

Meaning of 'fixed charge' and 'floating charge'

D6.2   One essential respect in which a fixed charge (which may be either a legal or an equitable charge) differs from an uncrystallised floating charge (which is necessarily an equitable charge) is that the company granting the fixed charge is not, without the consent of the holder, at liberty to deal with or dispose of the asset concerned even in the ordinary course of its business or even whilst it is not in default.

A fixed charge can be over a specified asset or category of assets. Future as well as existing assets may be the subject of a fixed charge, provided that the restriction against such dealing or disposal applies to them. It has been held, for example, that in such a situation there can be a valid fixed charge over future book-debts (*Siebe Gorman & Co Ltd v Barclays Bank Ltd [1979] 2 Lloyds Rep 142*).

The fact that a charge describes itself as a fixed charge may be indicative of the intention of the parties but is not decisive. Even the presence of an express restriction is not necessarily conclusive, although it provides a stronger indication of the parties' intention. It is conceivable that, reading the charging document (and any related documents) as a whole in the context of the nature of asset concerned, the court might hold that the charge is, in effect, a floating charge. For example:

(*a*) A fixed charge over all existing and future stock-in-trade and work-in-progress of a company may be incompatible with its ability to carry on its business or with its obligation in the charging document to do so in a proper and efficient manner, and may cast doubt on whether the charge is given in furtherance of its main objects mentioned in its memorandum of association (unless, perhaps, the charge is given in the context of the scaling down of the company's business).

(*b*) A fixed charge over all existing and future book and other debts may meet with similar objections (albeit with lesser force) unless it is in favour of a bank, particularly one which provides or contemplates providing the company with a continuing line of credit. Even in the case of a bank, the absence of a provision requiring payments of the proceeds of the debts, as they are realised, into an account with the bank may make the charge only a floating charge (see *Re Armagh Shoes Ltd [1984] BCLC 409* (a Northern Irish case) and contrast with *Re Keenan Bros Ltd [1986] BCLC 242* (Irish Supreme Court); see also *Re Yorkshire Woolcombers Association Ltd [1903] 2 Ch 284; Re Brightlife Ltd [1986] BCLC 418*). By contrast, in *Re Atlantic Medical Ltd [1992] BCLC 653*, where a company charged to a funder all present and future lease contracts under which the company granted leases or sub-leases of equipment to end-users, such charge expressed to be a fixed charge, the validity of the fixed charge was upheld notwithstanding that it did not require the company to pay all rental income receivable by it under the contracts into a bank account controlled by the funder. The court refused to draw a distinction between a charge over the lease contracts and a charge over the rental income receivable under it and to hold that even if the former was a fixed charge, the latter was only a floating charge. It stated that such a distinction would be unreal and that it did not matter that the company was free to use the rental income for the purposes of its business without the funder's consent. In the event the company did not do so. The income not so used was subject to a fixed charge. See, however, the *New Bullas* case below where the House of Lords held that parties can expressly agree such a distinction. Where such a charge containing such a provision is in favour of a party other than a bank, doubts may be raised whether the parties really intended that such a provision should be operated in practice, thereby depriving the charging company of its ability to recycle its book-debts in the ordinary course of its business. Draftsmen of charges have long struggled to achieve the twin objectives of freedom in trading and servitude in insolvency (a metaphor suggested by Fletcher Moulton LJ in *Evans v Rival Granite Quarries Ltd [1910] 2 KB 979* at 998).

(*c*) In *Re GE Tunbridge Limited [1994] BCC 563*, a company engaged in the business of sale and repairs of motor cars created a debenture in favour of an individual containing (i) a floating charge over new and used motor vehicles, spare parts and other assets acquired by the company for the purpose of resale and (ii) a fixed charge over freehold properties and 'all other assets (not being floating (charge) assets) now owned or hereafter acquired by (the company). . .'. The debenture contained the usual prohibition against the disposal (etc.) of the fixed charge assets without the debenture holder's consent. The question was whether the debenture effectively created a fixed charge over not only various chattels but also over intangible assets such as book debts. Sir Mervyn Davies held that the debenture created a charge on a class of present and future assets and clearly contemplated that the company was to carry on business in the ordinary way as far as those assets were concerned (see *Re Yorkshire Woolcombers Association* below). The debenture was not apt to create a specific (fixed) charge over the book debts or the chattels. It was unrealistic to suppose that a considerable number of chattels would not or might not be changed or removed from time to time. The debenture as a whole disclosed a situation where a floating charge arose despite the parties having supposed that they were creating a specific charge. The prohibition against alienation on its own did not convert what was otherwise a floating charge into a specific charge (see *Re Brightlife* below). The position might have been different had the debenture contained a schedule itemising particular assets that the parties regarded as susceptible of a fixed charge (see *National Provincial Bank of England v United Electric Theatres Limited* [*1916*] *1 Ch 132*).

A fixed charge over 'all present and future book-debts and other debts' may not necessarily include a fixed charge over bank credit balances and deposits of money (though, in law, they are debts due to the company), depending on how that expression is related to the other provisions of the charge; see, for example, *Re Brightlife Limited* [*1986*] *BCLC 418, per* Hoffmann J. In that case, the holder of the charge was not a bank and the charge contained no provision for the payment of the proceeds of recovery into a bank account held by the chargeholder. In a later case, *Re Permanent Houses Holdings Ltd* (*1989*) *5 BCC 151*, Hoffmann J clarified his comments in the *Brightlife* case by saying that he did not mean to say that in no circumstances could a cash (credit) balance at a bank be a 'book-debt'. However, as in the *Brightlife* case, he appeared to be of the view that on the true construction of the charging document, the cash balance at a bank, which is normally shown in books of account as 'cash at bank' rather than as an amount due from 'debtors' did not fall within the fixed charge over book and other debts. (But note the decision of the Northern Ireland Court of Appeal in *Northern Bank Ltd v Ross* [*1990*] *BCC 883*, in which it was held that to the extent that the moneys in the bank account represented payments received from debtors by means of cheques and credit card payments, they were 'book-debts'.) The receiver had also received money payable to the company under an indemnity agreement. This was conceded by H M Customs & Excise, a preferential creditor under the old legislation, to be subject to such fixed charge.

A fixed charge over existing and future book debts or other debts, contained in debentures created in favour of a bank, and stipulating a requirement for the payment of all sums recovered in respect of them into a separate and denominated account of the company with the bank and a prohibition against any withdrawal from that account without the consent of the bank, does not become a floating charge on the assignment of the debenture to a third party which is not a bank (*William Gaskell Group Ltd v Highley [1993] BCC 200*; decided under the old legislation).

A neat solution to the problems referred to in (*b*) above about the efficacy of a fixed charge over debts has been suggested in the decision of the Court of Appeal in *Re New Bullas Trading Ltd [1994] BCC 36*, a case where the holder of a charge was not a bank. In this case, unlike in the cases referred to in (*b*) above where the forms of fixed charge had treated book debts and the proceeds of their recovery indivisibly, the charge over debts, whilst they remained unrecovered, was expressed to be a fixed charge. However, the charge over the proceeds of their recovery was in essence to be a floating charge (in that although the proceeds were required to be paid into a designated account with a bank, they were to be released from the fixed charge and to stand subject to a floating charge unless the charge holder intervened or a specified event occurred). It was held that the debts which had remained unrecovered at the time of the receivers' appointment were validly subject to a fixed charge. It was not necessary for its validity that there should be a fixed charge even on the future proceeds of their recovery. Just as it was open for parties to provide for a fixed charge on future book debts, so it was open to them to provide that they should be subject to a fixed charge while they were uncollected and a floating charge on future realisation. The commercial realities of such a 'split charge' were summarised by Nourse LJ as follows:

> 'There being usually no need to deal with [a book debt] before collection, it is at that stage a natural subject of the fixed charge. But once collected, the proceeds being needed for the conduct of the business, it becomes a natural subject of the floating charge. While the company is a going concern, it is no less an advantage to the lender that the debt should be collected and the proceeds used in the business. But on insolvency, a crystallised floating charge on proceeds, which, in the event supposed, are more likely to have been dissipated, may be worthless; whereas a fixed charge enabling the lender to intercept payment to the company may be of real value'.

(See also *Tailby v Official Receiver (1888) 13 App Cas 523.*)

Certain recent Canadian cases suggest that the courts, at least in Ontario, will, in the context of the local legislation, treat a fixed charge on revolving collateral as in reality a floating charge (see *Re Urman (1983), 48 CBS (NS) 129 (Ont CA)*; *Re Zurich Insurance Company and Troy Woodworking Ltd (1984), 50 CBR (NS) 1, 61 OR (2d) 129 (CA)*; *Bank of Montreal v Titan Landco Inc (1989), 72 CBR (NS) 262 (BCSC)*; *Armstrong v Coopers & Lybrand Ltd (1987), 65 CBR (NS) 258 (Ont CA)*; and *Re National Bank of Canada and McArthur (1986), 53 OR (2d) 385 (Div Ct)*). However, in *Re Atlantic Computer Systems Plc [1992] 1 All ER 476*, assignments of sub-lease rentals which the company was left free to utilise in the ordinary course of business were held, on the facts, to be fixed charges rather than floating charges. Nicholls LJ, in his judgment in the Court of Appeal, stated:

> 'We have in mind that in practice, sums payable by the end users under these sub-leases were paid to the company and utilised by it in the ordinary course of business. In so far as this is relevant, it may well be that this was what the parties intended should happen. The company was to be at liberty to receive and use the instalments until AIB chose to intervene. We are unpersuaded that this results in these charges, on existing and defined property, becoming floating charges. A mortgage of land does not become a floating charge by a reason of the mortgagor being permitted to remain in possession and enjoy the fruits of the property charged for the time being. This is so even if the land is leasehold and the term is very short, and as such the asset charged is of a wasting character. So here; the mere fact that for the time being the company could continue to receive and use the instalments does not suffice to negative the fixed character of the charge . . . we have seen nothing to suggest that after the assignment the company was to be at liberty to deal with its rights under the sub-leases without the consent of AIB.'

The three essential characteristics of a *floating charge* are that

(i)   it is a charge on a class of assets,

(ii) that class will change in the ordinary course of business, and

(iii) it is contemplated that until some further step is taken by or on behalf of those interested in the charge, the company may carry on its business in the ordinary way as far as concerns the particular class (*Re Yorkshire Woolcombers Association [1903] 2 Ch 284*).

However, it does not follow that any deviation from those characteristics (including any addition of terms) will prevent the charge from being categorised as a floating charge. The position depends on the degree of deviation (see *Re Brightlife Ltd [1986] BCLC 418*). It would appear, however, that characteristic (iii) above is crucial and if it is substantially present, the charge over the assets concerned is likely to be a floating charge. For example, an Australian case, *Equus Financial Services Ltd v Boambee Bay Resort Property Ltd (in liquidation) (1991) 9 ACLC 779*, involved a charge, described as a 'floating charge', over a timeshare property. Bryson J, in the New South Wales Supreme Court, did not see any reason why a charge over specified land could not take effect as a floating charge if it was so described, even though it so happened that the charge was created by the very same words as those by which the instrument created a charge on land.

Although, as stated in (iii) above, the company is at liberty, until a crystallising event occurs, to deal with the charged assets in the ordinary course of its business, this does not mean, according to the decision of the Court of Appeal in Alberta in *CIBL v Coopers & Lybrand Ltd, Alberta CA [1989] 3 JIBL N-98*, that a subsequent legal charge granted by the company before crystallisation will have priority over the floating charge, if the holder of the legal charge had notice of the debenture and of the provision that the asset concerned could only be disposed of in the ordinary course of business. The granting of a legal mortgage does not fall within the ordinary course of business of a company, unless the business includes the business of granting mortgages.

The *Coopers & Lybrand* case is not binding authority in England and, in any case, needs to be put in its proper perspective in the light of certain English authorities. A subsequent *legal* charge takes priority over a prior equitable charge, such as a floating charge, unless the holder of the legal charge had notice of the earlier equitable charge. The question is, therefore, what constitutes notice for this purpose. The floating charge, in the normal course of events, would have been registered at the Companies Registry; and the holder of the subsequent legal charge, again in the normal course of events, would have made a search there and come to know of the existence of the prior charge. Even if no search had been made, he would, arguably, be deemed to have had constructive notice, because a company search is an inquiry which it was reasonable to expect him to make; particularly if he was a trader rather than a private individual, or if he was represented by solicitors.

The issue does not, however, end there. Notice of the existence of a floating charge is not notice of a prohibition in the floating charge against the creation of subsequent security ranking prior to or *pari passu* with the floating charge. As far as third parties are concerned, the essence of a floating charge is that until its active (as distinct from automatic or 'silent') crystallisation, the company remains free to dispose of the assets concerned in the ordinary course of its business. A possible doubt on this argument is cast by the proposition that under the current registration provisions there is no statutory requirement or authority for the inclusion of such a negative pledge in the particulars registered and, therefore, that any such inclusion made voluntarily (though under a well-established practice and without any objection from the Registrar) has no legal basis and cannot constitute constructive notice to the public or a subsequent encumbrancer.

However, in *Ian Chisholm Textiles Ltd v Griffiths* [1994] BCC 96 (a case where a retention of title clause, insofar as it might extend to finished products made out of the goods supplied, was held to be a registrable charge which was void for non-registration), the Deputy Judge expressed the view (*obiter*) to the effect that where the holder of such a (fixed) charge had actual notice of an earlier floating charge, he was deemed to have had notice of the prohibition in the earlier charge against the creation of a prior or *pari passu* charge and was therefore postponed to the prior chargeholder. (Compare and contrast the Scottish case of *AIB Finance Ltd v Bank of Scotland* referred to in D11.1(3) below.) In *Barclays Bank plc v Willowbrook Ltd* [1987] BCLC 717, the Court of Appeal held on the facts that the moneys representing a debt owed by a company to its associated company, which had granted to a bank a fixed charge over *inter alia* that debt, were held in trust for the bank since the existence of that charge was known to the recipients of those moneys. It has been held that where a specific charge is made expressly subject to a floating charge, the specific charge is postponed when the floating charge crystallises by the appointment of a receiver (*Re Robert Stephenson & Co Ltd [1913] 2 Ch 201 (CA);* see also *Re Camden Breweries Ltd (1912) 106 LT 598 (CA)*). The new provision of the Companies Act 1989 referred to at D2.5 above will, if and when brought into force, help put the issue beyond doubt (see also D11.1(3)).

'Ordinary course of business' has, however, been construed widely to include, for example, even the disposal of the whole of the undertaking or (where there are separate businesses) one whole business, if it is made in furtherance of the company's business activities (e.g. by way of amalgamation or rationalisation) rather than with a view to cessation of its activities (*Re Borax Co [1901] 1 Ch 326; Re H H Vivian & Co Ltd [1900] 2 Ch 654*). The grant of a specific charge has also been held to be in the ordinary course of business (*Cox Moore v Peruvian Corporation Ltd [1908] 1 Ch 604; Re Hamilton's Windsor Ironworks (1879) 12 Ch D 707*). See also *Dempsey & National Bank of New Zealand v Traders' Finance Corp Ltd [1933] NZLR 1258* (disposal by way of hire purchase); *Hamer v London, City & Midland Bank Ltd (1918) 87 LJKB 973* and *Reynolds Bros (Motor) Pty Ltd v Escanda Ltd (1983) 8 ACLR 422* (substantial sales).

Thus, the priority of a subsequent legal mortgage will not be postponed simply by reason of its holder having had actual or constructive notice of the existence of the earlier floating charge. The real question is whether the holder also had such notice of the terms of the charge, particularly the prohibition against the creation of subsequent securities ranking prior or *pari passu* with that charge. It is submitted that since the insertion of such a prohibition in modern floating charges, and the express (though voluntary and not mandatory) noting of that prohibition on the form of particulars registered at the Companies Registry, is an almost universal practice, the holder of the subsequent charge (or his solicitor) would be expected to look for such prohibition and would be deemed to have constructive notice. For similar reasons, the holder of a subsequent *specific equitable* charge would, arguably, be postponed to the earlier floating chargeholder. In reality, floating charges nowadays are semi-fixed charges in this sense.

A fixed charge over 'fixed plant and machinery' may not, depending on the language of the charging document, extend to items not firmly attached to the premises even if those items are, in accountancy terms, regarded as fixed assets (see, for example, *Re Hi-fi Equipment (Cabinets) Ltd (1987) 3 BCC 478*).

In *Re CCG International Enterprises Ltd [1993] BCC 580* it was held that a charge contained in a debenture in favour of a bank by way of assignment, 'by way of first fixed charge' over 'all policies of *assurance*' (as distinct from policies of insurance) did not go beyond policies which either had or included death as (or as part of) the triggering event, so that insurance moneys in respect of loss or damage to property was not within that fixed charge. However, it was also held that a subsequent clause in the charging document, requiring the chargor

(*a*)   to keep insured the property charged by way of fixed charge and to pay all moneys received in respect of such insurance into the chargor's account with the bank,

(*b*)   to ensure that the name and address of the bank was noted on all such policies of insurance, and

(*c*)   at the option of the bank, to apply such moneys either in making good the loss or damage, or in or towards the moneys secured by the debenture,

did have the effect of creating a fixed charge over such insurance moneys, since they were not at the free disposal of the chargor.

A fixed charge, contained in a debenture, over leasehold property does not confer on its holder a priority over the rights of a superior landlord who has given notice, under section 6 of the Law of Distress Amendment Act 1908, requiring the sub-tenants of the company to pay the sub-rents directly to the superior landlord, if the holder of the charge has not entered into possession prior to the service of the notice. The mere appointment of a receiver prior to the notice does not defeat the priority of the rights of the superior landlord, since the receiver, as agent of the company, does not acquire any better rights than the rights which the company had. This seems to be the effect of *Rhodes v Allied Dunbar Pension Services Ltd*; *Re Offshore Ventilation Ltd (1989) 5 BCC 160*. In that case, the court left open the question of whether the holder of the charge would have had priority if in addition to creating a fixed charge over the leasehold property, the debenture contained an express assignment, or a provision for automatic assignment, to the holder of the charge of the right to recover any rents accruing from the sub-tenants.

A debt owed by A to B cannot be the subject matter of a charge from B to A as security for any debt or other obligation owed by B to A (*Re Charge Card Services Ltd [1986] 3 WLR 697 (Ch D)*, a decision since doubted by the Court of Appeal in *Welsh Development Agency v Export Finance Co Ltd [1992] BCC 270*). However, depending on the circumstances, A may be entitled to exercise a right of set-off under the general law, or (if A is a bank) a banker's lien or right of combination of accounts (as to which see, for example, *Halesowen Presswork Assemblies Ltd v Westminster Bank Ltd [1970] 1 All ER 33*), or (if B is in liquidation) a statutory set-off under Rule 4.90 (as to which see C14.26 PART C: LIQUIDATIONS), or to rely on a 'flawed asset' contractual arrangement, if any, referred to in PART F: SPECIAL PROVISIONS FOR FINANCIAL MARKETS. Even if all this fails, it may be that once the amount of debt is released to B, that amount or any new book-debt or asset into which it is converted will, at that stage, be caught by the general (fixed or floating) charge (if any) which B may have granted to A. It should be noted in passing that a contractual right of set-off which is in excess of the right under the general law or Rule 4.90 will not be enforceable in a liquidation (*British Eagle International Airlines Ltd v Compagnie National Air France [1975] 2 All ER 390*—see *Re Charge Card* above).

Any recovery of money or assets which a liquidator of the company makes under the provisions relating to preferences (see C10.4 PART C: LIQUIDATIONS) does not fall within a floating charge (*Re Yagerphone Co Ltd [1935] Ch 392*, a case decided under the previous provisions relating to fraudulent preference). Presumably this principle will also apply to the new concept of transactions at an undervalue (see C10.2 PART C: LIQUIDATIONS); *quaere*, whether it applies to any recovery in respect of fraudulent trading (see C13.1 PART C: LIQUIDATIONS) and the new concept of wrongful trading (see C13.2 PART C: LIQUIDATIONS and D9.1 below) or whether a distinction will be drawn between antecedent transactions (such as preferences etc.) and malpractice (such as fraudulent trading etc.). However, in *Ross v Taylor* (*1985 SLT 387* (*Court of Session*), *Insolvency Intelligence 3, 189 page 21*), before a company went into receivership it had sold off its stock to a creditor, the price of which was set off by the creditor in reduction of the company's indebtedness to him. This would have, almost certainly, constituted an undue preference if the company had gone into liquidation within the vulnerable period. After his appointment, the receiver persuaded the creditor to return the goods and reverse the set-off. The company then went into liquidation and the liquidator argued that the goods reacquired by the receiver did not fall within the debenture. The court distinguished the facts from the facts of the *Yagerphone* case and held that the goods fell within the debenture as the reacquisition had taken place before the commencement of the liquidation.

What constitutes crystallisation?

D6.3   A floating charge crystallises when 'some event occurs or some act is done which causes it to settle and fasten on the subject matter of the charge within its grasp' (per Lord Macnaughten in *Illingworth v Houldsworth [1904] AC 355*) or, to put it differently, when the company ceases to be entitled to deal with or dispose of the class of assets concerned even in the ordinary course of business (see characteristic (iii) referred to in D6.2 above).

The law implies three events any one of which brings about this result: (i) winding up, (ii) appointment of a receiver under the charge concerned— it is not clear whether an appointment under any other charge, or a crystallisation of any other charge, over the same assets also has that effect—(see *Re Woodroffes (Musical Instruments) Ltd [1985] 2 All ER 908*) or (iii) cessation of business (*Re Brightlife*, above).

The parties may expressly agree on additional crystallising events, which involve intervention by the holder, such as the giving of a notice by the holder to the company converting the charge into a fixed charge (see *Re Woodroffes* or *Re Brightlife*, above)—at least in one instance, even before the Companies Act 1989 (see below) was enacted, the Registrar of Companies accepted for registration as a charge the fact of such conversion (contrast the decision of the New Zealand Supreme Court in *Re Manurewa Transport Co Ltd [1971] NZLR 909*, where it was held, apparently without argument, that the registration of the original floating charge amounted to the registration of the fixed charge into which it later crystallised).

Arguably, the parties may also validly agree on additional events, not involving any intervention by the holder, which will cause the floating charge to crystallise *automatically*, for example, a breach by the company of an undertaking not to create another charge (see *Re Manurewa*, above, to which Hoffmann J in *Re Brightlife*, above, appears to have lent support).

It remains to be decided whether the effect of a crystallisation on the rights of third parties varies according to whether the event giving rise to it is such as would normally come within the public domain (such as winding up, receivership or cessation of trading) or is a 'silent' (or automatic crystallisation) event. No such distinction was advocated in *Re Woodroffes* or *Re Brightlife*, above (where the event concerned was the giving of a conversion notice which was not registered with the Registrar of Companies) or *Re Manurewa*, above. In *B Hargreaves Ltd v Action 2000 Ltd* (referred to in *(1993) 6 Insolvency Intelligence 34*), a receivership set-off case, Judge Fox-Andrews QC held that the effect of the appointment of an administrative receiver and of the notice of the appointment given to the employer under a construction sub-contract, pursuant to which certain sums were due by the employer to the company, constituted an assignment to the debenture holder of the company's rights to receive the sums. However, such assignment took place 'subject to equities', such as any right of set-off which the employer might have. (This aspect of the case was not pursued before the Court of Appeal: *[1993] BCLC 1111*.) As far as subsequent charges are concerned, the priorities between them and the crystallised charge under which the receiver has been appointed may be governed by the ordinary rules.

It should be noted that under section 410 of the Companies Act 1985, as inserted by section 100 of the Companies Act 1989 (not yet in force), the Secretary of State may by regulations require notice to be given to the Registrar of Companies of (*a*) the occurrence of specified events affecting the nature of the security under a floating charge which has been previously registered and (*b*) the taking of specified actions in exercise of powers conferred by a fixed or floating charge previously registered, or conferred in relation to such a charge by an order of the court. The regulations may also make provision, *inter alia*, as to the consequences of failure to give notice. As regards the consequences of failure to give notice of an event causing a floating charge to crystallise, the regulations may include provisions to the effect that the crystallisation (i) shall be treated as ineffective until the prescribed particulars are delivered, and (ii) if the prescribed particulars are delivered after the expiry of the prescribed period, shall continue to be ineffective against such persons as may be prescribed, subject to the exercise of such powers as may be conferred by the regulations on the court. Such regulations are not to apply in relation to a floating charge created under the law of Scotland by a company registered in Scotland.

Chapter 7: Matters affecting assets available in receivership

Contracts of employment

D7.1   The appointment of a receiver does not automatically terminate an employee's contract of employment, unless the continuance of that particular employment is inconsistent with the role and functions of the receiver or unless any new agreement, or any variation of an old agreement, which the receiver enters into with him has the effect of superseding the old contract of employment (see *Griffiths v Secretary of State [1974] QB 468; Re Mack Trucks (Britain) Ltd [1967] 1 WLR 780*). Where the old contract is so superseded, he would be personally liable on the new agreement or the variation unless such personal liability is expressly and effectively excluded and the new agreement or variation is not a 'sham' (see the *Paramount* case referred to at D8.3 below).

Where a receiver incurs personal liability in the proper discharge of his functions, he has a right of indemnity in respect of such liability out of the receivership assets (see D8.2 and D8.3 below). This would have the effect of depleting the receivership assets correspondingly. In view of the *Paramount* case mentioned above, it is virtually impossible for him to avoid personal liability in respect of the contracts of employment continued beyond the period of 14 days after his appointment (subject to the limitation of liability, where he is an administrative receiver, laid down by the Insolvency Act 1994 discussed at D8.3 and subject to what is stated in the first paragraph above).

In relation to those employees whose employment he wishes to continue for a period less than such period of 14 days, although the receiver would have no personal liability to them (unless he assumes liability as contemplated in the first paragraph above) even if he says and does nothing, he may, in practice have to (i) write to them making his position clear (for example, by stating that their existing contracts with the company will continue on the same terms for a period not exceeding such period of 14 days, but that, although it is his intention to cause the company to pay their wages in respect of the post-appointment period as part of the receivership expenses, in so far as the funds of the company allow, he will not have any personal liability in respect of such wages and is not adopting their contracts of employment and (ii) to go on making payments thereunder to them in respect of the post-appointment period. As far as the employees whose services he does not wish to continue at all are concerned he would inform them that the company will not be able to continue to make payments under their contracts and that no funds are proposed to be made available out of the receivership assets for such payments and their contract must be treated as terminated (or repudiated) by the company.

Sections 188 to 198 of the Trade Union and Labour Relations (Consolidation) Act 1992 (which, as originally enacted in the Employment Protection Act 1975, implemented the EC Directive 75/129/EEC of 17 February 1975 in connection with collective redundancies) may be applicable to the company concerned. They impose a duty on the employer to give notice of any proposed redundancies to the recognised trade union (if any) and to the Secretary of State. The employer must consult with any such union and take into account and reply to any representations which it may make. The notice must be given, and the consultation must commence, at least 90 days (if 100 or more employees at one establishment are to be dismissed within 90 days or less) or at least 30 days (if 10 or more employees at one establishment are to be dismissed within 30 days or less) before the dismissals are to take effect. Even if there is no recognised trade union, a duty to consult employees would normally arise by virtue of those provisions (see also the Transfer of Undertakings (Protection of Employment) Regulations 1981 (SI 1981 No 1794), as read with the 1992 Act (see above) and the Trade Union Reform and Employment Rights Act 1993; and *Commission of the European Communities v United Kingdom [1994] IRLR 392* and *412*). However, if there are special circumstances rendering it impracticable to comply with any of these requirements, the employer must take such steps towards their compliance as are reasonably practicable in those circumstances.

However, to constitute 'special circumstances' the events in question must be out of the ordinary and uncommon. Insolvency, on its own, is not a special circumstance, particularly where it is due to a gradual run-down of the company's business; it depends entirely on the cause of the insolvency whether the circumstances can be described as special (*Clarkes of Hove Ltd v Bakers Union [1978] IRLR 366; Association of Patternmakers & Allied Craftsmen v Kirvin Ltd [1978] IRLR 318* (both receivership cases)); *Angus Jowett & Co v NUTGW [1985] IRLR 326*. In *Re Hartlebury Printers Ltd [1992] BCC 428*, Morritt J held that the mere fact that the employer company was in administration did not necessarily mean that such 'special circumstances' were present. Each case had to be looked at on its own merits. It is submitted that similar reasoning would apply to receiverships. The duty to consult arises once the employer has diagnosed a problem, an answer to which entails possible redundancies, and the stage is reached when there is a specific proposal for redundancies (*Hough v Leyland DAF Ltd [1991] IRLR 194*); compare and contrast *Usdaw v Leancut Bacon Ltd [1981] IRLR 295* (proposal must be in the mind of the employer); *Dansk Metalarbejderforbund v H Neilson and Son (in liquidation) [1985] 1 CMLR 91 (ECJ)* (employer 'planning' redundancies); the EC Directive (above) (employer 'contemplating' redundancies); *Sovereign Distribution Services v TGWU [1989] IRLR 334* ('potential or actual redundancy situation').

In *Longden v Ferrari Ltd and Kennedy International Ltd [1994] IRLR 157*, on 26 March 1991 the receivers' solicitors issued a draft contract to a prospective purchaser of the business of the company with a covering letter marked 'subject to contract', on 27 March the prospective purchaser provided the receivers with funds to finance continuation of the business pending the purchase, on 28 March the receivers dismissed non-essential employees and on 10 April the purchase was completed. The Employment Appeal Tribunal dismissed the employees' claim for unfair dismissal, holding that they had been dismissed because of financial restraints on the company and not for reasons connected with transfer of the business. (See also D9.16 below.) That case may be contrasted with *GMB v Rankin and Harrison [1992] IRLR 514*, a Scottish case on an appeal by a recognised trade union. On 19 July 1991 (four days after the receivers had confirmed to a representative of the union their intention to sell the business as a going concern, if possible), the receivers made 22 employees redundant without prior warning. They claimed they did this so as to reduce the workforce to facilitate the sale of the business. About a month later the remaining employees were made redundant, again without prior warning, no buyer of the business having been found. It later transpired that on 25 July a form HR1 had been sent by the receivers to the Department of Employment containing a statement that all employees would be dismissed within twelve weeks if no buyer was found in the meantime. The Employment Appeal Tribunal held that the circumstances did not constitute 'special circumstances', so as to justify a dispensation of the requirement to consult the union for the purposes of what was then section 101(2) of the Employment Protection Act 1975. There had been no sudden disaster or unexpected insolvency. The reduction of the workforce to make the business more saleable was not something special; it was a common incident in any form of insolvency, as were the inability to sell the business and lack of orders. Such circumstances might support a conclusion that closure was inevitable from the commencement of the receivership, but that was not the issue. Further the receivers could not be said to have taken all steps reasonable in the circumstances. (See also *Clarks of Hove Ltd v Bakers Union* above.)

It would appear that an employer need not consult with the employees if those employees have effectively waived their right to consultation. However, the mere fact that in a previous redundancy situation, some employees had said that they would have preferred to have been dismissed without consultation does not mean that any other employees on their subsequent redundancy have waived their rights to consultation, particularly where in the subsequent redundancy the employer adopts a vague and subjective criterion for selection of employees for redundancy (*Ferguson and Skilling v Prestwick Circuits Ltd [1992] IRLR 266 (Court of Session)*).

On the other hand, a finding by an industrial tribunal that an employee's dismissal without consultation was reasonable is not necessarily wrong by reason of the fact that there had been no deliberate decision by the employer that consultation would be useless (*Duffy v Yeomans and Partners, 12 July 1994 (CA, unreported)*).

Failure to consult, unless excused as above, may result in a protective award being made against the employer (section 189 of the 1992 Act) and may (in the case of failure to give notice to the Secretary of State) lead to prosecution of the company (section 194 of the 1992 Act). It is debatable whether the receiver can be made personally liable in respect of the award. He may be particularly at risk in respect of the redundancies caused by him of the employees whose employment he had continued for some time after his appointment. No unfair selection of employees for redundancy should be made so as to give rise to claims for unfair dismissal.

As to the effect of the Transfer of Undertakings (Protection of Employment) Regulations 1981 on the transfer of the company's undertaking, see D9.16 below. Where the Regulations apply, the liabilities to the employees in respect of the pre-transfer period will be transferred to the purchaser of the undertaking; and this is one of the factors which will have reduced the price which the purchaser might otherwise have offered. The end result is that the employees are, in effect, indirectly paid out of the pre-receivership assets as pre-preferential creditors in addition to what they may be entitled to as preferential creditors (see D7.4 below).

Redundancy Fund claims and national insurance contributions

D7.2   Under sections 122 to 127 of the Employment Protection (Consolidation) Act 1978 (as amended—see also the Employment Act 1989), certain types of claims of employees are, within specified limits (variable by statutory instrument—at the time of writing, the relevant instrument is the Employment Protection (Variation of Limits) Order 1992 (SI 1992 No 312)), required to be paid by the Secretary of State out of the National Insurance Fund in the event of the insolvency of the employer. 'Insolvency' includes a receiver or manager being appointed, by or on behalf of the holders of any debentures secured by a floating charge, of any property of the company comprised in or subject to the charge. A duty is imposed on, *inter alia*, a receiver to provide the Secretary of State, as soon as practicable after a request by him, with a statement of the amount of each such claim. The claims to which these provisions apply are

(i)   not more than eight weeks' arrears of pay (which expression is deemed to include a guarantee payment (sections 12 to 17 of the 1978 Act), remuneration on suspension on medical grounds (section 19 thereof), payment for time off (section 31(3) or 31A(4) thereof or section 169 of the Trade Union and Labour Relations (Consolidation) Act 1992), and remuneration under a protective award (section 189 of the Trade Union and Labour Relations (Consolidation) Act 1992)),

(ii)   salary for or in lieu of the minimum notice period (section 49 of the 1978 Act), subject to the deduction therefrom by the Secretary of State of an amount, by way of mitigation, equal to the tax that would have been payable if that amount were earned by way of salary (*Munday v Secretary of State for Employment, EAT 618/88, 6 November 1989*; see also *Westwood v Secretary of State for Employment [1984] IRLR 209*; *British Transport Commission v Gourley [1956] AC 185*; and *Secretary of State for Employment v Cooper [1987] ICR 766*),

(iii) holiday pay for period(s) not exceeding six weeks due during the twelve months preceding the insolvency,

(iv) any basic award of compensation for unfair dismissal (section 72 of the 1978 Act) and

(v) any reasonable sum by way of reimbursement of the whole or part of any fee or premium paid by an apprentice or articled clerk (section 122 thereof) (see also the Unfair Dismissal (Increase of Compensation Limit) Order 1993 (SI 1993 No 1348).

Further, under section 106 of the 1978 Act, claims of employees against the employer in respect of employer's payments (redundancy—section 106 (1A) and (1B) of that Act) are required in certain circumstances to be paid by the Secretary of State out of the National Insurance Fund in the event of the employer's insolvency. Where an employee makes an application to the Secretary of State under section 106, section 107 empowers the Secretary of State to serve a written notice on the employer, requiring him to provide the Secretary of State with such information and documents as the latter may reasonably require for determining whether the application is well-founded.

On making any payments to the employees out of the National Insurance Fund in respect of the claims referred to in the two preceding paragraphs, all rights and remedies of the employees against the employer are, to the extent of such payments, transferred to and vested in the Secretary of State. Although some of these claims, wholly or in part, might otherwise have fallen within the categories of preferential claims referred to in D7.4 (Category 5) below, it was held in *Re Urethane Engineering Products Ltd (1989) 5 BCC 614 (CA)*, that this did not make the Secretary of State's subrogated claim arising from payments in respect of those categories preferential in a receivership, as distinct from in a liquidation or bankruptcy. This was because section 125(2) of the 1978 Act, relating to the Secretary of State's subrogated preferential rights, only specified the provisions relating to preferential claims in a bankruptcy and in a winding-up (under the old legislation) and did not specify the provisions relating to preferential claims in a receivership involving a floating charge. The mere fact that the provisions dealing with preferential claims in a receivership (for example section 196 of the Companies Act 1985, now substituted) required that the debts which were in a winding-up were preferential under the companies legislation were to be preferential in a receivership, was not sufficient to read into the receivership provision section 125(2) which gave the Secretary of State a subrogated preferential right in a liquidation. In other words, the failure to state the receivership provision in that section was fatal to the Secretary of State's preferential rights.

The position under the Insolvency Act 1986 would have been, it is submitted, similar. Section 40 dealing with preferential claims in a floating charge receivership refers to section 386, as read with Schedule 6 which deals with categories of preferential claims under the 1986 Act generally.

Schedule 14 amends section 125(2) of the Employment Protection (Consolidation) Act 1978 by substituting references to sections 175 and 176 (preferential claims in a winding-up) and sections 329 and 348 (preferential claims in a bankruptcy) of and Schedule 6 (categories of preferential claims) to the 1986 Act. It is significant that it does not expressly insert a reference to section 40 of the 1986 Act in relation to preferential claims in a floating charge receivership. However, this anomaly has now been removed by the Employment Act 1989 with effect from 16 January 1990 by appropriate amendments to section 125(2) of the 1978 Act, so that a subrogated preferential claim is also available to the Secretary of State in a receivership.

The position as regards employers' national insurance contributions in respect of employees is that, where wages have been paid in respect of the relevant period preceding the receiver's appointment, the Department of Social Security may have a preferential claim (within certain limits) (see D7.4 below) or, where wages are paid in respect of the post-appointment period, the contributions in respect of them will be paid to the Department as an expense of the receivership. However, where wages have accrued before the appointment and remain unpaid, the contributions in respect of them are payable neither as a preferential claim nor as an expense of the receivership—the Department appears to have conceded this position.

(As to contracts other than contracts of employment, see D7.24 below; and as to post-appointment liabilities on contracts of employment, see D8.3 below.)

Preferential debts

Priority of preferential debts

D7.3 Where a receiver is appointed by or on behalf of the holders of any debentures of a company secured by a charge which, *as created*, was a floating charge and the company is not at the time in the course of being wound up, its preferential debts (see D7.4 below) must be paid out of the assets coming into the hands of the receiver in priority to any claims for principal or interest in respect of the debentures (section 40). The expression 'assets coming into the hands of the receiver' does not include assets which are never payable to the chargee or the receiver (for example, where there is a prior charge: *Re Lewis Merthyr Consolidated Collieries Ltd [1929] 1 Ch 498* at *511* and *512*—see, however, D10.4 below). If the company is already in the course of being wound up, section 40 will not apply (*Gosling v Gaskell [1897] AC 575 (HL)*); but see section 175 and C14.34 PART C: LIQUIDATIONS as to recourse for liquidation preferential debts to receivership floating charge assets. The payments made by the receiver to the preferential creditors are required to be recouped, as far as may be, out of the assets of the company available for payment of general creditors (section 40(3)). Subject to this, the priority provisions apply even if the company subsequently goes into liquidation; in fact, in such a case any further debts which are preferential *in the liquidation* may (to the extent that they cannot be met out of the liquidation assets) have to be paid out of the assets comprised in the charge which, *as created*, was a floating charge—see C14.34 PART C: LIQUIDATIONS, and also D10.2 below. Where the holder of a floating charge takes possession of the assets concerned, instead of appointing a receiver, section 196 of the Companies Act 1985 (as substituted by the Insolvency Act 1986, Schedule 13) has a similar effect.

It will be noted that the requirement applies in relation to a charge which *as created* was a floating charge. This attempts to close the loophole which previously existed, whereby preferential claims could (arguably) be defeated by a pre-receivership crystallisation of a charge which, at its inception, was a floating charge (see the reasoning in the *Christonette* case referred to at D10.3 below). Such crystallisation no longer adversely affects the position of preferential creditors. It is questionable whether a fixed charge over an asset executed pursuant to the terms of the original floating charge over that asset can still defeat preferential creditors as regards proceeds of disposal of that asset on the ground that the fixed charge so executed is a charge which *as created* is a *fixed* charge. It is submitted that unlike (arguably) in the case of a fixed charge which has no connection with the earlier floating charge, the answer must be in the negative. A subsequent fixed charge over assets which were previously subject to only a floating charge must be regarded as no more than a crystallised floating charge in such circumstances. Conversely, it is debatable whether, where a charge which *as created* was a *fixed* charge (and, hence, not *as created* a *floating* charge) is subsequently allowed to 'float' (in that the parties by their conduct operate it as if it is a floating charge), the preferential creditors' priority rights are triggered in relation to that charge. It is submitted that the answer could well be in the affirmative on the ground that the 'floated' charge, having been created voluntarily, was a new charge which from its inception was a floating charge.

Where a charge is in a hybrid form, that is, in the form of a floating charge as regards some assets and a fixed charge as regards others, preferential creditors would have priority only as regards the former: *Re Lewis Merthyr Consolidated Collieries* [*1929*] *1 Ch 498 (CA)*. Further, any surplus of proceeds of the assets comprised in the fixed charge, remaining after the holder of the hybrid charge has received full payment of the money secured by the charge, does not become part of the floating charge. It is not required to be applied in payment of preferential debts under section 40 and must be paid to the person entitled to the mortgaged property, that is, to the company itself or, if the company is in liquidation, to the liquidator or, if there is a subsequent charge over the same property, to the subsequent chargee (see *Re G L Saunders Ltd* [*1986*] *1 WLR 215*; but see D10.4 below). If the company is in liquidation, it would be for the liquidator to apply the assets in the liquidation, including the surplus above referred to, in discharge of the debts which *in the liquidation* are preferential under section 175. If there is a subsequent charge, and that surplus (or the property which it represents) is, by the terms of that charge at its inception, the subject of a floating charge, the subsequent chargee, or a receiver appointed by him, may be obliged to apply it in payment of debts which, at the time the chargee takes possession (section 196 of the Companies Act 1985, as substituted by the Insolvency Act 1986, Schedule 13) or appoints the receiver (section 40), are preferential (see also the examples set out in D10.4 below).

It will be noted that section 40 is not confined to administrative receivership. Where the receiver is an ordinary receiver (that is, because the charge, or his appointment, does not extend to the whole or substantially the whole of the company's property), the provisions for the payment of preferential debts still apply to any 'floating charge assets' comprised in his appointment. It will also be noted, however, that section 40 refers to a 'company'. The expression is confined to a company registered under the companies legislation so that there is no obligation to pay preferential debts out of any assets comprised in a floating charge created by, for example, an industrial and provident society registered under the Industrial and Provident Societies Act 1965 (or, arguably, an overseas company). (See D1.4(1) above.)

There is a positive duty on the receiver to pay preferential creditors of whom he has notice, in accordance with their statutory priority. If he makes a distribution without paying them or retaining a sufficient sum for payment to them, he is personally liable to them (see *Inland Revenue Commissioners v Goldblatt* [1972] *Ch 498*; *Westminster City Council v Haste* [1950] *Ch 442*).

Categories of preferential debts

D7.4   The preferential debts referred to in D7.3 above are those set out in Schedule 6 which remain unpaid at the date of the receiver's appointment ('the relevant date') (sections 40, 386 and 387). These fall into six categories and are summarised below (see also D7.6 below).

Category 1: Debts due to Inland Revenue

(*a*) PAYE deductions from emoluments paid during the twelve months next before the relevant date under section 203 of the Income and Corporation Taxes Act 1988 to the extent that they were not liable to be refunded by the company to the employees.

(*b*) Deductions required to be made for that period from payments to sub-contractors in the construction industry, under section 559 of the Income and Corporation Taxes Act 1988.

Category 2: Debts due to Customs and Excise

(*a*) Value Added Tax (which, as HM Customs and Excise have confirmed, does not include civil penalties, default surcharge and interest under section 76 of the Value Added Tax Act 1994), referable to the six months before the relevant date. Thus, where the whole of the accounting period (prescribed by regulations pursuant to the Value Added Tax Act 1994) to which the tax is attributable falls within the six-month period, the whole of that tax is preferential and, in any other case, the amount of preferential tax is the proportion of the tax equal to such proportion of the accounting reference period as falls within the six-month period. Where any pre-receivership VAT repayment is due to the company, it has been the practice of HM Customs and Excise to set it off against its preferential claim, if any. It should be noted that in the case of a group registration, the company may be liable on a joint and several basis for the VAT liability of another member of the group. If such liability of the company falls in the period mentioned above, it would be preferential (*Re Nadler Enterprises Ltd [1980] STC 457*). The company may be subrogated to the rights of HM Customs & Excise against the other member, upon discharging the liability, under section 5 of the Mercantile Law (Amendment) Act 1856 (for an analogy, see *Re Lamplugh Iron Ore Co Ltd [1927] 1 Ch 308*). As to value added tax on property held under a retention of title clause and returned to the supplier, see D8.5 below.

(*b*)   General betting duty or bingo duty, duty recoverable from an agent collecting stakes under section 12(1) of the Betting and Gaming Duties Act 1981 and gaming licence duty under section 14 of, or Schedule 2 to, that Act, which became due within twelve months next before the relevant date.

Category 3: Social security contributions

(*a*)   Class 1 or 2 contributions under the Social Security Contributions and Benefits Act 1992 or the Social Security Contributions and Benefits (Northern Ireland) Act 1992, which became due in the twelve months next before the relevant date.

(*b*)   Class 4 contributions assessed on the company up to 5 April next before the relevant date under either of those Acts and due to the Commissioners of Inland Revenue (rather than to the Secretary of State or a Northern Ireland Department), but not exceeding, in the whole, any one year's assessment. Where more than one year's assessments made up to that date remain unpaid, it would seem that the Commissioners can choose any one year's assessment (which would normally be that with the largest amount) for preferential ranking (see, e.g. *In Re Pratt [1951] Ch 225*).

Category 4: Occupational pension scheme contributions

Any sum owed by the company in respect of contributions to occupational pension schemes and state scheme premiums, pursuant to Schedule 3 to the Social Security Pensions Act 1975.

Category 5: Remuneration, etc. of employees

(*a*)   Amounts owed to a person who is or has been an employee of the company and payable by way of remuneration in respect of the whole or any part of the period of four months next before the relevant date, not exceeding the prescribed amount (at present £800 per employee—Insolvency Proceedings (Monetary Limits) Order 1986 (SI 1986 No 1996)).

(*b*) Amounts owed by way of accrued holiday remuneration, in respect of any period of employment before the relevant date, to a person whose employment by the company has been terminated, whether before, on or after that date.

(*c*) So much of the amount owed in respect of money advanced for the purpose as has been applied for the payment of a debt which, if it had not been paid, would have been preferential under (*a*) or (*b*) above.

(*d*) Amounts ordered (before or after the relevant date) to be paid by the company under the Reserve Forces (Safeguard of Employment) Act 1985 in respect of a default made by the company before that date in discharge of its obligations under that Act, not exceeding the prescribed amount (at present £800 per employee—Insolvency Proceedings (Monetary Limits) Order 1986 (SI 1986 No 1996)).

Notes to Category 5

(i) Whether or not a person is an employee is a question of fact (*Re London Casino Ltd [1942] WN 138* at *139*). One factor to be taken into account is whether he works under the control of the company or at its premises (*Re Ashley & Smith Ltd [1918] 2 Ch 378; Re G H Morison & Co Ltd (1912) 106 LT 731*). It has to be shown that there was a contract of employment (*Re General Radio Co Ltd [1929] WN 172*). Under the old legislation relating to preferential payments, the expression used was 'clerk or servant' instead of 'employee' as under the present legislation. In *Re Newspaper Proprietary Syndicate Ltd [1900] 2 Ch 349* it was held that a managing director was not a 'clerk or servant' (see also *McLean v Secretary of State for Employment (1992) 455 IRLIB 14*, where a managing director and majority shareholder of a family company, drawing a salary without a written contract of employment, was held not to be an 'employee' for the purposes of section 153 of the Employment Protection (Consolidation) Act 1978 which defines that expression as 'an individual who has entered into or works under a contract of employment'; and *Eaton v Robert Eaton Ltd and Secretary of State for Employment [1988] IRLR 83*, where it was ruled that in general terms the directors of a company would be regarded as holders of an office rather than employees, and that evidence would be required to refute that supposition for the purposes of that Act); but in *Re Beeton & Co Ltd [1913] 2 Ch 279*, where a director also held the position of a dress editress, she was held to be a 'clerk or servant'. A company secretary who devoted his whole time to the business of the company could be a 'clerk or servant', but not if he discharged the duties through a clerk appointed and paid by himself (*Cairney v Back [1906] 2 KB 746*; cf. *Re Scottish Poultry Journal Co (1896) 4 SLT 167*) or where he was also managing clerk to a firm of solicitors (*Re Clyde Football Co Ltd (1901) 8 SLT 328*). A wireless engineer who obtained orders for radios and installed them on commission and a regular newspaper contributor paid at a fixed salary did not fall into that category; but a chemist employed at a weekly wage to produce a perfume formula was held to be within that category despite the fact that he also had a regular engagement with another firm (*Re G H Morison & Co* above), as was an opera singer (*Re Winter Garden German Opera Ltd (1907) 23 TLR 662*). A 'labour only' sub-contractor was not a 'clerk or servant' (*Re CW & AL Hughes Ltd [1966] 1 WLR 1369*).

(ii) 'Remuneration' means wages or salary (whether payable for time or for piece work or earned wholly or partly by way of commission) in respect of services rendered to the company in the period concerned, and includes the items which are stated in D7.2 above (except any basic award of compensation for unfair dismissal) to be deemed to be included in 'arrears of pay'. Remuneration payable in respect of a period of holiday or of absence from work through sickness or other good cause is deemed to be wages or salary in respect of services rendered to the company in that period. Damages *in lieu of* proper notice in respect of dismissal before the relevant date are not 'wages or salary' (*Re VIP Insurance Ltd (1978) 3 ACLR 751*); but payments *in respect of* proper notice or salary due until the first date upon which the employment could be terminated are (*Re Leeds Twentieth Century Decorators (1962) CLY 365*).

(iii) Where a person's employment is terminated by or in consequence of the company going into liquidation or a receiver being appointed under a floating charge or debenture-holders taking possession under such a charge, holiday remuneration is deemed to have accrued in respect of any period of employment if, by virtue of his contract of employment or of any enactment (or any order or direction made under any enactment), that remuneration would have accrued in respect of that period, had his employment continued until he became entitled to be allowed the holiday.

(iv) Remuneration in respect of a period of holiday includes any sums which, if they had been paid, would have been treated for the purposes of the enactments relating to social security as earnings in respect of that period.

(v) The monetary limit of £800 per employee mentioned in (*a*) and (*d*) above appears to be gross (inclusive of PAYE and employees' social security contributions which are or would have been deductible from the payment due to him). There is no monetary limit in respect of accrued holiday remuneration under (*b*) above, nor any restriction as to the period to which it relates.

(vi) Where a person has made advances falling within (*c*) of Category 5 above, he is subrogated to the preferential rights of the employee only to the extent that the advances are applied in payment of remuneration during the four months preceding the relevant period but, in any case, not exceeding the gross sum of £800. The question is whether, within that limit, he is also subrogated in respect of the

PAYE and social security deductions made from the payment due to the employee concerned. It is submitted that he is only so subrogated if the amount of such deductions has actually been 'advanced' (for example, in the case of a bank overdraft account, by the amount being drawn from the account) *and* 'applied' (that is, paid over to the authorities).

The interaction between Category 5 and the Transfer of Undertakings (Protection of Employment) Regulations 1981 (referred to at D9.16 below) may be considered here. Since those regulations provide for the transfer of the employees' contracts of employment, and most of their outstanding and future rights, to any transferee of the undertaking in which they are employed, the question is whether the preferential rights of the employees or the subrogated lender are also transferred to the transferee and therefore cease to be the company's liability. The answer seems to be as follows.

(1)   If the transfer has taken place before the appointment of the receiver, the transferee would be solely responsible for the outstanding salaries (etc.) of the employees. Since the company would not have paid them, the advances made by the lender would not have been 'applied' for such payment. If the company voluntarily makes such payment, for example because the transferee fails or is unable to pay, the employees' claims would have been satisfied but the lender would not have a right of subrogation, because by implication the category only covers payments which are *legally* due by the company.

(2)   If the transfer takes place after the appointment of the receiver, the statutory and unconditional preferential rights of the employees or the lender would have been triggered upon the appointment being made; it cannot have been intended that those accrued *statutory* rights be subsumed by a subsequent transfer of the undertaking. The statutory provisions require the preferential claims to be determined by reference to the date of the appointment without regard to subsequent events. If the employees were paid before the appointment, the lender would have a subrogated right but the employees, having been paid, would not have a preferential claim going across to the transferee. If they were not so paid, they would have a preferential claim against the receivership company but the lender would not have a subrogated right as his advances would not have been 'applied', as at the date of appointment, for payment to the employees.

(vii) For an advance to be made 'for the purpose' mentioned in (c) of Category 5 above, it is not necessary to show that there was an express agreement or arrangement in this regard; it is sufficient if the purpose was in the contemplation of the parties (see *Re Primrose (Builders) Ltd* [1950] *1 Ch 561*; *Re Rampgill Mill Limited* [1967] *1 Ch 1138*).

(viii) If the lender holds security, he can appropriate the proceeds of its realisation against any non-preferential claim that he may have before appropriating them to the preferential claim (*Re William Hall (Contractors) Ltd [1967] 2 All ER 1150*). Further, where, for example, the lender, at the time of the borrower's liquidation, has one credit account, one overdrawn wages account and one overdrawn ordinary account, it would seem that the lender (at least where it is a bank) has a right (in the absence of any express or implied agreement to the contrary) to appropriate the credit balance first to the ordinary account, thereby maximising its preferential claim (see *Halesowen Presswork and Assemblies Ltd v Westminster Bank Ltd [1970] 1 All ER 33*, disapproving *Re EJ Morel (1834) Ltd [1962] Ch 21*, both liquidation cases). This may not apply where a debt, partly preferential and partly non-preferential, is owed to a creditor which is not a bank and there is no express or implied agreement as to appropriation. In such a case, any debt due to the company may be required to be appropriated *pro rata* between the preferential part and the non-preferential part (*Re Unit 2 Windows Ltd*—see D7.6 below).

Category 6: Levies on coal and steel production

The levies on the production of coal and steel referred to in Articles 49 and 50 of the ECSC Treaty and any surcharge referred to in Article 50(3) thereof and Article 6 of Decision 3/52 of the High Authority of the Coal and Steel Community (SI 1987 No 2093).

Set-off

Generally

D7.5

(1)　A set-off, where it arises, generally operates in favour of the debtor or creditor of the company rather than the company itself. The right. of set-off is based on the general law and is in some respects more restrictive than the statutory set-off operating in a liquidation (see C14.26 PART C: LIQUIDATIONS). Unlike in a liquidation, set-off is not mandatory and can be excluded by contract (*Hong Kong and Shanghai Banking Corporation v Kloeckner & Co AG [1989] 3 All ER 513*), although, depending on the circumstances, including the terms of the contract as a whole, such exclusion may be held to be unenforceable by virtue of section 13(1)(b) and (c) of the Unfair Contract Terms Act 1977 (see, for example, *Stewart Gill Ltd v Horatio Myer & Co Ltd [1992] 2 All ER 257*). A person who, immediately prior to the crystallisation of a floating charge, is indebted to the company is, subject as below, entitled to set off his indebtedness against any indebtedness of the company to him subsisting at that time. This right can be asserted even as against the holder of the charge or the receiver appointed under it (*Rother Iron Works Ltd v Canterbury Precision Engineers Ltd [1974] QB 1*), because neither the holder nor the receiver can have any better right than that which the company has. The right of set-off, which arises under the general law, must meet two essential requirements, which are (i) that there must be 'mutuality' between the two debts, at least in equity (*Brown v Gregory [1904] 1 Ch 410*; see also *Re Marwalt Ltd* referred to in D7.22(8) below) and (ii) that they must arise out of the same contract or out of contracts connected with each other. A counterclaim may be relied on as a set-off in equity only where it is so inseparably connected with the claim that the one ought not to be enforced without taking account of the other; but it need not actually serve to diminish the claim itself (see *Dole Dried Fruit and Nut Co v Trustin Kerwood Ltd [1990] 2 Lloyd's Rep 309 (CA)*).

(2) A bank cannot refuse to pay money held by it in credit merely because it has an arguable case that the account holder holds it as a nominee for someone who owes money to the bank (*Utlamchandami v Central Bank of India, The Independent, 31 January 1989; Bhogal v Punjab National Bank [1988] 2 All ER 296*).

(3) A bank is entitled to exercise its common law right of combination or its contractual right of set-off without infringing a restraint order made pursuant to the Drug Trafficking Offences Act 1986 (*Re K [1990] 2 All ER 562, per* Otton J).

(4) A shipowner's accrued right to advance payment of freight under a voyage charterparty survives his repudiation of the charter; and the charterers cannot set off their claim in respect of the repudiation against the freight (*Bank of Boston Connecticut v European Grain Shipping Ltd (The Dominique) [1989] 1 All ER 545*).

(5) A set-off between debts which arose before crystallisation can be asserted notwithstanding that the debt on either side is not a liquidated one, provided that it arises out of the same subject-matter (*Newfoundland Government v Newfoundland Rly Co (1887) 13 App Cas 199*).

(6) A set-off cannot be claimed where the debt owed by the company arose before crystallisation but that owed to the company arises after crystallisation under a separate contract entered into through the receiver. On a receiver's appointment (which causes crystallisation) the company's assets become assigned in equity to the holder of the charge. There is, therefore, no mutuality between the pre-receivership debt contracted for the company's benefit and the post-receivership debt contracted for the holder's benefit (*N W Robbie & Co Ltd v Witney Warehouse Co Ltd [1963] 1 WLR 1324 (CA)*; see also the New Zealand cases of *Felt and Textiles of New Zealand v R Hubrick Ltd [1968] NZLR 716; Rendell v Doors and Doors Ltd (in liquidation) [1975] 2 NZLR 191*).

(7) However, a claim in favour of the company which arises after the appointment, but relates to a contract entered into before the appointment, can be set off against a debt owed by the company at the time of appointment. In *Rother Iron Works Ltd v Canterbury Precision Engineers Ltd [1974] QB 1 (CA)*, the company had contracted before the receiver's appointment to sell goods to D for

£159, whilst already owing D £124 under a previous contract for the purchase of goods. The goods under the £159 contract were delivered to D after the appointment. It was held that although the company's right to sue for the £159 was embraced, when it arose, by the appointment of the receiver, the debenture holder, as equitable assignee, could not be in a better position to assert the rights under the contract than the assignor company; alternatively, that the obligation of D to pay £159 never came into existence, except subject to his right to set off the £124.

(8)   The *Rother Iron* case may be contrasted with *Business Computers Ltd v Anglo-African Leasing Ltd [1977] 2 All ER 741*. In the latter case, a pre-receivership debt due by A to the company, in respect of computers sold to A, was held to be capable of being set off against a hire purchase instalment due to A by the company before the receiver's appointment, in respect of another computer sold by the company to A and resold on hire-purchase terms to the company. It was not, however, capable of being set off against A's claim for damages for the repudiation of the hire-purchase agreement by the company after the receiver's appointment. After reviewing the relevant authorities, including the *Rother Iron* case, Templeman J said 'The result of the relevant authorities is that a debt which accrues due before notice of an assignment . . .' (that is, notice of the receiver's appointment) '. . . is received, whether or not it is payable before that date, or a debt which arises out of the same contract as that which gives rise to the assigned debt, or is closely connected with that contract, may be set off against the assignee. But a debt which is neither accrued nor connected may not be set off even though it arises from a contract made before the assignment'. In *Insituform (Ireland) Ltd v Insituform Group Ltd, The Times, 27 January 1992*, it was held that it was not enough for the purposes of an equitable set-off that a counterclaim by one party was in some way related to the transaction which gave rise to the claim by the other party. The counterclaim had to be so closely connected with the claimant plaintiff's demand that it would be manifestly unjust to allow a party to enforce judgment without taking into account the counterclaim. This still leaves open the question as to whether a contingent debt, as distinct from a debt which has arisen but has not become due for payment or been quantified, is capable of being set off. It would appear that the answer is in the affirmative (see *Re Charge Card Services Ltd [1986] 3 All ER 289*), but the position is not certain. In *Hargreaves Ltd v Action 2000 Ltd [1993] BCLC 1111*, the Court of Appeal held that a common law right of set-off was not available in respect of a sum which could only be ascertained following litigation or arbitration. For the purposes of such a right, the debt must be a liquidated debt. Further, since the claim to be set off arose out of another contract between the same parties, equitable set-off was not applicable; each contract had to be viewed separately.

(9)   A provision in a lease to the effect that the rent should be paid 'without any deductions' may not, depending on the context, be

sufficient to exclude the tenant's right to set off, against the rent
due, his claim for damages for the landlord's breach of covenants
(*Connaught Restaurants Ltd v Indoor Leisure Ltd [1994] 1 WLR
501*). However, a legal mortgagee's right to possession of the mortgaged property is unaffected by a right of set off claimed by the
mortgagor, regardless of whether the mortgagor is principal debtor
or surety and whether his cross-claim is liquidated, admitted or
exceeds the amount presently payable by him under the mortgage
or is in the nature of unliquidated damages giving a right to an
equitable set-off (*Ashley Guarantee plc v Zacaria [1993] 1 All ER
254*; see also *National Westminster Bank plc v Skelton [1993] 1 All
ER 242*; *Samuel Keller (Holdings) Ltd v Martins Bank Ltd [1971] 1
WLR 43*; *Mobil Oil Co Ltd v Rawlinson (1981) 43 P & CR 221*; *Lee-
Parker v Izzet [1971] 1 WLR 1688*; *Gilbert-Ash (Northern) Ltd v
Modern Engineering (Bristol) Ltd [1974] AC 689*; *Connaught Restaurants Ltd v Indoor Leisure Ltd* (above); and the other cases
referred to in *Estates Gazette*, 13 November 1993 at page 129).

(10) However, a contractual provision excluding a party's right of set-off
under the general law may, in certain circumstances, be unenforceable as being contrary to the provisions of the Unfair Contract
Terms Act 1977. *Stewart Gill Ltd v Horatio Myer & Co Ltd [1992]
QB 600* concerned the standard terms of contract of the supplier of a
conveyor belt system which expressly excluded the buyer's right to
withhold payment on the ground of 'any payment, credit, set-off,
counterclaim, allegation of incorrect or defective goods or for any
reason whatever'. It was held that although the Act primarily
applied to exclusion of liability, the effect of section 13 of that Act
was to apply it to the exclusion of a right or remedy as well; and,
further, that the exclusion failed the test of reasonableness laid
down in the Act and, hence, was not enforceable. See also
*Fastframe Franchises Ltd v Lohinski, 3 March 1993 (CA, unre-
ported)*), where execution of judgment was stayed pending a resolution of the defendant's counterclaim and the 'no set off' clause was
held to be unreasonable.

(11) As to the manner of appropriation of the amount of set-off, see, for
example, D7.4 (note (viii) to Category 5) above.

(12) As to a right of set-off as a defence against a landlord's distress, see
D7.13 below.

Crown set-off

D7.6

(1) The right of set-off between the Crown and a company in a receivership appears to be much more restricted than in a liquidation. In a
liquidation, the mandatory provisions of Rule 4.90 apply, while in a
receivership the position is governed by rules of court (RSC Ord 77
and CCR Ord 42) pursuant to section 35(2)(g) of the Crown Proceedings Act 1947, the effects of which are as follows.

(*a*)   Where the Crown sues for the recovery of taxes, duties or penalties, the defendant cannot assert any set-off or counterclaim. In proceedings of any other nature by the Crown, the defendant cannot assert any set-off or counterclaim in respect of refund of taxes, duties or penalties.

(*b*)   Where a department of the Crown sues, the defendant cannot, without the leave of the court, assert a set-off or counterclaim in respect of a subject-matter which does not relate to that department.

(*c*)   Where a department of the Crown is sued, it cannot, without the leave of the court, assert a set-off or counterclaim in respect of a subject-matter which does not relate to that department.

(2)   In practice, the question of set-off between a debt owed by the company to one government department and a debt owed by another department to the company is determined, where (1)(*b*) or (*c*) above applies, on the basis of whether, in the event of proceedings between the parties, the court would have granted the leave under section 35(2)(g). In *Smith v Lord Advocate (No 2) 1981 SLT 19*, Lord Avonside suggested that leave to the Crown would only be denied if the denial is justified by particular or cogent circumstances, such as where its departments are unlikely to suffer material prejudice or where the debts due to its departments are disputed and are of such number and complexity that they would not be resolved in the action concerned without undue and inequitable complication (see also *Re DH Curtis (Builders) Ltd [1978] Ch 162; R A Cullen Ltd v Nottingham Health Authority, The Times, 1 August 1986*). In relation to value added tax, there can be a valid set-off between a pre-receivership VAT liability and post-receivership VAT refund (*The Queen v C & E, QBD, 1 December 1988, Digest of Cases, Issue 49, p 839*; see also section 81 of the Value Added Tax Act 1994).

(3)   In a liquidation case, *Re Unit 2 Windows Ltd [1985] 1 WLR 1383* (cf. *Re Cushla Ltd [1979] 3 All ER 415*), it was held that moneys due by the Crown (through one department) must be set off *pro rata* between the preferential and non-preferential elements of the Crown's claim (through another department) against the company. However, HM Customs & Excise are understood to have adopted the practice that pre-insolvency repayments will be set off first against their preferential claims. Under Scots law, the Inland Revenue, to whom preferential and non-preferential debts were owing by the company, was allowed to set off primarily the non-preferential debts against a VAT payment due from HM Customs and Excise to the company (*Turner, Petitioner [1993] BCC 299*).

Lien

D7.7   If a lien (specific or general), or a right to assert a lien, on any asset of the company has arisen before crystallisation of the floating charge in which the asset is comprised, the receiver takes the asset subject to that lien or right. This is because, until crystallisation, the floating charge is an incomplete assignment of the asset in favour of the holder of the charge. However, if such lien or right arises after the presentation of a winding-up petition against the company, it is void, unless the court otherwise orders by virtue of section 127 of the Insolvency Act 1986 (see C8.4 PART C: LIQUIDATIONS). The essence of a valid lien is possession in the party claiming it. If he voluntarily gives up possession, lien is lost (except that an unpaid vendor of intangible assets may be able to exercise it regardless of 'possession'). Possession, for example possession of documents by a solicitor, must be an unqualified possession. This may not be the case where the documents are held in escrow (*Re Galden Properties Ltd (in liquidation) (1988) ILRM 559 (Irish Supreme Court)*).

In *Re Aveling Barford Ltd (1988) 4 BCC 448*, the receivers obtained an order under section 236 requiring the solicitors who had acted for the company and two of its associate companies to produce documents relating to the affairs of the company and to submit an affidavit containing an account of all their dealings with the companies. The solicitors applied to discharge the order on the ground that they had a lien over the documents for their unpaid fees. It was held that the lien was not a defence to the order for production of the documents. Although a lien could be asserted against a client, it could not be asserted against the third party entitled to production of documents as against the client, and the receivers, by virtue of section 236, were in that position. (Note that section 246(3), which preserves a lien on documents of title held as such, does not apply to receiverships.) This does not mean, however, that the documents produced, such as title deeds, must be delivered permanently to the receiver, thereby enabling him to defeat the lien, although if the solicitors are holding the title deeds to the order of the company's bank (usually the receiver's appointor) pursuant to an undertaking given by them to the bank, they cannot assert the lien as against the bank.

If the receiver (as the company's agent) enters into a transaction with another party which gives rise to a specific or general lien on the receivership assets which are or which later happen to be in the other party's possession in respect of a debt incurred under that transaction, it would seem that the receiver will be bound by it, as the transaction is entered into on account of the receivership assets.

If a right of general lien arises in favour of the other party in respect of a debt already owing to him, under a contract entered into by the company before the receiver's appointment (and (arguably) before the other party had notice of any pre-receivership crystallisation), and if the other party comes into possession of the company's assets *after* the appointment (or crystallisation) pursuant to that contract, then, again, the other party may be able to assert the lien. This can only be avoided if the receiver allows that other party into possession under a fresh contract which specifically excludes the right of lien. In *George Barker (Transport) Ltd v Eynon [1974] 1 WLR 462*, a carrier was owed over £3,000 by a company for goods which he had previously carried, and contracted to carry a further consignment of goods for a charge of £58. All contracts of carriage between the parties were governed by the Standard Conditions of the Road Haulage Association, which gave the carrier a general lien on all goods of the company which came into his possession in respect of any moneys owed to him, including the money owed in respect of any carriage already completed. Before the carrier obtained possession of the goods from the warehouse, a receiver of the company was appointed. The carrier refused to accept a new arrangement whereby he would complete the carriage subject to the receiver paying him the charge of £58. The carrier took delivery of the goods and asserted lien on them in respect of the £3,000. He then completed the carriage on the receiver undertaking to pay him the £3,000 if it was subsequently established that he was entitled to the lien. The Court of Appeal held that he was so entitled.

Where the company owns or has leased to it an aircraft, the aircraft may be liable to seizure for non-payment of air navigation charges or airport charges; and it would appear that the rights of the authorities would take precedence over the rights of the receiver's appointor. The legality in English law of the detention of an aircraft, pursuant to UK legislation, in order to secure the payment of air navigation charges owed by the company in respect of the aircraft, does not depend on the prior institution of proceedings, pursuant to an international treaty, to collect the charges from the company in the country where it is registered (*Irish Aerospace (Belgium) NV v European Organisation for the Safety of Air Navigation, The Times, 23 July 1991*). See also *Re Paramount Airways Ltd [1990] BCC 130*, an administration case (referred to in B4.1 PART B: ADMINISTRATION ORDERS).

A solicitor is entitled to a charge on any property of the company recovered or preserved through his instrumentality for his taxed costs in relation to the relevant suit or proceedings (see section 73 of the Solicitors Act 1974; see also *Re the Railways and Canal Commission, The Times, 1 June 1892* (where the solicitor's charge was held to have priority of the debenture holder's charge); *Scholey v Peck (1893) 1 Ch 709*).

(See also D7.23 below.)

Execution creditors

D7.8   A receiver's position against execution creditors in relation to assets comprised in the floating charge (as distinct from the fixed charge to which the execution creditor would normally be postponed) appears to be as follows.

Writ of fieri facias

D7.9

(1)   The effect of the delivery of the writ to the sheriff is to 'bind' the goods or chattels specified in it, but this does not necessarily confer

a proprietary interest in favour of the judgment creditor. Thus the delivery, even if made before crystallisation of the charge by the receiver's appointment, will not in itself confer priority on the execution creditor.

(2) The title of the holder of the charge also prevails where goods or chattels are seized, but not sold, before crystallisation (*Re Standard Manufacturing Co [1891] 1 Ch 627 (CA); Re Opera Ltd [1891] 3 Ch 260 (CA); Re London Pressed Hinge Co Ltd [1905] 1 Ch 576*).

(3) The position is not clear in cases where the goods or chattels have been both seized *and sold*, but the proceeds have not been paid over by the sheriff to the execution creditor, before crystallisation. It is submitted that the execution creditor will have priority. The judgments in *Robson v Smith [1895] 2 Ch 188* and *Taunton v Sheriff of Warwickshire [1895] 2 Ch 319* contain views to this effect, though they are not binding authority on the point. The reasoning there was that execution against goods is *completed* upon seizure and sale. If these views are correct, the position would be analogous to that in a liquidation under section 183, which entitles an execution creditor to retain the benefit of execution if it is completed by seizure and sale before the commencement of the winding up.

(4) Where a sheriff charged with the execution of a writ of *fieri facias* does no more than call at the debtor's premises and later reports his inability to gain access to the premises, this is not treated as a valid execution of the writ (*Re a Debtor (No 340 of 1992), The Independent, 13 September 1993*).

Garnishee order

D7.10

(1) A garnishee order nisi, when served on the company's debtor, requires the debtor to pay the debt only to the extent of meeting the claim of the company's judgment creditor at whose instance the order has been issued. The order does not create any charge or operate as an assignment or transfer of the debt.

(2) Even where the order is made absolute before crystallisation of the floating charge, the judgment creditor does not acquire priority over the holder of the floating charge unless money has actually been paid to that creditor before crystallisation. This is because even an uncrystallised floating charge covering the garnished debt is an equitable charge and the garnishor takes subject to all rights and equities then existing (*Cairney v Back [1906] 2 KB 746; Norton v Yates [1906] 1 KB 112*; see also *Coopers & Lybrand Ltd v National Carters Ltd 47 CBR (NS) 57 BCSC* (cf. D7.7 above)). The court has a discretion not to make a garnishee order absolute (*Wilson (Birmingham) Ltd v Metropolitan Property Developments Ltd [1975] 2 All ER 814*, where the court exercised that discretion in the case of an insolvency liquidation).

(3) A garnishee order prevents the company from assigning the debt except subject to the garnishee order (*Galbraith v Grimshaw [1910]*

AC 508). This may be compared and contrasted with the earlier decision in *Geisse v Taylor* [*1905*] *2 KB 658*, where a receiver appointed under a floating charge, which had been created in good faith (to secure money then borrowed) *after* a garnishee order was made absolute, was held to have priority over the garnishor in respect of the debt which had not yet been paid over to the garnishor.

Charging order

D7.11

(1) The position is now governed by the Charging Orders Act 1979. The procedure involves an order nisi followed by an order absolute. The former is made where the creditor can show just cause. The latter will be made unless it appears to the court that there is sufficient reason to the contrary. In the absence of any order made by statutory instrument under section 3(7) of that Act, the procedure is at present only available in respect of the types of assets mentioned in section 2(2) thereof, such as land, government stock, stock of a body corporate (other than a building society) incorporated in England and Wales, stock of a body corporate incorporated outside England and Wales on a register kept in England and Wales, units of a unit trust on a register in England and Wales, funds in court and interest under a trust.

(2) This procedure differs from a garnishee order in that a charging order *nisi* creates an immediate equitable charge. The charge is, however, defeasible in that the court may discharge a charging order (section 3(5) of that Act) or refuse to make absolute an order *nisi*, for example, where liquidation has supervened (*Roberts Petroleum Ltd v Bernard Kenny Ltd* [*1983*] *1 All ER 564*) or the company is insolvent (*Pritchard v Westminster Bank Ltd* [*1969*] *1 WLR 547 (CA)*; *Rainbow v Moorgate Properties Ltd* [*1975*]*1 WLR 788 (CA)*) or the rights of an innocent purchaser have supervened (see *Howell v Montrey, The Times, 17 March 1990*). The burden of proving that the order *nisi* should not be made absolute is on the debtor or others making that assertion (*Rosseel NV v Oriental Commercial and Shipping (UK) Ltd* [*1991*] *2 Lloyd's Rep 625*). Subject to the above considerations, a charging order (*nisi* or absolute) made before crystallisation prevails.

Other forms of execution

D7.12 The issue of a writ *in rem* against a ship for its arrest gives the plaintiff the status of a secured creditor (*Re Aro Co Ltd* [*1980*] *Ch 196*) and his title will prevail if the writ is issued before crystallisation (or perhaps before he has notice of it). On the other hand, the issue of a *Mareva* injunction (see *Mareva Compania Naviera v International Bulkcarriers SA* [*1975*] *2 Lloyd's Rep 509*) does not confer on the plaintiff such a status.

461

Distress

D7.13 A landlord who distrains for rent on goods or chattels (see the Law of Distress Amendment Act 1908 and the Distress for Rent Rules 1988 (SI 1988 No 2050)) before crystallisation of the floating charge (for example, by virtue of the appointment of a receiver) in respect of those goods or chattels has priority over the holder of the charge, and it appears that this may be so even if the distress, levied before crystallisation, is completed by sale only after crystallisation (*Re Roundwood Colliery Co [1897] 1 Ch 373*; see also *Purcell v Queensland Public Curator (1922) 31 CLR 220*). A distress levied over chattels which are already subject to the appointor's fixed charge, or a crystallised floating charge, does not prevail over that charge (*Re ELS Limited [1994] BCC 449* (also known as *Ramsbottom and another v Luton Borough Council and another*), where Ferris J applied the principles in *Biggerstaff v Rowatt's Wharf Ltd [1896] 2 Ch 93*; *NW Robbie & Co Ltd v Witney Warehouse Co Ltd [1963] 1 WLR 1324*; *George Barker (Transport) Ltd v Eynon [1974] 1 WLR 462* and *Roundwood Colliery Co (above)*, and refused to follow *Re Marriage Neave & Co [1896] 2 Ch 663*. As to the position in New Zealand where there is a fixed charge, see *Metropolitan Life Assurance Company of New Zealand Ltd v Essere Print Ltd (in receivership) (1990) 66 NZCL 775 (CA)*).

The same principle (that distress has priority over the holder of a charge) may apply to statutory distress, i.e.

(*a*) distraint by a local authority for community charge, council tax or non-domestic rates (Local Government Finance Act 1988, Schedule 4 paragraph 7, Schedule 9 paragraph 3; see also Community Charges (Administration and Enforcement Regulations) 1989 (SI 1989 No 438), Reg 39 *et seq.*, Local Government Finance Act 1992, and the Council Tax (Administration and Enforcement) Regulations 1992 (SI 1992 No 613) with effect from 1 April 1992; Non-Domestic Rating (Collection and Enforcement) (Local Lists) Regulations 1989 (SI 1989 No 1058), Reg 14 *et seq.*) (see also D8.11 below); and

(*b*) distraint by the Collector of Taxes for income tax, corporation tax, capital gains tax, interest on unpaid tax, unpaid PAYE deductions, national insurance contributions and deductions from sub-contractors in the construction industry (Taxes Management Act 1970, section 61, as amended by the Finance Act 1989; see also Income Tax (Employments) Regulations 1993 (SI 1993 No 744), Reg 54 and Income Tax (Sub-Contractors in the Construction Industry) Regulations 1993 (SI 1993 No 743), Reg 19); and

(*c*) distraint by the Collector of Customs and Excise for value added tax (Value Added Tax Act 1994, Schedule 11 paragraph 5(4); see also Value Added Tax (General) Regulations 1985, Reg 65 (as amended by SI 1985 No 1650, SI 1986 No 305 and SI 1987 No 1916)).

It is arguable that statutory distress has a different effect than that which a landlord's distress has and that the former has no priority over the holder of the charge. This is because unlike the landlord, who already has a contingent proprietary, possessory or security interest in the goods by virtue of his pre-existing ownership of the reversion of the leasehold premises on which the goods are located, the party levying the statutory distress has no such interest. It is also arguable (in deference to *Roundwood Colliery Co* cited above) that a distraining creditor does not acquire any proprietary interest in the assets distrained until their sale (whereupon he acquires such an interest in the proceeds of sale) and that if, before that happens, the interests of the debenture holder intervene (for example, by the appointment of a receiver, whereupon the goods become assigned in equity to the debenture holder—see the *N W Robbie* case cited in D7.5(6) above), the debenture holder takes priority. For the analogous position in a liquidation (where distress not completed before liquidation may be postponed to the rights of all the creditors, unless the court otherwise orders), see *Re Memco Engineering Ltd [1985] 3 All ER 267*.

A landlord may distrain in person but usually does so through a certificated bailiff (who must be authorised by the landlord in writing by means of a distress warrant in the prescribed form). Where goods are removed pursuant to a distress, Form 9 must be completed and a copy left on the premises. Often, goods distrained are left in the possession of the company at the premises under a 'walking possession' agreement by which the company undertakes to hold them in trust for the distrainer and not to remove or otherwise deal with them. Such an agreement must be in Form 8 and signed by the debtor. Any person who breaches the agreement is guilty of 'pound breach' and liable to triple damages (*Jones v Beirnstein [1900] 1 QB 100 (CA)*). No distress may be levied on certain types of assets, such as perishable goods, agricultural machinery and livestock, stock and work in progress relating to Crown contracts if there is a clause in the contract vesting them in the Crown, any goods in legal custody, for example, under a writ of *fieri facias* and, in the case of an individual debtor, certain types of tools and household goods (see the County Courts Act 1984, as amended by the Courts and Legal Services Act 1990).

The categories of assets over which distress may be levied may vary according to the specific legislation concerned. Assets belonging to subtenants and third parties may be removed by the bailiff in the case of a *distress by a landlord* but must be returned on the landlord being notified of their ownership. A landlord's distress can be levied only for rent (or sums treated as rent) and only on assets on the leasehold premises (including vehicles in a car park, if part of the premises) in respect of which the rent is due.

The bailiff or landlord can only enter peaceably, but if goods have been removed to other premises to avoid distraint, the other premises can be broken open to gain possession. A distraint can only be levied between sunrise and sunset. To be valid, a distress must consist of entry into premises and the seizure and impounding of goods. Although the seizure may be actual or constructive, there must first be a lawful entry onto the premises where the goods are lying. A mere posting of a notice of distress, with a 'walking possession' agreement signed by the bailiff, through the debtor's letter box in her absence is not sufficient (*Evans v South Ribble Borough Council [1992] 2 WLR 429*). The tenant's remedy for illegal, irregular or excessive distress is to apply to the court for appropriate relief or, in certain circumstances, for damages. In the case of excessive distress, the tenant can, by notice to the landlord, also ask for an appraisement by two independent persons. In *Steel Linings Ltd v Bibby & Co, The Times, 30 March 1993*, the Court of Appeal held that a person against whom excessive distress for unpaid non-domestic rates was levied was not barred by the relevant regulations (see above) from seeking a county court injunction to prevent the bailiff from selling the goods distrained; but to succeed he must establish a powerful *prima facie* case showing that the distress had in some way been unlawful.

Where the company as the tenant has a claim against the landlord for damages for nuisance and breach of covenant in respect of the property in question, the landlord may be restrained from levying or confirming a distress for rent due without allowing a set-off for such damages. The landlord should not be allowed to recover more by distress than he can by normal litigation. Injustice might be caused if the landlord in a weak financial position recovered the full amount and then distributed to his creditors leaving the tenant without an effective remedy (*Eller v Grovecrest Investments Ltd [1994] EGCS 28*).

A landlord may also be restrained from levying distress for new rent payable on renewal, and interim rent pending the grant of a new lease, as fixed by a court order, where the order is subject to a pending appeal: *Eren v Tarmac Ltd, 25 November 1993* (unreported, but see *Solicitors Journal*, 27 May 1994, page 524) where Nourse LJ in the Court of Appeal said,

'The whole purpose of distress is to enable the landlord to sell the goods . . . within a short time . . . the entitlement of the landlord to the proceeds, and indeed the entitlement of the tenant to the balance, if any, must be precisely established before the right arises. When I say precisely established I do not exclude a case, for example, where the rent can be precisely ascertained'.

Where a landlord of the company issued a notice under section 6 of the Law of Distress Amendment Act 1908 requiring the company's sub-tenants to pay the rent due to the company directly to the landlord, it was held that the landlord's rights prevailed over the rights of the debenture holder and the receiver (*Re Offshore Ventilation Ltd (1989) 5 BCC 160 (CA)*). The debenture holder had never gone into possession of the charged property and had not become entitled to the rents. The receiver's possession was as agent of the company and he had no better rights than the rights which the company itself had. (Note: It is possible that the effect of this case can be avoided by a debenture holder if the debenture expressly creates a fixed charge over all present and future rents, service charges etc. receivable by the company in relation to any freehold or leasehold property and requires all such receipts to be paid into a designated bank account controlled by the debenture holder.)

In the case of distress for non-domestic rates, the charging authority must first obtain a liability order from a magistrates' court. This it can only do after the ratepayer makes a default in payment of the rates after they have become due. Upon levying distress, a copy of Regulation 14 of and Schedule 3 to the 1989 Regulations (above), a memorandum setting out the amount due and a copy of any 'walking possession' agreement must be left at the premises; but the premises at which distress is levied need not be those to which the rates relate. If the ratepayer removes goods to avoid distress, he may be liable to be committed to prison.

Before the Collector of Taxes can levy distress, the taxpayer must have neglected or refused to pay the tax due after demand. No warrant of distress need be issued if the collector is accompanied by a bailiff. To effect a forced entry, the Collector must have a distress warrant from the General Commissioners and will be accompanied by police officers. No distress may be levied on third party goods as section 61 of the 1970 Act (above) refers to 'the goods and chattels of the person charged'. The goods may be removed or be the subject of a 'walking possession' agreement. A distraint notice together with an inventory of the goods concerned must be left at the premises. The tax, together with the costs of distraint, must be paid within five days to avoid sale. The Collector will have the goods appraised before sale.

A distress, other than a landlord's distress for rent, is, in effect, postponed to the right of the Collector to payment of unpaid tax for a period not exceeding twelve months (section 62 of the 1970 Act). A distress by HM Customs and Excise is governed by regulations similar to those applicable to a distress by the Collector of Taxes but it cannot be levied before the expiry of thirty days after demand.

HM Customs and Excise and the Inland Revenue appear to accept that they cannot levy distress on assets comprised in a fixed (or a crystallised floating) charge.

Forfeiture or termination of lease or contract

D7.14 A landlord's right to forfeit a lease held by the company for non-payment of rent or breach of other condition, or on the occurrence of any other event specified in the lease, is not affected by the receiver's appointment or any other form of crystallisation. (The lease may include receivership as one of the grounds for forfeiture.) However, if the landlord accepts rent for the current period after becoming aware of a breach which entitles him to forfeit, or otherwise conducts himself as if he treats the lease as continuing, he may be deemed to have waived his right of forfeiture (see, for example, *Iperion Investments Corporation v Broadwalk House Residents Ltd, Estates Gazette, 12 and 19 September 1992*). As to what may constitute acceptance of an offer to surrender a lease or intention to forfeit it, see *Re AGB Research plc [1994] EGCS 73*.

A forfeiture for non-payment may be avoided by (or a relief against forfeiture may be obtained conditional on) payment to him of the arrears of rent. It may be possible to obtain from the court relief against forfeiture effected on any other ground, on an application by or on behalf of the company or the holder of the charge under section 146 of the Law of Property Act 1925. A landlord who seeks forfeiture of a lease on the ground that the breach of a repairing covenant committed by the tenant would lead to substantial diminution in reversionary value, must prove his case on his application for leave to apply for forfeiture; and leave will not be granted if it appears on the evidence that the breach will lead to little diminution in value and that the purpose of forfeiture would be to benefit from redevelopment plans (*Associated British Ports v C H Bailey Plc [1991] 1 All ER 929 (HL)*). The court will usually require the tenant to remedy all breaches on its part which led to the forfeiture, insofar as they are capable of remedy. Where relief is claimed on the ground of change of circumstances following a long standing breach, the tenant will be required to show precisely where the money to rectify the breach is to come from and explain why it was not available earlier: *Darlington Borough Council v Denmark Chemists Ltd, The Times, 12 May 1992.* In *Billson v Residential Apartments Ltd [1993] EGCS 150*, at a re-trial, relief was refused on the ground that the intended and present use of the premises was in breach of the tenant's covenants, and the conversion of the premises by the tenant made it impossible to comply with the local authority's requirement without a considerable amount of cost.

The fact that the landlord has effected forfeiture by peaceable re-entry onto the leasehold premises (other than a public house—see below) is no bar to the grant of relief: *Billson v Residential Apartments Ltd [1992] 2 WLR 15 (HL)*; nor is the fact that the forfeiture was effected for illegal use of the premises contrary to the terms of the lease: *Van Haarlam v Kasner Charitable Trust [1992] NPC 11*.

It should be noted, however, that section 146 of the Law of Property Act 1925, relating to the circumstances in which relief against forfeiture of a lease may be available, is exhaustive and excludes any inherent jurisdiction of the court to grant relief (*Official Custodian of Charities v Parway Estates Developments Ltd [1984] 3 All ER 679; Billson v Residential Apartments Ltd [1991] 3 All ER 265 (CA)*). This means, for example, that in view of section 146(9) relief is not available in respect of premises used as a public house (which would include a wine bar).

By virtue of section 138(7) of the County Courts Act 1984, and sections 138(9A) and (9C) of that Act as inserted by section 55 of the Administration of Justice Act 1985, a mortgagee, like the lessee of a long lease, is entitled, in an action for possession by the lessor, to seek relief against forfeiture for non-payment of rent in the relevant county court or the High Court but is subject to the restriction of section 138(9A), as read with section 210 of the Common Law Procedure Act 1852, requiring an application for relief to be made within six months from the date of recover of possession (*United Dominions Trust Ltd v Shellpoint Trustees Ltd [1993] 4 All ER 310 (CA)*).

Relief may also be available against forfeiture clauses in an agreement for the sale of land or an agreement relating to chattels. In *Starside Properties*

Ltd v Mustapha [1974] 1 WLR 816, it was held that where the justice of the case required that relief by way of extension of time to pay stipulated sums which had been initially granted ought to be extended, the court had jurisdiction to do so; no distinction was to be drawn in that regard between cases of relief against forfeiture for non-payment of rent and other cases where relief against forfeiture was sought. In *Goker v NWS Bank Plc, The Times, 23 May 1990,* it was held that although the court had a general jurisdiction, extending beyond the statutory provisions, to provide relief from forfeiture to protect the hirer of chattels, it was unlikely to be used save in exceptional cases; but in the present case (*Starside*) the court was satisfied that no significant prejudice would result to the lender from the grant of relief. It should be noted that it is quite common, in contracts for the development of land, for the developer to agree to carry out a development on another party's land at the developer's own cost (probably financed by loans from the owner), in return for the owner's undertaking to sell the land to the developer upon completion of the development, subject to widely drawn forfeiture clauses relieving the owner of that undertaking if certain specified events or breaches occur. Where a forfeiture clause is invoked, this may result in considerable financial hardship to the developer. It is submitted that in certain circumstances relief against such forfeiture may be available, at least if the developer is in a position to put the owner in the same financial position as he would have been in if the breaches or events had not occurred.

A more recent case of relief against termination of a contract was *Transag Haulage Ltd v Leyland DAF Finance plc [1994] BCC 356.* The company in receivership held certain vehicles under hire purchase agreements, had kept up all payments and had not committed any breach. The owner of the vehicles sought to treat the agreements as terminated by virtue of a clause in the agreements providing for their automatic termination upon the company going into receivership and sought to repossess the vehicles. The receivers tendered to the owner a cheque in payment of the full sum remaining payable under the agreements. The owner neither cashed it nor returned it. Knox J, in granting relief against termination, held that equity should grant relief in the present case because payments had never been late and the owner would enjoy the benefit of early payment. Further, if forfeiture were allowed to stand, the owner would stand to make a windfall profit of £53,000 (in view of the rentals which had previously been paid) and the company would suffer a disproportionate loss. However, following the practice in landlord and tenant cases, the company had to pay the owner's costs of the proceedings.

The court, in exercising its jurisdiction to grant relief in cases of non-payment of rent is, of course, proceeding on the old principle of the court of equity which always regarded the condition of re-entry as being merely security for payment of the rent and gave relief if the landlord could get his rent (see *Chandles-Chandles v Nicholson [1942] 2 KB 321*). In *Barton Thompson & Co Ltd v Stapling Machines Co [1966] 1 Ch 499*, Pennycuick J adopted a cautious approach, saying that readiness to pay arrears within a time specified by the court was in law a necessary condition of the tenant's claim for relief.

Upon forfeiture or termination, the company may in certain circumstances be entitled to compensation from the landlord in respect of improvements (including erection of any buildings and any goodwill attaching) to the property carried out by the company or its predecessor tenant (section 1 of the Landlord and Tenant Act 1927). The company may also be entitled to remove tenants' fixtures but must make good any damage caused to the premises by such removal (see *Mancetter Developments Ltd v Garmanson Ltd [1986] BCLC 196*). Subject to this, buildings and fixtures form part of the landlord's reversion and belong to him.

Sitting tenants and occupants

D7.15 The receiver may find that the company's freehold or leasehold property is capable of being sold more advantageously if it is sold with vacant possession, but that there are sitting tenants who have contractual or statutory security of tenure or other protection against early eviction. However, where the employee of a company was living in a bungalow belonging to the company in order better to perform his duties, under a licence which provided that on the termination of his employment the licence would cease, it was held that he must vacate the bungalow on the termination of his employment (*Norris v Checksfield [1991] 4 All ER 327 (CA)*).

A tenant may also have the right under the Leasehold Reform Act 1967 (as amended) in certain circumstances to buy the freehold. A similar right (under Part I of the Landlord and Tenant Act 1987) can also be exercised in certain circumstances by the tenants of a block of flats, who may be qualified to buy the freehold reversion not only of the physical structure of the buildings but also of the gardens (*Denetower Ltd v Toop [1991] 3 All ER 661*). However, once the tenancy is surrendered, the right under the 1967 Act is lost even if the surrender is immediately followed by the grant of a new tenancy; section 23(3) of that Act (which allows the court to vary an agreement entered into by a tenant 'without the prior approval of the court for the surrender of the tenancy') applies only to an executory, as distinct from an executed (or completed) surrender (*Woodruff v Hambro, Estates Gazette, 30 March 1991*).

Planning control breaches

D7.16 If there has been any breach of the planning legislation in relation to any land or building owned or occupied by the company, the enforcement by the planning authorities of the planning obligations or restrictions (for example, by the demolition of any unauthorised structure) may result in considerable diminution in the realisable value of the land or building.

Retention of title claims

D7.17 The crystallisation of a floating charge or the appointment of a receiver does not affect the rights of a third party who has a valid retention of title claim (see D7.18 below) to any goods held by the company or to any proceeds of sale of such goods. The charge does not extend to those goods, but it may extend to such contractual rights of the company as still subsist under the relevant agreement. Such an agreement usually provides that the company's freedom to sell the goods in the ordinary course of business will terminate upon, *inter alia*, the appointment of a receiver. The only right of the company which usually continues is the right to acquire ownership of the goods on payment of the contract price, or such part thereof as remains outstanding, or (if the agreement so provides) on payment of all sums remaining unpaid to the third party under all contracts.

Usually, a hybrid form of charge contains only a floating charge over the company's stock-in-trade and work-in-progress. Therefore, if the receiver makes the outstanding payment so that the company acquires ownership of the goods under a retention of title agreement, the goods will be treated as subject only to a floating charge for the purposes of preferential claims (see D7.3 *et seq.* above). There may, therefore, be some advantage in making the company's contractual rights under such agreements subject to a fixed charge *ab initio* (see, e.g., D7.20(2) below).

Validity and effect of retention of title clause

D7.18   A retention of title clause, in an agreement for the supply of goods or raw materials on credit, is a device whereby the supplier can maintain his status akin to that of a secured creditor in relation to the goods or raw materials without the need to register the arrangement as a charge. Such clauses have become increasingly common after the decision in *Aluminium Industrie Vaassen BV v Romalpa Aluminium Ltd* [*1976*] *2 All ER 552* in which the basic validity of such a clause went unchallenged. The clause in that case was drawn in very wide terms and sought to retain title in not only the raw materials supplied but also in any manufactured articles into which they might be converted, until all moneys due to the supplier on whatever account had been paid. As it happened, no manufactured articles were involved and the validity of a retention of title to them did not fall to be determined. Such clauses have popularly come to be known as '*Romalpa* clauses'.

The subject is very complex. As Staughton J observed in *Hendy Lennox (Industrial Engines) Ltd v Grahame Puttick Ltd* [*1984*] *2 All ER 152* at *159*, the law in this area is 'presently a maze, if not a minefield, and one has to proceed with caution for every step of the way'. Case law on the subject is still in its infancy and a number of points remain unresolved. A detailed discussion of the subject is not within the scope of this chapter or, indeed, this book. The main points may be summarised as follows:

(1)   *Lex situs* usually determines the validity of a proprietary claim (including any registration formalities), but may, in turn, have to look to the proper law of the contract to the extent that the position depends on the intention of the parties and contractual relationship between them. Subject to this, the position under the English domestic law is as stated in the paragraphs which follow.

(2)   It is open to the parties to agree when property in the goods is to pass—see sections 17 and 19(1) of the Sale of Goods Act 1979. In the absence of an agreement, the question will be determined in accordance with the provisions of section 18 of that Act. A sub-purchaser in good faith will be protected by section 25 of the Sale of Goods Act 1979 (see, for example, *Four Point Garage Ltd v Carter* [*1985*] *3 All ER 12*).

(3)   It is possible to have a valid 'all-moneys' retention of title clause in relation to specific goods supplied. Ownership in goods in their original form may be reserved (subject to careful drafting of the relevant clause) not only until the goods in question are fully paid for but, for example, also until all sums owing to the supplier on all other accounts are fully paid (*Clough Mill Ltd v Martin* [*1984*] *3 All ER 982*). (For practical difficulties that may arise for a supplier where there is a 'specific' clause as distinct from an 'all moneys' clause, see D7.19 below.) In the Scottish case of *Armour v Thyssen* [*1990*] *3 All ER 481*, in allowing an appeal, the House of Lords upheld the validity of an 'all-moneys' clause and rejected the views of the Lord Ordinary and Court of Session that the clause constituted an imperfect security interest. The decision in *Emerald Stainless Steel Ltd v South Side Distribution Ltd 1983 SLT 162* was overruled. (See, however, the *Compaq Computer* case referred to in (8) below.) It should be noted that a specific charge over chattels is not required to be registered in Scotland (see section 410(4) of the Companies Act 1985), unlike in England (see section 396(1)(c) which requires registration of a charge which, if executed by an individual would require registration as a bill of sale, that is, where the charge is not accompanied by actual or constructive possession in the chargee). (Note that in relation to both England and Wales and Scotland, the Companies Act 1989 inserts new provisions relating to the registration of company charges into the Companies Act 1985 which will, when brought into force, replace the existing provisions of the 1985 Act.) In fact, the bills of sale legislation does not apply to Scotland, but it is understood that under its common law a valid security interest in chattels must involve actual or constructive possession.

(4)   To make his claim effective, the supplier must reserve both legal and beneficial/equitable ownership in the goods; otherwise the transaction might be regarded as a registrable charge which, in the absence of registration, would be void against the purchaser's creditors or a liquidator (see *Re Bond Worth Ltd* [*1979*] *3 All ER 919*; also *Stroud Architectural Systems Ltd v John Laing Construction Ltd* (*1993*) *Building LM 4.93, 3*, a case which involved a retention of title claim against a sub-contractor for building materials supplied, and where it was nevertheless recognised that a claim for conversion against the main contractor could lie if he is the debtor, and not the creditor, of the sub-contractor and if he received possession after the floating charge had crystallised). The words 'property in the goods shall not pass' or 'ownership in

the materials shall remain' would normally be sufficient (see *Clough Mill Ltd v Martin* (above) at *986, d, e*).

(5) To make effective the supplier's equitable right to trace the proceeds of sale of the goods, the terms and circumstances of the contract must be such as to expressly or impliedly constitute the buyer a bailee or fiduciary agent in respect of the goods (*Borden (UK) Ltd v Scottish Timber Products Ltd [1979] 3 All ER 961*). Where (4) above is complied with in clear terms and there is nothing else inconsistent with it, such bailment or fiduciary agency may be implied; but this is not always the case and it is advisable for the supplier to include express provisions in this regard. A provision requiring the purchaser to store the goods separately identified may also assist in this respect and also facilitate identification (see D7.19 below).

(6) Where title is retained to the goods supplied, the court will not infer from it that the retention extends to any finished product into which it is converted even if the character or appearance of the finished product essentially remains the same (see, for example, *Ian Chisholm Textiles Ltd v Griffiths [1994] BCC 96*). In any case, ownership can only be reserved while the goods remain in their original state. Once their character materially changes by the goods being admixed with other materials, or in a manufacturing process, in such manner that what emerges is a new product, the ownership will be lost (at least where the admixing or manufacturing process was carried out under an express or implied authority of the supplier); and in the absence of a registered charge, the supplier will lose his rights (*Borden (UK) Ltd v Scottish Timber Products Ltd* (above); *Ian Chisholm Textiles Ltd v Griffiths* (above), where the deputy judge stated that in such a case the title in relation to the finished product did, in a sense, *remain* with the supplier, albeit that the nature of the title was converted from that of beneficial owner to that of chargee, and, further (*obiter*) that any such charge arising after the date of the debenture under which the receiver was appointed would rank after the debenture (assuming that the debenture contained a restriction against the creation of any prior or *pari passu* charge), at least where the supplier had actual notice of the debenture). However, in the *Clough Mill* case (above), their Lordships were not so unequivocal in their views on this point. Goff LJ (at *989* and *990*) and Oliver LJ (at *993*) came to the conclusion that the clause was invalid largely on the grounds of expediency and of the true intention of the parties.

(7) Usually, a contract containing a 'Romalpa clause' expressly permits and, in any case, the courts readily imply in such a contract, a licence for the purchaser to use the goods in the ordinary course of his business. Such a licence is not inconsistent with the existence of a bailor/bailee relationship or the right to trace the proceeds of sale (*Clough Mill Ltd v Martin* (above) at *987, c–g*; see also *Hendy Lennox (Industrial Engines) Ltd v Grahame Puttick Ltd [1984] 2 All ER 152* and *Re Andrabell Ltd (in liquidation) [1984] 3 All ER 407*). The contract would normally specify

471

events, such as insolvency, including the appointment of a receiver, which would terminate the licence.

(8)   Where the goods, in their original state, have been resold by the purchaser in the ordinary course of business whilst he is a bailee or fiduciary agent, the sub-purchaser acquires a valid title, but the supplier's proprietary rights may be transferred from the goods to the proceeds of their sale (including any book debts generated by their sale on credit), which he is entitled to trace *in specie*. Whether or not, in a particular case, this happens will depend on whether, on the true construction of the contract, the purchaser is in a fiduciary relationship with the supplier. In the *Romalpa* case (see above) such a relationship was held to have existed and the court applied the equitable principles of tracing established in *Re Hallett's Estate* *(1880) 13 Ch D 696(CA)* (see also *Re Diplock [1948] Ch 465(CA)*). By contrast, in *Re Andrabell Limited [1984] 3 All ER 407*, where the relevant clause relating to the supply of travel bags read 'ownership of the goods . . . shall not pass . . . until the company has paid (to the supplier) the total purchase price . . .', the court rejected the supplier's argument that a fiduciary relationship was implied in the clause and that the supplier was entitled to trace the proceeds of sale. The court went on to say that on the facts there was no sufficient duty to account for the proceeds. Since there was no obligation to keep the moneys in a separate account, that was completely inconsistent with a duty to account.

In *E Pfeiffer Weinkellerei-Weineinkauf GmbH & Co v Arbuthnot Factors Ltd [1988] 1 WLR 150*, the relevant clause in the agreement read, 'All claims that he gets from the sale . . . with all rights including his profit amounting to his obligation towards [the supplier], will be passed on to [the supplier]. On demand the [purchaser] is obliged to notify the assignment of the claim to give [the supplier] in writing all necessary information concerning the assertion of [the supplier's] claim . . . In case of cash sales, the money that has come from a third person immediately becomes [the supplier's] . . . this money has to be separated from other money, it must be booked correspondingly and must be administered until called for'. It was held that where a buyer was permitted to sub-sell goods in the normal course of his business before paying the seller for them, the normal implication was that it would do so for its own account, not as a fiduciary who was obliged to account to the seller for all the proceeds of sale; that the clause set out comprehensively the nature of the interests which the plaintiff was to have by way of security in respect of debts created by sub-sales and its terms were inconsistent with the existence of such a fiduciary relationship; that the clause had effected an equitable assignment to the supplier of the future debts owed by sub-purchasers to the purchaser, up to the amount of any outstanding indebtedness of the purchaser to the supplier, which constituted a charge by way of security over the purchaser's book debts; and that, accordingly, the purported right of the supplier to the proceeds was void for want of registration. It will be seen that the main defect of the clause was to recognise that the proceeds and book debts generated from the sub-sales would initially arise in favour of the purchaser and then be passed to the supplier. A similar conclusion was reached in *Re Weldtech Equipment Ltd [1991] BCLC 393* in relation to goods located in England notwithstanding that the proper law of the contract was German law (see (1) above).

In *Tatung (UK) Ltd v Galex Telesure Ltd (1989) 5 BCC 25*, after reserving title to the goods supplied, the relevant clause went on to provide, 'and that the buyer shall be at liberty to sell the goods as principal . . . but the benefit of any such contract of sale and the proceeds . . . shall belong to the [supplier] absolutely'. The clause provided that the goods were to be held by the buyer as bailee for the supplier. The sums in issue were payments for hire of the goods received by the buyer from its customers. Phillips J held that the right to proceeds was void as an unregistered charge over book debts. He stated that the supplier's interest in that case arose from the express clause. He distinguished *Romalpa* (above) because in that case there was no express clause dealing with the proceeds of sale of the original goods so that the interest derived automatically under *Hallett's case ((1880) 13 Ch D 696)*. He held that the interest of the supplier to the proceeds was by way of security rather than an absolute interest. (Note that the buyer had liberty to sell the goods 'as principal'.) Phillips J went on to say that any contract which, by way of security for the payment of a debt, confers an interest in property defeasible upon payment of the debt or appropriates the property for the discharge of the debt, must necessarily be regarded as creating a mortgage or charge. The existence of the equity of redemption is quite inconsistent with the existence of a bare trustee-beneficiary relationship. Thus the position about proceeds of sale still remains unclear. It is debatable whether the supplier would have succeeded if the words 'as principal' and the express words reserving ownership to *proceeds* were omitted. Perhaps the express contractual provision regarding proceeds undermines or supersedes the equitable principles of tracing and constitutes a registrable charge over book debts, by conceding that book debts would arise in the company in the first instance and would immediately thereupon be held in trust for the supplier.

Another instance where an express provision relating to proceeds was not upheld was *Compaq Computer Ltd v Abercorn Group Ltd [1991] BCC 484*, where a retention clause was contained in a dealership agreement. The agreement contained an 'all moneys' clause in relation to goods supplied to the company. The company was permitted to sell the goods in the ordinary course of its business and was given 30 days' credit. In relation to proceeds, the agreement required the company to 'strictly account . . . for the full proceeds . . . as the seller's bailee or agent' and to 'keep a separate account of all such proceeds'. Mummery J held that there was no true fiduciary relationship despite a label to that effect attached to it. Reading the contract as a whole, the seller's interest in the proceeds was not absolute but was defeasible on the tender of the purchase price, and any profit made by the company on resale would belong to the company.

In *Carroll Group Distributors Ltd v G and J F Bourke Ltd [1990] ILRM 285*, the Irish High Court held that the proceeds of the subsales of goods supplied to the company were the subject of an unregistered charge rather than a trust for the suppliers. The retention clause required the company to hold the proceeds in trust for the supplier in an independent account to be maintained by the company. In the event, the company failed to maintain such an account and paid the proceeds into one of its own two accounts with its bank, the other account being overdrawn. The bank set off the moneys against the overdraft. On the facts, the court held that there was no effective trust created by the clause, but that even if there was a trust, there were no trust moneys remaining to be traced as a result of their dissipation by the set off.

It would seem that provided a genuine fiduciary relationship in respect of the goods (but not also expressly in respect of the proceeds) is imposed, the claim to the proceeds, if they are identifiable *in specie*, may succeed; but the court will have regard to the reality of the situation so that if in making a resale the company was intended to act on its own account, the claim to the proceeds may not succeed.

(9)   Where ownership of the goods is lost when their character changes (see (6) above), the supplier is not entitled to trace the proceeds of sale, not even such part of the proceeds as is attributable to the goods in their original form (*Borden (UK) Limited v Scottish Timber Products Ltd* (above)). In *Re Peachdart Ltd [1984] 1 Ch 131*, the seller retained ownership of the leather supplied by him and the right to trace any proceeds of sale by the buyer, including any goods made with the leather, with the creation of a fiduciary relationship between the buyer and the seller. It was held that on a true construction of the relevant conditions of sale, the parties intended that, once the leather had been appropriated into the handbag making process, the seller, whether as bailor or unpaid vendor, would cease to have exclusive title to the leather and instead would have a charge over the completed and uncompleted handbags including any proceeds of sale; that, since the charge had not been registered, it was void and, accordingly, the seller had no priority over the debenture holder and other creditors in respect of the proceeds of sale.

(10)   Where, however, an item of machinery (e.g. an engine) is incorporated into another item (e.g. a generating set), title is not lost, provided that the connections can be undone without causing damage to the other item (see *Hendy Lennox (Industrial Engines) Ltd v Grahame Puttick Ltd [1984] 2 All ER 152*). On the other hand, a contractual provision where a repairer seeks to reserve ownership

in a company's machine into which he incorporates parts, as security for the payment by the company of the repair charges, constitutes a registrable charge: *Specialist Plant Services Ltd v Braithwaite [1987] BCLC 1 (CA)*.

(11) A distinction should, perhaps, be drawn between the mixture of heterogeneous goods in a manufacturing process, in which the original goods lose their character and what emerges is a wholly new product, and the mixture of homogeneous goods, such as corn or oil. Title will survive, if at all, in the case of the latter to the extent of the quantity which belonged to the supplier (see the *Borden* case (above) at *970, g, h*, and *Indian Oil Corporation Ltd v Greenstone Shipping Co SA [1987] 3 All ER 893*, where it was also held that any doubt as to the quantity would be resolved in favour of the supplier).

(12) No *Romalpa* clause will be valid unless it is effectively incorporated in the contract in question. Where it is incorporated in the supplier's standard conditions, reasonable steps must be taken to bring it to the notice of the purchaser before or at the time he purchases the goods. Whether what is done is reasonable depends on all the circumstances, including the situation of the parties, the layout and content of the document and how unusual or stringent the term is. A retention of title term has become quite common in commercial transactions and is not to be treated as unusual (*John Snow & Co Ltd v DBG Woodcroft & Co Ltd [1985] BCLC 54*).

In *Harvey v Ventilatoren Fabrik Oelde GmbH, Financial Times, 11 November 1988 (CA)*, a German manufacturer supplied to the purchaser for erection two large machines with two sets of acknowledgements of the contract, asking the purchaser to sign and return one and retain the other. The one to be signed and returned had terms and conditions on its reverse which stated that German law applied. The terms and conditions were only in German. The other set did not contain any terms and conditions. The Court of Appeal held that the terms and conditions had not been brought to the purchaser's attention. As the other set did not contain any terms or conditions, the purchaser was entitled to assume that those contained in the first set did not form part of the contract.

Sometimes a purchaser may place an order containing his own standard conditions and excluding all other conditions, and the seller may send an acceptance or confirmation of the order containing his own standard conditions (including a *Romalpa* clause) and excluding all others. This gives rise to a 'battle of forms'. The position will be determined by analysing the sequence of events and ascertaining what was the last 'offer' or 'counter-offer' that was accepted, expressly or impliedly. (For an example, see *Sauter Automation Ltd v H C Goodman (Mechanical Services) Ltd, FT Law Reports, 14 May 1986*.) Even where a document in relation to a particular transaction does not incorporate the standard terms, they may still be held to be incorporated if there has been a course of dealings between the parties subject to those terms or the purchaser is aware that the supplier normally deals on standard terms: *Circle Freight International Ltd v Medeast [1989] 2 Lloyd's Rep 427 (CA)* where Taylor LJ said 'It is not necessary that terms should be specifically set out provided that they are conditions in common form or usual terms in the relevant business. It is sufficient if adequate notice is given identifying or relying upon the conditions and they are available on request. Other considerations apply if they are particularly onerous or unusual'.

(13) Where the goods supplied to the company under a retention of title clause bear the trademark of a third party, which was affixed with that third party's consent and which the company had a right to use under a contract with the third party, the supplier, upon retaking possession of the goods pursuant to that clause, is entitled to resell those goods bearing the trademark (without being liable to the third party for its infringement). This applies notwithstanding that the contract between the third party and the company has been terminated (*Accurist Watches v King [1992] FSR 80, Millett J, 29 October 1991*).

Practical problems

D7.19 In practice, the supplier's remedy under a valid retention of title clause, in the event of the purchaser's insolvency, can be effective only to the extent (if any) that he is able to identify the goods or proceeds *in specie* in the hands of the purchaser or its receiver, liquidator (etc.). Identification of goods can be extremely difficult where they do not bear distinctive marks, or where similar goods have been supplied by other suppliers, or where there have been successive supplies of similar goods by the same supplier but the retention clause is specific rather than general (that is, where title is reserved only until the particular goods are paid for rather than until all other supplies have been paid for) and some of the goods have been paid for (see, for example, *Ian Chisholm Textiles Ltd v Griffiths [1994] BCC 96*). The analogy of the 'first-in, first-out' rule in *Clayton's* case does not necessarily apply to goods, as it does (subject to some exceptions) to receipt and payment entries in an account.

Where a dispute arises between a retention of title claimant and the receiver, it is usual for the parties to prepare an agreed list of the goods in dispute, with their description, and to agree that the receiver may sell or use or otherwise dispose of them but will pay to the supplier their invoice value or, if less, their net realised value in the event of the supplier's title being established by agreement or determination by the court. Where the receiver offers an undertaking in these terms, the court is unlikely to grant an injunction to the supplier restraining the receiver from selling, using or otherwise disposing of the goods (see *Lipe Ltd v Leyland DAF Ltd [1993] BCC 385*).

Other third party proprietary claims

Hire purchase (etc.) agreements

D7.20

(1) In relation to any third party chattels held by the company under a hire-purchase or similar agreement, the receiver's position under the agreement, or by reason of its termination, is no better than the position in which the company would have been but for his appointment. The agreement would normally contain a provision entitling the owner to terminate the agreement and repossess the assets in the event of, *inter alia*, a receiver's appointment. However, relief from forfeiture of the hire-purchase goods may, in certain circumstances, be available. (See also D7.14 above.)

(2) Where, however, a substantial amount has already been paid by way of hire-purchase rentals, the receiver may consider realising the 'equity' in it by reaching fresh arrangements with the owner so that by discharging the outstanding liability (in some cases at a discounted figure) the receiver can acquire ownership of the assets in the name of the company. Alternatively, a novation of the agreement may be achieved by a purchaser of the business taking over the outstanding rights and obligations under the agreement with the owner's consent and paying the receiver an appropriate consideration for giving up the company's 'equity' in the assets. It must be noted that where the charge is a *fixed* charge on such *assets*, but only a *floating* charge on such an *agreement*, preferential creditors may rank before the receiver's appointor in relation to the consideration received for the novation. If the asset is first acquired in the name of the company by satisfying the outstanding liability and is then transferred to the purchaser, the appointor would, arguably, rank before the preferential creditors. (See the second paragraph of D7.17 above.)

Third party fixtures

D7.21 The receiver may find that a chattel which is held by the company under an outstanding hire-purchase or similar agreement has been sufficiently attached to the company's land or building so as to become a fixture. In such a case, competing claims in respect of the chattel may arise between the third party owner and the receiver's appointor as legal mortgagee of the land and, where the land is leasehold, the landlord. The law on the subject is not entirely clear. As to the position between the company (and, hence, the mortgagee) and the landlord, see the final paragraph of D7.14 above. The position between the third party owner and the landlord will not be the receiver's concern. That between the third party owner and the mortgagee will, arguably, be as follows.

(1) *Legal mortgage granted prior to affixation*

Where a legal mortgage over land is granted prior to affixation of the chattel, the legal mortgagee can claim the chatel as part of his security in priority to the rights of the owner of the chattel *unless*:

(*a*)   at the time of the mortgage, the legal mortgagee had notice of the contractual provision giving the chattel owner the right to enter and sever; or

(*b*)   the mortgagor had express authority from the mortgagee to affix the chattel to the property and had granted the chattel owner a right to remove them; or

(*c*)   the mortgagor had the mortgagee's implied authority (which can be negatived by express words) to affix the chattel, for example, where the legal mortgagee had left the mortgagor in possession and thus left him to carry on business thereon; or

(*d*)   the chattel owner has removed the chattel before the mortgagee goes into possession (the appointment of a receiver may not amount to entry into possession by the mortgagee for this purpose); or

(*e*)   in the case of unregistered land, the mortgage is not accompanied by a deposit of title deeds or has not been registered as a puisne mortgage under the Land Charges Act 1972.

(2)   *Legal mortgage granted after affixation*

If the mortgagee took without notice of the contractual provision, or if the title to the land is registered, he is not bound by, and can ignore, the right of severance and removal given to the chattel owner. His legal estate (or, in the case of registered land, the registered title) overrides the prior equitable interest arising under the contractual provisions.

Note: For a discussion of some of the above points with reference to hire-purchase and leasing agreements, see *The Conveyancer* Vol. 27, p. 30: *Hire Purchase, Equipment Leases and Fixtures* by Guest and Lever, and Chapter 32 of *Hire-Purchase Law and Practice (2nd edition)* by R M Goode.

Trust property

D7.22   Apart from funds which relate to retention of title claims (see D7.17 *et seq.* above), or which are clearly held under an express trust for another party, the following are further examples of where moneys held by the company may be subject to implied or constructive trust and, therefore, not part of the receivership assets.

(1)   Moneys paid by the company, pursuant to an effective voluntary arrangement, to the supervisor of the arrangement before the appointment of an administrative receiver and still held by the supervisor: *Re Leisure Study Group Ltd, 26 January 1993, per Harman J (unreported*, but see *Insolvency Law and Practice*, Vol 10 No 1 (1994) page 23), where it was held that on a true construction of the terms of the voluntary arrangement, the moneys were trust moneys and that as an agent of the company, the receiver was not entitled to the moneys. Note that this decision seems questionable

as one of general application in view of the fact that well drafted debentures prohibit any disposal by the company of any asset (even where it is subject only to a floating charge) otherwise than in the ordinary course of business. In ordinary course, the supervisor and the creditors would be aware of this prohibition.

(2)   Proceeds of factored book-debts (see, for example, *Lloyds and Scottish Finance Ltd v Cyril Lord Carpet Sales Ltd (1979) [1992] BCLC 609* where a block debt discounting agreement was, on a true interpretation of the intention of the parties, held to create an absolute assignment by way of sale, as distinct from a registrable charge over book debts).

(3)   Pre-payments received from customers and paid by a company in financial difficulties into a separate bank account with the intention of holding them in trust for those customers (*Re Kayford Ltd [1975] 1 WLR 279*; contrast *Re Multi Guarantee Co Ltd [1987] BCLC 257(CA)* and *Space Investments Ltd v Canadian Imperial Bank of Commerce Trust Company (Bahamas) Ltd [1986] 1 WLR 1072 (PC)*); also deposits in respect of any future breakages, received by a lessee company from short-term tenants, unilaterally put by it into a segregated 'tenants' account when its liquidation was imminent, the leases later having been surrendered to the landlord and the lessee company having undertaken to hold the deposits as agent for and to the order of the landlord in trust for the tenants (*Re Chelsea Cloisters Ltd 41 P&CR 98*).

(4)   Moneys paid to the company under a mistake of fact (*Chase Manhattan Bank NA v Israel-British Bank (London) Ltd [1979] 3 All ER 1025*) (*cf. Space Investments Ltd v Canadian Imperial Bank of Commerce Trust Co (Bahamas) Ltd [1986] 1 WLR 1072*).

(5)   Moneys advanced by a lender to the company for a specific purpose but remaining unused (*Barclays Bank Ltd v Quistclose Investments Ltd [1970] AC 567*; *Carreras Rothmans Ltd v Freeman Mathews Treasure Ltd [1985] Ch 207*; *General Communications Ltd v DFC New Zealand (High Court, Auckland, 4 November 1987 CP 634/86, unreported,* Tompkin J) (trust may be asserted against a receiver); *Dines Construction Ltd v Perry Dines Corporation Ltd (1989) 4 NZ CLC 65, 298* (specific purpose must be agreed at the outset and not subsequently); *Stanlake Holding Ltd v Tropical Capital Investment Ltd, FT Law Reports, 25 June 1991 (CA)* (trust not defeated merely because specific or real purpose was, unknown to the payer, fraudulent)). Also, moneys repaid to the company by a third party in connection with payments made to him by the company out of the moneys so advanced by the lender (*Re EVTR Ltd (1987) 3 BCC 389 (CA)*), but not the apartments in respect of which refundable deposits have been paid to the company and no contracts for their sale by the company have been exchanged (*Re Barrett Apartments Ltd [1985] IR 350 (Irish Supreme Court)*).

(6)   Moneys paid by investors to a company carrying on investment business in trust for credit to client account, including the benefit of

mortgages and interest attributable to such moneys, moneys paid into the client account to remedy the breach of trust and sums improperly transferred to (and remaining in) office account (*Re Berkeley Applegate (Investment Consultants) Ltd (1988) 4 BCC 274*). Also, where a company dealing in futures has maintained segregated bank accounts for its clients, moneys remaining or received on those accounts in respect of transactions effected on behalf of those clients and the benefit of any contracts and debts due by the other parties under those contracts representing such transactions (*Re Eastern Capital Futures Ltd (1989) 5 BCC 223*) and moneys received from a third party with knowledge that they had been extracted by fraud or in breach of trust vis-à-vis another party or where the recipient assisted in the fraud or breach of trust (see e.g. *Agip (Africa) Ltd v Jackson [1989] 3 WLR 1367*).

(7) Moneys held in a retention fund set aside by the company as employer under a building contract, which provided that the money would be held in trust by it for the contractor or other parties and kept in a separate bank account; but not if the company has failed to set aside such fund in breach of its obligations, even if the receiver's appointor had express notice of the contract at the time of taking the charge (*MacJordan Construction Ltd v Brookmount Erostin Ltd [1992] BCLC 350*, distinguishing *de Mattos v Gibson (1858) 4 de G and J 276*, as explained in *Swiss Bank Corp v Lloyds Bank Ltd* by Browne-Wilkinson J at first instance (*[1979] 2 All ER 853*; reversed, on a point of construction, by the Court of Appeal *[1980] 2 All ER 19*, whose decision was upheld by the House of Lords *[1981] 2 All ER 449*). However, where the company has failed to pay such moneys into a separate account, the court may issue a mandatory injunction to compel the employer to create a separate fund (*Wates Construction (London) Ltd [1991] 3 Constr LJ (CA)*) but, of course, using any moneys or assets (if any) other than those on which the charge held by the receiver's appointor already bites by virtue of crystallisation. The obligation to create a separate fund continues, notwithstanding that the employer has a claim for liquidated damages or defective work against the contractor, until that claim is resolved (*J F Finnegan Ltd v Ford Seller Morris Developments Ltd Nos 1 and 2 [1991] CILL 672 and 679*).

(8) Moneys received by the company merely as a conduit for transactions which are essentially between two other parties. See, for example, *Re Marwalt Ltd [1992] BCC 32* where, to obtain the benefit of the company's ECGD insurance cover, the company was used by B as a conduit for the export of goods to C and for the receipt of the price by means of letters of credit from C. The company had irrevocably instructed its bank to pay the proceeds of the letters of credit into a separate account for immediate transfer to B. It was held that the moneys beneficially belonged to B by way of absolute assignment and the company's receiver should pay it over to B. It was further held that the bank was not entitled to set off the money in the separate account against moneys due by the company to it in another account.

(9) A bribe accepted by the company as a fiduciary in breach of its duty to another party (see, for example, *Attorney-General for Hong Kong v Reid [1994] 1 AC 324*).

(10) The beneficial receipt by the company of the assets of another party from a third party, in breach of the third party's fiduciary duty to the owner, where the assets are traceable as representing the assets of the owner and the company knew that they were so traceable (*El Ajou v Dollar Land Holdings plc [1994] BCC 143 (CA)*).

The essence of a successful trust claim is the ability of the claimant to trace the fund or other assets concerned, or any other fund or asset into which they are converted. Where money is paid to a bank, the bank is generally free to deal with it and expend it for the general purposes of the bank. In the *Space Investments* case (above) the Privy Council refused to impose an equitable lien on all the property of the bank. For some other cases on tracing, see *James Roscoe (Bolton) Ltd v Winder [1915] 1 Ch 62*; *Attorney General for Hong Kong v Reid* (above); *Lord Napier and Ettrick v Hunter [1993] AC 713*; *Re Goldcorp Exchange Ltd [1994] 2 All ER 806*, where the Privy Council (hearing an appeal from New Zealand) stated that the law relating to the creation and tracing of equitable proprietary interests is still in a state of development.

Where trust funds belonging to several parties have been intermingled and are not sufficient to pay each claimant in full, the general rule is that each claimant is entitled to a *pro rata* interest in the balance or in any asset derived from the fund (*Sinclair v Brougham [1914] AC 398 (HL)*). Where trust funds have passed through an active current account at a bank, the 'first in first out' rule would apply (see *Clayton's Case (1816) 1 Mer 572*), so that, in the absence of any contrary intention on the part of the parties, competing trust fund claimants would have a right to be paid out of the balance of the account then remaining in the reverse order of the time their funds were deposited. If, on the application of that rule, it appears that the funds of a particular claimant do not exist in the account but have been used to acquire another asset, the claimant may have a right to that asset. (See *Re Diplock [1948] 1 Ch 465 (CA)*; *[1951] AC 251 (HL)*). Where the current account contains funds other than trust funds, the 'first in first out' rule is subject to the variation that regardless of the order of payments in, the non-trust funds are deemed to have been used before the trust funds. In *Re Eastern Capital Futures Ltd (1989) 5 BCC 223*, the court held, on the facts, that the parties had not intended that the 'first in first out' rule should apply in relation to the 'non-discretionary' investors who had invested funds through the company. The deficiency in their account had arisen as a result of some of the investors having failed to pay margin calls or as a result of losses made on futures contracts. It was impossible to presume any intention on the part of the non-discretionary investors that their payments into the segregated account or payment out of that account on their behalf should, as against the other investors, be treated on a 'first in first out' basis. The court ordered payment to the investors on a *pro rata* basis. (See also *Re Berkeley Applegate (Investment*

Consultants) Ltd (1988) 4 BCC 274 (investors' moneys invested in legal mortgages through clients' accounts with sufficient records of the sources of investment and destination of income—held that both the capital and the income belonged to the respective investors); and *Southern Cross Commodities Pty Ltd v Marlin 1991 SLT 85 (Scotland)* (rules as to tracing of mixed funds are that (1) the whole of the fixed fund is treated as trust property unless the non-trust fund can be distinguished and (2) property acquired with the mixed fund is treated as trust property to the extent of the trust's contribution).) As to tracing of funds for unjust enrichment, see *Lipkin Gorman v Karpnale Ltd [1991] 2 AC 548 (HL)*, where an employee had gambled away funds which he had embezzled from his employer—the employer was held entitled to recover from the casino as a *quasi-volunteer* (on the ground of unjust enrichment under unenforceable gaming contracts) the difference between the amount staked by the employee and his winnings.

(See also C12.9 PART C: LIQUIDATIONS.)

Where there is a surplus of funds at the conclusion of the receivership and there is a dispute between two claimants, one of whom is the liquidator of the company who has no funds to finance the costs of pursuing the dispute, the court has jurisdiction to order in advance of the resolution of the dispute that the costs incurred by the liquidator be paid out of the surplus (*Re Westdock Realisations Ltd (1988) 4 BCC 192*). See, however, *Re Biddencare Ltd [1993] BCC 757* where Mary Arden QC, sitting as a deputy High Court judge, in refusing a pre-emptive costs order, stated that such an order could clearly result in injustice if a party established a proprietary claim to assets which had been reduced by the payment of costs in resisting his claim. It was the other creditors in the liquidation who should bear the burden of unsuccessfully resisting the claim. On the facts, there was no countervailing factor of sufficient weight. Alternatively, the court was not satisfied that it was likely that an order would be made at the trial for the payment of the liquidators' costs out of the assets subject to the proprietary claim, even if the liquidator was successful, because this was hostile litigation.

Prior and subsequent charges

D7.23   (See also D10.1 *et seq.* below). Prior charges may include moneys deposited by the company in court in legal proceedings, whether voluntarily or pursuant to an order of the court. The other party has security over them until the hearing of the action (*W A Sherratt Ltd v John Bromley (Church Stretton) Ltd [1985] QB 1038*). Where a ship is involved, a third party may have acquired rights *in rem* against the ship. However, no security right arises until a judgment *in rem* is obtained (*The Cerro Colorado [1993] 1 Lloyd's Rep 58*). Where a charterparty agreement reserves a lien on cargoes and sub-freights, the charge on the sub-freights is a charge over book-debts requiring registration under sections 395 and 396 of the Companies Act 1985 (see *Re Welsh Irish Ferries Ltd [1986] Ch 471*). (But see now section 396(2)(g) of that Act, as inserted by section 93 of the Companies Act 1989 (to come into force on a date to be

announced) which will override the effect of the *Welsh Irish Ferries* case.)
The receiver must carefully investigate the validity (including regis-
trability—he has the right to bring proceedings to set aside an unregistered charge, as to which see *Curtain Dream plc v Churchill
Merchanting Ltd [1990] BCC 341*) and extent of all prior and (if there is
likely to be a surplus) subsequent charges (see, for example, the points
made in C12.9 and C12.10 PART C: LIQUIDATIONS some of which may apply
even where the company is not in liquidation or administration). (As to
priority between a floating charge and a subsequent fixed charge, see e.g.
D6.2 above.) The sale by a company of its interest in part of a loan is absolute notwithstanding a provision for the repurchase by it at the same
price. In the absence of a contrary intention, therefore, the transaction
will not create a registrable charge (*Chase Manhattan (Asia) Ltd v First
Bangkok City Finance Ltd, FT Law Reports, 15 July 1988*, a case decided
under the Hong Kong law).

One of the categories of charge requiring registration is a charge over book
debts. The only exception is that where a negotiable instrument has been
given to secure the payment of book debts to the company, the deposit of
that instrument for the purpose of securing an advance to the company is not
to be treated as a charge on those book debts. However, where there is
agreement between the company and its lender for such deposit and the
agreement has not been carried out by actual deposit, the lender cannot rely
on that agreement to assert his equitable charge (in the form of an agreement to create the charge) on that instrument (or the underlying book debts)
as against the liquidator, administrator or any intervening creditor acquiring
valid rights over that instrument (or the book debts) unless that agreement
has been registered as a charge on book debts (*Chase Manhattan Asia Ltd v
Official Receiver and Liquidator of First Bangkok City Finance Ltd [1990] 1
WLR 1181*, an appeal to the Privy Council from the Hong Kong decision
referred to in the preceding paragraph). This is a peculiar situation, where
the actual charge is not registrable but an agreement to create that charge is.
In other cases, if a charge is registrable, an agreement to create it is registrable but not otherwise.

A prior mortgage of a ship can be problematical as is illustrated by *'The
Shizelle' [1992] 2 Lloyd's Rep 444*. The case involved a British ship which,
due to its size, was not compulsorily registrable under the Merchant
Shipping Act 1894. Unknown to the purchasers of the ship, it was subject
to a pre-existing common law legal mortgage, created by the previous
owners who were individuals. This mortgage was exempt from registration under the 1894 Act and did not require registration under the Bills
of Sale Act 1878 (which expressly excluded registered or unregistered
ships from its scope), but would have required registration under section
395 of the Companies Act 1985 if it had been created by a company. The
new owners were held bound by that mortgage notwithstanding that they
were *bona fide* purchasers for value without actual or constructive notice
of the mortgage.

The court has no power to order that the costs expenses and remuneration of a receiver appointed by the court (otherwise than pursuant to a

charge) should be paid in priority to the sums secured under prior or paramount charges (*Choudri v Palta [1992] BCC 787*).

Where a lender has advanced money to the company to purchase a property on the term that the property on acquisition would be charged to the lender, and the company applies the money in such acquisition, the lender is subrogated to the unpaid vendor's lien which the vendor of the property had immediately before the receipt by him of the money; but such subrogated lien is treated as abandoned once the lender has obtained the charge, regardless of whether the charge is void for non-registration, because he gets what he had bargained for. Where such lien subsists, it takes priority over any mortgage or charge created by the company over the property on or after its acquisition, because such a mortgage or charge takes effect subject to the lien existing at the time of acquisition. The lien is valid without registration as a charge. (See *Connolly Brothers Ltd [1912] 2 Ch 25; Capital Finance Co Ltd v Stokes [1969] 1 Ch 261; Coptic Ltd v Bailey [1972] 1 All ER 1242; Burston Finance Ltd v Speirway Ltd [1974] 3 All ER 735; Paul v Speirway Ltd [1976] 2 All ER 587; Security Trust Co v Royal Bank of Canada [1976] 1 All ER 381; Orakpo v Manson Investments Ltd [1977] 3 All ER 1.*)

(See also D2.13 above.)

Outstanding contracts (other than employment contracts)

D7.24   The appointment of a receiver out of court, at least where and so long as he is the agent of the company, does not of itself automatically terminate any current contract or engagement of the company, unless the terms of the contract expressly or by a clear inference lead to that result. The receiver is not liable on the contract and, although he has no statutory power to disclaim it, he has at least the same right to repudiate it as the company had (and may, indeed, have a better right—see below), or he may simply refuse to perform it, leaving the other party to accept the repudiation or otherwise to pursue its remedy for damages as an unsecured creditor to rank for dividend in the event of liquidation (see, however, the following paragraph and D8.2 to D8.4 and D8.15 below).

The receiver's right to repudiate is, however, only exercisable if the repudiation does not adversely affect the realisation of the assets or seriously affect the trading prospects or goodwill of the company (if it is, at all, able to trade in future). Subject to this, the receiver is, indeed, in a better position as regards current contracts than the company itself, and can frustrate the contracts in circumstances where the company would not be entitled to do so (*Airline Airspares Ltd v Handley Page Ltd [1970] Ch 193*). In *Lathia v Dronsfield Ltd [1987] BCLC 321* and *Welsh Development Agency v Export Finance Co Ltd [1992] BCC 270* it was held that the receivers as agents for the company were, in carrying out their functions, immune from a claim for inducing a breach of contract by the company, unless they had not acted *bona fide* or had acted outside the scope of their authority (see, however, D8.15 below; and also compare and contrast a receiver's position with that of an administrator dealt with at B7.5 PART B: ADMINISTRATION ORDERS).

Even in cases where the company is holding an asset which it has contracted to sell to another party who has pre-paid the whole or part of the price, the receiver can refuse to perform the contract or deliver the asset, unless the legal or equitable ownership has passed to the purchaser and the purchaser has become entitled to specific performance.

As to the right of a counterparty to terminate a contract with the company and cases in which relief against termination may be available, see D7.14 above.

Goods sold but not delivered

D7.25 The receiver may find that the company has sold certain goods to its customers who have paid full price to the company but have not received delivery of the goods. The question in such cases is whether title to the goods has passed to the customers. If title has not passed, then the receiver can deal with the goods as part of his appointor's security and the only remedy which the customers have is to assert an unsecured, non-preferential, claim for damages for non-delivery against the company which the receiver is not required to be concerned about. If, however, title has passed to the customers, then the receiver must deliver the goods to them as assets not comprised in the charge. Whether or not in any given case title has passed is to be determined in accordance with the provisions of the Sale of Goods Act 1979 in the light of the terms of the relevant sale agreement and the subsequent events. The broad principle is that title passes when the parties intended that it should pass and that, subject to what the agreement provides in this regard, where goods are sold by description from an undivided bulk of that description (as distinct from a particular item of goods identified *in specie*), title only passes when particular goods *in specie* are appropriated to the particular contract, for example, by being segregated from the bulk.

An interesting example of the application of these principles occurred in *Re London Wine Company (Shippers) Limited [1986] PCC 121*. In that case, the company, a dealer in wine, had substantial stocks of wine which were deposited in various warehouses in England. It sold quantities of wine to customers but the wine remained warehoused and there was no appropriation from bulk to fulfil particular contracts. The customers received from the company a 'certificate of title' for wine for which they had paid. The certificate described each customer as 'sole and beneficial owner' of the wine in question and its purpose was to enable the customer to prove his title to third parties. Whilst the goods remained in the warehouse, the customer was charged for storage and insurance and the company reserved a right of lien for all moneys owing to it in respect of the goods. There was, however, no procedure for segregating or identifying specific cases of wine as the property of a particular customer and, certainly, no express representation to that effect.

On the date of the receiver's appointment under a fixed and floating charge, the company held stocks of wine in respect of which it had issued certificates of title and which related to three types of transaction:

(*a*) where a single purchaser of a particular wine by description had purchased the company's total stock of that wine which it had at the date of the purchase, but there had been no subsequent appropriation nor an acknowledgement by the company or the warehouseman that wine of that description was held to the purchaser's order;

(*b*) where there were a number of purchasers of wine of a particular description whose purchases together exhausted the whole of the company's stocks of wine of that description held at different warehouses but, again, there had been no subsequent appropriation or acknowledgement;

(*c*) where there were a number of purchasers of wine of a particular description whose purchases did not exhaust the company's stocks and there had been no subsequent appropriation but the company had given acknowledgements to the customer's mortgagees to the effect that appropriate quantities of wine were held to their order.

The court held that in none of the cases had title passed to the customers, as goods had not been 'ascertained' in the terms of the Sale of Goods Act 1979. As regards category (*a*), the description of the wine did not adequately link it with any given consignment or warehouse; and the mere fact that the company had at the date of the invoice only that amount of wine in stock was irrelevant to the contract, as the order could equally have been fulfilled from any other source. With regard to category (*b*), the acquisition of an undivided interest in a larger stock did not suffice to pass the property where there had been no appropriation to the contract. In any case, the underlying argument that there was an identifiable whole which had been appropriated in some way to fulfil the contracts which exhausted the entire parcel was, on the facts, not valid, since the company remained free to fulfil the contracts from any other source. As to category (*c*), although the circumstances surrounding the transaction gave rise to an estoppel against the warehouseman and the company, the estoppel did not confer upon the customers or the mortgagees an interest in the company's property *in specie* which could be asserted against the company or a transferee (such as the receiver's appointor as a chargee), since the dealing remained uncompleted. The remedy of the customer or the mortgagee was only to recover damages as an unsecured creditor.

The court also held that the company did not hold wine in any of the three categories in trust for its customers, as it was not possible to ascertain with certainty not only the interest of the beneficiary but also the property to which it was to attach, a principle which applied even where the subject matter was part of a homogeneous mass. The company could by appropriate words have declared itself a trustee of a specified proportion of the whole and thus have created an equitable tenancy in common between itself and a named beneficiary so as to give rise to a proprietary interest in the beneficiary in an undivided share of the whole.

It was further held that no proprietary right arose from the mere payment of the purchase price. A mere payment for goods, even in cases where the court would decree specific performance, did not result in the passing of a beneficial interest. The doctrine of equitable assignment as argued (which was in substance the same as that of the trust) required that the beneficial interest should pass to the buyer as soon as the goods became identifiable, notwithstanding that under the Sale of Goods Act, in the absence of express intention, property only passed when goods of that description, in a deliverable state, were appropriated to the contract. Moreover, the existence of a power in the court to decree a specific performance could only aid the customers if the decree was based on some proprietary interest in the goods, to which they were subject at the date when the charge crystallised (by the appointment of the receiver). There-fore, even if a specific performance could be decreed, the decree could not affect goods involved in the contract which were in the company's possession, because the decree could not create proprietary rights where none already existed.

As to some other cases on the question of passing off title to goods sold from a present or future bulk, see *Carlos Federspiel & Co SA v Charles Twigg & Co Ltd [1957] 1 Lloyd's Rep 240*; *Re Wait [1927] 1 Ch 606*; *Dublin City Distillery Ltd v Doherty [1914] AC 823*; *Laurie v Dudin & Sons [1926] 1 KB 223*; *Whitehouse v Frost (1810) 12 East 614*; *Waltons Stores (Interstate) Ltd v Maher (1988) 164 CLR 387*; *Commonwealth of Australia v Verwayen (1990) 95 ALR 321*; *Simm v Anglo-American Tele-graph Co (1879) 5 QBD 188* (cf. *Re Sharpe [1980] 1 WLR 219*; *Knights v Wiffen (1870) LR 5 QB 660*); *Mac-Jordan Construction Ltd v Brookmount Erostin Ltd [1992] BCLC 350*; and *Re Goldcorp Exchange Ltd [1994] 2 All ER 806 (PC)*).

Prior contractual or proprietary interests

D7.26 In *Freevale Ltd v Metrostore (Holdings) Ltd [1984] 1 All ER 495*, notwithstanding the appointment of a receiver, an order for specific per-formance was made against a company which had previously contracted to sell land. However, specific performance, being an equitable remedy, is at the discretion of the court and may be refused where it is incon-venient and unjust (see, for example, *National Westminster Bank plc v Hornsea Pottery Company Ltd and others (CA, 11 May 1984)*). If such ownership has passed, the receiver is in no better position than the com-pany, subject to any right of lien which the company may have for any unpaid amount of the price.

The receiver can also refuse to perform any contract entered into by the company for the supply of services even if the other party has made a prepayment.

(See also D7.27 and D8.15 below.)

In practice, the receiver may be able to obtain extra payment from the other party for completing a pre-receivership contract for the supply of goods or services, by entering into a fresh contract with it. This is because the other party may have to pay even more or may have to suffer more delay if he were to go to another supplier (see, however, D8.15 below).

Sometimes, the receiver may be able to reach a compromise with the other party to the contract for the benefit of the company. The compromise may include a waiver by the other party of his claims against the company. It would appear that such a waiver is not caught by section 10 of the Unfair Contract Terms Act 1977 (see *Tudor Grange Holdings Ltd v Citibank [1991] 4 All ER 1*).

Intellectual property

D7.27   The receiver may find that under a licensing agreement the company has granted a right to another party to use, in return for payment by the other party of periodic licence fees, the company's intellectual property (such as trade mark, patent, industrial process, design, copyright or know-how) for a period which has not expired. There seems to be no reason why the receiver cannot repudiate any outstanding obligations to perform any services under the licence, such as the continued provision of technical advice and back-up which involves the company in further expenditure.

What is not clear is whether, in the event of the receiver repudiating the entire outstanding agreement and the other party refusing to accept such repudiation, the other party ceases to be entitled to use the intellectual property for the remainder of the agreed period, assuming that it is willing to continue to pay the licence fees (perhaps, appropriately reduced to reflect the fact that the back-up service will not be available). It is arguable that, as against the company and the receiver, the other party is entitled to continue to use the intellectual property on that basis. However, unless, on the true construction of the agreement, the other party has acquired an equitable interest in the intellectual property itself, it is doubtful whether it can restrain the receiver from disposing of the intellectual property to a third party, or can continue to use it as against the third party (see, however, D8.15 below).

NHBC protection

D7.28   Houses, bungalows, maisonettes or flats which are newly built (or in the course of construction) will normally have the benefit of the NHBC Buildmark scheme, providing protection against defects by virtue of the building company's registration as a member of NHBC (National Housebuilders' Council). Where such dwellings are comprised in the receivership, the receiver may wish to maintain the registration. This would enable him to sell the dwellings with the benefit of the protection and thereby maximise realisation.

The problem is that the registration normally terminates automatically upon the company going into receivership or certain other forms of insolvency. It is usually possible to obtain a fresh registration, but only in the name of the receiver personally. This involves substantial risks for the receiver. For example, he would be required to give to the *purchaser*:

(a) a warranty, reinforcing the statutory liability under the Defective Premises Act 1972, that the dwelling has been, or will be, built in an efficient and workmanlike manner, with proper materials and so as to be fit for human habitation;

(b) an undertaking to remedy any defects, caused by any breach of the NHBC rules, notified within the initial guarantee period (usually two years from the date of completion of the sale);

(c) a transfer of the ten-year NHBC certificate (including the two-year period referred to above).

In addition, he would be required to give to the NHBC:

(i) an undertaking accepting full responsibility for the dwelling; and

(ii) either a bond executed by the receiver and his appointor (if a bank) or another bank, or a cash sum equal to 2.5 per cent of the full market value of the dwelling.

The receiver will normally have a right of recourse to the receivership assets in respect of any liability he may incur on account of these matters, but the assets may not be sufficient to provide a full recourse.

The registration which the receiver obtains may be either the 'Builders' registration or the 'Developers' registration. The former is appropriate where the company carries out the building of, or sells, dwellings. The latter is appropriate where the company sells, but does not carry out the building of, dwellings. Where partially constructed sites are to be completed and then sold as residential units with NHBC protection, the most satisfactory course may be to appoint a builder, which is registered with NHBC, as the company's main contractor.

Shares in private companies

D7.29 Where the company has a minority or 'deadlock' shareholding in a private company, the articles of association of the private company may contain restrictions against transfer and/or pre-emption rights in favour of the existing shareholder. There may be further restrictive provisions in the case of a shareholding in a joint venture company. These matters may severely prejudice the realisable value of the shares.

'Duress' payments

D7.30 If continued supply of goods or services from an existing supplier to the company is essential, the receiver may have no option but to accept the supplier's condition that all sums due in respect of pre-appointment supplies are paid for in full by the receiver before any further supplies are made. Such 'duress payments' have come to be regarded by receivers as a justifiable receivership expenditure in the larger interests of the receivership.

An unsuccessful attempt to challenge a supplier's right to extract such a duress payment was made by the administrative receiver in *Leyland DAF Ltd v Automotive Products plc [1993] BCC 389*. Automotive Products (AP), a substantial supplier of brake and clutch systems, had supplied parts of such systems to the company on a regular basis and in substantial quantities. AP threatened to discontinue further supplies if the receivers refused to pay moneys owed to it in respect of pre-receivership supplies, for which, of course, the receivers were not liable in law. In refusing the receivers' application for an injunction against AP carrying out the threat, Sir Donald Nicholls V-C stated that the common law position was clear: a party could not be forced to trade with another even if a long term contract was in existence. Mellish LJ had summarised the position in *Re Edwards, ex parte Chalmers (1873) 8 Ch App 289 at 291*:

'. . . the rights of a seller of goods when the purchaser becomes insolvent before the contract for sale has been completely performed . . . [are] that in such a case the seller, notwithstanding that he may have agreed to allow credit for the goods, is not bound to deliver any more goods under the contract until the price of the goods not yet delivered is tendered to him; and that, if a debt is due to him for goods already delivered, he is entitled to refuse to deliver any more till he is paid the debt due for those already delivered'. (See also *Rother Iron Works Limited v Canterbury Precision Engineers Limited [1974] QB 1*.)

The receivers, whilst not disputing the position under the common law, relied on Article 86 of the Treaty of Rome which provides:

'Any abuse by one or more undertakings of a dominant position within the common market or a substantial part of it shall be prohibited as incompatible with the common market insofar as it may affect trade between member States. Such abuse may, in particular, consist in:

(*a*)   directly or indirectly imposing unfair purchase or selling prices or other unfair trading conditions;

(*b*)   limiting production, markets or technical development to the prejudice of consumers;

(*c*)   applying dissimilar conditions to equivalent transactions with other trading parties, thereby placing them at a competitive disadvantage;

(*d*)   making the conclusion of contracts subject to acceptance by other parties of supplementary obligations which, by their nature or according to commercial usage, have no connection with the subject of such contracts.'

The receivers' case was that continuity of supply was vital to the company's ability to continue trading and that there was no other viable source of supply. The Vice-Chancellor said that although Article 86 conferred a direct right in respect of the individual concerned (see *Garden Cottage Foods Ltd v Milk Marketing Board [1984] 1 AC 130 at 141, per* Lord Diplock), to exert ordinary commercial pressure was not an abuse. To hold a dominant position was not of itself an abuse. The obligation to pay for goods was a normal feature of a commercial competitive market. Article 86 could not have been intended to stop a supplier exerting ordinary commercial pressure to obtain payment just because the supplier was in a dominant position. Citing *Hoffmann-La Roche & Co AG v EC Commission [1979] ECR 461* at *541 (para 91)*, the Vice-Chancellor said that abuse directed attention at the use by the dominant undertaking of methods different from normal commercial operators. In the present case, the company's difficulties arose not from the unreasonable conduct of AP but from its own insolvency. This was not a sufficient reason to compel AP to depart from normal commercial behaviour. (The decision of Sir Donald Nicholls V-C was upheld by the Court of Appeal.)

In the case of the supply of gas, electricity, water and telecommunication services (except cable programme services), an administrative receiver (but not an ordinary receiver) is entitled to insist that they should be continued without his having to pay for the past supplies; but he may be required to undertake to pay for the post-appointment supplies if the supplier so insists (see section 233 and A4.15 PART A: GENERAL).

Directors' right to enforce early sale

D7.31 It remains to be seen to what extent the provisions of section 91(2) of the Law of Property Act 1925 are properly applicable to the receivership of a company. That subsection provides that in any action for foreclosure, redemption, sale or raising and payment of mortgage money, the court, on the request of the mortgagee or any person interested in the mortgage money or the right of redemption, may direct a sale of the mortgaged property on such terms as it thinks fit, notwithstanding that any other person dissents or the mortgagee or any person so interested does not appear in the action. In *Palk v Mortgage Services Funding Plc [1993] Ch 330*, the Court of Appeal held that the court had an unfettered discretion to order the sale of mortgaged property, notwithstanding that the lender had refused to consent to the sale and that the sale would raise too little money to discharge the borrower's outstanding mortgage debt. In that case, the mortgagee had obtained an order for possession but the order had been suspended pending the borrower's application for an order of sale. The lender was proposing to let the property on short term lease and sell when the market improved but the sum due under the mortgage was increasing in respect of interest and other charges at a substantially higher rate than the rate of the rents receivable from the short term lettings. The borrower had negotiated a sale of the property for £283,000 although he needed £358,587 to redeem the mortgage. The court was of the view that a mortgagee did owe some duties to a mortgagor. Although it was not obliged to take steps to realise its security, if it did take steps to exercise its rights over the security, common law and equity alike had set bounds to the extent to which it could look after itself and ignore the mortgagor's interests. The morgagee had to act fairly towards the mortgagor. In that case the lender had embarked on a course of realisation which was likely to be highly prejudicial to the borrower's financial position.

It will be appreciated that the section would not apply unless there is pending before the court an action for any of the remedies described above. It is rare, where the mortgagor is a company, for the mortgagee to bring such an action and then appoint a receiver or to bring such an action during the receivership. However, where this has happened, it is conceivable that the directors of the company, in exercise of their residual functions (see D5.5 above) might successfully obtain an order for sale and thereby upset the receiver's plans for the realisation of the charged property. However, the court would no doubt carry out a balancing exercise between the interests of the mortgagor on the one hand and the mortgagee on the other hand.

Liquidation costs

(See D10.3 below.)

Receivers' right of recourse to assets

(See D4.10 above, and D8.1 *et seq.* and D10.1 below.)

Assets excluded by law from appointor's charge

(See D9.1 below.)

Chapter 8: Post-appointment liabilities

D8.1   Usually a charging document gives the receiver an extensive right of recourse to the receivership assets in respect of costs, expenses and liabilities properly incurred in the performance of his functions. This right augments the right of recourse which he has under the Insolvency Act 1986 (see, for example, sections 37(1)(b) and 44(1)(c) in relation to contractual liabilities and paragraph 13 of Schedule 1 in the case of an administrative receiver) and the Law of Property Act 1925 (see, for example, section 109(8) of that Act). However, there may be cases where the right of recourse is of little practical value because there are insufficient assets. Some types of such costs, expenses and liabilities are dealt with below. (See also the last paragraph of D7.2 above in respect of employers' national insurance contributions.)

New, novated or adopted contracts and receivership costs

Introduction

D8.2   An ordinary receiver (section 37) or an administrative receiver (section 44) is (in the case of the former, to the same extent as if he had been appointed by an order of the court) personally liable on any contract entered into by him in the performance of his functions (except insofar as the contract otherwise provides) and on any contract of employment adopted by him in the performance of those functions. He is not to be taken to have adopted a contract of employment by reason of anything done or omitted to be done within 14 days after his appointment; but before the decision of the Court of Appeal in the *Paramount Airways* case (see D8.3 below) it was believed that this did not necessarily mean that at the end of that period he was taken to have adopted it if the contract still continued; and that whether he had adopted a contract of employment or other contract depended on the facts of the case (see D8.3 and D8.4 below).

In *Hill Samuel & Co Ltd v Laing (1988) 4 BCC 9 (Court of Session)*, it was held that the receiver was personally liable for repayment of post-receivership advances made by the debenture holder to the company unless such liability had been excluded expressly or by implication.

Where the receiver does become personally liable, he is entitled in respect of that liability to idemnity out of (in the case of the ordinary receiver) 'the assets' or (in the case of the administrative receiver) 'the assets of the company'. However, where the receiver has not assumed personal liability, an employee whose contract is continued is not entitled to be paid his post-receivership salary as part of the receivership expenses, although if the receiver does make the payment (as he would normally do), he can recoup it out of the receivership assets (see *Nicoll v Cutts [1985] BCLC 322 (CA)*). (If the decision of the Court of Appeal in

Paramount Airways (see D8.3 below) is good law, it is inconceivable that in relation to an employee whose employment is continued beyond 14 days after the receiver's appointment, the receiver would be able to escape personal liability.) Such personal liability of the receiver (where it arises) does not limit any right to indemnity which he would otherwise have, nor limit his liability on contracts entered into or (in the case of the administrative receiver) adopted by him without authority, nor confer any right to indemnity in respect of that liability. Where, at any time, he vacates office, his remuneration and any expenses properly incurred by him, and any indemnity to which he is entitled out of the assets of the company, are to be charged on and paid out of any property of the company which is in his custody or under his control at that time, in priority to any charge or other security held by his appointor (sections 37, 44 and 45).

Contracts of employment

D8.3   Three important aspects of the effect of a receivership on contracts of employment are discussed below: the impact of the *Paramount Airways* decision, the effect of the Wages Act 1986, and the extent to which a receiver owes a duty of care to the employees of the business.

(A) *Paramount Airways and the Insolvency Act 1994*

The practice before the decision of the Court of Appeal in *Paramount Airways* (see below) was that a receiver would, as soon as practicable after his appointment, write to all parties with whom the company had outstanding contracts either repudiating them on behalf of the company (leaving the other party to pursue its own remedies as an unsecured creditor) or stating that the company intended to continue to perform them but that he should in no way be regarded as having adopted them or as being personally liable thereon. Where the services of employees were to be continued he would write to them within 14 days after his appointment (see D8.2 above) making it clear to them that their employment beyond that period would continue to be on behalf of the company on the same terms and that he would act only as the company's agent, would not adopt the contract or be personally liable thereon (see e.g. *Re Specialised Mouldings Ltd, 13 February 1987*, where Harman J approved such a practice).

However, in *Re Paramount Airways Limited (No 3) [1994] BCC 172*, a case concerning the administration procedure, the Court of Appeal, in upholding the decision of Evans-Lombe J in the Chancery Division (*[1993] BCC 662*) held, in effect, that if any administrator continues after the 14-day period of grace (mentioned in section 19(5) in common with sections 37 and 44 relating to administrative receivers), to employ staff, and pays them in accordance with their previous contracts, he will be held *impliedly* (emphasis supplied) to have adopted their contracts of employment (per Dillon LJ). The Court of Appeal's decision, in effect, gives the expression 'adopted' a meaning different from that previously understood. For example, in *Botibol v Botibol* [*1947*] *1 All ER 26*, Evershed J, dealing with the position of a court-appointed receiver, remarked:

'. . . it may be difficult to say that a receiver, acting strictly as such, can ever be sued in contract. On the other hand, a receiver may . . . adopt as his own a contract and render himself liable as on a novation of it'.

It is clear from the judgment of the Court of Appeal that the term 'adopted' is to be similarly construed in sections 37 and 44. The expression 'impliedly', emphasised above, might suggest that an administrator or a receiver can negative an implied adoption by express words to the contrary. However, Dillon LJ, in a later part of his judgment, referred to the practice of receivers and administrators of using such express 'non-adoption' language, following the *Specialised Mouldings* case (above) (which he did not find a helpful authority because of the absence of any report, transcript or note of reasons by which Harman J reached his conclusion). Dillon LJ said that the mere assertion (or 'ritual incantation') by an administrator *or* receiver that he is not adopting the contract was 'mere wind with no legal effect', because adoption was a matter not merely of words but of fact.

At the time of the revision of this chapter, an appeal by the administrators in the *Paramount Airways* case to the House of Lords against the decision of the Court of Appeal was pending. Meanwhile, in view of the far-reaching implications of that decision for administrators and receivers, who might be left with no choice but to close the business and dismiss the employees before the expiry of the 14-day grace period, emergency legislation was rushed through Parliament to partially counteract the harsher effects of that decision. The result was the Insolvency Act 1994, which came into force on 24 March 1994 but is retrospective to contracts of employment adopted on or after 15 March 1994. Insofar as it applies to receivers, it amends section 44 of the 1986 Act by restricting the personal liability of an *administrative receiver* in respect of contracts of employment adopted by him to 'qualifying liabilities'. A liability is a qualifying liability if:

(*a*)   it is a liability to pay a sum by way of wages or salary or contribution to an occupational pension scheme;

(*b*)   it is incurred while the administrative receiver is in office; *and*

(*c*)   it is in respect of services rendered wholly or partly after the adoption of the contract.

Where a qualifying liability relates to services rendered partly before and partly after the adoption of the contract, the administrative receiver's liability only extends to so much of the sum as is payable in respect of services rendered after the adoption. Wages or salary payable in respect of a period of holiday or absence from work through sickness or other good cause are deemed wages or salary in respect of services rendered in that period. A sum payable in lieu of holiday is deemed to be wages or salary in respect of services rendered in the period by reference to which the holiday entitlement arose. Here, the reference to wages or salary payable in respect of a period of holiday includes any sums which, if they had been paid, would have been treated for the purposes of the enactments relating to social security as earnings in respect of that period (section 2 of the 1994 Act).

Unfortunately, the 1994 Act does not similarly amend the corresponding section 37 of the 1986 Act, relating to receivers other than administrative receivers. Thus, an ordinary receiver continues to remain fully exposed to personal liability in respect of contracts of employment adopted by him (subject to his right of indemnity out of the receivership assets). (However, the Act does apply similar provisions to receivers in Scotland, as to which see D11.6 below.)

It will be noted that the 1994 Act does not protect administrators, administrative receivers or Scottish receivers in respect of potential liability under contracts of employment adopted by them before 15 March 1994. Their only hope is that the House of Lords overrules the Court of Appeal in *Paramount Airways* on the meaning of 'adopted'.

Hard on the heels of *Paramount Airways* came *Re Leyland Daf Ltd*; *Re Ferranti International plc [1994] BCC 658*, an administrative receivership case (Lightman J, Companies Court). It was held that the word 'adopted' in section 44 had the same meaning as that in section 19 as construed in *Paramount Airways*, namely 'treated as continuing in force'. Accordingly, the receivers were personally liable (co-extensively with the companies and subject to the rights of indemnity out of the receivership assets) in respect of all *contractual* (but not other) liabilities under the contracts of employment (which the receivers had caused the companies to continue), irrespective of the dates (whether before or after their appointment) on which the liabilities accrued, or the periods in respect of which they arose. However, the liabilities attached from the date of the adoption and were not retrospective to the date of the appointment. It was further held that there was no statutory prohibition against the employees contracting out of the protection afforded to them by section 44. Exclusion by the receivers of the statutory incident of personal liability required a contract to that effect between the receivers and the employees. The receivers' letters to the employees unilaterally declaring 'non-liability' were not sufficient. Even if the letters constituted an offer, it would be unrealistic and unfair to treat the continued performance by the employees of their contracts of employment as an acceptance of a new contract by way of variation excluding the statutory incident.

At the time of writing, an appeal in *Leyland Daf* to the House of Lords, by means of the 'leapfrog' procedure, was pending and was expected to be heard alongside the appeal in *Paramount Airways* on 5 December 1994.

Reference has been made above to the receiver's right of indemnity out of the receivership assets. There currently appears to be a difference of opinion between the Society of Practitioners of Insolvency and the British

Bankers Association on whether the indemnity extends not only to floating charge assets but also to fixed charge assets.

(See also D7.1 above.)

(B) *Effect of Wages Act 1986*

The receiver must bear in mind the provisions of the Wages Act 1986 relating to unlawful deductions from an employee's properly payable 'wages'. This expression does not include wages in lieu of notice (see *Delaney v RJ Staples [1992] 1 All ER 944 (HL)* and *Foster Wheeler (London) Ltd v Jackson [1990] ICR 757*; and see *Greg May (CF & C) Ltd v Dring [1990] IRLR 19 (EAT)*; *Gothard v Mirror Group Newspapers Ltd [1988] ICR 729 at 733)*. However, 'wages' does include commission, even where it is at the discretion of the employer (*Kent Management Services Ltd v Butterfield [1992] IRLR 394*) and supplements paid by way of bonus (*McCree v London Borough of Tower Hamlets [1992] IRLR 56*).

A deduction is unlawful unless it is required or authorised by statute or a relevant provision of the contract of employment or the employee has previously agreed or consented in writing to the making of it. Section 1(5) of the Wages Act sets out the categories of deduction which may be lawfully made. Included in them are any overpayment of wages and any overpayment of expenses incurred by the worker in carrying out his employment. An industrial tribunal has no jurisdiction to determine the legality of such a deduction even where the overpayment has resulted from a fraudulent expenses claim made by the employee: *SIP (Industrial Products) Ltd v Swinn [1994] IRLR 323*. A mistaken overpayment of agreed sick pay made to an employee on his early retirement may be deducted unless the employee has so altered his position in relation to the overpayment that the employer is estopped from claiming it (see, for example, *Home Office v Ayres [1992] IRLR 59*, an EAT decision which a later EAT declined to follow in *Sunderland Polytechnic v Evans [1993] ICR 392* in which it held that section 1(5)(e) of the Wages Act prevented it from having jurisdiction where any 'deduction' had been made on account of industrial action, regardless of whether the deduction was lawful; see also *Lipkin Gorman v Karpnale Ltd [1991] 2 AC 548* as to what may, or may not, amount to such estoppel). For a discussion of the principles applicable to a deduction for overpayment, see *Murray v Strathclyde Regional Council [1992] IRLR 396*. The mere fact that the employee has previously agreed to *repay* a loan made to him by the employer, or part of training fees paid for him by the employer, in the event of the employment being terminated by a specified date, does not mean that he has agreed to the deduction of the amount of such loan (or part of those fees) from his wages (*Potter v Hunt Contracts Ltd [1992] IRLR 108*). See also *Fairfield Ltd v Skinner [1992] ICR 837*, where the need for the tribunal to examine critically the factual justification for a deduction was emphasised. Non-payment of shift allowance in respect of the period of a production 'pause' to an employee whose contractual pay included a fixed shift allowance irrespective of actual hours worked may amount to an unlawful deduction (*British Steel plc v Elliott, Industrial*

Relations Legal Information Bulletin 425, 24 May 1991). A deduction of the balance of a private health insurance premium from the final wages of a departing employee (*Hall v Second Nature Ltd, IDS Brief 380 September 1988*—see *New Law Journal, 23 February 1990, page 243*) falls within section 1 of the Act.

An employee is entitled on his retirement to accrued holiday pay, in respect of holiday not taken during earlier periods, calculated at the rate of his holiday entitlement at the time of retirement (*Devon General Ltd v Seeney (1994) Industrial Relations Law Bulletin 499, 9*). The Act may also be breached where the employer reduces the employee's guaranteed overtime pay. The employee's consent cannot be inferred from the fact that he continues to work under protest (*McRuary v Washington Irvine Ltd (1994) Industrial Relations Law Bulletin 499, 9*). An agreement by an employee to authorise deductions in respect of conduct before the agreement is ineffective (*Discount Tobacco and Confectionery Ltd v Williamson [1993] ICR 371*).

In *Sim v Rotherham Metropolitan Borough Council [1986] ICR 897*, Scott J reviewed the earlier authorities which indicated that an equitable set-off could be made against wages due. Even where an employer claims to be entitled to an equitable set-off exceeding any wages that may be found to be due, the tribunal does have jurisdiction to hear evidence and investigate the circumstances to decide whether the employee can prove the essentials of his case and whether there have been deductions about which the tribunal can properly pronounce. (*New Centurion Trust Ltd v Welsh [1990] IRLR 123 (EAT)*).

Although the Act refers to 'deductions', the Employment Appeal Tribunal held in *Pename Ltd v Patterson [1989] IRLR 195* that where an employer withheld an entire week's wages from an employee who failed to give proper notice, there had been a contravention of the Act. The Act may also be contravened where the employer unilaterally withdraws a wages supplement (*McCree v Tower Hamlets London Borough Council [1992] IRLR 56*). Non-payment of wages was held to amount to a deduction. The contrary suggestion was made in *Rickard v BB Glass Supplies Ltd [1990] ICR 150*. However the principle in *Pename* was followed by the Employment Appeal Tribunal in *Greg May (CF & C) Ltd v Dring [1990] IRLR 19 (EAT)* and upheld by the Court of Appeal in *Delaney v Staples [1991] 1 All ER 609* (note that this aspect of the case did not form part of the House of Lords decision referred to above). The Court of Appeal preferred the reasoning in *Greg May v Dring* (above) and *Kournavous v JR Masterson & Sons (Demolition) Ltd [1990] IRLR 119* to that in *Barlow v Whittle [1990] IRLR 79* and *Alsop v Star Vehicle Contracts Ltd [1990] IRLR 83*, where the Employment Appeal Tribunal held that the Act 'is designed to deal with "deductions" not "non-payments"'.

Sums representing payments in lieu of notice are payable gross rather than net of deductions for tax and national insurance contributions. Such deductions are not unlawful under section 1(1) of the Wages Act 1986.

(C) *Receiver's duty of care*

A receiver owes a duty of care to all the employees of the business and must act reasonably in all the circumstances: *Larsen v Henderson* [*1990*] *IRLR 512*. In that case, Lord Sutherland in the Court of Session in Scotland stated:

> 'The fact that a receiver may have to take decisions which have an adverse effect on the employees does not, however, mean that he can ride roughshod over all the employees' rights . . . Accordingly, if there are two ways in which the receiver can achieve his desired end, he would have a duty to adopt that method which had the least adverse effect on the employees . . . '.

This proposition does not, however, mean that apart from as provided by statute, the receiver should materially subordinate the interests of the receivership to the interests of the employees.

As to the manner in which contracts of employment may affect realisation of assets, see D7.1 above.

Contracts generally

D8.4   As regards contracts for the supply to the company of goods and services which are to be continued, the receiver would also make it clear that neither he nor the receivership assets would be liable in respect of any claim for any pre-appointment supplies, or breaches by the company, but that it is intended that the post-appointment supplies would be paid for by him as the company's agent to the extent that assets are available in the receivership for the purpose (but see also below). Depending on the terms of the contract, the supplier may not be under an obligation to continue the supplies (as to which see D7.30 above).

In additon to continuing existing contracts, the receiver may also have to enter into new contracts. Such a contract is usually entered into in the name of the company through the receiver as its agent (for example, the party is expressed to be 'XYZ Ltd (in receivership) acting by its [administrative] receiver and agent ABC' and the attestation clause reads 'SIGNED for and on behalf of XYZ Ltd (in receivership) by ABC [administrative] receiver and agent'). It is important to include an express provision to the effect that the receiver will have no personal liability under or in connection with the contract. Further, as his agency ceases upon the company going into liquidation (see D5.2 above), it may be advisable to provide (in the alternative and without prejudice to the above) that any liability of the receiver and/or the company (see below) will, in any case, be limited to the funds for the time being in the receiver's hands as such receiver which may properly be applied in discharge thereof. A practice has lately also grown for the parties to recite in the contract circumstances tending to show that these exclusions and limitations of liability are reasonable for the purposes of the Unfair Contract Terms Act 1977, and for the parties to confirm that they regard them to be such. There still remains the problem about any liability in tort or under statute that may arise in respect of any post-receivership supplies of defective or unsafe products by the company. It may not be open to contract out of such liability and, in any case, any such contracting out would not be binding on subsequent third party users or sub-purchasers. The liability may fall not only on the company but also on the receiver personally. Wherever possible, an insurance cover against such liability should be maintained.

In addition to excluding his personal liability, the receiver also strives to ensure that he does not unnecessarily or unreasonably subject even the company to any liability under such a contract; otherwise he could risk a claim from a liquidator to the extent (if any) that a dividend to the unsecured creditors is reduced by reason of that liability. Further, if he causes the company to incur greater liabilities under post-appointment contracts than there are assets available for their discharge, he could risk personal liability for fraudulent trading, though perhaps not for wrongful trading unless he can be regarded as a 'shadow director' (see C13.1 *et seq.* PART C: LIQUIDATIONS).

For these reasons, it is usual for him to exclude, on the part of the company and himself, all warranties and representations as to title and other matters in relation to the assets which he is selling except, perhaps, where, in all the circumstances and having made due enquiries, he deems it reasonable to give any particular warranty or make any particular representation on behalf of the company. One warranty he may have to concede personally is that his appointment and the charge under which he is appointed are valid (although, as far as an administrative receiver is concerned, section 42(3) provides that a person dealing with him in good faith and for value is not concerned to inquire whether he is acting within his powers, and section 232 provides that, in common with certain other office-holders, his acts are valid notwithstanding any defect in his appointment, nomination or qualifications) and that he has not knowingly done (or omitted to do) anything which encumbers, or which adversely affects, the title to the assets which the company is selling.

Value added tax

D8.5   Any claim by HM Customs & Excise in respect of VAT charged by the receiver in the name of the company on taxable supplies lies only against the company and is *prima facie* postponed to the rights of the debenture holder. Section 109(8) of the Law of Property Act 1925 (which lays down the order of distribution of rents and profits collected by a receiver and provides for the discharge of taxes) governs the position as between the receiver himself and the debenture holder and confers no right on a third party (see e.g. *Liverpool Corpn v Hope* cited in D8.11 below). Thus, in theory, the receiver has a discretion whether or not to discharge the VAT claim. In *Re John Willment (Ashford) Ltd [1979] 2 All ER 615*, it was held that in fact he had no discretion, since by not making the payment he would cause the company to commit a criminal offence under the VAT legislation. However, failure to pay VAT is now no longer a criminal offence, since 1 October 1986. It would appear that the only way in which HM Customs and Excise can impose personal liability on the receiver is to register him as a taxable person under Regulation 11 of the Value Added Tax (General) Regulations 1985 (SI 1985 No 886). Upon such registration, he would be liable for VAT on all post-appointment supplies, including those made before registration. That Regulation empowers the Commissioners of Customs and Excise to treat, as a taxable person, any person carrying on a business in the course of which taxable supplies are or are intended to be made. There is no express reference to a receiver or any other insolvency office-holder. It is debatable whether a receiver, particularly where he is only a fixed charge (LPA) receiver can, as agent of the company, himself be regarded as carrying on the business. However, paragraph 7 of Schedule 4 to the Value Added Tax Act 1994 (together with Regulation 59 of SI 1985 No 886) requires any person, who disposes of any assets of a taxable person under a power of sale, to remit the appropriate amount of VAT directly to HM Customs and Excise. In *Sargent v Customs & Excise Commissioners [1994] 1 WLR 235*, Judge Paul Baker QC in the High Court held that a fixed charge receiver was accountable for VAT in respect of the assets sold. Apparently, the judge largely based his decision on section 109(8) of the Law of Property Act 1925 referred to at D8.11 below which, in the light of the authorities cited there, does not impose any obligation on a receiver. The decision is believed to be subject to a pending appeal.

The provisions of the VAT legislation relating to land, leases and buildings, which give rise to a liability to VAT in various circumstances, should be noted (including the Value Added Tax (Special Provisions) Order 1992 (SI 1992 No 3129), and the Value Added Tax Act 1994, Schedules 9 and 10)).

A statutory exemption from VAT is available, subject to certain conditions, in the case of the sale of a business and assets as a going concern (see D9.13 below).

Where the receiver discharges any pre-receivership debts (see, e.g. D7.17 to D7.20 and D7.30 above) which included VAT, or returns third party property previously invoiced with VAT to the company, the position will be as follows.

(*a*) The payment will be entered gross, as the parties would previously have already accounted for VAT input and output to the authorities. The VAT position will not be affected.

(*b*) Where the property is returned, the third party will claim a refund of VAT output previously accounted for to the authorities by issuing a credit note (see HM Customs & Excise VAT Guide Notice 700 Part VII); but this does not, in turn, give rise to a preferential claim by the authorities against the company by way of 'clawback' of the VAT input originally allowed, even if it was allowed within the preferential period (see D7.4 above). The claim which arises is only a non-preferential claim (because it arises after the receivership) and the receiver is not liable to pay it even as an expense of receivership (because no money representing VAT has been received in respect of that 'supply'—*Re Liverpool Commercial Vehicles Ltd* [*1984*] *BCLC 587*).

As to the present position on set off regarding value added tax, see D7.6(2).

See also PART H: TAXATION.

Attachment of earnings (or deduction from earnings) orders

D8.6 Where, prior to the appointment of a receiver under a debenture, the company has made deductions from an employee's salary pursuant to an attachment of earnings order (or deduction from earnings order) issued by a court, but has not paid over the deductions to the authorised officer, the receiver appears to have no obligation to make payment to the officer, as the deductions continue to form part of the assets charged by the debenture. However, if such deductions relate to any salary paid within four months preceding the receiver's appointment, then to the extent that such deductions, when aggregated with the amount of any other unpaid salary of that employee for that period, do not exceed £800, they would represent a preferential claim in favour of the employee to whom the order relates, against any floating charge assets available. Payment would be technically due to the employee but, since the judgment creditor of the employee who has obtained the order takes precedence, the receiver must remit it (out of any receivership funds available after deduction of or provision for the costs of receivership) to the officer concerned with an explanation on the above lines. The position appears to be analogous to that in respect of a garnishee order in respect of any debt due or any payment to be made or asset to be delivered by the company to a third party, as to which see *Re Combined Weighing and Advertising Machine Co (1889) 43 Ch D 99*; *Norton v Yates* [*1906*] *1 KB 112* and *Cairney v Back* [*1906*] *2 KB 746*; however, to the extent that any such claim is a non-proprietary or a non-preferential claim, the receiver would not be concerned to discharge it.

If the receiver continues the employment of the employee concerned after his appointment, the receiver must comply with the attachment order in respect of the post-appointment salary. The analogy of *Re John Willment (Ashford) Ltd* (see D8.5 above) may apply.

Statutory liabilities in respect of immovable property

D8.7 The main statutory provisions giving rise to possible liability of a receiver in relation to immovable assets over which he has been appointed are dealt with below. (As to possible environmental law liabilities, see D8.19 *et seq.* below).

(a) Public Health (etc.) Acts

D8.8 'Owner' is defined in section 343 of the Public Health Act 1936 as a person for the time being receiving the rack rent of the premises whether on his own account or as agent or trustee for any other person or who would so receive the same if the premises were let at a rack rent. Liability could arise under section 80 of the Environmental Protection Act 1990—summary proceedings for statutory nuisances. It is, however, limited under section 294 of the 1936 Act. Further, section 2(1) of the Health and Safety at Work (etc.) Act 1974 requires every employer to ensure, so far as reasonably practicable, the health, safety and welfare of his employees including *inter alia* the provision of plant and systems of work which are safe and without risks to health. This duty is owed to all his employees and not only to those engaged in the work involving the plant (*Bolton Metropolitan District Council v Malrod Insulations Ltd [1993] ICR 658*). Section 3(1) of that Act imposes a duty on every employer to conduct his undertaking so as to ensure, so far as reasonably practicable, that persons not in his employment who may be affected thereby are not exposed to risks to their health and safety. This includes the cleaning, repair and maintenance of plant, machinery and buildings necessary for carrying on business, whether it is done by the employer's own employees or by independent contractors (*R v Associated Octel Co Ltd [1994] IRLR 540 (CA)*, effectively overruling *RMC Roadstone Products Ltd v Jester [1994] IRLR 330 (DC)*). Under section 4(2) of that Act, a person who makes non-domestic premises available to those who are not his employees is under a duty to ensure, so far as reasonably practicable, that the premises and any plant and substance provided for use by them are safe and without risks to health.

It is debatable whether liability on a receiver's part for breach of statutory duty or in negligence may arise under those provisions and also under section 29(1) of the Factories Act 1961, which imposes a duty on an employer (which is a strict duty without proof of reasonable fore-seeability—see *Larner v British Steel plc [1993] 4 All ER 102*) to keep a place of work safe for any person working there. (See now the Workplace (Health, Safety and Welfare) Regulations 1992 (SI 1992 No 3004), implementing EC Directive 89/654.) Although the duty is imposed on the employer, and the liability of an administrative receiver in respect of contracts of employment adopted by him, following the *Paramount Airways* decision, is limited as set out in the Insolvency Act 1994 (see D8.3 above), it is unclear whether the receiver will be protected against any claim in tort where he has not taken steps to ensure compliance with section 29(1) of the 1961 Act or other similar legislation. See further D8.22 below.

(*b*) *Environmental law liabilities* (see D8.19 below)

(*c*) *Town and Country Planning Act 1971 (as amended)*

D8.9 'Owner' is defined in section 290. The definition differs from that in the Public Health Act 1936 in that it does not refer to an agent (though it does refer to a person as trustee). It is submitted that a receiver appointed out of court, being usually agent for the mortgagor, cannot be regarded as trustee for the mortgagor or the mortgagee at the same time for this purpose. Liability under this Act could arise particularly under sections 87 to 91 relating to enforcement notices and sections 96 to 99 relating to enforcement notices on listed buildings.

(d) *London Building Acts*

D8.10 The definition of 'owner' for the general purposes of the Acts is contained in section 5 of the London Building Act 1930, and 'includes every person in possession or receipt either of the whole or of any part of the rents or profits of any land or tenement or in the occupation of any land or tenement otherwise than as a tenant from year to year or for any less term or as a tenant at will'. A special definition applies to Part V of the London Building Acts (Amendment) Act 1939, dealing with means of escape in case of fire (section 33, following the wording of section 343 of the Public Health Act 1936). It has been held that a receiver is liable under Part V but not under Part XII of the 1939 Act (*Solomons v Gertzenstein [1954] 2 QB 243*).

(e) *Rates*

D8.11 Rating law has recently undergone a succession of changes, but has consistently maintained a distinction between the rating of occupied property and the rating of unoccupied property.

Under the General Rate Acts 1967 and 1984 (as from time to time amended and read with various statutory instruments made under them) the liability for rates on occupied property was imposed on the occupier. So long as the receiver was the agent of the occupier company, and he did not dispossess the company and take possession in an independent capacity as principal, there was no change of occupation (unless the charging instrument otherwise provided) (see *Ratford v Northavon District Council [1986] BCLC 397 (CA)*; *McKillop and Walters, The Times, 14 April 1994*, approving the following statement in *Palmer's Company Law*, Volume 2, paragraph 14.224:

'A receiver may be regarded as the occupier of company premises (jointly with the company) for the purposes of enforcing a statutory duty imposed on the occupier of premises . . . [see D8.26 below] . . . but not for the purposes of liability for rates'.).

Any provision in the charging document, and the provisions of section 109(8) of the Law of Property Act 1925, requiring payment of rates etc. out of the proceeds of the assets, only defines the position between the company and the mortgagee or chargee and does not enable the local authority to sue the receiver for rates (*Liverpool Corpn v Hope [1938] 1 KB 751*; *Re Kentish Homes Ltd [1993] BCC 212*). The occupation had to be actual and exclusive occupation, so that, where during a period of 'work in' by the company's employees, access to the premises was denied to the receiver, both he and the company could escape liability (*Re Briant Colour Printing Co Ltd [1977] 1 WLR 942*). By contrast, liability for empty rates was imposed on 'the person entitled to possession', though not actually in possession (see *Banister v London Borough of Islington*

(*1972*) *71 LGR 239*). However, the empty rates regime only applied to certain types of property and only in certain circumstances. The regime was contained, *inter alia*, in Schedules 1 to the 1967 and 1984 Acts, as modified by, *inter alia*, section 42 of the Local Government Planning and Land Act 1980, the Unoccupied Property Rate (Variation of Current Ceiling) Order 1980 (SI 1980 No 2012), Rating (Exemption of Unoccupied Property) Regulations 1967 (SI 1967 No 954) and Rating (Exemption of Unoccupied Industrial and Storage Hereditaments) Regulations 1985 (SI 1985 No 258)).

With effect from the financial year beginning with 1 April 1990, the Local Government Finance Act 1988 replaced the rating system described above, by a community charge, as regards domestic property, and a new system of rates on occupied and unoccupied non-domestic hereditaments. The community charge was of three types: personal community charge, standard community charge and collective community charge.

Personal community charge was payable by individuals by reference to their residence in a particular area (as distinct from their occupation or ownership of any particular premises within that area).

The standard community charge was payable by every person who had a freehold or leasehold interest in the whole of a domestic property or its self-contained part (not being his sole or main residence or designated for the purposes of collective community charges) situated in the relevant rating authority's area. Since the charge was levied by reference to ownership, no personal liability would normally have attached to the receiver of the company owning the interest (subject to what is stated below).

Collective community charge was payable by the person who had a qualifying freehold or leasehold estate in the whole of a designated dwelling, that is, a building, or part of a building used wholly or mainly as the sole or main residence of individuals most or all of whom resided there for short periods and were not undertaking full-time courses of education and where it would be difficult to collect payments in respect of personal community charges from individuals. Thus, again, liability depended on ownership of the relevant qualifying interest, and a receiver of the company owning it would not be personally liable (subject as stated below).

However, section 17 of the 1988 Act provided that where the person chargeable in respect of standard or collective community charge (being, in relation to the standard community charge, a company) had a management arrangement with another person (the manager), not being his employee, under which (in relation to a standard community charge) the manager was to collect payments for the use of the property in respect of which the charge arose or (in relation to a collective community charge) the manager was to collect payments for the residential accommodation in the designated dwelling or amounts by way of contribution in respect of the charge, both the person chargeable and the manager would be jointly and severally liable to pay the chargeable amount. It is arguable that upon his appointment the receiver could be regarded as such manager under the management arrangement, inasmuch as he would be collecting rents etc. On the other hand, if the company in receivership was the manager and not the owner, then, arguably, the receiver, as manager of such manager (as it were) would not be personally liable (see, for example, *Re Kentish Homes Ltd [1993] BCC 212*).

Part III of the 1988 Act dealt with the rating of non-domestic occupied and unoccupied hereditaments (see also the Non-Domestic Rating (Unoccupied Property) Regulations 1989 (SI 1989 No 2261). The rate liability for occupied hereditaments was on the person who was in occupation (section 43), and the *Ratford* case referred to above would be applicable. The liability in respect of unoccupied hereditaments was imposed on the 'owner' which was defined by section 65 as 'the person entitled to possession' of it. Therefore, arguably, the receiver or his appointor would be liable as the person entitled to possession of the premises concerned, if the *Banister* case (above) is still good law. It is submitted that the decision in that case was wrong. It was largely based on the decisions in *Richards v Kidderminster Overseers [1896] 2 Ch 212* and *Taggs Island Casino Hotel Ltd v London Borough of Richmond Upon Thames (1968) 14 RRC 119* where receivers had been held liable in respect of occupied property rates on the ground that upon their appointment, there had been a change of occupation. In other words, in imposing liability on receivers for *empty* property rates, *Banister* applied the analogy of liability on them for *occupied* property rates under those two cases. However, the *Ratford* case (decided by the Court of Appeal, see above) relating to *occupied* property rates has effectively overruled the *Richards* and *Taggs Island* cases (decided at first instance) by holding that, since a receiver is the agent of the company, there is no change of occupation. Thus, if a receiver can be in *actual occupation* as the company's agent without effecting a change of occupation, there seems to be no reason why he cannot also be *entitled to possession* as the company's agent without effecting a change of entitlement to possession. It is further submitted that, for these purposes, the agency survives liquidation on the principles of the *Sowman* and *Barrows* cases referred to at D5.2 above, since the receiver will be exercising his functions of dealing with the charged property. This view was echoed in *Re Leigh Estates (UK) Ltd [1994] BCC 292* by counsel for the company and opposing creditors, Miss Gloster QC; and the judge (Mr Richard Sykes QC), whilst expressing no opinion on the question, remarked that there may be a conflict between the decision of the Divisional Court in *Banister* and that of the Court of Appeal in *Ratford*.

The unoccupied property would be chargeable even if it was incapable of occupation owing to removal of sanitary fittings and plumbing in modernisation (*Easiwork Homes Ltd v Redbridge London BC [1970] 2 QB 406*).

With effect from the financial year beginning with 1 April 1993, the Local Government Finance Act 1992 has replaced the three-tier system of community charge in respect of domestic properties by the system of council tax on 'dwellings'. The liability for council tax lies with, in a descending order of priority, (i) the resident of the property who is also the freeholder, (ii) such resident who is also the leaseholder, (iii) the resident who is also a statutory or secure tenant, (iv) the resident who is also a licensee, (v) the resident or (vi) the owner. Here, the expression 'owner' does not include a person who is merely entitled to possession. It means a person who has a material interest which is not subject to an inferior material interest. For example, a freeholder would not be an 'owner' if he had let the property. 'Resident' means an individual, aged 18 or over, who has his sole or main residence in the dwelling. Again, where (vi) above applies to a company in receivership, the receiver will have no personal liability. The 1992 Act has *not* replaced the system of rating on occupied and unoccupied non-domestic property under the 1988 Act (see above).

It will be noted that both under the 1988 Act and the 1992 Act the rating authority has a power to levy distress as one of the means of collecting rates. However, any distress levied after the appointment of the receiver is unlikely to have priority over the rights of the receiver's appointor (see D7.13 above).

Income and corporation tax

D8.12 A receiver appointed out of court is not liable to account for any income tax or corporation tax on profits earned or capital gains realised during the course of the receivership. There is no statutory provision imposing such a liability on him. However, where he is in receipt of rent from the charged property, the Inland Revenue can, after issuing an assessment on the company, issue a notice requiring him as agent to pay the tax chargeable on the rent under section 23(7) of the Income and Corporation Taxes Act 1988. As rents are charged to the receiver's appointor, the receiver will be obliged, it seems, to pay the amount of the assessments from the rents still in his hands or thereafter coming into his hands. For further details regarding taxation in receivership see PART H: TAXATION.

Rent

D8.13 A receiver is not liable for pre-appointment or post-appointment rent but may, in practice, have to discharge the post-appointment rent so as to avoid distress or the pre-appointment or post-appointment rent so as to avoid forfeiture (see D7.13 and D7.14 above). Where there have been successive assignments of a lease, and the landlord sues the original tenant (who may be solvent) under its original covenant to pay rent for the remainder of the term (for example, because the present tenant is insolvent), the original tenant cannot compel an intermediate tenant (who also may be insolvent) to (i) sue its immediate successor intermediate tenant (who may be solvent) to force the latter to pay rent to the landlord, or (ii) assign to the original tenant the benefit of the covenant which he (the first mentioned intermediate tenant) has from the successor intermediate tenant. There is no direct *nexus* between the original tenant and the first intermediate tenant (see *Re Mirror Group (Holdings) Ltd [1992] BCC 973*). The practical significance of such a situation from the receiver's point of view would only arise if the company is either the first mentioned intermediate tenant or the present tenant. In the former case, it cannot be required to assist the original tenant. In the latter case, if the original tenant pays the rent to the landlord, the company might be in the happy position of being able to continue the lease without having to make payment, unless the original tenant is subrogated (by assignment or otherwise) to the rights of the landlord against the company as the present tenant.

Disposal at an undervalue, negligence and misfeasance

D8.14   A receiver, like a mortgagee, may become personally liable to the company or the guarantor of the debt secured by the charge for any loss which they may suffer if he fails to take reasonable care, in all the circumstances of the case, to obtain the true market value of a charged asset when he realises the asset in exercise of the power of sale. This duty of care is not based on the tort of negligence, but has been laid down by courts of equity because of the particular relationship between mortgagee and mortgagor; however, there is no warrant for extending the scope of that duty so as to include a beneficiary under a trust of the property of which the mortgagor is a trustee (*Parker-Tweedale v Dunbar Bank plc (No 1) [1990] 2 All ER 577*). The fact that the sale at the particular price is effected with the mortgagor's consent (perhaps given reluctantly) is no defence (*Rawlings v Barclays Bank plc [1900] EGCS 50 (CA)*). Where the chargee so interferes in the conduct of the receivership as to make the receiver his agent, he, too, may be liable to them. While the receiver is the company's agent, the chargee is not responsible for what the receiver does unless the chargee directs or interferes with the receiver's activities (*American Express International Banking Corp v Hurley [1985] 3 All ER 564; Standard Chartered Bank Ltd v Walker [1982] 3 All ER 938*). The agency terminates on liquidation (except for the purpose of *conveying* the asset—see D5.2 above) whereupon, unless the chargee is careful, there will be a danger of the receiver becoming his agent.

In *Downsview Nominees Ltd v First City Corporation Ltd [1993] BCC 46*, on an appeal from the Court of Appeal of New Zealand, the Privy Council laid down the following principles regarding a receiver's duty in relation to the charged assets:

(1)   A receiver, like a mortgagee, owes a duty to subsequent encumbrancers and to the mortgagor to use his powers for the sole purpose of securing repayment of the moneys owing under the mortgage, and a duty to act in good faith. There is no general duty in negligence to use reasonable care in dealing with the assets.

(2)   A dissatisfied subsequent mortgagee can require the prior mortgage to be assigned to him, and the mortgagor can redeem it, on payment of the sums due under it.

(3)   If a receiver decides at his discretion to manage, and does so in good faith, with the object of preserving and realising the assets for the benefit of the debenture holder, he is subject to no further or greater liability.

(4)   A receiver commits a breach of his duty if he abuses his powers by exercising them otherwise than for the special purpose of enabling the assets to be so preserved and realised.

A receiver is, however, under no obligation to continue the company's business before its sale so as to enhance realisation under the charge: see, for example, *Re B Johnson (Builders) Ltd [1955] Ch 634*.

A provision in the charging document entitling the mortgagee (or the receiver) to sell the charged property 'in such manner and upon such terms and for such consideration . . . as' the mortgagee (or the receiver) thinks fit without 'liability for loss howsoever arising in connection with such sale' does not relieve the mortgagee (or, arguably, the receiver) from the duty to act with reasonable care (*Bishop v Bonham (1988) 4 BCC 347, CA*).

In the absence of an express exclusion in any contract between the chargee and the receiver, the chargee may be entitled, under an implied term of the contract, to an indemnity from the receiver in respect of any breach of duty on the receiver's part (see the *American Express* case (above)).

Examples of breach of duty are: failure to take specialist advice or to advertise in specialist publications, depending on the nature of the asset (the *American Express* case (above)); advertising the sale poorly; (arguably) holding the sale at the wrong time (the *Standard Chartered* case (above) and see below); failure to bring the existence of any special features or matter, such as a planning permission, to the attention of the purchaser, which could reasonably have attracted a higher offer (*Cuckmere Brick Co Ltd v Mutual Finance Ltd [1971] 2 All ER 633*); or failure to trigger correctly the rent review procedure in a lease granted by the company and thereby to enhance realisation (*Knight v Lawrence [1991] BCC 411*). The duty is owed not only to the mortgagor but also to those who are immediately affected by his actions (*Knight v Lawrence*). There are several *dicta* to the effect that the mortgagee (and hence the receiver) can choose his own time for the sale (see, for example, the *Cuckmere Brick* case (above)) but Lord Denning MR said in the *Standard Chartered* case (above) (at *942*) that he did not think this meant that the mortgagee can sell at the worst possible time. It was at least arguable that, in choosing the time of sale, he should exercise a reasonable degree of care. Later in the same judgment, referring to the receiver's duty, he said (at *942*), 'It may be that the receiver can choose the time of sale within a considerable margin, but he should, I think, exercise a reasonable degree of care about it.'

A mortgagee is not obliged to do anything and is not under a duty to exercise his power of sale at any particular time or at all and does not become a trustee of the mortgaged property unless or until he has been paid in full. Nor is he obliged to carry on the company's business (*Re B Johnson (Builders) Ltd [1955] Ch 634*). Where the secured debt has been guaranteed, since the rights of a surety continue to depend on the principles of equity, it follows that unless the security is surrendered, lost, rendered imperfect or altered in condition by reason of what has been done by the mortgagee, the surety remains liable under his contract and the mortgagee is entitled to sue him instead of pursuing his claim against the mortgagor or selling the mortgaged property (*China and South Sea Bank Ltd v Tan Soon Gin [1990] 1 AC 536*). The mortgagee is not liable to a surety for a decline in value of the mortgaged property unless the mortgagee himself is personally responsible for the decline (*China and South Sea Bank Ltd v Tan Soon Gin*, as above).

Just as the receiver may be liable to the company and his appointor for failure to obtain a proper price, there is no reason why he should not also be liable to them for negligently causing loss of or diminution in the value of the receivership assets, for example, by failing to insure the assets which subsequently get lost, damaged or destroyed, or by failing to trigger a rent review provision in a lease for the benefit of the company as the lessor (see *Knight v Laurence [1991] BCC 411*) or by incurring unnecessary expenditure.

An administrative receiver may be liable to the company for misfeasance committed whilst in office; and, if the company is in liquidation, the court may make appropriate declarations against him on the application of the Official Receiver, the liquidator or any creditor or contributory under section 212 (see subsection (1)(b)).

Where a receiver has made sufficient realisation to discharge in full his appointor's claim, and all that remains before the termination of the receivership is his own remuneration, the amount of which the company's directors are disputing as excessive, they can successfully obtain an interlocutory injunction to restrain the receiver from selling any further property pending the determination of the dispute. This would reveal whether there is any need to realise any further property, as damages for wrongful sale of the further property may not be an adequate remedy (*Rottenberg v Monjack [1992] BCC 688*).

Interference with third party proprietary, statutory or contractual rights

D8.15   If a receiver interferes with the proprietary rights of a third party, however innocently (subject to the following paragraph), he may be liable to the third party for trespass or conversion (*Re Botibol [1947] 1 All ER 26* and *Said v Butt [1920] 3 KB 497*; and see *Re Goldburg (No 2) [1912] 1 KB 606*; *Re Gunsburg [1920] 2 KB 426*; *Re Herman [1915] HBR 41*; *Re Dombrowski (1923) 92 LJ Ch 415*; see also *Aspen Property v Ratcliffe (CA, 24 July 1993, New Law Fax Communication 97)*). It seems that the rightful owner may either treat the receiver as agent and claim all profits made by the receiver, but allow him to set up any claim for anything that he has usefully done as such agent, or claim damages for trespass or conversion; he cannot do both (*Re Simms [1934] Ch 1; Re Riddeough, ex p Vaughan (1884) 14 QBD 25*) (see also Torts (Interference with Goods) Act 1977). In an action to recover damages for conversion of goods under the 1977 Act, it was held that no general rule was applicable to determine the date at which the value of the goods should be assessed. But where goods had increased in value since their conversion, the owner might be entitled to be compensated by reference to their value at the date of judgment and not at the date of the conversion (*IBL Ltd v Coussens [1991] 2 All ER 133*). For examples of where third party property may be involved, see D7.8 to D7.23 above.

However, in the case of an administrative receiver, he now has limited statutory immunity from liability to any person in respect of any loss or damage resulting from the seizure or disposal, if at the time of the seizure or disposal he believes, and has reasonable grounds for believing, that he is entitled (in pursuance of an order of the court or otherwise) to seize or dispose of it, except insofar as that loss or damage is caused by (his) own negligence (section 234(3) and (4)(a)). He also has a lien on the property, or the proceeds of its sale, for such expenses as were incurred in connection with the seizure or disposal (section 234(4)(b)). However, as was held in *Welsh Development Agency v Export Finance Co Ltd [1992] BCC 270 (CA)*, subsections (3) and (4) of section 234 are confined to tangible property and do not protect the receiver with regard to the seizure and disposal of intangible property, such as book debts.

The decisions in *Airline Airspaces Ltd v Handley Page Ltd, Lathia v Dronsfield Ltd* and *Welsh Development Agency v Export Finance Co Ltd* (see D7.24 above) are not to be taken as authority to the effect that in no circumstances would a receiver be liable in tort for deliberately causing the company to commit a breach of a contract. There may be cases (which may include disposal of intellectual property in the circumstances described in D7.27 above) where the receiver may be said to be acting unreasonably or without sufficient justification. The point was left open in the *Welsh Development Agency* case and in *Re Botibol [1947] 1 All ER 26* (see also *Glamorgan Coal Co Ltd v South Wales Miners' Federation [1903] 2 KB 545 at 574–575; Dirassar v Kelly Douglas & Co Ltd (1966) 59 DLR (2nd) 452 at 481–482)*. In *Telematrix plc v Modern Engineers of Bristol (Holdings) plc and others [1985] BCLC 213*, where the receivers threatened to disregard a pre-receivership agreement by the company to assign the benefit of an option to the plaintiff, the court recognised that there was a possible cause of action against the receivers in tort for threatening to defeat the plaintiff's right to have the option assigned to it and that the receivers had been properly joined as co-defendants, and awarded the costs against them.

There may be outstanding contracts, such as licences of intellectual property granted to the company, or contracts relating to land, under which the company has undertaken certain obligations. Although the receiver is not obliged to cause the company to perform those obligations, or indeed any other part of the contract, it is conceivable that in appropriate cases, a negative injunction may be obtained against him and/or his appointor restraining them from doing acts prejudicial to the proprietary rights, or other rights in relation to the property concerned, of the other party to the contract. In *Swiss Bank Corporation v Lloyds Bank Ltd [1979] 2 All ER 853* (reversed, on a point of construction, *[1980] 2 All ER 19 (CA)*, affirmed *[1981] 2 All ER 449 (HL)*), where a borrower from a bank undertook with the bank to keep the securities which it purchased with the borrowed money in a separate account, and subsequently granted a charge over the securities to another bank, the following principle was stated by Browne-Wilkinson J:

> 'A person proposing to deal with property in such a way as to cause a breach of a contract affecting that property will be restrained by injunction from so doing if when he acquired that property he had actual knowledge of that contract . . . A plaintiff is entitled to such an injunction even if he has no proprietary interest in the property: his right to have his contract performed is a sufficient interest.'

Browne-Wilkinson J was referring to *de Mattos v Gibson (1858) 4 De G and J 276* at *282*, where Knight Bruce LJ had said:

> 'Reason and justice seem to prescribe that, at least as a general rule, where a man, by gift or purchase, acquires property from another, with knowledge of a previous contract, lawfully and for valuable consideration made by him with a third person, to use and employ the property for a particular purpose in a specified manner, the acquirer shall not, to the material damage of the third person, in opposition to the contract and inconsistently with it, use and employ the property in a manner not allowable to the giver or seller. This rule, applicable alike in general as I conceive to moveable and immoveable property, and recognised and adopted, as I apprehend, by the English law, may, like other general rules, be liable to exceptions "arising from special circumstances"'.

Browne-Wilkinson J regarded that case as authority 'that a person taking a charge on property which he knows to be subject to a contractual obligation can be restrained from exercising his rights under the charge in such a way as to interfere with the performance of that contractual obligation'. These principles were held not to apply in *MacJordan Construction Ltd v Brookmount Erostin Ltd [1992] BCLC 350* (see also D7.22(7) above) because

(i)   unlike in *de Mattos*, the contractual rights did not relate to a specific item of property, and

(ii)   the bank's charge was not, when granted, inconsistent with the plaintiff's contractual rights under the terms of the building contract—the terms of the charge did not, until crystallisation of the floating charge, prevent effect being given to those rights, and the plaintiff could not have obtained an injunction preventing the grant of the charge on the ground that it represented an interference with those rights.

It is debatable whether the company's knowledge at the time of the contract before receivership will be attributed to the receiver as its agent.

This seems unlikely. The crucial question may be whether the receiver's appointor, at the time when it obtained the charge under which the receiver is appointed, had actual knowledge. If it had, the appointor or the receiver may be restrained from enforcing the security over the property concerned in a way which would cause the breach.

In *Edwin Hill and Partners v First National Finance Corporation, The Times, 3 August 1988* (*CA*), a mortgagee who had insisted on the dismissal of the architects involved in connection with the charged property was held not to be liable to the architect for wrongful interference with his contract with the mortgagor. The mortgagee had an equal or superior interest in the matter. This decision may also apply to a receiver acting in good faith and having a legitimate interest. The decision was referred in *WA Ellis Services Ltd v Stuart Wood* (*1993*) *31 EG 78*. A lender to a company had taken a debenture from the company to secure the loan, well knowing that the company, because of its poor financial state, would thereby be precluded from paying commissions to an estate agent under an existing contract for future sales of flats by the agent on behalf of the company. The lender subsequently required the proceeds of the sales of flats to be paid by the solicitors directly to him (pursuant to his rights under the debenture) without deduction of the estate agent's commission. This was contrary to the previous practice. It was held that the lender was not liable to the estate agent for wrongful interference with the estate agent's contact with the company. Rejecting the estate agent's claim, Judge Antony Watson QC said:

> 'This is a proposition which, if correct, would affect many undertakings taking debentures who are aware that the company on whose assets the charge was placed owed money to other unsecured creditors. As a matter of principle, it seems to me that taking a debenture which might result in a contract with a third party being broken, in general would be too remote from the breach of contract to amount to the tort of unlawful interference with contract. Certainly it is too remote in this case since at the date of the debenture it was not even known whether commission would ever be payable . . .'.

The judge distinguished *Lathom v Greenwich Ferry* (*1895*) *72 LT 790* which, he said, was only authority for the proposition that when a mortgagee or receiver disposes of assets *under an order of the court*, the cost of realising that asset has priority over all other claims.

As to liability in respect of third party intellectual property, see D9.7 below. The receiver must bear in mind the provisions of the Data Protection Act 1984 (see, for example, section 20), the breach of which, in relation to any computerised information held by the company, may involve him as 'director or similar officer of the company' in personal civil and criminal sanctions.

(See also D7.26 above.)

Legal proceedings

D8.16 On his appointment, the receiver may find that an unsecured creditor of the company has obtained a *Mareva* injunction against the company to prevent a dissipation of its assets pending judgment, or execution of judgment, in an action which he has brought or is proposing to bring against the company to recover moneys due to him. While an injunction in itself does not create any security in favour of the plaintiff, if the injunction is subsisting, the receiver must take steps to have it discharged before disposing of any assets covered by his appointment which are also covered by the injunction; otherwise he might be technically in contempt of court. In *Capital Cameras Ltd v Harold Lines Ltd [1991] 1 WLR 54*, Harman J, on an application by the administrative receivers, in which their appointing bank was joined as a party, discharged the injunction, mainly on the ground that the appointment of an administrative receiver, who would be a licensed insolvency practitioner, and whose appointment would have crystallised the floating charge and thus made his appointor's rights as a fixed chargee intervene, removed the risk of dissipation of the assets. It is interesting to note that the court was prepared to accede to the receivers' application where it would not have acceded to the company's own application, notwithstanding that the receiver was making the application as an agent of the company. This is explainable on the basis that the grant, maintenance or variation of a *Mareva* injunction is within the discretion of the court, and the court would make such further orders as any change in the circumstances may warrant.

Where there is pending an injunction against a company, the receiver may be personally liable in contempt of court if he causes the company to breach it or does not prevent it from breaching it whereby taking reasonable steps he could have prevented it. He cannot escape liability on the basis that he was not a party to the proceedings in which the injunction was granted.

In legal proceedings to which the company and/or the receiver is a party, the court may make an order for costs against the receiver personally. Costs in all legal proceedings in the High Court are at the discretion of the court (Supreme Court Act 1981, s 51(1); RSC Ord 62, r 2(4)). Such an order against him may be made, for example, if he unnecessarily causes or prolongs such proceedings, or is guilty of misconduct or default therein, or where it is just and equitable to make such an order (see, e.g. *Bacal Contracting Ltd v Modern Engineering (Bristol) Ltd [1980] 2 All ER 655*) or where the receiver is properly joined as a defendant (e.g. where he might be personally liable in tort for threatening to defeat the plaintiff's equitable right acquired before the receiver's appointment and the receiver concedes the right (*Telematrix plc v Modern Engineers of Bristol (Holdings) plc and others [1985] BCLC 213*). Further, a receiver may find that the court (i) makes an order for security for costs against the company in receivership where it is a plaintiff and there is reason to believe that it will be unable to pay the costs of the defendant, if successful in his defence, and (ii) stays the proceedings until the security is given (pursuant to section 726 of the Companies Act 1985), although such an order may be refused if the effect would be to deprive the company of the chance to pursue a claim which has a good prospect of succeeding (see e.g. *Aquila Design (GRB) Products Ltd v Cornhill Insurance plc [1988] BCLC 134*, a liquidation case). See also *Europa Holdings Ltd v Circle Industries (UK) plc [1992] CILL 781* where, despite being satisfied that the plaintiff, a small construction company, would be unable to pay the costs of the defendant, a large company as employer under the contract, in the event of the defendant succeeding, the Court of Appeal refused to make an order for security for costs against the plaintiff. Dillon LJ said:

> 'The circumstances of the present recession make the issue of security for costs on claims involving the smaller companies in the construction industry a pressing one . . . This is a serious matter in the construction industry at the moment. It is not . . . in the least desirable that all small well-managed companies should be forced to abandon their claims for payment by building owners or main contractors because they cannot give security for the costs of expensive and protracted litigation'.

(Compare and contrast *Roburn Construction Ltd v William Irwin (South) and Co Ltd [1991] BCC 726; Ottotcha v Voest Alpine Intertrading GmbH, The Times, 21 September 1992*.) As to the operation of section 726 where there is a counterclaim by the defendant, see the article 'Claim and Counterclaim' by David Pittaway and Alastair Hammerton, barristers, in the *Law Society's Gazette*, Vol 90 No 16, 28 April 1993.

Pension scheme

D8.17   The provisions of section 57C of the Social Security Pensions Act 1975, as inserted by Schedule 4 to the Social Security Act 1990 which came into force on 11 November 1990, should be noted. They impose a duty on an insolvency practitioner, including an administrative receiver, where the company is an employer under an occupational pension scheme constituted by a *deed*, to satisfy himself that at all times at least one of the trustees of the scheme is an independent person and, if at any time he is not so satisfied, to appoint or secure the appointment of an independent person as a trustee of the scheme. For these purposes, a trustee is independent only if (i) he has no interest in the assets of the employer or of the scheme, otherwise than as trustee of the scheme and (ii) he is neither connected with nor an associate of the employer (within the meaning of sections 249 and 435 of the Insolvency Act 1986), the insolvency practitioner or the official receiver. If the administrative receiver fails to act, any member of the scheme can apply to the court requiring the administrative receiver to comply with his obligations. The latter is also under a duty to provide the trustees with information reasonably required for the purposes of the scheme.

It is not clear whether if the receiver fails to act he can become personally liable for any loss or damages suffered by the pension fund. There is no reason in principle why he should not be so liable, although it might be extremely difficult to prove a connection between his failure to act and the loss or damages. It is also not clear to what lengths the receiver should go to 'satisfy' himself that at least one of the trustees is independent. It is submitted that provided, from the answers which he receives to his enquiries of the trustees or proposed trustees as to their independence and from any information already in his possession or reasonably obtainable from sources in the public domain (for example, the Companies Registry), he finds nothing to doubt their independence, he would be protected.

It is arguable whether the section itself gives the receiver a power to appoint an independent trustee even where there is no such power in the company's favour under the terms of the scheme. The answer depends on the interpretation of the words '. . . to appoint under this paragraph, or to secure the appointment of . . .' in the section. It is submitted that the first phrase confers upon the receiver a substantive power, and not only imposes upon him a duty, to appoint an independent trustee. In any case, the receiver can, on behalf of the company, apply to the court under its inherent jurisdiction for the removal of a trustee and the appointment of another trustee—this would satisfy the receiver's obligation to appoint 'or secure the appointment of' an independent trustee. Where the appointment is made out of court, it would be advisable to make it by way of a deed so as to ensure that the trust fund legally vests in the new trustee jointly with any existing trustees (see section 40 of the Trustee Act 1925). Where the company has a power under the terms of the scheme to appoint new trustees, it would be advisable for the company, acting by the receiver, to join in for the purposes of confirming the change of trustees. This is not strictly necessary, in view of the power conferred by section 57C on him in his own right, but may help to minimise any contrary argument.

However, it seems that, apart from the limited purposes of that section, the receiver, as the company's agent, cannot exercise any power of the company, as employer, contained in its favour in the pension scheme trust deed. Arguably, those powers are of a fiduciary nature (see, for example, *Re Skeats' Settlement (1889) 42 Ch D 522, Mettoy Pension Trustees Ltd v Evans [1990] 1 WLR 1587*), although, perhaps, not truly fiduciary powers, such as those conferred on pension trustees, and which are not within the purview of the charge under which the receiver is appointed. There may, nevertheless, be some powers which are given to the company for its own benefit, rather than as trustee of the powers, and which can, therefore, be exercisable for the benefit of the receivership.

Section 57D(5) provides that any power of the trustees or managers under the scheme *and exercisable at their discretion* can *only* be exercised by the independent trustee. This also applies to any power of the employer (otherwise than as trustee or manager of the scheme), exercisable by him *at his discretion* but only as trustee *of the power*. It would seem that, once appointed, the independent trustee is for all purposes one of the trustees of the scheme so that, subject to section 57D(5) above, all functions and duties of the trusteeship are to be carried out by him in conjunction with the other trustees, and he is entitled to the benefit of all provisions of the scheme, for example, those giving trustees indemnities against and immunities from liability.

(See also D9.1 below.)

Duties under the companies legislation

D8.18   It would appear that the duties imposed on the directors and officers of a company by sections 226, 227, 233, 234 to 238, 241, 242, 242A, 363 and 366 of the Companies Act 1985, as amended by the Companies Act 1989, relating to the preparation, filing and presentation of annual accounts, reports and returns and the holding of annual general meetings do not apply to receivers (even if they are administrative receivers). This is because (i) directors continue to have residual functions in so far as the exercise of such functions does not in any way impinge prejudicially on the position of the receiver's appointor (see D5.5 above), (ii) a receiver is not an officer of the company for these purposes and (iii) it cannot have been intended that the requirements of the Insolvency Act 1986 relating to the preparation and filing of receipts and payments accounts and the holding of a creditors' meeting by an administrative receiver, and the disclosure by him of information to the creditors' committee, should run concurrently with the requirements of the companies legislation. However, where the receiver continues the business of the company he should maintain trading accounts, in addition to the statutory receipts and payments accounts, as stated in D5.5 above.

Environmental law liabilities

D8.19   Increasingly, a receiver is having to be wary of the impact of environmental law on the lands and buildings comprised in his appointment and on his personal position in relation to such lands and buildings. What follows is a summary of the relevant points.

(1) *Integrated Pollution Control ('IPC') and Air Pollution Control ('APC')*

D8.20   This is a new system of pollution control introduced by the Environmental Protection Act 1990 ('EPA 90'). The IPC and APC regimes first came into force in parts on 1 April 1991 and are being implemented on a rolling programme for different categories of new and old industrial processes.

Under the IPC regime, all firms in certain industries carrying out 'prescribed processes' are to use the 'best available techniques not entailing excessive cost'. This is likely to require progressive improvement of processes and their environment performance. The system is administered by Her Majesty's Inspectorate of Pollution. The Inspectorate have wide powers, including powers to revoke authorisations, enter premises and prohibit any process likely to result in pollution. The APC regime, which is administered by local authorities in parallel to the IPC regime, is aimed only at preventing or minimising pollution due to the release of substances into the air. (See Schedule 1 to EPA 90 and Schedule 1 to the Environmental Protection (Prescribed Processes and Substances) Regulations 1991 (SI 1991 No 472)).

Section 6 of EPA 90 states that no person may carry on a prescribed process after the date prescribed in relation thereto, otherwise than under, and in accordance with the terms of, an official authorisation. If the relevant authority is of the opinion that a person carrying on a prescribed process under an authorisation is contravening, or is likely to contravene, any condition of the authorisation, it may serve an enforcement notice upon him requiring him to remedy the contravention within a specified period (section 13). Further, section 14 requires the authority to serve a prohibition notice on any person carrying on a process under an authorisation, if in the authority's opinion its carrying on or the manner of its carrying on involves an imminent risk of serious pollution of the environment.

A contravention by the person concerned of *inter alia* section 6 referred to above, or of an enforcement or prohibition notice, is a criminal offence (section 23) and the court may order the person convicted of the offence to take remedial steps to clean up the site concerned (section 26). Where the commission of the offence causes any harm which it is possible to remedy, the relevant authority may also arrange for any reasonable steps to be taken towards remedying it and recover the costs of taking those steps from the person convicted of the offence (section 27).

As to the impact of these provisions on the receivership, see (7) below.

(2) *Waste management*

D8.21   This regime, also introduced by EPA 90, came into force in part on 1 April 1992 and as to most of the remainder, on 1 May 1994. The system is monitored by waste regulation authorities and waste disposal authorities, which, for most areas, are county councils. Their waste management functions are to be taken over by the proposed national Environment Agency when it is formed, currently anticipated in 1996.

As from 1 April 1992 a general duty is imposed on every person who imports, produces, carries, keeps, treats or disposes of controlled waste, or who, as a broker, has control of such waste, to look after the waste properly and to see that it is transferred to an authorised carrier or disposer and that the transfer is properly recorded. Failure to comply with this duty is a criminal offence. It is also a criminal offence to treat, keep or dispose of controlled waste in a manner likely to cause pollution of the environment or harm to human health (sections 33 and 34).

It is an offence for any person to deposit, treat, keep or dispose of controlled waste, or knowingly cause or permit controlled waste to be deposited, treated, kept or disposed of, without a waste management licence or otherwise than in accordance with the terms of such licence. A licence will be granted only to a 'fit and proper person' who is in occupation of the land in or on which the waste is treated, kept or disposed of, or operates a mobile plant by means of which the waste is treated or disposed of (section 36).

If waste is unlawfully deposited on a site, the relevant authority may serve notice of removal on the occupier. If the occupier fails to comply with the notice without reasonable excuse he will be guilty of an offence; however, he can apply to the magistrates' court for the requirement specified in the notice to be quashed, where he can show that he did not knowingly cause or permit the deposit. In certain circumstances (in particular to prevent pollution of land, water or air or harm to human health), the authority may itself remove the waste from the land or take any other necessary steps, and may recover the cost of so doing from the occupier of the land, or the person who deposited the waste (section 59, not yet in force).

A duty is also imposed (under section 61, yet to be implemented) on every waste regulation authority to clean up a site within its area where there are present noxious gases or noxious liquids which may cause pollution of the environment or harm to human health. This duty applies even if the gases or liquids have been present from a time before the new provisions come into force. To comply with its obligations, the authority has a duty to enter land, carry out the clean-up work and charge the costs back to the owner of the site. The authority may also enter any land which adjoins the land on which the waste was originally deposited to clean up that adjoining land and charge the costs to the 'owner', which in this context seems to refer to the owner of the adjoining land. The latter may, in turn, have a right of recourse under the general law against the owner of the original offending site. The 'owner' is not defined, but the term is likely to be widely construed.

As to the impact of these provisions on the receivership, see (7) below.

(3) *Statutory nuisance*

D8.22   The provisions relating to statutory nuisance, which were originally contained in the public health legislation, are now incorporated, with modifications, in Part III of EPA 90, as amended by the Noise and Statutory Nuisance Act 1993. They apply to any premises which are in such a state as to be, and any accumulation or deposit which is, prejudicial to health or a nuisance (section 79). The relevant local authority may serve an abatement notice on the 'person responsible' or, in relation to structural parts of the premises, on the 'owner'. If the person responsible cannot be found, or if preventive action is to be taken by the authority against possible future nuisance, the notice may be served on the 'owner or occupier'. A person served with an abatement notice may appeal against it to the magistrates' court. Failure to comply with such a notice is an offence (section 80).

If the notice is not complied with, the authority may carry out necessary works itself and recover the costs from 'the person by whose act or default the nuisance was caused' or the 'owner', regardless of whether he was the person responsible for causing or permitting the nuisance (section 81).

As to the impact of these provisions on the receivership, see (7) below.

(4) *Contaminated land*

D8.23   Substantial areas of contaminated land exist throughout the UK. Particularly in the industrial regions the previously great industries of coal, iron and steel and other metals have left a severe legacy to include extensive environmental harm and public danger. This can often affect ground and surface waters, leading to the abandonment of potential resources or extensive treatment. The health and safety of employees and members of the public generally can be prejudiced by poisonous residues and gases.

Section 143 of EPA 1990 was intended to enable the Secretary of State to establish registers of contaminated land to be kept by local authorities. However, during a number of consultation exercises it became clear that practical difficulties attended the making and maintaining of registers, such that in March 1993 the Secretary of State for the Environment announced that it was no longer intended to bring section 143 into force. At the same time he set in train a further study which has resulted in the consultation paper 'Paying for Our Past'. This discusses a wide range of issues pertaining to contaminated land including liability, the need for rationalisation of existing legislative arrangements, standards to which clean-up should be pursued and the strategy for proceeding to a pro- gramme of clean-up.

The existing legislation. By no means is there a lack of powers available to both central and local government to secure clean-up. For example:

(*a*)   EPA Part I gives HM Inspectorate of Pollution wide powers to impose conditions on authorisation (see (1) above). These powers seem to be sufficiently extensive to prevent pollution and possibly to require clean-up.

(*b*)   EPA 1990 Part II enables waste regulation authorities both to require clean-up of contamination through the conditions of a waste management licence and to refuse to allow the surrender of that licence because the condition of the land continues to offer the potential of pollution or harm to human health (see (2) above).

(*c*)   Contaminated land can be a statutory nuisance. Under EPA 1990 Part III environmental health authorities have powers to require abatement of nuisance and/or the execution of works (see (3) above).

(*d*)   The National Rivers Authority has powers to control and remedy pollution from contaminated land in circumstances where it is a threat to controlled waters under the Water Resources Act 1991 (see (5) below). Powers are also available to the Health and Safety

Executive under the Health and Safety at Work etc. Act 1974 sections 21 and 22 and even by the Town and Country Planning Act 1990 section 215 where the local authority may serve notices requiring the remedying of the condition of land adversely affecting the amenity of a locality.

All these powers offer to the regulator the opportunity to bring proceedings against the polluter, or the owner/occupier of the land, as the case may be. Coupled with this are powers for the regulators themselves to enter the land to carry out necessary works, recovering the cost from the person responsible.

As to the impact of these provisions on the receivership, see (7) below.

(5) *Water pollution*

D8.24   Section 161 of the Water Resources Act 1991 ('WRA 91'), which replaces section 115 of the Water Act 1989, empowers the National Rivers Authority to clean up 'controlled waters' and adjacent sites where any poisonous, noxious or polluting matter or any solid waste is present and to recover the costs from the person who caused or knowingly permitted the presence of such matter or waste on the land or in the water. Causing or knowingly permitting such matter or waste to enter controlled waters is also a criminal offence on the part of 'the owner or occupier' (see section 85).

As to the impact of these provisions on the receivership, see (7) below.

(6) *Future legal trends*

D8.25   At the European Community level, the amended proposal for a Directive on civil liability for damage caused by waste (COM (91) 219 Final) is effectively superseded by new proposals following the publication of a discussion paper on environmental liability by the EC Commission. One proposal which concerned bankers was aimed at imposing strict liability on a 'producer' of waste until the waste was delivered to a registered disposal installation. It was proposed that various categories of parties would be deemed to be producers, particularly, a person who was in 'actual control of the waste' at the time the damage was caused, unless he was able to name the original producer. It remains to be seen how far the final provisions are amended so as to alleviate the concerns of bankers.

The experience of financial institutions in the USA has worried lenders in the United Kingdom. Some fear that in the course of time the trends in the USA (which are briefly outlined below) could find their way into the legal systems of the United Kingdom.

Under the US Superfund legislation (CERCLA), there was an exemption in favour of lenders called 'the security interest exemption'. It was to the effect that where lenders held 'indicia of ownership' for the purposes of protecting their security they would not have any liability for clean-up provided that they exercised no management control. However, in *United States v Fleet Factors Corp* (*upheld on appeal, 901 F 2d 1550 (11th Cir 1990) and 111 S Ct 752 (1991)*), it was held that a lender could be liable for the costs of cleaning up pollution which had been generated by the debtor, if the lender was sufficiently involved in managing the debtor to 'affect hazardous waste disposal decisions if it (the lender) so chose'. Arguably, the point was not central to the decision in that case. The scope of that case was narrowed by *Re Bergsoe Metal Corp* (*910 F 2d 668 (9th Cir 1990)*) in which it was held that liability should not attach if the power to affect decisions was not actually exercised. A new rule, promulgated by the Environmental Protection Agency, restricts lenders' potential exposure to liability by defining more closely the relevant expressions, but with only limited effect. Further legislation to assist lenders was introduced but met considerable opposition; and its future is in doubt. There is also a general trend in the USA towards imposing personal criminal liability for environmental offences.

There is some judicial authority in the USA for imposing on a mortgagee responsibility for water clean-up costs. In the case in question, the mortgagee was held to have aided and abetted the borrower in the commission of an offence by reason of the mortgagee's 'influence and control', because 'it knew of the mortgagor's sewage problem and could have conditioned the loans on the fixing of the sewage problem'.

(7) Implications of the UK legislation on receivership

D8.26   The impact of the United Kingdom provisions summarised above on a receivership may be threefold:

(i) The market or realisable value of the land or premises concerned may be adversely affected to reflect the possible costs of compliance with the requirements which the company in receivership, or a purchaser of the land or premises, may have to incur, or simply because of the land being on the contaminated land register (see D8.23 above) even if it is not actually contaminated or likely to be contaminated.

(ii) The receiver may incur personal criminal penalties for the company's failure during the receivership to comply with the requirements.

(iii) The receiver may incur personal civil liability for any breach by the company during the receivership of those provisions.

As to criminal penalties, the receiver may not be able to rely on the defence that he was merely an agent of the company and that, therefore, the offence was committed by the company and not him. Section 157(1) of EPA 90 provides that where an offence under the Act, committed by a body corporate, is proved to have been committed with the consent or connivance of, or to have been attributable to, any neglect on the part of, any director, manager, secretary or other similar officer of the body corporate, or a person who was purporting to act in such capacity, he, as well as the body corporate, is guilty of that offence. In view of the wide powers of management and control usually conferred by the charging document and by law on an administrative receiver, and superimposed on the powers of the company's directors, it seems likely that he would be regarded as a 'manager or person purporting to act in such capacity'. Further, section 158 provides that where the commission by any person of any of the offences is due to the act or default of some other person, that other person may be charged with and convicted of an offence, regardless of whether the proceedings for the offence are taken against the first mentioned person. Section 217 of WRA 91 has a similar effect. Thus, a receiver may be regarded as the person due to whose act or omission the offence was committed. He may also become liable under section 59 of EPA 90 as an 'occupier' (see below) who knowingly caused or knowingly permitted the deposit of waste.

As noted above, there are provisions in both EPA 90 and WRA 91 imposing criminal liability on the part of the 'owner' or 'occupier' of the premises concerned. Although, in connection with the civil liability for rates on occupiers, it was held in *Ratford v Northavon District Council [1986] BCLC 397 (CA)* that a receiver, being agent of the company in receivership, was not an occupier, and hence not liable for rates, this principle may not apply to statutory provisions imposing, or any civil claim arising from, criminal liability on occupiers (or owners). In *Meigh v Wickenden [1942] 2 KB 160*, a receiver was appointed under a debenture with power to manage and carry on the business of the company. He had no knowledge of machines or the functioning of factories and, for all practical purposes, the directors of the company were left in control. An employee was injured as a result of a guard not being provided for a milling machine, contrary to the provisions of the Factories Act 1937. It was held that the receiver was an 'occupier of the factory' within the meaning of that Act and was, therefore, liable for the contravention. Viscount Caldecote CJ said:

> 'He was appointed, not to receive directions from directors, but to give directions. He might at any time remove them or appoint someone else to take over their duties . . . It may, indeed, be said with accuracy, I think, that he took the place of the directors and was responsible in their stead for the management of the affairs and business of the company, even while he permitted them to manage the business under him'.

He later added that the receiver was a 'complete master of the affairs of the company'. In a more recent Scottish case of *Lord Advocate v Aero Technologies Ltd (in Receivership) 1991 SLT 134*, a company trading in explosives had gone into receivership. During the receivership there was a contravention of the safety provisions of the Explosives Act 1875 which impose criminal liability for such contravention on 'occupiers'. It was held that for the purposes of that Act, the receiver was an occupier.

The expression 'owner', as used in EPA 90 has not been defined by that Act but is defined in WRA 91 and the Control of Pollution Act 1974. The latter, being the predecessor of EPA 90, should, arguably, be read *in pari materia* with EPA 90. The 1974 Act defines the expression 'owner' as 'the person for the time being receiving the rack rent of the premises . . . whether on his own account or as agent or trustee for another person, or who would so receive the rack rent if the premises were let at a rack rent'. Arguably, the receiver could fall within this definition.

A civil financial liability on the part of a receiver may arise for the tort of breach of statutory duty (which would be proved if the receiver is successfully convicted of an offence as discussed above), or under the tort of nuisance, if in either case, personal or financial injury is caused to any other person, or under the rule in *Rylands v Fletcher (1868) LR 3 HL 330* (although the scope of that rule has been narrowed by subsequent judicial decisions). That rule imposes strict liability (that is, liability without proof of fault) on the owner of land if he brings something dangerous on to it and it escapes on to adjoining land, causing damage to the adjoining land. In the Canadian case of *Gersten v Municipality of Toronto (1973) 41 DLR (3d) 464*, the rule was held to apply to landfill gas. In *Cambridge Water Company v Eastern Counties Leather plc [1994] 1 All ER 53*, the House of Lords attempted to put the position in a proper perspective. The plaintiffs' groundwater at a borehole had been contaminated as a result of seepage of a cleaning solvent, used at the defendants' tannery some thirteen miles away, into the ground beneath the tannery's concrete floor. The seepage was due to regular small spillages. The House of Lords held that:

(*a*)   the *Rylands v Fletcher* tort was essentially an extension of the tort of nuisance rather than a totally different type of tort;

(*b*)   liability in principle was strict, as in the tort of nuisance, notwithstanding that the defendant had exercised all due care to prevent the escape;

(*c*)   but the liability only extended to the type of damage that was reasonably foreseeable – in the present case, it had not been foreseeable.

The House of Lords also stated that nuisance actions depended on damage occurring to the plaintiffs' interests and there could be no actionable nuisance by virtue of the initial spillage but only when it caused damage – which, in the present case, occurred when the water available was rendered unuseable by its failure to meet the new standards imposed by the EC Directive and the relevant UK implementing regulations after the spillages had occurred.

In a Canadian case (*Panamericana de Bienes y Servicios SA v Northern Badger Oil & Gas Ltd, June 1991 (1991) 81 DLR (4th) 280, [1991] 5 WWR 577, 1 Alta LR (2d) 49, 2 OR (3d) 31 (CA)*), the Alberta Court of Appeal held a receiver, as manager of the oil wells with operating control of them, appointed by the court under a debenture, to be personally liable for the costs of complying with an abandonment order under the Oil and Gas Conservation Act, the purpose of which was to secure the observance of safe and efficient practices. However, in *Ontario v Tyre King Recycling Ltd (1992) 9 OR (3d) 318*, the Ontario Court held that a mortgagee not taking control or possession of the mortgaged property was not liable for environmental damages. In *King Township v Rolex Equipment Co Ltd (1992) 90 DLR (4th) 442, 8 OR (3d) 457 (Gen Div)*, the court gave the mortgagee who had not taken possession a choice of either removing the waste from the mortgaged property at its own cost (the owner having failed to remove it and having abandoned the property), or facing the appointment by the court of a receiver to remove the waste and charge the cost on the property. In the USA, a secured lender who participates in the management of the chargor company can face environmental liability (the US Comprehensive Environmental Response, Compensation and Liability Act, referring to lenders who hold 'indicia of ownership'). Originally, 'participation in management' was interpreted as active involvement in the company's day-to-day operations, but a number of judicial decisions (particularly *United States v Fleet Factors Corp (US Federal Court)* discussed in the article by R McQuiston in *British Journal of International Banking and Finance Law*, November 1993, 499) placed a broader interpretation, giving rise to serious concern for lenders and a spate of litigation. In April 1992, the US Environmental Protection Agency issued a Final Rule clarifying and specifying the range of activities that the lender could undertake without liability in this regard, such as policing the loan and undertaking a financial workout, on-site inspection and audit of environmental condition.

Chapter 9: Realisation of assets

General points

D9.1   The first task of a receiver in relation to assets is to obtain effective control of all the assets and (in the case of an administrative receiver) business and affairs comprised in his appointment, and to ensure that they are adequately protected and insured against fire, theft, loss and damage. He must also consider, where appropriate, taking out, *inter alia*, insurance against product liability and occupier's liability. The usually extensive powers contained in the charging document, the Law of Property Act powers and (in the case of an administrative receiver) the Insolvency Act powers (see D5.2 and D5.3 above) and other aids (see A4.15 *et seq*. PART A: GENERAL) should considerably facilitate his task of taking control and realising the assets. Some of the points relating to realisation of assets in a liquidation made in C12.1 *et seq*. PART C: LIQUIDATIONS may be relevant here. Other relevant matters relating to realisation are dealt with below.

(A)   *Ascertaining scope of assets available*

The receiver must distinguish between the following categories of assets (wherever applicable).

(1)   Assets which are, in any case, excluded from the charge on his appointment. Even where the charge is expressed to embrace all present and future assets of the company, it seems that the following will not fall within it.

    (i)   Any debt due by the appointor to the company (including any money deposited by the company with the appointor). This is because (arguably) there cannot be a charge over a debt in favour of the debtor himself (*Re Charge Card Services Ltd* [*1986*] *3 WLR 697*, a liquidation case, now doubted by the Court of Appeal in *Welsh Development Agency v Export Finance Co Ltd* [*1992*] *BCC 270*). The debt may, however, be the subject of a right of set-off (as recognised in that case) and the receiver should invite the appointor to deal with the debt by way of set-off. It should be noted, however, that the right is not as extensive as that in a liquidation (see C14.26 PART C: LIQUIDATIONS and cf. D7.5 and D7.6 above).

    (ii)   Any money recovered by a liquidator of the company in respect of fraudulent preference under the previous legislation (*Re Yagerphone Ltd* [*1935*] *Ch 392*). It is arguable whether this would apply to preferences and transactions at an undervalue (sections 238 to 241) under the new legislation. As regards recoveries by a liquidator for wrongful trading (section 214), see *Re Produce Marketing Consortium* (*1989*) *5*

BCC 569, where in determining the amount of the award, Knox J appears to have assumed that the benefit of the award would fall within the charge. The question must, however, be regarded as open; but see D7.3 above as to the receiver's right of recourse to liquidation funds in respect of preferential debts.

(2)   Assets subject to his appointor's charge which, as created, was a floating charge, and those subject to a charge which, as created, was a 'fixed charge'. The receiver may need to keep separate accounts of the proceeds of realisation (including accretion to and income from these categories of assets and also of the costs and expenses attributable to these two types of assets). It is only in relation to the former type of assets that preferential creditors have priority over the appointor (see D7.3 and D7.4 above; see also D6.2 above as to book debts).

(3)   Assets which are subject to prior and/or subsequent charges. The receiver will similarly need to keep separate accounts so as to determine the order and extent of distribution between various encumbrancers.

(4)   Assets which are subject to third party proprietary rights (see D7.8 to D7.23 above). These may not form part of the receivership assets.

(B)   *Pension surpluses*

The receiver should examine the position of any pension scheme which the company has established or in which it participates. In particular he should take steps to recover any surplus of funds to which the company may be entitled under the terms of the scheme.

Surplus funds in a terminated occupational pension scheme are held on resulting trust for the contributor, in the absence of express or implied contrary intention. Accordingly, where employers' obligations were to top up employees' contractually fixed contributions to the extent necessary to maintain benefits, surplus derived from employers' overpayments is returnable to them if there was no intention to exclude a resulting trust. Surplus derived from employees' contributions is not returnable to employees if impracticality or legislative requirements indicate an intention to exclude a resulting trust, and surplus derived from funds transferred from other schemes goes to the Crown as *bona vacantia* if circumstances and documentation show an intention to exclude claims by contributors. (*Davis v Richards & Wallington Industries Ltd [1990] 1 WLR 1511*; cf. *Jones v Williams, In re Dan Jones (Porth) Ltd Employees Pension Fund [1989] PLR 21*.)

Some schemes contain provisions giving trustees a discretion to use the surplus to augment the pension entitlements of employees. In so far as the receiver has any say or influence on behalf of the company in this regard, it is difficult to see how he can justify himself in agreeing to such augmentation (see, for example, *Mettoy Pension Trusts Ltd v Evans*

[1990] 1 WLR 1587; see also *Icarus (Hertford) Ltd v Driscoll [1990] PLR 1*). However, where the company has power under the terms of the scheme to give or withhold its consent to an amendment of the terms, that power is subject to an implied obligation of good faith. This does not preclude the company (or its receiver) from having regard to its own financial interests as long as that obligation is not breached; but a refusal of consent for some collateral purpose, such as putting pressure on the members of the scheme to abandon existing rights for the company's benefit, is not justified (*Imperial Group Pension Trust Ltd v Imperial Tobacco Ltd [1991] 1 WLR 589*).

It should be noted, however, that section 11(3) of the Social Security Act 1990 prohibits any payment to the employer out of the surplus until an amount of annual pension increase equal to five per cent or the specified percentage increase in the 'limited price indexation' (whichever is the lower) is secured for the member employees concerned. This applies even where the winding up of the scheme had commenced before the 1990 Act came into force. Subject to this and subject to the inclusion, for the purposes of such increases, of even those members who have since transferred to another scheme or had their benefits secured by the purchase of an annuity, the discretion as regards the disposal of the surplus is generally required to be exercised in favour of the employer where the employer is insolvent (see *Thrells v Lomas [1993] 2 All ER 546*).

(C)   *Recovery under antecedent transactions*

The receiver may also wish to investigate the possibility of recovering money or assets from third parties who may have acquired them under any pre-receivership transactions entered into by the company which were void or illegal, or are recoverable under any legal or equitable principles regarding restitution, subrogation and the like (other than the transactions which can only be challenged by a liquidator as preferences or transactions at an undervalue—see C10.1 *et seq.* PART C: LIQUIDATIONS) and moneys and assets from the officers of the company in respect of negligence or misfeasance in relation to the company's affairs (see C13.3 *et seq.* PART C: LIQUIDATIONS and (A)(1)(ii) above), but not for fraudulent trading or wrongful trading (which only arise in a liquidation).

However, a receiver may be able to make recovery in respect of a transaction at an undervalue if that transaction also constituted an *ultra vires* transaction or a breach of fiduciary duty or misfeasance on the part of the directors. A recent example where a receiver succeeded in obtaining a judgment for such a recovery was *Aveling Barford Ltd v Perion Ltd and others (1989) 5 BCC 677*. In that case the company in receivership and another company were controlled by the same person. At a time when the company was solvent on a balance sheet basis (ignoring a substantial debt due to an associated company), but had an accumulated deficit on profit and loss account of a substantial amount, the company transferred a property at a substantial undervalue to the other company. The sale was held to be in breach of fiduciary duty and liable to be set aside. The difference between the market value of the property and the value at which it was transferred was held to be a dressed-up distribution to that person (through the other company) and, the company having at the time no distributable reserves, an unauthorised return of capital which was *ultra vires* and incapable of validation by shareholder approval or ratification. The sale was not a genuine exercise of the company's power under its memorandum to sell its assets. It was a sale at a gross undervalue for the purpose of enabling a profit to be realised by an entity controlled by its sole beneficial shareholder.

(D)   *Calling up unpaid share capital*

A debenture containing fixed and floating charges usually also contains a fixed charge on the company's issued but unpaid share capital. Paragraph 19 of Schedule 1 to the Act empowers an administrative receiver to call up unpaid share capital; and this power is usually expressly contained in the debenture. A problem may however arise if the company's articles contain restrictions as to the amount and timing of any call that can be made on a share, or any conditions precedent. The receiver has no better rights in this regard than the rights which the company itself has under its memorandum and articles (see, for example, *Industrial Development Authority Ltd v William T Moran (1978) IR 159*). The articles may either reserve the power to make a call to the company in general meeting or, more usually, delegate their power to the directors, exercisable (by a board resolution) by giving the shareholders at least 14 clear days' notice (see, for example, article 12 of the Companies Act 1985 Table A). However, it is submitted that in either case the receiver will be entitled to make a call without the authority of a resolution of a general meeting or of the board of directors, provided that the debenture containing a charge over unpaid share capital was validly created pursuant to the provisions of the memorandum and articles, since those provisions taken with the terms of the debenture and paragraph 19 of Schedule 1 would have the effect of delegating the company's and the directors' powers to make a call to the receiver (see, for example, *South Australian Barytes Ltd v Wood (1978) South Australian State Reports 527*).

(E)   *Manner of realisation of assets*

The Law Society ethical guidelines about contract races in relation to the sale of freehold or leasehold property should be noted by the receiver's solicitors. In broad terms, the guidelines are to the effect that when and if on instructions the vendor's solicitors issue draft contracts to two or more prospective purchasers of the same property, they should inform each of the prospective purchasers of that fact (although their identity need not be disclosed).

As observed above, the receiver normally has extensive powers, rights and statutory aids to facilitate his task of realising the assets. He must, however, exercise a reasonable degree of care and skill in choosing the mode, time and terms of realisation (see D8.14 above). Now that it is the exclusive prerogative of those who have been licensed as insolvency practitioners to act as administrative receivers, perhaps an even higher degree of care and skill will be expected of them.

Among the courses available to the receiver as regards realisation of the assets are:

(*a*) to defer a sale until a more propitious date and, in the meantime,

    (i) derive income from the assets; and/or

    (ii) carry on the company's business with a view to making a trading profit and, thereby, preserving the goodwill of the business, pending (*c*) below; and

    (iii) as regards any uncompleted land development, complete the development with a view to a more advantageous realisation; or

(*b*) to sell the assets on a piecemeal basis (see, however, D8.14 above) at the outset or after (*a*) above; or

(*c*) to sell all the assets, undertaking and goodwill as a going concern at the outset or after (*a*) above, either directly or having first carried out a hive-down (see D9.4 below); and

(*d*) as regards any uncalled issue share capital comprised in the charge, to make calls in respect thereof on the members (see, for example, paragraph 19 of Schedule 1 in the case of an administrative receiver) and, as regards any debts due to the company, to recover them by action or otherwise.

Some of these methods are considered below.

Deriving income

D9.2 The receiver must weigh the short-term advantages of deriving income from the assets against any long-term damage that may be caused to the realisable value of those assets by any delay in their realisation or by any commitments he may have to enter into (e.g. the grant of leases or tenancies) in order to derive income. As to tax on income from land, see D8.12 above.

Carrying on business or development

D9.3 To be able to carry on the business of the company or carry out or complete any development on the company's land, the receiver may need to enter into new contracts, or continue old contracts, and may also have to raise finance, secured or unsecured. If the company has not gone into liquidation, he can do so as the agent and on behalf of and in the name of the company (but, in the case of an ordinary receiver, only if the charging document provides for his agency and gives him the necessary powers). See however, D8.4 above.

If the company is already in liquidation, the receiver cannot do any of the above-mentioned things as the company's agent, as his agency would have ceased for all purposes except for the purposes of selling and conveying property sold (see D5.2 to D5.4 above); he may be acting as principal, subject to his right of recourse against the receivership assets to the extent that such assets are available. He can still stipulate that his liability will be limited to the receivership assets for the time being available in his hands, but this may not be acceptable to the other party. The receiver's final recourse may be to any express indemnity which his appointor may have given (see D2.14 above).

Where finance is to be secured by a charge on the receivership assets, difficult questions may arise about priorities between different charges. A charging document usually empowers a receiver to borrow moneys on the security of the receivership assets. In the case of an administrative receiver, he also has power 'to raise or borrow money and grant security therefor over the property of the company' and to carry out 'works' (see paragraphs 3 and 12 respectively of Schedule 1). Although it is not made clear, there seems to be no doubt that he can create such security (whether as the company's agent or not) ranking in priority to the charge under which he has been appointed. What is doubtful is whether he can make such security rank in priority to any other existing charges; but the position appears to be as follows.

(*a*) Where he borrows as the company's agent from a lender other than his appointor, the new security will not rank ahead of any such existing charge (whether such a charge ranks before, after or *pari passu* with the appointor's charge), unless the holder of that charge consents. This would be the case even where the charge under which he is appointed empowers him to create a security ranking in front of all existing charges.

(*b*) Where he borrows from his appointor, and the charge held by the appointor either covers further advances or provides that such borrowing shall be treated as the appointor's expenses and, accordingly, covered by his charge, the appointor's priority in respect of the new advance, over any existing liability secured by a charge ranking after the appointor's charge, would depend on whether such borrowing can be 'tacked' as further advances under section 94 of the Law of Property Act 1925; see also section 30 of the Land Registration Act 1925. 'Tacking' is only possible if:

  (i) the appointor's charge is expressed to cover further advances *and* the appointor has no notice of any subsequent charge at the time of the further 'advance'; or

  (ii) the appointor's charge contains an *obligation* on his part to make further advances (on the security of his charge), notwithstanding that he has notice of a subsequent charge—in practice, such an obligation is likely to have ceased by reason of the company's default or receivership, depending on the terms of the charge; or

> (iii) an arrangement has been made with the subsequent mort-
> gagee that the moneys borrowed will rank in priority to the
> moneys secured by the subsequent charge.

The receiver's appointor, as mortgagee in possession, would be in a
stronger position to borrow or expend money to carry out development
on the land. A mortgagee is entitled to priority for any money he has
spent in improving the property insofar as the improvement enhances the
value of the property (*Henderson v Atwood* [*1894*] *AC 150* at *163*). This
entitlement can, perhaps, be extended by appropriate provisions in the
mortgage so that the whole of the money laid out in *developing* the
property can be added to the principal and recovered with interest, irrespective of whether the value added is as great as the expenditure. It is
submitted that such expenditure may not constitute further advances and
will not, therefore, involve the problems about tacking referred to in (*b*)
above.

Once the receiver's agency has terminated by liquidation, it is difficult to
see how, in any case, the development expenditure incurred by him (as
distinct from the appointor whose entitlement referred to above is not
affected) or any other borrowing made by him can be secured by a charge
ranking before the existing charges (other than the appointor's charge).

'Hive-down'

D9.4   A 'hive-down' is a device whereby the trading assets, business,
goodwill and undertaking of the receivership company ('the transferor
company') are transferred as a going concern to a newly-formed subsidiary of that company ('the transferee company'), but leaving all liabilities, to which the transferor company was subject at the transfer date,
with the transferor company. The consideration for the transfer ('the
hive-down consideration') is either an arm's-length consideration, to be
determined by a certificate from a firm of accountants and to be left outstanding on an open loan account as a debt due from the transferee company to the transferor company ('the hive-down value'), or further fully
paid shares in the transferee company to be issued to the transferor company. The former route is generally preferred. The accountants' certificate, to be effective, must be an unqualified certificate unless the
agreement otherwise provides (see, for example, *Shorrock Ltd v Meggitt
Plc* [*1991*] *BCC 471*). In effect, the receiver converts one form of assets
into another form of equal value, namely a book debt due by the transferee company or shares in the transferee company which would, by definition, reflect the value of the underlying assets.

The object of a hive-down is two-fold: first, to increase or preserve the
value of the business and assets in the hands of an outside purchaser, by
providing the transferee with the ability to offset, if possible (and
subject to statutory limitations), its future trading profits against the
transferor company's past trading losses for the purposes of corporation
tax; secondly, to present to the purchaser of the business a convenient

and attractive package in the form of the shares in the transferee company, for which he may be prepared to pay a higher price because of its going concern nature and the possible tax advantages. The consideration which the purchaser offers will reflect two elements. First, a nominal amount for the shares, to be settled in cash. Secondly, the value from the purchaser's point of view of the business and assets in the hive-down company ('the offered value'), to be settled by the purchaser providing the hive-down company with the necessary funds and procuring it to apply those funds to discharge its liability to the receivership company in respect of the hive-down consideration (see the preceding paragraph). This would necessitate a simultaneous amendment of the hive-down agreement by substituting the offered value for the hive-down value as the hive-down consideration. This is usually done by means of a supplemental agreement between the receivership company and the hive-down company.

The tax advantages

D9.5   The tax advantage arises by virtue of section 343 of the Income and Corporation Taxes Act 1988 (as amended). Under section 343 the transferee company is, in certain circumstances, able to use the past trading losses of the transferor company against its future profits as if the trade had always been carried on by the transferee company. The transferee company also takes over the capital allowances position of the transferor company, where the transfer is made on or after 19 March 1986. The losses which may be carried forward in the transferee company are restricted by deducting from the amount of the transferor company's trading losses the excess of 'relevant liabilities' over 'relevant assets'.

Broadly, 'relevant liabilities' are those liabilities which are not transferred to the transferee company and were 'outstanding and vested in the transferor' (not defined) immediately before the transfer. They do not include share capital, share premium account, reserves or loan stock (except where the amount is owed to a creditor carrying on a trade of lending money). Where the creditor concerned waives part of the liability, that part will be a relevant liability.

'Relevant assets' are those assets which were vested in the transferor company immediately before the transfer and not transferred with the trade, and the amount of any consideration given by the transferee to the transferor in respect of the transfer. The assets are to be valued for this purpose at a price which they might reasonably be expected to have fetched on a sale in the open market immediately before the transfer.

Even within those restrictions, relief is only available if the transfer takes place at a time when the group relationship subsists between the transferor and the transferee—such relationship will cease once the transferor goes into liquidation as upon liquidation the company ceases to be beneficial owner of its assets (including the shares in the hive-down company) (*IRC v Olive Mill Ltd [1963] 1 WLR 712*; *Ayerst v C & K Construction Ltd [1975] 3 WLR 16*). Beneficial ownership is also deemed to be lost for these purposes if prior to the hive-down there is already a binding contract for the sale of the shares in the hive-down company (*Wood Preservation Ltd v Prior (1968) 45 TC 112 (CA)*). (There can be complications if two separate trades are hived-down to two separate companies.) It is essential, therefore, that the transfer takes place before liquidation. Relief may also be lost on the ground of a major change in the nature or conduct of the transferee's business within three years before or after the shares are transferred to the purchaser or if there has been such transfer at any time after the scale of its activities has become small or negligible and before any considerable revival of the trade (section 768 of the Taxes Act 1988). (See also D9.7 below.)

Note: The above discussion of the tax treatment is a summary only. For a more detailed consideration, please consult *Tolley's Taxation in Corporate Insolvency* (see also PART H: TAXATION).

Liabilities of transferee company

D9.6   Although neither the receiver nor the receivership company would be liable for any losses or liabilities which the transferee hive-down company incurs, it is inevitable in practice that the receiver would have to ensure that, except due to circumstances which could not reasonably have been foreseen, the transferee company, being the creature of the receivership (transferor) company, does not become insolvent as regards third party creditors while it is still owned by the receivership company. The receivership company and the receiver may, in effect, have to underwrite the transferee company's deficiency. This is because of the provisions of the Insolvency Act 1986 relating to fraudulent trading, wrongful trading and misfeasance (as to which see C13.1 *et seq*. PART C: LIQUIDATIONS) and of the Company Directors Disqualification Act 1986. The receiver may have to rely on the indemnity given by his appointor (see D2.14 above) as regards any balance of the deficiency.

Assets to be transferred

D9.7   For the purposes of the tax relief referred to in D9.5 above, the effective date will be the date on which *beneficial* ownership of the assets passes to the transferee company. This will be the date on which an unconditional agreement for the sale is entered into or, where the sale is conditional, the date on which the condition is satisfied. The transfer of *legal* ownership may be delayed until a later date.

It is, however, necessary that all the assets required to maintain a going concern are available to the transferee company. Usually, all goodwill of the business, stock-in-trade, work-in-progress, intellectual property and assets which generate products and trading income are transferred. Book debts and other debts due to the transferor company are normally not transferred, but the transferee company undertakes to collect them for a fee on behalf of the transferor company. Nor is immovable property necessarily transferred; the transferee would be granted licence to occupy the business premises for a fee.

There may or may not be a tax advantage under section 178 of the Taxation of Chargeable Gains Act 1992 in hiving-down capital assets (perhaps into a separate group company having accumulated capital losses or gains), depending on the circumstances. The transfer of a capital asset to the transferee company which is still the transferor company's subsidiary is deemed to be for a consideration which produces neither a chargeable gain nor an allowable loss. However, once the transferee company ceases to be such a subsidiary on the shares in it being transferred to an independent third party, that asset is deemed to be disposed of by the transferee company at its market value. This may give rise to corporation tax on the capital gain, a factor which the purchaser of the shares would take into account in tailoring his offer for the shares. It is not essential that the capital asset be transferred to the hive-down company for the purposes of obtaining relief in respect of the trading losses, so long as the hive-down company has the use of that asset (for example, under a licence) to the extent that its use is necessary for the purposes of carrying on its trade.

Where leasehold property is involved in the sale, and the lease prevents the lessee from assigning (etc.) the lease without the landlord's consent, the sale may be expressed to be subject to the requisite consent of the landlord being available, the parties undertaking to make reasonable endeavours to obtain it. In practice, obtaining the landlord's consent quickly to avoid further deterioration in the value of the assets and complying with his requirements may present a major problem. Section 1(6) of the Landlord and Tenant Act 1988 has shifted the burden of proof on to the landlord so that the landlord has to show that his refusal to grant consent was reasonable. The Act also requires the landlord to respond to any written request for consent within a reasonable time, to give consent where it is reasonable to do so (stating any conditions to which that consent is subject) and, if consent is refused, to give reasons for the refusal. Section 1(5) of that Act must also be noted. It provides that it is reasonable for a person not to give consent to a proposed transaction only in the case where, if he withheld consent and the tenant completed the transaction, the tenant would be in breach of covenant. In *International Drilling Fluids Ltd v Louisville Investments (Uxbridge) Ltd* [1986] 1 All ER 332 (CA), decided before the passing of the 1988 Act, Balcombe LJ had laid down the following guidelines.

(1) The qualified covenant against assignment without the landlord's consent is intended to protect the landlord from his premises being used or occupied in an undesirable way, or by an undesirable tenant or assignee.

(2) The landlord's refusal to give consent must relate to the relationship of landlord and tenant with regard to the premises in question and not on any extraneous ground with a view to gaining some uncovenanted advantage.

(3) It is not necessary for the landlord to prove that the conclusions which led him to refuse the consent were justified; it is sufficient if the conclusions were such as might have been reached by a reasonable man in the circumstances.

(4) The purpose for which the assignee intends to use the premises may be a justification for withholding consent, even if the purpose is not prohibited by the lease.

(5) Where there is a disproportion between the benefit to the landlord and the detriment to the tenant, should the consent be withheld, it may be unreasonable for the landlord to refuse consent.

(6) However the position would depend on the circumstances of each case.

Since the 1988 Act shifts the burden on the landlord to show that his refusal of consent is reasonable, he would be deemed to have withheld consent unreasonably where he offers no explanation (see, for example, *Midland Bank plc v Chart Enterprises Inc [1990] 2 EGLR 59*). However, while the Act reverses the burden of proof, it does not alter the law in any other respect. If anything, the fact that the Act requires the landlord to respond within a reasonable time reinforces the existing legal principle that it is not necessary for the landlord to *justify* his reasons for refusal; he merely has to show that they are conclusions to which a reasonable landlord might, in the same circumstances, have come (*Air India v Balabel (1993) 30 EG 90*). The reasonableness or otherwise of any decision of the landlord must be judged by reference to the circumstances existing and known to the landlord at the time of the decision (*CIN Properties Ltd v Gill, Estates Gazette, 27 September 1993; Bromley Park Garden Estates Ltd v Moss [1982] 2 All ER 890*), and not at the time of the hearing of the case (cf. *Sonnenthal v Newton (1965) 109 SJ 333; Welch v Birrane (1974) 29 P&CR 102*).

In *Killick v Second Covent Garden Property Co Ltd [1973] 1 WLR 658*, the Court of Appeal held that merely because the user covenant precluded the assignee from using the premises as offices, it did not mean that a necessary consequence of the assignment was that there would be a breach of covenant. After the assignment had been made, the landlord would have the same rights to enforce the user covenant against the assignee as it had against the tenant. The landlord's refusal was held to be unreasonable. In *Orlanda Investments Ltd v Grosvenor Estate Belgravia (1989, unreported)*, where there had been long standing and extensive breaches of covenants to repair, the Court of Appeal held that the landlord was entitled to refuse his consent unless he could be reasonably satisfied that the proposed assignee would remedy the breaches. It would also be reasonable for the landlord to require security, either by way of performance and/or by way of deposit, for execution of the repairs. A landlord is not justified in withholding his consent on the ground of a breach of covenant on the part of the tenant, unless the breach is serious, or on the ground that there is a dispute as to breach which he has not substantiated (*Beale v Worth [1993] EGCS 135*).

Where the agreement relates to the sale of (or the grant of option to purchase—*Spiro v Glencrown Properties Ltd [1991] 2 WLR 931*) freehold or leasehold property, section 2 of the Law of Property (Miscellaneous Provisions) Act 1989 should be borne in mind. The section, which replaces section 40 of the Law of Property Act 1925, provides that a contract for the sale or other disposition of an interest in land can only be made in writing and by incorporating all the terms which the parties have expressly agreed in one document or, where contracts are exchanged, in each. The contract must be signed by each party and not just the party to be charged, as under the old provision. Great care is needed when, as often happens in practice, side letters supplementing the contract are issued. (It is not clear whether the doctrine of part performance which had been expressly preserved by the old provision would still apply.) However, it was held in *Record v Bell [1991] 1 WLR 853* that where, in order to induce the purchaser to exchange a contract for the sale of land which had been prepared, the vendor offered a warranty as to the state of his title, which the purchaser accepted, the offer and acceptance constituted a collateral contract outside the requirements of section 2.

A conveyance, transfer or assignment of any interest in freehold or leasehold property is required to be by deed (section 52 of the Law of Property Act 1925). The creation or disposal of interests in land is required to be in writing, as also are a declaration of trust representing any land or any interest therein and a disposition of an equitable interest or trust subsisting at the time of disposition (section 53 of the above Act, which does not affect the creation or operation of a resulting, implied or constructive trust). Interests in land created by parol have the force and effect of interests at will only, even if any consideration for such creation has been given (section 54 of the above Act). (See also *Crago v Julian [1992] 1 All ER 744.*)

Normally, an assignment by the company as tenant of a lease, even with the consent of the landlord, does not relieve the company as assignor, from the tenant's future obligations under the lease. Both the company and the assignee will remain liable for them to the landlord, although the landlord's claim against the company will be an unsecured, non-preferential claim ranking after the secured claim of the receiver's appointor. However, attempts should be made by the receiver, in negotiating the terms of the landlord's licence, to obtain an express release of the company's obligations. Where, however, the landlord subsequently grants a release to the assignee of any of its obligations, such release will also operate in favour of the company (see *Deanplan Ltd v Mahmoud [1992] 3 All ER 945*).

Where the landlord's consent is not readily available to the grant of the licence, it may be possible, depending on the terms of the lease, to grant a *non-exclusive* licence without committing a breach of the terms. (It is important that the licence should be for a time certain of less than six months, without any option for the licensee to renew or extend the duration of the licence, in view of the provisions of the landlord and tenant legislation). It will be noted, as mentioned above, that the Landlord and Tenant Act 1988 imposes an obligation on a landlord, who has stipulated in the lease that the tenant must not assign, underlet, charge or part with possession of the property, to give, within a reasonable time after his consent is sought, his consent (unless it is reasonable not to do so) and to specify any conditions of such consent or his reasons for withholding it. (A secure tenancy gives a tenant only personal rights and is not assignable (*City of London Corporation v Bourn, Estates Gazette Case Summaries 1989, 136*; and see Part IV of the Housing Act 1985)). Alternatively, the business may be carried on by the transferor company for the benefit of the transferee company against appropriate indemnities from the transferee company; but this may, conceivably, jeopardise the tax relief under section 343 of the Income and Corporation Taxes Act 1988.

It may be necessary, depending on the circumstances, to transfer outstanding contracts with customers and suppliers to satisfy the conditions on which tax relief under section 343 or 768 of the 1988 Act is available. This may be difficult. Novation generally requires the consent of the other party to the contract which may not be forthcoming within the time available. Where novation is not possible, it may be necessary for the transferor company to carry out the contract in its name but for the benefit of the transferee company (subject to any loss of the tax relief which this may cause). (See, further, D9.11 below.)

As the 'hive-down' company or its assets will eventually be sold (see D9.15 *et seq.*), the receiver must be particularly careful about the position of any intellectual property included in the sale. The intellectual property may be held under a licence agreement with its proprietor which contains prohibitions against disclosure of any trade or industrial secret involved in the intellectual property and against its transfer. A breach of such a prohibition could, conceivably, involve the receiver in personal liability in tort.

The transfer agreement

D9.8   The transfer agreement is usually on the terms that only such rights, title and interest (if any) as the transferor company may have in relation to the assets are sold. It expressly excludes all warranties and representations in relation thereto. Even the description 'beneficial owner' (which by virtue of sections 76 and 77 of the Law of Property Act 1925 would imply certain covenants as to title and absence of encumbrances and as to further assurances—note that section 76 is to be repealed and replaced, from a date to be appointed, by provisions in the Law of Property (Miscellaneous Provisions) Act 1994) is omitted in respect of the transferor company. In respect of particular types of assets, special safeguards for the transferor company may have to be included. For example, in respect of second-hand motor vehicles the transferee must undertake to put the vehicles in a roadworthy condition before using them. This may assist the transferor company to avoid any criminal liability under section 60 of the Road Traffic Act 1972 (as amended by the Road Traffic Act 1988) and, possibly, civil liability to third parties. (See also D9.15 below.) The agreement usually provides that any third property is expressly excluded from the sale.

Existing charges

D9.9   The transfer would normally be subject to all existing encumbrances (except the appointor's charge, and subject to the vendor procuring the release of other registered charges). However, it is advisable to make an exception in the case of any unregistered charge which, as against any creditor or liquidator of the company, may be potentially void by virtue of the Companies Act 1985 (as amended by the Companies Act 1989, although this amendment is not in force at the time of writing). This is because, if the transferee company takes the property concerned subject to that vulnerable charge, the charge would be valid as against the *transferee company's* creditors and liquidator if the acquisition subject to the charge is registered under the Companies Act 1985 as amended by the 1989 Act (but note that the 1989 Act amendments have not yet been brought into force).

Contracts of employment

D9.10   Normally, contracts of employment will not be transferred. The transferor company will retain such of the employees as are required for running the transferee company's business and will sub-contract their services to the transferee company on agreed terms. Regulation 5 of the Transfer of Undertakings (Protection of Employment) Regulations 1981 (SI 1981 No 1794) (made pursuant to EC Council Directive 77/187/EEC (OJ 1977, L61/26, 14 February 1977, the 'Acquired Rights Directive'), and amended by the Trade Union Reform and Employment Rights Act 1993—see D9.16 below) will not apply to the 'hive-down' at this stage. The regulation provides that the transfer from one person to another of an undertaking situated in the United Kingdom, or of part of such undertaking so situated, shall not operate so as to terminate the contracts of employment of the employees employed therein immediately before the transfer but shall have effect after the transfer as if the contracts were originally made between the employees and the transferee. In particular, on completion of the transfer, all the transferor's rights, powers, duties and liabilities under or in connection with such contracts (except in respect of an occupational pension scheme insofar as it relates to benefits for old age, invalidity and survivors) shall be transferred by virtue of the regulation to the transferee; and anything done by or in relation to the transferor before the transfer is completed in respect of those contracts or employees shall be deemed to have been done by or in relation to the transferee. However, Regulation 4 provides that where a receiver or a liquidator in a voluntary winding up transfers the company's undertaking to its wholly-owned subsidiary, the transfer shall for the purposes of the regulations be deemed not to have been effected until immediately before the transferee company ceases (otherwise than by reason of its being wound up) to be a wholly-owned subsidiary of the transferor company or the undertaking is transferred by the transferee company to another person. This means that the liabilities of the 'hive-down' company to the employees remain suspended until its shares are disposed of to an outside party by the receiver or liquidator (as to which see D9.15 *et seq.* below).

Other contracts

D9.11   The agreement may provide for the transfer of such right, title and interest as the company may have in its outstanding trade or building contracts with third parties and that the transferor company and the transferee company would endeavour to secure their novation by the third parties in favour of the transferee company (the purchaser). Pending novation, the purchaser would agree to perform, at its own cost, the company's part of the contracts in the company's name but for the purchaser's benefit and to keep the company indemnified in respect of them. In *Linden Gardens Trust Ltd v Lenesta Sludge Disposals Ltd; St Martins Property Corporation Ltd v Sir Robert McAlpine & Sons Ltd [1993] 3 WLR 408*, the House of Lords held that an employer under a contract on standard JCT terms (which prohibited an assignment of 'this contract' without the contractor's consent) was not entitled to assign the non-personal benefit of the contract, namely, a right of action against the contractor, without the contractor's consent. The right of action assigned was the right to have the building properly built and a subsequent claim for damages arising under the contract. That assignment was part of a larger transaction under which the employer had also assigned to the same party the lease of the land on which the building work was being carried out. It was further held that the employer, having made an ineffective assignment of the right of action, was entitled to pursue that right, notwithstanding that he had assigned the lease, and claim damages on the basis that the lease had not been assigned. It would appear that in a similar situation, a receiver of the employer may be able to get round this problem by causing the employer to allow the right of action to be pursued by the 'assignee' in the employer's name under a power of attorney granted to the 'assignee', on the basis that the benefit of any recovery will be held by the employer in trust for the 'assignee' and that the 'assignee' will indemnify the employer in respect of all costs and liabilities which the employer may incur as a result, such indemnity to be appropriately secured. Where, however, the employer is contractually permitted to assign his rights under the building contract to (for example) the owner of the site, the assignee may be able to recover damages for defective construction even though the assignor, not being the owner of the site, acting as principal (and not as the owner's agent), and having no liability to the owner in respect of the defect, would not have been able to recover them (*Darlington Borough Council v Wiltshier Northern Ltd, The Times, 4 July 1994*).

As far as any asset held by the company on hire purchase terms is concerned, the transfer may be of the benefit and burden of the relevant contract, subject to suitable indemnities from the purchaser. Alternatively, the purchaser may provide the receiver with funds, as additional purchase price, which the receiver can use to pay the finance company the 'settlement figure' required to obtain title to the asset, and the asset is then transferred to the purchaser. The latter course may have a marginal advantage if the asset concerned is subject to a fixed (as distinct from a floating) charge, in that the charge holder would rank before preferential creditors as regards the net proceeds of sale of that asset.

Stamp duty

D9.12 It would ordinarily be possible to obtain stamp duty relief in respect of the 'hive-down' under section 42 of the Finance Act 1930 (as amended by section 27(2) of the Finance Act 1967). That section, as amended, applies to any instrument as respects which it is shown to the satisfaction of the Commissioners that its effect is to convey or transfer a beneficial interest in property from one body corporate to another, and that one of them is beneficial owner of not less than 90 per cent of the issued share capital of another, or a third such body is beneficial owner of 90 per cent of the issued share capital of each. However, the Commissioners must also be satisfied that the instrument was not executed in pursuance of an arrangement whereby the consideration is provided or received directly or indirectly by a third party which is not so associated or whereby the beneficial interest was previously transferred, directly or indirectly, by such third party or whereby the transferor and the transferee were to cease to be so associated by reason of a change in the percentage of the issued share capital of the transferee in the beneficial ownership of the transferor or the third body corporate (Finance Act 1967, s 27(3)). Accordingly, it is advisable to effect the 'hive-down' before any sale to a purchaser is contemplated. (See, further, PART H: TAXATION.)

Value added tax

D9.13 No value added tax will be payable if the transfer amounts to the transfer of a business, or part of a business, as a going concern within article 5 of the Value Added Tax (Special Provisions) Order 1992 (SI 1992 No 3129). This applies if there has been no significant break in trading (apart from a short period of closure immediately before the transfer) and if the conditions set out in paragraph 3 of HM Customs & Excise VAT Leaflet 700/9/94 are satisfied, particularly the condition that the new owner is or becomes liable to be registered for the purposes of VAT. Neither the insolvency of the transferor nor the intention of the transferee are relevant for the operation of this relief. In *ECSG Ltd, LON/88/ 580 No 5204*, the tribunal held that a transfer of a going concern had occurred and there was no significant break, notwithstanding that the transferor was insolvent and had ceased trading before the transfer. See also *Spijkers v Gebroeders Benedik Abattoir cv [1986] 2 CMLR 296*, where it was held that a cessation of trading, or its substantial reduction before the transfer, did not prevent the transfer from being a transfer as a going concern, if the wherewithal to carry on the business, such as plant, building or employees, were available and transferred; and that a gap between transfer and resumption of trading, though relevant, was not conclusive against there being such a transfer. The vital question is whether the effect of the transaction is to put the transferee in possession of a business which he could carry on as a going concern even if he chooses not to do so (*Customs & Excise Commissioners v Dearwood Ltd [1986] STC 327*). The transfer of goodwill may be an important factor (see *Kenmir Ltd v Frizzell [1968] 1 WLR 329*), but is not decisive. Where the undertaking consists solely or substantially of stock-in-trade and most customers continue to trade with the transferee after the transferor has ceased trading, the transfer of the stock-in-trade may nevertheless constitute a transfer of a going concern. A bundle of assets constitutes a going concern if it comprises that which is necessary to trade, whether or not that business is profitable or has any goodwill (*Solar (Sales) Ltd, MAN/87/428 No 2988, VAT Tribunal*). One important consideration is whether the purchaser is using the assets transferred for substantially the same business (*Auchtertyre Farmers, EDN/87/109 No 2822, VAT Tribunal*).

It is the substance, and not merely the form, of the transaction which needs to be considered: *Gillet Pressings (Cardiff) Ltd [1994] Simon's Tax Intelligence 113*, where the VAT Tribunal held that the grant of a new lease of the business premises, previously occupied by the transferor, to the transferee had been organised in advance in contemplation of the transfer. The Tribunal stated that the main factors to be considered were: business premises; product and raw materials; the identity and type of suppliers, customers, persons controlling the business, and workforce; profit-making activities; and whether the business had been run down or closed at the time of transfer. On the facts, there had been a transfer of a going concern. The change of business activity following the transfer had been gradual and reflected a process of assimilation in the transferee's group. Although not all the former employees had been re-engaged, the transferee had employees of the same type. A temporary closure of the factory for cleaning and reorganisation was unimportant. See also *Grassby & Sons Ltd [1994] Simon's Tax Intelligence 133*, where the transfer, held to have been that of a going concern, included the benefit of a restrictive covenant, and the transferor had warranted that the business was being carried on as a going concern, although no premises or other business assets were transferred and the transferee had not re-engaged any of the transferor's employees. The VAT Tribunal held that the exclusion of some of the business assets did not prevent the transfer of a going concern in a case where what was sold was an existing economic activity.

The right to the relief described above is further qualified by the provisions of article 5(2) of the VAT (Special Provisions) Order 1992 (SI 1992 No 3129). The qualification applies to a sale of the whole or part of a business in so far as it consists of land or buildings. Its effect is that if the sale of the land or building would (but for the relief provisions described above) be standard rated (for example, where the vendor has elected that it be so rated or where the building is a new or uncompleted freehold building or civil engineering work), then the sale will be regarded as that of a going concern only if the *purchaser* both elects to waive the exemption and notifies in writing HM Customs & Excise of its election to be standard rated in respect of any future dealings with the land or building.

The receiver should be careful not to charge VAT where the relief applies. If he does charge it, he is liable to account for it to HM Customs & Excise (see Schedule 11, paragraph 5 to the Value Added Tax Act 1994) and the purchaser would not be entitled to set it off against his VAT output tax. Where the receiver is in doubt as to whether or not the relief applies, the safer course would be to obtain a cash deposit from the purchaser to cover any VAT that HM Customs & Excise determine is payable but should refrain, until such determination, from issuing a VAT invoice.

(For further analogous cases, see D9.16 below.)

If the disposal does not amount to the transfer of a business as a going concern, the VAT on the sale of each asset must be considered. For example, VAT will be payable on goodwill and on most second-hand goods such as plant and machinery. With effect from 1 August 1989 a receiver must charge VAT when selling a new freehold building (as defined in the Value Added Tax Act 1994, Schedule 9 Group 1) or on the surrender of a lease. The sale of an 'old' freehold building (one completed more than three years ago), and of freehold land, and the grant or assignment of a lease are exempt unless the company (or the receiver on its behalf) elects (or has elected already) to charge VAT. If an election has been made by the company to charge VAT in respect of the land or building (for instance so that VAT can be charged on rents) then the receiver must also charge VAT on the subsequent sale.

(See, further, PART H: TAXATION.)

Immunities and indemnities

D9.14 Finally, a 'hive-down' agreement would contain a provision to the effect that the receiver is acting as the company's agent and will not have personal liability or, alternatively, that, in any case, his and the company's liability would be limited to the assets for the time being available in the receivership. The purchaser would also undertake to indemnify the company and the receiver against any liability which they might incur in connection with the transfer to or use or disposal by the purchaser of any of the assets concerned. Such a liability may arise in relation to a number of assets, such as unsafe or defective premises, equipment, motor vehicles or stock; third party property delivered to the purchaser; computer data; intellectual property held under a licence; contracts not novated; leases; and so on.

It is also usual to have in such an agreement a provision to the effect that the agreement, together with any documents referred to in it, constitutes the whole agreement between the parties relating to its subject matter. The main object is to prevent the purchaser from relying on any representations made or assurances given to him outside the agreement. This may, however, also have the effect of preventing the parties from relying on any 'side letters' dealing with any outstanding ancillary matters exchanged between them at the time of the agreement or its completion. As such agreements are often entered into in haste, it is quite common for the agreement to be supplemented by such side letters for the benefit of either party. Care should, therefore, be taken to ensure that these side letters are not excluded from being treated as part of the agreement. In any case, it would appear that an 'entire agreement' clause may, in certain circumstances, be struck out as ineffective under section 3 of the Misrepresentation Act 1967, as substituted by section 8 of the Unfair Contract Terms Act 1977 (see *Goff v Gauthier, 27 March 1991, 62 P & CR 388 (Ch D; J A Gillard QC, deputy judge)*).

Sale of going concern

D9.15   The receiver should be wary of allowing unrestricted or unsupervised access to the company's trade secrets and employees to parties claiming to be prospective purchasers whose real motive may be to learn the trade secrets and recruit key employees of the company for the purposes of carrying on their own business in competition with the company. As a minimum, the receiver should establish the *bona fides* of prospective purchasers by requiring them to produce satisfactory bank references and getting them to execute appropriate undertakings regulating the terms on which they are allowed access. It may be noted here that even if an employee's contract of employment does not contain any restrictive covenant regarding the setting up of a competing business for the use of the company's trade secrets, the employee is under certain implied restrictions. In *Universal Thermosensors Ltd v Hibben [1992] 3 All ER 257*, it was held that the absence of such restrictive covenants merely meant that the employee was entitled to use for his own purposes, in any business set up in competition with the company, any information he carried in his head regarding the identity of the customers, customer contracts, the nature of the customers' product requirements, or the company's pricing policies, provided that he had acquired the information honestly in the ordinary course of his employment and had not, for instance, deliberately sought to memorise lists of names. What he was not entitled to do was to steal documents belonging to the company, or to use for his own purpose information, which could sensibly be regarded as confidential information, contained in such documents regarding the company's customers, or customer contracts, or customer requirements, or the prices charged. Nor was he entitled to copy such information onto scraps of paper and take those away and then use the information in his own business.

Where a 'hive-down' has not been carried out, the sale to an outside purchaser would be of the business assets owned by the receivership company, except any assets, such as book debts, which the parties agree to exclude. Where a 'hive-down' has previously been carried out, the assets of the receivership company to be sold may consist of (*a*) the shares in the 'hive-down' company and (*b*) any retained assets of the receivership company which were excluded from the 'hive-down' (see D9.7 above). The retained assets to be sold may include immovable property (subject to the consent of the landlord in the case of a leasehold), and the benefit, subject to the burden, of contracts (insofar as they are transferable or can in future be novated by express or implied agreement between the purchaser and the other parties to the contracts), but *not* book debts (which the receiver, or the purchaser, on behalf of the receivership company, will continue to collect). Any debt due by the 'hive-down' company to the receivership company (e.g. the loan account referred to in D9.4 above) will not be sold; the purchaser will undertake to pay it to the receivership company at completion. If the purchaser is contemplating the financing of such a payment out of the 'hive-down' company's assets, he and the receiver should note the provisions of sections 151 *et seq.* of the Companies Act 1985, which contain restrictions against financial assistance by a company (in this case the 'hive-down' company) for acquisition of its own shares.

Receivers may attempt to market the assets by various methods, such as negotiations with individual interested parties, invitation to tender and offer of sale by public auction. As to the first method, a collateral 'lock out' agreement, that is, an agreement by him with a prospective purchaser to the effect that he would not open or continue negotiations with, or consider an offer from, any other party for a specified period, may be binding on him (see *Pitt v PHH Asset Management Ltd [1993] 4 All ER 961 (CA)* and *Walford v Miles [1992] 1 All ER 453 (HL)* per Lord Ackner). By contrast, a 'lock-in' agreement, which seeks to bind the vendor to negotiate with the prospective purchaser in good faith is no more than an 'agreement to agree' which is too uncertain to be enforceable (*Walford v Miles* (above); *Courtney and Fairbairn Ltd v Tolani Bros (Hotels) Ltd [1975] 1 WLR 297*). As to the second method the case of *Blackpool and Fylde Aero Club Ltd v Blackpool Borough Council [1990] 1 WLR 1195* may be relevant. It was held by the Court of Appeal in that case that a party inviting submission of tenders within a specified period was contractually bound to consider all tenders submitted within that period, notwithstanding a condition in the invitation that the vendor was not bound to accept any tender. Failure to do so may result in a claim for damages by the tenderer concerned, and such damages may include his costs of fully equipping himself to ensure that he was in a strong position to win the contract (see the Australian case of *Commonwealth v Amann Aviation Pty Ltd (1991) 66 ALJR 12*). However, provided that the recipient gives some consideration to the tender and acts reasonably, it has no further obligation to the tenderer (*Fairclough Building Ltd v Borough Council of Port Talbot, 16 July 1992 (CA, unreported)*).

Effect of Transfer of Undertakings Regulations

D9.16 Upon completion of the sale to the outside purchaser, there will be automatically transferred to the purchaser (save as stated below) all contracts of employment between the receivership company and its employees, subsisting 'immediately before' the completion of the sale, and all liabilities thereunder (except those in respect of an occupational pension scheme; see, further, the last paragraph of this section). This automatic transfer takes place by virtue of Regulation 5 of the Transfer of Undertakings (Protection of Employment) Regulations 1981 (SI 1981 No 1794) (now amended), made pursuant to the EC Acquired Rights Directive 77/187 (see *Berg and Busschers v Besselsen [1989] IRLR 447*; see also D9.10 above).

Until the *Litster* case (see below) it was thought that the Regulation could be avoided if *before* such completion (regardless of how short the time gap was) the contracts were terminated (see *Secretary of State v Spence and others [1986] IRLR 248* where the Court of Appeal attempted to resolve the long judicial controversy on the point: as to which see *Premier Motors (Medway) Ltd v Total Oil Great Britain Ltd [1983] IRLR 471; Apex Leisure Hire v Barratt [1984] IRLR 224; Secretary of State for Employment v Anchor Hotel (Kippford) Ltd [1985] IRLR 452; Wendleboe v LJ Music ApS [1986] 1 CMLR 476 (European Court); Kestongate Ltd v Miller, The Times, 28 May 1986; Anderson v Dalkeith Engineering Ltd [1984] IRLR 429; Wheeler v Patel [1987] IRLR 211 (EAT); Brook Lane Finance Co Ltd v Bradley [1988] IRLR 283, EAT; P. Bork International A/S (in liquidation) v Foreningen Arbejtsledere I Danmark [1989] IRLR 41 (ECJ)*).

However, the question was finally resolved by the House of Lords in *Litster & Others v Forth Dry Dock & Engineering Co Ltd and Another [1989] IRLR 161*. The appeal was brought to the House of Lords by twelve former employees of a company in receivership. The receiver dismissed the employees one hour before selling the business and assets as a going concern. The purchaser did not re-engage those employees but, instead, engaged new employees at lower salaries. The House of Lords held that the appellants had been dismissed for reasons connected with the transfer and that the appellants were deemed to have been employed 'immediately before' the transfer. Regulation 5(3) was to be construed as if the words 'immediately before' were qualified by the words 'or would have been so employed if they had not been unfairly dismissed' in the circumstances described in Regulation 8(1). That Regulation provides that a person is to be treated as unfairly dismissed if the transfer or a reason connected with it is the reason or principal reason for his dismissal, but that where an 'economic, technical or organisational reason entailing changes in the workforce' of either the transferor or the transferee before or after the transfer is the reason or principal reason for dismissing that person, he is not to be treated as unfairly dismissed. In that case the House of Lords held that the dismissals were unfair for a reason connected with the transfer and the exception in Regulation 8(1) was not applicable to the facts of the case. Their Lordships found that this was the correct interpretation of the Regulations, having regard to the true intention of the EC Acquired Rights Directive (above) pursuant to which the Regulations had been made. (See also the European Court case of *P Bork International A/S v Foreningen Arbejtsledere*, above.)

In *DMG (Realisations) Ltd (August 1990, unreported)* an industrial tribunal accepted an argument that the dismissal of employees before a sale by a receiver, at the request of a purchaser, was a dismissal for an 'economic, technical or organisational' reason; this was because without the dismissal there would have been no sale. Of course, a decision of the tribunal is not binding, and it is submitted that the decision was wrong as being contrary to the spirit of the *Litster* case, and, also, it would seem, contrary to the decision of the Employment Appeal Tribunal in *Wheeler v Patel & J Goulding Group of Companies [1987] IRLR 211*. In *Ibex Trading Co Ltd v Walton [1994] IRLR 564*, the employees (who had declined to accept a cut in wages as part of the administrators' strategy for cutting costs), were dismissed on 16 October 1991, and an offer to purchase the business, received on 11 November 1991, resulted in the exchange of contracts on 13 February 1992. The dismissals were held not to be by reason of the transfer of business because at the time of dismissal, the transfer was no more than a possibility. However, the dismissals were held to be unfair by virtue of section 57(3) of the Employment Protection (Consolidation) Act 1978 (which sets out the criteria for determining whether a dismissal is unfair) for failure by the administrators to consult the employees; and accordingly, the transferor, *but not the transferee*, was liable. (See also *UK Security Services (Midland) Ltd v Gibbons, EAT 104/90.*) In the more recent case of *Longden v Ferrari Ltd and Kennedy International Ltd [1994] IRLR 157*, the facts of which are summarised in D7.1 above, the Employment Appeal Tribunal, in dismissing the employee's claim for unfair dismissal, also held that the employees had not been employed in the undertaking immediately before transfer. This was because the fact that there had been a succession of events causally linked to one another, and to the transfer itself, was not sufficient to establish that the transfer had been *effected* by a series of transactions within the meaning of the Regulations. At the European Community level, it has been held that the Directive referred to above does not apply to the transfer of undertakings, businesses or parts of businesses which occurs in the context of insolvency proceedings instituted with a view to the liquidation of the assets of the transferor under the supervision of the competent judicial authority (*see H B M Abels v The Administrative Board (Netherlands) [1987] 2 CMLR 406* (decided by the Court of Justice of the European Community)). However, that exception is not reflected in the Regulations referred to above made in the United Kingdom, although in a compulsory liquidation (and, arguably, in an insolvent voluntary liquidation), the winding-up order or resolution may, in certain circumstances, constitute termination of the contracts of employment (see C9.7 PART C: LIQUIDATIONS). Further, in *D'Urso v Ercole Marelli Elettromeccanica Generale SpA (in special administration) [1992] IRLR 136*, on a referral from an Italian court, the European Court of Justice held that the EEC 'Business Transfer' Directive did not apply to a transfer which occurred in the context of insolvency proceedings which were intended to realise the assets of the undertaking for the benefit of its creditors; but that the Directive did apply to transfers effected in the context of 'special administration' proceedings which were primarily aimed at securing the future viability of the whole or parts of an undertaking.

In any case, if the time gap between the dismissal and the transfer is short, then, according to the *Litster* case, the '*de minimis*' principle would apply so that the gap would be ignored. Further, note that dismissal takes effect on the expiry of the notice of dismissal or, where there is a summary dismissal, when the fact of dismissal is communicated to the employee (see *Brown v Southall & Knight [1980] IRLR 130*).

Only employees who have a current contract of employment can invoke the provisions (see Article 1(1) of the Acquired Rights Directive (above) and *Mikkelsen v Danmols Inventar A/S [1986] 1 CMLR 316; Wendelboe v L J Music ApS [1986] 1 CMLR 476*) but they include those who, but for their unlawful dismissal, would have been employees of the undertaking (*P Bork International* above).

As to what constitutes 'entailing changes in the workforce' (referred to in Regulation 8(1)—see above), some of the cases should be noted. In *Delabole Slate Ltd v Berriman [1985] IRLR 305 (CA)*, it was held that 'workforce' connotes the whole body of employees as an entity, so that the changes in the identity of individuals did not constitute changes in the workforce so long as the overall number and functions of the employees, looked at as a whole, remain unchanged. In *Crawford v Swinton Insurance Brokers Ltd [1990] IRLR 42*, the employee was employed by a company as a typist and clerk and was allowed to work at home. The business was transferred to another company which told the employee that in future there would be no requirement for typing and that she should consider a move to selling insurance. She was told that she would have to work normal office hours and that she would have to return her company car. She refused to accept the changes and resigned, claiming unfair dismissal. The Employment Appeal Tribunal decided that there did not have to be a change in the identity of any of the workforce for there to be an organisational reason for a dismissal. There could be a 'change in the workforce' if the same people were kept on but given entirely different jobs to do. What had to be looked at was the workforce as a whole, separate from the individuals that make it up. (The case was remitted to the industrial tribunal for reconsideration.) The expression 'entailing' quoted above was interpreted by the Court of Appeal in *Delabole Slate Ltd v Berriman* (above) to connote that the change in the workforce is *necessary*, so that a mere change in the identity of employees by the substitution of one set of workers for another does not constitute an *economic, technical or organisational reason*, even if the transferee can show a sound economic or organisational reason for doing so.

In this connection, the case of *Macer v Abafast Ltd [1990] IRLR 137* is also relevant. The employee had been employed by one company since June 1982. In June 1986 another company decided to acquire the business. In December 1986 he was dismissed, and on 12 January 1987 re-employed, by the original employer. Contracts for the acquisition were signed in February 1987 and he was dismissed by the new employer in September 1987. Completion of the transfer of the business under the contract took place in February 1988. The Employment Appeal Tribunal, taking guidance from the *Litster* case, held that for the purposes of paragraph 17(2) of Schedule 13 to the Employment Protection (Consolidation) Act 1978, the employment of the employee with the previous employer and with the new employer had been continuous so that the combined periods of service satisfied the qualification period for entitlement to redundancy payment. The reference to the 'time of transfer' in that paragraph ought not to be read as referring to a moment of time where there was a series of transactions in the transfer. To make an arbitrary rule that a gap of more than one week, or ten days, broke the continuity of employment, but that a gap of less than one week did not, allowed manipulation of the situation and was contrary to the intention of the legislation, which was to encourage and reward long service, and to seek to protect the employee from insolvency or death of the employer, or from insecurity due to a change of ownership of the business—not least where the employer was associated with a group of companies.

In *A & G Tuck Ltd v Bartlett [1994] IRLR 162*, the Employment Appeal Tribunal held that for the purposes of calculating whether the employee had the requisite two-year period of continuous employment to entitle him to claim compensation for unfair dismissal, the period of two weeks in which he nominally remained in the employment of the transferor before taking up his post with the transferee should not be taken to have broken the continuity of his employment. See also *Justfern Ltd v D'Ingerthorpe [1994] IRLR 164*, where the EAT held that a period of over a week during which the employee had claimed unemployment benefit, before taking up his employment with the transferee, did not break continuity.

The Regulations do not apply to a simple takeover of a company by another by the acquisition of the shares in the first company (*Initial Supplies Ltd v McCall 1991 SLT 67 (Court of Session, Outer House)*). This is provided that the takeover is not that of a company into which a receiver or liquidator had 'hived-down' the assets and undertaking of a receivership company—in that case the Regulations will apply on such takeover. (In other cases of 'hive-down', that is, not effected by a receiver or liquidator, the Regulations would have applied at the 'hive-down' stage; see D9.10 above.)

Where Regulation 5 applies, the effect of a transfer would be that the transferee assumes liability (if any) for the claims of the employees in respect of the dismissal prior to the transfer, rather than the employee being treated as then having entered into the employment of the transferee. In its original wording, the effect of Regulation 5 appeared to be that the transfer of the contracts of employment and liabilities thereunder was mandatory and was binding on the employees as well (except where their working conditions were so changed as to constitute constructive dismissal). In this respect the Regulation appeared to alter the common law principle that a contract of employment cannot be transferred without the consent of the parties (see *Nokes v Doncaster Amalgamated Collieries Ltd [1940] AC 1014*). However, in *Katsikas v Konstantinidas [1993] IRLR 179*, the European Court of Justice held that the Acquired Rights Directive (above) did not compel an employee to accept the transfer. Now, by virtue of section 33 of the Trade Union Reform and Employment Rights Act 1993 (see also below), Regulation 5 has been amended with effect from 30 August 1993 so as to enable an employee of the transferor to object to becoming employed by the transferee, by informing the transferor or transferee accordingly. In such a case, the employee's contract of employment will not be transferred to the transferee, and will terminate when the undertaking (or as the case may be, the part of it in which the employee is employed) is transferred; however, he will not be treated for any purpose as having been dismissed by the transferor.

The effect is not, however, only one way. The employee's obligations under the contract are also transferred including, for example, any restrictive covenants on his part, since the transferee is deemed retrospectively to be the owner of the undertaking transferred and hence to have *locus standi* to enforce the covenants with regard to customers of the transferred undertaking (*Morris Angel & Son Ltd v Hollande [1993] IRLR 169*).

The Regulation as originally worded was initially thought to apply only to a commercial venture. It was decided in a number of cases that where employees were employed by the company in connection with contracted out tendering for auxiliary services such as catering or cleaning services, this might not constitute a commercial venture of the company so that the change of contractor would not trigger the Regulation (see for example, *Expro Services Ltd v Smith [1991] IRLR 156*; *Port Talbot Engineering Co Ltd v Passmore [1975] IRLR 156*; *Caterleisure Ltd v Scottish Citybank Coaches Ltd, 14 October 1991, EAT 182/91 (unreported)*; see also *Stirling v Dietsmann Management Systems Ltd [1991] IRLR 368*; *O'Connor v Brian Smith Catering Services Ltd, EAT, 18 March 1992*; *Wren v Eastbourne Borough Council and UK Waste Control Ltd [1993] IRLR 425*; *Northern General Hospital National Health Service Trust v Gale [1994] ICR 426*; cf. *Rastill v Automatic Refreshment Services Ltd [1978] ICR 289* (decided in the context of the Employment Protection Act 1975)).

Section 33 of the Trade Union Reform and Employment Rights Act 1993 has made an important amendment to alter this position, by amending the definition of 'undertaking' in the Regulations so as to delete the exclusion of 'any undertaking or part of an undertaking which is not in the nature of a commercial venture'. The amendment also makes it clear that the Regulations, as they apply to the transfer of an undertaking in whole or in part, will apply 'whether or not any property is transferred to the transferee by the transferor'. However, even under the wording of the Regulations before the coming into force of that section, the Court of Appeal held in *Dines v Initial Health Care Services Ltd [1994] IRLR 336* that where a contract under which a company was providing services to a health authority was subsequently awarded to another company as a result of competitive tendering, and the other company engaged the employees who had thereupon been made redundant by the first company, there had been a transfer of an undertaking for the purposes of the Regulations. Accordingly, the employees' continuity of employment had been preserved and the second company was not entitled to vary unilaterally their terms and conditions. Neill LJ said that the European cases (decided in the context of EC Directive 77/187/EEC (the 'Acquired Rights Directive'), referred to above) demonstrated that the fact that another company took over the provision of certain services as a result of competitive tendering did not mean that the first business or undertaking necessarily came to an end. A transfer could take place in two phases, which, in the present case, were:

(*a*) the handing back of the services by the first company to the health authority, and

(*b*)   the grant or handing over of the services by the health authority to
the second company, which continued to be operated by essentially
the same labour force.

In *Belhaven Brewery Co Ltd v Berekis and others (1993) Industrial Relations Law Bulletin 484*, 9, certain public houses, in which four employees
worked, vested in a trustee in bankruptcy who entered into an agreement
with a brewery company for it to manage the public houses for a fixed fee.
It was held that the employees preserved their continuity of employment.

In *Schmidt v Spar- und Leihkasse der früheren Amter Bordesholm, Kiel
und Cronshagen [1994] IRLR 302*, the European Court (Fifth Chamber),
in interpreting the EC Directive referred to above, held that the fact that
an activity transferred from one undertaking to another was, for the
transferor, merely an ancillary activity and that the transfer concerned
only one employee and did not involve the transfer of any tangible assets,
could not have the effect of excluding that activity from the scope of the
Directive. See also *Kenny v South Manchester College [1994] IRLR 265*,
where it was held that the Regulations applied to the transfer of a prison
education service from a local education authority to a college following
competitive tendering. Sir Michael Ogden QC referred to the *Spijkers*
case (below), where Advocate-General Sir Gordon Slynn had stated that
a realistic and robust view was to be taken of Article 1 of the EC
Directive.

The transfer of the undertaking or part of it (see also *Green v Wavertree
Heating and Plumbing Co Ltd [1978] ICR 928*) must be a transfer as a
going concern. That is, where the business or part of the business in question retains its identity. In order to establish whether this is the case, it is
necessary to consider whether having regard to all the facts characterising
the transaction the business was disposed of as a going concern, as would
be indicated *inter alia* by the fact that its operations were actually continued or resumed by the new employer with the same or similar activities
(see the European Court case of *Spijkers v Gebroeders Benedik Abbatoir
cv [1986] 2 CMLR 296*). Whether there is a transfer as a going concern is a
question of fact for the industrial tribunal to decide; and, in the absence of
any material misdirection, a successful appeal from its finding of fact is
difficult (see *UCKATT v Brain [1981] ICR 452; Gilham v Kent County
Council (No 2) [1985] ICR 233; Neale v Hereford & Worcester County
Council [1986] ICR 471; Mannin Management Services Ltd v Ward (1989)
The Times, 9 February 1990 (CA)*). In making a finding of fact, the
industrial tribunal will look at the reality of the situation, regardless of the
label put by the parties on the transaction (see *Rencoule Joiners and
Shopfitters Limited v Hunt (1967) 2 ITR 475*).

Where the transfer is truly that of assets only, this will not be a transfer of
business as a going concern (*Woodhouse v Peter Brotherhood Ltd [1972] 2
QB 520; Melon v Hector Powe Ltd [1981] 1 All ER 313; cf. Kenmir Ltd v
Frizzell [1968] 1 WLR 329; Gibson v Motortune Ltd [1990] ICR 740;
Pittman v Davis Build plc (in liquidation) 9 October 1991, EAT 122/90
(unreported)*). Whether the same economic activities are carried on after

the transfer as were carried on before the transfer is also relevant; and if the activities are different, this may point to the transfer of assets only (*Woodhouse Applebee v Joseph Allnatt Centre EAT 292/80*; see also *Modiwear Ltd v Wallis Fashion Group EAT 535/80*). Also relevant is whether goodwill is transferred (*Ward v Haines Watts [1983] ICR 231*; *Modiwear v Wallis Fashion Group* (above)) or whether contracts with customers are transferred (*Rencoule v Hunt*, see above), or whether the transferor undertakes not to compete with the transferee (*Ault v Gregory (1967) 2 ITR 301*), whether the trading name of the transferor is transferred (*Bonsor v Patara (1967) 2 KIR 23*) and whether brand names are transferred (*Thompsons Soft Drinks Ltd v Quayle EAT 12/81*). Where an employee is employed in a body repair shop of an employer owning a garage business and only the body repair shop is transferred, this may not constitute transfer of a business or its part (see, for example *Gibson v Motortune Ltd [1990] ICR 740*, decided in the context of the Employment Protection (Consolidation) Act 1978). See also *ISS Mediclean v Searle and Wilson, EAT 711/91 (20 July 1992)*; for further analogous cases, see D9.13 above.

The Regulations do not appear to apply to employees of an associated company of the transferor company even if the associated company has made the services of the employees available to the transferor company (see, for example, *Banking, Insurance and Finance Union v Barclays Bank Plc [1987] ICR 495*) except, perhaps, where the associated company has no business of its own and is a front for the transferor companies. Difficult questions may arise where the transferor has a number of businesses, perhaps at the same premises. Where only some of the several businesses of a company are transferred, whether or not a particular employee is affected by the Regulations will depend on which particular business he has predominantly been working in. More difficult is the position of employees common to all the businesses, such as the head office administrative staff, secretaries and messengers. The answer is not clear.

As discussed above, the EC Directive referred to above also applies to a public sector entity which has no commercial characteristics. However, retention of identity is essential and the question is whether the functions performed by the transferor are in fact carried out or resumed by the new entity with the same or similar activities (*Dr Sophie Redmond Stichting v Bartol [1992] IRLR 366*; see also *Rask and Christensen v ISS Kantineservice A/S [1993] IRLR 133*; *Porter v Queen's Medical Centre [1993] IRLR 486*; see now also section 33 of the Trade Union Reform and Employment Rights Act 1993. See, further, *Marleasing SA v La Comercial Internacional de Alimentacion SA (Case No 106-89) (1990) [1993] BCC 421*, and the principles in *Francovich v Italian Republic [1992] IRLR 84*).

The Directive expressly excludes employees' rights to old-age, invalidity or survivors' benefits 'under supplementary company or inter-company pension schemes outside the statutory social security schemes in Member States'. The Regulations re-express this exclusion from transfer as that of any contract (etc.) relating to an 'occupational pension' within the meaning of the Social Security Pensions Act 1975 or any associated rights, liabilities etc. The Directive expressly requires Member States to adopt measures to protect the interests of persons no longer employed in the transferor's business at the time of the transfer in respect of rights conferring on them immediate or prospective entitlement to old-age benefits, including survivors' benefits under supplementary schemes referred to above. No such measures have been adopted in the United Kingdom by means of any implementing Act, statutory instrument or otherwise.

In *Perry v Intec Colleges Ltd [1993] IRLR 56*, the industrial tribunal held that words reflecting the Directive's requirements should be implied in the Regulations so as to transfer to the transferee the rights and obligations referred to in those requirements. However, in *Walden Engineering Co Ltd v Warrener [1993] IRLR 420*, the EAT rejected the *Perry* approach on three grounds:

  (i) the requirement in the Directive was addressed to Member States and did not create any liability on a transferor or transferee in the private sector;

 (ii) in view of *Webb v EMO Air Cargo (UK) Ltd [1993] IRLR 27 (HL)*, where the wording of UK legislation is clear, the tribunal would not feel able to import the requirements of the Directive into the Regulations;

(iii) 'supplementary . . . scheme', as used in the Directive, did not exclude the transferor's contracted-out group pension scheme.

(For excellent analyses of various questions arising under the Regulations, see 'Transfer and employee rights; the regulations' scope' by John McMullen, *The Law Society's Gazette*, 10 January 1990, 'Business Transfers and Statutory Continuity of Employment' by the same author in *Solicitors Journal*, 21 June 1991 and 'Transfer of Undertakings and Community Law' by Brian Napier, in *Solicitors Journal*, 26 February 1993.)

It is debatable whether the intention of the Directive has been sufficiently implemented by the UK Transfer of Undertakings Regulations referred to above. The proper course for raising this issue is not by way of judicial review but in an application to an industrial tribunal: *National Union of Public Employees, The Times (Scots Law Report), 5 May 1993*. Such a question was also successfully raised in the European Court of Justice in *Commission of the European Communities v United Kingdom [1994] IRLR 392*.

The liabilities transferred under the Regulations do not include a protective award made against the transferor under section 189 of the Trade Union and Labour Relations (Consolidation) Act 1992 (as to which see D7.2 above) because of the transferor's failure to consult a union over impending redundancies. The liability for such an award is personal to, and remains with, the transferor (*Angus Jowett & Co v NUTGW [1985] IRLR 326 (EAT)*). However, an employee's accrued right in respect of unfair dismissal prior to the transfer passes to the transferee, if the dismissal was connected with the transfer and was not for an economic, technical or organisational reason entailing changes in the workforce (*Green-Wheeler v Onyx (UK) Ltd (1993) Industrial Relations Law Bulletin 484, 8*).

Where an employee is dismissed in connection with a proposed transfer of auxiliary services in a competitive tendering process, although on a straightforward application of Regulation 5(2) the dismissal is deemed to have been carried out by the transferee, this does not mean that the act of dismissal is deemed to have been done by the transferee to the exclusion of the transferor. To hold otherwise would be inconsistent with the main objective of the Directive and the Regulations (*Allan v Stirling District Council [1994] IRLR 208*, a decision of the EAT in Scotland). Thus there may be circumstances where the transferor, too, can be liable in such a situation (but note that in *Ibex Trading Co Ltd v Walton [1994] IRLR 564*, the EAT in England indicated *obiter* that it would not have been prepared to follow *Allan*).

The sale agreement

D9.17 The agreement with the outside purchaser will again contain safeguards for the receiver and the receivership company and some of the provisions similar to those referred to in D9.8 and D9.14 above. Some of those safeguards may also be relevant to a sale of assets on a piecemeal basis. Excluded from the transfer will be the company's statutory records. The agreement will contain mutual rights of access to records, as appropriate.

The agreement will provide that the purchaser will pay VAT (if any) in addition to the purchase price, although exemption from VAT should be available on the ground that the transfer is that of a going concern (see D9.13 above). (As to preservation of VAT records, following such transfer, see section 49(1)(b) of the Value Added Tax Act 1994; see also the Value Added Tax (Accounting and Records) Regulations 1989 (SI 1989 No 2248).) VAT relief in respect of *fittings* to premises may also be available by extra-statutory concession, as if, like *fixtures*, they are part and parcel of the premises, provided that they are sold (whether or not as part of a going concern) with the premises and fixtures and no separate consideration is allocated to the fittings (see D9.13 above).

The vendor or transferor will be the company '(in receivership) acting by its [receiver] [administrative receiver] ABC'. Sometimes the receiver will be joined as a separate party 'merely for the purposes of receiving the benefit of the waivers and exclusions of liabilities herein in his favour contained.' The agreement will be signed 'For and on behalf of the Vendor/Transferor, ABC Receiver/Administrative Receiver,' followed by (if the company is not already in liquidation) 'attorney and agent'. The conveyance, transfer or assignment of land or any interest in it pursuant to the agreement will need to be by deed, and this applies even to the transfer of an oral periodic tenancy (see *Crago v Julian [1992] 1 All ER 744*).

Section 1 of the Law of Property (Miscellaneous Provisions) Act 1989 and section 130 of the Companies Act 1989, both of which came into force on

31 July 1990, make new provision for the execution of deeds by individuals and companies respectively by prescribing new requirements for the execution of a valid deed and introducing alternative forms of execution without the use of a seal or a common seal. Section 1(2) of the first-named 1989 Act provides that an instrument is not a deed unless (i) it makes it clear on its face that it is intended to be a deed by the person making it or, as the case may be, by the parties to it (whether by describing itself as a deed or expressing itself to be executed or signed as a deed or otherwise) and (ii) it is validly executed by that person or, as the case may be, by one or more of those parties. An instrument is validly executed as a deed by an individual if, and only if (*a*) it is signed (i) by him in the presence of a witness who attests the signature, or (ii) at his direction and in his presence and the presence of two witnesses each of whom attests to the signature, and (*b*) it is delivered as a deed by him or a person authorised to do so on his behalf. Section 1(5) provides that where a solicitor or licensed conveyancer or an agent or employee of a solicitor or licensed conveyancer, in the course of or in connection with a transaction involving the disposition or creation of an interest in land, purports to deliver an instrument as a deed on behalf of a party to the instrument, it shall be conclusively presumed in favour of a purchaser that he is authorised so to deliver the instrument.

Section 36A of the Companies Act 1985, as inserted by section 130 of the Companies Act 1989, provides that in England and Wales a document is executed by a company by the affixing of its common seal but the company need not have a common seal. (As to the execution of documents under the law of Scotland, see section 36B of the Companies Act 1985, as substituted by section 72(1) of the Law Reform (Miscellaneous Provisions) (Scotland) Act 1990.) Whether or not a company has a common seal, a document signed by a director and the secretary of a company, or by two directors of a company, and expressed (in whatever form of words) to be executed by the company has the same effect as if executed under the common seal of the company. A document executed by a company which makes it clear on its face that it is intended by the person or persons making it to be a deed has effect, upon delivery, as a deed; and it is presumed, unless a contrary intention is proved, to be delivered upon its being so executed. (As to the new forms of execution of deeds for the purposes of the Land Registration Act 1925, see the Land Registration (Execution of Deeds) Rules 1990 (SI 1990 No 1010).) There seems to be some doubt, however, whether the new forms of execution by an individual or by a company are applicable where the company executes a deed by its receiver, as distinct from by directors or a director and the secretary. Accordingly, until the position becomes clearer, it is recommended that the old forms of execution continue to be used, so that the document is executed, in the case of an administrative receivership, under the company's common seal or, in the case of an ordinary or administrative receivership, the words 'signed sealed and delivered as a deed' are preferred to the words 'signed as a deed'.

In the case of an ordinary receiver, the attestation clause in respect of the Vendor/Transferor may read:

may make it inevitable that some of the ancillary matters will be dealt with by side letters and supplemental agreements, notwithstanding that the main agreement may contain a provision to the effect that that document sets out the entire agreement of the parties. In *Record v Bell [1991] 4 All ER 471* it was held that for incorporation of any side letter or supplemental agreement to be effective under section 2, the signed (main) document must contain a reference to it and that, where that is the case, it is not necessary for the side letter or supplemental agreement to be signed. In *Tootal Clothing Ltd v Guinea Properties Management Ltd [1992] 41 EG 117*, it was held that the requirement as to effective incorporation only applies to executory contracts. Where, for example, an agreement to grant a lease is completed, a supplemental agreement, which is not effectively incorporated and under which the tenant is entitled to be reimbursed the costs of refurbishment carried out by him, can still be enforced.

Finally, in connection with the sale of assets, it should be noted that a mortgagee cannot, without the leave of the court, sell to himself either alone or with others, or to a trustee for himself, nor to any one employed by him to conduct the sale (see *Farrar v Farrars Ltd (1888) 40 ChD 395*; *Hodson v Dears [1903] 2 Ch 647*; *National Bank of Australasia v United Hand in Hand and Band of Hope Co (1879) 4 App Cas 391*). Equally, this restriction appears to apply to a sale by the receiver as the company's agent directly or indirectly to any of those parties or to himself (see, for an analogy, *Nugent v Nugent [1908] 1 Ch 546*. However, in *Tse Kwong Lam v Wong Chit Sen [1983] BCLC 88* (an appeal to the Privy Council from Hong Kong), it was held that there was no hard and fast rule forbidding a mortgagee from selling the mortgaged property to a company in which he was interested. However, he must show that the sale was in good faith, that he acted fairly, and that he took reasonable steps to secure the best price reasonably obtainable at the time of sale, although he was not obliged to postpone the sale in the hope of obtaining a better price or to adopt a piecemeal method of sale over a substantial period or at risk of loss. Normally, before such a sale, he must take expert advice on methods of sale to secure the best price obtainable and, if the sale is by auction, on the reserve price. If he fails to show that he obtained the best price obtainable, the sale would be set aside, but where it would be inequitable to do so, the mortgagor would be left to the remedy of damages. As to sale by tender, see the House of Lords guidelines on 'referential bids' in *Harvela Investments Ltd v Royal Trust Company of Canada (CI) Ltd [1986] AC 207*. See also the Australian case of *Re Vartex Petroleum Industries Pty Ltd*, referred to in [1990] 5 JIBL-N 1133.

Chapter 10: Conclusion of receivership

Allocation, marshalling and distribution of funds

Law of Property Act 1925 provisions

D10.1 Both in the case of an ordinary receiver and an administrative receiver, the charging document will, almost invariably, set out the order in which the proceeds of realisation should be distributed. Subject thereto, section 109(8) of the Law of Property Act 1925 applies; but see its limitations below. It provides that, subject to the provisions of that Act as to the application of insurance money, the receiver must apply all moneys received by him as follows:

(i) in discharge of all rents, taxes, rates and outgoings affecting the mortgaged property;

(ii) in keeping down all annual sums or other payments, and the interest on all principal sums, having priority to the mortgage;

(iii) in payment of his commission, and of the premium on insurances (if any) properly payable under the mortgage deed or the Act and the cost of executing necessary or proper repairs directed in writing by the mortgagee;

(iv) in payment of the interest accruing due in respect of the principal money due under the mortgage;

(v) in or towards discharge of the principal money *if so directed in writing* by the mortgagee; and

(vi) as to any residue, in payment to the person who, but for the possession of the receiver, would have been entitled to receive the income of which he is appointed receiver or who is otherwise entitled to the mortgaged property.

The following limitations of section 109(8) of the Law of Property Act 1925 must be noted:

(1) The receiver referred to in the section is the receiver only of *the income* of the property concerned (see section 109(3) of that Act) and, therefore, the order of payment laid down in section 109(8) only relates to the income which he may receive.

(2) The section only governs the position between the mortgagor and the mortgagee, and the mortgagee and puisne incumbrancers (*Yourell v Hibernian Bank [1918] AC 372* at *386–387*). It does not enable a third party involved in the order of payment to sue the receiver (*Liverpool Corporation v Hope [1938] 1 KB 751*, but see D8.5 above regarding value added tax).

(3) The categories of expenses to be paid out are limited.

(4)   The section does not deal with the discharge of any prior incumbrances.

Section 105 of the Law of Property Act 1925 deals with the order of payment out of the *proceeds of sale*, but it only applies where the mortgaged property is sold *otherwise than by the receiver*, as the receiver has no power of sale under that Act. The order of payment, subject to the terms of the charge, is as follows:

 (i)   discharge of prior incumbrances to which the sale is not made subject;

(ii)   costs, charges and expenses properly incurred by the mortgagee as incident to the sale or any attempted sale, or otherwise;

(iii)   mortgage money, interest, costs and other money due under the mortgage;

(iv)   as to the residue, the person entitled to the mortgaged property, or authorised to give receipts for the proceeds of sale.

Where the charging document contains express provisions as to the manner of application of the proceeds of realisation by the receiver or his appointor, they will prevail over the Law of Property Act provisions. Again, a third party involved in the order of payment has no right against the appointor or receiver, but the express provisions do not prejudice the rights of any prior incumbrancer or, as regards any residue, any subsequent incumbrancer.

Sometimes, where the receiver has realised sufficient assets to discharge the estimated amounts of his remuneration, receivership expenses, preferential debts and what is due to his appointor, he is asked by the company's directors or liquidator to pass the surplus funds or assets to them or him instead of delaying the release until the amounts are more precisely ascertained. In such a situation, the receiver should be careful not to accede to the request without appropriate indemnities and, if necessary, security, from the directors or the liquidator.

Recourse to liquidation assets re preferential debts

D10.2   What is stated in D10.1 above is subject to the provisions of the Insolvency Act 1986 regarding payment of both receivership preferential debts (section 40, see D7.3 *et seq.* above) and any liquidation preferential debts (section 175, see C14.34 PART C: LIQUIDATIONS) out of the assets comprised in a charge which, *as created*, was a floating charge before any payment to the appointor. These requirements are subject to the qualifications that the payments made in respect of the receivership preferential debts must be recouped, as far as may be, out of the company's assets available for general creditors (section 40(3)) and that recourse to the floating charge assets in respect of the liquidation preferential debts is to be had only so far as the assets available for general creditors are insufficient to meet them (section 175(2)(b)) (see also D10.3 below).

Discharge of liquidation costs

D10.3   It should also be noted that under Rule 4.218 of the Insolvency Rules 1986, the fees, costs and expenses listed there incurred in the *liquidation* (voluntary (as to which, see also section 115) or compulsory) of a company are required to be paid 'out of the assets'. Under the previous legislation, it was held that 'the assets of the company' referred to in the corresponding Rule 195 of the Companies (Winding-up) Rules 1949 (as amended) (which related to costs and expenses in a compulsory winding-up) included assets comprised in a floating charge (*Re Barleycorn Enterprises Ltd [1970] 2 All ER 155*) but only those which had not crystallised (by a receiver's appointment or otherwise) before the winding-up order (*Re Christonette International Ltd [1982] 3 All ER 225*). It would seem that the expression 'assets' in Rule 4.218 would be similarly construed. In view of the *Christonette* case, it was believed that there could be an advantage in providing in the charging document that the floating charge will automatically (or upon notice) crystallise upon a meeting being convened for a voluntary winding-up or a petition being presented for a compulsory winding-up. Such crystallisation could prevent such costs and expenses from being a burden on the assets comprised in the charge, although it would no longer defeat the priority of preferential creditors, since the wider effect of the *Christonette* case (in relation to preferential claims) has been removed by the words 'as created' (see D10.2 above). However, in *Re Portbase (Clothing) Ltd [1993] BCC 96*, Chadwick J refused to follow the *Christonette* case and held that a crystallisation before liquidation of a charge which, as created, was a floating charge did not prevent such claims from ranking ahead of the amount secured by the charge. It is submitted that that decision is incorrect, as there is no justification for allowing the security of a crystallised floating charge to be eroded more than as expressly provided by the legislation. The case comes very close to abolishing the judicial concept of crystallisation altogether. There seems no compelling reason for importing the new statutory definition of 'floating charge', for the purposes of those provisions of the 1986 Act which expressly refer to that expression, into the judicial definition of 'assets' which must refer to the 'assets' at the time the Rule begins to operate.

It would appear that 'assets', in relation to those comprised in a floating charge, must mean the net proceeds of realisation of such assets after the payment of or provision for

(i)   the costs of realisation, and

(ii)   the receiver's remuneration and costs (referable to those assets) and his liabilities (to the extent that he has a right of recourse to the receivership assets in respect of them),

but before the payment of or provision for the receivership and liquidation preferential debts (see D10.2 above), which under sections 40 and 175 have priority only over the claims of the debenture holders.

Marshalling and distribution of funds

D10.4 The receiver will also need to have regard to the rights of any prior, *pari passu*, or (as regards any residue) subsequent chargees and others having interests in the same asset. This may require 'marshalling' of funds. The equitable principle of 'marshalling' is, in effect, that where A has a first charge over, say, both property X and property Y to secure his claim, and B has a second charge over property Y only, then A must have recourse first to property X thus leaving B in a more advantageous position as regards property Y.

The interaction between the rights of preferential creditors and the position of successive chargees may produce a complex system of marshalling and distribution of funds. Two examples, taken first separately (see *Re Woodroffes (Musical Instruments) Ltd* [1985] 2 All ER 908; and *Re Portbase (Clothing) Ltd* [1993] BCC 96 distinguishing and/or not following the former) and then together, will illustrate this:

Example (1)
In relation to property X, A has a first fixed charge (*ab initio*), B a second floating charge and C a third fixed charge. B appoints a receiver but A and C take no action. The order of distribution of the net proceeds of sale of the property will be as follows:

  (i)   A

  (ii) Preferential creditors

  (iii) B

  (iv) C.

Example (2)
In relation to property Y, A has a first floating charge (*ab initio*) and B a second fixed charge (whether by virtue of express agreement (such as a deed of priority—see *Cheah Theam Swee v Equiticorp Finance Group Ltd* [1992] 2 WLR 108 which recognised the right of chargees to alter the priorities *inter se* of their respective charges) or by reason of his having had notice of the prohibitions in the first floating charge—see D6.2 above). B appoints a receiver but A takes no action. According to the *Woodroffes* case (above), the net proceeds of sale of the property will be distributed in the following order:

  (i)   A, to the extent of B's fixed charge

  (ii) Preferential creditors

  (iii) A, as to the balance of its claim

  (iv) B.

However, according to the *Portbase* case (above), where B's charge was created before A's charge and the priority of A's charge over B's charge was conceded by an agreement or deed of priority between the parties, the order will be as follows:

(i)   preferential creditors

(ii)   A

(iii)   B.

It is submitted that on this point (cf. D10.3 above) the *Portbase* decision is to be preferred to the *Woodroffes* decision. Under the latter, the position of preferential creditors can be adversely affected by a prior agreement between two chargeholders. This cannot be right. Under the former, such an agreement can confer an unexpected benefit on preferential creditors. This is acceptable as such a benefit is given at the expense of one of the chargeholders who must be presumed to have voluntarily concurred in that result. The *Portbase* decision is also consistent with the Australian case, *Waters v Widdows [1984] VR 503*.

Examples (1) and (2) together

(i)   Because of their duty to marshal *vis-à-vis* C, A and B must have recourse to their rights in example (2) in relation to Property Y before having recourse to those in example (1) in relation to Property X.

(ii)   It is not clear whether A is under a duty to marshal *vis-à-vis* the preferential creditors in the sense of having recourse to one fund before another, depending on which course (if any) produces a better result for the preferential creditors, without detriment to A. Nor is it clear whether the preferential creditors are under a similar duty *vis-à-vis* C.

Where the assets concerned are subject to a fixed charge in favour of the receiver's appointor but are subject to a prior or subsequent floating charge in favour of another party who has not appointed a receiver or entered into possession, it is debatable whether the onus is (*a*) on the receiver to give effect to the rights (if any) of preferential creditors under that other charge before satisfying the rights of the holder of that other charge, or (*b*) on the holder of that other charge to satisfy the rights of those creditors from the gross payment he receives from the receiver. The language of section 40 does not seem to have the effect of placing the onus on the receiver in this situation. It may be that when the holder of the other charge receives the gross payment from the receiver, the holder will be said to have taken 'possession' of the property comprised in his floating charge. The *Woodroffes* case cited above is not of much assistance here because the facts were materially different in this context.

Another type of marshalling was involved in *Brown v Cork [1985] BCLC 363 (CA)*. Several companies in a group had given cross-guarantees and charges to a bank in respect of the liability of each other. The receiver appointed under those charges was left with a surplus after satisfying the bank's claims. The companies were all in liquidation. It was held that the distribution of the surplus should be on the footing that each company was deemed to have discharged its own indebtedness first and to have borne, so far as it was able to do so, an equal share of the total liabilities under the guarantees; and that any debts due from one company to another could not be set off against what was due to each company from the receiver on the above basis. (See also *Re Ellesmere Brewery Co [1896] 1 QB 75* at *80*; *Deering v Lord Winchelsea (1787) 29 ER 1184*; *Ex parte Snowden (1881) 17 Ch D 44* at *48*; *Re St Clair Sampson Ltd, Ch D, 20 July 1984*; *Duncan, Fox & Co v North and South Wales Bank (1880) 6 App Cas 1, Re Parker, Morgan v Hill [1894] 2 Ch 400*; *Smith v Wood [1929] 1 Ch 14*; *Re A Debtor [1956] CLY 632*; section 5 of the Mercantile Law (Amendment) Act 1856).

As mentioned above, the holders of two mortgages over the same property can agree between themselves to vary the order of priority between the two mortgages. The charging company's consent is not necessary, since it is not adversely affected—it is not entitled to anything until all the mortgages on that property are satisfied in full: *Cheah Theam Swee v Equitycorp Finance Group Ltd [1992] 2 WLR 108* (an appeal to the Privy Council from the New Zealand Court of Appeal).

The receiver must ensure that he is satisfied that the amount of payment which he makes to his appointor is properly due under the appointor's charge. Usually a charging document empowers the chargee to add onto the amount secured all costs, expenses and charges reasonably and properly incurred in enforcing or preserving the security; but this does not include costs incurred by a third party in impugning the title to the mortgage or the exercise of the mortgagee's rights (*Parker-Tweedale v Dunbar Bank Plc (No 2) [1990] 2 All ER 588*).

Conclusions

D10.5 In summary, the receiver may need to treat separately the net proceeds of realisation of various categories of assets by reference to (*a*) the initial or subsequent character (i.e. fixed or floating) of each charge involved (see D10.2 and D10.3 above) and (*b*) priorities between various charges, interests and the assets to which they relate. A further difficulty which may arise is the treatment of any post-receivership trading receipts and the general costs and expenses of the receivership. Unlike in the case of income from a particular property, it may be difficult to attribute such trading receipts to specific underlying assets. The receipts may be the result of the use of a combination of assets, some of which were subject to a fixed charge and others subject to a floating charge or subject to another party's prior or subsequent charge. Similarly, it may be difficult, in arriving at the amount of net proceeds of realisation of various assets, to attribute certain types of post-receivership costs and expenses, including the receiver's remuneration, to specific underlying assets. The legal position on these matters is not entirely clear. In accountancy and commercial terms, it should be possible to make allocation of such receipts, costs and expenses in a way which produces a fair result; perhaps, as a last resort, on a *pro rata* basis according to the value of each asset concerned. A receiver might be well advised not to make any distribution in such a situation except in accordance with the directions of the court (see D4.8 above).

Procedural aspects (in either type of receivership)

D10.6   Where the receiver ceases to act, he must deliver to the Registrar of Companies, within one month after his ceasing to act (section 38(3)(b); but see Rule 3.32 which specifies two months in the case of an administrative receiver), an abstract in the prescribed form (Form 3.6 which applies to administrative receivers only) of receipts and payments from the end of the last period to which the preceding abstract has been delivered (see D4.10 above) or from the date of his appointment (as the case may be) to the date of his ceasing to act (section 38(3)(b)).

Where an *administrative* receiver vacates office, otherwise than by death, he must within 14 days after his vacation of office, send a notice to that effect to the Registrar of Companies (section 45(4); see also Rule 3.35(2)). On vacating office on completion of the receivership, or in consequence of his ceasing to be qualified as an insolvency practitioner, he must forthwith give notice of his doing so to the company (or, if it is in liquidation, to the liquidator) and to the members of the creditors' committee (if any).

Where an *ordinary* receiver ceases to act he must, on so ceasing, give the Registrar of Companies notice to that effect (section 405(2) of the Companies Act 1985 (replaced by section 409 of the Companies Act 1989 which will come into force on a date to be announced) and Form 405(2) in Schedule 3 to the Companies (Forms) Regulations 1985 (SI 1985 No 854)).

Chapter 11: Receivership in Scotland

Introduction

D11.1 What follows is only a summary of the position of floating charge receivers under the law of Scotland.

(1) Receivership under a floating charge in Scotland is governed by separate provisions in the Insolvency Act 1986, in particular sections 50 to 71, as read with sections 462 to 466 of the Companies Act 1985. They derive their origin from the Companies (Floating Charges and Receivers) (Scotland) Act 1972 (which was later incorporated in sections 462 to 487 of the Companies Act 1985, sections 467 to 487 having now been included, with modifications, in the provisions of the Insolvency Act 1986 mentioned above) and its predecessor, the Companies (Floating Charges) (Scotland) Act 1961. Only since the 1961 Act has it been possible for a Scottish company to create a floating charge, and only since the 1972 Act has it been possible under the law of Scotland for a receiver to be appointed under a floating charge over all or any of the property (including uncalled capital) of a company which is registered in Scotland (see section 51 as read with section 120(1)). Separate subsidiary legislation has been made under the Act in respect of receivership in Scotland. This is contained in Part 3 of the Insolvency (Scotland) Rules 1986 (SI 1986 No 1915), as amended by the Insolvency (Scotland) Amendment Rules 1987 (SI 1987 No 1921), ('the Rules') and the Receivers (Scotland) Regulations 1986 (SI 1986 No 1917) ('the Regulations'). Both the Rules and the Regulations contain prescribed forms.

(2) A receiver appointed under the law of either part of Great Britain (England and Wales, or Scotland) in consequence of the company having created a charge which, as created, was a floating charge may exercise his powers in the other part of Great Britain so far as their exercise is not inconsistent with the law applicable there (section 72). Where a floating charge created by an English company extends to its heritable property in Scotland, and an event (specified in the charging document) occurs crystallising that charge into a fixed charge (as far as the question of the validity of the security is concerned), the charge over the Scottish property continues to be a floating charge, so that a receiver appointed under that document has power to sell that property by virtue of the floating charge as crystallised. The crystallisation does not render the charge a void fixed charge as not having been created in accordance with the requirements of the law of Scotland (which does not recognise crystallisation as one of the modes of creating a fixed charge): *Norfolk House plc v Respol Ltd 1992 SLT 235*.

(3) Due to difficulties in creating a hybrid form of fixed and floating charge under the law of Scotland, Scottish general charges are often

purely floating charges. The only way in which a fixed security over corporeal movable property situated in Scotland can be created effectively is by the pledge of that property. For the pledge to be effective, the property must pass from the pledgor to the pledgee so as to give the pledgee absolute control over it. This means that the pledgee must have either actual possession or effective constructive possession. Normally, constructive possession would not be effective if the goods continue to be held by the pledgor. Where the property is held by an independent third party, the transfer of constructive possession can be effected by giving the pledgee an exclusive right of disposition and to receive delivery from the third party, and by giving the third party intimation of the transfer of ownership (see *Inglis v Robertson and Baxter [1898] AC 616*). However, fixed security, including heritable security, can be created over certain other categories of assets, subject to compliance with relevant formalities.

The only way in which a fixed security over book debts due from debtors resident in Scotland can be created is by an assignation followed by intimation to the debtors. If these formalities are not observed, other creditors can challenge the validity of the security (*Re Maudslay Sons and Field [1900] 1 Ch 602*). If the company creating the security is incorporated in Scotland, the assignation is required to be registered at Companies House in Edinburgh on Form 410, although before registering it, the Registrar will need to be satisfied that intimation has been sent to the debtors concerned. However, an unregistered assignment of book debts takes effect in equity if it is governed by English law and its terms effectively create a trust over the book debts sufficient to divest the assignor of the beneficial right to the debts, and will bind a liquidator (*Tay Valley Joinery Ltd v CF Financial Services Ltd (1987) 3 BCC 71*).

In *AIB Finance Ltd v Bank of Scotland [1994] BCC 184*, a company created a floating charge in favour of one party and a standard security (fixed charge) in favour of another, both on the same day. The floating charge contained a 'negative pledge', that is a prohibition against the creation of later charges ranking in priority to or *pari passu* with the floating charge. The floating charge was registered first together with (as is possible under the provisions applicable to Scotland) the 'negative pledge' clause. It was held that the floating charge took priority. This decision was arrived at without regard to the amending provisions of the Companies Act 1989 which are not yet in force (see D2.5 and D6.2 above).

Appointment of receiver

D11.2

(1)   A receiver under a floating charge can be appointed only by or at the instance of the holder of the charge. The holder may make the appointment out of court on the occurrence of any event which, by the terms of the charging instrument, entitles him to make that

appointment. Insofar as not otherwise provided by the charging document, he can appoint a receiver if:

(*a*)   the whole or any part of the principal sum secured by the charge remains outstanding for 21 days after demand;

(*b*)   a period of two months has expired during the whole of which interest due and payable under the charge has been in arrears;

(*c*)   an order has been made or a resolution passed to wind up the company; or

(*d*)   a receiver has been appointed by virtue of any other floating charge created by the company.

(Section 52(1)).

(2)   An appointment by the court can be made in similar circumstances (except that (1)(*d*) above does not apply) or where the court, on the application of the holder of the charge, pronounces itself satisfied that the position of the holder is likely to be prejudiced if no such appointment is made (section 52(2)).

(3)   The appointee must be a qualified insolvency practitioner (section 389) and must not be a body corporate, a firm according to the law of Scotland or an undischarged bankrupt (section 51(3)).

(4)   An out of court appointment is effected by the holder executing an instrument of appointment and filing a certified copy thereof (see Reg 4) with the Registrar of Companies, accompanied by a notice of appointment in the prescribed form, within seven days of execution (section 53, Form 1 (Scot) of the Regulations). The out of court appointment is not effective until it is accepted (not necessarily in writing) by the appointee before the end of the business day next following that on which the instrument of appointment is received by him or on his behalf (section 53(6), Rule 3.1). Subject to that, the appointment is deemed to be made on the day on, and at the time at, which the instrument is so received, as evidenced by a written docket by the appointee or on his behalf. Following the repeal of section 53(3) (by section 74 of the Law Reform (Miscellaneous Provisions) (Scotland) Act 1990) with effect from 1 December 1990, the instrument of appointment is validly executed, where the appointor is a company, if it is signed by a director, by the secretary or by a duly authorised person (i.e. in accordance with section 36B(2) of the Companies Act 1985, as substituted by section 72 of the 1990 Act). Where the appointor is any other person, the signature of the appointor is sufficient. The instrument of appointment can also be executed by any person duly authorised in writing by the holder or, in the case of the holders of a series of secured debentures, by any person authorised by resolution of the debenture holders (section 53(4)).

(5)   A court appointment is effected by the issue by the court of an interlocutor following a petition to the court. A copy of the interlocutor, certified by the clerk of the court, must be delivered by or on behalf

of the petitioning charge holder to the Registrar of Companies, accompanied by a notice in the prescribed form (Form 2 (Scot) of the Regulations), within seven days of the date of the interlocutor or such longer period as the court may allow (section 54).

Effect of appointment

D11.3 On the appointment of a receiver, the floating charge under which he is appointed attaches to the property then subject to the charge; and such attachment has effect as if the charge was a fixed security (but see D11.1(2) above) over the property to which it is attached (sections 53(7) and 54(6)). This does not imply an actual assignation with all the effects that would have on title. Title remains with the company and the receiver does not acquire any right, when suing in the company's name, to deny the ordinary defences (such as set-off and counterclaim) available to third parties against the company (*Callaghan (Myles J) Ltd v City of Glasgow District Council (1987) 3 BCC 337 (Court of Session)*). It should be noted that the charge may have already previously crystallised by reason of the company having gone into liquidation.

Powers of receiver

D11.4 In relation to the property which is attached by virtue of his appointment, the receiver has all the powers, if any, given to him by the charging document. In addition, he has all the powers specified in Schedule 2, insofar as they are not inconsistent with the provisions of the charging document. However, these powers are subject to the rights of any person who (*a*) has effectually executed diligence on the whole or any part of the property of the company prior to the appointment or (*b*) holds, over all or any part of the property of the company, a fixed security or floating charge having priority over, or ranking *pari passu* with, the floating charge under which the receiver is appointed. Any person dealing with the receiver in good faith and for value is not concerned to enquire whether the receiver is acting within his powers (section 55).

Precedence among receivers

D11.5 Receivers may be appointed under successive floating charges, but the appointee under the charge which has priority over the other charge exercises the powers of a receiver to the exclusion of the other receiver(s). Where a receiver is appointed under a prior charge, the powers of any other receiver are suspended until the prior charge ceases to attach to the property in question. Such suspension does not cause the floating charge concerned to cease to attach to the property. The receiver whose powers are suspended is entitled to an indemnity from the receiver under the prior charge in respect of his expenses, charges and liabilities which he may have incurred in the performance of his functions, before he releases the property from his control. In the case of different receivers appointed under charges ranking equally, they are deemed to have been appointed as joint receivers. Receivers who are appointed, or deemed to have been appointed, as joint receivers must act jointly unless the relative instrument(s) otherwise provide(s). The same receiver can be appointed under two or more floating charges (section 56).

Receiver's agency and liability

D11.6 A receiver is deemed to be the agent of the company in relation to the property concerned. Unlike in England and Wales, his agency is not terminated upon the company going into liquidation. The receiver is personally liable on any contract entered into by him in the performance of his functions, except insofar as the contract otherwise provides, and on any contract of employment adopted by him (but, in relation to a contract of employment adopted on or after 15 March 1994, only to the extent of any qualifying liability—for the meaning of which, see D8.3 above); however, he has a right of recourse against the property concerned. (He is not to be taken as having adopted a contract of employment by reason of anything done or omitted to be done within 14 days of his appointment.) Any existing contracts continue in force, subject to their terms, but the receiver does not incur any personal liability on them by virtue only of his appointment (section 57, as amended by the Insolvency Act 1994, which was rushed through Parliament following the Court of Appeal decision in *Re Paramount Airways Ltd (No 3)*—see D8.3 above).

Receiver's remuneration

D11.7 The remuneration is fixed by agreement between the receiver and the holder of the charge. Failing such agreement, or where the amount is disputed by other interested parties, the remuneration may be fixed by the Auditor of the Court of Session on application made to him (section 58).

Preferential debts

D11.8 The debts specified in Schedule 6 (i.e. preferential debts as defined by section 386) are required to be paid out of any assets coming into the hands of the receiver in priority to any claim for principal and interest by the holder of the charge. However, those debts are not preferential debts unless, by the end of six months after advertisement by him for claims in the *Edinburgh Gazette* and in a newspaper circulating in the district where the company carries on business, they have been intimated to him or have become known to him. Any payments made must be recouped as far as may be out of the assets of the company available for payment of ordinary creditors (section 59).

Order of distribution

D11.9

(1)   The order of distribution, as laid down by section 60(1) and (2) is as follows.

    (*a*)   The holder of any fixed security which is over property subject to the floating charge and which ranks prior to, or *pari passu* with, the floating charge.

(*b*)   All persons who have effectually executed diligence on any part of the property comprised in the floating charge.

(*c*)   Creditors in respect of all liabilities, charges and expenses incurred by or on behalf of the receiver.

(*d*)   The receiver in respect of his liabilities, expenses and remuneration, and any indemnity to which he is entitled.

(*e*)   The preferential creditors.

(*f*)   The holder of the charge under which he is appointed, in or towards satisfaction of the debt secured by that charge.

(*g*)   As to any balance, any other receiver or the holder of a fixed security which is over property subject to the floating charge; or the company or its liquidator (as the case may be).

(2)   In the case of doubt, or where a receipt or discharge cannot be obtained, the receiver must consign the amount in question in any joint stock bank of issue in Scotland in the name of the Accountant of the Court for behoof of the person or persons entitled thereto (section 60(3)).

Disposal of property

D11.10   Where the receiver is unable to obtain the consent of any creditor having a prior, *pari passu* or postponed security or interest or of any person who has executed effectual diligence, the court may, on the application of the receiver, authorise him to effect the sale subject, in certain circumstances, to terms as regards the application of the net proceeds or notional proceeds in satisfaction of the rights of the persons concerned and, in all cases, to any other terms which the court deems fit (section 61).

Miscellaneous provisions

D11.11   See section 62, Rules 3.10 and 3.11 and Form 3.3 (Scot) of the Rules and Reg 6 and Form 3 (Scot) of the Regulations (cessation of receiver's appointment), section 63 (court's power to give directions to and require indemnity for the receiver), section 64 (notification of appointment on stationery, etc.), section 65 and Form 4 (Scot) of the Regulations (notice to be given to the company by the receiver), section 66, Rules 3.2 and 3.3 and Form 3.1 (Scot) of the Rules and Form 5 (Scot) of the Regulations (statement of affairs), section 67, Form 3.5 (Scot) of the Rules and Reg 7 (report by receiver, and creditors' meeting), section 68 and Rules 3.4 to 3.8 (committee of creditors), section 69 (enforcement of receiver's duties), Rule 3.9, Form 3.2 (Scot) of the Rules (abstract of receipts and payments) and Rules 3.12 to 3.14 (VAT bad debt relief) which contain provisions similar to those applicable to receivers appointed in England and Wales.

Chapter 12: International aspects of receivership

D12.1 In the eyes of English law, the receiver's appointment under a general charge extends to foreign assets, assuming that the language of the charge has that effect (see, for example, *De Beers Consolidated Mines Ltd v British South Africa Co [1912] AC 52*). However, since English courts have, in practical terms, no extra-territorial jurisdiction *in rem* over foreign assets, the effectiveness of the receiver's position in relation to those assets will depend on whether the charge, insofar as it concerns those assets, is valid and enforceable under the laws of the country where they are situated (or notionally situated) (see, for example, *Re Maudslay Sons and Field [1900] 1 Ch 602*). It will also depend on whether the appointment of a receiver as a means of enforcing the charge, or his status as the company's agent, is recognised in that country and whether the English receiver is deemed to be validly appointed under its laws.

In many countries the concept of a floating charge is unknown. Some recognise such a charge over only limited categories of assets.

Insofar as the receiver is constituted and continues to be the company's agent under the laws of the country of its incorporation (e.g. England), a number of countries will recognise his status as the instrument through which the company can properly act to the exclusion of the directors. Accordingly, subject to the receiver establishing his credentials, they will recognise the receiver's acts to the same extent as the extent to which they would have recognised the acts of the directors. However, they may not generally recognise the substantive effect of his appointment which has an adverse bearing on the rights of any local or other competing creditors.

In the United States of America, although there is no decided case on the point, the better view is that a receiver appointed in England under a general charge does not qualify as a 'foreign representative' under section 101 of the USA Bankruptcy Reform Act 1978 (as amended by the Bankruptcy Code 1984) for the purposes of filing an involuntary case under section 303(b)(4), or a case ancillary to English proceedings under section 304(a), for the company's bankruptcy there. This is because his appointment is essentially contractual in nature for the benefit of his appointor and not under any 'foreign proceedings', that is, those for the purpose of liquidating the estate, adjusting debts by composition, extension or discharge or effecting a reorganisation. This deprives him of some useful remedies in relation to the company's assets situated in the USA, such as injunction, avoidance of antecedent transactions (including execution proceedings) by commencing bankruptcy proceedings there in respect of the company or other appropriate relief.

As to the question of whether a receiver appointed under a charge created by an overseas company over assets in England will be recognised in England, there is no reason in principle why he cannot be (see, for example, the observations of Mummery J in *Re International Bulk Commodities Ltd [1992] 3 WLR 238*, although in other respects that case was not followed in *Re Devon and Somerset Farmers Ltd [1993] BCC 410*; see also D1.4 above). Whether or not such a receiver can ever be an administrative receiver depends on the interpretation of the expression 'company' as used in section 29(2). According to Mummery J in *Re International Bulk Commodities Ltd*, 'company' includes an overseas company which validly creates the sort of charge contemplated by the section, while, according to *Re Devon and Somerset Farmers Ltd*, the expression is confined to a company formed and incorporated under the companies legislation of Great Britain.

In any given case the question of whether a receiver over English assets is validly appointed in the eyes of English law depends on some crucial points viewed under the British private international law system. *First*, the company concerned must have had legal capacity under the laws of the country of its incorporation to create the charge in question (including a floating charge, where relevant). *Secondly*, the company must have created the charge in pursuance of a valid exercise of its powers under the law of that country (including the company's constitution and rules). *Thirdly*, the charge must, as regards its proprietary aspects in relation to the assets in England, be in a form recognised under the laws of England. *Fourthly*, where the charge is required to be registered in England (as to which see D2.5 above), it must be duly registered. *Fifthly*, in so far as the contractual (as distinct from the proprietary) aspects of the charge are relevant, they must have the desired effect under the laws of the country governing those aspects.

As to co-operation between courts of United Kingdom *inter se* and between them and courts of other jurisdictions, see section 426 and A5.2 PART A: GENERAL above.

As stated in D1.4(1) above, it is possible in Great Britain to appoint an administrative receiver of a foreign company under a general charge in the English form created by that company.

It is to be hoped that future years will see some development of the receiver's international status, now that the Insolvency Act 1986 makes more detailed provisions regulating his status and functions, gives him power to use the company's seal and lays down a framework for co-operation between English and foreign courts on insolvency matters.

Part E: Voluntary Arrangements

1. Preliminary   **577**

Background and purpose   577
Scope and initiation of the procedure   579
The nominee's report   580

2. Creditors' and members' meetings for approval   **581**

General provisions   581
Summoning of meetings   581
The chairman of meetings   582
Attendance by company officers   582
Voting rights and requisite majorities and quorums   582
Proceedings to obtain agreement on proposal   585
Protection of secured and preferential creditors   586

3. Procedure after and effect of approval   **587**

Report of results and persons on whom proposal binding   587
The supervisor   588
Challenge of approval or implementation of proposal   588
Court's powers regarding implementation of the proposal   590
Handover of property etc. to supervisor   590
Position of post-proposal creditors   590
Supervisor's accounts, reports, fees, costs, charges and
    expenses and completion formalities   591

4. Taxation aspects   **592**

Part E: Voluntary Arrangements

Chapter 1: Preliminary

E1.1 This Chapter is to be read in conjunction with PART A: GENERAL and, if relevant, PART F: SPECIAL PROVISIONS FOR FINANCIAL MARKETS.

Background and purpose

E1.2 The Voluntary Arrangement procedure in its present form, as it applies to companies, was introduced for the first time by the Insolvency Act 1985 and is now embodied in the Insolvency Act 1986 (sections 1–7). Secondary legislation is mainly contained, in relation to companies registered in England and Wales, in Part 1 of the Insolvency Rules 1986 (SI 1986 No 1925), as amended by the Insolvency (Amendment) Rules 1987 (SI 1987 No 1919), 1989 (SI 1989 No 397), 1991 (SI 1991 No 495) and 1993 (SI 1993 No 602), and, in relation to companies registered in Scotland, in Part I of the Insolvency (Scotland) Rules 1986 (SI 1986 No 1915), as amended by the Insolvency (Scotland) Amendment Rules 1987 (SI 1987 No 1921). Unless otherwise stated, the sections and rules referred to are those of the 1986 Act and Rules (England and Wales), as amended, and the forms are those contained in Schedule 4 to those Rules. (The provisions in Scotland are similar to those applying in England and Wales.) The procedure came into force on 29 December 1986. It is not available in the case of oversea companies or other bodies not registered under the present or previous companies legislation.

The procedure is especially designed for use where a company is in liquidation or under an administration order (section 1(3)), but may be used in other cases by its directors. It is less cumbersome and more practical than the procedure under Part XIII of the Companies Act 1985 relating to arrangements and reconstructions. It does away with class meetings and approval of the court, although recourse to the court for appropriate relief in the case of need is available. It will be of particular value to small and medium-sized companies which urgently need to effect a composition or rescheduling without having to follow a complex, time-consuming procedure. However, as will be seen, the absence of an interim moratorium, and doubts raised by unsatisfactory legislative drafting as to whether a voluntary arrangement is binding on a creditor who did not receive a notice of the creditors' meeting, tend to undermine a wider use of this procedure.

With effect from 1 December 1994, the voluntary arrangement procedure, as it applies to companies, has also been made applicable, with modifications, to insolvent partnerships. The Insolvent Partnerships Order 1994 (SI 1994 No 2421) ('the 1994 Order'), replacing the Insolvent Partnerships Order 1986 (SI 1986 No 2142), provides that sections 1 to 7 of the 1986 Act, in their modified form as set out in Schedule 1 to the 1994 Order, apply to an insolvent partnership (Article 4). The following sections of the 1986 Act also apply, insofar as they relate to company voluntary arrangements: 233 (supply of gas, water, electricity etc.), 247, 248, 249 and 251 (interpretation), 386 and 387 (preferential debts), 388 to 398 (insolvency practitioners), 411, 413, 414 and 419 (subordinate legislation), 423 to 425 (debt avoidance), 426 to 434 (miscellaneous and general), 435 and 436 (interpretation) and 437 to 444 (final provisions) (Article 4). Further, where insolvency orders (that is, in the case of an insolvent partnership or a corporate member, a winding-up order or, in the case of an individual member of the partnership, a bankruptcy order) are made against an insolvent partnership *and* an insolvent member of that partnership in its/his capacity as such, sections 1 to 7 (company voluntary arrangement) apply to corporate members and sections 252 to 263 (individual voluntary arrangement) apply to individual members of the partnership, with the modification that any reference to the creditors of the company or of the debtor, as the case may be, includes a reference to the creditors of the partnership (Article 5(1)). It is not necessary for the application of those sections to a member of the partnership that there should be a winding-up order against the partnership, or an insolvency order against that member (Article 5(2)).

The company voluntary arrangement procedure is confined to companies formed and registered under the companies legislation of Great Britain, and now to insolvent partnerships but, it would appear, to only those partnerships over which the British courts would have winding-up jurisdiction. (This is despite the debate on whether the expression 'company', as used in the Act in relation to the administration and administrative receivership procedures, is confined to companies registered under the domestic companies legislation (see A5.2 PART A: GENERAL, B1.1 PART B: ADMINISTRATION ORDERS, and D1.4 PART D: RECEIVERS).)

The remainder of this part of the book deals with voluntary arrangements in relation to registered companies only. For detailed provisions on partnership voluntary arrangements, the reader should refer to the 1994 Order in full.

The Act does not impose a 'freeze' on the rights of unsecured creditors and others against assets owned or held by the company during the incubation period of the proposal for a voluntary arrangement. (This should be contrasted with the procedure for a voluntary arrangement in the case of an individual which has an in-built temporary moratorium—see sections 252 to 255.) The proposal can thus be seriously undermined if some creditors try to steal a march over others by levying and completing execution, attachment, distress etc. during that period. A proposal is, therefore, more likely to gain the requisite level of acceptance and be successful if it is made during a liquidation, administrative receivership or administration order, where in each case there would be a *de facto* or *de jure* 'freeze'. However, there is a general concern that for a small company to have to resort to such an additional cumbersome and expensive procedure, merely to obtain a temporary moratorium for the purpose of facilitating a simple voluntary arrangement, is like using a 'sledgehammer to crack a nut'. At the time of the revision of this chapter (September 1994), debate had been raging on the consultative paper on the reform of the corporate voluntary arrangement and administration procedures issued by the Department of Trade and Industry in December 1993. The principal proposal of the paper is to introduce an interim moratorium as part of the corporate voluntary arrangement.

Scope and initiation of the procedure

E1.3   A liquidator or administrator of a company or, where there is no liquidation or administration order, its directors (that is either all the directors or, where a proper board resolution has been passed, presumably all or some of the directors acting pursuant to that resolution—see the cases cited at B3.1 PART B: ADMINISTRATION ORDERS in relation to an application by directors for an administration order) may propose a composition in satisfaction of its debts, or a scheme of arrangement of its affairs, providing for its implementation under the supervision of a qualified insolvency practitioner ('the nominee') either as trustee or otherwise (section 1). The nominee may be the liquidator or the administrator himself where the proposal is made by him. Where the company is being wound up by the court, the liquidator must give notice of his proposal to the Official Receiver (Rules 1.10(2) and 1.1(3)). The provisions as to the preparation, contents and notice of the proposal to the intended nominee (except where he is the liquidator or administrator who has made the proposal) are contained in Rules 1.2, 1.3, 1.4, 1.10 and 1.12. As to a discussion of some types of terms of a proposal which may or may not be open to challenge, see E3.3 below; see also E2.7.

It will be noted that an *administrative receiver* has no power to make such a proposal. This is perhaps unfortunate. It may be advantageous, in suitable administrative receivership cases, to have a voluntary arrangement without a prior liquidation (which may involve extra expenses or otherwise adversely affect the value of the business or other assets). The administration procedure is not available during an administrative receivership and the directors may have lost all interest in the company's affairs on the appointment of the administrative receiver.

The corporate voluntary arrangement procedure does not apply to oversea companies, or companies or bodies not registered under the companies legislation of Great Britain. (See the definition of 'company' in section 735 of the Companies Act 1985 as incorporated in the Insolvency Act 1986 by the concluding paragraph of section 251 of the latter Act; see also *Re Devon and Somerset Farmers Ltd [1993] BCC 410*; contrast *Re International Bulk Commodities Ltd [1992] 3 WLR 238*, discussed at D1.4 PART D: RECEIVERS, and *Re Dallhold Estates (UK) Pty Ltd [1992] BCC 394*, discussed at A5.2 PART A: GENERAL.)

The nominee's report

E1.4   Unless he is the liquidator or administrator (who need not pre-pare a report), the nominee must within 28 days (or such longer period as the court may allow) after he is given notice of the proposal prepare and submit to the court a report. The report must include his opinion as to whether meetings of the company's members and creditors should be summoned and, if so, his suggestions about the date, time and place of such meetings (section 2, Rule 1.7). To enable the nominee (where he is not the liquidator or administrator) to prepare the report, the person/s intending to make the proposal must provide the necessary information, including (where the proposal has been made by the directors) the com-pany's statement of affairs (section 2, Rules 1.5, 1.6 and 1.12). Where the nominee has failed to submit a report as required by section 2, the court may direct the appointment of another insolvency practitioner in his place. Further, a modification to the proposal may confer the functions of the nominee on another insolvency practitioner (see E2.1 below).

Chapter 2: Creditors' and members' meetings for approval

General provisions

E2.1   Where the report contains a suggestion regarding meetings, and the nominee is not the liquidator or administrator, the person making the report must summon meetings in accordance with his suggestion unless the court otherwise directs. Where the nominee is the liquidator or administrator, no report will be submitted and the nominee must summon the meetings for such a time, date and place as he thinks fit (section 3). The meetings may approve the proposal with or without modifications or reject it. The modifications may include the appointment of an insolvency practitioner other than the nominee as supervisor (see E3.2 below), but must not include any modification by virtue of which the proposal ceases to be such as is mentioned in E1.3 above (section 4(1) and (2)).

Summoning of meetings

E2.2   Where the proposal has been made by the directors, the nominee must summon the meetings for a date not less than 14, nor more than 28, days from the date on which the nominee's report has been filed in court. He must send notices of the meetings at least 14 days before the date of the respective meetings (in the case of a creditors' meeting) to all creditors specified in the statement of affairs and any other creditors of whom he is otherwise aware and (in the case of a members' meeting) to all persons who, to the best of his belief, are members of the company. Each notice must specify the court to which the nominee's report has been delivered, state the effect of Rule 1.19(1),(3) and (4) (see E2.5 below) and must be accompanied by a copy of the proposal, a copy of the statement of affairs, or, if the nominee thinks fit, a summary of it (to include a list of creditors and the amounts of their debts), and the nominee's comments on the proposal (Rule 1.9). The same requirements apply where the proposal has been made by the administrator or liquidator (who will have received a statement of affairs from the directors during the course of the administration or liquidation proceedings) and either he or another insolvency practitioner is the nominee. There are, however, two differences: firstly, where he himself is the nominee he would not have filed the report (see E1.4 above) and, hence, the maximum period of 28 days stated above does not apply; secondly, the notices are not accompanied by his comments on the proposal (Rules 1.11 and 1.12).

The person summoning the meetings ('the convener') must, in fixing its venue, have regard primarily to the convenience of the creditors. (For commentary on a similar requirement, see 'Meeting the demands of creditors' by Chris Cope, *Accountancy Age*, 4 October 1990.) Meetings must be convened for commencement between 10.00 and 16.00 hours on a business day. The two meetings must be held on the same day and at the same place but the creditors' meeting must be fixed for a time in advance of the time for the members' meeting. Forms of proxy (Form 8.1) must accompany every notice (Rule 1.13: see also A5.2 PART A: GENERAL).

The chairman of meetings

E2.3   The convener (or, if he is unable to attend, another qualified insolvency practitioner, or an employee of the convener or his firm who is experienced in insolvency matters, nominated by the convener) will be the chairman of the two separate meetings (or any combined meetings— see E2.6 below) (Rule 1.14). Proxies can be in favour of the chairman; but he must not use any proxy to vote to increase or reduce the amount of the remuneration or expenses of the nominee or the supervisor (see E3.2 below), unless the proxy specifically directs him to vote that way (Rule 1.15).

Attendance by company officers

E2.4   At least 14 days' notice to attend the meetings must be given by the convener to all directors, and to any other officers or persons who have been directors or officers during the two years preceding the date of the notice, whose presence he requires. The chairman may exclude any present or former director or officer of the company from attendance at a meeting, either completely or for any part of it; and this applies even if a notice of the meeting has been given to him. (Rule 1.16)

Voting rights and requisite majorities and quorums

E2.5   Every creditor who was given notice of the creditors' meeting is entitled to vote at that meeting or any adjournment of it. (If this provision is interpreted literally, it would mean that a creditor who was entitled (or whom the convener intended) to be given notice but was not, cannot vote even if he chooses to attend the meeting of his own volition (personally or by proxy) and has notified his claim before the meeting (see (*a*) below). This would be a strange situation.) Votes are calculated according to the amount of the creditor's debt at the date of the meeting or (where applicable) at the date of the company's going into liquidation or of the administration order (Rule 1.17(1) and (2)).

The following points on the right of a creditor to vote in respect of his claim or part of his claim should be noted:

(*a*)   He cannot vote where the claim was not notified in writing to the chairman or the convener either at or before the meeting.

(*b*)   He cannot vote where the claim or part is secured. There has been some out-of-court controversy as to whether, where the debt is only partly secured, the creditor can vote in respect of the unsecured part or is deprived of a vote completely. However, in *Calor Gas Ltd v*

Piercy and others [1994] BCC 69, decided in the context of a similar rule (Rule 5.18(3)(b)) relating to individual voluntary arrangements) the deputy High Court judge held that, although the rule was ambiguous, on its true interpretation the creditor was entitled to vote in respect of the unsecured part.

(c)   Where the claim is in respect of a debt wholly or partly on, or secured by, a current bill of exchange or promissory note, he must estimate and deduct from his claim (for the purposes of voting, but not of any distribution under the arrangement) the value of his rights against every party (not being one against whom a bankruptcy order has been made or which has gone into liquidation) who is liable to him on the bill or note antecedently to the company.

(d)   He cannot vote if the claim is for an unliquidated amount or if its value is not ascertained, except where the chairman agrees to put an estimated minimum value on it for the purpose of entitlement to vote. In *Re Cranley Mansions Ltd: Saigol v Goldstein and another [1994] BCC 576*, Ferris J held that the expression 'agrees' requires some element of bilateral concurrence between the chairman and the creditor concerned. It was therefore not open to the chairman unilaterally to put an arbitrary value of £1 on the creditor's claim (as has been the practice among insolvency practitioners in such cases) without an invitation from the creditor or without some attempt being made to assess the value of the claim; otherwise the creditor would be at a dual disadvantage of not having sufficient voting strength which might determine the outcome of the proposals and yet being bound by the proposals (see E3.1 below). If such a claim is incapable of any valuation then, unless the creditor otherwise agrees, no value should be put, and no vote should be allowed, rather than a nominal value of £1 being put.

The mere fact that a creditor's claim under a guarantee given by the company is disputed by the company or the chairman of the meeting does not make the claim one for an unliquidated amount or one whose value is not ascertained. The proper course for the chairman, when in doubt whether to admit the claim because of a dispute, is (as stated below) to mark it as objected to and allow the creditor to vote subject to his vote being subsequently declared invalid if the objection is sustained (see *Re a Debtor (No 222 of 1990), ex parte the Bank of Ireland and others [1992] BCLC 137*, an individual voluntary arrangement case).

(e)   It is debatable whether the analogy of *Re British & Commonwealth Holdings plc (No 3) [1992] BCC 58* will apply here in relation to any contractual subordinated creditors. In that case, which concerned a scheme of arrangement under section 425 of the Companies Act 1985, contrary to popular belief, the efficacy of contractual subordination of debts in a future liquidation was upheld and a class meeting of subordinated creditors who stood to receive nothing under the terms of the scheme was dispensed with.

Any decision on the question of entitlement to vote is made by the chairman but is subject to appeal to the court. If he is in doubt whether a claim should be admitted or rejected, he must mark it as objected to and allow the creditor to vote, subject to the vote being subsequently declared invalid by the court on an appeal. Any appeal against the chairman's decision can be made by a creditor or member but must be made before the end of the period of 28 days beginning with the first day on which each of the reports referred to in E3.1 below has been made to the court. If the chairman's decision is reversed or varied or a creditor's vote is declared invalid, the court may order another meeting or make such order as it thinks just, but only if it considers that the matter is such as gives rise to unfair prejudice or material irregularity. The chairman is not liable for any costs incurred by the appellant (Rules 1.17 and 1.19). However, notwithstanding this, in *Re a Debtor (No 222 of 1990)* referred to in (*d*) above, Harman J in a subsequent judgment (*(No 2)* [*1993*] *BCLC 233*) made an order for costs against the chairman personally in exercise of his discretion under the Rules of the Supreme Court on the ground that the chairman, as nominee of the arrangement, had fallen far short of the professional standard expected of him.

At the creditors' meeting, a majority in excess of three-quarters in value of the creditors present in person or by proxy and voting is required to pass any resolution approving any proposal or modification (Rule 1.19(1)—but see below). (As to detailed provisions regarding proxies and corporate representation and restrictions against a proxy holder voting on a matter involving remuneration for himself or his associate, see Rules 8.1 to 8.7 and A6.1 PART A: GENERAL.) However, a resolution is invalid if those voting against it include more than half in value of the creditors, counting 'in the latter' only those (i) to whom notice of the meeting was sent, (ii) who are not excluded from voting as stated above and (iii) who are not, to the best of the chairman's belief, persons connected with the company (sections 249 and 435) (as to which the chairman may rely on the information provided by the company's statement of affairs or otherwise in accordance with Rules 1.1 to 1.30). The chairman's decision in this respect is subject to appeal as stated above (Rule 1.19(4) and (7)). The effect of (iii), as read with the quoted words, appears to be to require a two-stage count. At first stage, all votes, including those of the connected persons, which are cast at the meeting are counted. If more than three-quarters of those votes are cast for the resolution, the second stage becomes operative. At that stage, the value of all votes cast against, including those of connected persons present or represented and voting against, is compared with one-half of the total value of the claims of *all* the creditors (not necessarily only those present or represented and voting) who were entitled to vote, having regard to (*a*) and (*d*) above, except the value of the claims of all connected creditors whatever the manner of their voting, or voting entitlement status, and whether or not present or represented. If the votes cast against exceed one-half of such total value, the resolution is invalid.

As regards the meetings of members, they vote according to the rights attaching to their shares in accordance with the company's articles (Rule

1.18(1)). Where no voting rights attach to a member's shares, he is nevertheless entitled to vote for or against the proposal or any modification thereof (Rule 1.18(2)). The expression 'shares' includes any other interest which the person concerned may have as a member of the company. (Rule 1.18(3)). Subject to any express provision of the articles, a resolution at the meeting is passed if voted for by more than one-half in value of the members present in person or by proxy and voting (Rule 1.20(1)). (An amendment to Rule 1.20(1), as inserted by SI 1987 No 1919 with effect from 11 January 1988, makes it clear that the value of members is determined by reference to the number of votes conferred on each member by the company's articles). It is provided that in determining whether a majority has been obtained, any vote cast in accordance with Rule 1.18(2) (see the second sentence of this paragraph, above) is not to be counted (Rule 1.20(2)). The point of this latter provision is not clear.

The requisite quorum for a creditors' meeting is at least one creditor entitled to vote present or represented by a proxy or a corporate representative and that for a members' meeting at least two members present or so represented, in either case, subject as stated in A6.1 and A6.2 PART A: GENERAL.

Where under the proposal, as approved, at each meeting two or more insolvency practitioners are appointed to act as supervisors, a resolution may be passed by the creditors' meeting as to whether acts to be done in connection with the arrangement may be done by any one of them, or must be done by both or all. Such a resolution may even be passed by the creditors in anticipation of the arrangement being approved by the members' meeting. At either meeting a resolution may be moved for the appointment of some person other than the nominee to be supervisor (see E2.1 above) provided that there is produced to the chairman at or before the meeting that person's written consent to act (unless he is present and then and there signifies his consent) and his written confirmation that he is qualified to act as an insolvency practitioner in relation to the company (Rule 1.22). As to what happens if the resolutions of the two meetings on the choice of the supervisor conflict with each other, see E2.6 below.

Proceedings to obtain agreement on proposal

E2.6 The meetings of members and creditors may from time to time be adjourned. If the chairman thinks fit, for the purpose of obtaining the simultaneous agreement of the meetings to the proposal (with the same modifications, if any), the meetings may be held together (Rule 1.21(1)).

If the requisite majority for the approval of the arrangement (with the same modifications, if any) has not been obtained from both meetings, the chairman may, and must if it is so resolved, adjourn the meetings for not more than 14 days. Where the proposal of the arrangement has been made by the directors, notice of such adjournment must be given by the nominee to the court. If there are further adjournments, the final adjournment must not be to a day later than 14 days after the date on which the meetings were originally held. There must not be an adjournment of either meeting unless the other is adjourned to the same business day (Rule 1.21(2) to (5)).

If following any final adjournment of the meetings, the proposal (with the same modifications, if any) is not agreed by both meetings, it is deemed rejected (Rule 1.21(6)).

It should be noted that the proposal does not become effective or binding unless and until it is approved by both the meetings (held separately or together—see above). This seems to suggest that the proposal or any modifications thereto must be approved by both meetings in identical terms. There is no machinery for resolving any conflict between the decisions of the two meetings, even as to the choice of supervisor. It is debatable whether in every case the requirement for approval by a members' meeting is justified or desirable. Where the company is clearly insolvent and is likely to remain so after the implementation of the proposal, the members would have no tangible interest in opposing it and should not have a right to 'veto' it by either voting against it or simply refraining from attending the meeting, even to form a quorum of two members (as distinct from, ironically, a quorum of one creditor in the case of a creditors' meeting—see E2.5 above).

Protection of secured and preferential creditors

E2.7   A meeting cannot approve a proposal or modification which affects the right of a secured creditor to enforce his security, or under which a preferential debt (for details see D7.4 PART D: RECEIVERS) is to be paid otherwise than in priority to non-preferential debts or is discriminated as against another preferential debt, unless the secured or preferential creditor concerned concurs (section 4(3) and (4)).

However, the assets in the hands of the supervisor of the voluntary arrangement may constitute trust assets held by him as trustee for the creditors participating in the voluntary arrangement so that, for example, where those assets are comprised in a floating charge created by the company under which no receiver has been appointed, neither the holder of the charge nor a receiver subsequently appointed under it is entitled to those assets (see *Re Leisure Study Group Ltd, Chancery Division, 26 January 1993 (unreported), per* Harman J).

Chapter 3: Procedure after and effect of approval

Report of results and persons on whom proposal binding

E3.1   The results of the meetings of the creditors and the members are to be reported by the chairman thereof to the court within four days of the meetings being held and, immediately after reporting to the court, to certain other classes of persons (section 4(6), Rule 1.24, Form 1.1). The proposal, once approved by the meetings by the requisite respective majorities mentioned in E2.5 above, takes effect as if made by the company at the creditors' meeting. It becomes binding on every person who in accordance with the Rules had notice of, and was entitled to vote at, the meeting regardless of whether he was present or represented thereat (section 5(2)). On its literal interpretation, this provision suggests that a creditor who, though entitled (or intended by the convener) to be given notice, was not given notice is not bound by the proposal. In *Re a Debtor (No 64 of 1992)* [1994] *1 WLR 264*, Mr Colin Rimer QC, sitting as a Deputy Judge, in interpreting section 260 relating to individual voluntary arrangements and containing similar language, held that a creditor who did not actually receive the notice was not bound by the arrangement. 'Had notice' meant 'had received notice' rather than constructive notice, or presumed notice under Rule 12.16. The only presumption under that rule was as to the validity of the summoning and holding of the meeting; it did not purport to raise a presumption that a creditor had notice of the meeting when in fact he had none. Further, there was no case of constructive notice in the sense of the creditor being put on notice of matters which would or ought to lead him to discover the fact of the scheduled meeting. In this connection, *Re Thundercrest Ltd* [1994] *BCC 857 1994* may also be relevant, although it concerned a notice of provisional allotment by a company of shares. It was held that a provision that notice is deemed to have been effected at the expiration of 24 hours after its due posting could not be relied upon where a notice sent by recorded delivery had been returned to the sender.

It is submitted that if the above arguments are correct, the class of persons on whom it becomes binding is unduly restrictive. For example, a creditor who was excluded from voting under any of the provisions summarised in E2.5 above might not be bound by the approval and might take legal proceedings to enforce payment of his claim, thereby undermining the whole voluntary arrangement. Unclear legislative drafting has, again, given rise to confusion.

This confusion has been compounded by the decisions in two recent cases which have tended to restrict the categories of debts coming within the scope of the voluntary arrangement regime. In *Re Wisepark Ltd* [1994] *BCC 221*, it was held that a claim for costs of legal proceedings, which had not yet been awarded to the claimant by an order of the court in charge of those proceedings, was not a contingent liability within section 382. It was a claim which only came into existence when the court made an order for costs. Accordingly, such a claim could not be made in the voluntary arrangement; otherwise, it would fall to be adjudicated upon by the supervisor in the absence of agreement, thus involving him in effectively making an order for costs which was exclusively in the discretion of the court under section 51 of the Supreme Court Act 1981. Such a claim thereby survived the voluntary arrangement and could be pursued against the debtor company (if made good by the court order). Likewise, in *Burford Midland Properties Ltd v Marley Extrusions Ltd [1994] BCC 604*, the voluntary arrangement scheme was expressed to be binding on all creditors, present or potential, whether their claims were future, present or contingent or otherwise. It was held that rent becoming due to a landlord after the date the arrangement became effective was not within the scope of the arrangement, and the landlord was free to take recovery action. The basis of the decision was that, unlike arrears of rent, future rent was not an obligation to pay but was a right essentially of property.

The supervisor

E3.2   After the approval, the person who is for the time being carrying out the functions conferred, by virtue of the approval, on the nominee or, by virtue of section 2(4) or 4(2), on a person other than the nominee (see E1.4 and E2.1 above) becomes 'the supervisor' (section 7(2)).

Challenge of approval or implementation of proposal

E3.3   The nominee, his successor, or a creditor who was entitled to vote at the meeting, or the administrator or liquidator, may by application to the court challenge the approval on the ground that the proposal unfairly prejudices the interests of a creditor, member or 'contributory' (as to which see C5.30 PART C: LIQUIDATIONS) or that there has been some material irregularity at or in relation to the meeting. Any such application must be made within the period of 28 days from the date on which each of the reports (see E3.1 above) is filed. Note that there is no express right to challenge the proposal on the ground that it is outside the scope of the relevant statutory provisions. (*Quaere* whether this means that no such right is available at all or that the challenge can be pursued under the ordinary remedies, unfettered by the 28-day time limit.) The court may make various orders on the application (section 6, Rule 1.25, Form 1.2).

It is not clear what types of terms of a voluntary arrangement proposal may be outside the scope of section 1(1) (see E1.3 above) or may be 'unfairly prejudicial' within the meaning of section 6 (see preceding paragraph). For example—

(*a*)   As to the scope, bearing in mind the words in section 1(1) 'a composition in satisfaction of *its* (the company's) debts or a scheme of arrangement of *its* affairs', can the arrangement confer an incidental benefit on a third party (such as by restricting the right of the creditors to enforce their claims, connected with the company's affairs, against the third party without any or adequate consideration flowing from him)?

(*b*)   If different categories of unsecured non-preferential creditors are to rank for distribution in different orders, is this 'unfair prejudice'?

In the administration of *Primlaks (UK) Ltd, December 1989 (unreported and undecided)*, both such questions were involved but the matter was adjourned before judgment, pending a possible compromise.

In *Re FMS Financial Management Services Ltd (1989) 5 BCC 191*, a voluntary arrangement, proposed by the administrators and duly approved, related to a securities dealing company which had persuaded its clients to buy shares in a USA corporation which turned out to be worthless. Money and securities in relation to such purchases in the hands of the administrators which could be identified as belonging to particular clients were returned to those clients pursuant to an earlier direction of the court; and they were excluded from the voluntary arrangement as creditors. The remaining money and securities were to be divided among the remaining client creditors. All other money and assets were to be divided among the trade creditors not involved in the purchases. A question arose as to whether the clients who received the identified but worthless securities should not be treated as client creditors. (They appeared to have a strong claim in damages for misrepresentation.) On the administrators' application for directions, Hoffmann J directed that they should be so treated, as it would be a matter of reproach if they made such a claim only to find that the court had authorised distribution without leaving anything for them.

In *Re Mohammed Naeem, Law Society's Gazette, 20 December 1989*, a landlord claiming arrears of rent and having a right of forfeiture (subject to the power of the court to grant relief against it) was treated on the same basis as other unsecured non-preferential creditors in a voluntary arrangement of a bankrupt under different provisions of the Insolvency Act 1986 (relating to voluntary arrangements by individuals) which contained a similar 'unfair prejudice' provision. The landlord's challenge under that provision failed.

For an example of material irregularity at or in relation to the creditors' meeting, see *Re a Debtor (No 222 of 1990), ex parte the Bank of Ireland and others [1992] BCLC 137* (an individual voluntary arrangement case), where a refusal by the chairman to allow a disputed creditor's claim under a guarantee given by the debtor, on the ground that it was a claim for an unliquidated amount or a claim whose value had not been ascertained, was held to be a material irregularity and the voluntary arrangement was revoked.

In *Re a Debtor (No 259 of 1990) [1992] 1 WLR 226*, a case relating to an individual voluntary arrangement, Hoffmann J, in interpreting section 262(1)(a), which in all essential respects is similar to section 6 above, held (i) that the 'unfair prejudice' complained of must be brought about by the terms of the voluntary arrangement itself (as distinct from other factors such as the claims of some creditors, or past dealings by the debtor with property, being suspect) and that (ii) failure to give notice of the creditors' meeting to a creditor is not a 'material irregularity' unless his vote could have swung the decision of the meeting.

It is hoped that section 6 will be interpreted sufficiently flexibly to avoid injustice. For example, where the creditors' vote approving the arrangement was influenced by certain material factual statements contained in the voluntary arrangement document or made at the meeting which turn out to be incorrect, it would be unfair if the approval could not be challenged on the ground of material prejudice or material irregularity at or in relation to the meeting.

During the implementation of the proposal, any creditor or other person dissatisfied with any act, omission or decision of the supervisor may apply to the court for appropriate relief. The supervisor himself may apply to the court for directions (section 7(3) and (4)). In *Re Leisure Study Group Ltd*, referred to in E2.7 above, it was held that in the circumstances of the case recited there, the administrative receiver had no *locus standi* to make an application under section 7 in relation to the assets which the supervisor had received before the crystallisation of the floating charge.

Court's powers regarding implementation of the proposal

E3.4   If the company is being wound up or an administration order is in force, the court may stay (or sist) all proceedings in the winding up, or discharge the administration order, or give appropriate directions as to the conduct of the winding up or administration, for facilitating the implementation of the approved voluntary arrangement. The court must not, however, exercise its powers in these respects before the expiration of a period of 28 days from the date on which the reports of the result of the meetings were made to the court, or whilst an application to challenge the approval or implementation (see E3.3 above), or an appeal against such application, is pending (section 5(3) and (4)).

Handover of property etc., to supervisor

E3.5   After the approval of the arrangement, the directors, or any liquidator or administrator (if he is a person other than the supervisor), must forthwith do all that is required for putting the supervisor in possession of the assets included in the arrangement (Rule 1.23(1)). On taking possession, the supervisor must pay the liquidator or administrator (if any): (i) his fees, costs, charges and expenses properly incurred and payable under the Act or the Rules (as to which see E3.7 below) and (ii) any advances made in respect of the company together with interest on such advances as provided in Rule 1.23(2).

Position of post-proposal creditors

E3.6   It is not clear whether a person who advances money or supplies goods or services to a company which is not already in liquidation or receivership or under an administration order, or otherwise becomes its creditor under a contract entered into with it after the proposal is put forward and before it is approved or comes into effect, will be entitled to be paid in respect of such supply or contract in priority to existing creditors.

Presumably, specific provisions would be made in the proposal for the discharge of such claims before all other claims, as part of the expenses of the liquidation or administration (if already in force) or of the implementation of arrangements.

Supervisor's accounts, reports, fees, costs, charges and expenses and completion formalities

E3.7   Rules 1.26 to 1.29 and Form 1.4 deal with these matters. The fees, costs, charges and expenses that may be incurred for any of the purposes of the voluntary arrangement are (*a*) any disbursements made by the nominee prior to the approval of the arrangement, and any remuneration for his services as such agreed between himself and the company (or, as the case may be, the administrator or liquidator) and (*b*) any fees, costs, charges or expenses which (i) are sanctioned by the terms of the arrangement or (ii) would be payable, or correspond to those which would be payable, in an administration or winding up.

Not more than 28 days after the final completion of the voluntary arrangement, the supervisor must notify all the creditors and members who are bound by it that the arrangement has been fully implemented. The notice must be accompanied by the supervisor's report summarising all receipts and payments, and explaining any difference in the actual implementation as compared with the proposal as approved. Within the same period he must send to the Registrar of Companies and to the court a copy of the notice and a copy of the report. The time limit may be extended by the court.

Chapter 4: Taxation aspects

E4.1   Where the debt due by the company to a creditor represents a trading expense which the company has deducted in calculating its taxable profits or losses carried forward, any part of that debt waived or released by the creditor under a voluntary arrangement was previously required by section 94 of the Income and Corporation Taxes Act 1988 to be brought back into charge as a taxable receipt. In practice, this may not have resulted in any tax payable by the company if (as was often the case) it had sufficient accumulated tax losses against which the deemed taxable receipt could be wholly set. However, under section 144 of the Finance Act 1994, which amended section 94 above, any such debt waived or released on or after 30 November 1993 will not be required to be brought back. Further, that section of the 1994 Act also substitutes a new paragraph (j) in section 74 of the 1988 Act so that a creditor so waiving or releasing part of his debt is no longer required, before deducting that part from his taxable profits, to show that such part is not greater than that he would have lost if the company had gone into liquidation. These two changes remove some of the disincentives to debtors and creditors against the use of the voluntary arrangement procedure. As to other tax aspects of voluntary arrangements and the attitude of the fiscal authorities to voluntary arrangements, see the excellent article entitled 'Tax Aspects of Voluntary Arrangements' by Richard Setchim and Keith Jewitt in *(1991) 4 Insolvency Intelligence 27.*

As to VAT bad debt relief, the case of *AEG (UK) Ltd [1994] Simon's Tax Intelligence 135* may be noted here. In the terms of a corporate voluntary arrangement as duly approved, a creditor who had not voted in favour of the arrangement received redeemable preference shares, in respect of the debt due to him, which proved worthless. The VAT Tribunal held that it was not entitled to go behind the documentary evidence showing the approval of the arrangement and to enquire into the validity of the creditors' meeting. Accordingly, there was no outstanding amount of debt in respect of which the bad debt relief (as to which see D4.7 PART D: RECEIVERS) could be claimed.

(See also PART H: TAXATION.)

Part F: Special Provisions for Financial Markets

1. Introduction   **595**

Scope of the part   595
How financial markets work   596

2. Insolvency-related problems before CA 1989, Part VII   **598**

Preferences and transactions at an undervalue   598
'Cherry-picking'   598
Bilateral set-off   600
Specific performance   601
Fungibility   601
Disposition after commencement of formal insolvency   602
'Charge Card' case   602
'British Eagle' problem   603
Novation of contracts or market guarantee   603

3. Use of special contracts to minimise problems   **604**

Aggregation or unity clause   604
Acceleration clause   604
Quantification clause   605
Bilateral netting-off clause   605
'Flawed asset' clause   605
Individual charge (fixed and/or floating)   606

4. Use of market default rules to minimise problems   **607**

Closing out, reversal, quantification and bilateral netting-off   607
Market charge—fixed and/or floating and margins   607

5. Residual problems before CA 1989, Part VII   **608**

Preferences and transactions at an undervalue   608
'Cherry-picking'   608
Bilateral set-off   608
Specific performance   608
Fungibility   609
Disposition after commencement of insolvency   609
'Charge Card' case   609
'British Eagle' problem   609
Novation of contracts or market guarantee   609

6. CA 1989, Part VII—effect on general law of insolvency   **610**

Introduction   610
Application of Part VII   610

Meanings of a 'recognised investment exchange', 'recognised
    clearing house', 'overseas investment exchange' and
    'overseas clearing house'   612
Requirements as to default rules   612
Substantive provisions of Part VII which modify the general
    law of insolvency   613
Precedence of exchange or clearing house proceedings
    over insolvency proceedings   613
Duty of others to assist   614
Protection of assets   615
Provision for dividend in liquidation to market creditors   615
Modification of office-holder's functions   615
Default proceedings immune from stay of action,
    proceedings etc. in administration or liquidation   615
Completion of default proceedings   615
Net sum payable on completion of default proceedings   616
No disclaimer or rescission   616
Dispositions after commencement of compulsory winding-up
    not necessarily void   616
Preferences and transactions at an undervalue not
    necessarily voidable   617
Directions as to invoking default rules   617
Market charges protected from the impact of certain
    insolvency provisions   618
Enforcement of security in an administration   622
Disposition after commencement of compulsory winding-up
    —market charges   623
Modification of general insolvency law—other types of charges   624
Margins (market property) not affected by certain other interests 624
Priority of market charge over unpaid vendor's lien and of
    floating market charge over subsequent charges   624
Restrictions against enforcement by unsecured creditors
    against margins   625
Discretionary retrospective effect of Part VII   625
'The court' and cross-frontier insolvency   626
Indemnities for office-holders, markets etc.   626
Interaction with the Financial Services Act 1986   627

7. Overall effect of Part VII   **628**

Part F: Special Provisions for Financial Markets

Chapter 1: Introduction

Scope of the part

F1.1   This part deals with corporate insolvencies in financial markets and is to be read in conjunction with the other chapters on Insolvency in this book (PART A: GENERAL to PART E: VOLUNTARY ARRANGEMENTS).

This part focuses on Part VII of the Companies Act 1989 ('CA 1989'). Part VII was partially brought into force on 25 March 1991 by the Companies Act 1989 (Commencement No 9 and Saving and Transitional Provisions) Order 1991 (SI 1991 No 488), but only insofar as was necessary to enable regulations to be made under various provisions of Part VII. Those regulations (the Financial Markets and Insolvency Regulations 1991 (SI 1991 No 880)) came into force on 25 April 1991, at the same time as the substantive provisions of Part VII were (with certain exceptions) brought into force by the Companies Act 1989 (Commencement No 10 and Saving Provisions) Order 1991 (SI 1991 No 878). Those Regulations (which, as amended by the Financial Markets and Insolvency (Amendment) Regulations 1992 (SI 1992 No 716), are referred to below as 'the Regulations') supplement, amend or modify various provisions of Part VII. Unless otherwise stated, a reference in this part to a section or to a regulation is to a section of the Companies Act 1989 or, as the case may be, to a regulation in the Regulations.

The provisions of Part VII, as read with the Regulations, are considered in detail later in this part. However, to understand how Part VII modifies the general law of insolvency as it applies to financial markets, it will be useful to consider first how a financial market ('the market' which expression, as used in this part, means an investment exchange or a clearing house) works and what sort of insolvency-related problems have hitherto been involved in its workings. Accordingly, this part is arranged in the following order of main headings.

(*a*)   Introduction—how financial markets work.

(*b*)   Insolvency-related problems before CA 1989, Part VII.

(*c*)   Use of special contracts to minimise problems.

(*d*) Use of market default rules to minimise problems.

(*e*) Residual problems before CA 1989, Part VII.

(*f*) CA 1989, Part VII—effect on general law of insolvency.

(*g*) Conclusions.

How financial markets work

Terms governing market contracts

F1.2 Typically, on a given business day, a market member (in this chapter assumed to be a limited company and called 'the first party') enters into or performs a series of contracts on the market ('market contracts') with a number of other market members ('counterparties'). Some of these contracts are for the purchase, and others are for the sale, of securities (which expression in this chapter includes currencies, commodities, option contracts and futures) of types traded on the particular market for delivery at future dates.

All deals are either expressed to be or impliedly subject to the rules, custom and usages of that market. They are not usually covered by any special contracts between the parties. Market members are liable to each other as principals on all market contracts entered into between them, although in reality they may be acting for their clients as disclosed or undisclosed principals. In some markets, contracting members are required to deposit cash or readily realisable securities ('margins') as cover for any fluctuation in market prices in the event of non-performance by them.

In some of the markets where settlement and transfer of securities is effected electronically, there are also arrangements for a simultaneous electronic transfer of funds, representing the contract consideration ('assured payment'), by the transferee's bank, usually pursuant to pre-arranged banking facilities. Repayment of the facilities may be secured by a fixed and/or floating charge created by the transferee in favour of the bank but so that, unless and until the transferee has been declared a defaulter, any charge over the transferee's securities (or beneficial entitlement to securities) in the market or clearing house system does not bite in a way which would interfere with or prevent settlement of transactions in accordance with the market rules.

Role of the markets

F1.3 The markets provide their members with a centralised framework for recording, processing and clearing market contracts. Their governing bodies oversee compliance with, and, where necessary, enforce their default and disciplinary rules. The markets themselves are subject to the overall regulatory régime of the Financial Services Act 1986 (as amended, *inter alia*, by the Companies Act 1989) and the delegated legislation made under it. As a general rule, parties trading on the financial markets need authorisation, either directly by the Secretary of State or by being members of recognised self-regulating organisations ('SROs') under the Financial Services Act 1986. They are, therefore, also subject to detailed disciplinary rules made in that regard by the Secretary of State or the SROs. A party carrying on an investment business without being or continuing to be an authorised or exempt person may incur severe civil and criminal sanctions.

Multiplicity and interdependence of market contracts

F1.4   A counterparty relies on the first party to perform the contract on its due date and may in turn enter into a corresponding reverse transaction with another counterparty for performance on the same due date and so on. If the first party defaults, this may threaten a domino effect by jeopardising the ability of the first counterparty and the other counterparties down the line to perform (at all or without incurring substantial losses) their parts of the corresponding reverse transactions by delivery of securities or payment of consideration (as the case may be). If this were to occur on a large scale, the integrity of the market itself may be undermined. If a formal insolvency of the first party occurs, certain further problems under the general law of insolvency may arise for the counterparty. Some of these are discussed below.

Chapter 2: Insolvency-related problems before CA 1989, Part VII

F2.1   If no special contracts or market default rules were in existence, the following, *inter alia*, insolvency-related problems could arise for the counterparty in the event of the first party's formal insolvency such as liquidation, receivership, or administration.

Preferences and transactions at an undervalue

F2.2   These could arise, for example, in respect of contracts performed by the first party within (in the case of preferences) six months or (in the case of preferences in favour of 'connected persons' or undervalue transactions) two years before the commencement of its liquidation or administration, if, at the time or in consequence of the performance, the first party was or became unable to pay its debts within the meaning of section 123 of the Insolvency Act 1986 (which would be presumed to have been the case where the counterparty was a 'connected' person). In the case of a preference, it must be shown that in performing the contract, the first party was influenced by a desire to put the counterparty in a better position than the position it would be in if there were an insolvent liquidation. In the case of an undervalue transaction, it must be shown that the value which the first party received was significantly less than the value it gave. These conditions may, arguably, be satisfied if, by not performing the contract, the first party would have been better off, for example, because at the time of the performance the market price was more favourable to it than the original contract price, or because the counterparty had already previously performed its part and there was no fresh benefit to accrue to the first party by performing its part. A strong *bona fide* commercial justification on the part of the first party may negative such desire and may also provide a defence to the counterparty against a claim for an undervalue transaction. If a preference or claim for an undervalue transaction is established, the court may make appropriate orders to counteract its effect (IA 1986, ss 238 to 241, as amended by the Insolvency (No 2) Act 1994—see C10.2 to C10.6 PART C: LIQUIDATIONS and B9.1 to B9.6 PART B: ADMINISTRATION ORDERS).

'Cherry-picking'

F2.3   A formal insolvency of the first party does not, *per se*, terminate the counterparty's obligations under an outstanding contract. A receiver or administrator can repudiate the contract, without necessarily being liable for inducing its breach (*Lathia v Dronsfield Ltd [1987] BCLC 321*) or for specific performance (*Airline Airspaces Ltd v Handley Page Ltd [1970] Ch 193*) and a liquidator can, without being so liable, disclaim it under his statutory power (IA 1986, s 178). In certain circumstances an administrator may be restrained from committing a breach (see B7.5 PART B: ADMINISTRATION ORDERS). Further, where beneficial ownership of the asset involved in the contract has already passed to the counter-party, proceedings to obtain an order for specific performance to complete the counterparty's title may be permitted by the court as against a receiver, administrator or liquidator if such an order would otherwise have been made (see, for example, *Freevale Ltd v Metrostore (Holdings) Ltd [1984] 1 All ER 495*). If there is no repudi-ation or disclaimer, the counterparty must perform its part if the receiver, administrator or liquidator ('the office-holder') offers to or does perform the first party's part. In practice, where there are a number of outstanding contracts between the same parties, the office-holder may go 'cherry-picking', that is, abandon those contracts which are not favourable to the first party (leaving the counterparty with a claim for damages as an unsecured creditor) but insist on the perform-ance of those which are favourable to the first party.

If such a performance does take place, the counterparty must deliver the securities or make payment (as the case may be) according to the contract, without necessarily being entitled to appropriate the payment or securities by way of set-off against any claim it may have in respect of any abandoned contracts (see, e.g. *Ince Hall Rolling Mills v Dou-glas Forge & Co (1882) 8 QBD 179*; *Mersey Steel & Iron Co v Naylor Benzon & Co (1882) 9 QBD 648* at *669 (CA)*) and see also F2.4 below. If the counterparty refuses to perform, it may be liable in damages but in that case may have a better right of set-off. However, the office-holder is not obliged to disclose his decision to the counterparty in advance of the maturity date of any particular contract and may prefer to wait and see how market prices move (but, in a liquidation, the counterparty can end the uncertainty as outlined in the next para-graph). Arguably, in such a situation the counterparty cannot, in a receivership or administration, set off any debt due by it to the first party against a contingent claim it may have, on the assumption or possibility that the first party will not perform the unmatured contracts (see F2.4 below).

In a liquidation, the counterparty's position is better in three respects. Firstly, the right of set-off is wider—it covers contingent claims. Secondly, it can ask the court to rescind all the outstanding contracts under section 186 of the Insolvency Act 1986. The court may do so on such terms as to payment by or to either party of damages for non-performance of the contract, or otherwise as the court thinks just. Presumably, the words 'or otherwise as the court thinks just' enable the court to allow a set-off between damages payable in opposite directions under the different contracts so rescinded. Thirdly, the counterparty can end the uncertainty about disclaimer. This it can do, under section 178(5) of the Insolvency Act 1986, by applying to the liquidator in writing requiring him to make up his mind. If he fails to disclaim within 28 days thereafter or such longer period as the court may allow, he will lose his right to do so.

(See C12.6 and C12.7 PART C: LIQUIDATIONS and D7.5 and D7.23 PART D: RECEIVERS.)

Bilateral set-off

F2.4   Mention has already been made in F2.3 of the differences in the law of set-off between different insolvency procedures. In a receivership or administration, set-off is governed by the general law which is narrower in scope. However, it is debatable (although see Millett J's observations in *Re Charge Card Services Ltd [1986] 3 WLR 697*) whether a quantified claim can be set off against an unquantified or contingent claim (such as a counterparty's claim on the assumption or possibility that the first party will not perform an outstanding contract on its due date), as distinct from a quantified claim payable at a future date which, as *Business Computers Ltd v Anglo African Leasing Ltd [1977] 2 All ER 741* suggests, can be the subject of set-off. Further, as discussed in that case, set-off is only available between debts arising from the same contract or from different contracts closely connected with each other. Separate market contracts between the same parties but entered into on different dates or in respect of different securities may or may not be regarded as so connected.

In a liquidation, set-off is governed by Rule 4.90 of the Insolvency Rules 1986. In one respect, Rule 4.90, as read with Rules 12.3 and 13.12, is wider in scope, as it covers contingent and unquantified claims. However, in another respect it creates a new problem in that (arguably) a debt becoming due to the counterparty after it had notice of the presentation of a winding-up petition, or the convening of a creditors' meeting in a creditors' voluntary winding-up, cannot be set off by it (see C14.26 PART C: LIQUIDATIONS).

In a Guidance Notice dated 19 November 1993 which was entitled *Netting of Counterparty Exposure*, the Financial Law Panel issued a 'Statement of Law' recording a consensus of the views of leading practitioners in the fields of insolvency and banking law on the scope of set-off under Rule 4.90 in so far as it applies to banks' contracts for forward and spot foreign exchange, cross-currency and interest rate swaps, currency and interest rate options (including 'caps', 'floors' and 'collars'), forward rate agreements and similar commodity and equity-related derivatives and to loans by and deposits with a bank. The Guidance Notice stated: 'With the growth in complexity of routine financial transactions and the increase in the gross amount of obligations involved, banks have felt the need for a restatement of the principles of English Law on this subject' (netting). The relevant part of the 'Statement of Law' (which at best is only persuasive authority) states, 'Where a bank and its corporate customer enter into various transactions with each other prior to the customer's insolvent liquidation and the customer goes into liquidation before the transactions are closed mandatory set off applies. The bank will have a claim (or obligation) on a net basis only to receive from (or pay to) the liquidator the net amount in respect of the transactions taken as a whole'.

This robust view, interpreting Rule 4.90 more pragmatically, is to be welcomed; and it is hoped that it will be upheld by the courts. The 'Statement of Law' appears to apply even to cases where there is not in existence a master agreement between the parties which, as will be seen in Chapter 3 below, can help further strengthen the position of the parties.

Specific performance

F2.5   In a liquidation or administration, before the counterparty can bring or continue an action for specific performance, it would need to have the stay against legal proceedings lifted by the court (see C7.4, C7.5, C8.2, C8.3, and C9.2 to C9.4 PART C: LIQUIDATIONS and B4.1 and B4.2 PART B: ADMINISTRATION ORDERS). The court would not normally lift the stay unless the action is likely to succeed. (There are also restrictions in a liquidation against execution and distraining creditors retaining benefit of execution or distress.) In a receivership, there is no such stay (but see the next paragraph).

In any form of insolvency, even if the counterparty were to bring or continue the action, it may not succeed in the action unless it establishes that proprietary or possessory interest in security *in specie* had passed to it, or remained in it, before any liquidation or receivership supervened (see also F2.3 above). Contractually or under the market rules, or because of a repudiation or disclaimer (not followed by a vesting order of the court) of the contracts (see F2.3 above) this may not have happened or may have ceased to be the case; or, in view of the 'fungibility' problem (see F2.6 below), securities may not be traceable *in specie*. An administration, unlike a liquidation or receivership, does not prevent a subsequent passing of property. Therefore, once such a passing takes place, the counterparty may be in a better position to have the stay lifted and to succeed in the action. In a receivership, upon the appointment of an administrative receiver, the rights of the debenture-holder could have intervened and could prevent the passing of any property (see *N W Robbie & Co Ltd v Witney Warehouse Co Ltd [1963] 1 WLR 1324 (CA)* referred to at D7.5(6) PART D: RECEIVERS).

Fungibility

F2.6   Rarely, if ever, does a market contract relate to securities identifiable *in specie*. The transaction is by description of the particular class or type of securities. Often, a party may not even own securities of that class or type when it enters into a sale contract. The way certain market clearing systems work, securities in the system introduced by one party for the purpose of performing a particular contract are not necessarily those which ultimately reach the counterparty to that particular contract. The latter would receive its entitlement out of the general pool into which securities of the same type or class have been put on account of contracts between various members. Therefore, securities of the same type may be interchangeable or 'fungible'. This makes it difficult for a party to claim beneficial proprietary interest or an unpaid vendor's lien in any particular securities which are not in or have left its possession. (It should be noted that loss of possession *per se* would not have deprived it of its lien. It is the loss of identity which does so.)

However, in certain circumstances it may be possible under equitable principles for a fair distribution to be made among the various parties claiming beneficial interests to unidentified assets in an identified common fund or pool.

Disposition after commencement of formal insolvency

F2.7   Where the first party has put securities into the clearing system for the purposes of performing a market contract, and, before securities are delivered out to the counterparty by way of performance or otherwise become vested in it, the first party becomes insolvent, the securities may have to revert to the office-holder. This is because, in the case of a compulsory liquidation, any such delivery would constitute an invalid disposition, unless the court validates that disposition, under section 127 of the Insolvency Act 1986. (See C8.4 PART C: LIQUIDATIONS.) In all forms of winding-up, the company's property falls to be dealt with by the liquidator for distribution *pari passu* among its creditors (see C9.10, C11.25, C15.4 PART C: LIQUIDATIONS) and, if the vesting were to go ahead, this would (arguably) be contrary to that *pari passu* principle. In a receivership, any floating charge over such securities or commodities would have crystallised and the securities would have become assigned in equity to the charge-holder (*NW Robbie & Co Ltd v Witney Warehouse Co Ltd [1963] 3 All ER 613*, referred to at D7.5(6) PART D: RECEIVERS) before they could become vested in the counterparty. By contrast, an administrator may not be able to prevent the passing of the securities in the clearing system to the counterparty concerned because, arguably, he has no better rights than those which the company had.

'Charge Card' case

F2.8   Where the first party has deposited cash 'margins' with the counterparty as purported security for the performance of its obligations, the counterparty cannot assert a charge over the margins in the event of a default by the first party. This is the effect of the decision of Millett J in *Re Charge Card Services Ltd [1986] 3 WLR 697* (referred to at C14.26 PART C: LIQUIDATIONS and D9.1(A) PART D: RECEIVERS). Such margins are a debt owing by the counterparty to the first party and, according to that decision (which has been doubted by the Court of Appeal in *Welsh Development Agency v Export Finance Co Ltd [1992] BCC 270* and at first instance in *Re Bank of Credit and Commerce International SA (No 8) [1994] 1 BCLC 758*, but accepted in Australia in *Esanda Finance Corporation Ltd v Jackson (1993) 11 ACLC 138*), it is not conceptually possible for the counterparty to obtain a charge over a debt due by itself. Therefore, insofar as the counterparty has no valid right of set-off under the general law or under a properly drafted contractual provision (as to which see *Security over Cash Deposits—A Practice Recommendation* issued in July 1994 by the Financial Law Panel) or, in the case of liquidation of the first party, under the Insolvency Act 1986, it may be adversely affected.

'British Eagle' problem

F2.9   The case of *British Eagle International Airlines Ltd v Compagnie Nationale Air France [1975] 1 WLR 758* (referred to at C12.10 and C15.4 PART C: LIQUIDATIONS and D6.2 PART D: RECEIVERS) enunciated two principles applicable in a liquidation. One was that any contractual arrangement, under which in the event of the liquidation of one of the parties a multilateral set-off or a cross set-off between that party and other parties to the arrangement is to be effected, is void as being contrary to the mandatory requirements of the insolvency legislation as to *pari passu* distribution among all its creditors (including those who are not parties to that arrangement). The other, wider, principle of that case is believed to be that any contractual provision which seeks to make the rights of a party to property or money defeasible by reason of its liquidation is void for the same reason. Thus, a contractual multilateral set-off or a termination of a counterparty's money or property obligations to the insolvent party, solely because of its liquidation, may not be valid.

Novation of contracts or market guarantee

F2.10   In certain markets, a contract entered into between members is required to be registered with the clearing house concerned. The effect of such registration, in certain markets, may be to constitute either a novation of contract to, or an undertaking or guarantee to perform by, the clearing house itself, so that the clearing house itself is responsible to each party for the performance. In such a situation, in the event of the first party's insolvency, the clearing house may face problems similar to those faced by a counterparty, as described above, although the counterparty itself may be protected unless under its rules the clearing house has an ultimate right of recourse against the counterparty.

Chapter 3: Use of special contracts to minimise problems

F3.1   Insofar as there is no conflict with the market rules, a counter-party contemplating regular dealings with the first party may, in order to minimise the problem described above, enter into a master agreement with the first party which contains the following, among other, types of provision. Some of these types are addressed in a Guidance Note entitled *Netting of Foreign Exchange Transactions*, dated 28 September 1994, prepared by the Banking Law Sub-Committee of the City of London Law Society and circulated by the Financial Law Panel with its covering note dated 29 September 1994.

Aggregation or unity clause

F3.2   This clause is to the effect that (i) all transactions entered into between the parties are to be treated as one single contract so that the counterparty will not be obliged to perform its part of any particular outstanding transaction unless and until the first party performs its part of all the transactions maturing at the same time and is, at that time, in a position to perform its part of all the transactions maturing in the future, and that (ii) if certain specified pre-liquidation circumstances in relation to the first party exist at the time, the first party will be conclusively deemed unable to perform its part of the transactions maturing in the future. This clause, in combination with the acceleration and quantification clauses (see F3.3 and F3.4 below), may help relieve the 'cherry-picking' and set-off problems.

Acceleration clause

F3.3   This clause may provide that upon the occurrence of any of the specified pre-liquidation events, all outstanding transactions between the parties will be immediately terminated (automatically or upon the giving of notice by the counterparty), that the counterparty will be released from all its obligations under them and that all rights and obligations between the parties in relation to the termination will be immediately quantified into monetary rights and obligations in accordance with the formulae set out in the quantification clause (see F3.4 below). To avoid the *British Eagle* problem (see F2.9 above), it is important that the events of default are pre-liquidation events. Examples of such events are default in payment of any money due under a market contract, inability to pay debts within the meaning of section 123 of the Insolvency Act 1986, commencement of default proceedings by the market, appointment of a receiver or filing of an application for an administration order or imminence of any of those events.

Quantification clause

F3.4   This clause seeks to lay down a mutually fair basis for quantifying damages or compensation due by one party to the other in respect of each transaction terminated under the acceleration clause (see F3.3 above). The formula for quantification is normally based on the difference between the contract price and the market price prevailing on the date of termination—very much on the lines of default rules of the market relating to closing-out and netting-off (see F4.2 below).

Bilateral netting-off clause

F3.5   In view of the quantified netted-off position which the clauses mentioned above (F3.2 to F3.4) will produce, the residual set-off problems under the general law or Rule 4.90 are largely relieved but it is still useful and does no harm to have an express set-off clause. However, it should be stated to be without prejudice to rights of set-off available under the law. Before the *Charge Card* case (see F2.8 above) it was thought that if a contractual set-off clause was wider in scope than set-off available under the general law or, in the event of a liquidation, Rule 4.90 of the Insolvency Rules 1986, it might be void as an unregistered charge over book debts. After the *Charge Card* case this is no longer so. Therefore, there seems no reason why it should not be valid as against a receiver or administrator in relation to pre-receivership or pre-administration transactions. However, in a liquidation such a clause could be ineffective as being contrary to the wider anti-defeasance principle of the *British Eagle* case (see F2.9 above) in so far as the clause seeks better rights than those available in a liquidation.

'Flawed asset' clause

F3.6   This clause can be used in the place of the quantification and set-off clauses or those clauses can be expressed to be alternative to the 'flawed asset' clause (in case the latter does not work). A 'flawed asset' clause is a comparatively novel concept (not tested in the courts) and came about in response to the problems created by the *Charge Card* case (see F2.8 above), Rule 4.90 regarding set-off in a winding-up (see F2.4 above), the anti-defeasance principle of the *British Eagle* case (see F2.9 above) and the provisions as to avoidance of property dispositions made after the petition for a compulsory liquidation. The clause is mainly used in relation to cash margins, deposits and debts since, according to the *Charge Card* case, there cannot be a valid charge over them and since set-off under Rule 4.90 may not always be available.

The best way to explain the concept of 'flawed asset' is to contrast it with the concept of set-off. For there to be a set-off there must be at least two debts owed in opposite directions; but in the case of a 'flawed asset', there is, from the very beginning, only one single netted-off amount owing only in one direction at any given time. This way, the need to rely on an invalid set-off or a *Charge Card* type of invalid charge is rendered unnecessary. Further, there can be no question of a *British Eagle* type defeasance, as the latter presupposes the existence of a right and its subsequent dilution rather than the existence of a diluted right from the beginning. Great care is needed in structuring and drafting a 'flawed asset' clause.

Individual charge (fixed and/or floating)

F3.7   Here 'individual charge' means a charge taken by a counterparty for its own benefit, as distinct from a 'market charge' (see F4.3 below) which is taken by the market for the benefit of all its members and/or itself. A counterparty can, of course, secure its position better and minimise the problems discussed in F2.3 to F2.9 above (but not necessarily the bilateral set-off, fungibility and the *Charge Card* case problems) if it takes from the first party a fixed and/or floating charge over all or specified categories of present and/or future assets of the first party (in addition to any arrangements for margins or cash deposits). Any realisation of the assets comprised in the charge after the presentation of a compulsory winding-up petition is not caught by section 127 of the Insolvency Act 1986 (referred to at F2.7 above—see also D5.2 PART D: RECEIVERS). It should be noted, however, that an administrator of the first party would have a power to sell the assets comprised in the charge freed from that charge, although he would ultimately have to account for the net proceeds to the charge-holder and although in the first place, the holder of a general floating or fixed and floating charge would have an opportunity of preventing the appointment of an administrator by appointing an administrative receiver under that charge (see B6.1 and B6.2 PART B: ADMINISTRATION ORDERS).

In practice, the charge may have to be confined to certain categories of assets relating to the first party's business in securities; and it may have to be only a floating charge rather than a fixed charge so that the first party is able to carry on its business and, even then, so framed as not to impede the settlement and clearing systems of the market. However, any such charge may be held to be void as a preference, an undervalue transaction or an invalid floating charge as regards any liabilities under pre-charge contracts, if liquidation or administration commences within six months, twelve months or two years (as the case may be) (see B9.2 to B9.6, B9.8 to B9.10 PART B: ADMINISTRATION ORDERS, C10.2 to C10.6, C10.8 and C10.9 PART C: LIQUIDATIONS). Further, preferential creditors will rank ahead of the floating charge in the event of receivership, liquidation or enforcement (see D7.3 PART D: RECEIVERS). Often, for various practical and commercial reasons the first party may not be able to grant a charge, particularly a first charge, at all.

Chapter 4: Use of market default rules to minimise problems

F4.1   The default and settlement rules of most markets contain provisions intended to mitigate the effect of a default or an insolvency of a market member. Some examples are given below.

Closing out, reversal, quantification and bilateral netting-off

F4.2   There are provisions enabling the appropriate bodies supervising the markets to declare as a defaulter a member who has defaulted, or is likely to default, on any market transaction or has otherwise committed a serious disciplinary offence. The effect of such a declaration may be that securities or funds which have already been put in the clearing house pipeline by way of performance of contracts are allowed to go across to the parties concerned, but all rights and liabilities between the defaulter and all the counterparties under all outstanding transactions are discharged or settled and replaced by quantified money obligations in accordance with the formulae laid down in the rules. Debts arising in opposite directions between the same parties as a result are reduced to a net sum payable by or to the defaulting party. Thus, the rules would achieve a similar effect to that intended by the clauses of a special contract, except that the rules do not normally contain a 'flawed asset' concept (see F3.6 above).

Market charge—fixed and/or floating and margins

F4.3   In recent times some of the markets have introduced or contemplated introducing a requirement for all members trading on the market to create a charge (usually or largely a floating charge) in favour of the market for the benefit of or in trust for the market itself and all of its other members. Such a charge achieves a form of multilateral set-off which would survive the insolvency of a member provided that it is registered under section 395 of the Companies Act 1985 (to be amended by Part IV of the Companies Act 1989, which is not in force at the time of writing).

The charge has, of course, limitations similar to those in respect of an individual charge (see F3.7 above).

The rules of some of the markets require a provision of margins by one party to the other or, in the case of a novation or market guarantee, to the clearing house. The *Charge Card* case problem in this regard has already been adverted to in F2.8 above.

Chapter 5: Residual problems before CA 1989, Part VII

F5.1 The most important effect of the special clauses or default rules, when triggered, is to bring about an overall net crystallised and quantified position between the parties. (Indeed, a 'flawed asset' does not have to be triggered. It is in operation from its inception, notionally maintaining and updating such a position on a continuous basis.) This effect helps to resolve or minimise most, but not all, of the problems, more so, when an individual or a market charge is taken. The following review will illustrate this point.

Preferences and transactions at an undervalue

F5.2 Where there is no individual or market charge, these problems do not disappear in relation to recently-performed transactions. Where there is a first charge, the problems largely disappear, except as regards any pre-charge transactions and also where the charge is only a floating charge, as regards preferential creditors (see F2.2 above and D7.3 PART D: RECEIVERS).

'Cherry-picking'

F5.3 The special clauses (other than a 'flawed asset' clause) and/or the default rules will prevent 'cherry-picking' by a receiver or administrator but not by a liquidator unless the clauses or rules are triggered before liquidation or unless all the outstanding contracts are rescinded by the court (see F2.3 above). An office-holder can have no better rights than the rights which the first party had, except that in view of the *British Eagle* case anti-defeasance principle, any dilution of such rights occurring by reason of the clauses or rules being triggered after liquidation may not be binding on the liquidator. A 'flawed asset' clause and/or a first charge would remove any remaining problems (but see F3.7 above as to an administrator's right to dispose of charged assets).

Bilateral set-off

F5.4 Again, the clauses or rules will largely eliminate any residual problems, more so if there is a first charge, except where a wider right is sought than is available in a liquidation (see F2.4 above).

Specific performance

F5.5 The problem is not eliminated, but the crystallised net position produced by the clauses or the default rules will mitigate it and a first charge will render it irrelevant (see F2.5 above).

Fungibility

F5.6 This problem itself does not disappear insofar as a counterparty may wish to claim a beneficial proprietary or possessory interest in any particular market assets of the first party otherwise than under a charge (see F2.6 above).

Disposition after commencement of insolvency

F5.7 This problem is narrowed-down to cases where securities of the first party in the clearing house pipeline at the time of receivership or liquidation become vested in the counterparty after the commencement of any such procedure (see F2.7 above). A first charge would minimise this problem.

'Charge Card' case

F5.8 This problem persists in theory in relation to cash margins or deposits held by the counterparty, but any net sum found to be due to it by the operation of the clauses or rules (see F2.8 above) should (arguably) be capable of being set off against the margins or deposit. A 'flawed asset' clause, as distinct from a charge (which can never cover margins or deposits), would resolve it more conclusively.

'British Eagle' problem

F5.9 The multilateral set-off aspect of this problem remains unresolved by the clauses or default rules, unless a market charge is taken (see F2.9 above). The defeasance aspect can be avoided if the special clauses can get triggered before the commencement of liquidation or if an individual or a market charge is taken.

Novation of contracts or market guarantee

F5.10 The observations made above apply *mutatis mutandis* where transactions are novated to or underwritten by the market (see F2.10 above).

Chapter 6: CA 1989, Part VII—effect on general law of insolvency

Introduction

F6.1   The Financial Services Act 1986, with the delegated legislation made thereunder, is primarily aimed at the special protection of *investors*. However, the insolvency-related problems and the need to maintain the integrity of the markets discussed above indicate the necessity for some special statutory protection for the *markets and their members* as well. Part VII of the CA 1989 is intended to provide that protection. Section 154 states that Part VII has effect for the purposes of safeguarding the operation of certain financial markets by provisions with respect to:

(*a*)   the insolvency, winding-up or default of a party to transactions in the market (sections 155 to 172);

(*b*)   the effectiveness or enforcement of certain charges given to secure obligations in connection with such transactions (sections 173 to 176); and

(*c*)   rights and remedies in relation to certain property provided as cover for margins in relation to such transactions or subject to such a charge (sections 177 to 181).

The functions under Part VII of the CA 1989 previously exercised by the Secretary of State were transferred to the Treasury by the Transfer of Functions (Financial Services) Order 1992 (SI 1992 No 1315), with effect from 7 June 1992. However, certain functions under Part VII continue to be exercisable jointly by the Secretary of State and the Treasury.

Application of Part VII

F6.2   Part VII applies only to certain descriptions of contract connected with a 'recognised investment exchange' or 'recognised clearing house' (see F6.3 below)—section 155(1). Such contracts are referred to as 'market contracts'. In relation to a recognised investment exchange, Part VII applies to:

(*a*)   contracts entered into by a member of the exchange or 'designated non-member' of the exchange (i.e. a non-member of the exchange in respect of whom action may be taken under the default rules of the exchange), other than a recognised overseas investment exchange, which are either

  (i)   contracts made on the exchange, or on an exchange to whose undertaking the exchange has succeeded whether by amalgamation, merger or otherwise; or

  (ii)   contracts in the making of which the member or designated non-member was subject to the rules of the exchange or of an exchange to whose undertaking the exchange has succeeded whether by amalgamation, merger or otherwise; and

(*b*) contracts subject to the rules of the exchange entered into by the exchange for the purposes of or in connection with the provision of clearing services.

(Section 155(2) and (2A), as substituted by Regulation 3).

In relation to a recognised clearing house, Part VII applies to contracts subject to the rules of the clearing house entered into by the clearing house for the purposes of, or in connection with, the provision of clearing services for the recognised investment exchange (section 155(3)).

The Secretary of State (jointly with the Treasury) may by regulations provide for the application of Part VII in relation to:

(*a*) contracts connected with an overseas investment exchange or clearing house which is approved by him (section 170);

(*b*) contracts of any specified description in relation to which settlement arrangements are provided by a person for the time being included in a list maintained by the Bank of England for that purpose provided that the Secretary of State and the Treasury are satisfied that it is appropriate for the Bank of England to supervise the arrangements, having regard to the extent to which the contracts in question involve, or are likely to involve, money market investments or are otherwise of a kind dealt in by persons supervised by the Bank of England (section 171); and

(*c*) contracts of any specified description in relation to which settlement arrangements are provided by the Bank of England (section 172).

However, sections 170 to 172 have not yet been brought into force.

Section 187 deals with construction of references to parties to market contracts. Regulation 16 provides that for the purposes of that section, a member or designated non-member of a recognised investment exchange or a member of a recognised clearing house is to be treated as effecting 'relevant transactions' in a different capacity from other market contracts he has effected as principal. 'Relevant transaction' means—

(*a*) a market contract effected as principal by a member or designated non-member of a recognised investment exchange or a member of a recognised clearing house being a market contract—

    (i) which is an investment falling within paragraph 7, 8 or 9 of Schedule 1 to the Financial Services Act 1986 or falling within paragraph 11 of that Schedule in so far as that paragraph is relevant to any of those paragraphs; and

    (ii) in relation to which money received by the member or designated non-member is client money for the purposes of the Financial Services (Clients' Money) Regulations 1987 (see the Securities and Investment Board's releases Nos 54 and 85) or would be client money for those purposes were it not money which, in accordance with those Regulations, may be regarded as immediately due and payable to the member or designated non-member for his own account; and

(*b*)   a market contract which would be regarded as a relevant transaction by virtue of (*a*) above were it not for the fact that no money is received by the member or designated non-member in relation to the contract.

Meanings of a 'recognised investment exchange', 'recognised clearing house', 'overseas investment exchange' and 'overseas clearing house'

F6.3   These are the bodies in respect of which a recognition order, designating them as such, has been made under the provisions of the Financial Services Act 1986 ('FSA 1986'). However, section 156 of the Companies Act 1989 provides, subject to the discretion given to the Secretary of State on certain transitional matters, that in addition to meeting the requirements for such recognition set out in sections 39(4) and 40(2) of, and Schedule 4 to, the Financial Services Act 1986, such bodies must comply with the additional requirements set out in Parts I, II and III respectively of Schedule 21 to the Companies Act 1989, as modified by Regulation 17. A number of regulatory and enforcement provisions of FSA 1986 in relation to such bodies have been adapted to Part VII of the Companies Act 1989 (section 169).

Requirements as to default rules

F6.4   Schedule 21 sets out the requirements of section 156 as to the type of default rules (as defined by section 188) and provisions about notification and margins which such an exchange or clearing house (in this chapter each is continued to be referred to as the 'market') must have to obtain or maintain its recognition. Regulation 17 provides that the reference in sub-paragraph (1) of paragraph 2 of that Schedule to rights and liabilities between the parties as principals to unsettled market contracts does not include rights and liabilities in respect of margin or arising out of a failure to perform a market contract. Section 157 contains the procedure for amendment of such rules by the market and for the Treasury to veto any such amendment; but section 157 does not have effect in relation to a proposal made before that section came into force, i.e. 25 April 1991 (SI 1991 No 878).

These default rules are to be administered by the exchange or clearing house or a person or body appointed for the purpose by the exchange or clearing house. As these mandatory rules are very much on the lines of the special contract and default rules which have been outlined above (see F3.2 to F3.7, and F4.1 to F4.3 above) and are, in any case, already reflected to a large extent in the existing rules of many markets, they do not of themselves, unlike the substantive provisions dealt with in F6.5 *et seq*. below, significantly add to the protection already available. Multilateral set-off is not within the scope of these requirements and, in fact, would be inconsistent with them.

It will be noted that, as under those rules margins are to be treated and dealt with as clients' money for the purposes of the regulations made under section 55 of the Financial Services Act 1986, it is not possible to operate the 'flawed asset' concept as an answer to the *Charge Card* case and set-off problems referred to above. However, as will be seen, those problems are being resolved in a different way.

Substantive provisions of Part VII which modify the general law of insolvency

F6.5   Section 158 provides that the general law of insolvency has effect in relation to market contracts, and action to be taken under the rules of a market with respect to such contracts, subject to the provisions of sections 159 to 165 (see below). The Secretary of State, jointly with the Treasury, may make further provision by regulations modifying the law of insolvency in relation to such matters. His functions, except as to the making of orders and regulations, under Part VII may be delegated to a designated agency as stipulated under section 114 of the Financial Services Act 1986 (section 168).

So far as the provisions of sections 159 to 165 or any such further provisions relate to insolvency proceedings in respect of a person other than a defaulter (as defined by section 188), they apply in relation to (*a*) proceedings in respect of a member or designated non-member of a market and (*b*) proceedings in respect of a party to a market contract begun (i.e., a petition for an administration order or a winding-up presented or a voluntary winding-up resolution passed or an administrative receiver appointed) after a market has taken action under its default rules in relation to a party to the contract as principal. However, those provisions do not apply in relation to any other insolvency proceedings, notwithstanding that rights or liabilities arising from market contracts fall to be dealt with in the proceedings (section 158(2)).

A summary of some of the important substantive provisions of Part VII now follows, as amended and modified by the Regulations.

Precedence of exchange or clearing house proceedings over insolvency proceedings

F6.6   Section 159 provides that a market contract, the default rules or the rules as to settlement of market contracts of a market will not be regarded as invalid in law on the ground of inconsistency with the law relating to the distribution of assets on winding-up. The powers of a 'relevant (insolvency) office-holder' (as defined by section 189) or the powers of the court under the Insolvency Act 1986 or the Bankruptcy (Scotland) Act 1985 are not to be exercised in such a way as to prevent or to interfere with the settlement of a market contract in accordance with the market rules or any action taken under the default rules, but this does not prevent the office-holder from afterwards seeking to recover any amount under section 163(4) or 164(4) (see F6.13 and F6.15 below) or prevent the court from afterwards making an order mentioned in section 165(1) or (2) (but subject to section 165(3) and (4) and see F6.16 below).

Thus the defeasance problem under the *British Eagle* case principle is eliminated, but not necessarily the multilateral set-off problem (which, as stated in F6.4 above, is outside the scope of the mandatory default rules).

A debt or other liability arising out of a market contract which is subject to default proceedings (as defined by section 188) may not be proved, or (in Scotland) claimed, in a winding-up until the completion of the default proceedings (but see F6.9 and F6.13 below). Nor is such a debt or liability to be taken into account in the winding-up for the purposes of any set-off until the completion of the default proceedings. For these purposes default proceedings are taken to be completed when a report is made as stated in F6.12 below (section 159(4) and (5)). However, prior to the completion of default proceedings, where it appears to the chairman of the meeting of creditors that a sum will be certified under section 162(1) to be payable (see F6.12 below), section 159(4) does not prevent a proof or claim including or consisting of an estimate of that sum which has been lodged (or, in Scotland, submitted) from being admitted (or, in Scotland, accepted) for the purposes only of determining the entitlement of a creditor to vote at a meeting of creditors; and a creditor whose claim or proof has been lodged and admitted (or, in Scotland, submitted and accepted) for voting purposes, and which has not been subsequently wholly withdrawn, disallowed or rejected, is eligible as a creditor to be a member of a liquidation committee (section 159(4A), as inserted by Regulation 4).

The intention seems to be to ensure that only an ultimate bilaterally netted-off sum is provable against or payable to the insolvent first party. Multilateral set-off would be inconsistent with the provisions mentioned above and in F6.13 below. Normally, it is the quasi-judicial function of the office-holder to determine the validity and amount of a claim (including the question of set-off) against the first party (subject to his determination being challengeable in court). Now in relation to market contracts, the function is effectively being taken away from him and he will normally be bound by the determination made by the appropriate body or representative of the market in the course of the default proceedings.

Duty of others to assist

F6.7   Section 160 imposes a duty (as to which the Secretary of State, jointly with the Treasury, may make further provisions by regulations) on any person who has or had control of any assets of, or any documents of or relating to, a defaulter (as defined by section 188) to give the exchange or clearing house such assistance as it may reasonably require for the purposes of its default proceedings. This duty does not apply where insolvency proceedings relating to the defaulter in question had begun before the section came into force (i.e., 25 April 1991). This duty is also subject to any claim of legal professional privilege or confidentiality and his right to reasonable access to, and ultimate return of, any documents supplied by him. Where an office-holder is required to give such assistance, the expenses incurred by him in doing so are recoverable by him as part of the expenses incurred by him in the discharge of his duties (out of the assets in his hands). For the purposes of determining the priority of such expenses, sums in respect of time spent are to be treated as his remuneration, and other sums as his disbursements (or, in Scotland, outlays). Where the expenses cannot be so recovered, he is not obliged to assist unless the exchange or clearing house undertakes to meet them (section 160(4), as amended by Regulation 5).

Protection of assets

F6.8   Section 161(1) empowers the court on an application by the relevant office-holder to grant interlocutory relief against dissipation or misapplication of a defaulter's assets by a counterparty.

Provision for dividend in liquidation to market creditors

F6.9   Section 161(2) provides that a liquidator must not declare or pay any dividend to the creditors or make any return of capital to the contributories without retaining what he reasonably considers to be an adequate reserve in respect of any claims arising as a result of the default proceedings.

Modification of office-holder's functions

F6.10   Under section 161(3) the court may on an application by the relevant office-holder alter or dispense with such of his duties as are affected by the fact that default proceedings are pending or could be taken, or have been or could have been taken.

Default proceedings immune from stay of action, proceedings etc. in administration or liquidation

F6.11   Sections 10(1)(c), 11(3), 126, 128, 130 or 185 of the Insolvency Act 1986, which restrict the taking of certain legal proceedings and other steps in an administration or a liquidation (see C7.4, C7.5, C8.2, C8.3, C9.2 to C9.4 PART C: LIQUIDATIONS, B4.1, B4.2 PART B: ADMINISTRATION ORDERS, and also F2.5 above), do not affect any action taken by the market for the purpose of its default proceedings (section 161(4)).

Completion of default proceedings

F6.12   Section 162 requires that upon the default proceedings being completed, the exchange or clearing house must report to the Treasury on its proceedings, stating, in respect of each creditor or debtor, the sum certified by it to be payable from or to the defaulter or, as the case may be, that no sum is payable. There may be a single report or a number of reports as proceedings are completed with respect to transactions affecting particular persons. A copy of such a report must be supplied by the exchange or clearing house to the defaulter and any relevant office-holder acting in relation to the defaulter, and the Treasury must publish the notice of the receipt by them of the report for bringing it to the attention of the creditors and debtors of the defaulter. These requirements do not apply to a recognised overseas investment exchange or recognised overseas clearing house unless it has been notified by the Treasury that a report is required for the purposes of insolvency proceedings in any part of the United Kingdom (section 162(1A), as inserted by Regulation 6).

Net sum payable on completion of default proceedings

F6.13   Any net sum certified in the report is provable in the winding-up or payable to the liquidator, as the case may be, and is to be taken into account, where appropriate, for the purposes of Rule 4.90 of the Insolvency Rules 1986 (as amended) (set-off in the winding-up) (section 163(2)). (Section 163(3) makes similar provision for Scotland.) As the sum will be a netted-off amount anyway, it would seem that the need for a statutory set-off would normally only arise if there is also a non-market debt owing by one party to the other. Section 163(4) and (6) provides, however, that where, or to the extent that, a sum is so taken into account for the purposes of set-off which arises from a contract entered into at a time when the creditor had notice of a pending winding-up petition or of the summoning of a voluntary winding-up meeting of the creditors under section 98 of the Insolvency Act 1986 (see C4.6 PART C: LIQUIDATIONS), the value of any profit to the creditor arising from the sum being so taken into account to that extent is recoverable from him by the relevant office-holder as a pre-preferential debt, unless the court otherwise directs. However, this does not apply in relation to a sum arising from a contract effected under the default rules of the market (section 163(5)).

No disclaimer or rescission

F6.14   Section 164(1) provides that sections 178 and 186 of the Insolvency Act 1986 (which relate to the disclaimer of contracts by the liquidator, and to the power of the court to rescind outstanding contracts in a liquidation (see C12.6 PART C: LIQUIDATIONS and F2.3 above)), do not apply in relation to a market contract or a contract effected by the market for the purpose of realising margins. (In Scotland, a liquidator of the defaulter is bound by any market contract to which the defaulter is a party and by any contract for realising margins referred to above, notwithstanding any rule of law having effect in liquidations similar to that which section 42 of the Bankruptcy (Scotland) Act 1985 has in personal bankruptcy (section 164(2)).) This prevents 'cherry-picking' by the liquidator (see F2.3 above). The intention is that all outstanding positions should be exclusively dealt with under the default rules until the net position is arrived at.

Dispositions after commencement of compulsory winding-up not necessarily void

F6.15   Section 164(3) provides that section 127 of the Insolvency Act 1986 (avoidance of disposition made after commencement of compulsory winding-up) does not apply (*a*) to a market contract, or any disposition of property pursuant thereto, (*b*) to the provision of margins in relation to market contracts, (*c*) to contracts made by the market for realising margins in relation to such contracts or any disposition pursuant thereto or (*d*) to any disposition of property in accordance with the rules of the market as to application of margins.

This is subject to the qualification that if a person enters into a market contract, or accepts margins in relation to such a contract, having notice of a presentation of a winding-up petition in relation to the other party to the contract or the provider of the margin, the value of any profit to him arising from the contract or, as the case may be, the value or amount of the margin is recoverable from him by the relevant office-holder as a pre-preferential debt, unless the court otherwise directs (section 164(4) and (6)). This qualification does not apply where the party entering into the contract is a market acting in accordance with its rules or where the contract is effected under the default rules of the market but it applies in relation to the provisions of margin in relation to such a contract (section 164(5)).

Preferences and transactions at an undervalue not necessarily voidable

F6.16   Section 165 protects a market contract to which the market itself is a party or which is entered into under its default rules, and a disposition made in pursuance of such a contract, from the impact of sections 238 (transactions at an undervalue), 239 (preferences) and 423 (transactions defrauding creditors) and, in Scotland, sections 242 and 243 (gratuitous alienations and unfair preferences) and the common law relating to gratuitous alienations and fraudulent preferences. It provides that in relation to any such transaction, no order must be made or decree granted under any of those sections or, in Scotland, at common law on the ground of gratuitous alienation or fraudulent preference (section 165(1) and (2)). Where a margin is provided in relation to a market contract and no such order or decree has been, or could be, made in relation to that contract, these restrictions apply to the provision of the margin, any contract effected by the market for the purpose of realising the margin and any disposition in accordance with the rules of the market as to application of the margin (section 165(4)).

Directions as to invoking default rules

F6.17   Where a recognised UK market has not taken, but could take, any action under its default rules, the Treasury may direct it to do so, if after consultation with the exchange or clearing house he is satisfied that failure to take action would involve undue risk to investors or other participants in the market. Conversely, if the market is proposing to, or may, take action he may direct it not to do so (until a further direction to do so or revoking the earlier direction is made), if after such consultation he is satisfied that the taking of action would be premature or otherwise undesirable in the interest of investors or such participants. However, no direction not to take action may be given where a winding-up order has been made, a voluntary winding-up resolution passed or an administrator, administrative receiver or provisional liquidator has been appointed; and any previous direction not to take action will cease to have effect on the making or passing of such order, or appointment (or resolution). Where the market has taken or been directed to take action under its default rules, the Secretary of State may direct it to do or not to do such things under the rules as he may specify (section 166). Section 166 does not have effect to enable a direction to be given where insolvency proceedings relating to the person in question had begun before the section came into force (i.e. before 25 April 1991).

Where an administration or a winding-up order has been made or a voluntary winding-up resolution passed or a provisional liquidator appointed and the market has not taken action under its default rules in consequence of any such event or the matters giving rise to it, the Treasury must, on an application by the relevant office-holder, notify the market. Unless within three business days (as defined) of the receipt of the notice, the market takes action under its default rules or notifies the Treasury that it proposes to do so forthwith, the substantive provisions of Part VII (sections 158 to 165) do not apply in relation to market contracts to which the defaulting member or non-designated member is a party or to anything done by the market for the purposes of, or in connection with, the settlement of any such contract (section 167(3)). However, if before the end of that period the Secretary of State gives the market a direction under section 166(2)(a) to take action under its default rules (see above), the substantive provisions (sections 158 to 165) are not disapplied. No such direction may be given after the end of that period (section 167(4)). If the market notifies the Secretary of State that it proposes to take such action forthwith, it must do so and that duty is enforceable, on the Secretary of State's application, by injunction or, in Scotland, by an order under section 45 of the Court of Session Act 1988 (section 167(5)).

Market charges protected from the impact of certain insolvency provisions

F6.18   Sections 173 to 176 of CA 1989 (as modified by Regulations 7 to 15) deal with market charges (as defined) and seek to provide special protection for them and for their enforcement against the general law of insolvency (section 174). A market charge is defined by section 173 (as amended by Regulation 9) as a charge, fixed or floating, which is:

(*a*)   granted to the market for the purpose of securing debts or liabilities, in the case of an exchange, arising in connection with the settlement of market contracts or, in the case of a clearing house, arising in connection with its ensuring the performance of market contracts; or

(*b*)   granted in favour of The Stock Exchange, for the purposes of securing debts or liabilities arising in connection with short term certificates (that is, instruments issued by The Stock Exchange undertaking to procure the transfer of property of values and descriptions specified in them to or to the order of the persons to whom they are issued or their endorsees (or to persons acting on behalf of those persons or endorsees) and also undertaking to make appropriate payments in cash, in the event that the obligation to procure the transfer of property cannot be discharged in whole or in part); or

(c) granted to a person who agrees to make payment as a result of transfer or allotment of the beneficial interest in 'specified securities' i.e., those for the time being specified in Schedule 1 to the Stock Transfer Act 1982 or any right to such securities, made through the medium of the computer-based system established by the Bank of England and The Stock Exchange, to secure debts or liabilities of the transferee or allottee arising in connection therewith.

Charges to be treated (or not treated) as market charges

F6.19 The following points as to the scope of a market charge should be noted.

(1) A charge is not treated as a market charge to the extent that it is a charge (fixed or floating) on land or any interest in land, but so that a charge on a debenture forming part of an issue or series is not to be treated as a charge on land or any interest in land by reason of the fact that the debenture is secured by a charge on land or any interest in land. (Regulation 8).

(2) A charge granted in favour of a recognised investment exchange other than The Stock Exchange is to be treated as a market charge only to the extent that—

(a) it is a charge over property provided as margin in respect of market contracts entered into by the exchange for the purposes of or in connection with the provision of clearing services;

(b) in the case of a recognised UK investment exchange, it secures the obligation to pay to the exchange the net sum referred to in paragraph 9(2)(a) of Schedule 21 to CA 1989 (see F6.4 above) as it applies by virtue of paragraph 1(4) of that Schedule; and

(c) in the case of a recognised overseas investment exchange, it secures the obligation to reimburse the cost (other than fees and other incidental expenses) incurred by the exchange in settling unsettled market contracts in respect of which the charged property is provided as margin.

(Regulation 10(1)).

(3) A charge granted in favour of The Stock Exchange is to be treated as a market charge only to the extent that—

(a) it is a charge of the kind described in (2) above; or

(b) it is a Talisman charge (that is, a charge granted in favour of The Stock Exchange over property credited to an account within its settlement system, known as Talisman, maintained in the name of the chargor in respect of certain property beneficially owned by the chargor) and secures either or both of the following obligations:

(i)   the chargor's obligation to reimburse The Stock Exchange for payments (including stamp duty and taxes but excluding Stock Exchange fees and incidental expenses arising from the operation by The Stock Exchange of settlement arrangements) made by The Stock Exchange in settling, through Talisman, market contracts entered into by the chargor;

(ii) the chargor's obligation to reimburse The Stock Exchange the amount of any payment it has made pursuant to a short term certificate (as defined above).

(Regulation 10(2)–(4)).

(4)   A charge granted in favour of a recognised clearing house is to be treated as a market charge only to the extent that—

(*a*)   it is a charge over property provided as margin in respect of market contracts entered into by the clearing house;

(*b*)   in the case of a recognised UK clearing house, it secures the obligation to pay the clearing house the net sum referred to in paragraph 9(2)(a) of Schedule 21 to CA 1989 (see F6.4 above); and

(*c*)   in the case of a recognised overseas clearing house, it secures the obligation to reimburse the cost (other than fees or incidental expenses) incurred by the clearing house in settling market contracts in respect of which the charged property is provided as margin.

(Regulation 11).

(5)   A CGO Service charge (that is, a charge of the kind described in F6.18(*c*) above) is to be treated as a market charge only in the following circumstances:

(*a*)   if it is granted to a settlement bank (that is, a person who has agreed under a contract with the Bank of England to make payments of the kind mentioned in F6.18(*c*) above) by a person for the purposes of securing debts or liabilities of the kind mentioned in F6.18(*c*) above incurred by that person through his use of the CGO Service (that is the computer-based system mentioned in F6.18(*c*) above) as a CGO Service member (that is a person who is entitled by contract with the Bank of England to use the CGO Service); and

(*b*)   if it contains provisions which refer expressly to the CGO (that is, the Central Gilts Office of the Bank of England); and

(*c*)   to the extent that it is a charge over any one or more of the following:

(i) specified securities held with the CGO Service to the account of a CGO Service member or a former CGO Service member (that is, a person whose entitlement by contract with the Bank of England to use the CGO Service has been terminated or suspended);

(ii) specified securities which were held as mentioned in (i) above immediately prior to their being removed from the CGO Service consequent upon the person in question becoming a former CGO Service member;

(iii) sums receivable by a CGO Service member representing interest accrued on specified securities held within the CGO Service to his account or which were so held immediately prior to their being removed from the CGO Service consequent upon his becoming a former CGO Service member;

(iv) sums receivable by a CGO Service member or former CGO Service member in respect of the redemption or conversion of specified securities which were held within the CGO Service to his account at the time that the relevant securities were redeemed or converted or which were so held immediately prior to their being removed from the CGO Service member; and

(v) sums receivable by a CGO Service member or former CGO Service member in respect of the transfer by him of specified securities through the medium of the CGO Service; and

(*d*) to the extent that it secures the obligation of the CGO Service member or former CGO Service member to reimburse a settlement bank for the amount due from him to the settlement bank as a result of the settlement bank having discharged or become obliged to discharge payment obligations in respect of transfers or allotments of specified securities made to him through the medium of the CGO Service.

(Regulations 12 and 13).

(6) Where only a part of a charge meets the above requirements, that part is a market charge (section 173(2)).

(7) The Secretary of State (jointly with the Treasury) has a wide discretion to alter the meaning of 'market charges' for these purposes (section 173). The protection provided to a market charge is summarised below but again note that the Secretary of State (again jointly with the Treasury) has a wide discretion to alter that protection (section 174). (Note that section 174(1) does not apply where the relevant insolvency proceedings had begun before the section came into force, i.e. before 25 April 1991 (SI 1991 No 878).)

Enforcement of security in an administration

F6.20   Section 175 provides that the provisions of sections 10(1)(b) and 11(3)(c) of the Insolvency Act 1986 (restrictions against enforcement of security while a petition for an administration order is pending or the order is in force) do not apply to a market charge. However, the disapplication of sections 10(1)(b) and 11(3)(c) is to be limited in respect of a CGO Service charge (see F6.18 and F6.19 above) so that it has effect only to the extent necessary to enable there to be realised, whether through the sale of specified securities or otherwise, a sum equal to whichever is less of the following—

(*a*)   the total amount of payment obligations discharged by the settlement bank in respect of transfers and allotments of specified securities made during the 'qualifying period' (see below) to the relevant CGO Service member or former CGO Service member through the medium of the CGO Service, less the total amount of payment obligations discharged to the settlement bank in respect of transfers of specified securities made during the qualifying period by the relevant CGO Service member or former CGO Service member through the medium of the CGO Service; and

(*b*)   the amount (if any) described in F6.19(5)(d) above due to the settlement bank from the relevant CGO Service member or former CGO Service member.

Qualifying period' means the period beginning with the fifth 'business day' (as defined in section 167(3)) before the day on which a petition for the making of an administration order in relation to the relevant CGO Service member or former CGO Service member is presented and ending with the second business day after the day on which an administration order is made pursuant to that petition.

(Regulation 14).

Section 175 further provides that section 15(1) and (2) of the Insolvency Act 1986 relating to the administrator's power to deal with charged property apply to a market charge. It also provides that section 11(2) of that Act (receiver to vacate office when so required by administrator) does not apply to a receiver appointed under a market charge. However, where a market charge falls to be enforced after an administration petition or order and there exists another charge (over some or all of the same property) ranking in priority to or *pari passu* with the market charge, on the application of any person interested (Regulation 18), the court may order that after the enforcement of the market charge there should be taken such steps as it directs for ensuring that the chargee under the other charge is not prejudiced by such enforcement (section 175(2)).

Section 175 also provides that sections 43 (power of administrative receiver to dispose of charged property) and 61 (receiver's power in Scotland to dispose of an interest in property) of the Insolvency Act 1986 do not apply in relation to a market charge.

The disapplication of sections 15(1) and (2), 43 and 61 of the Insolvency

Act 1986, as described above, ceases to have effect in respect of a CGO Service charge or a Talisman charge after the end of the second business day after the day on which an administration order is made or, as the case may be, an administrative receiver or a receiver is appointed in relation to the chargor, in relation to property subject to the charge which—

(i) in the case of a CGO Service charge, is not, on the basis of a valuation made as described below, required for the realisation of whichever is the less of the sum referred to in (*a*) above and the amount referred to in (*b*) above (under Regulation 14) due to the settlement bank at the close of business on the second business day referred to above; and

(ii) in the case of a Talisman charge, is not, on the basis of a valuation made as described below, required to enable The Stock Exchange to reimburse itself for any payment it has made of the kind referred to in F6.19(3)(*b*) above.

For the purposes of (i) and (ii) above—

(A) the value of property is, except in a case falling within (B) below, such as may be agreed between whichever is the relevant of the administrator, administrative receiver or receiver on the one hand and the settlement bank or The Stock Exchange on the other; and

(B) the value of any investment for which a price for the second business day referred to above is quoted in the Daily Official List of The Stock Exchange is

(1) in a case in which two prices are so quoted, an amount equal to the average of those two prices, adjusted where appropriate to take account of any accrued interest; and

(2) in a case where one price is so quoted, an amount equal to that price, adjusted where appropriate to take account of any accrued interest.

(Regulation 15).

(Note that the provisions of section 175, including those described in F6.21 below, do not apply where the relevant insolvency proceedings had begun before the section came into force, i.e. before 25 April 1991 (SI 1991 No 878).)

Disposition after commencement of compulsory winding-up—market charges

F6.21 Section 175(4) provides that section 127 of the Insolvency Act 1986 (which relates to the avoidance of a disposition made after the commencement of a compulsory winding-up) does not apply to a disposition of property as a result of which the property becomes subject to a market charge, or any transaction pursuant to which that disposition is made. This is subject to the qualification that if a person (other than the chargee under the market charge) who is party to a disposition has notice at the time of the disposition that a petition has been presented for the winding-up, the value of any profit to him arising from the disposition is recoverable from him by the relevant office-holder as a pre-preferential debt, unless the court directs otherwise (section 175(5) and (6)). In a case falling within the protection of both section 175(4) (see above) and section 164(3) (see F6.15 above), the pre-preferential debt provision of section 164(4) applies and that of section 175(5) does not apply.

Modification of general insolvency law—other types of charges

F6.22   The Secretary of State (jointly with the Treasury) has power to make regulations modifying the general law of insolvency in relation to other types of charges to be specified, and action taken in enforcing them. The charges which he may specify are those in favour of overseas markets approved under section 170 (see F6.2 above), persons included in the list maintained by the Bank of England (see F6.2 above), the Bank of England itself and certain other persons, bodies, authorities and organisations (including international SROs) covered by the Financial Services Act 1986, where such charges are given for the purpose of securing debts or liabilities arising in connection with or as a result of the settlement of contracts or the transfer of assets, rights or interests on a financial market. He may also specify any description of charge granted for that purpose in favour of any other person in connection with exchange facilities or clearing services provided by a market or any such person, body, authority or organisation mentioned above (section 176). The powers to make regulations under sections 170 to 172 (see F6.2 above) and 176 include power to apply the provisions of sections 177 to 180 (see F6.23 to F6.25 below), to margins and charges in other cases (section 181). However, sections 176 and 181 have not yet been brought into force.

Margins (market property) not affected by certain other interests

F6.23   Section 177 provides that so far as necessary to enable property, held by the market as margin in relation to a market contract, to be applied in accordance with the market rules, it may be so applied notwithstanding any prior equitable interest or right, or any right or remedy arising from a breach of fiduciary duty, unless the market had notice of the interest, right or breach of duty at the time the margin was provided. It also provides that no right or remedy arising subsequently to the margin being provided may be enforced so as to prevent or interfere with the application by the market of the margin in accordance with its rules. A person to whom, pursuant to these provisions, the market disposes of the margin in accordance with those rules takes free of any such third party right, interest or remedy. The section does not apply where the property was held as margin at the time the section came into force (i.e. on 25 April 1991) (SI 1991 No 878).

Priority of market charge over unpaid vendor's lien and of floating market charge over subsequent charges

F6.24   Section 179 provides that where property subject to an unpaid vendor's lien becomes subject to a market charge, the charge has priority over the lien unless the chargee had actual notice of the lien at the time the property became subject to the charge. The section does not have effect where the property was subject to the relevant market charge at the time the section came into force (i.e. on 25 April 1991) (SI 1991 No 878).

The Secretary of State has power under section 178 by regulations to provide that a market floating charge has priority over charges subsequently created or arising, including a fixed charge. It is not clear whether any such regulations will or can have a retrospective effect on charges already in existence at the time the regulations come into force. Section 178 has not yet been brought into force.

Restrictions against enforcement by unsecured creditors against margins

F6.25   Section 180 prevents any unsecured creditor from (i) commencing or continuing any execution (or, in Scotland, carrying out or continuing any diligence) or other legal process for the enforcement of a judgment or order, or (ii) (except in Scotland) levying any distress, against any property (other than land) which is held by the market as a margin or is subject to a market charge, except with the consent of the exchange or clearing house or, where the margin is subject to a market charge, without the consent of the holder of that charge. Any injunction or other remedy granted with a view to facilitating the enforcement of any such judgment or order is not to extend to that property. The section does not have effect to prevent the continuation of any execution or other legal process commenced, or the continued levying of any distress begun, before the section came into force (i.e. before 25 April 1991) (SI 1991 No 878).

Where such consent is given the creditor is not further restricted by any of the provisions of the Insolvency Act 1986.

Discretionary retrospective effect of Part VII

F6.26   Section 182 confers certain powers on the court where a petition for winding-up or an administration order had been presented, or a voluntary winding-up resolution was passed in respect of a market member or a grantor of a market charge, on or after 22 December 1988 and before the commencement of section 182 (i.e. before 25 April 1991). In such a case the court may, on the application of the market or the grantee of the market charge made within three months after section 182 commences, make such order as it thinks fit for achieving, except so far as the assets of that member or grantor have been distributed before the making of the application, the same result as if the provisions of Schedule 22 (which applies the provisions of Part VII with modifications) had come into force on 22 December 1988 (section 182; subsection (6) of which spells out certain substantive transitional powers).

'The court' and cross-frontier insolvency

F6.27 For the purposes of proceedings under sections 161 (see F6.8 to F6.11 above), 163 (see F6.13 above), 164 (see F6.14 and F6.15 above), 175(5) (see F6.21 above) and 182 (see F6.26 above), 'the court' is the court which last heard an application in the proceedings under the Insolvency Act 1986 or the Bankruptcy (Scotland) Act 1985 in which the relevant office-holder is acting or, as the case may be, any court having jurisdiction to hear applications in those proceedings. For the purposes of section 175(2) (see F6.20—administration orders etc.), 'the court' is the court which has made the administration order or, as the case may be, to which the petition for an administration order has been presented. The rules regulating the practice and procedure of the court in relation to applications to the court in England and Wales under sections 161, 163, 164, 175 and 182 are the rules applying in relation to applications to that court under the Insolvency Act 1986 (Regulation 19).

Section 183 aims to ensure that foreign insolvency proceedings which would otherwise be recognised under section 426 of the Insolvency Act 1986 (co-operation with insolvency courts in other jurisdictions) are only recognised for the purposes of Part VII of the Companies Act 1989 in so far as they are not inconsistent with the provisions of that Part. However, the recognition or enforcement of a judgment under or by virtue of the Civil Jurisdiction and Judgments Act 1982 is not affected. For the purposes of section 426, the references to 'insolvency law' include provisions of Part VII or, in relation to countries or territories outside the United Kingdom, such of their laws as correspond to Part VII.

Indemnities for office-holders, markets etc.

F6.28 Where a relevant office-holder takes any action in relation to property of a defaulter which is liable to be dealt with in accordance with the market default rules and believes on reasonable grounds that he is entitled to take that action, he is not liable to any person in respect of any loss or damage resulting from that action except in so far as the loss or damage is caused by the office-holder's negligence.

Any failure by the market to comply with its own rules in respect of any matter does not prevent that matter being treated as done in accordance with those rules as long as the failure does not substantially affect the rights of any person entitled to require compliance with the rules.

No market, nor any officer, servant or member of the governing body of the market, is to be liable in damages for anything done or omitted in discharge or purported discharge of any functions of the market relating to, or matters arising out of, its default rules or any obligations to which it is subject by virtue of Part VII.

No delegate under paragraph 5 or 12 of Schedule 21, exercising his functions as such, nor any officer or servant of the delegate, is to be liable in damages for anything done or omitted in the discharge or purported discharge of those functions unless the act or omission is shown to have been in bad faith (section 184).

Interaction with the Financial Services Act 1986

F6.29 Section 72 of the Financial Services Act 1986 ('FSA') empowers the Secretary of State to present a petition for the winding up of an 'authorised person' (as defined by the FSA) where the authorised person is unable to pay its debts (within the meaning of section 123 or, as the case may be, section 221 of the Insolvency Act 1986) or it is just and equitable that that person should be wound up. Where the authorised person is a member of a recognised self-regulating organisation ('SRO') or a recognised professional body ('RPB'), the power can only be exercised with the consent of that organisation or body. Section 74 of the FSA empowers a SRO or RPB, or the Treasury, to present an administration petition in respect of a member of a SRO or RPB, or an appointed representative or an authorised person, in the circumstances set out in that section.

Further, section 67 of the FSA provides that the Treasury may impose a requirement that all assets, or all assets of a specified person or description (including overseas assets), belonging to an authorised person or appointed representative or belonging to investors but held by or to the order of an authorised person or appointed representative, be transferred and held by a trustee approved by the Treasury and be dealt with in accordance with the directions of the Treasury.

Where a winding-up or administration order is made, or a vesting of assets has taken place, pursuant to the above provisions, the provisions of Part VII dealt with above continue to apply insofar as the authorised person or appointed representative concerned has been involved in any market contracts or market charges. However, where assets have been vested in and are held by a trustee, the Treasury will need to issue alternative directions so as to facilitate the operation of Part VII.

Compensation fund

F6.30 It may be worth noting that compensation schemes have been established pursuant to section 54 of the FSA for the purpose of compensating investors in cases where an authorised person is unable (or likely to be unable) to satisfy claims in respect of any description of liability incurred by the authorised person in connection with his investment business. Where the authorised person is involved in market contracts and market charges, the compensation schemes may operate to supplement the Part VII provisions insofar as they do not result in investors being adequately compensated.

Chapter 7: Overall effect of Part VII

F7.1 As stated in F6.4 above, the default rules which a recognised investment exchange or clearing house is required to have are of the type which many of the exchanges or clearing houses have voluntarily adopted for a long time. What is significant is that they are now accorded statutory recognition, and protection from most of the problems which have been mentioned. A special contract between particular parties is rendered almost unnecessary except where a particular counterparty wishes to secure its position better than that of other counterparties by taking an individual charge or a 'flawed asset' provision over non-market assets.

The problem about multilateral set-off will still remain unless a market charge is taken. Such a charge can have statutory recognition and extra protection.

The 'fungibility' problem will remain in so far as a particular counterparty seeks to assert a proprietary interest over market assets. An unpaid vendor's lien will rank after any market charge.

The residual problems about 'cherry-picking', preferences, undervalue transactions and void dispositions regarding pre- or post-insolvency performance of transactions or creation of or dispositions under market charges, and about the *Charge Card* case in relation to cash margins, are effectively resolved to a large extent. It is in these areas that Part VII appears to achieve the most discernible results. Preferential creditors of a defaulter will still rank ahead of the market and its members as regards proceeds of a floating individual or market charge.

Complex practical problems can arise where there are in existence an individual charge, a market charge and a bank charge at the time an administration order is made. A market charge will not necessarily be a prior charge. Notwithstanding that, the administrator and the prior chargee will be powerless. The market charge can be enforced by the appointment of a receiver or otherwise, but not the prior charge. The administrator will have the statutory power to sell the assets freed from the prior charge, although not from the subsequent market charge, but he may not be able to exercise that power in practice. To do so could constitute interference with the default proceedings (see F6.6 and F6.23 above). Even if there is no market charge, the administrator and the other chargee may have to take a back seat until the default proceedings are completed for the benefit of market creditors. Any prospect of the relevant office-holder being able to dispose of the insolvent party's business as a going concern could be made more remote and non-market creditors may suffer as a result. There could thus be a conflict of interest between the market and the office-holder, but it is hoped that the two will strive to work in harmony to maximise the overall realisation of the defaulter's assets for the benefit of non-market as well as market creditors.

Part G: Dissolution and Revival

1. **Dissolution** **633**

   Methods of dissolution 633
   Striking-off by the Registrar of Companies—procedure
      under section 652 633
   Practical use of the section 652 procedure by a
      company's directors 634
   Cancellation of registration 635
   Striking off by the Registrar of Companies—procedure under
      sections 652A–652F 635

2. **Effect of dissolution** **638**

3. **Revival of a dissolved company** **641**

   Section 651: order declaring dissolution void 641
   Section 653 and 653(2A) to (2D) 645
   Procedure for application: section 651 or 653 647

Part G: Dissolution and Revival

Chapter 1: Dissolution

Methods of dissolution

G1.1   The existence of a company incorporated in England and Wales or in Scotland may be brought to an end:

(*a*)   by dissolution as the ultimate stage of

    (i)   a members' or creditors' voluntary winding up (see sections 94, 106 and 201 of the Insolvency Act 1986 (the 1986 Act) and PART C: LIQUIDATIONS); or

    (ii)   a compulsory winding-up (see sections 202 to 205 of the 1986 Act and PART C: LIQUIDATIONS); or

(*b*)   by dissolution as a result of the company's name being struck off the register by the Registrar of Companies pursuant to section 652 of the Companies Act 1985 (the 1985 Act), and sections 652A to 652F of that Act (as inserted by Schedule 5 to the Deregulation and Contracting Out Act 1994); or

(*c*)   by dissolution by the court without winding up under section 427 of the 1985 Act as part of a scheme of reconstruction or amalgamation.

See also G1.6 below.

Striking-off by the Registrar of Companies—procedure under section 652

G1.2   The procedure under section 652 of the 1985 Act may be invoked by the Registrar:

(1)   where he has reasonable cause to believe that the company is not carrying on business or is not in operation (section 652(1)); or

(2)   where the company is being wound up and he has reasonable cause to believe either that no liquidator is acting, or that the affairs of the company are fully wound up, and the returns required to be made by the liquidator have not been made for a period of six consecutive months (section 652(4)).

Where company is apparently not carrying on business nor in operation

G1.3   Where case (1) under G1.2 above applies, the procedure is as follows:

(*a*) the Registrar sends to the company by post a letter inquiring whether it is carrying on business or in operation (section 652(1));

(*b*) if he does not receive a reply within one month, he sends the company within 14 days thereafter a reminder by registered post giving the company a further month from the date of the reminder to respond (section 652(2));

(*c*) if he receives an answer that the company is not carrying on business or is not in operation, or does not receive a reply to the second letter within the further period of one month referred to in (*b*) above, he publishes in the *London Gazette* (or, where the company is registered in Scotland, in the *Edinburgh Gazette*—CA 1985, s 744), and sends to the company by post, a notice that at the expiration of three months from the date of that notice the name of the company will, unless cause is shown to the contrary, be struck off the register and the company will be dissolved (section 652(3));

(*d*) at the expiration of the period of three months referred to in (*c*), the Registrar may, unless cause to the contrary is previously shown by the company, strike its name off the register and must publish notice thereof in the *London* or *Edinburgh Gazette*, as appropriate. Upon the publication of the notice the company is dissolved (section 652(5)).

The right to show cause to the contrary is confined to the company. However, it is understood that in practice the Registrar is willing to take into account representations from a creditor, shareholder or a person otherwise having an interest in keeping the company in existence. Note that the operative words in section 652(5) are 'the Registrar may' and not 'the Registrar shall'. After the company is struck off, the remedy of such a person will be as stated in G3.3 below.

Where a company is being wound up

G1.4 Where case (2) under G1.2 above applies, the Registrar publishes in the *London* or *Edinburgh Gazette* and sends to the company or the liquidator, if any, the notice referred to in (*c*) above. The final step is as in (*d*) above (section 652(4) and (5)).

Practical use of the section 652 procedure by a company's directors

G1.5 Under the section 652 procedure, it has been possible for the directors informally to invite the Registrar invoke the procedure to strike off a company. Directors have often used this alternative as a cheaper method of dissolving a company than that through a winding up. This has normally been done by writing to the Registrar, informing him that the company is not carrying on business or in operation. The Registrar then informs the Inland Revenue, asking it if it has any objection to the striking-off. The Inland Revenue normally take five or six weeks to reply. If it does have an objection, the Registrar will put a stop on the striking-off of the company for a period of two years. If the Inland Revenue does not have any objection, the Registrar will proceed in the normal way as in

G1.3 above. He is only concerned with whether the company has ceased to carry on business or to be in operation—not whether the company has any assets or liabilities; but as the assets become *bona vacantia* upon dissolution (see G2.1 below), caution is advisable before the directors resort to this procedure.

The section 652 procedure (formerly section 353 of the 1948 Act) used to be the most common provision under which companies were dissolved after winding up by the court. The intention of the old legislation, in respect of winding up by the court, was that the liquidator should apply for a court order dissolving the company. In practice, however, the liquidator chose to have the company dissolved under section 652 and its precursor. This avoided the cost and delay of applying to the court, and allowed a longer period for applications to restore the company. The procedure for dissolution after a court winding up has now been simplified so as to provide for automatic dissolution after the delivery of specified documents to the Registrar. In this respect, the procedure has been assimilated to that following a voluntary winding up. Further, in a court winding up, the Official Receiver has been empowered to invoke an early dissolution procedure (see sections 201 to 205 of the 1986 Act and C16.7 PART C: LIQUIDATIONS).

Cancellation of registration

G1.6   Although not strictly an example of dissolution, this is another case where a company can cease to exist. In *R v Registrar of Companies ex p the Attorney-General (1980) [1991] BCLC 476* the High Court quashed a decision by the Registrar to register the business of a prostitute as a company called Lindi St. Clair (Personal Services) Ltd. Contracts made for sexually immoral purposes were against public policy and therefore the company should not have been registered—its purpose was illegal.

In *R v Registrar of Companies ex p Central Bank of India [1986] 1 All ER 105*, the Court of Appeal was of the opinion that only the Attorney-General could bring such proceedings.

The effect of cancellation is unclear. Article 12, paragraph 3 of the First Directive of the Council of the European Communities (Directive 68/151/EEC) requires that the nullity of a company shall not affect the validity of any commitments entered into by or with the company. This requirement has not yet been implemented by United Kingdom legislation.

Striking-off by the Registrar of Companies—procedure under sections 652A–652F

G1.7   These new sections (which are expected to come into force in July 1995) are specifically enacted to enable a private company to apply to be voluntarily struck off the register. Section 652A provides that on an application, in the prescribed form and containing the prescribed information, made on behalf of a private company by its directors or a majority of them, the Registrar may effect a striking off. Before doing so, he must, however, allow three months to elapse after publication by him of a notice in the *Gazette* inviting any person to show cause why he should not do so. Once the company is struck off, he must publish that fact in the *Gazette*. The section expressly provides that, notwithstanding the striking off, the liability (if any) of the directors, managing officers and members of the company, and the court's power to wind up the company, continue.

The right to make such an application is subject to a number of important restrictions. No application must be made where in the three previous months the company has

(*a*)   changed its name,

(*b*)   traded or otherwise carried on business,

(*c*)   made a disposal for value of property or rights held by it for the purposes of disposal for gain in the normal course of trading or carrying on business, or

(*d*)   engaged in any other activity, except one which is necessary or expedient for the purpose of making, or deciding whether to make, the application, or for concluding the affairs of the company, or for complying with any statutory requirement, or which is specified by the Secretary of State by order

(section 652B(1)).

A payment in respect of liability incurred in the course of trading or otherwise carrying on business is not caught by the above restrictions (section 652B(2)).

Further, no application must be made in any of the following circumstances:

 (i)   an application to the court under section 425 to sanction a compromise or arrangement has not been finally concluded;

 (ii)   a voluntary arrangement has been proposed but has not been finally concluded;

(iii)   an administration order is in force or a petition for such an order has been presented but not finally dealt with or withdrawn;

(iv)   the company is being wound up by the court or voluntarily, or a winding-up petition has been presented but has not been finally dealt with or withdrawn;

 (v)   there is a receiver or manager of the company's property; or

(vi)   the company's estate is being administered by a judicial factor

(section 652B(3)).

(As to the meaning of 'finally concluded', see section 652B(4) and (5).)

Important obligations are imposed on the persons who make the application on the company's behalf. They are required to ensure that a copy of the application is given to the members, employees, creditors, directors who have not joined in the application, managers or trustees of any employee pension fund and any other categories of persons specified by the Secretary of State by regulations (section 652B(6)). If, after the making of the application, any of the events referred to in the preceding two paragraphs above occurs, or if circumstances arise in which under section 84(1) of the Insolvency Act 1986 the company may be voluntarily wound up, the persons who are directors at the end of the day on which the event occurs must secure that the application is withdrawn (section 652C).

Chapter 2: Effect of dissolution

G2.1   The dissolution of a company has the following effects.

1. All property and rights vested in or held on trust for the company immediately before its dissolution (including leasehold property but not including property held by the company on trust for any other person), are deemed to be *bona vacantia* (CA 1985, s 654). As a result, the property and rights belong to the Crown (which expression is used here to include the Duchy of Lancaster or the Duke of Cornwall, as the case may be), subject to any order made by the court under section 651 or 653 of the 1985 Act (see below), and except as provided by section 655 of that Act (see also below). However, where the property is land subject to a rentcharge, the vesting does not subject the Crown to any liability in respect of any sums becoming due under the rentcharge, except liability in respect of any sums accruing due after the Crown has taken possession or control of the land or has entered into occupation thereof (section 658 of the Companies Act 1985 as read with section 180 of the 1986 Act).

2. Any property or rights so vested may, however, be disclaimed by the Crown by a notice executed (i) within twelve months of the date of vesting, or (ii) if any person has by written application required the Crown to decide whether or not to disclaim it, within three months after the receipt of such application or within such further period as may be allowed by the court (section 656 of the 1985 Act). A notice of disclaimer is required to be filed with the Registrar of Companies, copies of which will be published in the *London* or *Edinburgh Gazette* and be sent to any persons who have given the Crown representative notice that they claim to be interested in the property (section 656(5)). A disclaimer under section 656 has, as regards property in England and Wales, the same effect as if it was a disclaimer under section 178(4) and sections 179 to 182 of the 1986 Act made immediately before the dissolution (section 657(2) of the 1985 Act, and see C12.6 PART C: LIQUIDATIONS). This means, for example, that a person claiming an interest in the disclaimed property or having any liability in respect of it not discharged by the disclaimer can apply to the court, under the 1986 Act provisions referred to above, for an order vesting the property in him as if it had been disclaimed by a liquidator. However, in *Re No 1 London Ltd* [*1991*] *BCLC 501*, such an order was refused by Hoffmann J to the surety under a lease disclaimed by the Crown, because, as in the case of a disclaimer by a liquidator, the effect of the disclaimer was to discharge the surety's future, though not his existing or past, liability under the lease. The existing or past liability was not a liability 'in respect of the disclaimed property', as the disclaimed property was the unexpired term, in respect of which the surety had no liability.

    As regards property in Scotland, see section 657(3)–(7) of the 1985 Act.

3. Where the company has been struck off, the power of the court to wind up that company is not affected (section 652(6)(b)). However, the person seeking the winding-up order should ask for both restoration to the register and a winding up (*Re Cambridge Coffee Room Association Ltd [1952] 1 All ER 112*).

4. A pending action *by the company* (as distinct from against the company) ceases absolutely and for all time on the company's dissolution and is not revived by a subsequent order, under section 651, declaring the dissolution void (*Foster Yates & Thom Ltd v H W Edgehill Equipment Ltd (1978) 122 SJ 860*).

5. Where the company has assigned its right of action against a third party before dissolution, the right survives in favour of the assignee insofar as he is able to sue in his own name without joining the company. Examples are where the debt is purely equitable, or where section 136 of the Law of Property Act 1925 applies (absolute legal assignment by writing under the hand of the assignor).

6. A legal estate (including a leasehold estate) held by the company does not ordinarily come to an end (*Re Strathblaine Estates [1948] Ch 228*) (but will vest in the Crown, subject to its right of disclaimer— see 2. above). Where it does come to an end, section 181 of the Law of Property Act 1925 enables the court to create a corresponding estate and vest it in the person who would have been entitled to the estate which has determined.

7. In relation to any property held by the company on trust for any person the court may make a vesting order in favour of the beneficiary (see sections 44(ii)(c) and 51(ii)(c) of the Trustee Act 1925 and *Re Strathblaine Estates*, above).

8. No proceedings can be taken under section 212 of the 1986 Act against the directors or officers for misfeasance unless, it seems, fraud is alleged (*Coxon v Gorst [1891] 2 Ch 73*).

9. A creditor may have a right in damages against a liquidator if he has wilfully or negligently distributed the assets and caused the dissolution of the company without providing for the creditor's debt (*Pulsford v Devenish [1903] 2 Ch 625; Re Armstrong Whitworth Securities Co [1947] Ch 673*). Under the old legislation it was held that where a liquidator sold and purported to convey land to which the company had no title, and then, after due notice under Rule 106 of the Companies (Winding-up) Rules 1949 (see now Rule 11.3(2) of the Insolvency Rules 1986), proceeded to make a distribution to creditors and contributories and the company was dissolved before the purchaser realised the defect in title, the purchaser had no right of action against the contributories (*Butler and another v Broadhead and others [1974] 3 WLR 27*).

10. A solicitor who continues to represent a company after it has been dissolved may be liable to an opposing party for costs incurred after dissolution.

11. An action cannot be brought in the name of a dissolved company. This applies even where an insurer had become subrogated to the rights of the company before the dissolution by having discharged the company's claim for loss suffered as a result of the potential defendant's negligence. Further, in the absence of an express assignment to it of the company's right, the insurer cannot bring the action in his own name, as the right of subrogation does not have the effect of transferring the cause of action (*M H Smith (Plant Hire) Ltd v D L Mainwaring [1986] BCLC 342*).

12. A person who, before the dissolution of a company in liquidation, has not established (by judgment of a court or arbitrator's award) the existence of his claim (for example, for personal injuries) and its amount against the company is not entitled to be subrogated to the rights of the company against its insurers in respect of such claim under the Third Parties (Rights against Insurers) Act 1930 (*Bradley v Eagle Star Insurance Co Ltd [1989] 2 WLR 568*).

13. The Registrar may at any time after the expiration of two years from the date of dissolution direct that any documents in his custody relating to the dissolution be removed to the Public Record Office, and they can be disposed of in accordance with the enactments relating to that Office and the Rules made under them (section 712 of the 1985 Act; this section does not apply to Scotland).

Chapter 3: Revival of a dissolved company

G3.1   The following explains the procedure for and effect of reviving a dissolved company. The court has power under section 653 of the 1985 Act to restore to the register a company which has been struck off under section 652. Such restoration also results in the dissolution becoming void. The court also has overall power in the case of any dissolved company to declare a dissolution to have been void. Such a declaration also results in the company being put back on the register. Thus, in the case of a company that has been struck off the register, the court has jurisdiction under section 651 to declare the dissolution void as it has under section 653 to restore the company to the register (*Re Belmont & Co Ltd [1952] Ch 10*). The converse is not true, however, so that where a company has been dissolved as the ultimate stage of a winding up, or as part of a scheme of reconstruction or amalgamation under section 427 (see above), the court has jurisdiction under section 651, but not under section 653, to declare the dissolution void.

Although the effects of the dissolution of the company, whether as the ultimate stage of winding up or by striking off, are largely similar, the effects of subsequent restoration are somewhat different depending on whether it is made under section 651 or under section 653, as is also explained below.

Section 651: order declaring dissolution void

G3.2   By virtue of section 651, where a company has been dissolved the court may, on an application being made within the applicable time limit (see below) by the liquidator or any person who appears to the court to be interested, make an order upon such terms as it thinks fit, declaring the dissolution to have been void and thereupon such proceedings may be taken as might have been taken if the company had not been dissolved. Section 651 has been amended by section 141 of the Companies Act 1989, which came into force on 16 November 1989 (the date of Royal Assent). The amendment seeks to mitigate the effect of *Bradley v Eagle Star Insurance Co Ltd* referred to in item 12. of G2.1 above in cases of claims against the company in respect of personal injuries or fatal accidents, by inserting new subsections (4) to (7) in section 651.

Generally, as was the case previously, the time limit for making an application to declare the dissolution void is two years from the date of the dissolution (section 651(4)). However, the amendment extends the time limit indefinitely where such an application is made for the purposes of bringing proceedings against the company—

(*a*)   for damages in respect of personal injuries (including any sum claimed by virtue of section 1(2)(c) of the Law Reform (Miscellaneous Provisions) Act 1934 (funeral expenses)), or (*b*)   for damages under the Fatal Accidents Act 1976 or the Damages (Scotland) Act 1976 (section 651(5)).

Thus, the relevant claimant who has not established his claim before the dissolution of the company will not be deprived of any right of subrogation against the company's insurers under the Third Parties (Rights against Insurers) Act 1930 merely because two years have elapsed since the dissolution. Provided that before his claim becomes statute-barred, he successfully applies for the dissolution to be declared void and brings proceedings against the company which eventually succeed, any such right of subrogation will not be adversely affected. Section 651(5) provides that the court may decline the application if it appears to it that the proceedings would fail by virtue of any enactment governing limitation periods (but see the comments below on section 651(6)). 'Personal injuries' include any disease and any impairment of a person's mental or physical condition (section 651(7)).

The discretionary power of the court under section 651(5) to restore a company to the register, for the purpose of enabling the applicant to bring an action against the company for damages for personal injuries or death, is not necessarily barred because the primary limitation period for bringing such an action laid down by section 11 of the Limitation Act 1980 has expired, since an order could be made pursuant to section 33 of that Act overriding the primary period. The court should refuse a restoration order only if it is plain that a judge of the Queen's Bench Division would refuse to make an overriding order under section 33. Where the primary period had not expired at the date of dissolution of the company, and the court is satisfied that a section 33 order would succeed, the court may make an order under section 651(6) (see below) so as to avoid an unnecessary section 33 application (*Re Workvale Ltd [1992] 1 WLR 416*).

Section 651(6) provides that nothing in section 651(5) (above) affects the power of the court to direct that the period between the dissolution and the making of an order declaring it to be void is not to be counted for the purposes of the statutes of limitation. This assumes that the court has power to make such a 'limitation override' order. However, according to *Re Mixhurst Ltd [1993] BCC 748* (applying *Morris v Harris [1927] AC 252*), that assumption is misplaced and the court has no power, when declaring a dissolution void under section 651, to make a 'limitation override' order (except in the limited circumstances referred to in the previous paragraph, in the context of section 651(5)).

The assumption appears to have been based on the cases decided in the context of what is now section 653 relating to restoration following striking off (see G3.3 below), subsection (3) of which, unlike any part of section 651 relating to avoidance of dissolution following a winding up, expressly empowers the court to 'give such directions and make such provisions as seem just for placing the company and all other persons in the same position (as nearly as may be) as if the company's name had not been struck off'. The rationale for this difference in position seems to be that the striking off of a company is less likely to come to the notice of the public than its winding up and, except in rare cases, the position of all parties affected would have been dealt with in the winding up. In any case, the absence of the power to make a 'limitation override' order under section 651 is generally unlikely to operate harshly on a potential plaintiff. The period of limitation would have ceased to run on the commencement of the winding up, at least until the dissolution following the winding up (see *Re General Rolling Stock Company (1872) LR 7 Ch App 646*, and also C9.5 PART C: LIQUIDATIONS) and it is well established that on a dissolution being declared void, the company is restored to the state that it was in prior to the dissolution becoming effective (see below; and *Re Mixhurst* above).

In relation to a company dissolved more than two years before the commencement of that section (i.e. before 16 November 1987), an application may be made under the amended section 651(5) of the 1985 Act for the purpose of bringing the proceedings above referred to in relation to a company dissolved not more than 20 years before the date of commencement of section 141 (16 November 1969), even though the time limit (of two years) within which the dissolution might formerly have been declared void had already expired when section 141 came into force (CA 1989, s 141(4), (5)).

As indicated above (*Re Belmont & Co Ltd [1952] Ch 10*), the court's power under section 651 applies whether the dissolution occurs as the ultimate stage of a winding up, or occurs as a result of striking-off under section 652. For a person to be 'interested', he must have a proprietary or pecuniary interest in reviving the company. This does not include a solicitor to a proposed claimant (*Re Roehampton Swimming Pool Ltd [1968] 1 WLR 1693*). It *does* include a person who at the time of the dissolution was a creditor of the company. *Quaere* whether, unlike in the case of a striking-off (see the *Aga Estate* case referred to in G3.3 below), it suffices if he was only a *contingent* creditor (having regard to the rule that in the winding up which preceded the dissolution even a contingency would have to be provable, subject to the rule against double proof, if applicable)—see C14.9 PART C: LIQUIDATIONS.

The principles which the court will apply on an application to declare dissolution void were helpfully reviewed in *Re Forte's (Manufacturing) Ltd [1994] BCC 84*, where the Court of Appeal granted a landlord's application to revive a company (Forte) which had been dissolved following a members' voluntary liquidation. The purpose of the revival was to enable the landlord to lodge a claim in the liquidation for unpaid and future rent under a lease originally granted to the company and ultimately, following successive assignments, held by BCCI which had since gone into insolvent liquidation. In turn, the liquidator of Forte could claim the amount from the interim (solvent) assignee and distribute it by way of dividend for the benefit of the landlord.

Hoffmann J said that nowadays it would be more accurate to say that ordinarily the purpose of section 651 is to enable either (i) the liquidator to distribute an overlooked asset (*Re Servers of the Blind League [1960]*

1 WLR 564), or (ii) a creditor to make a claim which he had not previously made.

The further dictum in *Re Servers of the Blind League* (above) that the jurisdiction should not be exercised to put the applicant in a better position than he would have been if the liquidation had been properly conducted does not apply to cases where a claim in the original liquidation based on a contingency would have been lower than the claim which will be made following the revival. *Re Forte's (Manufacturing) Ltd* (above) does not expressly entirely rule out revival merely because the claim on revival would still be contingent. It is sufficient if the applicant's interest is more than 'merely shadowy': *Re Wood and Martin (Bricklaying Contractors) Ltd [1971] 1 WLR 293*.

On an application, the Registrar of Companies and the former liquidator should be joined as parties. Other parties having an interest may be allowed to be joined in if their presence is, in the words of RSC Order 15, rule 6(2)(b)(i) 'necessary to ensure that all matters in dispute . . . may be effectually and completely determined . . .' (*Re Forte's (Manufacturing) Ltd* (above)).

In *In re Townreach Ltd [1994] 3 WLR 983*, the court granted the Secretary of State's application to revive two companies. In relation to the first company, the court also made an order declaring valid a voluntary winding-up resolution which the company had purported to pass following its being struck off the register. The revival order in relation to the second company was made so as to enable the Secretary of State to invoke his investigatory powers under section 447 of the Companies Act 1985. It was held that the Secretary of State in those circumstances was a 'person interested' in the terms of section 651, that the court's power was not confined to cases where the dissolution followed liquidation but was also available where the dissolution occurred as a result of the striking off, and that the court had power to give consequential directions.

The effect of an order is that such proceedings may be taken as might have been taken if the company had not been dissolved, and all consequences flowing from the dissolution are themselves avoided. Therefore any property which had purportedly vested in the Crown as *bona vacantia* is treated as having never so vested; alternatively, such vesting is avoided by the restoration order. No order expressly vesting the property in the company is required (*Re C W Dixon Ltd [1947] Ch 251*). However, any purported corporate activity of the company carried out during the period of dissolution is not validated (*Morris v Harris [1927] AC 252*; contrast with the position where there is restoration under section 653—see below). Furthermore, as mentioned above, any action *by the company* (as distinct from against the company) which was pending at the time of dissolution is not revived.

The person on whose application the order is made must within seven days after the making of the order, or such further time as the court may allow, file with the Registrar of Companies an office copy of the order (section 651(3)).

Section 653 and 653(2A) to (2D): restoration to the register

G3.3   Where a company has been struck off the register by the Registrar under section 652 of the 1985 Act, and the company or any member or creditor feels aggrieved by such striking-off, the court may, on an application made by the aggrieved party before the expiration of 20 years from the publication of the notice in the *London* or *Edinburgh Gazette* referred to above, order the company to be restored to the register (section 653). For this purpose, a person is not a 'creditor' unless he was a creditor at the time the company was struck off the register. A surety who discharges the company's liability after the striking-off does not qualify (*Re Aga Estate Agencies Ltd [1986] BCLC 346*). The Registrar should be joined as a party (*Re Test Holdings (Clifton) Ltd* above). The court must be satisfied that the company was at the time of striking-off carrying on business or in operation, or otherwise that it is just that the company be restored to the register.

Where a company has been struck off the register under section 652A, on an application by any person to whom a copy of the application to strike off had been given pursuant to section 652B or 652C (see G1.7 above), made before the expiration of 20 years from publication in the *Gazette* of the notice of striking off, the court may order the company to be restored to the register if the court is satisfied that there was a breach of duty under section 652B(1) or (3), or with respect to the giving of notice under section 652B or 652C, or that for some other reason it is just to order restoration. A restoration may also be ordered on an application by the Secretary of State made within that 20-year time limit on the ground that it is in the public interest to do so (section 653(2A) to (2D) as inserted by the Deregulation and Contracting Out Act 1994; note that these provisions are expected to come into force in July 1995).

In *Re Portrafram Ltd [1986] BCLC 533*, A Ltd applied to be joined as a party to section 653 restoration proceedings under RSC Order 15 rule 6 on the ground that its presence was necessary to ensure that all matters in dispute in the cause or matter may be effectually and completely determined (RSC Order 15, rule 6(2)(b)(i)), and in order to oppose the restoration of B Ltd. In that case, an agent of B Ltd had contracted with A Ltd on behalf of B Ltd at a time when B Ltd had been struck off. A Ltd wished to preserve its claim against the agent for breach of warranty of authority and negligence, which claims would be effectively extinguished by the retrospective effect of a section 653 restoration order (see below). The court held that it had no jurisdiction to join A Ltd as a party. The section 653 proceedings are quasi-administrative in nature and the matters to be determined cannot properly be described as being 'in dispute'.

Where the application is made by a creditor, the company is not entitled to *appear* on the application. The right of the company to *apply* for the restoration is a convenient statutory provision but does not affect its nonexistence for other purposes. A member, too, may be refused a right to appear if he has no interest in the result (*Re H Clarkson (Overseas) Ltd (1987) 3 BCC 606*). The court may refuse to recognise an applicant as an 'aggrieved' person if the benefit to that person of restoring the company to the register is *de minimis* (*Re Lindsay Bowman Ltd* [*1969*] *1 WLR 1443*).

As to the restoration to the register of a company struck off by the Registrar of Companies after the presentation of a winding-up petition but before the making of a winding-up order see *Re Thompson and Riches Ltd* [*1981*] *2 All ER 477*. In that case the court granted a declaration that the dissolution, vesting the company's assets in the Crown, was void and the assets were instead to be vested in the Official Receiver as liquidator. The company may apply to set aside an order to restore the company to the register but only with the authority of a general meeting (see generally *Re Regent Insulation Co Ltd, The Times, 5 November 1981*).

Upon an office copy of the restoration order being filed with the Registrar of Companies, the company is deemed to have continued in existence as if its name had not been struck off. The court may give such directions and make such provisions as seem just for placing the company and all other persons in the same position as nearly as may be as if the name of the company had not been struck off (section 653(3)).

In contrast to the position where the dissolution is declared void under section 651, a restoration order under section 653 is effective to validate retrospectively all acts done in the name or on behalf of the company during the period between striking-off and restoration of the name to the register (*Tymans Ltd v Craven* [*1952*] *2 QB 100 (CA)*; see also discussion generally in *Morris v Harris* above). The court's powers under section 653(3) referred to above are complementary to the provision in the same subsection to the effect that the company is deemed to have continued in existence. The powers are not expository. The court cannot therefore use these powers to preserve any rights that creditors might have acquired by dealing with the company after the striking-off and by virtue of the fact that the company did not in fact exist (for example rights against directors for breach of warranty of authority). An example of the proper use of these powers is the insertion in the restoration order of a provision that in the case of creditors who were not statute-barred at the date of dissolution, the period between the date of dissolution and the date of restoration to the register is not to be counted for the purposes of any statutes of limitation (see *Re Donald Kenyon Ltd* [*1956*] *1 WLR 1397*). Such a provision will not, however, be inserted as a matter of routine but only if there are sufficient grounds for doing so (*Re Huntington Poultry Ltd* [*1969*] *1 WLR 204*). (See discussion generally in *Re Lindsay Bowman Ltd*, above.) In *Advance Insulation Ltd* (*1989*) *5 BCC 55* a subsequent challenge to such a provision failed because it was made too late. The ground for the challenge was that the provision deprived the company as a defendant in an action, begun after the restoration, of a defence under section 33 of the Limitation Act 1980 (under which the extension of the period of limitation was at the discretion of the court). Thus, any person desiring the revival of a company which has been struck off the register may wish to consider which of the two courses, namely an order declaring the dissolution to be void (section 651) or an order for restoration (section 653), is available and/or more advantageous to him, having regard to the subtle differences in effect and differences in time limits for application and in the categories of persons having a standing to apply.

The court has no jurisdiction to impose any penalty (such as an order for payment of costs incurred by the Registrar in the process of striking the company off the register) on a company or any other applicant, as a price of restoring the company to the register. However, the applicants will normally be jointly and severally liable for the Registrar's costs in the *restoration proceedings*. Where the company was in breach of its duty and at least one applicant was guilty of some default, the normal order for taxation of costs of those proceedings should be on a common fund basis, instead of the more usual party and party basis (*Re Court Lodge Development Co Ltd [1973] 1 WLR 1097*).

An order declaring the dissolution void or restoring the company to the register under section 651 or 653 respectively of the 1985 Act does not affect any disposition already made by the Crown, the Duchy of Lancaster or the Duke of Cornwall of property, or of any right or interest therein, vested in those bodies as *bona vacantia*. The purpose of this provision is to protect purchasers of property from those bodies. But the relevant body must account to the company for any consideration received for the property, right or interest or the value of any such consideration at the time of the disposition or, if no consideration was received, an amount equal to the value of the property, right or interest disposed of, as at the date of the disposition (see section 655 of the 1985 Act, which applies in relation to the disposition of property, rights or interests by the Crown, the Duchy of Lancaster or the Duke of Cornwall made on or after 22 December 1981, whether the company was dissolved before, on or after that date).

Procedure for application: section 651 or 653

G3.4   An application for restoration is usually made in the Chancery Division by originating summons under Order 102, rule 2 of the Rules of the Supreme Court 1965 (as amended). In England and Wales, notice of application for a declaration that a dissolution is void or for restoration to the register must be given to the Attorney-General through the Treasury Solicitor (see *Practice Notes [1928] WN 218* and *[1931] WN 199* and *Re Belmont & Co Ltd [1952] Ch 10*).

Under English procedure, the company must be made co-applicant and the Registrar of Companies a respondent where restoration to the register is sought (see also *Re Walter Wright [1923] WN 128*). The Registrar will normally insist, as a condition of his not opposing the application, at least where the applicant is the company itself, that all outstanding annual returns, accounts and other papers necessary to bring the public file up to date are filed before the hearing. This may involve the applicant in the payment of substantial late filing penalties. The costs of the Registrar and the Treasury Solicitor in connection with the application will normally be awarded against the applicant. Before granting the application, the court may require production of a letter of disclaimer signed on behalf of the Crown disclaiming its rights under the *bona vacantia* rule.

Part H: Taxation

1. Introduction   **651**

2. Tax planning   **652**

Termination of group relationship   652
Capital (chargeable) gains   653
New accounting period   654
Anti-tax avoidance provisions   654
Preferential debts in insolvency   654
Stamp duty relief on intra-group transfer   655
VAT relief on transfer of going concern   655
VAT group registration   656

3. Tax liabilities in insolvency   **657**

Corporation tax on income and trading profits   657
Corporation tax on capital (chargeable) gains   660
PAYE and national insurance contributions (etc.)   660
Stamp duty   661
Value added tax   661
Crown set-off   664
Relief from tax on debt waived in a voluntary arrangement   664

Part H: Taxation

Chapter 1: Introduction

H1.1   This Part considers two aspects of taxation: first, any opportunities for tax planning before the commencement of and during a corporate insolvency procedure; and, secondly, the nature and extent of tax liabilities falling to be dealt with within a corporate insolvency procedure. The references to the Taxes Act are to the Income and Corporation Taxes Act 1988.

It is not within the scope of this book to deal with either of these aspects in more than just the briefest outline. For detailed treatment, the reader should consult specialist textbooks, such as *Tolley's Taxation in Corporate Insolvency*.

Certain taxation aspects affecting particular corporate insolvency procedures, or all corporate insolvency procedures generally, have been touched upon earlier in this book at appropriate places: see, for example, A4.11 PART A: GENERAL; B5.18 PART B: ADMINISTRATION ORDERS; C2.4, C2.6, C14.8, and C15.9 PART C: LIQUIDATIONS; D4.7, D7.4, D7.6(2), D8.5, D8.12, and D9.4 to D9.13 PART D: RECEIVERS; and E4.1 PART E: VOLUNTARY ARRANGEMENTS.

Chapter 2: Tax planning

H2.1 Tax planning in the context of corporate insolvency procedures, actual or prospective, may require the following, among other, issues to be addressed.

Termination of group relationship

H2.2 For certain purposes of the tax legislation, the commencement of winding up, unlike the commencement of an administration or administrative receivership, has the effect of divesting the company of the beneficial ownership of its assets, including any shares in subsidiaries. One consequence of this is that the group relationship between the company and its subsidiaries, and that traced through the company, is severed (*IRC v Olive Mills Ltd [1963] 1 WLR 712; Ayerst v CK (Construction) Ltd [1976] AC 167*). Accordingly, the transfer of tax losses within the group is no longer possible.

Therefore, consideration should be given to the feasibility of effecting, before the commencement of winding up, any advantageous surrender of trading losses by way of group relief to the maximum possible extent, or carrying out an appropriate group restructuring by interposing a sub-holding company or by hiving down the company's business (as to which see C2.6 PART C: LIQUIDATIONS and D9.4 *et seq.* PART D: RECEIVERS).

These actions may be carried out by the directors, if the company is not in administration or administrative receivership; otherwise, they may be carried out by the administrator or the administrative receiver (but, again, before the commencement of winding up). Both these office-holders have power under paragraph 16 of Schedule 1 to the Insolvency Act 1986 to transfer business and property to subsidiaries; but where, for the purposes of any corporate acts in relation to any of the above actions, it is necessary to convene a meeting of the members, the office-holders may need the cooperation of the directors or an order of the court.

As stated above, a group relationship is not severed on the commencement of an administration or an administrative receivership, (so long as winding up has not commenced). However, any intra-group surrender of losses, for example, between the company and its subsidiary, or any hive-down of the company's business and assets to its subsidiary with a view to enabling the subsidiary to utilise the tax losses of the business, should be carried out before any arrangements (even if they fall short of a binding or unconditional contract) for the sale of the shares in the subsidiary are entered into. This is because the Inland Revenue has expressed the view that (i) such arrangements might be regarded as divesting the company of the beneficial ownership of the shares and (ii) that the approval by the creditors' meeting under section 24 of the Insolvency Act 1986 of the administrator's proposals (see B5.4 and B5.15 PART B: ADMINISTRATION ORDERS) which include a disposal of the shares might constitute such arrangements (see section 410 of the Taxes Act).

Capital (chargeable) gains

H2.3   The severance of the group relationship discussed in H2.2 above does not bring about a deemed disposal of chargeable assets for the purposes of corporation tax on capital gains (section 170(11) of the Taxation of Chargeable Gains Act 1992). Further, there is no such severance, as regards any future transactions involving chargeable assets, for capital gains tax purposes, so that there can still be intra-group transfers of assets without a chargeable gain or an allowable loss arising (section 171 of the Taxation of Chargeable Gains Act 1992). Nevertheless, there may be some practical advantage in effecting a transfer of chargeable assets before the commencement of winding up. For example, where the company has assets which are likely to give rise to a chargeable gain on disposal outside the group, they may be transferred to a group company which has unutilised capital losses; or where a disposal outside the group of the company's chargeable assets is likely to give rise to capital losses, and such losses are likely to remain unutilised by the company, the assets may be transferred to a group company which might be able to utilise such losses by setting them against any chargeable gains arising on the disposal outside the group of its own other chargeable assets.

Where the company is in receivership but not in liquidation, and the receiver proposes to dispose of an asset which may give rise to a chargeable gain, consideration should be given to effecting disposal before the company goes into liquidation. Although the receiver is neither personally liable for, nor obliged to discharge out of the receivership funds, any corporation tax on a chargeable gain arising on the disposal of the asset, whether before or during liquidation (see below), any chargeable gain arising on disposal by him during liquidation will be required to be discharged by the liquidator out of the liquidation funds in priority to the claims of preferential and ordinary creditors and (partly) his remuneration (see *Re Mesco Properties Ltd [1979] STC 788*; Rule 4.218(1)(o), (p) and (q) of the Insolvency Rules 1986; see also C15.2 PART C: LIQUIDATIONS).

It is not clear whether any corporation tax on a chargeable gain arising on the disposal of a chargeable asset by an administrator is required to be paid out of the administration funds—see below.

Where the liquidation of a solvent holding company is proposed, it may be advisable to get its subsidiary to pay to the holding company, before the commencement of its liquidation, as much dividend as can properly be paid. This will minimise the holding company's liability to corporation tax on any capital gain that may arise on the deemed disposal of the shares in the subsidiary arising as a result of the liquidation, and consequently leave more funds distributable among the shareholders of the holding company. No liability to advance corporation tax would arise in respect of any such dividend if there subsists a group income election. However, it may be more appropriate for a subsidiary which has any surplus franked investment income to pay the whole or an appropriate part of the dividend outside any election, in which case notice must be given to the paying company's Inspector of Taxes.

New accounting period

H2.4 On the commencement of winding up, a new accounting period begins (section 12(7) of the Taxes Act). This may affect the company's ability to make use of group relief and capital allowances, and calculation of the amount of losses available for set off against profits and gains etc. This point may be relevant in deciding on the date upon which winding up should be commenced (if the circumstances allow any flexibility at all in this regard). For these purposes, winding up commences on the passing of a resolution to wind up, or the presentation of a winding-up petition (if no such resolution has previously been passed) provided that a winding-up order on such a petition is eventually made. (Note: a cessation of trading after the commencement of winding up does not again bring to an end the accounting period. Accordingly, trading losses made during the winding up may be set off against post-cessation income from other sources, such as deposit interest.)

Unlike a winding up, neither an administration nor an administrative receivership brings about the start of a new accounting period under section 12 of the Taxes Act. This view has been accepted by the Inland Revenue.

Anti-tax avoidance provisions

H2.5 Where a voluntary liquidation of the company is proposed as part of a reconstruction under section 139 of the Taxation of Chargeable Gains Act 1992 (see also section 110 of the Insolvency Act 1986), whereby there is to be a transfer of the company's assets to another party in return for the issue of shares or securities or other intangible assets of that party for their distribution *in specie* among the shareholders of the company on a 'no-gain, no-loss' basis, it is strongly advisable to seek the Inland Revenue's advance clearance under section 139(5) of the 1992 Act.

Advance clearances from the Inland Revenue under other provisions of the tax legislation may be required in relation to other types of transaction entered into in connection with or contemplation of a liquidation, which have the effect of reducing tax liability on any party to the transaction.

Preferential debts in insolvency

H2.6 Certain types of fiscal claims against a company in liquidation, receivership or voluntary arrangement rank as preferential debts within certain limits determined by reference to appropriate periods preceding the liquidation or receivership or the coming into effect of the voluntary arrangement (see C14.34 PART C: LIQUIDATIONS, D7.3 PART D: RECEIVERS and E2.7 PART E: VOLUNTARY ARRANGEMENTS). Further, although there are no preferential debts in an administration, those in a compulsory liquidation, where the winding-up order is made immediately following the discharge of the administration order, are determined by reference to the appropriate periods preceding the date of the administration order (see C14.34 PART C: LIQUIDATIONS).

The requirements as to the determination of preferential debts by reference to appropriate periods preceding the relevant insolvency event may thus present an opportunity for reducing the amount ranking as a preferential debt by either advancing or delaying the commencement of the relevant procedure, where circumstances permit this flexibility.

Stamp duty relief on intra-group transfer

H2.7   The relief from stamp duty on intra-group transfers of assets, for example, by way of a hive-down of the company's business and assets to a subsidiary before liquidation, which is normally available under section 42 of the Finance Act 1930 (as amended) (see D9.12 PART D: RECEIVERS) can be adversely affected by virtue of section 27(3) of the Finance Act 1967, if at the time of the transfer or agreement to transfer, there exists a contract, or even a non-binding arrangement, for the sale of the shares in the subsidiary to a third party. Therefore, it may be advisable to effect any intra-group transfer or contract for the transfer of assets before any specific contract or arrangement for the sale of the shares comes into existence or is contemplated.

VAT relief on transfer of going concern

H2.8   Value added tax is not chargeable on the transfer (intra-group or to a third party, and whether before the commencement of or during an insolvency procedure) of a business or part of a business as a going concern provided that the requisite conditions for relief are satisfied (see D9.13 PART D: RECEIVERS). Two of those conditions are that there should have been no significant break in trading (apart from a short period of closure immediately before the transfer) and that the transferee is or becomes liable to be registered for the purposes of value added tax as a result of the transfer.

The right to the relief described above is qualified, in relation to any land or building included in the sale of the going concern, by paragraph 5(2) of the VAT (Special Provisions) Order 1992 (SI 1992 No 3129). If, but for the above relief provisions, the land or building would be standard-rated (which would be the case if the vendor has opted to tax the building or if it is a new or uncompleted freehold building or civil engineering work), then the sale, insofar as it concerns such land or building, would only be regarded as that of a going concern if the *purchaser* both

(i) elects to waive the exemption from VAT, and

(ii) notifies in writing HM Customs and Excise of his election to be standard-rated in respect of any future dealings with the land or building before the sale is made.

Consideration should be given, as part of tax planning, to the feasibility of compliance with the above conditions.

VAT group registration

H2.9 Intra-group transfers of assets, whether as a going concern or otherwise and whether before the commencement of or during any insolvency procedure, does not attract a charge to value added tax if at the time of the transfer there is in force a VAT group registration involving the transferor and the transferee. In appropriate cases it may, therefore, be advantageous to keep such registration alive where any such transfer is contemplated.

On the other hand, VAT group registration also exposes each member of the group to liability, jointly and severally with all the other members of the group, for any value added tax due by any member of the group to HM Customs and Excise. Thus, where a state of actual or potential insolvency exists in relation to any one or more of the members of the group, consideration may have to be given to the cancellation or appropriate alteration of the group registration so as to avoid such exposure as regards future taxable supplies.

Chapter 3: Tax liabilities in insolvency

H3.1   Various categories of liabilities arising before and after the effective date of an insolvency procedure, and the manner in which they are required to be dealt with in each insolvency procedure, are dealt with below.

Corporation tax on income and trading profits

Liability before insolvency

H3.2   Liability arising before, or in respect of the period before, the effective date of the insolvency procedure concerned ranks as an unsecured non-preferential liability.

However, where the Inland Revenue has levied statutory distress in respect of such liability prior to the commencement of the procedures, it may, in certain circumstances, gain priority (even over a floating charge-holder) to the extent of the net proceeds of the distress. (See B4.1 PART B: ADMINISTRATION ORDERS; C7.4, C7.5, C8.2, C8.3, C9.4 PART C: LIQUIDATIONS; D7.13 PART D: RECEIVERS; E2.7 PART E: VOLUNTARY ARRANGEMENTS; and H3.16 below.

In arriving at the amount of such liability, it may be possible to set against the investment income or trading profit, any relevant losses incurred by the company in preceding accounting periods to the extent that they have remained unutilised and to the extent that the relevant tax legislation allows such set off. (See also H3.16 below.) The liability might also be mitigated in an administration or administrative receivership (provided that liquidation has not commenced) by surrender of group relief, since the commencement of these procedures (unlike liquidation) does not sever group relationships for this purpose (except as stated in H2.2 above). However, difficulties as regards set off may arise in a liquidation by reason of the fact that a new accounting period begins on the commencement of liquidation (see H2.4 above).

Liability during insolvency generally

H3.3   The status of any liability arising as a result of trading carried on or investment income derived *during* an insolvency procedure varies according to the type of insolvency procedure involved, as discussed below.

Liability during liquidation

H3.4   In a liquidation, the liability will rank as an expense of the winding up, to be discharged by the liquidator out of the assets coming into his hands before any payment to preferential or non-preferential creditors (see C15.1 PART C: LIQUIDATIONS). This obligation of the liquidator is reinforced by section 108 of the Taxes Management Act 1970 which constitutes the liquidator a 'proper officer' for the purposes of accounting for such tax. See also H3.5, H3.6 and H3.7 below.

Liability during administration

H3.5   In an administration, such liability may, arguably, have to be discharged by the administrator as an expense of the administration out of the assets of the company, including those comprised in a charge which, as created, was a floating charge (see B7.7 PART B: ADMINISTRATION ORDERS). (Section 108 of the 1970 Act (see H3.4 above) does not apply to an administrator.)

Liability during liquidation and administration

H3.6   Such liability does not become the *personal* liability of the liquidator or (as confirmed by the Inland Revenue) the administrator (since each acts in a representative, statutory capacity, the administrator expressly as agent for the company), so that if no or insufficient assets have come into his hands he is not required to discharge the liability or the balance thereof out of his personal financial resources, unless

(*a*)   at the time the liability was incurred, he knew or ought reasonably to have known that no or insufficient assets would be coming into his hands, or

(*b*)   he has distributed or disposed of the assets coming into his hands (for purposes having less priority) without making provision for such liability.

It would appear, however, that in the light of the principles of *Re Mesco Properties Ltd [1979] STC 788* the court will not allow the liquidator or the administrator to complete the insolvency process without discharging such liability as an expense of the winding up or administration out of the assets in his hands, inasmuch as it would have been incurred for the benefit, or presumed benefit, of the liquidation or administration.

Liability during administrative receivership

H3.7   The position in an administrative receivership is substantially different. There is no concept of expense of receivership (corresponding to that in a liquidation or administration), such as can be enforced by a third party like the Inland Revenue; nor is any priority right conferred by the tax (or other) legislation on the Inland Revenue in respect of such liability. Further, the security rights of the debenture-holder over all the assets of the company intervene on the appointment by him of the administrative receiver, and the floating charge contained in the debenture crystallises into a specific charge on such appointment, before the liability in favour of the Inland Revenue arises. Accordingly, the administrative receiver is not required to discharge any such liability out of the receivership assets, although he may, at his discretion, discharge them if to do so appears to him to be in the overall interest of the receivership (see, for example, the general reasoning in *Re John Willment (Ashford) Ltd [1979] STC 288*).

Moreover, the administrative receiver has no personal liability in this regard even if the company was at the relevant time in liquidation (which has the effect of terminating his agency for the company for certain purposes, though not necessarily for the purposes of his function of dealing with and realising the charged assets—see D5.2 PART D: RECEIVERS). This is because the liability cannot be said to have been incurred under a contract entered into by him (without exclusion of personal liability) or contract of employment adopted by him (see D7.2 PART D: RECEIVERS). The liability may in any case have been incurred in the course of his dealing with the charged assets. Further, he is not a 'proper officer' for the purposes of section 108 of the Taxes Management Act 1970.

Liability during concurrent administrative receivership and liquidation

H3.8   If, at the time when in the course of the administrative receivership the liability arises, the company is not also in liquidation, such liability would be provable in a subsequent liquidation as an unsecured non-preferential liability. If at that time the company is already in liquidation, a difficult question arises as to whether it is required to be discharged by the liquidator as an expense of the winding up. It is one thing when the liability has been incurred for the benefit or presumed benefit of the liquidation at the instance of the liquidator. In that case, it is a proper expense of the winding up and should be so discharged as discussed in H3.4 above. It may be another thing when such liability, though incurred whilst the company is in liquidation, has been incurred for the benefit of the administrative receivership at the instance of the administrative receiver. It can hardly be described as an expense of the winding up. *Re Mesco Properties Limited* (see H3.6 above) made an exception in the case of liability to corporation tax on chargeable gains arising on a disposal made by a receiver whilst the company was in liquidation. This exception has been given express statutory recognition in Rule 4.218(1) (see H2.3 above). It seems arguable that there is no warrant for construing *Re Mesco Properties* more widely than Rule 4.218(1) expressly requires so as to include within its scope any liability to corporation tax on income or trading profits (as distinct from chargeable gains). On the other hand, it may be arguable that the reason for the express inclusion in that rule of corporation tax on chargeable gains is that it was intended to include such liability at a particular point in the 'pecking order' of the various types of liquidation expenses mentioned there; and that, accordingly, it cannot be assumed that corporation tax on income or trading profits was intended to be excluded completely as an item of expense of winding up falling in the general category and ranking in the 'pecking order' accordingly. There also remains the point that by virtue of section 108 of the Taxes Management Act 1970, he is a 'proper officer' (see H3.4 above) but it seems debatable whether that section applies to such a situation.

Liability during voluntary arrangement

H3.9   As regards any liability to corporation tax on income or trading profits arising during the course of a voluntary arrangement, either the terms of the arrangement will expressly provide for its discharge as an expense of the arrangement out of the assets comprised in the arrangement in priority to the claims of the preferential and non-preferential creditors, or the arrangement will not be binding as regards such liability, on the Inland Revenue. In the latter case, the Inland Revenue would be free to take appropriate enforcement action against the company, for example, by petitioning for its winding up and thereby bringing the voluntary arrangement to an end. Arguably, whilst the arrangement is in force the Inland Revenue might not succeed in levying execution or distress on the assets comprised in the arrangement if by its terms those assets expressly or impliedly constitute trust assets (see E2.7 PART E: VOLUNTARY ARRANGEMENTS).

Corporation tax on capital (chargeable) gains

H3.10   The position, broadly, is similar to that in respect of corporation tax on income and trading profits (see H3.2 *et seq.* above), except

(*a*)   that the combined effect of *Re Mesco Properties* and Rule 4.218(1) is expressly to constitute liability to corporation tax on chargeable gains, incurred in the course of an administrative receivership whilst the company is in liquidation, as an expense of the winding up in the 'pecking order' set out in that Rule, and

(*b*)   that section 26(2) of the Taxation of Chargeable Gains Act 1992 expressly provides that a receiver is not personally liable to taxation in respect of any gains made on the realisation of the assets of the company.

PAYE and national insurance contributions (etc.)

Liability arising before insolvency

H3.11   A claim against the company in respect of liabilities for PAYE, national insurance contributions, deductions from payments to sub-contractors in the construction industry, social security and occupational pension scheme contributions (etc.) incurred before the effective date of the insolvency procedure concerned is, in a liquidation, a floating charge receivership or a voluntary arrangement, a preferential claim within certain limits (see H2.6 above). To the extent that it is not preferential, it will rank as an unsecured non-preferential claim in those procedures (note that the administration procedure does not envisage the discharge of any pre-administration liabilities, preferential or otherwise, subject to the power of the administrator to discharge any of them in whole or in part if this is calculated to be in the overall interest of the administration). Such liabilities may have been the subject of a pre-insolvency statutory distress levied by the Inland Revenue, in which case the position will be as in H3.2 above; see also H3.16 below.

Liability arising during insolvency

H3.12 Insofar as such liabilities arise during an insolvency procedure, the position, broadly, is similar to that in respect of corporation tax on income and trading profits (see H3.2 *et seq.* above), except that a receiver, as well as an administrator, will be treated as the principal employer by virtue of Regulation 4(1) of the Income Tax (Employments) Regulations 1993 (SI 1993 No 744) and will be under an obligation to operate the PAYE system and account to the Inland Revenue for all income tax (PAYE) and national insurance contributions deducted from the emoluments paid to employees. This obligation is regarded by the Inland Revenue as a personal obligation which in an administration can, arguably, be enforced through the court under section 11 or 27 of the Insolvency Act 1986. (Note: the liquidator's obligation to account will arise in his capacity as a 'proper officer' under section 108.) The same applies to deductions at the basic rate of tax from payments made to subcontractors in the construction industry as required by section 559 of the Taxes Act and, by virtue of section 349 or 350 of that Act, to the withholding of tax on annual interest or other annual payments.

Stamp duty

H3.13 Section 190 of the Insolvency Act 1986 exempts from stamp duty certain types of documents relating to transactions entered into in the course of a compulsory or creditors' voluntary winding up of a company registered in Great Britain. The documents to which the exemption applies in the main are deeds, conveyances, assignments, surrenders and assurances relating to freehold and leasehold property of the company or any interest in it which after the execution of the relevant documents, either at law or in equity is or remains part of the company's assets.

Value added tax

Pre-insolvency transactions

H3.14 As far as liability to value added tax due in respect of pre-insolvency transactions is concerned, except to the extent that it ranks as a preferential debt in a liquidation, floating charge receivership or voluntary arrangement (see H2.6 above), it will rank as an unsecured non-preferential liability.

However, where HM Customs and Excise has levied statutory distress in respect of such liability (preferential or non-preferential) prior to the commencement of the insolvency procedures, its position is similar to that where the Inland Revenue has levied statutory distress in respect of corporation tax or PAYE etc. (see H3.2 above; and also H3.16 below).

Post-insolvency transactions

H3.15 As regards value added tax liability arising in respect of supplies made after the effective date of an insolvency procedure, the position is as follows.

(1) The appointment of a liquidator, administrator or receiver is required to be notified in writing on Form VAT 769 to HM Customs and Excise within 21 days of the appointment (see also A4.11 PART A: GENERAL). (This requirement does not apply in the case of a liquidator appointed after the discharge of an administration order, as the administrator would previously have complied with the requirement.) In any case, on learning of the appointment, for example, on the publication of a notice of the appointment in the *Gazette*, HM Customs and Excise will normally require such office-holder to comply with the company's obligations relating to value added tax as a person acting in a representative capacity (Regulation 63 of the Value Added Tax (General) Regulations 1985 (SI 1985 No 886), 'the 1985 Regulations'). In that event, the accounting period will be treated as having ended on the day immediately preceding the day of the appointment, and a return in respect of that period must be submitted by the office-holder within one month of the date of the appointment; otherwise a penalty may be charged unless he can establish a reasonable excuse. Thereafter, accounting in respect of subsequent periods must be done in the normal way.

(2) The effect is that VAT liability arising during an insolvency procedure (except a voluntary arrangement) must be discharged as an expense of the procedure out of the funds coming into the hands of the office-holder. The position in a voluntary arrangement will be as in H3.9 above. No personal liability on the part of the office-holder will arise except in the type of the circumstances described in H3.6 above.

(3) If a VAT refund arises during the course of an insolvency procedure, in respect of VAT supplies made to and by the company during the procedure, HM Customs and Excise is not entitled to set off any undischarged pre-procedure VAT liability of the company against such refund (section 81 of the Value Added Tax Act 1994). See, however, H3.16 below.

(4) As an alternative to the liability of an office-holder in his representative capacity as described above, a personal liability may also arise on his part (subject to his right of indemnity against the assets coming into his hands) where HM Customs and Excise invokes (which it sometimes does) Regulation 11 of the 1985 Regulations. Under that Regulation, it can, by notice in writing, treat an administrator, receiver or liquidator as a taxable person. (The expression 'receiver' includes both an administrative receiver and an ordinary (fixed charge or LPA) receiver: *Sargent v Customs and Excise Commissioners [1994] STC 11*.) The effect of such notice is to impose on the office-holder all statutory obligations relating to VAT as if he were a taxable person in the place of the company (see also section 46(4) of the Value Added Tax Act 1994 and *Sargent v Customs and Excise Commissioners* above).

(5) Where a company in receivership is a member of a group VAT registration, HM Customs and Excise may (but does not automatically) remove that company from the group registration and re-register it separately.

(6) In any case, where a group member becomes insolvent, HM Customs and Excise regard the group treatment as at an end from the relevant date of insolvency; and all the group members are automatically deregistered and then all solvent group members are automatically reregistered.

(7) Where the company which is in an insolvency procedure ceases to make taxable supplies, HM Customs and Excise must be notified within 30 days. Thereupon, HM Customs and Excise will, unless it accedes to a request for deferral, cancel the company's VAT registration. Despite such cancellation, the company is entitled to claim (on Form VAT 427) VAT on invoices in respect of supplies made to it within six months after cancellation (or such longer period as it may be allowed). In practice, such a claim is allowed to include VAT on the office-holder's remuneration and also, if relating to taxable supplies made by the company, his disbursements representing the fees of professional advisers, estate agents, surveyors and valuers.

(8) The VAT regime in respect of bad debt relief for creditors (see also A4.11 PART A: GENERAL, B5.18 PART B: ADMINISTRATION ORDERS, C14.8 PART C: LIQUIDATIONS, D4.7 PART D: RECEIVERS, and E4.1 PART E: VOLUNTARY ARRANGEMENTS) has now been modified. Relief is available if the following conditions, laid down by section 36 of the Value Added Tax Act 1994, are satisfied:

(*a*) the goods or services have been supplied for monetary consideration on or after 1 April 1989 and tax has been paid on the supply;

(*b*) the value of the supply is equal to or less than its open market value and, in the case of a supply of goods, the property in the goods has passed to the person to whom they were supplied or to a person who derives title from him;

(*c*) the whole or any part of the consideration for the supply has been written off in the supplier's books of accounts as a bad debt;

(*d*) a period of six months (beginning with the date of supply) has elapsed since the time of supply (before 1 April 1993, and in respect of supplies made prior to 1 April 1992, the waiting period was one year);

(*e*) a claim has not been made for bad debt relief under previous provisions for refunds in respect of bad debts; and

(*f*) a claim for a refund is made to HM Customs and Excise.

(9) The amount of the refund of VAT is determined by reference to the 'outstanding amount' which is either:

(*a*) an amount equal to the consideration written off in the accounts (if no payment has been received at the time of claim); or (*b*)   the amount by which the consideration written off exceeds the payment(s) received (if one or more payments have been received at the time of claim).

Crown set-off

H3.16   In certain circumstances, a fiscal authority can eliminate or minimise its loss in respect of any outstanding debt which became due by the company prior to the commencement of an insolvency procedure by exercising a Crown set-off, that is, by liaising with any other fiscal authority or Government department which may be owing to the company any refund or other debt which became due prior to such commencement, to ensure that the two debts are set off against each other. See D7.6 PART D: RECEIVERS.

Relief from tax on debt waived in a voluntary arrangement

H3.17   A company is no longer liable to tax in respect of any debt or part of a debt waived by a creditor as a term of the company's voluntary arrangement. Further, the creditor is no longer required, before deducting that debt or part debt from his taxable profits, to show that the amount waived is not greater than that which he would have lost if the company had gone into liquidation. (See E4.1 PART E: VOLUNTARY ARRANGEMENTS.)

Part I: Disqualification of Directors

1. **Preliminary**   **667**

2. **Circumstances triggering the disqualification process (section 1)**   **670**

   (1) Conviction of indictable offence (section 2)   670
   (2) Persistent breaches of companies legislation (section 3)   670
   (3) Fraud, etc., in winding up (section 4)   671
   (4) Summary conviction re companies legislation
        requirements (section 5)   671
   (5) Unfitness of directors of insolvent companies
        (sections 6 and 7)   672
   (6) Result of investigation under other statutory provisions
        (section 8)   674
   (7) Participation in fraudulent or wrongful trading (section 10)   674
   (8) Undischarged bankrupts (section 11)   674
   (9) Revocation of administration order against an individual
        (section 12)   675

3. **Scope of the court's discretion**   **676**

4. **Test of unfitness (section 9)**   **677**

5. **Principles for determining unfitness and length of disqualification**   **679**

   Determination of unfitness   679
   Determination of periods of disqualification   683

6. **Some cases on unfitness and periods of disqualification**   **685**

7. **Consequences of disqualification order**   **695**

   General effects (sections 1(1), 11 and 12)   695
   Leave applications (section 17)   696
   Consequences of contravention (sections 13 to 15)   697

8. **Procedural aspects**   **699**

   Notice of intended application (section 16(1))   699
   Period of limitation and its extension (section 7(2))   699
   Application for disqualification order (section 16; Rules 2 to 4,
       the 1987 Rules)   702
   Service and acknowledgement (Rule 5, the 1987 Rules)   702
   Evidence (Rules 3 and 6, the 1987 Rules)   703
   Hearing (section 16; Rule 7, the 1987 Rules)   705
   Striking out application for want of prosecution or sufficient case   707
   Effective date of disqualification order   707
   Costs   708
   Reviews and appeals   708

Part I : Disqualification of Directors

Chapter 1: Preliminary

I1.1   This Part is confined to the law relating to directors' disqualification, contained in the Company Directors Disqualification Act 1986 ('CDDA') and the associated delegated legislation consisting of the Companies (Disqualification Orders) Regulations 1986 (SI 1986 No 2067) ('the 1986 Regulations'), the Insolvent Companies (Report on Conduct of Directors) No 2 Rules 1986 (SI 1986 No 2134) ('the 1986 Rules') and the Insolvent Companies (Disqualification of Unfit Directors) Proceedings Rules 1987 (SI 1987 No 2023) ('the 1987 Rules').

CDDA, which came into force on 29 December 1986, supersedes less extensive director qualification provisions previously contained in the Companies Act 1985 and its predecessor Acts, subject to the savings contained in Schedule 2 and the transitional provisions and savings contained in Schedule 3 to the CDDA (sections 19 and 23(1)). Unless otherwise stated, the section numbers stated in this part are those of the CDDA.

The 1986 Regulations, which came into force on 29 December 1986 and superseded the Companies (Register of Disqualification Orders) (Fee) Regulations 1977 and the Companies (Disqualification Orders) Regulations 1985, deal with the requirements for various officers of the court to furnish to the Secretary of State particulars of disqualification orders made against individuals and bodies corporate and any leave granted in relation to disqualification orders and the variation or cessation of disqualification orders. In each case, particulars are to be supplied within a period of 14 days of the relevant order. The 1986 Rules, which also came into force on 29 December 1986, superseding, subject to transitional provisions, the Insolvency Companies (Reports on Conduct of Directors) Rules 1986 (SI 1986 No 611), contain detailed provisions regarding the reporting duties of insolvency office-holders. The 1987 Rules, which came into force on 11 January 1988 and superseded the Insolvent Companies (Disqualification of Unfit Directors) Proceedings Rules 1986 (SI 1986 No 612) contain the procedure for disqualification proceedings, but only those under sections 7 and 8 (see below).

It may be useful to be clear at the outset about the meanings of certain key expressions used in the CDDA.

(a)   'Company' means not only a company formed and registered in Great Britain but also, for the purposes of section 11 (see below), an unregistered company (including an insolvent partnership) and a company incorporated outside Great Britain which has an established place of business in Great Britain and, for the purposes of the other provisions of CDDA, any company which may be wound up under Part V of the Insolvency Act 1986 (an unregistered or overseas company having sufficient connection with Great Britain, irrespective of whether it has a place of business in Great Britain—see C5.8 PART C: LIQUIDATIONS) (section 22(2)). The Act also applies to a building society as if it were a company (section 22A).

(*b*)   'Director' includes any person occupying the position of director (for example a *de facto* director), by whatever name called, and in sections 6 to 9 (see below) includes a shadow director (section 22(4)). 'Shadow director' means a person on whose directions or instructions the directors of the company are accustomed to act (but so that a person is not deemed to be a shadow director by reason only that the directors act on advice given by him in a professional capacity) (section 22(5)). In *Re Tasbian Ltd (No 3)* [*1992*] *BCC 358*, on a preliminary issue, the Court of Appeal expressed the view that a chartered accountant and 'company doctor' was capable of being held to have been a *de facto* director or a shadow director where he had been appointed as a consultant to the company by a finance company which funded the company's business as a shareholder and debenture holder but (i) was paid by the company, (ii) negotiated an informal moratorium on behalf of the company with its creditors, (iii) monitored trading and assisted the board, (iv) negotiated with the DTI and the Inland Revenue and introduced the company to new factors, (v) became signatory to the company's bank account, (vi) advised the company on the transfer of the labour force to an associated company, and (vii) for the most part, was regarded by the *de jure* directors as a shadow, or even the managing, director. The expression 'director' is not confined to an individual. A disqualification order may be made against a company or other body corporate as a 'director' (note the expression 'person' and see section 14; also see *Re Bulawayo Market and Offices Co Ltd* [*1907*] *2 Ch 458*). The expression 'body corporate' has the meaning ascribed to it by section 740 of the Companies Act 1985 which provides that the expression does not include a corporation sole or a Scottish firm but includes a company incorporated elsewhere than in Great Britain (section 22(6) CDDA). Where an insolvent partnership is wound up as an unregistered company under Part V of the Insolvency Act 1986, sections 6 to 10, 15, 19(c) and 20 of and Schedule 1 to CDDA apply, in their modified form as set out in Schedule 8 to that Order, to an officer (that is, a member or a person having management or control of the business), present or past, of the partnership (paragraph 16 of the Insolvent Partnerships Order 1994 (SI 1994 No 2421)).

(*c*)   Various other expressions used in CDDA have meanings ascribed to them by the Insolvency Act 1986 or the Companies Act 1985 (as the case may be) (section 22).

CDDA applies to England and Wales and Scotland only but corresponding legislation is in force in Northern Ireland by virtue of the Companies (Northern Ireland) Order 1989 (SI 1989 No 2404). Section 6(1) (see I2.5 below) applies to any person, whether a British subject or a foreigner, irrespective of his presence in the jurisdiction at the time of the proceedings or when the activities took place; but the court retains a residual discretion under Rule 5 of the 1987 Rules (see I8.4 below) not to order service out of the jurisdiction if it is not satisfied that there is a good arguable case (*Re Seagull Manufacturing Co Ltd (No 2) [1993] BCC 833*, applying *Re Paramount Airways Ltd (No 2) [1992] BCC 416* and *Re Seagull Manufacturing Co Ltd [1993] BCC 241*).

Chapter 2: Circumstances triggering the disqualification process (section 1)

(1) Conviction of indictable offence (section 2)

I2.1 The court *may* make a disqualification order against a person where he is convicted of an indictable offence (whether on indictment or summarily) in connection with the promotion, formation, management or liquidation of a company, or with the receivership or management of a company's property. For this purpose 'the court' means (a) any court having jurisdiction to wind up the company in relation to which the offence was committed, or (b) the court by or before which the person is convicted of the offence, or (c) in the case of a summary conviction in England and Wales, any other magistrates' court acting for the same petty sessions area. 'Indictable offence' has the meaning (in relation to both England and Wales and Scotland) ascribed to it by Schedule 1 to the Interpretation Act 1978. The maximum period for which a person can be disqualified under this head is, where the disqualification order is made by a court of summary jurisdiction, 5 years and, in any other case, 15 years. In *R v Young [1990] BCC 549*, the Court of Appeal allowed an appeal against the disqualification of a person on his being found guilty of managing a company whilst an undischarged bankrupt but who was given a conditional discharge by the trial court. The factors which influenced the Court of Appeal were that he had since been discharged from bankruptcy, had a successful business record after his discharge and until his trial, had been given a lenient sentence and there had been delay in bringing the matter to court.

The reference to an indictable offence in connection with the 'management' of a company is not confined to the management of the internal affairs of the company. For example, section 2 has been held to apply where third parties, such as finance companies and insurance companies, were defrauded (*R v Corbin (1984) 6 Cr App R (S) 17; R v Appleyard (1985) 81 Cr App R 319*) and where a person was convicted of an offence of carrying on an unauthorised insurance business through the medium of a limited liability company (*R v Georgiou (1988) 4 BCC 322*). (See also I7.1 below.) However, the offence concerned must have some relevant factual connection with the management of the company (*R v Goodman [1992] BCC 625*).

(2) Persistent breaches of companies legislation (section 3)

I2.2 The court *may* make a disqualification order against a person for a maximum period of five years where he has been persistently in default in relation to the provisions of the companies legislation requiring any return, account or other document to be filed with, delivered or sent, or notice of any matter to be given, to the Registrar of Companies. Such persistent default may be conclusively proved by showing that in the five years ending with the date of the application he has been adjudged guilty (whether or not on the same occasion) of three or more defaults in relation to those provisions. He is treated as being adjudged guilty of such a default if (*a*) he is convicted (whether on indictment or summarily) of an offence consisting in a contravention of or failure to comply with the provision concerned (whether on his part or on the part of any company), or (*b*) a default order is made against him under (i) section 242(4) of the Companies Act 1985 (order requiring delivery of company accounts), (ii) section 245B of that Act (order requiring preparation of revised accounts), (iii) section 713 of that Act (enforcement of company's duty to make returns), (iv) section 41 of the Insolvency Act 1986 (enforcement of receiver's or manager's duty to make returns), or (v) section 170 of that Act (corresponding provision for liquidator in winding up) in respect of any such contravention of or failure to comply with that provision (whether on his part or on the part of any company).

For this purpose, 'the court' means any court having jurisdiction to wind up any of the companies in relation to which the offence or other default has been or is alleged to have been committed.

It would appear that the section does not prevent persistent default being proved otherwise than under the above provisions as to conclusive proof. However, 'persistent default' connotes some degree of continuation or repetition. A person may persist in the same default or may persistently commit a series of defaults. It is not necessary to show that he has been culpable in the sense of having deliberately disregarded the statutory requirements. The degree of culpability is, however, relevant to the question of whether a disqualification order should be made and, if so, for what period (*Re Arctic Engineering Ltd* (*1985*) *1 BCC 99,563*).

(3) Fraud, etc, in winding up (section 4)

I2.3   The court *may* make a disqualification order against a person for a maximum period of 15 years if, in the course of the winding up of a company, it appears that he has been guilty of an offence for which he is liable (whether he has been convicted or not) under section 458 of the Companies Act 1985 (fraudulent trading) or has otherwise been guilty, while an officer or liquidator of the company or receiver or manager of its property, of any fraud in relation to the company or of any breach of his duty as such officer, liquidator, receiver or manager. For this purpose, 'the court' means any court having jurisdiction to wind up any of the companies in relation to which the offence or other default has been or is alleged to have been committed; and 'officer' includes a shadow director. It will be noticed that the provision does not expressly apply to an administrator. It will also be noticed that a conviction for or a judgment in respect of fraudulent trading or fraud is not a prerequisite to the court making a disqualification order.

(4) Summary conviction re companies legislation requirements (section 5)

I2.4   Where a person is convicted of a summary offence (either on indictment or summarily) in consequence of a contravention of, or failure to comply with, any provision of the companies legislation requiring a return, account or other document to be filed with, delivered or sent, or notice of any matter to be given, to the Registrar of Companies (whether the contravention or failure is on the person's own part or on the part of any company), the court by which he is convicted (or, in England and Wales, any other magistrates' court acting for the same petty sessions area) *may* in specified circumstances make a disqualification order against him for a maximum period of five years. Those circumstances are that, during the five years ending with the date of the conviction, the person has been convicted (whether on indictment or summarily) of one or more similar offences, or has had one or more default orders (see I2.2 above) made against him, so that the aggregate number of default orders and offences (including the current summary conviction) totals three or more.

(5) Unfitness of directors of insolvent companies (sections 6 and 7)

I2.5 The court *shall* make a disqualification order against any person for a minimum period of 2 years and a maximum period of 15 years in any case where, on an application under section 6 pursuant to section 7, it is satisfied that

(*a*) he is or has been a director of a company which has at any time (whether while he was a director or subsequently) become insolvent (section 6(1)(a)) (that is, it has gone into liquidation at a time when its assets are insufficient for the payment of its debts and other liabilities and the expenses of the winding up, or an administration order is made in relation to it, or an administrative receiver of it has been appointed—section 6(2)), and

(*b*) his conduct as a director of that company (either taken alone or taken *together with* his conduct as a director of any other company or companies) makes him unfit to be concerned in the management of a company (section 6(1)(b)).

'*Together with*' indicates that there has to be some nexus between the conduct in relation to the other company or companies and the conduct in relation to the insolvent company (*Re Godwin Warren Control Systems plc [1992] BCC 557*). The words in italics enable the court to satisfy itself that the respondent is unfit by reference to his conduct as director of the insolvent company or (if not so satisfied) by reference to his conduct not only as director of that company but as director of other companies, but not solely by reference to his conduct as director of other companies. Those words do not *necessarily* enable the court to exonerate the respondent whose conduct in relation to the insolvent company shows serious failures by reference to his good conduct in relation to other companies (*Re Bath Glass Ltd (1988) 4 BCC 130*; but see *Re Polly Peck International plc (No 2) [1993] BCC 890* referred to in I5.5 below).

Section 7 provides that if it appears to the Secretary of State that it is expedient in the public interest that a disqualification order under section

6 should be made against any person, an application for such an order *may* be made by the Secretary of State or, if the Secretary of State so directs in the case of a person who is or has been a director of the company which is being wound up by the court in England and Wales, by the Official Receiver. Under the general power of delegation contained in section 400 of the Insolvency Act 1986, the Secretary of State can delegate his function of making an application to the Official Receiver even where the company concerned is not being wound up by the court. However, in that case the application must be made in the name of the Secretary of State and not (unlike where the company is being wound up by the court) in the name of the Official Receiver. If the application is wrongly made in the name of the Official Receiver, the error cannot be cured by an amendment, so that if the time limit for the making of the application has passed and has not been extended (see I8.2 below), a fresh application in the name of the Secretary of State cannot be made (*Re Probe Data Systems Ltd (1989) 5 BCC 384*).

Section 7(2) lays down an extendable time limit for making an application. It provides that, except with the leave of the court, an application for a disqualification order under section 6 shall not be made after the end of the period of two years beginning with the day on which the company of which that person is or has been a director became insolvent. Where two or more insolvency events have occurred in relation to the same company, the period of two years runs from the occurrence of the first of those events (*Re Tasbian Ltd [1990] BCC 318*). As to the procedure for an application for an extension of time, and factors influencing the court's attitude on such an application, see I8.2 below.

Section 7(3) and (4) imposes certain reporting duties on an insolvency office-holder of the company concerned, that is, the liquidator in a voluntary winding up, the Official Receiver in a compulsory winding up, the administrator and the administrative receiver. If it appears to the office-holder that the conditions laid down in section 6 for disqualification are satisfied as respects a person who is or has been a director of that company, the office-holder shall forthwith report the matter to the Secretary of State. Further, the Secretary of State or the Official Receiver may require the liquidator, administrator or administrative receiver to furnish him with such information with respect to any person's conduct as a director of the company, and to produce and permit inspection of such books, papers and other records relevant to the person's conduct as such a director, as the Secretary of State or the Official Receiver may reasonably require for the purpose of determining whether to exercise, or of exercising, any functions of his under section 7. The 1986 Rules contain more detailed provisions regarding these reporting duties, including various prescribed forms of report. Subject to the mandatory provisions contained in section 7(3) and (4) above, a report must in any case be furnished to the Secretary of State not later than the expiry of the period of six months from the relevant date (that is,

(i) the date of the passing of a voluntary winding-up resolution in a creditors' voluntary winding up, or

(ii)   the date on which the liquidator in a members' voluntary winding up forms the opinion that, at the time when the company went into liquidation, its assets were insufficient for the payment of its debt and other liabilities and the expenses of the winding up, or

(iii) the date of the appointment of the administrative receiver, or

(iv)   the date of the administration order,

as the case may be).

Rule 4(2) contains an option for the office-holder to voluntarily make a report earlier. If such optional report was submitted by a day one week before the expiry of the six-month period, then, subject to the above mandatory requirements of subsections (3) and (4), no further report need be submitted; nor if he has, since the relevant date, made optional reports under section 7(3) with respect to all the persons concerned. Such reports are privileged documents, not discoverable to the respondent: *Secretary of State for Trade and Industry v Sananes [1994] BCC 375.*

(6) Result of investigation under other statutory provisions (section 8)

I2.6   If it appears to the Secretary of State from a report made by inspectors under section 437 of the Companies Act 1985, or section 94 or 177 of the Financial Services Act 1986, or from information or documents obtained under section 447 or 448 of that 1985 Act or section 105 of that 1986 Act, or section 2 of the Criminal Justice Act 1987, or section 52 of the Criminal Justice (Scotland) Act 1987, or section 83 of that 1985 Act, that it is expedient in the public interest that a disqualification order should be made against any person who is or has been a director or shadow director of the company, he may apply to the court (that is, the High Court or, in Scotland, the Court of Session). On such an application, the court *may* make a disqualification order against that person for a maximum period of 15 years if it is satisfied that his conduct in relation to the company makes him unfit to be concerned with the management of a company.

(7) Participation in fraudulent or wrongful trading (section 10)

I2.7   Where the court makes a declaration under section 213 or 214 of the Insolvency Act 1986 that a person is liable to make a contribution to a company's assets, then, that court *may*, if it thinks fit, even without any application being made to it for a disqualification order, make a disqualification order against that person for a maximum period of 15 years.

(8) Undischarged bankrupts (section 11)

I2.8   It is an *offence* for an undischarged bankrupt to act as director of, or directly or indirectly to take part in or be concerned in the promotion, formation or management of, a company, except with the leave of the court by which he was adjudged bankrupt or, in Scotland, sequestration of his estates was awarded. The offence is an absolute offence without the need to establish *mens rea: R v Brockley [1994] BCC 131.* In England and

Wales, the leave of the court is not to be given unless notice of intention to apply for it has been served on the Official Receiver; and it is the official receiver's duty, if he is of the opinion that it is contrary to the public interest that the application should be granted, to attend on the hearing of the application and oppose it.

(9) Revocation of administration order against an individual (section 12)

I2.9   Where an individual is subject to an administration order under Part VI of the County Courts Act 1984, and fails to make any payment which he is required to make under that order, the court which is administering his estate under that order *may*, if it thinks fit, revoke the administration order and make an order directing that section 429 of the 1984 Act and section 12 of the CDDA should apply to him for such period, not exceeding two years, as may be specified in the order. The effect of this (as provided by section 12(2) of the CDDA) is that, except with the leave of the court which made the order, he is disqualified to act as director or liquidator of, or directly or indirectly take part or be concerned in the promotion, formation or management of, a company.

Chapter 3: Scope of the court's discretion

I3.1 The differences in the scope of the court's discretion under the above nine heads of disqualification provisions (I2.1 to I2.9 above) will be noted. Under heads (1), (2), (3), (4), (6) and (7), the court concerned has a discretion whether or not to make a disqualification order and is not tied down to a *minimum* period of disqualification. A qualification under head (8) is automatic throughout the period the person concerned remains an undischarged bankrupt. It is also automatic under head (9), although whether or not to revoke an administration order and apply section 12 of the CDDA is a matter of some discretion for the court. Under both heads (8) and (9), the court has discretion, on an application made by the person disqualified, to grant leave to do any act which he is otherwise prohibited from doing by virtue of the disqualification.

Only under heads (5) and (6) is the court expressly required to base its ultimate decision on the unfitness of the respondent to be concerned in the management of a company, although it seems inevitable that in exercising its discretion under heads (1), (2), (3), (4) and (7) whether to disqualify the person concerned, and under heads (8) and (9) whether to grant leave to act, one of the factors the court would take into consideration is the fitness or otherwise of the person to be concerned with the management of a company.

Under head (5), once the court is satisfied that the person concerned is unfit, it is mandatory for it to make a disqualification order for a period of not less than two years and not more than 15 years. By contrast, under head (6) even if the court is satisfied that the person is unfit, it still has a discretion whether or not to make a disqualification order and is not bound by any minimum period of disqualification. This may, for example, enable the court to take into account any extenuating circumstances, unlike under head (5). However, under both heads, it is a matter of discretion for the Secretary of State whether or not an *application* for disqualification is to be made to the court, although a party with sufficient interest may be able to challenge a decision of the Secretary of State in this regard by way of judicial review on the ground that it is perverse or otherwise improper: *R v Secretary of State for Trade and Industry, ex parte Lonrho plc [1992] BCC 325*.

No specific time limit has been laid down for the purposes of making an application for a disqualification order under any of the above heads, except head (5) under which no application can be made without the leave of the court after the expiration of two years from the date of the relevant insolvency event (see I8.2 below).

Chapter 4: Test of unfitness (section 9)

I4.1 Where it falls to a court to determine for the purposes of heads (5) or (6) (see I2.5 and I2.6 above) whether a person's conduct as a director or shadow director of any particular company or companies makes him unfit to be concerned in the management of a company, the court *must*, as respects his conduct as a director of that company or, as the case may be, each of those companies, have regard *in particular* to the matters mentioned in Part I of Schedule 1 to CDDA, and, where the company has become insolvent (as to the meaning of which, see section 6(2) and I2.5 above), also to the matters mentioned in Part II of that Schedule. These matters are set out below. (Note that the Secretary of State has power by order to modify Schedule 1, subject to transitional provisions.)

Part I—Matters applicable to all cases

(1) Any misfeasance or breach of any fiduciary or other duty by the director in relation to the company.

(2) Any misapplication or retention by the director of, or any conduct by the director giving rise to an obligation to account for, any money or other property of the company.

(3) The extent of the director's responsibility for the company entering into any transaction liable to be set aside under Part XVI of the Insolvency Act 1986 (provisions against debt avoidance).

(4) The extent of the director's responsibility for any failure by the company to comply with the following provisions of the Companies Act 1985: section 221 (companies to keep accounting records), 222 (where and for how long records to be kept), 288 (register of directors and secretaries), 352 (obligation to keep and enter up register of members), 353 (location of register of members), 363 (duty of company to make annual returns) or 399 and 415 (duty of company to register charges created by it), or for any failure by the directors to comply with section 226 or 227 (duty to prepare annual accounts), or 233 (approval and signature of accounts) of that Act.

Part II—Matters applicable where company has become insolvent

(5) The extent of the director's responsibility for the causes of the company becoming insolvent.

(6) The extent of his responsibility for any failure by the company to supply any goods or services which have been paid for (in whole or in part).

(7) The extent of his responsibility for the company entering into any transaction giving any preference which is liable to be set aside under section 127 or sections 238 to 240 of the Insolvency Act 1986,

or challengeable under section 242 or 243 of that Act or under any rule of law in Scotland.

(8) The extent of his responsibility for any failure by the directors of the company to comply with section 98 of the 1986 Act (duty to call creditors' meeting in creditors' voluntary winding up).

(9) Any failure by him to comply with any obligation imposed on him by or under section 22 (company's statement of affairs in administration), 47 (statement of affairs to administrative receiver), 66 (statement of affairs in Scottish receivership), 99 (directors' duty to attend meeting; statement of affairs in creditors' voluntary winding up), 131 (statement of affairs in winding up by the court), 234 (duty of anyone having property of the company to deliver it up) or 235 (duty to co-operate with liquidator, etc.) of the Insolvency Act 1986.

Chapter 5: Principles for determining unfitness and length of disqualification

Determination of unfitness

Purpose of disqualification order

I5.1 'It is well established that the purpose of a disqualification order is not primarily to punish the individual concerned . . .' (Warner J in *Re Tansoft Ltd [1991] BCLC 339* at *357*) but . . . 'to protect the public against the future conduct of companies by persons whose past records as directors of insolvent companies have shown them to be a danger to creditors and others' (Browne-Wilkinson V-C in *Re Lo-Line Electric Motors Ltd [1988] BCLC 698* at *703*).

In the same vein, Harman J in *Re Rolus Properties Ltd [1988] BCC 446* at *449* said, 'As I see this [the previous] legislation, it is not primarily punitive; it is primarily for the protection of the public against inadequate, dishonest or otherwise unfit persons being directors of companies'.

The report of the Cork Committee, which led to the present legislation, stated, 'A balance has to be struck. No one wishes to discourage the inception and growth of businesses, although both are unavoidably attended by risks to creditors. Equally a climate should exist in which downright irresponsibility is discouraged and in which those who abuse the privilege of limited liability can be made personally liable for the consequences of the conduct'. In *Re Douglas Construction Services Ltd (1988) 4 BCC 553*, Harman J said that it was important that the court in operating its jurisdiction to protect the public against those who abused limited liability, should be careful not to stultify all enterprise.

In this connection, it may also be relevant to note the views of Peter Joyce, Inspector General and the Chief Executive of the Insolvency Service Executive Agency which is responsible for instituting disqualification proceedings. In his editorial 'An essential means of coping with the financial failure' in *Butterworths Journal of International Banking and Financial Law*, September 1991, page 427, he states,

> 'In considering the exercise of the discretionary power to apply or direct an application by the Official Receiver, account has obviously to be taken of the courts' conclusions on unfitness, and what is considered and what is not considered to amount to unfitness in the circumstances of a particular case. Disqualification is directed to the protection of the trading community and the public rather than penalising individual directors (although the legislation provides the penalties of prosecution and personal liability for a company's debts, should a director act while disqualified). It is important in

that context that disqualification should not be seen as inhibiting genuine enterprise, with obvious implications for economic activity. Businesses fail for reasons not necessarily accompanied by impropriety. All that inevitably involves a striking of a fine, but important, balance in deciding which cases should be the subject of a direction . . . Directors should not be judged with the infallibility of 20:20 hindsight. All business involves some risk: decisions, particularly to trade on when debts to creditors are overdue for payment which prove only to make matters worse, should not by themselves bring disqualification and the consequences of that if there was a genuine, reasonably-based belief when the decisions were taken that they would lead to the company's recovery'.

He goes on to summarise the considerations which emerge from judgments in relation to one of the most common themes of disqualification proceedings, namely, the company continuing to trade whilst insolvent:

(1)   Was there a genuine effort to trade?

(2)   Did the company have a reasonable chance of succeeding?

(3)   How quickly did the directors respond when they saw things were starting to go wrong, and did they know things were going wrong?

(4)   Was it a commercial risk as distinct from mis-management or incompetence?

(5)   Was it a high risk, known to be so by creditors?

(6)   For what period did the company continue trading after the directors knew or should have known it was insolvent, with what effect and did they care?

Schedule 1 criteria not exhaustive

I5.2   It should be noted that the list in Schedule 1 of the matters the court is required to take into account (see I4.1 above) is not exhaustive. Other matters relevant to the issue of unfitness may be taken into account. The question has to be determined by reference to the conduct as a whole of the person concerned. The mere fact that a particular relevant matter has been proved does not necessarily lead to the conclusion that the person concerned is unfit or is a danger to creditors. For example, an isolated failure to file an annual return or instance of delay in producing accounts may not be sufficient to bring the matter under head (5) or (6) (see I2.5 and I2.6 above) (but a persistent default in that regard may bring it under head (2) —see I2.2 above), although it may add to the cumulative effect when considered with any other areas of misconduct. In determining unfitness or otherwise for the purposes of sections 6 to 9, no single offence has been specified as the condition to be satisfied. The court is to have regard to the respondent's conduct— this is a term of great generality. The court has to be satisfied that the respondent has been guilty of a serious failure or failures, whether deliberately or through incompetence, to perform those duties of directors which are attendant on the privilege of trading through limited liability companies. Any misconduct of the respondent *qua* director may be relevant even if it does not fall within a specified statutory provision (*Re Bath Glass Ltd* (*1988*) *4 BCC 130*, Peter Gibson J).

Categories of misconduct

I5.3   Various main labels of misconduct amounting to unfitness have emerged from the decided cases (considered in I6.1 below), such as mis-use of Crown debts, breach of standards of commercial morality, gross incompetence, danger to the public, serious failure or series of failures (deliberate or through incompetence) to perform those duties of direc-tors which are attendant on the privilege of trading through limited liability companies, very marked degree of incompetence or negligence, gross irresponsibility, speculative or *ultra vires* investments, disregard for statutory requirements, want of commercial probity, being a director of two or more companies successively going into liquidation and running undercapitalised companies. However, as Dillon LJ said in *Re Sevenoaks Stationers (Retail) Ltd* [*1991*] *Ch 164*, 'Unfitness is a concept of indeter-minate meaning which must not be replaced by judicial paraphrase.'

Responsibilities of directors

I5.4   Generally, there is no distinction between the responsibilities of executive directors and non-executive directors, at least as far as the requirements of the companies legislation as regards the preparation and filing of documents by the company or the directors are concerned. In *Dorchester Finance Company Ltd v Stebbing* (*1977*) [*1989*] *BCLC 498*, Foster J, dealing with the question of the liability of a director in negli-gence, said that executive and non-executive directors have the same duties under the company's legislation. Even the non-executive directors must show the necessary skill and care in the performance of their duties. They may be liable, for example, if they sign blank cheques and allow the executive director to do as he pleases with them. In *Euro RSCG SA v Conran, The Times, 2 November 1992*, a case concerning a restrictive cov-enant in a consultancy agreement against the consultant directly engaging in a competing consultancy business, Vinelott J said that the agreement would be breached if the consultant became a non-executive director of a competing company, because each director of a company, whether executive or non-executive, was responsible for the proper management of its affairs.

However, this does not mean that a non-executive director must be equated to an executive director in every respect for the purposes of the malpractice provisions of the Insolvency Act 1986 (see C13.1 *et seq.* PART C: LIQUIDATIONS above) or CDDA. For example, section 213 relating to fraudulent trading requires proof of knowing participation by the director concerned, section 214 relating to wrongful trading fixes the level of assumed expertise and the level of responsibility of a particular director by reference to the functions carried out by him and section 212 relating to misfeasance etc. can involve the relevance of the role of the particular director in the act or omission concerned. Further, it has been held that directors are entitled to trust persons in responsible positions (but see *Re Burnham Marketing Services Ltd [1993] BCC 518*, summarised below (number (22)) in I6.1). As Romer J said in *Re City Equitable Fire Insurance Co Ltd [1925] 1 Ch 407* at *429*, 'Business cannot be carried on upon principles of distrust'; and persons in responsible positions may be trusted until there is reason to distrust them (see *Norman and another v Theodore Goddard and others [1991] BCLC 1028*, a case involving the question of the standard of care on the part of a director in which section 214 of the Insolvency Act 1986 was referred to). In *Re Austinsuite Furniture Ltd [1992] BCLC 1047*, in holding that the failure of a director, with responsibility for manufacturing and production, to press for detailed information concerning the company's financial position was not sufficient to warrant his disqualification, Vinelott J said that to an extent the director was entitled to rely on his fellow director with greater business experience. Although his conduct was not free from criticism, as he was mainly responsible for the way in which the company's business was conducted, it was not appropriate to disqualify him.

As Peter Joyce in the article referred to in I5.1 above states: 'Responsibility of individual directors has to be established—what they did or did not do and what they knew and did not know (by choice or otherwise). The evidence has to be there: it is not sufficient—indeed, it would be wholly inappropriate—to proceed on the basis of unsubstantiated assumption, allegation and assertion'.

Guidelines in Polly Peck decision

I5.5   *Re Polly Peck International plc (No 2) [1993] BCC 890*, although it only concerned an application by the Secretary of State for an extension of time to bring disqualification proceedings, provides some insight into judicial thinking as to what conduct and other circumstances may or may not merit disqualification. Of the four respondents, one was the finance director, another a director based chiefly in the US and the other two non-executive directors. Together, they were less than one-third of the total number of directors, excluding the company's chairman Asil Nadir. The complaints against the respondents were that they had failed (*a*) to institute or ensure adequate financial controls and reporting procedures and monitor or set up proper procedures for monitoring expenditure incurred by, and funds provided to, the subsidiaries and (*b*) to obtain appropriate responses to questions regarding substantial funding needs of the subsidiaries from the company. The substance of the Secretary of State's case was 'not that they did not resign but that they failed as directors to procure that the omissions were rectified or to take the stance that "enough was enough" and that they would resign if the omissions and the lack of knowledge and control of the board which arose therefrom and of which they were well aware were not rectified . . .'. In rejecting the application for extension (see I8.2 below), Lindsay J held that:

(1)   there was no justification for lowering the threshold to be crossed by the complainant by construing the words in section 6(1)(b) 'unfit to be concerned in the management of the company' as if they were followed by the words 'without the leave of the court';

(2)   the relevant fitness to be determined under that section was in relation to companies generally;

(3)   evidence of past conduct within that section which would justify a finding of past unfitness *to the required level* would prove present unfitness to the same level unless the respondent satisfied the court otherwise;

(4)   the failures alleged in the present case could not properly be regarded as breaches of duty by *each individual respondent—the allegations confused the duty of the board as a whole with the duties of individual directors*; a director, who had not been individually charged by a board with the task of, for example, instituting adequate financial controls, might or might not be in breach of a duty to the company to use his best endeavours to procure their institution but not, without more, with their absence; were that not so, a director who had striven manfully to introduce them would be as much in breach as one who had resisted them;

(5)   in the circumstances, it was impossible to regard, as so serious a failure as to justify disqualification, the failure by the respondents (never a majority on the board at the time) to have cried 'enough is enough' and to have threatened their resignation, which, in the finance director's case, could have caused considerable loss in that ingredient of confidence so necessary to it and the effect of which upon Mr Nadir, in terms of bringing him to heel, was speculative;

(6)   the shortcomings alleged did not, in the light of indisputable facts, have the gravity required;

(7)   if that was wrong and there was misconduct which could amount to a serious failure, there was nothing in the evidence to suggest that such past failure would be likely to recur in any company of which any of the respondents was or was likely to become a director; and

(8)   had there been any doubt, the respondents would have to be given the benefit of it and, if no real likelihood of recurrence was shown, then the public interest was not diminished.

Analogy with section 727?

I5.6   It remains to be seen whether the court will refrain from disqualifying a person for conduct involving negligence, default or breach of duty or trust which, in a financial claim against him in a private action, would have merited relief under section 727 of the Companies Act 1985 (see C13.5 PART C: LIQUIDATIONS above).

Determination of periods of disqualification

I5.7   As stated above, for the purposes of section 6 of CDDA (see I2.5 above), the minimum period of disqualification is two years and the maximum period 15 years. In *Re Sevenoaks Stationers (Retail) Ltd* (above), Dillon LJ in the Court of Appeal suggested the following basis for determining the period of disqualification within that range. The potential 15-year period should be divided into three brackets. The top bracket of 10 years or over should be reserved for particularly serious cases where a director had already had one period of disqualification imposed on him and fell to be disqualified again. The minimum bracket of two to five years applied where, though disqualification was mandatory, the case was relatively not very serious. The middle bracket of six to ten years should apply for serious cases which did not merit the top bracket. See also *Re Tansoft Ltd [1991] BCLC 339 at 358* where Warner J followed these bands and *Re New Generation Engineers Ltd [1993] BCLC 435* where he stated that what the word 'relatively' required the court to do was to compare the seriousness or gravity of the charge against the director concerned with what, in the direct or indirect experience of the court, had happened in other cases.

In the *Sevenoaks Stationers* case (above), Dillon LJ emphatically disagreed with the Official Receiver's submission that the director could be 'sentenced' not only on the charges on which he had been 'convicted', but also on charges which were never made against him, if they happened to come out in the evidence given. That was inconsistent with the whole conception of giving notice of the charges (see below). It would in many cases stultify the statutory rule if, in fixing the disqualification period, other matters could be alleged of which no notice had been given. In this connection, it will be noted that the practice as required by the statutory rules is that the Official Receiver summarises in affidavits, or a report, the allegations of misconduct on which he is going to rely. As a result of evidence subsequently filed or for some other reason the Official Receiver might want to alter or add to the nature of the allegations. The court has the discretion to allow him to do so, provided that it does not cause injustice to the director concerned.

Chapter 6: Some cases on unfitness and periods of disqualification

I6.1   Set out below are brief summaries of a number of cases which illustrate how the principles discussed in Chapter 5 above, as to the determination of unfitness and the length of disqualification, have been applied by the courts. In each instance, the main features of the particular case are set out, followed by the decision as to disqualification, and judicial comments explaining that decision.

(1)   *Re Rolus Properties Ltd (1988) 4 BCC 446 (21 March 1986)*

Main features. Two companies compulsorily wound up, the first one due to failure of property speculation business following the great property crash of the seventies; no books kept or statutory returns filed and, as to the other company, no accounts prepared, audited or filed and no returns filed for an extensive period; a chartered secretary was employed.

Decision. Disqualified for two years.

Judicial comments. Absence of books was a matter of incompetence rather than dishonesty but showed the director's unfitness because of lack of understanding of paperwork; the substantial mitigating factor was that anyone who employed a chartered secretary to assist in the administration of the affairs of a company, large or small, had reasonable grounds for saying that he had taken proper steps to prepare all the necessary paperwork.

(2)   *Re Churchill Hotel (Plymouth) Ltd (1988) 4 BCC 112 (4 December 1987)*

Main features. Four companies going into insolvent liquidation, having traded unsuccessfully throughout with negligible capital and leaving large deficits and Crown debts; failure to comply with administrative requirements of the companies legislation.

Decision. No disqualification.

Judicial comments. The director knew or ought to have known that the Crown moneys deducted from wages were being used improperly to finance continued trading (*dicta* of Vinelott J in *Re Stanford Services Ltd (1987) 3 BCC 326 at 334* applied); however, he had not been guilty of any dishonesty nor was it a case where, having failed with one company, he had promptly started up the same business through another; other companies had substantial business and workforce and were up to date with filing obligations.

(3) *Re Bath Glass Ltd (1988) 4 BCC 130 (9 December 1987)*

Main features. Causing the company to continue to trade whilst insolvent to the detriment of creditors; substantial Crown debts.

Decision. No disqualification.

Judicial comments. The directors could be rightly criticised for certain aspects of their conduct; but there were certain countervailing points which weighed in the scales against those justified criticisms; imprudent and improper though their conduct had been, in all the circumstances it was not so serious as to make them unfit.

(4) *Re Majestic Recording Studios Ltd (1988) 4 BCC 519 (25 March 1988)*

Main features. Five companies in insolvent compulsory liquidation; A was a director of the first three, B of all the five; as to the first three, substantial deficits and Crown debts and no accounts and annual returns; A's defence was that he had no concern in or control over any financial matters and did not know why accounts and returns not filed; B accepted the court should disqualify him but applied for leave to act as a director of a sixth company which had survived since 1972 and was paying debts as they fell due and whose management was keeping better records and had made a promise, backed by accountants, to prepare up to date accounts.

Decision. A disqualified for three years, B for five years but with leave to continue to act as director of the sixth company.

Judicial comments. A had assumed position involving duties which could not be shirked by leaving everything to others; the public was entitled to be protected against someone who failed to observe duties attendant on the privilege of trading with the benefit of limited liability.

(5) *Re Western Welsh International System Buildings Ltd (1988) 4 BCC 449 (13 April 1988)*

Main features. Three companies successively wound up by the court; failure to keep proper books and produce proper accounts; trading whilst insolvent, continuing to accept customers' deposits when company unable to supply holiday chalets in Spain; Crown debts.

Decision. Disqualified for five years.

Judicial comments. Unfitness beyond question.

(6) *Re McNulty's Interchange Ltd [1989] BCLC 709 (8 July 1988)*

Main features. Two companies successively going into insolvent liquidation within five years; business of the second company purchased from receiver of the first; remuneration drawn but Crown debts not discharged.

Decision. Disqualified for 18 months.

Judicial comments. Re first company, no reason to believe earlier that there was insolvency; having relied on professional advice; not improper to draw remuneration in light of information then available; Crown authorities had agreed to accept payment by instalments; disqualification only justified where conduct dishonest, in breach of standards of commercial morality or grossly incompetent —commercial misjudgment not sufficient; re second company, acquisition of first company's business based on proper commercial decision but improper to continue to incur debts, receive remuneration and fail to pay Crown debts after the company became unable to market any products.

(7)   *Re C U Fittings Ltd (1989) 5 BCC 210 (15 December 1988)*

Main features. Two companies in insolvent liquidation; heavy losses in first company after collapse in the copper market; accountants advised parts of the business were viable; those parts were taken over by the second company; orderly winding down of the first company's remaining business went badly; appeal for help to main supplier failed; the complaint about the conduct re first company: allegation of lack of probity; re the second company: after it should have been plain that the company could not be saved, substantial amount of Crown debts incurred.

Decision. No disqualification.

Judicial comments. Conduct fell short of showing required lack of probity; Crown moneys not used as working capital for a trade that should not have been carried on; a misjudgment as to whether to realise the stock or go into liquidation to preserve preferential position of Crown debts did not amount to lack of commercial probity.

(8)   *Re Ipcon Fashions Ltd (1989) 5 BCC 773 (15 June 1989)*

Main features. Two companies in insolvent liquidation; transfer of business of the second to a third company; winding down of the second company's affairs before liquidation, paying self and wife salary but leaving Crown debts outstanding and continuing to incur liabilities to suppliers.

Decision. Disqualified for five years.

Judicial comments. Conduct particularly reprehensible and contrary to commercial morality. The law, for good reason, required a liquidator to be an independent and qualified insolvency practitioner, and the director was not entitled to take into his own hands, in effect, the liquidation of the company on the ground that the qualified insolvency practitioner's costs would have far exceeded the salaries paid to the director and his wife.

(9)   *Re Cladrose Ltd [1990] BCC 11 (6 October 1989)*

Main features. Three insolvent companies; total failure to produce audited accounts and file annual returns; the first director had relied on his co-director, a chartered accountant.

Decision. The first director not disqualified and the second director disqualified for two years.

Judicial comments. The first director's responsibility for the failures was slight and did not make him unfit; the second director was unfit but not for an extended period; as a chartered accountant, he could properly be relied upon by his fellow directors to have a better knowledge and understanding of company law.

(10)   *Re Keypak Homecare Ltd (No 2) [1990] BCLC 440 (21 December 1989)*

Main features. Preference in favour of one of the directors in respect of a loan made by him to the company; retention of Crown moneys; buying substantial stock on credit after trading ceased; transfer of stock to another company, formed by the directors, at an under-value.

Decision. Disqualified for three years.

Judicial comments. Mitigating factors: the loan had benefited the company to some extent, and the repayment was difficult to criticise as involving want of probity; only last quarter's VAT remained unpaid and the directors were operating within the parameters imposed by the Inland Revenue, which had agreed to accept payment of the substantial sums, due in respect of PAYE and National Insurance contributions, by instalments; therefore, although the retention of Crown moneys showed some want of probity, it was not serious; the manner of ordering and transferring of stock and the setting up of the new company were so misconceived as to amount to want of observance of proper standards.

(11)   *Re Austinsuite Furniture Ltd [1992] BCLC 1047 (1 March 1990)*

Main features. Several companies in insolvent liquidation; substantial Crown debts and pre-payments from customers; overpriced acquisition of loss making company; director S relying on director F's greater business experience; director S2, concerned only as director of one of the companies, aware of financial difficulties but relied on finance director and a manager with accounting qualifications.

Decision. F disqualified for seven years, S for five years and S2 not disqualified.

Judicial comments. Serious want of probity on F's part; S entitled to rely to an extent on F's experience but primarily responsible for the way in which the company's business was run and was paid excessive salary and had profited from a transaction; no want of probity on the part of S2, though not free from criticism re Crown moneys and failure to press for fuller financial disclosure.

(12) *Re T & D Services (Timber Preservation & Damp Proofing Contractors) Ltd [1990] BCC 592 (10 May 1990)*

Main features. Four companies going into compulsory liquidation with large deficiencies and having failed to keep proper accounting records and/or file accounts; all companies financed by retention of Crown monies; the last company's liabilities largely discharged out of monies paid by the respondent to the liquidator in settlement of proceedings for transaction at an undervalue and preference.

Decision. Disqualified for ten years.

Judicial comments. His conduct showed a serious want of probity; affairs conducted without regard to director's duty to see proper books of account were kept and returns promptly made; Crown debts had been allowed to build up over a long period.

(13) *Re Travel Mondial (UK) Ltd [1991] BCLC 120 (20 June 1990)*

Main features. Director of two companies going into insolvent liquidation and not having filed annual returns; third company formed with the same business and similar results.

Decision. Disqualified for nine years, order suspended for 21 days after its service since he had not appeared at the hearing (see Rule 8(2) of the 1987 Rules; see also I8.8 below).

Judicial comments. Serious case of misconduct—attempt to carry on the same business through the third company without having to pay creditors of the old business.

(14) *Re Melcast (Wolverhampton) Ltd [1991] BCLC 288 (17 July 1990)*

Main features. Two companies successively going into insolvent liquidation; neither director had accountancy experience; pursued policy of not paying Crown debts; failure by one to ensure representatives of the outside shareholders with financial expertise were brought in; failure to act on advice of insolvency specialist; continuing to trade whilst insolvent.

Decision. One disqualified for four years; the other for seven years.

Judicial comments. They had not benefited personally but ignored responsibilities as directors; the first one was not primarily a financial man and knew less than the other about the financial position but had not learnt from the first company's liquidation and had no concept of what being a director was.

(15) *Re Sevenoaks Stationers (Retail) Ltd [1991] Ch 164 (CA) (31 July 1990)*

Main features. Several companies in insolvent liquidation; A, a chartered accountant, and B, a former lorry driver, were directors; failure to make annual returns re two companies and to keep proper accounting records re two other companies; Crown debts outstanding.

Decision (on appeal). A's disqualification period reduced from seven to five years (B having been disqualified for three years).

Judicial comments. The non-payment of Crown debts was not automatically to be regarded as evidence of unfitness or breach of commercial morality—Hoffmann J in *Re Dawson Print Group Ltd [1987] BCLC 601* at *604* followed. The Crown authorities were not pressing for payment; the director took advantage of the forbearance and, instead of providing adequate working capital, was trading at the Crown's expense whilst the company was in jeopardy, it would be equally unfair to trade in that way at the expense of the other creditors, the Crown had been more exposed not from the nature of the debts but from the administrative problems in pressing for prompt payment; not a case of a 'rip-off' and pocketing proceeds; however, there had been incompetence or negligence in a marked degree on A's part for absence of proper financial control which was his responsibility.

(16)   *Re Tansoft Ltd [1991] BCLC 339 (1 October 1990)*

Main features. Compulsory insolvent winding up; non-payment of Crown debts, failure to ensure accounts and annual returns were filed; failure to submit statement of affairs to Official Receiver; failure to ensure adequate accounting records were kept and preserved; making a loan prohibited by section 330 of the Companies Act 1985; misapplying and misappropriating company moneys; negligent failure to take steps to recover proceeds of sale of assets; admission as director or former director of eight other companies that they had not filed annual returns and/or accounts.

Decision. Disqualified for seven years.

Judicial comments. Non-payment of Crown debts not to be treated as evidence of unfitness; but, in the case of one company, this made it reprehensible as it had made a loan to the director; failure re accounts and annual returns was not a trivial matter—those dealing with limited companies were entitled to have access to information in them; the fact that no disqualification of three other directors was sought was not an answer.

(17)   *Re Samuel Sherman plc [1991] 1 WLR 1070 (14 March 1991)*

Main features. Public limited company; deliberate, speculative, *ultra vires* and unsuitable investments; treating company as his own and ignoring shareholders; failure to keep accounting records; persistent and deliberate failure to prepare accounts in time; disregard for company legislation requirements; but did not act fraudulently or conceal the transactions.

Decision. Disqualified (under section 8) for five years.

Judicial comments. The circumstances could not be treated as other than a serious case.

(18) *Re ECM (Europe) Electronics Ltd [1991] BCC 268 (21 March 1991)*

Main features. Successful trade between 1983 and 1986; attempted expansion in 1987 leading to financial difficulties and collapse; allegations of (*a*) failure to file accounts for 1987; (*b*) excessive remuneration; (*c*) failure to co-operate with receivers; (*d*) attempted misuse of company name; (*e*) unjustified payments to wife; (*f*) holding shareholders' meeting without due notice; (*g*) making prohibited loan to himself (subsequently made good to the liquidator); (*h*) making payments to others which were of no benefit to the company (again, made good); (*i*) preferences.

Decision. No disqualification.

Judicial comments. No gross negligence or incompetence; (*a*) to (*f*) did not constitute lack of commercial propriety or serious failure of duties; not safe to act on (*i*); (*g*) and (*h*) could be criticised for irregular use of company funds, notwithstanding reparation but the falling off from the standards not of so blameworthy a character as to be stigmatised as a breach of commercial morality.

(19) *Re City Investment Centres Ltd [1992] BCLC 956 (18 July 1991)*

Main features. Five companies in insolvent liquidation; business connected with over-the-counter market, acquisition of an insolvent business without provision for adequate permanent capital; Crown debts; continuing to trade after knowledge or assumed knowledge of insolvency.

Decision. S disqualified for ten years and D and E for six years.

Judicial comments. S was in control of all companies and a shadow director of those from which he had resigned; D's conduct as 'compliance director' showed negligence in a very marked degree; no personal gain; the conduct of B displayed a woeful ignorance of duties of a director and negligence in a very marked degree; no personal gain; had co-operated fully with the Official Receiver.

(20) *Re Cargo Agency Ltd [1992] BCC 388 (17 January 1992)*

Main features. Wife director with salary of £15,000 and husband *de facto* director with consultancy fee of £35,000 a year; insolvent liquidation within 17 months of commencement of business; debts of £40,000 incurred after they should have realised that the company could not properly continue to trade.

Decision. Both disqualified for two years; and husband granted leave to be engaged as a general manager in his current employment but not to become a director.

Judicial comments. Husband had risked and lost his own £20,000 investment in the company; but the public at large had suffered by continued trading; not a serious case; husband's initial salary unreasonably high.

(21) *Re Godwin Warren Control Systems Ltd [1993] BCLC 80 (18 May 1992)*

Main features. Insolvent liquidation, debts £3m; the first director had recommended acquisition by the company of the business of another company without disclosing his financial interest in the vendor company.

Decision. The first director disqualified for six years; the other directors, for two years.

Judicial comments. Serious case of deliberate deception by the first director; the others had not set out to deceive for their own advantage, but had chosen not to raise or investigate inconsistencies.

(22) *Re Burnham Marketing Services Ltd [1993] BCC 518 (28 August 1992)*

Main features. £219,000 deficit; failure to remit Crown moneys, to keep proper accounting records and clients' money separate, to lodge accounts and keep statutory records; the respondent, as the company's owner, had appointed and relied on a managing director whom he had believed to be competent.

Decision. Disqualified for three years.

Judicial comments. No general rule that a director who entrusted the running of a company to others who ran it into insolvency was necessarily guilty of conduct which rendered him unfit; it was, however, essential that, as proprietor, he should have kept a close eye and tight rein on those whom he had appointed; was honest but was shown to have a fundamental disregard for his duties as a director by walking away from it; that was not merely a commercial misjudgment; he did make a belated effort to retrieve the situation.

(23) *Re Linvale Ltd [1993] BCLC 654 (13 November 1992)*

Main features. Two directors—not highly educated, and ignorant of financial matters in any technical sense—of three companies, which successively went into insolvent liquidation, incurring debts which in all probability would not be paid; using for their own purposes Crown moneys; honest in the sense that they did not deliberately seek to defraud; substantial deficiencies; accounts and records unsatisfactory.

Decision. Disqualified for five years.

Judicial comments. Element of recklessness in continuation of trading; 'Phoenix' aspect (an attempt to carry on the same business, leaving behind the creditors of the old business).

(24) *Re Swift 736 Ltd (Secretary of State for Trade and Industry v Ettinger) [1993] BCC 312 (16 February 1993)*

Main features. Husband and wife team; series of companies in insolvent liquidation; misuse of Crown debts; failure to file accounts and returns; absence of personal gain, husband having lost personal assets to the companies.

Decision. At first instance, the husband disqualified for three years and the wife for two years; the Court of Appeal increased the period for the husband to five years.

Judicial comments. Isolated lapses in filing documents might be excusable but not persistent lapses which showed a blatant disregard for that important aspect of accountability.

(25) *Re Synthetic Technology Ltd [1993] BCC 549 (23 March 1993)*

Main features. Director procuring the company to discharge his personal debts; wrongfully asserting personal ownership of company's assets in administration; drawing remuneration out of proportion to company's trading success and financial health; trading whilst insolvent; failure to file accounts; taking unwarranted risks with creditors' money; trading at the expense of moneys due to the Crown.

Decision. Disqualified for seven years and ordered to pay costs on standard basis only.

Judicial comments. The case was a serious case of its kind; deficiency disproportionately large to the company's size and capitalisation; the director had behaved in a markedly cavalier fashion.

(26) *Re Looe Fish Ltd [1993] BCC 348 (25 March 1993)*

Main features. Breach of duty as director by manipulating voting control so as to defeat attempts by rival factions to gain board control and thereby contravening companies legislation.

Decision. Disqualified for 2½ years (under section 8).

Judicial comments. By using power to allot shares improperly he displayed a clear lack of commercial probity; chose to play fast and loose to remain in control; case not among the most serious which might arise under section 8; no question of insolvency or personal gain or improper personal benefit.

(27) *Re Pamstock Ltd [1994] BCC 264 (24 November 1993)*

Main features. Company inadequately capitalised, reliant on borrowing from joint venture participators and the bank; consistently made losses resulting, by the end of 1986, in liabilities exceeding current assets; by the middle of June 1987, it was clear it could not survive; creditors kept at bay by issue of cheques which could not be met; business substantially financed by ever-increasing Crown debts; respondent specialised in providing financial advice and procuring venture capital finance to small and new companies, which often involved his accepting directorships; ceased being involved in the company's affairs since 1987–88; ensured a chartered accountant was appointed as company secretary to deal with statutory requirements; wound up compulsorily at the end of 1989; annual accounts and returns not filed.

Decision. Disqualified for two years.

Judicial comments. Not a case of a director who had taken large remuneration or other benefit at creditors' expense. The question, however, was not whether there was culpable misconduct in this sense—he had failed to put into place an adequate system of management and had allowed the company to trade beyond the point at which it should have ceased trading. To that extent he fell short of the standard. 'This case is one which has given me considerable anxiety . . . It (venture capital companies) is a field in which there are inevitably a proportion of casualties . . . companies are forced into liquidation not as a result of culpable misconduct or even a want of skill and care but because an expected market does not materialise or because of adverse circumstances which could not reasonably be foreseen', *per* Vinelott J.

(28) *Re Wimbledon Village Restaurant Ltd [1994] BCC 753 (18 March 1994)*

Main features. Three directors—lapses from the statutorily required standards by the first two directors demonstrated a failure to appreciate their responsibilities, a failure which damaged the interests of trade creditors. The third director retained a directorship simply as a means of protecting her position as the unlimited guarantor of the company's overdraft, but she failed to appreciate her wider responsibility to the company and creditors.

Decision. None disqualified.

Judicial comments. Not every impropriety should lead to a finding of unfitness. There was a significant measure of doubt as to whether the lapses properly attributable to the first two respondents were sufficiently serious to compel such a finding. The doubt must be resolved in their favour. As to the third respondent, although she had wholly misconceived her duties as a director, that did not inexorably lead to a finding of unfitness. The court had to consider her actual responsibility in relation to the allegations which had been proved.

(29) *Re Firedart Ltd (1994) 138 S J 16, 24 April 1994 (24 March 1994)*

Main features. Failure to keep accounting records.

Decision. Disqualified for six years.

Judicial comments. Accounting records are important both while a company is a going concern and in the event of liquidation: failure by directors to keep them in accordance with specified statutory requirements results in ignorance of accurate financial position and risk that the situation is worse than they think; creditors would suffer as a consequence; directors who permit this can expect to be found unfit.

Chapter 7: Consequences of disqualification order

General effects (sections 1(1), 11 and 12)

I7.1   The effect of a disqualification order is that during the period of disqualification the person concerned must not, without the leave of the court (see I7.2 and I7.3 below), be a director, liquidator or administrator of a company or a receiver or manager of a company's property or in any way, whether directly or indirectly, be concerned or take part in the promotion, formation or management of a company. The effect of the automatic disqualification of an undischarged bankrupt under section 11 or a person to whom section 12 applies on the revocation of an administration order (see heads (8) and (9), I2.8 and I2.9 above) is, *prima facie*, more limited in that he must not act as director of, or directly or indirectly take part in or be concerned in the promotion, formation, or management of, a company, except with the leave of the court. There is no express reference to his being disbarred from acting as liquidator, administrator or receiver or manager but he could fall foul of the disqualification provisions in so far as acting in any such capacity involves 'management' of the company; and, in any case, his authorisation, if any, as insolvency practitioner would almost certainly have been revoked. Further, section 31 of the Insolvency Act 1986 imposes penalties for an undischarged bankrupt acting as receiver or manager of the property of the company on behalf of debenture holders. This applies to both administrative receivers and non-administrative receivers but not to a receiver or manager acting under an appointment made by the court.

The expression 'take part in the . . . management of a company' has been construed widely so as to insulate the disqualified person from taking part in the management of company affairs generally. For example, his acting as an independent management consultant to a company falls within the prohibition (*R v Campbell [1984] BCLC 83*). However, it was held in the Australian case of *Re Magna Alloys & Research Pty Ltd (1975) CLC 40-227*, that a person who acted as marketing adviser, and in that capacity attended directors' meetings, could not be said to have taken part in the management of the company. A disqualified person who was the majority shareholder of the company was free to vote as a shareholder, even on a management matter, although there could be circumstances where he might so use his position on the question of management as to infringe the prohibition. According to another Australian case, *CCA v Brecht (1989) 7 ACLC 40*, the concept of 'management' required an involvement of some kind in the decision-making process of the company, and some degree of responsibility. See also *Re Clasper Group Services Ltd (1988) 4 BCC 673*, where the son of the controlling shareholder and director, who was employed as a management trainee with authority to sign company cheques, was held by Warner J not to have been concerned with or to have taken part in the management of the company, as he did not appear to have risen much above the status of an office boy and messenger. 'Management' includes both the internal and external management of a company (*R v Austen* (*1985*) *1 BCC 99,528*). (See also I2.1 above.)

Prima facie, a disqualification order, when made, operates to prohibit all activities mentioned in section 1 (or 11 or 12, as the case may be) except that leave to carry on any of those activities may subsequently be given. In practice, it is possible for the court to grant such leave at the same time as it makes the disqualification order, so that the order itself would, in effect, be one which imposes less than a total ban. See I7.2 below.

Leave applications (section 17)

I7.2   Where the application of the person disqualified is for leave to promote or form a company, the application should be made to any court with the jurisdiction to wind up companies (see C5.1 *et seq.* PART C: LIQUIDATIONS above); and where the application is for leave to be a liquidator, administrator or director of, or otherwise to take part in the management of, a company or to be a receiver or manager of a company's property, the application should be made to any court having jurisdiction to wind up *that* company. On the hearing of the application, the Secretary of State, the Official Receiver or the liquidator (if the disqualification order was made on his application) must appear and call the attention of the court to any matters which seem to him to be relevant, and may himself give evidence or call witnesses.

It is possible for an application for leave to be made in advance of a disqualification order for hearing at the same time as the application for disqualification order is heard, on the basis that leave is only sought if the court proceeds to make a disqualification order (see, for example, *Re Majestic Recording Studios Ltd* (*1988*) *4 BCC 519* (relevant part of the judgment not fully reported). This may save considerable time and costs. As to the costs of the Secretary of State where the application is not substantially opposed by him but he has incurred extra costs because the applicant was not ready, see *Re Dicetrade Ltd* [*1994*] *BCC 371*.

The court will seldom, if ever, grant leave in such wide terms as to substantially nullify the effect of the disqualification order. In considering an application for leave, it will take into account, *inter alia*, the gravity or otherwise of the applicant's conduct which led to his disqualification, how important it is for the applicant and those dependent on him and on the business of any company run by him that he should be allowed to carry on the activities in question and what safeguards would be available against those activities being carried on to the detriment of the public. Accordingly, an order granting leave would be so tailored as to allow the applicant to indulge in only those activities which, in the circumstances, it is reasonably necessary for him to carry on and as to provide appropriate safeguards for the public.

Cases on applications for leave

I7.3   In *Re Lo-Line Electric Motors Ltd* (*1988*) *4 BCC 415*, the applicant was granted leave to continue to be a director of his two family companies provided that another named person continued to be a director with voting control of those companies. The condition imposed in granting leave to the applicant to act as a director of a specified more successful company in *Re Majestic Recording Studios Ltd* (above) was that a chartered accountant should act as a co-director and that the accounts for the previous financial year (but not necessarily those for the earlier financial years) should be produced and filed. In *Re Chartmore Ltd* [*1990*] *BCLC 673* the condition on which leave to act as a director of a particular company was granted was that monthly board meetings should be held, attended by a representative of the auditors. In *Re DJ Matthews (Joinery Design) Ltd* (*1988*) *4 BCC 513*, in refusing leave to the applicant to act as a director of a company, the court indicated that such an application might be more sympathetically considered at a later stage if the company in question was one the liability of the members of which was unlimited. It is submitted that such a condition alone would not afford sufficient protection to the public. In *Re Cargo Agency Ltd* [*1992*] *BCC 388*, refusing leave, Harman J stated that leave should only be granted where there was a need for it and upon evidence of adequate protection from danger. The applicant in *Re Godwin Warren Control Systems plc* [*1992*] *BCC 557* was granted leave in relation to two companies (but not two other companies) where his conduct had amounted to 'an inadequate response to difficult circumstances rather than a planned course of wrongdoing'. The condition of the leave was that all the circumstances concerning his disqualification be brought to the attention of the boards of directors of those companies. In dismissing an application by an undischarged bankrupt for leave to act, the Northern Ireland High Court (Murray J) in *Re McQuillan* (*1989*) *5 BCC 137* said that the policy of the legislature was so strong against a bankrupt acting as a director or manager that it provided for his so acting without leave being a criminal offence punishable by imprisonment if necessary. Where the bankrupt simply had not made out the alleged need for his being allowed (and able to secure his appointment) to act as a director of the company in question, the court should not exercise its discretion to make an exception to the general policy of the legislature.

Consequences of contravention (sections 13 to 15)

I7.4   A contravention of a disqualification order involves both criminal penalties and personal financial liability.

If a person acts in contravention of a disqualification order or of section 12(2) (revocation of a county court administration order) or is guilty of an offence under section 11 (undischarged bankrupt) he is liable, on conviction on indictment, to imprisonment for not more than two years or a fine, or both or, on summary conviction, to imprisonment for not more than six months or a fine not exceeding the statutory minimum, or both (section 13). Where a body corporate is guilty of an offence of acting in contravention of a disqualification order, and it is proved that the offence occurred with the consent or connivance of, or was attributable to any neglect on the part of, any director, manager, secretary or other similar officer of the body corporate, or any person who was purporting to act in any such capacity, he, as well as the body corporate, is guilty of the offence and liable to be proceeded against and punished accordingly. Where the affairs of a body corporate are managed by its members, both sanctions apply in relation to the acts and defaults of a member in connection with his functions of management as if he were a director of the body corporate (section 14). For the meanings of 'body corporate' and 'officer', see sections 740 and 744 of the Companies Act 1985 as incorporated in CDDA by section 22(6).

Section 15 provides that a person is personally responsible for all the relevant debts of the company if at any time

(*a*) in contravention of a disqualification order or of section 11 (undischarged bankrupts) he is involved in the management of the company or

(*b*) as a person who is involved in the management of the company, he acts or is willing to act on instructions given without the leave of the court by a person whom he knows at that time to be the subject of a disqualification order or to be an undischarged bankrupt.

Such personal responsibility is joint and several with the company and any other person who, whether under section 15 or otherwise, is so liable. For this purpose, a person is involved in the management of the company if he is a director of the company or if he is concerned, whether directly or indirectly, or takes part, in the management of the company. For the purposes of (*b*), willingness to act is presumed, unless the contrary is shown, if the person involved in the management has previously acted on the instructions referred to there.

'Relevant debts' means, where (*a*) applies, such debts and other liabilities of the company as are incurred at a time when that person was involved in the management of the company and, where (*b*) applies, such debts and other liabilities of the company as are incurred at a time when that person was acting or was willing to act on instructions referred to there (section 15).

Chapter 8: Procedural aspects

Notice of intended application (section 16(1))

I8.1   A person intending to apply to the court having jurisdiction to wind up a company for a disqualification order must give not less than ten days' notice of his intention to the person against whom the order is sought. The period of ten days is to be calculated exclusive of the days on which the notice is given and on which proceedings are issued (*Re Jaymar Management Ltd [1990] BCC 303*, Harman J, who regarded the requirement to give notice as mandatory). However, it has been held in *Secretary of State for Trade and Industry v Langridge (Re Cedac Ltd) [1991] BCC 148 (CA)* (reversing the decision of Mummery J ([*1990] BCC 555*)), that this provision is directory and not mandatory, so that failure to give full ten days' notice is only a procedural irregularity which does not nullify the application. Nourse LJ dissented on the ground that *Howard v Boddington (1877) 2 PD 203* supported the proposition that, except when indicated to the contrary, a statutory provision, whose purpose was to protect an individual in regard to proceedings which might result in substantial interference with his freedom to pursue his trade, was mandatory not directory.

It is not entirely clear how such a notice would help the proposed respondent. Conceivably, it may give him a chance to apply to the court within the ten-day period for an injunction restraining the Secretary of State from issuing the proceedings. It is difficult to see him succeeding in this regard except, perhaps, in very rare cases where bad faith and abuse of the process can be established. Alternatively, the proposed respondent may take the advantage of the ten-day gap to make representations to the Secretary of State with a view to persuading him not to issue proceedings. The mere commencement of disqualification proceedings may cause substantial and permanent prejudice and detriment to the respondent even if in the event he is exonerated in the proceedings. If the two-year time limit is about to expire so as to leave the Secretary of State insufficient time to consider the representations, an offer may be made by the respondent to undertake to support the Secretary of State's application for an appropriate extension of time (although, in practice, the Secretary of State is known to have been reluctant to agree to delay instituting proceedings on the basis of such an undertaking). For these reasons, one may have considerable sympathy for the dissenting judgment of Nourse LJ.

Period of limitation and its extension (section 7(2))

I8.2   Except with the leave of the court, an application for a disqualification order under section 6 must not be made after the end of the period of two years beginning with the day on which the company of which the respondent is or has been a director become insolvent (see I2.5 above) (section 7(2)). No specific time limit has been prescribed for an application for a disqualification order under any of the other sections of CDDA.

Where two or more events mentioned in section 7(2) occur at different times in relation to the same company, for example liquidation followed or proceeded by administrative receivership or an administration order and its subsequent discharge followed by liquidation, the period of two years runs from the first of those events (*Re Tasbian Ltd (1989) 5 BCC 729; [1990] BCC 318*). Where the event concerned is winding up by the court, time begins to run from the date of the winding-up order and not the date of the winding-up petition (*Re Walter L Jacob & Co Ltd [1993] BCC 512*). An interim order made under section 9(4) of the Insolvency Act 1986 under the administration procedure is not an administration order proper so that time does not begin to run until an administration order is made under section 8 of that Act (*Secretary of State for Trade and Industry v Palmer [1993] BCC 650*, upheld by the Court of Session: *The Times, 4 November 1994*). An application filed on the first day the court office was open after the last day of the two-year period was not out of time: *Re Philipp and Lion Ltd [1994] BCC 261*.

The procedure for an application for an extension of time canvassed in *Re Crestjoy Products Ltd [1990] BCC 23* by Harman J, and followed in *Re Cedac Ltd [1990] BCC 555* by Mummery J, was that the applicant should issue an originating summons for leave and serve it on the respondent and that there should then be a hearing before the judge or, arguably, the registrar, with both parties present. This contrasts with the views of Millett J in *Re Probe Data Systems Ltd (No 2) [1990] BCC 21* where he suggested an *ex parte* application to the registrar in the first instance, accompanied by the whole of the applicant's evidence, with the discretion to the registrar, if he is satisfied that there was *prima facie* case for granting leave, to give directions to serve the respondent with the application and the supporting evidence.

Among the factors which the court is likely to consider on an application for an extension of time are the gravity of the allegations and the strength of the case against the respondent, the length of and the reasons for the delay (including delay within the two-year time limit), the extent, if any, to which the respondent might have contributed to the delay and the likelihood or otherwise of any unfair prejudice to the respondent because of the delay. Pressure of work and shortage of staff in the Secretary of State's office may not be a sufficient excuse for the delay, particularly where the application is made after, rather than before, the expiry of the two-year period (*Re Crestjoy* (above)). In *Re Cedac* (above), extension of time was granted on the ground that there had been no culpable or inordinate delay on the part of the Secretary of State. In *Re Probe Data Systems Ltd (No 3) [1992] BCC 110*, on an appeal by the respondent from the decision of the High Court granting extension of time to the Secretary of State, the Court of Appeal held that the registrar's error in disregarding the delay within the two-year period as irrelevant was not sufficient to impeach his decision. The delay was not such as to weigh very heavily in the balance. The rules set out in

Ladd v Marshall [1954] 1 WLR 1489 were not designed and did not have to be rigorously applied in the case of an application under section 7(2) which was of an interlocutory character. The appellant's evidence did not contain so incontrovertible an answer to the case against him as to justify the conclusion that the case was too weak to warrant the grant of leave.

This decision was followed by the Court of Appeal in *Re Tasbian Ltd (No 3) [1992] BCC 358*. The appellant had argued that there was insufficient evidence that he had been a *de facto* director or shadow director of the company and, alternatively, that the evidence was such that it did not justify the grant of leave to proceed out of time; and, further, that there was no sufficient explanation for the failure by the Secretary of State to commence proceedings in time and that leave should not have been given because the evidence explaining the delay was inaccurate. The Court of Appeal, in dismissing the appeal, held that the registrar and the judge were correct in saying that the evidence disclosed an arguable case and that the appellant was either a shadow or a *de facto* director, sufficient to preclude rejection of the application for extension of time on that ground. Some of the matters on which the Official Receiver relied were, taken by themselves, of little weight but others were more significant, in particular the allegation that the appellant monitored the company's trading and controlled its bank account through the bank mandate and was involved in the hive-down of the company's business. Taken overall, the judge was right that a sufficient explanation for the delay had been given. This was public interest litigation and, if the appellant had behaved in such a way as to render himself unfit to be a company director, it would not be right for the court to preclude the trial of that question merely because the Official Receiver had admittedly been inaccurate in certain facts put before the court to support the *ex parte* application.

In *Re Copecrest Ltd [1993] BCLC 1118*, Mervyn Davies J refused to grant an extension, stating that although there was an arguable case on the complaints of a grave nature made against the respondent, no good reason had been shown for an extension. An extension was also refused by Jacob J in *Re Packaging Direct Ltd [1994] BCC 213*. There had been both substantial and excessive delay—notice of intention had been given nine months before the two-year period expired but the application for leave was made nine weeks after the period expired—and the substantive case against the respondent was not sufficiently strong. The case should not be allowed to go forward simply because a particular point deserved to be properly argued. *Re Polly Peck International plc [1993] BCC 890* is an example of where the Secretary of State failed to obtain extension of time against four of the directors of the company in administration. Lindsay J, having found that there had been unreasonable periods of delay, reasoned thus:

(i) if the applicant's case was so weak that it could not lead to disqualification, the application for leave should be rejected even before a balancing of all the factors was embarked upon—that initial threshold (*Re Tasbian Ltd (No 3) [1992] BCC 358*) had not been crossed in the present case;

(ii) if the initial threshold was crossed, and it was necessary to consider the strength of the applicant's case as part of the balancing exercise, it was at best speculative and very weak against each of the respondents;

(iii) there was a case plainly arguable on the evidence as a whole that even if the respondents' shortcomings were seen as serious, they were not of a kind likely to recur in any company with which any of them would be likely to be associated, except in the quite exceptional circumstances of Polly Peck;

(iv) by reason of the applicant's failure to act within the two-year time limit, three of the respondents were to suffer some prejudice, and more prejudice was likely to follow;

(v) balancing the factors of delay, the reasons for it, the strength of the case and prejudice, there was no good reason for the extension in relation to three of the respondents; as for the fourth, the initial threshold was not crossed but even if it had been, the case against him was, on evidence, threadbare to a degree and too weak to warrant the grant of leave.

Application for disqualification order (section 16; Rules 2 to 4, the 1987 Rules)

I8.3   An application to a court with jurisdiction to wind up companies for a disqualification order under sections 2 to 5 (heads 1 to 4 (I2.1 to I2.4) above) may be made by the Secretary of State or the Official Receiver, or by the liquidator or any past or present member or creditor of the company in relation to which the respondent has committed or is alleged to have committed an offence or other default (section 16). An application for a disqualification order under section 7(1) or (8) should be made (*a*) in the High Court, by originating summons (Form 10 in Appendix A to the Rules of the Supreme Court, with such adaptation as may be appropriate), and in a county court, by originating application (also referred to below as a summons).

The Rules of the Supreme Court 1965 or (as the case may be) the County Court Rules 1981 apply, except where the 1987 Rules make provision to inconsistent effect.

At the time when the summons is issued, the applicant must file in court evidence in support of the application; and copies of the evidence are to be served with the summons on the respondent. (See further I8.5 below.) The summons must be endorsed with information set out in Rule 4 of the 1987 Rules.

Service and acknowledgement (Rule 5, the 1987 Rules)

I8.4   The summons must be served on the respondent by sending it by first class post to his last known address; and the date of service is, unless the contrary is shown, deemed to be the seventh day next following the date on which the summons was posted. When any process or document is to be served on any person who is not in England and Wales, the court may order service on him to be effected within such time limit and in such manner as it thinks fit, and may also require appropriate proof of such service.

The summons must be accompanied by a form of acknowledgement of service. The respondent must return that form to the court within 14 days from the date of service. For this purpose, the practice and procedure of the High Court relating to acknowledgements of service (including Form 15 in Appendix A to the Rules of the Supreme Court 1965, as modified) apply both in the High Court and, with necessary modifications, in the county court. The form of acknowledgement requires the respondent to indicate

(*a*) whether he contests the application on the ground that (i) he was not a director or shadow director of the company at the relevant time or (ii) his conduct as director or shadow director of that company was not as alleged,

(*b*) whether, in the case of any conduct of his, he disputes the allegation that such conduct makes him unfit, and

(*c*) whether, while not resisting the application for a disqualification order, he intends to adduce mitigating factors with a view to justifying only a short period of disqualification.

Evidence (Rules 3 and 6, the 1987 Rules)

I8.5   Evidence in support of the application to be filed and served with the summons can be by way of one or more affidavits, except that where the applicant is the Official Receiver, the evidence may be in the form of a written report (including one made by his deputy: *Re Homes Assured Corporation plc [1993] BCC 573*), with or without affidavits by other persons). Such report is to be treated as if it had been verified by affidavit and is to be *prima facie* evidence of any matter contained in it. The affidavit or affidavits or the report must include a statement of the matters by reference to which the respondent is alleged to be unfit.

The evidential status of the Official Receiver's report and annexures to it was considered in *Re City Investment Centres Ltd [1992] BCLC 956*. The report of the Official Receiver contained statements made by others either in the body of the report or in separate documents annexed to it. Morritt J stated that he could see no justification for distinguishing between the main body of the report and the documents which formed part by being annexed to it. He upheld the Official Receiver's submission that the words 'shall be *prima facie* evidence of any matter contained in it' were evidently intended to render any matter asserted in the report *prima facie* evidence of that matter whether or not it was otherwise admissible if contained in an affidavit. The apparent justification for the rule was that the Official Receiver would seldom have personal knowledge of the facts, and the weight to be attached to the assertion would be a matter for the court. The quoted words were obviously intended to confer on the report an evidential status in addition to that which an affidavit would have. The words 'any matter' were entirely general and did not warrant any restriction to statements which would have been admissible under the Civil Evidence Act 1968 if the requisite notices had been served. In assessing the weight to be attached to any particular matter, the court would no doubt consider the source of the Official Receiver's information as well as any other evidence and all the circumstances. (See also *Re Moonbeam Cards Ltd [1993] BCLC 1099*.)

The practice of the Official Receiver to include in his report every matter which could be the subject of a complaint, thus overloading the evidence with complaints of no substantial weight and going back over a very long time, came under some criticism by Vinelott J in *Re Pamstock Ltd [1994] BCC 264*, where he suggested that details about the respondent's relevant conduct with regard to other companies could be raised in a schedule or addendum without raising separate complaints, except where there was a serious failure for which he could be said to be responsible, whether alone or with others.

As to evidence in a county court and admissibility of (i) an administrator's affidavit containing hearsay matters and exhibiting documents from the company's records and (ii) a report under Rule 2.2 of the Insolvency Rules 1986, see *Re Circle Holidays International plc [1994] BCC 226*.

Evidence in the form of statements obtained under section 447 of the Companies Act 1985 by the Secretary of State when investigating the affairs of a company to determine whether it was expedient in the public interest to wind up the company, which although hearsay and admissible in winding-up proceedings, is also impliedly admissible in disqualification proceedings under section 8 of the CDDA (head (6)—see I2.6 above): *Re Rex Williams Leisure Plc [1994] BCC 551 (CA)*. Hoffmann LJ referred to the submission made on behalf of the respondent to the effect that there was a distinction between disqualification applications and public interest winding-up petitions, in that in the latter no particular facts had to be proved (since the evidence had merely to establish that it was in the public interest that the company should be wound up to enable the Official Receiver to investigate its affairs) whilst in the former the Secretary of State had to prove facts which showed that the director was unfit. In his Lordship's view, those distinctions went to weight rather than admissibility. In a disqualification application, hearsay evidence, untested by cross-examination of the informant, might be insufficient to satisfy the burden of proof against opposing evidence. It would depend on the facts and probabilities of each case. Once the Secretary of State knew from the opposing affidavits which material facts were seriously in dispute, he might well be advised to reinforce his case by affidavits from the appropriate informants. But that was no reason why the hearsay evidence under section 447 of the 1985 Act should not be admissible.

It would appear that, unlike under the old legislation, transcripts of private examination of the respondent under section 236 of the Insolvency

Act 1986 (see A4.19 PART A: GENERAL above) are admissible in disqualification proceedings by virtue of section 433 of that Act (*Re Keypak Homecare Ltd [1990] BCLC 440*). The same presumably applies to the notes of any interview under section 235 of that Act, although there is no express provision permitting its use for the purpose.

As in ordinary litigation, the respondent is entitled, under Order 24 of the Rules of the Supreme Court, to discovery of documents within the power of the Secretary of State, where he is the applicant. However, this entitlement does not extend to documents in the custody of an administrative receiver or former administrative receiver (*Re Lombard Shipping and Forwarding Ltd [1992] BCC 700*, where the Secretary of State and the receivers, though not willing to give full effect to Order 24, were willing to allow the respondent access to the documents for the purpose of preparing his defence).

In determining the length of the period of disqualification, the court will not take into account any charges not made in the application which come out in the course of the evidence given: *Re Sevenoaks Stationers (Retail) Ltd [1991] Ch 164 (CA)*, where it was stated that while the court had a discretion to allow the Official Receiver to adduce evidence not in his report (provided that that could be done without injustice), the period of disqualification should be fixed only by reference to matters properly proved.

The respondent must, within 28 days from the date of service of the summons, file in court any affidavit evidence in opposition to the application he wishes the court to take into consideration and must forthwith serve upon the applicant a copy of such evidence.

The applicant must, within 14 days from receiving the copy of the respondent's evidence, file in court any further evidence in reply he wishes the court to take into consideration and must forthwith serve a copy of that evidence upon the respondent.

Hearing (section 16; Rule 7, the 1987 Rules)

I8.6   The date fixed for the hearing of the application must not be less than eight weeks from the date of issue of the summons. The hearing must in the first instance be before the registrar in open court. The registrar must either determine the case on the date fixed or adjourn it. He must adjourn the case for further consideration if (*a*) he forms the provisional opinion that a disqualification order ought to be made, and that a period of disqualification longer than five years is appropriate or (*b*) he is of the opinion that questions of law and fact arise which are not suitable for summary determination. Where (*b*) above applies, he must direct whether the case is to be heard by the registrar or, if he thinks it appropriate, by a judge, for determination by him, state the reasons for the adjournment and give directions as to the manner in which and the time within which notice of the adjournment and the reasons for it are to be given to the respondent, the filing in court and the service of further evidence (if any) by the parties, such other matters as the registrar thinks necessary or expedient with a view to an expeditious disposal of the application and the time and place of the adjourned hearing. Where the case is adjourned other than to a judge, it may be heard by the registrar who originally dealt with the case or by another registrar.

Where the applicant is the Secretary of State, the Official Receiver or the liquidator, he must appear at the hearing and call the attention of the court to any matters which seem to him to be relevant and may himself give evidence or call witnesses. The respondent may appear and himself give evidence (section 16(1) and (3)). However, these rights to give evidence and call witnesses do not absolve the applicant or the respondent from the requirements to file and serve evidence before the hearing under Rules 3 and 6 of the 1987 Rules (see I8.5 above), subject to the discretion of the court, in exercise of its control over its own procedure, to permit otherwise in exceptional circumstances (see, for example, *Re Rex Williams Leisure plc [1994] BCC 551 (CA)*). Official Receivers and deputy Official Receivers have right of audience in any disqualification proceedings, whether the application is made by the Secretary of State or by the Official Receiver at his direction, and whether made in the High Court or a county court.

In addition to the summary procedure (under which the registrar himself can determine the application and make a disqualification order for a period not exceeding five years), another form of summary procedure before a judge has emerged in practice. In *Re Carecraft Construction Co Ltd [1993] BCC 336*, the judge was asked by the parties to determine the application on the basis of a schedule of agreed facts. The directors accepted that the court was likely to find that their conduct made them unfit to be concerned in the management of a company and would be bound to disqualify them for not less than two years. The Secretary of State accepted that such facts as were still in dispute would not be likely, if proved, to increase materially the seriousness of the accusations against the directors. He was content that the court should impose the minimum disqualification period of two years. Ferris J held that the court did have jurisdiction to adopt a summary procedure of this nature and that it was appropriate to do so in the present case. He proceeded to disqualify the directors for two years. This procedure was followed in *Re Aldermanbury Trust plc [1993] BCC 598* resulting in a lenient 'sentence'. It remains to be seen whether or not these cases mark the beginnings of a form of 'plea bargaining', extending to cases where the Secretary of State can, in suitable cases, invite the court not to make a disqualification order at all in the light of voluntary financial contributions made by the respondent to the liquidator for the benefit of the creditors.

In *Re Rex Williams Leisure plc [1993] BCC 79* at first instance, Sir Donald Nicholls V-C rejected the respondent's application for the postponement of the disqualification proceedings pending the outcome of a private action against the respondent involving the same complaints as those involved in the disqualification proceedings.

Striking out application for want of prosecution or sufficient case

I8.7   In *Re Manlon Trading Ltd, The Times, 15 August 1994*, the respondent successfully applied for the application for his disqualification made by the Secretary of State to be struck out for want of prosecution. The proceedings had been instituted on 7 June 1990, the day before the expiry of the two year period. Between 30 May 1991 and October 1992 the Official Receiver appeared to have taken virtually no steps to advance the proceedings towards a hearing. It was accepted on his behalf that that delay, of some 17 months, was inordinate and inexcusable and attributable to him. On 11 November 1992 the Official Receiver served on the respondent a notice of intention to proceed. Procedurally, all that remained to be done before the trial was for the Official Receiver to file his long overdue evidence. It was not done until 24 January 1994 when evidence of modest length and a further report containing very little new information and much argument was filed and served. By that time 15 months had expired since the service of the notice of intention to proceed. It was a common ground that the charges against the respondent were of a serious nature. Evans-Lombe J held that the approach of the court in applications to strike out cases brought under the CDDA could not be the same as the approach of the court to striking out applications in ordinary private litigation. It was inherent in the nature of proceedings under the CDDA that they would prejudice the business interests of the respondent so long as they remained pending. Accordingly, where there had been inordinate and inexcusable delay in the prosecution of such proceedings, they might be struck out without proof of specific prejudice to the respondent on the principles applicable to *inter partes* civil litigation. For another instance of striking out on the ground of inordinate and inexcusable delay, see *Re Noble Trees Ltd [1993] BCC 318*.

The court also has power to strike out an application for a disqualification order under Order 18, Rule 19 of the Rules of the Supreme Court on the ground that the application does not comply with Rule 3 of the 1987 Rules in that it does not contain sufficient evidence to make out a *prima facie* case against the respondent; but the court has a discretion to allow the applicant to submit further evidence under Rule 3 on the striking out application (*Re Jazzgold Ltd [1992] BCC 587*).

Effective date of disqualification order

I8.8   A disqualification order made under head (5) or (6) (I2.5 and I2.6 above) (section 7 or 8) takes effect 21 days after the date on which it is made, unless the court orders otherwise (Rules 1(3) and 9 of the 1987 Rules). The last phrase appears to empower the court both to shorten or to extend the 21-day period, although it is difficult to envisage circumstances in which the court would be justified in shortening it except at the request of the person disqualified. For instances of where the period was extended, see *Re T & D Services (Timber Preservation & Damp Proofing Contractors) Ltd [1990] BCC 592* (operation of the disqualification order deferred for two weeks so as to enable the person concerned to try to make alternative arrangements for the management of his company) and

Re Travel Mondial (UK) Ltd [1991] BCC 224 (direction that the disqualification order should not be enforced until 21 days after personal service of the order had been effected on the respondent who had not appeared or been represented at the hearing).

The court has no express power to suspend the operation of a disqualification order pending an appeal against the order except where the order has been made under section 7 or 8 (head (5) or (6)—I2.5 and I2.6 above), in which case such power is exercisable by virtue of Order 59, Rules 13(1) and 19(5) of the Rules of the Supreme Court, as applied to such a disqualification order by Rule 2, as read with Rule 1(3), of the 1987 Rules. The position, in effect, appears to be similar in relation to a disqualification order made under section 10 (following a finding of wrongful trading in the exercise of insolvency jurisdiction), since the Rules of the Supreme Court are made applicable to insolvency proceedings by Rule 7.51 of the Insolvency Rules 1986.

Costs

I8.9   Where the Secretary of State has discontinued an application for a disqualification order after affidavits have been put in on both sides but before trial, the ordinary rules as to costs apply, and the Secretary of State must pay the respondent's costs (*Secretary of State for Trade and Industry v Checketts and another (Re Southbourne Sheet Metal Co Ltd) [1992] BCC 797 (CA),* reversing the decision of Harman J *[1991] BCC 732).* Where the Secretary of State succeeds in obtaining a disqualification order but the respondent succeeds in substantially reducing the charges made good against him, the Secretary of State may be awarded costs only on the standard basis, and not on the indemnity basis. (*Re Synthetic Technology Ltd [1993] BCC 549).* In *Re Brooks Transport (Purfleet) Ltd [1993] BCC 766,* awarding costs to the Secretary of State on the indemnity basis on a successful application for disqualification, John V Martin QC (sitting as a deputy High Court judge) stated that the relevant consideration was whether, in the light of the conduct and nature of the defence and its outcome, it could be seen that the Crown had gone further than its public duty required. In the present case, the vast majority of the complaints made against the respondent were justified and the application had in no way overstated the case. The deputy judge followed *Re Synthetic Technology* (above) and refused to follow *Re Godwin Warren Control Systems plc [1992] BCC 557* (where the unsuccessful respondent had been required to pay only two-thirds of the Secretary of State's costs on the standard basis).

Reviews and appeals

I8.10   Rules 7.47 and 7.49 of the Insolvency Rules 1986 apply to director disqualification proceedings by virtue of section 21(2) of the CDDA (which deems sections 6 to 10, 15, 19(c) and 20 of, and Schedule 1 to, the CDDA to be included in Parts I to VII of the Insolvency Act 1986 for the purposes of, *inter alia,* section 411 (power to make insolvency rules) of that Act). It will be noted that the 1987 Rules are expressed to be made under section 411 of the Insolvency Act 1986 and section 21of the CDDA but that Rule 1(3) of the 1987 Rules limits the application of those Rules to applications made by the Secretary of State under section 7 or 8 of the CDDA (heads (5) or (6), I2.5 and I2.6, above).

Those Rules 7.47 and 7.49 read as follows—

'7.47 (1) Every court having jurisdiction under the (Insolvency Act 1986) to wind up companies may review, rescind or vary any order made by it in the exercise of that jurisdiction.

(2) An appeal from a decision made in the exercise of that jurisdiction by county court or by registrar of the High Court lies to a single judge of the High Court; and an appeal from a decision of that judge on such an appeal lies, with the leave of that judge or the Court of Appeal, to the Court of Appeal.

(3) A county court is not, in the exercise of its jurisdiction to wind up companies, subject to be restrained by the order of any other court, and no appeal lies from its decision in the exercise of that jurisdiction except as provided by this Rule.

(4) Any application for the rescission of a winding up order shall be made within seven days after the date on which the order was made.

7.49 (1) Subject as follows, the procedure and practice of the Supreme Court relating to appeals to the Court of Appeal apply to appeals in the insolvency proceedings.

(2) In relation to any appeal to a single judge of the High Court under . . . Rule 7.47(2) above . . ., any reference in the Rules of the Supreme Court to the Court of Appeal is replaced by a reference to that judge, and any reference to the registrar of civil appeals is replaced by a reference to the registrar of the High Court who deals with insolvency proceedings of the kind involved.

(3) In insolvency proceedings, the procedure under Order 59 of the Rules of the Supreme Court (appeal to the Court of Appeal) is by application, and not by summons.'

It was held by the Court of Appeal in *Re Tasbian Ltd (No 2)* [1990] BCC 322, and reaffirmed by it in *Re Probe Data Systems Ltd (No 3)* [1992] BCC 110, that contrary to the view of Peter Gibson J in *Re Time Utilising Business Systems Ltd* (1989) 5 BCC 851, Rules 7.47 and 7.49 of the Insolvency Rules 1986 applied to orders made under the CDDA. (See also *Re Tasbian (No 3)* [1991] BCC 435 and *Re Probe Data Systems Ltd (No 3)* [1991] BCC 428). The significance of these decisions is that, like in the case of orders made by the registrar in insolvency proceedings but unlike in the case of orders made by the registrar in ordinary civil litigation (see *Re Rolls Razor Ltd (No 2)* [1970] *Ch 576, per* Megarry J), an appeal from the order of the registrar under the CDDA to the judge is an appeal proper by way of rehearing and not by way of a hearing *de novo* (which is less restrictive as to the grounds for reversing the registrar's decision) and that a further appeal from the judge to the Court of Appeal requires leave, unlike in the case of an order in ordinary civil litigation. However, this difference is more theoretical than real in practice. Scott LJ in *Re Probe Data Systems* (above) explained it as follows:

(1)   Under *Rolls Razor Ltd (No 2)* (above), the Chancery judge will deal with the application *de novo* and not as an appeal. Under Rule 7.47 (2), on the other hand, the single judge will be performing an appellate function, reviewing the exercise of discretion by the High Court registrar or by the county court judge or registrar, as the case may be; but if Rule 7.47 (2) applies, so, also, will Rule 7.47 (1), under which a party dissatisfied by the initial decision can, if he or she chooses, ask for a review of (as distinct from appeal against) the decision. In any event, under Rule 7 of the 1987 Rules, the initial decision will, if the registrar so directs, be made by the judge rather than by the registrar. 'In my judgment, there is no significant disadvantage to the parties in having the procedure for disqualification proceedings regulated by Rule 7 (of the 1987 Rules) and Rule 7.47 of the Insolvency Rules'.

(2)   An appeal from a single judge to the Court of Appeal under Rule 7.47 (2) will require leave. If Rule 7.47 does not apply, the ordinary rules will determine whether or not leave to appeal from the High Court judge or the county court judge to the Court of Appeal is required. 'However, although the ability to appeal as of right and not simply by leave is a difference of substance, it is, in my opinion, a mile away from constituting a sufficient reason for treating *Tasbian Ltd (No 2)*, even if wrongly decided, as falling within the residual category of cases subject to the *per incuriam* rule'.

Re Tasbian Ltd (No 2) (above) was followed in *Re Langley Marketing Services Ltd [1991] BCLC 584*, where Hoffmann J held that an appeal from an order made under the CDDA by a district judge in the county court lay to the High Court and not to the county court judge.

Index

Accounts
office-holder filing   A4.12
Administration
    antecedent transactions,
    adjustment of
    —court, powers of   B9.6
    —extortionate credit
    transactions   B9.7
    —floating charges,
    avoidance of   B9.8–B9.10
    —gratuitous alienations   B9.3
    —lien on books, etc.,
    unenforceability   B9.11
    —power of   B9.1
    —transactions at undervalue   B9.2
    —unfair preferences   B9.5
    —void unregistered charges   B9.12
    —voidable preferences   B9.4
    availability of   A3.1
    corporation tax liability
    during   H3.5, H3.6
    creditor, application to court   B8.3
    creditors' committee
    —establishment of   B8.1
    —functions of   B8.1
    creditors' meeting
    —adjournment   B5.9
    —chairman   B5.8
    —minutes   B5.13
    —notice of   B5.7
    —procedure   B5.6
    —proposals, approval of   B5.5
    —quorum   B5.9
    —resolutions   B5.13
    —right to requisition   B8.2
    —voting   B5.10–B5.12
    distribution of funds,
    no provision for   B5.17
    financial markets,
    enforcement of security in   F6.20
    initial control and management   B5.2
    international elements   B10.1
    member, application to court   B8.3
    new procedure   A2.3
    stationery, notice on   B5.1
    VAT bad debt relief   B5.18
Administration order
    advertisement of   B3.3
    against individual, revocation of   I2.9
    application
    —effect on charge   D2.9
    —effects of   B4.1
    —hearing   B3.2
    —making   B3.1
    —rights of creditors and
    others, moratorium on   B4.1
    —serving   B3.1
    breakdown of trust, effect
    of   B2.1, B3.2
    charge, effect on   D2.10
    company subject to, winding up   C5.2
    conditions to be satisfied   B2.1
    discharge   B5.16, B8.3

Administration order – continued
    effects of   B4.1
    factors in deciding to grant   B2.1
    inability to pay debts   A1.2
    interim   B3.2
    introduction of   B1.1
    leave applications   B4.2
    legislation   B1.1
    liquidation, company in   B2.1
    notice of   B3.3
    petition
    —affidavit supporting   B3.1
    —application by   B3.1
    —costs of   B3.1
    —dismissal of   B3.2
    —filing and service of   B3.1
    —secured creditor,
    presented by   B2.1
    —sufficient interest in   B3.2
    report, Practice Note   B3.1
    reporting insolvency
    practitioner, reliance on   B2.1
    repossession of goods under
    hire-purchase agreement,
    restriction against   B4.1
    requirement to make   B3.2
    variation   B5.16
    winding-up petition
    —grant of   B2.1
    —presentation of   B4.1
Administrative receiver (see also *Receiver*)
    accounts and returns, filing   A4.12
    administrator distinguished   B1.1
    affairs in USA, position in
    relation to   A5.3
    agent, appointment of   D5.3
    appointment
    —general effects of   D5.1
    —notification of   D4.1
    assets, order of realisation   D10.1
    ceasing to act, procedure on   D10.6
    company, running   D5.5
    confidentiality of documents   A4.22
    Customs and Excise, informing
    of appointment   A4.11
    directors' conduct, report on   A4.9
    disqualification   A4.7
    financial services legislation,
    position under   A4.6
    guidance notes   A4.25
    information, right to   A4.18
    liens, unenforceability of   A4.20
    meaning   D1.4
    pension scheme, duties as to   A4.13
    personal liability   A4.8
    position of   D1.4
    powers of
    —generally   D5.3
    —sufficiency of   D5.4
    private examination   A4.19
    professional conflict of interest   A4.10
    property and debts, court
    orders as to   A4.21

Administrative receiver – continued
property and records,
  recovery of — A4.16
qualification — A4.5
report
—contents of — D4.4
—persons to which sent — D4.3
Restrictive Trade Practices
  Act, exemption from — A4.23
security for costs in recovery
  proceedings, relief against — A4.24
statutory aids — A4.14–A4.24
third party property,
  immunity and indemnity — A4.17
third party rights,
  interference with — D8.15
utility supplies — A4.15
voluntary arrangement
  proposal, no power to make — E1.3
Administrative receivership
  (see also *Receivership*)
availability of — A3.1
company's officers, position of — D5.5
corporation tax liability during — H3.7
—liquidation, concurrent with — H3.8
creditors' committee — D4.6
creditors' meeting — D4.5
directors, duties of — D5.5
statement of affairs — D4.2
VAT bad debt relief — D4.7
Administrator
accounts and returns, filing — A4.12
administrative receiver
  distinguished — B1.1
affairs in USA, position in
  relation to — A5.3
agency — B7.5
assets subject to charge,
  power of disposal — B6.1
—charge holders, protection of — B6.4
—implications of — B6.2
—transitional provisions — B6.3
claims, restrictions on third party — B4.1
confidentiality of documents — A4.22
contracts of employment,
  qualifying liabilities — B7.7
Customs and Excise, informing
  of appointment — A4.11
directions of court,
  seeking — B5.4, B7.3
directors' conduct, report on — A4.9
disqualification — A4.7
financial services legislation,
  position under — A4.6
general powers — B7.2
guidance notes — A4.25
information, right to — A4.18
initial control and management — B5.2
land subject to charge,
  power of disposal — B6.1
—implications of — B6.2
leave applications — B4.2
liability — B7.6
money, borrowing — B7.2
officer of company, as — B7.5
parties dealing with — B7.8
pension scheme, duties as to — A4.13
personal liability — A4.8
post-administration expenses
  and liabilities — B7.7

Administrator – continued
powers of company and
  officers, conflict with — B7.4
pre-administration contract,
  breach of — B7.2
private examination — A4.19
professional conflict of interest — A4.10
property and debts, court
  orders as to — A4.21
property and records,
  recovery of — A4.16
proposals by
—approval of — B5.5
—implementation of — B5.15
—revision — B5.15
—statement of — B5.4
qualification — A4.5
reasonably and fairly, acting — B4.1
receipts and payments,
  supply of abstract of — B7.10
release — B7.1
remuneration — B7.1, B7.9
rent and hire charges,
  payment of — B7.7
reports — B5.14
Restrictive Trade Practices
  Act, exemption from — A4.23
security for costs in recovery
  proceedings, relief against — A4.24
statement of affairs — B5.3
statutory aids — A4.14–A4.24
third party property,
  immunity and indemnity — A4.17
utility supplies — A4.15
vacancy in office — B7.1
winding-up petition, presenting — B7.2
Agency agreements
registrable charges — C12.10
Agent
administrator as — B7.5
moneys and assets in hands of — C12.17
receiver as — D5.2
—Scotland, in — D11.6
winding up, effect of — C9.8
Agricultural Marketing Boards
winding up
—grounds for — C5.12
—jurisdiction — C5.8
Air pollution
receiver, liabilities of — D8.20
Assets (see *Liquidation assets*
  and *Receivership assets*)
Association
winding up — C5.8
Attachment of earnings
receiver, payments by — D8.6
Authorised institutions
administration procedure — B2.1
insolvency of — A3.1
winding up
—grounds for — C5.16
—jurisdiction — C5.8
—protected deposits — C9.12

Book debts
charges over, registration — D7.23
lien (see *Lien*)
registrable charges — C12.10
rights over — C12.16

British Steel Corporation
  subsidiaries, grounds for
    winding up   C5.14
Building contracts
  liquidation, effect of   C12.19
Buildings
  NHBC protection,
    property with   D7.28

Cash
  third party rights   C12.15
Charges
  book debts, over   D7.23
  counterparty, taken by   F3.7
  fixed
  —debts, over   D6.2
  —fixed plant and
    machinery, over   D6.2
  —leasehold property, over   D6.2
  —meaning   D6.2
  —revolving collateral, on   D6.2
  floating (see *Floating charge*)
  hybrid   D7.3
  market
  —charges treated as   F6.19
  —dispositions after
    commencement of
    compulsory winding up   F6.21
  —floating, priority of   F6.24
  —general insolvency law,
    modification of   F6.22
  —protection from impact of
    insolvency provisions   F6.18
  —unpaid vendor's lien,
    priority over   F6.24
  market default rules   F4.3
  receivership (see *Receivership*)
  unregistered   C12.10
  —void   B9.12
  void, debt under   C14.25
Charging order
  execution creditor and
    receiver, position of   D7.11
Chattels
  rights over   C12.16
Co-operative societies
  winding up
  —grounds for   C5.13
  —jurisdiction   C5.8
Coal and steel
  production levies   D7.4
Company name
  winding up, re-use following   C9.1
Company officers
  administrative receivership,
    position in   D5.5
  administrator as   B7.5
  breach of statutory duty   C13.3
  —relieving provision   C13.5
  company secretary as   C13.4
  examination of   C11.22
  involvement in winding up   C11.21
  misfeasance by   C13.4
  —relieving provision   C13.5
  negligence by   C13.3
  —relieving provision   C13.5
  powers, conflict with
    administrator   B7.4
  voluntary arrangement
    meeting, attending   E2.4

Company registration
  cancellation of   G1.6
  restoration   G3.3
  —application for   G3.4
Company secretary
  officer, as   C13.4
Compulsory winding up
  accounts   C5.48
  administration order or
    voluntary arrangement,
    company under   C5.2
  agents
  —effect on   C9.8
  —moneys and assets in
    hands of   C12.17
  ancillary   C5.6
  assets and liabilities, effect on   C9.10
  assets of liquidation
    (see *Liquidation assets*)
  book debts, rights over   C12.16
  building contracts, effect on   C12.19
  chattels, rights over   C12.16
  commencement of   C5.1
  company's officers
  —examination of   C11.22
  —involvement of   C11.21
  contracts
  —effect on   C9.6
  —rescission of   C12.7
  contributories' liabilities   C12.20
  contributories' meeting, first   C5.49
  court, involvement of   C11.23
  creditors and contributories,
    involvement of   C11.19
  creditors' meeting
  —entitlement to vote   C11.13
  —first   C5.49, C11.3, C11.4
  —notice of   C11.5
  —proofs for voting, admission
    or rejection of   C11.14
  debts, inability to pay
  —corporate members of
    insolvent partnership   C5.23
  —oversea companies   C5.24
  —partnerships   C5.25
  —registered companies   C5.22
  —unregistered companies   C5.24
  derivative actions   C12.11
  directors' powers, cessation of   C8.1
  dissolution following   C9.11
  —early   C16.7, C16.8
  —notice of   C16.9
  —ordinary cases   C16.6
  —process of   C16.5
  distress, forfeiture or
    disfeasance following   C8.3
  documents exempt from
    stamp duty   C12.5
  employees, effect on   C9.7
  execution
  —creditors, relief for   C9.4
  —following order   C8.3
  —goods, land or debt, over   C9.3
  fixtures, rights over   C12.16
  foreign assets or proceedings,
    enforcement on   C5.6
  foreign court, assistance
    by or to   C5.6
  foreign proceedings, attitude to   C5.6
  generally   C1.5

Compulsory winding up – continued
goods and chattels taken
    in execution   C9.2
grounds for
—Agricultural Marketing
    Boards   C5.12
—authorised institutions   C5.16
—British Steel Corporation
    subsidiaries   C5.14
—co-operative societies   C5.13
—credit unions   C5.15
—debts, inability to pay   C5.22–C5.25
—insurance companies   C5.17
—investment business   C5.18
—just and equitable   C5.26
—most frequently relied on   C5.21
—partnerships   C5.19, C5.20, C5.23
—petition, founding   C5.9
—registered companies   C5.10
—special cases   C5.12–C5.20
—unregistered companies   C5.11
hearing
—appearances, notice of   C5.39
—powers of court   C5.42
information in   C5.48
initiation of   C5.1
jurisdiction
—bodies other than
    registered companies   C5.5
—cross-frontier recognition   C5.6
—England and Wales,
    companies registered in   C5.2
—Scotland, companies
    registered in   C5.3
—unregistered companies   C5.4
limitation against creditor,
    period of   C9.5
liquidation assets (see
    Liquidation assets)
liquidation committee
—appointment of   C5.51
—involvement of   C11.20
liquidator (see *Liquidator*)
malpractice, investigation of   C9.13
meetings
—chairman   C11.7
—company's personnel,
    attendance of   C11.8
—expense of summoning   C11.11
—final   C16.3
—notice of   C11.6
—proxy forms   C11.10
—quorum   C11.12
—record of proceedings   C11.17
—resolutions   C11.15
—venue   C11.9
Official Receiver,
    investigations by   C8.5
order
—formalities   C5.43
—rescission   C5.45
petition
—advertisement of   C5.36
—appearances   C5.39
—company, by   C5.28
—contributory   C5.30, C5.40
—creditor, by   C5.29
—disputed or unmatured
    debt, on   C5.29
—form of   C5.34

Compulsory winding up – continued
—majority of shareholders,
    class rights   C5.29
—Official Receiver, by   C5.32
—persons presenting   C5.27
—presentation of   C5.1, C5.34
—procedure   C5.33, C5.40
—requirements   C5.33
—restraining orders   C5.36
—Secretary of State, by   C5.31
—service of   C5.35
—substitution of petitioner   C5.38
—voluntary winding up
    in progress, where   C5.29
—withdrawal   C5.37
prior transactions
—adjustment of (see *Prior
    transactions, adjustment of*)
—investigation of   C9.13
proceedings, costs of   C5.44
prohibited company
    transactions   C12.9
proof of debt (see *Proof of debt*)
property
—disposition of   C8.4
—ownership of   C9.9
protected deposits   C9.12
re-use of company name,
    restriction on   C9.1
registered companies, of   C5.7
restraining orders   C5.36
section 127 order   C5.30
Secretary of State,
    investigations by   C8.5
special manager,
    appointment of   C11.29
statement of affairs   C5.48
stay of   C5.46
stay of actions and proceedings   C8.2
stocks, rights over   C12.16
unauthorised company
    transactions   C12.9
unclaimed funds and
    dividends, payment of   C16.11
unpaid share capital, calls on   C12.20
unregistered companies, of   C5.8
Contaminated land
receiver, liabilities of   D8.23
Contracts (see also *Market contracts*)
appointment of receiver, effect of
—generally   D7.24
—goods sold but not
    delivered, for   D7.25
—intellectual property,
    relating to   D7.27
—NHBC protection,
    property with   D7.28
—prior contractual or
    proprietary interests   D7.26
—private companies, transfer
    of shares in   D7.29
—repudiation, right of   D7.24
damages for breach, proof of   C14.22
hive-down, on   D9.11
receiver, termination by   D7.14
rescission by court   C12.7
winding up, effect of   C9.6
Contributories
liabilities   C12.20
meaning   C12.20

Contributories – continued
petition by — C5.30
winding up, involvement in — C11.19
Corporation tax
administration, liability
during — H3.5, H3.6
administrative receivership,
liability during — H3.7
—liquidation, concurrent with — H3.8
capital gains, on — H3.10
liability before insolvency — H3.2
liability during insolvency — H3.3
liquidation, liability
during — H3.4, H3.6
receiver, liability of — D8.12
voluntary arrangements,
liability during — H3.9
Credit unions
winding up
—grounds for — C5.15
—jurisdiction — C5.8
Creditors
deferred
—contractual deferment — C14.36
—statutory deferment — C14.35
execution, position of
receiver in relation to
—charging order, under — D7.11
—fieri facias, writ of — D7.9
—garnishee order, under — D7.10
—Mareva injunction, issue of — D7.12
—ship, writ *in rem* against — D7.12
ordinary, dividends to
—declaration, formalities
and restrictions — C15.7
—final — C15.6
—interim — C15.5
—ranking — C15.4
ordinary, division of
unsold assets among — C15.8
ordinary, meaning — C14.28
partnership, of — C14.37
petition by — C5.29
preferential — C14.34
—voluntary arrangements,
protection on — E2.7
proof of debt (see *Proof of debt*)
secured
—meaning — C14.29
—position of — C14.32
—types of — C14.30
—voluntary arrangements,
protection on — E2.7
two or more liquidations,
concurrent claims in — C14.33
unsecured — C14.31
winding up, involvement
in — C11.19
Creditors' voluntary winding up
company qualifying for — C4.1
conversion of members'
winding up to — C4.12
creditors' meeting — C4.6
distribution in specie,
authority to make — C4.2
filing and notification — C4.10
generally — C1.5
liquidation committee
—appointment of — C4.11
—nomination by members — C4.4

*Creditors' voluntary winding up –
continued*
liquidator
—appointment of — C4.8
—caretaker, position of — C4.9
—nomination by members — C4.3
list of creditors — C4.7
members' meeting
—commencement on — C4.1
—procedure — C4.5
statement of affairs — C4.7
Crown
company in receivership,
set-off between — D7.6
set-off — H3.16
Customs and Excise
debts due to, priority of — D7.4

Debt avoidance
powers as to — C10.10
Debts (see also *Proof of debt*)
fixed charge over — D6.2
preferential — H2.6
—categories of — D7.4
—coal and steel production
levies — D7.4
—Customs and Excise, due to — D7.4
—employees' remuneration,
etc — D7.4
—Inland Revenue, due to — D7.4
—occupational pension scheme
contributions — D7.4
—priority of — D7.3
—Scotland, in — D11.8
—social security contributions — D7.4
proof of (see *Proof of debt*)
Deduction of earnings
receiver, payments by — D8.6
Derivative actions
plaintiff in — C12.11
Directors
breach of statutory duty — C13.3
—relieving provision — C13.5
company, duty of care to — A3.1
conduct, report on — A4.9
disqualification (see
Disqualification of directors)
duty, scope of — C13.4
fraudulent trading (see
Fraudulent trading)
misfeasance by — C13.4
—relieving provision — C13.5
negligence by — C13.3
—relieving provision — C13.5
reasonably diligent person,
dual test of — A3.1
responsibility of — I5.4
wrongful trading (see
Wrongful trading)
Disclaimer
liquidator, by — C12.6
Discounts
proof of debt, deduction from — C14.16
Disqualification of directors
application for order
—acknowledgement
of summons — I8.4
—costs — I8.9
—evidence in support — I8.5
—extension of time for — I5.5, I8.2

Disqualification of directors – continued
—hearing   I8.6
—intended, notice of   I8.1
—limitation period   I8.2
—making   I8.3
—service of summons   I8.4
—striking out   I8.7
breach of trust of duty,
   conduct involving   I5.6
company, meaning   I1.1
default, conduct involving   I5.6
director, meaning   I1.1
discretion of court, scope of   I3.1
insolvency, definition   A1.2
leave to promote or form
   company, application for   I7.2, I7.3
legislation   I1.1
negligence, conduct involving   I5.6
order
—application for (see
   application for order)
—contravention,
   consequences of   I7.4
—effective date   I8.8
—general effects of   I7.1
—mandatory   I3.1
—purpose of   I5.1
—reviews and appeals   I8.10
periods of, determining   I5.7
proceedings, extension
   of time for   I5.5, I8.2
process, triggering
—administration order
   against individual, revocation
   of   I2.9
—companies legislation
   requirements, summary
   conviction on   I2.4
—companies legislation,
   persistent breaches of   I2.2
—directors of insolvent
   companies, unfitness of   I2.5
—fraud in winding up   I2.3
—fraudulent trading,
   participation in   I2.7
—indictable offence,
   conviction of   I2.1
—investigation under statutory
   provisions, results of   I2.6
—undischarged bankrupt
   as director   I2.8
—wrongful trading,
   participation in   I2.7
unfitness
—cases on   I6.1
—determination of   I5.1
—matters relevant to   I5.2
—misconduct, categories of   I5.3
—*Polly Peck* decision,
   guidelines in   I5.5
—responsibility of directors   I5.4
—test of   I4.1
Dissolution
compulsory winding up, on
—early   C16.7, C16.8
—notice of   C16.9
—ordinary cases   C16.6
—process of   C16.5
directors, practical use
   of procedure by   G1.5

Dissolution – continued
effect of   G2.1
methods of   G1.1
Registrar, striking off by
—company being wound
   up, where   G1.4
—company not carrying on
   business or in operation,
   where   G1.3
—procedure, invoking   G1.2
—voluntary   G1.7
registration, cancellation of   G1.6
restoration to register   G3.3
—application for   G3.4
revival after   G3.1–G3.4
—court, power of   G3.1
void, order declaring   G3.2
—application for   G3.4
voluntary winding up, on   C16.2
winding up, following   C9.11
Distress
compulsory winding up,
   following   C8.3
receivership, priority in   D7.13
voluntary winding up, following   C7.5

Employees
hive-down, contract
   of employment on   D9.10
receivership
—contracts of
   employment   D7.1, D8.3
—national insurance
   contributions   D7.2
—redundancies   D7.1, D7.2
—remuneration, priority of   D7.4
—Wages Act, provisions of   D8.3
Transfer of Undertakings
   Regulations, effect of   D9.16
winding up, effect of   C9.7
Environmental law, effect on
liabilities of receiver
air pollution control   D8.20
contaminated land   D8.23
criminal and civil   D8.26
future trends in   D8.25
integrated pollution control   D8.20
statutory nuisance   D8.22
UK legislation, implications of   D8.26
waste management   D8.21
water pollution   D8.24
Equipment leasing
registrable charges   C12.10
Escrow account
registrable charges   C12.10
Examination
private, rights of office-holder   A4.19
Extortionate credit transactions
court, powers of   C10.7
relief for   B9.7

Fieri facias, writ of
execution creditor and receiver,
   position of   D7.9
Financial assistance for purchase of shares
declaration of solvency   A1.2
Financial markets
authorised person, petition
   for winding up   F6.29
cherry-picking   F2.3, F5.3

Financial markets – continued
compensation funds — F6.30
corporate insolvency in
—administration, enforcement
of security in — F6.20
—application of provisions — F6.2
—*British Eagle* case,
position in — F2.9, F5.9
—cash margins, deposit
of — F2.8, F5.8
—counterparty, position of — F2.3
—court, meaning — F6.27
—cross-frontier — F6.27
—disclaimer of contracts — F6.14
—discretionary retrospective
effect of provisions — F6.26
—disposition after
commencement of — F2.7,
F5.7, F6.15
—duty to assist — F6.7
—effect of provisions — F7.1
—exchange or clearing house
proceedings, precedence of — F6.6
—general law, effect of special
provisions on — F6.1, F6.5
—legislation — F1.1
—market creditors, dividend
in liquidation to — F6.9
—office-holders, functions
and indemnities — F6.10, F6.28
—preferences — F2.2, F5.2, F6.16
—protection of assets — F6.8
—rescission of contracts — F6.14
—scope of provisions — F1.1
—transactions at undervalue — F2.2,
F5.2, F6.16
indemnities — F6.28
market charges
—charges treated as — F6.19
—dispositions after
commencement of
compulsory winding up — F6.21
—floating, priority of — F6.24
—general insolvency law,
modification of — F6.22
—protection from impact of
insolvency provisions — F6.18
—unpaid vendor's lien,
priority over — F6.24
market contracts (see
Market contracts)
market default
—bilateral netting-off clause — F4.2
—closing out — F4.2
—completion of proceedings — F6.12
—invoking rules,
directions as to — F6.17
—market charge,
requirement of — F4.3
—net sum payable on
completion of proceedings — F6.13
—requirements as to rules — F6.4
—reversal — F4.2
—rules, use of — F4.1–F4.3
—stay of action, etc,
not subject to rules on — F6.11
overseas clearing
house, meaning — F6.3
overseas investment
exchange, meaning — F6.3

Financial markets – continued
recognised clearing
house, meaning — F6.3
recognised investment
exchange, meaning — F6.3
role of — F1.3
set-off — F2.4, F2.9, F5.4
specific performance,
action for — F2.5, F5.5
unsecured creditors, restrictions
against enforcement
against margins — F6.25
Fixtures
rights over — C12.16
third party, disputes on
receivership — D7.21
Floating charge
adjustment of — C10.8, C10.9
assets subject to, disposal
of by administrator — B6.1
—charge holders, protection of — B6.4
—implications of — B6.2
—transitional provisions — B6.3
avoidance of — B9.8
crystallisation — D6.3
essential characteristics of — D6.2
invalid — B9.9
market, priority of — F6.24
meaning — D1.4, D6.2
value of goods and services — B9.10
Foreign currency
debt in, proof of — C14.17
Fraudulent trading
civil penalties — C13.1
criminal offences, as — C13.1
fraudulent intent — C13.1
meaning — C13.1
participation in,
disqualification for — I2.7
provisions, consideration of — A3.1
recovery — C13.1
single transaction as — C13.1

Garnishee order
execution creditor and
receiver, position of — D7.10
Going concern
disposal of company as — A3.1
sale of
—duties on — D9.15
—hive-down, effect of — D9.15
—marketing, methods of — D9.15
—sale agreement — D9.17
—transfer of undertakings
provisions — D9.16
VAT relief on transfer — H2.8
Gratuitous alienations
adjustment of — C10.3
challenge to — B9.3
Groups of companies
intra-group transfers,
stamp duty relief — H2.7
termination of group relationship
—capital gains on — H2.3
—effecting — H2.2
VAT registration — H2.9

Hire purchase agreement
receivership, disputes on — D7.20

Hive-down
  assets to be transferred — D9.7
  availability of — A3.1
  contracts of employment,
    effect on — D9.10
  contracts, effect on other — D9.11
  existing charges, effect on — D9.9
  immunities and indemnities — D9.14
  meaning — D9.4
  object of — D9.4
  pre-liquidation — C2.6
  property, transfer of — D9.7
  proposal for — B2.1
  receivership company, of — D9.4
  stamp duty relief — D9.12
  tax advantages — D9.5
  transfer agreement — D9.8
  transferee company,
    liabilities of — D9.6
  value added tax position — D9.13

Income tax
  receiver, liability of — D8.12
Inland Revenue
  debts due to, priority of — D7.4
Insolvency
  disqualification of
    directors — A1.2
  legislation
  —Act and Rules — A1.1
  —aims of — A2.3
  —background to — A2.2
  —delegated — A2.1
  —principal — A2.1
  —scope of — A2.4
  meaning
  —commercial and
    accountancy test — A1.3
  —general term, as — A1.4
  —specific statutory tests — A1.2
  onset of — A1.2
Insolvency practitioner (see
  also *Office-holder*)
  authorisation to act as — A4.2
  bond — A4.3
  caution, provision of — A4.3
  conduct — A4.1
  financial services legislation,
    position under — A4.6
  office-holder as — A4.5
  professional standards,
    monitoring — A4.2
  qualification — A4.1
  records kept by — A4.4
  security, provision of — A4.3
Insolvency proceedings
  appeals — A5.1
  co-operation between courts
  —international comity — A5.3
  —statutory provisions — A5.2
  court file, inspection of — A5.1
  jurisdiction — A5.1
Insurance company
  authorised, insolvency of — A3.1
  policyholders' claims — C14.23
  subrogated claims — C14.24
  winding up
  —grounds for — C5.17
  —protected deposits — C9.12

Insurance policies
  liquidator dealing
    with — C12.22
Intellectual property
  licensing agreements, effect
    of receivership — D7.27
  third party rights,
    interference with — D8.15
Interest, claim for — C14.19
Investment business
  assets, liquidator dealing with — C12.21
  winding up
  —grounds for — C5.18
  —jurisdiction — C5.8

Land
  subject to charge, disposal
    by administrator — B6.1
  —implications of — B6.2
Lessor
  claims of — C14.21
Liens
  books, papers and records,
    on, unenforceability — B9.11
  receivership assets or
    rights subject to — D7.7
  unenforceable — A4.20, C10.11
Liquidation (see also *Winding up*)
  alternatives to — C2.5
  appointment of receiver,
    effect on — D2.11
  assets (see *Liquidation assets*)
  corporation tax liability
    during — H3.4, H3.6
  fraudulent trading prior to — A1.2
  hive-down before — C2.6
  insolvent, liability of directors
    for debts — A1.2
  legislation
  —delegated — C1.3
  —principal — C1.2
  timing — C2.7
Liquidation assets
  antecedent transactions or
    matters, recovery in
    respect of — C12.8–C12.10
  collection of — C12.1
  consideration *in specie*, power
    to transfer for — C12.3
  dealings with — C12.12
  sale of — C12.14
  sale, power of — C12.2
  vesting order — C12.4
Liquidator
  administrative duties,
    enforcement of — C11.25
  appointment — C5.50
  assets (see *Liquidation assets*)
  business, sale of — C12.14
  cash, dealing with — C12.15
  continuation of business — C12.13
  disclaimer by — C12.6
  final return — C16.9
  freehold and leasehold
    property, dealing with — C12.18
  general functions of — C11.25
  immunity — C11.24
  insurance policies,
    dealing with — C12.22
  interim — C5.47

Liquidator – continued
  investment business assets,
    dealing with   C12.21
  meetings, summoning   C11.24
  Official Receiver as   C5.1, C5.47
  position of   C11.24
  provisional, appointment of   C5.41
  records, disposal of   C16.10
  release of   C16.4
  removal of   C11.28
  remuneration and costs   C11.27
  replacement of   C11.28
  specific powers and duties   C11.26
Market contracts
  acceleration clause   F3.3
  aggregation clause   F3.2
  bilateral netting-off clause   F3.5
  debt or liability arising from   F6.6
  flawed asset clause   F3.6, F5.1
  fungibility   F2.6, F5.6
  guarantee   F2.10, F5.10
  individual charges   F3.7
  margins affected by other
    interests   F6.23
  master agreement, provisions of   F3.1
  multiplicity and
    interdependence of   F1.4
  novation   F2.10, F5.10
  quantification clause   F3.4
  registration   F2.10
  terms governing   F1.2
  unity clause   F3.2
Mareva injunction
  company in receivership,
    against   D8.16
  effect of issue on creditor   D7.12
Meetings (see also *Administration,*
Compulsory winding up, Creditors'
voluntary winding up, Members'
voluntary winding up, Voluntary
arrangement, Winding up)
  corporate representation   A6.1
  proxies   A6.1
  quorum   A6.2
Members' voluntary winding up
  commencement of   C3.1
  company qualifying for   C3.1
  creditors' voluntary winding
    up, conversion to   C4.12
  declaration of solvency   C3.2
  —filing and notification   C3.8
  generally   C1.5
  liquidator
  —appointment of   C3.3
  —indemnity   C3.6
  meeting
  —commencement on   C3.1
  —impracticable to call, where   C3.7
  —procedure   C3.7
  —quorum   C3.7
  resolution   C3.1
  —filing and notification   C3.8
  transfer of assets for
    consideration *in specie*,
    authority for   C3.5
Misfeasance
  extra-territorial application   C13.6
  meaning   C13.4
  money or damages,
    recovery of   C13.4

Misfeasance – continued
  receiver, recovery of assets by   D9.1
  relieving provision   C13.5
Mortgagee
  charged property, taking
    possession of   D1.5
National insurance contributions
  liability arising before
    insolvency   H3.11
  liability arising during
    insolvency   H3.12
Negligence
  directors and officers, by   C13.3
  receiver, of   D8.14
Negotiable instruments
  proof in respect of   C14.15
Occupational pension schemes
  contributions, priority in
    receivership   D7.4
  receiver, examination by   D9.1
Office-holder
  accounts and returns, filing   A4.12
  affairs in USA, position in
    relation to   A5.3
  confidentiality of documents   A4.22
  Customs and Excise, informing
    of appointment   A4.11
  directors' conduct, report on   A4.9
  disqualification   A4.7
  financial markets and
  —functions   F6.10
  —indemnities   F6.28
  financial services legislation,
    position under   A4.6
  guidance notes   A4.25
  information, right to   A4.18
  liens, unenforceability of   A4.20
  pension scheme, duties as to   A4.13
  personal liability   A4.8
  private examination   A4.19
  professional conflict of interest   A4.10
  property and debts, court
    orders as to   A4.21
  property and records,
    recovery of   A4.16
  qualification   A4.5
  restrictive Trade Practices
    Act, exemption from   A4.23
  security for costs in recovery
    proceedings, relief
    against   A4.24
  statutory aids   A4.14–A4.24
  third party property, immunity
    and indemnity   A4.17
  utility supplies   A4.15
Official Receiver
  liquidator, as   C5.1, C5.47
  petition by   C5.32
  winding-up order,
    investigations
    following   C8.5
Oversea companies
  winding up   C5.4, C5.8
  —debts, inability to pay   C5.24
Partnership
  administration procedure,
    application of   B1.1

Partnership – continued
creditors of — C14.37
director disqualification
  procedure, application of — I1.1
voluntary arrangement
  procedure, application of — E1.2
winding up
  —debts, inability to pay — C5.25
  —grounds for — C5.19, C5.20, C5.23
  —jurisdiction — C5.4, C5.8
  —order — A4.6
PAYE
liability arising before
  insolvency — H3.11
liability arising during
  insolvency — H3.12
Pension scheme
independent trustee of — A4.13
receiver
  —duties of — D8.17
  —examination by — D9.1
Pledge
registrable charges — C12.10
Preferences
adjustment of
  —England and Wales — B9.4, C10.4
  —Scotland — B9.5, C10.5
court, powers of — C10.6
financial markets,
  insolvency in — F2.2, F5.2, F6.16
receiver, recovery of assets by — D9.1
Prior transactions, adjustment of (see
  also *Preferences* and *Transactions*
  at an undervalue)
debt avoidance — C10.10
extortionate credit transactions — C10.7
floating charges — C10.8, C10.9
gratuitous alienations — C10.3
legislation — C10.1
liens — C10.11
preferences — C10.4–C10.6
transactions at
  undervalue — C10.2, C10.6
Private company
shares in, effect of receivership
  on transfer — D7.29
Proof of debt
breach of contract,
  damage for — C14.22
consideration, enquiry into — C14.10
contingent claims — C14.14
debts not provable — C14.13
discounts — C14.16
double proof, rule against — C14.9
estoppel — C14.10
expunging by court — C14.6
final admission or rejection of — C14.4
foreign currency, debt in — C14.17
forms, supply of — C14.11
future time, debt payable at — C14.20
interest — C14.19
late creditors
  —exclusion of — C14.1
  —position of — C14.3
lessor's claims — C14.21
mutual credit and set-off — C14.26
negotiable instruments,
  in respect of — C14.15
notice to prove — C14.2
periodical payments — C14.18

Proof of debt – continued
policyholders' claims — C14.23
proof and prove, meaning — C14.12
provable debts — C14.13
rejection, appeal against — C14.5
security, disclosure of — C14.32
subrogated claims — C14.24
sums recovered abroad,
  accounting for — C14.27
unquantified claims — C14.14
variation of — C14.7
VAT bad debt relief — C14.8
void charge, debt under — C14.25
withdrawal of — C14.7
Property
compulsory winding up,
  disposition on — C8.4
disclaimer of — C12.6
freehold, liquidator
  dealing with — C12.18
leasehold, forfeiture of
  lease by receiver
  —planning control breaches,
    effect of — D7.16
  —powers — D7.14
  —sitting tenants and
    occupants, position of — D7.15
leasehold, fixed charge over — D6.2
leasehold, liquidator dealing
  with — C12.18
receiver, liabilities of
  —community charge, for — D8.11
  —council tax, for — D8.11
  —London Building
    Acts, under — D8.10
  —planning Acts, under — D8.9
  —Public Health Acts, under — D8.8
  —rates, for — D8.11
winding up, effect of — C9.9
Proxies
meetings, for — A6.1
Receiver
administrative (see
  Administrative receiver)
agent, as — D5.2
appointment
  —acceptance or
    confirmation of — D3.2
  —charging document,
    provisions of — D3.1
  —date of effect — D3.2
  —general effects of — D5.1
  —mode of — D3.1
  —notification of — D4.1
  —object of — D1.5
  —Scotland, in — D11.2, D11.3
assets (see *Receivership assets*)
attachment of earnings
  orders, payments under — D8.6
breach of duty by — D8.14
business, carrying on — D9.3
ceasing to act, procedure on — D10.6
charge under which appointed — D1.4
  —administration order,
    effect of — D2.10
  —application for administration
    order, effect of — D2.9
  —company, powers of — D2.2
  —directors, powers of — D2.3

Receiver – continued
—due execution   D2.4
—enforceability   D2.8
—illegality   D2.7
—liquidation, effect on   D2.11
—prior or subsequent
    charges, effect of   D2.13
—registration   D2.5
—scope of   D2.12
—validity   D2.1
—vulnerability   D2.6
companies legislation,
    duties under   D8.18
contract, termination of   D7.14
contracts, liability on
—employment   D8.3
—generally   D8.2
—supply of goods and
    services, for   D8.4
—Wages Act, provisions of   D8.3
contractual agency
    and powers of   A2.3
deduction of earnings
    orders, payments under   D8.6
development, carrying on   D9.3
directions, application
    to court for   D4.8
disposal at undervalue by   D8.14
duress payments,
    acceptance of   D7.30
duties, enforcement of   D4.11
eligible persons   D3.3
environmental law liabilities
—air pollution control   D8.20
—contaminated land   D8.23
—criminal and civil   D8.26
—future trends in   D8.25
—integrated pollution control   D8.20
—statutory nuisance   D8.22
—UK legislation,
    implications of   D8.26
—waste management   D8.21
—water pollution   D8.24
execution creditors, position against
—charging order, under   D7.11
—fieri facias, writ of   D7.9
—garnishee order, under   D7.10
—Mareva injunction, issue of   D7.12
—ship, writ in rem against   D7.12
foreign representative, as   D12.1
function of   D1.5
funds
—allocation   D10.1
—marshalling and
    distribution of   D10.4
immovable property, statutory
    liabilities for
—community charge, for   D8.11
—council tax, for   D8.11
—London Building
    Acts, under   D8.10
—planning Acts, under   D8.9
—Public Health Acts, under   D8.8
—rates, for   D8.11
income and corporation
    tax, liability for   D8.12
indemnity   D2.14
insurance money,
    application of   D10.1
international status   D12.1

Receiver – continued
lease, forfeiture of
—planning control breaches,
    effect of   D7.16
—powers   D7.14
—sitting tenants and
    occupants, position of   D7.15
legal proceedings
—bringing   D5.2
—position in   D8.16
liquidation costs, discharge of   D10.3
meaning   D1.2
misfeasance by   D8.14
negligence of   D8.14
pension scheme
—duties as to   D8.17
—examination of position of   D9.1
powers of
—generally   D5.3
—sufficiency of   D5.4
receipts and payments,
    abstract of   D4.10
references to   D1.4
remuneration   D4.9
rent, discharge of   D8.13
resignation   D4.1, D5.2
rights of recourse   D8.1
Scotland, in
—agency and liability   D11.6
—appointment   D11.2, D11.3
—powers of   D11.4
—precedence among   D11.5
—property, disposal of   D11.10
—regulations   D11.11
—remuneration   D11.7
third party rights,
    interference with   D8.15
unpaid share capital, calling up   D9.1
VAT, liability for   D8.5
Receivership
administrative (see *Administrative
    receivership*)
charges, fixed
—debts, over   D6.2
—fixed plant and
    machinery, over   D6.2
—leasehold property, over   D6.2
—meaning   D6.2
—revolving collateral, on   D6.2
charges, floating
—crystallisation   D6.3
—essential characteristics of   D6.2
—meaning   D6.2
charges, hybrid   D7.3
charges, nature of   D6.1
distress, effect of   D7.13
duress payments   D7.30
early sale, directors'
    right to force   D7.31
employees
—contracts of employment,
    effect on   D7.1
—national insurance
    contributions   D7.2
—redundancies   D7.1, D7.2
—remuneration, priority of   D7.4
hire purchase (etc.) agreements,
    claims under   D7.20
law on   D1.3
liens, assets or rights subject to   D7.7

Receivership – continued

outstanding contracts, effect on
—generally | D7.24
—goods sold but not
delivered, for | D7.25
—intellectual property,
relating to | D7.27
—NHBC protection,
property with | D7.28
—prior contractual or
proprietary interests | D7.26
—private companies,
transfer of shares in | D7.29
—repudiation, right of | D7.24
planning | D2.15
preferential debts
—categories of | D7.4
—coal and steel
production levies | D7.4
—Customs and Excise, due to | D7.4
—employees'
remuneration, etc | D7.4
—Inland Revenue, due to | D7.4
—occupational pension
scheme contributions | D7.4
—priority of | D7.3
—Scotland, in | D11.8
—social security contributions | D7.4
prior and subsequent
charges, effect of | D7.23
retention of title claims, and
—crystallisation of floating
charge, effect of | D7.17
—dispute as to | D7.19
—effectiveness of remedy | D7.19
—validity and effect of | D7.18
scope of text | D1.2
Scotland, in
—order of distribution | D11.9
—preferential debts | D11.8
—summary of | D11.1
set-off,
—Crown | D7.6
—generally | D7.5
stationery, notification on | D4.12
third party fixtures,
disputes as to | D7.21
trust, property subject to | D7.22
Receivership assets
antecedent transactions,
recovery under | D9.1
control, obtaining | D9.1
foreign, position of | D12.1
hive-down (see *Hive-down*)
income, deriving | D9.2
liquidation, recourse to
re preferential debts | D10.2
realisation
—liquidation costs,
discharge of | D10.3
—manner of | D9.1
—order of | D10.1
—separate treatment of | D10.5
sale of going concern
—duties on | D9.15
—hive-down, effect of | D9.15
—marketing, methods of | D9.15
—sale agreement | D9.17
—transfer of undertakings
provisions | D9.16

Receivership assets – continued
scope of, ascertaining | D9.1
Rescue
informal | A3.1
Retention of title
receivership, and
—crystallisation of floating
charge, effect of | D7.17
—dispute as to | D7.19
—effectiveness of remedy | D7.19
—validity and effect of | D7.18
registrable charges | C12.10
Returns
office-holder filing | A4.12

Sale and leaseback
registrable charges | C12.10
Scheme of arrangement
availability of | A3.1
Secretary of State
petition by | C5.31
winding-up order,
investigations following | C8.5
Set-off
financial markets, in | F2.4
fiscal authorities, by | H3.16
proof of debt | C14.26
receivership, in
—Crown | D7.6
—generally | D7.5
registrable charges | C12.10
Social security contributions
debts due, priority of | D7.4
Solvency
test of | A1.2
Stamp duty
hive-down, relief on | D9.12
intra-group transfers, relief on | H2.7
winding up, documents
exempt in | C12.5, H3.13
Stationery
administration, notice of | B5.1
receivership, notification of | D4.12
winding up, notification of | C11.1
Statutory duty
directors and officers,
breach by | C13.3
Statutory nuisance
receiver, liabilities of | D8.22
Stocks
rights over | C12.16

Tax planning
anti-tax avoidance | H2.5
generally | H1.1
group relationship, termination of
—capital gains on | H2.3
—effecting | H2.2
intra-group transfers,
stamp duty relief | H2.7
new accounting period | H2.4
preferential debts | H2.6
Transactions at an undervalue
adjustment of | C10.2
—third parties, position of | C10.6
court, powers of | C10.6
financial markets,
insolvency in | F2.2, F5.2, F6.16
receiver, recovery of assets by | D9.1

Transactions at an undervalue –
continued
  setting aside — B9.2
Transfer of undertakings
  sale of going concern, on — D9.16
Trust
  property subject to, effect
    of receivership — D7.22

United States
  concurrent proceedings in — A5.3
Unregistered companies
  bodies being — C5.8
  winding up
  —debts, inability to pay — C5.24
  —grounds for — C5.11
  —jurisdiction — C5.4, C5.8

Value added tax
  bad debt relief
  —administration, on — B5.18
  —administrative
    receivership, in — D4.7
  —voluntary arrangement, on — E4.1
  —winding up, on — C14.8
  group registration — H2.9
  hive-down, on — D9.13
  post-insolvency
    transactions, on — H3.15
  pre-insolvency transactions,
    on — H3.14
  receiver, charged by — D8.5
  refunds of — H3.15
  transfer of going concern,
    relief on — H2.8
Voluntary arrangement
  availability of — A3.1
  companies to which
    applying — E1.2, E1.3
  company subject to, winding up — C5.2
  completion formalities — E3.7
  corporation tax liability during — H3.9
  insolvent partnerships,
    application to — E1.2
  introduction of — E1.2
  legislation — E1.2
  limitations of procedure — B2.1
  meetings
  —chairman — E2.3
  —company officers,
    attendance by — E2.4
  —majorities — E2.5
  —notice of — E2.2
  —proposals, to approve — E2.1
  —quorum — E2.5
  —results, report of — E3.1
  —summoning — E2.2
  —voting rights — E2.5
  nominee
  —report — E1.4
  —role of — E1.3
  post-proposal creditors,
    position of — E3.6
  procedure
  —initiation of — E1.3
  —scope of — E1.3
  —use of — E1.2
  proposal
  —agreement, proceedings
    to obtain — E2.6

Voluntary arrangement – continued
  —approval of — E2.1
  —challenge to — E3.3
  —effective, becoming — E2.6
  —implementation,
    challenge to — E3.3, E3.4
  —persons on whom
    binding — E3.1
  —power to make — E1.3
  —unfairly prejudicial — E3.3
  secured and preferential
    creditors, protection of — E2.7
  supervisor
  —accounts — E3.7
  —appointment of — E2.5
  —assets, taking possession of — E3.5
  —charges — E3.7
  —costs — E3.7
  —expenses — E3.7
  —fees — E3.7
  —person being — E3.2
  —reports — E3.7
  taxation aspects — E4.1
  VAT bad debt relief — E4.1
  waived debt, relief from tax on — H3.17
Voluntary winding up
  agents
  —effect on — C9.8
  —moneys and assets
    in hands of — C12.17
  annual accounts — C11.18
  anti-tax avoidance — H2.5
  assets and liabilities, effect on — C9.10
  book debts, rights over — C12.16
  building contracts, effect on — C12.19
  business, cessation of — C7.1
  chattels, rights over — C12.16
  company's officers
  —examination of — C11.22
  —involvement of — C11.21
  conduct of directors,
    investigation of — C7.2
  contracts
  —effect on — C9.6
  —rescission of — C12.7
  contributories' liabilities — C12.20
  court, involvement of — C11.23
  creditors and contributories,
    involvement of — C11.19
  creditors' (see *Creditors'*
    voluntary winding up)
  creditors' meeting
  —entitlement to vote — C11.13
  —first — C11.3, C11.4
  —notice of — C11.5
  —proofs for voting, admission
    or rejection of — C11.14
  derivative actions — C12.11
  directors' powers, cessation of — C7.2
  dissolution following — C9.11, C16.2
  documents exempt from
    stamp duty — C12.5
  employees, effect on — C9.7
  execution
  —creditors, relief for — C9.4
  —goods, land or debt, over — C9.3
  execution or distress following — C7.5
  fixtures, rights over — C12.16
  goods and chattels taken
    in execution — C9.2

Index

Voluntary winding up – *continued*
limitation against creditor,
   period of   C9.5
liquidation committee,
   involvement of   C11.20
liquidator
—administrative duties,
   enforcement of   C11.25
—assets (see *Liquidation assets*)
—business, sale of   C12.14
—cash, dealing with   C12.15
—continuation of business   C12.13
—disclaimer by   C12.6
—freehold and leasehold
   property, dealing with   C12.18
—general functions of   C11.25
—immunity   C11.24
—insurance policies,
   dealing with   C12.22
—investment business
   assets, dealing with   C12.21
—position of   C11.24
—release of   C16.2
—removal of   C11.28
—remuneration and costs   C11.27
—replacement of   C11.28
—specific powers and duties   C11.26
malpractice, investigation of   C9.13
meetings
—annual   C11.18
—chairman   C11.7
—company's personnel,
   attendance of   C11.8
—expense of summoning   C11.11
—final   C16.1, C16.2
—notice of   C11.6
—proxy forms   C11.10
—quorum   C11.12
—record of proceedings   C11.17
—resolutions   C11.15
—suspension and
   adjournment   C11.16
—venue   C11.9
members' (see *Members'
   voluntary winding up*)
prior transactions,
   investigation of   C9.13
prohibited company
   transactions   C12.9
proof of debt (see *Proof of debt*)
property, ownership of   C9.9
protected deposits   C9.12
re-use of company name,
   restriction on   C9.1
special manager,
   appointment of   C11.29
stay of actions and
   proceedings   C7.4
stocks, rights over   C12.16
transfer of shares on   C7.3
unauthorised company
   transactions   C12.9
unpaid share capital, calls on   C12.20

Waste management
receiver, liabilities of   D8.21
Water pollution
receiver, liabilities of   D8.24
Winding up
agents, effect on   C9.8

Winding up – *continued*
alternatives to   C2.5
assets and liabilities,
   effect on   C9.10
assets, order of priority   C15.1
commencement, new
   accounting period on   H2.4
company
—reference to   C1.1
—solvent or insolvent   C1.4
—termination of existence   C2.3
compulsory (see *Compulsory
   winding up*)
contracts, effect on   C9.6
costs and expenses,
   payment of   C15.2
court, by (see *Compulsory
   winding up*)
court, meaning   C1.6
cross-frontier recognition   C1.6
dissolution following   C9.11
effect of   C6.1
employees, effect on   C9.7
execution
—creditors, relief for   C9.4
—goods, land or debt, over   C9.3
goods and chattels taken
   in execution   C9.2
initiation, reasons for   C2.1
just distribution, bringing about   C2.2
legislation
—delegated   C1.3
—principal   C1.2
limitation against creditor,
   period of   C9.5
malpractice, investigation of   C9.13
meetings
—chairman   C11.7
—company's personnel,
   attendance of   C11.8
—entitlement to vote   C11.13
—expense of summoning   C11.11
—first   C11.3, C11.4
—notice of   C11.5, C11.6
—proofs for voting,
   admission or rejection of   C11.14
—proxy forms   C11.10
—quorum   C11.12
—types of   C11.2
—venue   C11.9
members, distribution of
   surplus to   C15.9
modes of   C1.5
ordinary creditors, dividends to
—declaration, formalities
   and restrictions   C15.7
—final   C15.6
—interim   C15.5
—ranking   C15.4
—unsold assets, division of   C15.8
petition by administrator   B7.2
preferential creditors,
   payment to   C14.34
prior transactions
—adjustment of (see *Prior
   transactions, adjustment of*)
—investigation of   C9.13
proof of debt (see *Proof of debt*)
property, ownership of   C9.9
protected deposits   C9.12

Winding up – continued
  re-use of company name,
    restriction on   C9.1
  stamp duty relief   H3.13
  stationery, notification on   C11.1
  tax questions   C2.4
  timing   C2.7
  voluntary (see *Creditors'*
    voluntary winding up, Members'
    voluntary winding up, Voluntary
    winding up)

Wrongful trading
  civil liability   C13.2
  compensatory
    provisions   C13.2
  introduction of   C13.2
  participation in,
    disqualification for   I2.7
  provisions, consideration
    of   A3.1
  shadow directors, by   C13.2
  standard of care   C13.2